KT-131-994

BREWER'S
FAMOUS
QUOTATIONS

BREWER'S
FAMOUS
QUOTATIONS

NIGEL REES

WEIDENFELD & NICOLSON
LONDON

First published in Great Britain in 2006
by Weidenfeld & Nicolson

1 3 5 7 9 10 8 6 4 2

© Nigel Rees 2006

All rights reserved. No part of this publication may be reproduced, stored in a
retrieval system, or transmitted, in any form or by any means, electronic,
mechanical, photocopying, recording or otherwise, without the prior permission of
both the copyright owner and the above publisher.

The right of Nigel Rees to be identified as the author of this work has been
asserted in accordance with the Copyright, Designs and Patents Act 1988.

A CIP catalogue record for this book is available from the British Library.

ISBN-13   978 0 304 367993
ISBN-10   0 304 36799 0

Designed by Gwyn Lewis

Printed in Finland by WS Bookwell Ltd

Weidenfeld & Nicolson

The Orion Publishing Group Ltd
Orion House, 5 Upper Saint Martin's Lane, London, WC2H 9EA
www.orionbooks.co.uk

The Orion publishing group's policy is to use papers that are natural, renewable and
recyclable products and made from wood grown in sustainable forests. The logging
and manufacturing processes are expected to conform to the environmental
regulations of the country of origin.

Contents

Introduction

Traditionally, there have been two ways to go about compiling a dictionary of quotations. One has been to anticipate the kind of quotations that readers will be interested in and then to provide accurate wording and source material for them. The second has been to put forward quotations that the compiler has gathered together – possibly on a theme or themes – and that the reader may in time find useful or simply enjoyable.

Brewer's Famous Quotations is not quite either of these things. What it seeks to provide is the context for and ancillary information about quotations which do already exist – that is to say, which are written or spoken words that have already been quoted, but about which there is something to be said for their meaning to be properly appreciated. A complaint that can often be made about dictionaries of quotations – however substantial and 'comprehensive' they may be – is that they lack contextual commentary or, indeed, any commentary at all. There is a tendency for such books simply to deposit the minimum of information upon the page and then hurry on, however misleading (or inaccurate) this may be.

Accordingly, *Brewer's Famous Quotations* is, if you like, composed largely of footnotes. It provides information about the quotations that have been selected for inclusion and relates tales about their provenance, their ascriptions – and any other thing that may be relevant.

It stands to reason that if this technique were to be applied to the number of quotations, say, in the *Oxford Dictionary of Quotations* or in *Bartlett's Familiar*

Quotations, a very wieldy and impractical volume would result. So a selection process has been invoked. In order to make room for a good number of quotations that have been so far ignored by the major dictionaries (but that are known to be of interest to readers), a sizeable proportion of standard quotations has been jettisoned. Broadly, these are the quotations that are self-explanatory or about which there is nothing much to say. I have also tended not to include lines from songs and hymns that, although they may be familiar, are so more because of repeated performance than from actual quotation.

Alongside this process has been a parallel one of rejecting quotations that no one might think of using these days. Whereas most dictionary compilers have to rely on hunch, *Brewer's Famous Quotations* benefits from the knowledge of its compiler about what sort of quotations are of interest to readers or that have provoked debate or inquiry in the past. I am lucky to be able to speak with some confidence on this matter. Thirty years of work as deviser and presenter of the BBC Radio programme *Quote ... Unquote* has given me a good idea of the problem quotations. Since 1992, my editing of the subscription quarterly, the *'Quote ... Unquote' Newsletter*, together with its associated website www.btweb-world.com/quote-unquote has given me further working knowledge of these matters.

Accordingly, it is my hope that there will be very little dead wood in this book – the sort of quotation that is included by an editor just because it takes his or her fancy, or to meet the demands of political correctness, or that one can never imagine anyone in their right minds actually using. Foreign-language quotations are given in their original form only if they still tend to be quoted in that language rather than in English.

Inevitably, there will be one or two quotations in *Brewer's Famous Quotations* that will not meet these criteria. Some have been included when there is nothing much to say about them, because to exclude them would significantly reduce the work's usefulness as a reference work. Some have been included (when they might have been excluded by another editor) simply because they have formed the basis of questions or talking-points on *Quote ... Unquote*. But at least there is no question in these instances as to whether these sayings have been quoted at least once – if only on the radio show. Again, a special category of quotations has been given prominence that might not be justified anywhere else and that requires little in the way of annotation – observations on the art of quotation itself.

The *Brewer's Famous Quotations* aspect also comes to the fore in the way I have tried to reflect not just the origin, context and background of a quotation but the way it has been used. Accordingly, where appropriate, I record notable instances of a quotation being used in a significant way. In addition, I give numerous indications of the way quotations have been borrowed or put to work in different ways, especially as the titles of books, films, plays and broadcast programmes.

If there is one word that I hope the reader will not find too often in these pages, it is 'attributed'. On other occasions, I have felt that this word was better than nothing when no origin could be traced for a quotation. In this book, however, where so much effort has gone into source-finding, I thought it was justified to put the earliest secondary source when the actual origin of a saying proved impossible to find.

A slight change to the method used in this book's three predecessors – *Why Do We Quote ... ?* (Blandford Press, 1989), *Brewer's Quotations* (Cassell, 1995) and the *Cassell Companion to Quotations* (1998; also published as *Mark My Words – Great Quotations and the Stories Behind Them*, Barnes & Noble Books, 2002) – is that I have eschewed very much investigation of catchphrases and other forms of popular phraseology which modern practice has often been to include in dictionaries of quotations. These have been dealt with more than adequately in some other of my books, such as the *Dictionary of Catchphrases* (Cassell, second edition, 2005), the *Dictionary of Clichés* (Cassell, 1998 edition) and the *Dictionary of Word and Phrase Origins* (Cassell, third edition, 2002).

Many, many people have helped me in making this book. Substantial contributions to the text have come from: Marian Bock, Jaap Engelsman, Mark English, Thomas D. Fuller, Joe Kralich and Antony Percy – in most cases volunteering their own researches to add to what I had written in the earlier books. Others have either written to point out errors and to discuss points in these books; or they have written to me seeking a 'lost' quotation, hence alerting me to it; or they have been simply supportive in a general way to my (I hope benign) pedantry in this field.

I am indebted, for these different reasons, to: Sir Eric Anderson, Dr J.K.

Aronson, the late Paul Beale, H.E. Bell, Dr John Campbell, Professor Denis J. Conlon, T.A. Dyer, the late David Elias, Jean English, Ian Forsyth, Charles G. Francis, Mike Fraser, the late Ian Gillies, Jane Gregory, Patricia A. Guy, Raymond Harris, Donald Hickling, Michael Holroyd, the late Sir David Hunt, Sir Antony Jay, Jane Keskar – the Kipling Society, Miss M.L. King, Elizabeth Knowles, Oonagh Lahr, Michael R. Lewis, Dennis K. Lien, the late Leonard Miall, Professor Wolfgang Mieder, Jan Morris, Professor John Morris, the late Frank Muir, the late John G. Murray, Michael and Valerie Grosvenor Myer, Denis Norden, John Julius Norwich, John O'Byrne, Dermod Quirke, Claire Rayner, Tony Ring – the P.G. Wodehouse Society (UK), Brian Robinson, Derek Robinson, Anthony W. Shipps, Godfrey Smith, Muriel Smith, Chris Wain, Barbara Wild.

A final word may be necessary about where I have chosen to place certain quotations that are not obviously the result of something said or spoken by an identifiable person. I may not have been entirely consistent on this point. Rather than provide an entry for a song lyricist who may only have contributed one line to the language (and what's more he may have worked with a composer and any number of other lyricists), I have sometimes put such a quote in Anonymous. Where the true originator of a line or joke or film title (for example) may be in doubt – and may most safely be attributed to some sort of group effort – I have sometimes opened an entry under a film title. (Just consider who should really be credited with Groucho's lines from the Marx Brothers films or some of Bogart's misquoted lines from *Casablanca*.)

Where a line is frequently misattributed, should it appear in the entry for the correct source or the incorrect one? This is not a matter I have agonized over very greatly. It seems to me that as long as the quotation is discussed *somewhere* in the book it really does not matter where it is positioned. Although there is a good deal of cross-referencing, the only sure way of finding a line is by consulting the index. This should always be your route into the book.

Nigel Rees
LONDON, 2006

Abbreviations

Apperson: G.L. Apperson, *English Proverbs and Proverbial Phrases*, 1929

Bartlett: *Bartlett's Familiar Quotations* (15th edn), 1980, (16th edn), 1992, (17th edn), 2002

Benham: *Benham's Book of Quotations*, 1907, 1948, 1960

Bible: The Authorised Version, 1611 (except where stated otherwise)

Brewer: *Brewer's Dictionary of Phrase and Fable*, (2nd edn), 1894, (3rd edn), 1923, (13th edn), 1975, (14th edn), 1989

Burnam: Tom Burnam, *The Dictionary of Misinformation*, 1975; *More Misinformation*, 1980

CODP: *The Concise Oxford Dictionary of Proverbs*, 1982

DNB: *The Dictionary of National Biography* (and its supplements)

Mencken: *H.L. Mencken's Dictionary of Quotations*, 1942

ODP: *The Oxford Dictionary of Proverbs* (3rd edn), 1970

ODQ: *The Oxford Dictionary of Quotations* (2nd edn), 1953, (3rd edn), 1979, (4th edn), 1992, (5th edn), 1999, (6th edn), 2004

OED2: *The Oxford English Dictionary* (2nd edn), 1989, (CD-ROM version 3.0), 2002

PDQ: *The Penguin Dictionary of Quotations* (edited by J.M. & M.J. Cohen), 1960, 1992

PDMQ: *The Penguin Dictionary of Modern Quotations* (edited by J.M. & M.J. Cohen), 1971, 1980

PD20: *The Penguin Dictionary of Twentieth-Century Quotations* (edited by J.M. & M.J. Cohen), 1993, 1995

Partridge/Catch Phrases: Eric Partridge, *A Dictionary of Catch Phrases* (2nd edn, edited by Paul Beale), 1985

Partridge/Slang: Eric Partridge, *A Dictionary of Slang and Unconventional English* (8th edn, edited by Paul Beale), 1984

Pearson: Hesketh Pearson, *Common Misquotations*, 1937

RQ: *Respectfully Quoted* (edited by Suzy Platt, Congressional Reference Division), 1989

Safire: William Safire, *Safire's Political Dictionary*, 1978

Shakespeare: The Arden Shakespeare (2nd series)

The Dictionary

A

Diane ABBOTT British Labour politician (1953–)

1 Being an MP is a good job, the sort of job all working-class parents want for their children – clean, indoors and no heavy lifting. What could be nicer?

In an interview with Hunter Davies in *The Independent* (18 January 1994). Much the same claim had earlier been made by Senator Robert Dole about the US vice-presidency (ABC TV broadcast, 24 July 1988): 'It is inside work with no heavy lifting.' And then J.K. Galbraith, *Name-Dropping*, Chap. 8 (1999) had: '[John F.] Kennedy also knew how to identify himself with an audience and with the larger electorate. At the end of his 1960 campaign, he addressed a vast crowd in the old Boston Garden. As a member of his campaign staff, I was there. He asked himself, as though from the floor, why he was running for president. In reply, he listed some issues, all relevant to his audience, that needed attention; then he ended by saying that the presidency was a well-paid job with no heavy lifting. The largely working-class gathering responded with appreciation, affection and joy. He was one of them.'

Dean ACHESON American Democratic politician (1893–1971)

2 Great Britain … has lost an Empire and not yet found a role.

Speech at the Military Academy, West Point (5 December 1962). Acheson was a former Secretary of State (under President Truman) and the son of a British army officer who went to Canada, so the home truth was thus all the more painful when he went on to say: '[Britain's] attempt to play a separate power role – that is, a role apart from Europe, a role based on a "special relationship" with the United States, a role based on being the head of a "Commonwealth" … this role is about to be played out … Her Majesty's Government is now attempting, wisely in my opinion, to re-enter Europe.'

Lord Chandos, President of the Institute of Directors, protested that such words coming from one of President Kennedy's advisers were 'a calculated insult'. Prime Minister Harold Macmillan quietly observed that, in any case, the general drift of world affairs was against Britain or any other country trying to play 'a separate power role'. More than 30 years later, one can say that Britain's European 're-entry' is to some extent accomplished.

3 *Present at the Creation.*

Title of memoirs (1969). From a remark by Alfonso X, the Wise (1221–84), King of Castile, on studying the Ptolemaic system: 'Had I been present at the Creation, I would have given some useful hints for the better ordering of the universe.'

Thomas Carlyle had earlier quoted the remark in his *Life of Frederick the Great* (1858–65). In Bishop Berkeley's *Three Dialogues Between Hylas and Philonus* (1713), Philonus says: 'Why, I imagine that if I had been present at the Creation, I should have seen things produced into being; that is, become perceptible, in the order described by the sacred historian.'

J.R. ACKERLEY English writer (1896–1967)

4 I was born in 1896, and my parents were married in 1919.

My Father and Myself (1968), opening words. Compare the opening words of *Lady Sings the Blues* (1958), the autobiography of the American blues singer Billie Holiday (1915–59): 'Mom and Pop were just a couple of kids when they got married. He was eighteen, she was sixteen, and I was three.'

Lord ACTON English historian (1834–1902)

1 Power tends to corrupt and absolute power corrupts absolutely.

Letter to Bishop Mandell Creighton, dated 3 April 1887 (published 1904). It is often quoted as 'all power corrupts' – i.e. without the 'tends'. Acton had been anticipated by William Pitt, Earl of Chatham, speaking in the House of Lords (9 January 1770): 'Unlimited power is apt to corrupt the minds of those who possess it.' William Wordsworth's political tract *The Convention of Centra* (1809) stated: 'There is an unconquerable tendency in all power ... to injure the mind of him who exercises that power.' In 1839 Lord Brougham had written in *Historical Sketches of Statesmen of the Time of George III*: 'Unlimited power corrupts the possessor.' A.J.P. Taylor questioned the accuracy of the remark in a *New Statesman* article, in about 1955, calling it, 'Windy rot ... many an engine-driver is not corrupted' (which misses the point, surely?). Hence, however, the title of a Clint Eastwood film, *Absolute Power* (US 1997), about a corrupt US president.

Douglas ADAMS English novelist (1952–2001)

2 The last ever dolphin message was misinterpreted as a surprisingly sophisticated attempt to do a double-backwards-somersault through a hoop while whistling the 'Star Spangled Banner', but in fact the message was this: *So long and thanks for all the fish.*

The Hitch Hiker's Guide to the Galaxy, Chap. 23 (1979). Hence, *So Long and Thanks For All the Fish*, the title of the fourth volume in the 'trilogy' (1984).

3 'O Deep Thought Computer,' he said, 'the task we have designed for you to perform is this. We want you to tell us ...' he paused, '... the Answer!'
'The Answer?' said Deep Thought. 'The Answer to what?'
'Life!' urged Fook.
'The Universe!' said Lunkwill.
'Everything!' they said in chorus.

In the same book, Chap. 25. The answer to the question is 'Forty-two' (Chap. 27). In 1996 it was reported that Cambridge astronomers had found that 42 was the value of an essential scientific constant, the Hubble Constant – one that determines the age of the universe – source: *The Independent* (8 November 1996).

Adams's phrase was adapted to form an advertising slogan for *The Daily Telegraph* (current 1988): 'The Earth Dweller's Guide to Life, the Universe and Everything'. The format, from an untraced source, is now used to signify 'absolutely everything'. Compare the all-embracing title of my *The Quote ... Unquote Book of Love, Death and the Universe* (1980), which may have been suggested to me by the line in the first Adams book. Hence also, *Life, the Universe and Everything*, the title of the third novel of four in his 'trilogy' (1982).

4 It is a well-known fact, that those people who most want to rule people are, ipso facto, those least suited to do it ... Anyone who is capable of getting themselves made President should on no account be allowed to do the job.

The Restaurant At the End of the Universe, Chap. 28 (1980). Adams was not the first to suggest that politicians who seek office are the least proper people to hold it. Who said it first? Candidates include: Arthur C. Clarke (in his novel *Imperial Earth*, apparently), Isaac Asimov (but where?), Tolstoy (but where?), Sir Thomas More (*Utopia* – which does contain the line, 'If any man aspires to any office he is sure never to compass it'), and Plato, whose *Republic*, Pt 7, Bk 7, has: 'The state whose prospective rulers come to their duties with least enthusiasm is bound to have the best and most tranquil government, and the state whose rulers are eager to rule the worst.'

5 It was the Sunday afternoons he couldn't cope with ... As you stare at the clock the hands will move relentlessly on to four o'clock, and you will enter the long dark teatime of the soul.

Life, the Universe and Everything, Chap. 1 (1982). Hence, *The Long Dark Tea-time of the Soul*, title of a Dirk Gently novel (1988) by Adams. See also FITZGERALD 195:9; JOHN OF THE CROSS 256:5.

Franklin P. ADAMS American humorist (1881–1960)

6 Of a certain author it was said, 'A first edition of his work is a rarity but a second is rarer still.'

Quoted in *The Treasury of Humorous Quotations*, eds Esar & Bentley (1951). However, R.E. Drennan, *Wit's End* (1973, has it that when Alexander Woollcott was asked to sign a first edition of his book *Shouts and Murmurs*, he inquired rhetorically, 'What is rarer than a Woollcott first edition?' F.P. Adams produced the answer: 'A Woollcott *second* edition.' Drennan probably took this version from the telling in Harpo Marx, *Harpo Speaks*, Chap. 12 (1961). Also told of other people. As is often the case, Oscar Wilde seems to have been there first: 'While the first editions of most classical authors are those coveted by the bibliophiles, it is the second editions of my books that are the true rarities, and even the British Museum has not been able to secure copies of most of them' – in Hesketh Pearson, *The Life of Oscar Wilde*, Chap. 14 (1946).

John ADAMS American Federalist 2nd President
(1735–1826)

1 I agree with you that in politics the middle way is none at all.

Letter to Horatio Gates (23 March 1776). Compare MACMILLAN 303:6.

2 All great nations inevitably end up committing suicide.

What Adams wrote, precisely, in a letter to John Taylor (15 April 1814) was: 'Remember, democracy never lasts long. It soon wastes, exhausts, and murders itself. There never was a democracy that did not commit suicide.'

3 Thomas Jefferson still survives.

Dying words and, by a remarkable accident, untrue: Jefferson had died a few hours earlier. Both former presidents died on 4 July 1826, exactly 50 years since the founding of the Republic. *Brewer* (1975) has that his dying words were 'Independence for ever'.

Samuel ADAMS American revolutionary politician
(1722–1803)

4 What a glorious morning for America!

Thus is it usually quoted, but what Adams most likely said on hearing the sound of gunfire at Lexington (the opening battle of the War of American Independence) on 19 April 1775 was, 'What a glorious morning is this.'

Mrs Sarah Flower ADAMS English hymnwriter
(1805–48)

5 Nearer, My God, to Thee.

Title of hymn first published in 1841. This is often said to have been what the ship's band was playing when the *Titanic* sank in 1912. In the song 'Be British', written and composed by Paul Pelham and Lawrence Wright in the same year, there is a tear-jerking 'recitation after 2nd verse' enshrining the belief that the band played the hymn 'Nearer My God To Thee' as the ship went down. However, according to *Burnam* (1980), the band played ragtime until the ship's bridge dipped underwater, and then the bandmaster led his men in the Episcopal hymn 'Autumn'. This version of events was based on remarks by Harold Bride, the surviving junior wireless operator, reported in *The New York Times* (19 April 1912). As opposed to this, it has been suggested that the reporter misheard Bride who might have mentioned instead 'Aughton' – a hymn tune to which the words are more appropriately, 'And when my task on earth

is done ... E'en death's cold wave I will not flee.' Or he might have translated '*Songe d'Automne*', title of a waltz by Archibald Joyce, which was known to be in the band's repertoire. According to Walter Lord, *A Night to Remember* (1955), the 'Nearer My God To Thee' version was one of many rumours circulating within a few days of the ship sinking. It was, however, the one included in the film (UK 1958) of Lord's book.

Harold ADAMSON American songwriter (1906–80)

6 Comin' In On a Wing and a Prayer.

Title of song popular in the Second World War (published in 1943), and which derived from an alleged remark by a real pilot who was coming in to land with a badly damaged plane. Adamson's lyric (to music by Jimmy McHugh) includes the lines:

> Tho' there's one motor gone, we can still carry on
> Comin' in on a wing and a pray'r.

A film (US 1944) about life on an aircraft carrier was called simply *Wing and a Prayer*.

Joseph ADDISON English essayist and politician
(1672–1719)

7 And pleas'd th' Almighty's orders to perform, Rides in the whirlwind, and directs the storm.

Of the 1st Duke of Marlborough. *The Campaign* (1705) – a celebration of the Battle of Blenheim, fought the previous year. Addison's second line has become a figure of speech. Alexander Pope repeated it with comic effect in *The Dunciad* (1728). William Cowper in 'The Retirement' (1782) had: "Till he that rides the whirlwind checks the rein / Then all the world of waters sleeps again.' Henry Buckle in his *History of Civilisation in England* (1857) had: 'To see whether they who had raised the storm could ride the whirlwind.' Nowadays it simply means to deal with an extremely difficult situation: 'With his overall Commons majority already down to 18 and his Government fighting on several other damaging policy fronts, Mr Major is riding a whirlwind' – *Daily Mail* (21 May 1993).

8 The woman that deliberates is lost.

Cato, Act 4, Sc. 1, line 31 (1713). Most early uses of the phrase were about women, but the proverbial form is now 'He who hesitates is lost.' *CODP* has not found an earlier citation.

9 'We are always doing,' says he, 'something for Posterity, but I would fain see Posterity do something for us.'

The Spectator, No. 583 (20 August 1714). *Notes and Queries*

(Vol. 152) has it that, in 1723, the Oxford antiquary Thomas Hearne attributed to Dr Thomas Stafford (?1641–1723) the remark: 'Posterity? What good will Posterity do for us?' See also ROCHE 384:5.

See also HALE 226:1.

Alfred ADLER Austrian psychoanalyst (1870–1937)

1 Individual psychology holds that the most important key to the understanding of both personal and mass problems is the so-called sense of inferiority, or inferiority complex, and its consequences.

Quoted in *The New York Times* (20 September 1925). Adler had presented his theory that gave rise to the phrase 'inferiority complex' (repressed fear and resentment at being inferior) somewhat earlier: 'To be a human being means to possess a feeling of inferiority which constantly presses towards its own conquest ... The greater the feeling of inferiority that has been experienced, the more powerful is the urge for contest and the more violent the emotional agitation.'

Polly ADLER American brothel keeper (1900–62)

2 *A House Is Not a Home.*

Title of memoirs (1954). Adler was a notable New York madam in the 1920s and 1930s. She finally closed her bordello in 1945 and spent part of her twilight years writing memoirs. Then:

> One day I happened to be spraying a rose-bush in my back yard, and Dora [Maugham] ... was profoundly impressed by this spectacle of suburban domesticity.
>
> 'I wonder what the cops would say,' she mused, 'if they could see you now.'
>
> 'Oh,' said I, 'probably they'd be disappointed that my home is not a house.'
>
> Dora's reaction to this remark was so unusual ...
> 'Eyeow!' she squealed. 'Hold everything! ... Turn that around and you've got it!'
>
> 'What on earth are you talking about?'
>
> 'The perfect title for your book ...'
>
> So far as I was concerned, I told her, it was the most inspired piece of thinking anyone had done in a garden since the day Isaac Newton got conked by an apple.

Of course, 'house' here means 'brothel'. When the book was filmed (US 1964), there had to be a theme song incorporating the title, which managed coyly to avoid any suggestion as to what sort of 'house' was being talked about.

James AGATE English drama critic (1877–1947)

3 A professional is a man who can do his job when he doesn't feel like it; an amateur is one who can't [do his job] when he does feel like it.

From *Ego* (1935) – entry for 17 September 1933. The context was a lunch with the actor Cedric Hardwicke, who said: 'My theory of acting is that it is so minor an art that the only self-respect attaching to it is to be able to reproduce one's performance with mathematical accuracy.' The above was Agate's concurrence. Hardwicke added: 'It shouldn't make a hair's breadth of difference to an actor if he has a dead baby at home and a wife dying.'

There have been several other attempts to define the difference between amateurs and professionals, beyond the acting profession: 'Amateurs [musicians] practise until they can get it right; professionals practise until they can't get it wrong' – quoted by Harold Craxton, one-time professor at the Royal Academy of Music; 'Professionals built the *Titanic*; amateurs built the Ark' (Anon.).

George AIKEN American Republican politician (1892–1984)

4 The United States could well declare unilaterally that this stage of the Vietnam War is over – that we have 'won' in the sense that our Armed Forces are in control of most of the field and no potential enemy is in a position to establish its authority over South Vietnam.

Speech in US Senate (19 October 1966). Sometimes encapsulated as 'Aiken's Solution' in the form 'Claim victory and retreat', this was an attempt to persuade President Johnson to 'declare the United States the winner and begin de-escalation'. Commenting on the eventual 1973 withdrawal, Aiken said: 'What we got was essentially what I recommended ... we said we had won and we got out.'

Zoë AKINS American playwright (1886–1958)

5 *The Greeks Had a Word for It.*

Title of play (1929). For seemingly so venerable a phrase, it may come as a surprise to learn that this dates back no further than 1929. Although, as Akins said, 'the phrase is original and grew out of the dialogue', it does not appear anywhere in the text. Akins told Burton Stevenson that in dialogue cut from her play the 'word' was used to describe a type of woman. One character thinks that 'tart' is meant but another corrects this and says that 'free soul' is more to the point. Nowadays the phrase is used a trifle archly, as when one wishes to express disapproval and say, 'There's a name for that sort of behaviour.' Evidently there was a film (US 1932) with the title *The Greeks Had a Word for Them*.

Edward ALBEE American playwright (1928–)

1 *Who's Afraid of Virginia Woolf?*
Title of play (1962), supposedly taken from a graffito seen in Greenwich Village. In the play, the character Martha sings it to the tune of 'Who's Afraid of the Big Bad Wolf?' – that is her little joke.

See also DAVIS 163:2.

ALBERT German-born British Prince, Consort of Queen Victoria (1819–61)

2 Old mismanagement is no excuse for the continuance of it.
Letter to Lord Seymour (19 March 1851). Possibly not original and a statement used, with some rephrasing, by almost everyone who has ever spoken in favour of reform. Another version is: 'The antiquity of an abuse is no justification for its continuance.' In his play *Les Guèbres* (1769), Voltaire has: 'The more ancient the abuse the more sacred it is.'

Amos Bronson ALCOTT American teacher (1799–1888)

3 One must be a wise reader to quote wisely and well.
'Quotation', *Table Talk* (1877). Amos was the father of Louisa May Alcott, author of *Little Women* (1868).

Robert ALDEN American theologian (1937–)

4 There is not enough darkness in all the world to put out the light of even one small candle.
So attributed in *The David & Charles Book of Quotations* (1986). On the other hand, Bernard Levin describes this in *Conducted Tour* (1981) as 'an ancient proverb'. On yet another hand, a gravestone on the Oxford Road out of Henley-on-Thames has: 'JIMMY / A TINY MARMOSET / AUGUST 16TH 1937 / There isn't enough / Darkness in the world / To quench the light / Of one small candle.' It is believed that the memorial was raised by Jimmy's owner, a Miss Doris Jekyll. If this epitaph was applied near to the date of death it would preclude Alden's claim to authorship.

ALEXANDER THE GREAT King of Macedonia (356–323BC)

5 I am dying with the help of too many physicians.
Last words, attributed in *The Treasury of Humorous Quotations*, eds Esar & Bentley (1951); and earlier, in the form 'I die by the help of too many physicians', in H.L. Mencken's

Dictionary of Quotations (1942). No other evidence has been found to support this attribution. The idea, however, surfaces elsewhere in the classical world. The dying Emperor Hadrian (AD76–138) apparently came out with 'the popular saying "many physicians have slain a king"' (according to Chap. 69 of the Roman history by the Greek historian Dion Cassius). Pliny the Elder quoted an epitaph in AD77 that goes '*turba se medicorum periisse*' or, in another version, '*turba medicorum perii*' (translated as, 'the brawling of the doctors killed me'). There is also said to be a more recent Czech proverb, 'Many doctors, death accomplished.' In addition, Molière, in the opening line of Act 2 of *L'Amour Médecin*, comes close to the sense: '*Que voulez-vous donc faire, Monsieur, de quatre médecins? N'est-ce pas assez d'un pour tuer une personne?* [What do you want with four doctors? Isn't one enough to kill someone?]' One might also compare the fable of Aesop's variously entitled 'The Sick Man and the Doctor' or 'Favourable Omens' etc., in which a sick man goes to the doctor and describes a symptom, to which the doctor replies, 'Ah, that's a good sign.' This happens again and again with different symptons but the same reply from the doctor. Finally, a friend asks the sick man how he is doing, and the sick man replies, 'My friend, I am dying of good signs.'

See also PLUTARCH 361:6.

Mrs Cecil Frances ALEXANDER Irish poet and hymnwriter (1818–95)

6 All things bright and beautiful,
All creatures great and small,
All things wise and wonderful,
The Lord God made them all.
Hymn, 'All Things Bright and Beautiful' (1848). The English author James Herriot originally gave his books about life as a vet titles such as *It Shouldn't Happen To a Vet, Let Sleeping Vets Lie, Vets Might Fly* etc. When these titles were coupled together in three omnibus editions especially for the US market, Mrs Alexander's hymn was plundered for titles and they became *All Creatures Great and Small* (1972), *All Things Bright and Beautiful* (1973) and *All Things Wise and Wonderful* (1978). *The Lord God Made Them All* was given to a further original volume (1981). In 1997, I observed a food establishment off the A1 near Scotch Corner with the name 'All Pizzas Great and Small'.

7 The rich man in his castle,
The poor man at his gate,
God made them, high or lowly,
And ordered their estate.
In the same hymn. An omission rather than a misquotation. Mrs Alexander's hymn is in danger of becoming

known as the one from which a verse – the third – had to be dropped because of its apparent acceptance of an unacceptable *status quo*.

From Barbara Pym's novel *No Fond Return of Love* (1961): 'Dulcie sang in a loud indignant voice, waiting for the lines

The rich man in his castle, the poor man at his gate,
God made them, high or lowly, and ordered their estate.

but they never came. Then she saw that the verse had been left out. She sat down, feeling cheated of her indignation.'

Most modern hymnbook compilers omit the verse, and they started doing so about 1930. *Songs of Praise Discussed* (1933) calls it an 'appalling verse ... She must have forgotten Dives, and how Lazarus lay "at his gate"; but then she had been brought up in the atmosphere of a land-agent on an Irish estate. The *English Hymnal* led the way in obliterating this verse from the Anglican mind.' It remains in *Hymns Ancient and Modern* (Standard Edition, reprinted 1986), but it has disappeared from the *Irish Hymnal*. The authors of *The Houses of Ireland* (1975) note that by the 20th century 'the ecclesiastical authorities had decided that God's intentions are not to preclude movement within the social system. However, few of her contemporaries doubted that Mrs Alexander's interpretation was correct.'

Born in County Wicklow, Mrs Alexander was the wife of the Bishop of Derry and Archbishop of Armagh. The hymn was written while she was staying at Markree Castle, near Sligo. The 'purple-headed mountain' is thought to be a reference to Ben Bulben.

Nelson ALGREN American novelist and short-story writer (1909–81)

1 Never eat at a place called Mom's. Never play cards with a man called Doc. Never go to bed with a woman whose troubles are greater than your own.

A Walk on the Wild Side, essay 'What Every Young Man Should Know' (1956) – but *Bartlett* (1992) finds it only in H.E.F. Donahue, *Conversations with Nelson Algren* (1964), in which Algren says he was taught it by 'a nice old Negro lady'. *ODQ* (1992) and *ODMQ* (1991) both cite a *Newsweek* report (1956) rather than Algren's book itself. The wording varies.

Muhammad ALI (formerly Cassius Clay) American heavyweight boxing champion (1942–)

2 Float like a butterfly, sting like a bee.

His 'motto' from about 1964. Devised by an aide, Drew 'Bundini' Brown.

3 You don't want no pie in the sky when you die,
You want something here on the ground while you're still around.

Quoted in 1978. Based on HILL 238:3.

Alphonse ALLAIS French humorist (1854–1905)

4 There is no mystery about the authorship of Shakespeare's plays. They were not written by Shakespeare at all. They were all written by a total stranger, about whom all we know is that he was called Shakespeare.

Attributed by Miles Kington, from memory. But when was the transfer made to Shakespeare from Homer (see TWAIN 471:4)? Jerome K. Jerome, *My Life and Times* (1926), has: 'The Bacon stunt was in full swing about the same time, and again it was [Israel] Zangwill who discovered that Shakespeare's plays had all been written by another gentleman of the same name.'

Something akin to the observation is to be found in H.N. Gibson, *The Shakespeare Claimants* (1962). In outlining the Baconian theory, Gibson mentions the story that when Bacon felt his supposed authorship of *Richard II* was suspected by Queen Elizabeth I, 'to disarm her suspicions he hastily looked around for someone to use as cover. He had adopted the name "William Shakespeare" as a pseudonym for his secret works, and finding by an extraordinary coincidence an actor with a similar sounding name [Shakespere], he engaged him for the purpose.'

But if anyone can be credited with popularizing the saying about Homer adapted to Shakespeare, it is Robert Manson Myers, *From Beowulf to Virginia Woolf* (1954), a sort of literary *1066 And All That*: 'Until recently the so-called Shakespeare-Bacon Controversy remained a mute [sic] question, but it has finally been established, after the perusal of a rare manuscript found in a bottle, that Shakespeare never wrote Shakespeare's plays. Actually they were written by another man of the same name.'

Fred ALLEN American comedian (1894–1956)

5 A conference is a gathering of important people who singly can do nothing, but together can decide that nothing can be done.

Quoted in *The Treasury of Humorous Quotations*, eds Esar & Bentley (1951). Compare: 'A committee is a group of men who, individually, can do nothing, but collectively can meet and decide that nothing can be done', ascribed to 'Anonymous' in Prochnow & Prochnow, *Treasury of Humorous Quotations* (1969). See TREE 468:2.

Woody ALLEN American film actor, writer and director
(1937–)

1 Sex between a man and a woman can be wonderful – provided you get between the right man and
the right woman.
Attributed. Compare: 'I believe that sex is a beautiful thing
between two people. Between *five*, it's fantastic ...' on Allen's
record album, *The Nightclub Years 1964–1968* (1972).

2 The psychiatrist asked me if I thought sex was
dirty and I said, 'It is if you're doing it right.'
Film, *Take the Money and Run* (US 1969). Compare: 'Is sex
dirty? Only if it's done right' – film, *Everything You Always
Wanted To Know About Sex* (1972).

3 The lion and the calf shall lie down together, but
the calf won't get much sleep.
In *The New Republic* (31 August 1974). See BIBLE 77:1.

4 *Love and Death.*
Title of film (US 1975), a parody of *War and Peace* – see
TOLSTOY 467:2. Compare Oscar Wilde, *The Picture of Dorian
Gray* (1891): 'There was something fascinating in this son of
Love and Death.'

5 It's not that I'm afraid to die. I just don't want to be
there when it happens.
Death (1975). At the death of the comedian Spike Milligan in
2002, this was generally and mistakenly ascribed to him.
Whatever the case, Mark Twain, as so often, seems to have
got there first. In a sketch entitled 'The Latest Novelty –
Mental Photographs' (2 October 1869), Twain tells of being
sent a questionnaire on various subjects. He then gives
facetious answers, including: 'What is your Aim in Life? –
To endeavor to be absent when my time comes.'

6 Fun? That was the most fun I've ever had without
laughing.
On sex. Film, *Annie Hall* (US 1977), written with Marshall
Brickman. Alvy speaking. However, *Mencken* was recording 'Love [he probably meant sex] is the most fun you can
have without laughing' in 1942. Also attributed to
Humphrey Bogart in the form 'It was the most fun I ever
had without laughing.'

Leo S. AMERY English Conservative politician
(1873–1955)

7 Speak for England, Arthur!
Interjection, House of Commons (2 September 1939). On
the eve of war, Prime Minister Neville Chamberlain appeared
in the Commons and held out the prospect of a further
Munich-type peace conference and did not announce any
ultimatum to Germany. When the acting Labour leader,
Arthur Greenwood, rose to respond, a Conservative MP
shouted, 'Speak for England, Arthur!' For many years, it
was generally accepted that the MP was Amery and, indeed,
he wrote in *My Political Life* (Vol. 3, 1955): 'It was essential
that someone should ... voice the feelings of the House and
of the whole country. Arthur Greenwood rose ... I dreaded
a purely partisan speech, and called out to him across the
floor of the House, Speak for England.' (Note, no 'Arthur'.)
By 30 October, James Agate was writing in his diary (published in *Ego 4*) of the anthology for the forces he had been
busy compiling called *Speak for England*: 'Clemence Dane
gave me the title; it is the phrase shouted in the House the
other day when Arthur Greenwood got up to speak on the
declaration of the war.'
    However, writing up an account of the session in *his* diary,
Harold Nicolson (whose usual habit was to make his record
first thing the following morning) wrote: 'Bob Boothby cried
out, "*You* speak for Britain."' Boothby confirmed that he
had said this when shown the diary passage in 1964.
    The explanation would seem to be that after Amery spoke,
his cry was taken up not only by Boothby but by others on
the Tory benches. From the Labour benches came cries of
'What about Britain?' and 'Speak for the working classes!'
Interestingly, nobody claims to have said the exact words
as popularly remembered. The intervention went
unrecorded in *Hansard*. *Speak For England* later became the
title of a book (1976) by Melvyn Bragg – 'an oral history of
England since 1900'.

8 This is what Cromwell said to the Long Parliament
when he thought it was no longer fit to conduct
the affairs of the nation: 'You have sat too long
here for any good you have been doing. Depart, I
say, and let us have done with you. In the name
of God, go!'
Speech, House of Commons (7 May 1940). By this date,
criticism was growing of the British government's handling
of the war. Norway and Denmark had been lost to the Germans and yet a War Cabinet had not yet been formed. It
was obvious that things were getting very bad indeed. In a
dramatic speech Amery said, 'Somehow or other we must
get into the Government men who can match our enemies
in fighting spirit' and he had considered quoting something that Oliver Cromwell had said to John Hampden
'some three hundred years ago, when this House found
that its troops were being beaten again and again by the
dash and daring of the Cavaliers', namely, 'We cannot go

on being led as we are.' But, as Amery notes in his auto-biography, he chose this other Cromwell remark instead. 'I was not out for a dramatic finish, but for a practical purpose; to bring down the Government if I could.' And so he quoted Cromwell's words when dismissing the Rump of the Long Parliament in 1653. Chamberlain's government did indeed go. Churchill became Prime Minister and formed a National government three days later.

(Sir) Kingsley AMIS English novelist, poet and critic (1922–95)

1 *Lucky Jim.*

Amis's comic novel (1953) about a hapless university lecturer, Jim Dixon, takes its title from a not very relevant American song by Frederick Bowers (1874–1961) and his vaudeville partner Charles Horwitz (although it is usually ascribed to Anon.). It tells of a man who has to wait for his childhood friend Jim to die before he can marry the girl they were once both after. Then, married to the woman and not enjoying it, he would rather he was dead like his friend: 'Oh, lucky Jim, how I envy him.'

2 More will mean worse.

In *Encounter* (July 1960). Amis wrote about the expansion of higher education, especially on 'the delusion that there are thousands of young people who are capable of benefiting from university training but have somehow failed to find their way there'. He added: 'I wish I could have a little tape-and-loudspeaker arrangement sewn into the binding of this magazine, to be triggered off by the light reflected from the reader's eyes on to this part of the page, and set to bawl out at several bels: MORE WILL MEAN WORSE.'

When *The Times* misquoted this as 'more means worse' on one occasion, Amis fired off a broadside (22 February 1983): 'I think the difference is substantial, but let that go for now. You show by your misquotation that you couldn't be bothered to look up the reference, thereby ignoring the context, any arguments or evidence put forward, etc. Having garbled my remark you say roundly that in the event I was wrong. Not altogether perhaps. Laziness and incuriosity about sources are familiar symptoms of academic decline.'

3 Outside every fat man there was an even fatter man trying to close in.

One Fat Englishman (1963). Compare CONNOLLY 153:3.

4 *The Folk That Live On the Hill.*

Title of novel (1990). It would be interesting to know on what linguistic grounds Amis chose 'that' instead of 'who'. The song is actually called 'The Folks *Who* Live on the Hill'

and was written by Jerome Kern and Oscar Hammerstein II for the 1937 US film *High, Wide and Handsome*.

See also GORDON 218:1.

Maxwell ANDERSON American playwright (1888–1959)

5 But it's a long, long while
From May to December;
And the days grow short
When you reach September.

'September Song' (1938). Music by Kurt Weill. Compare WALKER 481:2.

Robert ANDERSON American playwright (1917–)

6 *Tea and Sympathy.*

Title of play (1953; film US 1956). *Brewer* (1995) defines the phrase as: 'A caring attitude, especially towards someone in trouble.' In Anderson's play, it is directed at a teenage boy at a New England boarding school by the housemaster's wife. To sort out his possible homosexuality, she goes to bed with him, and is reprimanded with: 'All you're supposed to do is every once in a while give the boys a little tea and sympathy.' The phrase undoubtedly predates the Anderson use, however.

Lancelot ANDREWES English bishop and scholar (1555–1626)

7 It was no summer progress. A cold coming they had of it, at this time of the year; just, the worst time of the year, to take a journey, and specially a long journey, in. The ways deep, the weather sharp, the days short, the sun farthest off *in solstitio brumali*, the very dead of winter.

Sermon 15, 'Of the Nativity' (1629). Paraphrased in T.S. Eliot's 'The Journey of the Magi' (1927) – see ELIOT 187:4.

8 The nearer the Church, the further from God.

In the same sermon. Compare DIAZ 167:7.

(Sir) Norman ANGELL English pacifist (1872–1967)

9 *The Great Illusion.*

Angell's anti-war book was first published in 1909 with the title *Europe's Optical Illusion*. A year later it was republished with this title. Angell was awarded the Nobel Peace Prize in 1933. Use of the phrase was further encouraged by its choice by Jean Renoir for his 1937 film *La Grande Illusion*, about French pilots captured by the Germans in the First World War.

1st Marquess of ANGLESEY English cavalry officer
(1768–1854)

1 By God! I've lost my leg!

At the Battle of Waterloo (1815), Lord Uxbridge (later to
become Marquess of Anglesey) said this to the Duke of
Wellington, who replied, 'Have you, by God?' and rode on.
The partly severed leg was amputated and buried in a garden
in the village of Waterloo. He consequently acquired the
nickname 'One-Leg'. Discussed in Elizabeth Longford,
Wellington: The Years of the Sword, Chap. 23 (1969). Lord
Angelsey, *One Leg: The Life and letters of Henry William Paget,
1st Marquess of Anglesey, K.G.* (1961), has 'the popular version': 'By God, sir, I've lost my leg!' 'By God, sir, so you have!'
David Howarth, *Waterloo: A Near Run Thing* (1959), has
'another even more evocative and even less likely version'
putting it the other way round: 'By God, sir, you've lost your
leg.' 'By God, sir, so I have.' Howarth also does not have the
Duke riding away but supporting 'Uxbridge in the saddle
until his aide-de-camp and some soldiers took him off his
horse and carried him away.'

ANIMAL CRACKERS American film 1930. Script by
Morrie Ryskind, from a musical by himself and George
S. Kaufman. With the Marx Brothers.

2 Hello, I must be going.

From the song, 'Hooray for Captain Spaulding', written by
Harry Ruby and Bert Kalmar, and sung by Groucho. Hence
Hello I Must be Going!, title of a record album (1982) by Phil
Collins.

Paul ANKA Canadian singer and songwriter (1941–)

3 And now the end is near
And so I face the final curtain,
My friend, I'll say it clear,
I'll state my case of which I'm certain.
I've lived a life that's full, I've travelled each
      and evr'y highway
And more, much more than this, I did it my way.

'My Way' (1965). Anka's English lyric (1969) replaced the
very different French one by Gilles Thibaut for the original
song '*Comme d'habitude*' (with music by Claude François
and Jacques Revaux). Anka was quoted in 1979 as saying: 'It
was three o'clock in the morning in New York. It was pour-
ing with rain and it came to me. And I said, "Wow, that's
it, that's for Sinatra" … and then I cried.' A clear-eyed look
at the lyrics reveals that they are at best not entirely literate, nor is their meaning clear. But that is the song's apparent strength – people can (and have) read into it whatever

they like – above all, a feeling of triumphant individualism,
that 'I' counts most of all. It gives them a feeling of self-
justification, even if without any real basis. Lord George-
Brown made an odd use of this song when he entitled his
1971 autobiography *In My Way*, but referring to 'My Way' he
undoubtedly was.

Noël ANNAN (later Lord Annan) English academic
and writer (1916–2000)

4 The day of the jewelled epigram is past and,
whether one likes it or not, one is moving into the
stern puritanical era of the four-letter word.

Quoted in *The Observer* (20 February 1966) as having been
spoken in the House of Lords. Compare what the future
Lord Curzon said on hearing Disraeli's speeches in the
House of Commons: 'There was an air of expectancy whenever he spoke. Men were on the look out for the jewelled
phrase, the exquisite epigram, the stinging sneer. He was like
the conjuror on a platform, whose audience with open
mouths awaited the next trick' – quoted in Kenneth Rose,
Superior Person (1969).

ANONYMOUS

5 Absinthe makes the tart grow fonder.

In Sir Seymour Hicks's *Vintage Years* (1943) this is given
as a toast proposed by one Hugh Drummond. It rides on
the back of 'absinthe makes the heart grow fonder', the
original pun, which has been ascribed (inevitably perhaps)
to Oscar Wilde, but also to Addison Mizner, the American
architect (1872–1933) and so quoted in *The Treasury of
Humorous Quotations*, eds Esar & Bentley (1951). The proverb
'absence makes the heart grow fonder' was first recorded
around 1850.

6 Ah! Ah! *ça ira, ça ira*
Les aristocrates à la lanterne.

Refrain of French revolutionary song, sung to the catchy
tune of '*Le Carillon national*', was first heard when the
Parisians marched on Versailles (5–6 October 1789). *Ça
ira*, though almost impossible to translate, means something like 'That will certainly happen', 'Things will work
out'. *À la lanterne* is the equivalent of the modern 'string
'em up' (*lanterne* being a street lamp in Paris useful for
hanging aristocrats). The inspiration for the first line of the
refrain may have been Benjamin Franklin's recent use of
the phrase in connection with the American Revolution
of 1776.

1 **All publicity is good publicity.**

An almost proverbial saying, certainly around in the 1960s but itself probably as old as the public-relations industry. Alternative forms include: 'There's no such thing as bad publicity', see BEHAN 58:5, 'There's no such thing as over-exposure – only bad exposure', 'Don't read it – measure it' and 'I don't care what the papers say about me as long as they spell my name right.' The latter saying has been attributed to the American Tammany leader 'Big Tim' Sullivan. *The Oxford Dictionary of Proverbs* (2004) includes it in the form 'Any publicity is good publicity', but finds no example before 1974. Earlier formulations include: James Agate in *Ego 7* (for 19 February 1944) quoting Arnold Bennett, 'All praise is good', and adds: 'I suppose the same could be said about publicity'; 'Publicity, darling, just publicity. Any kind is better than none at all' – Raymond Chandler in the *Black Mask* (26 December 1933); 'It has been my experience, sir, that the normal person enjoys seeing his or her name in print, irrespective of what is said about them' – P.G. Wodehouse, 'Jeeves Takes Charge' in *Carry On, Jeeves* (1925). See also COHAN 148:6.

2 **And what they could not eat that night,**
The queen next morning fried.

Referring to a bag pudding, well-stuffed with plums, this tantalizing couplet comes from a nursery rhyme, 'When good King Arthur ruled this land, / He was a goodly king.' *The Oxford Dictionary of Nursery Rhymes* (1951) finds a version about 1799.

3 **Any reform that does not result in the exact opposite of what it was intended to do must be considered a success.**

Quoted by Katharine Whitehorn in *The Observer* (1992), but untraced. However, Samuel Taylor Coleridge wrote in *Biographia Literaria* (1815–16): 'Every reform, however necessary, will by weak minds be carried to an excess which will itself need reforming.' Peter F. Drucker (1909–), the American management consultant and author, has written: 'Look at governmental programs for the past fifty years. Every single one – except for warfare – achieved the exact opposite of its announced goal.' Compare also what Garrett Hardin (1915–), an American biologist, wrote in the February 1974 issue of *Fortune*: 'You can never do merely one thing. The law applies to any action that changes something in a complex system. The point is that an action taken to alleviate a problem will trigger several effects, some of which may offset or even negate the one intended.'

4 **Behind every great man stands a woman.**

An unascribed saying that takes several forms and is probably most often encountered nowadays in parodied versions. Working backwards, here are some of the parodies: 'Behind every good man is a good woman – I mean an exhausted one' – the Duchess of York, speech, September 1987; 'As usual there's a great woman behind every idiot' – John Lennon (quoted 1979); 'Behind every successful man you'll find a woman who has nothing to wear' – L. Grant Glickman (quoted 1977) *or* James Stewart (quoted 1979); 'We in the industry know that behind every successful screenwriter stands a woman. And behind her stands his wife' – Groucho Marx (quoted 1977); 'The road to success is filled with women pushing their husbands along' – Lord (Thomas R.) Dewar, quoted in Stevenson, *The Home Book of Quotations* (1967); 'And behind every man who is a *failure* there's a woman, too!' – John Ruge, cartoon caption, *Playboy* (March 1967); 'Behind every successful man stands a surprised mother-in-law' – Hubert Humphrey, speech (1964).

An early example of the basic expression occurs in an interview with Lady Dorothy Macmillan, wife of the then just retired British Prime Minister (7 December 1963). In the *Daily Sketch*, Godfrey Winn concluded his piece with the typical sentiment (his capitals): 'NO MAN SUCCEEDS WITHOUT A GOOD WOMAN BEHIND HIM. WIFE OR MOTHER. IF IT IS BOTH, HE IS TWICE BLESSED INDEED.'

The *Evening Standard* (18 April 1961) carried an advertisement showing a spaceman (Yuri Garagrin was in the news at that time) drifting off into space with the slogan, 'Behind every great man there's a bottle of Green Shield' (Worthington beer). In the film *The Country Girl* (US 1954), William Holden spoke the lines: 'That's what my ex-wife used to keep reminding me of, tearfully. She had a theory that behind every great man there was a great woman.' In *Love All*, a little-known play by Dorothy L. Sayers, which opened at the Torch Theatre, Knightsbridge, London, on 9 April 1940, and closed before the end of the month, was this: 'Every great man has a woman behind him ... And every great woman has some man or other in front of her, tripping her up.' Even earlier, Sayers herself referred to it as an old saying in *Gaudy Night*, Chap. 3 (1935). Harriet Vane is talking to herself, musing on the problems of the great woman who must either die unwed or find a still greater man to marry her: 'Wherever you find a great man, you will find a great mother or a great wife standing behind him – or so they used to say. It would be interesting to know how many great women have had great fathers and husbands behind them.'

1 **Bell, book and candle.**

As in the title of John Van Druten's play (1950; film US 1958) about a publisher who discovers his girlfriend is a witch, this refers to a solemn form of excommunication from the Roman Catholic Church. *Bartlett* (1980) says the ceremony has been current since the 8th century AD. There is a version dating from AD1200 which goes: 'Do to the book [meaning, close it], quench the candle, ring the bell.' These actions symbolize the spiritual darkness the person is condemned to when denied further participation in the sacraments of the church.

Sir Thomas Malory in *Le Morte d'Arthur* (1485) has: 'I shall curse you with book and bell and candle.' Shakespeare has the modern configuration in *King John*, III.ii.22 (1596): 'Bell, book and candle shall not drive me back.'

2 **Better the chill blast of winter than the hot breath of a pursuing elephant.**

Said to be a 'Chinese saying' and included in *Livres Sans Nom*, five anonymous pamphlets (1929–33) by Geoffrey Madan (though not in all versions). As with most such sayings, authenticity is in doubt (compare CONFUCIUS 152:1). In any case, might not Madan have invented it himself? The matter is discussed in *The Lyttelton Hart-Davis Letters*, Vol. 4 (1982).

3 **Between the revolution and the firing squad there is always time for a bottle of champagne.**

A Russian prince is supposed to have said this – as suggested in *The Sunday Times* (2 June 1996). This interesting parallel was produced by Derek Robinson. He remembered the following passage from Claud Cockburn's autobiography *In Time of Trouble* (1956) where the old rogue is describing Washington DC in June 1931 when President Hoover announced a one-year suspension of payment of debts between governments (because of the spread of the Depression to Europe). 'Violent wrangling' broke out over the exact terms of the moratorium between Washington and Paris. 'When "agreement in principle" was finally reached, M. Paul Claudel invited a number of American officials and others to the French Embassy to celebrate the event ... In the drawing-room at the Embassy M. Claudel greeted them. "Gentlemen," he said simply, "in the little moment that remains to us between the crisis and the catastrophe, we may as well take a glass of champagne."' (Claudel, though a diplomat, is now remembered as poet, playwright and essayist.) Then at the time of Munich (1938), Cockburn recalls that a Russian journalist, Mikhail Koltzov, quoted the Claudel story back at him (Cockburn). Could this be the original of the 'Russian prince'? Derek adds: 'I'm sure I recall a French general being quoted as saying something

similar when Dien Bien Phu – which was where he was in command – was about to fall [1954]. In his case, I think it was more like: "Gentlemen, in the short time we have between the crisis and the calamity, we might as well drink a glass of champagne."'

4 **The British, as usual, will fight to the last Frenchman.**

Anthony Rhodes, *Propaganda: The Art of Persuasion in World War II* (1976): 'Already in the "phony war" of 1939–40 the [German] Propaganda Ministry was organizing broadcasts to France, sowing discord between the Western Allies. The French were told that the British had sent only six divisions, and that the eighty French divisions would have to bear the brunt of the fighting. The British, as usual, would fight "to the last Frenchman".' A German newsreel included in the documentary *Le Chagrin et la Pitié* contains this passage (in German): 'This is the war of the Franco-English plutocrats. They began this war rashly without taking any heed of the consequences, to fight for the English Lords. Not only to the last Frenchman, but to the last French house.' This may date from 1940/1. Note how in the film *Passage to Marseilles* (US 1943), Sydney Greenstreet as a Nazi sympathizer gets to say: 'The British will fight to the very last drop of French blood.'

Thomas D. Fuller (2005) summarized earlier uses of the jibe: 'The phrase is referred to by Sir Edmund Ironside (a WWI general who was appointed chief of the imperial general staff when WWII broke out) in his diary entry for September 30, 1939, thusly: "Daladier [the French Prime Minister] has been talking to the British Ambassador in Paris and telling him that the appearance of even one Regiment of British in the Maginot Line would hearten up the French and stop the [German] propaganda that the British are willing to fight to the last Frenchman." This is from *Time Unguarded: The Ironside Diaries 1937–1940* (1963). Earlier still is a reference (in a secondary, not primary, source) in "Cartoons of the Third Reich", an article by W.A. Coupe in *History Today*, Vol. 48 (September 1998): "Goering, in a speech of September 9th, 1939, had revived the hoary notion from 1914 that 'Britain would fight to the last Frenchman.'"' The 1914 reference is, if not confirmed, at least robustly seconded (by another secondary source) in David French, *The Strategy of the Lloyd George Coalition 1916–1918*, Chap. 7 (1995): "In 1914 the British had intended to fight to the last Frenchman ..." I haven't yet found a primary source to confirm 1914, but I have one for 1918. In a January 20, 1918 letter from Kurt Hahn, a German Foreign Service officer who later became private secretary to Prince Max von Baden, to Lieutenant Colonel von Haeften, we find: "To believe that the British will come to an understanding with us on

Belgium is to despise your enemy. It is the same mood in which people say that the British will fight to the last Frenchman." This is quoted in *The Memoirs of Prince Max of Baden*, Vol. 1, Chap. 3 (1928).'

1 Champagne for your real friends, real pain for your sham friends.

An Edwardian toast that the painter Francis Bacon (1909–92) acquired from his father, according to Daniel Farson, *The Gilded Gutter Life of Francis Bacon* (1993). But it is of earlier provenance. In R.S. Surtees, *Jorrocks's Jaunts and Jollities* (1838), the famous fox-hunter Mr Jorrocks gives a dinner party during the course of which he comments on champagne and Surtees has him pronouncing it 'shampain'. 'Mr. Jorrocks then called upon the company in succession for a toast, a song, or a sentiment. Nimrod gave, "The Royal Stag-hounds"; Crane gave, "Champagne to our real friends, and real pain to our sham friends" ... and Mr Spiers, like a patriotic printer, gave "The Liberty of the Press", which he said was like fox-hunting – "if we have it not we die" – all of which Mr Jorrocks applauded as if he had never heard them before, and drank in bumpers.'

2 Channel storms. Continent isolated.

The original of this English newspaper headline remains untraced (if, indeed, it ever existed). In Maurice Bowra's *Memories 1898–1939* (1966) he recalled Ernst Kantorowicz, a refugee from Germany in the 1930s: 'He liked the insularity of England and was much pleased by the newspaper headline, "Channel storms. Continent isolated", just as he liked the imagery in, "Shepherd's Bush combed for dead girl's body".'

As an indicator of English isolationism, the phrase does indeed seem to have surfaced in the 1930s. John Gunther in his *Inside Europe* (1938 edition) had: 'Two or three winters ago a heavy storm completely blocked traffic across the Channel. "CONTINENT ISOLATED", the newspapers couldn't help saying.' The cartoonist Russell Brockbank drew a newspaper placard stating 'FOG IN CHANNEL – CONTINENT ISOLATED' (as shown in his book *Round the Bend with Brockbank*, published by Temple Press, 1948). By the 1960s and 1970s, and by the time of Britain's attempts to join the European Community, the headline was more often invoked as: 'FOG IN CHANNEL. EUROPE ISOLATED.'

3 Che sera sera.

In 1956 Doris Day had a hit with the song 'Whatever Will Be Will Be', the title being a translation of this foreign phrase which was also used in the choruses. She had sung it in the re-make of Alfred Hitchcock's *The Man Who Knew Too Much* in that year. Ten years later Geno Washington and

the Ram Jam Band had a hit with a song entitled '*Que Sera Sera*'. So is it *che* or *que*? There is no such phrase as *che sera sera* in modern Spanish or Italian, though *che* is an Italian word and *sera* is a Spanish one. *Que sera? sera?* in Spanish translates as 'what will be? will be?' which is not quite right; *lo que sera, sera* makes sense but is not the wording of the song. However, in Christopher Marlowe's *Dr Faustus* (published 1604) Faustus's first soliloquy has: 'What doctrine call you this? Che sera, sera, / What will be, shall be.' This is an old spelling of what would be, in modern Italian *che sara, sara*. In *Dr Faustus*, however, it is probably Old French.

The *idea* behind the proverbial saying is simpler to trace. 'What must be, must be' can be found as far back as Chaucer's 'Knight's Tale' (about 1390): 'When a thyng is shapen, it shal be.' However, *che sera sera* is the form in which the Duke of Bedford's motto has always been written and so presumably that, too, is Old French or Old Italian.

4 Cometh the hour, cometh the man.

John 4:23 has 'But the hour cometh, and now is' and there is an English proverb 'Opportunity makes the man' (though originally, in the 14th century, it was 'makes the *thief*'), but when did the phrases come together? Andrew Marvell's poem 'The First Anniversary of the Government Under His Highness the Lord Protector [Oliver Cromwell]' (1655) has: 'If these the times, then this must be the man.' Thomas Carlyle's *History of the French Revolution*, Pt 3, Bk 7, Chap. 7 (1837) has: 'In old Broglie's time, six years ago, this Whiff of Grapeshot was promised; but it could not be given then; could not have profited then. Now, however, the time is come for it, and the man.' Harriet Martineau entitled her biography of Toussaint L'Ouverture (1840) *The Hour and the Man*. An American, William Yancey, said about Jefferson Davis, President-elect of the Confederacy in 1861: 'The man and the hour have met', which says the same thing in a different way. P.G. Wodehouse in *Aunts Aren't Gentlemen* (1974) has: 'And the hour ... produced the man.'

Earlier, at the climax of Sir Walter Scott's novel *Guy Mannering*, Chap. 54 (1815), Meg Merrilies says, 'Because the Hour's come, and the Man.' In the first edition and in the *magnum opus* edition that Scott supervised in his last years the phrase is emphasized by putting it in italics.

Then, in 1818, Scott used 'The hour's come, but not [sic] the man' as the fourth chapter heading in *The Heart of Midlothian*, adding in a footnote: 'There is a tradition, that while a little stream was swollen into a torrent by recent showers, the discontented voice of the Water Spirit [or Kelpie] was heard to pronounce these words. At the same moment a man, urged on by his fate, or, in Scottish language, *fey*, arrived at a gallop, and prepared to cross the water. No remonstrance from the bystanders was of power to stop him – he plunged into the stream, and perished.' Both these examples appear to be hinting at some earlier core saying that is still untraced. Frank Muir pointed out (1990) that 'The hour brings forth the man' is a variant.

It appears from a survey of ten British newspapers in recent years that the saying is especially a weapon (or cliché) in the sportswriter's armoury. From *Today* (22 June 1986): 'Beating England may not be winning the World Cup, but, for obvious reasons, it would come a pretty close second back in Buenos Aires. Cometh the hour, cometh the man? Destiny beckons. England beware.' From *The Times* (13 August 1991): '"Graham [Gooch] is a very special guy," [Ted] Dexter said. "It has been a case of 'Cometh the hour, cometh the man.' I do not know anyone who would have taken the tough times in Australia harder than he did."' From *The Scotsman* (29 February 1992): 'In the maxim of "Cometh the hour, cometh the man", both the Scotland [Rugby Union] manager, Duncan Paterson, and forwards coach, Richie Dixon, indicated yesterday the need to look to the future.'

The reason why the phrase is so popular with sportswriters may be because it was notably used (about himself) by Cliff Gladwin, the Derbyshire and England cricketer, during the first test match against South Africa at Durban (20 December 1948). England were 117 for 8 requiring 128 to win, when Gladwin walked out to bat, remarking to Dudley Nourse, the South Africa captain, as he did so: 'Cometh the hour, cometh the man!' The last ball of the match hit Gladwin on the thigh and he and Alec Bedser ran a leg-bye to win the match for England.

1 Comfort the afflicted, and afflict the comfortable.

This is a good example of a quotation formula that can be applied to more than one subject, to the extent that it is difficult to say what it was originally directed at. However, although *Mencken* (1942) has 'Anon.' saying, 'The duty of a newspaper is to comfort the afflicted and afflict the comfortable', and newspapers seem likely to have been the original subject of the remark, in John K. Winkler, *W.R. Hearst: An American Phenomenon* (1928), is this: 'For forty years he has carried out, rather literally, the dictum of Mr Dooley [i.e. the creation of Finley Peter Dunne] that the mission of a modern newspaper is to "comfort the afflicted and afflict the comfortable".'

In the film *Inherit the Wind* (1960), Gene Kelly gets to say to Fredric March: 'Mr Brady, it's the duty of a newspaper to comfort the afflicted and to flick the comfortable.' To Michael Ramsey, the former Archbishop of Canterbury (1904–88), has been attributed this version: 'The duty of the church is to comfort the disturbed and to disturb the comfortable.' Clare Booth Luce introduced Eleanor

Roosevelt at a 1950 dinner, saying: 'No woman has ever so comforted the distressed – or so distressed the comfortable' – also said to be in *Anna Eleanor Roosevelt: Memorial Addresses in the House of Representatives, Joint Committe on Printing*.

2 Dance to your daddy.
My little babby ...
In a little dishy,
You shall have a fishy when the boat comes in.

Nursery rhyme (first recorded about 1806). Hence, *When the Boat Comes In*, title of a BBC TV drama series (1975–7).

3 Der spring is sprung
Der grass is riz

I wonder where dem boidies is?
Der little boids is on der wing,
Ain't dat absoid?
Der little wings is on der boid!

Entitled 'The Budding Bronx', this is described as by 'Anon (New York)' in Arnold Silcock's *Verse and Worse* (1952). Beyond that no source has been found.

4 Do not stand at my grave and weep.
I am not there, I do not sleep.
I am the thousand winds that blow.
I am diamond glints on snow.
I am the sunlight on ripened grain.
I am gentle autumnal rain.
When you waken in the morning hush.
I am the soft uplifting rush
Of quiet birds in circled flight.
I am the soft stars that shine at night.
Do not stand at my grave and cry –
I am not there. I did not die.

A poem that the British soldier Stephen Cummins left behind him when he was killed by an IRA landmine in Londonderry in 1989. In November 1995 when these words were reprised on the BBC TV programme *Bookworm* – read by the dead soldier's father – there were apparently 10,000 requests from viewers for the text of the poem. What is not clear is who wrote it, though it could have been Cummins himself. Debbie Turley, his fiancée, was quoted in 1989 as saying, 'He used to write every day and he was always writing poems.'

Barbara King, calligrapher of Llandeilo, stated (1996) that she had looked into the copyright position. It transpired that, before Cummins used it in his farewell note, an American called Marilyn Rhinehart had sent the poem to Terry Boyle, a Republican prisoner of Strabane (with the last line reading, 'While Ireland lives I will not die'). Another very similar poem with just a few divergences in the text has been found as written by an Englishwoman, Mary E. Frye, in 1932.

1 **Do right and fear no man.**

CODP dates this saying from about 1450 in the form 'The beste wysdom that I Can [know], Ys to doe well, and drede no man.' But has anybody notable taken the motto to themselves? A book of mottoes that I have lists several along the lines of 'do right and fear not/naught/nothing' but not this precise form. Nowadays it tends to get quoted as the first part of a saying that ends '… don't write and fear no woman'. This 'Epigram' from the Cincinnati *Enquirer* (about 1918) is attributed to the columnist Luke McLuke (J.S. Hastings) by *The Home Book of Proverbs, &c.*, ed. Burton Stevenson (1948). Elbert Hubbard is credited with 'Wrong no man and write no woman' in *The Treasury of Humorous Quotations*, eds Esar & Bentley (1951).

2 **The dove says, Coo, coo, what shall I do?**
I can scarce maintain two.
Pooh, pooh, says the wren, I have ten,
And keep them all like gentlemen.

Nursery rhyme (recorded by 1853), of which there is more than one version. *The Oxford Dictionary of Nursery Rhymes* (1951) suggests that 'What shall I do? I can scarce maintain two' is how country folk interpret a dove's (or pigeon's) cooing, 'referring to the fact she seldom has more than two eggs in each brood. This is in contrast to the wren who rears a family of fourteen, fifteen, or sixteen.'

3 **Early to bed, early to rise,**
Never get tight, and advertise.

Prof. Wolfgang Mieder has explored updates of 'Early to bed and early to rise' in *Proverbs Are Never Out of Season* (1993). He found this in *Life* Magazine, No. 833 (1893) as a recipe for success. More recently, 'Early to bed, early to rise, work like hell and advertise' has been ascribed to the American entrepreneur, Dr Scholl. A caption to a *Punch* cartoon (13 January 1989) was: '[Father to son] Remember this: early to bed, early to rise, work like hell and computerize.'

All these are variations on the proverb 'Early to bed and early to rise, makes a man healthy, wealthy and wise.' This was in use by 1639, but in 1496 it was already being described as an old English proverb, in the form 'Who so will rise early shall be holy, healthy and zealy' [meaning happy or fortunate]. James Thurber, however, said: 'Early to rise and early to bed, makes a male healthy and wealthy and dead.' Yet another version, from English playgrounds, is: 'Early to rise and early to bed, / Makes life so boring, I wish I was dead.'

4 *Et in Arcadia ego.*

One finds these words associated with tombs, skulls and Arcadian shepherds in classical paintings, but not before the 17th century. Most notably the phrase occurs in two paintings by the French artist Nicolas Poussin, both of which depict shepherds reading the words carved on a tomb. One painted 1626–8 hangs in Chatsworth House, Derbyshire; the other, *The Shepherds of Arcady*, 1630–5, in the Louvre. Just before this, however, the Italian artist Guercino had painted a painting known as '*Et in Arcadia ego*', which hangs in the Galleria Corsino, Rome. This was painted no later than 1623.

Is the inscription meant to suggest that, in death, the speaker is in Arcadia – the Greek name for a place of rural peace and calm taken from an actual area in the Peloponnese? Or is he saying he was formerly there? '*Et in Arcadia ego vixi*' ('I lived') or '*Et in Arcadia fui pastor*' ('I was a shepherd') are variants. Or is it Death speaking – 'Even in Arcadia, I, Death, cannot be avoided'?

L.A. Moritz of University College, Cardiff, wrote in a letter to *The Times* (27 January 1982), 'The Latin cannot mean what Goethe and many others … took it to mean: "I too was in Arcadia." Its only possible meaning is "Even in Arcadia am I" … this association of the pastoral Arcadia with death goes back to Virgil's tenth *Eclogue*, which first placed idyllic shepherds in an Arcadian landscape.'

Erwin Panofsky pointed this out first in *Philosophy and History, Essays presented to E. Cassirer* (1936), in which he claimed that since the 18th century the English had had an instinct not shared by Continentals for making a special kind of sense out of the classical tag. '"Even in Arcadia I, Death, hold sway" … while long forgotten on the Continent remained familiar' in England, he asserted, and ultimately 'became part of what may be termed a specifically English or "insular" tradition – a tradition which tended to retain the idea of a *memento mori*. Skulls juxtaposed with roses could be conventionally employed as an emblem of the omnipotence of Death, whose power is not finally to be excluded even from the sequestered "safe" world of pastoral.'

In German literature, the phrase first appeared in *Winterreise* (1769) by Johann Georg Jacobi: 'Whenever, in a beautiful landscape, I encounter a tomb with the inscription: "I too was in Arcadia", I point it out to my friends, we stop a moment, press each other's hands, and proceed.' The phrase was later used by Goethe as the motto of his *Travels in Italy* (1816).

In England, Sir Joshua Reynolds painted a picture in 1769 on which a tomb can be seen with the words inscribed. In Evelyn Waugh's *Brideshead Revisited* (1945), the narrator, while an undergraduate at Oxford, adorns his rooms with a 'human skull lately purchased from the School of Medicine which, resting in a bowl of roses, formed, at the moment, the chief decoration of my table. It bore the motto "*Et in Arcadia ego*" inscribed on its forehead.' (Book One of the novel is entitled '*Et in Arcadia Ego*'.)

1 Everyman, I will go with thee and be thy guide,
In thy most need to go by thy side.

From the *Everyman* morality play, written sometime between 1509 and 1591. These legendary lines are spoken by Knowledge and thus have been an appropriate choice as a slogan to promote the Everyman's Library series of book reprints of the classics. These have been published by J.M. Dent in Britain since the 1900s (and by E.P. Dutton in the US). Compare MILTON 322:8 and SIDNEY 431:3.

2 Every man likes the smell of his own farts.

Quoted in *Viking Book of Aphorisms*, eds Auden & Kronenberger (1962), and described as of Icelandic origin. Might it have been the editors' invention? See also AUDEN 44:4. Earlier, Erasmus's *Adagia* had this: '*Suus cuique crepitus bene olet*' – quoted in Montaigne, *Essais*, ed. Céard, Bk 3, Chap. 8, which has it as: '*Stercus cuique suum bene olet*' (with faeces instead of fart).

3 The Father, the Son and the Pigeon.

A French rhyme that appeared in the introduction to *Some Limericks* (1928), privately printed by Norman Douglas (published 1969 as *The Norman Douglas Limerick Book*):

Il y avait un jeune homme de Dijon
Qui n'avait que peu de religion.
Il dit: 'Quant à moi,
Je déteste tous les trois,
Le Père, et le Fils, et le Pigeon.'

Which may be translated:

There was a young man of Dijon
Who had only a little religion.
He said, 'As for me,
I detest all the three,
The Father, the Son and the Pigeon.'

To talk of the Holy Ghost in these terms seems to have been nothing new, even in the 1920s. Lord Berners describing his time at Eton in the 1890s in *A Distant Prospect* (1945) tells of a friend called Manston: 'At first I was inclined to be shocked by his irreverence – for instance, when he had said that the Trinity put him in mind of a music-hall turn – the Father, the Son and the Performing Pigeon.'

4 *Forget-Me-Not Lane.*

Title of a play (1971) by Peter Nichols. Derived from the Flanagan and Allen song 'Down Forget-Me-Not Lane' (1941) written by Horatio Nicholls, Charlie Chester and Reg Morgan.

5 For want of a nail, the shoe is lost; for want of a shoe, the horse is lost; for want of a horse, the rider is lost.

Proverbial expression (known by the 17th century) about the perils of penny-pinching or lack of attention to detail. Hence, the title of a novel, *For Want of a Nail* (1965) by Melvyn Bragg.

6 Friday night too tired, Saturday night too drunk, Sunday night too far away.

The lament of an anonymous (Australian) sheep-shearer's wife. Hence, *Sunday Too Far Away*, title of a film (Australia 1977).

7 Georgie Porgie, pudding and pie,
Kissed the girls and made them cry;
When the girls came out to play,
Georgie Porgie ran away.

Nursery rhyme (first recorded 1844). Hence, *Kiss the Girls and Make Them Cry*, title of a BBC TV drama series (1979).

8 *God Protect Me from My Friends.*

Title of a book (1956) by Gavin Maxwell about Salvatore Giuliano, the Sicilian bandit. From the proverbial expression: 'I can look after my enemies, but God protect me from my friends.' *CODP* traces this to 1477 in the forms 'God keep/save/defend us from our friends' and says it now often appears simply as, 'Save us from our friends'. It is common to many languages. 'With friends like these/with a Hungarian for a friend, who needs enemies?' are but two versions.

The diarist Chips Channon (21 February 1938) has: 'This evening a group of excited Communists even invaded the Lobby, demanding Anthony [Eden]'s reinstatement. God preserve us from our friends, they did him harm.' *The Morris Dictionary of Word and Phrase Origins* (1977) finds a quotation from Maréchal Villars who, on leaving Louis XIV, said: 'Defend me from my friends; I can defend myself from my enemies.' In 1821, George Canning rhymed: 'Give me the avowed, the erect, the manly foe, / Bold I can meet – perhaps may turn his blow! / But of all plagues, Good Heaven, thy wrath can send, / Save, save, Oh, save me from the candid friend!' Charlotte Brontë also used the idea in a letter (untraced) in response to a patronizing review of one of her books.

1 *The Good, the Bad and the Ugly.*

English title of the Italian 'spaghetti Western' *Il Buono, il Bruto, il Cattivo* (1966), co-written and directed by Sergio Leone. Colonel Oliver North, giving evidence to the Washington hearings on the Irangate scandal in the summer of 1987, said: 'I came here to tell you the truth – the good, the bad, and the ugly.' Two headlines, both from *The Independent* (16 September 1996): 'The Good ... the Bad ... and the Ugly: The Premiership's Leading Scorers'; 'The Good, the Bad and the Spoilt: How Children React'.

2 A great man! Why, I doubt if there are six his equal in the whole of Boston.

On Shakespeare. Said to W.E. Gladstone by an unnamed Bostonian. Quoted in the book *Quote ... Unquote* (1978). *Mencken* (1942) has it that Gladstone got it from Lionel A. Tollemache (23 December 1897) as: 'There are not ten men in Boston equal to Shakespeare.'

3 Hark the herald angels sing
Mrs Simpson's pinched our king.

Within days of the abdication of King Edward VIII in December 1936 schoolchildren were singing this. A letter from Clement Attlee on 26 December included the information that his daughter Felicity had produced the 'ribald verse which was new to me' – quoted in Kenneth Harris, *Attlee* (1982). Iona and Peter Opie in *The Lore and Language of Schoolchildren* (1959) comment on the rapidity with which the rhyme spread across the country. The constitutional crisis did not become public until 25 November, the King abdicated on 10 December, 'yet at a school party in Swansea given before the end of term ... when the tune played happened to be "Hark the Herald Angels Sing", a mistress found herself having to restrain her small children from singing this lyric, known to all of them, which cannot have been composed more than three weeks previously'.

4 Has anyone here been raped and speaks English?

The absurdity of the war correspondent's job was encapsulated by a question heard during the war in the Congo (1960). Thousands of frightened Belgian civilians were waiting for a plane to take them to safety from the newly independent ex-Belgian colony when a BBC television reporter walked among them with his camera team and posed this question. The incident was reported – and used as the title of a book *Anyone Here Been Raped and Speaks English* (1978) – by the American journalist Edward Behr, who commented: 'The callous cry summed up for me the tragic, yet wildly surrealist nature of the country itself.'

5 Hear no evil, see no evil, speak no evil.

Bartlett (1980) describes this as a legend related to the Three Wise Monkeys and carved over the door of the Sacred Stable, Nikko, Japan, in the 17th century. The three monkeys are shown with their paws over, respectively, their ears, eyes and mouth. This is referred to in a poem 'The Three Wise Monkeys' by Pauline Carrington Rust Bouvé (1860–1928) – 'The three wise monkeys of Nikko, / Who see, speak, hear but the good!' 'Hear, see, keep silence' (often accompanied by a sketch of the Three Wise Monkeys) is the motto of the United Grand Lodge of Freemasons in the form '*Audi, Vide, Tace*'.

The motto of Yorkshiremen is said to be:

Hear all, see all, say nowt,
Aight all, sup all, pay nowt,
And if ever tha does owt for nowt
Do it for thisen.

A Noel Gay song written in 1938 for Sandy Powell, the Yorkshire comedian, had the title 'Hear all, see all, say nowt'. *See No Evil* was the American title of the film *Blind Terror* (UK 1971); *See No Evil, Hear No Evil* was the title of a film (US 1989).

6 He died as he lived – at sea.

On Ramsay MacDonald, the British Labour Prime Minister, who died during a cruise (1937). Quoted in Atyeo & Green, *Don't Quote Me* (1981). However, Hesketh Pearson, *Lives of the Wits* (1962), has this: 'Whistler had an unforgiving nature, and on hearing some years later that [William Stott, a disciple] had expired during an ocean voyage he merely remarked: "So he died at sea, where he always was."'

7 Here lies a poor woman who always was tired,
For she lived in a place where help wasn't hired,
Her last words on earth were, 'Dear friends,
    I am going,
Where washing ain't done nor cooking nor
    sewing,
And everything there is exact to my wishes,
For there they don't eat, there's no washing of
    dishes,
I'll be where loud anthems will always be ringing
(But having no voice, I'll be out of the singing).
Don't mourn for me now, don't grieve for me
    never,
For I'm going to do nothing for ever and ever.'

Sometimes referred to as 'The Maid-of-all-Works' Epitaph' or 'The Tired Woman's Epitaph', this has two possible sources. As 'an epitaph for Catherine Alsopp, a Sheffield washerwoman, who hanged herself, 7 August 1905', it was composed by herself and included in E. Jameson, *1000 Curiosities of Britain* (1937). But a letter in *The Spectator* (2 December 1922) from a correspondent at the British Museum asserted that the inscription was once to be found in a churchyard in Bushey, Hertfordshire. A copy of the text was made before 1860, but the actual stone had been destroyed by 1916. It was also discussed in *Notes and Queries* for March 1889 and *Longman's Magazine* for January 1884. *Benham* (1907) states that it had been quoted 'before 1850'.

1   Here lies Fred,
    Who was alive and is dead:
    Had it been his father,
    I had much rather;
    Had it been his brother,
    Still better than another;
    Had it been his sister,
    No one would have missed her;
    Had it been the whole generation,
    Still better for the nation:
    But since 'tis only Fred,
    Who was alive and is dead, –
    There's no more to be said.

Epitaph on Frederick Louis, Prince of Wales (1707–51), eldest son of George II and father of George III, quoted by Horace Walpole in an appendix to his *Memoirs of George II* (1847). Frederick quarrelled with his father and was banished from court. Compare from *Frobisher's New Select Collection of Epitaphs ...* (?1790), 'On a tombstone in Cornwall: Here lies honest Ned, / Because he is dead. / Had it been his father ...' *A Collection of Epitaphs ...* (1806) has from 'a headstone in the church-yard of Storrington in the County of Sussex: Here lies the body of Edward Hide; / We laid him here because he died. / We had rather it had been his father. / If it had been his sister, / We should not have miss'd her. / But since 'tis honest Ned / No more shall be said ...' Peter Haining, *Graveyard Wit* (1973), has a version beginning 'Here lies HONEST NED ...' from 'Kirkby Stephen parish church, Westmorland'.

2   Here lies the loyal Duke of Newcastle and his Duchess his second wife by whom he had no issue her name was Margaret Lucas youngest sister to the Lord Lucas of Colchester a noble family for all the brothers were valiant and all the sisters virtuous.

Inscription on the monument of the 1st Duke and Duchess of Newcastle in the North Transept of Westminster Abbey. The monument was erected during the lifetime of William (Cavendish), 1st Duke (1592–1676), his second wife,

Margaret (1623–73), having predeceased him. His duchess was quite a figure in her own right. She wrote plays, letters, verses, a biography of her husband, and an autobiography. *All the Brothers Were Valiant* became the title of a film (US 1953) based on a novel by Ben Ames Williams.

3   Here we go round the mulberry bush.

Derives from the refrain sung in the children's game (first recorded in the mid-19th century, though probably earlier) in which the participants hold hands and dance in a ring. There are numerous variations, using various fruits. Hence, however, the title of the novel (1965; film UK 1967) by Hunter Davies.

    One theory of the rhyme's origin is that a mulberry tree stood in the middle of the exercise yard at Wakefield Prison in Yorkshire. The prisoners would have to go round and round it on a 'cold and frosty morning'. This may be, however, no more than a coincidence.

4   He was my man, but I done him wrong.

From the famous anonymous American ballad 'Frankie and Johnny' (which *Mencken* dates around 1875). There are numerous versions (200 is one estimate) and it may be of Negro origin. 'Frankie and Johnnie were lovers' (or husband and wife) but he (Johnnie) went off with other women – 'He was her man, but he done her wrong.' So, to equal the score, Frankie shoots him and has to be punished for it (in some versions in the electric chair):

> Frankie walked up to the scaffold, as calm as a girl
> could be,
> She turned her eyes to Heaven and said 'Good Lord,
> I'm coming to Thee;
> He was my man, but I done him wrong.'

Bartlett (1980) draws a comparison with Shakespeare, *The Rape of Lucrece* (line 1462): 'Lucrece swears he did her wrong' and *King Lear* (I.ii.161): 'Some villain hath done me wrong.'

    When Mae West's play *Diamond Lil* was transferred to the cinema screen in 1933, it was renamed *She Done Him Wrong* – surely an allusion.

5   Hey diddle diddle,
    The cat and the fiddle,
    The cow jumped over the moon;
    The little dog laughed
    To see such craft,
    And the dish ran away with the spoon.

Traditional nursery rhyme. The question is, how did the penultimate line get changed (in some cases) to 'to see such sport' and, especially, to 'to see such fun' (neither of which rhymes) and thus become sufficiently popular for *To See*

Such Fun to be used as the title of a show starring Tommy Cooper that was presented at the London Palladium in 1971?

The Opies in their nursery-rhyme survey make no mention of the 'fun' version. Research shows that 'sport' is in three standard nursery-rhyme books published in about 1750, 1850 and 1950. Of the 90–100 newish nursery-rhyme books in the Poetry Library published 1981–2000, only seven had 'fun'. In a smaller but older collection (1875–1983) only one (privately published in 1964) had 'fun'. So where, when and how did 'to see such fun' establish its small hold? In America? Well, *The Annotated Mother Goose* (1962) – an American book – merely states that 'to see such fun' is now the usual form.

Compare, however, what is to be found in the first part of J.R.R. Tolkien's *The Lord of the Rings* – viz. *The Fellowship of the Ring* (1954). In the book (but not in the film) Frodo has a song (written by Bilbo) that he sings at the inn called 'At the Sign of the Prancing Pony'. Its verse 12 is:

With a ping and a pong the fiddle-strings broke!
  the cow jumped over the Moon,
And the little dog laughed to see such fun,
And the Saturday dish went off at a run
  with the silver Sunday spoon.

Tolkien seems to have accepted that 'to see such fun' was the correct version of the rhyme he incorporated into his own 'song'.

1 Hickory, dickory, dock,
The mouse ran up the clock.
The clock struck one,
The mouse ran down,
Hickory, dickory, dock.

Children's counting rhyme, first recorded in about 1744, possibly derived from the sheep-counting method, 'hevera, devera, dick'. Hence, *Hickory Dickory Dock*, British title of a Hercule Poirot novel (1955) by Agatha Christie. In the US the book is known as *Hickory Dickory Death*.

2 The higher the monkey climbs, the more he shows his tail.

'The egotistical surgeon is like a monkey; the higher he climbs the more you see of his less attractive features' is an anonymous saying applied to anyone in any profession who has achieved high rank. On BBC Radio *Quote ... Unquote* (29 March 1994), John Oaksey recalled that his father, Geoffrey Lawrence (Lord Oaksey; 1880–1971), had said the same sort of thing about judges and other high-ups in the legal profession, drawing a parallel rather with orangutans. The basic proverbial saying (as above) was discussed in *Notes and Queries* (1887).

3 Hitler
Has only got one ball!
Goering
Has two, but very small!
Himmler
Has something similar,
But poor old Goebbels
Has no balls at all!

This was the title of an anonymous song (sung to the tune of 'Colonel Bogey') that was in existence by 1940. As with 'Not tonight, Josephine' (335:8), the basis for this assertion about the sexuality of a political figure is obscure. The rumour had been widespread in Central Europe in the 1930s, and Martin Page in *Kiss Me Goodnight, Sergeant Major* (1973) wrote of a Czech refugee who had referred in 1938 to the fact that Hitler had been wounded in the First World War, since when '*ihm fehlt einer* [he lacks one]'. Perhaps it was no more than a generalized slight against the Nazi leader's virility, which conveniently fitted the tune and also permitted a 'Goebbels / no balls' rhyme. There had earlier been a 19th-century American ballad about a trade-union leader that began: 'Arthur Hall / Has only got one ball'.

4 Home is where the heart is.

The first appearance of this proverbial expression may well have been in an 1870 American play by J.J. McCloskey, but even then it was 'Home, *they say*, is where the heart is', so it was obviously an established saying by then. *Mencken* (1942) has it as an 'American saying, author unidentified'. Hence, *Where the Heart Is*, title of a film (US 1990), directed by John Boorman.

5 How different – how very different from the home life of our own dear Queen!

One night Sarah Bernhardt (1844–1923) essayed the role of Cleopatra in Shakespeare's *Antony and Cleopatra* during a London season sometime in the reign of Queen Victoria. In the scene where Cleopatra receives the news of Mark Antony's defeat at the Battle of Actium, she stabbed the messenger who brought her the news, 'stormed, raved, frothed at the mouth, wrecked some of the scenery in her frenzy and finally, as the curtain fell, dropped in a shuddering convulsive heap'. As the applause died down, an American visitor overhead a middle-aged British matron saying the above to her friend in the next seat. So attributed by Irvin S. Cobb in *A Laugh a Day Keeps the Doctor Away ...* (1921).

1 If anything can go wrong, it will.

Most commonly known as 'Murphy's Law', this saying dates back to the 1940s. *The Macquarie Dictionary* (1981) suggests that it was named after a character that always made mistakes in a series of educational cartoons published by the US Navy. *CODP* hints that it was invented by George Nichols, a project manager for Northrop, the Californian aviation firm, in 1949. He developed the idea from a remark by a colleague, Captain Edward A. Murphy Jr of the Wright Field-Aircraft Laboratory: 'If there is a wrong way to do something, then someone will do it.'

The most notable demonstration of Murphy's Law is that a piece of bread when dropped on the floor will always fall with its buttered side facing down (otherwise known as the Law of Universal Cussedness). This, however, pre-dates the promulgation of the Law. *Punch* (2 February 1856) had this observation: 'Such is Life. A Little School-girl makes the following pathetic inquiry: "Did you ever know a piece of bread and butter fall on the ground but it was sure to fall on the buttered side?"' In 1867, A.D. Richardson wrote in *Beyond Mississippi*: 'His bread never fell on the buttered side.' In 1884 James Payn composed the lines:

I never had a piece of toast
Particularly long and wide,
But fell upon the sanded floor
And always on the buttered side.

The corollary of this aspect of the Law is that bread always falls buttered side down *except when demonstrating the Law* …

Some have argued that the point of Captain Murphy's original observation was constructive rather than defeatist – it was a prescription for avoiding mistakes in the design of a valve for an aircraft's hydraulic system. If the valve could be fitted in more than one way, then sooner or later someone would fit it the wrong way. The idea was to design it so that the valve could be fitted only the right way. Murphy's Law is also referred to as Sod's Law.

2 I feel no pain, dear mother, now
But oh, I am so dry!
O take me to a brewery
And leave me there to die.

PDQ (1992) gives this as an anonymous 'shanty', but really it is just a parody of an old weepie, 'The Collier's Dying Child' – sometimes known as 'Little Jim' – by the English poet Edward Farmer (?1809–76), of which the eighth verse is:

I have no pain, dear mother, now
But oh! I am so dry:
Just moisten poor Jim's lips once more;
And, mother, don't you cry!

3 If you can remember the sixties you weren't really there.

'Who said "If you can remember the sixties you weren't really there"? I can't remember' – Nancy Banks-Smith in *The Guardian* (2 June 1987), making it clear that this was an established saying by that date, but it was oddly popular at that time: '"If you can remember the sixties, you weren't really there," said a guy from Jefferson Airplane' – *Today* (2 June 1987); 'The best quote about the period came from a leading American hippie – now, I think, something huge on Wall Street – who said: "If you can remember the sixties, you weren't there." There's a lot of truth in that, though I think he's pointing at certain kinds of substance' – *The Independent* (11 March 1989). This hippie might well have been Jerry Rubin.

4 If you want to be happy for a day, go fishing. If you want to be happy for a week, get married. If you want to be happy for a month, kill a pig. If you want to be happy and contented for all time, smoke a pipe.

Quoted by Lord Mason, convenor of the Lords and Commons Pipesmokers' Club in March 1995, but untraced. On the other hand, this version described as a 'Chinese proverb' was heard in 1993: 'If you wish to be happy for an hour, drink wine; if you wish to be happy for three days, get married; if you wish to be happy for eight days, kill your pig and eat it; but if you wish to be happy for ever, *become a gardener*.'

5 I know why the sun never sets on the British Empire: God wouldn't trust an Englishman in the dark.

In Nancy McPhee, *The Book of Insults* (1978), this is ascribed to 'Duncan Spaeth' (is this John Duncan Spaeth, the US educator?) Clearly it plays upon NORTH 344:3. This is attributed to Lincoln in Emanuel Hertz, *Lincoln Talks* (1939). An Irish Republican placard held up during Prince Charles's visit to New York in June 1981 had the slogan: 'The sun never sets on the British Empire because God doesn't trust the Brits in the dark.'

6 I'll tell you a story
About Jack a Nory,
And now the story's begun;
I'll tell you another
Of Jack and his brother,
And now my story is done.

Nursery rhyme first recorded in 1760. Hence, *Jackanory*, the title of the BBC TV story-telling series for children (from the 1960s onwards).

1 In good King Charles's golden days,
When loyalty no harm meant;
A furious High-Churchman I was,
And so I gained preferment.

Song 'The Vicar of Bray' in *The British Musical Miscellany* (1734), referring to a person who changes allegiance according to the way the wind blows. The original was a vicar of Bray, Berkshire, in the 16th century who is supposed to have changed his religious affiliation from Roman Catholic to Protestant more than once during the reigns of Henry VIII, Edward VI, Mary I and Elizabeth I. However, there were, in fact, several vicars at Bray in this period. Whatever the case, by the time of Thomas Fuller's *Worthies* (1662) there was a proverb: 'The Vicar of Bray will be Vicar of Bray still.' As for the song, it was probably written at the beginning of the 18th century and describes a different (perhaps completely fictional) vicar of Bray who changed his religion to suit the different faiths of monarchs from Charles II to George I. Can there have been two such turncoat vicars – or was the song merely an updating of the circumstances of the actual first vicar?

Hence, the play *In Good King Charles's Golden Days* (1939) by George Bernard Shaw, about a visit of Charles II to Isaac Newton in 1680 (and introducing other well-known names from that time).

2 Is it kind? Is it true? Is it necessary?

In George Seaver's *Edward Wilson of the Antarctic* (1963), it is stated that Wilson's widow had this motto printed on her mantelshelf to remind herself to curb her sharp tongue. In the Dorothy L. Sayers novel *Gaudy Night* (1935), it is said (with the first two queries reversed) by that arch-quoter, Lord Peter Wimsey. As such it bears a certain resemblance to part of the Four Way Test 'of the things we think, say or do' that Rotarians in the US devised in 1931: 'Is it the *truth*? Is it *fair*? Will it be *beneficial* to all concerned?' The most likely origin, however, is a poem called 'Three Gates' written in 1855 by Beth Day and said to be 'after the Arabian':

If you are tempted to reveal
A tale to you someone has told
About another, make it pass
Before you speak, three gates of gold.
These narrow gates: First, 'Is it true?'
Then, 'Is it needful?' In your mind
Give truthful answer. And the next
Is last and narrowest, 'Is it kind?'
And if to reach your lips at last
It passes through these gateways three,
Then you may tell the tale, nor fear
What the result of speech may be.

3 Is there a life before death?

This graffito was reported from Ballymurphy in Ireland in about 1971, and is confirmed by Seamus Heaney's poem 'Whatever You Say Say Nothing' from *North* (1975), which has:

Is there a life before death? That's chalked up
In Ballymurphy ...

The saying may not be Irish in origin: 'Is there life before death?' is the epigraph to Chap. 9 of Stephen Vizinczey's novel *In Praise of Older Women* (1966), where it is credited to 'Anon. Hungarian'.

4 I told you I was sick.

This epitaph on a hypochondriac was quoted by the American writer Paul Theroux on BBC Radio *Quote ... Unquote* (22 December 1981), although he did not say where he had got it from. Subsequently, I may have heard that it was supposed to have originated, rather vaguely, in 'the southern US'. The only report I received that anything like this epitaph had appeared anywhere at all in the US came when I was told that it is/was carved on the Hermine (Hermione?) E. and Thomas P. Connelly gravestone in the Forest Hill cemetery in East Derry, New Hampshire. There is as yet no confirmation of this. Further research turned up other mentions of this 'sick' version: Another version appears in Robert Ramsay and Randall Toye's *The Goodbye Book*, published by Van Nostrand Reinhold (1979). Ramsay and Toye are pretty careful about giving sources for their material so it is disappointing that their only note on 'I told you I was sick' reads 'In a Georgia cemetery'. It also turned up in Ed Morrow's *The Grim Reaper's Book of Days: A Cautionary Record of Famous, Infamous and Unconventional Exits*, a Citadel Press Book, published by Carol Publishing Group (1992). Under 18 June 1979 it has: 'Key West, Florida. B.P. Roberts died at age 50. His tombstone reads: "I TOLD YOU I WAS SICK".'

In 2004, Robert Deis of Cudjoe Key, Florida, confirmed that a large white crypt in the Key West cemetery does indeed have a facing tablet that says: 'I TOLD YOU I WAS SICK. B.P. Roberts, May 17, 1929 – June 18, 1979'. He added that, according to local legend, B. Pearl Roberts was, in fact, a waitress who people viewed as a laughable hypochondriac, but she apparently got the last laugh. So at least we know the epitaph had some scattered popularity by 1979 and in more than one place.

In 2002, when the comedian Spike Milligan died, it was reported that he wanted 'I told you I was *ill*' to be his epitaph. At first, possibly due to family disputes and clerical disapproval, it looked as though the words would not be appearing over his grave in St Thomas's churchyard, Winchelsea, East Sussex. *I Told You I Was Ill* was the title of a Milligan memorial tribute at Guildhall, London (15 September 2002). Whatever the case, it should be obvious from the foregoing that Milligan did not originate the joke. By 2004, however, it was revealed that Milligan now rested under a Celtic cross but with his epitaph tastefully put in Irish Gaelic: *'Duirt me leat go raibh me breoite'*, together with the English words, 'Love, light, peace'.

In the same year, Anne Tayler wrote to me: 'In the 1960s, I shared an office with a man called Frank Granville Barker [the music critic] and he told this story, with the inscription being: "I told you I *wasn't feeling very well*", which I think is funnier.'

1 **It's not the heat, it's the humidity.**

One of S.J. Perelman's prose pieces had the punning title 'It's Not the Heat, It's the Cupidity'. What was the allusion there? Presumably the same as contained in the title of a revue put on by Combined Services Entertainment in the Far East (around 1947) and featuring the young actor Kenneth Williams. It was called *It's Not So Much the Heat, It's the Humidity*, though in his memoirs he simply calls it *Not So Much the Heat*. Whatever the form, it was a common expression in the Second World War.

There is a case, however, for supporting an earlier Anglo-American origin. In the first paragraph of *Sam the Sudden* (1925), P.G. Wodehouse describes the inhabitants of New York on a late August afternoon: '[one half] crawling about and asking those they met if this was hot enough for them, the other maintaining that what they minded was not so much the heat as the humidity'. In *Are You a Bromide?* (1906) by Gelett Burgess, the remark is given as the sort of thing a bromide (someone addicted to clichés) would say.

2 **It's worse than a crime, it's a blunder!**

There is no doubting that this was said about the execution of the Duc d'Enghien in 1804. Napoleon, suspecting the Duc of being involved in royalist conspiracies against him, had him found guilty and executed, an act that hardened opinion against the French Emperor. But who said it? Comte Boulay de la Meurthe (1761–1840) was credited with the remark in C.-A. Sainte-Beuve's *Nouveaux Lundis*, Vol. 12 (1870), but among other names sometimes linked to it are Talleyrand, Joseph Fouché and Napoleon himself.

In French, the remark is usually rendered as: '*C'est pire qu'un crime; c'est une faute!*' *Pearson* (1937) has what he seems to think is the more correct translation: 'It is more than a crime; it is a political fault', from the *Memoirs of Fouché*.

3 **It takes seventy-two muscles to frown, but only thirteen to smile.**

A saying included in Celia Haddon, *The Yearbook of Comfort and Joy* (1991). 'This reminder,' she says, 'came from a newsletter sent to traffic wardens.' But it is quite old and probably of American origin. Keith Waterhouse, *Billy Liar* (1959), has it as a quotation on a calendar: 'It takes sixty muscles to frown, but only thirteen to smile. Why waste energy?'

4 **It was the wrong kind of snow.**

The archetypal limp excuse, now a part of British folklore. In *The Independent* (16 February 1991), it was ascribed to Terry Worrall, British Rail's director of operations. He had been attempting to explain why snow had disrupted services, even though a 'big chill' had been correctly forecast. In an interview with the BBC Radio *Today* programme on 11 February (presumably after he had made the original remark), he said, 'We have had a particular problem with this type of snow ... it has ... been very dry and powdery and it has actually penetrated all the protection that we have on our traction motors, beneath our multiple units and on some of our locomotives.' Alternatively, he may have been fed the description by the presenter, Peter Hobday, and asked if he agreed with it.

The other most often quoted excuse for disruption on British railways is '[There were] leaves on the line'. In the autumn, damp falling leaves have been known to form a layer on the rails and thus hinder the safe passage of wheels over them. The excuse was cited as though it was already an established one in *The Guardian* (22 December 1984).

5 **I write in order to find out what I think.**

The kind of thing that any writer might say. 'Rebecca West once said she wrote to find out what she thought' – Steven Bach, *Final Cut*, Foreword (1985). The British novelist Ian McEwan in *The Times* (27 June 1987): 'Writers divide between those who simply write to find out exactly what it is that they think, and those who have to think of the sentence first, then put it down, and constantly agonize about the gap between the thought and the language that's going to embody the thought.' David Lodge, *The Practice of Writing* (1997): 'You discover what it is you have to say in the process of saying it.'

However, there is also this line, which really says the same thing, in E.M. Forster's *Aspects of the Novel* (1927): 'That old lady in the anecdote ... was not so much angry as contemptuous ... "How can I tell what I think till I see what I say?"' Which may be the same as Graham Wallas, *The Art of Thought* (1926): 'The little girl had the making of a poet in her who, being told to be sure of her meaning before she spoke, said, "How can I know what I think till I see what I say?"'

Some near-misses and allusions: according to *The Treasury of Humorous Quotations*, eds Esar & Bentley (1951), Horace Walpole wrote: 'I never understand anything until I have written about it.' Alphonse Daudet has a character in *Numa Roumestan* (1881) say: '*Quand je ne parle pas, je ne pense pas.*' To the poet Louis Macneice is attributed: 'How do I know what I think till I hear what I say.' And when US journalist James Reston died in 1995 it was recalled what he said when his newspaper did not appear because of a strike: 'How can I know what I think if I can't read what I write?'

1 *A Kestrel for a Knave.*
The novel with this title by Barry Hines (1968) – filmed simply as *Kes* (UK 1969) – tells of a boy misfit who learns about life through training his kestrel hawk. The title comes from *The Boke of St Albans* (1486) and it is also in a Harleian manuscript: 'An Eagle for an Emperor, a Gyrfalcon for a King; a Peregrine for a Prince, a Saker for a Knight, a Merlin for a Lady; a Goshawk for a Yeoman, a Sparrowhawk for a Priest, a Musket for a Holy water Clerk, a Kestrel for a Knave.' This amounts to a feudal ranking of hunting birds.

2 *The Killing Fields.*
Title of a film (UK 1984) concerning the mass murders carried out by the Communist Khmer Rouge, under Pol Pot, in Cambodia between 1975 and 1978, when possibly 3 million people were killed. The mass graves were discovered in April 1979. In the film the phrase was seen to refer, literally, to paddy fields where prisoners were forced to work and where many of them were callously shot. The film was based on an article 'The Death and Life of Dith Pran' by Sydney Schanberg, published in *The New York Times* Magazine (20 January 1980), which tells of the journalist's quest for a reunion with his former assistant. The article has the phrase towards the beginning: 'In July of 1975 – two months after Pran and I had been forced apart on April 20 – an American diplomat who had known Pran wrote me a consoling letter. The diplomat, who had served in Phnom Penh, knew the odds of anyone emerging safely from a country that was being transformed into a society of terror and purges and "killing fields".' So it appears that the coinage is due to the unnamed diplomat.

Compare the phrase 'killing *ground(s)*', which has entered the military vocabulary as a strategic term for an area into which you manoeuvre the enemy before finishing them off and which has been current since the Second World War. In a non-military sense, the phrase was used by Rudyard Kipling in his poem 'The Rhyme of the Three Sealers' (1893) about seal hunting.

3 *Le roi est mort, vive le roi!* [The king is dead – long live the king!]
This declaration was first used in 1461 on the death of King Charles VII of France. Julia S.H. Pardoe in her *Louis the Fourteenth and the Court of France in the Seventeenth Century* (1847) describes how that king's death (in 1715) was announced by the captain of the bodyguard from a window of the state apartment: 'Raising his truncheon above his head, he broke it in the centre, and throwing the pieces among the crowd exclaimed in a loud voice, "*Le Roi est mort!*" Then seizing another staff, he flourished it in the air as he shouted, "*Vive le Roi*".' The custom ended with the death of Louis XVIII (1824). The expression is now used allusively to denote a smooth transition of power of any sort. From *The Independent* (25 January 1988): 'The cry went up: "The Liberal Party is dead. Long live the Liberal Party." It was hard to distinguish the wake from the marriage feast.'

4 The less things change, the more they remain the same.
'Old Sicilian proverb', quoted in Richard Condon, *Prizzi's Honour* (1982). Clearly based on '*Plus ça change, plus c'est la même chose* [the more it changes, the more it is the same thing]' – usually ascribed to the French novelist and journalist, Alphonse Karr (1808–90) in *Les Guêpes* (January 1849) – see KARR 264:2. Compare LAMPEDUSA 278:1.

5 Life is just a bowl of cherries.
Title of song (1931), words by Lew Brown, music by Ray Henderson, in the musical *Scandals of 1931*. Origin of the modern proverbial expression. Hence, *If Life Is a Bowl of Cherries, What Am I Doing In the Pits?*, the title of a book (1979) by Erma Bombeck.

6 Life's a bitch, and then you die.
This is a popular saying of untraced origin, though probably North American. A development of it, known both in the US and the UK is 'Life's a bitch, *you marry a bitch*, and then you die.' Citations in print are not very plentiful. Working backwards: during the summer of 1991, the Body Shop chain in the UK was promoting sun-tan products with a window display under the punning slogan 'Life's a beach – and then you fry'. (Another pun: 'Life's a bleach – and then you dye'.) A caption to an article in the London *Observer* (23 September 1990) about frozen food was the equally punning 'Life's a binge and then you diet'. In Caryl Churchill's play about the City, *Serious Money* (first performed March 1987), we find: 'I thought I'd be extremely rich. / You can't be certain what you'll get. / I've heard the young say Life's a bitch.' The earliest citation found so far comes from *The Sunday Times* of 21 December 1986: 'Life

is a bitch, then you die. So says the pilot of a flying fuel tank who last week took off to circumnavigate the globe with his girlfriend.'

Other suggested origins – Woody Allen's film *Love and Death* (1975) and the 1983 re-make of Jean-Luc Godard's *À Bout de Soufle* (in which the Jean-Paul Belmondo character originally died saying, '*La vie – c'est dégeulasse* [Life's a drag]') – have not proved fruitful. The films *Pretty in Pink* (US 1986) and *Less Than Zero* (US 1987) have also been suggested as possible sources.

'Life's a *beach*' seems to have taken on a life of its own as a slogan, especially in Australia, but probably developed from 'Life's a bitch', rather than the other way round.

Attention might be drawn to *An Essay on Woman* by 'Pego Borewell Esq.', which was published in about 1763 as a bawdy parody of Alexander Pope's *An Essay on Man*. It is thought to have been written by the politician John 'Friend of Liberty' Wilkes and one Thomas Potter, working in some form of collaboration. Wilkes was expelled from Parliament on account of it. Interestingly, the poem starts like this:

Let us (since life can little more supply
Than just a few good fucks, and then we die)
Expatiate freely ...

Something of the same spirit comes through here. 'Life's a bitch and then you die' has not been found before the mid-1980s. *The Observer* Magazine (2 August 1998) claimed that when the couturier Balenciaga closed the door of his salon for the last time in 1968 he declared: 'Life's a dog.' As he was Spanish-born and worked in Paris, he might have said this in either Spanish or French. A proverbial expression in either language?

On British troops in the First World War:

1 Lions led by donkeys.

Popularized as a result of being used as the epigraph to *The Donkeys* (1961) by Alan Clark, in this form:

Ludendorff: The English soldiers fight like lions.
Hoffman: True. But don't we know that they are lions led by donkeys.

Max Hoffman (1869–1927) and Erich Ludendorff (1865–1937) were German generals. The remarks have sometimes been given with the speakers reversed. Clark gave the source as the memoirs of Field Marshal von Falkenhayn – but the exchange and, indeed, the memoirs remain untraced. It has been suggested on more than one occasion that Clark might have invented it himself. In *The Spectator* (14 June 1997), Ronald Spark berated Clark (by then better known as a philandering politician and diarist) on this matter: 'I myself have written to Alan Clark for elucidation. With his usual combination of charming manners and pseudo-aristocratic pretensions, he has not

deigned to reply. In this mysterious affair the only clearly identified donkey seems to be Master Clark, except that he was cunning enough to devise an arresting title for a less than impressive book.'

Clark told *ODQ* to consult the Liddell Hart archive, as he had discussed it with Liddell Hart (the historian). Its archivist, Kate O'Brien, duly supplied *ODQ* with details of some relevant correspondence, which included a reference to the following source: 'Unceasingly they [the French forces] had had drummed into them the utterances of *The Times*: "You are lions led by jackasses." Alas! The very lions had lost their manes. [*On leur avait répété tout le long de la campagne le mot du* Times: – *Vous êtes des lions conduits par des ânes! – Hélas! les lions mêmes avaient perdus leurs crinières.*]' – Francisque Darcey (sometimes Sarcey), *Paris During the Siege*, Chap. 3, translated from *Le Siège de Paris* (both editions 1871). It has not proved possible to trace *The Times* usage, however. Whatever the case, this usage refers to the French troops fleeing from Sedan having undergone crushing defeats with the Prussians at their heels.

From this and from rumoured attributions to Napoleon, it is clear that what we have here is probably a military saying, modified to suit particular circumstances. The proverb 'An army of stags led by a lion would be more formidable than one of lions led by a stag' was cited by W.F. Butler in his *Sir Charles Napier* (1890) and this would appear to be based on Plutarch. K.F.W. Wander has something similar in *Deutsches Sprich-wörter-Lexikon*, Vol. 3 (1873): '*Hundert Löwen verlieren, wenn ein Schaf sie anführt.* [A hundred lions lose, when led by a sheep.]' In 1997, the British Channel 4 TV series *The Crimean War* contained a reference to a letter sent home by a British soldier quoting a Russian officer who had said that British soldiers were 'lions commanded by asses'. This was immediately after the French and British attempt to storm the fortress of Sebastopol had failed. If verified, this citation would take the saying back to 1854–5.

Indeed, Michael Hargreave Mawson, who was the 'expert reader' for the book associated with the Channel 4 documentary on the Crimean War, has stated that the phrase was attributed to a Russian sergeant and apparently communicated to a sergeant of the British 46th Regiment of Foot on 18 June 1855, during a ceasefire for the recovery of bodies. It was mentioned in two separate letters home, both dated 25 June 1855, one from Lieutenant-Colonel David Wood, Royal Artillery, and the other from Capt. George Frederick Dallas, 46th Regiment of Foot (Mawson is a descendant of Dallas). This information is from *The Journal of the Society for Army Historical Research* (Notes and Documents Section).

1 Little Jack Horner
Sat in the corner,
Eating a Christmas pie.
He put in his thumb,
And pulled out a plum,
And said, What a good boy am I?

A tradition has grown up that in the 16th century, at the time of the Dissolution of the Monasteries, the Abbot of Glastonbury sent his steward Jack Horner to London. In an attempt to appease King Henry VIII, Horner was bearing a Christmas pie containing the title deeds of 12 manors. But Horner 'put in his thumb' and pulled out the other kind of 'plum' – the deeds to the Manor of Mells in Somerset – and put them to his own use. A *Thomas* Horner *did* take up residence in Mells shortly after the Dissolution and his descendants lived there until late in the 20th century – source: Iona & Peter Opie, *The Oxford Dictionary of Nursery Rhymes* (1951).

2 Little Miss Muffet
Sat on a tuffet,
Eating her curds and whey;
There came a big spider,
Who sat down beside her
And frightened Miss Muffet away.

Nursery rhyme, known since 1805. People like to think that Miss Muffet was Patience, the daughter of Dr Thomas Muffet, an entomologist who died in 1604. But entomologists study insects, which have six legs. Spiders have eight legs. Therefore the employment of Miss Muffet's father is no explanation for her intimate experience with the spider. If he had been an arachnologist that might have been relevant. Hence, *Along Came the Spider*, the title of a cop film (US 2001) based on a James Patterson novel with the some title (1993).

3 Mairzy doats and dozy doats.

One of the more impenetrable graffiti jokes was (at least on first seeing it), the scribbled addition to a notice in Liverpool proclaiming: 'Mersey Docks and Harbour Board ... and little lambs eat ivy.' This was recorded in 1944. The graffiti-writer had cleverly spotted that a Scouser (Liverpudlian) would pronounce Mersey, 'mairzy' and that the rhythm of 'Mersey Docks and Harbour Board' exactly matched the first line of a nonsense song popular in Britain and America at the time called 'Mairzy Doats and Dozy Doats (Mares Eat Oats and Does Eat Oats)'. It went:

I know a ditty nutty as a fruit cake
Goofy as a goon and silly as a loon ...

Mairzy doats and dozy doats

And liddle lamzy divey.
A kiddley divey too,
Wouldn't you?

The song was 'written' by Milton Drake, Al Hoffman and Jerry Livingston but, as the Opies point out in their *Oxford Dictionary of Nursery Rhymes* (1951), there is a 'catch' which, when said quickly, appears to be in Latin:

In fir tar is,
In oak none is,
In mud eels are,
In clay none are.
Goat eat ivy
Mare eat oats.

Say the Opies: 'The joke may be traced back 500 years to a medical manuscript in Henry VI's time.'

4 A man's gotta do what a man's gotta do.

A statement of obligation, as in film Westerns. *Partridge/ Catch Phrases* dates popular use of this saying from about 1945, but its origin remains untraced, although an early example occurs in John Steinbeck's novel *The Grapes of Wrath*, Chap. 18 (1939): 'I know this – a man got to do what he got to do.' The film *Shane* (US 1953), based on a novel by Jack Shaeffer, is sometimes said to contain the line, but does not (nor does the book). The John Wayne film *Stagecoach* (1939) does not include it either, as some people state. By the 1970s, several songs had been recorded with the title.

5 May you live in interesting times.

Robert F. Kennedy, speaking in Cape Town, South Africa, on 7 June 1966, said: 'There is a Chinese curse which says, "May he live in interesting times." Like it or not, we live in interesting times ...' This has since become a very popular observation, almost a cliché, though any Chinese source remains untraced. It is said to have been found (though this is not the case) in the quasi-Chinese novel *The Wallet of Kai Lung* by Ernest Bramah (1900), where it is the first of three progressively awful curses. The others are 'May you come to the attention of those in high places' and 'May the gods grant your prayers'. In Nancy McPhee, *The Book of Insults* (1978), it is billed as an 'old Scottish curse'.

6 Money can't buy you happiness, but you can be miserable in comfort.

Untraced. Denis Conlon points out that the gist appears in exchanges between Topaze (the schoolmaster who gets rich by falling in with shady businessmen) and Tamise in Marcel Pagnol's *Topaze* (1930) – 'L'argent ne fait pas le bonheur ...' Perhaps this precise saying occurred in one of the two English-language film versions?

1 A more efficient conduct of the war.

A phrase from the First World War, though its precise origin remains untraced. A.J.P. Taylor in his *English History 1914–45* (1965) has: 'The Coalition government, which Asquith announced on 26 May 1915, claimed to demonstrate national unity and to promote a more efficient conduct of the war.' Writing of the following year (1916) in *Clementine Churchill* (1979), Mary Soames has 'more vigorous and efficient prosecution of the war'. Is it also sometimes given as 'more energetic' conduct? Compare, from Lord Home, *The Way the Wind Blows* (1976): 'Sir Roger Keyes [in 1939] ... made an impassioned speech in favour of more urgent conduct of the war.'

2 *Morituri te salutant* [We who are about to die salute you].

(Literally, 'those who are ...'). Words addressed to the Emperor by gladiators in ancient Rome on entering the arena. The practice seems to have been mentioned first in Suetonius, *Claudius*. In time, the phrase was extended to anyone facing difficulty, and then ironically so.

3 A mugwump is a sort of bird that sits on a fence with his mug on one side and his wump on the other.

A *mugquomp* in the language of the Algonquin (American Indians) describes a great chief or person of high rank (and was so recorded by 1663). In 1884, however, the word was popularized and used to describe 'the little men attempting to be big chiefs' who felt unable to support James Blaine as the Republican candidate for the US presidency and transferred their allegiance to the Democrat, Grover Cleveland. Hence, in American political parlance, the word mugwump came to describe a 'bolter' or someone who held himself self-importantly aloof. More generally, it has been used to describe a fool.

The above definition of the mugwump as a bird derives from the *Blue Earth* (Minnesota) *Post* in the early 1930s.

4 My friend's friend is my enemy.

This expression was invoked, for example, at the time of the Suez crisis (1956). It might have been President Nasser of Egypt referring to the United States (the friend) and Israel (the friend's friend). There seem to be many precedents. *Mencken* (1942) lists a legal maxim, 'The companion of my companion is not my companion [*Socii mei socius meus socius non est*]', but compare the French proverb, 'The enemy of my enemy is my friend.' Kingsley Amis entitled a book of short stories *My Enemy's Enemy* (1962). The original insight has been traced to the *Arthasastra*, a

pre-4th century BC Sanskrit text on statecraft by the guru Kautilya. Contrast the supposedly Flemish proverb, 'The friends of my friends are my friends.'

5 My mother said
That I never should
Play with the gypsies
In the wood
Because she said
That if I did
She'd smack my bottom
With a saucepan lid!

Nursery rhyme recorded in about 1875. There is more than one version, but none from much before the 1860s. Hence, *My Mother Said I Never Should*, the title of a play (1989) by Charlotte Keatley.

6 My name is George Nathaniel Curzon,
I am a most superior person.
My cheek is pink, my hair is sleek,
I dine at Blenheim once a week.

Written by an anonymous hand in *The Masque of Balliol* (in about 1880). Hence, *Superior Person*, the title of Kenneth Rose's biography of the Conservative politician and imperial administrator, Lord Curzon (1969).

7 The Navy's here!

On the night of 16 February 1940, 299 British seamen were freed from captivity aboard the German ship *Altmark* as it lay in a Norwegian fjord. The destroyer *Cossack*, under the command of Captain Philip Vian, had managed to locate the German supply ship, and a boarding party discovered that British prisoners were locked in its hold. As Vian described it, Lieutenant Bradwell Turner, the leader of the boarding party, called out: 'Any British down there?' 'Yes, we're all British,' came the reply. 'Come on up then,' he said, 'The Navy's here.'

The identity of the speaker is in doubt, however. Correspondence in *The Sunday Telegraph* (February/March 1980) revealed that Turner denied he had said it, that Leading Seaman James Harper was another candidate, and that Lieutenant Johnny Parker was the most likely person to have said it (and he had certainly claimed that he did).

The Times (19 February 1940) gave a version from the lips of one of those who had been freed and who had actually heard the exchange: 'John Quigley of London said that the first they knew of their rescue was when they heard a shout of "Any Englishmen here?" They shouted "Yes" and immediately came the cheering words, "Well, the Navy is here." Quigley said – "We were all hoarse with cheering when we heard those words."'

1 The noise and the people!

Describing what it was like to be in battle, a certain Captain Strahan exclaimed, 'Oh, my dear fellow, the noise ... and the people!' According to *ODQ* (1979), quoting the *Hudson Review* (Winter, 1951), he said it after the Battle of Bastogne in 1944. Various correspondents have suggested it was earlier in the war than this, however. Roy T. Kendall wrote (1986): 'I heard this phrase used, in a humorous manner, during the early part of 1942. It was related to me as having been said by a young Guards officer, newly returned from Dunkirk, who on being asked what it was like used the expression: the inference being, a blasé attitude to the dangers and a disdain of the common soldiery he was forced to mix with.' Tony Bagnall Smith added that the Guards officer was still properly dressed and equipped when he said it, and that his reply was: 'My dear, the noise and the people – how they smelt!'

ODQ (1992) appears to have come round to the earlier use regarding Dunkirk, in the form 'The noise, my dear! And the people!' It finds it already being quoted in Anthony Rhodes, *Sword of Bone*, Chap. 22 (1942).

Another originator is said to be Lord Sefton, a Guards officer at Dunkirk (suggested in correspondence in the *London Review of Books* beginning 29 October 1998). In the same correspondence, an assertion reappeared that it was something said by the actor Ernest Thesiger at a dinner party in 1919 regarding his experiences as a soldier in the Battle of the Somme.

2 *Non, je ne regrette rien* [No, I regret nothing].

Title of song (1960), words by Michael Vaucaire, music by Charles Dumont, popularized by Edith Piaf (1915–63). A favourite song of many people because, like 'My Way', it seems to assert one's individuality. Broadcaster – and at that time satirist – David Frost chose it as his favourite record on BBC Radio's *Desert Island Discs* in 1963. On 23 April 1993, Britain's Chancellor of the Exchequer, Norman Lamont, used the phrase with regard to his handling of the economy, when speaking during the Newbury by-election. The Conservatives lost the seat and he was sacked on 27 May.

3 *Not As a Stranger.*

The title of a novel (1954) by Morton Thompson and the film (US 1955) appear not to be consciously quoting anything. The song that came out of the film goes, 'Not as a stranger, dear, but my own true love ...' However, the title phrase does occur in the 1928 Episcopal Prayer Book's translation of Job 19:25–7 (the Burial of the Dead): 'I know that my redeemer liveth ... and though this body be destroyed, yet shall I see God: whom I shall see for myself, and mine eyes shall behold, and not as a stranger.' The Anglican Prayer Book takes from the Authorised Version of the Bible the less striking 'and not another'.

4 *Nunc scripsi totum, pro Christo da mihi potum* [I have now written everything, for the sake of Christ give me a drink].

In the preface to *Blue Guide Belgium and Luxembourg* (8th edition, 1993), it was suggested that this was written in the margin of a medieval manuscript or of the Domesday Book or in the Little Domesday (a set of working notes). In the University of Durham Library, however, there is a medieval manuscript (MS Cosin V.III.11 Recipes, etc.), dating from about 1435–56, that contains this: 'To make Frumente. Tak clene whete & braye yt wel ... For to claryfyen hony ... tak of e whye with a sklyse. *Nunc scripsi totum pro cristo da mihi potum.*' Some would suggest, in fact, that this was a fairly common monk's signing-off phrase to mark the end of a day's work in the scriptorium.

5 Oh, wash me in the water
That you washed the colonel's daughter in
And I shall be whiter
Than the whitewash on the wall.

Song popular among British troops in France during the First World War. This would appear to be a parody of (or at least inspired by) one of the Sankey and Moody hymns, 'The Blood of the Lamb', which has the chorus:

Wash me in the Blood of the Lamb
And I shall be whiter than snow!
(Whiter than the snow!
(Whiter than the snow!)
Wash me in the Blood of the Lamb
And I shall be whiter than snow, (the snow!)

Compare BIBLE 72:9.

6 Old Noah once he built the Ark
There's one more river to cross.
And patched it up with hick'ry bark
There's one more river to cross.
One more river, and that's the river of Jordan,
One more river
There's one more river to cross.

From the traditional song 'One More River to Cross' (also known as 'Noah's Ark'), which refers to the Jordan. Hence, *One More River*, the title of a film (US 1934) based on John Galsworthy's 1933 novel *Over the River* (which was how the film was known in the UK).

1 Once aboard the lugger and the girl is mine.

In 1908, A.S.M. Hutchinson (1879–1971) entitled a novel *Once Aboard the Lugger – the History of George and Mary*, but he was merely alluding to an established 'male catchphrase either joyously or derisively jocular', as *Partridge/Catch Phrases* notes. It may have come originally from a late Victorian melodrama – either *My Jack and Dorothy* by Ben Landeck (in about 1890) or from a passage in *The Gypsy Farmer* by John Benn Johnstone (who died in 1891): 'I want you to assist me in forcing her on board the lugger; once there, I'll frighten her into marriage.' The phrase also occurred later, in the music-hall song 'On the Good Ship Yacki-Hicki-Doo-La', written and composed by Billy Merson in 1917, of which the chorus (in the version he recorded himself in 1933) is:

> Then I snap my fingers ha ha ha ha!
> Then I snap the other one ho ho ho ho!
> I don't care should the lady pine,
> Once aboard the lugger and the girl is mine.
> Then I set my sails and sail away.
> No pirate e'er was cooler.
> Wher'er I go I fear no foe.
> On the good ship 'Yacki Hicki Doola'.

Benham (1948) has a different version, as often. According to him 'Once aboard the lugger and all is well' was said to have been an actor's gag in *Black Eyed Susan*, a nautical melodrama (in about 1830). *Punch* (16 August 1890) has this cartoon caption: 'W.H. Smith as "The Rover of the Seas." "Once more on board the lugger, and I am free!"'

2 One flew east, one flew west,
One flew over the cuckoo's nest.

Nursery rhyme (chiefly known in this version and in the US). Hence, *One Flew Over the Cuckoo's Nest*, title of the novel (1962) by Ken Kesey (film US 1975). Another version:

> Charley, Barley, buck and rye
> What's the way the Frenchmen fly?
> Some fly east, and some fly west
> And some fly over the cuckoo's nest.

3 One man's terrorist is another man's freedom fighter.

It seems as though this view was established by the time of the 1964 New York version of the revue *Beyond the Fringe*. Paxton Whitehead (taking over from Jonathan Miller) played the Duke of Edinburgh (something not then allowed on the London stage) and had him talk about his attending the independence celebrations in Kenya that had taken place in December 1963. Of Jomo Kenyatta, the first president, he says: 'That was when we thought he was a Mau-Mau terrorist. Now of course we realize that he was a freedom fighter.'

Earlier, Joseph Conrad, *The Secret Agent*, Chap. 4 (1907), had written: 'The terrorist and the policeman both come from the same basket. Revolution, legality – counter-moves in the same game; forms of idleness at bottom identical.' Harold Nicolson had written in his published diaries (entry for 29 October 1956): 'When people rise against foreign oppression, they are hailed as patriots and heroes; but the Greeks whom we are shooting and hanging in Cyprus are dismissed as terrorists. What cant!' Later, Hugh Gaitskell's widow Dora wrote in a letter to *The Guardian* (23 August 1977): 'All terrorists, at the invitation of the Government, end up with drinks at the Dorchester.' In 1985, President Reagan famously saluted Nicaraguan Contras as 'our brothers, these freedom fighters'.

4 One, two,
Buckle my shoe;
Three, four,
Knock at the door.

Children's counting rhyme, first recorded in about 1821. Hence, *One Two Buckle My Shoe*, title of a novel (1940) by Agatha Christie.

5 On Ilkla Moor Bah t'at.

The most famous – and impenetrable – of Yorkshire songs comes in two versions. The older, said to have been written by Thomas Clark to the hymn tune 'Cranbrook' in 1805, was sung in a spirited way:

> Wheear baht thee bahn when I been gone? [*repeated three times*]
> Wheear baht?
> On Ilkla Moor bah t'at [*repeated twice*]
> Bah t'at, bah t'at.
>
> Then thou wilt catch a cold and dee
> In Lonnenfuit bah t'buit [*repeated twice*]
> Bah t'buit, bah t'buit.
>
> Then we shall cum and bury thee
> Inn Saltruble Docks bah t'socks [*repeated twice*]
> Bah t'socks, bah t'socks.
>
> Then worms'll cum and eat up thee
> On Ikla Moor bah t'at [etc.]
>
> Then doocks'll cum and eat them worms
> In Lonnenfuit bah t'buit [etc.]
>
> Then we shall cum and eat them doocks
> In Saltruble Docks bah t'socks [etc.]
>
> Then we shall catch th'auld cold and dee
> On Ilka Moor bah t'at [etc.]

(Salter Hebble Docks and Luddenden Foot are canal points on the Hebble and Calder rivers near Halifax.)

A later (and now more popular) version, is sung more dolefully. It has a second verse, beginning 'I've been a courting Mary Jane', and a final verse sung thus:

Then we shall all 'av 'etten thee
That's how we get our owen back
This is the moral of this tale
Doan't go a-courtin Mary Jane.

This version was reputedly composed on an outing to Ilkley Moor by the choir of Ebenezer Chapel, Halifax, in 1886. The meaning of the old saga is roughly this: 'You've been on Ilkley Moor without a hat, courting Mary Jane. You'll catch your death of cold, and we shall have to bury you. The worms will eat you up, and the ducks will eat up the worms. Then we shall eat the ducks, so we shall have eaten you.'

1 **The opera ain't / isn't over till the fat lady sings.**
Relatively few modern proverbs have caught on in a big way but, of those that have, this one has produced sharp division over its origin. It is also used with surprising vagueness and lack of perception. If it is a warning 'not to count your chickens before they are hatched', it is too often simply employed to express a generalized view that 'it isn't over till it's over'.

So how did the saying come about? A report in *The Washington Post* (13 June 1978) had this version: 'One day three years ago [i.e. 1975], Ralph Carpenter, who was then Texas Tech's sports information director, declared to the press box contingent in Austin, "The rodeo ain't over till the bull riders ride." Stirred to that deep insight, San Antonio sports editor Dan Cook countered with, "The opera ain't over till the fat lady sings."' Two days before this (i.e. 11 June 1978), *The Washington Post* had more precisely quoted Cook as coming up with his version *the previous April*, 'after the basketball playoff game between the San Antonio Spurs and the Washington Bullets, to illustrate that while the Spurs had won once, the series was not over yet. Bullets coach Dick Motta borrowed the phrase later during the Bullets' eventually successful championship drive, and it became widely known and was often mistakenly attributed to him.'

Another widely shared view is that the saying refers to Kate Smith, a handsomely proportioned American singer in the 1930s and 1940s. Her rendition of Irving Berlin's 'God Bless America' signified the end of events like the political party conventions and World Series baseball games. Hence, possibly, the alternative version: the 'game's not over till the fat lady sings'. On the other hand, it has been argued that American national anthems ('The Star-Spangled Banner' and 'America the Beautiful', among others) are usually sung at the *start* of baseball games, which would

remove the point from the saying. If the 'opera' version can actually be said to mean anything, it derives from a hazy view of those sopranos with a 'different body image' who get to sing a big number before they die and thus bring the show to a close. But they do not do this invariably. In *Tosca*, for example, the heroine makes her final death plunge over the battlements without singing a big aria. The end of Wagner's opera *Siegfried* is, however, signalled by the arrival of Brünnhilde, who does indeed sing and is often played by a well-proportioned singer. Whatever the case, allusive use of the proverb is widespread – especially just the second part of it. The Fat Lady Sings was the name of an Irish (pop) band, formed *circa* 1990. After winning the US presidential election in November 1992, Bill Clinton appeared at a victory party in Little Rock bearing a T-shirt with the slogan 'The Fat Lady Sang', which presumably meant no more than, 'It's over.' In July 1992, tennis champion Andre Agassi, describing the surprise climax of his Wimbledon final, said, 'I knew that it might just go to 30–30 with two more aces. I didn't hear the fat lady humming yet.' The American singers En Vogue had a song called 'It Ain't Over Till The Fat Lady Sings' about this time, and there were several books with approximate versions of the phrase for their titles.

As is to be expected with a proverbial expression, the *idea* behind 'the fat lady' is nothing new. In Eric Maschwitz's memoir *No Chip on My Shoulder* (1957), he recalled Julian Wylie, 'The Pantomime King': 'He had a number of favourite adages about the Theatre, one of which I have always remembered as a warning against dramatic anti-climax: "Never forget," he used to say, "that once the giant is dead, the pantomime is over!"' Which is a corollary if ever there was one.

However, proof that this 'opera' version is merely a derivative of some earlier American expression appears to be provided by *A Dictionary of American Proverbs* (1992), which lists both 'The game's not over until the last man strikes out' and 'Church is not out 'til they sing'. *Bartlett* (1992) finds in *Southern Words and Sayings* (1976) by F.R. and C.R. Smith, the expression 'Church ain't out till the fat lady sings.'

2 **A picture is worth a thousand words.**
This famous saying, which occurs, for example, in the song 'If', popularized by Bread in 1971, is sometimes said to be a Chinese proverb. *Bartlett* (1980) listed it as such in the form 'One picture is worth more than ten thousand words', and compared what Turgenev says in *Fathers and Sons* (1862): 'A picture shows me at a glance what it takes dozens of pages of a book to expound.'

But *CODP* points out that it originated in an American paper *Printers' Ink* (8 December 1921) in the form 'One look is worth a thousand words.' It was later reprinted in the better-known form in the same paper (10 March 1927) and there ascribed by its actual author, Frederick R. Barnard, to a Chinese source ('so that people would take it seriously', as he told Burton Stevenson in 1948).

1 **A politician is an animal who can sit on a fence and yet keep both ears to the ground.**

Anonymous saying. Quoted in *Mencken* (1942). A commonly evoked criticism – from *The Observer* (8 September 1996): '[Archbishop Robert Runcie] was once described in a speech in the General Synod by the then Bishop of Leicester as a man who enjoyed "sitting on the fence with both ears to the ground". It helped him to accommodate both sides in every argument, but in the long term had the effect of destroying trust in his own statements.'

2 **A politician is a person who approaches every subject with an open mouth.**

Another of those quotations that floats continually in search of a definite source and could have been said by anyone and everybody. Was it Oscar Wilde? Or Adlai Stevenson? Or Arthur Goldberg? The first two sources are given by different contributors to *Kindly Sit Down*, a compilation of after-dinner speech jokes by politicians (1983), collected by Jack Aspinwall. Writing the foreword, Margaret Thatcher put this: 'It was after all, the late Governor Adlai Stevenson who defined a politician as one who approached every question with an open mouth.' Unfortunately, another of the book's contributors, Roger Moate, ascribed it rather to Oscar Wilde.

PDMQ (1971) gives Stevenson as the source, adding Goldberg (on diplomats) in 1980. Earlier Leon A. Harris in *The Fine Art of Political Wit* (1966) had plumped for Stevenson. In the absence of any hard evidence, one feels inclined to award the palm to Stevenson.

3 *Post coitum omne animal triste est* [Every creature is sad after sexual intercourse].

A post-classical Latin proverb, according to *ODQ* (1979) – on the grounds that it does not appear in classical texts. However, Laurence Sterne in *Tristram Shandy* (1762) ascribes it to Aristotle, presumably because Aristotle did write: 'Why do young men, on first having sexual intercourse, afterwards hate those with whom they have just been associated?' The ascription to Aristotle occurs earlier in Hogarth's pair of engravings *Before and After* (December 1736), which shows a man and woman before and after intercourse. On the floor in the latter picture lies a volume of Aristotle open at the page where 'Omne Animal Post Coitum Triste' is clearly visible. The Roman author Pliny also wrote: 'Man

alone experiences regret after first having intercourse.' Aristotle would, of course, have been writing in Greek, and in the *Problemata* – which is based on his original texts – there is quite a close Greek approximation to the well-known Latin text: *'Kai meta ta aphrodisia hoi pleistoi athumoteroi ginontai'*, which has been translated as: 'Also after sexual intercourse most people tend to be despondent' or 'After sexual intercourse most men are rather depressed.'

4 **The postillion has been struck by lightning.**

Said to be a useful expression from an old phrase book. Hence, *A Postillion Struck by Lightning*, title of the first volume of Dirk Bogarde's autobiography (1977). Describing a holiday in early childhood (the 1920s presumably), he mentions an old phrase book (seemingly dated 1898) that contained lines like: 'This muslin is too thin, have you something thicker?'; 'My leg, arm, foot, elbow, nose, finger is broken'; and 'The postillion has been struck by lightning.' Which phrase book is this? Not *English as She is Spoke*, in which the 'postillion' line does not occur. In the third volume of Bogarde's autobiography, *An Orderly Man* (1983), describing the writing of the first, he says: 'My sister-in-law, Cilla, on a wet camping holiday somewhere in northern France ... once sent me a postcard on which she said ... she had been forced to learn a little more French than the phrase "Help! My postillion has been struck by lightning!" I took the old phrase for the title of my book.'

A similarly untraced Russian/English phrase book is said to have included: 'Don't bother to unsaddle the horses, lightning has struck the innkeeper.' In Karl Baedeker's *The Traveller's Manual of Conversation in Four Languages* (1836 edn) he has found: 'Postillion, stop; we wish to get down; a spoke of one of the wheels is broken.' In an 1886 edition I have found: 'Are the postillions insolent?; the lightning has struck; the coachman is drunk.' From these examples it is quite clear that the preposterous phrase could quite likely have appeared in Baedeker or similar, but where?

A writer in *The Times* (30 July 1983) noted: '"Look, the front postillion has been struck by lightning" ... supposed to feature in a Scandinavian phrase book: but it may well be apocryphal.' *Punch* (22 April 1970) contains a headline with the earliest allusion found so far: 'My postillion has been struck by the vice-consul.'

A later discovery: *More Comic and Curious Verse* (1956) contains a poem 'Ballad of Domestic Calamity' by M.H. Longson, apparently extracted from *Punch* (3 July 1935). The last line is 'For our postillion has been struck by lightning' and an introductory note explains: '"Our postillion has been struck by lightning" is one of the "useful Common Phrases" appearing in a Dutch manual on the speaking of English.' One is reminded that Dirk Bogarde was of Dutch ancestry. Somewhat surprisingly, it transpires that Longson had even written memoirs – *A Classical Youth and other pieces* (1985) – in which he actually described his finding the phrase: 'I first became acquainted with him [the postillion] in a column of the *New Statesman* in the late winter of 1934.' A search for this possibly helpful lead has so far proved unavailing.

1 Power to the people.

A slogan of the Black Panther movement in the US. Shouted, and with clenched fist raised, this cry was publicized by the Black Panthers' leader, Bobby Seale, in Oakland, California, July 1969. Also used by other dissident groups, as illustrated by Eldridge Cleaver: 'We say "All Power to the People" – Black Power for Black People, White Power for White People, Brown Power for Brown People, Red Power for Red People, and X Power for any group we've left out.' It was this somewhat generalized view of 'People Power' that John Lennon appeared to promote in the 1971 song 'Power to the People (Right on!)'.

2 Pray, Mrs Mouse, are you within?
Heigh ho! says Rowley.

From the nursery rhyme 'A Frog He Would A-wooing Go' (first recorded 1611). Hence, *Mrs Mouse Are You Within?*, the title of a play (1968) by Frank Marcus. *Private Eye* (No. 299, June 1973) quoted what the elderly 10th Duke of Marlborough had said on returning from one of his honeymoons: 'I'm afraid Mr Mouse didn't come out to play.'

3 Regulations [are] written for the obedience of fools and the guidance of wise men.

It is not clear how this saying originated but it is spoken in this form (prefaced with 'Some') by a man called Harry Day in Paul Brickhill, *Reach for the Sky* (1954), his biography of Douglas Bader. The passage was repeated in the film (UK 1956):

Harry Day (as supervising officer, to Bader): You know my views of some regulations. They're written for the obedience of fools and the guidance of wise men.

Day apparently made the observation when Bader's squadron was in training for the team aerobatics display in the annual Hendon air show. Day was acting squadron commander. Compare what is attributed to General Douglas MacArthur: 'Rules are mostly made to be broken and are too often for the lazy to hide behind' – William A. Ganoe, *MacArthur Close-Up* (1962).

4 *Revenons à ces moutons* [Let's get back to these sheep].

Sometimes quoted as '*Retournons à nos moutons*', as by Rabelais in *Pantagruel* (1545). The meaning is, 'let us get

back to the subject'. In an anonymous 15th-century play entitled *La Farce de Maître Pierre Pathelin*, a woollen draper charges a shepherd with maltreating his sheep, but continually wanders from the point in court. The judge attempts to bring him back with this phrase – alluding perhaps to Martial: '*Jam dic, Postume, de tribus capellis*'?

5 Rings on her fingers and bells on her toes.

From the nursery rhyme 'Ride a cock-horse to Banbury Cross' (first recorded 1784). Hence, *Rings On Their Fingers*, the title of a BBC TV comedy series (from 1979) about live-in lovers who decide to get married.

6 Sarcasm is the lowest form of wit.

There is no doubt that this proverbial expression exists: 'Sarcasm is supposed to be the lowest form of wit. Never mind. It has its moments' – Greville Janner, *Janner's Complete Letterwriter* (1989). But it is hard to say where it came from. Thomas Carlyle remarked in *Sartor Resartus*, II.iv (1834) that 'Sarcasm is the language of the devil.' The more usual observation is that 'Punning is the lowest form of wit', which probably derives from Dryden's comment on Ben Jonson's 'clenches' – 'the lowest and most grovelling kind of wit'. At some stage the comment on the one has been applied to the other. The saying is definitely *not* Dr Johnson's definition of wit in his *Dictionary*.

7 Say it ain't so, Joe!

A small boy is reputed to have said this to the American baseball player 'Shoeless Joe' Jackson as he came out of a grand jury session in 1920 about corruption in the 1919 World Series. Jackson, of the Chicago White Sox, had been accused with others of deliberately losing the Series at the behest of gamblers. A journalist called Hugh Fullerton reported a boy asking, 'It ain't so, Joe. Is it?' and him replying, 'Yes, kid, I'm afraid it is.' Over the years, the words rearranged themselves into the more euphonious order. Ironically, Jackson denied that the exchange had ever taken place – using any set of words.

8 Say not in grief that he/she is no more
But in thankfulness that he/she was.

These words, spoken at many a memorial or thanksgiving service, have been variously described as a Jewish prayer and/or from the Talmud. The underlying thought is almost a commonplace, however. General George S. Patton said in a speech in Boston, Mass. (7 June 1945): 'It is foolish and wrong to mourn the men who died. Rather we should thank God that such men lived.' In 1992, *The Times* quoted the Queen Mother as having said of her husband King George VI's death in 1952: 'One must feel gratitude for what has been, rather than distress for what is lost.' Another suggestion is that the lines may have been said by or about Pushkin.

And, although it is not quite the same thing, that well-known quotation-scruncher, Margaret Thatcher, incorporated this in a VE-Day message to the Kremlin in May 1985: 'It is right that we should look back and pay tribute with pride and *thankfulness* for the heroism of those in both our countries who fought in a common cause, and with *grief* for the terrible sufferings involved.'

1 Seems Like Old Times.

Title of a song (written in about 1946) by John Jacob Loeb and Carmen Lombardo. It had been preceded by 'It Seems Like Old Times' (1939) by Sammy Stept and Charles Tobias. Hence, however, *Seems Like Old Times*, the title of a film (US 1980) and of a book (1989) by Alan Coren (made up of his old pieces from *The Times*).

2 Set a thief to catch a thief.

Already quoted as an old saying in Richard Howard's *The Committee* (1665). Hence, *To Catch a Thief*, title of a film (US 1955). Compare SHAKESPEARE 416:9.

3 Sing a song of sixpence,
A pocket full of rye;
Four and twenty blackbirds,
Baked in a pie.

From the nursery rhyme, first recorded in about 1744, and capable of any number of allegorical interpretations. The belief that it sprang from the occasion when Henry James Pye was appointed Poet Laureate in 1790 is clearly erroneous, given that the rhyme had appeared 50 years previously. Hence, however, *A Pocket Full of Rye*, title of a Miss Marple novel (1953) by Agatha Christie, who also used 'Sing a Song of Sixpence' (1934) and 'Four and Twenty Blackbirds' (1960) from the same source for the titles of short stories.

4 *The Singer Not the Song.*

Title of novel (1959) by Audrey Erskine Lindop (film UK 1960). The story concerns the relationship between a Mexican outlaw and a priest. He accepts the priest but not his message. Lindop took the title from a West Indian calypso 'Come With Me My Honey', credited to David/Whitney/Kramer (as recorded, for example, by Edmundo Ros in September 1944): 'The singer not the song, that's the sound of calypso Joe.' Compare, from W.S. Gilbert, *Iolanthe*, Act I (1882), 'Thou the singer; I the song', from Strephon and Phyllis's duet 'None Shall Part Us From Each Other'.

5 The situation in Germany is serious but not hopeless; the situation in Austria is hopeless but not serious.

Described as 'an Austrian proverb collected by Franklin Pierce Adams' in A. Andrews, *Quotations for Speakers and Writers* (1969). Hence, *Situation Hopeless But Not Serious* – the title of a film (US 1965).

6 [The Skibbereen Eagle has] got its eye both upon him and on the Emperor of Russia.

The 1898 edition of *Brewer* states: 'It was the *Skibbereen*, or *West Cork Eagle* newspaper, that solemnly told Lord Palmerston that it had "got its eye both upon him and on the Emperor of Russia." This terrible warning has elevated the little insignificant town of Skibbereen in the southwest coast of Ireland, quite into a Lilliputian pre-eminence. Beware, beware, ye statesman, emperors, and thrones, for the *Skibbereen Eagle* has its eye upon you!' No date of publication or any other evidence, of course.

7 Socialism is no more than the family writ large.

Quoted in 1995 by the sociologist Michael Young, who commented: 'My memory was that it was part of an election broadcast that Clement Attlee made in 1945 or 1950 or 1951. I was employed myself then as Head of the Research Department of the Labour Party and was responsible for the broadcasts ... but someone has checked this for me and it looks as though it's not the case.'

8 So Deep Is the Night.

Title of song (1939) by Sonny Miller, first featured in the 1940 film *Hear My Song*, though originally Mario Melfi's setting of Chopin's Étude in E Major, Op. 10, No. 3, which appears to have had French words under the title 'Tristesse'. Compare the film title (US 1946), *So Dark the Night*.

9 *Somebody's Husband, Somebody's Son.*

The title of Gordon Burn's (1984) book about the 'Yorkshire Ripper' murder investigation is taken from something said during the prolonged police hunt for the killer. George Oldfield, leading the police hunt, appeared on the Jimmy Young radio show on 9 February 1978 and 'urged the predominantly female audience to search their collective conscience and report any man of their acquaintance who they suspected of behaving oddly. Husband, father, brother, son – it shouldn't matter.' After another killing, a Yorkshire clergyman, the Revd Michael Walker, told his congregation on Palm Sunday, 1979, 'He [the Ripper] needs help, he is somebody's child, husband or father.' In 2004, BBC TV presented a series about the children of celebrities entitled *Somebody's Daughter, Somebody's Son*.

1 The son of a duck is a floater.

Arab saying. Dr Rosalind Miles commented (1995): '"Son of a duck" means far more than the literal "like father like son". It means more like the US Western proverb "There is no education in the second kick of a mule." It also applies to projects and suggestions – i.e. a second or subsequent idea from someone whose ideas or efforts have bombed before will bomb again.'

The Son of a Duck Is a Floater is the title of a collection of Arab sayings with English equivalents published in 1985 by Primrose Arnander and Ashkhain Skipwith. The 1992 sequel was *Apricots Tomorrow* – the title taken from the Arab saying 'Tomorrow [there] will be apricots', which means 'Never do today what you can possibly put off till tomorrow.' This comes from the story in the *Arabian Nights* about the princess's servant who was instructed to pick the ripening fruit every evening and so preserve her mistress's life and honour. Arnander and Skipwith give the Western equivalents 'Tomorrow never comes' and 'Jam tomorrow ...'

2 Spake as he champed the unaccustomed food,
This may be wholesome but it is not good.

'Anon. 1852' is the only hint given in *The Making of Verse: A Guide to English Metres* (1934) by Robert Swan and Frank Sidgwick, where this appears among examples of heroic couplets. In *The Dublin Review* (July 1937), J. Lewis May, while discussing 'Flashed from his bed the electric tidings came' (see AUSTIN 45:5), says: 'The name of the inventor of these immortal lines has not been handed down, but one may hazard a guess that they proceeded from the same source as those on another prince, also a subject for the Newdigate [prize poem at Oxford] – to wit, Nebuchadnezzar, "Who murmured – as he ate the unaccustomed food – / It may be wholesome, but it is not good."' *Everyman's Dictionary of Quotations and Proverbs* (1951) ascribes this full version to Goldwin Knox, historian (1823–1910): 'King Nebuchadnezzar was turned out to grass / With oxen, horses and the savage ass. / The King surveyed the unaccustomed fare / With an inquiring but disdainful air / And murmured as he cropped the unwanted food, / "It may be wholesome but it is not good."'

3 Starkle, starkle, little twink,
Who the hell you are, you think?
I'm not under the alcofluence of incohol,
Though some thinkle peep I am.
I fool so feelish. I don't know who is me
For the drunker I sit here, the longer I get.

Drunken parody of 'Twinkle, twinkle, little star', popular in the 1940s. Said to have been published in the small

magazine *Argosy* (in about 1943) and also to have appeared in 'The Line Book' at RNAS Yeovilton, Somerset, in 1944. A musical version was recorded by the British comedian Charlie Drake in 1959. A more sober parody, also current by the mid-1940s, is this:

Scintillate, scintillate, globule vivific,
Fain would I fathom thy nature specific.
Loftily poised in the ether capacious
Strongly resembling a gem carbonaceous.

Compare CARROLL 123:6.

4 Ten little nigger boys went out to dine;
One choked his little self, and then there were
nine.

'Ten Little Niggers' – Frank Green's British version (1869) of the American rhyme. Actually 'Ten Little Injuns' was the title of the original piece, written by the US songwriter Septimus Winner (in about 1868). Hence, however, *Ten Little Niggers*, title of a novel (1939) by Agatha Christie, which has been dramatized and thrice filmed. Understandably, the US title of the book became *Ten Little Indians*, and the UK 1966 film also had this more acceptable title. *And Then There Were None* was the title of the US 1945 film – in the UK, *Ten Little Niggers* – and also of the UK 1974 film.

5 There are three kinds of lie: a small lie, a big lie and politics.

Anonymous Russian, quoted in *Time* Magazine (25 March 1985). Prefaced by, 'As one of your [i.e. presumably American] writers said ... ' Sometimes said to be a Jewish proverb in the form, 'One is a lie, two are lies, but three is politics.'

6 There are three sides to every argument: my side, your side and the truth.

Modern proverbial saying, variously ascribed: ' ... to every case' is said to be 'an old lawyer' advising his pupil; ' ... to every argument' was 'a quote from a bloke in the pub'; from the *Financial Times* (25 October 1986): 'As everyone knows there are always three sides to the story of any marriage: His, Hers and the Truth. Here we have Hers [Dylan Thomas's widow's] with nothing kept back this time.' In the film *The Marrying Kind* (US 1952), a judge (Madge Kennedy) tells Judy Holliday, who is seeking a divorce, 'There are three sides to every story: yours, his and the truth.'

7 There is so much that is bad in the best of us
And so much that is good in the worst of us
That it doesn't behoove any of us
To talk about the rest of us.

Two versions of a verse known as 'Charity', by Anon. This is what appeared in *Heart Throbs (in Prose and Verse Dear to the American People) contributed by readers of National Magazine* (1904–5). In *Everyman's Dictionary of Quotations and Proverbs* (1951), a version is attributed to Edward Wallis Hoch, American politician (1849–1925). Another version is to be found written up in the Common Room of Sackville College, a Jacobean almshouse in East Grinstead, Sussex, but this, too, is anonymous and undated.

1 **This must be the first time a rat has come to the aid of a sinking ship.**

A BBC spokesman on puppet Roland Rat's success in reversing the fortunes of TV-am, a rival breakfast television station (1983). Not entirely original however – see CHURCHILL 140:5.

2 **Three blind mice, see how they run!**
They all ran after the farmer's wife,
Who cut off their tails with a carving knife,
Did you ever see such a thing in your life,
As three blind mice?

Nursery rhyme, known by 1609. *Three Blind Mice* was the title of a James Patterson thriller (1979), first published as *The Jericho Commandment*. See also KING 271:1.

3 **The tie that binds.**

This proverbial expression (sometimes 'the ties that bind') may possibly have originated in a hymn written by John Fawcett, an English Baptist minister, in 1782:

Blest be the tie that binds
Our hearts in Christian love:
The fellowship of kindred minds
Is like to that above.

The story goes that Fawcett had already set out on the road leaving a chapel where he had been minister, but his congregation prevailed on him to return. When he got back to his manse he sat down right away and wrote the hymn. It is used prominently in Thornton Wilder's play *Our Town* (1938) and occasioned a parody (probably American):

Blest be the tie that binds
Our collar to our shirt,
For it is the only thing that hides
A little rim of dirt.

Other references: in *Punch* (20 May 1843) there is a cartoon of two dogs tethered by their kennels and the caption: 'There is a tie that binds us to our homes.' In the journal *Lux Mundi* (1889): 'The ties which bind men in the relation of brotherhood and sonhood are the noblest.' A film (US 1996) about

adoption, with Keith Carradine and Daryl Hannah, had the title *The Tie That Binds*. Also *Ties That Bind* was the title of a novel (2000) by Pam Rhodes.

4 **Tinker, tailor, soldier, sailor, rich man, poor man, beggar man, thief.**

From the children's fortune-telling rhyme, first recorded in something like this form in 1883. Hence, *Tinker Tailor Soldier Spy*, the title of a spy novel (1974) by John Le Carré. *Rich Man, Poor Man* was the title of a novel (1970) by Irwin Shaw, to which the sequel was *Beggarman, Thief* (1977).

5 **Today Germany, tomorrow the world!**

The slogan for the National Socialist Press in Germany of the early 1930s, '*Heute Presse der Nationalsozialisten, Morgen Presse der Nation* [Today the press of the Nazis, tomorrow the nation's press]', reached its final form in '*Heute gehört uns Deutschland – morgen die ganze Welt* [Today Germany belongs to us – tomorrow the whole world]'. Although John Colville in *The Fringes of Power* states that by 3 September 1939 Hitler 'had already ... proclaimed that "Today Germany is ours; tomorrow the whole world"', an example of Hitler actually saying it has yet to be found. However, in *Mein Kampf* (1925) he had said: 'If the German people, in their historic development, had possessed tribal unity like other nations, the German Reich today would be the master of the entire world.'

The phrase seems to have come from the chorus of a song in the Hitler Youth 'songbook':

Wir werden weiter marschieren
Wenn alles in Scherben fällt
Denn heute gehört uns Deutschland
Und morgen die ganze Welt

– which may be roughly translated as:

We shall keep marching on
Even if everything breaks into fragments,
For today Germany belongs to us
And tomorrow the whole world.

Another version replaces the second line with '*Wenn Scheiße vom Himmel fäll*' [When shit from Heaven falls]'. Sir David Hunt recalled hearing the song in 1933 or possibly 1934. See also EBB 181:3.

6 **Tomorrow will be Friday,**
But we've caught no fish today.

Lines from the song 'Tomorrow Will Be Friday', popular around 1900, about a group of monks on a Thursday who are finding it difficult to cater for the morrow. Words by F.E. Weatherley, music by J.L. Molloy (and sung originally by Mr F. Barrington Foote). There is a painting (1880) with the same title by Walter Dendy Sadler in the collection of Tate Britain; it is also known as *Thursday*.

1 To save the town, it became necessary to destroy it.
An unnamed American major on the town of Ben Tre, Vietnam, during the Tet Offensive, according to an AP dispatch headed 'Major Describes Move' in *The New York Times* (8 February 1968). A token of the futility of American activities in Vietnam. In 1970, there was a 'psychedelic biker comedy' movie with the title *Gas-s-s-s! Or It Became Necessary to Destroy the World in Order to Save It.*

2 To the world he was a soldier
To me he was the world.
Said to be on a Second World War grave in the Western Desert (as reported by Colin Smith in *The Observer*, 8 November 1981), but also found elsewhere. On the grave in Brookwood Military Cemetery, Surrey, of Wing Commander H.J. Fish, RAF, who died on 19 October 1945, age 30, there is: 'TO THE WORLD / HE WAS JUST A PART / TO ME HE WAS THE WORLD.'

3 The twelfth day of Christmas,
My true love sent to me
Twelve lords a-leaping,
Eleven ladies dancing,
Ten pipers piping,
Nine drummers drumming,
Eight maids a-milking,
Seven swans a-swimming,
Six geese a-laying,
Five gold rings,
Four calling birds,
Three French hens,
Two turtle doves, and
A partridge in a pear tree.
A rhyme, also known in French, first recorded in English *circa* 1780. The numbering of the gifts varies from version to version. Hence, for example, *Ten Lords A-Leaping*, title of a crime novel (1995) by Ruth Dudley Edwards. Most discussion has been about the last line, chiefly because the game bird is a famously low flyer and is never seen in trees. A popular suggestion (which also explains some of the other gifts listed in the song) is that a 'partridge in a pear tree' is a corruption of the Latin *parturit in aperto* ('she gave birth in the open'), referring to Mary's delivery of Christ in a stable. Similarly, the shepherds coming down from the hills (*descendens de collibus*) could explain the phrases 'three French hens' and 'four colly/calling birds'. Another ingenious explan-

ation for 'partridge in a pear tree' is that it is a mixture of the English and French words for 'partridge' – 'a partridge, *une perdrix*'.

4 Until we meet again.
A staple sentiment of the bereaved, to be found on many gravestones. One can't help wondering, however, whether its popularity, particularly on war graves, has anything to do with the enormous success of Vera Lynn's song 'We'll meet again, don't know where, / Don't know when, / But I know we'll meet again some sunny day' (1939), written by Ross Parker and Hugh Charles. However, in 1918 there had been a song with the title 'Till We Meet Again', which was a great success for its writers Richard Whiting and Ray Egar. Before that was the hymn 'God be with you till we meet again', written by Jeremiah Eames Rankin, American minister (1828–1904).
    From the grave in Brookwood Military Cemetery, Surrey, of Sergeant D.J. Ansell, 'wireless operator/air gunner, Royal Air Force', who died on 23 September 1944, aged 34 years is this: 'HE IS ALWAYS IN OUR HEARTS / UNTIL WE MEET AGAIN.' 'Always In My Heart' was, incidentally, the title of a song (1942) by Kim Gannon and Ernesto Lecuona, popularized by Deanna Durbin.

5 Uprose the Monarch of the Glen
Majestic from his lair,
Surveyed the scene with piercing ken,
And snuffed the fragrant air.
Hence, *The Monarch of the Glen*, title of a much-reproduced painting (1851) by Sir Edwin Landseer, showing a stag rampant on a small rock (and now in the possession of John Dewar & Sons Ltd, the whisky firm). When the painting was first exhibited at the Royal Academy, the catalogue entry contained a poem only identified as 'Legends of Glenorchay', which ended thus.

6 We are the unwilling, led by the unqualified, doing the unnecessary for the ungrateful.
Slogan said to have been seen written on GI helmets in Vietnam. In the June 1980 issue of *Playboy* was a slightly different version from 'the Ninth Precinct': 'We the willing, led by the unknowing, are doing the impossible for the ungrateful. We have done so much for so long with so little, we are now qualified to do anything with nothing.' Somebody bitter about police salaries had amended the last line to read, 'to do anything for nothing'.
    Compare: 'What is a committee? A group of the unwilling, picked from the unfit, to do the unnecessary' – Richard Harkness, *New York Herald Tribune* (15 June 1960).

1 We give thee hearty thanks, most merciful Father, for our founder, John Harrison, and all other our benefactors, by whose benefits we are here brought up to godliness and good learning.

Thus begins the Founder's Prayer that I heard spoken by the headmaster every day in the late 1950s and early 1960s at the Merchant Taylors' School, Crosby, near Liverpool. I believe it then went on: 'And we beseech thee to give us grace so to use these thy blessings to the honour and glory of thy holy name and for the good of thy church and people', although I am not certain of this.

It had occurred to me that this might have been based on a template circulated among similar institutions requiring some form of founder's prayer. I have not managed to confirm this. However, in *The College Graces of Oxford and Cambridge*, compiled by Reginald Adams (1992) — and by a remarkable coincidence — I came across this grace from New College, Oxford, where I was an undergraduate after leaving Merchant Taylors'. It is said to be used on 'Election day' of scholars from Winchester College, which has the same founder: '*Agimus tibi gratias pro Fundatore nostro, Gulielmo de Wykeham, reliquisque quorum beneficiis hic ad pietatem et ad studia literarum alimur; rogantes ut nos, his donis tuis ad nominis tui honorem recte utentes, ad resurrectionis tuae gloriam perducamur immortalem, per Jesum Christum Dominum nostrum* [We give thee thanks for our Founder, William of Wykeham, and for the others by whose benefits we are here brought up to godliness and learning; beseeching thee that we, using these thy gifts to the honour of thy name, may pass on to the immortal glory of thy resurrection, through Jesus Christ our Lord].'

In fact, other Oxford and Cambridge college graces (before dinner) also frequently contain the standard phrases that ended up in my school's Founder's Prayer, including, 'We give thee hearty thanks ... for our Founder and all other our benefactors ... by whose benefits we are here brought up to godliness and learning ... beseeching thee that, using these thy gifts ... ' and so on. A template, as I said.

2 We have ways of making you talk.

The threat by an evil inquisitor to his victim appears to have come originally from 1930s Hollywood villains and was then handed on to Nazi characters from the 1940s onwards. In the film *The Lives of a Bengal Lancer* (1934) Douglas Dumbrille, as the evil Mohammed Khan, says, 'We have ways to make men talk.' A typical 'Nazi' use can be found in the British film *Odette* (1950) when the eponymous French Resistance worker played by Anna Neagle) is threatened with unmentioned nastiness by one of her captors. Says he: 'We have ways and means of making you talk.' Then, after a little stoking of the fire with a poker, he urges her on

with: 'We have ways and means of making a woman talk.'

Later, used in caricature, the phrase saw further action in TV programmes like *Rowan and Martin's Laugh-In* (in about 1968), when it was invariably pronounced with a German accent. Frank Muir presented a comedy series for London Weekend Television with the title *We Have Ways of Making You Laugh* (1968).

3 The Welsh are the Italians in the rain.

Quoted by the writer Elaine Morgan on BBC Radio *Quote ... Unquote* (1983). An earlier version spoken, though probably not coined, by the journalist René Cutforth was: 'The Welsh are the Mediterraneans in the rain', which was quoted by Nancy Banks-Smith in *The Guardian* (17 October 1979).

4 What a difference a day makes.

Almost proverbial, yet not listed in any proverb books. The phrase either expresses surprise at someone's rapid recovery from a mood that has laid them low, or the old thought that time is a great healer. Did it begin in a song? 'What a Difference a Day Made' was a hit for Esther Phillips in 1975 (though translated in 1934 by Stanley Adams from the Spanish lyric '*Cuando Vuelva a Tu Lado*' by Maria Grever.) Dinah Washington popularized a blues with the title 'What a Difference a Day Makes' before 1963.

5 What a wonderful bird the frog are!
When he walk, he fly almost;
When he sing, he cry almost.
He ain't got no tail hardly, either.
He sit on what he ain't got almost.

A leading article in *The Times* (20 May 1948) ascribed these lines to the pen of an African schoolgirl, causing one reader to write in and say he had always believed they had come from the mouth of a French Canadian. He also said he had an idea that he had first seen them in the *Manchester Guardian* 'about twenty years ago'.

The version that appears in Arnold Silcock's *Verse and Worse* (1952) is also ascribed to 'Anon (French Canadian)' and is fractionally different:

What a wonderful bird the frog are –
When he stand he sit almost;
When he hop, he fly almost.
He ain't got no sense hardly;
He ain't got no tail hardly either.
When he sit, he sit on what he ain't got almost.

6 When captains courageous whom death could
  not daunt,
Did march to the siege of the city of Gaunt,

They mustered their soldiers by two and by three,
And the foremost in battle was Mary Ambree.

Ballad, 'Mary Ambree'. Hence, *Captains Courageous*, title
of a novel (1897) by Rudyard Kipling.

1 *Who Pays the Ferryman?*

Title of a BBC TV drama series (1977) by Michael J. Bird,
about a former Greek Resistance fighter in Crete. Not a
quotation but an allusion to the Greek legend of Charon
who demanded a fee to ferry the dead across the River
Styx.

2 Who were you with last night?
Out in the pale moonlight.

Song, 'Who Were You With Last Night?' (1912), written by
the British composer of music-hall songs, Fred Godfrey
(1889–1953) with Mark Sheridan. Compare the lines
from John Masefield's 'Captain Stratton's Fancy': 'And some
are all for dancing by the pale moonlight'; and from the
much later film *Batman* (US 1989): 'Have you ever danced
with the devil in the pale moonlight?' The phrase 'in the
pale moonlight' occurs earlier in Charles Dickens, *The Old
Curiosity Shop*, Chap. 43 (1840). See also GILBERT 213:4;
SCOTT 397:4.

3 With drums and guns, and guns and drums
The enemy nearly slew ye.
My darling dear, you look so queer,
Oh, Johnny, I hardly knew ye.

'Johnny, I hardly knew Ye', an Irish folk song. Hence: *Johnnie I Hardly Knew You*, the title of a novel (1977) by Edna
O'Brien; *Johnny, We Hardly Knew Ye*, the title given to a
volume (1972) by Ken O'Donnell and Dave Powers commemorating the death of President Kennedy (who was of
Irish descent); *Daddy, We Hardly Knew You*, title of a memoir
of her father (1989) by Germaine Greer.

4 With twenty-six soldiers of lead, I can conquer the
world.

The typographer F.W. Goudy (1865–1947) wrote in *The Type
Speaks*, 'I am the leaden army that conquers the world – I am
TYPE' – but he was probably re-working an old riddle. *ODQ*
(1979) finds in Hugh Rowley's *Puniana* (1867) the saying,
'With twenty-six lead soldiers [the characters of the alphabet
set up for printing] I can conquer the world', and points to
the (probably independently arrived at) French riddle: '*Je
suis le capitaine de vingt-quatre soldats, et sans moi Paris serait
pris,*' to which the answer is '*A*'. ('I am the captain of
twenty-four [sic] soldiers and without me Paris would be
taken' – remove the '*a*' from '*Paris*' and it becomes '*pris*' or

'taken'.) But is the French alphabet at this time presumed to
have had only 25 letters? If so, which was the missing letter
– K or W perhaps?

The phrase has been used as the title of a spiritual quest
book, *Twenty-Six Lead Soldiers*, by Dan Wooding (1987): 'A
top Fleet Street journalist and his search for the truth ...'
Wooding attributes the saying to 'Karl Marx or Benjamin
Franklin'.

5 Women's faults are many,
Men have only two:
Everything they say
And everything they do.

The observation regarding quotations or jokes that there is
always an earlier example if only you can find it, is particularly true of graffiti. The rash of feminist graffiti of the
1970s (spreading in time to T-shirts, buttons, and so on)
produced this popular verse. How ironic, therefore, that
Mencken (1942) has this well-documented rhyme from the
18th century – and note the change of gender:

We men have many faults:
Poor women have but two –
There's nothing good they say,
There's nothing good they do.
Anon.: 'On Women's Faults' (1727)

6 *Yield To the Night.*

Title of a film (UK 1956), from a novel by Joan Henry, about
a convicted murderess. The source is untraced – except that
it occurs in a translation of a passage in Bk 7 of Homer's
Iliad: 'But night is already at hand; it is well to yield to the
night.'

7 You don't have to be mad to work here – but it
helps.

Popular slogan on signs made for hanging in offices and
workplaces, especially in the 1960s/70s. Preceded by the
word 'methinks', it is spoken in Peter Nichols, *The National
Health*, Act 1, Sc. 4 (1969).

Jean ANOUILH French playwright (1910–87)

8 *Ring Round the Moon.*

Christopher Fry's adaptation of Anouilh's play *L'Invitation
au château* ('the invitation to the castle/château') was first
performed in 1950 (following the Paris production of 1947).
The English title alludes to the proverb 'Ring around the
moon, brings a storm soon' (sometimes, '... rain comes
soon'). This is a modern version of 'When round the moon
there is a brugh [halo], the weather will be cold and rough'

(*ODP* has it by 1631). In Longfellow's 'The Wreck of the Hesperus' there occurs the line 'Last night the moon had a golden ring, and tonight no moon we see!' as though this presages bad weather (as indeed it does in the poem).

ARCHELAUS Macedonian King (reigned 413–399BC)

1 In silence.

His reply when asked by a barber how he would like his hair cut. Quoted by W. & A. Durant in *The Story of Civilization* (1935–64). Possibly said, rather, by a successor, Philip II. Plutarch, however, in his *Moralia*, attributes it to Archelaus. Curiously, this is the caption to a Bernard Partridge cartoon entitled 'A DAMPER' in *Punch* (27 February 1897):

Chatty Barber: 'Ow would you like to be shaved, sir? *Grumpy Customer:* In perfect silence, please.

ARCHILOCHUS Greek poet (7th century BC)

2 The fox knows many things – the hedgehog one *big* thing.

A somewhat obscure opinion, but note how it is used by Isaiah Berlin in *The Hedgehog and the Fox: An Essay on Tolstoy's View of History* (1953): 'Scholars have differed about the correct interpretation of these dark words, which may mean no more than that the fox, for all his cunning, is defeated by the hedgehog's one defence ... There exists a great chasm between those, on one side, who relate everything to a single central vision ... and, on the other side, those who pursue many ends, often unrelated and even contradictory ... The first kind of intellectual and artistic personality belongs to the hedgehogs, the second to the foxes.' Benham (1948) gives it as an anonymous proverb: '*Ars varia vulpis, est una echino maxima* [The fox is versatile in its resources, but the hedgehog has one, and that chief of all].' Note how Erasmus renders the idea in *Adagia* (1500): 'The fox has many tricks, and the hedgehog has only one [i.e. it can roll itself up into a ball for protection], but that is the best of all.' Apparently Archilochus is so quoted in Plutarch, *Moralia*, 'The Cleverness of Animals'.

ARCHIMEDES Greek mathematician and inventor (?287–212BC)

3 Give me but one firm spot on which to stand, and I will move the earth.

On the action of a lever. Quoted in Pappus of Alexandria, *Synagoge*.

4 *Eureka* [I've got it]!

Leaping out of his bath having discovered the principle of water displacement. Quoted in Vitruvius Pollio, *De Architectura* (1st century BC). Archimedes's Principle is: 'When a body is immersed in water (or a fluid), its apparent loss of weight is equal to the weight of the water (or fluid) displaced.'

5 Wait till I have finished my problem.

Or, 'Stand away, fellow, from my diagram.' Last words. When the city of Syracuse was taken by the Romans, Archimedes was ordered by a soldier to follow him. Engaged as he was on a mathematical problem by drawing figures in the sand, he gave one or both of these responses. The soldier killed him. Quoted in Barnaby Conrad, *Famous Last Words* (1961). A common traditional form of what Archimedes is supposed to have said is '*Noli turbare circulos meos* [Do not disturb my circles].' Valerius Maximus gives the phrase as '*Noli, obsecro, istum disturbare* [Please, do not disturb this].' A slightly different wording is given by Porfirius.

Hannah ARENDT German-born American philosopher (1906–75)

6 It was as though in those last minutes he was summing up the lessons that this long course in human wickedness had taught us – the lesson of the fearsome, word-and-thought-defying banality of evil.

The final phrase was Arendt's key observation when writing about the trial of Adolf Eichmann, the Nazi official who was executed as a war criminal by Israel in 1962. Her book *Eichmann in Jerusalem* (1963) was subtitled 'A Report on the Banality of Evil'. Her essay was controversial in arguing that Europe's Jews might have been complicit in their own destruction and that Eichmann was not an abnormal monster but a mechanical one, unable to pit a personal morality against the Nazi system.

Richard ARENS American lawyer (1913–69)

7 Are you now or have you ever been a member of a godless conspiracy controlled by a foreign power?

Quoted in Peter Lewis, *The Fifties* (1978), this is Arens's version of the more usual question, 'Are you now or have you ever been a member of the Communist Party?', put to those appearing at hearings of the House of Representatives Committee on un-American Activities (approximately 1947–57), especially by J. Parnell Thomas. It was the stock phrase of McCarthyism, the pursuit and public ostracism of suspected US Communist sympathizers at the time of the war in Korea in the early 1950s. Senator Joseph McCarthy was the instigator of the 'witch hunts' that led to the black-listing of people in various walks of life, notably the film business. *Are You Now Or Have You Ever Been?* was the title of a radio/stage play (1978) by Eric Bentley.

ARISTOPHANES Greek comic playwright (?450–?385BC)

1 How about 'Cloudcuckooland [*Nephelococcygia*]'?
The Birds. This suggested name for the capital city of the birds (in the air) came to be included in the expression 'to live in cloud-cuckoo land', meaning 'to have impractical ideas'. Another 19th-century translation of the Greek was 'cloud cuckoo borough' (joke) and meaning 'never never land'. In 1943 Rommel was given the task by Hitler of completing the, up to that time, fictional Atlantic Wall. After his initial examination of what had been done so far, he proclaimed that it was a 'figment of Hitler's *Wolkenkuck-sheim* [cloud-cuckoo-land]'. This German translation has also been given as '*Wolkenkuckucksheim*'. The English phrase was listed as a current cliché in *The Times* (28 May 1984). 'The decision to standardize the names of authors may be a big stride for the book world. But it is only a small step towards that cloud-cuckoo-land where everybody speaks and writes English according to the same rules' – *The Times* (30 May 1994); 'Fund managers have questioned RJB's assessment of the market after 1998 when contracts with power generators, coal's biggest customer, expire. One banker advising an under-bidder said the RJB predictions "were in cloud-cuckoo-land"' – *The Sunday Times* (27 November 1994); 'Mr Watkinson said that the RMT's claim for 6 per cent [pay rise] meant that the [union's] leadership was "living in cloud cuckoo land"' – *The Independent* (27 May 1995).

ARISTOTLE Greek philosopher (384–322BC)

2 Tragedy is thus a representation of an action that is worth serious attention, complete in itself and of some amplitude ... by means of pity and fear bringing about the purgation of such emotions.
Poetics, Chap. 6. Hence, the word *catharsis* (Greek for 'cleansing, purging') that Aristotle used is now applied to the purification of the emotions, especially through drama.

3 A gentleman should be able to play the flute, but not too expertly.
Attributed to Aristotle – possibly an encapsulation of the point he makes in Bk 8 of his *Politics*, where he says that children of free men should learn and practise music only

until they are able to feel delight in it and should not become professional musicians because this would make them vulgar.

Reginald ARKELL English poet (1882–1959)

4 There is a lady, sweet and kind
As any lady you will find.
I've known her nearly all my life;
She is, in fact, my present wife.

In daylight, she is kind to all,
But, as the evening shadows fall,
With jam-pot, salt and sugar-tongs
She starts to right her garden's wrongs.
An extract from Arkell's poem 'The Lady with the Lamp', which appeared in his *Green Fingers* (1934). 'There is a lady sweet and kind' is also the first line of a poem attributed to Thomas Ford (died 1648).

(Sir) John S. ARKWRIGHT English lawyer and poet (1872–1954)

5 O valiant hearts, who to your glory came
Through dust of conflict and through battle
flame;
Tranquil you lie, your knightly virtue proved,
Your memory hallowed in the land you loved.

Proudly you gathered, rank on rank, to war,
As who had heard God's message from afar;
All you had hoped for, all you had, you gave
To save mankind – yourselves you scorned
to save.
'The Supreme Sacrifice' (1919). In the 1950s this moving hymn suffered a backlash and was dropped from Remembrance Day services by those who believed it was insufficiently critical of militarism. It is best sung to the already-existing tune 'Ellers' by E.J. Hopkins. The hymn contains *OED2*'s earliest citation for the phrase 'supreme sacrifice', which, alas, became a cliché for death.

Neil ARMSTRONG American astronaut (1930–)

6 Tranquillity Base here – the Eagle has landed.
The *Apollo 11* space mission that first put a man on the surface of the moon in July 1969 provided another phrase in addition to – and before – Armstrong's famous 'first' words (below). As the lunar module touched down, this was what he announced. Nobody at Mission Control had known that Armstrong would call the landing site 'Tranquillity Base', although the name was logical enough: they touched down in the Sea

of Tranquillity; *Eagle* was the name of the lunar module (referring to the American national symbol). *ODQ* (1992), basing itself on an inaccurate report in *The Times*, had the words spoken by Buzz Aldrin. Confusingly, the writer Jack Higgins later used the phrase *The Eagle Has Landed* as the title of a 1975 thriller about a German kidnap attempt on Winston Churchill during the Second World War.

1 **That's one small step for a man, one giant leap for mankind.**

Armstrong claimed that this was what he actually said when stepping on to the moon's surface for the first time at 10.56 p.m. (EDT) on 20 July 1969. Six hundred million television viewers round the world watched, but what were his first words going to be? It seemed to him that every person he had met in the previous three months had asked him what he was going to say or had made suggestions. Among the hundreds of sayings he was offered were passages from Shakespeare and whole chapters from the Bible.

'I had thought about what I was going to say, largely because so many people had asked me to think about it,' Armstrong reflected afterwards in *First on the Moon* (1970). 'I thought about [it] a little bit on the way to the moon, and it wasn't really decided until after we got to the lunar surface. I guess I hadn't actually decided what I wanted to say until just before we went out.'

What the six hundred million *heard* was another matter. The indefinite article before 'man' was completely inaudible, thus ruining the nice contrast between 'a man' (one individual) and 'mankind' (all of us). However, this was how the line was first reported and, indeed, exactly how it sounds on recordings. There is no perceptible gap between 'for' and 'man'.

It is probably the most misheard remark ever. *The Times* of 21 July had it as: 'That's one small step for man but [*sic*] one giant leap for mankind.' *The Observer* 'Sayings of the Week' column on the Sunday following the landing had: 'That's one small step for man, one giant leap for all [*sic*] mankind.' And reference books have continued the confusion ever since. Several follow the version – 'One small step for [...] man, one big step [*sic*] for mankind' – which appeared in the magazine *Nature* in 1974.

When he returned to earth, the astronaut spotted the near-tautology in a transcript of the mission and tried to put over a correct version. It was explained that the indefinite article 'a' had not been heard because of static on the radio link or because 'tape recorders are fallible'. But it is just as possible that Armstrong fluffed his mighty line. If the 20th century's most *audible* saying could result in such confusion, what hope is there for the rest?

Thomas D. Fuller wrote (1999): 'Mr Armstrong hails from Wapakoneta, Ohio, which is about 150 miles from where I grew up. My Ohio ears have no difficulty whatever in hearing Mr Armstrong's statement on the moon as "for a man". Most Americans, or at least Midwesterners, would have no difficulty in interpreting "Jeer jet?" as "Did you eat yet?" despite an abundance of elision. It seems a little odd to make (as we would say in the States) a Federal case about what was at best a dialectical delivery.' This seems a fair point. Armstrong said the 'a' (as he has always claimed he did) but we cloth-eared non-Ohioans simply did not hear it.

(Sir) Robert ARMSTRONG (later Lord Armstrong)
English civil servant (1927–)

2 **It is perhaps being economical with the truth.**

On 18 November 1986 Armstrong, then the British Cabinet Secretary, was being cross-examined in the Supreme Court of New South Wales. The British government was attempting to prevent publication in Australia of a book about MI5, the British secret service. Defence counsel Malcolm Turnbull asked Sir Robert about the contents of a letter he had written that had been intended to convey a misleading impression. 'What's a "misleading impression"?' inquired Turnbull. 'A sort of bent untruth?'

Sir Robert replied: 'It is perhaps being economical with the truth.' This explanation was greeted with derision not only in the court but in the world beyond, and it looked as if a new euphemism for lying had been coined. In fact, Sir Robert had prefaced his remark with: 'As one person said ...' and, when the court apparently found cause for laughter in what he said, added: 'It is not very original, I'm afraid.'

Indeed not. The Earl of Dalkeith MP had referred to Harold Wilson's post-devaluation broadcast (see 502:1) in a House of Commons question (4 July 1968): 'Would he openly admit that he either made a gross miscalculation, misled the people, or at least had been over-economical with the truth?' Dr E.H.H. Green, writing to *The Guardian* on 4 February 1987, said he had found a note penned by Sir William Strang, later to become head of the Foreign Office, in February 1942. Describing the character of the exiled Czech President Beneš, Strang had written: 'Dr Benes's methods are exasperating; he is a master of representation and ... he is apt to be economical with the truth.'

The notion thus appears to have been a familiar one in the British Civil Service for a very long time. Samuel Pepys apparently used the precise phrase in his evidence before the Brooke House Committee in its examination of the Navy Board in 1669–70.

Mark Twain wrote: 'Truth is the most valuable thing we have. Let us economize it' – *Following the Equator* (1897).

In March 1988 Armstrong said in a TV interview that he

had no regrets about having used the phrase. And he said again, it was not his own, indeed, but Edmund Burke's. The reference was to Burke's *Two Letters on Proposals for Peace* (1796): 'Falsehood and delusion are allowed in no case whatsoever. But, as in the exercise of all the virtues, there is an economy of truth.' Compare CLARK 144:6.

Matthew ARNOLD English poet and essayist
(1822–88)

1 Others abide our question. Thou art free.
We ask and ask – Thou smilest and art still,
Out-topping knowledge.

'Shakespeare' (1849). From P.G. Wodehouse, *Thank You, Jeeves* (1934): '"Jeeves," I said, "As I have often had occasion to say before, you stand alone." "Thank you, sir." "Others abide our question. Thou art free." "I endeavour to give satisfaction, sir."'

2 A God, a God their severance ruled!
And bade betwixt their shores to be
The unplumb'd, salt, estranging sea.

'To Marguerite – Continued' (1852). The last sentence of *The French Lieutenant's Woman* (1969) by John Fowles (unattributed at that point, though it has been earlier) is: 'And out again, upon the unplumb'd, salt, estranging sea.'

3 Beautiful city! so venerable, so lovely, so unravaged by the fierce intellectual life of our century, so serene! ... whispering from her towers the last enchantments of the Middle Age ... home of lost causes, and forsaken beliefs, and unpopular names, and impossible loyalties!

Preface, *Essays in Criticism*, First Series (1865). On Oxford. James Morris, *Oxford* (1965), comments: 'Matthew Arnold said it was still "whispering the last enchantments of the Middle Ages", but Max Beerbohm thought he must have been referring to the railway station.' And adds: 'It is no such Arcady now, and its University no longer whispers those last enchantments. It is a turmoil, always dissatisfied, always in disagreement.'

4 And that sweet city with her dreaming spires,
She needs not June for beauty's heightening.

'Thyrsis' (1866). On Oxford. Morris (in the same book as above) comments: 'Nor does she. The particular magic of Oxford rides out the seasons ... all four seasons suit Oxford, and each enhances the look of her in a different way.' For appalling wordplay on this, see RAPHAEL 376:2.

5 The sea is calm to-night,
The tide is full, the moon lies fair
Upon the straits ...
For the world, which seems
To lie before us like a land of dreams.

'Dover Beach' (1867). The last two lines here were famously misquoted by Lyndon Johnson in a speech in the summer of 1965. He (or his speechwriter) put 'lie out' and attributed the poem to Robert Lowell, who had merely used the lines as epigraph to his book *The Mills of the Kavanaughs*. See also JOHNSON 257:4.

6 And we are here as on a darkling plain
Swept with confused alarms of struggle and
   flight,
Where ignorant armies clash by night.

From the same poem. Hence, the film title *Clash By Night* (US 1952) and, just possibly, the title of Norman Mailer's non-fiction work *Armies of the Night* (1968).

7 Let the long contention cease!
Geese are swans, and swans are geese.

'The Last Word' (1867). The 'geese/swans' comparison is in a long tradition. Three years before this, Cardinal Newman had written in his *Apologia*: 'He was particularly loyal to his friends, and, to use the common phrase, "all his geese were swans".' Horace Walpole said of Sir Joshua Reynolds, 'All his own geese are swans, as the swans of others are geese' (letter to the Countess of Upper Ossory, 1 December 1786). 'All their geese are swans' occurs in 'Democritus to the Reader' in Robert Burton, *The Anatomy of Melancholy* (1621). 'All his geese are swans' was a proverbial expression by 1529.

8 The pursuit of perfection, then, is the pursuit of sweetness and light. He who works for sweetness and light, works to make reason and the will of God prevail.

Culture and Anarchy, Chap. 1 (1869). *The Lyttelton Hart-Davis Letters* (for 25 January 1956) affirms that Arnold believed this conjunction of sweetness and light was the *sine qua non* of all real civilization. Compare SWIFT 450:4.

9 *L'homme sensuel moyen dont la patrie est la France et la ville Paris, et dont l'idéal est la vie libre, gaie, plaisante de Paris* [The averagely sensual man whose natural home is France and in particular the city of Paris, and whose ideal is the free, gay, pleasant life you can have in Paris].

In *Mixed Essays* (1879) – although not found in the original

English version. In seeking the origin of the literary term *un homme moyen sensuel* to denote the expectations of the averagely sensual reader, all roads lead to Matthew Arnold, the English poet and critic, though whether he actually coined the phrase is hard to say. He usually put the words in the order *homme sensuel moyen* – for example in his piece on George Sand in *Mixed Essays* (1879). Othon Guerlac, *Les Citations françaises* (1931), credits Arnold with originating the expression, but critic Harry Levin states that it 'is never used in the sensual land of France'.

Daisy ASHFORD English child author (1881–1972)

1 Mr Salteena was an elderly man of 42 and was fond of asking peaple to stay with him.

The Young Visiters, Chap. 1 (1919). This story of romance and high society was written when Daisy was nine. It was published, complete with crude spellings and interesting punctuation, when she was 38. Because there was an introduction by J.M. Barrie, it has sometimes been wrongly believed that he was the actual author. Other choice extracts: 'I do hope I shall enjoy myself with you ... I am parshial to ladies if they are nice I suppose it is my nature. I am not quite a gentleman but you would hardly notice it' (Chap. 1); 'I am very fond of fresh air and royalties' (Chap. 5).

2 Well one never knows (he murmerd to himself) and as one of the poets says, great events from trivil causes spring.

From the same book, Chap. 7. Bernard Clark is probably alluding to Pope, *The Rape of the Lock*, Canto 1, line 2: 'What mighty contests rise from trivial things.'

H.H. ASQUITH (later 1st Earl of Oxford and Asquith) British Liberal Prime Minister (1852–1928)

3 You had better wait and see.

To a persistent inquirer about the Parliament Act Procedure Bill, in the House of Commons (4 April 1910). In fact, this was the fourth occasion on which Asquith had said 'Wait and see'. On 3 March he had replied 'We had better wait and see' to Lord Helmsey concerning the government's intentions over the Budget and whether the House of Lords would be flooded with Liberal peers to ensure the passage of the Finance Bill. So he was clearly deliberate in his use of the words. His intention was not to delay making an answer but to warn people off. Roy Jenkins commented in *Asquith* (1964): 'It was a use for which he was to pay dearly in the last years of his premiership when the phrase came to be erected by his enemies as a symbol of his alleged inactivity.'

In consequence, Asquith acquired the nickname 'Old Wait and See', and during the First World War French

matches that failed to ignite were known either as 'Asquiths' or 'Wait and sees'.

It was, of course, an old phrase: Daniel Defoe has it in *Robinson Crusoe* (1719): 'However, we had no remedy, but to wait and see what the issue of things might present.'

4 [Balliol men are distinguished from lesser souls by their] tranquil consciousness of effortless superiority.

This is the version of Asquith's remark given by John Jones in his *Balliol College: A History 1263–1939*. Frances Bennion wrote to *Oxford Today* (Hilary Term 1992) to point out that the British Labour politician Denis Healey – an old member of the college – had misquoted this in his memoirs, *The Time of My Life* (1989), as, 'the conscious tranquillity of effortless superiority'. Which is not quite the same thing.

5 Another little drink wouldn't do us any harm.

The boozer's jocular justification for another snort is, in fact, rather more than a catchphrase. It is alluded to in Edith Sitwell's bizarre lyrics for 'Scotch Rhapsody' in *Façade* (1922):

There is a hotel at Ostend
Cold as the wind, without an end,
Haunted by ghostly poor relations ...
And 'Another little drink wouldn't do us any harm,'
Pierces through the sabbatical calm.

The actual origin is in a song with the phrase as title, written by Clifford Grey to music by Nat D. Ayer, and sung by the comedian George Robey in *The Bing Boys Are Here* (1916). The song includes a reference to the well-known fact that Prime Minister Asquith was at times the worse for drink when on the Treasury Bench (hence his nickname of Old Squiffy):

Mr Asquith says in a manner sweet and calm:
And another little drink wouldn't do us any harm.

6 It is fitting that we should have buried the Unknown Prime Minister by the side of the Unknown Soldier.

At the Westminster Abbey funeral of Andrew Bonar Law (5 November 1923). Hence, *The Unknown Prime Minister*, the title of Law's biography (1955) by Robert Blake.

Margot ASQUITH (later Countess of Oxford and Asquith) Wife of H.H. Asquith (1864–1945)

7 Kitchener is a great poster.

Sir Philip Magnus, *Kitchener: Portrait of an Imperialist* (1958), ascribes this remark to Margot but in *More Memories*, Chap. 6 (1933), she herself attributed it to her daughter Elizabeth (1897–1945).

1 My dear old friend King George V told me he would never have died but for that vile doctor, Lord Dawson of Penn.

An observation that Lady Asquith made several times in her old age, but especially to Lord David Cecil (and recorded first by Mark Bonham Carter in his introduction to *The Autobiography of Margot Asquith*, 1962 edn). It turns out to be not so preposterous as might appear. On 20 January 1936, King George V lay dying at Sandringham. At 9.25 p.m., Lord Dawson of Penn, the King's doctor, issued a bulletin: 'The King's life is moving peacefully towards its close' – see DAWSON 163:3. This was taken up by the BBC and repeated until the King died at 11.55 p.m. In December 1986, Dawson's biographer suggested in *History Today* that the doctor had in fact hastened the King's departure with lethal injections of morphine and cocaine at the request of the Queen and the future Edward VIII. Dawson's notes reveal that the death was induced at 11 p.m. not only to ease the King's pain but to enable the news to make the morning papers, 'rather than the less appropriate evening journals'. *The Times* was advised that important news was coming and to hold back publication. So Dawson of Penn *might* have had a hand in the King's death, though quite how George V communicated his view of the matter to Margot Asquith is not known.

2 The 't' is silent – as in 'Harlow'.

Margot Asquith was noted for the sharp remarks she made about people, but her most famous shaft was probably said by someone else. The story goes that Margot went on a visit to the United States (*that* is not in dispute), where she met Jean Harlow. The film actress inquired whether the name of the Countess (which she was by this time, the 1930s) was pronounced 'Margo' or 'Margott'. '"Margo",' replied the Countess, 'the "t" is silent – as in "Harlow".' The story did not appear in print until T.S. Matthews' *Great Tom* in 1973.

Then, in about 1983, a much more convincing version of its origin was given. Margot *Grahame* (1911–82) was an English actress who, after stage appearances in Johannesburg and London, went to Hollywood in 1934. Her comparatively brief career as a film star included appearances in *The Informer*, *The Buccaneer* and *The Three Musketeers* in the mid-1930s. It was when she was being built up as a rival to the likes of Harlow (who died in 1937) that Grahame herself claimed the celebrated exchange had occurred. She added that it was not intended as a put-down. She did not realize what she had said until afterwards.

Grahame seems a convincing candidate for speaker of the famous line. However, when her star waned people attributed the remark to the other, better known and more quotable source.

Clement ATTLEE (later 1st Earl Attlee) British Labour Prime Minister (1883–1967)

3 You have no right whatever to speak on behalf of the Government. Foreign Affairs are in the capable hands of Ernest Bevin. His task is quite sufficiently difficult without the embarrassment of irresponsible statements of the kind which you are making ... a period of silence on your part would be welcome.

Quoted in *British Political Facts 1900–75*. From a letter to Harold Laski, Chairman of the Labour Party NEC (20 August 1945). Just after the Labour government had come to power, Laski had been giving a constant flow of speeches and interviews, not always in accord with party policy. The put-down was typical of Attlee's clipped way, and also reflected his own more reticent way with words.

4 Few thought he was even a starter
There were many who thought themselves smarter
But he ended PM, CH and OM
An Earl and a Knight of the Garter.

Of himself. Lines written on 8 April 1956, quoted in Kenneth Harris, *Attlee* (1982). Of modest demeanour (hence CHURCHILL 140:6), Attlee was a man of considerable achievement as he gently points out here.

W.H. AUDEN Anglo-American poet (1907–73)

5 Private faces in public places
Are wiser and nicer
Than public faces in private places.

Dedication, *Orators* (1932). Hence, possibly, *Public Faces*, title of a book (1932) by Harold Nicolson. The actress Sian Phillips entitled the two volumes of her autobiography, *Private Places* (1999) and *Public Faces* (2001).

6 *The Dog Beneath the Skin.*

Title of play (1935), written with Christopher Isherwood. According to Humphrey Carpenter's biography of Auden (1981), the title was suggested by Rupert Doone and probably alludes to ELIOT 186:4.

7 August for the people and their favourite islands.

'Birthday Poem' (1935). Hence, *August for the People*, title of a play (1961) by Nigel Dennis.

8 This is the Night Mail crossing the Border
Bringing the cheque and the postal order,

Letters for the rich, letters for the poor,
The shop at the corner, the girl next door.

'Night Mail' (1935). Commentary for Post Office Film Unit documentary film. 'We were experimenting,' Auden said, 'to see whether poetry could be used in films, and I think we showed it could.' The first draft contained lines that Harry Watt, the director, felt 'could not be matched with adequate images on the screen – lines such as "Uplands heaped like slaughtered horses" ... Watt observed: "No picture we put on the screen could be as strong as that"' – source: Humphrey Carpenter, *W.H. Auden* (1981). Nevertheless, the cut line has not been forgotten and is still quoted.

1 And make us as Newton was, who in his
   garden watching
The apple falling towards England, became
   aware
Between himself and her of an eternal tie.

'O Love, the interest itself' (1936). Hence, probably, *Falling Towards England*, title of a volume of memoirs (1985) by the Australian-born writer, Clive James (although he does not cite the poem in his book). Julian Mitchell's 1994 play about a family in the early part of the 20th century has the similar title, *Falling Over England*.

2 Look, stranger, at this island now.

'Look, Stranger' (1936). Hence, *Look, Stranger!*, the title of a BBC TV documentary series (1976). This use revealed an interesting state of affairs. Auden's famous poem has two versions of its first line: 'Look, stranger, at this island now' and ' ... on this island now'. 'At' is the original reading in the title poem of the collection *Look, Stranger!* published in the UK (1936). But the US title of the collection was *On This Island*. The text of the poem was changed to 'on' for the 1945 *Collected Poems*, published in the US. Just to complicate matters, the poem's title was changed variously to 'Seascape' and 'Seaside'.

The reason for all this is that when he was inaccessible in Iceland, his publishers Faber & Faber (in the person of T.S. Eliot) applied the title *Look, Stranger!* to the collection that Auden wanted called 'Poems 1936'. He said the Faber title sounded 'like the work of a vegetarian lady novelist' and made sure that it was subsequently dropped.

3 Stop all the clocks, cut off the telephone,
Prevent the dog from barking with a juicy bone,
Silence the pianos and with muffled drum
Bring out the coffin, let the mourners come.

... He was my North, my South, my East and West,
My working week and my Sunday rest,

My noon, my midnight, my talk, my song;
I thought that love would last for ever. I was
   wrong.

From 'Funeral Blues', originally in *The Ascent of F6* (1937), a play jointly written with Christopher Isherwood. Set to music, a pastiche blues, by Benjamin Britten for the original production, the original words mocked the death of a political leader. Auden then rewrote the poem as more of a love song, and it had a separate existence for many years as one of Britten's *Cabaret Songs*. Then in 1994, the text was spoken at the funeral 'of another bugger' in the UK film *Four Weddings and a Funeral*. Seldom can a poem have become so immediately known and popular.

4 He disappeared in the dead of winter:
The brooks were frozen, the airports almost
   deserted,
And snow disfigured the public statues;
The mercury sank in the mouth of the dying
   day.
What instruments we have agree
The day of his death was a dark cold day ...
Mad Ireland hurt you into poetry.
Now Ireland has her madness and her
   weather still,
For poetry makes nothing happen ...
Earth, receive an honoured guest:
William Yeats is laid to rest.
Let the Irish vessel lie
Emptied of its poetry.

'In Memory of W.B. Yeats' (1939). Carpenter (in the same biography) comments: 'Yeats had been an important influence on Auden's poetic style during the 1930s, but Auden did not have an unmitigated admiration for him ... By contrast the poem was scarcely critical of Yeats; in fact it was not really about him, but about the nature and function of poetry – and thus really about Auden himself.'

5 In the deserts of the heart
Let the healing fountain start,
In the prison of his days
Teach the free man how to praise.

From the same poem. The last two lines are quoted on the memorial slab to Auden in Poets' Corner, Westminster Abbey. The memorial was unveiled on 2 October 1974. Auden is actually buried at Kirchstetten, Austria.

6 There is no such thing as the State
And no one exists alone;
Hunger allows no choice

To the citizen or the police;
We must love one another or die.

'September 1, 1939' (1940). Auden became embarrassed by the last line here in 'the most dishonest poem I have ever written' because it was 'a damned lie' – we must all die in any case. When the editor of a 1955 anthology pleaded with Auden to include the entire text of the poem, Auden agreed provided that 'We must love one another *and* die' was substituted. The poem does not appear in his *Collected Poems* (1976 edn).

1 Defenceless under the night
Our world in stupor lies;
Yet, dotted everywhere,
Ironic points of light
Flash out wherever the Just
Exchange their messages.

From the same poem. See BUSH 113:2.

2 Perfection, of a kind, was what he was after,
And the poetry he invented was easy to
    understand;
He knew human folly like the back of his hand,
And was greatly interested in armies and
    fleets;
When he laughed, respectable senators burst
    with laughter,
And when he cried the little children died in
    the streets.

'Epitaph on a Tyrant' (1940). The last line echoes J.L. Motley's description of William of Orange in *The Rise of the Dutch Republic* (1856): 'As long as he lived, he was the guiding-star of a whole brave nation, and when he died the little children cried in the streets.'

3 Lay your sleeping head, my love,
Human on my faithless arm.

'Lullaby' (1940). Carpenter (in the same biography) comments: '[This poem] became, in the years that followed, the most famous of all his short lyrics ... [this and other poems] are not usually even explicitly homosexual: their subject is the impermanence of all love, whatever sex the loved may be.'

4 Most people enjoy the sight of their own hand-writing as they enjoy the smell of their own farts.

'Writing', *The Dyer's Hand* (1962). See also ANONYMOUS 15:2.

5 Thoughts of his own death,
like the distant roll
of thunder at a picnic.

'Marginalia', V (1965–8). Sometimes quoted as, 'Thoughts of death are like distant thunder at a summer picnic.'

6 In a brothel, both
The ladies and gentlemen
Have nicknames only.

An epigrammatic verse in the collection *About the House* (1966). Hence, *Both the Ladies and the Gentlemen* – title of a memoir (1975) by William Donaldson about being a pimp and brothel-keeper.

7 My face looks like a wedding-cake left out in the rain.

No, it was not said by someone else *about* Auden – as stated, for example, in L. Levinson, *Bartlett's Unfamiliar Quotations* (1972). The poet himself said to a reporter: 'Your cameraman might enjoy himself, because my face looks like a wedding-cake left out in the rain' (cited in Humphrey Carpenter, *W.H. Auden*, 1981). However, according to Noël Annan in *Maurice Bowra: a celebration* (1974), Bowra once referred to E.M. Forster's *work* as a wedding-cake left out in the rain.

Someone once said of Auden's face, 'If a fly walked over it, it would break its leg' – quoted on BBC Radio *Quote ... Unquote* (5 June 1980). In *The Poet Auden* by A. L. Rowse (1987), this remark is ascribed to Lord David Cecil.

Émile AUGIER French poet and playwright (1820–89)

8 Marquis: *Mettez un canard sur un lac au milieu des cygnes, vous verrez qu'il regrettera sa mare et finira par y retourner.*
Montrichard: *La nostalgie de la boue!* [Longing to be back in the mud].

In the play *Le Mariage d'Olympe* (1855), Augier gave this as an explanation of what happens when you put a duck on a lake with swans: he will miss his own pond and eventually return to it. The phrase has been taken up in many situations where there is a desire for degradation. At the very end of D.H. Lawrence's *Lady Chatterley's Lover* (1928), Sir Clifford says to Lady Connie: 'You're one of those half-insane, perverted women who must run after depravity, the *nostalgie de la boue.*'

AUGUSTINE OF HIPPO North African Christian theologian and saint (AD354–430)

1 A stiff prick hath no conscience.

Ascribed confidently by John Osborne in *Almost a Gentleman* (1991), this remark remains unverified, though, in one sense, it would not be surprising given Augustine's interesting activities prior to conversion. After all, he did write '*Da mihi castitatem et continentiam, sed noli modo* [give me chastity and continence – but not yet]' in his *Confessions* (397–398). The proverbial status of the remark was, however, evident by the 1880s when 'Walter' in *My Secret Life* (Vol. 1, Chap. 12) wrote: 'I thought how unfair it was to her sister, who was in the family way by me ... but a standing prick stifles all conscience.' Indeed, 'a *standing* prick has no conscience' is an equally well-known variant. *Partridge/Catch Phrases* adds that this proverbial view is sometimes completed with, '... and an itching cunt feels no shame', just to even out the matter.

Compare: 'Another writer whom [Wilde] did not spare was his old teacher J.P. Mahaffy, two of whose books Wilde reviewed ... [he] might have treated Mahaffy nostalgically, but the erect pen has no conscience' – Richard Ellman, *Oscar Wilde* (1987).

Further confirmation of the proverbial nature of this kind of saying is to be found in the diary of Samuel Pepys, where on 15 May 1663 he writes of hearing from Sir Thomas Crew that: 'the King [Charles II] doth mind nothing but pleasures and hates the very sight or thoughts of business. That my Lady Castlemayne rules him; who he says hath all the tricks of Aretin [erotic writer Pietro Aretino] that are to be practised to give pleasure – in which he is too able, hav[ing] a large —— [Pepys's blank]; but that which is the unhappiness is that, as the Italian proverb says, *Cazzo dritto non vuolt consiglio.*' This may be translated as 'A stiff prick doesn't want any advice.'

Marcus AURELIUS Roman Emperor (AD121–180)

2 Does aught befall you? It is good. It is part of the destiny of the Universe ordained for you from the beginning. All that befalls you is part of the great web.

This is a particular translation of *Meditations*, Bk 10, Sect. 5, much favoured by Jeeves in the P.G. Wodehouse stories. *The Mating Season*, Chap. 4 (1949), has Jeeves saying to Bertie Wooster: 'I wonder if I might call your attention to an observation of the Emperor Marcus Aurelius. He said [as above].' This is then repeated word for word by Bertie to Gussie Fink-Nottle in Chap. 9, and then Gussie reminds Bertie of the last sentence. Another translation of the passage is: 'Whatever may happen to you was prepared for you from all eternity; and the implication of causes was from eternity spinning the thread of your being.'

Jane AUSTEN English novelist (1775–1817)

3 *Pride and Prejudice.*

The title of Austen's novel (written as *First Impressions*, 1797, published 1813) has been said to derive from the second chapter of Edward Gibbon's *The Decline and Fall of the Roman Empire* (published 1776). Writing of the enfranchisement of the slaves, Gibbon writes: 'Without destroying the distinction of ranks a distant prospect of freedom and honours was presented, even to those whom pride and prejudice almost disdained to number among the human species.'

More to the point, the phrase occurs no fewer than three times, in bold print, towards the end of Fanny Burney's *Cecilia* (1787): '"The whole of this unfortunate business," said Dr Lyster, "has been the result of Pride and Prejudice ... Yet this, however, remember; if to Pride and Prejudice you owe your miseries, so wonderfully is good and evil balanced, that to Pride and Prejudice you will also owe their termination."' This seems the most likely cue to Jane Austen. On the other hand, *OED2* provides six citations of the phrase 'pride and prejudice' before Burney, one of which has capital Ps.

4 It is a truth universally acknowledged, that a single man in possession of a good fortune, must be in want of a wife.

Pride and Prejudice (1813), opening words – probably the most imitated and parodied of all such.

Alfred AUSTIN English Poet Laureate (1835–1913)

5 Flash'd from his bed the electric tidings came, 'He is no better, he is much the same.'

Lines often ascribed to Austin, as in A. & V. Palmer, *Quotations in History* (1976), and sometimes remembered as 'Across/along the electric wire the message came ...' The couplet is quoted as an example of bathos and of a Poet Laureate writing to order at his worst. As such, it needs some qualification, if not an actual apology to the poet's shade. D.B. Wyndham Lewis and Charles Lee in their noted selection of bad verse, *The Stuffed Owl* (1930), interestingly included a similar couplet, but ascribed it to a 'university poet unknown', and quite right, too. F.H. Gribble had included the slightly different version, 'Along the electric wire ...' in his *Romance of the Cambridge Colleges* (1913).

What is not in dispute is that the lines were written to mark the Prince of Wales's illness in 1871. Unfortunately, to spoil a good story, it has to be pointed out that Austin never wrote them (though he *did* match them in awfulness on other occasions) and he did not become Poet Laureate until 1896, following in the illustrious footsteps of Tennyson. As J. Lewis May observed in *The Dublin Review* (July 1937), in an article about Austin as 'a neglected poet', the couplet was written 'when the then Prince of Wales (he who afterwards became King Edward VII) had recovered from the attack of typhoid fever which had caused the gravest anxiety throughout the country, [and] the subject set for the Newdigate Prize Poem at Oxford was "The Prince of Wales's illness"; whereupon some wag, with consequences of which he never dreamed, produced the following couplet, as a specimen of the sort of thing that might be sent in by competitors for the coveted guerdon ... The name of the inventor of those immortal lines has not been handed down.'

The Editor of *The Author* (Spring 1993) questioned whether Austin had really attracted 'universal derision' (my phrase) because of his supposed authorship of the lines. To which I replied that, almost invariably, Austin was linked to them, with or without an 'attributed to' or other qualification, in such dictionaries of quotations as *PDQ* (1960), the *Bloomsbury Dictionary of Quotations* (1987) and Robin Hyman's *Dictionary of Famous Quotations* (1962). Even *ODQ* (1992) *mentions* Austin, although it places the couplet under 'Anonymous'.

As for Austin generally, Mrs Claude Bettington recalled in *All That I Have Met* (1929) that he had said to her in all seriousness one day, 'My child, have you ever noticed how many great men are called *Alfred* – Alfred the Great, Alfred Tennyson?' As a dutiful niece, she added, 'And *you*, Uncle Alf.' Mrs Bettington goes on: 'No one could fathom why he was made Poet Laureate, since his only claim to fame was his exquisite prose. I therefore asked a niece of Lord Salisbury point blank, "Why on earth did your uncle give the laureateship to Uncle Alfred?" She answered, "Because it was absolutely the only honour Mr Austin would accept from the Government for his long years of service to the Conservative cause."'

(Revd) W(ilbert) AWDRY English clergyman and author (1911–97)

1 After pushing [trucks] about here for a few weeks you'll know almost as much about them as Edward. Then you'll be a Really Useful Engine.
Thomas the Tank Engine (1946). Accordingly, since the 1980s, the composer Andrew Lloyd Webber has presided over a business empire called the Really Useful Group.

2 We are nationalized now, but the same engines still work the Region. I am glad, too, to tell you that the Fat Director, who understands our friends' ways, is still in charge, but is now the Fat Controller.
Introduction, *James the Red Engine* (1948). In fact, the gentleman in question has twice undergone a name change. Initially, indeed, he was shown very much as a director of a private railway company, wearing striped pants, tail coat and top hat, but the nationalization of Britain's railways in the late 1940s did necessitate the change from 'director' to 'controller'. Then again, in the 1990s, when a hugely successful TV film version was made of the stories, sales to the politically correct US market necessitated that the character be referred to not by the fat-ist 'Fat Controller' but by Awdry's actual name for the character, 'Sir Topham Hatt'.

George AXELROD American screenwriter (1922–2003)

3 *The Seven Year Itch.*
Title of play (1952; film US 1955) – a term for the urge to be unfaithful to a spouse after a certain period of matrimony. *OED2* provides various examples of this phrase going back from the mid-20th to the mid-19th century, but without the specific matrimonial context. For example, the 'seven-year itch' describes a rash from poison ivy that was believed to recur every year for a seven-year period. Then one has to recall that since biblical days seven-year periods (of lean or fat) have had especial significance, and there has also been the army saying, 'Cheer up – the first seven years are the worst!'

But the specific matrimonial application was not popularized until Axelrod's play. 'Itch' had long been used for the sexual urge but, as Axelrod commented on BBC Radio *Quote ... Unquote* (15 June 1979): 'There was a phrase which referred to a somewhat unpleasant disease but nobody had used it in a sexual [he meant 'matrimonial'] context before. I do believe I invented it in that sense.'

Oddly, there is no mention in reference books of 'itch' being used in connection with venereal diseases. Nonetheless, the following remark occurs in Robert Lewis Taylor, *W.C. Fields: His Follies and Fortunes* (published as early as 1950): 'Bill exchanged women every seven years, as some people get rid of the itch.'

B

Francis BACON (1st Baron Verulam and Viscount St Albans) English philosopher and politician (1561–1626)

1 I have taken all knowledge to be my province.

Letter to Lord Burghley (1592). Bacon also wrote: '*Nam et ipsa scientia postestas est* [Knowledge is itself power]' in *De Haeresibus* (1597). Sir James Murray, first editor of what became *The Oxford English Dictionary*, wrote 'Knowledge is power' (in English) on the flyleaf of his copy of Cassell's *Popular Educator* – quoted in Elizabeth Murray, *Caught in the Web of Words* (1977).

2 My *Essays*, which of all my other works have been most current, for that as it seems they come home to men's business and bosoms.

Dedication of the 1625 edition of his *Essays*. Business = concerns; bosoms = emotions.

3 Question was asked of Demosthenes, *What was the chief part of an orator?* He answered, *Action.* What next? *Action.* What next again? *Action.*

'Of Boldness', in the same work. Bacon is quoting Cicero, who gives these replies in *Orator* 3:56 and *Brutus* 17:56. For some reason the translation 'action' has been preferred over the more literal 'delivery', which, however, makes the meaning clearer. Demosthenes, Athenian orator and politician (384–322BC), reputedly gave these as the three most important qualities in an orator. Quoted by Kenneth Tynan in 'A Tribute to Mr Coward' (1953). In Boswell's *Life of Johnson* (1791) – for 3 April 1773 – Dr Johnson 'repeated his usual paradoxical declamation against action in publick speaking. "Action can have no effect upon reasonable minds."' When Mrs Thrale pointed out Demosthenes's recipe, he retorted: 'Demosthenes, Madam, spoke to an assembly of brutes; to a barbarous people.'

4 If the mountain won't come to Mohammed, Mohammed must go to the mountain.

Now meaning, if you can't get your own way, you must bow to the inevitable. What Bacon actually wrote in the same essay, where the proverb probably made its first appearance in English, was: 'If the hill will not come to Mahomet, Mahomet will go to the hill.' Bacon had it in the form of a Spanish proverb in his commonplace book, but the source ultimately is the *Hadith* – the traditional sayings of Mohammed that are not to be found in the Koran. The saying would seem to refer to the occasion when Mohammed asked for miraculous proof of his teaching and ordered Mount Safa (a hill near Mecca) to come to him. When it did not, he took this as a sign of God's mercy – because they would have been buried by the mountain if it had moved – and instead went to the mountain to give thanks.

5 Men fear death as children fear to go into the dark; and as that natural fear in children is increased with tales, so is the other.

'Of Death', in the same work. Bacon also alludes to Seneca's saying: '*Pompa mortis magis terret quam mors ipsa* [The trappings of death terrify us more than death itself].' See also FIELDING 194:1.

6 If a man be gracious and courteous to strangers, it shows he is a citizen of the world.

'Of Goodness, and Goodness of Nature', in the same work. Cicero had the phrase 'citizen of the world' as '*civem totius mundi*', meaning 'one who is cosmopolitan, at home anywhere'. Similarly, Socrates said, 'I am a citizen, not of Athens or Greece, but of the world.' *OED2* finds the English phrase in Caxton (1474). Later, *The Citizen of the World* was the title of a collection of letters by Oliver Goldsmith purporting to be those of Lien Chi Altangi, a philosophic Chinaman living in London and commenting on English life and characters. They were first published as 'Chinese Letters' in the *Public Ledger* (1760–1), and then again under this title in 1762.

James Boswell, not unexpectedly, in his *Journal of a Tour to the Hebrides* (1786) reflects: 'I am, I flatter myself, completely a citizen of the world ... In my travels through Holland, Germany, Switzerland, Italy, Corsica, France, I never felt myself from home; and I sincerely love "every kindred and tongue and people and nation".'

1 He that hath wife and children, hath given hostages to fortune; for they are impediments to great enterprises, either of virtue or mischief.

'Of Marriage and Single Life', in the same work. The idea is that such a man has placed himself at a disadvantage since he must do nothing to affect their well-being adversely. An argument *against* marriage. This is probably the origin of the expression 'hostage to fortune' for what one creates by delivering one's future into the hands of fate, usually by making some specific move or decision.

2 He was reputed one of the wise men that made answer to the question, when a man should marry: *A young man not yet, an elder man not at all.*

In the same essay. The allusion is to Thales of Miletus, as recounted in Plutarch, *Table-Talk*, III.6.3. This was advice that Bacon himself took and then did not take. He did not marry until he was quite old, in his forties, when he wed the daughter of an alderman.

3 Let diaries therefore be brought in use ... Let him also keep a diary.

'Of Travel', in the same work. Bacon is urging the keeping of, specifically, travel diaries rather than the more general type.

4 *What is Truth?* said jesting Pilate, and would not stay for an answer.

'Of Truth', in the same work. The allusion is to Pilate's question to Jesus Christ, as reported in John 18:38. 'Jesting' is Bacon's additional comment. Hence, *Jesting Pilate*, title of a travel book (1926) by Aldous Huxley.

5 It is the wisdom of the crocodiles, that shed tears when they would devour.

'Of Wisdom for a Man's Self', in the same work. The legend that crocodiles shed tears in order to lure victims to their deaths was established by the year 1400. In an account of a 1565 voyage by Sir John Hawkins (published by Richard Hakluyt, 1600), there is: 'In this river we saw many crocodiles ... His nature is ever when he would have his prey, to cry and sob like a Christian body, to provoke them to come to him, and then he snatcheth at them.' Shakespeare makes reference to crocodile tears in *Antony and Cleopatra*, *Othello* and *Henry VI*. Hence, the modern use of 'crododile tears' to denote a false display of sorrow.

See also ELIZABETH I 188:6.

Francis BACON Irish-born British painter (1909–92)

6 *Three Screaming Popes.*

This is not the title of any painting by Bacon, but of a musical work inspired by his three paintings of Popes which, in turn, were based on the Velázquez portrait 'Pope Innocent X'. The English composer Mark-Anthony Turnage (1960–), whose orchestral work with the title was first performed in 1989, says his initial idea was 'to write a piece which distorted a set of Spanish dances as Bacon had distorted and restated the Velázquez'. Bacon's paintings tend to be referred to dryly along the lines of *Study after Velázquez's Portrait of Pope Innocent X* (1953).

See also WERTENBAKER 488:6.

(Sir) Robert BADEN-POWELL (later 1st Baron Baden-Powell) English soldier (1857–1941)

7 Be Prepared ... the meaning of the motto is that a scout must prepare himself by previous thinking out and practising how to act on any accident or emergency so that he is never taken by surprise; he knows exactly what to do when anything unexpected happens.

Scouting for Boys (1908). 'Be prepared' is the motto of the Boy Scout movement and shares its initials with those of its founder (who was often referred to by its members as 'B-P'). The words first appeared in a handbook and mean that Scouts should always be 'in a state of readiness in mind and body' to do their duty. Winston Churchill wrote in *Great Contemporaries* (1937): 'It is difficult to exaggerate the moral and mental health which our nation has derived from this profound and simple conception. In those bygone days the motto Be Prepared had a special meaning for our country. Those who looked to the coming of a great war welcomed the awakening of British boyhood.'

With permission, the words were subsequently used as an advertising slogan for Pears' soap.

1 It is called in our schools 'beastliness', and this is about the best name for it ... should it become a habit it quickly destroys both health and spirits; he becomes feeble in body and mind, and often ends in a lunatic asylum.

On masturbation in the same work, although 'beastliness' has also been taken to refer to homosexuality.

Walter BAGEHOT English constitutional historian (1826–77)

2 The soldier ... of today is ... a quiet, grave man ... perhaps like Count Moltke, 'silent in seven languages'.

'Checks and Balances', *The English Constitution* (1867). The source of Bagehot's quotation is unknown, but it is yet another interesting description of the taciturn German, Helmuth Graf von Moltke (1800–91). 'Moltke' is, in consequence, a name given to a taciturn, unsmiling person. Michael Wharton ('Peter Simple' columnist of *The Daily Telegraph*) described in *The Missing Will* (1984) how he was so nicknamed, as a child, by his German grandfather after the famous general, 'who seldom spoke and was said to have smiled only twice in his life'. Geoffrey Madan's *Notebooks* (1981) recorded that these two occasions were 'once when his mother-in-law died, and once when a certain fortress was declared to be impregnable'.

3 A severe though not unfriendly critic of our institutions said that 'the cure for admiring the House of Lords was to go and look at it'.

'The House of Lords', in the same work. Note that this was not necessarily Bagehot's own view, as it is sometimes taken to be.

4 Nations touch at their summits.

In the same chapter. Possibly the origin of the modern concept of summit conferences – meetings of the chief representatives of anything, usually political leaders of major world powers. In which case, the usage was revived by Winston Churchill – see CHURCHILL 142:4.

5 The best reason why Monarchy is a strong government is, that it is an intelligible government. The mass of mankind understand it, and they hardly anywhere in the world understand any other.

'The Monarchy', in the same work. Much quoted in the debates over the continuation of the British monarchy in the 1980s and 1990s.

6 A princely marriage is the brilliant edition of a universal fact, and as such, it rivets mankind.

In the same part. Much quoted at the time of the marriage of the Prince of Wales to Lady Diana Spencer in 1981.

7 Our royalty is to be reverenced, and if you begin to poke about it you cannot reverence it ... Its mystery is its life. We must not let in daylight upon magic.

In the same part. Compare DE GAULLE 166:1.

8 The sovereign has, under a constitutional monarchy such as ours, three rights – the right to be consulted, the right to encourage, the right to warn.

In the same part. Referring specifically to the British sovereign.

Sydney D. BAILEY English writer (1916–)

9 It has been said that this minister [the Lord Privy Seal] is neither a Lord, nor a privy, nor a seal.

British Parliamentary Democracy (3rd edn, 1971). The *ODMQ* (1991) curiously elevates Bailey to the status of originator of this joke when it is obvious that even he is not claiming it. The observation was already widely known by the time of Bailey's book, not least from its use on BBC TV's *The Frost Report* (1966–7). It was possibly inspired by Voltaire's joke that the Holy Roman Empire was neither holy, nor Roman, nor an empire (*Essai sur l'histoire générale et sur les moeurs et l'esprit des nations*, 1756). By the late 1960s there was also an observation current that the YMCA was joined by those who were neither young, male nor Christian. The Lord Privy Seal is now the title of a Cabinet minister, sometimes one without portfolio. His job was formerly to keep the Great Seal of England, which was put on official documents.

Bruce BAIRNSFATHER British cartoonist (1888–1959)

10 Well, if you knows of a better 'ole, go to it.

Caption to cartoon published in *Fragments from France* (1915) depicting the gloomy soldier 'Old Bill' sitting in a shell crater in the mud on the Somme during the First World War. The cartoon series was enormously popular. A musical (London 1917; New York 1918) and two films (UK 1918; US 1926), based on the strip, all had the title *The Better 'Ole*.

Howard BAKER American Republican politician (1925–)

1 What did the President know, and when did he know it?

At the US Senate Watergate Committee hearings during the summer of 1973, Baker, the vice-chairman – an earnest lawmaker from Tennessee – became famous when he framed this essential question about Richard Nixon. He repeated it several times, and the answer led to Nixon's downfall. Later, during the investigations into the Iran-Contra affair, when President Reagan repeatedly said he knew nothing of the matter (1987), Washingtonians joked: 'What did Reagan know, and when did he forget it?'

James BALDWIN American novelist (1924–87)

2 *The Fire Next Time.*

Title of novel (1963). It is explained in the concluding sentence: 'If we do not now dare everything, the fulfilment of that prophecy, re-created from the Bible in song by a slave, is upon us: *God gave Noah the rainbow sign, No more water, the fire next time!*' As a warning of the use of fire in racial clashes it anticipated 'Burn, baby, burn!', the Black extremist slogan used following the August 1965 riots in the Watts district of Los Angeles, when entire blocks were burned down and 34 people killed.

Monica BALDWIN English writer (?1896–1975)

3 *I Leap Over the Wall.*

Title of book (1949) that described 'a return to the world after twenty-eight years in a convent'. The author traced the title to a Baldwin family motto, '*Per Deum Meum Transilio Murum* [By the help of my God I leap over the wall]', which derived from the escape of an earlier Baldwin: 'Nearly 400 years ago, my ancestor Thomas Baldwin of Diddlesbury leaped to freedom from behind the walls of the Tower of London ... His name with an inscription and the date "July 1585" can still be seen where he carved it on the wall of his cell in the Beauchamp Tower.' He added the motto to his arms and it was taken up again by Stanley Baldwin when he took his earldom. There may be an echo in it, too, of 2 Samuel 22:30, 'By my God have I leaped over a wall.'

Noël Coward in his published diary mentions having read Monica Baldwin's book and gives this critical comment: 'Very interesting, I must say. It has strengthened my decision not to become a nun.'

Stanley BALDWIN (later 1st Earl Baldwin of Bewdley) British Conservative Prime Minister (1867–1947)

4 They are a lot of hard-faced men ... who look as if they had done well out of the war.

The members of the House of Commons who had been returned in the 1918 general election were so described by a 'Conservative politician', according to John Maynard Keynes, the economist, in *The Economic Consequences of Peace* (1919). Baldwin is taken to be the man who said it. In his biography (1969) by Keith Middlemas and John Barnes, Baldwin is also quoted as having noted privately on 12 February 1918: 'We have started with the new House of Commons. They look much as usual – not so young as I had expected. The prevailing type is a rather successful-looking business kind which is not very attractive.'

The playwright Julian Mitchell, surveying the members of Mrs Thatcher's government in 1987, remarked that they looked like 'hard-faced men who had done well out of the peace'.

5 The papers conducted by Lord Rothermere and Lord Beaverbrook are not newspapers in the ordinary acceptance of the term. They are engines of propaganda, for the constantly changing policies, desires, personal wishes, personal likes and dislikes of two men ... What the proprietorship of these papers is aiming at is power, and power without responsibility – the prerogative of the harlot throughout the ages.

Attacking the press lords during a by-election campaign in London (18 March 1931). Baldwin's cousin, Rudyard Kipling, had originated the remark many years previously. He had also already used it in argument with Beaverbrook. It is often misquoted: in Frank S. Pepper, *Handbook of 20th Century Quotations* (1984), it is given as 'the *privilege* of the harlot'. There are also those who would say that it is not actually the harlot who has the power without the responsibility – it is the harlot's customer. Hence, however, *The Prerogative of the Harlot*, title of a book (1980) by Hugh (Lord) Cudlipp, about Fleet Street.

Harold Macmillan recalled that his father-in-law, the Duke of Devonshire, exclaimed at this point in Baldwin's speech: 'Good God, that's done it, he's lost us the tarts' vote.' Compare STOPPARD 448:2.

6 The bomber will always get through.

Speech, House of Commons (10 November 1932). This remark has to be seen in the context of the times – the First World War had introduced the completely new concept of airborne bombardment. Said Baldwin in full: 'I think it is well for the man in the street to realize that there is no power on earth that can protect him from being bombed. Whatever people may tell him, the bomber will always get through. The only defence is in offence, which means that you have to kill more women and children more quickly than the enemy if you want to save yourselves.' In a speech to the House of Commons (30 July 1934) Baldwin provided a corollary: 'Since the day of the air, the old frontiers are gone. When you think of the chalk cliffs of Dover; you think of the Rhine. That is where our frontier lies.'

1 There is a wind of nationalism and freedom blowing round the world, and blowing as strongly in Asia as elsewhere.

Speech, London (4 December 1934). Compare MACMILLAN 305:4.

2 I shall be but a short time tonight. I have seldom spoken with greater regret, for my lips are not yet unsealed.

Speech in the House of Commons on the Abyssinia crisis (10 December 1935). He was playing for time with what, he admitted, was one of the stupidest things he had ever said. Popularly quoted as 'My lips are sealed.' The cartoonist Low portrayed him for weeks afterwards with sticking plaster over his lips. Meaning 'I am not giving anything away', and deriving originally, perhaps, from the expression to seal up *another* person's lips or mouth, to prevent betrayal of a secret; *OED2* has the expression by 1782.

3 I put before the whole House my own view with appalling frankness ... supposing I had gone to the country and said ... that we must rearm, does anybody think that this pacific democracy would have rallied to that cry at that moment? I cannot think of anything that would have made the loss of the election from my point of view more certain.

Speech in the House of Commons (12 November 1936). Winston Churchill had reproached him for failing to keep his pledge that parity should be maintained against air forces within striking distance of British soil. Why had this happened? Churchill commented on the reply in *The Second World War*, Vol. 1 (1948): 'This was indeed appalling frankness. It carried naked truth about his motives into indecency. That a prime minister should avow that he had not done his duty in regard to national safety because he was afraid of losing the election was an incident without parallel in our Parliamentary history.' G.M. Young wrote: 'Never I suppose in our history has a statesman used a phrase so fatal to his own good name and at the same time, so wholly unnecessary, so incomprehensible.'

In *Baldwin* (1969), Keith Middlemas and John Barnes are at pains to assert that these judgements were made very much after the event and that the speech did not set off a horrified reaction at the time.

4 Once I leave, I leave. I am not going to speak to the man on the bridge, and I am not going to spit on the deck.

Statement to the Cabinet (28 May 1937) later released to the press, when Baldwin stepped down, flushed with success over his handling of the Abdication Crisis. Earlier, on his inauguration as Rector of Edinburgh University in 1925, Baldwin had expressed a view of the limitations on the freedom of a former Prime Minister in similar terms: 'A sailor does not spit on the deck, thereby strengthening his control and saving unnecessary work for someone else; nor does he speak to the man at the wheel, thereby leaving him to devote his whole time to his task and increasing the probability of the ship arriving at or near her destination.'

When Harold Wilson resigned as Prime Minister, he quoted Baldwin's 'Once I leave ... ' words in his own statement to the Cabinet (16 March 1976), also later released to the press.

5 Do not run up your nose against the Pope or the NUM [National Union of Mineworkers]!

Quoted by Lord Butler in *The Art of Memory* (1982). Compare MACMILLAN 306:5.

6 You will find in politics that you are much exposed to the attribution of false motive. Never complain and never explain.

To Harold Nicolson (21 July 1943), alluding to DISRAELI 174:5.

Arthur BALFOUR (later 1st Earl of Balfour) British Conservative Prime Minister (1848–1930)

7 His Majesty's Government looks with favour upon the establishment in Palestine of a national home for the Jewish people.

Although Balfour had been Prime Minister (1902–5), he became Foreign Secretary in Lloyd George's wartime Cabinet. Just before the British army in Palestine took Jerusalem in 1917, Balfour sought to curry favour with Jews in the United States and Central Europe by promising that Palestine should become a national home for the Jews and issued what has become known as the Balfour Declaration on 2 November 1917. This acted as a spur to Zionism and paved the way for the founding of the modern state of Israel in 1948. The declaration was contained in a letter addressed to the 2nd Lord Rothschild, a leader of British Jewry. The ambiguous rider was: 'Nothing shall be done which may prejudice the civil and religious rights of existing non-Jewish communities in Palestine.'

Hence, *Dear Lord Rothschild*, title of Miriam Rothschild's biography (1983) of her uncle, taken from the first words of Balfour's letter.

1 In that oration there were some things that were true, and some things that were trite: but what was true was trite, and what was not trite was not true.

Remark quoted in Winston Churchill, 'Arthur James Balfour', *Great Contemporaries* (1937). For a remark with a similar structure, compare MACMILLAN 305:5.

2 Nothing matters very much and very few things matter at all.

Quoted in *PDMQ* (1971), but there appears to be no other source for this much-quoted observation. Compare what Bishop Creighton (1843–1901) said when reassuring an anxious seeker after truth, that it was 'almost impossible to exaggerate the complete unimportance of everything' – quoted in *The Lyttelton Hart-Davis Letters* (for 2 May 1956).

Honoré de BALZAC French novelist (1799–1850)

3 The county where women die of love.

Of Lancashire. This extraordinary statement was quoted once by A.J.P. Taylor (who might have had an interest: he was born there). One of Balzac's biographers, Graham Robb, traced it to the novel *Le Lys dans la vallée* (1836), where it is uttered by the Lancastrian Lady Arabella Dudley to her lover, Felix de Vandenesse. It is thought that Balzac's authority was his English lover, Sarah Lovell. But she came from Bath, Somerset.

Tallulah BANKHEAD American actress (1903–68)

4 There's less in this than meets the eye.

A frequently employed critical witticism, which derives its modern popularity from the use made of the words by Bankhead to Alexander Woollcott about the play *Aglavaine and Selysette* by Maurice Maeterlinck on 3 January 1922. Quoted in Woollcott, *Shouts and Murmurs* (1922). However, in his journal, James Boswell attributed a version to Richard Burke, son of Edmund (1 May 1783): 'I suppose here *less* is meant than meets the ear.'

5 Cocaine habit-forming? Of course not. I ought to know. I've been using it for years.

Tallulah (1952). Compare: 'Typhoid is a terrible disease; it can kill you or damage your brain. I know what I'm talking about, I've had typhoid.' – Comte Maurice de Mac-Mahon, quoted in Bechtel & Carrière, *Dictionnaire de la Bêtise* (1983).

W.N.P. BARBELLION English essayist and diarist (1889–1919)

6 On the bus the other day a woman with a baby sat opposite, the baby bawled, and the woman at once began to unlace herself, exposing a large red udder, which she swung into the baby's face. The infant, however, continued to cry and the woman said, 'Come on, there's a good boy – if you don't, I shall give it to the gentleman opposite.'

The Journal of a Disappointed Man (1919). This was included in my book *Eavesdroppings* (1981) as an early example of an 'overheard', but it was subsequently discovered that – like so much else – it probably began life as a *Punch* cartoon caption. In the edition of 11 May 1904 (Vol. 126), 'THE UNPROTECTED MALE' shows a man in an omnibus being addressed thus: '*Mother (after vainly offering a bottle to refractory infant)* "'ERE, TIKE IT, WILL YER! IF YER DON'T 'URRY UP, I'LL GIVE IT TO THE GENTLEMAN OPPOSITE!"'

Maurice BARING English writer (1874–1945)

7 If you would know what the Lord God thinks of money, you have only to look at those to whom He gave it.

Attributed by Dorothy Parker, according to Malcolm Cowley (ed.), *Writers at Work*, First Series (1958). Compare: 'We may see the small value God has for riches, by the people he gives them to' – Alexander Pope, *Thoughts On Various Subjects* (1727).

8 We see the contrast between the genius which does what it must and the talent which does what it can.

An Outline of Russian Literature, Chap. 3 (1914). Contrasting Mozart and Salieri in Pushkin's play *Mozart and Salieri*.

Clive BARNES English-born American theatre and ballet critic (1927–)

9 This is the kind of show that gives pornography a dirty name.

On *Oh! Calcutta!* Review in *The New York Times* (18 June

1969). What we may have here is a kind of format for criticism where something not very reputable in the first place is given a 'bad name'. In the film *Please Don't Eat the Daisies* (US 1960), David Niven, playing a drama critic, speaks the line: 'This poor failure gives poor failures a bad name.'

P(hineas) T. BARNUM American showman (1810–91)

1 There's a sucker born every minute.

No evidence exists that Barnum ever used this expression – not least, it is said, because 'sucker' was not a common term in his day. He did, however, express the view that 'The people like to be humbugged', which conveys the same idea. There was also a song of the period, 'There's a New Jay Born Every Day' (jay = gullible hick). By whatever route, Barnum took the attribution. A.H. Saxon in his *P.T. Barnum: The Legend and the Man* (1889) reportedly ascribes the saying to Joseph 'Paper Collar Joe' Bessimer, the American con man of the 1880s.

Going further back, '*Populus vult decipi* [People wish to be deceived]' is attributed to Cardinal Carafa (died 1591), legate of Pope Paul IV. Understandably, in the musical *Barnum* (Broadway 1980), there is a rousing song 'There's a Sucker Born Ev'ry Minute'.

(Sir) James BARRIE Scottish playwright (1860–1937)

2 Second to the right, and then straight on till morning.

Peter Pan, Act 1 (1904). Peter Pan responds to Wendy's question, 'Where do you live?' Second 'star' is understood. She comments: 'What a funny address!' This turns out to be the way to Neverland. Hence, *Straight On Till Morning*, title of film (UK 1972).

3 To die will be an awfully big adventure.

In the same play, Act 3, Sc. 1. Peter Pan speaking. Peter Llewellyn Davies, the original of Peter Pan, supposedly said this first, though Andrew Birkin, *J.M. Barrie and the Lost Boys* (1979), credits it to his brother George. Hence, however, *An Awfully Big Adventure*, the title of a novel by Beryl Bainbridge (1989; film UK 1995) – about a small repertory company in Liverpool which is putting on a seasonal production of *Peter Pan*. See also FROHMAN 203:2.

4 *Floreat Etona* [May Eton flourish].

In the same play, Act 5, Sc. 1. Spoken by the villain Captain Hook (an Old Etonian), just before he is eaten by a crocodile. It is the motto of Eton College (founded 1440) in Berkshire. The Etonian allusions were added to the play when the Davies boys were going through the school. In the novel version, *Peter Pan and Wendy* (1911), Hook merely

cries, 'Bad form.' The motto was earlier used as the title of a painting (1882) by Elizabeth, Lady Butler depicting an attack on Laing's Neck (against the Boers in South Africa, 1881), after this eyewitness account: 'Poor Elwes fell among the 58th. He shouted to another Eton boy (adjutant of the 58th, whose horse had been shot) "Come along, Monck! Floreat Etona! we must be in the front rank!" and he was shot immediately.'

5 Someone said that God gave us memory so that we might have roses in December.

Rectorial Address, St Andrews University (3 May 1922). Anthony C. Shipps again reminded me that not every quotation query is a new one – far from it. He showed me an inquiry from 'E.E.' in the 'Queries and Answers' column of *The New York Times Book Review* (8 April 1928): 'I wrote to [Barrie] and he replied he is not the author of it nor does he know who is.' See also STUDDERT KENNEDY 449:2.

6 *Without Drums or Trumpets.*

There is a story told about Barrie's advice to a young writer who did not know what title to give his work. 'Are there any trumpets in it?' Barrie asked, and got the answer 'No.' 'Are there any drums in it?' he asked. 'No.' 'Then why not call it *Without Drums or Trumpets*?' Untraced. A similar story is told about the French playwright, Tristan Bernard (1866–1947) in Cornelia Otis Skinner's *Elegant Wits and Grand Horizontals* (1962). Somebody did take the advice: the Dutch author Jeroen Brouwers published a novel entitled *Zonder trommels en trompetten* ('Without drums and trumpets'; 1973); and the English translation of Alec Le Vernoy's Second World War memoirs was entitled *No Drums – No Trumpets* (1983).

Michael BARSLEY English writer and broadcaster (died ?1978)

7 'Twas Danzig, and the Swastikoves
Did heil and hittle in the reich,
All nazi were the lindengroves,
And the neuraths jewstreich.

Grabberwocky and Other Fights of Fancy, first published as a booklet in December 1939. It states inside that Barsley's poem had first been published in the magazine *Time and Tide*, though it may also have been broadcast by the BBC in a radio programme called *Adolf in Blunderland* shortly after the outbreak of war. In this it was performed in a choral version to the tune of '*Gaudeamus Igitur*' (which, in fact, it fits rather well). The phrase 'neuraths jewstreich' plays not only on the name of Julius Streicher, the infamous Jew-baiter, but also on that of Baron Konstantin von Neurath

(1873–1956) who, at the time, was Nazi 'Protector of Bohemia and Moravia' until he was dismissed by Hitler for being 'too lenient'. See also CARROLL 124:4.

Bernard BARUCH American financier (1870–1965)

1 Let us not be deceived – we are today in the midst of a cold war.

The final phrase describes any tension between powers, short of all-out war, but specifically that between the Soviet Union and the West following the Second World War. In this latter sense it was popularized by Baruch, the American financier and Presidential adviser in a speech in South Carolina (16 April 1947). A year later he was able to note a worsening of the situation to the extent that he could tell the Senate War Investigating Committee: 'We are in the midst of a cold war which is getting warmer.'

The phrase was suggested to Baruch in June 1946 by his speechwriter Herbert Bayard Swope, former editor of the New York *World*, who had been using it privately since 1940. The columnist Walter Lippmann gave the term wide currency and is sometimes mistakenly credited with coining it. Swope clearly coined it; Baruch gave it currency.

Edgar BATEMAN English songwriter (late 19th century)

2 Oh it really is a wery pretty garden,
And Chingford to the eastward can be seen;
Wiv a ladder and some glasses
You could see to 'Ackney Marshes,
If it wasn't for the 'ouses in between.

Song, 'The 'Ouses in Between' (1894), popularized by Gus Elen (1862–1940), which had lyrics by Bateman and music by George Le Brunn (1862–1905). Hence, *The Houses in Between*, title of a novel (1951) by Howard Spring, who mentions in a foreword a music-hall song containing the words, 'You could see the Crystal Palace – if it wasn't for the houses in between.' The full lyrics given in *The Last Empires*, ed. Benny Green (1986), do not include mention of the Crystal Palace, but no doubt verses were added and subtracted over the years.

H.M. BATEMAN British cartoonist (1887–1970)

3 The Man Who ...

... committed some solecism or other. Caption format for a series of cartoons in the 1920/30s, e.g.: 'The Man Who Missed the Ball on the First Tee at St Andrews', 'The Man Who Lit His Cigar Before the Royal Toast', 'The Girl Who Ordered a Glass of Milk at the Café Royal', and, 'The Man Who Asked for "A Double Scotch" in the Grand Pump Room

at Bath'. All the cartoons show the perpetrator of the solecism as a shrivelled, embarrassed little figure while all around are experiencing paroxysms of dismay.

H.E. BATES British novelist and short story writer (1905–74)

4 Perfick wevver.

The Darling Buds of May, Chap. 1 (1958). Pa Larkin's use of 'perfick' (a Kentish pronunciation of 'perfect') extends through all the novels about the Larkin family. Hence, perfick wevver = perfect weather. The expression 'Perfick!' again had a vogue in the spring of 1991 when the stories were dramatized for British TV with huge success. At that time, 'Perfick' was the *Sun*'s headline over a front-page story about the new council tax (Pa Larkin is a notable income-tax dodger); the Family Assurance Society promoted a tax-free investment with the word as headline in newspaper adverts in May 1991 (revealing, at the same time, that the word had been registered as a trade mark by Yorkshire Television, the programme's producer).

Charles BAUDELAIRE French poet (1821–67)

5 *Hypocrite lecteur, – mon semblable, – mon frère!* [Hypocrite reader, my likeness, my brother!]
'Au Lecteur', *Les Fleurs du mal* (1857). T.S. Eliot quotes the French in 'The Burial of the Dead', *The Waste Land* (1922).

6 *Là, tout n'est qu'ordre et beauté,*
Luxe, calme et volupté.
[Everything there is simply order and beauty,
Luxury, peace and sensual indulgence.]
'L'Invitation au voyage', in the same work. Hence, '*Luxe, calme et volupté*', the title of a painting by Henri Matisse (1904–5) showing nude bathers on the beach at St Tropez.

7 *Il faut épater les bourgeois* [One must shock the bourgeois].
Attributed remark. To Baudelaire's contemporary, Alexandre Privat d'Anglemont (?1820–59) is attributed the similar, '*Je les ai épatés, les bourgeois* [I shocked them, the bourgeois]'.

L. Frank BAUM American author (1856–1919)

8 *The Wizard of Oz.*

Actually the title of Baum's 1900 children's classic is *The Wonderful Wizard of Oz*. It was shortened for the 1939 film and also for some later editions of the book. Baum wrote another 13 volumes about Oz and 26 further titles were added after his death. Legend has it that Baum took the name 'Oz' from the label 'O–Z' on a filing cabinet. It has been observed how similar are Dorothy's adventures to those of *Alice in Wonderland* (1865). In each case, the heroine endures a succession of (mostly) unpleasant encounters and finally escapes back home – Dorothy to Kansas after a cyclone has blown her to Oz, Alice to her sister after she has fallen down a rabbit hole.

Note these other alterations between book and film:

1 **The road to the City of Emeralds is paved with yellow brick.**

That is what Baum put. He also wrote of 'the road of yellow brick'. The phrase 'Yellow Brick Road' only comes from the song 'Follow the Yellow Brick Road' in the film. *Follow the Yellow Brick Road* was the title of a TV play by Dennis Potter (1972). 'Goodbye Yellow Brick Road' was the title of a song (1973) by Bernie Taupin and Elton John. The song 'Over the Rainbow' (by E.Y. Harburg with music by Harold Arlen) does not derive from anything in the book.

2 **Toto, I have a feeling we're not in Kansas any more.**

Again, this is a line from the film, not the book, but one that has achieved catchphrase status. Judy Garland as Dorothy says it on arrival in the Land of Oz, concluding, 'We must be over the rainbow.'

3 **The Wicked Witch of the West.**

This *was* the name of a character in *The Wonderful Wizard of Oz* (there was also one of the East; those of the North and South were good witches). It produced a wonderfully alliterative way of describing women not liked. Allan Massie wrote of Margaret Thatcher: 'It would not convert those for whom she is She Who Must Be Obeyed and the Wicked Witch of the West rolled into one' – quoted in Michael Cockerell, *Live From Number 10* (1989).

4 **Close your eyes and tap your heels together three times. And think to yourself, 'There's no place like home.'**

On how to get from the Land of Oz back to Kansas. Said at the end of the film by Glinda, the (Good) Witch of the South. In the book she says: 'All you have to do is to knock the heels together three times and command the shoes to carry you wherever you wish to go.'

(Sir) Arnold BAX English composer (1883–1953)

5 **You should make a point of trying every experience once, excepting incest and folk-dancing.**

Often wrongly ascribed to Sir Thomas Beecham and others

– including Bax himself. Anthony Powell attributes it to Guy Warrack in his diary entry for 30 July 1988. In fact, it was said by 'a sympathetic Scotsman' and quoted *by* Bax in his book *Farewell, My Youth* (1943).

6 **You know you are getting old when the policemen start looking younger.**

Not said *by* Bax. What he says *of Arnold Bennett* in the same book is: '[He] once remarked that his earliest recognition of his own middle age came at a certain appalling moment when he realized for the first time that the policeman at the corner was a mere youth.' This realization has also been attributed to Sir Seymour Hicks (1871–1949), the actor, in connection with *old* age – in C.R.D. Pulling, *They Were Singing* (1952), for example. The source for this may be Hicks's own *Between Ourselves* (1930).

Thomas Haynes BAYLY English poet and playwright (1797–1839)

7 Oh! no! we never mention her,
Her name is never heard;
My lips are now forbid to speak
That once familiar word …

From sport to sport they hurry me
To banish my regret,
And when they win a smile from me,
They think that I forget.

Song, 'Oh! No! We Never Mention Her' (1844). A 'lost' quotation until traced to its source (1997). The second of these verses is alluded to, anonymously, in P.G. Wodehouse, *Psmith in the City*, Chap. 14 (1910): 'From ledger to ledger they hurry me to stifle my regret. And when they win a smile from me they think that I forget.'

BEACHCOMBER See MORTON, J.B.

(Sir) David BEATTY (later 1st Earl Beatty) English admiral (1871–1936)

8 **There seems to be something wrong with our bloody ships today, Chatfield.**

The Battle of Jutland on 31 May–1 June 1916 was the only major sea battle of the First World War. It was, on the face of it, an indecisive affair. The British grand fleet under its Commander-in-Chief, Sir John Jellicoe, failed to secure an outright victory. Admiral Beatty, commanding a battlecruiser squadron, saw one ship after another sunk by the Germans. At 4.26 on the afternoon of 31 May, the *Queen Mary* was sunk with the loss of 1266 officers and men. This was what led Beatty to make the above comment to his Flag Captain, Ernle Chatfield. Sometimes the words 'and with our system' have been added to the remark, as also 'Turn two points to port' (i.e. nearer the enemy) and 'Steer two points nearer the enemy', but Chatfield denied that anything more was said – source: *ODQ* (1953, 1979).

Ultimately, the battle marked the end of any German claim to have naval control of the North Sea and, in that light, was a British victory, but Jutland was a disappointment at the time and has been chewed over ever since as a controversial episode in British naval history.

Mark Hanbury BEAUFOY English politician and sportsman (1854–1922)

1 If a sportsman true you'd be
Listen carefully to me.

Never, never let your gun
Pointed be at any one;
That it may unloaded be
Matters not the least to me.

'A Father's Advice to His Son' – a rhyme written in about 1900 and published in *The Field* in 1922. Compare from Nancy Mitford, *The Blessing* (1951), a grandfather giving a grandson his first real gun: 'And just remember this,' he says, 'Never never let your gun pointed be at anyone. That it may unloaded be matters not a rap to me!' In the next chapter, the grandson repeats the text to admonish a burglar who is pointing a (dummy) gun at him. *The Faber Book of Useful Verse* (1981) has this in the form: 'Never, never let your gun / Pointed be at anyone. / All the pheasants ever bred / Won't make up for one man dead.'

Simone de BEAUVOIR French writer (1908–86)

2 *On ne naît pas femme: on le devient* [One is not born a woman: one becomes one].

Le Deuxième Sexe (1949–50). She explains: 'No biological, psychological or economic fate determines the figure that the human female presents in society; it is civilization as a whole that determines this creature.'

1st Baron BEAVERBROOK (Maxwell Aitken)
Canadian-born British politician and newspaper proprietor (1879–1964)

3 Our cock won't fight.

To Winston Churchill, of Edward VIII during the Abdication Crisis. He meant, of course, that the King (whom they were supporting) would not pursue the course they wanted him to – namely, to cling on to the crown at all costs. The

source for this is Frances Donaldson, *Edward VIII* (1974). The notion of a reluctant cock is venerable, indeed. *OED2* finds no less than three words – *cradden, coward* and *fugie* – for such a bird. But the phrase itself occurs in Scott's *Ivanhoe*, Bk 2, Chap. 21 (1819): 'Cedric found the mind of his friend Athelstane so fully occupied that it had no room for another idea ... It was a desperate case therefore. There was obviously no more to be made of Athelstane; or, as Wamba expressed it, in a phrase which has descended from Saxon times to ours, he was a cock that would not fight.'

4 Let me say that the credit belongs to the boys in the back rooms. It isn't the man who sits in the limelight like me who should have the praise. It is not the men who sit in prominent places. It is the men in the back rooms.

As Minister of Aircraft Production, Beaverbrook paid tribute to the Ministry's research department in a broadcast on 19 March 1941. This version of the text has been taken direct from a recording and differs from that usually given – as for example in *ODQ* (1992).

In North America the phrase 'back-room boys' can be traced back to the 1870s at least, but Beaverbrook may be credited with the modern application to scientific and technical boffins. His inspiration for the phrase was quite obviously Marlene Dietrich singing his favourite song 'The Boys in the Back Room' in the film *Destry Rides Again* (1939). Written by Frank Loesser and Frederick Hollander, this is more properly called 'See What the Boys in the Back Room Will Have'. According to A.J.P. Taylor, Beaverbrook believed that 'Dietrich singing the Boys in the Backroom is a greater work of art than the Mona Lisa.' Also in 1941, Edmund Wilson entitled a book, *The Boys in the Back Room: Notes on California Novelists*. A British film with Arthur Askey was entitled *Back Room Boy* (1942).

An even earlier appearance of the bar phrase occurs in the Marx Brothers film *Animal Crackers* (1930): 'Let's go and see what the boys in the back room will have.' In 1924, Dorothy Parker is said to have cabled to her friends at the Round Table concerning the flop of a show she had written with Elmer Rice: 'Close Harmony did a cool ninety dollars at the matinée. Ask the boys in the back room what they will have.'

5 Who's in charge of the clattering train?

Beaverbrook was notorious for interfering with the running of his newspapers. His favourite inquiry as his mighty media machine rumbled on was: 'Who is in charge of the clattering train?' Ominously, this quotation was based on a remembering of the anonymous poem 'Death and His Brother Sleep', which includes the lines:

Who is in charge of the clattering train?
The axles creak, and the couplings strain ...
For the pace is hot, and the points are near,
And Sleep hath deadened the driver's ear;
And signals flash through the night in vain.
Death is in charge of the clattering train!

It is possible that Beaverbrook borrowed the expression from Winston Churchill, who also quoted the poem in the first volume of *The Second World War* (1948), saying, 'I had learnt them from a volume of *Punch* cartoons which I used to pore over when I was eight or nine years old at school in Brighton.' That would have been in 1882–3. In fact, the poem did not appear in *Punch* until 4 October 1890. It concerns a railway collision at Eastleigh. Due to fatigue, the driver and stoker had failed to keep a proper look-out.

A.J.P. Taylor states that Beaverbrook's quotation was not quite accurate, but then proceeds to print an inaccurate version himself, beginning 'Who is in charge of the *rattling* train ... ' – *Beaverbrook* (1972).

For the title of the poem, see SHELLEY 428:3.

See also *DAILY EXPRESS* 161:1; KIPLING 274:4.

H.C. BEECHING English clergyman and writer (1859–1919)

1 First come I; my name is Jowett.
There's no knowledge but I know it.
I am the Master of this College:
What I don't know isn't knowledge.

A contribution to the mostly anonymous 'The Masque of Balliol', which was current at Balliol College, Oxford in the 1870s. Jowett was Master of Balliol from 1870.

(Sir) Max BEERBOHM English writer and caricaturist (1872–1956)

2 Often, even in his heyday, his acting and his waggishness did not carry him very far. Only mediocrity can be trusted to be always at its best. Genius must always have lapses proportionate to its triumphs.

Obituary of the British music-hall comic Dan Leno in the *Saturday Review* (5 November 1904) – the earliest found formulation of the thought that 'only the mediocre are always at their best'. Among those also credited with it have been Jean Giraudoux and W. Somerset Maugham. The Giraudoux attribution appears without source in Robert Byrne's *The 637 Best Things Anybody Ever Said* (1982). In his introduction to *The Portable Dorothy Parker* (1944), Maugham chooses his words carefully (Parker was, of course, still alive) in discussing the uneven quality of her output. With (for him), unusual tact, Maugham wrote: 'Only

a very mediocre writer is always at his best, and Dorothy Parker is not a mediocre writer.' Compare what the film director Ernst Lubitsch (1892–1947) is quoted as having said: 'I sometimes make pictures which are not up to my standard, but then it can only be said of a mediocrity that all his work is up to his standard' – quoted in Leslie Halliwell, *The Filmgoer's Book of Quotes* (1973).

3 'I don't,' she added, 'know anything about music, really. But I know what I like.'
Zuleika Dobson, Chap. 16 (1911). In Chap. 9, Beerbohm had already commented of his heroine at a college concert: 'She was one of the people who say, "I don't know anything about music really, but I know what I like."' Earlier, Gelett Burgess had identified 'I don't know much about Art, but I know what I like' as a philistine's platitude (also applied to literature) in *Are You a Bromide?* (1907). Henry James, *The Portrait of a Lady*, Chap. 24 (1881), had already had: 'I don't care anything about reasons, but I know what I like.'

See also BENSON 62:7; LINCOLN 287:6.

Ludwig van BEETHOVEN German composer (1770–1827)

4 *Muss es sein? Es muss sein* [Must it be? It must be].
Epigraph to the final movement of his String Quartet in F Major, Op. 135 (1826), which was more or less his last completed composition. Accordingly, some deep philosophical significance has been read into the words, or at least a parallel with the musical resolution at this point, but Robert Simpson in *The Beethoven Companion* (1973) quotes Joseph Kerman as treating it as a 'not very good joke': when someone who owed Beethoven money asked, '*Muss es sein?*', Beethoven, 'with some lack of originality', replied, '*Es muss sein!*'

5 England is a land without music.
It seems he never said it. *Das Land ohne Musik* was, however, the title of a British-bashing book by Oscar A. Schmitz, published at the start of the First World War. The book had nothing to do with music, but depicted England as a country 'without a soul'. The criticism has also been ascribed to Felix Mendelssohn, a frequent visitor to Britain, with even less reason – source: letter from Arthur Jacobs in *The Independent* Magazine (1 February 1992).

Land Without Music was, coincidentally, the title of a film operetta (UK 1936; US title *Forbidden Music*) about a Ruritanian ruler who bans music because her subjects are too busy singing to make money. The cast included Richard Tauber, Jimmy Durante and Diana Napier.

1 *Plaudite, amici, comedia finita est* [Applaud, my friends, the comedy is over].

Words on his deathbed, quoted in 'Bega', *Last Words of Famous Men* (1930). Compare RABELAIS 375:4. However, 'I shall hear in heaven' are the last words as attributed in Barnaby Conrad, *Famous Last Words* (1961).

Mrs (Isabella) BEETON English writer (1836–65)

2 First catch your hare.

In the proverbial sense this means, 'You can't begin to do something until you have acquired a necessary basic something (which may be difficult to acquire).' *CODP* finds the equivalent thought in about 1300 in Latin: 'It is commonly said that one must first catch the deer, and afterwards, when he has been caught, skin him.'

For a long time the saying was taken to be a piece of practical, blunt good sense to be found in Mrs Beeton's *Book of Household Management* (1861), but it does not appear there. In Mrs Hannah Glasse's *The Art of Cookery made plain and easy* (1747), however, there is the practical advice, 'Take your hare when it is cased [skinned].' In 1747 also, La Varenne in *La Cuisine française* offered a hare stew: '*Pour faire un civet, prenez un lievre* [To make a ragout , first catch a hare].' From an edition of the *York Herald and County Advertiser* (1808): 'Our new books of cookery are becoming a little more particular than formerly in their directions; one of them, in ordering a species of pudding, begins thus – "Take your maid, and send her for a peck of flour' etc. This is something like Mrs Glasse's receipt for dressing a carp, "First catch your fish."' In Thomas Love Peacock, *Melincourt*, Chap. 23 (1817), there is: 'Grovelgrub, you know the old receipt for stewing a carp: "First, catch your carp."' 'First catch your hare' had become the familiar form by 1855 when it appeared in Thackeray's *The Rose and the Ring.*

Similar proverbs include: 'Catch your bear before you sell its skin', 'Never spend your money before you have it' and 'Don't count your chickens before they are hatched.' Going right back, Bracton recorded in *De legibus et consuetudinibus Angliae* (about 1250): 'It is a common saying that it is best first to catch the deer/stag, and afterwards, when he has been caught, to skin him.'

3 A place for everything and everything in its place.

The Book of Household Management, Chap. 2 (1861). A prescription for orderly domestic arrangements. One feels that Mrs Beeton was probably more interested in domestic order than in making delicious food. The saying was not original to her, however, as is plain from these earlier uses: George Herbert had the basic idea in his *Outlandish Proverbs* (1640): 'All things have their place, knew we how to place them.'

Captain Marryat in *Masterman Ready*, Pt 2, Chap. 1 (1842) has: 'In a well-conducted man-of-war ... everything in its place, and there is a place for every thing.' Then there is this Wellerism from *Yankee Blade* (18 May 1848): '"A place for everything in its place," as an old lady said when she stowed the broom, bellows, balls of yarn, cards, caps, curry-comb, three cats and a gridiron into an old oven.' Samuel Smiles quoted it, notably, in *Thrift*, Chap. 5 (1875), and is sometimes credited with the coinage.

Brendan BEHAN Irish playwright (1923–64)

4 The bells of hell go ting-a-ling-a-ling
For you but not for me,
Oh death, where is thy sting-a-ling-a-ling,
Or grave, thy victory?

Behan made notable use of this in Act 3 of his play *The Hostage* (1958), but he was, in fact, merely adopting a song popular in the British Army in 1914–18. Even before that, though, it was sung – just like this – as a Sunday School chorus. It may have been in a Sankey and Moody hymnal, though it has not been traced. The basic element is from 1 Corinthians 15:55: 'O death, where is thy sting? O grave, where is thy victory?'

5 There's no such thing as bad publicity except your own obituary.

Quoted in the *Sunday Express* (5 January 1964) and in Dominic Behan, *My Brother Brendan* (1965). See also ANONYMOUS 10:1.

6 I saw a notice which said 'Drink Canada Dry' and I've just started.

Attributed remark. Quoted in *The 'Quote ... Unquote' Book of Love, Death and the Universe* (1980), but probably a joke ascribed to any famous drinker. The following version was used in his act by the 1950s American comedian Pat Henning: 'He was a drinkin' man, my fadder. One day he's standin' onna banks of the river, wonderin' what the hell folks can do with all that water, when suddenly he sees a great sign on the other side DRINK CANADA DRY. [Pause] So he went up there.'

7 Critics are like eunuchs in a harem: they know how it's done, they've seen it done every day, but they're unable to do it themselves.

Quoted in Laurence J. Peter, *Quotations for Our Time* (1977). Compare Kenneth Tynan in *The New York Times* Magazine (9 January 1966): 'A critic is a man who knows the way but can't drive the car.' Robin May in *The Wit of the Theatre* (1969) describes all such remarks as based on the observation that 'the critic knows how it is done but can't do it himself' and adds, 'there is an early version in Farquhar' (without saying what it is) and that the idea probably goes back to the 'ancient Greeks'. And compare Coleridge's *Biographia Literaria*, Chap. 3 (1817): 'The multitudinous public ... sits nominal despot on the throne of criticism. But, alas! as in other despotisms, it but echoes the decision of its invisible ministers, whose intellectual claims to the guardianship of the Muses seem, for the greater part, analogous to the physical qualifications which adapt their oriental brethren for the superintendence of the harem.'

Alexander Graham BELL Scottish-born American inventor (1847–1922)

1 Mr Watson, come here: I want you.

First intelligible words transmitted by telephone (10 March 1876). Bell said them three days after receiving his patent on his invention. He had just spilled acid on his clothes and was calling to his assistant, Thomas A. Watson, for help. Interesting how, from the word go, the telephone was used in a peremptory manner – sources: Thomas A. Watson, *Exploring Life* (1922) and John J. Carty, *The Smithsonian Report for 1922*.

H.E. BELL English university administrator (1925–)

2 Parents are the very last people who ought to be allowed to have children.

Ted Bell has an unusual problem – a remark has been fathered on him and he does not know whether he is entitled to claim paternity. In March 1977, as Senior Assistant Registrar in charge of undergraduate admissions at the University of Reading, he was speaking to a mixed group of people about the increasing complexity of the selection procedures and the variety of guidance available to prospective students. 'In this respect, being a parent of three children myself,' he noted (1992), 'I happened to say that in my view, "Parents are the very last people who ought to be allowed to have children." Reporters were present (I had invited them), the words appeared in *The Guardian*, and they were repeated in "Sayings of the Week" in *The Observer*. Later, in 1980, they appeared under my name in the second edition of *The Penguin Dictionary of Modern Quotations*.'

In truth, Bell was merely saying what oft had been thought but ne'er so pithily expressed. According to *The Treasury of Humorous Quotations* (1951), Bernard Shaw (inevitably) was credited with making the same point in rather more words: 'There may be some doubt as to who are the best people to have charge of children, but there can be no doubt that parents are the worst.' In fact, that was a misattribution. In Shaw's *Everybody's Political What's What?*, Chap. 19 (1944), he quotes *William Morris* ('great among the greatest Victorians as poet, craftsman, and practical man of business, and one of the few who remained uncorrupted by Victorian false prosperity to the end'). Speaking 'as a parent and as a Communist', Morris had said: 'The question of who are the best people to take charge of children is a very difficult one; but it is quite certain that the parents are the very worst.' In the same book, Shaw does himself say very nearly the same thing: 'Parentage is a very important profession, but no test of fitness for it is ever imposed in the interest of the children.'

An unverified suggestion is that 'Parents are the last people on earth who ought to have children' appears in Samuel Butler's *Notebooks*. This is according to *Medical Quotations* (1989). *Punch* (12 April 1933) has a cartoon by T. Derrick with the caption of a schoolmaster chiding the parents of a small boy and saying: 'This proves what I've always maintained; parents are precisely the people who ought not to have children.' Compare SWIFT 450:4.

Mary Hayley BELL English novelist (1911–2005)

3 *Whistle Down the Wind.*

Title of novel (1958; film UK 1961). It comes from an expression with a number of alternative meanings. (1) To abandon or to cast off lightly (after the releasing of a hawk down wind, from the fist, by whistling), as in Shakespeare's *Othello* (III.iii.266): 'I'd whistle her off, and let her down the wind.' This is what you do in falconry when you are turning a hawk loose – you send it into or against the wind when it is pursuing prey. (2) To vanish. From J.M. Barrie, *What Every Woman Knows*, Act 3 (1908): 'Where's your marrying now? ... all gone whistling down the wind.' Noël Coward was quoted in *Panorama* Magazine (Spring 1952) as saying: 'I marched down to the footlights and screamed: "I gave you my youth! Where is it now? Whistling down the wind! *où song les neiges d'antan?*" ... And I went madly on in French and Italian.' (3) Something to be avoided on board ship. The superstition is that whistling, because it sounds like the wind, can raise the wind, as if by magic – though this may more properly be 'whistle up the wind', as in 'to whistle for something'. (Whistling backstage at the theatre is also said to bring bad luck.) Nevertheless, in the seafaring novels (1970–2000) of Patrick O'Brian, the hero 'Lucky' Jack Aubrey is sometimes said to 'whistle down the wind' in order to raise wind to fill his sails. So perhaps there is also the meaning (4) 'to summon' – as also here from Frank Harris, *Oscar Wilde, His Life and Confessions*, Chap. 21 (1930): 'A man should be able to whistle happiness and hope down the wind and take despair to his bed and heart, and win courage from his harsh companion.'

Mary Hayley Bell said in 1980 that she had not been aware of the Shakespeare use until Len Deighton pointed it out to her. The relevance of the title to a story of children who believe that a murderer on the run is Jesus Christ may not be immediately apparent.

Francis BELLAMY American clergyman and editor (1856–1931)

1 I pledge allegiance to my flag and the republic for which it stands, one nation indivisible, with liberty and justice for all.

The Pledge of Allegiance to the Flag was put into this form by Bellamy in 1892, omitting any mention of God or the United States. A dispute as to who wrote it – he or James Upham – was decided in Bellamy's favour in 1939, some years after his death. In 1923 'my flag' was changed to 'the flag of the United States', and the words 'of America' were added one year later. 'Under God' was added to 'one nation' in 1954, though this ran counter to the wish of America's founders, who opposed the institutionalizing of religion. The wording is now: 'I pledge allegiance to the flag of the United States of America and to the republic for which it stands, one nation under God, indivisible, with liberty and justice for all.' Hence, the title of a 1979 film about the US legal system, *And Justice for All*. The idea of 'justice for all' is, however, one that goes back to the Greeks. It also gave rise to MATHEW 318:3.

Hilaire BELLOC French-born British poet and writer (1870–1953)

2 Blood understood the Native mind,
He said: 'We must be firm but kind.'
A mutiny resulted.
I never shall forget the way
That Blood upon this awful day
Preserved us all from death.
He stood upon a little mound,
Cast his lethargic eyes around,
And said beneath his breath:
'Whatever happens we have got
The Maxim Gun, and they have not.'

'The Modern Traveller', Pt 6 (1898), which narrates the more or less nefarious adventures of a scoundrel named Blood. Sometimes misquoted with the alliterative 'Gatling gun' in the last line.

3 When I am dead, I hope it may be said:
'His sins were scarlet, but his books were read.'

Belloc wrote this jocular epitaph for himself in 'On his

Books', *Sonnets and Verse* (1923). Compare from Isaiah 1:18: 'Though your sins be as scarlet, they shall be as white as snow.' Belloc is buried in a family grave at the Church of Our Lady of Consolation, West Grinstead, Sussex, but, understandably, without this inscription. A few yards away, a plaque on the tower commemorates him, noting that he had been a member of the congregation for 48 years. The tower and spire were completed in 1964, 'in grateful recognition of his zealous and unwavering profession of our Holy Faith which he defended in his writings and noble verse'. Then follow his lines from 'The Ballade to Our Lady of Czestochowa' quoted below.

4 This is the Faith that I have held and hold
and This is That in which I mean to die.

'The Ballade to Our Lady of Czestochowa', in the same work. See above.

5 Like many of the Upper Class
He liked the Sound of Broken Glass.

'About John who Lost a Fortune Throwing Stones', *New Cautionary Tales* (1930). Compare WAUGH 483:4.

Saul BELLOW Canadian-born novelist (1915–2005)

6 All a writer has to do to get a woman is to say he's a writer. It's an aphrodisiac.

Believed to have come from a BBC TV interview in the 1970s. Compare KISSINGER 275:4; NAPOLEON 336:1.

7 The Papuans have had no Proust and the Zulus have not yet produced a Tolstoy.

Unverified statement from an interview given by Bellow in 1988. In *The New Yorker* (7 March 1994), this was found unacceptable by Alfred Kazin, a politically correct writer, who said: 'My heart sank when I heard that Bellow once said, "Who is the Tolstoy of the Zulus? The Proust of the Papuans?"' Apparently, however, Bellow did not say 'When the Zulus produce *War and Peace* I'll take them seriously' either. When censured for this view, in whatever way expressed, Bellow replied: 'There's no Bulgarian Proust. Have I offended the Bulgarians too?' – source: Keith Botsford in *The Independent* (31 March 1994).

Robert BENCHLEY American humorist (1889–1945)

8 I must get out of these wet clothes and into a dry martini.

This was a line much enjoyed by Benchley and delivered by him to Ginger Rogers in the film *The Major and the Minor* (1942). It was in the form 'Why don't you get out of that wet coat and into a dry Martini?', according to Harry Haun's *The Movie Quote Book* (1980). Robert Drennan, *Wit's End* (1972), has: 'Let's get out of these wet clothes and into a dry martini.' Sometimes also attributed to Alexander Woollcott, the line may actually have originated with Benchley's press agent in the 1920s or with his friend Charles Butterworth. In any case, apparently, Mae West also adopted the line, as screenwriter, in *Every Day's a Holiday* (1937).

1 See Hebrews 13:8.

A capsule criticism of the play *Abie's Irish Rose*, which ran so long (1922–7) that Benchley was incapable of saying anything new about it in the weekly edition of *Life* Magazine. The text he alluded to read: 'Jesus Christ the same yesterday, and today, and for ever.' Quoted in Diana Rigg, *No Turn Unstoned* (1982).

Between 1975 and 1990, when *A Chorus Line* was running on Broadway, the capsule criticism space for it in *The New Yorker*'s listings was given over to reprinting paragraphs from *War and Peace*.

Julien BENDA French writer and philosopher (1867–1956)

2 *La Trahison des clercs* [The intellectuals' betrayal].

Title of book (1927). The phrase denotes a compromise of intellectual integrity by writers, artists and thinkers.

Stephen Vincent BENÉT American poet (1898–1943)

3 I shall not rest quiet in Montparnasse.
I shall not lie easy at Winchelsea.
You may bury my body in Sussex grass,
You may bury my tongue at Champmédy.
I shall not be there, I shall rise and pass.
Bury my heart at Wounded Knee.

In his poem 'American Names' (1927) Benét celebrates the 'sharp names that never get fat' of American places: extraordinary names such as 'Medicine Hat', and 'Lost Mule Flat'. He contrasts them with the names of other possible burial places in Europe – Montparnasse (where there is a famous cemetery) in Paris, Winchelsea (the 'ancient town' of Rye in Sussex and linked to Henry James), and Champmédy (the significance of which escapes one). *Bury My Heart At Wounded Knee* became the title of a book (1970) by Dee Brown, a survey of American Indian history.

4 Oh, where are you coming from, soldier, gaunt soldier,
With weapons beyond any reach of my mind,

With weapons so deadly the world must grow older
And die in its tracks, if it does not turn kind?

'Song for Three Soldiers', published in *The Atlantic Monthly* (October 1943). It is quoted anonymously in the Peter Watkins film, *The War Game*. Made for the BBC in 1965, it was kept off the TV screen for 20 years lest it upset the populace with its depiction of the effects of an imaginary nuclear attack on Britain (which was, of course, the intention). The poem crawls across the screen at one point and it was many years before it was identified.

Tony BENN British Labour politician (1925–)

5 Broadcasting is really too important to be left to the broadcasters and somehow we must find some new way of using radio and television to allow us to talk to each other.

Speech, Bristol (18 October 1968), when Minister of Technology. Compare CLEMENCEAU 146:1; DE GAULLE 165:4.

6 If voting changed anything they would make it illegal.

Has been dubiously ascribed to Benn. Whatever else he may be, he is neither anti-democratic nor cynical. Fred Metcalf in *The Penguin Dictionary of Modern Humorous Quotations* (1987) merely places the slogan as on a 'badge, London, 1983'. In Rennie Ellis's *Australian Graffiti Revisited* (1979), there is a photograph of a wall slogan in Carlton, Victoria: 'IF VOTING COULD CHANGE THINGS, IT WOULD BE ILLEGAL.' This may predate the original publication of the book in 1975. In 1987, Ken Livingstone, then a Labour MP, published a book with the title *If Voting Changed Anything, They'd Abolish It*.

Alan BENNETT English playwright and actor (1934–)

7 Life, you know, is rather like opening a tin of sardines. We're all of us looking for the key.

'Take a Pew', *Beyond the Fringe* (1961). Bennett's parody of an Anglican church sermon included this banal simile and more than one mangled quotation – see BIBLE 68:5 and RICE 382:5. It was said that a record of the sermon used to be played as a warning to trainee priests, but clearly most of them did not get the message.

8 They are rolling up the maps all over Europe. We shall not see them lit again in our lifetime.

Forty Years On, Act 1 (1969). Alluding to GREY 223:3 and PITT 360:1.

1 All women dress like their mothers, that is their tragedy. No man ever does. That is his.
In the same act. Alluding to WILDE 495:5.

2 Two of the nicest people if ever there was one.
In the same play, Act 2. On the political thinkers, Sidney and Beatrice Webb. Alternatively, 'Two nice people if there was one.' This line does not appear in the published script of Bennett's play, though it was spoken in the original production. Having quoted the first version in my book *Quote ... Unquote* (1978), I was interested to see it picked up in Kenneth Williams's anthology *Acid Drops* (1980) credited to *Arnold* Bennett.

3 Sapper, Buchan, Dornford Yates, practitioners in that school of Snobbery with Violence that runs like a thread of good-class tweed through twentieth-century literature.
In the same act. In its obituary (21 January 1983) for Colin Watson, the detective story writer, *The Times* mentioned his book *Snobbery with Violence* (1971) – a survey of the modern crime story – 'from which the phrase comes'. As usual, there is an earlier example of the phrase in use: in Bennett's play. In his preface to the published text of *Forty Years On and Other Plays* (1991), Bennett states that he thought he *had* invented the phrase, but was then told it had been used before – it was the title of a pamphlet by the New Zealand eccentric, Count Potocki de Montalk: *Snobbery with Violence. A Poet in Gaol* was published in 1932.

4 You only have to survive in England and all is forgiven you ... if you can eat a boiled egg at ninety in England they think you deserve a Nobel Prize.
On ITV, on the *South Bank Show* (1984). In his TV film *An Englishman Abroad* (1989), this reappears as: 'In England, you see, age wipes the slate clean ... If you live to be ninety in England and can still eat a boiled egg they think you deserve the Nobel Prize.'

Arnold BENNETT English novelist (1867–1931)

5 Mrs Laye ... told a good thing of a very old man on his dying bed giving advice to a youngster: 'I've had a long life, and it's been a merry one. Take my advice. Make love to every pretty woman you meet. And remember, if you get 5 per cent on your outlay it's a good return.'
Diary entry for 24 May 1904, published in *The Journals* (1971). *The Treasury of Humorous Quotations*, eds Esar & Bentley (1951), has this as though said by Bennett himself,

in the form: 'Make love to every woman you meet; if you get five per cent on your outlay, it's a good investment.' See also BAX 55:5.

A.C. BENSON English writer (1862–1925)

6 Land of Hope and Glory, Mother of the Free,
How shall we extol thee, who are born of thee?
Wider still and wider shall thy bounds be set;
God who made thee mighty, make thee
    mightier yet.
'Land of Hope and Glory' is the title popularly given to the Finale of Sir Edward Elgar's *Coronation Ode* (1902), originally written for performance at the time of the Coronation of Edward VII. Elgar, having written the basic *Ode*, invited Benson to fit words to the big tune in the Trio of the 'Pomp and Circumstance March No. 1', which had first been performed the previous year. It is said that the idea for this came from the King himself. In 1914 Benson recast the words as a war song, but these have not endured in the way the originals have done.
Hence, *Hope and Glory*, the title of a film (UK 1987).

7 *From a College Window.*
Title of essay collection (1906). In a book called *A Victorian Boyhood*, L.E. Jones refers to Benson, who taught at Eton and became Master of Magdalene College, Cambridge: 'This was long before the days when sitting at his College window at Magdalene, he was killed dead by the straightest and most lethal arrow ever aimed by the gentle "Max".' This slight allusion is to *A Christmas Garland* (1912), in which Max Beerbohm produced a number of amusing parodies of his contemporaries. What is considered by some to be the book's best parody is that of Benson's windy and waffly essay style. Benson apparently took it amiss – hence, the 'lethal arrow'. And 'sitting at his College window'? – from the title of this book.

Stella BENSON English novelist and poet (1892–1933)

8 Call no man foe, but never love a stranger.
To the Unborn, St. 3 (1935). Hence, presumably the title of Harold Robbins's novel *Never Love a Stranger* (1948; film US 1958).

E. Clerihew BENTLEY English novelist, journalist and poet (1875–1956)

9 Sir Christopher Wren
Said, 'I am going to dine with some men.
If anybody calls
Say I am designing St Paul's.'

Biography for Beginners (1905). An example of a 'clerihew', the four-line, amusing biographical verse form he invented at the turn of the century. This volume was published under the name 'E. Clerihew'. There was a second run of these verses in the late 1930s in *Punch*, when they were illustrated by his son, Nicolas.

Lloyd BENTSEN American Democratic Senator (1921–)

1 I served with Jack Kennedy. I knew Jack Kennedy. Jack Kennedy was a friend of mine. Senator, you're no Jack Kennedy.

To Dan Quayle, who had evoked the name of John F. Kennedy in a vice-presidential TV debate during a presidential election (6 October 1988). Compare: 'Mr Blair, I know Margaret Thatcher. Margaret Thatcher is a friend of mine. When Margaret Thatcher was rebuilding this country, you opposed everything she did. Mr Blair, you're no Margaret Thatcher' – Brian Mawhinney, British Conservative Party chairman at Bournemouth conference (8 October 1996).

Lord Charles BERESFORD English politician (1846–1919)

2 VERY SORRY CAN'T COME. LIE FOLLOWS BY POST.

Beresford is supposed to have telegraphed this message to the Prince of Wales (presumably the future Edward VII) after receiving a dinner invitation at short notice. It is reported by Ralph Nevill in *The World of Fashion 1837–1922* (1923). The same joke occurs in Marcel Proust, *Le Temps retrouvé* (published in 1927, after his death in 1922), in the form: 'One of those telegrams of which M. de Guermantes has wittily fixed the formula: "Can't come, lie follows" [*Une de ces dépêches dont M. de Guermantes avait spirituellement fixé le modèle: "Impossible venir, mensonge suit"*].'

George BERKELEY Irish philosopher and Anglican bishop (1685–1753)

3 If a tree falls in a forest, and no one is there to hear it, it makes no sound.

Which philosopher said this? Not Kant, apparently, though it was one of his preoccupations. Berkeley also seems a likely bet. In his writings on 'subjective idealism', he holds that there is no existence of matter independent of perception. But in his three best-known works, *Essays Towards a New Theory of Vision*, *A Treatise Concerning the Principles of Human Knowledge* and *Three Dialogues Between Hylas and Philonous*, the precise example does not occur. However, *Principles*, 1.23, has: 'Surely there is nothing easier to imag-

ine than trees, for instance, in a park, or books existing in a closet, and nobody by to perceive them'; in the *Dialogues* there is: 'Can a real thing which is not *audible*, be like a *sound?*' Perhaps these have become linked to the idea expressed by Monsignor Ronald Knox in the limerick attributed to him:

> There was once a man who said 'God
> Must think it exceedingly odd
> If he finds that this tree
> Continues to be
> When there's no one about in the Quad.'

The editor of *The Book of Cloyne* (1994 edn) comments: 'Berkeley's philosophy will always be tagged to the lines about the tree that might disappear when there was no one to see it and God's remark that it would not because he was always on the lookout. "To be," said Berkeley, "is to be perceived."'

The background to this is that it all started with Aristotle. In *De Anima*, he said that if there are flowers in the forest but nobody to smell them, they have no scent, because trees cannot smell. Berkeley refuted Aristotle. First he conceded that '*Esse est percipi* [To be is to be perceived]', but then he argued that the flowers do have scent (and the tree does crash) because God not only sees all, but also smells all and hears all. So, when a tree falls in the forest, and there's no one to hear it, does it make a sound? Berkeley would say it does, because God hears it.

4 The peasant starves in the midst of plenty.

The Book of Cloyne (1994 edn), concerning the town in Ireland where Berkeley was bishop, quotes a certain George Cooper as having written this in 1799 (i.e. after Berkeley's death), while Berkeley is also credited with being the first to make use of the phrase. Unverified. Compare: Richard Chamption Rawlins, *An American Journal 1839–40* (2002), entry for 26 October 1839: 'Glad to leave Gorrings, where the waiters are scanty in number and wanting in sense. You might almost starve in the midst of plenty, if you did not keep up a constant call until you secured a waiter.'

See also COWPER 157:10.

Irving BERLIN American composer and lyricist (1888–1989)

5 Puttin' on the Ritz.

Title song of film (US 1930). Lines include: 'If you're blue and you don't know where to go / Why don't you go to where fashion sits / Puttin' on the Ritz? ... Dressed up like a million-dollar trouper / Trying hard to look like Gary Cooper, sooper dooper ... Come let's mix where Rockefellers / Walk with sticks or umberellas [sic] in their mitts / Puttin' on the Ritz.' The verbal phrase is defined by *OED2* as 'to assume an air of superiority'. It had been used previously by Ring Lardner in 1926.

1 *As Thousands Cheer.*

Title of show (1933) with words and music by Berlin. Hence, *As Thousands Cheer: The Life of Irving Berlin*, title of book (1990) by Laurence Bugneer. There was a film *Thousands Cheer* (US 1943). A natural enough phrase found in newspaper reports but somehow still echoic of the Berlin use. From the *Daily Mail* (18 December 1993): 'When Maiden returned to Southampton in 1990, the triumph was enormous. A band played Tina Turner's "You're Simply The Best" as the girls sailed into the marina and thousands cheered and wept.' From *The Mail on Sunday* (27 February 1994): '... So when Paul O'Callaghan laid into an impersonation of Noel Edmonds's brain, thousands cheered.'

2 I'm dreaming of a white Christmas.

'White Christmas', *Holiday Inn* (film US 1942), in which it is sung by Bing Crosby. His recording of the song is the biggest-selling single record of all time. A re-make of the film called *White Christmas* followed in 1954. *OED2*'s first recorded use of the term 'white Christmas' (= a snowy one) is from *Two Years Ago* (1857) by Charles Kingsley.

3 *Annie Get Your Gun.*

Title of musical (1946). Even if it was utterly suitable for the tale of Annie Oakley, the gun-toting gal, this title appears to have been an allusion. The song 'Johnny Get Your Gun' – with lyrics along the lines of 'Johnny get your gun, get your gun, get your gun, / Keep them on the run, on the run, on the run' – was written by 'F. Belasco' (Monroe H. Rosenfeld) and published in New York in 1886; it was a popular American song of the First World War. Dalton Trumbo's film *Johnny Got His Gun* (US 1971) was about a horrendously mutilated soldier in the same war.

4 There's No Business Like Show Business.

Title of song in *Annie Get Your Gun* (1946). Later the title of a musical film (1954) and the origin of a quasi-proverbial modern expression.

5 The Hostess with Mostes' on the Ball.

Title of song, *Call Me Madam* (1950). Compare FORREST 198:6.

See also PERKINS 357:3.

BERNARD OF CLAIRVAUX French theologian and saint (1090–1153)

6 Love me, love my dog.

Meaning 'if you are inclined to take my side in matters generally, you must put up with one or two things you don't like at the same time', this comes from one of St Bernard's sermons: '*Qui me amat, amat et canem meum* [Who loves me, also loves my dog]'. A good illustration comes from an article by Valerie Bornstein in *Proverbium* (1991): 'I told my mother that she must love my father a lot because she tolerated his snoring! ... She became aggravated with me and stated the proverb "*Aime moi, aime mon chien.*" She told me that when you love someone, you accept all the things that go along with them, their virtues and faults.'

Alas, this was a different St Bernard to the one after whom the breed of Alpine dog is named. It was said (or quoted) by St Bernard of Clairvaux rather than St Bernard of Menthon (who died in 1008).

Lord BERNERS English writer and composer (1883–1950)

7 He's always backing into the limelight.

On T.E. Lawrence. Quoted in *ODQ* (1979). Winston Churchill said the same thing, according to his secretary, Montague Brown (speech to the International Churchill Society, 25 September 1985): 'He had the art of backing uneasily into the limelight. He was a very remarkable character and very careful of that fact.' *ODQ* (2004) reported that Bernard Shaw had also been found saying something like it: 'The diaries of the German diplomat, Count Harry Kessler, tell of a meeting with Shaw in November 1929. Lawrence had apparently complained that every move of his was followed by the Press, eliciting the Shavian response, "You always hide just in the middle of the limelight."' Which of these is the original is anyone's guess.

Lawrence ('Yogi') BERRA American baseball player and coach (1925–)

8 The game isn't over till it's over.

His comment on a National League pennant race (1973), when he was managing the New York Mets. It is claimed that *Sports Illustrated* investigated this and found that Berra's actual comment was 'You're not out of it till you're out of it.' Nowadays, the expression is more usually: 'It isn't over until it's over.'

'Berraisms' like Goldwynisms have been put into his mouth more often than they have emerged from it unaided. Berra was a star with the New York Yankees, and took part in a record 14 World Series (1946–63). He went on to manage the New York Yankees, the New York Mets and the

Houston Astros – as has been said, 'a great catcher and hitter, was three times nominated Most Valuable Player in the American League, but is perhaps most famous for his verbal confusions'.

Some of the more unlikely ones are: 'It was déjà vu all over again', 'When you come to a fork in the road, take it' and 'If people don't want to come out to the ball park, nobody's going to stop 'em' – all attributed in *Bartlett* (1992); and 'The future ain't what it used to be' – attributed in *ODQ* (1999). Not to mention: 'We made too many wrong mistakes', 'Baseball is ninety per cent mental, the other half is physical', 'Prediction is a difficult art – particularly when it involves the future' and 'Always go to other people's funerals, otherwise they won't go to yours.' Of those he has admitted to, 'Nobody ever goes there anymore, it's too crowded' had been said by others before him, but 'You can observe a lot by watching' is wisdom through tautology.

(Sir) John BETJEMAN English Poet Laureate (1906–84)

1 *Ghastly Good Taste.*
Title of book (1933), subtitled 'a depressing story of the Rise and Fall of English Architecture', in which Betjeman concludes: 'We have seen in this book how English architecture emerged from the religious unity of Christendom to the reasoned unity of an educated monarchic system, and then to the stranger order of an industrialized community. As soon as it became unsettled, towards the end of the 19th century, "architecture" *qua* architecture became self-conscious.' Th is probably applies equally to design in general.

2 Come, friendly bombs, and fall on Slough.
It isn't fit for humans now.
'Slough' (1937). In reply to a correspondent (9 January 1967), published in *John Betjeman Letters: Volume Two 1951 to 1984* (1995), the poet explained the precise nature and cause of his aversion: 'The town of Slough was not, when those verses were written, such a congestion as it is now and I was most certainly not thinking of it but of the Trading Estate ... which had originated in a dump that now stretches practically from Reading to London ... The chain stores were only then just beginning to deface the High Street, but already the world of "executives" with little moustaches, smooth cars and smooth manners and ruthless methods was planted in my mind along the fronts of those Trading Estate factories.'

3 Miss J. Hunter Dunn, Miss J. Hunter Dunn,
Furnish'd and burnish'd by Aldershot sun.
'A Subaltern's Love-Song' (1945). Miss Hunter Dunn was a real person. Betjeman surmised that she came from Alder-

shot and was a doctor's daughter and was correct on both counts. The title notwithstanding, Betjeman said it was really *his* love song.

4 Phone for the fish knives, Norman,
As Cook is a little unnerved.
'How to Get on in Society' (1954). The poem concerns 'Non-U' language and behaviour – that is to say 'genteel' rather than the 'U' language and behaviour of the upper-classes. In the latter milieu, special knives for eating are frowned upon, the full word 'telephone' is preferred, and so on. See ROSS 388:2.

Aneurin BEVAN Welsh Labour politician (1897–1960)

5 Listening to a speech by [Neville] Chamberlain is like paying a visit to Woolworths; everything in its place and nothing over sixpence.
In *Tribune* (1937). 'Nothing over sixpence' was the slogan of Woolworth's stores in the UK until the Second World War pushed prices well above this limit.

6 Playing on a fuddled fiddle, somewhere in the muddled middle.
Of J.B. Priestley during the Second World War. From Alan Watkins in *The Observer* (28 September 1987): 'Dr David Owen has a bit of a cheek saying that the new SDP ought not to be "playing on a fuddled fiddle, somewhere in the muddled middle". The words were most recently used by Mr Roy Jenkins of the old SDP. They were first used by Bevan of J.B. Priestley during the last war. Mr Jenkins acknowledges his debt to Bevan. Dr Owen should likewise acknowledge his debt to Mr Jenkins. There is nothing new under the sun.'

7 No amount of cajolery, and no attempts at ethical or social seduction, can eradicate from my heart a deep and burning hatred for the Tory Party that inflicted those experiences on me. So far as I am concerned they are lower than vermin.
The fiery left-winger was on the eve of his most substantial achievement – launching the postwar Labour government's National Health Service – when on 4 July 1948 he spoke at a rally in Belle Vue, Manchester. He contrasted Labour's social programme with the days of his youth between the wars when the Means Test reigned, when he had had to live on the earnings of his sister and when he had been told to emigrate. As abuse goes, it was traditional stuff. In Swift's *Gulliver's Travels* (1726), the King of Brobdingnag considers Gulliver's fellow countrymen to be 'the most pernicious race of little odious vermin that nature

ever suffered to crawl upon the face of the earth'. Nevertheless, in 1948, Bevan's words caused a storm. Outside his home someone daubed 'VERMIN VILLA – HOME OF A LOUD MOUTHED RAT', and the Tory press went to town. *The Sunday Times* commented: 'Nothing said at a political meeting for a long time has been more talked about or will be longer remembered.' The *Sunday Dispatch* headlined: 'THE MAN WHO HATES 8,093,858 PEOPLE' (the number who had voted for the Conservatives at the previous election). Prime Minister Attlee quietly warned Bevan: 'Please be a bit more careful in your own interest.'

The Minister was not allowed to forget his remarks for a long while. As Michael Foot described in his biography of Bevan: 'Adult members of Conservative associations founded Vermin Clubs, pinned vermin badges on their breasts, or invaded Bevan's meetings with the chant "vermin, vermin" ... Harold Laski guessed that [Bevan's use of the word 'vermin'] was worth two million votes to the Tories. If the claim was true, the one casual word was responsible for deciding in advance the outcome of the 1950 election.'

1   The language of priorities is the religion of socialism.
Speech at Labour Party Conference in Blackpool (8 June 1949). On BBC Radio *Quote ... Unquote* (1 May 2000), Peter Kellner remarked how this would make as much or as little sense if you moved any of the nouns round.

2   *In Place of Fear.*
Title of book about disarmament (1952). Compare CASTLE 128:2.

3   We know what happens to people who stay in the middle of the road. They get run over.
Quoted in *The Observer* (9 December 1953). But you can't keep a good line down. According to Kenneth Harris, *Thatcher* (1988), Margaret Thatcher once said to James Prior: 'Standing in the middle of the road is very dangerous, you get knocked down by traffic from both sides.' And a TV play called *A Very British Coup* (1988) had a fictional Prime Minister saying, 'I once tried the middle of the road ... but I was knocked down by traffic in both directions.'

4   I know that the right kind of leader for the Labour Party is a desiccated calculating machine who must not in any way permit himself to be swayed by indignation ... He must speak in calm and objective accents and talk about a dying child in the same way as he would about the pieces inside an internal combustion engine.

During a *Tribune* group meeting held at the Labour Party Conference in Scarborough (29 September 1954), countering Clement Attlee's plea for a non-emotional response to German rearmament. The characterization as a 'desiccated calculating machine' came to be applied to Hugh Gaitskell, who beat Bevan for the leadership of the Labour Party the following year. In 1959, however, Bevan told Robin Day in a TV interview: 'I never called him that. I was applying my words to a synthetic figure, but the press took it up and it's never possible to catch up a canard like that, as you know.' After the interview was over, he added: 'Of course I wasn't referring to Hugh Gaitskell. For one thing Hugh is not desiccated – he's highly emotional. And you could hardly call him a calculating machine – because he was three hundred millions out' – source: Michael Foot, *Aneurin Bevan*, Vol. 2 (1973).

5   I am not going to spend any time whatsoever in attacking the Foreign Secretary. Quite honestly I am beginning to feel extremely sorry for him. If we complain about the tune, there is no reason to attack the monkey when the organ grinder is present.
Wishing to address the Prime Minister (Harold Macmillan) rather than the Foreign Secretary (Selwyn Lloyd) in a post-Suez debate, House of Commons (16 May 1957). The saying has also been attributed to Winston Churchill during the Second World War – replying to a query from the British Ambassador as to whether he should raise a question with Mussolini or with Count Ciano, his Foreign Minister – but this is unverified. Evidence that the idea behind this remark existed already can be found in the caption to a cartoon by Chas Grave (1886–1944) in *Punch* (23 January 1924):

Tommy (describing his experience of being up before the Colonel). I WAS TELLIN' THE C.O. WOT 'APPENED WHEN THE SERGEANT-MAJOR INTERRUPTED ME, SO I TURNED ROUND AN' I SED, 'NOW LOOK 'ERE, SERGEANT-MAJOR,' I SEZ, 'WHEN I'M TALKIN' TO THE ORGAN-GRINDER I DON'T WANT THE BLEEDIN' MONKEY TO CHIP IN.'

One might compare the proverb 'Better speak to the master, than the man' that *Apperson* has in 1661 and which is presumably on the same theme.

6   If you carry this resolution ... you will send a British Foreign Secretary – whoever he was – naked into the conference chamber.
Speech, Labour Party Conference (3 October 1957) – as Shadow Foreign Secretary – in opposition to a motion proposing unilateral disarmament. By taking this point of view, he shocked those normally on his side.

1 Yesterday, Barbara [Castle] quoted from a speech which I made some years ago, and she said that I believed that Socialism in the context of modern society meant the conquest of the commanding heights of the economy ...

Speech, two-day Labour Conference (November 1959) – referring to the areas of activity which Labour would have to nationalize to bring about fundamental change. Hugh Gaitskell, the party leader, also quoted the phrase 'commanding heights of the economy', apparently, but no one has been able to find Bevan's original coinage, least of all his most recent biographer, John Campbell. Alan Watkins in a throwaway line in his *Observer* column (28 September 1987) said 'the phrase was originally Lenin's'. In his 'white heat of technology' speech in October 1963, Harold Wilson referred to 'the commanding heights of British industry'. At the Labour Party Conference in October 1989, Neil Kinnock also revived the phrase format, saying that education and training were 'the commanding heights of every modern economy'.

2 I read the newspaper avidly. It is my one form of continuous fiction.

Quoted in *The Times* (29 March 1960). Compare JEFFERSON 255:4.

Ernest BEVIN English Labour politician (1881–1951)

On being told that another Labourite was 'his own worst enemy':

3 Not while I'm alive, he ain't.

Reputedly levelled at Aneurin Bevan, Herbert Morrison, Emanuel Shinwell and others. Quoted by Michael Foot in *Aneurin Bevan*, Vol. 2 (1973), who footnoted: 'Perhaps once he had made it he recited it about all of them. Impossible to determine who was the original victim.' Douglas Jay in *Change and Fortune* (1980) added that it was 'made, I have little doubt, though there is no conclusive proof – about Bevan ... I could never discover direct evidence for this oft-told story.' Earlier, in about 1939, the American Senator Walter George may have said, 'Roosevelt is his own worst enemy' and 'Cotton Ed' Smith may have replied, 'Not so long as I am alive!' It is believed that in the James Cagney film *The Fighting 69th* (US 1940), there occurs the exchange: 'He's his own worst enemy' – 'Not while I'm around, he's not.'

4 My policy is to be able to take a ticket at Victoria Station and go anywhere I damn well please.

On his foreign policy when Labour Foreign Secretary, and so quoted in *The Spectator* (20 April 1951). Francis Williams

in his biography of Bevin (1952) has a slightly different version – said to a diplomat about the most important objective of his foreign policy: 'Just to be able to go down to Victoria station and take a ticket to where the hell I like without a passport.'

5 It was clitch after clitch after clitch.

On the cliché-ridden content of a speech by another politician (possibly Anthony Eden). Quoted in Willard R. Espy, *An Almanac of Words at Play* (1975) – where it is said by Bevin of Aneurin *Bevan*.

6 The real tragedy of the poor is the poverty of their aspirations.

Attributed in 1960 to Adam Smith in this form, but unverified. Keir Hardie has also been suggested as the originator. Since 1987, however, it has frequently been attributed to Bevin, though with no precise source as yet (also to Aneurin Bevan, though with even less backing) and about any number of subjects – the poor, the working class, Britain, the trade unions. 'There was a marvellous remark by Ernest Bevin when he said that what characterized Britain was a poverty of aspiration – and it's true' – *The Times* (19 May 1987). Sometimes the word 'ambition' is substituted: 'John Edmonds, secretary of GMB, the general union, recalled Ernest Bevin's observation 50 years ago that the greatest failing of Britain's trade unions was their poverty of ambition which made them set their sights too low' – *The Guardian* (6 September 1990). 'My family were the same as any other working class family in those days; they suffered from what I shall call the poverty of ambition' – Sir Bernard Ingham, *The Times* (18 May 1991); 'Only the Morgan Motor Company refused to follow his advice to expand – a course of action which Sir John [Harvey Jones] cites as evidence of the poverty of ambition of small and medium-sized British companies' – *Financial Times* (21 April 1993). Perhaps on a balance of probabilities Bevin wins this one over Bevan.

The BIBLE

Except where stated these quotations are in the form to be found in the Authorized Version or King James Bible (1611).

7 It was the expectation of many ... upon the setting of that bright Occidental Star, Queen Elizabeth of most happy memory, some thick and palpable clouds of darkness would so have overshadowed this land, that men should have been in doubt

which way they were to walk ... The appearance of Your Majesty, as of the Sun in his strength, instantly dispelled those supposed and surmised mists.

Epistle Dedicatory (to King James I). Compare DISRAELI 173:8 on the use of a trowel.

OLD TESTAMENT

GENESIS

1 In the beginning God created the heaven and the earth. And the earth was without form, and void; and darkness was upon the face of the deep. And the Spirit of God moved upon the face of the waters. And God said, Let there be light: and there was light.

Genesis 1:1. Hence, *fiat lux*, motto of several institutions including Moorfields Eye Hospital, London.

2 So God created man in his own image, in the image of God created he him

Genesis 1:27. Hence, Michelangelo, 'The Creation of Man', from the Sistine Chapel ceiling (1511–12). Compare BRIGHT 101:3

3 And the Lord God planted a garden eastward in Eden.

Genesis 2:8. Compare 4:16: 'And Cain went out from the presence of the Lord, and dwelt in the land of Nod, on the east of Eden.' Hence, *East of Eden*, title of a novel (1952; film US 1955) by John Steinbeck – about two brothers vying for their father's love (like Cain and Abel).

4 And the Lord God caused a deep sleep to fall upon Adam, and he slept: and he took one of his ribs, and closed up the flesh instead thereof; And the rib, which the Lord God had taken from man, made he a woman, and brought her unto the man.

Genesis 2:21–3, stating that God made woman from one of Adam's ribs. Hence, *Adam's Rib*, the title of a film (US 1949) about husband and wife lawyers opposing each other in court (also of a 1923 Cecil B. DeMille marital film with biblical flashbacks), and *Spare Rib*, the title of a British feminist magazine (founded 1972) – a punning reference to the cuts of meat known as 'spare ribs'.

5 Esau selleth his birthright for a mess of potage.

The expression 'to sell one's birthright for a mess of potage', meaning to sacrifice something for material comfort, has biblical origins but is not a quotation of a verse in the Bible.

It appears as a chapter heading for Genesis 25 in one or two early translations of the Bible, though not in the Authorized Version. The nearest wording in the text is at 25:33–4: 'And he sold his birthright unto Jacob. Then Jacob gave Esau bread and pottage of lentiles.'

The word 'mess' is used in its sense of 'a portion of liquid or pulpy food'. 'Potage' is thick soup (compare French *potage*).

6 Behold, Esau my brother is a hairy man, and I am a smooth man.

Genesis 27:11. This was the unlikely text preached upon by Alan Bennett's Anglican clergyman in the revue *Beyond the Fringe* (1961), which has become a model for how not to do it. One hopes it was intentional that the clergyman ascribed the text to 2 Kings 14:1.

EXODUS

7 And I am come to deliver them out of the hand of the Egyptians ... unto a land flowing with milk and honey.

Exodus 3:8, God speaking – hence, the phrase 'land flowing with milk and honey', referring to any idyllic, prosperous situation.

8 And thou shalt say unto him, The Lord God of the Hebrews hath sent me unto thee, saying, Let my people go, that they may serve me in the wilderness.

Exodus 7:16. Compare 8:1–2: 'And the Lord spake unto Moses, Go unto Pharaoh, and say unto him, Thus saith the Lord, Let my people go, that they may serve me. And if thou refuse to let them go, behold, I will smite all thy borders with frogs ... ' A soft-porn stage revue in London (1976) had the title *Let My People Come*. Compare SAHL 392:3.

9 Would to God we had died by the hand of the Lord in the land of Egypt, when we sat by the flesh pots, and when we did eat bread to the full.

Exodus 16:3, said by the Israelites. Hence, 'the fleshpots of Egypt', now meaning 'any place of comparative luxury'. Clementine Churchill wrote to Winston on 20 December 1910: 'I do so wish I was at Warter with you enjoying the Flesh Pots of Egypt! It sounds a delightful party ...' – quoted in Mary Soames, *Clementine Churchill* (1979).

10 Thou shalt have no other gods before me.

Exodus 20:3. How many words are there in the Ten Commandments? The question is neither rhetorical nor uttered because one is too lazy to count them oneself. The test is whether one is talking about Exodus 20:2–17 or Deuteronomy 5:6–21, and then which language you are using and which translation. Raymond Harris declared (1995): 'As the Ten Commandments were written in Hebrew, I thought you would like to know that 120 words were used.' He also points out that the numbering of the commandments varies with different religions and, depending whether one includes 'I am the Lord thy God' as the first commandment, there may or may not be ten in all. But 'ten commandments' are referred to several times in the Old Testament.

Dr J.K. Aronson added (1995): 'By my count the version in Exodus has 172 [Hebrew] words and the version in Deuteronomy 189 words. The corresponding numbers of English words in the Authorized Version are 319 and 372, and in the Revised English Bible 301 and 348.' So, this is a considerably more complicated matter than at first appears. The word count very much depends on whether you restrict it to the actual commandments or whether you include the incidental observations.

1 Honour thy father and thy mother.

Exodus 20:12. Hence, *Honour Thy Father*, the title of a book (1972; film US 1973) about the Mafia, by Gay Talese.

2 Thou shalt not covet thy neighbour's house, thou shalt not covet thy neighbour's wife.

Exodus 20:17. Hence, the title of Gay Talese's study of sexual mores in the US, *Thy Neighbour's Wife* (1980).

3 Thou shalt not commit adultery.

Exodus 20:14. The 1631 'Wicked Bible' through one of the more notable printer's errors advised readers, 'Thou shalt commit adultery.'

LEVITICUS

4 And the goat shall bear upon him all their iniquities unto a land not inhabited: and he shall let go the goat in the wilderness.

Leviticus 16:22. In Jewish tradition, on the Festival of the Day of Atonement, a goat was driven into the wilderness taking with it the sins of the congregation. This practice was notably portrayed in William Holman Hunt's painting 'The Scapegoat' (1854–5). A cartoon based on this appeared in *Punch* (25 October 1922) after David Lloyd George, no longer Prime Minister, had said, 'If I am driven alone into the wilderness ...' Indeed, he was in the political wilderness for the rest of his life, as he never again held high office. Lloyd George may also have been portrayed as a goat because of his Welshness, his shaggy white hair and because

of his other goat-like tendencies. Anyway, hence *Lloyd George the Goat in the Wilderness 1922–1931*, the title of a biography (1977) by John Campbell.

5 Thou shalt love thy neighbour as thyself.

Leviticus 19:18. Not one of the Ten Commandments, as might be supposed, however, in Matthew 22:39 Jesus says of 'Thou shalt love thy neighbour as thyself' that it is one of the two commandments upon which 'hang all the law and the prophets'. *Love Thy Neighbour* was the title of an ITV sitcom (1972–6) and spin-off film (UK 1973), concerning English/West Indian families living next door to each other.

NUMBERS

6 What hath God wrought!

Numbers 23:23. Quoted by Samuel F.B. Morse, American inventor (1791–1872), in the first telegraph message he sent to his partner, Alfred Vail, from the Old Supreme Court Chamber in Washington DC to Baltimore (24 May 1844). Quoted in Stuart Berg Flexner, *Listening To America* (1982).

DEUTERONOMY

7 He kept him as the apple of his eye.

Deuteronomy 32:10. Hence, 'apple of one's eye' for what one cherishes most. The pupil of the eye has long been known as the 'apple' because of its supposed round, solid shape. To be deprived of the apple is to be blinded and lose something extremely valuable.

JUDGES

8 Out of the eater came forth meat, and out of the strong came forth sweetness.

Judges 14:14. Samson's riddle. His wife (not Delilah) wheedles the answer out of him and gives it to those whom he had challenged with the riddle. The answer is honey from a swarm of bees he had observed in the carcass of a lion he had killed. Hence, 'Out Of The Strong Came Forth Sweetness', a slogan for Lyle's Golden Syrup in the UK (current from the 1930s). Later, the Tate & Lyle company completely reversed the phrase by saying 'Out Of Sweetness Came Forth Strength' as part of its occasionally necessary campaigns featuring 'Mr Cube' to ward off nationalization of the British sugar industry.

1 SAMUEL

1 God save the king.

1 Samuel 10:24, referring to Saul. The third line of the British national anthem occurs several times in the Bible – also in 2 Samuel 16:16, 2 Kings 11:12 and 2 Chronicles 23:11. The national anthem is of obscure composition. It was possibly written by Henry Carey – and sung by him as his own composition, 1740 – or taken from an old Jacobite drinking song in about 1725, or dates back to the 17th century. Benham (1948) comments: 'The words of "God Save the King" appear in the Gentleman's Magazine (October 1745). John Bull (?1563–1628), composer, singer, and organist at Antwerp Cathedral in 1617, has been credited with composition of the words and music.' The British Inheritance, A Treasury of Historic Documents (2000) refers to a document in the music section of the British Library, which is dated 1745 and contains 'A Loyal Song' with these words:

> God save Great George our King,
> Long Live our noble King
> God save the King.
> God save Great George our King,
> Long live our noble King
> God save the King.
> Send him victorious ...

The book states: 'The first recorded performances of the National Anthem took place at Drury Lane and Covent Garden in September 1745, when Thomas Arne's arrangement of God Save the King was loudly sung on several successive nights until the dangers of the Jacobite rebellion were past.'

2 And Saul went in to cover his feet.

1 Samuel 24:3. David was hiding from Saul in a cave when into the cave came Saul to evacuate his bowels. Most modern versions of the Bible say, 'to relieve himself'. The Revised Authorized Version (1982) has: 'Saul went in to attend to his needs.' The Living Bible (Illinois, 1971) has, memorably: 'Saul went in to a cave to go to the bathroom.'

3 After whom is the king of Israel come out? after whom dost thou pursue? after a dead dog, after a flea.

1 Samuel 24:14. Yes, fleas are mentioned twice in the Bible, both here and at 26:20.

2 SAMUEL

4 The beauty of Israel is slain upon thy high places: how are the mighty fallen! Tell it not in Gath, publish it not in the streets of Askelon; lest the daughters of the Philistines rejoice.

2 Samuel 1:19–20. This is part of David's lamentation over the deaths of Saul and Jonathan, his son. 'How are the mighty fallen' is repeated twice more in the chapter. Publish It Not ... was the title of a book (1975) by Christopher Mayhew and Michael Adams, subtitled 'the Middle East cover-up'.

5 Saul and Jonathan were lovely and pleasant in their lives, and in their death they were not divided.

2 Samuel 1:23. Taken from the lament of David for Saul and Jonathan, the line 'in their death they were not divided' has often been used by epitaph writers, although not always with total appropriateness. They are the last words of George Eliot's novel The Mill on the Floss (1860), being the epitaph on the tomb of Tom and Maggie Tulliver, brother and sister, who have been drowned. Of course, the original couple, Jonathan and Saul, were of the same sex, father and son, and died on the battlefield. When Joseph Severn, the friend of John Keats, died in 1879, his son Walter suggested that the text on the grave in the Protestant Cemetery, Rome, should be, 'In their death they were not divided.' He was told that this 'must seem highly inappropriate to anyone who recollects the original application of the phrase ... [and] as more than sixty years elapsed between Keats's death and your father's'. On the memorial plaque to the British-born actors Dame May Whitty (1865–1948) and Ben Webster (1864–1947) in St Paul's Church, Covent Garden, London, the full text is used ('They were lovely and pleasant...'): they were husband and wife.

The film They Were Not Divided (UK 1950) is about British and American soldiers and friends who die during the advance on Berlin during the Second World War.

6 By my God have I leaped over a wall.

2 Samuel 22:30. See BALDWIN 50:3.

1 KINGS

7 I enter into the way of all flesh.

1 Kings 2:2 – in the 1609 Douai Bible translation, repeating an old mistranslation of 'the way of all the earth' (which is what the Authorized Version has) and meaning either 'to die' or 'to experience life'. Hence, The Way of All Flesh, title of a novel (1903) by Samuel Butler.

1 To your tents, O Israel: now see to thine own house, David.

1 Kings 12:16. See ROSEBERY 387:8.

2 Behold, there ariseth a little cloud out of the sea, like a man's hand.

1 Kings 18:44. In the New English Bible the passage is rendered as, 'I see a cloud no bigger than a man's hand.' When something is described as such, it is not yet very threatening – as though a man could obliterate a cloud in the sky by holding up his hand in front of his face – and the context is usually of trouble ahead perceived while it is still apparently of little consequence.

The Revd Francis Kilvert, in his diary for 9 August 1871, has: 'Not a cloud was in the sky as big as a man's hand.' In a letter to Winston Churchill on 14 December 1952, Bob Boothby MP wrote of a dinner at Chartwell: 'It took me back to the old carefree days when I was your Parliamentary Private Secretary, and there seemed to be no cloud on the horizon; and on to the fateful days when the cloud was no bigger than a man's hand, and there was still time to save the sum of things.'

2 KINGS

3 Go up, thou bald head; go up, thou bald head.

2 Kings 2:23. One of the more comical effusions in the whole Bible; it is how 'little children out of the city' mocked Elisha. The New English Bible has them saying, 'Get along with you, bald head, get along.' Comical, except that he 'cursed them in the name of the Lord', and two she-bears came out of a wood and mauled 42 of them ...

2 CHRONICLES

4 And they buried him in the city of David among the kings, because he had done good in Israel, both toward God, and toward his house.

2 Chronicles 24:16, concerning Jehoida, a 130-year-old man. Hence, 'They buried him among the kings, because he had done good toward God and toward his house' – the text placed on the tomb of the Unknown Soldier in Westminster Abbey in 1920.

EZRA

5 And I, even I Arta-xerxes the king, do make a decree to all the treasurers which are beyond the river, that whatsoever Ezra the priest, the scribe

of the law of the God of heaven, shall require of you, it be done speedily.

Ezra 7:21. Not very quotable perhaps – but this verse contains all the letters of the alphabet, except J ...

ESTHER

6 Then said the king unto her, What wilt thou, queen Esther? and what is thy request? it shall be even given thee to the half of the kingdom.

Esther 5:3. Possible origin of the expression 'Even unto half my kingdom', as much quoted by P.G. Wodehouse. Also at Esther 5:6 and 7:2. The (American) Revised Standard Version (1946–52) has 'even half of my kingdom', which is nearer to the Wodehouse allusions. It is more likely, however, that Wodehouse was quoting Mark 6:23: 'And he [Herod] sware unto her [Salome], whatsoever thou shalt ask of me, I will give it thee, unto the half of my kingdom.' This reappears in Lord Alfred Douglas's translation (1894) of Oscar Wilde's *Salomé* where Herod offers 'Even to the half of my kingdom' to Salomé if she will dance for him.

JOB

7 Man is born unto trouble, as the sparks fly upward.

Job 5:7. Hence, *Sparks Fly Upward*, title of the autobiography (1981) of the actor, Stewart Granger. Frank (Lord) Chapple, the former trade-union leader, called his autobiography (1984) *Sparks Fly*. Chapple had been leader of the Electricians' Union and 'sparks' has been the nickname given to members of that trade since before the First World War.

8 Man that is born of a woman is of few days, and full of trouble.

Job 14:1. *Not* 'Man that is born of woman'. Also Job 15:4 and 25:4.

9 Miserable comforters are ye all.

Job 16:2. Hence, 'Job's comforter' – an expression used to describe one who seeks to give comfort but who, by blaming you for what has happened, makes things worse. Job received rebukes from his friends and, as a result, characterized them thus.

10 My bone cleaveth to my skin and to my flesh, and I am escaped with the skin of my teeth.

Job 19:20. Note that it is '*with* the skin of my teeth'. To escape by the skin of one's teeth now means to do so by a very narrow margin indeed. *The Skin of Our Teeth* was the title of a play (1942) by Thornton Wilder.

1 The price of wisdom is above rubies.

Job 28:18. Compare Proverbs 31:10.

2 Thus far shalt thou go and no further.

Job 38:11 actually has: 'Hitherto shalt thou come, but no further: and here shall thy proud waves be stayed.' Charles Stewart Parnell, the champion of Irish Home Rule, said at Cork in 1885: 'No man has a right to fix the boundary of the march of a nation; no man has a right to say to his country, Thus far shalt thou go and no further.' George Farquhar, the Irish-born playwright has this in *The Beaux' Stratagem*, Act 3, Sc. 3 (1707): 'And thus far I am a captain, and no farther.'

3 He swalloweth the ground with fierceness and rage: neither believeth he that it is the sound of the trumpet. He saith among the trumpets, Ha, ha; and he smelleth the battle afar off, the thunder of the captains, and the shouting.

Job 39:24–5. It is a *horse* that is being talked about. Hence, *Ha! Ha! Among the Trumpets*, the title of a collection of stories (1945) by Alun Lewis.

PSALMS

See also under BOOK OF COMMON PRAYER 96:2 – 98:3.

4 Out of the mouth of babes and sucklings hast thou ordained strength because of thine enemies.

Psalm 8:2. Matthew 21:16 has: 'Out of the mouth of babes and sucklings thou has perfected praise.' Note 'mouth' not 'mouths' in both cases.

5 The lines are fallen unto me in pleasant places; yea, I have a goodly heritage.

Psalm 16:6. Hence, *In Pleasant Places*, the title of Joyce Grenfell's second volume of memoirs (1979). She concludes: 'Flying home with a stop-over in South Africa, I thought about the way the lines have continued to fall unto me in pleasant places.' She also has this verse as her epigraph: But what does it mean? *OED*, in defining 'lines' as one's 'appointed lot in life', states that it is 'in echoes of Ps. 16:6, where the reference seems to be to the marking out of land for a dwelling-place'. Compare from Kenneth Grahame, *The Wind In the Willows*, Chap. 4 (1908): 'He

must be wise, must keep to the pleasant places in which his lines were laid and which held adventure enough, in their way, to last for a lifetime.'

6 Deliver my soul from the wicked, which is thy sword: From men which are thy hand, O Lord, from men of the world, which have their portion in this life.

Psalm 17:14. Hence, the expression 'man of the world'. From 'irreligious, worldly', the term has come to mean (less pejoratively) 'one versed in the ways of the world' and has been used as a title of a novel by Henry Mackenzie (1773) and a comedy by Charles Macklin (1871). See also GOLD-SMITH 216:4.

7 Thou preparest a table before me in the presence of mine enemies: thou anointest my head with oil; my cup runneth over.

Psalm 23:5. Hence, 'my cup runneth over' has come to mean 'I am overjoyed; my blessings are numerous.' In her book *Does She … Or Doesn't She?* (1975), the advertising agent Shirley Polykoff describes how she once suggested 'Her Cup Runneth Over' as a joke slogan to a corset manufacturer. 'It took an hour to unsell him,' she adds.

8 Weeping may endure for a night, but joy cometh in the morning.

Psalm 30:5. Hence, *Joy in the Morning*, title of a novel (1947) by P.G. Wodehouse.

9 Wash me, and I shall be whiter than snow.

Psalm 51:7. The expression meaning 'of extreme purity, innocence or virtue' is of long standing, as also the similar 'whiter than white'. Shakespeare in *Venus and Adonis*, line 398 (1592) has: 'Teaching the sheets a whiter hew than white.' Precisely as 'whiter than white', the phrase was known by 1924. There is a firm belief in advertising circles that this later phrase has been used as a slogan, possibly in the form 'Washes Whiter Than White' for an unidentified washing powder/detergent in the UK (1950s?). From *Campaign* (3 January 1986): 'How Mrs Thingy discovered that Bloggo could wash her floor whiter than white'; (8 August 1986): 'It could have been something startling and whiter-than-white from Procter and Gamble'; (30 January 1987): 'The classic ad where A.N. Other Housewife pulls the whiter-than-white shirt from her machine and gasps with cataclysmic delight when she finds that the baby sick has been washed clean away.'

1 My heart is sore pained within me: and the terrors of death are fallen upon me.
Fearfulness and trembling are come upon me, and horror hath overwhelmed me.
And I said, O that I had wings like a dove! for then would I flee away, and be at rest.

Psalm 55:4–6. 'O for the wings of a dove' is the title of Mendelssohn's famous vocal setting. Compare: 'Oh, had I the wings of a dove, / How soon would I taste you again! [society, friendship and love]' – William Cowper, 'Verses Supposed to be Written by Alexander Selkirk' (1782). Also: 'Alas for the breaking of love / And the lights have died out in the West, / And, oh, for the wings of a dove, / And, oh, for the haven of rest' – quoted by the Revd Francis Kilvert in his diary (22 April 1872), but untraced. Hence, presumably, *The Wings of the Dove*, title of a novel (1902; film UK 1998) by Henry James.

2 Moab is my washpot; over Edom will I cast out my shoe.

Psalm 60:8. One of the strangest sentences in the Bible. The New English Bible translation may make it clearer: (God speaks from his sanctuary) 'Gilead and Manasseh are mine; Ephraim is my helmet, Judah my sceptre; Moab is my wash-bowl, I fling my shoes at Edom; Philistia is the target of my anger.' In other words, God is talking about useful objects to throw, in his anger. (Moab was an ancient region of Jordan.) The actor and writer Stephen Fry entitled his memoirs *Moab Is My Washpot* (1997). In *The Independent* (18 August 1999) he explained his choice of title as having more to do with the following sentence ('Philistia, triumph thou because of me'), which he interprets as concerning 'vanquishing the Philistines. My adolescent self saw life as a war between the athlete and the aesthete, the inner life and the outer life. But then, I was something of a wanker.'

3 He shall have dominion also from sea to sea.

Psalm 72:8. Perhaps these words led to the line in the poem 'America the Beautiful' (1893) by Katharine Lee Bates (1859–1929):

America! America!
God shed his grace on thee
And crown thy good with brotherhood
From sea to shining sea!

The words have also been set to music, creating yet another American national anthem. The motto of the Dominion of Canada (adopted 1867) is, however a direct quote, albeit in Latin: '*A mari usque ad mare* [From sea to sea]'.

4 They that dwell in the wilderness shall bow before him; and his enemies shall lick the dust.

Psalm 72:9. No, the Bible does not have 'to kick the dust' for 'to die'. That usage is nicely illustrated by a passage from Thoreau's *Walden* (1854): 'I was present at the auction of a deacon's effects ... after lying half a century in his garret and other dust holes ... When a man dies he kicks the dust.' Nor does the Bible have 'kiss the dust'. *OED2* mentions neither of these expressions, though it does find 'bite the dust' in 1856. What Psalm 72 has is '*lick the dust*' – though this is suggesting humiliation rather than death.

5 The days of our years are three score years and ten.

Psalm 90:10. Seventy was not a person's allotted span in biblical times but was simply a good age to live to.

6 I am like a pelican of the wilderness.

Psalm 102:6. The Book of Common Prayer has: 'I am become like a pelican *in* the wilderness.' It is a prayer of the afflicted man who 'poureth out his complaint before the Lord'. Hence, *A Pelican In the Wilderness*, the title of a book (2002) by Isobel Colegate on the subject of 'hermits, solitaries and recluses'.

7 As for man, his days are as grass: as a flower of the field, so he flourisheth.

Psalm 103:15. Hence, *The Flowers of the Field*, title of a First World War novel (1980) by Sarah Harrison – also alluding to 'The Flowers of the Forest', see COCKBURN 148:3.

8 To bind his princes at his pleasure; and teach his senators wisdom.

Psalm 105:22. When John Wesley visited the Irish Parliament building in Dublin, he was appalled by its splendour at a time when Ireland was suffering. He wrote in his journal (4 July 1787): 'But what surprised me above all, were the kitchens of the house, and the large apparatus for good eating. Tables were placed from one end of a large hall to the other; which, it seems, while the parliament sits, are daily covered with meat at four or five o'clock, for the accommodation of the members. Alas, poor Ireland! Who shall teach thy very senators wisdom? War is ceased; *Sed saevior armis, / Luxuria incubuit!* [But luxury, more direful than war, oppresses thee!]' Compare also Sir John Masterman's *To Teach the Senators Wisdom, or, an Oxford Guidebook*, published in 1952.

1 They that go down to the sea in ships, that do business in great waters.

Psalm 107:23. The Anglican Book of Common Prayer has, rather, '*occupy* their business in the great waters'. The 'go down to the sea' here may have a bearing on MASEFIELD 318:1.

2 My soul fainteth for thy salvation ... for I am become like a bottle in the smoke.

Psalm 119:81–3. Hence, *A Bottle in the Smoke*, title of a novel (1990) by A.N. Wilson. The first section of Robertson Davies' novel *World of Wonders* (1975) also has this title.

3 The Lord is thy shade upon thy right hand. The sun shall not smite thee by day, nor the moon by night.

Psalm 121:5–6. Hence, *Nor the Moon by Night*, title of a film (UK 1958) about a game warden in Africa. In the US the film was called *Elephant Gun*.

4 By the rivers of Babylon, there we sat down, yea, and wept.

Psalm 137:1. A No.1 hit of 1977 for Boney M, the Jamaica/Antilles/Montserrat group, was 'Rivers of Babylon', based on this quotation. See also BOOK OF COMMON PRAYER 98:1.

5 If I take the wings of the morning, and dwell in the uttermost parts of the sea; even there shall thy hand lead me, and thy right hand shall hold me.

Psalm 139:9–10. This text is on the tombstone of Charles A. Lindbergh (1902–74), the American aviator, on the island of Maui, Hawaii. Lindbergh made the first non-stop solo flight across the Atlantic in 1927. *Wings of the Morning* (UK 1937) was also Britain's first film in Technicolor, a romantic story starring Henry Fonda and the songs of John McCormack.

PROVERBS

6 Wisdom is the principal thing; therefore get wisdom: and with all thy getting get understanding.

Proverbs 4:7. Hence, the title of Henry Handel Richardson's book *The Getting of Wisdom* (1910; filmed Australia 1977).

7 But her end is bitter as wormwood, sharp as a two-edged sword.

Proverbs 5:4. Hence, 'bitter end' in general use, meaning 'the last extremity; the absolute limit' – a common phrase by the mid-19th century. Another explanation given for the phrase hardly allows bitterness to enter into it: the nautical 'bitt' is a bollard on the deck of a ship, on to which cables and ropes are wound. The end of the cable that is wrapped round or otherwise secured to the bollard is the 'bitter end'.

8 Wisdom hath builded a house, she hath hewn out her seven pillars.

Proverbs 9:1. Hence, the title *Seven Pillars of Wisdom* as applied by T.E. Lawrence to his memoir of the Arabian campaign in the First World War (published 1926/35). The relevance of the title is not totally apparent and Lawrence does not explain. However, his brother A.W. Lawrence noted in a preface: 'The title was originally applied by the author to a book of his about seven cities. He decided not to publish this early book because he considered it immature, but he transferred the title as a memento.'

9 Give instruction to a wise man, and he will be yet wiser.

Proverbs 9:9. 'Give counsel unto a wise man, he will be yet wiser' appeared inside the covers of the 'Teach Yourself' series of books for a number of years.

10 He that troubleth his own house shall inherit the wind.

Proverbs 11:29. Hence, *Inherit the Wind*, title of a film (US 1960) about the 1925 Scopes 'Monkey Trial' (concerning the teaching of evolution in schools), and which is explained in dialogue. The film was based on a stage play by Jerome Lawrence and Robert E. Lee.

11 Better is a dinner of herbs where love is, than a stalled ox and hatred therewith.

Proverbs 15:17. The meaning becomes clearer in the New English Bible translation: 'Better a dish of vegetables if love go with it than a fat ox eaten in hatred.' Hence, the title of Catherine Cookson's novel, *A Dinner of Herbs* (1980). 'Saki' wrote a short story entitled 'The Stalled Ox' in *Beasts and Super-Beasts* (1914): when an ox invades a lady's house, it enables the artist Eshley to paint a picture entitled 'Ox in a Morning-room, Late Autumn', and for him to comment: 'I forget how the proverb runs ... We seem to have all the ingredients for the proverb ready to hand.'

12 A man's heart deviseth his way: but the Lord directeth his steps.

Proverbs 16:9. See THOMAS à KEMPIS 463:2.

1 Pride goeth before destruction, and an haughty spirit before a fall.

Proverbs 16:18. The proverb 'Pride goeth before a fall' might seem to be a telescoped version of this, but apparently developed on its own. *CODP* cites Alexander Barclay's *The Ship of Fools* (1509), 'First or last foul pride will have a fall', and Samuel Johnson wrote in a letter (2 August 1784), 'Pride must have a fall.' At some stage the biblical wording must have been grafted on to the original proverb. One of Swift's clichés in *Polite Conversation* (1738) is: 'You were afraid that Pride should have a Fall.'

2 The hoary head is a crown of glory, if it be found in the way of righteousness.

Proverbs 16:31. Hoary = grey or white with age. The New English Bible (1970) renders this as: 'Grey hair is a crown of glory, and it is won by a virtuous life.'

3 As cold waters to a thirsty soul, so is good news from a far country.

Proverbs 25:25. Hence, possibly, *From a Far Country*, title of a TV film (1981) comprising dramatized episodes from the early life of Pope John Paul II. The source, in fact, could lie in several places in the Old Testament where there are examples of 'from a far land' and 'from a far country': in Deuteronomy 29:22, 2 Kings 20:14, Isaiah 39:3 and so on.

Compare William Caxton in England's first printed book, *Dictes or Sayengis of the Philosophres* (1477), which has: 'Socrates was a Greek born in a far country from here.' Lines 517–8 of Coleridge's 'The Rime of the Ancient Mariner' (1798) are: 'He loves to talk with marineres / That come from a far countree.' H.D. Thoreau, *On the Duty of Civil Disobedience* (1849), describes going to prison thus: 'It was like travelling into a far country, such as I had never expected to behold, to lie there for one night.' 'A Man from a Far Countree' is the title of one of Edith Sitwell's poems in *Façade* (1923). *Crowned In a Far Country* was the title of a book (1986) by Princess Michael of Kent about people who married into the British Royal Family.

4 As a dog returneth to his vomit, so a fool returneth to his folly.

Proverbs 26:11. Compare 2 Peter 2:22 (see 86:5 below). See also BYRON 115:7.

5 Who can find a virtuous woman? for her price is far above rubies.

Proverbs 31:10. Compare Job 28:18.

ECCLESIASTES

6 The sun also riseth, and the sun goeth down, and hasteth to his place where he arose.

Ecclesiastes 1:5. Famous as the title of an Ernest Hemingway novel, *The Sun Also Rises* (also known as *Fiesta* in the UK), about expatriates in Europe (1926; film US 1957). It promoted the Hollywood joke, 'The son-in-law also rises', possibly inspired by Louis B. Mayer's promotion of his daughter's husband William Goetz to a key position at MGM – quoted in Leslie Halliwell, *The Filmgoer's Book of Quotes* (1973). More recently there has been a book about the Japanese economy called *The Sun Also Sets* (1990) by Bill Emmott, the title playing on Japan's sobriquet, 'The Land of the Rising Sun'.

7 There is no new thing under the sun.

Ecclesiastes 1:9. Often rendered as 'There is nothing new under the sun.'

8 To everything there is a season, and a time to every purpose under the heaven:
A time to be born, and a time to die; a time to plant, and a time to pluck up that which is planted;
A time to kill, and a time to heal; a time to break down, and a time to build up;
A time to weep, and a time to laugh; a time to mourn, and a time to dance;
A time to cast away stones, and a time to gather stones together; a time to embrace, and a time to refrain from embracing;
A time to get, and a time to lose; a time to keep, and a time to cast away;
A time to rend, and a time to sew; a time to keep silence, and a time to speak;
A time to love, and a time to hate; a time of war, and a time of peace.

Ecclesiastes 3:1–8. Hence, among many borrowings from this passage, *A Time to Love and a Time to Die*, title of a film (US 1958), from a novel by Erich Maria Remarque entitled *Zeit zu leben und zeit zu sterben* (1954). This is a blending of 'a time to love, and a time to hate' from 3:8 and 'a time to be born, and a time to die' (3:2). *A Time to Dance* was the title of a novel (1990) by Melvyn Bragg; while *A Time to Kill* is a novel (1989) by John Grisham (film US 1996).

1 Evil under the sun.

Used as the title of an Agatha Christie thriller about murder in a holiday hotel (1941; film UK 1982), it is not explained in the text, although Hercule Poirot, the detective, remarks before any evil has been committed: 'The sun shines. The sea is blue ... but there is evil everywhere under the sun.' Shortly afterwards, another character remarks: 'I was interested, M. Poirot, in something you said just now ... It was almost a quotation from Ecclesiastes ... "Yea, also the heart of the sons of men is full of evil, and madness is in their heart while they live."' But Ecclesiastes (which finds everything 'under the sun') gets nearer than that: 'There is a sore evil which I have seen under the sun, namely, riches kept for the owners thereof to their hurt' (5:13); and 'There is an evil which I have seen under the sun' (6:1, 10:1). Were it not for the clue about Ecclesiastes, one might be tempted to think that Christie had once more turned to an old English rhyme for one of her titles. In this one, the phrase appears exactly:

> For every evil under the sun,
> There is a remedy or there is none;
> If there be one, try and find it;
> If there be none, never mind it.

2 Sorrow is better than laughter: for by the sadness of the countenance the heart is made better. The heart of the wise is in the house of mourning; but the heart of fools is in the house of mirth.

Ecclesiastes 7:3–4. Hence, *The House of Mirth*, title of an Edith Wharton novel (1905) about a failed social climber.

3 The race is not to the swift, nor the battle to the strong ... but time and chance happeneth to them all.

Ecclesiastes 9:11. Hence, *Time and Chance*, title of the autobiographies of Group Capt. Peter Townsend (1978) and James (Lord) Callaghan, the former British Prime Minister (1987).

4 Dead flies cause the ointment of the apothecary to send forth a stinking vapour.

Ecclesiastes 10:1. Hence, probably, the expression 'a fly in the ointment', meaning 'some small factor that spoils the general enjoyment of something'.

5 Cast thy bread upon the waters: for thou shalt find it after many days.

Ecclesiastes 11:1. The origin of the expression 'to cast one's bread upon the waters', meaning 'to reap as you shall sow'. Oddly expressed, the idea is that if you sow seed or corn in a generous fashion now, you will reap the benefits in due course. The New English Bible translates this passage more straightforwardly as 'Send your grain across the seas, and in time you will get a return.'

6 Or ever the silver cord be loosed, or the golden bowl be broken, or the pitcher be broken at the fountain, or the wheel broken at the cistern.

Ecclesiastes 12:6. Hence, *The Golden Bowl*, title of a novel (1904) by Henry James. There is an actual golden bowl that is used emblematically in the novel. It is not solid gold and contains a flaw.

7 Of making many books there is no end; and much study is a weariness of the flesh.

Ecclesiastes 12:12. Does the first half of this verse mean that (as is certainly the case nowadays) too many titles are published, or does it mean that the production of a lot of books is a never-ending task? Discuss.

SONG OF SOLOMON

8 The flowers appear on the earth; the time of the singing of birds is come, and the voice of the turtle is heard in our land.

Song of Solomon 2:12 – referring to spring. The turtle here is not the thing with a shell that ends up in soup, but the turtle dove, a more poetic image.

9 Take us the foxes, the little foxes, that spoil the vines.

Song of Solomon 2:15. Hence, *The Little Foxes*, title of a play (1939; film US 1941) by Lillian Hellman – in which she writes about a family of schemers.

ISAIAH

10 They shall beat their swords into plowshares, and their spears into pruninghooks: nation shall not lift up sword against nation, neither shall they learn war any more.

Isaiah 2:4. Compare Micah 4:3 (78:4 below).

11 Then said I, Lord, how long?

Isaiah 6:11. Hence, 'How long, O Lord, how long?', now used in mock exasperation. The prophet has a vision in which God tells him to do various things and he reports: 'Then said I, Lord, how long?' The more familiar version occurs, for example, in schoolboy verse by G.K. Chesterton (in about 1890): 'Not from the misery of the weak, the madness of the strong, / Goes upward from our lips the cry, "How long, oh Lord, how long?"'

1 The wolf also shall dwell with the lamb, and the leopard shall lie down with the kid; and the calf and the young lion and the fatling together. And a little child shall lead them.
Isaiah 11:6. So the simplified version, 'the lion shall lie down with the lamb' is incorrect. Compare ALLEN 7:3.

2 Watchman, what of the night?
Not a street cry. In Isaiah 21:11–12 the watchman replies, unhelpfully: 'The morning cometh, and also the night.' Used as the title of a Bernard Partridge cartoon in *Punch* (3 January 1900). Set to music several times, notably by Sir Arthur Sullivan. The line is also in Swinburne's poem 'A Watch in the Night', part of *Songs Before Sunrise* (1904).

3 Let us eat and drink; for tomorrow we shall die.
Isaiah 22:13. Ecclesiastes 8:15 has: 'A man hath no better thing under the sun, than to eat, and to drink, and to be merry', and Luke 12:19: 'Take thine ease, eat, drink and be merry.' Luke 15:23 has simply: 'Let us eat, and be merry.' *Brewer* (1975) calls it, however: 'A traditional saying of the Egyptians who, at their banquets, exhibited a skeleton to the guests to remind them of the brevity of life.'

4 The desert shall rejoice, and blossom as the rose.
Isaiah 35:1. Hence, 'to make the desert bloom', which the modern state of Israel has made come true. Adlai Stevenson also alluded to the phrase in a speech at Hartford, Connecticut (18 September 1952): 'Man has wrested from nature the power to make the world a desert or to make the deserts bloom.' The exact phrase does not appear in the Bible, though Isaiah has the above and, at 51:3: 'For the Lord shall comfort Zion ... and he will make ... her desert like the garden of the Lord.' Cruden's *Concordance* (1737) points out: 'In the Bible this word [desert] means a deserted place, wilderness, not desert in the modern usage of the term.'

5 They shall mount up with wings as eagles; they shall run, and not be weary.
Isaiah 40:31. The words are written in gold on red granite in English and Chinese on the memorial to Eric Liddell (1902–45) in Weifang, Shandong Province, China. Liddell's refusal to race for his country on a Sunday in the 1924 Olympic Games – probably losing himself a second gold medal in the process – was celebrated in the 1981 film *Chariots of Fire*. The son of Scots missionaries, he was born in

China and duly returned there after the Olympics to work for the London Missionary Society. He died of a brain tumour in the Japanese internment camp at Weifang. The memorial was not set up until June 1991 – source: report by Andrew Higgins in *The Independent* (10 June 1991).

6 There is no peace, saith the Lord, unto the wicked.
Isaiah 48:22. Compare Isaiah 57:21: 'There is no peace, saith my God, to the wicked.' Not simply 'No peace for the wicked'.

7 They make haste to shed innocent blood.
Isaiah 59:7. Hence, *Innocent Blood*, title of a crime novel (1980) by P.D. James.

JEREMIAH

8 Is there no balm in Gilead?
Jeremiah 8:22. Meaning, 'Is there no remedy or consolation?' In the so-called 'Treacle Bible', it is curiously translated as: 'Is there no treacle at Gilead? Is there no physitian there?' 'Balm of Gilead' has also been used as a slang expression for money, and for illicitly distilled whisky.

9 Let us cut him off from the land of the living, that his name may be no more remembered.
Jeremiah 11:19. Hence, the phrase 'in the land of the living' in general slang use, meaning 'alive'. A cliché by the mid-20th century. One might say of a person referred to: 'Oh, is he still in the land of the living?'

DANIEL

10 And whoso falleth not down and worshippeth shall the same hour be cast into the midst of a burning fiery furnace.
Daniel 3:6. 'Burning fiery furnace' also occurs at 3:20, 3:21 and 3:23. Hence, *The Burning Fiery Furnace*, the title of Benjamin Britten / William Plomer's 'parable for church performance' (1966) about the incident.

11 True, O king.
When someone makes an obvious remark, perhaps even a pompous one, other people will sometimes comment, 'True, O King!' In *The Diaries of Kenneth Williams* (1993) – the entry for 5 January 1971 – the comic actor recounts being told on TV by an Irishman that he was a bore: 'I smiled acquiescence and said "How true, O King!"' The source for this expression is not absolutely certain but may well derive

from the story of Nebuchadnezzar and the gentlemen who were cast into the fiery furnace. 'Did not we cast three men bound into the midst of fire?' Nebuchadnezzar asks (Daniel 3:24). 'They answered and said unto the king, True, O king.'

The nearest Shakespeare gets is the ironical 'True? O God!' in *Much Ado About Nothing* (IV.i.68), though he has any number of near misses like 'true, my liege', 'too true, my lord' and 'true, noble prince'.

Another version is 'True, O King! Live for ever', the second phrase also appearing in Daniel at 6:21.

1 And this is the writing that was written, MENE MENE, TEKEL, UPHARSIN.

Daniel 5:25. Meaning 'God hath numbered thy kingdom, and finished it ... Thou art weighed in the balances, and art found wanting ... Thy kingdom is divided, and given to the Medes and Persians.' The origin of the phrase 'the writing (is) on the wall'. This way of expressing a hint, sign or portent, often doom-laden, derives – though not the precise phrase – from King Belshazzar's being informed of the forthcoming destruction of the Babylonian Empire through the appearance of 'A handwriting on a wall' (as the Authorized Version's chapter heading has it). Compare FITZGERALD 195:7.

The phrase became established in the 19th century. Lieutenant-General Sir Ian Hamilton, *A Staff Officer's Scrap Book during the Russo-Japanese War* (1907), has: 'I have today seen the most stupendous spectacle it is possible for the mortal brain to conceive – Asia advancing, Europe falling back, the wall of mist and the writing thereon.' In a BBC broadcast to Resistance workers in Europe (31 July 1941), 'Colonel Britton' (Douglas Ritchie) talked of the 'V for Victory' sign that was being chalked up in occupied countries: 'All over Europe the V sign is seen by the Germans and to the Germans and the Quislings it is indeed the writing on the wall.'

HOSEA

2 They have sown the wind, and they shall reap the whirlwind.

Hosea 8:7. Hence, presumably, *Reap the Wild Wind*, title of a film (US 1942).

JOEL

3 I will restore to you the years that the locust hath eaten, the cankerworm, and the caterpillar, and the palmerworm, my great army which I sent among you.

Joel 2:25. From Winston Churchill, *The Second World War*, Vol. I (1948), 'The Locust Years 1931–1935', heading to Chap. 5: (note) 'Sir Thomas Inskip, Minister for Co-ordination of Defence, who was well versed in the Bible, used the expressive phrase about this dismal period, of which he was the heir: "The years that the locust hath eaten."' In November 1936, Stanley Baldwin had told the House of Commons: 'I want to say a word about the years the locusts have eaten ...'

And hence, presumably, *The Day of the Locust*, title of Nathanael West's novel (1939) about the emptiness of life in Hollywood in the 1930s. The relevance of the title to the book is not totally clear. Locusts are, however, usually associated with times when waste, poverty or hardship are in evidence. They also go about in swarms committing great ravages on crops. The climax of the novel is a scene in which Tod, the hero, gets crushed by a Hollywood mob. In addition to the above, Revelation 9:3 has: 'There came out of the smoke locusts upon the earth: and unto them we give power'; Revelation 9:4: 'Locusts give power to hurt only those men which have not the seal of God in their foreheads.'

MICAH

4 Nation shall speak peace unto nation.

The motto of the BBC (decided upon in 1927) echoes Micah 4:3: 'Nation shall not lift up a sword against nation' (compare Isaiah 2:4). In 1932, however, it was decided that the BBC's primary mission was to serve the home audience and not that overseas. Hence, '*Quaecunque*' [whatsoever] was introduced as an alternative reflecting the Latin inscription (composed by Dr Montague Rendall, an ex-headmaster of Winchester College) in the entrance hall of Broadcasting House, London, and based on Philippians 4:8: 'Whatsoever things are beautiful and honest and of good report ... ' '*Quaecunque*' was also taken as his own motto by Lord Reith, the BBC's first Director-General, who never liked the Corporation's 'peace' motto. In 1948, the 'peace' motto was nevertheless reintroduced by the BBC.

HABBAKUK

5 He who runs may read.

This expression is an alteration of Habbakuk 2:2, 'That he may run that readeth it', but is no more easily understandable. The New English Bible translates it as 'ready for a herald to carry it with speed' and provides the alternative 'so that a man may read it easily'. *OED2* has citations from 1672, 1784 and 1821, but possibly the most famous use is in John Keble's hymn 'Septuagesima' from *The Christian Year* (1827):

There is a book, who runs may read,
Which heavenly truth imparts,
And all the lore its scholars need,
Pure eyes and Christian hearts.

Given the obscurity, one of the more unlikely uses of the phrase has been as an advertising slogan for *The Golden Book* in the 1920s, according to E.S. Turner in *The Shocking History of Advertising* (1952).

Apocrypha (Old Testament)

2 ESDRAS

1 For the world hath lost his youth, and the times begin to wax old.

2 Esdras 14:10 might just be the origin of the wistful expression 'When the world was young', a harking back not just to 'long ago' but also to a time more innocent than the present. Precisely as *When the World Was Young*, it was used as the title of a painting (1891) by Sir Edward John Poynter PRA, which shows three girls in a classical setting, relaxing by a pool. Seemingly the earliest use of the expression in poetry is in Elkanah Settle, *The Empress of Morocco* (1673): 'Since Nature first made Man wild, savage, strong, / And his Blood hot, then when the world was Young: / If Infant-times such Rising-valours bore, / Why should not Riper Ages now do more?' Compare KINGSLEY 271:3.

ECCLESIASTICUS

2 Speak, you who are older, for it is fitting that you should,
but with accurate knowledge, and
do not interrupt the music.

A curious passage from Ecclesiasticus 32:3, in a modern translation. The meaning is made clearer by the New English Bible version of the concluding words in this section concerning 'Counsels upon social behaviour': 'Where entertainment is provided, do not keep up a stream of talk; it is the wrong time to show off your wisdom.'

3 Let us now praise famous men, and our fathers that begat us.

Ecclesiasticus 44:1. Hence the title of the book *Let Us Now Praise Famous Men* by James Agee and Walker Evans (1939), an account of the Depression in the US.

4 Rich men furnished with ability, living peaceably in their habitations.

Ecclesiasticus 44:6. See CHURCHILL 142:1.

5 Their bodies are buried in peace; but their name liveth for evermore.

Ecclesiasticus 44:14. Hence, 'Their name liveth for evermore', the standard epitaph put over lists of the dead in the First World War and chosen by Rudyard Kipling. He was invited by the Imperial War Graves Commission to devise memorial texts for the dead and admitted to 'naked cribs of the Greek anthology'. He also used biblical texts, as here.

Earlier, the diarist Francis Kilvert had written (31 January 1875): 'So Charles Kingsley is dead. "His body is buried in peace, but his name liveth for evermore." We could ill spare him.'

1 MACCABEES

6 Arm yourselves, and be ye men of valour, and be in readiness for the conflict.

1 Maccabees 3:58. Judas Maccabeus, Jewish patriot and leader of the revolt of the Maccabees, says it. Quoted by Winston Churchill in his first broadcast as Prime Minister (19 May 1940). The passage continues: 'For it is better for us to perish in battle than to look upon the outrage of our nation.'

NEW TESTAMENT

MATTHEW

7 I indeed baptize you with water ... but he that cometh after me ... shall baptize you with the Holy Ghost and with fire.

Matthew 3:11. John the Baptist speaking. Hence, the phrase 'baptism of fire' to describe a difficult initial experience, originally a soldier's first time in battle (compare the French *baptême du feu*). 'The first American troops to receive a baptism of fire in Europe in this war were the men of the United States Ranger Battalion who fought in the Dieppe raid today' – *The New York Times* (20 August 1942).

8 Ye are the salt of the earth: but if the salt have lost his savour, wherewith shall it be salted?

Matthew 5:13. From Christ's description of his disciples. Hence, 'salt of the earth', a phrase now meaning 'the best of mankind'. Christ was suggesting, rather, that they should give the world an interesting flavour, be a ginger group, and not that they were simply jolly good chaps. The New English Bible conveys this meaning better as 'you are salt to the world'.

1 Ye are the light of the world. A city that is set on an hill cannot be hid.

Matthew 5:14. See REAGAN 378:1.

2 Till heaven and earth pass, one jot or one tittle shall in no wise pass from the law, till all be fulfilled.

Matthew 5:18. Hence, 'every jot and tittle' meaning 'the least item or detail'. 'Jot' is *iota*, the smallest Greek letter (compare 'not one iota') and 'tittle' is the dot over the letter *i* (Latin *titulus*).

3 And whosoever shall compel thee to go a mile, go with him twain.

Matthew 5:41 – which, in the New English Bible, has Jesus Christ advising: 'If a man in authority makes you go one mile, go with him two.' A possible origin of the expression 'to go the extra mile', meaning 'to make an extra special effort to accomplish something'. President George H. W. Bush used this American military/business expression at the time of the Gulf War (1991), referring to his attempts to get a peaceful settlement before resorting to arms. Later that same year, Bush, expressing sorrow for baseball star Magic Johnson, who had been found to be HIV-positive, said: 'If there's more I can do to empathize, to make clear what AIDS is and what it isn't, I want to go the extra mile' – *The Independent* (9 November 1991). The expression had been around long before that, however. In a revue song by Joyce Grenfell, 'All We Ask Is Kindness' (1957), there is: 'Working like a beaver / Always with a smile / Ready to take the rough and smooth / To go the extra mile.'

4 No man can serve two masters ... Ye cannot serve God and mammon.

Matthew 6:24. Hence, presumably, the title of Carlo Goldoni's 1745 play *Il servitore di due padroni* (*The servant of two masters*).

5 Consider the lilies of the field, how they grow; they toil not, neither do they spin. And yet I say unto you, That even Solomon in all his glory was not arrayed like one of these.

Matthew 6:28–9. Hence, *Lilies of the Field*, title of a film (US 1963) from a novel by William E. Barrett. *Consider the Lilies* is the title of two novels, both published in 1968: one was by Auberon Waugh, and the other by the Scottish poet Iain Crichton Smith.

6 Therefore all things whatsoever ye would that men should do to you, do you even so to them: for this is the law and the prophets.

Matthew 7:12 – from Christ's Sermon on the Mount. *Not* 'Do as you would be done by', or any of the other derivatives. By the 17th century this was known as 'The Golden Rule' or 'The Golden Law'. (The 'rule of three' in mathematics was, however, known as the Golden Rule a century earlier.) Compare *The Law and the Profits*, title of a book (1960) by C. Northcote Parkinson.

7 Strait is the gate, and narrow is the way, which leadeth unto life, and few there be that find it.

Matthew 7:14. Hence, 'the straight and narrow' – the idea of a straight and narrow path of law-abiding behaviour or goodness from which it is easy to wander. Hence also, *Strait is the Gate*, the 1924 translation of André Gide's 1909 novel *La Porte étroite*.

8 Beware of false prophets, which come to you in sheep's clothing, but inwardly they are ravening wolves.

Matthew 7:15. The concept of the wolf in sheep's clothing probably finds its earliest form in Aesop's fable about the wolf that puts on a sheepskin to trick a shepherd but then gets slaughtered by mistake for the shepherd's supper. For 'a sheep in sheep's clothing', see CHURCHILL 140:6.

9 By their fruits ye shall know them.

Matthew 7:20 in the part of the Sermon on the Mount about being beware of false prophets. Meaning 'you can judge people by the results they produce'.

10 The foxes have holes, and the birds of the air have nests; but the Son of man hath not where to lay his head.

Matthew 8:20. A variant is 'fowl(s) of the air' (Genesis 1:26), though much more commonly one finds 'fowls of the heavens' in (mostly) the Old Testament. Compare the 'fish(es) of the sea', which occurs at least three times in the Old Testament (e.g. Genesis 1:26). 'All the beasts of the forest' is biblical, too (Psalm 104:20), though more frequent is 'beasts of the field' (e.g. Psalm 8:7).

The phrase later made a notable appearance in the nursery rhyme 'Who Killed Cock Robin?' (first recorded in 1744): 'All the birds of the air / Fell a-sighing and a-sobbing, / When they heard the bell toll / For poor Cock Robin.' It has been suggested that this is connected with the downfall of Sir Robert Walpole's ministry in 1742.

11 What went ye out into the wilderness to see? A reed shaken with the wind.

Matthew 11:7. Christ referring to John the Baptist (though in fact John had a firm belief, from the first, that was not shaken). Hence, also *A Reed Shaken By the Wind* (1963), the title of a travel book by Gavin Maxwell.

1 A prophet is not without honour, save in his own country, and in his own house.

Matthew 13:57. Usually rendered as 'A prophet is without honour in his own country.' Meaning 'you tend not to be appreciated where you usually live or are known'.

2 O thou of little faith, wherefore didst thou doubt?

Matthew 14:31. Christ speaking. This description (sometimes 'O ye of little faith') also occurs at Matthew 6:30, 8:26, 16:8 and Luke 12:28. Usually Christ is upbraiding his disciples or others for their doubts.

3 They be blind leaders of the blind. And if the blind lead the blind, both shall fall into the ditch.

Matthew 15:14. Hence, 'the blind leading the blind', meaning 'the ignorant are incapable of helping anybody similarly incapacitated'. A form of words that seemingly demands parody. In 1958 Kenneth Tynan quoted people saying of *The New Yorker* that it was 'the bland leading the bland'. See TYNAN 472:7.

4 The sky is red and lowring. O ye hypocrites, ye can discern the face of the sky; but can ye not discern the signs of the times?

Matthew 16:3. Christ speaking. Hence, the expression used by everyone from Thomas Carlyle – as a book title, *Signs of the Times* (1829) – to the pop singer Prince – an album title *Sign 'o' the Times* (1987) – to describe portents or general indications of current trends.

5 Get thee behind me, Satan.

Matthew 16:23. Jesus Christ rebukes Peter with the phrase for something he has said. Nowadays, an exclamation used in answer to even the mildest call to temptation.

6 It is easier for a camel to go through the eye of a needle than for a rich man to enter into the kingdom of God.

That is how Christ's words appear in Matthew 19:24 – also in Mark 10:25 and Luke 18:25, though the latter has 'through a needle's eye'. Note that the Koran contains a similar view, and in Rabbinical writings there is the expression 'to make an *elephant* pass through the eye of a needle', which also appears in an Arab proverb. But why this camel/elephant confusion? Probably because the word for 'camel' in the older Germanic languages, including Old English, was

almost like the modern word for 'elephant' (OE *olfend* 'camel'). In this biblical saying, however, it is possible that neither camel nor elephant was intended. The original Greek word should probably have been read as *kamilos*, 'a rope', rather than *kamelos*, 'a camel'. The difficulty of threading a rope through the eye of a needle makes a much neater image.

Another theory is that Christ was alluding to the Needle's Eye, the name given to a narrow defensive postern in the walls of Jerusalem, which admitted one man at a time, or to a gate in the walls of that city through which a camel might pass but only without its baggage. If Jerusalem is taken as symbolizing heaven, the point is that a fully loaded camel cannot pass through the narrow gate. All the excess baggage (the rich man's wealth) must first be unloaded and given to someone else. So, 'It is easier for a *laden* camel to pass through The Eye of *the* Needle than it is for a rich man to enter the kingdom of heaven.' As such, this seems an early precursor of 'You can't take it with you.'

7 At the eleventh hour.

Meaning 'at the last moment', the origin of this phrase lies in the parable of the labourers, of whom the last 'were hired at the eleventh hour' (Matthew 20:9). The expression was used with a different resonance at the end of the First World War. The Armistice was signed at 5 a.m. on 11 November 1918 and came into force at 11 a.m. that day – 'at the eleventh hour of the eleventh day of the eleventh month'.

8 Woe unto you, scribes and Pharisees, hypocrites! for ye are like unto whited sepulchres, which indeed appear beautiful outward, but which are full of dead men's bones, and of all uncleanness.

Matthew 23:27. Hence, the expression 'whited sepulchre', meaning a person 'coated in white' who pretends to be morally better than he, in fact, is – also 'holier than thou'.

9 Well done, thou good and faithful servant.

Matthew 25:21. Hence, *The Good and Faithful Servant*, a TV play (1967) by Joe Orton (about a commissionaire who has given 50 years of loyal service to a company).

10 The poor are always with us.

That is the phrase as we would most likely say it now, but it is to be found in three different forms in three gospels: in Matthew 26:11 ('For ye have the poor always with you'), Mark 14:7 ('For ye have the poor with you always'), and John 12:8 ('For the poor always ye have with you'). Compare these allusions: *The Rich Are Always With Us* was the title of a film (US 1932) and *The Rich Are With You Always*, the title of a novel (1976) by Malcolm Macdonald.

MARK

1 If a house be divided against itself, that house cannot stand.

Mark 3:25. See JOHNSON 257:7.

2 My name is Legion: for we are many.

Mark 5:9. In other words, 'we are innumerable' – what the untamed 'man with an unclean spirit' tells Jesus, who has said, 'Come out of the man, thou unclean spirit' and asked, 'What is thy name?' After Jesus expels the devils from the man, he puts them into a herd of swine which jump into the sea. The man is then referred to as 'him that was possessed with the devil, and had the legion'.

3 Beware of the scribes ... Which devour widows' houses, and for a pretence make long prayers.

Mark 12:38–40. Hence, *Widowers' Houses*, title of a play (1892) by Bernard Shaw.

LUKE

4 Physician, heal thyself.

Luke 4:23. Christ himself refers to this as a proverb. He is in the synagogue back home at Nazareth and he is treating it as something his hearers will taunt him with. Much later, Samuel Smiles explained it rather tellingly: 'How can a man teach sobriety or cleanliness, if he be himself drunken or foul?' In other words, practise what you preach before you try to convert others. Also used as the moral in some versions of Aesop's fable 'The Quack Doctor' or 'The Quack Frog'.

5 Forbid him not: for he that is not against us is for us.

Luke 9:50. Jesus speaking. See also Luke 11:23 below, and STALIN 440:10.

6 A certain man went down from Jerusalem to Jericho, and fell among thieves.

Luke 10:30. The parable of the good Samaritan. Hence, presumably, the construction 'a good man fallen among —'. From R.M. Wardle, *Oliver Goldsmith* (1957): 'It was Goldsmith's misfortune that he was a jigger fallen among goons.' John Stonehouse called Edward Heath, 'A good man fallen among bureaucrats' (House of Commons, 13 May 1964). And when former journalist Michael Foot was leader of the British Labour Party, the *Daily Mirror* described him in an editorial (28 February 1983) as 'a good man fallen among politicians'. See also LENIN 282:7.

7 He that is not with me is against me.

Luke 11:23. See also Luke 9:50 above, and STALIN 440:10.

8 Therefore whatsoever ye have spoken in darkness shall be heard in the light; and that which ye have spoken in the ear in closets shall be proclaimed upon the housetops.

Luke 12:3. Hence, the expression 'to proclaim from the housetops', meaning 'to announce loudly and publicly'.

9 Go out quickly into the streets and lanes of the city, and bring in hither the poor, and the maimed, and the halt and the blind.

Luke 14:21. From the parable of the great supper. 'Halt' here means 'lame, crippled, limping'.

10 And it came to pass, that the beggar died, and was carried by the angels into Abraham's bosom.

Luke 16:22. Hence, 'Abraham's bosom' as a term for the place where the dead sleep contentedly. This alludes to Abraham, the first of the Hebrew patriarchs.

11 It were better for him that a millstone were hanged about his neck, and he cast into the sea, than that he should offend one of these little ones.

Luke 17:2. Jesus speaking. Probably origin of the expression 'a millstone around one's neck', referring to a person or thing that is a burden to one.

12 The stones cry out.

Luke 19:40. Probable source for the title of a BBC radio programme, *The Stones Cry Out But the People Stand Firm*, broadcast during the Second World War. Presumably this was about London in the Blitz. Other allusions to the biblical passage may include a book called *The Stones Cry Out* by Molyda Szymusiak (1987) – a 12-year-old girl's story of the 'chaos and cruelty of her Cambodian childhood 1975–80'. Then there is this description, based on contemporary accounts, of Armistice Day 1920 and the burial of the Unknown Warrior, which appeared in *The Observer* (14 November 1993): 'From the Cenotaph, the carriage bearing the Unknown Warrior made its way to Westminster Abbey, where inside waited 1000 widows and bereaved mothers; 100 nurses wounded or blinded in the war; and a guard of honour made up of 100 men who had won the Victoria Cross ... The highest ranking commanders from the war were among the pallbearers: Haig, French and Trenchard; the King, George V, scattered earth from France on to the coffin. "All this," commented one observer, "was to stir such memories and emotions as might have made the very stones cry out."'

Also recalled from a tourist brochure seen in Provence in 1959, referring to what old buildings may have to tell us: '*Les pierres parlent à ceux qui savent les entendre* [the stones speak to those who know how to listen to them].'

JOHN

1 He that is without sin among you, let him first cast a stone at her.

John 8:7. Jesus Christ is being encouraged to support the punishment of 'the woman taken in adultery'. Often misquoted as: 'Let him cast the first stone ...' Now, a common jibe at people who are proponents of punishment and vengeance.

2 Then spake Jesus again unto them, saying, I am the light of the world: he that followeth me shall not walk in darkness, but shall have the light of life.

John 8:12. Hence, *The Light of the World*, title of a painting (1854) by Holman Hunt, showing Jesus Christ with a lantern, knocking on a door in a tree (to represent the soul). The painting is in the chapel of Keble College, Oxford, and another version is in St Paul's Cathedral, London. This is also the title of an oratorio (1873) by Sir Arthur Sullivan.

3 And ye shall know the truth, and the truth shall make you free.

John 8:32. Hence, the title of a book (1995) by David Icke, *And the Truth Shall Set You Free*.

4 Jesus wept.

John 11:35 is the shortest verse in the Bible (the shortest sentence would be 'Amen'). It occurs in the story of the raising of Lazarus. Jesus is moved by the plight of Mary and Martha, the sisters of Lazarus, who break down and weep when Lazarus is sick. When Jesus sees the dying man he, too, weeps.

Compare Victor Hugo's centenary oration on Voltaire (1878): 'Jesus wept; Voltaire smiled. Of that divine tear and of that human smile the sweetness of present civilization is composed.'

Like it or not, the phrase has also become an expletive to express exasperation. The most notable uttering was by Richard Dimbleby, the TV commentator, on 27 May 1965. In a broadcast in which everything went wrong during a Royal visit to West Germany, Dimbleby let slip this oath when he thought his words were not being broadcast.

A graffito from the 1970s, from the advertising agency that lost the Schweppes account, was: 'Jesus wepped.'

5 Greater love hath no man than this, that a man lay down his life for his friends.

John 15:13. See THORPE 466:2.

6 Pilate saith unto him, What is truth?

John 18:38. See BACON 48:4.

7 Then cried they all again, saying, Not this man, but Barabbas. Now Barabbas was a robber.

John 18:40 – in which Pilate is asking the crowd whether Jesus should be the prisoner customarily released at Passover. Hence, *Now Barabbas ...*, title of a film (UK 1949) about prisoners, based on a play (1947) by William Douglas-Home, but also known as *Now Barabbas was a Robber*. See also BYRON 116:1.

8 The soldiers, when they had crucified Jesus took ... his coat: now the coat was without seam, woven from the top throughout.

John 19:23. Hence, *The Seamless Robe*, title of a book, subtitled 'Broadcasting Philosophy and Practice' (1979) by Sir Charles Curran, a former Director-General of the BBC. The phrase was meant to describe 'the impossibility of separating out any one strand of the job from another ... It was impossible to disentangle, in the whole pattern, one thread from another.'

ACTS OF THE APOSTLES

9 And he went on his way rejoicing.

This expression used in allusion to Acts 8:39 should be treated with caution. It refers to a eunuch – a high official of the Queen of Ethiopia – who has been baptized by Philip the Deacon.

10 It is hard for thee to kick against the pricks.

Acts 9:5. Hence, 'kick against the pricks', meaning to resist futilely. Prick here refers to something like a spur used to urge on a horse. Hence also, *More Pricks than Kicks*, a collection of short stories (1934) by Samuel Beckett.

11 These that have turned the world upside down are come hither also.

Acts 17:6. Compare 'Behold, the Lord maketh the earth empty, and maketh it waste, and turneth it upside down' (Isaiah 24:1) as an origin for the phrase 'the world turned upside down'. This is (1) a popular name for English inns; (2) the title of an American tune played when the English surrendered at Yorktown (1781); (3) a figure of speech, as in Robert Burton's *The Anatomy of Melancholy* (1621–51): 'Women wear the breeches ... in a word, the world turned upside downward'; (4) the title of a well-known tract dating from the English Civil War concerning 'ridiculous fashions' (1646). Compare the French expression *la vie à l'envers* ('life upside down/the wrong way round'), used as the title of a film (1964).

1 And it came to pass, that, as I made my journey, and was come nigh unto Damascus about noon, suddenly there shone from heaven a great light round about me.

Acts 22:6. St Paul's conversion to a fervent belief in Christ – previously he had been a Pharisee persecuting the Christians. This gives us two expressions: 'road to Damascus' meaning 'the occasion of a change of heart, conversion or sudden realization; a turning point'; and 'to see the light'.

ROMANS

2 For the wages of sin is death; but the gift of God is eternal life through Jesus Christ our Lord.

Romans 6:23, St Paul speaking. 'For sin pays a wage, and the wage is death' is the New English Bible's version. The strength of expression derives from the perfectly correct singular verb 'is', where the hearer might be more comfortable with 'are'. There may possibly be an allusion in *The Wages of Fear*, English title of the film *Le Salaire de la Peur* (France/Italy 1953).

3 If God be for us who can be against us?

Romans 8:31. Compare Luke 11.23. See STALIN 440:10.

4 Vengeance is mine, saith the Lord.

No, he doesn't, nor does Paul the Apostle in his Epistle to the Romans (12:19). Paul writes: 'Dearly beloved, avenge not yourselves, but rather give place unto wrath: for it is written, Vengeance is mine; I will repay, saith the Lord. Therefore if thine enemy hunger, feed him; if he thirst, give him drink: for in so doing thou shalt heap coals of fire on his head.'

Paul is quoting 'To me belongeth vengeance, and recompence', which occurs in Deuteronomy 32:35 and is also alluded to in Psalm 94:1 and Hebrews 10:30.

5 Let every soul be subject unto the higher powers. For there is no power but of God: the powers that be are ordained of God.

Romans 13:1. Hence, the term 'powers that be', now used to describe any form of authority exercising social or political control. The New English Bible has: 'the existing authorities are instituted by him'.

I CORINTHIANS

6 When I was a child, I spake as a child, I understood as a child, I thought as a child: but when I became a man, I put away childish things. For now we see through a glass, darkly; but then face to face ... And now abideth faith, hope, charity, these three; but the greatest of these is charity.

1 Corinthians 13:11–13. Hence, *In a Glass Darkly*, the US title given to the novel *Murder Reflected* (1965) by Janet Caird, to a novel by Agatha Christie (1939), and to a collection of stories by Sheridan LeFanu (1872). *Through a Glass Darkly* was the English title of an Ingmar Bergman film (1961) and of a poem by Arthur Hugh Clough (1869). The word 'charity', as used here and in the previous entry, derives from the Latin Vulgate use of *caritas*, meaning 'charitable acts of love', and is what appears in the Authorized Version. Cranmer and two of his fellow translators had earlier argued for 'faith, hope and love', but lost out to advocates of 'charity'. The New English Bible (1961) duly substituted the word 'love' for 'charity' in this and the previous passage. Although reading from the Authorized Version at the funeral of Diana, Princess of Wales (6 September 1998), the British Prime Minister similarly substituted the word 'love' for charity throughout.

7 The last enemy that shall be destroyed is death.

1 Corinthians 15:26. Hence, *The Last Enemy*, title of a book (1942) by Richard Hillary, about his experiences as an RAF pilot when he was burned in the Battle of Britain.

8 O death, where is thy sting? O grave, where is thy victory?

1 Corinthians 15:55. See BEHAN 58:4.

GALATIANS

9 Be not deceived; God is not mocked: for whatsoever a man soweth, that shall he also reap.

Galatians 6:7. 'God is not mocked' is a favourite text of the super-religious when confronted with any form of blasphemy. The New English Bible chooses rather to say that, 'God is not to be fooled', which does not convey the same element of abusiveness towards the deity.

PHILIPPIANS

1 For I am in a strait betwixt the two, having a desire to depart, and to be with Christ; which is far better.

In St Paul's Epistle to the Philippians 1:23, he compares the folly of living with the wisdom of dying. Hence, 'With Christ, which is far better' is quite a common text on gravestones, though it can seem rather ungenerous to those who survive. 'Better than what?' one is tempted to ask.

2 Who shall change our vile body, that it may be fashioned like unto his glorious body.

Philippians 3:21. Referring to Christ's resurrection. Also part of the interment service in the Anglican Book of Common Prayer. Hence, *Vile Bodies*, title of a novel (1930) by Evelyn Waugh.

3 The peace of God, which passeth all understanding, shall keep your hearts and minds through Christ Jesus.

This 'grace' comes as Paul is signing off his letter (4:7), though the final verse (4:23) is: 'The grace of our Lord Jesus Christ be with you all.' See also JAMES I 252:6; LUTYENS 298:3.

I THESSALONIANS

4 Remembering without ceasing your work of faith, and labour of love.

I Thessalonians 1:3. Hence, the expression 'labour of love', meaning 'work undertaken through enjoyment of the work itself rather than for any other reward'. Also to be found in Hebrews 6:10.

I TIMOTHY

5 A bishop then must be blameless, the husband of one wife ... Not given to wine, no striker, not greedy of filthy lucre.

I Timothy 3:2–3. The New English Bible translates 'no striker' as 'not a brawler'. Filthy lucre is 'money', though the original Greek suggests more 'dishonourable gain'. The phrase is also used by Paul, in the same context, in Titus 1:7 and 1:11, and in I Peter 5:2. The word 'lucre' also occurs in the Old Testament (I Samuel 8:3).

6 The love of money is the root of all evil.

I Timothy 6:10. Not simply 'money is the root of all evil'.

HEBREWS

7 He being dead yet speaketh.

Hebrews 11:4. A popular gravestone inscription – as, for example, on the grave of the Revd Francis Kilvert (1840–79), an Anglican curate at Langley Burrell, Wiltshire, and afterwards at Clyro near the Welsh border. He was then vicar of Saint Harmon and moved to Bredwardine two years before his early death. He died a month or so after marrying. As such, he would now be completely forgotten but for the diary that he kept from 1870 to his death. Having been pruned first by his widow, selections were published in 1938–40. How appropriate therefore that the inscription on the white stone cross over Kilvert's grave at Bredwardine should be this text, chosen, presumably, by his widow, unaware how apt it was to be for a posthumously published diarist.

8 Wherefore seeing we also are compassed about with so great a cloud of witnesses ...

Hebrews 12:1. Hence, *Clouds of Witness*, title of a detective novel (1926) by Dorothy L. Sayers.

9 For here have we no continuing city, but we seek one to come.

Of heaven. Hebrews 13:14. A request from a correspondent in Ireland wanting to know the 'author of the quotation "We have not here a lasting city" and the title of the book or poem, if any, in which it appeared' was instructive. At first glance it was not a very notable saying, but that has never stopped one from appealing to somebody, somewhere. The solution, however, was interesting, if only because it reminds us that there are more translations of the Bible than we may care to realize, and more ways of expressing the simplest thought than we might think possible.

It was soon spotted that the query was probably a version of what is as above in the Authorized Version. The Revised Version says, 'For we have not here an abiding city'; the Good News Bible says, 'For there is no permanent city for us here on earth'; the Jerusalem Bible has, 'For there is no eternal city for us in this life'; the New English Bible has, 'For we have no permanent home'; the New International Bible has, 'For here we do not have an enduring city, but we are looking for the city that is to come.'

Relaying this information back to the original questioner, I soon heard from him that he had now found *his* version in the Douai-Rheims Bible (1609): 'For we have not here a lasting city, but we seek one that is to come.' Next day I happened to be reading Chapter 3 of Churchill's *History of the English-Speaking Peoples* (Vol. 1) in which he quotes the verse, in the Authorized Version, of course. In T.S. Eliot's *Murder in the Cathedral* (1937) we find the line: 'Here is no continuing city, here is no abiding stay.'

JAMES

1 The tongue is a little member, and boasteth great things ... But the tongue can no man tame; it is an unruly evil, full of deadly poison.

James 3:5 and 8. Hence, the expression 'unruly member' for the tongue.

1 PETER

2 All flesh is as grass, and all the glory of man as the flower of grass. The grass withereth, and the flower thereof falleth away.

1 Peter 1:24. Compare Isaiah 40:6.

3 Wives, be in subjection to your husbands ... husbands ... giving honour unto the wife, as unto the weaker vessel.

1 Peter 3:1–7. Hence, *The Weaker Vessel*, title of a book (1984) by Antonia Fraser about 'woman's lot in seventeenth century England'.

4 The end of all things is at hand.

1 Peter 4:7. Origin of the phrase 'the end is nigh', the traditional slogan of placard-bearing religious fanatics. But, although 'nigh' is a biblical word, this phrase does not occur as such in the Authorized Version. Rather: 'The day of the Lord ... is nigh at hand (Joel 2:1); 'the kingdom of God is nigh at hand' (Luke 21:31); and the above.

2 PETER

5 The dog is turned to his own vomit again.

2 Peter 2:22. Compare Proverbs 26:11 (see 75:4 above). See also BYRON 115:7.

REVELATION

6 Be thou faithful unto death, and I will give thee a crown of life.

Revelation 2:10. Hence, *Faithful Unto Death*, title of a painting by Sir Edward John Poynter PRA, showing a centurion staying at his sentry post during the eruption of Vesuvius that destroyed Pompeii in AD 79. In the background,

citizens are panicking as molten lava falls upon them. The picture was inspired by the discovery of an actual skeleton of a soldier in full armour excavated at Pompeii in the late 18th or early 19th century. Many such remains were found of people 'frozen' in the positions they had held as they died. Bulwer-Lytton described what might have happened to the soldier in his *Last Days of Pompeii* (1834). Poynter painted the scene in 1865; it now hangs in the Walker Art Gallery, Liverpool.

7 And I looked, and behold a pale horse: and his name that sat on him was Death.

Revelation 6:8 has given a phrase much used in titles: Katherine Anne Porter's novel *Pale Horse, Pale Rider* (1939), Agatha Christie's novel *Pale Horse* (1961), and Emeric Pressburger's film script *Behold a Pale Horse* (1964).

Hence, *The Four Horsemen of the Apocalypse*, title of a novel (1916, films US 1921, 1961) by Vicente Blasco Ibáñez, referring to the agents of destruction, famine and pestilence which appear on different coloured horses in Revelation 6. There is a white horse and a red horse; a black horse, and a pale horse.

8 And when he had opened the seventh seal, there was silence in heaven about the space of half an hour.

Revelation 8:1. Hence, *The Seventh Seal*, title of a film (1957) by Ingmar Bergman.

9 And I saw an angel come down from heaven, having the key of the bottomless pit.

Revelation 20:1, where 'the bottomless pit' is Hell. The phrase is quoted in Milton, *Paradise Lost*, Bk 6, line 864 (1667):

> Headlong themselves they threw
> Down from the verge of Heaven, eternal wrath
> Burnt after them to the bottomless pit.

William Pitt the Younger, British Prime Minister (1783–1801, 1804–6) was nicknamed 'the Bottomless Pitt', on account of his thinness. A caricature attributed to James Gillray with this title shows Pitt as Chancellor of the Exchequer introducing his 1792 budget. His bottom is non-existent.

10 The street of the city was pure gold.

Revelation 21:21 – a vision of the new Jerusalem. Probable origin of the expression that the streets of some cities are metaphorically 'paved with gold'. John Bunyan, *Pilgrim's Progress* (1684) has:

> Now as they walked in this land, they had more rejoicing

than in parts more remote from the kingdom to which they were bound; and drawing near to the city, they had yet a more perfect view thereof. It was builded of pearls and precious stones, also the street thereof was paved with gold; so that by reason of the natural glory of the city, and the reflection of the sunbeams upon it, Christian with desire fell sick.

In the story of Dick Whittington, he makes his way to London from Gloucestershire because he hears the streets are paved with gold and silver. The actual Dick Whittington was thrice Lord Mayor of London in the late 14th and early 15th centuries. The popular legend does not appear to have been told before 1605. *Benham* (1948) comments on the proverbial expression 'London streets are paved with gold' – 'A doubtful story or tradition alleges that this saying was due to the fact that in about 1470, a number of members of the Goldsmiths' Company, London, joined the Paviors' Company.' George Colman the Younger in *The Heir-at-Law* (1797) wrote:

Oh, London is a fine town,
A very famous city,
Where all the streets are paved with gold,
And all the maidens pretty.

The Percy French song 'The Mountains of Mourne' (1896) mentions 'diggin' for gold in the streets [of London]'. From G.K. Chesterton, *William Cobbett* (1925): 'He had played the traditional part of the country boy who comes up to London where the streets are paved with gold.' In the Marx Brothers film *Go West* (US 1940), Chico says: 'He's goin' West, and when he gets off the train he's gonna pick up some gold and send it to me. They say that the gold is layin' all over the streets.'

The streets of *heaven* are also sometimes said to be paved with gold – though not specifically as such in the Bible. There is, however, a spiritual where the 'streets in heaven am paved with gold'.

Apocrypha (New Testament)

ACTS OF ST JOHN

1 The heavenly spheres make music for us. All things join in the dance.

This is the unattributed text on the grave of Imogen Holst in the churchyard of St Peter and St Paul's, Aldeburgh, Suffolk. She was a musical educationalist, conductor, composer (especially of songs) and arranger of folksongs. She collaborated with Benjamin Britten, whose grave is but a few feet in front of hers. Her father, the composer Gustav Holst (1874–1934), unwittingly provided his daughter's

epitaph. It comes from a text he prepared and translated himself from the Greek of the Apocryphal Acts of St John for his *Hymn of Jesus* (1917). The passage concerns Jesus 'before he was taken by the lawless Jews', calling on his disciples to 'sing a hymn to the Father', at which they join hands in a ring and dance. Rosamund Strode of the Holst Foundation has commented: 'Since to Imogen dancing was every bit as important as music (and indeed she once hoped to be a dancer), the two lines seemed to us appropriate in every possible way.'

Vulgate

2 *Dominus illuminatio mea, et salus mea, quem timebo?* [The Lord is the source of my light and my safety, so whom shall I fear?]

Psalm 26. The first three words, in Latin, are the motto of the University of Oxford.

3 *Non nobis, Domine, non nobis; sed nomini tuo da gloriam* [Not unto us, Lord, not unto us; but to thy name give glory].

Psalm 113 (second part):1. '*Non Nobis Domine*' is also the title of a vocal cannon said to be by William Byrd (1543–1623) and sung at banquets as an after-dinner grace.

4 *De profundis clamavi ad te, Domine; Domine, exaudi vocem meam* [Out of the depths I have cried to thee, Lord; Lord, hear my voice].

Psalm 129:1. Hence, *De Profundis*, title of Oscar Wilde's letter of self-justification (published 1905).

5 *Quo vadis?* [Whither goest thou?/Where are you going?]

These words are the Vulgate's version of John 13:36: 'Simon Peter said unto him, Lord, whither goest thou? Jesus answered him, Whither I go, thou canst not follow me now'; and of John 16:5, in which Christ comforts his disciples before the Crucifixion. The words also occur in Genesis 32:17 and in the Acts of St Peter among the New Testament Apocrypha in which, after the Crucifixion, Peter, fleeing Rome, encounters Christ on the Appian Way. He asks Him, '*Domine, quo vadis?* [Lord, whither goest thou?]' and Christ replies, '*Venio Romam, iterum crucifigi* [I am coming to Rome to be crucified again].'

Quo Vadis? was famously used as the title of a film (US 1951, and of two previous Italian ones) and of an opera (1909) by Jean Nouguès, all of them based on a novel with the same title (1896) by a Pole, Henryk Sienkiewicz (1846–1916).

1 *Ecce homo* [Behold the man].

John 19:5. Said by Pontius Pilate. Hence, the title of a sculpture (1934) by Jacob Epstein.

See also STERNE 445:2; WESLEY 489:2

Isaac BICKERSTAFFE Irish playwright (?1735–?1812)

2 I care for nobody, no, not I,
And nobody cares for me.

This should be 'I care for nobody, not I, / If no one cares for me', if one is quoting from Bickerstaffe's comic opera *Love in a Village*, Act 1, Sc. 2 (1762). Is the misquoted version easier to sing?

Ambrose BIERCE American journalist (1842–?1914)

Of Oscar Wilde:

3 He had nothing to say and he said it.

Attributed remark, but unverified. In Wilde's own *The Picture of Dorian Gray* there is: 'Women ... never have anything to say, but they say it charmingly', and in Hesketh Pearson's *Life* (1954 edn) the biographer comments: 'His astonishing conversational gifts were thoroughly appreciated only in social and political circles ... despite such outspoken comments on the politicians as: "The Lords Temporal say nothing, the Lords spiritual have nothing to say, and the House of Commons has nothing to say and says it."' (This last is from *The Soul of Man Under Socialism*.) Similarly, a review in *The Times* (5 May 1937) of a book by A.A. Milne said: 'When there is nothing whatever to say, no one knows better than Mr Milne how to say it.' Compare also: 'The magic of [Bernard] Shaw's words may still bewitch posterity ... but it will find that he has nothing to say' – A.J.P. Taylor in *The Observer* (22 July 1956). 'Berlioz says nothing in his music but he says it magnificently' – James Gibbons Huneker, *Old Fogy* (1913). And before all this, from Charles Dickens, *Little Dorrit*, Bk 1, Chap. 10 (1855–7): 'And although one of two things always happened; namely, either that the Circumlocution Office had nothing to say and said it, or that it had something to say of which the noble lord, or right honourable gentleman, blundered one half and forgot the other; the Circumlocution Office was always voted immaculate by an accommodating majority.'

4 Quotation, n. The act of repeating erroneously the words of another. The words erroneously repeated.

The Cynic's Word Book (later re-titled *The Devil's Dictionary*) (1906).

Josh BILLINGS (Henry Wheeler Shaw) American humorist (1818–85)

5 Love iz like the meazles.

From the 'Affurisms' in *Josh Billings: His Sayings* (1865). He goes on: 'We kant have it bad but onst, and the later in life we have it the tuffer it goes with us.' Compare JEROME 256:1; JERROLD 256:3.

6 'Vote early and vote often' is the Politishun's golden rule.

From *Josh Billings' Wit and Humour* (1874), which seems merely to be recalling an adage. Indeed, earlier, William Porcher Miles had said in a speech to the House of Representatives (31 March 1858): '"Vote early and vote often", the advice openly displayed on the election banners in one of our northern cities.'

    Safire (1978) ignores both these sources but mentions that historian James Morgan found 'in his 1926 book of biographies' that the original jokester was John Van Buren (who died in 1866), a New York lawyer and son of President Martin Van Buren.

Laurence BINYON English poet (1869–1943)

7 They shall grow not old, as we that are left grow old:
Age shall not weary them, nor the years condemn.
At the going down of the sun and in the morning
We will remember them.

The poem 'For the Fallen' was first printed in *The Times* (21 September 1914) and subsequently in Binyon's *The Four Years*. Spoken at numerous Armistice Day and Remembrance Day services since, the opening phrase is frequently rendered wrongly 'They shall *not grow old* ...' – as, for example, on the war memorial at Staines, Middlesex, though this was apparently corrected (albeit visibly) in about 1986. The UK National Inventory of War Memorials (which has 48,000 on its database) reported in 2003 that 76 show the incorrect quotation, whereas 125 show it correctly. When Binyon's poem was set to music by Edward Elgar in the choral and orchestral work *The Spirit of England* (1915–17), 'they shall not grow old' was used, presumably because it sounds better when enunciated in song.

    As to the assertion that the last word in line 2 should be 'contemn', not 'condemn', certainly 'contemn' makes more sense as it means 'to despise or treat with disregard'. Despite an exhaustive search through Binyon's published anthologies, no copy of the poem using 'contemn' was found. So how did the confusion start? Indeed, one might add, that Binyon, who lived until 1943, would surely have protested at the printings if he had really intended 'contemn'.

Nigel BIRCH (later Lord Rhyl) British Conservative MP (1906–81)

1 My God! They've shot our fox!

On the resignation of the Labour Chancellor Hugh Dalton. Remark (13 November 1947), reported in Harold Macmillan, *Tides of Fortune*, Chap. 3 (1969). In other words, the Conservatives had been deprived of their legitimate prey. Shooting the fox is the ultimate type of bad form on the hunting field as it deprives the participants of the thrill of the chase. It is not clear to what extent this expression existed prior to Birch's use. In Ian Fleming, *On Her Majesty's Secret Service*, Chap. 23 (1963), James Bond says, 'I want this man for myself … I don't want someone else to shoot my fox.'

See also BROWNING 105:5.

John BIRD English actor (1936–)

2 *That Was the Week That Was.*

Title of BBC TV's famous 'satire' series (1962–3), also used in the US. In *A Small Thing – Like an Earthquake* (1983), the producer Ned Sherrin credits the coinage to the actor John Bird, who was originally going to take part in the programme. It was in conscious imitation of the 'That's Shell – That Was' advertisements of the early 1930s. Often abbreviated to 'TW3'.

Norman BIRKETT (later Lord Birkett) English barrister and judge (1883–1962)

3 I do not object to people looking at their watches when I am speaking. But I strongly object when they start shaking them to make sure they are still going.

Quoted in *The Observer* (30 October 1960). However, in *Joyce Grenfell Requests the Pleasure* (1976), Grenfell writes: 'It made me think of my father's story of Edward Marsh, who said he didn't mind if anyone looked at his watch when he was lecturing, but he didn't much like it when they looked at it a second time and shook it to see if it was still going.' As Eddie Marsh died in 1953 and Joyce Grenfell's father died in 1954, there may be grounds for wondering if Birkett really originated the joke.

Augustine BIRRELL English Liberal politician and writer (1850–1933)

4 That great dust-heap called 'history'.

'Carlyle', *Obiter Dicta* (1884–7). Compare TROTSKY 468:6.

(Sir) John BIRT (later Lord Birt) English broadcasting executive (1944–)

5 There is a bias in television journalism. It is not against any particular party or point of view – it is a bias against understanding.

Birt, who later became Director-General of the BBC and famous for promoting a dry, analytical approach to current-affairs broadcasting, was working in the commercial sector when he coined the phrase 'bias against understanding'. In 1986 he told me: 'The problem of authorship that you raise is difficult. The phrase first appeared in the article in *The Times* of 28 February 1975. This article was written by me but was the result of a dialogue of years with Peter Jay. Subsequently we went on to write together a series of articles on the same subject. I don't think it would be wrong of me to claim authorship of the phrase; but it would only be just to acknowledge Peter's role.'

6 *The Harder Path.*

Title of autobiography (2002). As epigraph Birt has 'When the road through the mountains forks, take the harder path' as a 'Himalayan saying'. In Chap. 11, he writes: 'I discovered something basic about myself in those years in the 1980s working as an ITV Controller: I was not prepared to tolerate the blatantly unsatisfactory; I had a compulsion to sort things out, a willingness to take the harder path.'

Thomas Brigham BISHOP American writer (1835–1905)

7 John Brown's body lies a-mouldering in the grave.

Bishop is but one of several suggested authors of the song 'John Brown's Body'. Brown was hanged in 1859, and the song was being sung by 1861. The phrase 'a-mouldering in the grave' was not original to him. In Henry Austen's 'Biographical Notice' of his sister Jane, which prefaced the first (posthumous) edition of *Persuasion* and *Northanger Abbey* (1818), he writes of her: 'The hand which guided that pen is now mouldering in the grave.' Earlier, Shelley in *Queen Mab* (1813) had had: 'All around the mouldering relics of my kindred lay.' In a letter to Lady Beaumont (21 May 1807), William Wordsworth had written: 'Long after we … are mouldered in our graves.' Even earlier connections between 'moulder' and graves occur in Gray's 'Elegy' (1751): 'Heaves the turf in many a mouldering heap' – GRAY 221:4 – and Hervey's *Meditations* (1746): 'Your grandeur mouldering in an urn.'

Otto von BISMARCK Prusso-German statesman
(1815–98)

1 Blood and iron.

When Bismarck addressed the Budget Commission of the Prussian House of Delegates on 30 September 1862, what he said was: 'It is desirable and it is necessary that the condition of affairs in Germany and of her constitutional relations should be improved; but this cannot be accomplished by speeches and resolutions of a majority, but only by iron and blood [*Eisen und Blut*].' On 28 January 1886, speaking to the Prussian House of Deputies, he did, however, use the words in the more familiar order: 'This policy cannot succeed through speeches, and shooting-matches and songs; it can only be carried out through blood and iron [*Blut und Eisen*].'

The words may have achieved their more familiar order, at least to English ears, through their use by A.C. Swinburne in his poem 'A Word for the Country' (1884): 'Not with dreams, but with blood and with iron, shall a nation be moulded at last.' (Eric Partridge, while identifying this source correctly in *A Dictionary of Clichés*, 1966 edn, ascribes the authorship to Tennyson ...) On the other hand, the Roman orator Quintillian (1st century AD) used the exact phrase '*sanguinem et ferrum*'.

2 When a lady says no, she means perhaps ...

In October 1982, Lord Denning, then a senior British jurist, was quoted as having commented on the difference between a diplomat and a lady, at a meeting of the Magistrates Association, in these words: 'When a diplomat says yes, he means perhaps. When he says perhaps, he means no. When he says no, he is not a diplomat. When a lady says no, she means perhaps. When she says perhaps, she means yes. But when she says yes, she is no lady.'

Whether Denning claimed it as his own is not recorded, but in Hans Severus Ziegler's *Heitere Muse: Anekdoten aus Kultur und Geschichte* (1974), the passage appears in a (possibly apocryphal) anecdote concerning Bismarck at a ball in St Petersburg. His partner, whom he had been flattering, told him, 'One can't believe a word you diplomats say' and provided the first half of the description. Then Bismarck replied with the second half. The popular form of this would be:

When a gentleman says 'yes' he means 'maybe',
When a gentleman says 'maybe' he means 'no',
And when a gentleman says 'no' he's no gentleman.

When a lady says 'no' she means 'maybe',
When a lady says 'maybe' she means 'yes',
And when a lady says 'yes' she's no lady.

3 God protects fools, drunks and the United States of America.

Untraced. But, there is a French proverb that states: 'God helps three sorts of people, fools, children and drunkards.' As 'children, sailors and drunken men', this was known in English by 1861 – in Thomas Hughes, *Tom Brown at Oxford*. W. Eric Gustafson commented (1995): 'My history teacher, the great Henry Wilkinson Bragdon, used to ascribe to Bismarck the saying that "There is a special providence that protects idiots, drunkards, children, and the United States of America." I have even quoted it in my own writing, but I can't find it in the standard quotation books.' On 9 January 1995, *US News and World Report* quoted Daniel P. Moynihan as saying of the avoidance of casualties in the Haitian intervention: 'The Lord looks after drunks and Americans.'

4 If you like laws and sausages, you should never watch either one being made.

Widely attributed to Bismarck, but unverified. A slightly different version, 'Laws are like sausages; you should never watch them being made', has been credited to the French revolutionary statesman Honoré Gabriel de Riqueti, Comte de Mirabeau (1749–91).

(Sir) William BLACKSTONE English jurist (1723–80)

5 That the king can do no wrong, is a necessary and fundamental principle of the English constitution.

Commentaries on the Laws of England (1765). The concept was not original, however. John Selden's *Table-Talk* (1689) has, 'The King can do no wrong, that is no Process can be granted against him'; and one is told (unverified) that Judge Orlando Bridgeman said it in the trial of the regicides after the restoration of the monarchy in 1660. But Bridgeman did go on to say that ministers *could* do wrong *in the king's name* and the fault should, therefore, be held against the ministers. In the same year, Cunelgus Bonde in his *Scutum regale; the royal buckler, or vox legis, a lecture to the traytors who most wickedly murthered Charles the I*, wrote: 'The King can do no wrong; Therefore cannot be a disseisor [dispossessor].'

Even earlier, John Milton in *Eikonoklastes* (1649) had written: 'As the King of England can doe no wrong, so neither can he do right but ... by his courts.' In other words, it was a venerable idea, even by the time Blackstone expressed it, as is attested by the legal maxim (of no known date) to the same effect, expressed in Latin: '*Rex non potest peccare*.'

Later, in 1822, giving judgement in the case of 'the goods of King George III, deceased', Mr Justice John Nicholl said: 'The king can do no wrong; he cannot constitutionally be supposed capable of injustice.' And, *mutatis mutandis*, Richard Nixon tried to assert the same principle on behalf of the American Presidency in his TV interviews with David Frost in May 1977, saying: 'When the President does it, that means it is not illegal.'

Tony BLAIR British Labour Prime Minister (1953–)

1 Labour is the party of law and order in Britain today. Tough on crime and tough on the causes of crime.

Speech, Labour Party conference (30 September 1993) as Shadow Home Secretary. The 'tough' phrase had been used by Blair for the first time earlier in the year and had been supplied by his colleague, Gordon Brown. When he became the Labour leader in the summer of 1994, there followed any number of 'tough on ... tough on the causes of ... ' imitations and parodies. Chris Smith MP said of the Labour Party's position on cleaning up historic buildings, in 1994: 'We're tough on grime and tough on the causes of grime.'

2 Ask me my three main priorities for government, and I tell you: education, education and education.

Speech. Labour Party conference (1 October 1996) – the year before he became Prime Minister. Earlier examples of this slogan include what Oliver Tambo, former National Chairman of the ANC in South Africa, is reported to have said when asked what message he had for his comrades. Shortly before he died in 1993, Tambo, who had been a science teacher himself at one time, replied: 'Education, education, education.' Before that, the slogan was attributed to Lenin in the form, 'Education, education and more education.' And long before that, the French historian Jules Michelet wrote in *Le Peuple* (1846): 'What is the first part of politics? Education. The second? Education. And the third? Education.' In Anthony Trollope's *The Last Chronicle of Barset*, Chap. 32 (1867), the lawyer Toogood advises Mr Crawley on his many children: 'Educate, educate, educate; that's my word.'

3 They liked her, they loved her, they regarded her as one of the people ... She was the People's Princess, and that is how she will stay ... in our hearts and in our memories forever.

TV statement at Sedgefield, on hearing of the death of Diana, Princess of Wales (31 August 1997). The phrase was suggested to Blair by his press secretary, Alastair Campbell, though it had already been used regarding the Princess by journalists. Also, in 1984, *The People's Princess* had been the title of a book by S.W. Jackman about Princess Mary, Duchess of Teck, the 'crowd-pleasing' mother of Queen

Mary. There is, of course, a long history of usage of the formula in egalitarian and/or communistic contexts – we have had the People's Car (*Volkswagen*, known as such by 1938) and then the People's War, not to mention Bureau, Court, Army and much else. The People's Palace (a London educational institution for the working class) was being referred to as such by 1854, though not formally opened until 1887. Flora Thompson's *Lark Rise* (1939), recalling her Victorian country childhood, tells us that Prime Minister Gladstone was referred to as 'The People's William' – as in the song: 'God bless the people's William, / Long may he lead the van / Of Liberty and Freedom, / God bless the Grand Old Man.'

4 This is not a time for sound bites. We've left them at home ...

During the final stages of negotiations over the Northern Ireland 'Good Friday' peace agreement (8 April 1998). He went on to say, 'I feel the hand of history upon our shoulders.'

Eubie BLAKE American jazz musician (1883–1983)

5 If I'd known I was gonna live this long, I'd have taken better care of myself.

The centenarian boogie-woogie pianist, ragtime composer and lyricist, was so quoted in *The Observer* (13 February 1983). Unfortunately, five days after marking his centennial, Blake died. Even so, his felicitous remark was not original. In *Radio Times* (17 February 1979), Benny Green quoted Adolph Zukor, founder of Paramount Pictures, as having said on the approach to his hundredth birthday: 'If I'd known how old I was going to be I'd have taken better care of myself.' Zukor died in 1976, having been born in 1873.

William BLAKE English poet and painter (1757–1827)

6 Such such were the joys,
When we all girls & boys,
In our youth time were seen,
On the Ecchoing Green.

'The Ecchoing Green', *Songs of Innocence* (1789). Hence, 'Such, such were the joys', the title of an essay on his prep school days by George Orwell, written 1947 and published in *The Partisan Review* (September/October 1952) and *Such, Such Were the Days*, a collection of his essays published in New York (1953). Hence, *The Echoing Green*, title of a book on cricket by John Arlott (1952).

1 When the green woods laugh with the voice
    of joy,
And the dimpling stream runs laughing by;
When the air does laugh with our merry wit,
And the green hill laughs with the noise of it.

'Laughing Song', in the same work. Hence, *When the Green Woods Laugh*, the title of a novel (1960) by H.E. Bates.

2 Never seek to tell thy love
Love that never told can be;
For the gentle wind does move
Silently, invisibly.

I told my love, I told my love,
I told her all my heart;
Trembling, cold, in ghastly fears –
Ah, she doth depart.

Soon as she was gone from me
A traveller came by
Silently, invisibly –
Oh, was no deny.

The poem, written in about 1791, was found not in a published source but in what used to be called 'the Rossetti MS' and now 'Blake's MS Note-book'. The other version (as preferred by recent editions of *ODQ* for example) has the opening couplet as: 'Never *pain* to tell thy love'. The last line was given (until *ODQ* dropped it) as: 'He took her with a sigh.'

So what did Blake intend and who did the re-writing? Fortunately, we have David Erdman's facsimile edition of Blake's Note-book, from which we can see that the poet himself changed the first line to 'Never pain to tell thy Love' and substituted 'O was no deny' for 'He took her with a sigh'. Nor did Blake have any of the punctuation in the above version. And, as Erdman shows, he actually marked the whole of the first verse to be deleted. No wonder later editors felt they were entitled to print their own versions and (some of them) revise inconsistencies like 'does' and 'doth'. But it is reasonably clear what Blake intended, and neither *Bartlett* nor *ODQ* gets it wholly right.

3 The reason Milton wrote in fetters when he wrote of Angels and God, and at liberty when of Devils and Hell, is because he was a true Poet, and of the Devil's party without knowing it.

'The Voice of the Devil', Plate 6, note, *The Marriage of Heaven and Hell* (?1790–3). Referring to Milton's alleged shortcomings in *Paradise Lost*.

4 The tygers of wrath are greater than the horses of instruction.

In the same work. Passion lends more energy – and more insight – than rational thought (where wrath = passion).

5 If the doors of perception were cleansed, every thing would appear to man as it is, infinite.

'A Memorable Fancy', in the same work. The doors of perception = the senses. Has also been derived from Blake's 'There are things that are known, and things that are unknown; in between the doors' (unverified). Aldous Huxley used *The Doors of Perception* as the title of a book (1954) about his experiments with mescaline and LSD. This view was seized upon by proponents of drug culture in the 1960s and from it was also derived the name of the US vocal/ instrumental group The Doors.

6 The morning comes, the night decays, the watchmen leave their stations.

'America, a Prophecy' (1793). Blake supported the American Revolution and wrote this in support. Hence, *Watchmen in the Night: presidential accountability after Watergate* (1975) by Theodore C. Sorenson. Compare BIBLE 77:2.

7 Fiery the Angels rose, & as they rose deep
    thunder roll'd
Around their shores: indignant burning with
    the fires of Orc
And Boston's Angel cried aloud as they flew
    thro' the dark night.

From the same work – the verse to Plate 11. Quoted in the film *Blade Runner* (US 1982) by 'Roy Batty', as: 'Fiery the angels fell; deep thunder rolled around their shores, burning with the fires of orc.'

8 Tyger Tyger, burning bright
In the forests of the night:
What immortal hand or eye
Could frame thy fearful symmetry?

'The Tyger', *Songs of Experience* (1794). Hence, *Forests of the Night*, title of a crime novel (1987) by Margaret Moore and *In the Forests of the Night* by James Riddell (1948), the latter title also used by John Simpson (1993).

9 Every night and every morn
Some to misery are born.
Every morn and every night
Some are born to sweet delight,

Some are born to sweet delight,
Some are born to endless night.

'Auguries of Innocence', line 119 (?1803). Hence, *Endless Night*, title of a novel (1967) by Agatha Christie.

1 And did those feet in ancient time
Walk upon England's mountains green?
And was the holy Lamb of God
On England's pleasant pastures seen?

And did the Countenance Divine
Shine forth upon our clouded hills?
And was Jerusalem builded here
Among these dark Satanic mills?

Blake's short preface to his poem *Milton* (1804–10) has come to be called 'Jerusalem' as a result of the immensely popular musical setting (1916) by Sir Hubert Parry, which has become an alternative British national anthem. It should not be confused with Blake's other poem with the title *Jerusalem: The Emanation of the Giant Albion*. Because of the musical setting's magnificent hymn-like nature, it would not be surprising if most people believed the 'feet' were those of Jesus Christ, but this is not the case. Additionally, because of the poem's date, it might be assumed that the 'dark Satanic mills' had something to do with the Industrial Revolution.

In fact, as F.W. Bateson points out in *English Poetry* (1950), the poem would appear to be an 'anti-clerical paean of free love'. It originally came at the end of a prose preface, Bateson notes, in which Blake attacked the practice of drawing on 'Greek or Roman models'. The phrase 'in ancient time' alludes to the legend that Pythagoras derived his philosophical system from the British Druids. So, Blake is saying, it is foolish to rely on classical models when these originally derived from primitive Britain.

Another interpretation of the piece is that it relates to the legend of Joseph of Arimathea's visit to England with the Holy Grail. Blake might be asking how close the ancient Britons were to the early Christians and, therefore, how close was Blake's generation to God?

As for the significance of the name 'Jerusalem', Blake refers to this in a later Prophetic Book: 'Jerusalem is nam'd Liberty / Among the sons of Albion.' Rather than indicating some Utopian ideal, 'Jerusalem' stands for something much more abstract – sexual liberty, Bateson thinks.

Another passage in *Milton* makes it clear that the 'dark Satanic mills' are nothing industrial but rather the altars of the churches on which the clergy of Blake's time were plying 'their deadly Druidic trade', in Bateson's phrase. They have, however, been interpreted as bearing some rural prejudice against city-dwellers and also as representing the universities of Oxford and Cambridge ...

It is no wonder that the meaning of the poem is so widely misunderstood when it can be perceived only through a thicket of footnotes. As sung, it is a meaningless but joyful assertion of rather vague higher thoughts – a vision of the better world to which the dead have gone and of the nobler society that could be created here on earth if only we could get round to it. Hence, *And Did Those Feet?* – title of a TV play (1965) by David Mercer.

2 Bring me my bow of burning gold:
Bring me my arrow of desire:
Bring me my spear: O, clouds unfold!
Bring me my chariot of fire.

In the same poem. Hence, *Chariots of Fire*, the title of a film (UK 1981) about the inner drives of two athletes (one a future missionary) in the 1924 Olympics. Appropriately for a film whose basic themes included Englishness (though one of the runners was a Scot), Christianity and Judaism, the title comes from Blake's poem, which is sung in Parry's setting at the climax of the film. Note the singular 'chariot' in the original. 'Chariots of fire' in the plural occurs in 2 Kings 6:17: 'And the Lord opened the eyes of the young man; and he saw: and, behold, the mountain was full of horses and chariots of fire round about Elisha.'

3 I will not cease from mental fight,
Nor shall my sword sleep in my hand,
Till we have built Jerusalem,
In England's green and pleasant land.

In the same poem. Hence, *Green and Pleasant Land*, title of film (UK 1955). Unfortunately, this phrase became a cliché by the mid-20th century and was included in the parody of sportswriters' clichés in the book *That Was The Week That Was* (1963). 'How is it that, if the New Zealand flatworm's habit of slurping up the good old British earthworm will devastate this green and pleasant land, New Zealand seems a very green and pleasant land, far from an arid wasteland?' – *The Independent* (17 January 1995). 'As the environment is increasingly threatened by developers, the concerned classes are rising up to save our green and pleasant land. Sheila Hale reports from the front line' – by-line, *Harpers & Queen* Magazine (May 1995).

F.R. Leavis, the literary critic, entitled his autobiography *Nor Shall My Sword* (1972).

4 This life's five windows of the soul
Distort the Heavens from pole to pole,
And leads you to believe a lie
When you see with, not thro', the eye.

The Everlasting Gospel (?1818). Here, Blake seems to be saying that the five *senses* (or perhaps two eyes, two ears, and a nose?) are the windows of the soul. In some texts, it is 'life's dim windows of the soul'.

In *Zuleika Dobson* (1911) Max Beerbohm wrote: 'It needs no dictionary of quotations to remind me that the eyes are the windows of the soul.' But who was credited with that coinage in his dictionary of quotations? It has been suggested that Plato originated the concept in the Dialogues (255d), in Jowett's translation: 'So does the stream of beauty, passing through the eyes which are the windows of the soul, come back to the beautiful one.' But usually the first writer to be credited with speaking along these lines is Guillaume du Bartas (1544–90), who wrote in 1578 of 'these lovely lamps, these windows of the soul'. Shakespeare, *Richard III* (V.iii.116), has Richmond mention, 'the windows of mine eyes' (but here windows = eyelids, and the eyes are being looked out of rather than in through). Théophile Gautier combined the notions in his poem *À deux beaux yeux* (1838): '*Ils sont si transparents qu'ils lassient voir votre âme* [Eyes so transparent that they permit your soul to be seen].' Queen Elizabeth I reputedly spoke of 'not wishing to open windows into men's souls' – see ELIZABETH I 188:6.

1   I give you the end of a golden string;
    Only wind it into a ball,
    It will lead you in at Heaven's gate,
    Built in Jerusalem's wall.

Jerusalem (1820). This use of the phrase 'Heaven's gate' is one of the contenders for the naming of Michael Cimino's 1980 film with the title *Heaven's Gate*, famous for having lost more money than any other film to date – about £34 million. In it, 'Heaven's Gate' is the name of a roller-skating rink used by settlers and immigrants in Wyoming in 1891. Conceivably, the name is meant to be taken as an ironic one for the rough situation many of the characters find themselves in as they arrive to start a new life.

The idea of a 'gate to heaven' goes back to the Bible. For example, Genesis 28:17 has: 'This is none other but the house of God, and this is the gate of heaven.' Psalm 78:23 has: 'He commanded the clouds from above, and opened the doors of heaven.' Shakespeare twice uses the phrase. In *Cymbeline* (II.iii.20) there is the song, 'Hark, hark, the lark at heaven's gate sings', and Sonnet 29 has 'Like to the lark at break of day arising / From sullen earth sings hymns at heaven's gate.'

Browning uses the phrase and Steven Bach in his book *Final Cut* (1985) about the making of the film cites two more possible sources: the Wallace Stevens poem with the title 'The Worms at Heaven's Gate' and this passage from Blake.

2   Great things are done when men and mountains meet. This is not done by jostling in the street.

MS Note-Book (no date). For his time, this might seem a slightly unusual comment in support of communing with nature. It is often claimed that, in the 18th century, mountains were things to be feared and the blinds would be drawn down in the carriage so that they could not be seen. There is little or no proof of this, however, and earlier poets, such as Thomas Gray, had responded to them with awe and admiration.

Lesley BLANCH English writer (1907–)

3   *The Wilder Shores of Love.*

Title of a biographical study (1954) in which Blanch describes four 19th-century women 'who found fulfilment as women along wilder *Eastern* shores'. Describing Jane Digby (whose fourth husband was an Arab Sheik), Blanch writes: 'She was an Amazon. Her whole life was spent riding at breakneck speed towards the wilder shores of love.' Hence, presumably, such usages as: 'The wilder shores of PC [political correctness]' – *The Independent* (21 July 1992); 'The consultant, alone in triumph upon the wilder shores of dermatology, raised his eye-glass to me and averred ...' – Duncan Fallowell, *One Hot Summer in St Petersburg* (1994); 'Gladstone's third major excursion to the wilder shores of political rashness came in May 1864' – Roy Jenkins, *Gladstone* (1995).

Philip P. BLISS American hymn writer (1838–76)

4   Dare to be a Daniel,
    Dare to stand alone,
    Dare to have a purpose firm!
    Dare to make it known!

From the hymn 'Stand by a purpose true' – No. 7 in *Sacred Songs and Solos*, edited by Ira D. Sankey. Hence, *Dare To Be a Daniel*, title of a memoir (2004) by Tony Benn.

Alfred BLUNT English bishop (1879–1957)

5   The benefit of the King's Coronation depends under God upon ... the faith, prayer and self-dedication of the King himself ... We hope that he is aware of this need. Some of us wish that he gave more positive signs of such awareness.

Press comment on the relationship between King Edward VIII and Wallis Simpson finally burst through following these innocuous remarks made on 1 December 1936 by the Bishop of Bradford. Speaking at a diocesan conference, he was dealing with a suggestion that the forthcoming Coronation should be secularized and with criticism that the King was not a regular churchgoer. The *Yorkshire Post* linked the bishop's words to rumours then in circulation. Dr Blunt claimed subsequently that his address had been written six weeks earlier, without knowledge of the rumours, and added: 'I studiously took care to say nothing of the King's private life, because I know nothing about it.'

Ivan BOESKY American financier (1937–)

1 Greed is all right ... Greed is healthy. You can be greedy and still feel good about yourself.

Part of a commencement address when receiving an honorary degree at the University of California at Berkeley on 18 May 1986. Boesky also said, 'Seek wealth, it's good.' In December 1987 he was sentenced to three years imprisonment for insider dealing on the New York Stock Exchange. *Bartlett* (1992) has: 'Greed is good! Greed is right! Greed works! Greed will save the U.S.A.!' See also *WALL STREET* 481:5.

Humphrey BOGART American film actor (1899–1957)

2 Tennis, anyone?

Wrongly said to have been Bogart's sole line in his first appearance in a stage play. A wild-goose chase was launched by Jonah Ruddy and Jonathan Hill in their book *Bogey: The Man, The Actor, The Legend* (1965). Describing Bogart's early career as a stage actor (in about 1921) they said: 'In those early Broadway days he didn't play menace parts. "I always made my entrance carrying a tennis racquet, baseball bat, or golf club. I was the athletic type, with hair slicked back and wrapped in a blazer. The only line I didn't say was, 'Give me the ball, coach, I'll take it through.' Yes, sir, I was Joe College or Joe Country Club all the time." It was hard to imagine him as the originator of that famous theatrical line – "Tennis anyone?" – but he was.'

It is clear from this extract that the authors were adding their own gloss to what Bogart had said. *Bartlett* (1968) joined in and said it was his 'sole line in his first play'. But Bogart had denied ever having said it (quoted in Goodman, *Bogey: The Good-Bad Boy*, 1965, and in an ABC TV film of 1974 using old film of him doing so).

Alistair Cooke in *Six Men* (1977) is more cautious: 'It is said he appeared in an ascot and blue blazer and tossed off the invitation "Tennis, anyone?"', but Cooke adds that Bogart probably did not coin the phrase.

3 Even the dead can talk.

Line spoken in a 1951 film called *Murder, Inc.* (known in the US as *The Enforcer*) and celebrated in the Pete Atkins/

Clive James song 'Driving Through Mythical America'.

Mendoza (Everett Sloane): I'll have a better memory: you looking like a chump in that courtroom today.
Ferguson (Bogart): If you think you can get away with this, you're crazy. You think you can shut people up by killing them, but you're wrong. Even the dead can talk. Maybe not in a courtroom, but they'll be talking to you, Mendoza. At night when you're trying to sleep ...
Mendoza: I don't have to listen to this.

See also *ALLEN* 7:6; *CASABLANCA* 127:1–2; *TO HAVE AND HAVE NOT* 466:6.

John B. BOGART American journalist (1845–1921)

4 If a man bites a dog, that is news ...

As a definition of news, this has been variously ascribed – chiefly, in the form, 'When a dog bites a man, that is not news, because it happens so often. But if a man bites a dog, that is news,' to Bogart, city editor of the New York *Sun*, 1873–90, who once said it to a young reporter. The chief source for this is F.M. O'Brien, *The Story of the Sun*, Chap. 9 (1918). According to O'Brien, Bogart 'absorbed the Dana idea of news and the handling thereof', alluding to Charles A. Dana, the editor of the same paper from 1868 to 1897, to whom the saying has also been ascribed in the form: 'If a dog bites a man, it's a story; if a man bites a dog, it's a good story.' But *The Macmillan Book of Proverbs* ..., ed. Burton Stevenson (1948), has: 'Edward P. Mitchell, Dana's assistant for many years, stated positively that Bogart was the author.' Hence, whatever the case, *Man Bites Dog*, title of a newspaper play reviewed in *Time* Magazine (8 May 1933).

William BOLITHO British writer (1890–1930)

5 The shortest way out of Manchester is notoriously a bottle of Gordon's gin.

'Caliogstro and Seraphina', *Twelve Against the Gods* (1930). However, *The Times* (21 June 1921) was writing: 'Certainly if drink, in the proverbial saying, has proved on occasion "the shortest way out of Manchester" ... ' – evidence of a much earlier source.

Robert BOLT English playwright and screenwriter (1924–95)

6 *Thomas More*: Why not be a teacher? You'd be a fine teacher. Perhaps a great one.
Rich: And if I was, who would know it?
More: You, your pupils, God.

A Man For All Seasons, Act 1 (1960). In the film (UK 1966), the last line becomes, 'You. Your pupils. Your friends. God.

Not a bad public that.' In *What I Saw At the Revolution* (1990), Peggy Noonan describes her first assignment as a speechwriter for President Reagan – to write something with which he would announce the Teacher of the Year. She was tipped off to use this quotation (albeit in the form, '"You, your students, God …" Or words to that effect … Look it up.') She used it. 'The President to my pride and disappointment did not change a word.'

(Sir) David BONE Scottish novelist (1874–1959)

1 It's 'Damn you, Jack – I'm all right!' with you chaps.
From *The Brassbounder* (1910), one of Bone's many novels set on the sea and based on his own experiences (he rose to be Commodore of the Anchor Line). *Partridge/Catch Phrases* suggests this saying (certainly not Bone's coinage) may have arisen in about 1880 in the form 'Fuck you, Jack, I'm all right.' The bowdlerized versions 'typified concisely the implied and often explicit arrogance of many senior officers towards the ranks' in the navy, hence, the use of 'Jack', the traditional name for a sailor since about 1700. Hence, *I'm All Right Jack*, title of a film (UK 1959) co-written and directed by John Boulting.

The BOOK OF COMMON PRAYER 1662 version

2 We have erred and strayed from thy ways like lost sheep. We have followed too much the devices and desires of our own hearts.
From the General Confession in Morning/Evening Prayer. Compare Psalm 140:8 (Authorized Version): 'Grant not, O Lord, the desires of the wicked: further not his wicked device; lest they exalt themselves.' Hence, *Devices and Desires*, title of a novel (1989) by P.D. James.

3 From thence he [Christ] shall come to judge the quick and the dead.
In the Apostles' Creed in Morning Prayer. 'Quick' meaning 'alive'. To Lord Dewar (1864–1930), a British industrialist, is credited the joke that there are 'only two classes of pedestrians in these days of reckless motor traffic – the quick, and the dead'. George Robey ascribed it to Dewar in *Looking Back on Life* (1933). A *Times* leader in April that same year merely ventured: 'The saying that there are two sorts of pedestrians, the quick and the dead, is well matured.'

4 Our Father, which art in heaven, Hallowed be thy Name. Thy kingdom come. Thy will be done, in earth as it is in heaven. Give us this day our daily bread. And forgive us our trespasses, As we

forgive them that trespass against us. And lead us not into temptation; But deliver us from evil: For thine is the kingdom, The power and the glory, For ever and ever. Amen.
From the Lord's Prayer (and so called in the Prayer Book) in Morning and Evening Prayer. The translation, as found in the service of Morning Prayer (which differs slightly from that in Matthew 6:9–13), has provided the following titles (among others): *Give Us This Day* (film UK 1949), *Our Daily Bread* (film US 1934), *The Power and the Glory* (film US 1933) and Graham Greene's novel (1940). *World Without End* is the title of a film (US 1956). *Deliver Us From Evil* is the title of a book (1953) by Hugh Desmond, and *Thine Is The Kingdom* of unrelated books by Heini Arnold, Thomas Dooley and Paul Marshall. *The Power and the Kingdom* is the title of a novel by Michael Williams (1989), while Gay Talese's book (1971) about *The New York Times* with the title *The Kingdom and the Power* is presumably an allusion.

5 Give peace in our time, O Lord.
From Morning and Evening Prayer. See also CHAMBERLAIN 129:4.

6 In Quires and Places where they sing, here followeth the Anthem.
From the Rubric after the Third Collect in Morning Prayer. Hence, *Places Where They Sing*, title of a novel (1970) by Simon Raven.

7 From fornication, and all other deadly sin; and from all the deceits of the world, the flesh and the devil, Good Lord, deliver us.
The Litany. Hence, the expression 'The world, the flesh, and the devil' with the words in the order given – as used, for example, in a 1959 film title. There was also a film (US 1926) called *Flesh and the Devil*. Again, in the Collect for the Eighteenth Sunday after Trinity, we find: 'Lord, we beseech thee, grant thy people grace to withstand the temptations of the world, the flesh, and the devil.'

The same combination also occurs in the Catechism, where the confirmee is asked what his Godfathers and Godmothers had promised for him at his baptism: 'First, that I should renounce the *devil* and all his works, the pomps and vanity of this wicked *world*, and all the sinful lusts of the *flesh*.'

In the 16th and 17th centuries, the words were also grouped together in a different order to denote 'our ghostly enemies' – as, for example, 'the devil, the world, and the flesh' (1530).

1 Incline our hearts to keep this law.

From the response to the recital of the Commandments during the service of Holy Communion. Hence, *Incline Our Hearts*, title of a novel (1988) by A.N. Wilson.

2 Lift up your hearts.

One of the versicles and responses in the Communion. The phrase is '*Sursum corda*' in the Ordinary of the Mass in the Roman Catholic Missal. Compare the line 'Lift up your heart, lift up your voice' in John Wesley's hymn 'Rejoice, the Lord is King!' (1746). *Lift Up Your Hearts* was the title of a long-running BBC radio series, a short burst of uplift in the mornings, broadcast from 1939 to 1965 on the Home Service. A clergyman I knew when I was a boy used to say, 'I'm just off to do a series of lift-ups on the BBC ...'

3 N. or M.

In the Catechism the guide answer to the first question 'What is your name?' is not intended to indicate where a male or female Christian name should be inserted. 'N' is the first letter of the Latin *nomen* ('name') and 'M' is a contraction of 'NN' standing for the plural *nomina* ('names'). So it just means 'name or names'.

Agatha Christie used the title *N or M?* for a spy story published in 1941.

4 Wilt thou obey him, and serve him, love, honour and keep him in sickness and in health; and, forsaking all other, keep thee only unto him, so long as ye both shall live?

From the question posed to the Woman in the Solemnization of Matrimony, to which the answer is 'I will.' Hence, the film titles *Love, Honour and Obey* (UK 2000), *Forsaking All Others* [sic] (US 1934), and *I Will ... I Will ... for Now* (US 1976).

5 To have and to hold from this day forward, for better for worse, for richer for poorer, in sickness and in health, to love and to cherish, till death us do part, according to God's holy ordinance.

From the man's marriage vow in the Solemnization of Matrimony, where mistakes are often made in the wording, i.e. it is *not* 'till death do us part'. Originally, the phrase was 'till death us depart' = 'separate completely', the English form of the French word *departir*. This explains why 'do' appears where one might expect to find 'does' or 'doth'. Hence, titles of the films *To Have and to Hold* (US 1998), *From This Day Forward* (US 1946, UK 2000), *For Better For Worse* (UK 1954) and *Till Death Us Do Part* (UK 1968), the latter based on the notable British TV comedy series (1964–74). This last also resulted in a sequel, *In Sickness and in Health* (from

1985). *To Love and To Cherish* was the title of a romance novel by Barbara Goolden (1966?).

6 I am the Resurrection and the Life.

The Burial of the Dead. Sentence taken from John 11:25.

7 I know that my Redeemer liveth.

The Burial of the Dead. Sentence from Job 10:25–7. Also in Handel's *Messiah*.

8 We bring nothing into the world and we carry nothing out.

The Burial of the Dead. Sentence after 1 Timothy 6:7; Job 1:21.

9 In the midst of life, we are in death.

In the same part, alluding to 2 Corinthians 4:11. Hence, 'In the midst of life we are in debt', attributed to Ethel Mumford and quoted in *The Treasury of Humorous Quotations*, eds Evan Esar & Nicolas Bentley (1951).

10 He shall keep the simple folk by their right: defend the children of the poor, and punish the wrong doer.

It is from Psalm 72:4 — not in any Bible version but as it is in the Book of Common Prayer. One might ask, surely everyone and not just the poor, requires the protection of the law against the criminal? High up over the door of the Old Bailey in London, is the version: 'Defend the children of the poor and punish the wrongdoer.' A case perhaps of the quoter forcing through a not entirely appropriate saying just because it had Biblical origins.

11 Whose feet they hurt in the stocks: the iron entered into his soul.

Prayer Book version of Psalm 105:18. In the Bible, it is: 'Whose feet they hurt with fetters: he was laid in iron.' Although 'the iron entered into his soul' is a mistranslation of the Hebrew, it has given us the phrase meaning 'he has become embittered, anguished'. It was used notably by David LLOYD GEORGE, see 292:1. The English title of Jean-Paul Sartre's novel *La Mort dans L'âme* (1949) is *Iron in the Soul*.

12 All good things come to an end.

The proverbial expression meaning 'pleasure cannot go on for ever' would seem to be a corruption of the Prayer Book version of Psalm 119:96: 'I see that all things come to an end: but thy commandment is exceeding broad' (note the lack of 'good'). The original Bible text is: 'I have seen an end of all perfection: but thy commandment is exceeding broad.' But there are versions of the proverb going back to 1440, and, as 'Everything has an end', the idea appears in Chaucer's *Troilus and Criseyde* (1385).

1 **By the waters of Babylon we sat down and wept.**
The metrical versions of the Psalms in the Prayer Book differ significantly in wording and verse numbering from the Psalms in the Bible. This is the Prayer Book version of Psalm 137:1, of which the original is: 'By the rivers of Babylon, there we sat down, yea, we wept, when we remembered Zion.' See also BIBLE 74:4.

The 'waters' version is the much preferred usage. Horace Walpole (in a letter, 12 June 1775) has: 'By the waters of Babylon we sit down and weep, when we think of thee, O America!' Hence, also *By Grand Central Station I Sat Down and Wept*, title of a poetic novel (1945) by Elizabeth Smart.

2 **O put not your trust in princes, nor in any child of man: for there is no help in them.**
The Prayer Book version of Psalm 146:2 is different from the Bible's 146:3, which is: 'Put not your trust in princes, nor in the son of man, in whom there is no help.'

3 **Be pleased to receive into thy Almighty and most gracious protection the persons of us thy servants, and the Fleet in which we serve.**
From Forms of Prayer to be used at Sea. Hence, *In Which We Serve*, title of the Noël Coward naval film (UK 1942).

John Wilkes BOOTH American actor and assassin (1838–65)

4 *Sic semper tyrannis!* The South is avenged.
Booth shot President Lincoln in his box at the Ford Theatre, Washington DC, on 14 April 1865. Then, falling from the box on to the stage, he addressed the audience with the Latin words meaning, 'May this always be the fate of tyrants' (which is what Brutus is supposed to have exclaimed when murdering Julius Caesar); it is also the motto of the State of Virginia. The rest of the cry may be apocryphal but was reported in *The New York Times* the following day.

'When Abraham Lincoln was murdered / The one thing that interested Matthew Arnold / Was that the assassin shouted in Latin / As he leapt on the stage. / This convinced Matthew / That there was still hope for America' – Christopher Morley, *Points of View* (untraced).

Jorge Luis BORGES Argentinian novelist (1899–1986)

5 The Falklands thing was a fight between two bald men over a comb.
ODMQ (1991) and *ODQ* (1992) may have caused readers to think that it was Borges who originated the remark about 'two bald men fighting over a comb'. Not so. Borges was quoted by *Time* Magazine on 14 February 1983 as having characterized the previous year's Falklands conflict between Britain and Argentina in these words. *Time* is unable to say for sure where it acquired this quotation, though it has had a good rummage among its yellowing files. It may have picked it up from the Spanish paper *La Nación* (28 June 1982), which was apparently quoting from an interview with Borges that had appeared in *Le Monde* the previous day.

But the basic expression about bald men fighting over combs had very definitely been around before 1983. Robert Nye wrote in *The Times* (18 June 1981): 'I think it was Christopher Logue who once characterized the drabness of the English Movement poets of the 1950s as being like the antics of two bald men fighting for possession of a comb.'

The saying occurs even earlier in *Mencken* (1942) – as 'Two bald-headed men are fighting over a comb' (listed as a 'Russian saying') – and in Champion's *Racial Proverbs* (1938).

Cesare BORGIA Italian cardinal, politician and military leader (1476–1507)

6 *Aut Caesar, aut nihil* [Either Caesar or nothing].
The motto of Borgia, who was the bastard son of Pope Alexander VI and brother to Lucrezia Borgia. Meaning 'either I'm boss or I'm not interested', it was inscribed on his sword.

Pierre BOSQUET French general (1810–61)

7 *C'est magnifique – mais ce n'est pas la guerre* [It is magnificent, but it is not war].
This remark was made by Maréchal Bosquet about the Charge of the Light Brigade at the Battle of Balaclava (25 October 1854). It is the source of several witticisms. *Punch* during the First World War said of margarine: '*C'est magnifique, mais ce n'est pas le beurre* [butter]'; in *Oxford Life* (1957), Dacre Balsdon quotes a 'bright young man in a novel' who said of the façade of Worcester College, Oxford, which has a splendid clock on it, '*C'est magnifique, mais ce n'est pas la gare* [station]'. The joke had earlier been applied to Waterhouse Tree Court at Caius Colllege, Cambridge. There is also this limerick:

A waitress who lived in Nanterre
Shaved the whole of her pubic parts bare.

Said the chef in surprise
When this sight met his eyes
'Magnifique, mais ce n'est pas la guerre.'

F.W. BOURDILLON English poet (1852–1921)

1 The night has a thousand eyes,
And the day but one;
Yet the light of the bright world dies,
With the dying sun.

'Light', *Among the Flowers* (1878). Hence, 'The Night Has a Thousand Eyes', title of a story (1945) by Cornell Woolrich (about a vaudeville entertainer who can predict the future). It was adapted as a film (US 1948), and gave rise to several songs. The phrase 'Night hath a thousand eyes' had occurred earlier, however, in the play *The Maydes Metamorphosis* (1600) by John Lyly.

Lord BOWEN English judge (1835–94)

2 We must ask ourselves what the man on the Clapham omnibus would think.

Apparently this famous man was first evoked by Lord Bowen when hearing a case of negligence. The coinage was ascribed to him, after his death, in a 1903 law report. The term refers to the ordinary or average person, the man in the street, particularly when his/her point of view is instanced by the Courts, newspaper editorials etc. Quite why he singled out this particular bus route we shall never know. It sounds suitably prosaic, of course, and the present 77A to Clapham Junction does pass though Whitehall and Westminster, thus providing a link between governors and governed. There is evidence to suggest that the 'Clapham omnibus' in itself had already become a figure of speech by the mid-19th century. In 1857, there was talk of the 'occupant of the knife-board of a Clapham omnibus'. Compare Lord Palmerston's characterization of the typical John Bull as a 'fat man with a white hat in the twopenny omnibus' – G.W.E. Russell, *Collections and Recollections*, Chap. 5 (1898).

E.E. BOWEN English schoolmaster (1836–1901)

3 Forty years on, when afar and asunder
Parted are those who are singing today,
When you look back, and forgetfully wonder
What you were like in your work and your play.

'Forty Years On' (1872) – the Harrow Football Song (which is also the Harrow School Song). Hence, *Forty Years On*, title of Alan Bennett's chronicle play of the 20th century (1968), set in a boys' public school.

Omar BRADLEY American general (1893–1981)

4 This strategy would involve us in the wrong war, at the wrong place, at the wrong time, and with the wrong enemy.

On General Douglas MacArthur's proposal to carry the Korean war into China. Senate inquiry (May 1951).

John BRAHAM English singer and songwriter (1774–1856)

5 England, home and beauty.

'The Death of Nelson', from the opera *The Americans* (1811) by Braham and S.J. Arnold, was one of the most popular songs of the 19th century. Here are the lyrics that suggest the phrase 'England, home and beauty', though the words do not appear exactly in this order:

> 'Twas in Trafalgar bay,
> We saw the Frenchmen lay,
> Each heart was bounding then,
> We scorn'd the foreign yoke
> For our ships were British Oak,
> And hearts of Oak our men.
>
> Our Nelson mark'd them on the wave,
> Three cheers our gallant Seamen gave,
> Nor thought of home or beauty (*rpt.*)
> Along the line this signal ran,
> 'England expects that every man
> This day will do his duty!' (*rpt.*)

Charles Dickens has Captain Cuttle quote 'Though lost to sight, to memory dear, and England, Home, and Beauty!' in *Dombey and Son*, Chap. 48 (1844–6), though these words do not appear in the text consulted (there may be other versions).

Braham was not alone in perceiving the rhyming delights of 'duty' and 'beauty'. In Gilbert and Sullivan's *Trial by Jury* (1875), 'Time may do his duty' is rhymed with 'Winter hath a beauty', at which point, Ian Bradley in his annotated edition remarks: 'This is the first of no fewer than fifteen occasions, exclusive of repetitions, when the words "duty" and "beauty" are rhymed in the Savoy Operas ... *HMS Pinafore* holds the record with four separate songs in which the words are rhymed.'

Home and Beauty (simply) was the title of a play (1919) by Somerset Maugham, concerning the complications surrounding a First World War 'widow' who remarries and whose original husband then turns up (in the US the play was known as *Too Many Husbands*).

John BRAINE English novelist (1922–86)

1 *Room at the Top.*
Braine merely popularized this phrase as the title of his novel (1957; film UK 1958). Much earlier, in reply to advice not to become a lawyer because it was an overcrowded profession, Daniel Webster (1782–1852) had replied, 'There is always room at the top.'

Ernest BRAMAH English writer (1868–1942)

2 As it is truly said, 'Although there exist many thousand subjects for elegant conversation, there are persons who cannot meet a cripple without talking about feet.'
In *The Wallet of Kai Lung*, 'The Transmutation of Ling', Chap. 4 (1900). Compare: 'I cried because I had no shoes, until I met a man who had no feet' – sometimes described as a Zen saying. See ANONYMOUS 11:2; CONFUCIUS 152:1; MAO ZEDONG 310:3.

Louis D. BRANDEIS American jurist (1856–1941)

3 Publicity is justly commended as a remedy for social and industrial diseases. Sunlight is said to be the best of disinfectants; electric light the most efficient policeman.
In *Harper's Weekly* (20 December 1913). Compare the saying, 'Rain is the best policeman of all', heard from a senior police officer after London's Notting Hill Carnival had been rained off on the August Bank Holiday in 1986. Meaning that the incidence of crime falls when the rain does (as it also does in very cold weather).

Marlon BRANDO American film actor (1924–2004)

4 An actor's a guy who, if you ain't talking about him, ain't listening.
Quoted in *The Observer* (January 1956). In fact, Brando appears to have been quoting George Glass (1910–84) – source: Bob Thomas, *Brando* (1973.)
See also SCHULBERG 395:5.

(Sir) Richard BRANSON English entrepreneur (1950–)

5 I believe in benevolent dictatorships, provided I am the dictator.
His favourite remark. He was quoted as saying it in *The Observer* (25 November 1984) and again in *The Independent* (11 March 1989).

Bertolt BRECHT German playwright (1898–1956)

6 Food comes first, then morals [*Erst kommt das Fressen, dann kommt die Moral*].
Die Diegroschenoper (*The Threepenny Opera*), Act 2, Sc. 3 (1928). Variously translated: 'Eats first, morals after.' W.H. Auden wrote a poem entitled 'Grub First, Then Ethics (Brecht)' (1958).

7 The alienation effect.
Brecht's term ('*Verfremdungseffekt*' in German) for a theory of drama, first promoted in 1937, in which the audience has to be reminded that the play it is watching *is* a play and not real. The effect is to distance the watchers from the players, to prevent too much emotional involvement and to reject the traditional make-believe element in theatre.
Not an entirely new technique. How else to explain this from Shakespeare? In *Twelfth Night*, III.iv.127 (1600): 'If this were played upon a stage now, I could condemn it as an improbable fiction.' Then again, from the Wilkie Collins novel, *No Name* (1862–3): '"Very strange!" he said to himself, vacantly. "It's like a scene in a novel – it's like nothing in real life."'

8 *The Resistible Rise of Arturo Ui.*
Title of play (1941) – in German *Der aufhaltsame Aufstieg des Arturo Ui* – and origin of the phrase 'resistible rise', sometimes misquoted as 'irresistible rise'.

Charles Henry BRENT Canadian-born American bishop (died 1929)

9 What is dying? I am standing on the sea shore. A ship sails to the morning breeze and starts for the ocean. She is an object of beauty and I stand watching her till at last she fades on the horizon, and someone at my side says, 'She is gone.' Gone where? Gone from my sight, that is all; she is just as large in the masts, hull and spars as she was when I saw her, and just as able to bear her load of living freight to its destination. The diminished size and total loss of sight is in me, not in her; and just at the moment when someone at my side says, 'She is gone,' there are others who are watching her coming, and other voices take up a glad shout, 'There she comes' – and that is dying.
Ascribed to Brent in *All In the End Is Harvest* (an anthology of readings for funerals) (1984). Brent became Chief of Chaplains to the US expeditionary force in the First World War, and later became Bishop of Western New York.

Nicholas BRETON English poet and writer
(?1545–?1626)

1 *A Mad World, My Masters.*
Title of prose dialogue (1603). *A Mad World, My Masters* became the title of a comedy by Thomas Middleton, published in 1608. Hence, *A Mad World My Masters*, the title of a volume of memoirs (2001) by John Simpson, the BBC's World Affairs Editor. Also, if not the inspiration for, then a very early forerunner of, the film title *It's a Mad, Mad, Mad, Mad World* (US 1963).

Raymond BRIGGS English children's illustrator and author (1934–)

2 *When the Wind Blows.*
Title of illustrated book about the aftermath of a nuclear holocaust (1982). From 'When the wind blows the cradle will rock', a line from the nursery rhyme 'Hush-a-bye, baby, on the tree top' (known since 1765), or from 'Grass never grows when the wind blows', a proverb.

John BRIGHT English Radical politician (1811–89)

3 He is a self-made man and worships his creator.
Mencken (1942) has, rather, Henry Clapp saying this in 1858 about Horace Greeley, and dates Bright's use of the saying about Benjamin Disraeli ten years later, to about 1868. Leon Harris, *The Fine Art of Political Wit* (1965) has *Disraeli* saying it about *Bright*. Alluding to BIBLE 68:2.

4 This regard for the liberties of Europe, this care at one time for the Protestant interest, this excessive love for the balance of power, is neither more nor less than a gigantic system of outdoor relief for the aristocracy of Great Britain.
Speech at Birmingham (12 May 1858). A. & V. Palmer, *Quotations in History* (1976), has the date rather as 29 October (taken from *Life and Speeches*, Vol. 1, 1881). *The Oxford Dictionary of Political Quotations* (1996) prefers: 'A gigantic system of out-relief for the British aristocracy.' A criticism of Britain's foreign policy, though sometimes remembered as 'the foreign service' or 'diplomacy'. In other words, it kept the aristocracy off the streets and in useful employment. Outdoor relief was the name given to charitable relief given in the 19th century outside of a charitable institution.

5 England is the mother of parliaments.
That is what Bright said in a speech in Birmingham on 18 January 1865. Frequently misused, even at the highest levels. The phrase is *not* 'Westminster is the mother of parlia-

ments'. Westminster is, rather, one of her children. Icelanders may well object that they have a prior claim to the title anyway, having established the first parliament long in advance, but the point is that Britain's parliamentary system has been copied in so many of her colonies and around the world.

Colonel BRITTON (nom de guerre of Douglas Ritchie) British propagandist (1905–67)

6 The night is your friend. The V is your sign.
During the Second World War the resistance movements in occupied Europe were encouraged from London by broadcasts over the BBC. In an English-language broadcast on 31 July 1941, 'Colonel Britton', as he was known, said: 'It's about the V – the sign of victory – that I want to talk to you now. All over Europe the V sign is seen by the Germans and to the Germans and the Quislings it is indeed the writing on the wall. It is the sign which tells them that one of the unknown soldiers has passed that way. And it's beginning to play on their nerves. They see it chalked on pavements, pencilled on posters, scratched on the mudguards of German cars. Flowers come up in the shape of a V; men salute each other with the V sign separating their fingers. The number five is a V and men working in the fields turn to the village clocks as the chimes sound the hour of five.'
In the same broadcast, the 'Colonel' also encouraged the use of the V in Morse code, three short taps and a heavy one: 'When you knock on a door, there's your knock. If you call a waiter in a restaurant, call him like this: "Eh, *garçon!*" [*taps rhythm on wine glass*] ... Tell all your friends about it and teach them the V sound. If you and your friends are in a café and a German comes in, tap out the V sign all together.' The Morse code for V is also the rhythm of the opening phrase of Beethoven's Symphony No. 5, and the musical phrase was used in BBC broadcasts to occupied Europe to reinforce the message.
From these broadcasts emerged an evocative slogan: 'You wear no uniforms and your weapons differ from ours – but they are not less deadly. The fact that you wear no uniforms is your strength. The Nazi official and the German soldier don't know you. But they fear you ... The night is your friend. The V is your sign.' (Cole Porter's song 'All Through the Night', 1934, had earlier contained the lines: 'The day is my enemy / The night is my friend.') Hence, presumably, later, *The Night Was Our Friend*, title of a play (1950) by Michael Pertwee.
Winston Churchill spoke of the V sign as a symbol of 'the unconquerable will of the people of the occupied territories'. These kinds of broadcasts were also used for sending coded messages to resistance workers in France:

'*Le lapin a bu un apéritif*', '*Mademoiselle caresse le nez de son chien*', and '*Jacqueline sait le latin*' are examples of signals used to trigger sabotage operations or to warm of parachute drops.

Jacob BRONOWSKI Polish-born British mathematician and scientist (1908–74)

1 The hand is more important than the eye ... The hand is the cutting edge of the mind.

TV series, *The Ascent of Man* (1973). Since this use, the term 'cutting edge' has become a cliché for what is considered to be at the forefront of attention or activity. The term is derived from the ancient notion that the sharp edge is the most important part of a blade, but *OED2*'s earliest example is only from 1966.

Charlotte BRONTË English novelist (1816–55)

2 Reader, I married him.

Jane Eyre, Chap. 38 (1847). Of Mr Rochester, who has employed Jane as a governess and is now free to marry her through the death by fire of his mad first wife. These words are not the last in the book, as might be supposed, but the opening words of the final chapter.

Rupert BROOKE English poet (1887–1915)

3 Unkempt about those hedges blows
An English unofficial rose.

'The Old Vicarage, Grantchester' (1912). Hence, *An Unofficial Rose*, title of a novel (1962) by Iris Murdoch.

4 These I have loved.

'The Great Lover' (1914). This is a 'list' poem in which Brooke mentions some of his 'favourite things' (rather as the song with that title did in the much later musical *The Sound of Music*). Hence, the title of the BBC radio record programme *These You Have Loved*, which has a history going back to 1938 when Doris Arnold introduced a selection of favourite middle-of-the-road music. The title was still being used 40 years later. Brooke's 'loves' included 'white plates and cups' and 'The cool kindliness of sheets, that soon / Smooth away trouble; and the rough male kiss / Of blankets.'

5 If I should die, think only this of me:
That there's some corner of a foreign field
That is for ever England. There shall be
In that rich earth a richer dust concealed;
A dust whom England bore, shaped, made
   aware,

Gave, once, her flowers to love, her ways to
   roam,
A body of England's, breathing English air,
Washed by the rivers, blest by suns of home.
And think, this heart, all evil shed away,
A pulse in the eternal mind, no less
Gives somewhere back the thoughts by
   England given;
Her sights and sounds; dreams happy as her
   day;
And laughter, learnt of friends; and gentleness,
In hearts at peace, under an English heaven.

'The Soldier' (1914). This very soon made a perfect epitaph for the poet himself, who died of acute blood poisoning at Lemnos on 23 April 1915, and was buried in a foreign field. He was then a sub-lieutenant in the Royal Naval Division and was on his way by boat to fight in the Dardanelles. According to Edward Marsh's *Memoir*, at Brooke's burial a pencil inscription in Greek was put on a large white cross at the head of his grave, stating: 'Here lies the servant of God, Sub-Lieutenant in the English Navy, who died for the deliverance of Constantinople from the Turks.' Eventually (in 1983), a marble plaque bearing the whole poem was erected on the Greek island of Skyros where the poet is buried; this may have replaced an earlier plaque bearing a quotation from the same poem.

Hence, *Forever England*, the UK title given to the re-issue of the film version of C.S. Forester's novel *Brown on Resolution* (1929; film UK 1935). In the US however, the film was know as *Born for Glory*. Hence also, *Under An English Heaven*, title of a novel about Second World War Britain by Robert Redcliffe (2002).

Gary BROOKER English musician and songwriter (1945–)

6 We skipped the light fandango
And turned cartwheels cross the floor ...
And so it was that later
As the miller told his tale
That her face just ghostly
Turned a whiter shade of pale ...
One of sixteen vestal virgins
Who were leaving for the coast ...

Song, 'A Whiter Shade of Pale' (1967). In fact, Brooker wrote the music and Keith Reid wrote the lyrics. The song was performed by their group, Procul Harum (sometimes spelt 'Procol Harum'). It *appears* to contain several allusions. 'We skipped the light fandango' echoes the expression 'to trip the light fantastic', for 'to dance', which in turn echoes Milton's 'L'Allegro' ('Come, and trip it as ye go / On the light fantastic toe', 323:1) or *Comus* ('Come, knit hands, and beat the ground / In a light fantastic round', 323:3). 'Skipped the light fantastic out of town' appears in Tennesse Williams, *The Glass Menagerie* (1944). 'As the miller told his tale' presumably refers to the 'Miller's Tale' in Chaucer's *Canterbury Tales*, though Keith Reid said (1994) that he had never read Chaucer in his life. And 'One of sixteen Vestal Virgins / Were leaving for the coast' presumably refers to 'The Coast', i.e. the eastern/western seaboards of the US.

The song as a whole – and especially the title – is a paradigm of the drug-influenced creativity of the 1960s. The title – according to Reid in *Melody Maker* (3 June 1967) – was overheard at a gathering: 'Some guy looked at a chick and said to her, "You've gone a whiter shade of pale."'

Thomas BROOKS English Puritan divine (1608–80)

1 *Heaven on Earth, or a Serious Discourse touching a well-grounded Assurance of Mens Everlasting Happiness.*

Title of book (1654). The phrase 'heaven on earth', meaning 'a perfect, very pleasant, ideal place or state of affairs', is not biblical. This is the only citation for the precise phrase in *OED2*, but earlier similar occurrences are plentiful: 'For if heaven be on this earth, and ease to any soul, / It is in cloister or in school' – William Langland, *The Vision of Piers Plowman*, B text (?1377–9). 'A heaven on earth I have won by wooing thee' – Shakespeare, *All's Well That Ends Well*, IV.ii.66 (1603).

From *The Guardian* (5 June 1986): 'The Prime Minister yesterday promised her party "a little bit of heaven on earth" produced by further tax cuts ... Mrs Thatcher was in lyrical mood at the Conservative Women's Conference in London, talking of her vision of a society of satisfied consumers.' This was a slogan that did not catch on at all.

Lord BROUGHAM Scottish jurist and politician (1778–1868)

2 It adds a new terror to death.

Pearson (1937) insists that what Brougham said in a 'speech on an ex-chancellor' was 'Death was now armed with a new terror', but he gives no source for the remark. What was being talked about? Biography, and in particular what Lord Campbell wrote in *Lives of the Lord Chancellors* (1845–7) without the consent of the subjects' heirs or executors. Lord Lyndhurst (three times Lord Chancellor, who died in 1863) said, 'Campbell has added another terror to death' (quoted 1924).

On the other hand, the lawyer and politician Sir Charles Wetherell (who died in 1846) is also quoted as having said of Lord Campbell: 'Then there is my noble and biographical friend who has added a new terror to death' – quoted in Lord St Leonards, *Mispresentation in Campbell's Lives of Lyndhurst and Brougham* (1869). So everyone seems to have been saying it.

Pearson adds that before all this, the expression had been used in relation to the bookseller Edmund Curll (1683–1747), who used to churn out cheap lives of famous people as soon as they were dead. John Arbuthnot had called him 'One of the new terrors of death' (in a letter to Swift, 13 January 1733).

Later came the remark attributed to Sir Herbert Beerbohm Tree (also by Pearson, as it happens, in his biography of the actor, 1956) on the newly invented gramophone: 'Sir, I have tested your machine. It adds new terror to life and makes death a long-felt want.'

'Capability' BROWN English garden landscaper (1715–83)

3 Nature abhors a straight line.

Attributed in *Broadlands, The Home of Lord Mountbatten* (guide book, 1988). Compare RABELAIS 375:1.

Helen Gurley BROWN American journalist (1922–)

4 *Sex and the Single Girl.*

Title of book (1962; film US 1964). Hence, 'sex and the (single) ––', a journalistic headline format. Fritz Spiegl, *Keep Taking the Tabloids!* (1983), identified it in the following actual headlines: 'Sex and the single Siberian', 'Sex and the kindly atheist', 'Sex and the girl reporter' and 'Sex and the parish priest'.

Jerry BROWN American Democratic politician (1938–)

5 We carry in our hearts the true country and that cannot be stolen. We follow in the spirit of our ancestors and that cannot be broken.

In a speech (October 1991), the former Governor of California announced his candidacy for the Democratic nomination for the Presidency (which he did not get – it went to Bill Clinton). Unusually for a politician, Brown had always been associated with rock music and musicians. On this occasion, he quoted from the song 'The Dead Heart' (1988), by the Australian rock group Midnight Oil, which has rather, 'We follow in the *steps* of our *ancestry* ...' Brown did not openly acknowledge the borrowing in his speech, though an information sheet given to reporters did – source: *The Guardian* (26 October 1991).

Thomas BROWN English satirist (1663–1704)

1 I do not love thee, Dr Fell.
The reason why I cannot tell;
But this I know, and know full well,
I do not love thee, Dr Fell.

On the Dean of Christ Church, Oxford, when Brown was an undergraduate there. Ward Lock's *Oxford* (1936–7) has: 'With the Restoration came Doctor John Fell ... whose name is chiefly known to the world through a not very brilliant adaptation of Martial's *Non amo te, Sabidi*. The writer could have probably given a very definite reason for his dislike. Doctor Fell seems to have been a man with a strong sense of duty, who also saw to it that others did *their* duty – according to his conception. He had the doubtful honour of expelling Locke, the philosopher, at the King's behest, and Penn, the founder of Pennsylvania, for non-conformity.'

(Sir) Thomas BROWNE English author and physician (1605–82)

2 That children dream not in the first half year, that men dream not in some countries, are to me sick men's dreams, dreams out of the ivory gate, and visions before midnight.

'On Dreams' (no date). Hence, *Visions Before Midnight*, title of a volume of collected TV criticism (1977) by Clive James.

3 When the living might exceed, and to depart this world could not be properly said to go unto the greater number.

Epistle Dedicatory, *Hydriotaphia* (*Urn-Burial*) (1658). Hence, the expression 'to join the great majority', meaning 'to die'. *OED2* does not find use of 'to join/pass over to the majority', in this sense, before 1719 (Edward Young, *The Revenge*: 'Death joins us to the great majority'), though it does relate it to the Latin phrase '*abiit ad plures*' – Petronius, *Satyricon*, 'Cena Tremalchionis', Chap. 42, Sect. 5.

On his way out in 1884, the politician Lord Houghton quipped, 'Yes, I am going to join the Majority and you know I have always preferred Minorities.' Compare NIXON 344:1.

4 Man is a noble animal, splendid in ashes, and pompous in the grave.

In the same work, Chap. 5. Referring to epitaphic inscriptions on gravestones and memorials.

Elizabeth Barrett BROWNING English poet (1806–61)

5 How do I love thee? Let me count the ways ...
I love thee with a love I seemed to lose

With my lost saints – I love thee with the breath,
Smiles, tears, of all my life! – and, if God
  choose,
I shall but love thee better after death.

Sonnets from the Portuguese, No. 43 (1850). Hence, *Let Me Count the Ways*, title of novel (1996) by Deborah Bosley.

(Sir) Frederick 'Boy' BROWNING English soldier (1896–1965)

6 I think we might be going a bridge too far.

Reported remark to Field Marshal Montgomery on 10 September 1944. Hence, the expression, 'a bridge too far'. Since Cornelius Ryan's 1974 book with the title about the 1944 airborne landings in Holland and the subsequent film (UK/US 1977), the phrase has passed into the language. It is now frequently used allusively when warning of an unwise move. For example: 'A BRIDGE TOO NEAR. A public inquiry opened yesterday into plans to re-span the Ironbridge Gorge in Shropshire' – *The Times* (20 June 1990); 'Ratners: A bid too far?' – *The Observer* (8 July 1990); 'The Government is poised to announce legislation to ban [pub lotteries], but is its decision justified? Fran Abrams asks why ministers believe that this is a punt too far' – *The Independent* (13 November 1997).

Operation Market Garden was designed to capture 11 bridges needed for the Allied invasion of Germany – an attempt that came to grief at Arnhem, with the Allies suffering more casualties than in the landings at Normandy. On 10 September 1944, in advance of the action, Lieutenant-General 'Boy' Browning, Corps Commander, is said to have protested to Montgomery, who was in overall command: 'But, sir, we may be going a bridge too far.' This incident was recorded by Major-General Roy Urquhart in his (ghost-written) memoir, *Arnhem* (1958). The remark was hardly noticed when the book was published and remained so until Ryan picked it up and launched it with brilliant success as a latter-day aphorism. It has gone into the dictionaries of quotations (as said in advance of the operation to Monty) and, in the film, was solemnly delivered by Dirk Bogarde (Browning) to Sean Connery (Urquhart), as a retrospective view: 'Well, as you know I've always thought that we tried to go a bridge too far.'

The military historian Colonel Geoffrey S. Powell MC, author of *The Devil's Birthday: The Bridges to Arnhem* (1984), summarized exactly why there is now a strong belief that Browning never said any such thing (1996): 'It was Nigel Hamilton in the third volume of his masterly biography of Montgomery, *Monty: The Field Marshal 1944–1976* (1986), a book based on Monty's own papers, who once and for all dealt with the myth of the expression "a bridge too far". He wrote: "Neither ... Urquhart, nor Brigadier Hackett ... ever heard Browning use the phrase ... Besides it was not in Browning's nature to speculate pessimistically ... Even if Browning *had* felt the operation to be too ambitious he was not a man to say so."

'[In any case] Cornelius Ryan's book is littered with inaccuracies. His account of Browning's conversation with Monty, in which much is made of Browning's alleged remark is, of course, utterly imaginary as such a meeting never took place. But Ryan clearly based this imaginary interview on Urquhart's similar account on page 4 of *Arnhem*. For Urquhart's anecdote, I cannot fully account. Browning would not have passed on such a discouraging remark before the battle, one that forecast probable ruin to Urquhart's division. It seems more than likely that it arose in some post-battle and informal conversation, half remembered by Urquhart, and recounted by Browning as an excuse for the operation's failure.'

Clearly, at this date, no absolute verification is possible as no minutes of any meeting between Browning and Montgomery exist and Browning left no statement on the matter (having destroyed all his papers). Indeed, as Colonel Powell considers, 'It is a pity that no proper biography of Browning ever appeared, but Daphne du Maurier [his widow] denied aspirant authors access to his papers.' He did not die until 1965, which presumably would have enabled him to rebut anything he did not like in Urquhart's 1958 book but, as Colonel Powell indicates, the phrase did not become controversial until Cornelius Ryan got to work on it many years later.

Robert BROWNING English poet (1812–89)

1 The year's at the spring
And day's at the morn;
Morning's at seven;
The hill-side's dew-pearled;
The lark's on the wing;
The snail's on the thorn:
God's in his heaven –
All's right with the world!

'Pippa Passes' (1841). From P.G. Wodehouse, *Much Obliged, Jeeves* (1971): 'The snail's on the wing and the lark's on the thorn, or rather the other way round, as I've sometimes heard you say.'

2 What's become of Waring?
Since he gave us all the slip,
Chose land-travel or seafaring
Boots and chest or staff and scrip,
Rather than pace up and down
Any longer London town?

'Waring' (1842) – portrait of a friend called Domett. Hence, the title of Anthony Powell's novel *What's Become of Waring* (1939).

3 Oh, to be in England
Now that April's there ...
In England – now!

'Home-Thoughts, from Abroad' (1845). Hence, *Oh! To Be In England*, the title of a novel (1963) by H.E. Bates.

4 I sprang to the stirrup, and Joris, and he;
I galloped, Dirck galloped, we galloped all three.

'How They Brought the Good News from Ghent to Aix' (1845). Browning sets it in '16––' during the wars in the Netherlands, but, according to the *Browning Cyclopedia*, ed. Edward Berdoe (1898): 'There is no actual basis in history for the incidents in this poem, though there is no doubt that in the war in the Netherlands such an adventure was likely enough.' So there is no point in asking what was the good news or what was the occasion.

Sellar and Yeatman (of *1066 and All That*) produced a splendid parody entitled 'How I Brought the Good News from Aix to Ghent (or Vice Versa)', which concludes with the messenger sending a telegram – in *Horse Nonsense* (1933).

5 Never glad confident morning again.

'The Lost Leader' (1845). To be found very near the top of any list of overused, misused quotations, this comes from Browning's poem in which Wordsworth is regretfully portrayed as a man who had lost his revolutionary zeal.

A correct – and devastating – use of the phrase came on 17 June 1963 when the British government under Prime Minister Harold Macmillan had been rocked by the Profumo scandal. In the House of Commons, Tory MP Nigel Birch said to Macmillan: 'I myself feel that the time will come very soon when my Right Hon. Friend ought to make way for a much younger colleague. I feel that that ought to happen. I certainly will not quote at him the savage words of Cromwell, but perhaps some of the words of Browning might be appropriate in his poem on "The Lost Leader", in which he wrote:

... Let him never come back to us!
There would be doubt, hesitation and pain.
Forced praise on our part – the glimmer of twilight,
Never glad confident morning again!

"Never glad confident morning again!" – so I hope that the change will not be too long delayed.' Birch was right. A few months later Macmillan was out of office; a year later, so was the government.

In November 1983, on the 20th anniversary of President Kennedy's assassination, Lord Harlech, former British Ambassador in Washington, paid tribute thus in *The Observer* Magazine: 'Since 1963 the world has seemed a bleaker place, and for me and I suspect millions of my contemporaries he remains the lost leader – "Never glad confident morning again".' Harlech may have wanted to evoke a leader who had been lost to the world, but surely it was a mistake to quote a *criticism* of one?

Also in November 1983, in *The Observer*, Paul Johnson wrote an attack (which he later appeared to regret) on Margaret Thatcher: 'Her courage and sound instincts made her formidable. But if her judgement can no longer be trusted, what is left? A very ordinary woman, occupying a position where ordinary virtues are not enough. For me, I fear it can never be "glad confident morning again".'

Still at it in 1988 was Shirley Williams. When part of the SDP united with the Liberals, she used the words about David Owen, the SDP's once and future leader.

1   What of soul was left, I wonder,
    When the kissing had to stop?

'A Toccata at Galuppi's' (1855). Hence, *When the Kissing Had to Stop* (1960) by Constantine FitzGibbon, about a Russian takeover of Britain.

2   Ah, did you once see Shelley plain,
    And did he stop and speak to you
    And did you speak to him again?
    How strange it seems, and new!

The first line of 'Memorabilia' (1855) is often misquoted as '*And* did you once see Shelley plain?' A man called Stubbs wrote the following parody:

> And did you once find Browning plain?
> And did he really seem quite clear?
> And did you read the book again?
> How strange it seems, and queer.

Beau BRUMMELL   English dandy (1778–1840)

3   Tell me, Alvanley, who is your fat friend?

A famous question to Lord Alvanley about the Prince Regent. Brummell, almost a dandy by profession, had fallen out with the Prince of Wales. He is said to have annoyed the Prince by ridiculing his mistress and also by saying once to his royal guest at dinner, 'Wales, ring the bell, will you?' When they met in London in July 1813, the Prince cut Brummell but greeted his companion. As the Prince walked off, Brummell put his question in ringing tones. Quoted in Captain Jesse, *Life of George Brummell* (1844).

The nicely alliterative phrase 'fat friend' occurs as early as Shakespeare, *The Comedy of Errors* (V.i.414): 'There is a fat friend at your master's house.' But in the novel *Handley Cross* (1843) by R.S. Surtees there is: 'When at length *our fat friend* got his horse and his hounds ... together again'; and in Anthony Trollope's *Castle Richmond* (1860): 'Is it not possible that one should have one more game of rounders? Quite impossible, *my fat friend*.' In 1972, there was a play by Charles Laurence called *My Fat Friend*. The play was about a fat girl and her experiences when she lost weight (it was originally going to be called *The Fat Dress*).

William Jennings BRYAN   American Democratic politician (1860–1925)

4   We will answer their demand for a gold standard by saying to them: You shall not press down upon the brow of labour this crown of thorns. You shall not crucify mankind upon a cross of gold.

Speech to the Democratic Convention on 8 July 1896. One of the most notable examples of American oratory, the 'Cross of Gold' speech, as it became known, contained an impassioned attack on supporters of the gold standard (Bryan championed a looser monetary policy based on silver). Bryan had said virtually the same in a speech to the House of Representatives on 22 December 1894. He won the nomination and fought the Presidential election against William J. McKinley, who supported the gold standard. Bryan lost. The US formally went on to the gold standard in March 1900, under McKinley. Somerset Maugham wrote in 1941 – included in *A Writer's Notebook* (1949): 'Democracy seldom had a ruder shock than when a phrase – you shall not crucify mankind upon a cross of gold – nearly put an ignorant and conceited fool in the White House.'

A 'Cross of Gold'-type speech is sometimes called for when a politician (such as Edward Kennedy in 1980) is required to sweep a Convention with his eloquence. See also HOOVER 243:9.

John BUCHAN (later Lord Tweedsmuir)   British politician and writer (1875–1940)

5   Tommy in such a situation was a tower of strength, for, whatever his failings in politics, I knew no one I would rather have with me to go tiger-shooting.

The Power-House, Chap. 4 (1916). Compare HEALY 231:5.

6   *The Courts of the Morning.*

Title of an adventure novel (1929) – a translation of *Los Patios de la Mañana*, a geographical hill feature in the fictitious South American republic of Olifa, where the book is set: 'In the Courts of the Morning there was still peace.

The brooding heats, the dust-storms, the steaming deluges of the lowlands were unknown. The air was that of a tonic and gracious autumn slowly moving to the renewal of spring.' Whether the name has anywhere been given to actual hills, is not known.

1 An atheist is a man who has no invisible means of support.

'Memory Hold the Door' (1940). Quoted in H.E. Fosdick, *On Being a Real Person* (1943) – not said *by* Fosdick as claimed by *PDMQ* (1971).

Richard BUCKLE English ballet critic (1916–2001)

2 John Lennon, Paul McCartney and George Harrison are the greatest composers since Beethoven, with Paul McCartney way out in front.

On The Beatles. Review in *The Sunday Times* (29 December 1963). Compare MANN 309:5; PALMER 351:5.

Ivor BULMER-THOMAS (formerly Ivor Thomas)
British Labour, then Conservative, MP (1905–93)

3 If ever he [Harold Wilson] went to school without any boots it was because he was too big for them.

Thomas made this jibe in a speech at the Conservative Party Conference (12 October 1949) – a remark often wrongly ascribed to Harold Macmillan. It followed a press dispute involving Wilson the previous year – see WILSON 499:5.

Edward BULWER-LYTTON (1st Baron Lytton)
English novelist and politician (1803–73)

4 The pen is mightier than the sword.

According to a piece in the London *Evening Standard* Diary following the Gorbachev–Reagan summit in November 1987, Parker Pens broke new ground by placing an advertisement in the *Moscow News* to draw attention to the fact that the treaty had been signed with one of its fountain pens. The advertisement's Russian slogan, translated directly, was, 'What is written with the pen will not be chopped up with an axe', which the *Standard* thought was the equivalent of 'The pen is mightier than the sword.'

Unfortunately, the *Standard* announced that 'The pen is ... ' was the most famous maxim attributed to Cardinal Richelieu. But no. That was merely a line said by Richelieu in Edward Bulwer-Lytton's play *Richelieu*, Act 2, Sc. 2 (1839):

Beneath the rule of men entirely great,
The pen is mightier than the sword.

– which is not quite the same as Richelieu himself having originated it. As for the idea, it was not, of course, Bulwer-

Lytton's either. *CODP* finds several earlier attempts at expressing it, to which one might add this 'corollary' from Shakespeare's *Hamlet*, II.ii.344: 'Many wearing rapiers are afraid of goose-quills.' Cervantes, *Don Quixote* (Pt 1, Bk 4, Chap. 10), has, in Motteux's translation: 'Let none presume to tell me that the pen is preferable to the sword.' The saying has also been ascribed to Abu Thammam, an Arab poet during the Abbasid era, about 150 years after the time of the Prophet Mohammed. It was apparently part of a poem praising the Khalifah after the capture of Amuriah.

See also SCHULTZ 396:2.

Alfred BUNN English theatrical manager and librettist (?1796–1860)

5 I dreamt I dwelt in marble halls
With vassals and serfs at my side,
And of all who assembled within those walls
That I was the hope and the pride.

Song, 'The Gypsy Girl's Dream' from *The Bohemian Girl*, Act 2 (1843), with music by Michael Balfe. Arline, daughter of the Count, sings it to Thaddeus, 'a proscribed Pole'. The Balfe–Bunn work has been described as the most popular British opera of the 19th century. This song was parodied by Lewis Carroll in *Lays of Mystery, Imagination, and Humour* (1855): 'I dreamt I dwelt in marble halls, / And each damp thing that creeps and crawls / Went wobble-wobble on the walls.' A painting presumably by George Belcher, who became ARA in 1931 and RA in 1945, entitled *I Dreamt I Dwelt in Marble Halls*, was hung in the Royal Academy, London, possibly in the late 1930s.

Henry Cuyler BUNNER American humorous writer (1855–96)

6 Shake was a dramatist of note;
He lived by writing things to quote.

Henry Cuyler Bunner, American humorous writer (1855–96). Said to be in 'Shake, Mulleary and Go-ethe' (untraced). Quoted (in prose form) in *The Treasury of Humorous Quotations*, eds Esar & Bentley (1951).

John BUNYAN English writer and preacher (1628–88)

7 It beareth the name of Vanity-Fair, because the town where 'tis kept, is lighter than vanity.

The Pilgrim's Progress, Pt 1 (1684). Hence, *Vanity Fair*, title of the novel (1847–8) by William Thackeray. John Sutherland in his introduction to the World's Classics edition says of Thackeray's title that it, 'came upon him unawares in the middle of the night'. He 'jumped out of bed and ran three times round his room, uttering as he went, "Vanity Fair, Vanity Fair, Vanity Fair."' Before this, he had referred to the book as *Novel Without a Hero* and *Pen and Pencil Sketches of English Society* – both of which survive as sub-titles in the final version. *Vanity Fair* has also been used as the title of magazines, notably the one published in New York from 1914 to 1936.

1 **A man that could look no way but downwards, with a muckrake in his hand.**

From the same work, Pt 2. 'In *Pilgrim's Progress*, the Man with the Muck-Rake is set forth as the example of him whose vision is fixed on carnal instead of on spiritual things. Yet he also typifies the man who in this life consistently refuses to see aught that is lofty, and fixes his eyes only on that which is vile and debasing.' So said President Theodore Roosevelt in a speech (14 April 1906). This led to the term 'muckraker' being applied to investigative journalists who seek out scandals, especially about public figures.

2 **So he passed over, and the trumpets sounded for him on the other side.**

From the same part. Referring to 'Mr Valiant-for-Truth'. Hence, *The Sound of Trumpets*, title of a novel (1998) by John Mortimer.

Winston BURDETT American journalist

3 **I don't want to be quoted, and don't quote me that I don't want to be quoted.**

Burdett was a CBS news correspondent, quoted thus in Barbara Rowes, *The Book of Quotes* (1979). A circumspect journalist when on the receiving end of his colleagues' attentions.

Anthony BURGESS English novelist and critic (1917–93)

4 **Who ever heard of a clockwork orange? ... The attempt to impose upon man, a creature of growth and capable of sweetness, to ooze juicily at the last round the bearded lips of God, to attempt to impose, I say, laws and conditions appropriate to a mechanical creation, against this I raise my sword-pen.**

A Clockwork Orange (1962; film UK 1971). This passage hints at the reason for the unusual title. The book describes an attempt to punish its criminal hero, Alex, by turning him into a 'mechanical man' through forms of therapy and brainwashing. But Burgess several times explained that he had taken the title from a cockney expression 'to be queer as a clockwork orange' (i.e., homosexual). This was not known

to many but has been in use since the mid-1950s, according to Paul Beale in *Partridge/Slang*. As such, its relevance to the story, which has no overt homosexual element, is debatable. Denis Conlon added: 'I can confirm that this phrase was used in the late 1950s and early sixties, but, as I recall, it then took the form of "*daft* as a clockwork orange". Prof. Conlon also commented: 'When he [Burgess] pointed out that "oran" is Malay for "man" he was probably correct from the point of view of Raj Malay, but on a more humble level the word for "man" was usually encountered under the form "orang" as in "orang-utan" or "orang asli". In that form there is an even closer connection with *Clockwork Orange*.'

1st Lord BURGHLEY (William Cecil) English courtier and politician (1520–98)

5 **What! all this for a song?**

Burghley or Burleigh (the name is variously spelt) was Lord High Treasurer to Elizabeth I. He exclaimed this when told by the Queen to pay Edmund Spenser the sum of £100 for some poems. Related by Thomas Birch in 'The Life of Mr Edmund Spenser' in a 1751 edition of *The Faerie Queene*. To get something 'for a song' now means that one has purchased it at very little cost.

See also SHERIDAN 429:11.

John William BURGON English poet and clergyman (1813–88)

6 **Match me such marvel, save in Eastern clime, – A rose-red city – 'half as old as Time'!**

This famous couplet from Burgon's poem 'Petra' (1845) palpably contains a quotation. It comes from the epilogue to the poem *Italy* (1838) by Samuel Rogers: 'By many a temple half as old as time.' Compare the parody contained in the travelogue sketch 'Balham – Gateway to the South', written by Frank Muir and Denis Norden in 1948 for a BBC Third Programme comedy show called *Third Division*:

> Broadbosomed, bold, becalm'd, benign
> Lies Balham foursquare on the Northern Line.
> Matched by no marvel save in Eastern scene,
> A rose-red city half as gold as green.

(Golders Green is a London suburb.) This was re-recorded by Peter Sellers on his album *The Best of Sellers* (1959).

Edmund BURKE Irish-born statesman and philosopher (1729–97)

7 **Truth is stranger than fiction.**

Pearson (1937) points out that if quoting Burke's *On Conciliation with America* (1775) this should properly be

'Fiction lags after truth.' By the time of Byron's *Don Juan*, Canto 14, St. 101 (1819–24), the saying was in the form: ''Tis strange, but true; for truth is always strange – / Stranger than fiction.' By the mid-19th century, the version 'Fact is stranger than fiction' had also emerged.

1 The people are the masters.

Speech, House of Commons (11 February 1780). Compare SHAWCROSS 427:7.

2 The age of chivalry is past.

Should be 'The age of chivalry is gone', if alluding to Burke's *Reflections on the Revolution in France* (1790). The misquotation is probably caused by confusion with the proverb 'The age of miracles is past', which was current by 1602.

3 The only thing necessary for the triumph of evil is for good men to do nothing.

So Burke said, or at least is often quoted as having done. *Bartlett* (1968) cited it in a letter from Burke to William Smith (9 January 1795), but on checking found that this did not exist. In his book *On Language* (1980), William Safire describes his unavailing attempts to find a proper source. In the House of Commons on 23 April 1770 Burke said, 'When bad men combine, the good must associate; else they will fall one by one, an unpitied sacrifice in a contemptible struggle' – which seems be heading somewhere in the right direction and is also to be found in *Thoughts on the Cause of the Present Discontents* (1770). But, for the moment, we have here another of those quotations which arrive apparently from nowhere, and get quoted and re-quoted without justification. On the other hand, it is fair to assume that Burke would not have wished to disown it. Compare what John Stuart Mill said later in 'On Education', his inaugural address on being installed as Rector of St Andrews University, Scotland (1 February 1867): 'Bad men need nothing more to compass their ends than that good men should look on and do nothing.'

4 The great unwashed.

Meaning 'working-class people, the lower orders', this term is said (by *Safire*, 1978) to have been used originally by Burke (though untraced), and has also been attributed to Lord Brougham, perhaps echoing Shakespeare's reference to 'another lean unwash'd artificer' in *King John*, IV.ii.201 (1596). Bulwer-Lytton in *Paul Clifford* (1830) uses the full phrase. Thackeray has it in *Pendennis* (1848–50). Thomas Carlyle in his *History of the French Revolution* (1837) has: 'Man has set man against man, Washed against unwashed.'

5 Somebody has said, that a king may make a nobleman but he cannot make a gentleman.

Letter to William Smith (29 January 1795). See also WILSON 502:3.

Johnny BURKE American songwriter (1908–64)

6 Every time it rains, it rains
Pennies from heaven.

'Pennies from Heaven' (1937). Music by Arthur Johnston. Hence, *Pennies From Heaven*, title of a TV drama series by Dennis Potter (1978; film US 1981).

George BURNS American comedian (1896–1996)

7 *Burns*: Say goodnight, Gracie.
Allen: Goodnight, Gracie.

Possibly apocryphal exchange between Burns and his wife (Gracie Allen) – either in their radio shows or their TV series, *The George Burns and Gracie Allen Show* (1950–8). Burns wrote in *Gracie: A Love Story*, Chap. 5 (1988): 'And my line, "Say good night, Gracie," to which she replied "Good night," was certainly one of the most famous catchphrases in entertainment history. It's a show business myth that Gracie replied to my request to "Say good night, Gracie," by saying, "Good night, Gracie." In fact, that's probably one of the most misquoted lines in theater history. Maybe she said it once, but I don't remember it. She simply said, "Good night." There were many reasons for that, the main one was that I just never thought of "Good night, Gracie." And now that I've thought of it, from now on she will have said it.'

8 The secret of acting is sincerity – and if you can fake that, you've got it made.

Usually attributed to Burns – as, for example, in Michael York, *Travelling Player* (1991). Fred Metcalf in *The Penguin Dictionary of Modern Humorous Quotations* (1987) has Burns saying, rather: 'Acting is about honesty. If you can fake that, you've got it made.' However, Kingsley Amis in a devastating piece about Leo Rosten in his *Memoirs* (1991) has the humorist relating 'at some stage in the 1970s' how he had given a Commencement address including the line: 'Sincerity. If you can *fake that* ... you'll have the world at your feet.' So perhaps the saying was circulating even before Burns received the credit. Or perhaps Rosten took it from him? An advertisement in *Rolling Stone* in about 1982 offered a T-shirt with the slogan (anonymous): 'The secret of success is sincerity. Once you can fake that you've got it made.' Fred MacMurray was quoted in *Variety* (15 April 1987): 'I once asked Barbara Stanwyck the secret of acting. She said: "Just be truthful – and if you can fake that, you've got it made."'

Robert BURNS Scottish poet (1759–96)

1 Wee, sleekit, cow'rin', tim'rous beastie.

'To a Mouse' (1785) – 'on turning her up in her nest with the plough, November 1785.' Sleekit = sleek.

2 The best laid plans o' mice an' men
Gang aft a-gley.

From the same poem. Hence, *Of Mice and Men*, title of a novel (1937; film US 1939) by John Steinbeck. A-gley = off the right line, awry.

3 O wad some Pow'r the giftie gie us
To see oursels as others see us!
It wad frae mony a blunder free US
And foolish notion.

'To a Louse' (1786). Hence, the peculiar resonance of the phrase 'to see ourselves as others see us'.

4 Man's inhumanity to man
Makes countless thousands mourn.

'Man Was Made to Mourn' (1786), though the thought that lies behind it is, of course, a very old one. The first line provided John Arlott, the English journalist and radio cricket commentator (1914–91) with a bright comment on one occasion. At Lord's, a South African googly bowler named 'Tufty' Mann was tying a Middlesex tail-end batsman named George Mann into such knots that the crowd was reduced to laughter. When it occurred for the fourth time in a single over, Arlott, apparently without a moment's thought, reported, 'So what we are watching here is a clear case of Mann's inhumanity to Mann.' Reported in *The Daily Mail* (3 September 1980).

5 The Poetic Genius of my Country found me, as the prophetic bard Elijah did Elisha – at the *plough* – and threw her inspiring mantle over me. She bade me sing the loves, the joys, the rural scenes and rural pleasures of my natal Soil, in my native tongue. I tuned my wild, artless notes, as she inspired. She whispered me to come to this ancient metropolis of Caledonia, and lay my Songs under your honoured protection. I now obey her dictates ... I do not approach you, my Lords and Gentlemen, in the usual style of dedication, to thank you for past favours; that path is so hackneyed by prostituted Learning, that honest Rusticity is ashamed of it. Nor do I present this Address with the venal soul of a servile Author, looking for a continuation of those favours: I was bred to the Plough, and am independent ...

'To the Noblemen and Gentlemen of the Caledonian Hunt', prefacing the 1787 'Edinburgh' edition of his poems. The Caledonian Hunt was an association of noblemen and country gentlemen who shared a keen interest in field sports, races, balls and social assemblies. This has been described as 'the start of the Burns myth'. It has also been written that Burns said this, obsequiously, only to please the Hunt, who topped the subscribers' list.

A large, seated statue of Burns with the following version of the text below it is to be found in Victoria Embankment Gardens, London (a city he never visited): 'The Poetic Genius of my Country found me at the Plough and threw her inspiring Mantle over me. She bade me sing the Loves, the Joys, the Rural Scenes and Rural Pleasures of my Native Soil, in my Native Tongue. I tuned my Wild, Artless Notes as She inspired.'

6 O whistle, an' I'll come to you, my lad.

From the poem of that title (?1788). Compare FLETCHER 197:6. 'Oh, Whistle and I'll Come To You My Lad' became the title of a short story in *Ghost Stories of an Antiquary* (1904) by M.R. James, in which the wind is 'whistled up'.

7 Should auld acquaintance be forgot,
And never brought to mind?
Should auld acquaintance be forgot,
And auld lang syne.

CHORUS
For auld lang syne, my jo,
For auld lang syne,
We'll tak a cup o' kindness yet
For auld lang syne.

The song 'Auld Lang Syne' is traditionally massacred and half-remembered, if remembered at all, at farewell ceremonies and on New Year's Eve. It is not just inebriation that leads Sassenachs into gibbering incomprehensibility – there is widespread confusion as to what the words mean, how they should be pronounced and – indeed – what the correct words are.

In fact, Burns adapted 'Auld Lang Syne' from 'an old man's singing' in 1788. The title, first line and refrain had all appeared before as the work of other poets, mostly by the early 18th century. Nevertheless, what Burns put together is now the accepted version. 'For *the sake of* auld lang syne' should *not* be substituted at the end of verse and chorus. 'Auld lang syne' means, literally, 'old long since' i.e. 'long ago'. Hence, 'syne' should be pronounced with an 's' sound and not as 'zyne'. 'My jo' is a term of endearment – 'my dear'.

1 We twa hae run about the braes,
And pou'd the gowans fine;
But we've wandered mony a weary fit,
Sin' auld lang syne.

In the same poem. A 'gowan' is a daisy (Scots word recorded since the 16th century), indeed any white or yellow field flower. 'Pluck' would be more widely understood than 'pou' (the Scots version of 'pull'), which explains why P.G. Wodehouse uses it in the several allusions to 'pluck the gowans fine' in the Jeeves books. Sometimes, in any case, 'pu't' or 'pu'd the gowans fine' is printed in versions of the poem.

Incidentally, Wilkins Micawber quotes the line in Dickens, *David Copperfield*, Chap. 28 – adding, 'I am not exactly aware ... what gowans may be, but I have no doubt that Copperfield and myself would frequently have taken a pull at them, had it been feasible.'

2 Ae fond kiss, and then we sever;
Ae fareweel, and then for ever!

'Ae Fond Kiss' (1792). 'Ae' = 'one'. Hence, the title of a film, *Ae Fond Kiss* (UK 2004), about a love affair between a Muslim Pakistani and a Scots Roman Catholic in Glasgow.

3 A Workhouse! ah, that sound awakes my woes,
And pillows on the thorn my racked repose!
In durance vile here must I wake and weep,
And all my frowzy couch in sorrow steep.

'Epistle from Esopus to Maria' (1795–6). From P.G. Wodehouse, *The Code of the Woosters* (1938): 'It was nice to feel that I had got my bedroom to myself for a few minutes, but against that you had to put the fact that I was in what is known as durance vile and not likely to get out of it.' 'In durance vile' also has a quasi-legal meaning – 'in awful confinement'.

4 Scots, wha hae wi' Wallace bled,
Scots, wham Bruce has aften led,
Welcome to your gory bed,
Or to victorie.

'Scots, Wha Hae' is the title given to, and a phrase from the first line of, a battle song. It is sometimes subtitled 'Robert Bruce's March to Bannockburn' or 'Robert Bruce's Address to his army, before the battle of Bannockburn', and was published in 1799. 'Wha hae' is not an exclamation ('Scots wu-hey!') but simply means 'who have'. 'Wham' in the next line means 'whom'.

A further comment, from James Murray (creator of *OED*) in 1912: 'Even Burns thought that Scotch was defiled by "bad grammar" and tried to conform his Scotch to

English grammar! Transforming e.g. the Scotch "*Scots 'at hae*" to *Scots wha hae* which no sober Scotch man in his senses ever naturally said.'

5 John, don't let the awkward squad fire over me.

Burns's dying words are said to have been these, presumably referring to his fear that literary opponents might metaphorically fire a volley of respect, as soldiers sometimes do, over a new grave – in their case by burbling inept and embarrassing paeans. Reported in A. Cunningham, *The Works of Robert Burns; with his Life* (1834).

As for the phrase 'awkward squad' on its own, Sloppy in *Our Mutual Friend* (1864–5) is described by Charles Dickens as 'Full-Private Number One in the Awkward Squad of the rank and file of life'. Of military origin and used to denote a difficult, uncooperative person, the phrase originally referred to a squad that consisted of raw recruits and older hands who were put in it for punishment, but seems to have been used in other contexts for quite some time.

See also SPECTOR 438:3.

Edgar Rice BURROUGHS American author (1875–1950)

6 Me Tarzan, you Jane.

A box-office sensation of 1932 was the first sound Tarzan film, *Tarzan the Ape Man*. It spawned a long-running series and starred Johnny Weismuller, an ex-US swimming champion, as Tarzan, and Maureen O'Sullivan as Jane. At one point the ape man whisks Jane away to his tree-top abode and indulges in some elementary conversation with her. Thumping his chest, he says, 'Tarzan!'; pointing at her, he says, 'Jane!' So, in fact, he does not say the catchphrase commonly associated with him, though Weissmuller did use the words in an interview for *Photoplay Magazine* (June 1932) – 'I didn't have to act in "Tarzan, the Ape Man" – just said, "Me Tarzan, you Jane"' – so it is not surprising the misquotation arose.

Interestingly, this great moment of movie dialogue appears to have been 'written' by the British playwright and actor Ivor Novello. In the original novel, *Tarzan of the Apes* (1914) by Edgar Rice Burroughs, the line does not occur – whatever it says in *PDMQ* (1980), not least because, in the jungle, Tarzan and Jane are able to communicate only by writing notes to each other.

Benjamin Hapgood BURT American songwriter (1880–1950)

7 One evening in October, when I was one-third sober,
An' taking home a 'load' with manly pride;

My poor feet began to stutter, so I lay down in
   the gutter,
And a pig came up an' lay down by my side;
Then we sang 'It's all fair weather when good
   fellows get together,'
Till a lady passing by was heard to say:
'You can tell a man who "boozes" by the
   company he chooses'
And the pig got up and slowly walked away.

Song, 'The Pig Got Up and Slowly Walked Away' (1896),
to music by F.V. Bowers. It is yet to be confirmed whether
Burt originated these lines or whether they were based on
something by another hand. This is the version as sung by
Frank Crumit on disc (in 1934). The *Oxford Book of Comic
Verse* (1995) has a version by Anonymous that is substantially the one in *More Comic and Curious Verse* (1956):

   It was an evening in November,
   As I very well remember,
   I was strolling down the street in drunken pride.
   But my knees were all a-flutter,
   And I landed in the gutter
   And a pig came up and lay down by my side.

   Yes, I lay there in the gutter
   Thinking thoughts I could not utter,
   When a colleen passing by did softly say
   'You can tell a man who boozes
   By the company he chooses' –
   And the pig got up and slowly walked away.

While the *Oxford Book of American Light Verse* (1979) has
yet another version:

   It was early last December,
   As near as I remember,
   I was walking down the street in tipsy pride;
   No one was I disturbing
   As I lay down by the curbing,
   And a pig came up and lay down by my side.

   As I lay there in the gutter
   Thinking thoughts I shall not utter,
   A lady passing by was heard to say:
   'You can tell a man who boozes
   By the company he chooses';
   And the pig got up and slowly walked away.

(Sir) Richard BURTON English explorer and writer (1821–90)

1 Prostitutes for pleasure, concubines for service,
wives for breeding ... A melon for ecstasy.

When the late Pearl Binder (Lady Elwyn-Jones) appeared,
with octogenarian aplomb, on BBC Radio *Quote ... Unquote*

in 1984, she chose as a favourite quotation what she claimed
Burton had borrowed from Demosthenes: 'Prostitutes for
pleasure, concubines for service, wives for breeding.' Alan
Brien, who was in attendance, chimed in with, 'And a melon
for ecstasy.'

The Demosthenes remains unconfirmed. What slightly
off-colour, old joke did we have here? *A Melon for Ecstasy*
was the title of a novel (1971) by John Fortune and John
Wells, and presumably alluded to the same core remark.
Fortune has subsequently described it as 'a Turkish proverb'.
Apparently, the novelist John Masters ascribed to a 'Pathan
tribesman' the saying 'A woman for duty, a boy for pleasure, a goat for ecstasy', whereas Stephen Fry in *Paperweight*
(1992) credits this to the Greeks. At the same time, 'A
woman for duty, a boy for pleasure, a melon for ecstasy'
has been described as 'an old Arab saying'. Compare also
John Gay, 'The Toilette' (1716): 'A miss for pleasure, and a
wife for breed.'

Robert BURTON English clergyman and writer (1577–1640)

2 As if they had heard that enchanted horn of
Astolpho, that English duke in Ariosto, which
never sounded but all his auditors were mad, and
for fear ready to make away [with] themselves ...
they are a company of giddy-heads, afternoon men.

The Anatomy of Melancholy (1621). This is the final part of the
quotation from 'Democritus to the Reader' given by Anthony
Powell as the epigraph to his novel with the title *Afternoon
Men* (1931). The phrase also occurs earlier in 'Democritus to
the Reader' in the sentence, 'Beroaldus will have drunkards, afternoon men, and such as more than ordinarily
delight in drink, to be mad.'

See also ARNOLD 40:7.

George BUSH American Republican 41st President (1924–)

3 Oh, the vision thing.

As Bush debated with other potential Republican candidates for the presidency, he said: 'On vision – you have to
have a vision. Mine is that education should be the No. 1
thing' – *The Washington Post* (15 January 1988). But, shortly
before this, he had coined the phrase 'vision thing', unin-
tentionally characterizing his own lack of an overarching
view of what he might do with the presidency. His very use
of the word 'thing' seemed to confirm his pragmatic, tongue-
tied, earthbound stance. *Time* Magazine had picked up the
phrase by 27 January 1987 – which may or may not be correct. In 1993 *The Vision Thing* became the title of a BBC TV

play by Mark Lawson about a British Prime Minister who does have visions and is consequently eased out of office.

1 **My opponent won't rule out raising taxes, but I will. And the Congress will push me to raise taxes, and I'll say no, and they'll push again. And I'll say to them, read my lips, no new taxes.**

Although popularized by Bush in his speech accepting the Republican nomination at New Orleans on 18 August 1988, the expression 'read my lips' was not new. According to William Safire in an article in *The New York Times* Magazine (September 1988), the phrase is rooted in 1970s rock music (despite there being a song with the title copyrighted by Joe Greene in 1957). The British actor/singer Tim Curry used the phrase as the title of an album of songs in 1978. Curry said he took it from an Italian-American recording engineer who used it to mean, 'Listen and listen very hard, because I want you to hear what I've got to say.' Subsequently, several lyricists in the 1980s used the phrase for song titles. A football coach with the Chicago Bears became nicknamed Mike 'Read My Lips' Ditka, and there has been a thoroughbred race horse so named. Safire cites a number of American politicians who used the phrase, also in the 1980s. In the film *Breathless* (1983), a scrap dealer says it to the Richard Gere character, encouraging him to believe that there is no money in the yard worth taking.

Needless to say, Bush *did* have to raise taxes in due course.

2 **I will keep America moving forward, always forward – for a better America, for an endless enduring dream and a thousand points of light.**

From the same acceptance speech, and used many times throughout the 1988 campaign, the words 'thousand points of light' were put on his lips by speechwriter Peggy Noonan. But what did they mean? The phrase was said to symbolize individual endeavour and voluntary charity efforts across the country (later, in June 1989, President Bush announced details of his 'Points of Light Programme', costing $25 million, to encourage a voluntary crusade to fight poverty, drugs and homelessness). But Bush never seemed too sure what he was saying. On one occasion, he called it 'one thousand points of life'. Herblock, the cartoonist, drew a drunk at a bar pledging his vote to Bush because he had promised '1000 pints of Lite'. Perhaps it was supposed to echo Shakespeare, *The Merchant of Venice*, V.i.90 (1596): 'How far that little candle throws his beams! / So shines a good deed in a naughty world.' Light often comes in thousands: 'It was but for an instant that I seemed to struggle with a thousand mill-weirs and a thousand flashes of light' – Charles Dickens, *Great Expectations*, Chap. 54 (1860–1). In *Conducted*

Tour (1981), Bernard Levin describes an English pantomime when parents were asked to take out matches and cigarette lighters – 'the vast shell of the Coliseum's auditorium was alive with a thousand tiny points of light'.

In her memoir *What I Saw at the Revolution* (1990), Noonan makes mention of several earlier uses of the phrase or parts of it. She does not appear to have been aware of C.S. Lewis's *The Magician's Nephew* (1955): 'One moment there had been nothing but darkness, next moment a thousand points of light leaped out ...', or of Thomas Wolfe's *The Web and the Rock* (1939): 'Instantly he could see the town below now, coiling in a thousand fumes of homely smoke, now winking into a thousand points of friendly light its glorious small design', though she had read it as a teenager. A speech by a turn-of-the-century engineer was also found urging the electrification of Venice so that it would be filled with 'a thousand points of light'.

Oddly, Noonan does not draw attention to one possible point of inspiration. Having admitted earlier that she is a fan of Auden's poem 'September 1, 1939' – see AUDEN 44:1 – she overlooks the line, 'Ironic points of light'.

See also WELLS 488:4.

George W. BUSH American Republican 43rd President (1946–)

3 **Either you are with us, or you are with the terrorists.**

Address to joint session of Congress (20 September 2001). Sometimes summarized as 'You're either with us or against us in the fight against terror' and known as 'the Bush doctrine'. This had, however, been said by others in the administration within days of the terrorist attacks on 11 September. By early 2002 Bush was saying, 'Many nations are realizing [that] when we say you're either with us or against us, we mean it.' Compare STALIN 440:10.

4 **The battle has been joined on many fronts. We will not tire and we will not fail. The United States did not ask for this conflict but we will win it.**

Broadcast address (7 October 2001). Compare CHURCHILL 136:2.

5 **States like these ... constitute an axis of evil, arming to threaten the peace of this world.**

State of the Union address (29 January 2002). Referring to Iraq, Iran and North Korea. The rhetorical phrase was half-coined by speechwriter David Frum who, attempting to imitate Franklin D. Roosevelt's 'date which will live in infamy', 386:7, came up with 'axis of hatred', but this was altered by the chief speechwriter Michael Gerson. The coinage was criticized for seeming to say that the three countries were somehow colluding in terrorism whereas they did not have anything to do with each other. In particular it exacerbated relations between the US and North Korea.

R.A. BUTLER (later Lord Butler) English Conservative politician (1902–82)

1 The best Prime Minister we have.

In December 1955, Butler, passed over (not for the last time) for the Conservative Party leadership, was confronted by a Press Association reporter just as he was about to board an aircraft at London Airport. Criticism was growing over the performance of Anthony Eden, the Prime Minister selected in preference to him. The reporter asked, 'Mr Butler, would you say that this is the best Prime Minister we have?' Butler's 'hurried assent' to this 'well-meant but meaningless proposition' was converted into the above statement. 'I do not think it did Anthony any good. It did not do me any good either' – *The Art of the Possible* (1971). In due course, Butler himself became known as 'the best Prime Minister we *never* had'.

2 Politics is the art of the possible.

Butler's memoirs entitled *The Art of the Possible* (1971) caused him to be credited with this view. However, in the preface to the paperback edition (1973) he pointed out that the thought appeared first to have been advanced in modern times by Bismarck in 1866–7 (in conversation with Meyer von Waldeck: '*Die Politik ist keine exakte Wissenschaft, wie viele der Herren Professoren sich einbilden, sondern eine Kunst* [Politics is not a science, as many professors declare, but an art]'). If he said precisely the phrase as used by Butler, it would have been: '*Die Politik ist die Lehr vom Möglichen.*' Others who had touched on the idea included Cavour, Salvador de Madriaga, Pindar and Camus. To these might be added J.K. Galbraith's rebuttal: 'Politics is not the art of the possible. It consists in choosing between the disastrous and the unpalatable' – letter to President Kennedy (March 1962), quoted in *Ambassador's Journal* (1969).

3 I think the Prime Minister has to be a butcher, and know the joints. That is perhaps where I have been not quite competent in knowing the ways that you cut up a carcass.

Interviewed on BBC TV by Kenneth Harris – transcript in *The Listener* (28 June 1966). Possibly alluding to GLADSTONE 214:4.

Samuel BUTLER English author (1835–1902)

4 Dusty, cobweb-covered, maimed, and set at naught, Beauty crieth in an attic, and no man regardeth. O God! O Montreal!

'Psalm of Montreal' (1878). This poem arose from an incident in which a discobolus (a statue of a discus-thrower) in the Montreal Museum of Natural History was banished from public view. When asked why, a custodian replied that such things were 'rather vulgar'. Butler concluded that Montreal's inhabitants were as yet too busy with commerce to care greatly about the masterpieces of old Greek art.

5 It was very good of God to let Carlyle and Mrs Carlyle marry one another and so make only two people miserable instead of four, besides being very amusing.

Letter to Miss E.M.A. Savage (21 November 1884). As part of their long correspondence, Miss Savage had written to Butler on 18 November: 'Are you not glad that Mr and Mrs Carlyle were married to one another, and not to other people? They certainly were justly formed to meet by nature.' In my very first quotation book I mistakenly attributed to Tennyson a view on the marriage of Thomas and Jane Carlyle. When it was suggested that the marriage had been a mistake – because with anyone but each other they might have been perfectly happy – I said that Tennyson had opined: 'I totally disagree with you. By any other arrangement *four* people would have been unhappy instead of *two*.' The remark should have been credited to Butler. My inaccurate version was taken up by *The Faber Book of Anecdotes* (1985). However, I now know why I made the misattribution. In *The Autobiography of Margot Asquith* (1936) she recounts a meeting with Tennyson at which they discussed the Carlyles. She said, 'With anyone but each other, they might have been perfectly happy.' He said: 'I totally disagree with you. By any other arrangement four people would have been unhappy instead of two.' This exchange occurred in 1885 (if Margot Asquith was not inventing the whole episode), which is very close to the year of Butler's letter. In the end, perhaps one might allow that both men independently had the same bright view.

6 It is bad enough to see one's own good things fathered on other people, but it is worse to have other people's rubbish fathered upon oneself.

Notebooks (in about 1890). The perils of being worthy of quotation.

1 Greater luck hath no man than this, that he lay down his wife at the right moment.

In the same book. Compare BIBLE 83:5.

2 'Tis better to have lost than never to have lost at all.

The Way of All Flesh, Chap. 77 (1903). Compare A.H. Clough, 'Peschiera' (1854): ''Tis better to have fought and lost, / Than never to have fought at all.' Compare TENNYSON 455:5.

3 Have you brought the cheque book, Alfred?

Butler, though dying, was engaged in the purchase of the freehold of a house in Hampstead. To Alfred Emery Cathie, his clerk, 'servant and friend', he said, 'Have you brought the cheque book, Alfred?' Butler took off his spectacles and put them down on the table. 'I don't want them any more,' he said, his head fell back, and he died – source: Philip Henderson, *Samuel Butler: the Incarnate Bachelor* (1953.)

See also BELL 59:2; FORSTER 199:3.

Lord BYRON English poet (1788–1824)

4 A man must serve his time to every trade
Save censure – critics all are ready made.
Take hackneyed jokes from Miller, got by rote,
With just enough of learning to misquote.

English Bards and Scotch Reviewers, line 63 (1809). Joe Miller (1684–1738) lent his name (posthumously and unwittingly) to a book of old jokes compiled by John Mottley and called *Joe Miller's Jest-Book*. Accordingly, a 'Joe Miller' became the term for an old joke, as though it had come from the Mottley collection.

5 I awoke one morning and found myself famous.

On the success of the first two cantos of *Childe Harold* in 1812. Quoted in Thomas Moore, *The Letters and Journals of Lord Byron* (1830).

6 When one subtracts from life infancy (which is vegetation), – sleep, eating, and swilling – buttoning and unbuttoning – how much remains of downright existence? The summer of a dormouse.

Journal (7 December 1813). 'If I ever write an autobiography, Byron has found me the title' – Kenneth Tynan, letter of 17 November 1972 (also in his diary for the same date). Hence, *The Summer of a Dormouse*, the title of a novel (1967) by Monica Stirling, and also memoirs (2000) by John Mortimer. *ODQ* (1992) has 'all this buttoning and unbuttoning' from an anonymous '18th-century suicide note'.

7 I will keep no further journal ... to prevent me returning, like a dog, to the vomit of memory.

In the same work (19 April 1814). He did not, of course, keep to this. Compare: 'To write a diary every day is like returning to one's own vomit' – Enoch Powell, interview in *The Sunday Times* (6 November 1977). The image of a dog returning to its vomit is biblical in origin: see BIBLE 75:4 and 86:5 (Proverbs 26:11 and 2 Peter 2:22).

8 The Assyrian came down like the wolf on the fold.

'The Destruction of Sennacherib', St. 1 (1815). Byron based this poem on 2 Chronicles 32 and 2 Kings 19, where Sennacherib, King of Assyria, gets his comeuppance for besieging Jerusalem in this manner.

9 So, we'll go no more a-roving
So late into the night,
Though the heart be still as loving,
And the moon be still as bright.

Poem (written in 1817). The second line is often misquoted as 'so far into the night'. Byron appears to have imitated a song called 'The Jolly Beggar', which is attributed to King James V of Scotland: 'And we'll gang nae mair a roving / Sae late into the night / And we'll gang nae mair a roving, boys, / Let the moon shine ne'er so bright.'

10 There was a sound of revelry by night.

Childe Harold's Pilgrimage, Canto 3, St. 11 (1818). Referring to the Duchess of Richmond's ball in Brussels on the night before the Battle of Waterloo (1815) – or rather, as Lord Wavell points out in *Other Men's Flowers* (1944), on Thursday 15 June, which was on the eve of the battles of Ligny and Quatre Bras and three days before Waterloo.

11 On with the dance! let joy be unconfined;
No sleep till morn, when Youth and Pleasure meet
Tho chase the glowing hours with flying feet.

In the same work, Canto 3, St. 12. Hence, from *The Independent* (13 September 1996): 'Mr Kenyon will take a more relaxed attitude to the atmosphere of the last night [of the Proms] than his predecessor, who last year forbade "extraneous" noises. Mr Kenyon said: "I am a 'let joy be unconfined' man myself."'

12 Butchered to make a Roman holiday.

In the same work, Canto 4, St. 141. Mark Twain seems to think this is a cliché of travel writing – in *The Innocents Abroad*, Chap. 27 (1869). *Punch* (19 August 1882) has 'butchered to make a Spanish holiday'. Hence, somewhat inappropriately, *Roman Holiday*, the title of a film (US 1953) in which Audrey Hepburn plays a princess visiting Rome and falling for a reporter who interviews her.

1 Now Barabbas was a publisher.

The story has it that when John Murray, Byron's publisher, sent the poet a copy of the Bible in return for a favour, Byron sent it back with the words 'Now Barabbas was a robber' (St John 18:40, see BIBLE 83:7) altered to, 'Now Barabbas was a publisher ...' This story was included in Kazlitt Arvine's *Cyclopedia of Anecdotes of Literature and the Fine Arts*, published in Boston, Massachusetts, in 1851. In 1981, the then head of the firm, John G. (Jock) Murray, told me that those involved were in fact the poet Coleridge and *his* publishers, Longmans. But when I asked for evidence in 1988, he could only say that, 'I have satisfied myself that it was not Byron.' The copy of Byron's Bible which exists has no such comment in it. He also drew my attention to the fact that in Byron's day publishers were more usually called booksellers.

Mencken, on the other hand, gave Thomas Campbell (1777–1844) as the probable perpetrator, so did *Benham*, and so did Samuel Smiles in *A Publisher and his Friends: Memoir and Correspondence of the late John Murray*, Vol. 1, Chap. 14 (1891). Certainly, Campbell seems to have taken the required attitude. At a literary dinner he once toasted Napoleon with the words: 'We must not forget that he once shot a bookseller' – quoted by Lord Macaulay in his diary for 12 December 1848. Mark Twain recalled this in one of his letters: 'How often we recall, with regret, that Napoleon once shot at a magazine editor and missed him and killed a publisher. But we remember with charity, that his intentions were good.'

2 'Whom the gods love die young' was said of yore.

Don Juan, Canto 4, St. 12 (1819–24). Indeed, Menander the Greek and Plautus said it in times BC. *Whom the Gods Love* was the title of a film (UK 1936) about Mozart. Related to this saying is what Euripides and other classical authors put in the form: 'Whom the Gods wish to destroy, they first make mad.' Sophocles in *Antigone* (?450 BC) quotes as a proverb: 'Whom Zeus would destroy, he first makes mad.' Compare CONNOLLY 153:1.

3 There is a tide in the affairs of women,
Which, taken at the flood, leads – God knows where.

In the same work, Canto 6, St. 2. See SHAKESPEARE 412:14.

4 Now Hatred is by far the longest pleasure;
Men love in haste, but they detest at leisure.

In the same work, Canto 13, St. 6. Hence, the title of a novel *The Longest Pleasure* (1986) by Anne Mather.

5 Posterity will ne'er survey
A nobler grave than this.
Here lie the bones of Castlereagh.
Stop, Traveller ── .

'Epitaph' (1821). Byron wrote this epitaph on Viscount Castlereagh (1769–1822) apparently the year *before* the Foreign Secretary's death by suicide. Castlereagh is actually buried in Westminster Abbey and attracted the poet's enmity either because Byron supported Napoleon or on account of Castlereagh's assumed role in the Peterloo Massacre of 1819 (which also inspired SHELLEY 429:5). In any case, the statesman was singularly unpopular: it is said that a great cheer went up when his coffin was carried into Westminster Abbey.

See also BURKE 108:7.

C

Julius CAESAR Roman general and politician (?100–44BC)

1 Caesar's wife must be above suspicion.

It was Julius Caesar *himself* who said this of his wife Pompeia when he divorced her in 62BC. In North's translation of Plutarch's *Lives* – which is how the saying came into English in 1570 – Caesar is quoted thus: 'I will not, sayd he, that my wife be so much as suspected.' Pompeia was Caesar's second wife. According to Suetonius, in 61BC she took part in the women-only rites of the Feast of the Great Goddess. But it was rumoured that a profligate called Publius Clodius attended wearing women's clothes and that he had committed adultery with Pompeia. Caesar divorced Pompeia, and at the subsequent inquiry into the desecration, when asked why he had done so, he gave this response. He later married Calpurnia.

An example of the phrase in use occurs in Lord Chesterfield's letters (published 1774): 'Your moral character must be not only pure, but, like Caesar's wife, unsuspected.' This should not be confused with what a newly elected mayor – quoted by G.W.E. Russell in *Collections and Recollections* (1898) – once said. During his year of office, he said, he felt he should lay aside all his political prepossessions and be, like Caesar's wife, 'all things to all men'.

2 *Gallia est omnis divisa in partes tres* [Gaul as a whole is divided into three parts].

De Bello Gallico, Bk 1, Sect. 1. Hence the expression that something is 'divided into three parts, like Caesar's Gaul'. He goes on to be drily specific: '... one of which is inhabited by the Belgae, another by the Aquitani, and the third by the people who call themselves Celts and whom we call Gauls'.

3 *Iacta alea est* [The die is cast].

What Julius Caesar is supposed to have said when he crossed the Rubicon (a small stream on the east coast of northern Italy), marking the start of the war with Pompey (49BC). The stream marked the southern boundary of Cisalpine Gaul and crossing it meant the fateful decision had been made and there was no turning back. Hence, the expression, 'to cross the Rubicon'. The words were reported by Suetonius in *Lives of the Caesars*, and were originally spoken in Greek, not Latin. The expression has been known in English since at least 1634. Here 'die' is the singular of 'dice'.

4 *Veni, vidi, vici* [I came, I saw, I conquered].

According to Suetonius, *Lives of the Caesars*, this was an inscription displayed in Latin after Caesar's triumph over Pontus (a part of modern Turkey) in 47BC – a campaign that lasted only five days. 'This referred not to the events of the war ... but to the speed with which it had been won.' Plutarch states that it was written in a letter by Caesar, announcing the victory of Zela (in Asia Minor), which concluded the Pontic (Black Sea) campaign. In North's 1579 translation of Plutarch, it says: 'Julius Caesar fought a great battle with King Pharnaces and because he would advertise one of his friends of the suddenness of this victory, he only wrote three words unto Anicius at Rome: *Veni, Vidi, Vici*: to wit, I came, saw, and overcame. These three words ending all with like sound and letters in the Latin, have a certain short grace, more pleasant to the ear, than can well be expressed in any other tongue.' Shakespeare alludes to Caesar's 'thrasonical brag' in four plays, including *Love's Labour's Lost*, IV.i.68 (1592–3) and *As You Like It*, V.ii.30 (1598).

1 *Et tu, Brute?* [Even you, Brutus?]

Julius Caesar's supposed dying words to Brutus, on realizing that his old friend was one of his assassins in 44 BC, were made famous through Shakespeare's use of the Latin in the form, '*Et tu, Brute? – Then fall Caesar!*' in the play *Julius Caesar* (III.i.77). The Latin words are not found in any classical source, but they do occur in English drama just before Shakespeare. *The True Tragedie of Richard Duke of Yorke* (printed in 1595) has 'Et tu, Brute, wilt thou stab Caesar too?' The origin of the phrase lies probably in Suetonius's account of the assassination, in which Caesar is made to say in *Greek*, 'And thou, my son.' The 'son' has been taken literally – as, according to Suetonius, Caesar had had an intrigue with Brutus's mother and looked upon Brutus as his likely son.

Chips Channon wrote in his diary (7 April 1939): 'The Italians are occupying Albania ... "Et tu Benito?" – for Mussolini had only recently assured us that he had no territorial claims whatsoever on Albania.'

James CAGNEY American actor (1899–1986)

2 You dirty rat!

Although impersonators of James Cagney always have him saying 'You dirty rat!' it may be that he never said it like that himself. However, in Joan Wyndham's wartime diaries – *Love Lessons* (1985) – her entry for 1 October 1940 begins: 'Double bill at the Forum with Rupert. *Elizabeth and Essex*, and a gangster film where somebody actually *did* say "Stool on me would ya, ya doity rat!"' What film could this have been? Note her surprise that the line was uttered at all.

The nearest Cagney seems to have got to uttering the phrase with which he is most associated was in the films *Blonde Crazy* (1931), where he says, 'You dirty, double-crossing rat'; and *Taxi* (1931), where he says, 'Come out and take it, you dirty yellow-bellied rat, or I'll give it to you through the door.' In the Cagney film *Each Dawn I Die* (US 1939), Ed Pawley as Dale gets to say, 'Listen, you dirty rats in there!'

In a speech to an American Film Institute banquet on 13 March 1974, Cagney said to Frank Gorshin, a well-known impersonator: 'Oh, Frankie, just in passing: I never said [in any film] "Mmm, you dirty rat!" What I actually did say was "Judy! Judy! Judy!"' See GRANT 219:5.

(Sir) Michael CAINE English actor (1933–)

3 Not many people know that.

It is rare for a personal catchphrase to catch on (as opposed to phrases in entertainment, films and advertising that are engineered to do so). But it has certainly been the case with the one that will always be associated with Caine. Peter Sellers started the whole thing off when he appeared on BBC TV's *Parkinson* show on 28 October 1972. The edition in question was subsequently released on disc ('Michael Parkinson Meets the Goons'), thus enabling confirmation of what Sellers said: ' "Not many people know that" ... this is my Michael Caine impression ... You see Mike's always quoting from *The Guinness Book of Records*. At the drop of a hat he'll trot one out. "Did you know that it takes a man in a tweed suit five and a half seconds to fall from the top of Big Ben to the ground? Now there's not many people know that!"'

It was not until 1981–2 that the remark really caught on. Caine was given the line to say as an in-joke (in the character of an inebriated university lecturer) in the film *Educating Rita* (1983), and he put his name to a book of trivial facts for charity with the slight variant *Not a Lot of People Know That!* in 1984.

See also NAUGHTON 337:4.

James CALLAGHAN (later Lord Callaghan) British Labour Prime Minister (1912–2005)

4 We say that what Britain needs is a new Social Contract. That is what this document is all about.

Referring to *Labour's Programme* (1972). While it was in Opposition from 1970 to 1974, the British Labour Party developed the idea of a social 'compact' between government and trade unions. In return for certain 'social' measures, like price subsidies, the unions would moderate their wage demands. This, in turn, meant that unpopular voluntary or statutory incomes policies could be abandoned. The use of the words 'social contract' differed from that of Rousseau, Hobbes and Locke in that these earlier political philosophers were thinking in terms of a compact between a government and a whole people, rather than with just one section of it.

Coinage of the term 'social contract', in this specific sense, has been credited to Dennis (later Lord) Lyons (who died in 1978), a public-relations consultant who advised the Labour Party in five general elections. Callaghan used the phrase at the Labour Party Conference on 2 October 1972, and Anthony Wedgwood Benn had used the term in a 1970 Fabian pamphlet, *The New Politics*. Jean-Jacques Rousseau's *Du contrat social* was published in 1762.

5 *Bid ben, bid bont* [He who commands, must be a bridge].

When Callaghan became Prime Minister in 1976, his first public engagement was at a luncheon in Cardiff before opening a new bridge over the River Taff. He said that he was to be guided by this Welsh proverb. 'I am to be a bridge between the Government and people, a bridge that links both together so that there is an easy understanding between us.' On 10 April 1976 *The Times* in its report of the speech managed to make nonsense of the Welsh. Subsequently, in 1983, when George Thomas, former Speaker of the House of Commons, became Viscount Tonypandy, he took the words for his motto. They come indirectly from *The Mabinogion*, the collection of ancient Welsh folk stories, in which the tale is told of a king, leading an invasion of Ireland, who came to a river without a bridge. '"There is none," said he, "save that he who is chief, let him be a bridge. I will myself be a bridge." And then was that saying first uttered, and it is still used as a proverb. And then, after he had lain himself down across the river, hurdles were placed upon him, and his hosts passed through over him.' The Welsh form here is, apparently, '*A fo ben, bid bont*' – i.e. 'If he *be* a chief, let him be a bridge.'

1 Now, now, little lady, you don't want to believe all those things you read in the newspaper about crisis and upheavals, and the end of civilization as we know it. Dearie me, not at all.
This example of Callaghan's patronizing style when dealing, as Prime Minister, with the then Leader of the Opposition, Margaret Thatcher, was quoted in all seriousness by *Newsweek* Magazine. It was, in fact, a parody written by John O'Sullivan that had appeared in *The Daily Telegraph* (10 June 1976).

2 A lie travels round the world while truth is putting on her boots.
In November 1976 Callaghan said in the House of Commons: 'A lie can be halfway round the world before the truth has got its boots on.' From time to time since, this has been credited to him as an original saying, as by *PDMQ* (1980) and *ODMQ* (1991). To Mark Twain has been attributed, 'A lie can travel half way round the world while the truth is putting on its shoes' – though this is probably no more than another example of the rule, 'When in doubt, say Mark Twain said it.'
A more certain user of the expression was C.H. Spurgeon (1834–92), the noted 19th-century Baptist preacher, though even he cited it as an 'old proverb' when saying: 'A lie will go round the world while truth is pulling its boots on' – *Gems from Spurgeon* (1859). *Benham* (1948) suggests, however, that 'A lie travels round the world while Truth is putting on her boots' is 'probably [Spurgeon's] own' and ascribes it to his *John Ploughman's Almanack*.
The *Dictionary of American Proverbs* (1992) gives the variations: 'A lie can go around the world and back while the truth is lacing up its boots', 'A lie can travel round the world while the truth is tieing up its shoestrings', 'A lie can go a mile before truth can put its boots on' and 'A lie will travel a mile while truth is putting on its boots.'

3 Either back us or sack us.
Speech, Labour Party Conference (5 October 1977). This became a format phrase in British politics, usually suggested as something spoken by an individual than a whole government. From *The Independent* (25 October 1989): 'The Chancellor of the Exchequer [Nigel Lawson] was last night challenged by the Opposition to stand up to the Prime Minister, say "Back me or sack me" and end confusion over who is running the economy ... "It is time to say (to the Prime Minister) either back me or sack me" ... Mr Smith said.' Compare MAJOR 308:5.

4 There I was waiting at the church ...
As speculation mounted over an October general election in 1978, Callaghan teased the Labour Party Conference in September by saying: 'The commentators have fixed the month for me, they've chosen the date and the day, but I advise them, "Don't count your chickens before they're hatched." Remember what happened to Marie Lloyd. She fixed the day and the date, and then she told us what 'appened. As far as I remember it went like this: "There was I, waiting at the church ... All at once, he sent me round a note. Here's the very note. This is what he wrote. 'Can't get away to marry you today. My wife won't let me.'"'
Unfortunately, it wasn't Marie Lloyd's song. It was Vesta Victoria's. ('Waiting at the Church' had words by Fred W. Leigh, who died in 1924, and music by Henry W. Pether, who died in 1925.) In the end, Callaghan did not call an election until the following May, by which time the 'winter of discontent' had undermined his chances of re-election. Given his record on misquotations, perhaps this was appropriate punishment.

5 Crisis, what crisis?
Callaghan may be said to have been eased out of office by a phrase he did not (precisely) speak. Returning from a sunny summit meeting in Guadeloupe to Britain's 'winter of discontent' on 10 January 1979, he was asked by a journalist at a London airport press conference (and I have been back to the original tapes to verify this): 'What is your general approach and view of the mounting chaos in the country at the moment?' Callaghan replied: 'Well, that's a judgement that you are making. I promise you that if you look at it from the outside (and perhaps you are taking rather a parochial view), I don't think that other people in the world would share the view that there is mounting chaos.'

Next day, *The Sun* carried the headline: 'Crisis? What crisis?' Callaghan lost the May 1979 general election, and the editor of *The Sun* was given a knighthood by the incoming Prime Minister.

Some people insist on recalling that Callaghan said something much more like 'Crisis? What crisis?' on the TV news. When told that these words do not survive on film, these people begin to talk about conspiracy theories. But the impression he created was a strong one. In *The Diaries of Kenneth Williams* (1993), the comedian noted in his entry for 10 January (the day of Callaghan's return and not of the *Sun* headline, which he would not have seen anyway): 'Saw the news. Callaghan arrived back from Guadeloupe saying, "There is no chaos" which is a euphemistic way of talking about the lorry drivers ruining all production and work in the entire country, but one admires his phlegm.'

1 The minority parties have walked into a trap ... It is the first time in recorded history that turkeys have been known to vote for an early Christmas.

Speech, House of Commons (28 March 1979) – from a recording rather than *Hansard*. During a debate that ended in a no-confidence motion that sank his government and also led to a general election defeat the next month, Callaghan derided the Liberal Party and the Scottish National Party in these terms. He described the phrase as a 'joke going about the House'.

See also DRYDEN 178:8; SUN 449:4.

(Baron) Pierre de CAMBRONNE French general (1770–1842)

2 *Merde!*

At the Battle of Waterloo in 1815, Cambronne, the commander of Napoleon's Old or Imperial Guard is *supposed* to have declined a British request for him to surrender with the words, '*La garde meurt mais ne se rend jamais/pas* [The Guards die but never/do not surrender].' However, it is quite likely that what he said, in fact, was, '*Merde! La garde meurt ... [Shit! The Guards die ...]*' At a banquet in 1835 Cambronne specifically denied saying the more polite version. That may have been invented for him by Rougemont in a newspaper, *L'Indépendent*.

In consequence of all this, *merde* is sometimes known in France as *le mot de Cambronne*, a useful euphemism when needed. Unfortunately for Cambronne, the words he denied saying were put on his statue in Nantes, his hometown.

Mrs Patrick CAMPBELL English actress (1865–1940)

3 It doesn't matter what you do, as long as you don't do it in the street and frighten the horses.

Although Ted Morgan's biography of Somerset Maugham (1980) actually attributes this to King Edward VII on the subject of the double standard of sexual morality, it is generally accepted as having been said by Mrs Pat. But what gave rise to the remark? Another version, as in Daphne Fielding's *The Duchess of Jermyn Street* (1964), is: 'It doesn't matter what you do *in the bedroom* as long as you don't do it in the street and frighten the horses.' Yet another, as in *ODQ* (1979), is, 'I don't mind where people *make love*, so long as they ...'

Margot Peters, in her otherwise painstakingly footnoted biography *Mrs Pat* (1984), gives no reason for stating her belief that it was 'when told of a *homosexual affair* between actors' that the actress uttered: 'I don't care what people do, as long as they don't do it in the street and frighten the horses.' More precisely, in *Brendan Behan's New York* (1964) is this remark: 'My attitude to homosexuality is rather like that of the woman who, at the time of the trial of Oscar Wilde, said she didn't mind what they did, so long as they didn't do it in the street and frighten the horses.'

4 The deep, deep peace of the double-bed after the hurly-burly of the chaise longue.

On marriage. Quoted in Alexander Woollcott, 'The First Mrs Tanqueray', *While Rome Burns* (1934).

5 My Stella used to sing a song which I told her was silly, and she declared was funny – your last letter reminds me more of it than others –

He's mad, mad, mad,
He's clean gone off his nut
He cleans his boots with strawberry jam
He eats his hat whenever he can
He's mad, mad, mad.

Letter to Bernard Shaw (29 July 1912), included in *Bernard Shaw and Mrs Patrick Campbell: Their Correspondence* (1952). Stella was her daughter. Hence, *Boots With Strawberry Jam*, title of a musical (1968) with book and lyrics by Benny Green based on the correspondence.

6 You are a terrible man, Mr Shaw. One day you'll eat a beefsteak and then God help all women.

On the grounds that he was a vegetarian. Quoted in Arnold Bennett, *The Journals* (18 June 1919). Alexander Woolcott, *While Rome Burns* (1934), has a slightly different version: 'Some day you'll eat a pork chop, Joey, and then God help all women.'

1 'Quoth the raven ... '

After a dull weekend, Mrs Pat took pen in hand and wrote this in the hostess's elaborate visitor's book. Also ascribed to John Barrymore. This version is from Bennett Cerf, *Shake Well Before Using* (1948). See POE 362:2.

Thomas CAMPBELL Scottish poet (1777–1844)

2 To live in hearts we leave behind
Is not to die.

'Hallowed Ground' (1825). This is probably the original of a sentiment frequently to be found on gravestones – for example, on that of RAF Aircraftsman 1st Class G.C.E. Hodges, who was killed in the Second World War on 18 September 1944, aged 42, and who lies in Brookwood Military Cemetery, Surrey. His grave has: 'TO LIVE IN THE HEARTS / OF THOSE WE LOVE / IS NOT TO DIE.' Another variation is: 'He lives for ever in the hearts of those who loved him.'

3 What though my wingèd hours of bliss have
been,
Like angel-visits, few and far between?

The Pleasures of Hope, 2, line 378 (1799). 'Our semi-tautological phrase "few and far between" is a corrupt formulation by the nineteenth-century Scottish poet Thomas Campbell of an old folk saying to the effect that the visits of angels to our world are "brief and far between"' – *The Observer* (26 June 1988). Campbell, in any case, was echoing what the Scottish poet Robert Blair had written in *The Grave* (1743): 'Its Visits, / Like those of Angels, short, and far between.' William Hazlitt pointed this out. Byron alludes to one or both of these in an 1821 *Diary* entry: 'Whenever an American requests to see me (which is *not* infrequently), I comply ... because these trans-atlantic visits, "few and far between", make me feel as if talking with Posterity from the other side of the Styx.'

The phrase 'few and far between' had existed before this in a different context. R. Verney wrote a letter in about July 1668 saying 'Hedges are few and between' – *Memoirs of the Verney Family* (IV.iii.89).

4 On Linden, when the sun was low,
All bloodless lay the untrodden snow,
And dark as winter was the flow
Of Iser, rolling rapidly.

'Hohenlinden' (1802). The fourth line features in several anecdotes. In 1877, a writer to the New York *World* referred to a lost letter by John Keats to his brother George in which Keats reported that he had heard Charles Lamb say this to Thomas Campbell, having fallen downstairs – *Notes and*

Queries, Vol. 206 – though the writer himself did not believe in the existence of this letter. W.W. Keen, the American surgeon (1837–1932), included in his memoirs (1915–17) the anecdote of the learned butler who, as he was falling downstairs, replied to his master's inquiry as to what was going on: ''Tis I, sir, rolling rapidly.' A learned butler, indeed, to pun in such circumstances.

See also BYRON 116:1.

George CANNING British Tory Prime Minister (1770–1827)

5 I called the New World into existence, to redress the balance of the old.

In a speech in the House of Commons on the affairs of Portugal (12 December 1826), Canning sought to justify his foreign policy in the face of French intervention to suppress liberal revolts in Spain. He said: 'If France occupied Spain, it was necessary ... to avoid the consequences of the occupation ... I sought materials for compensation in another hemisphere. Contemplating Spain as our ancestors had known her, I resolved that if France had Spain, it should not be Spain with the Indies.'

Eric CANTONA French footballer (1966–)

6 When the seagulls follow the trawler, it is because they think sardines will be thrown into the sea.

Quoted in *The Observer* (2 April 1995). When a jail term for kicking a spectator was commuted to community service, Cantona said only this at a press conference and then walked out of it. He was referring to the undue interest paid in him by journalists. Compare what has been credited to Malcolm Muggeridge: 'Journalists follow authority as sharks follow a liner, dining on the scraps that are thrown overboard' (unverified); and to Bernard Shaw: 'To the born editor, news is great fun, even as the capsizing of a boat in Sydney Harbour is great fun for the sharks' – in a letter to Kingsley Martin, quoted by Martin in a 1956 edition of Granada TV *What The Papers Say* and re-quoted in *The Listener* (4 April 1976). '[This] is neither "French philosophy" nor "pretentious gibberish". It is, rather, a good old-fashioned metaphor – the birds follow trawlers, expecting food, and the media follow footballers expecting titbits of information. Perhaps it is time to lay to rest the myth of Mr Cantona's impenetrable remarks' – Benjamin John Sheriff, letter (dated 15 April 2003) to the editor of *The Times*.

Francesco CARACCIOLO Neapolitan diplomat (1752–99)

1 In England there are sixty different religions, and only one sauce.

Attributed in *Notes and Queries* (December 1968). Compare from Dorothy L. Sayers, *Unnatural Death*, Chap. 11 (1927): 'Was it Voltaire who said that the English had three hundred and sixty-five religions and only one sauce?'

Thomas CARLYLE Scottish historian and philosopher (1795–1881)

2 The soul politic.

In contrast to the 'body politic' (the nation in its corporate character, the state), this phrase was used by Margaret Thatcher in speeches in the 1980s. But Carlyle had anticipated her in *Signs of the Times* (1829).

3 Silence is golden.

This encouragement to silence is from the German: '*Sprechen ist silbern, Schweigen ist golden*' and best known in Carlyle's English translation, 'Speech is silver(n), silence is golden' – *Fraser's Magazine* (June 1834). The original is sometimes given in the form, '*Reden ist Silber, Schweigen ist Gold*' ('*Reden*' = 'to speak'). Proverb research points to an Arab origin.

4 The whiff of grapeshot can, if needful, become a blast and tempest.

History of the French Revolution, Vol. 1, Bk 5, Chap. 3 (1837). Carlyle also uses the phrase 'whiff of grapeshot' as a chapter title (Vol. 3, Bk 7, Chap. 7), and on one other occasion (apparently quoting Napoleon). The expression refers to the ease with which Bonaparte and the artillery dispersed the Paris insurrection of the Vendémiaire in 1795, by firing at or over it.

5 The most terrified man in Paris or France is ... seagreen Robespierre ... 'A Republic?' said the Seagreen, with one of his dry husky unsportful laughs, 'What is that?' O seagreen Incorruptible, thou shalt see!

In the same work, Vol. 2, Bk 5, Chap. 4. Accordingly, 'the seagreen incorruptible' became a nickname of Robespierre, the French revolutionary leader who established the Reign of Terror (1793–4) but was executed in it himself. There was no connection between Robespierre's greenness and his incorruptibility. He was green because of poor digestion, and he was incorruptible because he was a fanatic.

6 Genius is an infinite capacity for taking pains.

Carlyle did not quite say this in his life of *Frederick the Great* (1858–65) but, rather, 'Genius ... which means transcendent capacity of taking trouble, first of all.' Disraeli, Samuel Butler and Leslie Stephen are among those credited with the idea or simply with using it. By 1870, Jane Ellice Hopkins in *Work Amongst Working Men* was saying, 'Gift, like genius, I often think only means an infinite capacity for taking pains.'

James Agate in *Ego 6* (1944) calls Carlyle's remark, 'The most misleading pronouncement ever made by a great man', and suggests that a better definition of genius would be: 'That quality in a man which enables him to do things that other people cannot do, and without taking pains.' Indeed, it can be argued that 'taking pains' has nothing to do with genius at all. Mental, spiritual and physical energy may have more to do with it. Compare EDISON 182:4.

Lewis CARROLL (Charles Lutwidge Dodgson) English writer (1832–98)

7 *Alice in Wonderland.*

Incorrect title. It should be *Alice's Adventures in Wonderland* (1865). However, as with *Through the Looking Glass and What Alice Found There* (1872), it is quoted almost as extensively as Shakespeare and the Bible. In addition, the books are alluded to for their particular characters and incidents, and as a whole to denote a mad, fantastic world. Even while Carroll was still alive, *Punch* was parodying 'Alice in Blunderland' (22 November 1890), and already in the year of Carroll's death, S.D. Collingwood was writing: 'With the exception of Shakespeare's plays, very few, if any, books are so frequently quoted in the daily Press as the two "Alices"' – *The Life and Letters of Lewis Carroll*, Chap. 3 (1898).

8 How doth the little crocodile
Improve his shining tail,
And pour the waters of the Nile
On every golden scale!

Alice's Adventures in Wonderland, Chap. 2 (1865). A parody of 'Against Idleness and Mischief' (1715) by Isaac Watts, which goes:

How doth the little busy bee
Improve each shining hour,
And gather honey all the day
From every opening flower!

It appears that Johnny Mercer (1909–76) found the title-lyric of his song 'My Shining Hour' (first sung in the film *The Sky's the Limit*, 1943) in the same place.

1 Everybody has won, and *all* must have prizes.

In the same book, Chap. 3. The Dodo, at the end of the Caucus-Race. Hence, *All Must Have Prizes*, title of a book (1996) on the British education system by Melanie Phillips.

2 'You are old, father William,' the young man said,
'And your hair has become very white;
And yet you incessantly stand on your head –
Do you think, at your age, it is right?'

Alice's recitation from the same book, Chap. 5, is a parody of a much more sober piece – 'The Old Man's Comforts and How He Gained Them' (1799) by Robert Southey:

'You are old, father William,' the young man cried,
'The few locks which are left you are grey;
You are hale, father William, a hearty old man;
Now tell me the reason, I pray.'

3 Speak roughly to your little boy,
And beat him when he sneezes;
He only does it to annoy,
Because he knows it teases.

In the same book, Chap. 6. Said to be a parody of G.W. Langford (dates unknown) or David Bates, a mid-19th-century Philadelphian: 'Speak gently; it is better far / To rule by love than fear; / ... Speak gently to the little child; / Its love be sure to gain ...'

4 She was a little startled by seeing the Cheshire Cat sitting on a bough of a tree a few yards off ... 'Well! I've often seen a cat without a grin,' thought Alice; 'but a grin without a cat! It's the most curious thing I ever saw in all my life!'

In the same chapter. Hence, the expression 'to grin like a Cheshire Cat', meaning 'to smile very broadly'. The 'Cheshire Cat' is most famous from its appearances in *Alice* – where it has the ability to disappear leaving only its grin behind – but the beast had been known since about 1770. Carroll, who was born in Cheshire, probably knew that Cheshire cheeses were at one time moulded in the shape of a grinning cat. From Andrew Roberts, *Eminent Churchillians* (1994): 'British power was slowly disappearing during the Churchillian Era, leaving, like the Cheshire Cat, only a wide smile behind.'

5 Why is a raven like a writing desk?

In the same book, Chap. 7, the Hatter poses this riddle at the 'Mad Tea-Party', but Carroll stated positively that there was no answer. Nevertheless, various people have tried to supply one: 'a quill' – what a raven and a writing desk would have had in common in the last century (Christo-pher Brown of Portswood, Southampton); 'they both begin with the letter R' (Leo Harris); 'because it can produce a few notes, tho they are very flat; and it is never put with the wrong end in front' – these were Lewis Carroll's own possible solutions (1896 edition); 'because the notes for which they are noted are not noted for being musical notes' (Sam Loyd); 'Edgar Allan Poe' – he wrote on both a raven and a writing desk (Sam Loyd); 'because bills and tales (tails) are among their characteristics; because they both stand on their legs; conceal their steels (steals); and ought to be made to shut up' (Sam Loyd); 'because it slopes with a flap' (A. Cyril Pearson); 'because there is a "B" in "both"' (Dr E.V. Rieu). Some of these solutions are included in *The Annotated Alice*, ed. Martin Gardner (1960).

6 Twinkle twinkle little bat!
How I wonder what you're at! ...
Up above the world you fly,
Like a tea-tray in the sky.

The Hatter's song in the same chapter is a parody of Jane Taylor's poem 'The Star' (1806):

Twinkle, twinkle, little star.
How I wonder what you are!
Up above the world so high,
Like a diamond in the sky.

Compare ANONYMOUS 32:3.

7 Oh, 'tis love, 'tis love that makes the world go round.

This is the proverb the Duchess speaks in the same book, Chap. 9. W.S. Gilbert in *Iolanthe* (1882) has a song made up of proverbial sayings and includes:

In for a penny, in for a pound –
It's love that makes the world go round.

Ian Bradley in his *Annotated Gilbert and Sullivan* (Vol. 1) notes how a previous commentator wondered if this had to do with the old saying: 'It's drink that makes the world go round', and also finds it in *Our Mutual Friend* by Charles Dickens (published in the same year as *Alice*). But earlier than these was a French song (published 1851, but recorded as early as 1700):

C'est l'amour, l'amour
Qui fait le monde
À la ronde.

There is an English song, 'Love Makes the World Go Round' by Noel Gay, but that was not written until about 1936. Compare EBB 181:2.

1 Change lobsters again!

From the 'Lobster Quadrille' passage in the same book, Chap. 10. Hence, *Change Lobsters and Dance*, the English title of the autobiography (1974) of the film actress Lilli Palmer (called originally *Dicke Lilli, gutes Kind*). Perhaps deemed appropriate because Palmer quite frequently changed her marriage partners. The precise words for the title do not appear in *Alice*, though the instruction 'change lobsters' does. 'Won't you change partners and dance with me' is a line from the song 'Change Partners', an Irving Berlin song from *Carefree* (1938).

2 'Will you walk a little faster?' said a whiting
   to a snail,
   'There's a porpoise close behind us, and he's
   treading on my tail.'

In the same chapter. A parody of 'Will you walk into my parlour...' in 'The Spider and the Fly'. See HOWITT 246:5.

3 'Tis the voice of the Lobster: I heard him declare
   You have baked me too brown, I must sugar
   my hair.

In the same chapter. Alice's attempt to recite *The Sluggard*, an improving poem by Isaac Watts, which actually begins: ''Tis the voice of the sluggard; I heard him complain, / "You have wak'd me too soon, I must slumber again."'

4 'Twas brillig, and the slithy toves
   Did gyre and gimble in the wabe;
   All mimsy were the borogoves,
   And the mome raths outgrabe.

Through the Looking-Glass and What Alice Found There, Chap. 1 (1872). This opening stanza of the poem 'Jabberwocky' first appeared in a periodical that Carroll wrote and published for his brothers and sisters in 1855. There it is headed 'Stanza of Anglo-Saxon Poetry' and the following translations given of the difficult words: brillig = the close of the afternoon; slithy = smooth and active; tove = a species of badger; gyre = scratch like a dog; gimble = screw out holes in anything; wabe = side of a hill; mimsy = unhappy; borogove = extinct kind of parrot; mome = grave; rath = species of land turtle; outgrabe = squeaked. The word 'borogove' has been described as the most misquoted word in all literature. Almost inevitably it comes out as 'borogrove', or, as pronounced by Frank Muir on one occasion, *borro-gwove*. A much-parodied poem – compare BARSLEY 53:7.

5 The Jabberwock, with eyes of flame,
   Came whiffling through the tulgey wood,
   And burbled as it came.

In the same chapter. Carroll subsequently explained the name Jabberwock as meaning 'the result of much excited discussion'; whiffling is not a Carrollian invention, but means something like blowing; tulgey (his invention) = thick, dense, dark; burbling, though an established word, was derived, according to Carroll, from an amalgam of 'bleat', 'murmur' and 'warble'.

6 One, two! One, two! And through and through
   The vorpal blade went snicker-snack!

In the same chapter. No point in seeking a meaning for the word 'vorpal' – Carroll himself said it had none. However, hence *The Vorpal Blade*, title of a novel (2001) by Colin Forbes.

7 'And hast thou slain the Jabberwock?
   Come to my arms, my beamish boy!
   O frabjous day! Callooh! Callay!'
   He chortled in his joy.

In the same chapter. Beamish (an old word) = shining brightly; frabjous (Carroll's invention) = fair and joyous; chortled (Carroll's invention, surprisingly perhaps) = chuckled and snorted.

8 'The time has come,' the Walrus said,
   'To talk of many things:
   Of shoes – and ships – and sealing-wax –
   Of cabbages and kings –
   And why the sea is boiling hot –
   And whether pigs have wings.'

In the same chapter, the 'Walrus and the Carpenter' episode. As a result, the phrase 'cabbages and kings' was taken by the American writer O. Henry for the title of his first collection of short stories published in 1904, and there was a book entitled *Of Kennedys and Kings: Making Sense of the Sixties* by Harris Wofford (1980). It has been the title of more than one TV series, including the ITV version (1979–82) of the BBC Radio quiz *Quote ... Unquote*. However, the conjunction of 'cabbages' and 'kings' pre-dates Carroll. In Hesketh Pearson's *Smith of Smiths* he quotes the Revd Sydney Smith saying about a certain Mrs George Groce (in an 1840 letter): 'She had innumerable hobbies, among them horticulture and democracy, defined by Sydney as "the most approved methods of growing cabbages and destroying kings".'

1 But answer came there none –
And this was scarcely odd, because
They'd eaten every one.

In the same chapter. 'But answer came there none' is a phrase that also appears in Scott, *The Bridal of Triermain* (1813) and almost in Shakespeare – 'But answer made it none', *Hamlet*, I.ii.215 (1600–1).

2 The rule is, jam tomorrow and jam yesterday – but never jam today.

In the same book, Chap. 5. The White Queen wants Alice to be her maid and offers her twopence a week and jam every other day, except that she can never actually have any – it's never jam today. An early version of Catch-22 (see HELLER 233:3). Nowadays, the phrase is used quite often in connection with the unfulfilled promises of politicians. But did Carroll adopt an older phrase?

Others recall being taught that this was an academic joke. In Latin there are two words meaning 'now': *nunc* and *iam*. The former is used in the present tense, whereas the latter is the correct word for past and future tenses, i.e., yesterday and tomorrow, so it is correct to say *iam* for tomorrow and *iam* for yesterday but never *iam* for today.

3 He's an Anglo-Saxon Messenger – and those are Anglo-Saxon attitudes.

In the same book, Chap. 7. Alice observes the Messenger, 'skipping up and down, and wriggling like an eel, as he came along'. When she expresses surprise, this is the King's explanation. Harry Morgan Ayres in *Carroll's Alice* (1936) suggests that the author may have been spoofing the Anglo-Saxon scholarship of his day. He also reproduces drawings of Anglo-Saxons in various costumes and attitudes from the Caedmon manuscript in the Bodleian Library, Oxford.

Hence, *Anglo-Saxon Attitudes*, the title of Angus Wilson's novel (1956) about a historian investigating a possible archaeological forgery.

4 It's as large as life, and twice as natural!

In the same chapter. Haigha says this of Alice. Until *Alice*, the expression was normally 'As large as life and *quite* as natural'.

5 But I was thinking of a plan
To dye one's whiskers green,
And always use so large a fan
That they could not be seen.
So having no reply to give
To what the old man said,

I cried, "Come, tell me how you live!"
And thumped him on the head.

In the same book, Chap 8. From the White Knight's song. Hence, *Come, Tell Me How You Live*, title of a novel (1946) by Agatha Christie.

6 'Friends, Romans and Countrymen, lend me your ears!'
(They were all of them fond of quotations:
So they drank to his health, and they gave him three cheers,
While he served out additional rations.)

The Hunting of the Snark, Fit the Second (1876) – The Bellman's Speech. Initially alluding, of course, to SHAKESPEARE 412:11, though with 'and' added before 'Countrymen'.

7 'My father and mother were honest, though poor – '
'Skip all that!' cried the Bellman in haste.

In the same work, Fit the Third: The Baker's Tale. Hence, *Skip All That*, title of memoirs (1997) by the writer and broadcaster, Robert Robinson, who notes: 'I think the Bellman put paid to the Baker's story at this point because he thought he was going to hear more than he wanted to: he may have felt the Baker's opening gambit to be a preliminary to many a shy boast. So 'Skip all that' is a wise injunction, though if it is too studiously observed no book of memoirs would ever get written.'

8 I am fond of children (except boys).

Letter to Kathleen Eschwege (24 October 1879), in Stuart Dodgson Collingwood, *The Life and Letters of Lewis Carroll* (1898). Carroll's fondness for little girls (not least Alice Liddell) has become notorious. Here he seems to be saying he is aware of his predilection. Collingwood comments on Carroll's 'aversion almost amounting to terror' of boy-nature: 'Nevertheless, on the few occasions on which I have seen him in the company of boys, he seemed to be thoroughly at his ease, telling them stories and showing them puzzles.'

9 Is all our Life, then, but a dream?

Introductory poem to *Sylvie and Bruno* (1889). In Poets' Corner, Westminster Abbey, Dodgson/Carroll is remembered by a stone (unveiled 17 December 1982) bearing this line. Compare the concluding line of the end-poem to *Through the Looking Glass*: 'Life, what is it but a dream?'

See also BUNN 107:5; SHAWCROSS 427:7.

Edward CARSON (later Lord Carson) Northern Irish lawyer and politician (1854–1935)

1 My only great qualification for being put at the head of the Navy is that I am very much at sea.

Quoted in I. Colvin, *Life of Lord Carson* (1936). Compare WALPOLE 482:3.

Rachel CARSON American biologist (1907–64)

2 *The Silent Spring.*

Title of book (1962) – an early flowering of the environmental movement. The book aroused public awareness of the destruction of wildlife and the danger to the food chain caused by the use of dangerous pesticides, as in this passage: 'Over increasingly large areas of the United States, spring now comes unheralded by the return of birds, and the early mornings are strangely silent where once they were filled with the beauty of bird song.'

Howard CARTER English archaeologist (1873–1939)

3 As my eyes grew accustomed to the light, details of the room within emerged slowly from the mist, strange animals, statues and gold – everywhere the glint of gold ... Lord Carnavon, unable to stand the suspense any longer, inquired anxiously, 'Can you see anything?' it was all I could do to get out the words, 'Yes, wonderful things.'

The Tomb of Tut-ankh-Amen (1933). The most exciting archaeological find of the 20th century was that of the tomb of Tutankhamun in November 1921. Carter, backed by his patron, the 5th Earl of Carnarvon, had been digging fruitlessly for many years in Egypt's Valley of the Kings. Then he hit upon a flight of steps beneath the ruins of old workmen's huts. Carter wired for Carnavon to join him. Three days of digging were needed to clear the entrance passage. On 26 November another sealed door appeared. It was through the hole which he made in this door that Carter glimpsed the treasure. He described the moment in a thrilling passage. Carter originally wrote '*marvellous* things' in his diary.

Jimmy CARTER American Democratic 39th President (1924–)

4 Why not the best?

Carter's official slogan, used as the title of a campaign book and song as he ran for the presidency in 1976, originated with an interview he had had with Admiral Hyman Rickover when applying to join the nuclear submarine programme in 1948. 'Did you do your best [at Naval Academy]?'

Rickover asked him. 'No, sir, I didn't *always* do my best,' replied Carter. Rickover stared at him for a moment and then asked: 'Why not?'

5 Jimmy who?

The question was posed when Carter came from nowhere (or at least from the Governorship of Georgia) to challenge Gerald Ford, successfully, for the US Presidency in 1976. It acquired almost the force of a slogan. *Jimmy Who?* was the title of a campaign biography published in 1976.

6 I've looked on a lot of women with lust. I've committed adultery in my heart many times. God recognizes I will do this and forgives me.

Interviewed in *Playboy* (November 1976). The American electorate, perceiving a useful working relationship with the Almighty, voted in Carter as their President that same month.

7 He is competent, honest, trustworthy, a man of integrity. Bert, I'm proud of you.

Of Bert Lance, the director of Carter's Office of Management and Budget, as pressure mounted for him to be fired because of his banking activities in 1977. Carter had appointed Lance from the chairmanship of the Calhoun First National Bank in their mutual home state of Georgia, but irregularities in Lance's conduct were alleged and, after prolonged hearings, he was forced to resign. He was found not guilty on a list of charges, but paid a fine to avoid a retrial on the remaining ones.

8 Hawae the lads!

On a visit to the northeast of England in 1977, President Carter (no doubt put up to it by the British Prime Minister, James Callaghan) used the traditional Geordie greeting when addressing a crowd. It means something like 'Come on, lads!' – a cry of encouragement – and also appears in the forms 'Haway' (or 'Howay') and 'Away' (or 'A-wee'). According to Frank Graham's *New Geordie Dictionary* (1979), it is a corruption of 'hadaway' as in 'hadaway wi'ye', which means the opposite, 'begone!'

Sydney CARTER English songwriter (1915–2004)

9 Dance then, wherever you may be,
I am the Lord of the Dance, said he,
And I'll lead you all wherever you may be,
And I'll lead you all in the dance, said he.

'Lord of the Dance' (1967), referring to Jesus Christ and employing the image of life as a dance. Carter's words are sung to an old Shaker tune, 'Simple Gifts', written by Joseph Brackett Jr in 1848; Aaron Copland had used this tune in his ballet score *Appalachian Spring* (1944). Hence, *Lord of the Dance*, title of a dance show (1996), choreographed by and featuring Michael Flatley.

CASABLANCA American film 1942. Script by Julius J. Epstein, Philip G. Epstein and Howard Koch, from an unproduced play *Everybody Comes To Rick's* by Murray Burnett and Joan Alison. With Humphrey Bogart as Rick, Ingrid Bergman as Ilsa, Dooley Wilson as Sam and Claude Rains as Captain Louis Renault.

1 **Play it again, Sam.**

Of course, Humphrey Bogart never actually says this in the film when talking to Sam, played by Dooley Wilson. Sam is the night club pianist and reluctant performer of the sentimental song 'As Time Goes By'. At one point Ingrid Bergman, as Ilsa, *does* have this exchange with him:

Ilsa: Play it once, Sam, for old time's sake.
Sam: I don't know what you mean, Miss Ilsa.
Ilsa: Play it, Sam. Play 'As Time Goes By'.

Later on Bogart, as Rick, also tries to get Sam to play it:

Rick: You know what I want to hear.
Sam: No, I don't.
Rick: You played it for her, [and] you can play it for me.
Sam: Well, I don't think I can remember it.
Rick: If she can stand it, I can. Play it.

All one can say is that the saying was utterly well established by the time Woody Allen thus entitled his play *Play It Again Sam* (1969; film US 1972) about a film critic who is abandoned by his wife and obtains the help of Bogart's 'shade'. By listing it under Allen's name, *Bartlett* (1980 and 1992) might be thought to suggest that Allen coined the phrase. It would be interesting to know by which year it had really become established. Ian Gillies (1996) recalled that in 1943 the Jack Benny radio programme went to North Africa to entertain the troops. When he returned, two of the shows were based on the idea of a reporter asking him, 'When you toured North Africa, were you in Algiers?' and 'Were you in Casablanca?' Each led to a film parody. In that of *Casablanca*, Benny played the Bogart part and 'Rochester' (Eddie Anderson) Dooley Wilson. As has now been confirmed with a recording of the original broadcast on 17 October 1943, 'Ricky' (increasingly inebriated) keeps on saying: 'Go ahead, Sam, play that song. Sam, sing it, boy. Sing it, Sam. Sing it, Sam, sing that song that keeps breaking my heart.' Above all, he exclaims: 'Sam, Sam, play that song for me again, will you?' This is certainly closer to the catchphrase than anything uttered in the film and, to my mind, is reasonable proof that Jack Benny really did help create the phrase. Presumably, rather more people heard the radio show than had seen the film at that point.

2 **Drop the gun, Louis.**

Alistair Cooke writing in *Six Men* (1977) remarked of Bogart: 'He gave currency to another phrase with which the small fry of the English-speaking world brought the neighbourhood sneak to heel: "Drop the gun, Looey!"' Quite how Bogart did this, Cooke does not reveal. We have Bogart's word for it: 'I never said, "Drop the gun, Louie"' – quoted in Ezra Goodman, *Bogey: The Good-Bad Guy* (1965). The line was, however, celebrated in the song 'All Right, Louie, Drop the Gun' (1949). This was written by Ray Carter and Lucile Johnson and tells how the singer's boy/girl friend likes watching Western movies and has a tendency to come out with the phrase at odd moments. It would seem it was an established phrase by the time it was incorporated in the song – perhaps it was a cliché of Westerns – and, as far as *Casablanca* goes, it is just another of those lines that people would like to have heard spoken but that never were. Towards the end of the film what Rick says is: 'Not so fast, Louis.' Ironically, it is *Louis* who says: 'Put that gun down.'

3 *Louis*: **Major Strasser has been shot. Round up the usual suspects.**

Soundtrack. In the final scene, 'Round up the usual suspects' is a line spoken by Renault, the Vichy French police chief in the Moroccan city, who is, in his cynical way, appearing to act responsibly in the light of the fact that a German officer, Major Strasser, has been shot. But Strasser was shot by Rick before Renault's very eyes.

It is remarkable that, of all the many memorable lines from *Casablanca*, it took until the early 1990s for this one to catch on. Indeed, as allusions go and referring to 'the people you would expect, the customary lot', it almost became a cliché – as was perhaps confirmed by the release of a film called *The Usual Suspects* (US 1995), which involved a police identity parade.

Examples of the catchphrase in use range from straightforward quotation in 1983 to more recent unattributed allusions: 'All the usual suspects will be out at Fontwell tomorrow, when the figure-of-eight chase course will throw up its usual quota of specialist [horse-racing] winners' – *Independent on Sunday* (17 January 1993). A BBC Radio Scotland discussion show was called *The Usual Suspects* in 1993 – a rather revealing title given that the journalists and hacks who take part are inevitably just the sort of people you would expect to hear invited on to such a show.

In 1992 Howard Koch appeared to concede the coining of the phrase to his co-scriptwriters Julius J. Epstein and Philip G. Epstein.

See also HUPFELD 248:4.

CASSANDRA (Sir William Connor) English journalist (1909–67)

1 As I was saying when I was interrupted, it is a powerful hard thing to please all the people all the time.

In September 1946 'Cassandra' resumed his column in the *Daily Mirror* after the Second World War with quite a common form of words. In June of that same year, announcer Leslie Mitchell is also reported to have begun BBC TV's resumed transmissions with: 'As I was saying before I was so rudely interrupted.' The phrase sounds as if it might have originated in music-hall routines of the 'I don't wish to know that, kindly leave the stage' type. Eamonn De Valera, the Irish politician, is said to have started a public speech at Ennis in 1924, 'As I was saying before I was interrupted ...' – referring to the fact that he had been arrested at the same venue a year before. A.A. Milne, in *Winnie-the-Pooh* (1926), has: '"AS – I – WAS – SAYING," said Eeyore loudly and sternly, "as I was saying when I was interrupted by various Loud Sounds, I feel that – "'

Long before any of these, Fary Luis de León, the Spanish poet and religious writer, is believed to have resumed a lecture at Salamanca University in 1577 with, '*Dicebamus hesterno die* ... [We were saying yesterday].' He had been in prison for five years.

Ted CASTLE (later Lord Castle) English journalist (1907–79)

2 *In Place of Strife.*

This was Castle's suggested title for an ill-fated Labour government White Paper on industrial-relations legislation put forward by his wife, Barbara Castle, Secretary of State for Employment, on 17 January 1969. It was clearly modelled on Aneurin Bevan, *In Place of Fear*, the title of a book about disarmament (1952); see BEVAN 66:2.

Harry CASTLING British songwriter (?–1930)

3 Let's all go down the Strand – have a banana!

From the song, 'Let's All Go Down the Strand' (1904), written with C.W. Murphy. The words 'Have a banana' were interpolated by audiences. Although not part of the original lyrics, they were included in later versions.

Wynn CATLIN Unidentified (1930–)

4 Diplomacy is the art of saying 'Nice Doggie!' till you can find a rock.

Quoted in Laurence J. Peter, *Quotations for Our Time* (1977). Could this have anything to do with Wynelle Catlin, author of *Old Waffles* (1975) – Texas farm-life fiction?

CATO the Elder (or 'the Censor') Roman politician and orator (234–149BC)

5 *Delenda est Carthago* [Carthage must be destroyed].

Cato punctuated or ended his speeches to the Roman Senate with this slogan for eight years, from about 157BC, realizing the threat that the other state posed. It worked – Carthage was destroyed (in 146BC) and Rome reigned supreme, though Cato had not lived to see the effect of his challenge. He did have the decency to precede the slogan with the words '*ceterum censeo* [in my opinion]'.

6 Scipio is the soul of the council; the rest are vain shadows.

Quoted in Plutarch's *Life of Cato*. Alluded to, for example, in John Moore's *Portrait of Elmbury* (1945), in which the author returns to Elmbury after four years' absence to find that his old classics master has been elected to the town council. 'You must show me proper respect,' he says, 'Scipio is the soul of the Council; the rest are vain shadows.'

Edith CAVELL English nurse (1865–1915)

7 This I would say, standing as I do in view of God and Eternity: I realize that patriotism is not enough; I must have no hatred or bitterness towards anyone.

Bartlett (1992) is not alone in describing these, inaccurately, as her 'Last words [12 October 1915], before her execution by the Germans'. Cavell was a British Red Cross nurse who, without question, broke the rules of war by using her job to help Allied prisoners escape from German-occupied territory. She was condemned by a German court martial for 'conducting soldiers to the enemy' and shot. Her 'message to the world' was not in the form of 'last words' spoken before the firing squad but was said the previous day (11 October 1915) to an English chaplain, the Revd Stirling Gahan, who visited her in prison.

CERVANTES (Miguel de Cervantes Saavedra) Spanish novelist (1547–1616)

8 Many a time we look for one thing, and light on another.

Don Quixote, Pt 1, Chap. 16 (1605). Numerous proverbial expressions took their first English form through Peter Motteux's translation (1700–3), for example: 'I have always heard it said, that to do a kindness to clowns, is like throwing water into the sea' and 'To withdraw is not to run away, and to stay is no wise action' (Pt 1, Chap. 23).

1 *El Caballero de la Triste Figura* [The Knight of the Doleful Countenance].
In the same work, Pt 1, Chap. 19. Sancho Panza's description of Don Quixote. Smollett translates this as 'Knight of the Sorrowful Countenance' and Shelton, 'Knight of the Ill-favoured Face'.

Richard CHALLONER English bishop (1691–1781)

2 [Sanctity] does not so much depend upon doing extraordinary actions, as upon doing our ordinary actions extraordinarily well.
In a letter to *The Independent* Magazine (22 May 1993), David Pocock pointed out that when, in an earlier issue, Stephen Bayley had written concerning Peter Boizot (founder of the Pizza Express restaurant chain in Britain), 'Doing ordinary things extraordinarily well is a true mark of genius', he had unwittingly invoked Challoner's remark.

Neville CHAMBERLAIN British Conservative Prime Minister (1869–1940)

3 How terrible, fantastic, incredible it is that we should be digging trenches and trying on gas masks here because of a quarrel in a faraway country between people of whom we know nothing.
On Czechoslovakia. Radio broadcast (27 September 1938). An unverified suggestion has been made that he had been anticipated in this kind of shortsighted view of foreign affairs by Sir John Simon, as Foreign Secretary, in a House of Commons speech referring to the Japanese invasion of Manchuria in 1931.

4 My good friends, this is the second time in our history that there has come back from Germany to Downing Street peace with honour. I believe it is peace for our time. Go home and get a nice quiet sleep.
On returning from signing the Munich Agreement, Chamberlain spoke from a window at 10 Downing Street – 'Not of design but for the purpose of dispersing the huge multitude below' – according to his biographer Keith Feiling. Two days before, when someone had suggested the Disraeli phrase 'peace with honour' (see 174:3), Chamberlain

had impatiently rejected it. Now, according to John Colville, *Footprints in Time* (1976), Chamberlain used the phrase at the urging of his wife.
Chamberlain's own phrase 'peace for our time' is often misquoted as 'peace *in* our time' – as by Noël Coward in the title of his 1947 play set in an England conquered by the Germans. Perhaps Coward, and others, were influenced by the phrase from the Book of Common Prayer, 'Give peace in our time, O Lord'. The year before Munich, *Punch* (24 November 1937) showed 'Peace in our time' as a wall slogan.

5 This morning the British Ambassador in Berlin handed the German Government a final note stating that, unless we heard from them by eleven o'clock that they were prepared at once to withdraw their troops from Poland, a state of war would exist between us. I have to tell you that no such undertaking has been received, and that consequently this country is at war with Germany.
Radio broadcast from Downing Street, London (3 September 1939). This was the first occasion on which a people had been told by radio that its country was at war with another. Most of the British nation apparently heard the broadcast having been alerted that it would contain the news that it did. Chamberlain went on to say: 'You can imagine what a bitter blow it is to me that all my long struggle to win peace has failed ...' In the film *In Which We Serve* (UK 1942), when sailors are shown listening to the broadcast on a wireless, this produces the response from one of them: 'It's not exactly a bank holiday for us ...'

6 Whatever may be the reason, whether it was that Hitler thought he might get away with what he had got without fighting for it, or whether it was that, after all, the preparations are not sufficiently complete, one thing is certain – he missed the bus.
Speech to Conservative Central Council (5 April 1940). Chamberlain made this boastful observation unwisely just as the 'phoney war' period (of little or no action) was coming to an end. Five days later Hitler invaded Norway. Chamberlain was ousted as Prime Minister within the month. Nevertheless, it is a notable use of the expression 'to miss the bus'. This first appears in *OED2* in 1886 as 'to miss the omnibus', having probably developed from an earlier expression 'to miss the boat'.

Nicolas-Sébastien CHAMFORT French writer (1741–94)

1 Most anthologists of poetry or quotations are like those who eat cherries or oysters, first picking the best and winding up by eating everything.

Quoted in Prochnow & Prochnow, *Treasury of Humorous Quotations* (1969). A salutary reminder to all editors of dictionaries of quotations.

Raymond CHANDLER American novelist (1888–1959)

2 *The Big Sleep.*

Title of novel (1939). A synonym for death – as also is his *The Long Goodbye* (1954).

3 She gave me a smile I could feel in my hip pocket.

Farewell, My Lovely (1940). But what does this line mean? A winning smile, presumably – but is the reference to the hip pocket meant to suggest something about money (where the wallet might be kept) or about guns or about the other things that men keep in their trousers?

4 Down these mean streets a man must go who is not himself mean; who is neither tarnished nor afraid.

Chandler wrote this of the heroic qualities a detective should have in 'The Simple Art of Murder' – in the *Atlantic Monthly* (December 1944), reprinted in *Pearls Are a Nuisance* (1950). However, the phrase 'mean streets' was not original. In 1894, Arthur Morrison had written *Tales of Mean Streets* about impoverished life in the East End of London. The usage was well established by 1922 when the *Weekly Dispatch* was using the phrase casually: 'For him there is glamor in the mean streets of dockland.' Hence, title of the film *Mean Streets* (US 1973).

George CHAPMAN English playwright (?1559–1634)

5 I am ashamed the law is such an ass.

Revenge for Honour (published 1654). Compare DICKENS 171:6.

CHARLES I English King (1600–49)

6 I go from a corruptible to an incorruptible crown, where no disturbance can have place.

Last words before his execution, quoted in David Hume, *History of England ...*, Chap. 22 (1778). He is also said to have remarked to Bishop Juxon, 'Remember.' Quoted in Barnaby Conrad, *Famous Last Words* (1961).

CHARLES II English King (1630–85)

7 He had been, he said, an unconscionable time dying; but he hoped that they would excuse it.

Last words, reported in Lord Macaulay, *History of England* (1849).

See also ROCHESTER 385:1.

CHARLES British Prince (1948–)

8 Yes ... whatever that may mean.

When asked if he was 'in love' upon getting engaged to Lady Diana Spencer. In TV news interview (February 1981). Compare from D.H. Lawrence, *Lady Chatterley's Lover*, Chap. 10 (1928): '"It's just love," she [Constance] said cheerfully. "Whatever that may be," he [Mellors] replied.'

9 A kind of vast municipal fire station ... I would understand better this type of high-tech approach if you demolished the whole of Trafalgar Square, but what is proposed is like a monstrous carbuncle on the face of a much-loved and elegant friend.

Speech to the Royal Institute of British Architects (30 May 1984), describing the proposed design for a new wing of the National Gallery in London. It had an effect: the design was scrapped and replaced by another one.

The Prince's ventures into architectural criticism have not gone unnoticed, and the image of a 'monstrous carbuncle' ('a red spot or pimple on the nose or face caused by habits of intemperance' – *OED2*) has become part of the critical vocabulary. A report in *The Independent* (1 March 1988) about plans for a new lifeboat station dominating the harbour at Lyme Regis concluded by quoting a local objector: 'They've called this building a design of the age. What we've got here is a Prince Charles Carbuncle, and we don't like carbuncles down on Lyme harbourside.' The Prince's step-mother-in-law, the Countess Spencer, had earlier written in a book called *The Spencers on Spas* (1983) of how 'monstrous carbuncles of concrete have erupted in gentle Georgian squares'. In *Barnaby Rudge*, Chap. 54 (1841), Charles Dickens had written: 'Old John was so red in the face ... and lighted up the Maypole Porch wherein they sat together, like a monstrous carbuncle in a fairy tale.' Even before this, in 1821, William Cobbett had characterized the whole of London as 'the Great Wen of all' – a 'wen' being a lump or protuberance on the body, a wart – see COBBETT 148:2.

Paddy CHAYEFSKY American playwright and screen-writer (1923–81)

1 I want you to get up right now and go to the window, open it and stick your head out and yell: 'I'm as mad as hell, and I'm not going to take this any more!'

Film *Network* (US 1976) – in which Peter Finch plays a TV pundit-cum-evangelist who exhorts his viewers to get mad with these words. From *New Society* (25 November 1982): 'Some years ago the irascible Howard Jarvis, author of California's Proposition 13 (the one that pegged property taxes), coined the immortal political slogan: I'm mad as Hell and I'm Not Taking Any More.' Well, no, he obviously didn't. In 1978 Jarvis (1902–86), the California social activist, merely adopted the slogan and came to be associated with it. As a result, 57 per cent voted to reduce their property taxes. Dire warnings about the effect on government if tax revenues were pegged were not borne out and Proposition 13 paved the way for Reaganomics three years later. Jarvis entitled a book *I'm Mad as Hell* but duly credited Chayevsky with the coinage of his slogan. He added: 'For me, the words "I'm mad as hell" are more than a national saying, more than the title of this book; they express exactly how I feel and exactly how I felt about the ... countless other victims of exorbitant taxes.'

CHER American singer and actress (1946–)

2 Stripped, washed and brought to my tent.

Cher spent a certain amount of time in March 1988 denying, apropos some toy-boy lover, that she had ever ordered him, metaphorically speaking, to be stripped, washed and brought to her tent. The allusion here was not very precise. Presumably, the suggestion was that she had behaved as, say, an Arab prince might to an underling (either male or female). Perhaps she acquired the line from some film about sheikhs and harems. Compare from Christopher Marlowe, *Tamburlaine Pt 2*, Act 4, Sc. 1 (1590): 'Then bring those Turkish harlots to my tent / And I'll dispose them as it likes me best.'

4th Earl of CHESTERFIELD English politician and writer (1694–1773)

3 The pleasure is momentary, the position ridiculous, the expense damnable.

Chesterfield's alleged remark about sex is well known but has not been found in any of his works, not even in the letters of advice (1774) to his natural son for which he is best remembered. It may be that the original utterance was in French – by Voltaire, perhaps, or La Rochefoucauld – in the form *'Le plaisir est court et la position ridicule.'* It appears

increasingly likely that the authorship has been imposed on Chesterfield as someone who had a reputation for handing out views like this. In fact, it doesn't sound like him. In the 1981 book *Toasts* by Paul Dickson it was attributed – in the form 'The pleasure is momentary; the expense is exorbitant; the position ridiculous' – to G.K. Chesterton. A most unlikely originator, and his name was probably mistaken for Chesterfield's.

The earliest source found to date is an unsigned piece in the journal *Nature*, Vol. 227 (22 August 1970). It begins: 'Lord Chesterfield once remarked of sexual intercourse "the pleasure is momentary, the position ridiculous, and the expense damnable".' Another example of an anonymous saying ascribed to a convenient author? An earlier unattached allusion is contained in a letter from Evelyn Waugh to Nancy Mitford (5 May 1954): 'Of children as of procreation – the pleasure momentary, the posture ridiculous, the expense damnable.' Compare D.H. Lawrence, *Lady Chatterley's Lover*, Chap. 12 (1928): 'It was quite true, as some poets said, that the God who created man must have had a sinister sense of humour, creating him a reasonable being, yet forcing him to take this ridiculous posture ... Men despised the intercourse act, and yet did it.' Which poets?

4 The chapter of knowledge is a very short, but the chapter of accidents is a very long one.

Letter to Solomon Dayrolles (16 February 1753). Possibly a phrase in general use even then, meaning 'a series of unforeseen happenings or misfortunes'. Hence, *A Chapter of Accidents*, title of the autobiography (1972) of Goronwy Rees. In 1837, John Wilkes was quoted by Southey as saying: 'The chapter of accidents is the longest chapter in the book.'

G.K. CHESTERTON English poet, novelist and critic (1874–1936)

5 'My country, right or wrong' is a thing no patriot would ever think of saying except in a desperate case. It is like saying, 'My mother, drunk or sober.'

The Defendant (1901). See DECATUR 164:3.

6 Am in Market Harborough. Where ought I to be?

This is often misquoted as 'Am in Wolverhampton' – for example, in my *The 'Quote...Unquote' Book of Love, Death and the Universe* (1980) and several other places. Chesterton was noted for being disorganized, and according to one biographer, Maisie Ward in *Return to Chesterton* (1944), a hundred different places have been substituted for 'Market Harborough' in the telling of this story. Chesterton's wife, Frances, on this occasion cabled the answer 'Home' – because, as she exclaimed, it was easier to get him home and start him off again. Yes, Market Harborough was the original and is confirmed by Chesterton's own *Autobiography*, Chap. 16 (1936): 'Of those days the tale is told that I once sent a telegram to my wife in London, which ran: "Am in Market Harborough. Where ought I to be?" I cannot remember whether this story is true; but it is not unlikely or, I think, unreasonable.'

1 *The Man Who Was Thursday.*

Title of a short novel (1908), subtitled 'a Nightmare'. It was a fantasy with an anarchist background. The seven members of the Central Anarchist Council are named after the days of the week. Hence, all the many later newspaper headlines of 'The Man Who Was – ' variety.

2 The prime truth of woman, the universal mother ... that if a thing is worth doing, it is worth doing badly.

'Folly and Female Education', *What's Wrong with the World* (1910). Obviously, a cynical variation of the proverbial 'If a job [*or* thing] is worth doing, it's worth doing well' – which *CODP* finds Lord Chesterfield using by 1746. When the Prince of Wales made his maiden speech to the House of Lords (13 June 1974), he began by ascribing this to Oscar Wilde. Frank Muir pointed out this solecism to *The Times* and added, 'If a thing is worth quoting, it is worth quoting badly.'

The father of someone I know always used to say: 'If a thing's worth doing, it's worth doing *well enough*.'

3 I tell you naught for your comfort,
Yea, naught for your desire,
Save that the sky grows darker yet
And the sea rises higher.

The Ballad of the White Horse (1911). Hence, *Naught for Your Comfort*, title of a book (1956) by Bishop Trevor Huddleston – a classic denunciation of apartheid in South Africa by an Anglican priest.

4 Talk about the pews and steeples
And the cash that goes therewith!
But the souls of Christian peoples ...
Chuck it, Smith!

Antichrist, or the Reunion of Christendom (1912). Here, Chesterton satirizes the pontificating of F.E. Smith (later 1st Earl of Birkenhead) on the Welsh Disestablishment Bill. Thus Chesterton popularized – although he did not coin – the phrase 'Chuck it —— !' meaning, 'abandon that line of reasoning, that posturing'. *Partridge/Slang* guesses that it is of 20th-century origin.

A more recent example from the BBC's *World at One* radio programme in May 1983 during the run-up to a general election: Labour politician Roy Hattersley complained that he was being questioned only on the ten per cent of the Labour Party manifesto with which he disagreed. Robin Day, the interviewer, replied: 'Chuck it, Hattersley!'

5 I think I will not hang myself today.

'A Ballade of Suicide' (1915). This short poem is about a suicide who finds reasons for putting off the deed. In *Lyrics on Several Occasions* (1959), Ira Gershwin notes that the title of his song *I Don't Think I'll Fall in Love Today* (written in 1928) was inspired by this line.

6 The only way of catching a train I ever discovered is to miss the train before.

Quoted in *The Treasury of Humorous Quotations*, eds Esar & Bentley (1951). P. Daninos, 'Le Supplice de l'heure', *Vacances à tous prix* (1958) has: 'Chesterton taught me this: the only way to be sure of catching a train was to miss the one before it.'

7 When a man stops believing in God he doesn't then believe in nothing, he believes in anything.

Unverified, but widely quoted. The chief problem of verification is the immense number of GKC's books and newspaper articles that it could be in – if, indeed, it is. Aidan Mackey of the G.K. Chesterton Study Centre wrote in the March 1996 issue of *The Chesterton Society Newsletter*: 'I have been asked for the source by the BBC (twice), *The Sunday Telegraph*, by many writers and researchers, and by Mrs Thatcher's private office. I now believe that we must make a concerted effort to locate it, and to this end I seek help. I have been, very hastily, through 28 books but I work under pressure, and these should be checked again by at least one other reader ...

'It has been suggested to me that it is not a genuine quotation at all, but one which GKC had once or twice expressed, and that it has, with time, hardened into something else. However, I and others, are certain that this is genuine. I am positive that I have read it in one of his books, not in a fugitive piece, and will even tempt fate by saying that the words [as above] are as near accurate as makes no difference.'

Another line of inquiry was opened by David Torvell (1996), who said he recognized the statement as coming from one of the 'Father Brown' stories: 'The context was a "locked-room murder" attributed to supernatural causes. Fr Brown refused to accept what he regarded as atheist woolly-mindedness and successfully looked for human and mechanical agents.' This refers to: 'The Miracle of Moon Crescent' from *The Incredulity of Father Brown* (1923): '"By the way," went on Father Brown, "don't think I blame you for jumping to preternatural conclusions. The reason's very simple, really. You all swore you were hard-shelled materialists; and as a matter of fact you were all balanced on the very edge of belief – of belief in almost anything.'" To which one might add that in the adjacent story, 'The Oracle of the Dog' can be found: 'It's the first effect of not believing in God that you lose your common sense.'

Professor Denis J. Conlon, Chairman of the Chesterton Society, commented (1996): 'There's general agreement that it does sound like the typical Father Brown aphorism, and GKC put many remarks about the superstitions of agnostics into his mouth. Unfortunately, not the one we are looking for, although one must always take into account that the stories as collected did vary a little from the versions originally published in magazines.

'I am beginning to think that it might have been something he said during one of his countless talks, lectures and debates. The earliest citation so far unearthed is in Emile Cammaerts's *Chesterton: The Laughing Prophet* first published in 1937, but Cammaerts does not give his source.'

What Cammaerts does do is to insert, in the middle of some direct quotation, the paraphrase, 'The first effect of not believing in God is to believe in anything.' It may be upon this that all the subsequent quoters have constructed their versions.

1 Paradox has been defined as 'Truth standing on her head to get attention'.

'When Doctors Agree', *The Paradoxes of Mr Pond* (1937). But who was the definer? In 1999, Denis Conlon of the Chesterton Society recalled that Dean Inge had once described GKC himself as 'a fat clown who crucifies truth upside-down.' Brian Robinson, however, found the most likely original. In *The Romantic Nineties* (1926), Richard Le Gallienne wrote of Oscar Wilde: 'Paradox with him was only Truth standing on its head to attract attention.' Compare the story told about George Orwell. When the young Eric Blair was 11 years old, he saw three children playing in a field – one of whom, Jacintha Buddicom, was to have great influence on him. Wanting to get to know them, he used a simple stratagem to gain their attention, and when they came across the field to him and asked him why he was standing on his head, he replied, 'You are noticed more if you are standing on your head than if you are the right way up.'

2 *Termino nobis donet in patria.*

The Latin text on Chesterton's grave in the Roman Catholic cemetery at Beaconsfield, Buckinghamshire, is taken from the final stanza of the Lauds hymn for the Feast of Corpus Christi. The entire office was written by St Thomas Aquinas, and Chesterton was said to have known large parts of it by

heart. As Father Ian Brady, editor of *The Chesterton Review*, pointed out (1992), the words would also have been familiar to Chesterton because they formed part of the hymn sung at the once-popular short devotional service of Benediction – a hymn that began with the words, '*O salutaris hostia*', and concluded with this prayer to the Holy Trinity:

> *Uni trinoque Domino*
> *sit sempiterna gloria,*
> *qui vitam sine termino*
> *nobis donet in patria.*
> [Everlasting glory be to the Lord, Three in One, who gives us life without end in heaven.]

In Maisie Ward's *Return to Chesterton* (1944) there is a letter from one of Chesterton's Beaconsfield friends in which Chesterton is quoted as saying that he regarded the phrase '*in patria*' as a perfect definition of heaven. 'Our native land,' he said, 'it tells you everything.' Father Brady added that perhaps the fact that Chesterton died on the Sunday within the Octave of Corpus Christi also influenced the choice of these words for his monument. The words were also an especial favourite of Chesterton's friend and colleague, Hilaire Belloc. It is said that Belloc was unable to hear the closing lines of the hymn without being moved to tears.

See also CORNFORD 154:6; TENNYSON 455:8.

Agatha CHRISTIE (later Dame Agatha) English detective novelist (1890–1976)

3 I believe that a well-known anecdote exists to the effect that a young writer, determined to make the commencement of his story forcible and original enough to catch the attention of the most blasé of editors, penned the first sentence: '"Hell!" said the Duchess.'

These are the opening lines of *The Murder on the Links* (1923). 'Hell! said the Duchess' also became the opening words of Michael Arlen's *The Green Hat* (1924) and *Hell! Said the Duchess* the title of 'A Bed-time Story' by Arlen (1934). *Partridge/Catch Phrases* dates the longer phrase, 'Hell! said the Duchess when she caught her teats in the mangle', to about 1895 and says it was frequently used in the First World War.

Compare the suggested newspaper headline containing all the ingredients necessary to capture a reader's attention (sex, royalty, religion etc.): 'Teen-age Dog-loving Doctor-priest in Sex-change Mercy-Dash to Palace' (a joke current by 1959 and quoted in *The Lyttelton Hart-Davis Letters*, Vol. 4, 1959). Hence, *PDMQ* (1980)'s attribution of 'Teenage sex-change priest in mercy dash to Palace' to Magnus Linklater in the BBC Radio programme *Between the Lines* (18 September 1976) is misleading.

Yet another version is: '"Hell!" said the Duchess, "I'm pregnant, whodunnit?"'

1 **An archaeologist is the best husband any woman can have; the older she gets, the more interested he is in her.**

Attributed, for example, in Laurence J. Peter, *Quotations for Our Time* (1977). Christie was married to the archaeologist Sir Max Mallowan, and so it seemed quite feasible when she was quoted as saying this in a news report (8 March 1954), also quoted in *The Observer* (2 January 1955). However, according to G.C. Ramsey, *Agatha Christie: Mistress of Mystery* (1967), she vehemently denied having said it, insisting that it would have been a very silly remark for anyone to make, and neither complimentary nor amusing.

Frank S. Pepper in his *Handbook of 20th Century Quotations* (1984) placed the remark in Christie's *Murder in Mesopotamia* (1936), but it is not be found in that book.

Charles CHURCHILL English poet (1731–64)

Of actors:

2 **The strolling tribe, a despicable race,**
Like wand'ring Arabs, shift from place to place.

The Apology, lines 206–7 (1761), a satire on theatrical personalities of his day. Cited by Bryan Forbes in his Foreword to *That Despicable Race* (1980).

Lord Randolph CHURCHILL English politician (1849–94)

3 **Ulster will not be a consenting party; Ulster at the proper moment will resort to the supreme arbitrament of force; Ulster will fight and Ulster will be right.**

Public letter to a Liberal-Unionist (7 May 1886). Hence, the slogan 'Ulster will fight and Ulster will be right' used by the Ulster Volunteers opposing Irish Home Rule (1913–14). From Randolph Churchill, *Winston Churchill: Youth* (1966): 'This famous slogan became the watchword of Ulster; it pithily explains why Ulster is still a part of the United Kingdom of Great Britain and Northern Ireland.'

4 **An old man in a hurry.**

On W.E. Gladstone. In an address to the electors of South Paddington (19 June 1886): 'This monstrous mixture of imbecility, extravagance and political hysterias, better known as "the bill for the future government of Ireland" [the Home Rule Bill] – this farrago of superlative nonsense – is to be put into motion – for this reason and no other: to gratify the ambitions of ...'

5 **The duty of an opposition is to oppose.**

In W.S. Churchill, *Lord Randolph Churchill* (1906). A political attitude cited when an opposition party appears to take up a contrary position just for its own sake. Harold Wilson's criticism of the EEC when in opposition to the Conservative government in the early 1970s was said to reflect it. When Labour returned to power it renegotiated Britain's terms of membership and put the results before a referendum in 1975.

Randolph CHURCHILL English journalist and politician (1911–68)

6 **I should never be allowed out in private.**

In a letter to a hostess whose dinner party he had ruined with one of his displays of drunken rudeness. Quoted in Brian Roberts, *Randolph* (1984). In a letter to his father (16 October 1952), Randolph wrote: 'It is not for nothing that I coined the "mot" about myself: "Randolph should never be allowed out in private."'

(Sir) Winston CHURCHILL British Conservative Prime Minister (1874–1965)

7 **The conditions of the Transvaal ordinance under which Chinese Labour is now being carried on do not, in my opinion, constitute a state of slavery. A labour contract into which men enter voluntarily for a limited and for a brief period, under which they are paid wages which they consider adequate, under which they are not bought or sold and from which they can obtain relief on payment of seventeen pounds ten shillings may not be a desirable contract ... but it cannot in the opinion of His Majesty's Government be classified as slavery in the extreme acceptance of the word without some risk of terminological inexactitude.**

In 1906 the status of Chinese workers in South Africa was mentioned in the King's speech to Parliament as 'slavery'. An Opposition amendment of 22 February of the same year was tabled regretting, 'That Your Majesty's ministers should have brought the reputation of this country into contempt by describing the employment of Chinese indentured labour as slavery'. Churchill, as Under-Secretary at the Colonial Office, replied by quoting what he had said in the previous election campaign. Subsequently, the phrase 'terminological inexactitude' has been taken, almost invariably, as a humorously long-winded way of indicating a 'lie', but the context shows that this is not the meaning. One of the first to misunderstand it, however, was Joseph Chamberlain. Of 'terminological inexactitude' he said: 'Eleven syllables, many of them of Latin or Greek derivation, when one good English word, a Saxon word of a single syllable, would do!' Following Churchill's coinage, *Punch* Magazine ran a series of 'terminological exactitudes' from 6 May 1908.

1   Nothing in life is so exhilarating as to be shot at without result.

The Malakand Field Force (1898) – referring to his time in India. Quoted by Ronald Reagan after the attempt on his life in 1981. Compare Prince Andrew, interviewed in *The Times* (14 November 1983): 'Asked whether his Falklands experience had helped shape his character, the prince replied: "That is a very difficult question to answer. I think being shot at is one of the most character-forming things of one's life."'

2   If you were my wife, I'd drink it.

To Lady Astor, who had said, 'If you were my husband, I'd poison your coffee' (in about 1912). Quoted in Consuelo Vanderbilt Balsan, *Glitter and Gold* (1952), and Elizabeth Langhorne, *Nancy Astor and Her Friends* (1974). The exchange is used in the film *Paradise Alley* (US 1961) in which Margaret Hamilton shouts at her neighbour, 'If you were my husband, I'd give you poison!' and Billy Gilbert retorts, 'If I were your husband, I'd take it!'

3   I can only say to you let us go forward together and put these grave matters to the proof.

Speech on Ulster (14 March 1914) – first appearance of a Churchill stock phrase. Compare 'Let us go forward together in all parts of the Empire, in all parts of the Island' (speaking on the war, 27 January 1940); and 'I say, "Come then, let us go forward together with our united strength"' (in his 'blood, sweat and tears' speech, 13 May 1940). A cliché from then on. It occurs along with other rhetorical clichés during the 'Party Political Speech' (written by Max Schreiner) on the Peter Sellers comedy album *The Best of Sellers* (1958): 'Let us assume a bold front and go forward together.'

4   They say you can rat, but you can't re-rat.

On 'crossing the floor' of the House of Commons more than once. Reported in John Colville, *The Fringes of Power*, Vol. 1 (1985) – entry for 26 January 1941. The remark may date from 1923/4 when Churchill rejoined the Conservatives, having earlier left them to join the Liberals.

5   It was with a sense of awe that they [the German leaders] turned upon Russia the most grisly of all weapons. They transported Lenin in a sealed truck like a plague bacillus from Switzerland into Russia.

The World Crisis: The Aftermath, Chap. 4 (1929). Lenin was indeed shipped back to Russia to foment revolution in 1917, but was put in a sealed train so that his 'plague' would not be caught by the countries he passed through. A choice description that Churchill would seem to have originated. An earlier outing for the image occurred in Churchill's House of Commons speech (5 November 1919): 'Lenin was sent to Russia by the Germans in the same way that you might send a phial containing a culture of typhoid or cholera to be poured into the water supply of a great city, and it worked with amazing accuracy.'

6   It is a good thing for an uneducated man to read books of quotations.

My Early Life, Chap. 9 (1930). He goes on: 'Bartlett's *Familiar Quotations* is an admirable work, and I studied it intently. The quotations when engraved upon the memory give you good thoughts. They also make you anxious to read the authors and look for more.'

7   I once went to bed with a man to see what it was like.

According to Ted Morgan, *Somerset Maugham* (1980), this was Churchill's reply when asked by Maugham if he had ever had any homosexual affairs. Maugham asked him who the man was. Churchill replied, 'Ivor Novello.' 'And what was it like?' 'Musical.' The source for this story was Alan Searle, one of Maugham's acolytes. Churchill's daughter, Mary Soames, questioned it when it was included in my *Dictionary of 20th Century Quotations* (1987), and it is surely of dubious veracity.

8   I cannot forecast to you the action of Russia. It is a riddle wrapped in a mystery inside an enigma.

Radio broadcast (1 October 1939). Not, as might appear, a general reflection on the Russian character but a specific response to the Soviet occupation of East Poland, in league with Germany, on 18 September.

9   I would say to the House, as I said to those who have joined this Government: I have nothing to offer but blood, toil, tears and sweat.

Speech to the House of Commons (13 May 1940) upon becoming Prime Minister. Note the order of the last five words. There are echoes in these of earlier speeches and writings. The combination makes an appearance in John Donne's line from *An Anatomy of the World* (1611): ''Tis in vain to do so or mollify it with thy tears or sweat or blood.' Byron follows with 'blood, sweat and tear-wrung millions' in 1823. Theodore Roosevelt spoke in an 1897 speech of 'the blood and sweat and tears, the labour and the anguish, through which, in the days that have gone, our forefathers moved to triumph'. The more usual order of the words was later enshrined in the name of the 1970s American band. Churchill seemed to avoid this configuration, however. In 1931, he had already written of the Tsarist armies: 'Their sweat, their tears, their blood bedewed the endless plain.'

Possibly the closest forerunner of Churchill's 'backs to the wall' exhortation was Giuseppe Garibaldi's impromptu speech to his followers on 2 July 1849 before Rome fell to French troops. The speech was not taken down at the time, so this version is made up of various accounts. Seated upon a horse in the Piazza of St Peter's, he declared: 'Fortune, who betrays us today, will smile on us tomorrow. I am going out from Rome. Let those who wish to continue the war against the stranger, come with me. I offer neither pay, nor quarters, nor provisions; I offer hunger, thirst, forced marches, battles and death [fame, sete, marcie forzate, battaglie e morte]. Let him who loves his country with his heart, and not merely his lips, follow me.' As precedents go, this is obviously quite a close one, and it is probable that Churchill had read G.M. Trevelyan's series of books about Garibaldi, published at the turn of the century, in which the lines occur. Having launched such a famous phrase, Churchill referred to it five more times during the course of the war, though he did not always use all four keywords or in the original order.

Indeed, right from the start, people seem to have had difficulty in getting the order of the words right. The natural inclination is to put 'blood', 'sweat' and 'tears' together. Joan Wyndham in *Love Lessons – A Wartime Diary* (1985) concludes her entry for 13 May 1940 with: 'Later we listened to a very stirring speech by Churchill about "blood, toil, sweat and tears".' There is a slight suspicion that this diary may have been 'improved' somewhat in the editing, but not, obviously, to the point of imposing accuracy. Boller & George's *They Never Said It* (1989), dedicated to exposing quotation errors, has Churchill saying, 'blood *and* toil, tears and sweat'.

1 You ask, what is our aim? I can answer in one word: victory, victory at all costs, victory in spite of all terror, victory, however long and hard the road may be.
In the same speech. Compare CLEMENCEAU 146:11.

2 We shall not flag or fail. We shall go on to the end ... We shall fight on the beaches, we shall fight on the landing grounds, we shall fight in the fields and in the streets, we shall fight in the hills; we shall never surrender.
Speech to the House of Commons (4 June 1940). At the end of May, some 338,000 Allied troops had been evacu-

ated from the Dunkirk area of northern France – a formidable achievement celebrated as a victory although it was a retreat. Churchill tried to check the euphoria in this speech. He ended thus, however, on a note of hope. Note, not 'fight *them* on the beaches ...' Compare BUSH 113:3.

3 If we can stand up to [Hitler], all Europe may be free and the life of the world may move forward into broad, sunlit uplands.
Speech, House of Commons (18 June 1940). In Churchill's long speaking career there was one thematic device he frequently resorted to for his perorations. It appears in many forms but may be summarized as the 'broad, sunlit uplands' approach. In his collected speeches there are some 13 occasions when he made use of this construction. 'The level plain ... a land of peace and plenty ... the sunshine of a more gentle and a more generous age' (1906); 'I earnestly trust ... that by your efforts our country may emerge from this period of darkness and peril once more in the sunlight of a peaceful time' (at the end of a speech on 19 September 1915 when Churchill's own position was precarious following the failure of the Gallipoli campaign); in his 'finest hour' speech, Churchill hoped that, 'the life of the world may move forward into broad, sunlit uplands' (1940); 'it is an uphill road we have to tread, but if we reject the cramping, narrowing path of socialist restrictions, we shall surely find a way – and a wise and tolerant government – to those broad uplands where plenty, peace and justice reign' (1951 – prior to the general election).

4 What General Weygand called the Battle of France is over. I expect that the Battle of Britain is about to begin.
In the same speech. The urge to give names to battles – even before they are fought and won – is well exemplified by this coinage. The 'Battle of Britain' duly became the name by which the decisive overthrowing of German invasion plans by 'the Few' is known. The order of the day, read aloud to every pilot on 10 July, contained the words: 'The Battle of Britain is about to begin. Members of the Royal Air Force, the fate of generations is in your hands.' Another Churchill coinage – 'The Battle of Egypt' in a speech (10 November 1942) – caught on less well.

5 If we fail, then the whole world, including the United States, including all that we have known and cared for, will sink into the abyss of a new Dark Age made more sinister, and perhaps more protracted, by the lights of perverted science. Let us therefore brace ourselves to our duties, and so bear ourselves that, if the British Empire and its

Commonwealth last for a thousand years, men will still say, This was their finest hour.

In the same speech. The various versions of this famous concluding passage raise questions as to precisely what Churchill did or did not say on this and other occasions. The first point to make about this (and almost every other Churchill speech) is that it was entirely premeditated. As Jock Colville, his secretary at the time, recalled in *Action This Day* (1968): 'The composition of a speech was not a task Churchill was prepared to skimp or to hurry; nor, except on some convivial occasion, was he willing to speak impromptu. He might improvise briefly, but only to elaborate or clarify, and he stuck closely to the text he had prepared ... Quick as was his wit and unfailing his gift for repartee, he was not a man to depart in the heat of the moment from the theme or indeed the words that he had laboriously conceived in set-speech form.'

Churchill dictated his speeches to a typist. The finished speech would be laid out on many sheets of paper, with plenty of spacing, and then the whole lot was fastened firmly together so that it wouldn't end up on the floor. He would read from detailed notes which were set out in what was known as Speech Form which meant rather like a hymn-sheet or, as someone said, like the psalms, and made them easier to read.

It would seem, however, that these 'notes' were almost a word-for-word text and this came in useful when (as on 18 June) he repeated his House of Commons speech in the evening for radio listeners to the BBC. But when one talks of Churchill's famous 'Finest Hour' speech one is, in fact, referring to any one of several versions: (1) the notes from which he spoke, (2) the transcript of the parliamentary speech made by *Hansard* reporters, (3) any transcripts made of the radio 'talk', (4) the version used when Churchill re-recorded some of his speeches for the Decca record company after the war was over. No wonder that published versions of the speeches differ in many details from each other and from Churchill's notes (which have been published).

It has to be said that these discrepancies are not very major, but they are interesting. At the peroration, did he say exactly what is in his notes and which is broadly speaking *Hansard*'s version and also what is to be found cited in *ODQ* (1992) – namely, 'duty' for 'duties', 'lasts' for 'last'?

Or did he say what is to be found, for example, in the book *Churchill Speaks*, his 'Collected Speeches in Peace and War', ed. Robert Rhodes James (1981), and which is given above? This version accords with what Churchill put in his *History of the Second War*, Vol. 2 (1949), and also with what he speaks on the Decca recording made after the war. This presumably met with his approval. It is also the version in *Bartlett* (1992). But we still cannot be sure it was what he

said at the time. *ODQ* also puts, rather, 'British *Commonwealth* and its *Empire*' in that order. If nothing else, this only goes to prove how difficult it is to quote correctly – even one of the most famous speeches of all.

The Finest Hours was the title of a documentary film (UK 1964) about Churchill's life.

1 Set Europe ablaze.

Instruction on the establishment of the Special Operations Executive to co-ordinate acts of subversion against enemies overseas. This ringing call was one of the last Churchillisms to become publicly known. E.H. Cookridge wrote in *Inside S.O.E.* (1966): 'The Special Operations Executive was born on 19 July 1940 on the basis of a memo from Winston Churchill "to coordinate all action by way of subversion and sabotage against the enemy overseas". Or, as the Prime Minister later put it "to set Europe ablaze".' The title of the first chapter of Cookridge's book is 'Set Europe Ablaze'.

2 Never in the field of human conflict was so much owed by so many to so few.

On RAF pilots in the Battle of Britain. Speech, House of Commons (20 August 1940). Churchill's classic tribute was made well before the battle had reached its peak. There is a clear echo of Shakespeare's lines 'We few, we happy few, we band of brothers' in *Henry V. Benham* (1948) quotes Sir John Moore (1761–1809) after the fall of Calpi (where Nelson lost an eye): 'Never was so much work done by so few men.'

Another pre-echo may be found in Vol. 2 of Churchill's own *A History of the English-Speaking Peoples* (1956, but largely written before the war). In describing a Scottish incursion in 1640 during the run-up to the English Civil War, he writes: 'All the Scots cannon fired and all the English army fled. A contemporary wrote that "Never so many ran from so few with less ado." The English soldiers explained volubly that their flight was not due to fear of the Scots, but to their own discontents.'

Earlier outings of the phraseology in Churchill's own speeches include: 'Never before were there so many people in England and never before have they had so much to eat' (Oldham by-election, 1899); and 'Nowhere else in the world could so enormous a mass of water be held up by so little masonry' (of a Nile dam, 1908).

The bookish phrase 'in the field of human conflict' tended to be dropped when Churchill's speech was quoted. It is interesting that Harold Nicolson, noting the speech in his diary, slightly misquotes this passage: '[Winston] says, in referring to the RAF, "never in the history of human conflict *has* so much been owed by so many to so few".' Much later, Terry Major-Ball was one of those who repeated the first of these errors in *Major Major* (1994): 'Never in the history of human conflict has a private soldier been so relieved,' he writes.

The immediate impact of Churchill's phrase was unquestionable, however, and is evidenced by a letter to him of 10 September from Lady Violet Bonham Carter (from the Churchill papers, quoted by Martin Gilbert in Vol. 6 of the official biography): 'Your sentence about the Air-war – "Never in the history [*sic*] of human conflict has [*sic*] so much been owed by so many to so few" – will live as long as words are spoken and remembered. Nothing so simple, so majestic & so true has been said in so great a moment of human history. You have beaten your old enemies "the Classics" into a cocked hat! Even my Father [H.H. Asquith] would have admitted that. How *he* would have loved it!'

By 22 September, Churchill's daughter Mary was uttering a *bon mot* in his hearing about the collapse of France through weak leadership: 'Never before has so much been betrayed for so many by so few' – recorded by John Colville, *The Fringes of Power*, Vol. 1 (1985).

1 Like the Mississippi, it just keeps rolling along. Let it roll. Let it roll on full flood, inexorable, irresistible, benignant, to broader lands and better days.

On co-operation with the US. In the same speech. Alluding to HAMMERSTEIN 226:6.

2 Here is the answer which I will give to President Roosevelt ... Give us the tools, and we will finish the job.

Radio broadcast (9 February 1941). Churchill ended his speech by quoting the verse from LONGFELLOW 294:4 that President Roosevelt had sent him in January. Churchill's prime objective at this time (Pearl Harbor did not take place until December) was to bring the United States into the war or, at least, to wring every possible ounce of assistance out of it. Hence, the famous rallying cry with which he concluded. In May, Churchill also replied to Roosevelt's quotation with his own taken from CLOUGH 147:6.

3 As far as I can see, you have used every cliché except 'God is love' and 'Please adjust your dress before leaving.'

On a long-winded memorandum by Anthony Eden. This is quoted in Maurice Edelman, *The Mirror: A Political History* (1966) together with Churchill's comment: 'This offensive story is wholly devoid of foundation.' In 1941, Churchill took the unusual course of writing to Cecil King of the *Daily Mirror* about the matter. The columnist 'Cassandra' had used the story, though labelling it apocryphal and saying he had

taken it from *Life* Magazine. *Reader's Digest* in August 1943 certainly carried this version by Allan A. Michie: 'Asked once to look over a draft of one of Anthony Eden's vague speeches on the post-war world, he sent it back to the Foreign Minister with this curt note: "I have read your speech and find that you have used every cliché known to the English language except 'Please adjust your dress before leaving.'"'

4 [He is] like a female llama surprised in her bath.

On Charles de Gaulle. Quoted in Lord Moran, *The Struggle for Survival* (1966), which also includes his denial that he ever said it.

5 The Cross of Lorraine is the heaviest cross I have had to bear.

On Charles de Gaulle. In France the Resistance movement had a symbol – the Cross of Lorraine – and when Charles de Gaulle was told that Churchill had made this remark in reference to him, he commented: 'If we consider that the other crosses Churchill had to bear were the German army, submarine warfare, the bombing of Britain and the threat of annihilation, then when he says that the heaviest of all these was de Gaulle, it is quite a tribute to a man alone, without an army, without a country, and with only a few followers' – Romain Gary, *Life* Magazine (December 1958). According to Colonel Gilbert Rémy, *Ten Years with De Gaulle* (1971), the film producer Alexander Korda asked Churchill in 1948, 'Winston, did you really say that of all the crosses you ever had to bear, the heaviest was the Cross of Lorraine?' and Churchill replied, 'No, I didn't say it; but I'm sorry I didn't, because it was quite witty ... and so true!'

6 They *must* float up and down with the tide. The anchor problem must be mastered. The ships must have a side-flap cut in them, and a drawbridge long enough to overreach the moorings of the piers. Let me have the best solution worked out. Don't argue the matter. The difficulties will argue for themselves.

In Vol. 5 of Churchill's *The Second World War* (1952) there is a facsimile of the minute he issued to Lord Louis Mountbatten, Chief of Combined Operations, on 30 May 1942, describing his ideas for the Mulberry Harbours project. The spur is in a hand-written note addressed to the 'CCO or deputy'.

7 Now this is not the end. It is not even the beginning of the end. But it is, perhaps, the end of the beginning.

In the same speech. Of the Battle of Egypt. The formula seems to have a particular appeal, judging by the number of times it has been recalled. One occasion that comes to mind is when Ian Smith, the Rhodesian leader, broadcast a speech containing – or so it seemed at the time – a commitment to majority rule, after Dr Henry Kissinger's shuttle diplomacy in the autumn of 1976.

Note that Talleyrand went only half-way when he said, 'It is the beginning of the end [*Voilà le commencement de la fin*]' either after Napoleon's defeat at Borodino (1812) or during the Hundred Days War (20 March–28 June 1815).

In *F.E. Smith, First Earl of Birkenhead* (1983), John Campbell observes that Churchill was sitting next to F.E. when Smith addressed an all-party meeting in London on 11 September 1914. The Battle of the Marne, he said, was not the beginning of the end, 'it is only the end of the beginning'. And, Campbell suggests, Churchill 'remembered and tucked [it] away for use again twenty-seven years later'.

1 The soft under-belly of the Axis.

The phrase 'soft under-belly', for a vulnerable part, appears to have originated with Churchill. Speaking in the House of Commons on 11 November 1942, he said: 'We make this wide encircling movement in the Mediterranean ... having for its object the exposure of the under-belly of the Axis, especially Italy, to heavy attack.' In his *The Second World War*, Vol. 4 (1951), he describes a prior meeting with Stalin in August 1942, at which he had outlined the same plan: 'To illustrate my point I had meanwhile drawn a picture of a crocodile, and explained to Stalin with the help of this picture how it was our intention to attack the soft belly of the crocodile as we attacked his hard snout.'

Somewhere, subsequently, the 'soft' and the 'underbelly' must have joined together to produce the phrase in the form in which it is now used.

2 The proud German Army by its sudden collapse, sudden crumbling and breaking up, has once again proved the truth of the saying 'The Hun is always either at your throat or at your feet.'

Speech to the US Congress (19 May 1943). Compare, from J.R. Colombo, *Popcorn in Paradise* (1979), what Ava Gardner said about a well-known American film critic: 'Rex Reed is either at your feet or at your throat'; from Marlon Brando in *Playboy* (January 1979): 'Chaplin reminded me of what Churchill said about the Germans: either at your feet or at your throat.'

3 No socialist Government conducting the entire life and industry of the country could afford to allow free, sharp, or violently worded expressions of public discontent. They would have to fall back on some form of Gestapo.

Party political radio broadcast (4 June 1945). In the run-up to the general election that he lost, Churchill attempted to reinforce his view of a socialist future with a misjudged reference to the Gestapo. Evidently his wife had begged him to leave out the passage, but, in what was a significant miscalculation and a possible token of waning powers, Churchill went ahead and was duly much criticized by his political opponents, though he did also receive some support.

4 At the moment it seems quite effectively disguised.

On his defeat in the 1945 general election, to his wife who had told him it might be a blessing in disguise. Quoted in his *The Second World War*, Vol. 6 (1954). Meaning 'a misfortune which turns out to be beneficial', this phrase has been in existence since the early 18th century.

Despite this comment, Churchill seems to have come round to something like his wife's point of view. On 5 September 1945 he wrote to her from an Italian holiday: 'This is the first time for very many years that I have been completely out of the world ... Others having to face the hideous problems of the aftermath ... It may all indeed be "a blessing in disguise".'

5 Neither the sure prevention of war, nor the continuous rise of world organization will be gained without what I have called the fraternal association of the English-speaking peoples. This means a special relationship between the British Commonwealth and Empire and the United States.

Speech at Fulton, Missouri (5 March 1946). The term 'special relationship', used to describe affiliations between countries or regions (the earliest *OED2* citation is for one between Britain and Galicia in 1929), but particularly referring to that supposed to exist between Britain and the US on the basis of historical ties and a common language, was principally promoted by Churchill in his attempts to draw the US into the 1939–45 war, though whether he used the phrase prior to 1941 is not clear. In the House of Commons on 7 November 1945 Churchill said: 'We should not abandon our special relationship with the United States and Canada about the atomic bomb.' In his Fulton speech, he also asked: 'Would a special relationship between the United States and the British Commonwealth be inconsistent with our over-riding loyalties to the World Organization [the UN]?'

6 From Stettin in the Baltic to Trieste in the Adriatic, an iron curtain has descended across the Continent.

In the same speech. A famous reference to an imaginary division between the Eastern and Western blocs in Europe, caused by the hard-line tactics of the Soviet Union after the Second World War. Churchill had already used the phrase 'iron curtain' in telegrams to President Truman and in the House of Commons.

Before him there were any number of uses, all alluding to the iron 'safety' curtains introduced in theatres as a fire precaution in the 18th century (and still sometimes referred to as 'the iron' in theatrical circles). In his novel *The Food of the Gods* (1904), H.G. Wells had written: 'An iron curtain had dropped between him [the scientist Redwood] and the outer world.' When Germany invaded Belgium in 1914, Queen Elisabeth of Belgium, who was the daughter of a German duke and married the future King Albert of Belgium in 1900, is reported to have said that between the Germans and herself '*un rideau de fer*' had descended. In the specific Soviet context, Ethel Snowden was using the phrase as early as 1920 in her book *Through Bolshevik Russia*. Describing her arrival in Petrograd with a Labour Party delegation, she said: 'We were behind the "iron curtain" at last!' Joseph Goebbels, Hitler's propaganda chief, wrote in an article for the weekly *Das Reich* (23 February 1945): 'Should the German people lay down their arms, the agreements between Roosevelt, Churchill and Stalin would allow the Soviets to occupy all Eastern and South-Eastern Europe together with the major part of the Reich. An iron curtain would at once descend on this territory.' These remarks were reprinted in British newspapers at the time.

1 *The Sinews of Peace.*

Churchill's speech at Fulton had this title – an allusion to the phrase '*nervi belli pecunia*' from Cicero's *Philippics* where the 'sinews of war' meant 'money'. The 'sinews of peace' recommended by Churchill in dealing with the Soviet Union amounted to recourse to the newly formed United Nations Organization.

2 One is a majority.

Any number of British parliamentarians have used this expression to lessen the importance of only achieving a small majority in an election or parliamentary vote. It is fair to assume that a proportion of them attributed the phrase to Churchill (as Margaret Thatcher did in April 1988). *The Observer* Magazine had '"One vote is enough" – Churchill' in a compendium of election sayings on 5 April 1992. Possibly Churchill *did* say it, but if he did, he was quoting or alluding. It was Benjamin Disraeli who wrote, 'As for our majority ... one is enough' in Chapter 64 of his novel *Endymion* (1880). Accordingly, Andrew Roberts writes in *Eminent Churchillians* (1994): 'Despite Disraeli's famous comment, which Churchill made his own, that "One is Enough", the new Prime Minister felt himself politically insecure.'

Compare, from the US, 'One with the law is a majority' in Calvin Coolidge's Speech of Acceptance (27 July 1920),

and 'One man with courage makes a majority', often ascribed to Andrew Jackson. Also, Wendell Phillips in a speech at Brooklyn on 1 November 1859 said: 'One, on God's side, is a majority.' Later, John F. Kennedy, when elected President in 1960, remarked: 'The majority is narrow, but the responsibility is clear. There may be difficulties with Congress, but a majority of one is still a majority.' *A Majority of One* was the title of a play and film (US 1961).

3 And you, madam, are ugly. But I shall be sober in the morning.

To Bessie Braddock MP, who had told him he was drunk. Quoted in Sykes & Sproat, *The Wit of Sir Winston* (1965), without naming Braddock. She was named in Leslie Frewin, *Immortal Jester* (1973). The same idea apparently occurs in the W.C. Fields film *It's a Gift* (US 1934) where Fields says: 'I'll be sober tomorrow, but you'll be crazy for the rest of your life.'

4 There, but for the grace of God, goes God.

Churchill did not deny having made this remark about the Labour politician, Sir Stafford Cripps. It was quoted in Willans & Roetter, *The Wit of Winston Churchill* (1954), but had already been noted by Geoffrey Madan, who died in July 1947 – see his *Notebooks* (published in 1981).

In so speaking, Churchill was adapting a remark made by John Bradford (who died in 1555) on seeing criminals going to their execution: 'There, but for the grace of God, goes John Bradford.' This is normally now rendered proverbially as 'There, but for the grace of God, go I.'

5 It [is] the first time that [I have] heard of a rat actually swimming out to join a sinking ship.

On Air Vice-Marshal Bennett who had joined the Liberals. Quoted in Malcolm Muggeridge, *Like It Was* (1981) – diary entry for 14 February 1948. Later, Ralph Yarborough said of John B. Connally's 1973 switch from Democratic to Republican party in pursuit of the presidential nomination: 'It is the only case on record of a *man* swimming toward a sinking ship' – quoted in *The Washington Post* (18 January 1988).

6 A sheep in sheep's clothing.

On Clement Attlee. Quoted in Willans & Roetter, *The Wit of Winston Churchill* (1954). According to *Safire* (1980), however, Churchill told Sir Denis Brogan that he had said it not about Attlee but about Ramsay MacDonald, with rather more point. If so, it would appear that he was quoting a joke made by the humorous columnist Beachcomber in about 1936. Aneurin Bevan alluded to this same source in about 1937 – 'Beachcomber once described Mr Ramsay

MacDonald as ... It applies to many of the front-bench men with whom the Parliamentary Labour Party is cursed' – quoted in Michael Foot, *Aneurin Bevan*, Vol. 1 (1962).

Sir Edmund Gosse is supposed to have said the same of T. Sturge Moore, the 'woolly-bearded poet', in about 1906 – and was quoted as such by Ferris Greenslet in *Under the Bridge* (1943). 'A wolf in sheep's clothing' is an expression from a fable by Aesop; see also Mark 7:15.

1 An empty taxi arrived at 10 Downing Street, and when the door was opened Attlee got out.

On Clement Attlee. Succeeded by the Labour leader after the 1945 general election, Churchill was obliged to oppose the man who had been his deputy in the wartime coalition. So this was another joke that went the rounds about the time. When John Colville told Churchill it was being attributed to him, he commented gravely, 'after an awful pause': 'Mr Attlee is an honourable and gallant gentleman, and a faithful colleague who served his country well at the time of her greatest need. I should be obliged if you would make it clear whenever an occasion arises that I never would make such a remark about him, and that I strongly disapprove of anybody who does.' This denial was reported in Kenneth Harris, *Attlee* (1982). François Dournon, *Dictionnaire des mots et formules célèbres* (1994), suggests that the remark really originates with Aurélien Scholl (1833–1902), who is supposed to have said: '*Une voiture vide s'arrête. Sarah Bernhardt en descend*' – source: Gilbert Guilleminault, *La Jeunesse de Marianne* (no date). And from the *carnets* of Ludovic Halévy (May 1879): '*Mot bien drôle ce matin, dans "Le Figaro", sur Sarah Bernhardt: "Un fiacre vide s'arrête devant le Théâtre Français. Sarah Bernhardt en descend"*' – source: *La Revue des Deux-Mondes* (15 December 1937).

2 [Clement Attlee is] a modest man who has a good deal to be modest about.

Quoted in the *Chicago Sunday Tribune Magazine of Books* (27 June 1954) – perhaps in a review of Willans & Roetter, *The Wit of Winston Churchill* (1954). Earlier, in the film *Sitting Pretty* (US 1948), Clifton Webb delivers the line: 'Your husband has a great deal to be modest about.'

3 Don't talk to me about naval tradition. It's nothing but rum, sodomy, and the lash.

Quoted in Sir Peter Gretton, *Former Naval Person* (1968) – on the occasion when a naval officer objected that a wartime operation the Prime Minister was supporting ran against the traditions of the Royal Navy. In Harold Nicolson's diary (17 August 1950), this appears as: 'Naval tradition? Monstrous. Nothing but rum, sodomy, prayers and the lash.' Hence, *Rum, Bum and Concertina*, the title of a volume of

George Melly's autobiography (1977), which he prefers to derive from 'an old naval saying': 'Ashore it's wine, women and song, aboard it's rum, bum and concertina.'

4 Do not criticize your government when out of the country. Never cease to do so when at home.

Attributed remark, but unverified. An unwritten rule for members of a political party in power – and also, to some extent – in opposition. Quite frequently ignored. The original of the remark is probably this passage from a speech in the House of Commons (18 April 1947): 'When I am abroad I always make a rule never to criticize or attack the Government of my country. I make up for lost time when I come home.'

5 He's not as nice as he looks.

On Ian Mikardo MP. Quoted by Richard Boston on BBC Radio *Quote ... Unquote* (4 January 1976). Said to have been spoken to Christopher Soames, Churchill's PPS. According to Matthew Parris, *Scorn* (1994): 'Sir Edward Heath told us that this remark was made after a debate in the House of Commons in which Mr Mikardo "pressed the Prime Minister about anti-Semitic practices at the Mid-Ocean Club, Bermuda, somewhat to the irritation of the Prime Minister".' Perhaps it should be explained that Mr Mikardo was no oil painting, as the saying has it.

6 In war, resolution; in defeat, defiance; in victory, magnanimity; in peace, goodwill.

Churchill's history *The Second World War* was published in six volumes between 1948 and 1954. He took as the motto of the work some words that had occurred to him just after the First World War, as Eddie Marsh, at one time his Private Secretary, recalled: 'He produced one day a lapidary epigram on the spirit proper to a great nation in war and peace ... (I wish the tones in which he spoke this could have been "recorded" – the first phrase a rattle of musketry, the second "grating harsh thunder", the third a ray of the sun through storm-clouds; the last, pure benediction).'

In 1941 Churchill said the words had been devised (and rejected) as an inscription for a French war memorial, in the form: 'In war fury, in defeat defiance ...' Perhaps he had been inspired by one of the Latin quotations he knew – '*parcere subiectis et debellare* [spare the conquered and subdue the proud]' – Virgil, *Aeneid*, Bk 6, line 854. In *My Early Life* (1930) he had earlier given his rejected inscription just as it appears here in the head phrase.

7 *The Gathering Storm.*

Title of Vol. 1 of his history *The Second World War*, published in 1948. The phrase had already been used about the approach of the war by Anthony Eden in a speech to the National Association of Manufacturers in New York in 1938. Robert Burns, in 'Tam o'Shanter' (1791), has: 'Gathering her brows like gathering storm, / Nursing her wrath to keep it warm.' See also below 142:2.

1 The years from 1931 to 1935, apart from my anxiety on public affairs, were personally very pleasant to me. I earned my livelihood by dictating articles which had a wide circulation ... I lived in fact from mouth to hand ... Thus I never had a dull or idle moment from morning till midnight, and with my happy family around me dwelt at peace within my habitation.

Referring to his 'exile' at Chartwell in the 1930s, in Chap. 5 of *The Gathering Storm*, the first volume of Churchill's *The Second World War* (1948). Churchill would have known he was alluding to Ecclesiasticus 44:6: 'Rich men furnished with ability, living peaceably in their habitations' (from the passage beginning 'Let us now praise famous men'.)

2 I felt as if I were walking with destiny, and that all my past life had been but a preparation for this hour and this trial.

On becoming Prime Minister in 1939. In the same chapter. Hence, *A Walk With Destiny*, title of a TV drama documentary play by Colin Morris (1974). In the US it was known as *The Gathering Storm* (see above 141:7).

3 I would kick him up the arse, Alfred.

On being asked what he would do if he saw Picasso walking ahead of him down Piccadilly. Quoted by Sir Alfred Munnings in a speech at the Royal Academy dinner (1949). A report in the *Times* Diary (29 March 1983) recalled that Munnings, as President, had invited Churchill, who had just been admitted to the Academy. He supposedly ruffled the politician's feathers by saying in his speech: 'Seated on my left is the greatest Englishman of all time. I said to him just now: "What would you do if you saw Picasso walking ahead of you down Piccadilly?" – and he replied: "I would kick him up the arse, Alfred."'

Alas, the BBC recording of the event fails to confirm that Munnings ever said this. Not a born speaker, to put it mildly, what he said was, 'Once he said to me, "Alfred, if you met Picasso coming down the street, would you join with me in kicking his something-something?" I said, "Yes, sir, I would!"'

The *Times* report also suggested that, 'as the laughter died, Munnings yelled at the top of his voice: "Blunt, Blunt [i.e. Sir Anthony Blunt, the art connoisseur later unmasked as a

traitor] – you're the one who says he prefers Picasso to Sir Joshua Reynolds!"' If he did yell it he was very quiet about it, because the barb is not audible on the recording.

Another version of Churchill's view of this exponent of modern art (whom he disliked) was that he would tell Picasso to shove his paint brushes up his arse. This was related by the war artist Arnold MacCulloch.

4 It is not easy to see how things could be worsened by a parley at the summit, if such a thing were possible.

Quoted in *The Times* (15 February 1950). This was apparently the start of the modern use of the term 'summit meeting/conference', but see also BAGEHOT 49:4.

5 The trees do not grow up to the sky.

A favourite proverb of Churchill's – but what does it mean? John Colville quotes him as saying it on 6 January 1953 in a situation where he is recommending a 'wait-and-see' policy. The full version seems to be, 'The trees are tall but they do not reach to the sky.' In other words, 'trees may be tall, but they're not that tall' or, metaphorically, 'no person is that important, however grand they may appear'. Later in the same year, on 9 November, in his speech to the Lord Mayor's Banquet, Churchill said: 'Another old saying comes back to my mind which I have often found helpful or at least comforting. I think it was Goethe who said, "The trees do not grow up to the sky." I do not know whether he would have said that if he had lived through this frightful 20th century where so much we feared was going to happen did actually happen. All the same it is a thought which should find its place in young as well as old brains.' In *The Second World War*, Vol. 2, Chap. 19 (1949), Churchill writes: 'There is a useful German saying, "The trees do not grow up to the sky."'

Is this a case of ascribing to Goethe any foreign-language quote of which the speaker doesn't really know the source? Wolfgang Mieder and George B. Bryan supply the answer in *The Proverbial Winston S. Churchill. An Index to Proverbs in the Works of Sir Winston Churchill* (1995). Listed are no less than 13 occasions on which Churchill used the proverb in his writing or speeches. Mieder and Bryan note how close the meaning of the words is to 'Pride goeth before a fall' (Proverbs 16:18), how it derives from a German original '*Est ist dafür gesorgt, daß die Bäume nicht in den Himmel wachsen*' (though sometimes this is in the form '*God takes care that* the trees don't grow up to the sky'), and how although Goethe probably didn't originate it, he used the proverb in his autobiography *Dichtung und Wahrheit* (1811). Earlier it occurs in Martin Luther's *Tischreden* (table talk) and in one of the collections of proverbs (1528–48) of Johann Agricola

Of course, people *do* manufacture these folk proverbs. Anon. devised one for the Soviet leader Nikita Khrushchev: 'Great oafs from little ikons grow.' Lyndon Irving sent this one into a *New Statesman* competition (though it has been ascribed to Dr Walter Heydecker): 'No leg is too short to reach the ground'. In *Unauthorized Versions* (1990), Kenneth Baker says: 'I am reminded of a competition for the most meaningless Russian proverb, of which the winning entry was, "The tallest trees are closest to the sky."' This is probably a reference to the game played by Claud Cockburn who won it once – according to his son, Patrick, in *The Independent* (29 May 1996) – with the 'fine old Norwegian saying, "The tree is taller than the highest wave."'

1 Talking jaw to jaw is better than going to war [or To jaw-jaw is always better than to war-war].
At a White House lunch (26 June 1954). Compare MACMILLAN 305:1.

2 The portrait is a remarkable example of modern art. It certainly combines force and candour. These are qualities which no active member of either house can do without or should fear to meet.
Speech, Westminster Hall (30 November 1954). For his 80th birthday, both Houses of Parliament presented Churchill with a portrait painted by Graham Sutherland. He did not like it but accepted the picture with a gracefully double-edged compliment. Lady Churchill's dislike of the portrait took a more practical form: she had it destroyed.

3 I look as if I was having a difficult stool.
Remark on the same portrait, quoted in Ted Morgan, *Somerset Maugham* (1980), but earlier in *The Lyttelton Hart-Davis Letters* (1978) – for 20 November 1955. Other versions of this criticism are: 'How do they paint one today? Sitting on a lavatory!' (said to Charles Doughty, secretary of the committee that organized the tribute), and 'Here sits an old man on his stool, pressing and pressing.'

4 I am not a pillar of the church but a buttress – I support it from the outside.
When Churchill was reproached for not going to church. Recalled by Montague Browne in a speech to the International Churchill Society, London (25 September 1985). Note, however, that it was said of John Scott, Lord Eldon (1751–1838): 'He may be one of its [the Church's] buttresses, but certainly not one of its pillars, for he is never found within it' – H. Twiss, *Public and Private Life of Eldon* (1844). *ODQ* (1992) adds that this remark was later attributed to Lord Melbourne.

Long before Churchill used it, the joke had become the caption to a cartoon in *Punch* (24 January 1880). A squire responds to a vicar who has commented on his non-attendance at services, disqualifying him from being a pillar of the church: 'If I'm not a pillar, I'm one of the buttresses – always to be found outside, you know!!'

See also BERNERS 64:7; BEVAN 66:5; HEALEY 231:4; KENNEDY 268:2; MARVELL 314:3; MURROW 333:1.

Count Galeazzo CIANO Italian politician (1903–44)

5 As always, victory finds a hundred fathers, but defeat is an orphan.
Mussolini's foreign minister (and son-in-law) made this diary entry on 9 September 1942 (translation published 1946). President Kennedy quoted the 'old saying' following the Bay of Pigs disaster in April 1961.

Colley CIBBER English playwright (1671 1757)

6 Off with his head – so much for Buckingham.
In his 1700 edition of Shakespeare's *Richard III*, Cibber extended 'off with his head' by the last four words. It proved a popular and lasting emendation. However, when Shakespeare used the original phrase at III.iv.76, Richard of Gloucester is speaking about Hastings. The extra phrase was included in Laurence Olivier's film of Shakespeare's play (UK 1955). In Boswell's *Life of Johnson* (1791) – for 15 May 1776 – John Wilkes is quoted as saying: 'If I had displeased the Duke [of Argyle], and he had wished it, there is not a Campbell among you but would have been ready to bring John Wilkes's head to him in a charger. It would have been only "Off with his head! So much for Aylesbury."' I was then member for Aylesbury.' (Aylesbury is in the county of Buckingham.)
  In 'Private Theatres' (1835), one of the *Sketches by Boz*, Charles Dickens describes the parts on offer to amateur actors who at that time could pay to take certain roles in plays: 'For instance, the Duke of Glo'ster is well worth two pounds ... including the "off with his head!" – which is sure to bring down the applause, and it is very easy to do – "Orf with his ed" (very quick and loud; – then slow and sneeringly) – "So much for Bu-u-u-uckingham!" Lay the emphasis on the "uck"; get yourself gradually into a corner, and work with your right hand, while you're saying it, as if you were feeling your way, and it's sure to do.'

7 Perish that thought!
In the same play, an interpolation into Act 5. First recorded use of the expression, now usually 'perish the thought'. Cibber's *The Tragical History of King Richard III* is a sub-

stantial reworking of Shakespeare's play. He brings in related material from *Henry VI* and even a line from *Richard II* (see 419:11), presumably on the basis that he thought it was rather a good one. However, he manages to leave out the first four lines of Shakespeare's 'Now is the winter of our discontent ...' speech. Like Shakespeare he repeats 'A horse! A horse! My kingdom for a horse!' (420:6) but, on the repeat, puts '*An* horse! *an* horse! my kingdom for *an* Horse ...'

1 Conscience avaunt, Richard's himself again:
Hark! the shrill trumpet sounds, to horse, away,
My soul's in arms, and eager for the fray.
Another of Cibber's Act 5 interpolations, this was one of the many Cibber and Garrick lines incorporated in Laurence Olivier's film of *Richard III* (1955).

2 Stolen sweets are best.
The Rival Fools (1709). See also HUNT 248:1; TRENET 468:3.

CITIZEN KANE American film 1941. Script by Herman J. Mankiewicz and Orson Welles. With Orson Welles as Kane, Dorothy Comingore as Susan and George Coulouris as Thatcher.

3 *Kane*: Rosebud!
Soundtrack. His dying word, the first word in the film, and referred to *passim*, as finding out what it meant to him is a theme of the picture. It is finally glimpsed written on the side of a snow-sledge – a powerful talisman of childhood innocence, or a 'symbol of maternal affection, the loss of which deprives him irrecoverably of the power to love or be loved' (Kenneth Tynan). Orson Welles himself issued a statement (14 January 1941) explaining: '"Rosebud" is the trade name of a cheap little sled on which Kane was playing on the day he was taken away from his home and his mother. In his subconscious it represented the simplicity, the comfort, above all the lack of responsibility in his home, and also it stood for his mother's love which Kane never lost.'

4 *Kane*: Dear Wheeler, you provide the prose poems. I'll provide the war.
Soundtrack. Kane, replying to a war correspondent's message, 'Could send you prose poems about scenery but ... there is no war in Cuba.' This is based on an 1898 exchange between the newspaper artist Frederic Remington and his proprietor, William Randolph Hearst (1863–1951). Remington asked to be allowed home from Cuba because there was no war for him to cover. Hearst cabled: 'Please remain. You furnish the pictures and I will furnish the war.' Hearst was, of course, the model for Kane.

Alan CLARK English Conservative politician (1928–99)

5 The trouble with Michael is that he had to buy all his furniture.
On Michael Heseltine. *Diaries* (1993) – entry for 17 June 1987. Although sometimes attributed to Clark himself, he was actually quoting Michael Jopling MP. But the jibe was not particularly new. Dorothy Parker, reviewing Emily Post's *Etiquette* (December 1927), wrote of the typical characters Mrs Post devised to illustrate her admonitions (Mrs Worldly, Mr Bachelor, and so on): 'Let them be dismissed by somebody's phrase (I wish to heaven it were mine) – "the sort of people who buy their silver".' Douglas Sutherland, *The English Gentleman* (1978) has: 'Gentlemen do not buy furniture. They inherit it.'

6 Economical with the *actualité*.
Under cross-examination at the Old Bailey during the Matrix Churchill arms-to-Iraq trial (November 1992). A whimsical twist on the euphemism 'economical with the truth' – see ARMSTRONG 39:2 – but more or less meaningless – *actualité* does not mean truth but rather 'topicality' or 'news'. Clark was displaying his ignorance. Perhaps he had meant to use *vérité* instead?

Brian CLARK British playwright (1932–)

7 *Whose Life Is It Anyway?*
Title of play (1978; film US 1981) about a paraplegic who resists his carers' determination to keep him alive. Hence, the format phrase 'whose — is it anyway?' A BBC Radio 4/Channel 4 TV improvisatory game was given the title *Whose Line Is It Anyway?* (by 1989). By 1993, *The Independent* Magazine was campaigning for the abolition of it as a headline cliché. Among a blizzard of examples, it cited: 'WHOSE QUEEN IS IT ANYWAY?' – London *Evening Standard* (18 March 1993) – and 'WHOSE WOMB IS IT ANYWAY?' – *Northern Echo* (9 November 1992).

8 Don't half-quote me to reinforce your own prejudices.
Kipling (1984) – put in the mouth of Rudyard Kipling.

(Sir) Kenneth CLARK (later Lord Clark) English art historian (1903–83)

9 *Another Part of the Wood.*
Title of the first volume of Clark's autobiography (1974) and taken from the stage direction to Act 3, Sc. 2 of Shakespeare's *A Midsummer Night's Dream*. Scene locations such as this were mostly not of Shakespeare's own devising but

were added by later editors. Clark said he wished also to allude to the opening of Dante's *Inferno*: 'I found myself in a dark wood where the straight way was lost.' Lillian Hellman had earlier entitled one of her plays, *Another Part of the Forest* (1946).

Roy CLARKE British writer (1930–)

1 *Last of the Summer Wine.*
Title of a long-running BBC TV comedy series (1974–) about a trio of former school friends in a Yorkshire village finding themselves elderly and unemployed . Not a quotation, according to its writer. In *Radio Times* (February 1983), Clarke described it as: 'Merely a provisional title which seemed to suit the age group and location. I expected it to be changed but no one ever thought of anything better.'

The phrase 'summer wine', on its own, had already been used in a song, 'If I Thought You'd Ever Change Your Mind' by John Cameron, which was recorded in 1969 by Kathe Green ('... feed you winter fruits and summer wine ...').

'Last of the wine' had also been used earlier to describe things of which there is only a finite amount or of which the best is gone. From a programme note by composer Nicholas Maw for *The Rising of the Moon*, Glyndebourne Festival Opera (1970): 'In a recent television interview, Noël Coward was asked if he thought it still possible to write comedy for the stage. Did his own generation not have the "last of the wine"?' In the 1950s, Robert Bolt wrote a radio play and Mary Renault a novel (1956) both with the title *The Last of the Wine* .

Karl von CLAUSEWITZ Prussian soldier (1780–1831)

2 War is nothing but a continuation of politics with the admixture of other means.
Vom Kriege (1832–4). Usually rendered as: 'War is the continuation of politics by other means.' Compare, 'Writing is the continuation of politics by other means' – Philippe Sollers, 'Tel Quel: Théorie d'Ensemble', *Ecriture et Révolution* (1968).

Eldridge CLEAVER American political activist (1935–)

3 If you're not part of the solution, you're part of the problem.
CODP's earliest citation for this (anonymous) modern proverb is Malcolm Bradbury's novel *The History Man* (1975). But there is little doubt that Cleaver said it in a 1968 speech in San Francisco. It may even be included in his *Soul on Ice* (1968). One form of Cleaver's remark is: 'What we're saying today is that you're either part of the solution or you're part of the problem.' Another: 'There is no more neutrality in the world. You either have to be part of

the solution, or you're going to be part of the problem.'
Compare: 'If you're not part of the steamroller, you're part of the road' – attributed to Michael Eisner, Chairman of Walt Disney, in 1993.

Georges CLEMENCEAU French Prime Minister (1841–1929)

4 *J'Accuse* [I accuse].
The Dreyfus Affair in France arose in 1894 when Captain Alfred Dreyfus, who was Jewish, was dismissed from the army on trumped-up charges of treason. Condemned to life imprisonment on Devil's Island, he was not reinstated until 1906. In the meantime, the case had divided France. The writer Émile Zola (1840–1902) came to the defence of Dreyfus with two open letters addressed to the President of the French Republic and printed in the paper *L'Aurore*. In these letters, Zola accused the French military and civil authorities of lying. The first, under the banner headline '*J'Accuse!*' was published on 13 January 1898, each concluding paragraph beginning with the words. For example: 'I accuse Lieutenant Colonel du Paty de Clam of having been the diabolic agent of the judicial error and of having for three years bolstered his dastardly deed with the strangest, most culpable machinations. I accuse the three expert graphologists – Messrs. Bel-homme, Varinard and Couard – of having prepared fraudulent and deceitful analyses, unless a medical examination should prove them to be afflicted with impaired vision and judgement ...' The second letter, more moderate in tone, followed on 22 January. As he anticipated, Zola was convicted of libel on the basis of the letters and fled to England.

It is a small point, perhaps, but Clemenceau, who played a prominent part in the campaign with Zola, claimed in a letter (19 June 1902) that: 'It was I who gave the title "*J'accuse*" to Zola's letter.' He also said that he had written most of the second letter – source: D.R. Watson, *Clemenceau* (1974).

Uses of the term: in 1919, Abel Gance made a film for Charles Pathé with the title *J'Accuse*, but it was not about the Dreyfus Affair. In it, the dead returned en masse from the First World War to accuse the survivors. Another version of the film was made before the outbreak of the Second World War. *I Accuse* became the title of a British film (1958), which was about the case, with José Ferrer as Dreyfus and Emlyn Williams as Zola.

In time, 'j'accuse' became a term of limited use given to any kind of crusading writing, especially in a newspaper. Frank Brady wrote in *Citizen Welles*, Chap. 12 (1989), about a statement ascribed to Orson Welles in a magazine called *Friday* that the character 'Citizen Kane' was based on William Randolph Hearst: 'After giving an outline of what the film was really about, in his opinion, Welles finished up his j'accuse against *Friday* with an interpretation and an attempt at self-protection.' Graham Greene entitled his short book on organized crime in the South of France *J'Accuse: the dark side of Nice* (1982).

1 *La guerre, c'est une chose trop grave pour la confier à des militaires* [War is too serious a business to be left to the generals].

In France, parliament had suspended its sittings at the outbreak of the First World War and the conduct of the war had been entrusted to the government and to Joffre and the General Staff. By 1915, however, opinion was changing. It may have been about this time that Clemenceau, who became French Prime Minister again in 1917, uttered this, his most famous remark. It was, apparently, quoted by Aristide Briand to David Lloyd George: 'D. was very much taken with a remark of Briand's to the effect that "this war is too important to be left to military men". It is exactly D.'s view, but unfortunately he never thought of putting it quite in that way. I like D. to be the person to put things in a particular clever way. Briand, however, seems to have the knack' – *Lloyd George: A Diary by Frances Stevenson*, ed. A.J.P. Taylor (1971), entry for 23 October 1916.

Later, it was quoted in Suarez, *Soixante Années d'histoire française: la vie orgueilleuse de Clemenceau* (1932; a later edition dates this to 1887, but without any source) and Hampden Jackson, *Clemenceau and the Third Republic* (1946). It is also attributed to Clemenceau in the film *Dr Strangelove ...* (US 1963).

The notion has also been ascribed to Talleyrand (Briand quoted him as such to Lloyd George during the First World War) and, indeed, Clemenceau may have said it himself much earlier (in 1886 even). Subsequently, the format of the saying has been applied to many other professions. See BENN 61:5; DE GAULLE 165:4; MACLEOD 302:5. In 1990 Helmut Sihler, president of a West German chemical company, said, 'The environment is too important to be left to the environmentalists.'

2 My home policy? I wage war. My foreign policy? I wage war. Always, everywhere, I wage war.

Speech to the Chamber of Deputies (8 March 1918). Compare CHURCHILL 136:1.

3 America is the only country in history which miraculously has gone directly from barbarism to degeneration without the usual interval of civilization.

So ascribed to Clemenceau by Hans Bendix in *The Saturday Review of Literature* (1 December 1945). No more substantial attribution appears to exist.

4 If you don't vote Socialist/Communist before you are twenty, you have no heart – if you do vote Socialist/Communist after you are twenty, you have no head.

The saying to this effect may derive from what Bennett A. Cerf attributed to Clemenceau in *Try and Stop Me* (1944). It is supposedly what Clemenceau said when told his son had just joined the Communist Party: 'My son is twenty-two years old. If he had not become a Communist at twenty-two I would have disowned him. If he is still a Communist at thirty, I will do it then.'

Another suggested source is Dean Inge, the 'Gloomy Dean' of St Paul's (who died in 1954). And then there is the remark, attributed loosely to Benjamin Disraeli, in Laurence J. Peter's *Quotations for Our Time* (1977): 'A man who is not a Liberal at sixteen has no heart; a man who is not a Conservative at sixty has no head.'

Pass the Port Again (1980) has this version, ascribed to Maurice Maeterlinck: 'If a man is not a Socialist at twenty he has no heart. If he is a Socialist at thirty, he has no brain.' *The Oxford Book of Ages* (1985) ascribes to Aristide Briand (1862–1932) the similar: 'The man who is not a socialist at twenty has no heart, but if he is still a socialist at forty he has no head.'

The matter may have been resolved by *Benham* (1948), who ascribes this to François Guizot (1787–1874), French historian and statesman (under Louis Philippe): '*N'être pas republicain à vingt ans est preuve d'un manque de coeur; l'être après trente ans est preuve d'un manque de tête* [Not to be a republican at twenty is proof of want of heart; to be one at thirty is proof of want of head].' *Benham* adds: 'M. Clemenceau adapted this saying, substituting *socialiste* for *republicain*.'

Putting it another way, Will Durant, the American teacher, philosopher and historian (1885–1982), said, 'There is nothing in Socialism that a little age or a little money will not cure.' The American poet Robert Frost wrote in 'Precaution' (1936): 'I never dared be radical when young / For fear it would make me conservative when old.'

Compare what Bernard Shaw said in a lecture at the University of Hong Kong in February 1933: 'Steep yourself in revolutionary books. Go up to your neck in Communism, because if you are not a red revolutionist at 20, you will be at 50 a most impossible fossil. If you are a red revolutionist at 20, you have some chance of being up-to-date at 40.'

5 Oh, to be seventy again!

Said to have been exclaimed on his 80th birthday (i.e. in 1921) when walking down the Champs-Élysées with a friend and a pretty girl passed them – quoted by James Agate, *Ego 3* (1938) – diary for 19 April 1938. The same remark is ascribed to Oliver Wendell Holmes Jr (1841–1935), the American jurist, on reaching his 87th year (by Fadiman & van Doren in *The American Treasury*, 1955). In the film biography of Holmes, *The Magnificent Yankee* (US 1950), it becomes, 'Do you know what I think when I see a pretty girl? ... Oh, to be eighty again.' (Perhaps this was derived from the Emmet Lavery play and the Francis Biddle book upon which the film is based.) Bernard de Fontenelle (1657–1757), the French writer and philosopher, is said in great old age to have attempted with difficulty to pick up a young lady's fan, murmuring, 'Ah, if I were only eighty again!' – Pedrazzini & Gris, *Autant en apportent les mots* (1969).

Grover CLEVELAND American Democratic 22nd and 24th President (1837–1908)

1 We love him for the enemies he has made.

A curious campaign slogan for Cleveland was derived from a speech made by Governor Edward Stuyvesant Bragg (1827–1912), when seconding Cleveland's presidential nomination (9 July 1884): 'They love him most for the enemies he has made.' With the slogan, however, Cleveland won the first of his two separate presidential terms. Compare ROOSEVELT 386:4.

Bill CLINTON (William Jefferson Clinton) American Democratic 42nd President (1946–)

2 When I was in England [as a Rhodes Scholar], I experimented with marijuana a time or two, and I didn't like it, and I didn't inhale and I never tried it again.

From a report in *The Washington Post* (31 March 1992). During his campaign for the Presidency, Clinton had to fend off criticisms that not only had he been to Oxford (anathema to the incumbent President, George Bush), but also had not fought in Vietnam and was generally associated with 1960s habits. While seeking the Democratic nomination, Clinton appeared on TV with a rival candidate, Jerry Brown. The two men were asked if they had ever violated state, federal or international laws. Under 'pinpoint questioning that closed all avenues of escape', according to the *Post*, he finally confessed to the above banality.

3 It's the economy, stupid.

Although he did not actually say it himself, this slogan became very much associated with Clinton during his campaign for election in 1992. It was coined by James Carville, who orchestrated the campaign, and simply meant that the team must remember that the economy was the issue of most importance to the electorate.

4 I did not have sexual relations with that woman, Ms Lewinsky.

Statement on TV (26 January 1998). Seven months later he admitted, 'Indeed, I did have a relationship with Ms Lewinsky that was not appropriate. In fact, it was wrong.' Neither remark was made under oath, but the possible conflict with statements that he had made under oath in a separate sexual harassment case led to an unsuccessful attempt to impeach him in 1999.

5 It depends on what the meaning of the word 'is' is. If 'is' means 'is and never has been', that is one thing. If it means 'there is none', that was a completely true statement.

In grand jury testimony (1998), when asked about an earlier deposition during the Paula Jones case that 'there is absolutely no sex of any kind' between the President and Monica Lewinsky. Among the other quotations that *Bartlett* (2002) listed under Clinton's name were: 'I'll be with you until the last dog dies', 'I feel your pain', and the previous quotation above.

Arthur Hugh CLOUGH English poet (1819–61)

6 Say not the struggle naught availeth,
The labour and the wounds are vain,
The enemy faints not, nor faileth,
And as things have been, things remain ...

For while the tired waves, vainly breaking,
Seem here no painful inch to gain,
Far back, through creeks and inlets making,
Comes silent, flooding in, the main.

And not by eastern windows only,
When daylight comes, comes in the light,
In front, the sun climbs slow, how slowly,
But, westward, look, the land is bright.

'Say Not the Struggle Nought Availeth' (1855). In a radio broadcast on 3 May 1941, hinting at future American involvement in the war, Winston Churchill responded to the quotation – see LONGFELLOW 294:4 – sent to him by President Roosevelt by quoting from Clough. 'I have,' he said by way of introduction, 'some other lines which are less well known but which seem apt and appropriate to our fortunes tonight, and I believe they will be so judged wherever the English language is spoken or the flag of freedom flies.' He quoted the second two verses above in the form shown.

Hence, *The Land Is Bright*, title of a play (1941) by George S. Kaufman and Edna Ferber.

1 Thou shalt not kill; but need'st not strive
Officiously to keep alive.
Do not adultery commit;
Advantage rarely comes of it.
Thou shalt not steal; an empty feat,
When it's so lucrative to cheat ...

Clough's 'The Latest Decalogue' (1862) was an *ironical* version of the Ten Commandments – so the first two lines here were not serious advice to doctors (in which sense they have sometimes been quoted, however).

William COBBETT English radical writer (1762–1835)

2 But what is to be the fate of the great wen of all?
The monster, called ... 'the metropolis of empire'?

In 'Rural Rides: The Kentish Journal' in *Cobbett's Weekly Political Register* (5 January 1822). Cobbett asked this of London. A 'wen' is a lump or protuberance on a body; a wart. However, the name in reference to London appears to have existed before Cobbett. Jane Austen in a letter to someone at Hendon (22 November 1814) wrote: 'Should you [guess] that you were within a dozen miles of the We[n from] the atmosphere?' Even earlier, Dean Tucker writing of London in 1783, had: 'No better than a wen or excrescence upon the body politic.' Compare CHARLES 130:9.

Alison COCKBURN Scottish poet and songwriter (1713–94)

3 For the flowers of the forest are a' wade away.

'The Flowers of the Forest' (1765 – though believed to have been written 20 years before). The poem was apparently inspired by a commercial disaster in which seven local lairds were bankrupted in one year. 'Wade/wede' means 'weeded', but sometimes the phrase is rendered as 'withered away'. The line also appears in 'The Flowers of the Forest' (?1755) by the Scottish poet and songwriter, Jean Elliot (1727–1805). *The Dictionary of Scottish Quotations* (1996) notes: 'Based on a traditional version of which only a fragment survives, this song was written as a lament for the Battle of Flodden (9 September 1513) in which James IV and thousands of his men were slain by the English.' What the connection is between the Cockburn and Elliot versions (so close in time) is not clear. According to the *Oxford Dictionary of Music* (1985), the Cockburn was originally sung to a different tune but is now 'generally sung to an old tune' (i.e. the traditional one used by Elliot for her version) ... 'the flowers are young men, the Forest [i.e. the Ettrick Forest] a district of Selkirk and Peebles: the poem commemorates their death in battle. The tune, played by pipers, is a regular and moving feature of the Remembrance Day ceremony at the Cenotaph in Whitehall, London.' See also BIBLE 73:7.

Claud COCKBURN English journalist (1904–81)

4 Small earthquake in Chile. Not many dead.

In his book *In Time of Trouble* (1956), also incorporated in his *I Claud ...* (1967), Cockburn claimed to have won a competition for dullness among sub-editors on *The Times* with this headline in the late 1920s: 'It had to be a genuine headline, that is to say one which was actually in the next morning's newspaper. I won it only once.' At Cockburn's death it was said, however, that an exhaustive search had failed to find this particular headline in the paper. It may just have been a smoking-room story. However, the idea lives on: it became (perhaps inevitably) the title of a book (1972) by Alastair Horne about the Allende era in Chile. The journalist Michael Green called a volume of memoirs *Nobody Hurt in Small Earthquake* (1990), and the cartoonist Nicholas Garland called his 'Journal of a year in Fleet Street', *Not Many Dead* (1990). In 2000 Mark English made the intriguing discovery that in 1929 (when Cockburn started work on *The Times* in London before becoming its correspondent in New York and Washington) there occurred two similar entries in the paper's 'Telegrams in Brief' column: 'An earthquake was felt yesterday between Illapel, to the north, and Talca, to the south, in Chile. No damage was done' (6 August 1929); 'An earthquake shock was felt in Melilla [which is in Chile] on Wednesday, but no one was injured' (16 August 1929). Could Cockburn have embroidered the story in the telling and asserted that the 'Telegrams in Brief' were in fact headlines?

William Sloane COFFIN American clergyman (1924–)

5 Even if you win the rat-race, you're still a rat.

When consulted at his home in Vermont (July 1995), the Revd Coffin said that to the best of his knowledge he did originate this statement in the above form. He thought up the quip 'in the 1950s or 1960s' when he was chaplain either at Williams College or at Yale University. He added the caveat that he originated the statement 'as far as I know'. The line is often attributed to the American actress Lily Tomlin who, in turn, ascribes it to the writer, Jane Wagner.

George M. COHAN American songwriter and entertainer (1878–1942)

6 I don't care what you say about me, as long as you say *something* about me, and as long as you spell my name right.

Quoted in John McCabe, *George M. Cohan* (1973). See other observations on publicity under ANONYMOUS 10:1.

Al COHN American musician (1925–88)

1 A gentleman knows how to play the accordion, but doesn't.

Cohn was a saxophonist. Unverified. However, *Reader's Digest* (March 1976) quoted Anon. in *The Wall Street Journal*: 'A true gentleman is a man who knows how to play the bagpipes – but doesn't.' This has also been ascribed to G.K. Chesterton. Compare ARISTOTLE 38:3.

Irving COHN American songwriter (1898–1961)

2 Yes, we have no bananas,
We have no bananas today.

Song 'Yes, We Have No Bananas' (1923), to music by Frank Silver (1892–1960). According to Ian Whitcomb in *After the Ball* (1972), the title line came from a cartoon strip by Tad Dorgan and not, as the composers were wont to claim, from a Greek fruit-store owner on Long Island. Alternatively, it was a saying picked up by US troops in the Philippines from a Greek pedlar. In Britain, Elders & Fyffes, the banana importers, embraced the song and distributed 10,000 hands of bananas to music-sellers with the slogan: 'Yes! we have no bananas! On sale here.'

Desmond COKE English writer and schoolteacher (1879–1931)

3 All rowed fast, but none so fast as stroke.

In *Sandford of Merton*, Chap. 12 (1903), Coke wrote: 'His blade struck the water a full second before any other: the lad had started well. Nor did he flag as the race wore on: as the others tired, he seemed to grow more fresh, until at length, as the boats began to near the winning-post, his oar was dipping into the water nearly twice as often as any other.' This is deemed to be the original of the modern proverbial saying (which is used, for example, in its 'all rowed fast' form in 'The Challenge' episode of the TV adaptation of *The Forsyte Saga* (1967)).

The 'misquotation' is sometimes thought to have been a deliberate distortion of something written earlier than Coke, by Ouida, 'designed to demonstrate the lady's ignorance of rowing, or indeed of any male activity' – Peter Farrer in *Oxford Today* (Hilary, 1992). The *Oxford Companion to English Literature* (1985) refers to the ridicule Ouida suffered for 'her inaccuracies in matter's of men's sports and occupations', of which this must be one.

Mary Elizabeth COLERIDGE English poet (1861–1907)

4 Be still, my beating heart, be still!

First line of 'All One' (1910). In the 20th century, 'Be still my beating heart' became almost a catchphrase, a cynical comment on an account of young love or a romantic incident. But where did it originate? Psalm 4:4 has 'Commune with your own heart upon your bed, and be still.' 'Oh my soul, my beating heart' is in Mark Twain, *Innocents Abroad* (1869). 'My beating heart', on its own, appears in innumerable verses between 1700 and 1900. Additionally, the phrase appears to have been a stock piece of rhetoric used by dramatists at the beginning of the 18th century. 'Oh! yet lye still, my beating Heart' wrote Nicholas Rowe in *The Royal Captive* (1708). Still earlier: 'Ha! hold my Brain; be still my beating Heart' – William Mountfort, *Zelmane* (1705).

Further evidence of just how common this kind of phrase was in 19th-century verse: Josephine in the Gilbert and Sullivan opera *HMS Pinafore*, Act 1 (1878), says: 'Oh, my heart, my beating heart'. And from Dr Daly in *The Sorcerer*, Act 1 (1877) there is: 'Be still, my fluttering heart!' A little later than these is the song entitled 'Be Still, My Heart! (I can tell who's knocking at my door)' (1934).

Samuel Taylor COLERIDGE English poet and writer (1772–1834)

5 Water, water everywhere,
And all the boards did shrink;
Water, water, everywhere
Nor any drop to drink.

'The Rime of the Ancient Mariner' (1798). Often misquoted as 'Water, water, everywhere / And not a drop to drink.'

6 Nothing great was ever achieved without enthusiasm. For what is enthusiasm but the oblivion and swallowing-up of self in an object dearer than self, in an idea more vivid.

The Statesman's Manual (1816). Emerson included the first sentence in his *Essays* (First Series), 'Circles' (1841).

7 On awaking he ... instantly and eagerly wrote down the lines that are here preserved. At this moment he was unfortunately called out by a person on business from Porlock.

From Coleridge's introductory note to 'Kubla Khan' (1816) describing how he, the poet, was interrupted in writing out the two or three hundred lines that had come to him in his sleep, when staying in Somerset. The incident happened in 1797 after Coleridge had taken opium and fallen asleep. Hence, the expression 'person from Porlock' to describe any kind of distraction, but especially from literary or other creative work. Thus Stevie Smith's poem "Thought about "The Person from Porlock"" (1962):

I long for the Person from Porlock
To bring my thoughts to an end,
I am growing impatient to see him,
I think of him as a friend.

1 In Xanadu did Kubla Khan
A stately pleasure-dome decree.

'Kubla Khan'. The 'stately pleasure-dome' has become a cliché of journalism and pop music. *The Pleasure Dome* was the title of a collection of Graham Greene's film criticism (1972). *Welcome to the Pleasure Dome* was the title of an album and a song by Frankie Goes to Hollywood (1985). 'We would be turning ourselves into not just a non-reproductive society but an unproductive, hedonistic society. Here comes the stately pleasure dome' – *The Sunday Times* (1 May 1994). 'Politics govern artistic activity in France and Italy. President Mitterrand a stately pleasure dome decreed, and thence stem all the Bastille's problems' – *The Times* (12 September 1994).

2 And here were forests ancient as the hills,
Enfolding sunny spots of greenery.
But O, that deep romantic chasm which slanted
Down the green hill athwart a cedarn cover!
A savage place! as holy and enchanted
As e'er beneath a waning moon was haunted
By woman wailing for her demon-lover!
And from this chasm, with ceaseless turmoil
    seething,
As if this earth in fast thick pants were breathing,
A mighty fountain momently was forced.

In the same poem. The 'fast thick pants' have occasioned much schoolboy laughter over the years. C.S. Lewis evidently posed the question whether the pants were 'woollen or fur' – according to *My Oxford* (1977).

3 ... Five miles meandering with a mazy motion
Through wood and dale the sacred river ran,
Then reach'd the caverns measureless to man,
And sank in tumult to a lifeless ocean:
And 'mid this tumult Kubla heard from far
Ancestral voices prophesying war!
The shadow of the dome of pleasure
Floated midway on the waves;
Where was heard the mingled measure
From the fountain and the caves.
It was a miracle of rare device,
A sunny pleasure-dome with caves of ice!
... A damsel with a dulcimer
In a vision once I saw:

... And close your eyes with holy dread,
For he on honey-dew hath fed,
And drunk the milk of Paradise.

In the same poem. Ransacked by the architectural historian James Lees-Milne for the titles of his published diaries in 12 volumes: *Ancestral Voices* (1975), *Prophesying Peace* (1977), *Caves of Ice* (1983), *Midway on the Waves* (1985), *A Mingled Measure* (1994), *Ancient As the Hills* (1997), *Through Wood and Dale* (1998), *Deep Romantic Chasm* (2000), *Holy Dread* (2001), *Beneath a Waning Moon* (2003), *Ceaseless Turmoil* (2004) and, finally, *Milk of Paradise* (2005). In punning homage, Tom Sharpe gave the title *Ancestral Vices* to one of his comic novels (1980).

4 That willing suspension of disbelief for the moment, which constitutes poetic faith.

Biographia Literaria, Chap. 14 (1817). The 'willing suspension of disbelief', essential to the appreciation of many of the arts, not just poetry, has been called 'one of the most famous phrases ever coined' and describes the state of receptiveness and credulity required by the reader or 'receiver' of a work of literature, as well as the acceptance of dramatic and poetic conventions. In the original context, Coleridge was writing of two possible subjects for poetry: 'In this idea originated the plan of the Lyrical Ballads; in which it was agreed, that my endeavours should be directed to persons and characters supernatural, or at least romantic; yet so as to transfer from our inward nature a human interest and a semblance of truth sufficient to procure from these shadows of imagination that willing suspension of disbelief for the moment, which constitutes poetic faith.'

5 I wish our clever young poets would remember my homely definitions of prose and poetry; that is prose = words in their best order; poetry = the best words in the best order.

In the same work – entry for 12 July 1827. Earlier Jonathan Swift had written in *A Letter to a Young Gentleman, Lately entered into Holy Orders* (9 January 1720): 'Proper words in proper places, make the true definition of a style.' Compare: 'Good prose is the selection of the best words; poetry is the best words in the best order; and journalese is any old words in any old order' – Anon., quoted by Adam Brewer in a letter to *The Times* (21 August 1987).

Michael COLLINS Irish politician (1890–1922)

6 Think what I have got for Ireland. Something which she has wanted these past seven hundred years. Will anyone be satisfied with the bargain? Will anyone? I tell you this – early this morning

I signed my death warrant. I thought at the time how odd, how ridiculous – a bullet may just as well have done the job five years ago.

Letter (6 December 1921), written after he had signed a peace treaty with the British Government. Subsequently, when head of the Irish Provisional Government, he was killed by his own anti-treaty compatriots in March 1922. In *Michael Collins*, Chap. 8 (1990), Tim Pat Coogan suggests that Collins had already made this point when at 2.30 a.m. that morning: '[Lord] Birkenhead turned to Collins after putting his name to the document and said, "I may have signed my political death warrant tonight." The younger man replied, "I may have signed my actual death warrant."'

Norman COLLINS English broadcasting executive and novelist (1907–82)

1 *London Belongs To Me.*

Title of novel (1945; film UK 1948 – known in the US as *Dulcimer Street*). Compare the later title *Paris Nous Appartient* ('Paris belongs to us') (film France 1961). Will Fyffe's song 'I Belong to Glasgow' (1920) – which contains the lines 'But when I get a couple of drinks on a Saturday, / Glasgow belongs to me' – predates these titles, however.

George COLMAN (the Younger) English playwright (1762–1836)

2 Oh, London is a fine town,
A very famous city,
Where all the streets are paved with gold,
And all the maidens pretty.

The Heir-at-Law (1797). See also BIBLE 86:10.

3 Says he, 'I am a handsome man, but I'm a gay deceiver.'

Love Laughs at Locksmiths, Act 2 (1808). By the time of Tennessee Williams's play *The Glass Menagerie* (1948), 'gay deceivers' had become a slang term for 'falsies'.

Charles COLSON American Watergate conspirator (1931–)

4 I would walk over my grandmother if necessary [to get something done].

This was a view attributed to Colson rather than anything he ever actually said himself, but he subsequently muddied the water by appearing to endorse the sentiment. An article in *The Wall Street Journal* in 1971 had portrayed Colson, a special counsel of President Nixon, as someone who, in the words of another Washington official, would be prepared

to walk over his grandmother if he had to. In 1972, when Nixon sought re-election as US President, Colson misguidedly sent a memo to campaign staff that stated: 'I am totally unconcerned about anything other than getting the job done ... Just so you understand me, let me point out that the statement ... "I would walk over my grandmother if necessary" is absolutely accurate.' This was leaked to *The Washington Post*.

Subsequently convicted for offences connected with Watergate and then emerging as a born-again Christian, Colson tried unavailingly to point out that he had never really said it. In his book *Born Again* (1977) he wrote: 'My mother failed to see the humour in the whole affair, convinced that I was disparaging the memory of my father's mother ... Even though both of my grandmothers had been dead for more than twenty-five years (I was very fond of both).' Such are the penalties for tangling with figures of speech.

In an earlier age – the 1880s – the editor of the *Pall Mall Gazette*, W.T. Stead, famous for his exposé of the child-prostitution racket, said: 'I would not take libel proceedings if it were stated that I had killed my grandmother and eaten her.' Another even earlier image often invoked was of 'selling one's own grandmother'. In the film *The Philadelphia Story* (US 1940), a character exclaims: 'I'd sell my grandmother for a drink.'

Barber B. CONABLE Jr American Republican politician and banker (1922–)

5 I guess we have found the smoking pistol, haven't we?

The term 'smoking pistol/gun' was popularized during the Watergate affair. Conable said this of a tape of President Nixon's conversation with H.R. Haldeman, his chief of staff, on 23 June 1972, which contained a discussion of how the FBI's investigation of the Watergate burglary could be 'limited'. The phrase simply means 'incriminating evidence', as though a person found holding a smoking gun could be assumed to have committed an offence with it – as in Conan Doyle's Sherlock Holmes story 'The "Gloria Scott"' (1894): 'Then we rushed on into the captain's cabin ... and there he lay ... while the chaplain stood, with a smoking pistol in his hand.'

CONFUCIUS Chinese philosopher (551–479BC)

6 There is no spectacle more agreeable than to observe an old friend fall from a roof-top.

Sometimes it is a 'neighbour': 'Even a virtuous and high-minded man may experience a little pleasure when he sees his neighbour falling from a roof.' The earliest citation to hand dates only from 1970, and one suspects that, like so many other Confucian sayings, it has nothing whatever to do with the Chinese philosopher who, nevertheless, undoubtedly did exist and did say a number of wise things (some through his followers). Even when not prefaced by 'Confucius, he say ...' there is a tendency – particularly in the US – to ascribe any wry saying to him. In John G. Murray, *A Gentleman Publisher's Commonplace Book* (1996), the above precise form is ascribed to 'Kai Lung' – by which he presumably means Ernest Bramah's fictional Chinese philosopher.

With regard to this one, similar thoughts have occurred to others: 'Philosophy may teach us to bear with equanimity the misfortunes of our neighbours' – Oscar Wilde, *The English Renaissance of Art* (1882); 'I am convinced that we have a degree of delight, and that no small one, in the real misfortunes and pains of others' – Edmund Burke, *On the Sublime and Beautiful* (1756); and, especially, *'Dans l'adversité de nos meilleurs amis, nous trouvons toujours quelque chose qui ne nous déplaît pas* [In the misfortune of our best friends, we find something that is not displeasing to us]' – Duc de La Rochefoucauld (1665).

1 I was complaining that I had no shoes till I met a man who had no feet.

Ascribed to Confucius in Patricia Houghton, *A World of Proverbs* (1981), but unverified. Has also been described as a 'Zen saying'. Compare BRAMAH 100:2. 'There was the man who complained because he had no shoes, until he met a man who had no feet' – quoted in Jacob M. Braude, *Speakers' Encyclopedia* (1955); 'I had no shoes, and I murmured, till I met a man who had no feet' – described as 'Arabic' in Viscount Samuel, *A Book of Quotations* (1947). It has also been attributed to R.W. Emerson. But, rather, Emerson's source may be the first appearance of the saying. In *The Rose Garden* or *Gulistany*, the Persian poet Sheikh Muslih'ud-Din Sadi of Shiraz (*circa* 1213–91), wrote: 'I had never complained of the vicissitudes of fortune, nor murmured at the ordinances of heaven, excepting on one occasion, that my feet were bare, and I had not wherewithal to shoe them. In this desponding state I entered the metropolitan mosque of Cufah, and there I beheld a man that had no feet. I offered up praise and thanksgiving for God's goodness to myself, and submitted with patience to my want of shoes.'

William CONGREVE English playwright (1670–1729)

2 See how love and murder will out.

The Double Dealer (1694). The proverb 'murder will out' (i.e. will be found out, will reveal itself) goes back at least to 1325, and 'truth will out' to 1439. Later, Hannah Cowley in *The Belle's Stratagem* (1782) has: 'Vanity, like murder, will out.'

3 Music has charms to soothe a savage breast.

The Mourning Bride (1697). Opening line. Not 'hath charms' and not 'savage beast'.

4 Heaven has no Rage, like Love to Hatred turned, Nor Hell a Fury, like a Woman scorned.

In the same play. Hence, the expression 'Hell hath no fury like a woman scorned.' The fury of a disappointed woman had been characterized along these lines before Congreve, but insofar as he coined this proverbial expression, it should be noted that his text is as above.

5 As I am a person I can hold out no longer.

The Way of the World, Act 5, Sc. 1 (1700). Lady Wishfort speaking. Person = 'a person of distinction'. She uses the phrase in the form 'as I'm a person' several times in the course of the play.

James M. CONNELL Irish-born songwriter (1852–1929)

6 The people's flag is deepest red; It shrouded oft our martyred dead, And ere their limbs grew stiff and cold, Their heart's blood dyed its every fold. Then raise the scarlet standard high! Within its shade we'll live or die. Tho' cowards flinch and traitors sneer, We'll keep the red flag flying here.

'The Red Flag' (1889). According to a record sleeve-note by the Workers' Music Association Ltd, Connell reminisced in 1920 about 'a series of great struggles which got him into the mood which enabled him to write the song'. His inspirations were the Irish Land League, the Russian revolutionaries, the hanging of the Chicago anarchists and the English dockers' strike of 1889. Connell apparently intended the words to be sung to the jaunty tune of 'The White Cockade', a Scottish reel. Instead, in the British Labour movement, it has traditionally been sung to the dirge-like German hymn tune, 'Der Tannenbaum' (known in Britain as 'Maryland').

Billy CONNOLLY Scottish comedian (1942–)

7 Still you can't worry too much about the future. Life is not a rehearsal.

Gullible's Travels (1983). But probably no more than a popular modern proverb. In December 1980 I spotted this in the Eight-O Club, Dallas, Texas, and included it in my *Graffiti 3* (1981): 'This is not a dress rehearsal, this is real life.' An earlier formulation is this, from Sybille Bedford's novel, *A*

Compass Error, 'Prologues' (1968): 'You see, when one's young one doesn't feel part of it yet, the human condition; one does things because they are not for good; everything is a rehearsal. To be repeated ad lib, to be put right when the curtain goes up in earnest. One day you know that the curtain was up all the time. That *was* the performance.'

Cyril CONNOLLY English writer and critic (1903–74)

1 Whom the gods wish to destroy they first call promising.
Enemies of Promise (1938). Compare BYRON 116:2.

2 There is no more sombre enemy of good art than the pram in the hall.
In the same book.

3 Imprisoned in every fat man a thin one is wildly signalling to be let out.
The Unquiet Grave (1944). Five years earlier, however, George Orwell had written: 'I'm fat, but I'm thin inside. Has it ever struck you that there's a thin man inside every fat man, just as they say there's a statue inside every block of stone?' (see ORWELL 348:4).

Great minds think alike. The coincidence was pointed out in a letter to *Encounter* in September 1975. Not to be outdone, Kingsley Amis twisted the idea round in 1963 (see AMIS 8:3). And Timothy Leary was quoted in 1979 as having said: 'Inside every fat Englishman is a thin Hindu trying to get out.' See also WHITEHORN 492:1.

4 Vulgarity is the garlic in the salad of charm.
Epigraph, ascribed to 'St Bumpus', of 'Told in Gath', Cyril Connolly's excellent parody of Aldous Huxley, contained in *The Condemned Playground* (1945).

5 She looked like Lady Chatterley above the waist and the gamekeeper below.
Of Vita Sackville-West. In Peter Quennell's *Customs and Characters* (1982), he says of the poet's appearance that it was 'strange almost beyond the reach of adjectives ... she resembled a puissant blend of both sexes – Lady Chatterley and her lover rolled into one, I recollect a contemporary humorist observing ... her legs, which reminded [Virginia] Woolf of stalwart tree trunks, were encased in a gamekeeper's breeches and top-boots laced up to the knee.'

Quennell may have been alluding to the rather more pointed remark that Vita looked 'like Lady Chatterley above the waist and the gamekeeper below'. In fact, by 'contemporary humorist' he probably meant Connolly, who went

with him on a joint visit to Sackville-West at Sissinghurst in 1936. Certainly, that is the form in which Connolly's remark is more usually remembered.

Joseph CONRAD Polish-born novelist (1857–1924)

6 The horror! The horror!
Heart of Darkness (1902). Dying words of Mr Kurtz, an ivory trader in Africa, who has obtained a brutal hold over the local tribesmen and has seen into the dark heart of human existence. The utterance was duly carried over to the film *Apocalypse Now* (US 1979), based on Conrad's story.

7 Of course government in general, any government anywhere, is a thing of exquisite comicality to a discerning mind.
Nostromo, Pt 2, Chap. 3 (1904).

Shirley CONRAN English journalist and novelist (1932–)

8 Life is too short to stuff a mushroom.
Superwoman (1975). The epigraph to her home-hints volume is in the tradition of such remarks. Richard Porson (1759–1808), Regius Professor of Greek at Cambridge, is quoted by Thomas Love Peacock in *Gryll Grange* (1861) as having said, 'Life is too short to learn German.'

Peter COOK English humorist (1937–95)

9 You know, I go to the theatre to be entertained ... I don't want to see plays about rape, sodomy and drug addiction ... I can get all that at home.
Caption to cartoon by Roger Law in *The Observer* (8 July 1962). However, the words 'I go to the theatre to be entertained. I want to be taken out of myself. I don't want to see lust and rape, incest and sodomy I can get all that at home' also occur in the sketch 'Frank Speaking' credited to Cook and Alan Bennett in *Beyond the Fringe*. This sketch is also described as 'Lord Cobbold/The Duke' and credited to Cook and Jonathan Miller. By the time of Leslie Halliwell, *The Filmgoer's Book of Quotes* (1973), this was being quoted as: 'I don't like watching rape and violence at the cinema. I get enough of that at home!'

COOL HAND LUKE American film 1967. Script by Donn Pearce and Frank Pierson. With Strother Martin as Captain and Paul Newman as Luke.

10 *Captain (to Luke)*: What we've got here is failure to communicate. Some men you just can't reach.
Soundtrack. The line 'What We've Got Here Is A [*sic*] Failure

To Communicate' was used to promote the film. *What We Have Here Is A Failure To Communicate* was the title of a book on advertising (1975) by Barry Day.

Calvin COOLIDGE American Republican 30th President (1872–1933)

1 If you don't say anything, you won't be called on to repeat it.

A comment from the famously taciturn President on the business of quotation. Quoted in Laurence J. Peter, *Quotations for Our Time* (1977).

2 After all, the chief business of the American people is business.

Speech to the American Society of Newspaper Editors (17 January 1925). *ODQ* (1979) simply had, 'The business of America is business', but this was revised in the 1992 edition. Coolidge went on: 'They are profoundly concerned with producing, buying, selling, investing, and prospering in the world. I am strongly of the opinion that the great majority of people will always find these are moving impulses in our life.' But Coolidge also had a non-materialistic viewpoint. In another speech, he said: 'We do not need more material development, we need more spiritual development.'

3 I do not choose to run.

That is not quite what Coolidge said, and, in any case, he didn't actually *say* it. Having been President since 1923, his words to newsmen at Rapid City, South Dakota, on 2 August 1927 were: 'I do not choose to run for President in 1928.' And rather than speak, 'Silent Cal' handed slips of paper with these words on them to waiting journalists. For some reason, the unusual wording of the announcement caught people's fancy and the phrase was remembered. In 1928, there was a silly song recorded in New York about a recalcitrant wristwatch. It was performed by Six Jumping Jacks with Tom Stacks (vocal) and was called 'I Do Not Choose To Run'. The dedication of Frank Nicholson's *Favorite Jokes of Famous People* (1928) is to: 'A famous man whose favorite joke is not included in this collection ... he did not choose to pun.'

A.E. COPPARD English short-story writer and poet (1878–1957)

4 Again they were quiet, voiceless, and thus in fading light they came to their homes. But how windy, dispossessed and ravaged, roved the darkening world! Clouds were borne frantically across the heavens, as if in a rout of battle, and the lovely earth seemed to sigh in grief at some calamity all unknown to men.

The Field of Mustard (1926). The title short story of this somewhat Hardy-esque collection describes three forty-something 'disvirgined' women as they gather kindling from a wood and then muse on life and men against the symbolic backdrop of a mustard field. The poetic passage comes at the end of the tale and is tied to the land rather than the sea. Hence, nevertheless, *In Fading Light*, the title of a film (UK 1989) about a North Shields fishing community. In the film, the passage becomes: 'In fading light they homeward came – windy, dispossessed and ravaged – and all the lovely ocean sighed in grief. For darkness drove the world but some calamity drove the men.'

Richard CORBET English poet and bishop (1582–1635)

5 Farewell, rewards and Fairies,
Good housewives now may say,
For now foul sluts in dairies
Do fare as well as they.

'The Fairies' Farewell'. 'Fairies' refers to Roman Catholics. Hence, however, *Rewards and Fairies*, the title of a children's book (1910) by Rudyard Kipling.

Frances CORNFORD English poet (1886–1960)

6 O why do you walk through the fields in gloves,
Missing so much and so much?
O fat white woman whom nobody loves.

'To a Fat Lady Seen from a Train' (1910). *The Oxford Companion to English Literature* (1985) describes this short poem as 'curiously memorable though undistinguished'. Part of the fascination must lie in the fact that we must all have wondered at some time about the people we glimpse from trains. It was Cornford's assumptions about the fat white woman, however, that caused G.K. Chesterton to provide the other side of the story. His 'The Fat White Woman Speaks' was published in *New Poems* (1932):

Why do you flash through the flowery meads,
Fat-headed poet that nobody reads;
And how do you know such a frightful lot
About people in gloves as such?

Beachcomber (J.B. Morton) also wrote a riposte, 'The Fat Lady Seen from a Train Replies to the Scornful Poet', and D.B. Wyndham Lewis in his *News Chronicle* 'Timothy Shy' column, *Beyond the Headlines*, came up with 'Mrs Overweight, "To a Thin Girl Seen from the Fields"' under the heading 'Stout Girl Hits Back' (late 1940s):

O, why do you whizz through the fields in trains,
Missing so much and so much?
O thin, pale girl with the Bloomsbury brains,
Why do you whizz through the fields in trains? [etc.]

Francis CORNFORD English academic (1874–1943)

1 Nothing should ever be done for the first time.

Microcosmographia Academica (1908). The precise wording is: 'Every public action, which is not customary, either is wrong, or, if it is right, is a dangerous precedent. It follows that nothing should ever be done for the first time.' Francis Cornford, who was married to Frances Cornford, was Professor of Ancient Philosophy at Cambridge.

Compare: 'The conservative in financial circles I have often described as a man who thinks nothing new ought ever to be adopted for the first time' – Frank A. Vaderlip, *From Farm Boy to Financier* (1935).

Anne-Marie Bigot de CORNUEL French society hostess (1605–94)

2 No man is a hero to his valet.

In *Lettres de Mlle Aïssé à Madame C* (1787) – letter of 1728. The apparent origin of this proverbial expression.

William CORY English poet and schoolmaster (1823–92)

3 Jolly boating weather,
And a hay-harvest breeze,
Blade on the feather,
Shade off the trees.
Swing, swing together,
With your bodies between your knees.

Cory wrote the 'Eton Boating Song' in 1863, and it was published two years later in *The Eton Scrap Book*, a school magazine. The phrase *Blade on the Feather* was taken as the title of a TV play (1980) by Dennis Potter, whose main character was an Old Etonian author and spy. 'On the feather' is a rowing term for when the oar's blade is returned horizontally at the end of a stroke, and out of the water.

4 He is one of those who like the palm without the dust.

In the 1860s Cory wrote this of one of his pupils, the future Prime Minister, Lord Rosebery, then aged 15. The comment was published in Johnson's *Letters and Journals* in 1897 and came to haunt Rosebery. As Robert Rhodes James notes in *Rosebery* (1963), it has been seized upon by countless persons as the key to the aristocratic politician's complex personality. The allusion is to Horace, the Roman author, who talked

of 'the happy state of getting the victor's palm without the dust of racing'. '*Palma non sine pulvere* [no palm without labour]' is a motto of the Earls of Liverpool, among others.

Émile COUÉ French psychologist (1857–1926)

5 *Tous les jours, à tous (les) points de vue, je vais de mieux en mieux* [Every day and in every way I am getting better and better].

(Sometimes rendered 'every day in every way' ... *or* 'day by day in every way ...'.) Coué was the originator of a system of 'Self-Mastery Through Conscious Auto-Suggestion', which had a brief vogue in the 1920s. His patients had to repeat the words over and over, and they became a popular catchphrase of the time. Physical improvement did not necessarily follow. Couéism died with its inventor, though there have been attempted revivals. In John Galsworthy, *The White Monkey*, Pt 3, Chap. 3 (1924), a woman is described as trying to influence her unborn baby's sex by 'repeating, every evening before falling asleep, and every morning on waking the words: "Day by day, in every way, he is getting more and more male."' John Lennon alluded to the slogan in his song 'Beautiful Boy' (1980).

(Sir) Noël COWARD English entertainer and writer (1899–1973)

6 Just know your lines and don't bump into the furniture.

This advice to actors was attributed to Spencer Tracy by *Bartlett* (1980) but to Coward in the 1992 edition. In Leslie Halliwell, *The Filmgoer's Book of Quotes* (1973), Alfred Lunt is credited with the line: 'The secret of my success? I speak in a loud clear voice and try not to bump into the furniture.' In *Time* Magazine (16 June 1986) it was reported that President Reagan had offered a few hints on appearing before the cameras to a White House breakfast for Senators: 'Don't bump into the furniture,' he said, 'and in the kissing scenes, keep your mouth closed.' Coward seems to be the originator, and Dick Richards, *The Wit of Noël Coward* (1968), has it that he said it during the run of his play *Nude With Violin* (1956–7). *The Sayings of Noel Coward*, ed. Philip Hoare (1997), has this from a 'speech to the Gallery First-Nighter's Club, 1962': 'Speak clearly, don't bump into people, and if you must have motivation think of your pay packet on Friday.'

7 Poor Little Rich Girl.

The title of the Coward song from *Charlot's Revue* (1926) is not original. The phrase had been used as the title of a Mary Pickford film of 1917 (which was re-made in 1936).

1 Dear 338171 (May I call you 338?)

Writing to T.E. Lawrence in the RAF (when Lawrence was hiding under the name 'Shaw'). Included in *Letters to T.E. Lawrence*, ed. D. Garnett (1938). The letter was dated 25 August 1930 and sent from the Adelphi Hotel, Liverpool, where Coward was staying on the tour of his play *Private Lives*. Lawrence replied on 6 September: 'It is very good to laugh: and I laughed so much, and made so many people laugh over your "May I call you 338" that I became too busy and happy to acknowledge your letter.' A pedant has pointed out to me that the really individual part of one's number in the services is at the end, so Coward should have put: 'May I call you 171?'

2 Very flat, Norfolk.

Private Lives, Act 1 (1930). Amanda is honeymooning with her second husband at the same hotel as her first, Elyot, is honeymooning with his new wife. In a wonderfully clipped conversation that nevertheless hints that they are probably still in love, Elyot remarks that he met his new wife at a house party in Norfolk. This is Amanda's famously dismissive response.

3 Strange how potent cheap music is.

In the same Act. Amanda speaking. Some texts of the play (as quoted by *Bartlett* and *ODQ*, for example) employ 'extraordinary', but 'strange' is what Gertrude Lawrence says on the record she made with Coward of the relevant scene in 1930. The line may be popular for two reasons. Coward's voice can be heard quite clearly in it and there is an in-joke – he, as playwright, is referring to one of his own compositions ('Someday I'll Find You'), which is being played at that moment.

4 You're looking very lovely, you know, in this damned moonlight.

In the same play, Act 3. Elyot speaking. Again, Coward himself on the 1930 *Noel and Gertie* record album delivers this line differently to the published text – 'You're looking very lovely in this damned moonlight, *Amanda*' – and this is the way it is usually parodied.

5 Let's drink to the hope that one day this country of ours, which we love so much, will find dignity and greatness and peace again.

The toast from *Cavalcade* (1931). See also THATCHER 458:4.

6 In Bangkok at twelve o'clock
They foam at the mouth and run.

But mad dogs and Englishmen
Go out in the midday sun.

Song, 'Mad Dogs and Englishmen', *Words and Music* (1932). In *The Life of Noël Coward* (1976), Cole Lesley commented on the 'Mad Dogs' phrase: 'Many fans had been sending slight traces of its origins from obscure books of travel, the earliest in *Rough Leaves from a Journal* by Lt.-Col. Lovell Badcock, published in 1835: "It happened to be during the heat of the day, when dogs and English alone are seen to move." The first mention of mad dogs we ever came across was an 1874 *Guide to Malta* by the Revd G.N. Goodwin, Chaplain to the Forces there: "Only newly arrived Englishmen and mad dogs expose themselves to it."'

In *The Noël Coward Song Book* (1953), the composer wrote: 'I have sung it myself *ad nauseam*. On one occasion it achieved international significance. This was a dinner party given by Mr Winston Churchill on board HMS *Prince of Wales* in honour of President Roosevelt on the evening following the signing of the Atlantic Charter ... The two world leaders became involved in a heated argument as to whether "In Bangkok at twelve o'clock they foam at the mouth and run" came at the end of the first refrain or at the end of the second. President Roosevelt held firmly to the latter view and refused to budge even under the impact of Churchillian rhetoric. In this he was right and when, a little while later, I asked Mr Churchill about the incident he admitted defeat like a man.'

Hence, title of film *Mad Dogs and Englishmen* (UK 1995).

7 The Party's Over Now.

Title of song in the same show. 'The Party's Over' was later (1956) the title of a song by Betty Comden and Adolph Green, to music by Jule Styne. See also CROSLAND 159:4.

8 I believe that since my life began
The most I've had is just
A talent to amuse.

Song, 'If Love Were All', *Bitter Sweet* (1932). *A Talent To Amuse* became the title of Sheridan Morley's biography of Coward in 1969. Cole Lesley comments in *The Life of Noël Coward* (1976): 'It is Manon in *Bitter Sweet*, not Noël, who sings [this] ... he himself never thus underrated his many gifts or "summed them up" (and neither can anybody else) in those four words.' Compare this in Byron's *Don Juan*, Canto 13, St. 86 (1819–24): 'There was the *preux Chevalier de la Ruse*, / Whom France and Fortune lately deign'd to waft here, / Whose chiefly harmless talent was to amuse.' A collection of Nancy Mitford's writings, edited by Charlotte Mosley, was published as *A Talent to Annoy* in 1986.

1 *Design for Living.*

Title of play (1932). This, although dealing with what later would be called 'trendy' people, had nothing to do with fashion. It was about a *ménage-à-trois*, so the 'living' was in that sense. However, the phrase is often used in magazine journalism for headlines when the practical aspects of furniture and even clothes design are being discussed. The Flanders & Swann song 'Design for Living' in *At The Drop of a Hat* (1957) concerned trendy interior decorating and furnishing.

2 The Stately Homes of England
How beautiful they stand,
To prove the upper classes
Have still the upper hand.

Although this is one of Coward's best-known songs (from the show *Operette*, 1938), it is based on the ballad 'The Homes of England' (1827) by Mrs Felicia Dorothea Hemans:

The stately homes of England,
How beautiful they stand!
Amidst their tall, ancestral trees,
O'er all the pleasant land.

Abraham COWLEY English poet and essayist (1618–67)

3 God the first garden made, and the first city Cain.

In the poem *The Garden* (1664). Compare COWPER 157:6.

William COWPER English poet (1731–1800)

4 I am monarch of all I survey,
My right there is none to dispute;
From the centre all round to the sea
I am lord of the fowl and the brute.

'Verses Supposed to be Written by Alexander Selkirk' (?1779). Selkirk was the original of Robinson Crusoe. The first line is nowadays used as a light-hearted proprietorial boast. Jane Austen wrote in a letter (23/24 September 1813): 'I am now alone in the Library, Mistress of all I survey – at least I may say so & repeat the whole poem if I like it, without offence to anybody.' Kenneth Tynan, writing about Noël Coward in *Panorama* (Spring 1952), said: 'He is, if I may test the trope, monocle of all he surveys.'

5 God moves in a mysterious way
His wonders to perform;
He plants his footsteps in the sea,
And rides upon the storm.

Hymn, 'Light Shining Out of Darkness', *Olney Hymns* (1779). Hence, the modern – often ironical – comment, 'God moves in a mysterious way ...' after some unexpected outcome to events.

6 God made the country, and man made the town.

'The Sofa', *The Task* (1785). A proverbial expression in classical times. Varro: '*Nec mirum, quod divina natura dedit agros, ars humana aedificavit urbes.*' From the *East Anglian Daily Times* (20 May 1922): 'God made the country, man the town, the devil the little country town.' Compare COWLEY 157:3.

7 England, with all thy faults, I love thee still –
My country!

'The Timepiece', in the same poem. Byron later made use of this in *Beppo*, St. 47 (1818): '"England! with all thy faults I love thee still," / I said at Calais, and have not forgot it.' Cowper is really talking about the weather. See also MCCORMICK 301:1.

8 Variety's the spice of life,
That gives it all its flavour.

In the same poem. The apparent origin of this proverb.

9 I was a stricken deer, that left the herd
Long since.

'The Garden', in the same poem. Hence, *The Stricken Deer*, title of a study of Cowper (1929) by David Cecil. The phrase 'stricken deer' appeared earlier in Shakespeare, *Hamlet*, III.ii.265 (1600–1).

10 Now stir the fire, and close the shutters fast,
Let fall the curtains, wheel the sofa round,
And, while the bubbling and loud-hissing urn
Throws up a steamy column, and the cups,
That cheer but not inebriate, wait on each,
So let us welcome peaceful ev'ning in.

'The Winter Evening', in the same poem. 'The cup that cheers' (the container is usually in the singular) means 'tea' (usually) in preference to alcohol. Antedating this is a piece from *Siris* (1744) by Bishop George Berkeley: '[Tar water] is of a nature so mild and benign and proportioned to the human constitution as to warm without heating, to cheer but not inebriate.'

George CRABBE English poet (1754–1832)

11 I hear those voices that will not be drowned calling.

Although Crabbe's long poem *The Borough* provided Benjamin Britten and his librettist, Montagu Slater, with the story for their opera *Peter Grimes* (1945), this line in Act 2, Sc. 2 is not from it and is presumably Slater's own. In 2003, the words 'I hear those voices that will not be drowned' were written on Maggie Hambling's steel sea-shell sculpture – a tribute to the composer – on the beach at Aldeburgh, Suffolk, where he used to live.

Mrs CRAIK (Dinah Maria Mulock) English novelist (1826–87)

1 Each in his place is fulfilling his day, and passing away, just as that Sun is passing. Only we know not whither he passes; while whither we go we know, and the Way we know, the same yesterday, today and for ever.

Words to be found on the marble tablet to Mrs Craik in Tewkesbury Abbey. The quotation comes from the final chapter of the most celebrated of her novels, *John Halifax, Gentleman* (1857), which is set in and around Tewkesbury. Shortly before Halifax dies, Phineas Fletcher, the narrator, tells how new tenants of the old family house are going to turn it into an inn. Halifax says, 'What a shame! I wish I could prevent it. And yet, perhaps not ... Ought we not rather to recognize and submit to the universal law of change? how each in his place is fulfilling his day, and passing away ...' The final phrase is a quotation from Hebrews 13:8.

Thomas CRANMER English archbishop and martyr (1489–1556)

2 This was the hand that wrote it, therefore it shall suffer first punishment.

During his trial for treason and heresy, Cranmer signed seven recantations of his faith. As he was being burned at the stake (in Oxford), he thrust his right hand first into the flames as it was this hand with which he had signed the recantations. Quoted in John Richard Green, *A Short History of the English People* (1874). Other versions include the exclamation, 'That unworthy hand!' and 'This hand hath offended!'

Mrs Edmund CRASTER English poet (died 1874)

3 A centipede was happy quite,
Until a frog in fun
Said, 'Pray, which leg comes after which?'
This raised her mind to such a pitch,
She lay distracted in a ditch
Considering how to run.

'The Puzzled Centipede'. Quoted in *PDQ* (1960). It is not clear whether the following verse (known by 1948) is by Mrs Craster or another hand:

While lying in this sorry plight
A ray of sunshine caught her sight,
And pondering its beauties long
She burst into a happy song:
Unthinking she began to run,
And quite forgot the croaker's fun.

Julia CRAWFORD Irish writer (1799–1860)

4 Kathleen Mavourneen! the grey dawn is breaking,
The horn of the hunter is heard on the hill.

'Kathleen Mavourneen', in *The Metropolitan Magazine* (1835). Could the second line have inspired STEVENSON's phrase 447:5? The ballad also includes the line 'It may be for years and it may be for ever', hence in Ireland a hire-purchase agreement is known as a Kathleen Mavourneen.

Quentin CRISP English homosexual celebrity (1908–99)

5 I became one of the stately homos of England.

The Naked Civil Servant (1968). Alluding to Mrs Hemans's poem 'The Homes of England' – see COWARD 157:2.

6 Mr Melly had to be obscene to be believed.

Remark about George Melly, the critic and jazz singer, who recalled it on BBC Radio *Quote ... Unquote* (27 May 1997). This set a number of distant bells ringing in my memory and I eventually remembered seeing this couplet by G.C. Norman quoted in *Yet More Comic and Curious Verse*, ed. J.M. Cohen (1959):

Poor Mr Graham Greene is greatly grieved.
He has to be obscene to be believed.

Obscenity was hardly one of Greene's most characteristic qualities, and the whole thing was clearly built around the Greene/obscene rhyme. The similar seen/obscene pun also occurs in *Graffiti 2* (1980): 'Graffiti should be obscene and not heard'; and, from New York, in Reisner & Wechsler's *Encyclopedia of Graffiti* (1974): 'Women should be obscene and not heard.' Well, nothing new, etc. In his 1976 biography, H. Montgomery Hyde has Oscar Wilde saying: 'Little boys should be obscene and not heard.' Which probably brings us back to Quentin Crisp and George Melly ...

Oliver CROMWELL English soldier and Parliamentarian (1599–1658)

7 Put your trust in God, my boys, and keep your powder dry.

Thus Cromwell during his Irish campaign in 1649. There is some doubt whether he really said it at all, as it was ascribed to him long after his death by a certain Valentine Blacker (1778–1823) in an Orange ballad, 'Oliver's Advice' (published 1856). The part about keeping one's powder dry is no more than sensible advice from the days when gunpowder had to be kept dry if it was to be used at all. The overall idiomatic injunction means, 'remain calm and prepared for immediate action', 'be prudent, practical, on the alert'.

Playing upon the word 'powder', *Keep Your Powder Dry* was the title of a 'female flagwaver' film (US 1945) – about female WACS.

1 I desire you would use all your skill to paint my picture truly like me, and not flatter me at all; but remark all these roughnesses, pimples, warts, and everything as you see me; otherwise I will never pay a farthing for it.

According to Horace Walpole's *Anecdotes of Painting in England*, Vol. 3 (1763), this is what Cromwell said to the portrait painter, Sir Peter Lely. The anecdote was first recorded in 1721 and gave rise to the expression 'warts and all', for the plain, unvarnished truth. It is now thought more likely that Cromwell made the remark to Samuel Cooper, the miniaturist, whom Lely copied.

2 I beseech you, in the bowels of Christ, think it possible you may be mistaken.

From his Letter to the General Assembly of the Kirk of Scotland (3 August 1650). However strange it may sound to modern ears, the bowels were once thought to be the seat of tender and sympathetic emotions – kindness, mercy, pity, compassion and feeling. Hence, to refer to Christ's bowels was to heighten the imagery. John Wycliffe wrote in 1382: 'I covet you all in the bowels of Christ ...' Bowels, in this sense, are often evoked in the Bible, mostly in the Old Testament – again, often with puzzling effect on modern sensibilities: 'My beloved put in his hand by the hole of the door, and my bowels were moved for him' (Song of Solomon 5:4).

See also AMERY 7:8.

Anthony CROSLAND English Labour politician (1918–77)

3 If it's the last thing I do, I'm going to destroy every fucking grammar school in England. And Wales, and Northern Ireland.

After a dinner with four teachers' associations in about 1965. Quoted in Susan Crosland, *Tony Crosland* (1982). As Education Secretary in Harold Wilson's Labour government, Crosland propelled the meritocratic move to destroy the old grammar schools and replace them with comprehensive schools, supposedly less dependent on privilege. Susan Crosland elaborated in a letter to *The Independent* (24 February 2001): '[He] did not use four-letter words habitually ... [the remark] occurred in a conversation at home with his wife, me.'

4 With its [the local-government world's] usual spirit of patriotism and its tradition of service to the community's needs, it is coming to realize that, for the time being at least, the party is over.

Speech at a civic luncheon at Manchester (9 May 1975). A warning that Britain's local authorities should not carry on with lavish spending plans when the country's economy, as a whole, was in crisis. Compare COWARD 156:7.

Richard CROSSMAN English Labour politician (1907–74)

5 Already I realize the tremendous effort it requires not to be taken over by the Civil Service. My Minister's room is like a padded cell, and in certain ways I am like a person who is suddenly certified a lunatic and put safely into this great vast room, cut off from real life ... Of course, they don't behave quite like nurses because the Civil Service is profoundly deferential – 'Yes, Minister! No, Minister! If you wish it, Minister! Yes, minister.'

The Diaries of a Cabinet Minister, Vol. 1 (1975). *Yes Minister* was the title of a BBC TV comedy series (1980–5) about the relationship between British government ministers and the Civil Service. It has been said (for example, in *The Listener* (*circa* 1985) that the title came from this description by Crossman, a minister in Labour governments of the 1960s and 1970s, of his first day in office as a Cabinet minister, in October 1964. Antony Jay (co-author with Jonathan Lynn of the TV series) said in 1993: 'I think the Crossman attribution is probably fair. We didn't have it consciously in mind when we thought up the title, but the *Diaries* were one of our set texts and I feel that it was an echo of it that was running through our minds when we gave the series that title, though the original idea predated Crossman.'

e.e. cummings American poet (1894–1962)

6 who knows if the moon's
a balloon, coming out of a keen city
in the sky – filled with pretty people?
'& N &' (1925). Hence, *The Moon's A Balloon*, title of David Niven's first volume of autobiography (1972).

7 nobody, not even the rain, has such small hands.
'somewhere I have never travelled' (1931). It is also said to be the epigraph of Tennessee Williams's play *The Glass Menagerie* (1945), though not in all editions. It also features in Woody Allen's film *Hannah and Her Sisters* (US 1986) – where the Michael Caine character buys a book of e.e. cummings's poetry for the Barbara Hershey character and urges her to read the poem (as a means to seducing her).

John Philpot CURRAN Irish judge (1750–1817)

1 The price of liberty is eternal vigilance.

Speaking on the right of election of the Lord Mayor of Dublin (10 July 1790), what Curran said precisely was: 'The condition upon which God hath given liberty to man is eternal vigilance; which condition if he break, servitude is at once the consequence of his crime, and the punishment of his guilt.' Not said by Thomas Jefferson, as is popularly supposed. The American abolitionist Wendell Phillips said in 1852: 'Eternal vigilance is the price of liberty.'

Compare 'The price of pedantry is eternal vigilance' – Oliver Mason, in a letter to *The Independent* (28 January 1987).

George CURZON (later 1st Marquess Curzon)
English Conservative politician (1859–1925)

2 Gentlemen do not take soup at luncheon.

Attributed remark (1912), quoted in E.L. Woodward, *Short Journey* (1942). Curzon was a snob and had an eccentric view of social behaviour. From the same source: 'Gentlemen never wear brown in London' (said to a fellow Cabinet member on the clothes of a colleague). However, in *The Oxford Book of Oxford*, the first of these remarks is said to have been made in 1921 when Curzon was Chancellor of the University of Oxford. Queen Mary was to be awarded an honorary degree and Curzon was asked to approve of the luncheon to which she was to be invited at Balliol. 'He returned it to the bursar with a single comment written in the corner.'

3 This omnibus business is not what it is reported to be. I hailed one at the bottom of Whitehall and told the man to take me to Carlton House Terrace. But the fellow flatly refused.

On his first trip by bus. This is among the 'Curzonia' included in *The Oxford Book of Political Anecdotes* (1986), though it is not quite clear what the original source was. In fact, it is surely doubtful whether Curzon, the 'most superior person', *ever* went anywhere by bus. This may be yet another example of an old story being fixed on an obviously suitable subject. As always, the origin of the tale could lie in *Punch*. On 10 April 1901 there was a cartoon by Everard Hopkins with this caption: 'A GIRLISH IGNORANCE. *Lady Hildegarde, who is studying the habits of the democracy, determines to travel by Omnibus. Lady Hildegarde.* "CONDUCTOR, TELL THE DRIVER TO GO TO NO. 104, BERKELEY SQUARE, AND THEN HOME!"'

4 Ladies never move.

When instructing his second wife on the subject of love-making. Quoted in *The Oxford Book of Political Anecdotes* (1986). No precise source is given, however. The book of *New Statesmen* competition winners called *Salome, Dear, Not in the Fridge!* (1968 – edited by Arthur Marshall) prefers, 'A lady does not move' (and proceeds to provide the circumstances in which it *might* first have been said).

Note, however, that a completely different source for the story is given by Rupert Hart-Davis in *The Lyttelton Hart-Davis Letters* (for 19 August 1956). When researching Cora, Lady Strafford, a thrice-married American, he discovered that: 'Before one of her marriages (perhaps the second – to Lord Strafford) she thought it would be a good thing to get a little sex-instruction, so she went over to Paris and took a few lessons from a leading cocotte. On her wedding night she was beginning to turn precept into practice when her bridegroom sternly quelled her by saying: "Cora, *ladies don't move!*"' Alas, he does not give a source for this version either.

See also ANNAN 9:4.

D

DAILY EXPRESS London-based newspaper, founded 1900

1 Britain will not be involved in a European war this year, or next year either.

A front-page headline (30 September 1938). Contrary to popular myth, this was the only time the paper predicted as much in a headline although, occasionally, the view that 'There will be no European war' appeared in leading articles. While the statement turned out to be true up to the comma, Lord Beaverbrook, the paper's proprietor, unfortunately insisted on the 'or next year either'. He said: 'We must nail our colours *high* to the mast.' Something like the phrase 'Britain will not be involved in a European war' appeared eight times in the *Express* between September 1938 and August 1939 – source: A.J.P. Taylor, *Beaverbrook* (1966).

A copy of the paper bearing the message '*Daily Express* holds canvass of its reporters in Europe. And ten out of twelve say NO WAR THIS YEAR' was later shown with ironic effect in Noël Coward's film *In Which We Serve* (1942). It was seen bobbing up and down amid the wreckage of a British destroyer that had been torpedoed by the Germans. As a result, Beaverbrook launched a campaign to try to suppress the film.

DAILY MIRROR London-based newspaper, founded 1903

2 Whose finger on the trigger?

'WHOSE FINGER?' was the actual front-page headline on 25 October 1951 – general-election day – and the culmination of a campaign to ensure that the Labour Government was re-elected and the Conservatives under Winston Churchill not allowed back. Earlier, on the 21 September, the paper had asked, 'Whose finger do you want on the trigger when the world situation is so delicate?' The choice was between Churchill and Clement Attlee. Churchill's response

(in a speech, 6 October 1951) was: 'I am sure we do not want any fingers upon any trigger. Least of all do we want a fumbling finger ... But I must tell you that in any case it will not be a British finger that will pull the trigger of a Third World War. It may be a Russian finger or an American finger, or a United Nations Organization finger, but it cannot be a British finger ... the control and decision and the timing of that terrible event would not rest with us. Our influence in the world is not what it was in bygone days.' As it happens, the *Mirror* was unable to stir the electorate and the Conservatives came back to power under Churchill. The Prime Minister then issued a writ for libel against the newspaper because he took the view that the slogan implied that he was a warmonger. The case was settled out of court.

3 Enough is enough.

Front-page headline (10 May 1968) over an article by Cecil H. King, Chairman of the International Publishing Corporation, referring to the government of Harold Wilson. But it resulted in King's fall from power rather than the government's. See also MACMILLAN 305:2.

4 A good man fallen among politicians.

On Michael Foot, then Labour party leader. Editorial (28 February 1983). See BIBLE 82:6.

Édouard DALADIER French politician (1884–1970)

5 *C'est une drôle de guerre* [It's a phoney war].

At first, when war was declared in September 1939, nothing happened. Chamberlain talked of a 'Twilight War' and on 22 December Daladier, the French Prime Minister, used this expression (spelled 'phony' in the US). On 19 January 1940, the *News Chronicle* had a headline: 'This is Not a Phoney

War: Paris Envoy.' And Paul Reynaud employed the phrase in a radio speech on 3 April 1940: '"It must be finished", that is the constant theme heard since the beginning. And that means that there will not be any "phoney peace" after a war which is by no means a "phoney war".' Though speaking French, Reynaud used the phrase in English.

Daniel DALY American soldier (1874–1937)

1 Come on you sons of bitches! Do you want to live for ever?

According to Stuart Berg Flexner, *I Hear America Talking* (1976), Marine Sergeant Daly is remembered for having shouted this during Allied resistance at the Battle of Belleau Wood in June 1918 (during the First World War). *Mencken* (1942) has it from 'an American sergeant ... addressing soldiers reluctant to make a charge', in the form: 'What's the matter with you guys? Do you want to live for ever?' Otherwise the saying remains untraced.

   Whatever the case, Daly was not the first military man to use this form of encouragement. Frederick the Great (1712–86) demanded of hesitating Guards at Kolin (18 June 1757), '*Ihr Racker/Hunde, wollt ihr ewig leben?* [Rascals/Dogs, would you live for ever?]' (or '*immer leben?*'). *Mencken* concludes that the cry is 'probably ancient', anyway.

DANTE ALIGHIERI Italian poet (1265–1321)

2 *Nel mezzo del cammin di nostra vita*
Mi ritrovai per una selva oscura,
Che la diritta via era smarrita.
[In the middle of the journey of our life
I came to myself within a dark wood
Where the straight way was lost].

'Inferno', Canto 1, line 1, *La Divina Commedia* (?1320). This would be at the age of 35 – half of the biblical three score years and ten. The 'dark wood' represents sin and error. See also CLARK 144:9.

3 *Lasciate ogni speranza voi ch'entrate!* [All hope abandon, ye who enter here!]

In the same poem, Canto 3, line 9. Words written over the entrance to Hell. 'Abandon hope all ye who enter here!' is a popular though less accurate translation.

Georges DANTON French revolutionary leader (1759–94)

4 *De l'audace, encore de l'audace, toujours de l'audace!* [Boldness (or daring), more boldness, always boldness!]

Speech to the Legislative Committee of General Defence (2 September 1792), reported in *Le Moniteur* (4 September). This was Danton's recipe for effective resistance against foreign invaders. He concluded: 'Thus will France be saved.'

Clarence DARROW American lawyer (1857–1938)

5 I have never wanted to see anybody die, but there are a few obituary notices I have read with pleasure.

Quoted in *The Treasury of Humorous Quotations*, eds Evan Esar & Nicolas Bentley (1951). The earliest source found for this frequently attributed remark.

Harry DAUGHERTY American Republican supporter (1860–1941)

6 [A group of senators] bleary eyed for lack of sleep [will have to] sit down about two o'clock in the morning around a table in a smoke-filled room in some hotel and decide the nomination.

In *The New York Times* (21 February 1920). Daugherty's prediction concerning the 'smoke-filled room' refers to the choosing of the Republican Party's Presidential candidate in Chicago the following June, if – as in fact happened – the Convention failed to make up its mind. Daugherty, the chief supporter of Warren Harding (the eventual winner), denied that he had ever used the phrase 'smoke-filled'. *ODMQ* (1991) cites a news report dated 12 June 1920 from Kirke Simpson of the Associated Press: '[Warren] Harding of Ohio was chosen by a group of men in a smoke-filled room early today as Republican candidate for President.' But this is clearly alluding to an already established phrase.

   The room in question was Suite 408–409–410 (previously rooms 804–5) of the Blackstone Hotel in Chicago. Whoever coined the phrase, it vividly evokes cigar-smoking political bosses coming to a decision after much horse-trading.

(Sir) John DAVIES English poet (1569–1626)

7 What mean the mermaids when they dance and sing
But certain death unto the mariner?

'Orchestra, or a Poem of Dancing', St. 101 (1594). An early reference to the legendary capacity of mermaids to lure mariners to their deaths. They are generally shown singing alone, mirror in hand, combing their hair 'With a comb of pearl / On a throne', as Tennyson later put it. At Zennor in Cornwall 'for several centuries' there has been told the story of a mermaid's singing that so beguiled the squire's son, Matthew Trewhella (who was also a church chorister), that he went off with her and was never seen again. It is said that their voices are still heard on calm nights. See also ELIOT 186:3.

Bette DAVIS American film actress (1908–89)

1 Yes, I killed him. And I'm glad, I tell you. Glad, glad, glad!

In the 1940 film version of W. Somerset Maugham's play *The Letter*, Davis plays a woman who has killed a man in what seems to have been self-defence. According to Leslie Halliwell in *The Filmgoer's Book of Quotes* (1973), she utters the memorable line – 'Yes, I killed him. And I'm glad, I tell you. Glad, glad, glad!' – but this is not to be found in the film. Might the line have been used on posters rather than in the film itself? After all, Halliwell notes in his book, 'They even used the line as catch-phrase on the posters.' If so, an example has not been found. The line does not appear in Maugham's play. It is, however, mentioned in 'I Love a Film Cliché', a list song (1974) by Dick Vosburgh and Peter Lomax included in the show *A Day in Hollywood, A Night in the Ukraine* (1980). The only fictional character to have used anything like the expression is Pollyanna in the novels of Eleanor H. Porter. Her favourite word is 'glad'. In *Pollyanna Grows Up* (1914), she says: '"Oh, how splendid! Now you've really got folks – folks that care, you know. And you won't ever have to explain that he wasn't born [to] your folks, 'cause your name's the same now. I'm so glad, *glad*, GLAD!"' (Chap. 2); '"Why, Jimmy, I'm glad, glad, GLAD for – everything now!"' (Chap. 30).

2 What a dump!

In the film *Beyond the Forest* (US 1949). The phrase is memorably quoted by Elizabeth Taylor in the film of Edward Albee's *Who's Afraid of Virginia Woolf?* (US 1966) as coming from a Bette Davis movie – and, indeed, a discussion of the phrase's film origins also occupies the opening minutes of the 1962 stage play. *Beyond the Forest* is the melodramatic film where Davis plays the discontented wife of a small-town doctor, has an affair and comes to a sticky end. She also says of the small town in Wisconsin: 'If I don't get out of here, I'll just die! Living here is like waiting for the funeral to begin.'

The line 'What a dump!' had, however, already been used in Otto Preminger's 1945 *Fallen Angel*. Dana Andrews, suspected of murdering Linda Darnell, holes up in a seedy San Francisco hotel with his wife. Andrews exclaims, 'What a dump!' without, it must be admitted, the memorably explosive consonants of both Miss Davis and Miss Taylor.

But how much farther back can we take the phrase? *Partridge/Slang* with its famously wobbly dating suggests about 1919. A more definite indication comes from Eugene O'Neill's play *Ah Wilderness!*, III.i.84 (1933): 'Christ, what a dump!'

Lord DAWSON OF PENN English physician (1864–1945)

3 The King's life is moving peacefully towards its close.

On Monday, 20 January 1936, King George V lay dying at Sandringham – not Buckingham Palace, as stated in *ODQ* (1992). At 9.25 p.m., Lord Dawson, the King's doctor, issued this bulletin, which he had drafted on a menu-card. It was taken up by the BBC. All wireless programmes were cancelled and every quarter of an hour the announcer, Stuart Hibberd, repeated the medical bulletin until the King died at 11.55 p.m. and the announcement was made at 12.15. On the 21st, James Agate entered in his diary – *Ego 2* (1936) – that he 'heard afterwards that the Queen drafted this [bulletin]'.

It seems to be a difficult statement to get right. Harold Nicolson, the King's official biographer (1952), has 'to its close' rather than 'towards'. Chips Channon in his diary (entry for 20 January 1936) has: 'The life of the King is moving slowly to its close.' George Lyttelton wrote to James Agate to point out what he perceived to be an error in the passage already quoted from *Ego 2* (1936): 'Page 321. "The King's life is moving peacefully *to* (not 'towards') its close." I could swear to this. Surely the beauty of the sentence would be severely damaged by *ds* coming before "its" ' – *Ego 6* (1944).

But no. The above version, preceded by the words, 'This is London. The following bulletin was issued at 9.25 ...' has been checked against the BBC Sound Archives recording. Indeed, in *Ego 7* (1945) – for 23 May 1944 – Agate authenticated the wording similarly. He told Lyttelton: 'In Noël Coward's film *This Happy Breed*, which I saw tonight, a lower middle-class family listens to the wireless on that January evening. You can distinctly hear Stuart Hibberd say, "The King's life is moving peacefully towards its close." The thing is obviously a record. *Now* what have you to say for yourself?' Lyttelton was reasonably contrite – but persuaded Hibberd to check with his diary just the same. Compare ASQUITH 42:1.

C. DAY LEWIS Anglo-Irish poet and critic (1904–72)

4 Eye of the wind, whose bearing in
A changeful sky the sage
Birds are never wrong about
And mariners must gauge.

When Peter Scott, the artist and naturalist, came to write his autobiography (published 1961), he set his heart on calling it *The Eye of the Wind*, but nowhere could he find a poem or passage of suitable prose containing the words. Eventually, in desperation, he asked Day Lewis to write a poem from which he could quote them.

OED2 has citations for the exact phrase going back to 1725 and for 'the wind's eye' to 1562. 'In the wind's eye' means 'in the direction of the wind'; 'into the wind's eye' means 'to windward'.

1 *Shall I be gone long?*
For ever and a day.
To whom there belong?
Ask the stone to say.
Ask my song.

An epitaph written for himself in 1944. It is now to be found on the poet's grave in the churchyard of St Michael, Stinsford, Dorset (near Thomas Hardy's heart). 'It directs the pilgrim back to the poems where he still breathes', according to Sean Day-Lewis in the biography of his father, *C. Day-Lewis*, 1980. (The hyphen was not used in his pen name.)

Ralph DEAKIN English journalist (1888–1952)

2 Nothing is news until it has appeared in the columns of *The Times*.

In *I, Claud* (1967) Claud Cockburn described the 'Foreign and Imperial News Editor' of the London *Times*: 'Mr Deakin was believed to be the originator of the statement that nothing was news until it had appeared in the columns of *The Times*, and at that period he gave – from his shining shoes to the beautifully brushed bowler on the rack behind him – an impression of mental and physical discretion and complacency which could have been offensive had it not been, in its childish way, touching.'

The equivalent complacency, not to say pomposity, in the BBC was enshrined in the remark, 'The BBC does not have scoops' – thought to have been the philosophy of Tahu Hole (1908–85), an austere New Zealander who was Editor of BBC News from 1948 to 1958.

Stephen DECATUR American naval officer (1779–1820)

3 My country, right or wrong!

Correctly, Decatur's toast at a public dinner in Norfolk, Virginia (April 1816) was: 'Our country! in her intercourse with foreign nations, may she always be in the right; but our country, right or wrong!' This is sometimes referred to as 'Decatur's Toast'. Compare CHESTERTON 131:5.

(Baron) Pierre DE COUBERTIN French founder of the modern Olympics Games (1863–1937)

4 *L'important dans ces olympiades, c'est moins d'y gagner que d'y prendre part ... L'important dans la vie ce n'est point le triomphe mais le combat; l'essentiel ce n'est pas d'avoir vaincu mais de s'être bien battu* [The most important thing in the Olympic Games is not winning but taking part [just as] the most important thing in life is not the triumph but the struggle; the essential thing in life is not conquering but fighting well].

Speech (24 July 1908) at a banquet for officials of the Olympic Games that were currently being held in London. Although widely credited with this ringing motto, it is just possible the Baron may not have been its originator. According to François Dournon, *Dictionnaire des mots et formules célèbres* (1994), the Baron prefaced his remarks with: '*Dimanche dernier, lors de la cérémonie organisée à Saint-Paul en l'honneur des athlètes, l'évêque de Pennsylvanie l'a rappelé en termes heureux ...*' This refers to a sermon preached in St Paul's Cathedral the previous Sunday by Ethelbert Talbot (1848–1928), Bishop of Central Pennsylvania, who happened to be in London at the time for a liturgical conference. Dournon's source for *this* is Th. A. Cook, 'The fourth Olympiad: being the official report ...' (1909). So did the Baron really take the passage from the bishop?

A report of the banquet in the following day's *Times*, does not report the keynote passage, though it does quote what the Baron had to say on the subject of 'fair play' (and apparently in English). The 'hear, hears' that greeted his remarks are faithfully recorded.

In 2002, the International Society of Olympic Historians managed to dig up Talbot's sermon in the files of the American Episcopal Church in Texas. The relevant section from Talbot is: 'The Games themselves are better than the race and the prize. St. Paul tells us how insignificant is the prize ... though only one may wear the laurel wreath, all may share the equal joy of the contest' (an interesting interpretation of Corinthians 9:24). This is not really very close to what de Coubertin said. Another Olympic historian, David C. Young, wrote a very thorough article on the matter, showing that de Coubertin himself had already said something similar in 1894, when trying to convince the unwilling Greek authorities to organize the first modern Games. On 16 November 1894 de Coubertin said, at the Parnassus Literary Society in Athens: '*Le déshonneur ne consisterait pas ici à être battu; il consisterait à ne pas se battre.*'

Young tried to explain why in 1908 de Coubertin pretended to be quoting Talbot: he would have tried to comment, as diplomatically as possible, on the frequent clashes between American athletes and British officials. But de Coubertin simply mixed up his own earlier phrase from 1894 with an inaccurate memory of what Talbot said in St. Paul's. Whatever the case, Young supposes that de Coubertin's original phrase closely followed something that he may very well have read at school. In Ovid's *Metamorphoses*,

Bk 9, lines 5–6, it says: *'Nec tam / Turpe fuit vinci quam contendisse decorum est.'* In the translation by Dryden and others, this is rendered as: 'Nor was it still so mean the prize to yield, / As great, and glorious to dispute the field.' Less poetically, it would be something like: 'The shame of defeat counted for less than the honour of having struggled.'

After 1908, de Coubertin repeated 'his' words on many occasions thereafter (apparently with no further acknowledgement to Bishop Talbot), until they gradually developed into the official Olympic creed (even if they were ignored by many of the competing athletes). Important stages were Los Angeles 1932, when the words appeared on the scoreboard in English as a message from de Coubertin, and Berlin 1936, when a recording of his voice was played in the stadium (and preserved in a recording by the Swedish Broadcasting Corporation): *'Important aux Jeux Olympiques, ce n'est pas tant d'y gagner que d'y avoir pris part; car l'essentiel dans la vie, ce n'est pas tant de conquérir que d'avoir bien lutté.'* Thus was born a modern proverb. Compare RICE 382:5.

Charles DEDERICH American addiction specialist (1913–)

1 Today is the first day of the rest of your life.

Slogan (?1969) – also known in the form 'Tomorrow is ...' and as a wall slogan, graffito etc. Attributed to Dederich, founder of of the Synanon anti-drug and alcohol centres in the US. 'Today Is the First Day of the Rest of *My* Life' was apparently sung in a late 1960s musical *The Love Match* (by Maltby & Shire).

Charles DE GAULLE French general and President (1890–1970)

2 *La France a perdu une bataille! Mais la France n'a pas perdu la guerre!* [France has lost a battle, but France has not lost the war!]

This memorable line appeared in a proclamation dated 18 June 1940 and circulated later in the month, but it was not spoken in de Gaulle's famous broadcast appeal of that date, from London, to Frenchmen betrayed by Pétain's armistice with the Germans. Earlier, on 19 May 1940, Winston Churchill, in his first broadcast to the British people as Prime Minister, had said: 'Our task is not only to win the battle – but to win the war' (meaning the battle *for* Britain).

3 *Maintenant, elle est comme les autres* [Now she is like the others].

Jean Lacouture in his biography (1965) of de Gaulle recorded the remark the future French President made at the grave-

side of his mentally disabled daughter, Anne, who died shortly before her 20th birthday in 1948. Mme Yvonne de Gaulle had written to a friend when Anne was born: 'Charles and I would give everything, everything, health, fortune, promotion, career, if only Anne were a little girl like the others.' Hence, the particular nature of the later, poignant remark. 'Is this the most moving thing ever said by a Great National Hero?' – *The Diaries of Kenneth Tynan*, ed. John Lahr (2001), for 5 June 1974.

4 Politics is too important to be left to the politicians.

Quoted in Clement Attlee, *A Prime Minister Remembers* (1961). See also BENN 61:5; CLEMENCEAU 146:1; MACLEOD 302:5.

5 *Comment voulez-vous gouverner un pays qui a deux cent quarante-six variétés de fromage?* [How can you govern a country which produces 246 different kinds of cheese?]

There are many versions of de Gaulle's aphorisms, but this is probably an accurate summing up of his view of the French people, although the number of cheeses varies: 246 is Ernest Mignon's version in *Les Mots du Général* (1962); *ODQ* (1979) has 265 – the occasion given for this version is the 1951 election when de Gaulle's political party, though the largest, still did not have an overall majority.

Compare the older view of the writer and gourmet Alexandre Balthazar Grimod de la Reynière (1758–1838): *'On connoit en France 685 manières differentes d'accommoder les oeufs* [In France, there are 685 different ways of using eggs]'.

6 *Je vous ai compris ... Vive l'Algérie française!* [I have understood you ... Long live French Algeria!]

De Gaulle became President in 1958 amid the turmoil created by resistance from French colonialists to the idea of Algerian independence. He eventually led his country in quite the opposite direction to the one expected of him, but from the beginning he spoke with a forked tongue. On 4 June he flew to Algiers and told a rally 'I have understood you' – which could have meant anything – at the same time as *'Vive l'Algérie française!'* – which could have been taken to imply that he supported the continuation of colonial rule.

7 *La réforme, oui; la chienlit, non* [Reform, yes, bedshitting, no].

In private de Gaulle had a colourful way of describing his political opponents – for example, he would call them *pisse-vinaigres* ('vinegar pissers') and 'eunuchs of the Fourth Republic' or *'politichiens'*. Returning from a visit to Romania at the time of the May 1968 student uprising in France, he asked the Minister of Education: 'What about your students – still the *chienlit*?' Quite what this meant was much debated at the time. The polite dictionary definition is 'carnival masquerade' or 'ridiculous disguise', but if spelt *chie-en-lit* it can mean 'bed-shitting', which seems more appropriate in the context. A day or two later, on 19 May, de Gaulle used the expression again at a Cabinet meeting while giving his view of the students' demands, as above. It was his Prime Minister, Georges Pompidou, who passed the remark to the press. One of the many banners appearing in the streets at the time responded with a cartoon of the President and the charge '*La chienlit c'est lui!*' This was outside the Renault factory at Billancourt where workers were staging a sit-in.

1 **Where there is mystery, there is power.**

Or 'Where there is no mystery there is no power.' This unverified statement was made by de Gaulle to André Malraux in the context of a discussion about the importance of politicians not exposing themselves too frequently on television. But nowhere in the culture minister's writings could this be found, and a call to *The André Malraux Review* failed to elicit any helpful response. However, in de Gaulle's book *Le Fil de l'Épée*, Chap. 3 (1932), translated as *The Edge of the Sword*, there is this assertion: 'The true leader, like the great artist, is a man with an inborn propensity which can be strengthened and exploited by the exercise of his craft. First and foremost, there can be no prestige without mystery, for familiarity breeds contempt. All religions have their holy of holies, and no man is a hero to his valet ... Nothing more enhances authority than silence. It is the crowning virtue of the strong, the refuge of the weak, the modesty of the proud, and pride of the humble, the prudence of the wise and the sense of fools.' So de Gaulle really did believe this, although of course when television came along, he did not eschew the medium entirely. But he didn't overdo it. A lesson for all politicians today. Compare BAGEHOT 49:7.

R.F. DELDERFIELD English novelist (1912–72)

2 *A Horseman Riding By.*

Title of novel (1966). Just possibly an allusion to YEATS 510:9.

3 *God Is an Englishman.*

The title of Delderfield's novel (published in 1970) might derive from a saying attributed to Bernard Shaw – in Prochnow & Prochnow, *Treasury of Humorous Quotations* (1969): 'The ordinary Britisher imagines that God is an Englishman.' But, however expressed, the arrogant assumption is almost traditional. Harold Nicolson recorded in his diary for 3 June 1942 that three years previously, R.S. Hudson,

the Minister of Agriculture, was being told by the Yugoslav minister in London of the dangers facing Britain. 'Yes,' replied Hudson, 'you are probably correct and these things may well happen. But you forget that God is English.'

Working backwards: in his introduction to *The British Character* (1951) by 'Pont', E.M. Delafield writes: 'Most Englishmen, if forced into analysing their own creeds – which Heaven forbid – are convinced that God is an Englishman – probably educated at Eton.' James Morris in *Farewell the Trumpets* has a Dublin balladeer at the time of the 1916 Easter Rising singing: 'God is not an Englishman and truth will tell in time.' The closing line of the Gilbert and Sullivan opera *HMS Pinafore* (1878) is 'That he is an Englishman!', but it is sung to such grandiose music that it tends to sound like, '*He* is an Englishman!'

God's Englishness is also expressed in other ways: in a June 1977 edition of BBC Radio *Quote ... Unquote*, Anna Ford (a clergyman's daughter) mentioned the (apocryphal?) priest who prayed: 'Dear God, as you will undoubtedly have read in the leader column of *The Times* this morning ...'

And then God is sometimes included in other groups. R.A. Austen-Leigh's *Eton Guide* (1964) points out that on the south wall of Lower Chapel an inscription begins, 'You who in the chapel worship God, an Etonian like yourselves ...' When H.M. Butler, Master of Trinity College, Cambridge, said, 'It was well to remember that, at this moment, both the Sovereign and the Prime Minister are Trinity men', Augustine Birrell replied: 'The Master should have added that he can go further, for it is obvious that the affairs of the world are built upon the momentous fact that God is also a Trinity man' – quoted by Harold Laski in a letter to Oliver Wendell Holmes (4 December 1926). In *As We Are*, Chap. 1 (1932), E.F. Benson wrote of 'people with broad lands and exalted titles, who in their hearts knew that God was the real head of the Tory party'.

On BBC Radio *Quote ... Unquote* in July 1987, the actor Brian Glover drew attention to the adage: 'God is a Yorkshireman.' By way of contrast, there is apparently a Greek saying – presumably of reassurance – which states: 'Never mind, God isn't an Albanian.'

4 *To Serve Them All My Days.*

The title of Delderfield's 1972 novel about a schoolmaster sounds as if it *ought* to be a quotation, but contains no more than echoes of several religious lines: 'And to serve him truly all the days of my life' from the Catechism in the Book of Common Prayer; 'To serve thee all my happy days' from the hymn 'Gentle Jesus, meek and mild' in the Methodist Hymnal; the Devon carol, 'We'll bring him hearts that love him / To serve him all our days'; and the Sunday school hymn, 'I must like a Christian / Shun all evil ways, / Keep the faith of Jesus, / And serve him all my days.'

Jack DEMPSEY American heavyweight boxer (1895–1983)

1 Honey, I just forgot to duck.

Dempsey said this to his wife on losing his World Heavy-weight title to Gene Tunney during a fight in Philadelphia (23 September 1926). In his *Autobiography* (1977) Dempsey recalled: 'Once I got to the hotel, Estelle managed to reach me by telephone, saying she'd be with me by morning and that she'd heard the news. I could hardly hear her because of the people crowding the phone. "What happened, Ginsberg?" (That was her pet name for me.) "Honey, I just forgot to duck."' The line was recalled by ex-sports commentator Ronald Reagan when explaining to *his* wife what had happened during an assassination attempt in 1981.

Alan DENT Scottish critic and writer (1905–78)

2 This is the tragedy of a man who could not make up his mind.

From the introduction to Dent's film adaptation of Shake-speare's *Hamlet* (1948). Laurence Olivier spoke the words but did not write them, as is suggested by *ODQ* (1992). Dent's capsule comment was criticized on the grounds that *Hamlet* is not so much about a man who could not make up his mind as about one who could not bring himself to take necessary action.

G.V. DESANI Indian-born novelist and philosopher (1909–2001)

3 Geography is everywhere.

In the days when humorous graffiti were all the rage, I was sent a photograph of a curious daub on a brick wall in the middle of a field in Bedworth, Warwickshire. It proclaimed: 'GEOGRAPHY IS EVERYWHERE – G.V. DESANI.' The identity of the given author of this profound thought puzzled me, but latterly I have learned that Desani actually existed. His novel *All About H. Hatterr* was published to acclaim in 1948. Until his retirement he was a visiting professor at the University of Austin, Texas. The last line of *Hatterr* is the (seemingly very Indian), 'Carry on, boys, and continue like hell!'

Colin DEXTER English novelist (1930–)

4 *The Jewel That Was Ours.*

Title of novel (1991). Not a quotation, despite the placing of a verse by 'Lilian Cooper, 1904–1981' as the book's epigraph:

Espied the god with gloomy soul
The prize that in the casket lay,
Who came with silent tread and stole
The jewel that was ours away.

Cooper was Dexter's mother-in-law and long dead by the time he appended her name to his manufactured verse, as he told me in 1998. In the same book, extreme scepticism should be exercised over: 'Almost all modern architecture is farce' – *Reflections*, Diogenes Small (1797–1805). Just look at those dates. Beware, too, anything ascribed by Dexter to a certain Viscount Mumbles ...

Serge DIAGHILEV Russian ballet impresario (1872–1929)

5 *Etonne-moi!* [Astonish me!]

Said to Jean Cocteau, the French writer and designer, in Paris in 1912. Cocteau had complained to Diaghilev that he was not getting enough encouragement and the Russian exhorted him with the words, 'Astound me! I'll wait for you to astound me.'

In Cocteau's *Journals* (published 1956) he comments: 'I was at the absurd age when one thinks oneself a poet, and I sensed in Diaghilev a polite resistance.' When Cocteau received the command he felt it was one he could, and should, obey. In due course, he may be said to have done so.

DIANA British Princess (1961–97)

6 I'd like to be a queen of people's hearts ... but I don't see myself being Queen of this country.

Interviewed on BBC TV *Panorama* (20 November 1995). In answer to the question, 'Do you think you will ever be Queen?' From *The Independent* (18 December 1995): 'The Princess of Wales seems certain to land in next year's dictionaries of quotations for her wish to be "the queen of people's hearts". It was a memorably spontaneous phrase. Or was it? Searching through the remaindered section of his record collection, Eagle Eye is stunned to find the lyrics from a 1987 composition by an amateur songwriter, Basilio Magno, who lives in Spain and is now 72. It is entitled Sweet Lady Di and includes the phrase: "She'll remain a queen in every Briton's heart."'

After the Princess's death, an attempt was made to register 'Queen of Hearts' as a trademark, along with her title and image, to safeguard its use on memorabilia.

Porfirio DÌAZ Mexican President (1830–1915)

7 *Pobre México, tan lejos de Dios y tan cerca de los Estados Unidos* [Poor Mexico, so far from God, so close to the United States].

Attributed in *Bartlett* (1980). Frank McLynn, *Villa and Zapata: a biography of the Mexican Revolution* (2000), states that it is doubtful that Dìaz ever said it – 'It sounds too witty for him.' Compare ANDREWES 8:8.

Thomas DIBDIN English songwriter (1771–1841)

1 Oh! what a snug little Island,
A right little, tight little Island!

Song, 'The Snug Little Island', from a musical play, *The British Raft* (1797), said to have been written in the late 18th century when Britain was threatened by French invasion. In a letter (27 November 1816), Lord Byron wrote: 'I would never willingly dwell in the "tight little island".' *Tight Little Island* was the US title of the film (UK 1948) of Compton Mackenzie's novel *Whisky Galore*.

Charles DICKENS English novelist (1812–70)

BLEAK HOUSE 1852–3

2 This is a London particular ... A fog, miss.

Chap. 3. The name 'London particular' was given to London's one-time notorious fogs because they were very characteristic of, or particular to, London. Possibly originally from a Madeira wine imported especially for the London market and thence applied to the fog because of its colour.

3 'Well!' said Mr Boythorn '... I am looked upon about here, as a second Ajax defying the lightning. Ha ha ha ha!'

Chap. 18. Compare, from Oscar Wilde's New York lecture 'The English Renaissance of Art' (9 January 1882): 'The English [artists'] models form a class entirely by themselves. They are not so picturesque as the Italian, nor so clever as the French, and they have absolutely no tradition, so to speak, of their order. Now and then some old veteran knocks at the studio door, and proposes to sit as Ajax defying the lightning, or as King Lear upon the blasted heath.' Now the Ajax referred to in all this is not the famous warrior of the siege of Troy, but the lesser-known Ajax the Lesser, son of Oileus, who was there nevertheless and raped Priam's daughter Cassandra after dragging her from a statue of Athena. This so annoyed the goddess that she shipwrecked Ajax on his way home. He clung to a rock, defied the goddess, not to mention the lightning, and was eventually washed off and drowned by Neptune. The question is, how and when did the allusion turn into a phrase? In the description of Ajax's death in Homer's *Odyssey*, the lightning incident is not mentioned but in Virgil's *Aeneid*, Bk 1, line 42, he is found being dealt with by Zeus's bolts (in Dryden's translation):

She, for the fault of one offending foe,
The bolts of Jove himself presum'd to throw:
With whirlwinds from beneath she toss'd the ship,

And bare expos'd the bosom of the deep;
Then, as an eagle gripes the trembling game,
The wretch, yet hissing with her father's flame,
She strongly seiz'd, and with a burning wound
Transfix'd, and naked, on a rock she bound.

The wretch, of course, being Ajax the Lesser. Earlier, the matter was mentioned, though less specifically, by Euripides in his *Trojan Women*. Early in the play (around line 77) we find (in E.P. Coleridge's translation):

Athena: Dost not know the insult done to me and to the shrine I love?
Poseidon: Surely, in the hour that Aias tore Cassandra thence ...
Athena: When they have set sail from Ilium for their homes. On them will Zeus also send his rain and fearful hail, and inky tempests from the sky; yea, and he promises to grant me his levin-bolts [lightning bolts] to hurl on the Achaeans and fire their ships.

Finally, the incident is alluded to in Ovid's *Metamorphoses* (Bk 14; here in translation):

After fam'd Ilium was by Argives won,
And flames had finish'd, what the sword begun;
Pallas, incens'd, pursu'd us to the main,
In vengeance of her violated fane [shrine, temple].
Alone Oileus forc'd the Trojan maid,
Yet all were punish'd for the brutal deed.
A storm begins, the raging waves run high,
The clouds look heavy, and benight the sky;
Red sheets of light'ning o'er the seas are spread,
Our tackling yields, and wrecks at last succeed.

There are a number of representations in art of Ajax the Lesser going about his rapes and so on, but the search is still on for the lightning-defying pose.

4 [Chadband] 'Why can't we not fly, my friends?'
[Mr Snagsby] 'No wings.'

Chap. 19. Compare from Lord Berners, *First Childhood* (1934): 'My [model flying machine] elicited a reproof from the Headmaster, who happened to see it [in about 1893]. "Men," he said, "were never meant to fly; otherwise God would have given them wings." The argument was convincing, if not strikingly, having been used previously, if I am not mistaken, by Mr Chadband.'

5 'It's turned very dark, sir. Is there any light a–comin?'
'It is coming fast, Jo.'
Fast. The cart is shaken all to pieces, and the rugged road is very near its end.
'Jo, my poor fellow!'

Chap. 47. Describing the last moments of Jo, the crossing sweeper. Quoted as 'The cart is shaken all to pieces, and the rugged road is at its end' in Colin Dexter's *The Way Through the Woods* (1992). Dexter has confirmed this.

A CHRISTMAS CAROL 1843

1 'Bah,' said Scrooge. 'Humbug!'

Stave 1. Ebenezer Scrooge, an old curmudgeon, userer and miser, has this view of the Christmas spirit until frightened into changing his ways by the appearance of a ghost and sundry visions. The derivation of the word 'humbug' meaning 'deception, sham' is uncertain, but it suddenly came into vogue in about 1750.

2 'God bless us every one!' said Tiny Tim, the last of all.

Stave 3. Tiny Tim is the younger son in the Cratchit family and a cripple. The converted Scrooge is concerned to save him. Tiny Tim's exclamation is the sentimental highpoint of the story and is repeated as the last line of the story.

THE CRICKET ON THE HEARTH 1846

3 *The Cricket on the Hearth.*

Title of Dickens's Christmas book for 1846. The cricket, so described, influences the main character to overcome a misunderstanding. Dickens probably took the idea from a ballad in what is known to be one of his favourite works – Goldsmith's *The Vicar of Wakefield* (1766):

The cricket chirrups on the hearth,
The crackling faggot flies.

Earlier, in Milton's 'Il Penseroso' (1632), there had been:

Far from all resort of mirth,
Save the cricket on the hearth.

The inevitable joke was made by Sidney Chawsen Woodhouse in the title of his book *The Critic On the Hearth, and other plays and dialogues* (1929).

DAVID COPPERFIELD 1850

4 'In case anything turned up,' which was his favourite expression.

Chap. 11. Of Wilkins Micawber, an optimistic failure, who lives on the breadline but is convinced that his fortunes will soon be on the mend. The character is based in part on Dickens's father. His financial analysis in Chap. 12 is impeccable: 'Annual income twenty pounds, annual expenditure nineteen nineteen and six, result happiness. Annual income twenty pounds, annual expenditure twenty pounds ought and six, result misery.'

5 My mother is likewise a very umble person. We live in a numble abode.

Chap. 16. Uriah Heep speaking. 'Humble abode' is a self-deprecating term for where one lives. Appropriately, two of the most unctuous characters in all literature use it. Heep, as here, and earlier Mr Collins in Jane Austen's *Pride and Prejudice*, Chap. 14 (1813): 'The garden in which stands my humble abode, is separated only by a lane from Rosings Park, her ladyship's residence.'

6 Accidents will happen in the best-regulated families.

This proverbial expression is best remembered in the form delivered in Chap. 28: '"Copperfield," said Mr Micawber, "accidents will occur in the best-regulated families; and in families not regulated by ... the influence of Woman, in the lofty character of Wife, they must be expected with confidence, and must be borne with philosophy."' Dickens had earlier used the saying in *The Pickwick Papers* (1836–7) and *Dombey and Son* (1844–6). However, the saying is not original to him. Scott wrote in Chap. 49 of *Peveril of the Peak* (1823): 'Nay, my lady ... such things will befall in the best regulated families.'

CODP finds 'P. Atall' writing in *Hermit in America* (1819), 'Accidents will happen in the best regulated families.' Even earlier, George Colman in *Deuce is in Him* (1763) has the more basic, 'Accidents will happen.'

7 I got to know what umbleness did, and I took to it. I ate umble pie with an appetite.

Chap. 39. Uriah Heep. The expression 'to eat humble pie', meaning 'to submit to humiliation' came about because the 'humbles' or 'umbles' were those less appealing parts of a deer (or other animal) that had been killed in a hunt. They would be given to those of lower rank and perhaps served as 'humble pie' or 'umble pie'. A coincidence then that 'humble pie' should have anything to do with being 'humble'. Recorded in use by 1830. *An umble pie* was a mistaken split of *a numble pie*, from *numbles*, the offal of a deer, from Old French *nombles*.

8 The partner of his joys and sorrows – I again allude to his wife.

Chap. 42. Mrs Micawber, referring somewhat archly to herself (as also 'the bosom of affection – I allude to his wife') in a letter to David, using an already existing, if looser, formula. Earlier, Scott in *The Talisman*, Chap. 6 (1825) has: 'The Almighty, who gave the dog to be companion of our pleasures and our toils ...' and in Motteux's 1703 translation of *Don Quixote*, Sancho Panza refers to his horse Dapple as 'my faithful companion, my friend, and fellow-sharer in my toils and miseries'. Later, P.G. Wodehouse in *Ring for Jeeves*, Chap. 9 (1953), has Rory refer to Monica (to whom he is married) as 'my old partner of joys and sorrows'.

See also BURNS 111:5.

DOMBEY AND SON 1846–8

1 What the Waves were always saying.

Heading of Chap. 16. Nowhere in the novel does Dickens use the precise words, 'What are the *wild* waves saying?', though the book is fairly awash with the idea of a 'dark and unknown sea that rolls round all the world' (Chap. 1, end). At the end of Chap. 8, in Brighton, young Paul Dombey says to his sister, Florence, 'I want to know what it says ... The sea, Floy, what is it that it keeps on saying?' Then, a line or two later: 'Very often afterwards, in the midst of their talk, he would break off, to try to understand what it was that the waves were always saying; and would rise up in his couch to look towards that invisible region, far away.'

The quotation in question is actually the title line of a Victorian song with words by J.E. Carpenter (1813–85) and music by Stephen Glover (1813–70):

What are the wild waves saying,
Sister, the whole day long:
That ever amid our playing,
I hear but their low, lone song?
Not by the seaside only,
There it sounds wild and free;
But at night when 'tis dark and lonely,
In dreams it is still with me.

The song is a duet between the characters Paul and Florence Dombey, and based on an incident in Dickens's novel. *Punch* had the phrase 'What are the wild waves saying?' on 21 October 1848. Compare this: an advertisement for Igranic wireless coils, dating from the early 1920s, which plays upon the idea of radio waves and asks, 'What are the wild waves saying?'

GREAT EXPECTATIONS 1860–1

2 What larks!

Kenneth Tynan wrote to Cecil Beaton: 'Can you sing bass? Kensington's Boris Christoff – what larks!' – letter (1 January 1953). In *The Kenneth Williams Diaries* (1993) – entry for 30 August 1970 – the actor writes: 'Tom played the

piano and all the girls danced with us & I stuck me bum out and oh! what larks Pip!' Ned Sherrin dedicates his *Theatrical Anecdotes* (1991), 'For Judi [Dench] and Michael [Williams]: "What larks!"' All these refer to the characteristic phrase of Joe Gargery, the blacksmith, who looks after his brother-in-law and apprentice, Pip, in the boy's youth. Chap. 13 has him saying 'calc'lated to lead to larks' and Chap. 57, 'And when you're well enough to go out for a ride – what larks!' In Chap. 7, Pip writes it down with the spelling 'WOT LARX'. The recent use of the phrase probably has more to do with the 1946 film of the book in which Bernard Miles played Joe. As he sees Pip off on a stagecoach, he says, 'One day I'll come to see you in London and then, what larks, eh?' and similarly, after Pip's breakdown, 'You'll soon be well enough to go out again, and then – what larks!' Even here, the name Pip is not actually included in the phrase.

LITTLE DORRIT 1857

3 Lady here is extremely anxious that there should be no Row. Lady – a mother of mine, in point of fact – wishes me to say that she hopes no Row.

Bk. 2, Chap. 3. Sparkler (Mrs Merdle's son by her first marriage) attempts to head off an argument by saying this. In a rather roundabout way, this explains why Lord Peter Wimsey (in the novels by Dorothy L. Sayers) applies the name 'Mrs Merdle' to the succession of Daimler motor cars he owns. Mrs Merdle's connection with motor cars is not immediately apparent. The solution depends on finding the first mention of her in the Sayers novels. This occurs in *Unnatural Death*, Chap. 6 (1927), when Lord Peter takes delivery of a new Daimler: 'With a racing body. Specially built ... useful ... gadgets ... no row – hate row ... like Edmund Sparkler ... very anxious there should be no row ... Little Dorrit ... remember ... call her Mrs Merdle ... for that reason.' Even this is not very explicit. The whole thing depends on a pun. Lord Peter is using the word 'row' in the sense of noise: the Daimler has a 'smooth, uncanny silence'. In Dickens, 'row' is as in 'argument'.

4 Once a gentleman, and always a gentleman.

Bk 2, Chap. 28. Referring to Rigaud. The seemingly modern 'once a — always a — ' format derives from an old series of proverbs, 'Once a knave/whore/captain, always a ...' Dr Johnson used 'once a coxcomb, and always a coxcomb' in an anecdote included in Boswell's *Life of Johnson* (1791) for the year 1770. S.T. Coleridge wrote an article with the title *Once a Jacobin Always a Jacobin* (21 October 1802). William Cobbett quoted 'once a parson always a parson' in his *Rural Rides* (for 11 October 1826).

NICHOLAS NICKLEBY 1838–9

1 As she frequently remarked when she made any such mistake, it would be all the same a hundred years hence.

Chap. 9. Mrs Squeers. Compare JOHNSON 259:2.

2 Language was not powerful enough to describe the infant phenomenon.

Chap. 23. 'The infant phenomenon' was the stage billing of Ninetta Crummles (who has been ten years old for at least five years). The term also appears earlier in *The Pickwick Papers*, Chap. 26 (1836–7), when Sam Weller says to Master Bardwell: 'Tell her I want to speak to her, will you, my hin-fant fernomenon?' This suggests that the phrase was in general use before this novel came to be written or was something Dickens had picked up from an actual case. In 1837 the eight-year-old Jean Davenport was merely billed as 'the most celebrated juvenile actress of the day'. George Parker Bidder (born 1806), who possessed extraordinary arithmetical abilities, had been exhibited round the country as a child, billed as 'the calculating phenomenon'.

3 All is gas and gaiters.

Chap. 49. The Gentleman in the Small-Clothes speaking. Gaiters (leg coverings below the knee) have traditionally been associated with bishops. Hence, *All Gas and Gaiters*, the title of a BBC TV comedy series about the clergy (1966–70).

THE OLD CURIOSITY SHOP 1840–1

4 Does Little Nell die?

A query not from the book but *about* its child heroine, Nell Trent. She attempts to look after her inadequate grandfather and to protect him from various threats, but her strength gives out. According to one account, 'Does Little Nell die?' was the cry of 6000 book-loving Americans who hurried to the docks in New York to ask this question of sailors arriving from England. Another version is that it was longshoremen demanding 'How is Little Nell?' or 'Is Little Nell dead?' As the novel was serialized, they were waiting for the arrival of the final instalment of the magazine to find out what had happened to the heroine. Little Nell's death came to typify the heights of Victorian sentimental fiction. Oscar Wilde later commented: 'One must have a heart of stone to read the death of Little Nell without laughing' – quoted in Ada Leverson, *Letters to the Sphinx from Oscar Wilde and Reminiscences of the Author* (1930).

OLIVER TWIST 1837

5 Please, sir, I want some more.

Chap. 2. Oliver requests more food in the workhouse.

6 If the law supposes that ... the law is a ass – a idiot.

Chap. 51. Strictly speaking, if one is quoting Dickens, what Mr Bumble says, is not 'the law is *an* ass'. He is dismayed that the law holds him responsible for his wife's actions. Compare CHAPMAN 130:5.

OUR MUTUAL FRIEND 1864–5

7 *Our Mutual Friend.*

The title refers to the novel's hero, John Harmon, who feigns death and whose identity is one of the mysteries of the plot. This is a rare example of Dickens using an established phrase for a title (he usually chooses the invented name of a character). 'Our mutual friend' was an expression established by the 17th century, but Dickens undoubtedly further encouraged its use. Some have objected that 'mutual friend' is a solecism, arguing that it is impossible for the reciprocity of friendship to be shared with a third party. Even before Dickens took it for a title, a correspondent was writing to the journal *Notes and Queries* in 1849 and asking: 'Is it too late to make an effective stand against the solecistic expression "mutual friend"?' *The Oxford Dictionary for Writers and Editors* (1981) points out that it is an expression used also by Edmund Burke, George Eliot and others, and that 'the alternative "common" can be ambiguous'.

8 A fair day's wages for a fair day's work is ever my partner's motto.

Bk 1, Chap. 13. Not original to Dickens. T. Attwood in a speech in the House of Commons (14 June 1839) said: 'They only ask for a fair day's wages for a fair day's work', which is probably the first time the slogan was uttered. In any case, Benjamin Disraeli had used the slogan before Dickens in his novel *Sybil* (1845).

See also NASH 337:2.

THE PICKWICK PAPERS 1837

9 It's over, and can't be helped, and that's one consolation, as they always say in Turkey, ven they cut the wrong man's head off.

Chap. 23. Sam Weller speaking. Hence, the term 'wellerism' (a term known by 1839) for a form of comparison in which a saying or proverbial expression is attributed to an amusingly inapposite source. E.g. '"That's an antelope," observed the small boy when he heard that his mother's sister had run away with the coachman.' Mieder & Kingsbury in their *Dictionary of Wellerisms* (1994) note that a wellerism usually consists of three parts: a statement, a speaker who makes this remark, and a phrase or clause that places the utterance in a new light or an incompatible setting: '"Every little helps," quoth the wren when she pissed in the sea.' This last was recorded in 1605 and demonstrates that the type was known long before Dickens gave Sam Weller a fondness for uttering these jocular remarks. Dickens did, however, popularize the form.

A TALE OF TWO CITIES 1859

1 It was the best of times, it was the worst of times, it was the age of wisdom, it was the age of foolishness, it was the epoch of belief, it was the epoch of incredulity, it was the season of Light, it was the season of Darkness, it was the spring of hope, it was the winter of despair, we had everything before us, we had nothing before us, we were all going direct to Heaven, we were all going direct the other way.

First words of Bk 1, Chap. 1. One of the most memorable opening sentences to a novel ever written. Hence, many allusions get made to it. For example, the headline 'Best of Thames, Worst of Thames' over a review of books about the current condition of London in *The Observer* (22 December 1996).

2 It is a far, far better thing that I do than I have ever done; it is a far, far better rest that I go to, than I have ever known.

Bk 3, Chap. 15. These words, appearing at the end of the novel, are sometimes said to be Sydney Carton's last words as he ascends the scaffold to be guillotined. But he does not actually speak them. They are prefaced with: 'If he had given any utterance to his [last thoughts], and they were prophetic, they would have been these ...'

One editor refers to this as, 'A complicated excursus into the pluperfect subjunctive.' In dramatizations, however, Carton has actually *said* the lines – as did Sir John Martin-Harvey in the play *The Only Way* (1898) by F. Wills. One of the slogans devised by Dorothy L. Sayers in *Murder Must Advertise* (1933) was for margarine: 'It's a far, far butter thing ...'

DIOGENES Greek philosopher (?400–?325BC)

3 Stand out of my sun a little.

When asked by Alexander the Great if he lacked anything. Reported in Plutarch, *Parallel Lives*, in Thomas North's translation (1579). Sometimes rendered as 'Give me more light.'

Walt DISNEY American cartoon film-maker (1901–66)

4 All the world owes me a living.

The Grasshopper and the Ants (1934). This expression was so ascribed to Disney when it was used as the epigraph of Graham Greene's novel *England Made Me* (1935). The cartoon film in question – one of the first 'Silly Symphonies' – is based on the Aesop fable 'Of the ant and the grasshopper' (as it is called in Caxton's first English translation, 1484), which tells of a grasshopper asking an ant for corn to eat in winter. The ant asks, 'What have you done all the summer past?' and the grasshopper can only answer, 'I have sung.' The moral is that you should provide yourself in the summer with what you need in winter. Disney turns the grasshopper into a fiddler and gives him a song to sing (written by Larry Morey to music by Leigh Harline):

> Oh! the world owes me a living
> Deedle, diedle, doedle, diedledum.
> Oh! the world owes me a living
> Deedle, diedle, doedle, diedleum, etc.

This develops in time to:

> Oh, the world owes us a living ...
> You should soil your Sunday pants
> Like those other foolish ants,
> So let's play and sing and dance ...

And then, when the error of his ways has been pointed out to him, the grasshopper sings:

> I owe the world a living ...
> I've been a fool the whole year long.
> Now I'm singing a different song,
> You were right and I was wrong.

This song became quite well known and presumably helped John Llewellyn Rhys choose *The World Owes Me a Living* as the title for his 1939 novel about a redundant Royal Flying Corps hero who tries to make a living with a flying circus (filmed 1944). It is a little odd rendered in this form, because on the whole it is not something a person would say about himself. More usually, another would say, pejoratively, 'The trouble with you is, you think the world owes you a living.' The phrase *was* used before Disney. W.G. Sumner wrote in *Earth Hunger* (1896): 'The men who start out with the notion that the world owes them a living generally find that the

world pays its debt in the penitentiary or the poorhouse.'
Sumner was an American economist, but the phrase may
not have originated in the US.

Benjamin DISRAELI (1st Earl of Beaconsfield)
British Conservative Prime Minister (1804–81)

1 Read no history: nothing but biography, for that
is life without theory.

Contarini Fleming (1832). Compare EMERSON 190:3.

2 I will sit down now, but the time will come when
you will hear me.

When Disraeli gave his maiden speech in the House of
Commons (7 December 1837), he wanted to take the House
by storm. His subject was the validity of certain Irish elections, but he was greeted with hisses, catcalls and hoots of
laughter. The above was his concluding sentence. Samuel
Smiles in *Self-Help* (1859) wrote of the occasion: 'It was
spoken of as "more screaming than an Adelphi farce".
Though composed in a grand and ambitious strain, every
sentence was hailed with "loud laughter". "Hamlet" played
as a comedy were nothing to it. But he concluded ... writhing
under the laughter with which his studied eloquence had
been received, he exclaimed, "I have begun several times
many things, and have succeeded in them at last. I shall sit
down now ...'

3 'Two nations; between whom there is no intercourse and no sympathy; who are as ignorant of
each other's habits, thoughts, and feelings, as if
they were dwellers in different zones, or inhabitants of different planets; who are formed by a
different breeding, are fed by a different food, are
ordered by different manners, and are not
governed by the same laws.' 'You speak of — ' said
Egremont, hesitatingly, 'THE RICH AND THE
POOR.'

Sybil, or The Two Nations, Bk 2, Chap. 5 (1845). Disraeli did
not speak of 'One Nation' – that was the title of a pamphlet
published in 1950 by a group of Tories including Iain
Macleod, Angus Maude and Enoch Powell. According to
Alan Watkins in the *Independent on Sunday* (21 January
1996): 'The title was suggested by Maude, though some
think the phrase was supplied to him by Macleod. The
group, chiefly members who looked up to R.A. Butler, took
their name from the pamphlet rather than the other way
round.' Tony Blair, the Labour Party leader, revived the
phrase in 1996.

4 The question is this: Is man an ape or an angel?
Now I am on the side of the angels.

Speech on evolution to the Oxford Diocesan Society
(25 November 1864).

5 I have climbed to the top of the greasy pole.

On becoming Prime Minister (1868). Quoted in W.
Monypenny and G. Buckle, *The Life of Benjamin Disraeli*
(1920).

6 When a man fell into his anecdotage it was a sign
for him to retire from the world.

Lothair, Chap. 28 (1870). Earlier, however, his father, Isaac
Disraeli, had noted in his *Curiosities of Literature* (1839):
'Among my earliest literary friends, two distinguished themselves by their anecdotical literature: James Petit Andrews,
by his "Anecdotes, Ancient and Modern", and William
Seward, by his "Anecdotes of Distinguished Persons". These
volumes were favourably received, and to such a degree,
that a wit of that day, and who is still a wit as well as poet,
considered that we were far gone in our "Anecdotage".' The
word 'anecdotage' in a less critical sense had been used by De
Quincey in 1823 simply to describe anecdotes collectively.

7 Many thanks; I shall lose no time in reading it.

To an author who had sent him an unsolicited manuscript.
Quoted in Wilfrid Meynell, *The Man Disraeli* (1903). G.W.E.
Russell, *Collections and Recollections*, Chap. 31 (1898), has
the remark but merely ascribes it to an eminent man 'on
this side of the Atlantic'.

8 Everyone likes flattery; and when you come to
Royalty you should lay it on with a trowel.

To Matthew Arnold. Quoted in G.W.E. Russell, *Collections
and Recollections*, Chap. 23 (1898). The most notable example of Disraeli's own use of the trowel must be his saying
'We authors, Ma'am' to Queen Victoria when she published
her Highland journals and on several other occasions
(asserted by Monypenny and Buckle, *Life of Disraeli*,
1910–20, though G.W.E. Russell had already had it in the
work cited).

The figure of speech 'To lay it on with a trowel', meaning
'to be generous in supplying something – usually when
engaged in flattery', was an old one even in the 19th century. 'That was laid on with a trowel' appears in Shakespeare's *As You Like It*, I.ii.98 (1598), which the Arden
edition glosses as 'slapped on thick and without nicety, like
mortar'. The trowel in question is not a garden one, but of
the kind used by bricklayers or by painters for spreading
paint thickly.

1 The wisdom of the wise and the experience of the ages are perpetuated by quotations.

Comment on the art of quotation. Quoted in Laurence J. Peter, *Quotations for Our Time* (1977).

2 The Church of England is the Tory Party at prayer.

This description is often attributed to Disraeli. However, Robert Blake, the historian and author of *Disraeli* (1966), told *The Observer* (14 April 1985) that he could not say who had said it first and that a correspondence in *The Times* some years before had failed to find an answer. According to Robert Stewart's *Penguin Dictionary of Political Quotations* (1984), Agnes Maude Royden, the social reformer and preacher, said in an address at the City Temple, London (1917): 'The Church should no longer be satisfied to represent only the Conservative Party at prayer' – but even this sounds as though it was alluding to an already established saying.

3 Lord Salisbury and myself have brought you back peace – but a peace I hope with honour.

Speech on returning from the Congress of Berlin (16 July 1878). Compare CHAMBERLAIN 129:4.

4 A sophistical rhetorician, inebriated with the exuberance of his own verbosity, and gifted with an egotistical imagination that can at all times command an interminable and inconsistent series of arguments to malign an opponent and to glorify himself.

Of Gladstone, in a speech to a banquet in the Knightsbridge Riding School (27 July 1878), quoted in *The Times* (29 July). Commonly rendered in the form: 'Sir, you are intoxicated by the exuberance of your own verbosity.' In *Scouse Mouse* (1984), George Melly describes how this was ascribed to *Dr Johnson* by a headmaster called W.W. Twyne. A common mistake.

5 Never complain and never explain.

Quoted in John Morley, *Life of Gladstone* (1903) – specifically about attacks in Parliament. The following must have been referring back to, or at least echoing, Disraeli: according to an article in the *Oxford Chronicle* (7 October 1893), a favourite piece of advice given to young men by Benjamin Jowett, who became Master of Balliol College, Oxford, in 1870, was, 'Never regret, never explain, never apologize.' However, in *The Oxford Book of Oxford* this is given as 'Never retreat. Never explain. Get it done and let them howl.' Compare BALDWIN 51:6; GRACIAN 218:4; HUBBARD 246:6.

6 Yes, I am a Jew, and when the ancestors of the right honourable gentleman were brutal savages in an unknown island, mine were priests in the temple of Solomon.

Bartlett gives this as an assertion made by Disraeli to Daniel O'Connell (for which no source is given). Compare what Judah P. Benjamin (1811–84) said in reply to a US senator: 'The gentleman will please remember that when his half-civilized ancestors were hunting the wild boar in the forests of Silesia, mine were the princes of the earth' – Ben Perley Poore, *Reminiscences of Sixty Years in the National Metropolis* (1886).

7 There are lies, damn lies – and statistics.

Although sometimes attributed to Mark Twain – because it appears in his posthumously published *Autobiography* (1924) – this should more properly be ascribed to Disraeli, as indeed Twain took trouble to do: his exact words being, 'The remark attributed to Disraeli would often apply with justice and force: "There are three kinds of lies: lies, damned lies, and statistics."' On the other hand, the remark remains untraced among Disraeli's writings and sayings, and Lord Blake, Disraeli's biographer, does not know of any evidence that Disraeli said any such thing and thinks it most unlikely that he did. So why did Twain make the attribution? Leonard Henry Courtney, the British economist and politician (1832–1918), later Lord Courtney, gave a speech on proportional representation 'To My Fellow-Disciples at Saratoga Springs', New York, in August 1895, in which this sentence appeared: 'After all, facts are facts, and although we may quote one to another with a chuckle the words of the Wise Statesman, "Lies – damn lies – and statistics," still there are some easy figures the simplest must understand, and the astutest cannot wriggle out of.' This speech was reproduced in *The National Review*, No. 26, in the same year. Subsequently, Courtney's comment was reproduced in an article by J.A. Baines on 'Parliamentary Representation in England illustrated by the Elections of 1892 and 1895' in *Journal of the Royal Statistical Society*, No. 59 (1896): 'We may quote to one another with a chuckle the words of the Wise Statesman, lies, damn lies, and statistics, still there are some easy figures which the simplest must understand but the astutest cannot wriggle out of.'

It would be a reasonable assumption that Courtney was referring to Disraeli by his use of the phrase 'Wise Statesman', though the context is somewhat complicated. For some reason, at this time allusions to rather than outright quotations of Disraeli were the order of the day. Compare the remark to an author who had sent him an unsolicited manuscript, 'Many thanks; I shall lose no time in reading it', which is merely ascribed to an 'eminent man on this side of the Atlantic' by G.W.E. Russell, *Collections and Recollections*, Chap. 31 (1898).

Comparable sayings: Dr Halliday Sutherland's autobiographical *A Time to Keep* (1934) has an account of Sir Henry Littlejohn, 'Police Surgeon, Medical Officer of Health and Professor of Forensic Medicine at the University [Edinburgh] ... Sir Henry's class at 9 a.m. was always crowded, and he told us of the murder trials of the last century in which he had played his part. It was Lord Young [judge] who said, "There are four classes of witnesses – liars, damned liars, expert witnesses, and Sir Henry Littlejohn."' Hence, *Lies, Damn Lies, and Some Exclusives* – title of a book about British newspapers (1984) by Henry Porter; and 'There are lies, damned lies ... and Fianna Fáil party political broadcasts' – Barry Desmond MEP, (Irish) Labour Party director of elections, in November 1992.

1 She would only ask me to take a message to Albert.

These are not Disraeli's last words. During his final illness, it was suggested that he might like to receive a visit from Queen Victoria. 'No, it is better not,' he replied, 'She would only ask me to take a message to Albert.' That is a perfectly genuine quotation and is confirmed by Robert Blake in his life, *Disraeli* (1966). The last authenticated words Disraeli uttered were: 'I had rather live but I am not afraid to die' – quoted in Wintle & Kenin, *The Dictionary of Biographical Quotation* (1978).

See also CHURCHILL 140:2; SMITH 435:5.

Henry Austin DOBSON English poet (1840–1921)

2 Time goes, you say? Ah no!
Alas, Time stays, we go.

The Paradox of Time, St 1 (1875). A translation of: '*Le temps s'en va, le temps s'en va, ma dame; / Las! le temps non, mais nous, nous en allons*' – credited to the French poet Jean Passerat (1534–1602) and also, more probably, to Pierre de Ronsard (1524–85), in his *Pièces retranchées*.

Ken DODD English comedian and singer (1927–)

3 The trouble with Freud is that he never played the Glasgow Empire Saturday night.

On Freud's theory that a good joke will lead to great relief and elation. In the ATV programme *The Laughter Makers* and so quoted in *The Times* (7 August 1965). Dodd's remark has appeared in several versions since that date. For example, with the addition of 'after Rangers and Celtic had both lost' in *The Guardian* (30 April 1991). *The Observer* (17 March 2002) had this version: 'It was Freud who described humour as being as incongruous as a buckled wheel, but the trouble with Freud is he never played the old Glasgow Empire on a

wet Monday night after both Celtic and Rangers had lost on the previous Saturday.' Some say it was Aristotle whose definition of comedy was the buckled wheel. Not confirmed.

Aelius DONATUS Roman grammarian (4th century AD)

4 *Pereant qui ante nos nostra dixerunt!* [Damn those who have made my remarks before me!]

Quoted in this form in *The Treasury of Humorous Quotations*, eds Esar & Bentley (1951). Originally quoted by St Jerome in *Commentary on Ecclesiastes*: 'The same idea is said by the comic poet [Terence, in *Prolog. Eunuchi*]: "Nothing is said which has not been said before." Whence my teacher Donatus when he was speaking of that verse, said, "Confound those who have said our remarks before us."'

John DONNE English poet and divine (1572–1631)

5 Licence my roving hands, and let them go,
Behind, before, above, between, below.
O my America, my new found land,
My kingdom, safeliest when with one man
   manned.

'To His Mistress Going to Bed', *Elegies* (?1595). The word play in the third line was relatively topical. Newfoundland had been discovered by John Cabot in 1497 and had [some 12 years before] been claimed for Queen Elizabeth I by Sir Humphrey Gilbert in 1583.

6 She, and comparisons are odious.

'The Comparison', in the same collection. Compare SHAKESPEARE 419:2.

7 Come live with me, and be my love,
And we will some new pleasures prove
Of golden sands, and crystal brooks,
With silken lines, and silver hooks.

'The Bait', *Songs and Sonnets* (1611).

8 Go, and catch a falling star
Get with child a mandrake root,
Tell me, where all past years are.
Or who cleft the Devil's foot.

'Song', in the same work. Since at least 1563 a 'falling star' has been another name for a meteor or shooting star. Here, the catching is clearly just one of four impossible tasks. 'Catch a falling star' was also the title of a 1958 song, popularized by Perry Como:

Catch a falling star and put it in your pocket,
Never let it fade away.

1 This bed thy centre is, these walls thy sphere.

In the same work. Hence, *This Bed Thy Centre*, title of novel (1935) by Pamela Hansford Johnson – 'the authoress had intended it satirically. The novel was an early feminist outcry against the sexual and domestic subordination of women' – John Bayley, *Iris* (1998).

2 But I do nothing upon my self, and yet I am mine own *Executioner*.

'Meditation 12', *Devotions Upon Emergent Occasions* (1624). Hence, *Mine Own Executioner*, title of a novel (1945; film UK 1947) by Nigel Balchin.

3 No man is an Island, entire of it self; every man is a piece of the Continent, a part of the main; if a clod be washed away by the sea, Europe is the less, as well as if a promontory were, as well as if a manor of thy friends or of thine own were; any man's death diminishes me, because I am involved in Mankind. And therefore never send to know for whom the bell tolls; it tolls for thee.

'Meditation 17', in the same work. Hence, the title of the novel *For Whom the Bell Tolls* (1940; film US 1943) by Ernest Hemingway, set in the Spanish Civil War. Hemingway's approach to the matter of choosing the title is described in a letter to Maxwell Perkins (21 April 1940), included in *Ernest Hemingway Selected Letters 1917–1961*, ed. Carlos Baker (1981): 'I think it has the magic that a title has to have. Maybe it isn't too easy to say. But maybe the book will make it easy. Anyway I have had thirty some titles and they were all possible but this is the first one that has made the bell toll for me. Or do you suppose that people think only of tolls as long distance charges and of Bell as the Bell of the telephone system? If so it is out. The Tolling of the Bell. No. That's not right.'

The same passage is the likely source for the modern funerary cliché 'His death diminishes us all', for example, 'Sir William's death diminishes us all' was how André Previn commented on the death of William Walton in March 1983. 'One must not be too hard on Mr Previn,' commented *The Guardian*. 'Music is his chosen medium, not words.'

(Sir) Alec DOUGLAS-HOME (formerly Earl of Home, later Lord Home) British Conservative Prime Minister (1903–95)

4 When I have to read economic documents I have to have a box of matches and start moving them into position to illustrate and simplify the points to myself.

Interviewed in *The Observer* (16 September 1962), when Foreign Secretary in Harold Macmillan's government. It was by such remarks as these that Douglas-Home projected an image of a likeable buffoon, which he was not (buffoon, that is – he was certainly likeable). When he became Prime Minister he still fostered the image: 'There are two problems in my life. The political ones are insoluble and the economic ones are incomprehensible' – speech (January 1964).

5 As far as [being] the 14th Earl is concerned, I suppose Mr Wilson, when you come to think of it, is the 14th Mr Wilson.

TV interview (21 October 1963). In response to WILSON 500:7.

6 *The Way the Wind Blows.*

Title of memoirs (1976). He explains that it was what a gamekeeper said of his family's abilities: 'The Home boys always seem to know which way the wind blows', and he adds, '[He] was not thinking of me as a political trimmer, but simply stating a fact of our family life ... on the right interpretation of wind or weather depended the action of the day.' A proverbial expression of 1546 was 'I knew which way the wind blew.' See also DYLAN 180:6.

Ernest DOWSON English poet (1867–1900)

7 They are not long, the weeping and the laughter, Love and desire and hate ... They are not long the days of wine and roses; Out of a misty dream Our path emerges for a while, then closes Within a dream.

'*Vitae Summa Brevis Spem Nos Vetar Incohare Longam*' (1896). Hence, *The Days of Wine and Roses*, title of a film (US 1962) about an alcoholic (though the phrase is often used to evoke romance). Hence, also, *The Weeping and the Laughter*, the title of a novel (1988) by Noel Barber, and of autobiographies by J. Maclaren-Ross (1953) and Viva King (1976).

8 *Non Sum Qualis Eram* [I am not what I was].

Title of poem (in full '*Non Sum Qualis Eram Bonae Sub Regno Cynarae*') (1896), also known as 'Cynara'. She is a woman to whom the poet professes faithfulness even when consorting with others. *Non sum qualis eram bonae / Sub regno Cinarae* [I am not what I was in the reign of the good queen Cinara]' appeared much earlier in Horace, *Odes*, IV.i.3.

1 I have forgot much, Cynara! Gone with the wind.

In the same poem. Hence, *Gone With the Wind*, title of Margaret Mitchell's famous novel (1936; film US 1939), where the phrase refers to the southern United States before the American Civil War, as is made clear by the on-screen prologue to the film: 'There was a land of Cavaliers and Cotton Fields called the Old South. Here in this patrician world the Age of Chivalry took its last bows. Here was the last ever seen of the Knights and their Ladies fair, of Master and Slave. Look for it only in books, for it is no more than a dream remembered, a Civilization gone with the wind.'

2 I have been faithful to thee, Cynara! in my fashion.

In the same poem. Compare 'Always True To You In My Fashion', the song by Cole Porter from *Kiss Me Kate* (1948), which echoes, consciously or unconsciously, this line.

3 For Lord I was free of all Thy flowers, but I
   chose the world's sad roses,
And that is why my feet are torn and mine eyes
   are blind with sweat.

Impenitentia Ultima (1896). In *Seven Pillars of Wisdom* (1926), T.E. Lawrence described being thrown to the ground from a camel: as he lay 'passively waiting for the Turks to kill me', he recalled these 'verses of a half-forgotten poem', but he does not own up to the source.

(Sir) Arthur Conan DOYLE Scottish-born writer
(1859–1930)

4 It is cocaine ... a seven per cent solution. Would you care to try it?

The Sign of Four, Chap. 1 (1889). Hence, *The Seven Per Cent Solution*, title of a novel (1974; film US 1976) by Nicholas Meyer, about Sherlock Holmes being treated by Sigmund Freud for a persecution complex and cocaine addiction.

5 Quick, Watson, the needle!

Not uttered by Holmes in the books, but it is in the film *The Hound of the Baskervilles* (US 1939). Known a good bit before this: P.G. Wodehouse in a letter (22 December 1922) wrote: 'I wonder what an osteopath does if a patient suddenly comes apart in his hands. ("Quick, Watson, the seccotine!")'

6 You will remember that I remarked the other day ... that for strange effects and extraordinary combinations we must go to life itself, which is always far more daring than any effort of the imagination.

'The Red-Headed League', *The Adventures of Sherlock Holmes* (1892). Holmes talking. Hence the title *Life Itself!* of Elaine Dundy's memoir (2001).

7 It is quite a three-pipe problem, and I beg that you won't speak to me for fifty minutes.

In the same story. Holmes is saying that the case requires sufficient thought to accompany the smoking of three fills of his famous pipe.

8 He is the Napoleon of crime, Watson.

Of 'Ex-Professor Moriarty of mathematical celebrity' in 'The Final Problem', *The Memoirs of Sherlock Holmes* (1894). Holmes continues: 'He is the organizer of half that is evil and of nearly all that is undetected in this great city ... He has a brain of the first order. He sits motionless, like a spider in the centre of its web, but that web has a thousand radiations, and he knows well every quiver of each of them.' Compare ELIOT 188:1.

9 Elementary, my dear Watson!

This, the most celebrated Sherlock Holmes phrase, appears nowhere in Conan Doyle's writings, though the great detective does exclaim just 'Elementary' to Dr Watson in 'The Crooked Man', in the same work. Conan Doyle brought out his last Holmes book in 1927. His son Adrian (in collaboration with John Dickson Carr) was one of those who used the phrase in follow-up stories – as have adapters of the stories in film and broadcast versions. In the 1929 film *The Return of Sherlock Holmes* – the first with sound – the final lines of dialogue are:

   Watson: Amazing, Holmes!
   Holmes: Elementary, my dear Watson, elementary.

This may have put the catchphrase squarely in the language, but it appears already to have been a phrase in 1915. In *Psmith Journalist*, Chap. 19, P.G. Wodehouse wrote: '"Elementary, my dear Watson, elementary," murmured Psmith. Even earlier, in *Psmith in the City*, Chap. 8 (1910), Psmith is already reaching towards the finished phrase: 'Then I am prepared to bet a small sum that he is nuts on Manchester United. My dear Holmes, how – ! Elementary, my dear fellow, quite elementary.'

10 'Is there any other point to which you would wish to draw my attention?' 'To the curious incident of the dog in the night-time.' 'The dog did nothing in the night-time.' 'That was the curious incident,' remarked Sherlock Holmes.

'Silver Blaze', *The Memoirs of Sherlock Holmes* (1894). A much quoted example of an absence of fact that could provide an important clue in detection. Possibly most usually alluded to now as 'the dog that did not bark in the night'. Hence the title of Mark Haddon's novel *The Curious Incident of the Dog in the Night-Time* (2003).

1 Come, Watson, come! The game is afoot.
'The Abbey Grange', *The Return of Sherlock Holmes* (1904). Compare SHAKESPEARE 409:6.

(Sir) Francis DRAKE English sailor and explorer (?1540–96)

2 There must be a beginning of any great matter, but the continuing unto the end until it be thoroughly finished yields the true glory.
Dispatch to Sir Francis Walsingham before the raid on Cadiz (1587). Hence, the title of a documentary film *The True Glory* (UK/US 1945) about the end of the Second World War. In a speech on 15 August 1945, about the surrender of Japan, Winston Churchill said: 'This is the true glory, and long will it gleam upon our forward path.' It was also a favourite phrase of Margaret Thatcher. She paraphrased it in a speech (21 May 1980), and later alluded to the rest of Drake's dispatch in an address to the 1922 Committee of backbench MPs (19 July 1984), as reported here in *The Guardian*: 'After reminding them of their success in the recent Euro-elections, and pointing out that few people during last year's general election could have foreseen a 19-week pit strike, she declared that it was not the beginning of the struggle that mattered. It was the continuation of the fight until it was truly concluded.'

3 The singeing of the King of Spain's beard.
Drake's own phrase for his impish attack on the Spanish fleet and stores at Cadiz in 1587, which delayed the sailing of the Armada until the following year. Reported in Francis Bacon, *Considerations touching a War with Spain* (1629): 'I remember Drake, in the vaunting style of a soldier, would call the enterprise the singeing of the King of Spain's beard.'

4 There is plenty of time to win this game, and to thrash the Spaniards too.
An example of world-class insouciance. Possibly apocryphal, but this is what everyone would like to believe was said by Drake as he played bowls on Plymouth Hoe when the Armada was sighted (20 July 1588). So attributed in the *Dictionary of National Biography* (1917). His game of bowls was first mentioned in a preface to the 1736 edition of Sir Walter Raleigh's *History of the World*. The saying, sometimes rendered as 'There is time to finish the game and beat the Spaniards afterwards', is 'the work of a later embroiderer', according to another source.

Ruth DRAPER American monologist and entertainer (1884–1956)

5 Of course he [Dante] was a genius, wasn't he – like Shakespeare? ... He and Dante seem to have known *everything* ... known what would always be true ... Wonderful, I imagine that we're going to find that this is *full* of quotations.
Sketch, 'The Italian Lesson' (1930s?).

Michael DRAYTON English poet (1563–1631)

6 Fair stood the wind for France
When we our sails advance,
Nor now to prove our chance
Longer will tarry ...
'Agincourt', *To the Cambro-Britons* (1619). Hence, *Fair Stood the Wind for France*, title of a novel (1944) by H.E. Bates. Before Drayton, in Christopher Marlowe's *Edward II* (1593), there had been: 'Fair blows the wind for France.'

Allen DRURY American novelist (1918–98)

7 *Advise and Consent.*
Title of novel (1959; film US 1962) about Washington politics. Taken from Senate Rule 38: 'The final question on every nomination shall be, "Will the Senate advise and consent to this nomination?"' In the US Constitution (Art. 2, Sect. 2), dealing with the Senate's powers as a check on the President's appointive and treaty-making powers, the phrase is rather '*Advice* and consent'. Originally, George Washington as President went in person to the Senate Chamber (22 August 1789) to receive 'advice and consent' about treaty provisions with the Creek Indians. Vice-President Adams used the words, 'Do you advise and consent?' Subsequent administrations have sent written requests.

John DRYDEN English poet and playwright (1631–1700)

8 A man so various that he seemed to be
Not one, but all mankind's epitome.
Stiff in opinions, always in the wrong;
Was everything by starts, and nothing long:
But, in the course of one revolving moon,
Was chemist, fiddler, statesman and buffoon.
Absalom and Achitophel (1681). In July 1978, the British Prime Minister, James Callaghan, as Rogue Quotationist, used this passage to attack Margaret Thatcher and the Conservative front bench in the House of Commons. Mrs Thatcher was at one time a chemist, but that is about the only link. Besides, Dryden was writing about a *man* in a

work that dealt with the Exclusion Crisis, with various public figures given biblical names. 'Zimri', described here, was George Villiers, 2nd Duke of Buckingham (1628–87). He was a politician, Cabal member and close friend of Charles II. It has been urged that it is his personal qualities rather than his political ones that are described in these lines.

1 Happy the man, and happy he alone,
He, who can call today his own:
He who, secure within, can say,
Tomorrow do thy worst, for I have lived today.

Translation of Horace's *Odes*, Bk 3, No. 29. These became the Narrator's closing lines in John Osborne's screenplay for the film *Tom Jones* (UK 1963).

2 Arms, and the man I sing, who, forced by fate,
And haughty Juno's unrelenting hate,
Expelled and exiled, left the Trojan shore.

Translation of Virgil's *Aeneid* (1697) – opening lines. Hence, *Arms and the Man*, title of a play (1894) by Bernard Shaw. Between times, Thomas Carlyle had suggested in *Past and Present* (1843) that a true modern epic was technological rather than military, and had written: 'For we are to bethink us that the Epic verily is not *Arms and the Man*, but *Tools and the Man*.' See also VIRGIL 478:6.

3 None but the brave deserves the fair.

Alexander's Feast (1697). Hence, *None But the Brave*, title of a film (US 1965) about the Second World War. Earlier Sir Edwin Landseer's painting *None But the Brave Deserve the Fair* (1838) had shown two stags fighting while anxious hinds look on.

4 Like pilgrims to th'appointed place we tend;
The world's an inn, and death the journey's end.

Palamon and Arcite (1700). See SHERRIFF 430:7.

Alexander DUBČEK Czechoslovak politician (1921–92)

5 Give socialism back its human face.

Slogan used frequently in 1968 – sometimes 'Socialism [or Communism] with a human face' – when a brief flowering of independence in Czechoslovakia gave rise to the 'Prague Spring'. The phrase was first suggested to Dubček, Communist Party First Secretary, by Radovan Richta in a private conversation – according to Robert Stewart in the *Penguin Dictionary of Political Quotations* (1984). A party group in the Ministry of Foreign Affairs referred to Czech foreign policy acquiring 'its own defined face' – *Rudé právo* (14 March 1968). The slogan was later applied to domestic affairs.

The experiment was quashed when the Soviet Union invaded the country in August 1968. Dubček was later removed from power.

Joachim DU BELLAY French poet (1522–60)

6 *Heureux qui comme Ulysse a fait un beau voyage* [Happy he who, like Ulysses, has made a great journey].

Les Regrets, Sonnet 31 (1558). Used as an inscription on the headstone of the grave of Sir Henry 'Chips' Channon (1897–1958), the American-born socialite and Conservative MP, who achieved posthumous fame through the publication of his diaries. He is buried at Kelvedon in Essex. Robert Rhodes James, editor of *Chips: The Diaries of Sir Henry Channon* (1967), refers to 'the words [from a sonnet] of Du Bellay which had been his special favourite'. The translation continues: 'Or like that man [Jason] who won the Fleece and then came home, full of experience and good sense, to live the rest of his time among his family.'

Much depends on the translation. Another: 'Happy the man who's journeyed much, like Ulysses. / Or like the traveller who won the Golden Fleece, / And has returned at last, experienced and wise, / To end his days among his family in peace.' George Seferis (1900–71), 'On a Line of Foreign Verse', develops the idea: 'Fortunate he who's made the voyage of Odysseus. / Fortunate if on setting out he's felt the rigging / Of a love strong in his body, spreading there like / Veins, where the blood throbs ... / ... To see once more the smoke / Ascending from his warm hearth and the dog grown / Old waiting by the door.'

Alexandre DUMAS (Dumas Père) French novelist (1802–70)

7 *Tous pour un, un pour tous* [All for one and one for all].

Motto of the Three Musketeers, made famous in the novel *Les Trois Mousquetaires* (1844–5). Earlier, Shakespeare in his poem *The Rape of Lucrece*, lines 141–4 (1594) had written:

The aim of all is but to nurse the life
With honour, wealth and ease, in waning age;
And in this aim there is much thwarting strife
That one for all, or all for one we gage [= pledge].

More prosaically, 'Each for all and all for each' has been used in Britain as a slogan of the Co-operative Wholesale Society.

Daphne DU MAURIER (later Dame Daphne)
English novelist (1907–89)

1 Last night I dreamt I went to Manderley again.

Rebecca (1938). Opening words, spoken by the unnamed narrator who is the second wife of Mr de Winter. The story tells of the mystery surrounding her predecessor, and is set in Manderley, a house that eventually meets its end. That is why she can only dream of going back to it.

Paul Laurence DUNBAR   American poet (1872–1906)

2 But a plea, that upward to heaven he flings –
I know why the caged bird sings!

'Sympathy', *Lyrics of Hearthside* (1899). Webster in *The White Devil* has: 'We think caged birds sing, when indeed they cry.' Hence, the titles of two volumes of autobiography by Maya Angelou: *I Know Why the Caged Bird Sings* (1969) and *A Song Flung Up To Heaven* (2002).

William DUNBAR   Scottish poet and priest (?1460–?1520)

3 *Timor mortis conturbat me.*
Fear of death disturbs me.

'Lament for the Makaris' [= makers, i.e. poets]. The poem is an elegy for life's transitoriness, as well as mourning the loss of Dunbar's fellow poets, including Chaucer and Gower.

Will DURANT   American writer (1885–1981)

4 There is nothing in Socialism that a little age or a little money will not cure.

Unverified. Compare CLEMENCEAU 146:3.

Leo DUROCHER   American baseball manager (1906–91)

5 Nice guys finish last.

In his autobiography with the title *Nice Guys Finish Last* (1975), Durocher recalled that what he had said to reporters concerning the New York Giants in July 1946 was: 'All nice guys. They'll finish last. Nice guys. Finish last.' However, Frank Graham of the New York *Journal-American* had written down something slightly different: 'Why, they're the nicest guys in the world! And where are they? In seventh place!' As the last place at that time was eighth, seventh was no big improvement. Hence, the title of Ralph Keyes's book on misquotations *Nice Guys Finish Seventh* (1992).

Bob DYLAN   American singer and songwriter (1941–)

6 How many roads must a man walk down
Before you can call him a man? ...
The answer, my friend, is blowin' in the wind.

Song, 'Blowin' in the Wind' (1962).

7 The Times They Are A-Changin'.

Title of song (1963).

8 Keep a clean nose
Watch the plain clothes
You don't need a weather man
To know which way the wind blows.

Song, 'Subterranean Homesick Blues' (1965). Hence, 'Weathermen', the original name of a violent radical group in the US (current in 1969), which then became known as the Weather Underground.

9 All Along the Watchtower.

A 1968 Dylan song begins: 'All along the watchtower, princes kept the view.' This is probably after Isaiah 21:5, prophesying the fall of Babylon: 'Prepare the table, watch in the watchtower, eat, drink: arise ye princes, and anoint the shield.' *The Watchtower*, magazine of the Jehovah's Witnesses, presumably takes its name from the same source.

10 If I had a good quote, I'd be wearing it.

When asked for 'a good quote' by a French journalist on a cold night. Quoted in *The Times* (July 1981).

E

Clint EASTWOOD American film actor (1930–)

1 Go ahead, make my day!

This popular laconicism was originally spoken by Eastwood as a cop, himself brandishing a .44 Magnum, to a gunman he is holding at bay in *Sudden Impact* (US 1983). At the end of the film he says (to another villain, similarly armed), 'Come on, make my day.' In neither case does he add 'punk', as is sometimes supposed, e.g. from *The Independent* (14 July 1993): 'When Clint Eastwood said "Go ahead, punk, make my day" ...'). This may come about from confusion with *Dirty Harry* (US 1971) in which Eastwood holds a .44 Magnum to the temples of a criminal and says 'Ask yourself one question: "Do I feel lucky?" Well, do ya, punk?'

In March 1985 President Ronald Reagan told the American Business Conference: 'I have my veto pen drawn and ready for any tax increase that Congress might even think of sending up. And I have only one thing to say to the tax increasers. Go ahead – make my day.' The phrase may have been eased into Reagan's speech by having appeared in a parody of the *New York Post* put together by editors, many of them anti-Reagan, in the autumn of 1984. Reagan was shown starting a nuclear war by throwing down this dare to the Kremlin – source: *Time* Magazine (25 March 1985).

Fred EBB American songwriter (1932–2004)

2 Money makes the world go around.

Song, 'Money, Money', from the musical *Cabaret* (1966; film US 1972), with music by John Kander. The modern proverbial phrase derives, apparently, from this musical. As with 'Tomorrow Belongs To Me' (below), we may have to thank the writers of *Cabaret* for either creating an instant 'saying' or, in this instance, for introducing to the English language something that has long been known in others.

'Money makes the world go around' is clearly built on the well-established proverb ''Tis love that makes the world go round' – see CARROLL 123:7 – but it is not recorded in either *ODP* or *CODP*. The nearest these get is, 'Money makes the mare to go.' The thought is not new, of course: 'I know what makes the world go round. It isn't money. It's love' – J.B. Priestley, *The Good Companions*, Bk 2, Chap. 5 (1929).

'Money makes the world go around' appears in the English-language key to the *Flemish Proverbs* picture by David Teniers the Younger (1610–90), at Belvoir Castle. The painting shows an obviously wealthy man holding a globe. The key may, however, be modern.

3 The babe in his cradle is closing his eyes, the
    blossom embraces the bee,
But soon says a whisper, 'Arise, arise',
    Tomorrow belongs to me.
O Fatherland, Fatherland, show us the sign your
    children have waited to see,
The morning will come when the world is mine,
    Tomorrow belongs to me.

Song, 'Tomorrow Belongs to Me', in the same musical. Has this ever been used as an actual political slogan, either as 'Tomorrow belongs to me' or 'to us'? Harold Wilson in his final broadcast before the 1964 general election said, 'If the past belongs to the Tories, the future belongs to us – all of us.' At a Young Conservative rally before the 1983 general election, Margaret Thatcher asked: 'Could Labour have organized a rally like this? In the old days perhaps, but not now. For they are the Party of Yesterday. Tomorrow is ours.'

What one *can* say is that, in *Cabaret*, Ebb wrote a convincing pastiche of a Hitler Youth song, so much so that the song was denounced as a real Nazi anthem. Ebb told *The Independent* (30 November 1993): 'The accusations against "Tomorrow Belongs to Me" made me very angry ... "I knew that song as a child," one man had the audacity to tell me. A rabbinical person wrote me saying he had absolute proof it was a Nazi song.'

The *idea*, rather, seems likely to have been current in Nazi Germany. A popular song, '*Jawohl, mein Herr*', featured in the 1943 episode of the German film chronicle *Heimat* (1984), included the line, 'For from today, the world belongs to us.' Compare also the Hitler Youth song '*Heute gehort uns Deutschland. / Morgen die Ganze Welt* [Today Germany belongs to us. Tomorrow the whole world]' – dealt with under 'Today ... tomorrow the world' – ANONYMOUS 33:5. Note also that 'Tomorrow – for us!' is a translation used by the mutineers in Eisenstein's film *The Battleship Potemkin* (Soviet Union 1929).

The nearest the slogan appears to have been actually used by any (admittedly right-wing) youth organization is referred to in this report from *The Guardian* (30 October 1987): 'Contra leader Adolfo Calero ... was entertained to dinner on Wednesday by Oxford University's Freedom Society, a clutch of hoorays ... [who] got "hog-whimpering" drunk ... and songs like "Tomorrow Belongs To Us" and "Miner, Cross that Picket Line" were sung on the return coach trip.'

The same paper, reporting a meeting addressed by the SDP leader, Dr David Owen (1 February 1988), noted: 'Down, sit down, he eventually gestured; his eyes saying Up, stay up. It reminded you of nothing so much as a Conservative Party conference in one of its most Tomorrow-belongs-to-us moods.' In each of these last two examples, it is the song from the musical that is being evoked, of course, rather than any Nazi original.

Umberto ECO Italian novelist (1932–)

1 *Il Nome della Rosa* [The Name of the Rose].

Title of novel (1981; film US 1986). But what does it mean? Eco's own *Reflections on The Name of the Rose* (1985) explains how the title derives from the Latin hexameter with which the book ends: '*Stat rosa pristina nomine, nomina nuda tenemus.*' This comes from a satirical poem *De contemptu mundi* by the 12th-century monk, Bernard of Cluny. Broadly speaking, the title has to do with the passing of things. The dying rose is merely another symbol of this – and only its name remains. Incidentally, Eco states in *Reflections*: 'A title must muddle the reader's ideas, not regiment them.'

(Sir) Arthur EDDINGTON British astrophysicist (1882–1944)

2 If as we follow the arrow we find more and more of the random element in the world, then the arrow is pointing towards the future; if the random

element decreases the arrow points towards the past ... I shall use the phrase 'time's arrow' to express this one-way property of time which has no analogue in space.

The Nature of the Physical World (1928). Hence, *Time's Arrow: or the Nature of the Offence*, title of a novel (1991) by Martin Amis.

(Sir) Anthony EDEN (later 1st Earl of Avon) British Conservative Prime Minister (1897–1977)

3 We are not at war with Egypt. We are in an armed conflict; that is the phrase I have used. There has been no declaration of war.

Speaking in the House of Commons (1 November 1956) about Britain's response to the Egyptian takeover of the Suez Canal, Eden seemed curiously punctilious about his words, urging that it was not an act of war. Possibly he was obsessed by the thought of becoming a warmonger when, as he said in a TV and radio broadcast two days later, 'All my life I have been a man of peace, working for peace, striving for peace, and negotiating for peace. I have been a League of Nations man and a United Nations man. And I am still the same man, with the same convictions, and the same devotion to peace. I could not be other even if I wished, but I am utterly convinced that the action we have taken is right.'

Thomas Alva EDISON American inventor (1847–1931)

4 Genius is one per cent inspiration and ninety-nine per cent perspiration.

Quoted in *Harper's Monthly Magazine* (September 1932), also reportedly in a *Life* of Edison, Chap. 24 (1932) (possibly the former was quoting from the latter), having originally been said by him in about 1903. Earlier, the French naturalist, the Comte de Buffon (1707–88), was quoted in 1803 as having said, 'Genius is only a greater aptitude for patience.' Compare CARLYLE 122:6.

J.M. EDMONDS English poet and academic (1875–1958)

5 Went the day well? we died and never knew;
But well or ill, England, we died for you.

'On Some who died early in the Day of Battle' in 'Four Epitaphs', published in *The Times* (6 February 1918). Later popularized in the form:

Went the day well?
We died and never knew.
But, well or ill,
Freedom, we died for you.

This appears as the anonymous epigraph on screen at the

start of the 1942 British film *Went the Day Well?* (re-titled *48 Hours* in the US). At the time the film was released, some thought it was a version of a Greek epitaph. Based on a story by Graham Greene entitled 'The Lieutenant Died Last', the film tells of a typical English village managing to repel Nazi invaders. The epigraph thus presumably refers to the villagers who die defending 'Bramley End'. Penelope Houston in her 1992 British Film Institute monograph on the film describes it as a quotation from an anonymous poem that appeared in an anthology of tributes to people killed in the war to which Michael Balcon, head of Ealing Studios, contributed a memoir of the dead director Pen Tennyson. But Edmonds was the poet. It is said that it was based on a suggestion given him by Sir Arthur Quiller-Couch, who in turn got it from a Romanian folksong – *Notes and Queries* (Vol. 100).

1 When you go home, tell them of us and say, 'For your tomorrow these gave their today.'

'For a British graveyard in France', another suggested epitaph by Edmonds, which appeared in *The Times Literary Supplement* (4 July 1918). By the Second World War, however, it was frequently stated that 'the words are a translation from the Greek'. Famously, this version appeared on the 2nd British Division's memorial at Kohima War Cemetery, Assam (now Nagaland), in India (and on many other war graves round the world):

> When you go home
> Tell them of us and say
> For your tomorrow
> We gave our today.

Many people still appear to think that it is an allusion to the Greek poet Simonides – see 432:4. The second line of Edmonds's original should not read 'for your tomorrows', as in *ODMQ* (1991) and *ODQ* (1992). The verse appears as epigraph to the 1959 film *Yesterday's Enemy* about the Burma campaign – and, apparently, inspired the title.

The BBC received a somewhat crusty letter from Edmonds (by this time a Fellow of Jesus College, Cambridge), dated 23 July 1953, in which he said, 'I thought the Greek origin of my epitaph used – and altered – at Kohima had been denied in print often enough; but here it is again. It is no translation, nor is it true to say it was suggested by one of the beautiful couplets which you will find in *Lyrica Graeca* (Loeb Classical Library), though I *was* at work on that book in 1917 when my Twelve War Epitaphs were first printed in *The Times* and its *Literary Supplement* ... The epitaph, of course, should be used only abroad. Used in England its "home" may be just round the corner – which makes the whole thing laughable.'

EDWARD III English King (1312–77)

2 *Honi Soit Qui Mal Y Pense* [Evil be to him who evil thinks].

The motto of the Order of the Garter, founded by Edward (in ?1348) is traditionally said to derive from something uttered by him as he adjusted the Countess of Salisbury's garter when it fell down. The tale was current by the reign of Henry VIII and was included in Polydore Vergil's *Anglicae Historiae* (1534–55). Another translation would be: 'May evil be [to] who thinks bad of it', where *soit* is the subjunctive whilst *y* translates as 'of it' – the 'it' being the act of replacing the garter in question.

Accordingly, the version given by Sellar and Yeatman in their comic history *1066 and All That* (1930) is not so wide of the mark: 'Edward III had very good manners. One day at a royal dance he noticed some men-about-court mocking a lady whose garter had come off, whereupon to put her at her ease he stopped the dance and made the memorable epitaph: "*Honi soie qui mal y pense*" ("Honey, your silk stocking's hanging down").' Byron is also said to have re-translated the motto as, 'On his walk he madly puns.'

EDWARD VII British King (1841–1910)

3 We are all socialists nowadays.

Edward is said to have said this, when Prince of Wales, in a speech at the Mansion House, London, on 5 November 1895 – though no record exists of him making any such speech on that day. His biographer, Sir Philip Magnus, makes no mention of him doing so either. *ODQ* dropped the entry after pointing out in the Corrigenda to the 1941 edition that the saying should more correctly be ascribed to Sir William Harcourt (1827–1904). Harcourt is quoted as saying it in *Fabian Essays* (1889, edited by Bernard Shaw), i.e. six years before the supposed 1895 speech. Harcourt was Lord Rosebery's (Liberal) Chancellor of the Exchequer and an impassioned enemy of the House of Lords. He introduced estate duty, a major reform in death duties, in his Budget of 1894. Oscar Wilde told an interviewer in the spring of 1894: 'We are all of us more or less Socialists nowadays' – Almy, 'New Views of Mr O.W.' in *Theatre* (1894). Compare THORPE 466:3.

EDWARD VIII (later Duke of Windsor) British King (1894–1972)

4 Something must be done.

In November 1936 the King went to South Wales to tour the depressed areas and moved the public with his expressions of concern. At the Bessemer steel works at Dowlais, where 9000 men had been made unemployed, hundreds sang an old Welsh hymn. Afterwards the King was heard to say to an official: 'These works brought all these people here. Something must be done to find them work' (or 'get them at work again'); occasionally quoted as 'something ought to be done'. Followed the next day by the promise, 'You may be sure that all I can do for you, I will', the King's words were taken as an indication of his concern for ordinary people and of his impatience with established authority.

Although his distress at what he saw in South Wales was no doubt genuine, the King's assurances might look less hollow if we did not now know that by then he had already informed his family and the Prime Minister of his decision to abdicate.

1 **I have found it impossible to carry the heavy burden of responsibility and to discharge my duties as King as I would wish to do without the help and support of the woman I love.**

Edward abdicated on 11 December 1936. That evening, before he left the country, 'His Royal Highness Prince Edward', as he was introduced, took the opportunity of broadcasting a message to his former subjects. Nothing in Edward's short reign became him like the leaving of it. He later commented – in *A King's Story* (1951): 'It has become part of the Abdication legend that the broadcast was actually written by Mr Churchill. The truth is that, as he had often done before with other speeches, he generously applied the final brush strokes.' Such phrases as 'bred in the constitutional tradition by my father' and 'one matchless blessing ... a happy home with his wife and children' are the two most obvious of those strokes. They were applied to a basic text drawn up by Edward's lawyer, Walter Monckton. The BBC's chief, Sir John (later Lord) Reith, who introduced the broadcast from Windsor Castle, noted that he had 'never [seen] so many alterations in a script'.

The moving speech could be heard by all his subjects over the wireless, a unique event. However relieved people may subsequently have been that Edward's reign was not prolonged, for the moment they were touched, if not reduced to tears, by the courageous tones in which the broadcast was delivered and by the protestations of love and duty it included.

2 **England ... the waste ... the waste.**

These, if truly the Duke of Windsor's dying words, might seem to be appropriate, insofar as their meaning can be guessed at. Their provenance is, however, not recorded. A biographer of the Duchess of Windsor suggests rather that what the ex-King said on his deathbed in Paris was 'Darling' and 'Mama, mama, mama, mama'. On the other hand, Bryan & Murphy's *The Windsor Story* (1979) states that there were no last words.

See also GEORGE V 210:3.

Oliver EDWARDS English lawyer (1711–91)

3 **I have tried too in my time to be a philosopher; but I don't know, cheerfulness was always breaking in.**

Quoted in James Boswell, *Life of Johnson* (1791) – for 17 April 1778. Hence, *Cheerfulness Breaks In*, the title of a novel (1941) by Angela Thirkell.

John D. EHRLICHMAN American presidential aide (1925–99)

4 **It'll play in Peoria.**

About 1968, during the Nixon election campaign, Ehrlichman is credited with devising this yardstick for judging whether policies would appeal to voters in 'Middle America'. He later told *Safire* (1978): 'Onomatopoeia [presumably he meant 'alliteration'] was the only reason for Peoria, I suppose. And it ... exemplified a place, far removed from the media centres on the coasts where the national verdict is cast.' Peoria is in Illinois. David Shulman has noted (1997): 'As early as 1911, Peoria was known as "The Central City" and was regarded as typical America or representative of the average American' – and offers this citation from *These Eventful Years* (1924): 'Playgoers in Peoria could not hope to see as good a performance of a play as was to be seen in Broadway.'

5 **I think we ought to let him hang there. Let him twist slowly, slowly in the wind.**

Richard Nixon's henchmen may have acted wrongly and, for much of the time, spoken sleazily. Occasionally, however, they minted political phrases that have lingered on. Ehrlichman, Nixon's Assistant for Domestic Affairs until he was forced to resign over Watergate in 1973, came up with one saying that caught people's imagination. In a telephone conversation with John Dean (Counsel to the President) on 7–8 March 1973 he was speaking about Patrick Gray (Acting Director of the FBI). Gray's nomination to take over the FBI post had been withdrawn by Nixon during Judiciary Committee hearings – though Gray had not been told of this. Ehrlichman suggested he be left in ignorance – and in suspense.

From *The Guardian* (28 January 1989): 'The foreign press observed with admiration the way President Bush stressed in words that he was not ditching the beleaguered Mikhail Gorbachev by playing his China card, while making it clear he was doing exactly that, and leaving the Soviet leader to twist a little longer in the wind.'

Max EHRMANN American writer (died 1945)

1 Go placidly amid the noise and haste, and remember what peace there may be in silence. As far as possible without surrender be on good terms with all persons. Speak your truth quietly and clearly; and listen to others, even the dull and ignorant; they too have their story. Avoid loud and aggressive persons, they are vexations to the spirit.

There can have been few bedroom walls during the great poster-hanging craze of the late 1960s that did not bear a copy of a text called 'Desiderata' ('things desired'), reputedly found in Old St Paul's Church, Baltimore, and dating from 1692. Les Crane spoke the words on a hit record in 1972. However, 'Desiderata' had nothing to do with Old St Paul's. That was a fanciful idea incorporated in the first US edition of the poster. Nor did 1692 come into it. The words were written by Max Ehrmann in 1927 and copyright was renewed in 1954 by Bertha K. Ehrmann. In 1983 the poster was still on sale as 'from 1692', but carrying the correct copyright lines.

Albert EINSTEIN German-born physicist (1879–1955)

2 God does not play dice with the universe.

What he actually wrote to Max Born (on 4 December 1926, in German) was simply: 'At any rate, I am convinced that *He* does not play dice.' This was his way of objecting to quantum mechanics, in which physical events can only be known in terms of probabilities. What he was saying was, there is no uncertainty in the material world. Compare: 'I cannot believe that God plays dice with the cosmos', so ascribed in *The Observer* (5 April 1954).

(Sir) Edward ELGAR English composer (1857–1934)

3 To my friends pictured within.

Dedication, the *Enigma Variations* (1899). Each variation bears a dedication by name, nickname or initials to a friend or relative of the composer. Each of these has now been identified. For example, No. 9, 'Nimrod' portrays A.J. Jaeger of Novello's, the music publishers, and an old friend of Elgar's.

4 My idea is that there is music in the air, music all around us, the world is full of it and you simply take as much as you require.

Quoted in R.J. Buckley, *Sir Edward Elgar* (1904). The phrase 'music in the air', of which this may be the first appearance, was taken as the title of (probably) more than one

BBC radio series after the 1920s when music was rather 'on the air'. *Music in the Air* was also the title of a film (US 1934) about an opera singer, based on a play by Oscar Hammerstein II and Jerome Kern.

5 The Starlight Express.

Title of incidental music composed for a play (1915) by Violet Pearn, based on Algernon Blackwood's *Prisoner in Fairyland*. In 1984, Andrew Lloyd Webber composed a musical called simply *Starlight Express*.
See also KAZANTZAKIS 264:6.

George ELIOT (Mary Ann Evans) English novelist (1819–80)

6 The first condition of human goodness is something to love; the second something to reverence.

Said by Amos Barton in *Scenes of Clerical Life*, Chap. 10 (1858). When the novelist was commemorated in Poets' Corner, Westminster Abbey, this quotation was placed on her memorial. 'It is a quotation of which we are particularly fond,' said the Secretary of the George Eliot Fellowship, which was responsible for the worldwide appeal for funds to place the memorial stone in 1980, 'and it describes, we feel, George Eliot's own philosophy.'

7 The happiest women, like the happiest nations, have no history.

The Mill on the Floss, Bk 6, Chap. 3 (1860). Eliot adapted a proverbial expression to her own ends. In the form 'Happy the people whose annals are blank in history-books!', the saying was ascribed to Montesquieu by Thomas Carlyle in his *History of Frederick the Great* (1858–65). In *The French Revolution – A History* (1838), Carlyle had written: 'A paradoxical philosopher, carrying to the uttermost length that aphorism of Montequieu's, "Happy the people whose annals are tiresome," has said, "Happy the people whose annals are vacant."'

Theodore Roosevelt said in a speech (10 April 1899): 'It is a base untruth to say that happy is the nation that has no history. Thrice happy is the nation that has a glorious history. Far better it is to dare mighty things, to win glorious triumphs, even though checkered by failure, than to take rank with those spirits who neither enjoy much nor suffer much because they live in the grey twilight that knows neither victory nor defeat.' The earliest form of the proverb found by *CODP* is in Benjamin Franklin, *Poor Richard's Almanack* (1740): 'Happy that Nation, – fortunate that age, whose history is not diverting.'

1 Oh may I join the choir invisible
Of those immortal dead who live again
In minds made better by their presence.

Poem, 'Oh May I Join the Choir Invisible' (1867). The second two lines appear on Eliot's grave in Highgate Cemetery, London. A setting of the poem was sung by the graveside at her funeral. Hence, *The Choir Invisible*, title of a novel (1897) by James Lane Allen. Joining the choir invisible subsequently became a euphemism for dying, as in Monty Python's 'Dead Parrot' sketch – see 326:7.

See also BIBLE 70:5.

T.S. ELIOT American-born English poet, playwright and critic (1888–1965)

2 No! I am not Prince Hamlet, nor was meant to be;
Am an attendant lord, one that will do
To swell a progress, start a scene or two.

'The Love Song of J. Alfred Prufrock', *Prufrock* (1917). Hence, *Not Prince Hamlet*, title of an autobiography (1989) by the critic and translator of plays, Michael Meyer.

3 I grow old ... I grow old ...
I shall wear the bottoms of my trousers rolled.
Shall I part my hair behind? Do I dare to eat a peach?
I shall wear white flannel trousers, and walk upon the beach.
I have heard the mermaids singing, each to each.
I do not think that they will sing to me.

In the same poem. Hence, the two film titles: *I've Heard the Mermaids Singing*, a Canadian film (1987) about a gauche girl who develops a crush on her (female) boss, and – even more allusively – *Eat the Peach* (Ireland, 1986). *To Eat a Peach* was the title of a novel by Calder Willingham (US 1960s). See also DAVIES 162:7.

4 Webster was much possessed by death
And saw the skull beneath the skin;
And breastless creatures under ground
Leaned backwards with a lipless grin.

'Whispers of Immortality' (1920). Hence, *The Skull Beneath the Skin*, title of a crime novel (1982) by P.D. James.

5 *The Waste Land.*

Title – a double quotation from Malory's *Morte D'Arthur* and from St Augustine's *Confessions*. Also the June 1915 issue of *Poetry Chicago*, which published 'The Love Song of J. Alfred Prufrock', also had a poem called 'The Waste Land' by Madison Cawein.

6 April is the cruellest month, breeding
Lilacs out of the dead land, mixing
Memory and desire, stirring
Dull roots with spring rain.

The Waste Land (1922) – opening words. Frequently misquoted, often with 'August' being substituted, possibly out of confusion with *August is a Wicked Month*, title of a novel (1965) by Edna O'Brien. Or, rather, the observation is much abused allusively: 'After the highs and lows of Christmas and the winter holidays, February always seems to me the cruellest month' – *The Daily Telegraph* (15 February 1992); 'Sometimes March can be the cruellest month' – *Northern Echo* (18 February 1992); 'August used to be the cruellest month' – *The Times* (25 August 1992); 'June is the cruellest month in politics' – *The Times* (5 June 1993); 'August has always been the cruellest month' – *The Times* (25 August 1993). Hence, however, *The Cruellest Month*, title of a detective novel (1991) by Hazel Holt. *Lilacs Out of the Dead Land* was the title of a novel (1971) by Rachel Billington.

7 And I will show you something different from either
Your shadow at morning striding behind you
Or your shadow at evening rising to meet you;
I will show you fear in a handful of dust.

In the same poem, Pt 1. As acknowledged, *A Handful of Dust*, the novel (1934) by Evelyn Waugh, takes it title from this. Compare, 'The heat of life in the handful of dust' in Joseph Conrad's novel *Youth* (1902). Earlier, a 'handful of earth' was a symbol of mortality.

8 O O O O that Shakespeherian Rag.
It's so elegant
So intelligent.

In the same poem, Pt 2. In *The Waste Land*, Eliot provides notes to explain the numerous allusions. However, he neglects to mention that lines 128–30 are taken from a popular song 'That Shakespearian Rag' published in 1912 by the Edward Marks Music Corp. (in the US) and written by Gene Buck, Herman Ruby and David Stamper. The chorus goes: 'That Shakespearian Rag, most intelligent, very elegant.' This was pointed out by Ian Whitcomb in *After the Ball* (1972).

9 When lovely woman stoops to folly and
Paces about her room again, alone,
She smoothes her hair with automatic hand,
And puts a record on the gramophone.

In the same poem, Pt 3. From *The Observer* Magazine (28 November 1993): 'For some reason, T.S. Eliot's line "When lovely woman stoops to folly" comes to mind.' Yes, but as he acknowledged in the extensive notes to *The Waste Land*, it is a reference to the song in Goldsmith's *The Vicar of Wakefield* (1766):

When lovely woman stoops to folly
And finds too late that men betray,
What charm can soothe her melancholy,
What art can wash her guilt away?

Kate Hardcastle in Goldsmith's play *She Stoops to Conquer* (1773) also 'stoops', but not to folly, as the Epilogue points out:

Well, having stooped to conquer with success,
And gained a husband without aid from dress,
Still as a Barmaid, I could wish it too,
As I have conquered him to conquer you.

Mary Demetriadis once reworked the couplet for a *New Statesman* competition:

When lovely woman stoops to folly
The evening can be awfully jolly.

1 [The critic] must compose his differences with as many of his fellows as possible in the common pursuit of true judgement.

Essay, 'The Function of Criticism' (1923). Hence, *The Common Pursuit*, title of a book of essays by the critic F.R. Leavis (1952). In turn, it became the title of a play (1984) by Simon Gray about a group of Cambridge undergraduates and graduates who produce a literary magazine called *The Common Pursuit*.

2 We are the hollow men
We are the stuffed men
Leaning together ...

Between the idea
And the reality
Between the motion
And the act
Falls the shadow.

The Hollow Men (1925). Hence, *Falls the Shadow*, title of a novel (1996) by Gemma O'Connor.

3 This is the way the world ends
Not with a bang but a whimper.

In the same poem – last words. The phrase 'not with a bang but a whimper' is now widely used to express anticlimax, and is frequently alluded to. For example, from Richard Aldington, *The Colonel's Daughter* (1931): 'I wish you'd all

shoot yourselves with a bang, instead of continuing to whimper.' From a G.K. Chesterton broadcast, reproduced in *The Listener* (18 March 1936): 'In the youth where we laughed, and sang. / And *they* may end with a whimper / But *we* will end with a bang.' From *The Times* (16 December 1959): 'Here the world ends neither with a bang nor a whimper, but with a slow, resigned sigh at its own criminal imbecility.' In the film *Goodbye Charlie* (US 1964), Tony Curtis delivers a funeral oration about a man who was shot when he was found in bed with the killer's wife: 'Anyway, he's gone, and he went – to paraphrase Mr Eliot – not with a whimper, but a bang.' *Not With a Bang* was the title of an ITV series (1990), and *The Observer* (8 July 1990) reported: 'After some 70 hours Ernest Saunders finally left the Southwark witness box on Thursday afternoon not with a bang or whimper but more with a chorus of the familiar refrains which had echoed ... '

The joke variation, 'This is the way to World's End / Not with a Banger but a Wimpy' was ascribed to his father-in-law, Professor Robert Gorham Davis of Columbia University, New York, by Michael Flanders in the introduction to a verse anthology *London Between the Lines* (1973).

'I should be glad,' Eliot remarked, a little ruefully, in 1964, 'to hear no more of a bang and a whimper.'

4 'A cold coming we had of it,
Just the worst time of the year
For a journey, and such a long journey:
The ways deep and the weather sharp,
The very dead of winter.'

Journey of the Magi (1927) – opening words. As the quotation marks show this is a conscious quotation of ANDREWES 8:7, though in fact a paraphrase.

5 Time present and time past
Are both perhaps present in time future,
And time future contained in time past.

'Burnt Norton' (1935), *Four Quartets*. Hence, one might suppose, *Time Present*, title of a play (1968) by John Osborne – except that the text is prefaced with 'a time to embrace and a time to refrain from embracing ...' from Ecclesiastes.

6 Sudden in a shaft of sunlight
Even while the dust moves
There rises the hidden laughter
Of children in the foliage.

In the same poem. Hence, *Hidden Laughter*, title of a play (1990) by Simon Gray.

1 Macavity, Macavity, there's no one like Macavity,
There never was a Cat of such deceitfulness and
  suavity.
He always has an alibi, and one or two to spare:
At whatever time the deed took place – MACAVITY
  WASN'T THERE!
And they say that all the Cats whose wicked
  deeds are widely known
(I might mention Mungojerrie, I might mention
  Griddlebone)
Are nothing more than agents for the Cat who
  all the time
Just controls their operations: the Napoleon of
  Crime!

'Macavity: the Mystery Cat', *Old Possum's Book of Practical
Cats* (1939). Compare DOYLE 177:8.

2 In my beginning is my end ...
In my end is my beginning.

'East Coker' (1940), *Four Quartets*. As to the second of these
phrases, compare '*En ma fin git mon commencement*' – a
motto reputedly embroidered with an emblem of her mother
by Mary, Queen of Scots (1542–87).

3 The moment of the rose and the moment of
  the yew-tree
Are of equal duration.

'Little Gidding' (1942), *Four Quartets*. Hence, *The Rose and
the Yew Tree*, title of a novel (1947) by Mary Westmacott
(Agatha Christie).

4 Those who say they give the public what it wants
begin by underestimating public taste, and end
up by debauching it.

The Report of the Committee on Broadcasting 1960 (1962)
states that the Pilkington Committee was told this. It has
been ascribed to T.S. Eliot – but he is not listed as someone who gave evidence to the committee.

ELIZABETH I English Queen (1533–1603)

5 I don't keep a dog and bark myself.

Quoted in Frederick Chamberlin, *The Sayings of Queen Elizabeth* (1923), who says: 'High authority vouches for this
Saying, but I have not seen the original.'

6 The heart and stomach of a king.

What Elizabeth is supposed to have said in a speech to her
army of 20,000 gathered at Tilbury during the approach
of the Spanish Armada in 1588 is: 'My loving people, we
have been persuaded by some that are careful for our safety
to take heed how we commit ourselves to armed multi-
tudes, for fear of treachery. But I assure you I do not desire
to live to distrust my faithful and loving people. Let tyrants
fear. I have always so behaved myself that, under God, I
have placed my chiefest strength and safeguard in the loyal
hearts and goodwill of my subjects; and therefore I am come
amongst you, as you see, resolved, in the midst and heat of
the battle, to live or die amongst you all, to lay down for my
God, and for my kingdom, and for my people, my honour
and my blood, even in the dust.

'I know I have the body of a weak and feeble woman, but
I have the heart and stomach of a king, and of a king of
England too; and think foul scorn that Parma or Spain, or
any prince of Europe, should dare to invade the borders of
my realm; to which, rather than any dishonour shall grow
by me, I myself will take up arms, I myself will be your general, judge, and rewarder of every one of your virtues in the
field. I know already for your forwardness you have deserved
rewards and crowns; and we do assure you, in the word of
a prince, they shall be duly paid you.'

In *History Today* (May 1988) Felix Barker contended that
the Queen might never have used these words because of
the absence of any contemporary accounts of her doing so.
The sole source is an undated letter to the Duke of Buckingham (not published until 1691) from Leonel Sharp, a
chaplain who was at Tilbury but who had a reputation for
being 'obsequious and ingratiating' – according to the *Dictionary of National Biography*. The only contemporary
account of the speech is by a poet called James Aske, but it
contains none of the above phrases. Why did no one else
quote the good bits at the time, Felix Barker wondered, if
they had in fact been used? For reasons of delicacy presumably, when Flora Robson came to give the speech in
the film *Fire Over England* (1937), she found herself saying,
'But I have the heart and valour of a king' rather than the
traditional 'heart and stomach'.

7 I would not open windows into men's souls.

Elizabeth is often cited as saying this, when in fact the
phrase is most likely Francis Bacon's rationalization of her
religious tolerance. In drafting a letter for her, he was
attempting to say that the Queen, while not liking to do so,
was forced into it by the people she had to deal with – source:
letter from Professor William Lamont, University of Sussex,
in *The Observer* (13 November 1988). Sir Christopher Hatton
(1540–91), Elizabeth's Lord Chancellor, is said to have commented, similarly: 'The queen did fish for men's souls, and
had so sweet a bait that no one could escape her network.'
Frederick Chamberlin, *The Sayings of Queen Elizabeth* (1923)

has, 'For I make no windows into the hearts of men', as said to Walsingham, 'to whom she had remarked that she only required the papists to obey the laws'.

1 **My lord, we have forgot the fart.**

John Aubrey (1626–97) in his *Brief Lives* records that, 'The Earl of Oxford, Edward de Vere, making of his low obeisance to Queen Elizabeth, happened to let a fart, at which he was so abashed and ashamed that he went to travel, seven years.' On his return, the Queen welcomed him home with this remark. There is, coincidentally, a parallel story in the *Arabian Nights' Entertainment*: 'How Abu Hasan Brake Wind' tells of the poor chap who had too much to eat and drink at his wedding-banquet and 'let fly a fart, great and terrible' in front of the guests and before he was able to make it to the bridal chamber. In his embarrassment he instantly exiled himself for ten years. On his return he overheard a girl asking her mother about her birth date. The mother replied: 'Thou was born, O my daughter, on the very night when Abu Hasan farted.' At this he said to himself, 'Verily thy fart hath become a date, which shall last for ever and ever' and went off into exile for the remainder of his life.

2 **God may pardon you, but I never can.**

Remark to the dying Countess of Nottingham in 1603, quoted in David Hume, *The History of England* (1759). The Countess had failed to execute the commission of returning a ring from the Earl of Essex to the Queen. When the Queen found out, she upbraided the Countess on what turned out to be her deathbed.

3 **The word 'must' is not to be used to princes. Little man, little man! if your father had lived, ye durst not have said so much; but ye know I must die and that makes ye so presumptuous.**

To Robert Cecil on her deathbed (1603), when he had told her that 'to content the people you must go to bed'. Quoted in Frederick Chamberlin, *The Sayings of Queen Elizabeth* (1923), who adds: 'Cecil was a hunchback and very short.'

ELIZABETH II British Queen (1926–)

4 **I declare before you all that my whole life, whether it be long or short, shall be devoted to your service, and the service of our great imperial family to which we all belong.**

On her 21st birthday. Radio broadcast from South Africa (21 April 1947). The script, according to *The Guardian*

(4 November 1997), was written by 'the hard-bitten courtier, Sir Alan Lascelles'. Misquoted in William Shawcross, *Queen and Country* (2002) as 'great imperial Commonwealth'.

5 **My husband and I.**

George VI had quite naturally spoken the words 'The Queen and I', but something in his daughter's drawling delivery turned her version into a joke. It first appeared during her second Christmas broadcast (made from New Zealand) in 1953 – 'My husband and I left London a month ago' – and still survived in 1962: 'My husband and I are greatly looking forward to visiting New Zealand and Australia in the New Year.' By 1967 the phrase had become 'Prince Philip and I'. At a Silver Wedding banquet (20 November 1972), the Queen allowed herself a little joke: 'I think on this occasion I may be forgiven for saying "My husband and I".' Compare the title of the Rodgers and Hammerstein musical *The King and I* (1951). In 1988, the phrase was used as the title of an ITV comedy series with Mollie Sugden.

6 **1992 is not a year I shall look back on with undiluted pleasure. In the words of one of my more sympathetic correspondents, it has turned out to be an *Annus Horribilis*.**

Speaking at a lunch in the City of London on 24 November 1992 to mark her 40th year on the British throne, the Queen reflected her current mood: she had a cold, part of Windsor Castle had been burned down four days previously, and the marriages of three of her children had collapsed or were collapsing. She states that she had the phrase from a correspondent and this person is believed to be her former Principle Private Secretary, Sir Edward Ford, who had written it in a Christmas card. He was asked for permission to use it. The more usual phrase is, of course, modern (as opposed to classical) Latin's *annus mirabilis* ('wonderful year'), given common currency by Dryden's poem *Annus Mirabilis* (1667) about the year 1665–6, which witnessed two naval victories over the Dutch and the Great Fire of London.

Lord ELLENBOROUGH English lawyer (1750–1818)

7 **The greater the truth, the greater the libel.**

Benham (1948) has: 'Lord Ellenborough (about 1789) seems to have originated this saying. He amplified it by the explanation: "If the language used was true, the person would suffer more if it was false." Burns, in some lines written at Stirling, attributes the saying to Lord Mansfield (1704–93).' *Benham* also includes Thomas Campbell's version in 'A Case of Libel': 'That the greater the truth, the worse the libel.'

Duke ELLINGTON American bandleader, pianist and composer (1899–1974)

1 There'll be some changes made.

In the early 1990s, Alistair Cooke asserted in three different *Letter from America* broadcasts on BBC Radio that: '"There'll be some changes made", *as Duke Ellington used to say*.' In fact, Ellington never recorded the song with that title (written by Overstreet and Higgins in 1929). Most likely, Cooke was confusing it with the Mercer Ellington/Ted Person composition of 1939, 'Things Ain't What They Used To Be'.

Paul ÉLUARD French poet (1895–1952)

2 *Bonjour tristesse* [Good-day sadness].

'*À peine défigurée*' (1932). Hence, *Bonjour Tristesse*, title of the novel (1954; film UK 1957) by Françoise Sagan.

Ralph Waldo EMERSON American poet and essayist (1803–82)

3 There is properly no history; only biography.

'History', in *Essays* (1841). Emerson is advocating the primacy of experience over second-hand knowledge, and that all you might read or hear means nothing to you as a person until you experience it or its analogue. Compare DISRAELI 173:1.

4 All mankind love a lover.

'Love', in the same work. Hence, the more modern rendering, 'All the world loves a lover.' In 1958 there was a popular song by Richard Adler and Robert Allen, 'Everybody Loves a Lover'. Compare the proverb, 'Everybody loves a Lord', which *CODP* finds by 1869.

5 I hate quotations.

ODQ (1979) had Emerson writing this in his journal for May 1849. Even toilers in the quotation vineyard feel like echoing this thought from time to time when they hear yet another person about to launch into some over-familiar line with, 'As the poet has it …' or 'As Bernard Shaw once said …'

Oddly enough, and ironically, what *ODQ* had (the entry was dropped from the 1992 edition) is a *misquotation*. What Emerson actually wrote was: '*Immortality*. I notice that as soon as writers broach this question they begin to quote. I hate quotation. Tell me what you know' – *Journals and Miscellaneous Notebooks*, Vol. 6. So it is 'quotation' not 'quotations'. There is a difference.

6 The louder he talked of his honour, the faster we counted our spoons.

'Worship', *The Conduct of Life* (1860). Dr Samuel Johnson had anticipated this remark. 'If he [Macpherson] does really think that there is no distinction between virtue and vice, why, Sir, when he leaves our houses let us count our spoons' – James Boswell, *Life of Johnson* (1791) – 14 July 1763.

7 Next to the originator of a good sentence is the first quoter of it. Many will read the book before one thinks of quoting a passage. As soon as he has done this, that line will be quoted east and west.

'Quotation and Originality', *Letters and Social Aims* (1876). From the same source: 'By necessity, by proclivity – and by delight, we all quote.'

8 If a man write a better book, preach a better sermon, or make a better mousetrap than his neighbour, tho' he build his house in the woods, the world will make a beaten path to his door.

Sarah Yule claimed (in 1889) that she had heard Emerson say this in a lecture. Elbert Hubbard also claimed authorship. Either way, this is a remark alluded to whenever people talk of 'beating a path to someone's door' or a 'better mousetrap'. In his journal for February 1855, Emerson had certainly entertained the notion: 'If a man … can make better chairs or knives … than anybody else, you will find a broad hard-beaten road to his house, though it be in the woods.' See also COLERIDGE 149:6.

Robert EMMET Irish politician (1778–1803)

9 Let no man write my epitaph; for as no man who knows my motives dare now vindicate them, let not prejudice or ignorance asperse them. Let them rest in obscurity and peace! Let my memory be left in oblivion, my tomb remain uninscribed, until other times and other men can do justice to my character. When my country takes her place among the nations of the earth, *then*, and *not till then*, let my epitaph be written.

Speech from the dock at his trial for leading a muddled insurrection against the British in July 1803. Tried and found guilty on 19 September, he was executed the next day. After this, his headless body was taken from Kilmainham Gaol, Dublin, to one of the burial grounds at the Royal Hospital nearby, but the exact place of its burial is not known. Another theory is that Emmet lies in an unmarked grave in St Michan's churchyard or that of St

Paul's. Hence, either way, there is still no epitaph over it. The film *Let No Man Write My Epitaph* (US 1960) is apparently unconnected.

(Dame) Edith EVANS English actress (1888–1976)

1 Death is my neighbour now.

According to *PD20* (1995), this was a remark in a 'BBC radio interview, a week before her death [which was on] 14 October 1976'. Not the case, apparently. Evans's last broadcast was on 15 August 1976 – a choice of her favourite prose and poetry in the series *With Great Pleasure*. Far from making this remark herself, 'the last words she ever spoke in public' – according to Bryan Forbes, *Ned's Girl* (1977), were from a poem 'Two Ways' 'by her great friend, Richard Church' (1893– 1972):

> Some are afraid of Death.
> They run from him, and cry
> Aloud, shrinking with fear
> When he draws near.
> Others take their last breath
> As though it were a sigh
> Of sheer content, or bliss
> Beneath a lover's kiss.
> Perhaps it is not much,
> After life's labour,
> That summoning touch
> Of Death, our neighbour.

Hence, *Death Is Now My Neighbour*, title of an Inspector Morse novel (1996) by Colin Dexter, who explained in 1997 how he had taken the title from the Edith Evans usage. In the Introduction to Sir Walter Scott's *A Legend of Montrose* (1819), is to be found this somewhat literal use: 'His [the old soldier More M'Alpin's] morning walk was beneath the elms of the churchyard; "for death," he said, "had been his next-door neighbour for so many years, that he had no apology for dropping the acquaintance."' So, even if Dexter probably did use it as a result of Edith Evans quoting the Richard Church poem, as explained earlier, the idea is, naturally,

not exactly a new one. Indeed, Aline Templeton had used *Death Is My Neighbour* as the title of a crime novel in 1984.

EVERSLEY See SHAW-LEFEVRE.

W.N. EWER English journalist and poet (1885–1976)

2 How odd
    Of God
    To choose
    The Jews.

A frequently misattributed rhyme – perhaps because it was composed in an informal setting and not published originally in written form – is the one by the foreign correspondent, W.N. Ewer. It was published subsequently in *The Week-End Book* (1924). In a letter to *The Observer* (13 March 1983), Alan Wykes, Honorary Secretary of the Savage Club in London, described the rhyme's origins: 'In the Savage Club, one of the guests was trying to make his mark with the Jewish pianist Benno Moiseiwitsch, who was not a man to be trifled with. "Is there," asked this Hooray Henry, "Any anti-Semitism in the club?" To this Benno snarled back: "Only amongst the Jews." Trilby Ewer, on the fringe of this conversation, thereupon coined the quatrain, which has since passed into history.'

Mencken (1942) ascribes the saying to Howland Spencer (1915). There has been more than one corollary or rejoinder. This, published in 1924, was by Cecil Browne:

> But not so odd
> As those who choose
> A Jewish God
> Yet spurn the Jews.

Another, quoted in the early 1960s, went:

> Who said he did?
> Moses. But he's a yid.

Other responses include: 'How strange / Of man / To change / The plan' and 'Oh no / It's not. / God knows / What's what.'

F

Henry FAIRLIE English journalist (1924–90)

1 I have several times suggested that what I call the 'Establishment' in this country is today more powerful than ever before. By the 'Establishment' I do not mean only the centres of official power – though they are certainly part of it – but rather the whole matrix of official and social relations within which power is exercised … the 'Establishment' can be seen at work in the activities of, not only the Prime Minister, the Archbishop of Canterbury and the Earl Marshal, but of such lesser mortals as the Chairman of the Arts Council, the Director-General of the BBC, and even the editor of the *Times Literary Supplement*, not to mention dignitaries like Lady Violet Bonham Carter.

As a nickname for a conservative, partly hereditary, secretive, self-perpetuating ruling class, the term 'Establishment' was brought to prominence by Fairlie in a series of articles for *The Spectator* in 1955. On 23 September, he wrote the above. Hugh Thomas, editing a book on the phenomenon called *The Establishment* (1959), stated: 'The word was, however, in use among the thoughtful at least a year previously; I recall myself employing it while passing the Royal Academy in a taxi in company with Mr Paul Johnson of the *New Statesman* in August 1954.' An earlier example of the phrase's use among the 'thoughtful' has, indeed, come to light in A.J.P. Taylor's *Essays in English History*. In one on William Cobbett (originally a review in the *New Statesman*, in 1953) he wrote: 'Trotsky tells how, when he first visited England, Lenin took him round London and, pointing out the sights, exclaimed: "That's *their* Westminster Abbey! That's *their* Houses of Parliament!" Lenin was making a class, not a national emphasis. By "them" he meant not the

English, but the governing classes, the Establishment so clearly defined and so complacently secure.' *OED2* has other citations of the phrase in its modern sense going back to 1923, to which might be added one in George Eliot's *Daniel Deronda*, Bk 2, Chap. 12 (1876).

George FARQUHAR Irish playwright (1678–1707)

2 My Lady Bountiful.

The Beaux' Stratagem, Act 1, Sc. 1 (1707). Hence the expression 'lady bountiful' (now only applied ironically) for a woman who is conspicuously generous to others less fortunate than herself (particularly within a small community or village).

David FARRAGUT American naval commander (1801–70)

3 Damn the torpedoes! Full speed ahead!

At the Battle of Mobile Bay (5 August 1864). During the American Civil War, Farragut fought on the Federal side and took part in the siege of Vicksburg. At Mobile Bay, he made a quick decision to chance passing through a minefield, suspecting that most of the torpedoes (= mines) were duds through long immersion. As a consequence, the Confederate boat *Tennessee* and two land forts were forced to capitulate. Farragut was appointed the US Navy's first vice-admiral in 1864 and its first admiral in 1866.

William FAULKNER American novelist (1897–1962)

4 The long hot summer.

Coinage of this phrase follows the film title *The Long Hot Summer* (1958) and that of the spin-off TV series (1965–6).

The film was based on 'The Hamlet', a story by Faulkner published in 1928 which contained the chapter heading 'The Long Summer' (that is, no 'hot'). So it is not correct to say that Faulkner 'coined' the longer phrase. *Bartlett* (1980 and 1992) suggests that there was a film with the longer title in *1928*. Some mistake surely?

The full phrase had appeared before all this – for example, in the opening chapter of Wilkie Collins, *The Woman in White* (1860): 'It was the last day of July. The long, hot summer was drawing to a close.' But the bright phrase rapidly turned into a journalist's cliché following the 1967 riots in the black ghettos of 18 US cities, notably Detroit and Newark. In June of that year Martin Luther King warned: 'Everyone is worrying about the long hot summer with its threat of riots. We had a long cold winter when little was done about the conditions that create riots.'

Guy FAWKES English conspirator (1570–1606)

1 Desperate diseases require desperate remedies.

Commonly ascribed to Fawkes on 6 November 1605 (the day following his arrest for attempting to blow up the Houses of Parliament), 'A desperate disease requires a dangerous remedy' (*DNB* wording) was apparently said by him to James I, one of his intended victims. The King asked if he did not regret his proposed attack on the Royal Family. Fawkes replied that one of his objects was to blow the Royal Family back to Scotland. He was subsequently tried and put to death.

What he said, however, appears to have been a version of an established proverbial saying. In the form, 'Strong disease requireth a strong medicine', *ODP* traces it to 1539. In *Romeo and Juliet*, IV.i.68 (1594), Shakespeare has 'I do spy a kind of hope, / Which craves as desperate an execution / As that which we would prevent' – and alludes to the saying on two other occasions. 'Desperate cases need the most desperate remedies' has also been ascribed to Hippocrates, *Aphorisms*.

Federico FELLINI Italian film director and writer (1920–93)

2 *La Dolce Vita.*
The Sweet Life.

The title of Federico Fellini's 1960 Italian film passed into the English language as a phrase suggesting a high-society life of luxury, pleasure and self-indulgence – a precursor of the Swinging Sixties. Meaning simply 'the sweet life', it is not clear how much of a set phrase it was in Italian before it was taken up by everybody else. Compare the long-established Italian phrase *dolce far niente* [sweet idleness].

Georges FEYDEAU French playwright (1862–1921)

3 In comedy there are only two main parts. He who slaps and he who gets slapped. It is never the one who slaps who gets the laughs.

On rejecting a request from Lucien Guitry to write a farce for him. Retold in *Ned Sherrin In His Anecdotage* (1994). One wonders what the connection is, if any, between this remark and *He Who Gets Slapped* – the English title of the play (1914) by the Russian dramatist Leonid Andreyev.

Eric FIELD English advertising practitioner (alive 1914)

4 Your King and Country need you.

Field Marshal Lord Kitchener was appointed Secretary of State for War on 6 August 1914, two days after the outbreak of the First World War. He set to work immediately, intent on raising the 'New Armies' required to supplement the small standing army of the day, which would not be adequate for a major conflict. In fact, advertising for recruits had started the year before, and the *month* before, Field, of the Caxton Advertising Agency, had received a call from a Colonel Strachey, who 'swore me to secrecy, told me that war was imminent and that the moment it broke out we should have to start at once'. That night, Field wrote an advertisement with this slogan and only the royal coat of arms as illustration. The day after war was declared – 5 August – it appeared prominently in the *Daily Mail* and other papers.

The alliterative linking of 'king' and 'country' was traditional. Francis Bacon (1625) wrote: 'Be so true to thyself, as thou be not false to others; specially to thy King, and Country.' In 1913, J.M. Barrie included in his play *Quality Street*: 'If ... death or glory was the call, you would take the shilling, ma'am ... For King and Country.'

5 Your Country Needs You!

This version of Field's slogan, accompanied by the famous drawing of Kitchener with staring eyes and pointing finger, was taken up by the Parliamentary Recruiting Committee for poster use (issued 14 September 1914). The slogan and Alfred Leete's drawing were widely imitated abroad. In the US James Montgomery Flagg's poster of a pointing Uncle Sam bore the legend 'I want *you* for U.S. Army'. The British slogan also became a catchphrase used when telling a man he had been selected for a dangerous or disgusting task.

Henry FIELDING English novelist and judge (1707–54)

6 To fill up a work with these scraps may, indeed, be considered as a downright cheat on the learned world, who are by such means imposed upon to

buy a second time in fragments and by retail, what they already have in gross, if not in their memories, upon their shelves.

Tom Jones, Bk 12, Chap. 1 (1749). On the quotation industry. Fielding, in one of his many addresses to the reader, is discussing why, when translating passages from the ancient classics, he does not give the original language or details of sources. The chapter heading is: 'Shewing what is to be deemed Plagiarism in a modern Author, and what is to be considered as lawful Prize.'

1 It hath been often said, that it is not death, but dying, which is terrible.

Amelia, Bk 3, Chap. 4 (1751). Clearly, from the 'It hath been often said', this is not something that is original to Fielding. It keeps on being said, too. The 1950s TV personality Gilbert Harding said to John Freeman in a *Face to Face* interview: 'I am not afraid of death. I am afraid of dying. I should be very glad to be dead, but I don't look forward to the actual process of dying.' In John Mortimer's *In Character* (1983), Cardinal Basil Hume quoted Monsignor Ronald Knox as having said, 'Everyone's afraid of dying but no one is afraid of being dead.' See also BACON 47:5; SMITH 436:2.

FIELD OF DREAMS American film, 1989. Written and directed by Phil Alden Robinson. With Kevin Costner as Ray Kinsella.

2 If you build it, he will come.

Costner portrays an Iowa farmer who hears a voice (played by 'Himself', according to the credits) which tells him this repeatedly. So he creates a baseball pitch in his field so that 'Shoeless Joe' Jackson, the discredited Chicago White Sox player of 'Say it ain't so, Joe' fame (see ANONYMOUS 30:7), can come back from the dead and be rehabilitated. Subsequent messages received – too complicated to explain here – are 'Ease his pain' and 'Go the distance'.

The Observer (5 June 1994) quoted James Cosgrove of AT&T as saying: 'In the movie *Field of Dreams* there is the phrase "If you build it, they will come."' Well no, there isn't.

A neater allusion to the original phrase occurs in the movie *Wayne's World 2* (1993), in which the ghost of rock star Jim Morrison inspires the teenagers to put on a rock concert called 'Waynestock'. When Morrison is asked whether big-name groups will actually show up, he intones, 'If you book them, they will come.'

W.C. FIELDS American comedian (1879–1946)

3 On the whole I'd rather be in Philadelphia.

What the comedian actually submitted as a suggested epitaph to *Vanity Fair* Magazine in 1925 was: 'Here lies W.C. Fields. I would rather be living in Philadelphia.' This does not appear on his actual gravestone (which bears his name and dates only). The saying may have evolved from an older expression 'Sooner dead than in Philadelphia'. In the film *My Little Chickadee* (US 1940), Fields is about to be strung up by a lynch mob and says, 'I'd like to see Paris before I die ... Philadelphia will do.'

One of the quips trotted out by President Reagan when he was lying in hospital, wounded by an assassin's bullet, in March 1981 was, 'All in all, I'd rather be in Philadelphia.' The following week, the London *Times* noted that historians of humour are unclear where Fields got the quip from: 'Some believe it was made originally by ... George Washington who became dissatisfied with New York after he was chosen President in 1789. As a result of this chance remark, which he may have made to Alexander Hamilton, the capital was moved to Philadelphia.

'A chronically restless man, Washington later made a joke that has survived less well: "Come to think of it, I'd rather be on the Potomac," he told Aaron Burr. It was then that the present-day capital was built and named after him.'

4 It ain't a fit night out for man or beast.

Film, *The Fatal Glass of Beer* (US 1933). In a letter from Fields (8 February 1944) quoted in *W.C. Fields by Himself* (1974), he states that the catchphrase was first used by him in a sketch in Earl Carroll's *Vanities* and then as the title of a picture he made for Mack Sennett. He concluded: 'I do not claim to be the originator of this line as it was probably used long before I was born in some old melodrama.' Compare the old weather lore rhyme that includes: 'When the wind is in the east, / 'Tis neither good for man or beast.'

5 Never give a sucker an even break.

This saying has been attributed to various people, but has largely become associated with Fields. He is believed to have ad-libbed it in the musical *Poppy* (1923) and certainly spoke it in the film version (1936). The words are not uttered, however, in the film called *Never Give a Sucker an Even Break* (1941). *Bartlett* (1992) attributes the saying to Edward Francis Albee (1857–1930).

6 Any man who hates children and dogs can't be all bad.

Or 'Anybody who hates dogs and babies can't be all bad.' Often ascribed to the comedian – for example, by *Radio Times* (12 August 1965) – it was, in fact, said *about* Fields by Leo Rosten (1908–97) at a Masquers' Club dinner (16 February 1939).

1 Boiled or fried?

When asked whether he liked children. Quoted on BBC Radio *Quote ... Unquote* (22 June 1977). Perhaps based on *Fields for President*, ed. Michael M. Taylor (1971), in which the answer to the question whether he liked children is, 'I do if they're properly cooked.' In fact this is a line from *Tillie and Gus* (US 1933).

2 Looking for loopholes.

To the actor Thomas Mitchell who came to visit Fields in a sanatorium during his last illness, was amazed to see him thumbing through the Bible, and asked, 'What are you doing?' Fields died on Christmas Day 1946, and his actual last words were: 'Goddamn the whole friggin' world and everyone in it but you, Carlotta' (a reference to his mistress). Quoted in my book *Quote ... Unquote* (1978) – source unknown.

Millard FILLMORE American 13th President (1800–74)

3 Peace at any price.

'Peace at any price; peace and union' was the slogan of the American (Know-Nothing) Party in the 1856 US presidential election. The party supported ex-President Fillmore, and the slogan meant that it was willing to accept slavery for blacks in order to avoid a civil war. Fillmore lost to James Buchanan.

It has been suggested that the phrase had been coined earlier (in 1820 or 1848) by Alphonse de Lamartine, the French foreign affairs minister in his *Méditations poétiques* in the form 'La paix à tout prix.' However, the Earl of Clarendon quoted an 'unreasonable calumny' concerning Lord Falkland in his *History of the Rebellion* (written in 1647): 'That he was so enamoured on peace, that he would have been glad the king should have bought it at any price.' When Neville Chamberlain signed his pact with Hitler in 1938, many praised him for trying to obtain 'peace at any price'.

Edward FITZGERALD English poet (1809–93)

4 A book of verses underneath the bough,
A jug of Wine, a loaf of bread – and Thou
Beside me singing in the wilderness –
Oh, wilderness were paradise enow!

The Rubáiyát of Omar Khayyám, St. 12 (1879). Fitzgerald revised his poem so many times that it is difficult to settle for one version. The 1859 lines (where it is St. 11) were: 'Here with a loaf of bread beneath the bough, / A flask of wine, a book of verse – and Thou ...' Burnam (1980) makes the point that in Fitzgerald's somewhat free translation, the 'thou' could refer to either sex. In Victorian times, the

assumption was female, but a literal translation would make it clear that the person being addressed was, in fact, a 'comely youth'.

In a sense, Fitzgerald mistranslated in both versions. The original Persian coupling was the traditional 'kebab' (meat on a skewer) and 'sherab' (wine), but Fitzgerald did not speak the language and relied on friends for help.

5 Ah, take the cash in hand and waive the rest;
Oh, the brave music of a *distant* drum!

In the same work, St. 12 (1859). 'Nor heed the rumble of a distant drum!' is the 1879 version. A quotation scornfully applied by Aneurin Bevan to those who 'wanted to escape from awkward present conflicts altogether' and quoted by Michael Foot in his biography of Bevan.

6 I sometimes think that never blows so red
The rose as where some buried Caesar bled.

In the same work, St. 20 (1859). Hence, *So Red the Rose*, title of a film (US 1935) set during the American Civil War.

7 The Moving Finger writes; and, having writ,
Moves on: nor all thy Piety nor Wit
Shall lure it back to cancel half a Line,
Nor all thy Tears wash out a Word of it.

In the same work, St. 51 (1851). Hence, *The Moving Finger*, title of a 'Miss Marple' novel (1943) by Agatha Christie. Later the US title became *Murder In Our Midst*. Could this be because four other writers (including E. Phillips Oppenheim) had already used *The Moving Finger*?

F. Scott FITZGERALD American novelist (1896–1940)

8 Then wear the gold hat, if that will move her;
If you can bounce high, bounce for her too,
Till she cry 'Lover, gold-hatted, high-bouncing lover,
I must have you!'

As the epigraph to *The Great Gatsby* (1925), this is attributed to one 'Thomas Parke D'Invilliers'. He remains untraced, so one wonders whether perhaps it was Fitzgerald in disguise? He did, after all, write poetry himself, some of which has been published. As Thomas Parke D'Invilliers's appears as a poet character in Fitzgerald's *This Side of Paradise* (1920), this would appear to be the case.

9 In a real dark night of the soul it is always three o'clock in the morning.

The Crack-Up (1936). See JOHN OF THE CROSS 256:5.

See also HEMINGWAY 234:3.

Bob FITZSIMMONS New Zealand-bred boxer in the US (1862–1917)

1 The bigger they are, the further they have to fall.
Referring to an opponent of larger build (James L. Jeffries), prior to a fight in San Francisco (9 June 1899) and quoted in the *Brooklyn Daily Eagle* (11 August 1900). Also attributed to John L. Sullivan. Probably of earlier proverbial origin in any case and more usually, 'The bigger they come, the harder they fall.' Hence, presumably, *The Harder They Fall*, title of a novel by Budd Schulberg and a film (US 1956) about boxing. *The Harder They Come* was the title of a film (Jamaica 1972).

Michael FLANDERS English writer and entertainer (1922–75)

2 Ma's out, Pa's out – let's talk rude:
Pee, po, belly, bum, drawers.
From 'a very rude song' (?1956), supposedly based on a child's remark. This would seem to be confirmed by 'Pa's out and ma's out, let's talk dirt / Pee-poh-belly-bottom-drawers' – quoted by Robert Graves in *Occupation Writer* (1950).

3 Eating people is wrong.
Song, 'The Reluctant Cannibal', *At the Drop of a Hat* (1957), with music by Donald Swann. Used as the title of a novel by Malcolm Bradbury (1959).

Gustave FLAUBERT French novelist (1821–80)

4 We shall find life tolerable once we have consented to be always ill at ease.
Quoted in *The Times* (23 June 1969) by Bryan Forbes, at that time newly appointed head of production at Elstree Studios: 'As an everyday working rule for anybody contemplating an existence in the British film industry, it is not without a certain valid cold comfort.' Forbes also notes that he had already used the quotation as an epigraph in his 'first published work', presumably *Truth Lies Sleeping* (1950). Otherwise untraced.

James Elroy FLECKER English poet (1884–1915)

5 Four great gates has the city of Damascus ...
Postern of Fate, the Desert Gate, Disaster
Cavern, Fort of Fear ...
Pass not beneath, O Caravan, or pass not singing.
Have you heard
That silence where the birds are dead yet something pipeth like a bird?

'The Gates of Damascus' (1913). Hence, *Postern of Fate* (1973), title of a novel by Agatha Christie.

Ian FLEMING English novelist and journalist (1908–64)

6 A martini, shaken not stirred.
This example of would-be sophistication became a running joke in the immensely popular James Bond films of the 1960s and 1970s. However, the *idea* stems from the very first book in the series, *Casino Royale* (1953), in which Bond orders a cocktail of his own devising. It consists of one dry Martini 'in a deep champagne goblet', three measures of Gordon's gin, one of vodka – 'made with grain instead of potatoes' – and half a measure of Kina Lillet. 'Shake it very well until it's ice-cold.' Bond justifies this fussiness a page or two later: 'I take a ridiculous pleasure in what I eat and drink. It comes partly from being a bachelor, but mostly from a habit of taking a lot of trouble over details. It's very pernickety and old-maidish really, but when I'm working I generally have to eat all my meals alone and it makes them more interesting when one takes trouble.'

This characteristic was aped by the writers of the first Bond story to be filmed – *Dr No* (1962). A West Indian servant brings Bond a vodka and Martini and says: 'Martini like you said, sir, and not stirred.' Dr No also mentions the fad, though the words are not spoken by Bond himself. In the third film, *Goldfinger* (1964), Bond (played by Sean Connery) does get to say 'a Martini, shaken not stirred' – he needs a drink after just escaping a laser death-ray – and there are references to it in *You Only Live Twice* (1967) and *On Her Majesty's Secret Service* (1969), among others.

The phrase was taken up in all the numerous parodies of the Bond phenomenon on film, TV and radio, though – curiously enough – it may be a piece of absolute nonsense. According to one expert, shaking a dry Martini 'turns it from something crystal-clear into a dreary frosted drink. It should be stirred quickly with ice in a jug.'

The *ODMQ* (1991) claimed to have discovered the source for this remark in one of Fleming's novels – *Dr No* (1958) ('Bond said ... Martini – with a slice of lemon peel. Shaken and not stirred, please'), and this was taken up by *Bartlett* (1992). But it appears in the novels earlier than that: 'The waiter brought the Martinis, shaken and not stirred, as Bond had stipulated' – *Diamonds are Forever* (1956).

7 *Diamonds are Forever.*
Title of book (1956), alluding to the advertising slogan 'A Diamond is Forever' for De Beers Consolidated Mines (since 1939).

1 The licence to kill for the Secret Service, the double-o prefix, was a great honour.

Dr No (1958). Eventually there was a Bond film with the title *Licence to Kill* (UK 1989) – there had already been an imitation Bond film called *Licensed to Kill* (UK 1965). Compare these earlier uses: in Thomas Love Peacock's first novel *Headlong Hall* (1816), a phrenologist gives advice on how to decide your son's future career – 'If the development of the organ of destruction point out a similarity between the youth and the tiger, let him be brought to some profession (whether that of a butcher, a soldier, or a physician, may be regulated by circumstances) in which he may be furnished with a licence to kill ...'; then William Godwin Jnr (son of the philosopher-novelist) in *Blackwood's Edinburgh Magazine* (October 1833): 'My Lord of the thirty thousand acres expired on a couch of down ... each moment of his fluctuating existence watched by an obsequious practitioner, "licensed to kill", whose trade it is to assuage the pangs of death ...' The quotation marks make it look like an established joke at the expense of doctors. In 1881, Arthur Conan Doyle made a rough sketch of himself on learning that he had obtained his diploma as a Bachelor of Medicine. He entitled it 'Licensed to kill' and it was reproduced in *The Strand Magazine* (October 1923). In Saki's posthumously published short story 'The Cupboard of the Yesterdays', one character says, 'In old bygone days we had the wars in the Low Countries always at our doors, as it were; there was no need to go far afield into malaria-stricken wilds if one wanted a life of boot and saddle and licence to kill and be killed.'

2 *You Only Live Twice.*

Title of novel (1964). In an epigraph, Fleming puts: 'You only live twice: / Once when you are born / And once when you look death in the face' as 'after' Matsuo Bashō, the Japanese poet (1644–94).

3 Older women are best because they always think they may be doing it for the last time.

Quoted in John Pearson, *The Life of Ian Fleming* (1966). Compare Benjamin Franklin's *Reasons for Preferring an Elderly Mistress* (1745): '8th and lastly. They are so grateful!'

4 *Tomorrow Never Dies.*

Title of film (US/UK 1997). After *Never Say Never Again*, this was the first Bond film title not to be taken from an Ian Fleming story nor to have a Fleming association (*Goldeneye* was the name of Fleming's house in Jamaica). Whether the title has any meaning is, of course, another matter: the villain of the piece is a media mogul and *Tomorrow* is on the masthead of one of his publications. The plot hinges on the mogul's creation of wars and other news events so that his paper can get scoops on them. Presumably, the title also alludes lightly to the proverb 'Tomorrow never comes' (a warning against procrastination).

5 *The World Is Not Enough.*

Title of film (US/UK 1999). Though not a title invented by Fleming, it derives from a line in his novel *On Her Majesty's Secret Service* (1963, film UK 1969). At the College of Heralds, Sir Hilary Bray is showing the Bond family coat of arms, on which the Latin motto is 'The World Is Not Enough'. In the film, the Latin is shown as '*Orbis non sufficie*'. Indeed, '*Non sufficit orbis*' is the motto of the Bond family of Dorset and, in this form, would appear to be a quotation from Juvenal. *The World Is Not Enough* was also used as the title of a 1948 translation of *Argile et cendres* (1946) by the novelist Zoé Oldenbourg (1916–).

See also KAEL 264:1; SHAKESPEARE 410:6.

John FLETCHER English playwright (1579–1625)

6 Whistle and she'll come to you.

Wit Without Money, Act 4, Sc. 4 (?1614). Compare BURNS 110:6.

7 Nothing can cover his high fame but Heaven;
No pyramids set off his memories,
But the eternal substance of his greatness.

The False One (?1620). This is the epitaph on the grave of Sir Thomas Beecham (1879–1961), the orchestral conductor. He was originally buried in Brookwood Cemetery, near Woking, but was re-interred at the parish cemetery of Limpsfield, Surrey, in April 1991. Beecham arranged music for several productions of Fletcher's plays and gave the Oxford Romanes Lecture on the playwright in 1956.

Dario FO Italian playwright (1926–)

8 *Can't Pay Won't Pay.*

The English title (1978) of the play *Non si paga, non si paga!* (1974), as translated by Lino Pertile. In 1990, it was adopted as a slogan by those objecting to the British Government's Community Charge or 'poll tax' and by other similar protest groups. Hence, *Can't Cook, Won't Cook*, title of a British TV cookery show (1990s).

Ferdinand FOCH French soldier (1851–1929)

9 *Mon centre cède, ma droite recule, situation excellente. J'attaque!* [My centre gives way, my right retreats; situation excellent. I shall attack!]

Remark to General Joffre, during the second Battle of the

Marne (July/August 1918). In R. Recouly, *Foch* (1919), the remark is given during the first Battle of the Marne, September 1914.

Michael FOOT British journalist and Labour politician (1913–)

1 *Guilty Men.*

Title of a tract, 'which may rank as literature' (A.J.P. Taylor), written with Frank Owen and Peter Howard under the collective pseudonym 'Cato'. Published in July 1940, it taunted the appeasers who had brought about the situation where Britain had had to go to war with Germany. The preface contains this anecdote: 'On a spring day in 1793 a crowd of angry men burst their way through the doors of the assembly room where the French Convention was in session. A discomforted figure addressed them from the rostrum. "What do the people desire?" he asked. "The Convention has only their welfare at heart." The leader of the angry crowd replied, "The people haven't come here to be given a lot of phrases. They demand a dozen guilty men."'

The phrase 'We *name* the guilty men' subsequently became a cliché of popular 'investigative' journalism. The 'guilty men' taunt was one much used in the 1945 general election by the Labour Party, and was referred to in a speech by Winston Churchill in the House of Commons (7 May 1947).

2 I say this in the utmost affection ... he has passed from rising hope to elder statesman without any intervening period whatsoever.

Of David Steel. Speech in the House of Commons (28 March 1979) – taken from a recording rather than *Hansard*. Foot, as Leader of the House, was ending the debate that resulted in the Labour Government's defeat on a motion of no confidence (and led to its general election defeat the following month). The Liberals, led by the youngish David Steel, had until quite recently been part of the 'Lib–Lab' pact that had helped keep Labour in office. But then it collapsed.

Foot never relinquished his journalist's habit of using a good line whenever an opportunity presented itself. In 1952 he had written a profile of Peter Thorneycroft, the Conservative politician, who, he said, had, 'passed the stage of rising hope to elder statesman without any intervening period whatever'.

3 Is it always his desire to give his imitation of a semi-housetrained polecat?

This was Foot, when leader of Britain's Labour Party, talking about Norman Tebbit, the prickly Conservative Party Chairman. Foot said it at an eve-of-poll rally in Ebbw Vale in 1983. He noted that he had said it first in the House of Commons

'a few years ago' – indeed, on 2 March 1978. Foot lost the general election overwhelmingly. Tebbit continued to bite people in the leg for a few years more.

Henry FORD American industrialist (1863–1947)

4 History is bunk.

In the course of a libel action against the *Chicago Tribune*, which came to court in the spring of 1919 – an editorial had described Ford as an 'anarchist' and an 'ignorant idealist' – the motor magnate found himself as much on trial as the defendant. Cross-examined for no fewer than eight days, Ford was continually tripped up by his ignorance. He could not say when the United States came into being. He suggested 1812 before 1776. He was asked about a statement reported by Charles N. Wheeler in an interview with Ford on 25 May 1916: 'History is more or less bunk. It's tradition.' Ford explained: 'I did not say it was bunk. It was bunk to me ... but I did not need it very bad.' The *Tribune* was found guilty of libel – and fined six cents.

5 Any customer can have a car painted any colour that he wants so long as it is black.

An expression indicating that there is no choice. Ford is supposed to have said it about the Model T Ford, which came out in 1909. Quoted in his *My Life and Work* (written with Henry Crowther, 1922). Hill and Nevins in *Ford: Expansion and Challenge* (1957) have him saying: 'People can have it any colour – so long as it's black.' However, in 1925 the company had to bow to the inevitable and offer a choice of colours. Dr Harry Corbett of Bayswater, Australia, commented (1996): 'Initially, the T model was available in several colours but when Ford changed to a different painting technique the product used was only available in the colour black. The early finishing technique was a carryover from the carriage industry and resulted in curing times of up to four weeks. This meant that huge numbers of cars had to be stored during the finishing process. From what I can gather, Ford changed to a faster drying product – which was only available in black – to rid himself of the warehousing difficulties.'

Nathan B. FORREST American general (1821–77)

6 Firstest with the mostest.

To describe anything as 'the mostest' might seem exclusively American. However, *OED2* finds English dialect use in the 1880s, and *Partridge/Slang* recognizes its use as a jocular superlative without restricting it to the US. As such, it is a consciously ungrammatical way of expressing extreme degree. Whether this was consciously the case with the

Confederate general, Nathan B. Forrest, is very much in doubt. He could hardly read or write, but he managed to say that the way to win battles was to be 'Firstest with the mostest', or that you needed to 'Git thar fustest with the mostest'. *Bartlett* (1992) gives this last as the usual rendering of the more formally reported words: 'Get there first with the most men.' In Irving Berlin's musical *Call Me Madam* (1950) there is a song with the title 'The Hostess with the Mostes' on the Ball'. One assumes that Berlin's use, like any evocation of 'the mostest' nowadays, refers back to Forrest's remark.

E.M. FORSTER English novelist (1879–1970)

1 He was passionately in love with her; therefore she could do exactly as she liked. 'It mayn't be heaven below,' she thought, 'but it's better than Charles.'

Where Angels Fear to Tread, Chap. 3 (1905). The idea of marriage as a heaven or paradise below might seem to be a well-meaning 19th-century view of the matter, but in Neville Coghill's translation (1951) of Chaucer's 'The Merchant's Tale', he puts: 'For wedlock is so easy and so clean / It is a very paradise on earth.' In Chaucer's original, the second line is: 'That in this world it is a paradys.' In his 'A Chapter on Ears', Charles Lamb quotes the lines of 'Dr [Isaac] Watts' (1674–1748): 'I have been there, and still would go; / 'Tis like a little heaven below' – but here the reference is to chapels rather than marriage.

2 *A Room With a View.*

Title of novel (1908). Noël Coward's song with the title did not appear until *This Year of Grace* (1928).

3 'Life,' wrote a friend of mine, 'is a public performance on the violin, in which you must learn the instrument as you go along.' I think he puts it well.

A Room With a View, Chap. 19. Note the casual way in which 'Mr Emerson', a fictional character, airily attributes it to 'a friend of mine'. Might he have been referring to Edward Bulwer-Lytton (1st Baron Lytton), English novelist and politician (1803–73), who is quoted in *The Treasury of Humorous Quotations*, eds Esar & Bentley (1951), as having said: 'Life is like playing a violin solo in public and learning the instrument as one goes on'? Later this seems to have been quoted by Samuel Butler during a speech at the Somerville Club (27 February 1895), though it is presented as his own thought in *Further Extracts from the Note-Books of Samuel Butler* (1934). A pity the Bulwer-Lytton is not more precise.

4 'Only connect ...'

Epigraph to *Howard's End* (1910). Goronwy Rees wrote in *A Chapter of Accidents* (1972): 'It could be said that those two words, so misleading in their ambiguity, had more influence in shaping the emotional attitudes of the English governing class between the two world wars than any other single phrase in the English language.' The words also occur in the body of Forster's book (Chap. 22): 'Only connect! That was the whole of her sermon. Only connect the prose and the passion, and both will be exalted, and human love will be seen at its height. Live in fragments no longer. Only connect, and the beast and the monk, robbed of the isolation that is life to either, will die.' Forster's message was that barriers of all kinds must be dismantled if the harmony lacking in modern life was to be discovered.

5 Personal relations are the important thing for ever and ever, and not this outer life of telegrams and anger.

In the same novel, Chap. 19. Alluded to in *Peter Hall's Diaries* (1983) – entry for 30 December 1973: 'Jenny and Christopher to Paris to see their mother. The holidays feel over. Back into the world of telegrams and anger ...'

6 *A Passage to India.*

Title of novel (1924). Forster acknowledged that this was derived from a poem called 'Passage to India' (1871) in Walt Whitman's *Leaves of Grass.*

7 I hate causes, and if I had to choose between betraying my country and betraying my friend, I hope I should have the guts to betray my country.

'What I Believe', *Two Cheers for Democracy* (1938). This was quoted by the traitor Anthony Blunt when trying to persuade friends not to tell the British authorities what they knew about the 1951 defectors, Burgess and Maclean. Goronwy Rees (as above) replied to Blunt: 'Forster's antithesis was a false one. One's country [is] not some abstract conception which it might be relatively easy to sacrifice for the sake of an individual; it [is] itself made up of a dense network of individual and social relationships in which loyalty to one particular person formed only a single strand.' Blunt, Burgess and Maclean were part of the between-the-wars generation at Cambridge influenced by Forster's thinking.

8 I do not believe in Belief ... Lord I disbelieve – help thou my unbelief.

In the same essay. Compare Mark 9:24.

(Sir) George FOSTER Canadian politician (1847–1931)

1 In these somewhat troublesome days when the great Mother Empire stands splendidly isolated in Europe.

A speech in the Canadian House of Commons (16 January 1896) was the occasion of the coining of the phrase 'splendid isolation', which was the headline in the London *Times* over its subsequent account. Foster was MP for North Toronto. 'A flattering Canadian conception of Britain's lonely magnificence' – Jan Morris in *Farewell the Trumpets* (1978). The 1st Lord Goschen picked up the phrase in a speech at Lewes (26 February 1896): 'We have stood here alone in what is called isolation – our splendid isolation, as one of our colonial friends was good enough to call it.'

H.W. FOWLER English lexicographer (1858–1933)

2 A writer expresses himself in words that have been used before because they give his meaning better than he can give it himself, or because they are beautiful or witty, or because he expects them to touch a chord of association in his reader, or because he wishes to show that he is learned and well read. Quotations due to the last motive are invariably ill-advised; the discerning reader detects it and is contemptuous; the undiscerning is perhaps impressed, but even then is at the same time repelled, pretentious quotations being the surest way to tedium.

A Dictionary of Modern English Usage (1926).

(Sir) Norman FOWLER (later Lord Fowler) English Conservative politician (1938–)

3 I have a young family and for the next few years I should like to devote more time to them while they are still so young.

Letter of resignation to the Prime Minister (3 January 1990). Margaret Thatcher replied the same day: 'I am naturally very sorry to see you go, but understand your reasons for doing so, particularly your wish to be able to spend more time with your family.' At the same time, Peter Walker also resigned from the Cabinet, giving as his reason that he wished to 'spend more time with my family', and the phrase became a cliché of political resignations.

Charles James FOX English Liberal politician (1749–1806)

4 No Greek: as much Latin as you like; never French in any circumstances: no English poet unless he has completed his century.

Fox's advice on the use of quotations in House of Commons speeches. Quoted in G.W.E. Russell, *Collections and Recollections*, Chap. 11 (1898). Russell comments on the changing fashions in parliamentary oratory: 'Quoting Virgil will be the next thing to disappear. In the last Parliament we often had Latin quotations, but never from a member with a new constituency. I have heard Greek quoted here, but that was a long time ago, and a great mistake. The House was quite alarmed.'

FRANCIS OF ASSISI Italian monk and saint (1181–1226)

5 Lord, make me an instrument of your peace.
Where there is hatred, let me sow love.
Where there is injury, pardon.
Where there is doubt, faith.
Where there is despair, hope.
Where there is darkness, light.
Where there is sadness, joy.

O Divine Master, grant that I may not so much seek
To be consoled as to console,
To be understood as to understand,
To be loved as to love.

For it is in giving that we receive,
It is in pardoning that we are pardoned,
It is in dying that we are born to eternal life.

Bartlett (1980) has a fuller version and a different translation, saying no more than that the words are 'attributed' to St Francis. In 1988 this was the version entitled 'Prayer for Peace' that was available (unattributed) in Britain on prayer cards. There was even a version on a tea towel on sale at York Minster. At the Basilica of St Francis at Assisi, it was, of course, available in any number of languages. Actually, there is some doubt as to whether St Francis had anything to do with the prayer at all. The Rt Revd Dr J.R.H. Moorman (1905–89), a former Bishop of Ripon, wrote to the *Church Times* stating that the prayer was written in France in 1912 – source: *The Observer* (7 September 1986).

The first few lines of the prayer were quoted by Margaret Thatcher on becoming British Prime Minister (4 May 1979). According to Sir Ronald Millar, one of her speechwriters, it was he who at four o'clock on Mrs Thatcher's first morning as Prime Minister gave her the words to read out, 'ignoring the advice of harder-nosed associates who thought the sentiments too trite even for that emotional occasion' – *The Sunday Times* (23 November 1980). It was inevitable that the quotation would in time be held against her.

FRANCIS II Austrian Holy Roman Emperor (1768–1835)

1 But is he a patriot for me?

A distinguished servant of the Austrian Empire was being recommended to Francis II as a sterling patriot, so the last Holy Roman Emperor asked this. A. & V. Palmer, *Quotations in History* (1976), ascribing this to his other title of 'Francis I of Austria', add: 'Remark on being told of the patriotic qualities of a candidate for high office, *c*.1821'. Hence, the title of John Osborne's play *A Patriot for Me* (1965).

Benjamin FRANKLIN American politician and scientist (1706–90)

2 Fish and visitors smell in three days.

Poor Richard's Almanack (1736). In Whit Stillman's film *Barcelona* (1994), one of the characters – perhaps intentionally – misascribes this famous proverb to Dr Johnson. A pity that he didn't ascribe the saying to America's own Dr Johnson, Benjamin Franklin. Even so, *CODP* finds the idea (without the fish) in Plautus and the first English reference (with the fish) in Lyly's *Euphues* (1580). Wolfgang Mieder in *Proverbs Are Never Out of Season* (1993) has provided a useful corrective to the view that Franklin was a great coiner of proverbs. In fact, of the 1044 proverbs in *Poor Richard's Almanack*, only 5 per cent can be said to have been coined by Franklin himself.

3 Here Skugg
Lies snug
As a bug
In a rug.

Letter to Miss Georgiana Shipley (26 September 1772) on the death of her pet squirrel. However, lest it be thought that, by its inclusion in dictionaries of quotations, Franklin originated the phrase 'snug as a bug in a rug', note that there are earlier uses. In an anonymous work *Stratford Jubilee* (commemorating David Garrick's Shakespeare Festival in 1769) we find:

If she [a rich widow] has the mopus's [money]
I'll have her, as snug as a bug in a rug.

Probably, however, it was an established expression even by that date, if only because in 1706 Edward Ward in *The Wooden World Dissected* had the similar 'He sits as snug as a Bee in a Box', and in Thomas Heywood's play *A Woman Killed with Kindness* (1603) there is: 'Let us sleep as snug as pigs in pease-straw.'

A little after Franklin's use: in the July 1816 edition of the *New Monthly Magazine*, among the curious epitaphs printed from Waddington in Yorkshire (now in Lancashire) was one, 'In memory of WILLIAM RICHARD PHELPS, late Boatswain of H.M.S. *Invincible*. He accompanied Lord Anson in his cruise round the world, and died April 21, 1789.' It reads:

When I was like you,
For years not a few,
On the ocean I toil'd,
On the line I have broil'd,
In Greenland I've shiver'd,
Now from hardship deliver'd,
Capsiz'd by old death,
I surrender'd my breath.
And now I lie snug
As a bug in a rug.

4 We must indeed all hang together, or, most assuredly, we shall all hang separately.

At the signing of the Declaration of Independence (4 July 1776), though possibly not original. Remark to John Hancock. Quoted in *A Book of Anecdotes*, ed. Daniel George (1958.)

5 Never pick a quarrel with someone who buys their ink in barrels.

Or, 'Never disagree with anyone who buys ink by the barrel' – i.e., with a journalist or professional arguer. This was attributed to Franklin by *The Observer* (27 July 1992), but remains unverified. Yet another version of this American saying is: 'Never pick a fight with anyone who buys ink by the barrel and paper by the ton.'

6 The body
of Benjamin Franklin, printer,
(Like the cover of an old book,
Its contents worn out,
And stript of its lettering and gilding)
Lies here, food for worms!
Yet the work itself shall not be lost,
For it will, as he believed, appear once more
In a new
And more beautiful edition,
Corrected and amended
By its Author!

An epitaph suggested for himself and written in about 1728. *Benham* (1948) compares the Revd Joseph Capen (19th century), 'Lines on Mr John Foster': 'Yet at the resurrection we shall see / A fair edition, and of matchless worth, / Free from erratas, new in heaven set forth.' *Benham* also suggests that the idea was borrowed from the Revd Benjamin Woodbridge, chaplain to Charles II, who wrote these 'Lines of John Cotton' (1652): 'O what a monument of glorious worth, / When in a new edition he comes forth, / Without erratas, may we think he'll be / In leaves and covers of eternity!'

In fact, Franklin lies with his wife under a simple inscription in Christ Church, Philadelphia: 'Benjamin and Deborah Franklin 1790.'

1 **Dost thou love life? Then do not squander time; for that's the stuff life is made of.**
Poor Richard's Almanac (1746) – June. As noted above, there is no telling whether this saying was original to Franklin. It is notably shown inscribed on a sundial in one of the early scenes in the film *Gone With the Wind* (US 1939) in the form: 'DO NOT SQUANDER TIME. / THAT IS THE STUFF LIFE IS MADE OF' – but without attribution.

See also FLEMING 197:3.

Malcolm FRASER Australian Liberal Prime Minister (1930–)

2 **Life is not meant to be easy.**
Fraser was Prime Minister of Australia 1975–83. The phrase was very much associated with him, and was used as the title of a biography by John Edwards in 1977. Douglas Aiton asked Fraser in an interview for the London *Times* (16 March 1981) if he had ever actually said it. Fraser replied, 'I said something very like it. It's from *Back to Methuselah* by Bernard Shaw ... A friend I was visiting in hospital asked me why I didn't give up politics and return to the good life [on his sheep farm]. I said life wasn't meant to be like that. That would be too easy. So that's what it grew from. I wouldn't mind a cent for every time it's been quoted or misquoted. It's the best thing I ever said.' Presumably, Shaw would agree.

Fraser's derivation of the line from Shaw was probably an afterthought, however. The play has, 'Life is not meant to be easy, my child; but take courage: it can be delightful.' In a Deakin lecture on 20 July 1971, which seems to have been his first public use of the phrase, Fraser made no mention of the source. Referring rather to Arnold Toynbee's analysis of history, Fraser said: 'It involves a conclusion about the past that life has not been easy for people or for nations, and an assumption for the future that that condition will not alter. There is within me some part of the metaphysic, and thus I would add that life is not meant to be easy.'

It is not, of course, a startlingly original view. In A.C. Benson's essays *The Leaves of the Tree* (1912), he quotes Brooke Foss Westcott, Bishop of Durham, as saying: 'The only people with whom I have no sympathy ... are those who say that things are easy. Life is not easy, nor was it meant to be.' Compare KENNEDY 268:1.

Samuel FREEMAN American jurist (alive late 19th century)

3 **Never walk when you can ride, never sit when you can lie down.**
Freeman apparently served in the US Supreme Court from 1862 to 1890. Claire Rayner, the British 'agony aunt', has a longer version, acquired from the Sister Tutor who trained her as a nurse back in the 1950s: 'Nurse, never stand when you can sit, never sit when you can lie down, and never lie if there's any chance they might find you out.' Compare from H.L. Mencken, *Happy Days* (1940): 'I long ago associated with the Chinese doctrine that it is foolish to do anything standing up that can be done sitting down, or anything sitting down that can be done lying down'; and the letter Coleridge wrote to John Thelwall (14 October 1797): '... at other times I adopt the Brahman Creed, & say – It is better to sit than to stand, it is better to lie than to sit, it is better to sleep than to wake – but Death is the best of all!' – in E.L. Griggs, *Collected Letters of Samuel Taylor Coleridge*, Vol. 1 (1956).

Notes and Queries, 5th Series, 7 (1877), printed a query along the lines: 'It is better to be sitting than standing, / It is better to be in bed than sitting, / It is better to be dead than in bed.' This produced a reply that, 'The lines asked for are, I believe, an imperfect version of a Hindoo proverb which runs thus: "It is better to walk than to run: it is better to stand than to walk: it is better to sit than to stand: it is better to lie than to sit."' Compare GEORGE V 210:3.

Marilyn FRENCH American novelist (1929–)

4 **Whatever they may be in public life, whatever their relations with men, in their relations with women, all men are rapists, and that's all they are. They rape us with their eyes, their laws and their codes.**
Said by a character whose daughter has been raped in *The Women's Room* (1977). From *The Observer* (3 March 1996): 'Talk to French about that quotation, and she seethes with exasperation. Because she never said those words. One of the characters in her first, massive bestseller *The Women's Room* did. And, she fumes: "Nobody holds up Iago's speeches and blames Shakespeare for them."'

Sigmund FREUD Austrian psychiatrist (1856–1939)

5 **The great question that has never been answered and which I have not yet been able to answer, despite my thirty years of research into the feminine soul, is 'What does a woman want?'**
From a letter to Marie Bonaparte, quoted in Ernest Jones, *Sigmund Freud: Life and Work* (1955). The question became a rallying cry in the resurgence of feminism from the 1970s

onwards. *What Do Women Want? Exploding the Myth of Dependency* was the title of a book by Luise Eichenbaum and Susie Orbach (1983). The same question is posed to the protagonist of Chaucer's 'The Wife of Bath's Tale' when the answer is: 'Wommen desiren to have sovereynetee / As wel over hir housbond as hir love, / And for to been in maistrie hym above.'

Milton FRIEDMAN American economist (1912–)

1 There is no such thing as a free lunch.

In the US the concept of the 'free lunch' dates back to at least 1840, according to Flexner (1976). It might have amounted to no more than thirst-arousing snacks like pretzels in saloon bars, but even so it was not strictly speaking 'free', because you had to buy a beer to obtain it. Quite at what point the saying 'There ain't no such thing as a free lunch' – meaning 'there's always a catch' or 'don't expect something for nothing' – arose is hard to say. The *ODMQ* (1991) found this in *The Moon is a Harsh Mistress*, a science fiction novel (1966) by Robert A. Heinlein: 'Oh, "tanstaafl". Means "There ain't no such thing as a free lunch." And isn't,' I added, pointing to a FREE LUNCH sign across room, 'or these drinks would cost half as much. Was reminding her that anything free costs twice as much in the long run or turns out worthless.'

But it was misleading of the *ODMQ* to proffer this as if it were the original coinage when the observation that free lunches have hidden costs was already well established. In the epilogue to his *America* (1973) Alistair Cooke ascribes the phrase 'There is no free lunch' to 'an Italian immigrant, when asked to say what forty years of American life had taught him'. The saying 'There is no such thing as a free lunch' is quoted by Burton Crane in *The Sophisticated Investor* (1959).

Milton Friedman, along with other economists of the University of Chicago school, gave the saying new life in the 1970s, using it in articles, lectures and as the title of a book (1975) to support his monetarist theories. But he did not coin the phrase either, even if it came to be much associated with him.

Charles FROHMAN American theatrical producer (1860–1915)

2 Why fear death? It is the most beautiful adventure of life.

These were Frohman's last words before going down with the *Lusitania* in 1915. The words were reported by survivors and quoted in I.F. Marcosson and D. Frohman, *Charles Frohman* (1916). Undoubtedly Frohman was alluding to the line 'To die will be an awfully big adventure' in J.M. Barrie's

play *Peter Pan* (1904), which he had first produced on the London stage. See BARRIE 53:3.

3 For it is not right that in a house the muses haunt mourning should dwell. Such things befit us not.

These words are on the fountain monument to Frohman near the church (but outside the churchyard) of All Saints, Marlow, Buckinghamshire. Frohman used to spend weekends at Marlow and, indeed, expressed a wish to die and to be buried there. The monument shows a nude maiden in marble, and the inscription runs round the base. J. Camp in *Portrait of Buckinghamshire* (1972) comments: 'His memorial is a graceful tribute to the female form, and a reminder of the pleasure his stage presentations gave to so many on both sides of the Atlantic in late Victorian and Edwardian days.' As I have only lately discovered, the text is taken from a translation of fragments by Sappho, the Greek lyric poet of the late 7th century BC – also sometimes rendered as 'For it is not right that in the house of song ...' and taken to be her dying words. Henry T. Wharton in *Sappho* (1895) has the poet 'blaming her daughter' and translates the passage, 'For lamentation may not be in a poet's house: such things befit us not.' He also quotes Frederick Tennyson's version: 'In the home of the Muses / 'Tis bootless to mourn.'

(Sir) David FROST English broadcaster (1939–)

4 Hello, good evening, and welcome.

Frost probably did not use this greeting as host of BBC TV's *That Was the Week That Was* (1962–4), but may have introduced it in *Not So Much a Programme, More a Way of Life* (1964–5). As 'Hello, good evening, [...] welcome', the catchphrase had already been used in an impersonation of Frost on the *Private Eye* record 'The Rites of Spring' (1 April 1965), so was obviously established by this date. It became a greeting well known on both sides of the Atlantic when Frost was commuting back and forth to host TV chat shows in London and New York, and in particular *The Frost Programme* on ITV (1966). *ODMQ* (1991) and *ODQ* (1999) wrongly ascribe *The Frost Programme* to BBC Television, whereas it was a Rediffusion production. The phrase was later used as the title of a BBC 'Wednesday Play' about a TV interrogator (16 October 1968).

The greeting may have been contrived to say three things where only one is needed, but it became an essential part of the Frost impersonator's kit (not to mention the Frost self-impersonator's kit). Frost was still saying it in 1983 when, with a small alteration, it became 'Hello, good *morning* and welcome!' at the debut of TV-am, the breakfast-TV station.

Robert FROST American poet (1874–1963)

1 My apple trees will never get across
And eat the cones under his pines, I tell him.
He only says, Good fences make good
neighbours.

'Mending Wall', *North of Boston* (1914). This thought is an old one, as *Burnam* (1975) noted. 'E. Rogers' (1640), in a letter quoted in the Winthrop Papers, wrote: 'A good fence helpeth to keepe peace between neighbours; but let us take heed that we make not a high stone wall, to keep us from meeting.' And *Apperson* has, from the same year, a proverb: 'Love your neighbour yet pull not down your hedge.' However, as Frost's poem makes clear, this is not the poet's point of view. It is the neighbour ('an old-stone savage armed') who says the line. Frost is pointing out that good fences do not necessarily make good neighbours at all: 'Before I built a wall I'd ask to know / What I was walling in or walling out.'

2 'Home is the place where, when you have to
go there,
They have to take you in.'

From his poem 'The Death of a Hired Man' (1914). Note the quotation marks. Compare THATCHER 462:10.

3 Two roads diverged in a yellow wood,
And sorry I could not travel both
And be one traveller, long I stood
And looked down one as far as I could
To where it bent in the undergrowth ...

Two roads diverged in a wood, and I –
I took the one less travelled by,
And that has made all the difference.

'The Road Not Taken', *Mountain Interval* (1916). Hence, *In a Yellow Wood*, the title of Gore Vidal's second novel (1947). *The Road Less Travelled* was taken as the title of a popular work of psychotherapy by M. Scott Peck (1978) and *The Road Taken* became the title of a memoir (2004) by the British broadcaster Michael Buerk.

4 The woods are lovely, dark and deep.
But I have promises to keep,
And miles to go before I sleep,
And miles to go before I sleep.

'Stopping by Woods on a Snowy Evening' (1923). Frost suffered misquotation at the hands of President Kennedy, who used the poem as a rousing, uplifting end to speeches. However, until Jacqueline Kennedy pointed it out to her husband, he would frequently combine the poem with another (by Emerson) and say: 'I'll hitch my wagon to a star / But

I have promises to keep.' Or he would work in the venue of his speech, as in 'Iowa is lovely, dark and deep' – source: Theodore C. Sorensen, *Kennedy* (1965).

Hence, *Promises to Keep*, title of a memoir (1971) by Chester Knowles, and of an unrelated film (US 1985), and of a novel (1988) by George Bernau.

Compare from Shakespeare, *Titus Andronicus*, II.i.128 (1591): 'The woods are ruthless, dreadful, deaf and dull' – pointed out by Anthony Powell in a diary entry for 23 February 1988.

5 Some say the world will end in fire,
Some say in ice.
From what I've tasted of desire,
I hold with those who favour fire.

'Fire and Ice' (1923). Here fire = desire, ice = hate, either of which is strong enough to kill. The word combination has appealed to many. A.E. Housman in *A Shropshire Lad* (1896) has: 'And fire and ice within me fight / Beneath the suffocating night.' Dante's *Inferno* has: 'Into the eternal darkness, into fire and into ice.' Psalm 148:7 in the Book of Common Prayer has 'fire and hail'. Latterly, the fire–ice combination has been used to refer to the death of the planet Earth by atomic warfare or a new ice age. The ice skaters Jayne Torville and Christopher Dean had a routine with the title in the late 1980s.

Mitsuo FUCHIDA Japanese pilot (1902–)

6 Tora-tora-tora.

Fuchida was the leader of the Japanese attack on the US Pacific Fleet at Pearl Harbor (7 December 1941). On confirming that the fleet was indeed being taken by surprise at dawn, he uttered this codeword to signal that the rest of the Japanese plan could be put into operation. 'Tora' means 'tiger'. Source: Gordon W. Prange, *At Dawn We Slept*, Chap. 61 (1982). Hence, *Tora! Tora! Tora!*, title of a film (US 1970) about the events leading up to Pearl Harbor.

Francis FUKUYAMA American government official (1953–)

7 What we may be witnessing is not the end of the Cold War but the end of history as such; that is, the end point of man's ideological evolution and the universalization of Western liberal democracy.

The 'end of history' was a concept promoted by Fukuyama in the summer 1989 edition of the American journal *National Interest* to describe Western democracy's perceived triumph over Communism in Eastern Europe. 'He gained a lot of publicity,' wrote Michael Ignatieff in the *Indepen-*

dent on Sunday (22 October 1995) 'by stating the obvious: that the death of Communism had removed the last systematic challenge to the triumph of the capitalist system ... In fact, of course, History continued, not least because there is not one capitalist system but many, and the reckoning between them was far from over.'

The idea had been touched on before, but for different reasons. From Graham Swift, *Waterland* (1983): 'Alluding rapidly to certain topics of the day ... the perilous and apparently unhaltable build-up of nuclear arms ... "The only important thing about history, I think, sir, is that it's got to the point where it's probably about to end."' Compare also SELLAR 399:1.

J. William FULBRIGHT American Democratic politician (1905–95)

1 A policy that can be accurately, though perhaps not prudently, defined as one of 'peaceful coexistence'.

Speech in the Senate (27 March 1964), but the phrase had long been current. In 1920 Lenin had spoken of 'peaceful cohabitation with the peoples, with the workers and peasants of all nations'. In the 1950s and 1960s, the possibility of fair competition between Eastern and Western ideologies was also much mooted, though whether the Soviets and the Americans meant quite the same thing by the phrase is doubtful.

2 We must dare to think 'unthinkable' thoughts. We must learn to explore all the options and possibilities that confront us in a complex and rapidly changing world. We must learn to welcome and not to fear the voices of dissent. We must dare to think about 'unthinkable' things because when things become unthinkable, thinking stops and action becomes mindless.

In the same speech. A little earlier, Herman Kahn had written a book with the title *Thinking the Unthinkable* (1962). The sort of thing Fulbright had in mind was collaboration with the Soviets on various schemes.

3 *The Arrogance of Power.*

Title of book (1967) questioning the basis of US foreign policy, particularly in Vietnam and the Dominican Republic. In the previous year, Fulbright, the Democratic chairman of the Senate Foreign Relations Committee, had given lectures establishing his theme: 'A psychological need that nations seem to have ... to prove that they are bigger, better or stronger than other nations.'

R. Buckminster FULLER American architect (1895–1983)

4 I am a passenger on the spaceship, Earth.

Operating Manual for Spaceship Earth (1969). The concept of planet Earth as a spaceship was designed to underline that we are travelling through space on our own, with our survival dependent upon a fragile economy and a polluted environment. The idea was not totally original: in 1965 Adlai Stevenson told UNESCO: 'We travel together, passengers on a little space ship, dependent on its vulnerable reserves of air and soil.' Marshall McLuhan added: 'There are no passengers on Spaceship Earth. Only crew.'

Sam FULLER American film writer and director (1912–97)

5 The film is like a battleground ... love ... hate ... action ... violence ... death ... in one word: emotions.

This is a maxim spoken by Fuller in a cameo appearance in Jean-Luc Godard's film *Pierrot le Fou* (France 1966). He appears in the film as a visiting director and makes his pronouncement at a party. It has been wrongly attributed to Nicholas Ray.

Thomas FULLER English preacher and historian (1608–61)

6 Here lies Fuller's Earth.

A punning epitaph suggested for himself by the author of *The History of the Worthies of England*. T. Webb in *A New Select Collection of Epitaphs* (1775) mentions it. Fuller was buried in the church of which he had been rector, at Cranford, west London, but the grave no longer survives. His actual epitaph was a sober Latin text.

Thomas FULLER English writer and physician (1654–1734)

7 Be you never so high the law is above you.

Gnomologia (1732). During a landmark ruling in the British High Court in January 1977, Lord Denning quoted Fuller's words 'to every subject of this land, however powerful' in the matter of the 'South African mail boycott case'. He ruled that the Attorney-General, Sam Silkin, could not suspend or dispense with the execution of the law.

See also REAGAN 379:6.

G

Hugh GAITSKELL English Labour politician (1906–63)

1 There are some of us ... who will fight ānd fight and fight again to save the party we love.

Speech as leader of the British Labour Party at the party conference (3 October 1960). When, against the wishes of the party leadership, the conference looked like taking what Gaitskell called the 'suicidal path' of unilateral disarmament, 'which will leave our country defenceless and alone', he was faced with making the most important speech of his life – for his leadership was at stake. Many delegates who were free to do so changed their votes, but the Party executive was still defeated. Nevertheless, Gaitskell reduced his opponents to a paper victory, and the phrase is often recalled in tribute to a great personal achievement. The coinage has been claimed by Brian Walden, the broadcaster and one-time Labour MP. Compare DANTON 162:4, which is sometimes rendered as: 'Dare! and dare! and dare again!'

2 It does mean, if this is the idea, the end of Britain as an independent European state ... it means the end of a thousand years of history.

In a speech to the Labour Party Conference (3 October 1962), Gaitskell gave this view of a proposal that Britain should join the European Economic Community. It is always dangerous these days to use the phrase 'thousand years'. Speaking on European unity (14 February 1948), Winston Churchill said: 'We are asking the nations of Europe between whom rivers of blood have flowed, to forget the feuds of a thousand years.'

John Kenneth GALBRAITH Canadian-born American economist (1908–)

3 *The Affluent Society.*

Title of book (1958) about the effect of high living standards on economic theories that had been created to deal with scarcity and poverty. The result stemmed from an imbalance between private- and public-sector output. 'In a community where public services have failed to keep abreast of private consumption things are very different. Here, in an atmosphere of private opulence and public squalor, the private goods have full sway.' For example, there might be more cars and TV sets but not enough police to prevent them from being stolen. Martin Luther King in a 1963 letter from gaol used the phrase thus: 'When you see the vast majority of your twenty million Negro brothers smouldering in an airtight cage of poverty in the midst of an affluent society ... then you will understand why we find it difficult to wait.' The notion was not new to the mid-20th century, however. Tacitus, in his *Annals* (?AD115) noted that 'many, amid great affluence, are utterly miserable', and Cato the Younger (95–46BC), when denouncing the contemporary state of Rome, said: '*Habemus publice egestatem, privatim opulentiam*' [public want, private wealth]. Then again, Sallust wrote in *The War with Catiline* (?42BC): 'We have public poverty and private opulence.'

The punning tag of 'effluent society', a commonplace by the 1980s, had appeared in Stan Gooch's poem 'Never So Good' in 1964.

1 The Great Wall, I've been told, is the only manmade structure on earth that is visible from the moon. For the life of me I cannot see why anyone would go to the moon to look at it, when, with almost the same difficulty, it can be viewed in China.

In *The Sunday Times* Magazine (23 October 1977) – a prime example of Galbraith's laconic style. At the time, China had not opened itself up to tourism. The idea of 'the Wall of China' being 'the only work of man visible from the moon' was current by August 1939, when it was mentioned in the *Fortnightly Review*. Compare Herbert A. Giles, *The Civilization of China* (1911): 'The famous Great Wall, which dates back to a couple of hundred years before Christ, and which has been glorified as the last trace of man's handiwork on the globe to fade from the view of an imaginary person receding into space.' Additionally, an article entitled 'Discerned at the Moon: 250 Years of an Urban Myth' by Tony Wilmott appeared in *Polybius To Vegetius: Essays On the Roman Army and Hadrian's Wall* (privately published by the Hadrianic Society in 2002). The article is said to include a full discussion of early references to the Great Wall, including assertions about its visibility from the moon. The earliest such reference appears to be a letter that the antiquarian William Stukeley wrote in 1754. Stukeley wrote that Hadrian's Wall is exceeded in length only 'by the Chinese wall, which makes a considerable figure upon the terrestrial globe, and may be discerned at the moon'. This letter was published in *The Family Memoirs of Rev. William Stukeley*, ed. W.C. Lukis, Vol. III, published by the Surtees Society, London (1887).

See also BUTLER 114:2; TYNAN 472:7.

Galileo GALILEI Italian astronomer and physicist (1564–1642)

2 *Eppur si muove* [But it does move].

Muttered comment after his recantation of the theory that the earth moves around the sun, probably in 1633. First reported in Giuseppe Baretti, *The Italian Library* (1757), the remark seems most unlikely ever to have passed Galileo's lips. Baretti reports that 'the celebrated *Galileo*, who was in the inquisition for six years, and put to the torture, for saying, *the earth moved*. The moment he was set at liberty, he looked up to the sky and down to the ground, and, stamping with his foot, in a contemplative mood, said, *Eppur si move* [*sic*]; that is, *still it moves*, meaning the earth.' A Spanish painting dating from around 1643 is said to show Galileo in prison, with the text '*Eppur si move*', but this has not been confirmed.

Mahatma GANDHI Indian politician (1869–1948)

3 The things that will destroy us are ...
politics without principle;
pleasure without conscience;
wealth without work;
knowledge without character;
business without morality;
science without humanity; and
worship without sacrifice.

Attributed statement. As 'The seven [social] sins ... wealth without works ... politics without principle ... worship without sacrifice' etc., this has been ascribed by Arun Gandhi to his grandfather, Mahatma Gandhi, and is so quoted by Jim Wallis in the introduction to *The Soul of Politics: A Practical and Prophetic Vision for Change* (1994). Additionally, *RQ* (1989) states that Jimmy Carter quoted the words in his eulogy at the funeral of Hubert Humphrey (16 January 1978). President Carter spoke of finding the words engraved on the wall of Gandhi's memorial during a trip to India. There remains doubt as to whether Gandhi really originated it. Perhaps it is of American origin.

4 That would be a good idea.

When asked what he thought of modern civilization. In *Good Work* (1979), E.F. Schumacher describes seeing a newsreel film of Gandhi's visit to England in 1930. Disembarking at Southampton he was swamped by journalists, one of whom put this question to him (sometimes reported as 'what do you think of *Western* civilization?') and got this reply.

Greta GARBO Swedish-born film actress (1905–90)

5 I want to be alone.

Garbo claimed in *Life* Magazine (24 January 1955) that 'I only said, "I want to be *let* alone"' – i.e. she wanted privacy rather than solitude. Oddly, as Alexander Walker observed in *Sex in the Movies* (1968), 'Nowhere in anything she said, either in the lengthy interviews she gave in her Hollywood days when she was perfectly approachable, or in the statements on-the-run from the publicity-shy fugitive she later became, has it been possible to find the famous phrase, "I want to be alone." What one can find, in abundance, later on, is "Why don't you let me alone?" and even "I want to be left alone", but neither is redolent of any more exotic order of being than a harassed celebrity. Yet the world prefers to believe the mythical and much more mysterious catchphrase utterance.'

What complicates the issue is that Garbo herself *did* employ the line several times on the screen. For example, in the 1929 silent film *The Single Standard* she gives the brush-off to a stranger and the subtitle declares: 'I am walking alone because I want to be alone.' And, as the ageing ballerina who loses her nerve and flees back to her suite in *Grand Hotel* (1932), she actually *speaks* it. Walker calls this 'an excellent example of art borrowing its effects from a myth that was reality for millions of people'.

The phrase was obviously well established by 1932 when the impressionist Florence Desmond spoke it on record in her sketch 'The Hollywood Party'. In 1935 Groucho Marx uttered it in *A Night at the Opera*. Then Garbo said in *Ninotchka* (1939), 'Go to bed, little father. We want to be alone.' So it is not surprising that the myth has taken such a firm hold, and particularly since Garbo became a virtual recluse for the second half of her life.

1 **I think I go home.**

At one time, 'I tink I go home', spoken in a would-be Swedish accent, was as much part of the impressionist's view of Garbo as 'I want to be alone'. A caricatured Garbo was shown hugging Mickey Mouse in a cartoon film in the 1930s. She said, 'Ah tahnk ah kees you now' and 'Ah tink ah go home.' One version of how the line came to be spoken is told by Norman Zierold in *Moguls* (1969): 'After such films as *The Torrent* and *Flesh and the Devil*, Garbo decided to exploit her box-office power and asked Louis B. Mayer for a raise – from three hundred and fifty to five thousand dollars a week. Mayer offered her twenty-five hundred. "I tank I go home," said Garbo. She went back to her hotel and stayed there for a full seven months until Mayer finally gave way.'

Alexander Walker in *Garbo* (1980) recalls, rather, what Sven-Hugo Borg, the actress's interpreter, said of the time in 1926 when Mauritz Stiller, who had come with her from Sweden, was fired from directing *The Temptress*: 'She was tired, terrified and lost ... as she returned to my side after a trying scene, she sank down beside me and said so low it was almost a whisper, "Borg, I think I shall go home now. It isn't worth it, is it?"'

Walker comments: 'That catchphrase, shortened into "I think I go home", soon passed into the repertoire of a legion of Garbo-imitators and helped publicize her strong-willed temperament.'

James A. GARFIELD American Republican 20th President (1831–81)

2 **My fellow citizens, the President is dead, but the government lives and God omnipotent reigns.**

Speech, New York (15 April 1865), on Lincoln's assassination, when Garfield was a Congressman. Apparently, he was attempting to calm down a panicky New York crowd. Burke A. Hunsdale, *President Garfield and Education* (1882), has a different version: 'Fellow citizens! God reigns, and the Government at Washington still lives!' Garfield was himself assassinated the year he became President, in 1881.

3 *From Log Cabin to White House.*

Title of a biography (1881) of Garfield by the Revd William Thayer. Earlier Presidents, such as Henry Harrison and Abraham Lincoln, had used their log-cabin origins as a prop in their campaigns. Subsequently, most presidential aspirants have sought a humble 'log cabin' substitute to help them on their way.

John Nance GARNER American Democratic Vice-President (1868–1967)

4 **[The Vice-Presidency] isn't worth a pitcher of warm piss.**

Usually bowdlerized to 'warm spit', as apparently it was by the first journalist who reported it and (invariably) by Alistair Cooke. Garner was Vice-President (1933–41) during F.D. Roosevelt's first two terms. Furthermore, Garner said, in 1963, that the job 'didn't amount to a hill of beans'. Both remarks are quoted in O.C. Fisher, *Cactus Jack* (1978).

Theo Lippman Jr in the *San Francisco Chronicle* (25 December 1992) provided this further Garner story: he was walking down the halls of the Capitol one day when the circus was in Washington. A fellow came up to him and introduced himself. 'I am the head clown in the circus,' he said. Very solemnly, Garner replied, 'And I am the Vice-President of the United States. You'd better stick around here a while. You might pick up some new ideas.'

David GARRICK English actor (1717–79)

5 **Any fool can play tragedy, but comedy, sir, is a damned serious business.**

Attributed, and, in the form 'Comedy is a very serious thing', in conversation with the actor Jack Bannister. The date 1778 was applied to this by Richard Briers. Hence, *A Damned Serious Business*, title of the later memoirs (1990) of Sir Rex Harrison – who does not, however, give a source for the observation. Probably a more accurate rendering of this tale occurs in *Garrick and His Circle* (1906) by Mrs Clement Parsons, in which it is related that when *Charles Bannister* tired of tragic parts and begged to be allowed to do comedy, Garrick told him: 'No, no! You may humbug the town some time longer as a tragedian, but comedy is a serious thing.'

Heathcote William GARROD English academic (1878–1960)

1 Madam, I am the civilization they are fighting to defend.

On being asked why he was not fighting to defend civilization in the First World War. Attributed by Dacre Balsdon in *Oxford Then and Now* (1970). Garrod was a classical scholar and literary critic. Note how the line was incorporated in Hugh MacDiarmid's poem 'At the Cenotaph' (1935): 'Keep going to your wars, you fools, as of yore; / I'm the civilization you're fighting for.' Compare: during the First World War, a patriotic hostess pointedly asked the more than portly G.K. Chesterton, 'Why are you not out at the Front?' He replied to her, gently: 'Madam, if you go round to the side, you will find that I am.' An old story, recounted for example by A.N. Wilson in *Hilaire Belloc* (1984).

Paul GAVARNI French caricaturist and illustrator (1801–66)

2 *Les enfants terribles* [the terrible children/the little terrors].

Title of series of prints (1842). Subsequently the title of a novel (1929) by Jean Cocteau. An *'enfant terrible'* is now an adult (usually) whose questionable behaviour draws attention to him.

John GAY English poet and playwright (1685–1732)

3 A miss for pleasure, and a wife for breed.

'The Toilette' (1716). Compare BURTON 112:1.

(Sir) Eric GEDDES British Conservative politician (1875–1937)

4 The Germans, if this Government is returned, are going to pay every penny; they are going to be squeezed as a lemon is squeezed – until the pips squeak. My only doubt is not whether we can squeeze hard enough, but whether there is enough juice.

Calls for reparations or 'indemnities' at the end of the First World War were fierce. Geddes, who had lately been First Lord of the Admiralty, said this in an electioneering speech at the Beaconsfield Club, Cambridge (10 December 1918). The previous night at the Guildhall, Cambridge, he had said the same thing in a slightly different way as part of what was obviously a stump speech: 'I have personally no doubt we will get everything out of her that you can squeeze out of a lemon and a bit more … I will squeeze her until you can hear the pips squeak … I would strip Germany as she has stripped Belgium.'

The slang term 'pipsqueak' for an insignificant little person was current before this (by 1910). In the First World War it was also the name given to a high-velocity German shell which made the noise in flight. Presumably Geddes constructed his idiom out of these elements. See also HEALEY 231:3.

Arnold van GENNEP French ethnographer (1927–)

5 *Rites de passage* [Rites of Passage].

Title of a book (1909) about the transitional stages through which people pass between birth and death. The most notable *rite de passage* is probably some experience (maybe of a ritual nature) that a boy has to go through before achieving manhood. It might have to do with a demonstration of his physical skills or involve some confirmation of his sexual maturity.

The concept is now well known, especially as the name given to a genre of films. From *Flicks* Magazine (April 1994): 'Brad Pitt and Craig Sheffer play Paul and Norman in Robert Redford's *A River Runs Through It*, a nostalgic "rites of passage" drama … it's only when they're fishing that they find the true harmony that eludes them elsewhere.'

Rites of Passage is the title of a novel (1980) by William Golding.

GEORGE I British King (1660–1727)

6 I hate all Boets and Bainters.

Quoted in Lord Campbell, *Lives of the Chief Justices* (1849), and so ascribed in *ODQ* and other dictionaries. However, as it is said that George I never learned to speak English (even German-accented), a more believable account is that George II (1683–1760), who did speak English, was the one who said it. The context was that the King was discussing Hogarth's picture *The March to Finchley* (painted 1749–50, engraved and printed 1750–1). John Ireland's *Hogarth Illustrated* (1790) recounts that the picture was indeed brought to *George II* for approval: 'Before publication it [the print] was inscribed to his late Majesty, and the picture taken to St James's, in the hope of royal approbation. George the Second was an honest man, and a soldier, but not a judge of either a work of humour, or a work of art … [Hence] his disappointment on viewing the delineation. His first question was addressed to a nobleman in waiting – "Pray, who is this Hogarth?" "A painter, my liege." "I hate bainting and boetry too! neither the one nor the other ever did any good! Does the fellow mean to laugh at my guards?"'

The painting was returned to Hogarth, who dedicated it instead to the King of Prussia. Obviously this is a story that could have been aimed at both father and son (in Lord Campbell's *Lives of the Justices*, the line is delivered by George

I in the context of a poem being read), but Ireland's anecdote is rooted in a particular circumstance and is written closer to the events described, so I favour it.

Robert Louis Stevenson in *Virginibus Puerisque* (1881) puts, 'You will marry no one who is not like George the Second, and cannot state openly a distaste for poetry and painting.'

GEORGE II British King (1683–1760)

1 Mad is he? Then I hope he will *bite* some of my other generals.

Replying to the Duke of Newcastle, who had said that General Wolfe was a madman. Quoted in Henry Beckles Wilson, *The Life and Letters of James Wolfe* (1909).

GEORGE V British King (1865–1936)

2 Wake up England!

In a speech at the Guildhall, London (5 December 1901) – four days before he was created Prince of Wales – the then Duke of York, on returning from an Empire tour, warned against taking the Empire for granted: 'To the distinguished representatives of the commercial interests of the Empire ... I venture to allude to the impression which seemed generally to prevail among our brethren overseas, that the old country must wake up if she intends to maintain her old position of pre-eminence in her Colonial trade against foreign competitors.' This statement was encapsulated by the popular press in the phrase 'Wake up, England!' which George did not precisely say himself. *Punch* was still using the phrase the following year (in Vol. 123).

3 Never miss an opportunity to relieve yourself; never miss a chance to sit down and rest your feet.

In *A King's Story* (1951), George's son and heir (who became the Duke of Windsor) wrote: 'Perhaps one of the only positive pieces of advice that I was ever given was that supplied by an old courtier who observed: "Only two rules really count. Never miss an opportunity to relieve yourself; never miss a chance to sit down and rest your feet."' The 'old courtier' may well in fact have been George V himself, to whom this advice has also been attributed directly. A correspondent who wished to remain anonymous told me in 1981 that a naval officer of her acquaintance who was about to accompany Prince George, Duke of Kent, on a cruise, was asked by George V to make sure that the Prince was properly dressed before going ashore. He also advised: 'Always take an opportunity to relieve yourselves.' Another correspondent suggested, rather, that King Edward VII had been the first to say this when he was Prince of Wales.

On the other hand, more than a century earlier, the 1st Duke of Wellington had said: 'Always make water when you can.'

4 Bugger Bognor!

What the King said in reply to a suggestion that his favourite watering place be dubbed Bognor Regis (in about 1929). They are not his dying words, as often supposed – for example by Auberon Waugh in his *Private Eye* diary entry (9 August 1975), which stated: 'Shortly before the King died, a sycophantic courtier said he was looking so much better he should soon be well enough for another visit to Bognor, to which the old brute replied "Bugger Bognor" and expired.' The first recorded telling of this version that I have found is in a letter from R.K. Parkes to the *New Statesman* (3 March 1967).

The dating above is given by Kenneth Rose in his biography *George V* (1983), where it is linked to the King's recuperative visit to Bognor after his serious illness in the winter of 1928–9: 'A happier version of the legend rests on the authority of Sir Owen Morshead, the King's librarian. As the time of the King's departure from Bognor drew near, a deputation of leading citizens came to ask that their salubrious town should henceforth be known as Bognor Regis.

'They were received by Stamfordham, the King's private secretary, who, having heard their petition, invited them to wait while he consulted the King in another room. The sovereign responded with the celebrated obscenity, which Stamfordham deftly translated for the benefit of the delegation. His Majesty, they were told, would be graciously pleased to grant their request.'

5 How is the Empire?

This is the leading contender for the King's *actual* last, dying words. But, oddly enough, there are several others. On Monday 20 January 1936, a few members of the Privy Council gathered in the King's bedroom at Sandringham to witness the signing of a proclamation constituting a Council of State. The King was so weak it took a long time. To the Privy Councillors he murmured: 'Gentlemen, I am sorry for keeping you waiting like this – I am unable to concentrate' – this is sometimes given as his last utterance – in Barnaby Conrad, *Famous Last Words* (1961), for example.

The King died just before midnight. The next day, Stanley Baldwin, the Prime Minister, broadcast a tribute which included a different version of the deathbed words: 'There is one thing I can tell you without any impropriety, for though much, and most indeed, of what passes near the end is sacred ... I think I may tell you this. The King was having brief intervals of consciousness, and each time he became conscious it was some kind enquiry or kind observation of someone, some words of gratitude for kindness shown. But he did say to his Secretary [Lord Wigram] when he sent for him, "How is the Empire?" – an unusual phrase in that form. And the Secretary said: "All is well, sir, with the Empire," and the King gave him a smile and relapsed once more into unconsciousness.'

Other accounts make it clear that the wonderfully imperial inquiry arose *before* the Privy Council meeting. One of them suggests that only the word 'Empire' was audible and the rest merely assumed by the King's Secretary. Lord Dawson, the King's physician, reported in his diary yet another version of the last words: 'God damn you.' Could this possibly relate to Margot Asquith's celebrated dictum? (42:1). See also DAWSON 163:3.

GEORGE VI British King (1895–1952)

1 Abroad is bloody.

Quoted in W.H. Auden, *A Certain World* (1970). Compare MITFORD 324:4.

See also HASKINS 229:7; LINCOLN 288:3.

Ira GERSHWIN American lyricist (1896–1983)

2 Someone To Watch Over Me.

Title of song, *Oh! Kay* (1926). Music by George Gershwin, as in all the following. Hence, *Someone To Watch Over Me*, title of film (US 1987) about a bodyguard who falls for the woman he is minding.

3 Nice Work, If You Can Get It.

Title of song, *A Damsel in Distress* (1937). Perhaps a phrase taken from the Depression years – and the origin of the later admiring comment said enviously when one comes across something attractive that one would like to get one's hands on. Ira Gershwin in *Lyrics on Several Occasions* (1959) says he thought he had obtained the phrase from a cartoon by the *Punch* cartoonist George Belcher that had been *rejected* for publication. It showed two London charwomen discussing the daughter of a third. 'She's become an 'ore,' says the first. 'Nice work, if you can get it,' says the second.

4 I was a stranger in the city ...
But as I walked through the foggy streets alone,
It turned out to be the luckiest day I've known.

A foggy day in London Town
Had me low and had me down.
I viewed the morning with alarm.
The British Museum had lost its charm.
How long, I wondered, could this thing last?

But the age of miracles hadn't passed,
For, suddenly, I saw you there –
And through foggy London Town
The sun was shining ev'rywhere.

Song, 'A Foggy Day (in London Town)', in the same film. It was sung by Fred Astaire as 'Jerry Halliday', an American in London. A coincidence: in the dancer Isadora Duncan's *My Life*, Chap. 7 (1928), she describes how, in her earlier years, 'We spent the entire month of August between the Kensington Museum and the British Museum Library.' Then, when autumn comes: 'We had our first taste of London fog, and a régime of penny soups had perhaps rendered us anaemic. Even the British Museum had lost its charm ...' If Ira Gershwin had consciously taken this line from Isadora, I am sure he would have mentioned it in *Lyrics On Several Occasions* (1959), in which he describes the genesis of almost all his song lyrics. Later, David Lodge had to call his novel *The British Museum Is Falling Down* (1965) because he could not get permission to call it *The British Museum Had Lost Its Charm*.

5 They all laughed at Christopher Columbus
When he said the world was round;
They all laughed when Edison recorded sound.

Song, 'They All Laughed', in the same film. Said by Ira to have been inspired by the advertisement slogan 'They Laughed When I Sat Down At the Piano, But When I Started to Play ...' – used for the US School of Music piano tutor (from 1925).

Edward GIBBON English historian (1737–94)

6 Such was the public consternation when the barbarians were hourly expected at the gates of Rome.

Nowadays, the phrase 'barbarians at the gates' is commonly used to describe a situation when the end of civilization is alleged to be at hand. In 1990 it was used as the title of a book by Bryan Burrough about goings-on in Wall Street (subtitled 'The Fall of RJR Nabisco'), suggesting that unregulated behaviour had broken out. It is just one of those ideas that seems always to have been there, but there is a good example (as above) in Bk 1 of Gibbon's *Decline and Fall of the Roman Empire* (1776–88). From *The Sunday Times* (19 June 1988): 'The ragbag, pseudo-scholarship on display here suggests that the barbarians are not at the gate, they are sitting in the professors' chairs.' At the time of the Suez crisis, Harold Macmillan 'saw – in one of his favourite images – the Russians moving in from the east as the barbarians at the gates of Constantinople' – Anthony Sampson, *Macmillan*, Chap. 7 (1967).

1 After a powerful struggle, I yielded to my fate. I sighed as a lover, I obeyed as a son.

From *Memoirs of My Life and Writings*, Chap. 4, note (1796). As a young man, Gibbon fell for Mlle Suzanne Curchod (later the wife of Jacques Necker, the French statesman) at Lausanne, Switzerland, in 1757. But he did not get married to her because of his father's objections. Possible sources for Gibbon's phrase have been found in Corneille's *Polyeucte*, 'J'en aurais soupiré, mais j'aurai obéi', and, less plausibly, in Dryden's *Aureng-Zebe*, 'I to a Son's and Lover's praise aspire' – source: *Notes and Queries*, Vol. 234.

Stella GIBBONS English novelist (1902–89)

2 Something nasty in the woodshed.

Cold Comfort Farm (1933), *passim*. Hence, the phrase for any unnamed unpleasantness. In the novel, the phrase is used to refer to a traumatic experience in someone's background, e.g., from Chap. 10: 'When you were very small ... you had seen something nasty in the woodshed.' Hence, from Beryl Bainbridge's novel *Another Part of the Wood* (1968): 'They had all, Joseph, brother Trevor, the younger sister ... come across something nasty in the woodshed, mother or father or both, having it off with someone else.' Kyril Bonfiglioli entitled a novel *Something Nasty in the Woodshed* (1976).

3 The life of the journalist is poor, nasty, brutish and short. So is his style.

In the same novel. Compare HOBBES 241:2.

4 What a pleasant life might be had in this world by a handsome, sensible old lady of good fortune, blessed with a sound constitution and a firm will.

In Malcolm Bradbury's script for the TV film of *Cold Comfort Farm* (1995), Flora Poste advises aunt Ada Doom in these terms. Mr Mybug attributes the remark to Jane Austen – but in Gibbons's original (Chap. 22), it is not ascribed to her, though mention is made of various Austen works in the course of the book. A possible source is in *Emma*, Chap. 10: 'A single woman of good fortune is always respectable, and may be as sensible and pleasant as anybody else!'

Fred GILBERT British composer and singer (1849–1903)

5 As I walk along the Bois de Boulogne with an independent air.

Song, 'The Man Who Broke the Bank in Monte Carlo' (published 1900 – though first performed by Charles Coborn in 1891). Hence, *With an Independent Air*, title of the autobiography (1977) of Howard Thomas, the British broadcasting executive and early participant in Independent Television.

(Sir) W.S. GILBERT English writer and lyricist (1836–1911)

6 The other night, from cares exempt,
I slept – and what d'you think I dreamt?
I dreamt that somehow I had come
To dwell in Topsy-Turveydom –

Where vice is virtue – virtue, vice:
Where nice is nasty – nasty, nice:
Where right is wrong and wrong is right –
Where white is black and black is white.

'My Dream' (first published 1870), later in *The Bab Ballads*. Hence, title of the film *Topsy-Turvy* (US/UK 1999), Mike Leigh's take on the tensions in the great creative partnership of Gilbert and Sullivan, particularly during the writing and production of *The Mikado* (1885). 'Topsy-turvy' or 'topsy turvey' is a very old coinage for 'upside down' – *OED2* has it by the 16th century and is unable to explain the etymology of the word. Although it only occurs once in the G&S operas, it is certainly a very Gilbertian word, and can be found several times in his *Bab Ballads*. The reason for bestowing the title on the film would appear to have something to do with an (actual?) incident when *The Times* dubbed Gilbert, 'The King of Topsy-Turvydom'. It has proved impossible to locate this reference, if indeed it existed. Notoriously touchy on all subjects, WSG apparently took this as an insult. He wished to be taken *seriously* as a comic writer.

7 She may very well pass for forty-three
In the dusk with a light behind her!

Trial by Jury (1875). Music by Sir Arthur Sullivan, as for all the following. Ian Bradley writes in *The Annotated Gilbert and Sullivan*, Vol. 2 (1984): 'Gilbert had a thing about women in their forties. Poor Ruth in *The Pirates of Penzance* is mocked by Frederic for being forty-seven ... while Marco is warned by Gianetta in *The Gondoliers* not to address any lady less than forty-five.'

8 I pray you, pardon me, ex-Pirate King,
Peers will be peers, and youth must have its fling.

The Pirates of Penzance, Act 2 (1879). The proverb 'Youth must have its fling', meaning 'let the young enjoy themselves while they can', also appears in Gilbert's lyrics for *The Mikado* (1885): 'But youth, of course, must have its fling.' Gilbert greatly enjoyed proverbs and, indeed, wrote two songs completely made up of them. In this instance, he appears to have created a more memorable version of the older proverbs 'Youth will have his course' (known from the 16th century) and 'Youth will be served' (though this latter did not appear until the early 19th century). In *The Water Babies* (1863), Charles Kingsley has:

When all the world is young lad
And all the trees are green:
... Young blood must have its course, lad
And every dog his day.

John Ray's *Compleat Collection of English Proverbs* (1670) has 'Youth will have its swing' (as a version of 'youth will have its course'), which means much the same as 'fling'.

1 A wandering minstrel I –
A thing of shreds and patches.
Of ballads, songs and snatches,
And dreamy lullaby!

The Mikado, Act 1 (1885). Presumably an allusion to what Hamlet says of Claudius: 'A king of shreds and patches' (in comparison to Gertrude's first husband, his father, a complete husband), in Shakespeare, *Hamlet*, III.iv.103 (1600–1).

2 To sit in solemn silence in a dull, dark, dock,
In a pestilential prison, with a life-long lock,
Awaiting the sensation of a short, sharp, shock,
From a cheap and chippy chopper on a big
    black block.

In the same Act. Other use: in a speech at the Conservative Party Conference (10 October 1979), William Whitelaw, as Home Secretary, outlined a new method of hard treatment for young offenders. They were to be given 'a short, sharp shock'. This expression had apparently been used by other Home Secretaries before him, however. Hence, *A Short Sharp Shock*, title of a play (1980) by Howard Brenton and Tony Howard – originally called *Ditch the Bitch* and referring to Margaret Thatcher.

In fact, it was a phrase Thatcher had herself used long before. In a speech to the Standing Committee in support of an amendment to restore flogging (14 February 1961), she had said of R.A. Butler's Criminal Justice Bill: 'If, instead of giving him [an offender] a short, sharp lesson, we encourage in him a feeling of self-justification, we may completely blot out all feeling of guilt or shame ... The method of a short, sharp shock ... no longer seems to be the aim of detention centres.'

3 Are you old enough to marry, do you think?
Won't you wait till you are eighty in the shade?

In the same operetta, Act 2. Ko-Ko asks Katisha. There is also a song 'Charming Weather' in Lionel Monckton's *The Arcadians* (1908) with the lines, 'Very, very warm for May / Eighty in the shade they say, / Just fancy!' 'Eighty in the shade' is otherwise no more than a catchphrase used to express extreme temperature.

4 When I am lying awake at night, and the pale moonlight streams through the latticed casement, strange fancies crowd upon my poor mad brain, and I sometimes think that if we could hit upon some word for you to use whenever I am about to relapse – some word that teems with hidden meaning – like 'Basingstoke' – it might recall me to my saner self.

So says the character Mad Margaret in *Ruddigore* (1887). The mention of the place still raises a laugh, being one of those English names which, from sound alone, is irresistibly funny. Others would include Chipping Sodbury, Godalming, Scunthorpe, Wigan and Surbiton. More recently Neasden has joined the select band. However, it has been suggested that the once-modest Hampshire town had another claim upon the laughter of the original *Ruddigore* audience. Possibly the Conservative Party had recently held its annual conference there? Ian Bradley in his *Annotated Gilbert and Sullivan: 2* (1984) makes no mention of this theory and dismisses a suggestion that it was because Basingstoke had a well-known mental hospital, on the grounds that this had not been built in 1887. He relays another theory that Gilbert's father had featured the town in his novel *The Doctor of Beauvoir*, and that his father and sister lived in Salisbury, which would have necessitated his passing through Basingstoke when paying visits.

A magazine called *Figaro* reporting on rehearsals for *Ruddigore* in December 1886 made mention of a character called Mad Margaret 'with that blessed word Barnstaple' – which suggests that Basingstoke was not Gilbert's first choice.

Basingstoke had already rated a mention in Shakespeare – *Henry IV, Part 2*, II.i.169 (1597), but with rather less comic result.

5 In a contemplative fashion,
And a tranquil frame of mind,
Free from every kind of passion,
Some solution let us find.
Let us grasp the situation,
Solve the complicated plot –
Quiet, calm deliberation
Disentangles every knot.

The Gondoliers, Act 2 (1889). When Harold Macmillan was Prime Minister (1957–63) he wrote this out in longhand as a motto for his Private Office and the Cabinet Room when at 10 Downing Street, as reported in Anthony Sampson, *Macmillan*, Chap. 8 (1967).

1 Funny without being vulgar.

A Quaker singer, David Bispham, noted in his *Recollections* (1920) that he had heard Gilbert say something like this to Sir Henry Beerbohm Tree about his Hamlet. On the stage of the Haymarket Theatre, London, after the first performance, Gilbert said: 'My dear fellow, I never saw anything so funny in my life, and yet it was not in the least vulgar.'

At the time, the line quickly went round in its abbreviated form, and apparently Tree put up a brave show of not being offended. He wrote to Gilbert on 25 March 1893: 'By the bye, my wife told me that you were under the impression that I might have been offended at some witticism of yours about my Hamlet. Let me assure you it was not so. On the contrary, it was I believe *I* who circulated the story. There could be no harm, as I knew you had not seen me act the part, and moreover, while I am a great admirer of your wit, I have also too high an opinion of my work to be hurt by it.'

Hesketh Pearson in his 1956 biography of Tree seems to think this letter shows the actor claiming not only to have circulated the story against himself but to have *invented* it. On the other hand, Pearson in his biography of Gilbert and Sullivan does report that Bernard Shaw told him that Gilbert complained shortly before his death (1911) of the way ill-natured witticisms had been fathered on him and instanced the description of Tree. There seems little doubt, though, that he did say it.

Shaw himself had used the phrase in a review of a pantomime in *London Music* on 23 January 1897: 'Pray understand that I do not want the pantomime artists to be "funny without being vulgar". That is the mere snobbery of criticism. Every comedian should have vulgarity at his fingers' ends.'

J.B. Booth in *Old Pink 'Un Days* (1924) recalled an exchange in a London theatre after Pavlova's successes when a large lady from Oldham or Wigan was attempting to pass herself off as a Russian dancer. 'What do you think of her?' asked one. Came the reply, 'Funny without being Volga.'

Eric GILL English sculptor, engraver and typographer (1882–1940)

2 *Trousers and the Most Precious Ornament.*

Title of book (1937). According to Fiona McCarthy, *Eric Gill* (1989), this book is: 'A grand defence of male supremacy, a plea for the reconsideration of the penis, tucked away into men's trousers, "all sideways, dishonoured, neglected, ridiculed and ridiculous – no longer the virile member". The dishonoured penis was a terrible indictment of the world's lost potency, the onset of commercialization and destructiveness. In their craziness and funniness Gill's penis-power writings remind one of the cunt-power movement of the 1970s. This is Eric Gill in pursuit of Germaine Greer.'

3 When will revolutionary leaders realize that 'culture' is dope, a worse dope than religion; for even if it were true that religion is the opiate of the people, it is worse to poison yourself than to be poisoned, and suicide is more dishonourable than murder. To hell with culture, culture as a thing added like a sauce to otherwise unpalatable stale fish!

Quoted in Herbert Read, *To Hell With Culture* (1941) – hence its title.

W.E. GLADSTONE British Liberal Prime Minister (1809–98)

4 The first essential for a Prime Minister is to be a good butcher.

In *Great Contemporaries* (1937), Winston Churchill states that H.H. Asquith quoted Gladstone as saying this when offering Churchill a Cabinet post in 1908. Asquith added: 'There are several who must be pole-axed now.' It has also been attributed to Lord Salisbury – the particular circumstance was that a minister had collapsed and died after Salisbury dismissed him. The saying may have re-entered political parlance when it was quoted by Richard Nixon when interviewed (1977) by David Frost about Watergate. He was seeking to explain his reluctance to sack his aides Ehrlichman and Haldeman: 'I suppose you could sum it all up the way one of your British Prime Ministers summed it up, Gladstone, when he said that the first requirement for a Prime Minister is to be a good butcher ... I will have to admit I was not a good butcher.' Nixon also wrote in *Leaders* (1982): 'If [a leader] cannot be a good butcher himself, he needs someone who can be ... In my own administration Bob Haldeman got a reputation for ruthlessness. One reason was that he performed for me a lot of the butcher's tasks that I could not bring myself to perform directly.'

5 If you add the candle ends together you get a whole candle.

Quoted by John Major, but unsourced. A heavily ironical piece from *The Guardian* (4 December 1992): 'There were scenes of wild enthusiasm, bordering on delirium, in the streets of London yesterday as [Prime Minister] John Major spoke out once more – with all the passion at his command – on the topic of the Citizen's Charter. Oh, yes. It has been criticized for dealing with a lot of little things. But, said Mr Major, quoting the less colourful Mr Gladstone, "... if you add the candle ends together you get a whole candle".'

'Saving candle ends' has long been a proverbial expression for making petty economies. It is possible to melt the stubs of candles down and make new candles from the wax. *OED2* has a citation from 1668, referring to filching candle ends and laying them away, and another from 1732: 'When Hopkins dies, a thousand lights attend / Who living, sav'd a candle's end' – Alexander Pope, *Moral Essays – Epistle III to Allen Lord Bathhurst* (1732).

In the days when candles were a major expense in grand houses, the candle ends were a perquisite of certain servants, to be re-used or sold. So Gladstone was perhaps defending himself from accusations of 'saving candle ends' by arguing that 'many a mickle maks a muckle'.

Ellen GLASGOW American novelist (1874–1945)

1 *In This Our Life.*

Title of novel (1941; filmed US 1942) about a neurotic girl who, according to one plot summary, 'steals her sister's husband, leaves him in the lurch, dominates her hapless family and is killed while on the run from the police'. Glasgow's novel gives no clue as to the relevance of the title, and does not even have a quotation as an epigraph, but the 'this our life' formula goes back to the 16th century at least. Within one scene, Shakespeare's *As You Like It*, II.i, has 'And this our life' and 'Yea, and of this our life'. Even earlier, the Preface to Thomas Cranmer's Book of Common Prayer (1549) employs the phrase 'in this our time'. So perhaps it was from some religious source? The Revd Francis Kilvert, the diarist, used the expression 'in that her young life' on 26 March 1872. The exact phrase is in MEREDITH 320:8. It also occurs earlier in Thomas Carlyle's *Sartor Resartus* (1831): 'To me, in this our life ... which is an internecine warfare with the Time-spirit, other warfare seems questionable.' And exactly also in Thomas Heywood's poem *The Hierarchy of the Blessed Angels* (1635). All this would seem to indicate that it was just an old phrase rather than a quotation when used as the title of Glasgow's novel.

William Henry, 1st Duke of GLOUCESTER English Duke (1743–1805)

2 Another damned, thick, square book! Always scribble, scribble, scribble! Eh! Mr Gibbon?

Quoted in Henry Best, *Personal and Literary Memorials* (1829). Also ascribed to King George III and to a Duke of Cumberland. The remark was addressed to Edward Gibbon, the historian (1737–94), whose *Decline and Fall of the Roman Empire* was published in many volumes (1776–88).

Jean-Luc GODARD French film director (1930–)

3 *La photographie, c'est la vérité. Le cinéma: la verité vingt-quatre fois par seconde* [Photography is truth. And cinema is truth twenty-four times a second].

In film, *Le Petit Soldat* (France 1960). The cinematographic version of 'the camera cannot lie'.

4 Movies should have a beginning, a middle and an end, but not necessarily in that order.

ODQ (1992) has this as being said to Georges Franju and quoted in *Time* Magazine (14 September 1981), but 'Every film should have a beginning, a middle and an end – but not necessarily in that order' was quoted in Len Deighton, *Close Up* (1972). Indeed, even earlier, as an exchange between Clouzot and Godard, it has been given as taking place at Cannes (May 1965).

A.D. GODLEY English classicist (1856–1925)

5 What is this that roareth thus?
Can it be a motor bus?

There are many versions of Godley's macaronic that beginneth thus. *ODQ* (1992), which prints only part of it, gives the source as a letter Godley sent to C.R.L. Fletcher on 10 January 1914, reprinted in *Reliquiae* (1926). The magazine *Oxford Today* (Michaelmas 1992) took the trouble to find a complete, definitive version:

> What is this that roareth thus?
> Can it be a Motor Bus?
> Yes, the smell and hideous hum
> Indicat Motorem Bum!
> Implet in the Corn and High
> Terror me Motoris Bi:
> Bo Motori clamitabo
> Ne Motore caedar a Bo –
> Dative be or Ablative
> So thou only let us live:
> Whither shall thy victims flee?
> Spare us, spare us, Motor Be!
> Thus I sang; and still anigh
> Came in hordes Motores Bi,
> Et complebat omne forum
> Copia Motorum Borum.
> How shall wretches live like us
> Cincti Bis Motoribus?
> Domine, defende nos
> Contra hos Motores Bos!

The references to the Corn and High locate the poet in Oxford, where he taught most of his life. Motor buses were first introduced to Oxford by William Morris and Frank Gray only in 1912, so Godley would seem to have developed a rapid dislike of them.

Joseph GOEBBELS German Nazi leader (1897–1945)

1 We can do without butter, but, despite all our love of peace, not without arms. One cannot shoot with butter, but with guns.

From the translation of a speech given in Berlin (17 January 1936). When a nation is under pressure to choose between material comforts and some kind of war effort, the choice has to be made between 'guns *and* butter'. Some will urge 'guns *before* butter'. Later that same year, Hermann Goering said in a broadcast, 'Guns will make us powerful; butter will only make us fat', so he may also be credited with the 'guns or butter' slogan. But there is a third candidate. Airey Neave in his book *Nuremberg* (1978) stated of Rudolf Hess: 'It was he who urged the German people to make sacrifices and coined the phrase: "Guns before butter".'

Hermann GOERING German Nazi leader (1893–1946)

2 When I hear the word Culture, I reach for my pistol.

Although Goering is often linked with this remark, it comes, in fact, from a play by an unsuccessful Nazi playwright, Hanns Johst (1890–1978), who was president of the Reich Chamber of Literature, a group of authors, translators and publishers that excluded those who refused to toe the party line. In 1933 he wrote *Schlageter*, a play about a martyr of the French occupation of the Ruhr after the First World War. A storm trooper's line '*Wenn ich Kultur hore ... entsichere ich meinen Browning*' is more accurately translated as 'When I hear the word "culture", I release the safety catch of [or 'I cock'] 'my Browning [an automatic pistol].'

Johann Wolfgang von GOETHE German poet, novelist and playwright (1749–1832)

3 Distrust all those in whom the urge to punish is strong.

Attributed remark. Sir Ludovic Kennedy claimed on BBC Radio *Quote ... Unquote* (in 1983) that he had read this in Goethe's *Conversations With Eckermann* (1837, translated 1839). Johann Peter Eckermann did, of course, publish his long conversations and correspondence with Goethe; indeed, he is sometimes likened to Johnson's Boswell. But this remark has not been found in his book. On the contrary, among the conversations mostly on literary and artistic

matters, is this on 19 February 1831: 'I am always for rigid adherence to a law, especially at a time like ours, when out of weakness and excessive liberality one is always conceding too much.' This might be thought to conflict with the supposed 'punishment' pronouncement.

On the other hand, there is this, not by Goethe but by Nietzsche: verse 17 in the 'Tarantula' chapter of *Also Sprach Zarathustra* (1883–92): '*Also aber rathe ich euch, meine Freunde: misstraut Allen, in welchen der Trieb, zu strafen, mächtig ist! / Das ist Volk schlechter Art und Abkunft; aus ihren Gesichtern blickt der Henker und der Spürhund.*' Two English translations of the verse: 'Mistrust everyone in whom the impulse to punish is strong!'; 'Distrust all in whom the impulse to punish is powerful!' The second of these, ascribed to Nietzsche, is included in *Quotations for Our Time*, ed. Laurence J. Peter (1977).

Oliver GOLDSMITH Irish-born playwright and writer (1730–74)

4 *The Citizen of the World.*

Title of a collection of letters by Goldsmith purporting to be those of Lien Chi Altangi, a philosophic Chinaman living in London, commenting on English life and characters. First published as 'Chinese Letters' in the *Public Ledger* (1760–1), and then again under the above title in 1762. See also BACON 47:6.

5 But soon a wonder came to light
That show'd the rogues they lied;
The man recover'd of the bite,
The dog it was that died.

'Elegy on the Death of a Mad Dog' (1766). Hence, *The Dog It Was That Died*, title of a radio play (1983) by Tom Stoppard.

6 Sweet Auburn, loveliest village of the plain,
Where health and plenty cheered the labouring
    swain ...
Ill fares the land, to hast'ning ills a prey,
Where wealth accumulates, and men decay ...
A bold peasantry, their country's pride,
When once destroy'd, can never be supplied.

The Deserted Village (1770). Goldsmith's view of the depopulation of villages caused by the enclosure acts of the 18th century and the drift to the cities. In many cases, the 'bold peasantry' had been forced into emigration. Later, a film by Bill Bryden about people leaving the island of St Kilda, off the west coast of Scotland, was given the title *Ill Fares the Land* (1982).

1 At church, with meek and unaffected grace,
His looks adorn'd the venerable place;
Truth from his lips prevailed with double sway,
And fools, who came to scoff, remained to pray.

In the same poem. Origin of the expression 'fools who come to scoff and remain to pray', meaning people who undergo some kind of conversion or change of heart. Compare from Clive James, *The Crystal Bucket* (1981): 'I came to mock *Dallas* but stayed to pray.'

2 There is some fun going forward.

She Stoops to Conquer, Act 1, Sc. 1 (1773). Tony Lumpkin speaking. Hence, *There Is Some Fun Going Forward*, the somewhat unexpected title of a compilation album (material recorded 1969–72) from Dandelion Records, the label co-established by John Peel, the English disc jockey.

3 The very pink of perfection.

In the same scene. Miss Neville speaking. The first use of this phrase. Mrs Malaprop's abuse of the 'the very pinnacle of politeness', three years later, may be related. See SHERIDAN 430:1.

4 As for murmurs, mother, we grumble a little now and then, to be sure. But there's no love lost between us.

In the same play, Act 4, Sc. 1. Tony Lumpkin says this to his mother, Mrs Hardcastle. The editor of the New Mermaids edition (1979) states that Goldsmith coined the phrase 'No love lost', but this is true neither of the literal sense nor of the current ironic, opposite one. *OED2* finds uses of the phrase in both senses over a century before Goldsmith's play.

See also DICKENS 169:3; ELIOT 186:9.

Barry M. GOLDWATER American Republican politician
(1909–98)

5 I would remind you that extremism in the defence of liberty is no vice. And let me remind you also that moderation in the pursuit of justice is no virtue.

Accepting his party's nomination for the presidency, San Francisco Convention (16 July 1964). Goldwater's extremist tag-line did him no good in the subsequent election. As Johnson's speech would have been before the actual election (presidential elections are in November), perhaps recast thus: Lyndon Johnson, who was running for the Democrats, rejoined: 'Extremism in pursuit of the Presidency is an unpardonable vice. Moderation in the affairs

of the nation is the highest virtue' – speech, New York (31 October 1964). Johnson won the election with a landslide. Perhaps Goldwater would have done better to quote Thomas Paine's *The Rights of Man* (1792) directly: 'A thing moderately good is not so good as it ought to be. Moderation in temper is always a virtue; but moderation in principle is always a vice.' To give him his due, Goldwater disclaimed any originality, saying the idea could be found in Cicero and in Greek authors.

Sam GOLDWYN Polish-born American film producer
(1882–1974)

6 An oral [*or verbal*] contract isn't worth the paper it's written on.

Samuel Goldwyn Jr, interviewed in *TV Times* (13 November 1982), commented on the 'twenty-eight' genuine sayings attributed to his father and included this as one. Carol Easton in *The Search for Sam Goldwyn* (1976) claims that what he actually said about fellow mogul Joseph L. Mankiewicz was: 'His verbal contract is worth more than the paper it's written on.' The original attribution was by Alva Johnston in *The Great Goldwyn* (1937) – who also cites: 'That's the way with these directors, they're always biting the hand that lays the golden egg.'

7 In two words – impossible!

Sam Goldwyn Jr has expressed doubts as to the authenticity of this one and, according to Alva Johnston, *The Great Goldwyn* (1937), the joke appeared in a humour magazine late in 1925, and was subsequently imposed upon Goldwyn. *Mencken* (1942) has: 'I can answer in two words – im possible', and ascribes it to 'an American movie magnate, 1930'. Curiously, however, this is to be found in *Punch* (10 June 1931) – caption to a cartoon by George Belcher: 'Harassed Film-Producer. "This business can be summed up in two words: IM-POSSIBLE."'

8 You've still only got the mucus of a good idea.

Attributed by Terry Wogan on BBC Radio, *Quote ... Unquote* (29 May 1980), but probably another invention. In a P.G. Wodehouse story set in Hollywood, 'The Castaways' (1933), Mr Schnellenhamer, the film mogul, says of a script he has bought, 'It has the mucus of a good story. See what you can do with it.'

9 Include me out.

This apparently arose when Goldwyn and Jack L. Warner were in disagreement over a labour dispute. Busby Berkeley, who had made his first musical for Goldwyn, was discovered moonlighting for Warner Brothers. Goldwyn said to

Warner: 'How can we sit together and deal with this industry if you're going to do things like this to me? If this is the way you do it, gentlemen, include me out!'

Scott Berg, working on the official biography, told *The Sunday Times* (3 May 1981) that he claimed the ability to tell which Goldwynisms are genuine and suggested this one *might* be, as Goldwyn himself appeared to acknowledge when speaking at Balliol College, Oxford, on 1 March 1945: 'For years I have been known for saying "Include me out" but today I am giving it up for ever.' On the other hand, Boller & George, *They Never Said It* (1989), report Goldwyn as having denied saying it, claiming rather to have said to members of the Motion Picture Producers and Distributors of America: 'Gentlemen, I'm withdrawing from the association.'

Adam Lindsay GORDON Australian poet (1833–70)

1 I've had my share of pastime, and I've done my
      share of toil,
And life is short.

'The Sick Stockrider' (written 1869). The quotation is sometimes completed with: '... And none will weep when I go forth, / Or smile when I return.' But this is, in fact, one line and should read: 'And none will grieve when I go forth, or smile when I return.' This is from 'Virginia', one of Lord Macaulay's *Lays of Ancient Rome* (1842).

2 Life is mostly froth and bubble,
Two things stand like stone,
Kindness in another's trouble,
Courage in your own.

Ye Wearie Wayfarer, 'Fytte 8' (1866), also known as 'A Metaphysical Poem'. Often loosely quoted by Diana, Princess of Wales – which gave rise to this parody by Kingsley Amis: 'Life is mainly toil and labour. / Two things see you through: / Chortling when it hits your neighbour / Whingeing when it's you' – in *The Observer* (14 November 1999).

Elizabeth GOUDGE English novelist (1900–84)

3 *Green Dolphin Street.*

Title of her novel *Green Dolphin Country* (1944) when it was published in the US (1945). It was then filmed under this title (US 1947). The film included a specially written song 'On Green Dolphin Street', with a rather brief lyric by Ned Washington and music by Bronislaw Kaper. The tune became famous, particularly in the Miles Davis rendition. Hence, *On Green Dolphin Street*, the title of a novel (2001) by Sebastian Faulks. This is the tale of a relationship in early 1960s Washington DC. The title is taken from the recording by Miles Davis, which is playing when the adulterous couple kiss. Another complication: *The Elizabeth Goudge Reader* (New York 1946) was re-titled *At the Sign of the Dolphin: an Elizabeth Goudge Anthology* when it was published in the UK (1947).

Baltasar GRACIAN Spanish philosopher (1601–58)

4 Don't give explanations to those who haven't asked for them. And although they are asked for, it is folly to give them too eagerly. To offer excuses before they are called for is to incriminate yourself, and to bleed yourself when you are healthy is to attract malady and malice. Excusing yourself beforehand awakens suspicions that were fast asleep. The prudent person should never blink before the suspicions of others: that would be looking for offence. He should try to dissimulate with a firm, righteous manner.

'Manual of the Art of Discretion', Para. 246 (1646). An early formulation of the 'never complain, never explain' philosophy – see DISRAELI 174:5. 'Never complain' might just be said to be covered by this in para. 138: 'Leave things alone ... It takes little to muddy a stream. You can't make it grow clear by trying to, only by leaving it alone. There is no better remedy for disorder than leaving it alone to correct itself.'

David GRAHAM English broadcaster (1911–99)

5 That this House will in no circumstances fight for its King and Country.

Hitler came to power in January 1933. On 9 February, the Oxford Union Debating Society carried this motion by 275 votes to 153. Graham was the Librarian that term and worded the motion and later took up a career in the BBC External Services. It has been suggested that this pacifist rather than disloyal motion, although adopted by an unrepresentative group of young people, encouraged Hitler to believe that his programme of conquests would go unchallenged by the British. There appears to be no evidence that Hitler ever referred to the Oxford Union debate, though Goebbels and his propaganda ministry certainly knew of it. As a result, Churchill wrote in *The Second World War*, Vol. 1 (1948): 'In Germany, in Russia, in Italy, in Japan, the idea of a decadent, degenerate Britain took deep root and swayed many calculations.' Erich von Richthofen confirmed this view in *The Daily Telegraph* (4 May 1965): 'I am an ex-officer of the old Wehrmacht and served on what you would call the German General Staff at the time of the Oxford resolution. I can assure you, from personal knowledge, that no other factor influenced Hitler more and decided him on his course than that "refusal to fight for King and Country", coming from what was assumed to be the intellectual élite of your country.'

Sir John Colville, Churchill's Private Secretary during the war, recalled in a letter to *The Times* (12 February 1983): 'At Tübingen University in July 1933, I was contemptuously informed by a group of Nazi students that my contemporaries and I would never fight; and the Oxford debate was quoted in evidence.'

On the other hand, Sir Hugh Greene, Berlin correspondent of *The Daily Telegraph* (1934–9) commented in 1983: 'Obviously one did not have the opportunity of discussing the matter with Hitler personally, but one did talk from time to time with high Nazi officials and members of the German armed forces. I am sure that the subject was never mentioned. Why should Hitler concern himself with Oxford undergraduates when he could base his thinking on the attitude of British ministers?' Mussolini is said, however, to have referred to the debate several times.

Harry GRAHAM British writer and journalist (1874–1936)

1 The days passed slowly, one by one;
I fed the ducks, reproved my wife,
Played Handel's Largo on the fife,
Or gave the dog a run.

Poem, 'Creature Comforts', following the opening line, which is: 'For years I led a dreary life!' It is not often that I find an answer without being prompted to do so by a query but such was the case when I read Miles Kington's introduction to *When Grandmama Fell Off the Boat* (1986), a collection of Grahams 'Ruthless Rhymes' and other verse. Miles recounts how a friend of his once wrote to Dame Agatha Christie to inquire about four lines of poetry quoted by one of her characters. Dame Agatha wrote back to say she could not remember the author's name. But the Harry Graham book showed that the lines were his.

Philip L. GRAHAM American newspaper publisher (1915–63)

2 News [or journalism] is the first [rough] draft of history.

From *The Washington Post* (24 November 1985): 'The summit coverage was textbook stuff of the "journalism-as-first-draft-of-history" variety'; (28 February 1988): 'A daily newspaper such as the *Post* is, as someone once put it, the first rough draft of history'; (10 July 1988): 'The newspaper, *Post* executives have often reminded us, is merely a "first rough draft of history".' From the editor of Britain's ITN in *The Times* (21 December 1990): 'Journalism is the

first draft of history.' From *The Times* (27 April 1991): 'When foreign governments want to know what matters are weighing on the minds of the US establishment, they have always turned to the *New York Times*, the sober "grey lady" which has been recording America's first draft of history for the past 140 years.' From *The Washington Post* (29 September 1991): 'Daily journalism is "the first rough draft of history", in the phrase of former *Washington Post* publisher, Philip Graham.'

The phrase has also been attributed to Ben Bradlee (1921–), a noted editor of *The Washington Post*. Perhaps the real originator was Douglas Cater (1923–), American writer and assistant to President Lyndon B. Johnson, who wrote in *The Fourth Branch of Government* (1959): 'The reporter [is] one who each twenty-four hours dictates a first draft of history.'

Kenneth GRAHAME Scottish-born writer (1859–1932)

3 The Piper at the Gates of Dawn.

The Wind in the Willows, Chap. 7 (1908). Heading to chapter. Grahame describes a lyrical, not to say mystical, experience that Mole and Ratty have when they hear the god Pan piping at dawn. Hence, the title of the first album recorded by Pink Floyd in 1967.

4 'Like Summer Tempests came his Tears'.

In the same novel, heading to Chap. 11. Grahame puts '*his* Tears' because it refers to Toad, but in the original, Tennyson's *The Princess* (1847), where it is in a song at the beginning of Canto VI, the subject is *female*. Also, the 'tempest' is singular and the verse reads: 'Rose a nurse of ninety years, / Set his child upon her knee – / Like summer tempest came her tears – / "Sweet my child, I live for thee."'

Cary GRANT English-born film actor (1904–86)

5 Judy ... Judy ... Judy!

Impersonators always put this line in Grant's mouth – as alluded to by CAGNEY 118:2 – but Grant always denied that he had ever said it and had a check made of all his films. According to Richard Keyes, *Nice Guys Finish Seventh* (1992), Grant once said: 'I vaguely recall that at a party someone introduced Judy [Garland] by saying, "Judy, Judy, Judy," and it caught on, attributed to me.'

There may be another explanation. Impersonators usually seek a key phrase which, through simple repetition, readily gives them the subject's voice. It is possible that one of these impersonators found that saying 'Judy' helped summon up Grant's distinctive tones, and it went on from there. Besides, many an impersonator, rather than aping his subject, simply impersonates fellow impersonators.

John Woodcock GRAVES British huntsman and songwriter (1795–1886)

1 D'ye ken John Peel with his coat so grey,
D'ye ken John Peel at the break o' day,
D'ye ken John Peel when he's far, far away
With his hounds and his horn in the morning.

Song, 'John Peel' (1820). Peel was an actual huntsman in Cumbria, known to Graves, and his coat was very definitely grey (the colour 'Skiddaw grey' was long favoured by Lakeland huntsmen). So, it is wrong to sing 'coat so *gay*', though presumably this usage came about because people would rather imagine the most famous huntsman of all wearing the more usual hunting pink.

2 Yes, I ken John Peel, and Ruby too,
Ranter and Ringwood, Bellman and True,
From a find to a check, from a check to a view,
From a view to a death in the morning.

In the same song. Hence, the title of Anthony Powell's 1933 novel *From a View to a Death*. Compare *A View to a Kill*, title of a James Bond film (UK 1985). The original title of the short story by Ian Fleming (published in 1960 in *For Your Eyes Only*) was '*From* a View To a Kill'.

In foxhunting terminology, a 'check' is a loss of scent, a 'view (halloo)' is the huntsman's shout when a fox breaks cover, and a 'kill' or a 'death' is self-explanatory. This verse from Graves's song also provided the title of a film (UK 1988) based on a novel by Desmond Lowden, *Bellman and True* (1975). Although Bellman and True are mentioned in the list of hounds, the book and film are about a bellman in the criminal sense: that is, a man who disables alarm systems so that robberies can take place.

Robert GRAVES English poet (1895–1985)

3 *Goodbye To All That.*

Title of autobiography (1929). Apparently, 'all that' meaning 'all that sort of thing' was in the language before it was popularized by Graves in the title of his farewell to participation in the First World War and to an unhappy period in his private life, but the cod volume of English history *1066 And All That* (1930) by Sellar and Yeatman further popularized it. In a Prologue to the 1957 edition of his book, Graves noted: 'The title became a catch-word, and my sole contribution to Bartlett's *Dictionary of Familiar Quotations*.'

4 Far away is close at hand
Close joined is far away,
Love shall come at your command
Yet will not stay.

'Song of Contrariety' (1923). Hence, in part, the graffito 'Far away is close at hand in images of elsewhere.' For a number of years in the 1970s, train passengers going in and out of Paddington Station in London were beguiled or puzzled by these words painted up at the side of the track. This elegant graffito became almost famous – not least when Michael Wharton, the 'Peter Simple' humorous columnist on *The Daily Telegraph*, discussed the work of the unknown artist as if he were an Old Master. On 22 June 1978 he wrote: 'Dr Anita Maclean-Gropius's monumental catalogue raisonné, "The Master of Paddington" (Viper and Bugloss, £65), published last year, dealt in detail with all the works confidently or tentatively attributed to the Master and his School. It was, of course, savaged in a long review by Dr J.S. Hate, Keeper of Graffiti at the Victoria and Albert Museum, in the *British Journal of Graffitology* ...' When Michael Wharton came to collect some of his 'Peter Simple' pieces in 1995, he called it *Far Away Is Close at Hand*.

I myself mentioned the graffito and Peter Simple's interest in it in my first collection *Graffiti Lives, OK* (1979), and eventually got round to photographing it in May 1981 just as builders were demolishing the wall upon which it was painted, to enable the redevelopment of land behind it. In 2004 I was more than intrigued to be contacted by Helen Issler who claimed (very convincingly) that the 'Master of Paddington' was, in fact, two people: her husband, Dave Hall, and his brother Geoff. They had painted it, she said, 'one Christmas Eve (no trains) in probably 1974 or thereabouts'. It was placed so that it was 'visible on the Oxford line' – pointedly so, as both Dave and Helen are Oxford graduates.

Helen confirmed the Graves allusion in the first six words but fascinatingly suggested that the last four came from something written by the poet Ruth Padel (who, as it happens, had been at Oxford with Helen and Dave). But what was it? I contacted Ruth Padel and asked for her assistance. At first she could only think that her very first publication was a pamphlet called *Alibi* (1985) – and 'alibi', of course, means 'elsewhere' in Latin.

But then the light dawned. Ruth remembered she had written an article entitled 'Imagery of the Elsewhere: Two Choral Odes of Euripides' in *Classical Quarterly* (December 1974). Dave Hall said, 'Yes, that was it. I don't think I ever read the *Classical Quarterly* article, but it was a great title.' As to what it means and as to why it struck a great chord with many people who viewed it, Ruth commented: 'Well, it is by a railway line, carrying people far away. And metaphor, according to Aristotle, means carrying across from one place to another. Those choral odes of Euripides were basically about going away.'

Thomas GRAY English poet (1716–71)

1 Alas, regardless of their doom,
The little victims play!
No sense have they of ills to come,
Nor care beyond to-day.

'Ode on a Distant Prospect of Eton College' (1747). From this title comes *A Distant Prospect* (1945), a volume of autobiography by Lord Berners (who had attended Eton).

2 Where ignorance is bliss,
'Tis folly to be wise.

In the same poem. Hence, the proverbial expression. There was a BBC radio show in the late 1940s with the title *Ignorance is Bliss*, and a film *Folly To Be Wise* (UK 1952).

3 The curfew tolls the knell of parting day,
The lowing herd wind slowly o'er the lea,
The ploughman homeward plods his weary way,
And leaves the world to darkness and to me.

Now fades the glimmering landscape on the sight,
And all the air a solemn stillness holds,
Save where the beetle wheels his droning flight,
And drowsy tinklings lull the distant folds.

'Elegy Written in a Country Churchyard' (1751). One of the most quoted poems in the English language, feeding numerous phrases into allusive speech. From P.G. Wodehouse, *Right Ho, Jeeves* (1934): '"But what can I say about the sunset?" asked Gussie. "Well, Jeeves got off a good one the other day. I met him airing the dog in the park one evening, and he said, 'Now fades the glimmering landscape on the sight, sir, and all the air a solemn stillness holds.' You might use that."'

4 Beneath those rugged elms, that yew-tree's shade,
Where heaves the turf in many a mouldering heap,
Each in his narrow cell for ever laid,
The rude forefathers of the hamlet sleep.

In the same poem. See also BISHOP 89:7.

5 Let not ambition mock their useful toil,
Their homely joys, and destiny obscure;
Nor grandeur hear with a disdainful smile,
The short and simple annals of the poor.

The boast of heraldry, the pomp of pow'r,
And all that beauty, all that wealth e'er gave,
Awaits alike th'inevitable hour,
The paths of glory lead but to the grave.

In the same poem. Hence, *Paths of Glory*, title of a novel (1935; film US 1957) by Humphrey Cobb. See also WASHINGTON 483:2.

6 Can honour's voice provoke the silent dust,
Or flatt'ry soothe the dull cold ear of death?

In the same poem. Hence, *Silent Dust*, title of a film (UK 1949) based on a play called *The Paragon*.

7 Full many a flower is born to blush unseen,
And waste its sweetness on the desert air.

In the same poem. Taken up by the poet Charles Churchill: 'Nor waste their sweetness in the desert air' appears in *Gotham* (1764).

8 Far from the madding crowd's ignoble strife,
Their sober wishes never learn'd to stray;
Along the cool sequestered vale of life
They kept the noiseless tenor of their way.

In the same poem. Hence, the title of Thomas Hardy's novel *Far From the Madding Crowd* (1874; film UK 1967). 'Madding' here means 'frenzied, mad' – not 'maddening'.

Horace GREELEY American editor and politician (1811–72)

9 Go West, young man!

At one time, it was held that the originator of the saying was John Babson Lane Soule, who first wrote it in the Terre Haute (Indiana) *Express* in 1851 when, indeed, the thing to do in the United States was to head westwards, where gold and much else lay promised. However, Horace Greeley repeated it in *his* newspaper, the *New York Tribune*, and, being rather more famous – a candidate for the Presidency and all – it stuck with him. The original sentence was, 'Go west, young man, and grow up with the country.' To 'go west' meaning 'die' is a completely separate coinage. It dates back to the 16th century and alludes to the setting of the sun.

However, Thomas D. Fuller, writing in *The Indiana Magazine of History*, Vol. 100, No. 3 (September 2004) stated: 'It was the motto of nineteenth-century America, the watchword of Manifest Destiny. Despite its fame, however, works of reference give the phrase confusingly contradictory origins.' So, was it said by Horace Greeley, editor and politician, or – as the misinformation lobby would have us believe – by John Babson Lane Soule, an Indiana newspaper editor? Fuller ruled: 'I have examined this assertion with some care, and have concluded that it is a fiction dating in print to no earlier than 1890. Before that date, the primary source historical record contains not a shred of evidence that Soule had anything to do with the phrase.'

On the other hand, if Greeley *was* the source, 'proof is maddeningly elusive. I have not been able to find any writing by Greeley where this exact phrase appears ... [but] it is impossible to suppose that he did not repeat it many times over, and in many contexts.'

1 The moment a newspaperman tires of his own campaign is the moment the public begins to notice it.
Attributed to Greeley by the British journalist and editor, Harold Evans, in the *Independent on Sunday* (29 December 1991). A version has also been encountered in connection with Richard Nixon's view of a politician getting over his policies: 'When you get tired of saying it, that's when they're just beginning to listen.'

Benny GREEN English writer and broadcaster (1927–98)

2 Live music is an anachronism, and now is the winter of our discothèque.
Remark recalled on BBC Radio *Quote ... Unquote* (1 June 1977). Alluding to SHAKESPEARE 420:3.

Germaine GREER Australian-born writer and feminist (1939–)

3 No sex is better than bad sex.
Quoted in my book, *Nudge Nudge Wink Wink* (1986). 'Better No Sex Than Bad Sex' was the headline over an article by Greer in *The Sunday Times* Review (13 January 1984), possibly tied to the publication of her book *Sex and Destiny: The Politics of Fertility* (1984), in which the remark does not appear.

GREGORY I Rome-born Pope (AD ?540–604)

4 *Non Angli sed Angeli* [not Angles but Angels].
Pope Gregory is said to have uttered these words when he set eyes on fair-haired slaves from Deira (modern Yorkshire) offered for sale in the market place in Rome sometime in the late 6th century. In fact, the earliest surviving version of this story, recorded by the historian Bede over a hundred years later in AD720, offers rather different words, albeit with a similar meaning: 'They have angelic faces, and it is right that they should become joint-heirs with the angels in heaven.' According to Bede, Pope Gregory went on to make two more puns about Deira and its king, Aelle. He was evidently proud of his wordplay. But who later polished the Pope's punnery to create the snappy 'Not Angles but Angels'?
There is an even older English telling than Bede's: the *Life of Gregory the Great*, written some time before Bede's *History* by an anonymous monk of Whitby, has the same

anecdote, but in this earlier version Gregory, not yet Pope, comes across a group of boys '*de nostra natione forma et crinibus candidati albis*', and asks about their nationality. When the answer comes back '*Anguli*', he responds '*Angeli Dei*', and then carries on with the rest of his routine about Aelle and Deira, much as in Bede. Sir Frank Stenton, *Anglo-Saxon England* (1947 edn), dates this incident between 574 and 578, i.e. about 20 years before Gregory got around to dispatching Augustine to Kent. He says, 'There is no need to reject this famous story, for it contains nothing that is improbable, and it belongs to the oldest stratum of tradition about Gregory's life', and adds of the anonymous *Life* that 'At the points where it differs from Bede its statements generally seem preferable.'
As to how and when the crisped-up pun first appeared upon the scene: the earliest citation I have found so far is in James T. Fields, *Yesterdays With Authors* (1871), in which he describes Thackeray in St Paul's Cathedral and quotes from 'one of his books': '[I] think in all Christendom there is no such sight as Charity Children's day. *Non Angelei [sic], sed angeli*. As one looks at that beautiful multitude of innocents: as the first note strikes: indeed one may almost fancy that cherubs are singing.'
Sellar and Yeatman in *1066 And All That* (1930) have the much more amusing: 'Noticing some fair-haired children in the slave market one morning, Pope Gregory ... on being told that they were Angels, made the memorable joke – "Non Angli, sed Angeli" ("*not* Angels, but *Anglicans*") and commanded one of his Saints called St Augustine to go and convert the rest.'

Lady (Augusta) GREGORY Irish writer (1852–1932)

5 *The Rising of the Moon.*
Title of one-act play (1907). Shared by a film (Ireland 1957) and by an opera (Glyndebourne 1970) with libretto by Beverley Cross and music by Nicholas Maw. All these works (with Irish themes) borrow the title of an Irish patriotic song. This was written by John Keegan Casey (1846–70) and called, precisely, 'The Rising of the Moon A.D. 1798': 'And a thousand blades were flashing / At the risin' of the moon.' The date 1798 was the year of the United Irishmen's Rebellion, and the phrase came to be synonymous with rising of the Irish themselves.

Stephen GRELLET French missionary (1773–1855)

6 I expect to pass through this world but once; any good thing therefore that I can do now, or any kindness that I can show to any fellow-creature, let me do it now; let me not defer or neglect it, for I shall not pass this way again.

Born Etienne de Grellet du Mabillier, in France, he eventually settled in the US. Now sometimes referred to as a Quaker 'saint', he is widely quoted as having said this. It is not to be found in any of his writings, however, and has been attributed to others. *Benham* (1907) exhaustively explores the alternatives and mentions William C. Gannett in *Blessed be Drudgery* (1897) as having: 'The old Quaker was right ...' (and then quoting as above). The Pre-Raphaelite artist Holman Hunt is said to have been inspired to paint his picture of Christ, *The Light of the World* (1854) – there are versions in Keble College, Oxford and St Paul's Cathedral – by this quotation.

Arthur Marshall, in *Life's Rich Pageant* (1984), quotes Maurice Bowra (1898–1971), the Oxford don, as having said at lunch in the Reform Club (with a bishop sitting within earshot): 'I expect to pass through this world but once and therefore if there is anybody that I want to kick in the crutch I had better kick them in the crutch *now*, for I do not expect to pass this way again.'

Joyce GRENFELL English entertainer (1910–80)

1 George – don't do that.

'Nursery School Sketches' (1953). This line came from the sketch in which Grenfell played a slightly harassed but unflappable teacher. Part of its charm lay in the audience's never knowing precisely what it was that George was being asked not to do. When the nursery-school sketches were re-printed in a book called *George – Don't Do That* (1977), the line appeared in the one entitled 'Free Activity Period'. In her book *In Pleasant Places*, Chap. 1 (1979), she noted: 'In my series of nursery-school sketches I always introduced a five-year-old character called George. He is apparently misbehaving and in every sketch I admonish him in that high, bright adult voice that is used to divert attention from some undesirable behaviour ..."George – don't do that ..." The misdeed remains unspecified to this day. In America after I had done the sketches on television [on *The Ed Sullivan Show*] I was continually asked what was George doing, but I always answered that I thought it best not to know. And I didn't.'

2 The sordid topic of coin.

A delightful term for the matter of payment due or cash. Not from any sketch but mentioned by her in discussing a woman who inspired the creation of one of her characters. In *Joyce Grenfell Requests the Pleasure* (1976), she writes about the wife of an Oxbridge vice-chancellor who featured in three monologues called 'Eng. Lit.' The character was based partly on Grenfell's own expression while cleaning her teeth, partly on the playwright Clemence Dane (Winifred Ashton)

and partly on the idiosyncratic speech patterns of Hester Alington, wife of the Dean of Durham, and a distant relative of Grenfell's husband. 'On a postcard addressed to a shoeshop in Sloane Street she had written: "Gently fussed about non-appearance of dim pair of shoes sent to you for heeling" ... And when Viola [Tunnard, Grenfell's accompanist] and I went to Durham to perform in aid of one of her charities she introduced the paying of our expenses: "My dears, we have not yet touched on the sordid topic of coin ... "' See also STOPPARD 448:6.

(Sir) Edward GREY (later Viscount Grey of Fallodon) British Liberal politician (1862–1933)

3 The lamps are going out all over Europe; we shall not see them lit again in our lifetime.

Grey was Foreign Secretary at the outbreak of the 1914–18 War, and with this statement tolled the knell for the era that was about to pass. In *Twenty-five Years* (1925) he recounted: 'A friend came to see me on one of the evenings of the last week – he thinks it was on Monday August 3. We were standing at a window of my room in the Foreign Office. It was getting dusk, and the lamps were being lit in the space below on which we were looking. My friend recalls that I remarked on this with the words ...'

Mervyn GRIFFITH-JONES British lawyer (1909–79)

4 Is it a book that you would even wish your wife or your servants to read?

When Penguin Books Ltd was tried at the Old Bailey in October 1960 for publishing an unexpurgated edition of D.H. Lawrence's novel *Lady Chatterley's Lover* (1928), the jury and the public at large were entertained by the social attitudes revealed by Griffith-Jones, senior prosecuting counsel, especially by the question (above) posed in his opening address on the first day of the trial.

Gerald Gardiner, in his closing speech for the defence, commented: 'I cannot help thinking that this was, consciously or unconsciously, an echo from an observation which had fallen from the Bench in an earlier case: "It would never do to let members of the working class read this." I do not want to upset the Prosecution by suggesting that there are a certain number of people nowadays who as a matter of fact don't *have* servants. But of course that whole attitude is one which Penguin Books was formed to fight against.'

The publishers were found not guilty of having published an obscene book, and from the trial is usually dated the permissive revolution in British sexual habits (if not in social attitudes).

Philip GUEDALLA British writer (1889–1944)

1 The work of Henry James has always seemed divis-
ible by a simple dynastic arrangement into three
reigns: James I, James II, and the Old Pretender.
'Men of Letters: Mr Henry James', *Collected Essays* (1920).
Guedalla also used this device in his introduction to *The
Queen and Mr Gladstone* (1933). There were really three
Queen Victorias, he wrote: 'The youngest of the three was
Queen Victoria I ... distinguished by a romping sort of inno-
cence ... She was succeeded shortly after marriage by Victoria
II ... [bearing] the unmistakable impress of her married life
... [Then] the Queen became Queen-Empress ... her third
and final manner.'

2 History repeats itself. Historians repeat each other.
'Some Historians' in the same collection. Also ascribed to
Arthur Balfour by his biographer, Kenneth Young. Rupert
Brooke stated in a letter from Rugby (4 June 1906), 'As a
motto I made up a little epigram "History repeats itself;
Historians repeat one another."' Actually it was Oscar Wilde
who originated it – as 'History never repeats itself. The historians repeat each other. There is a wide difference' – at
least according to Richard Ellman, *Oscar Wilde*, Chap. 5
(1987), though he does not give a precise source and it has
proved impossible to trace the remark in Wilde's works,
despite the assistance of Merlin Holland, his grandson.

Texas GUINAN American nightclub hostess (1884–1933)

3 Fifty million Frenchmen can't be wrong.
A good deal of confusion surrounds this phrase. As a slightly
grudging expression it appears to have originated with
American servicemen during the First World War, justifying
support for their French allies. The precise number of millions was variable. *Partridge/Catch Phrases* suggests that it
was the last line of a First World War song 'extolling

the supreme virtue of copulation, though in veiled terms'.
Partridge may, however, have been referring to a song with
the title (by Rose, Raskin & Fisher), which was not recorded
by Sophie Tucker until 15 April 1927. Cole Porter's
musical *Fifty Million Frenchmen* opened in New York on
27 November 1929. An unrelated US film with this three-
word title was released in 1931.

Where the confusion has crept in is that Guinan was
refused entry into France with her girls in 1931 and said:
'It goes to show that fifty million Frenchmen *can* be wrong.'
She returned to America and renamed her show *Too Hot
for Paris*. Perversely, *ODQ* (1979, 1992) has her saying 'Fifty
million Frenchmen *can't* be wrong' in the *New York World-
Telegram* on 21 March 1931, and seems to be arguing that
she originated the phrase as she had been using it 'six or
seven years earlier'. Sometimes it is quoted as '*forty
million Frenchmen ...* '

Bernard Shaw also held out against the phrase. He insisted: 'Fifty million Frenchmen can't be right.'

Thom GUNN English-born poet (1929–)

4 He turns revolt into style.
Poem, 'Elvis Presley' (1957). Hence, *Revolt into Style*, the
title of a book about the pop arts in Britain (1970) by George
Melly.

Nell GWYN English actress and courtesan (1650–87)

5 Pray, good people, be civil. I am the Protestant whore.
Remark made at Oxford during the Popish Terror (1681),
when an angry crowd mistook her carriage for that of
King Charles II's French Catholic mistress. Quoted in
B. Bevan, *Nell Gwyn* (1969). Also recalled in the form, 'Good
people, let me pass, I am the *Protestant* whore.' See also
CHARLES II 130:7.

H

(Sir) Henry Rider HAGGARD English writer (1856–1925)

1 She who must be obeyed.

The original 'she' in Haggard's novel *She* (1887) was the all-powerful Ayesha, 'who from century to century sat alone, clothed with unchanging loveliness, waiting till her lost love is born again'. But also, 'she was obeyed throughout the length and breadth of the land, and to question her command was certain death'.

From the second of these two quotations we get the use of the phrase by barrister Horace Rumpole regarding his formidable wife in the 'Rumpole of the Bailey' stories by John Mortimer (in TV plays from 1978 and novelizations therefrom). Hence, too, one of the many nicknames applied to Margaret Thatcher – 'She-Who-Must-Be-Obeyed', used, for example, by Denis Healey in a speech to the House of Commons (27 February 1984).

(Sir) Douglas HAIG (later 1st Earl Haig) British soldier (1861–1928)

2 With our backs to the wall, and believing in the justice of our cause, each one of us must fight on to the end.

The expression 'backs to the wall', meaning 'up against it', dates back to at least 1535, but it was memorably used when the Germans launched their last great offensive of the First World War. On 12 April 1918 Haig, as British Commander-in-Chief on the Western Front, issued an order for his troops to stand firm: 'Every position must be held to the last man: there must be no retirement.' A.J.P. Taylor in his *English History 1914–1945* (1966) commented: 'In England this sentence was ranked with Nelson's last message. At the front, the prospect of staff officers fighting with their backs to the walls of their luxurious châteaux had less effect.'

David HALBERSTAM American journalist (1934–)

3 *The Best and the Brightest.*

In Halberstam's book with this title (1972) the phrase applies to the young men from business, industry and the academic world whom John F. Kennedy brought into government in the early 1960s but who were ultimately responsible for the quagmire of American involvement in the Vietnam War. The alliterative combination is almost traditional: 'Political writers, who will not suffer the best and brightest of characters ... to take a single right step for the honour or interest of the nation' – *Letters of Junius* (1769); 'Best and brightest, come away!' – Shelley, 'To Jane: The Invitation' (1822) – originally the letter poem 'The Pine Forest of the Cascine Near Pisa'; 'Brightest and best of the sons of the morning' (see HEBER 232:6); 'The best, the brightest, the cleverest of them all!' – Trollope, *Dr Thorne*, Chap. 25 (1858).

H.R. HALDEMAN American government official (1926–93)

4 Once the toothpaste is out of the tube, it is awfully hard to get it back in.

Remark to John Dean on the Watergate affair (8 April 1973) and reported in *Hearings Before the Select Committee on Presidential Campaign Activities: Watergate and Related Activities*, Vol. 4 (1973). The remark has been wrongly attributed to his colleague, John D. Ehrlichman, and to President Nixon, but it is probably not an original expression in any case. Indeed, according to his daughter Heather, Lord Baden-Powell, the founder of the Scout Movement, would reply to those who said that Scouting was impossible for them: 'Nothing is impossible, except putting toothpaste back into the tube' – Heather King, *Baden-Powell, A Family Album* (1986).

Nathan HALE American revolutionary (1755–76)

1 I only regret that I have but one life to lose for my country.

Before his execution by the British for spying (22 September 1776). Quoted in Henry Phelps Johnston, *Nathan Hale, 1776*, Chap. 7 (1914). The words are carved beneath his statue in the Connecticut State Capitol building, Hartford. Compare from Joseph Addison, *Cato*, Act 4, Sc. 1 (1713): 'What pity is it / That we can die but once to serve out country!'

Mary Lee HALL Unknown poet

2 If I should die and leave you here awhile,
Be not like others, sore undone, who keep
Long vigils by the silent dust, and weep.
For my sake – turn again to life and smile,
Nerving thy heart and trembling hand to do
Something to comfort other hearts than thine.
Complete those dear unfinished tasks of mine
And I, perchance, may therein comfort you.

(Line 6 usually has 'comfort *weaker* hearts'.) This passage was read by Lady Sarah McCorquodale at the funeral service of her sister, Diana, Princess of Wales, at Westminster Abbey (6 September 1997). It was being anthologized under the title 'Turn Again to Life' by 1965 and is probably of American origin. In Celia Haddon's *Love Remembered* (1997) and Agnes Whitaker's *All In the End is Harvest* (1977), it is said to be by 'A. Price Hughes'. Haddon believes it is to be found under this name in a 1920s book. 'If I should die' is, of course, the opening phrase of Rupert Brooke's 'The Soldier' (1914).

(Sir) Peter HALL English theatre director (1930–)

3 We do not necessarily improve with age: for better or worse we become more like ourselves.

Quoted in *The Observer* (in about 1988). Almost a proverbial expression by this time. In my *Eavesdroppings* (1981), I quoted this from Miss Bernice Hanison of Haywards Heath: 'On the London Underground, I heard one of those carrying, well-bred, female voices saying to her companion: "I don't know about you, but as we get older I always find we get more and more like ourselves."'

Friedrich HALM (Baron von Münch-Bellinghausen) German playwright (1806–71)

4 Two minds with but a single thought,
Two hearts that beat as one.

What *Pearson* (1937) says Halm actually wrote near the end of Act 2 of *Der Sohn der Wildnis* is, 'Two *souls* with but a

single thought ...' – as in Maria Lovell's translation of the play, under the title *Ingomar the Barbarian* (1854). The original German is, indeed, '*Zwei Seelen und ein Gedanke*'. But the 'two minds' version is the one that entered the English language. *Partridge/Catch Phrases* draws attention to the similar phrase 'Great minds think alike' – which may have influenced the English form.

The British music-hall mind-reading act The Zancigs (the wife died in 1916, the husband in 1929) had as bill matter: 'Two Minds With But A Single Thought'. Compare the variation 'two minds with *not* a single thought': Kenneth Horne contributed an article entitled 'TMWNAST' to the *Radio Times Annual* (1954): 'The title of this article is how Murdoch and I would write it in our script if it were a catchphrase ... It is quite true that when Murdoch and I get together to write our epic stuff we are two minds with not a single thought.'

Gail HAMILTON American writer (1838–96)

5 The total depravity of inanimate things.

In *ODQ* (edns 1–3), this was attributed to Gail Hamilton, real name Mary Abigail Dodge (believed to be an American teacher, essayist and journalist). Katherine C. Walker wrote an article with the phrase as title in *The Atlantic Monthly* (September 1864), but though it is filled with tales of inanimate objects thwarting, tripping up and generally obstructing the fulfilment of expectations in normal life, Walker fails to put the phrase in quotes or attribute the phrase to anyone.

Oscar HAMMERSTEIN II American lyricist (1895–1960)

6 Ol' Man River
He just keeps rollin' along.

'Ol Man River', *Show Boat* (1927). Music by Jerome Kern, as for the following. See also CHURCHILL 138:1.

Kurt HAMMERSTEIN-EQUORD German soldier (1878–1943)

7 I divide my officers into four classes as follows: the clever, the industrious, the lazy, and the stupid. Each officer always possesses two of these qualities. Those who are clever and industrious I appoint to the General Staff. Use can under certain circumstances be made of those who are stupid and lazy. The man who is clever and lazy qualifies for the highest leadership posts. He has the requisite nerves and the mental clarity for difficult decisions. But whoever is stupid and industrious must be got rid of, for he is too dangerous.

Quoted in *Infantry Journal Reader*, ed. J.I. Greene (1943). Hammerstein-Equord was born in Hinrichshagen, Germany, on 26 September 1878. He joined the German Army and was attached to the General Staff during the First World War. A close friend of Kurt von Schleicher, Hammerstein-Equord was appointed Chief of the General Staff of the Reichswehr in 1930. He was extremely hostile to the Nazi Party and warned Paul von Hindenburg about the dangers of appointing Adolf Hitler as chancellor. Hammerstein-Equord's opposition to Hitler was well known, and in February 1934 he was dismissed from office. During the Second World War he was involved in several plots to overthrow Hitler. He died in Berlin on 25 April 1943.

Christopher HAMPTON English playwright (1946–)

1 Masturbation is the thinking man's television.

The Philanthropist (1970). An amusing variant on the 'thinking man's/person's/woman's — ' theme. As long ago as 1931, Pebeco toothpaste in the US was being promoted as 'The Toothpaste for Thinking People'. However, Frank Muir (1920–98) set the more recent trend (now almost a cliché) when he talked of British broadcaster Joan Bakewell as 'the thinking man's crumpet', in the 1960s. Much later, Chantal Cuer, a French-born broadcaster in Britain, said she had been described as 'the thinking man's croissant'. And how about these for originality? 'Frank Delaney – the thinking man's Russell Harty' – *The Sunday Times* (16 October 1983); 'Frank Delaney – the thinking man's Terry Wogan' – *The Guardian* (17 October 1983); 'the thinking woman's Terry Wogan, TV's Frank Delaney' – *Sunday Express* (30 October 1983). And still it goes on. Janet Suzman, the actress, has been described as 'the thinking man's Barbara Windsor'. From *The Independent* (28 January 1989): 'One member of the Government said: "[Kenneth Clarke's] the thinking man's lager lout".' From *The Observer* (29 January 1989): 'It was chaired by Nick Ross, the thinking woman's newspaper boy.' Also, from *The Observer* (13 September 1987): 'His performance as a trendy and hung-up LA painter in *Heartbreakers* made him the thinking woman's West Coast crumpet' – which brings us back more or less to where we started. In February 1989, the American magazine *Spy* drew up a long list of examples of American variations on the theme: *Hobbies* magazine in 1977 had described Descartes as 'The thinking man's philosopher'; *Boating Magazine* (1984) described the Mansfield TDC portable toilet as 'the thinking man's head'; *Horizon* (1965) called Lake Geneva, 'the thinking man's lake'; and *Esquire* (1986) had called actor William Hurt, 'the thinking man's asshole'.

2 *Philip (bewildered):* I'm sorry. (*Pause.*) I suppose I am indecisive. (*Pause.*) My trouble is, I'm a man of no convictions. (*Longish pause.*) At least, I think I am.

In the same play. This re-emerged later as a graffito: 'I used to be indecisive – but now I'm not so sure' – contributed by Brian Johnston to BBC Radio *Quote … Unquote* (21 August 1979), but see also PERTWEE 357:5.

3 Asking a working writer what he thinks about critics is like asking a lamppost how it feels about dogs.

Quoted originally in *The Sunday Times* Magazine of 16 October 1977. Sometimes this remark is ascribed to John Osborne, and with good reason. Osborne wrote it on a postcard to Hampton after the poor critical reception of the latter's play *Treats* (1976).

George Frederic HANDEL German-born British composer (1685–1759)

4 I did think I did see all Heaven before me – and the great God himself!

When Handel had completed composing Part 2 of *Messiah* – which includes the Hallelujah Chorus – his servant found him at the table, tears streaming from his eyes. This was his comment, reported by Miss Laetitia Hawkins, daughter of the music historian (and on the authority of Dr Allott, Dean of Raphoe). Quoted in Derek Watson, *Dictionary of Musical Quotations* (1991). *Messiah* was composed between 22 August and 14 September 1741, and first performed the following April.

5 See, the conquering hero comes!
Sound the trumpets, beat the drums!

Lines written by Thomas Morell, English clergyman (1703–84), which occur both in Handel's oratorio *Judas Maccabaeus* (1747) and also in *Joshua* (1748). Hence, presumably, *Hail the Conquering Hero*, title of a film (US 1944).

Otto HARBACH American lyricist (1873–1963)

6 Smoke Gets in Your Eyes.

Title of song, *Roberta* (1933). Music by Jerome Kern.
See also MACMILLAN 306:1.

Joan HARBEN English actress (1909–53)

7 It's being so cheerful as keeps me going.

Harben would utter this catchphrase in the character of 'Mona Lott', a gloomy laundrywoman with a dreary, flat voice, in *ITMA*, the BBC's immensely popular radio comedy show (1939–49). When told to 'keep her pecker up' by the star of the show, Tommy Handley, she would reply, 'I always do, sir, it's being so cheerful as keeps me going.' Her family was always running into bad luck, so she had plenty upon which to exercise her cheerfulness. Scripts for the show were by Ted Kavanagh and Handley himself. The catchphrase had earlier appeared in a *Punch* cartoon during the First World War (27 September 1916): 'Wot a life. No rest, no beer, no nuffin. It's only us keeping so cheerful as pulls us through.'

E.Y. HARBURG American lyricist (1898–1981)

1 It's only a paper moon,
Sailing over a cardboard sea,
But it wouldn't be make-believe
If you believed in me.

Song, 'It's Only a Paper Moon', *The Great Magoo* (1932). Written with Harold Arlen and Billy Rose. Hence, *Paper Moon*, title of a film (US 1973).

2 Somewhere over the rainbow, skies are blue,
And the dreams that you dare to dream really do come true.

Song, 'Over the Rainbow', *The Wizard of Oz* (1939). Music by Harold Arlen. See also BAUM 54:8.

3 Follow the Yellow Brick Road.

Title of song, in the same film. Hence, 'Goodbye Yellow Brick Road', the title of a song (1973) by Bernie Taupin and Elton John. See also BAUM 55:1.

Warren G. HARDING American Republican 29th President (1865–1923)

4 America's present need is not heroics but healing, not nostrums but normalcy, not revolution but restoration, not agitation but adjustment, not surgery but serenity, not the dramatic but the dispassionate, not experiment but equipoise, not submergence in internationality but sustainment in triumphant nationality.

The slogans 'Back to Normalcy' and 'Return to Normalcy with Harding' were both based on a word extracted from a speech Harding made in Boston, Massachusetts (14 May 1920). Out of such an alliterative bog stuck the word 'normalcy', a perfectly good Americanism, though it has been suggested that Harding was actually mispronouncing the word 'normality'. He himself claimed that 'normalcy' was what he had meant to say, having come across it in a dictionary.

Oliver HARDY American film comedian (1892–1957)

5 Well, here's another nice mess you've gotten me into.

Hardy's exasperated cry to his partner Stan Laurel (1890–1965) after some piece of ineptitude was spoken in several of their films – notably in *The Sons of the Desert* (US 1933). Both *ODMQ* (1991) and *ODQ* (1992) place the saying under Laurel's name (because Laurel wrote the scripts) while acknowledging that it was always said *to* him. John P. Fennell in *Film Quotes: Great Lines from Famous Films* (1991) even has: 'Another fine mess you've got us in, *Ollie*.' It is one of the few film catchphrases to register because there was a sufficient number of Laurel and Hardy features for audiences to become familiar with it. Latterly, it has often been remembered as 'another fine mess', possibly on account of one of the duo's 30-minute features (released in 1930) being entitled *Another Fine Mess*. *The Independent* (21 January 1994) carried a letter from Darren George of Sheffield – clearly a Laurel and Hardy scholar – which stated that 'nice mess' was what was 'invariably' spoken and that in *Another Fine Mess* 'the duo inexplicably misquote themselves'. Note that in W.S. Gilbert, *The Grand Duke*, Act 1 (1896), there occurs the line, 'Well, a nice mess you've got us into!' Even earlier, a Tenniel cartoon in *Punch* (27 February 1864), concerning Lord John Russell, includes the phrase: 'A nice mess you have got yourself into!'

Thomas HARDY English novelist and poet (1840–1928)

6 A time there was ...
Before the birth of consciousness,
When all went well ...
But the disease of feeling germed,
And primal rightness took the tinct of wrong.

'Before Life and After' (1909). Hence, *A Time There Was*, title of a 'suite on English folk tunes' (1974) by Benjamin Britten. Also *A Time There Was: a profile of Benjamin Britten* (1980), for London Weekend Television.

William HARGREAVES English songwriter (1846–1919)

7 I'm Burlington Bertie
I rise at ten thirty and saunter along like a toff,
I walk down the Strand with my gloves on my hand,
Then I walk down again with them off.

From the song, 'Burlington Bertie from Bow' (1915), and not to be confused with the earlier 'Burlington Bertie' (1900) by Harry B. Norris. That song, performed by Vesta Tilley, is about a 'swell'. Hargreaves was writing about a more down-at-heel character (for his wife Ella Shields, the male impersonator, to perform). It is a kind of parody, but is probably better known now than the original.

1 The Prince of Wales' brother, along with some
other,
Slaps *me* on the back, and says 'Come and see
mother.'
I'm Bert, Bert, and Royalty's hurt when they ask
me to dine,
I say 'No –
I've just *had* a banana with Lady Diana,
I'm Burlington Bertie from Bow.'

In the same song. The implication in the penultimate line of this verse is that Bertie has just had sex with someone – 'banana' is a slang word for 'penis'. A slight misquotation from the song – 'I had a banana / With Lady Diana' – is given by Allen Walker Read in *Lexical Evidence from Folk Epigraphy ... a Glossarial Study of the Low Element in the English Vocabulary* (1935).

Jean HARLOW American film actress (1911–37)

2 Would you be shocked if I put on something more
comfortable?

'Do you mind if I put on something more comfortable?' and 'Excuse me while I slip into something more comfortable' are just two of the misquotations of this famous line. 'Pardon me while I slip into something more comfortable' was perpetrated by Denis Gifford in *The Independent* (22 July 1995) and 'Would you be shocked if I changed into something more comfortable?' appeared in *The Times* (3 March 2005). What Jean Harlow as Helen actually says to Ben Lyon as Monte in *Hell's Angels* (1930) is, of course, by way of a proposition, and she duly exchanges her fur wrap for a dressing gown.

Joel Chandler HARRIS American writer (1848–1908)

3 Tar-baby ain't sayin' nuthin', en Brer Fox, he lay low.

'The Wonderful Tar-Baby Story', *Uncle Remus and His Legends of the Old Plantation* (1881). In Kenneth Harris's biography of Clement Attlee (1982), he says at one point that the former British Prime Minister was, 'lying low, like Brer Rabbit, and saying nuffin'. This is a fairly common conflation of what Harris actually wrote. In fact, the phrase 'en Brer Fox, he lay low' is a phrase repeated rhythmically throughout the piece, as Frank Muir has noted, 'like a line in a Blues song'.

Lorenz HART American lyricist (1895–1943)

4 Thou swell, thou witty, thou sweet, thou grand.

Song, 'Thou Swell', in *A Connecticut Yankee* (1927) with music by Richard Rodgers. Hence, *Thou Swell Thou Witty*, title of his collected lyrics, ed. by Dorothy Hart (1976).

5 We'll have Manhattan ...

Song, 'Manhattan', *Garrick Gaieties* (1925). Music by Richard Rodgers. Hence, *I'll Take Manhattan*, title of a novel (1986) by Judith Krantz. Although acknowledging the Rodgers and Hart song, it only alludes to it.

L.P. HARTLEY English novelist (1895–1972)

6 The past is a foreign country: they do things
differently there.

The Go-Between (1953), opening words. Compare Christopher Morley's earlier statement: 'Life is a foreign language: all men mispronounce it' – *Thunder on the Left*, Chap. 14 (1925).

Minnie Louise HASKINS English teacher and writer (1875–1957)

7 And I said to the man who stood at the Gate of the
Year, 'Give me a light that I may tread safely into
the unknown.' And he replied, 'Go out into the
darkness, and put your hand into the Hand of God.
That shall be to you better than light, and safer
than a known way.'

Introduction to poem, *The Desert* (1908). If one were to look for an equivalent British example of President Reagan's quoting of J.G. Magee's 'High Flight' poem at the time of the *Challenger* disaster in 1986 (307:3) – that is to say, an outstanding choice of quotation in a head of state's speech – the most obvious, and possibly only, candidate would be found in King George VI's Christmas radio broadcast of 1939.

The King, hampered by a severe speech impediment, was scarcely a man noted for what he said. Yet, when he quoted an obscure poet that year, he captured the public imagination as few other Royals had done (and certainly have not done since). He concluded his message by quoting (anonymously) words written by Haskins, a retired lecturer at the London School of Economics.

One can imagine how the nation collectively responded to the King's difficult delivery of the words, especially given that this was the first Christmas of the war. The King added: 'May that Almighty Hand guide and uphold us all.'

Haskins did not hear the broadcast herself, but was soon inundated with writing offers. Her reprinted poem sold 43,000 copies, she was ushered into *Who's Who* and merited an obituary in *The Times* – all testimony to the power of being quoted by the right person at the right time. One assumes that the King's speech was written for him by a member of the Royal Household. According to the King's official biographer, John Wheeler-Bennett, the poem had merely been 'sent to him shortly before the text of his broadcast was completed'. The words of the poem were inscribed on the gate of the King's memorial chapel in St George's, Windsor.

R.S. HAWKER English clergyman (1803–75)

1 And shall Trelawny die?
Here's twenty thousand Cornish men
Will know the reason why.

The refrain from Hawker's 'Song of the Western Men' (1845) refers to Bishop Sir Jonathan Trelawny of Bristol. In 1688 Trelawny was sent to the Tower by King James II with six other bishops on charges of seditious libel. They were acquitted. Hawker said he took the whole refrain from an old Cornish ballad but, if so, it has not been discovered.

John HAWKESWORTH English TV playwright (1920–)

2 By the Sword Divided.

Hawkesworth gave this title to a BBC TV historical drama series (1983–5) set in the English Civil War. He commented (1991): 'When I first wrote down the idea for a story about the Civil War I called it 'The Laceys of Arnescote' ... [but] I decided the title didn't convey the sort of Hentyish swashbuckling style that we were aiming at, so I thought again. The title "By the Sword Divided" came to me as I was walking along a beach in Wales.'

The phrase sounds like a quotation, but apparently is not. In dealing with the Civil War period, Macaulay in his *History of England*, Chaps. 1–2 (1848) came close with: 'Thirteen years followed during which England was ... really governed by the sword'; 'the whole nation was sick of government by the sword'; 'anomalies and abuses ... which had been destroyed by the sword'.

Ian HAY British novelist and playwright (1876–1952)

3 The First Hundred Thousand.

Title of war novel (1915), subtitled 'Adventures of a typical regiment in Kitchener's army'. The book begins with a poem (Hay's own, presumably):

We're off a hundred thousand strong.
And some of us will not come back.

A.J.P. Taylor in his *English History 1914–45*, describing a period of 'patriotic frenzy' in the Great War, says that the 'spirit of 1915 was best expressed by Ian Hay, a writer of light fiction, in *The First Hundred Thousand* – a book which

treated soldiering as joke, reviving "the best days of our lives" at some imaginary public school'.

4 What do you mean, funny? Funny peculiar, or funny ha-ha?

Hay's play *Housemaster*, Act 3 (first performed 1936 – not the novel published in the same year, where it does not appear) is usually given as the origin of this popular expression. Earlier, however, in the American Meriel Brady's novel *Genevieve Gertrude*, Chap. 7 (1928), there had been:

'I liked that song, myself,' he said, 'even if it isn't classical. It's funny, anyhow.'
Genevieve Gertrude raised her hand.
'Do you mean funny peculiar, or funny ha-ha?' she inquired politely.
...''Cause,' explained his mentor gravely, 'our teacher don't allow us to say funny when we mean peculiar. It's bad English, you know.'

There is also a tantalizing play on words to be found in Mary Vivian Hughes, *A London Family Between the Wars*, Chap. 6 (1940) – referring to the 1920s:

'Haven't you brought me any funny stories this time?'
'Not much. There's one thing I heard – "not sunny but pecoola" as you used to say when you were tiny.'

The first, if not the second, of these quotes is clear proof that the phrase existed before Ian Hay popularized it further. Mae West in her autobiography, *Goodness Had Nothing To Do With It*, Chap. 9 (1959), writing of the period before her play *Pleasure Man* opened in New York (17 September 1928), quotes a male friend as saying: 'Men can get funny over a woman. Funny peculiar that is.'

J. Milton HAYES British writer (1884–1940)

5 There's a one-eyed yellow idol to the North of
Khatmandu;
There's a little marble cross below the town;
And a brokenhearted woman tends the grave
of 'Mad' Carew,
While the yellow god for ever gazes down.

'The Green Eye of the Yellow God' (1911), written with Cuthbert Clarke. This recitation piece (often misascribed to Kipling) has been much parodied, though it can hardly have been written in total seriousness in the first place. The British music-hall comedian Billy Bennett (1887–1942) once performed 'The Green Tie of the Little Yellow Dog' before King George V: 'There's a cock-eyed yellow poodle to the North of Gongapooch [Hindustani for 'arseholes'], / There's a little hot-cross-bun that's turning green, / There's a double-jointed wop-wop doing tricks in Who-flung-dung, / And you're a better man than I am Gunga-Din.'

Abraham HAYWARD English essayist (1801–84)

1 He writes too often and too fast ... If he persists much longer in this course, it requires no gift of prophecy to foretell his fate – he has risen like a rocket, and he will come down like a stick.

Of Charles Dickens. Hayward was reviewing *Pickwick Papers* for *The Quarterly Review* (October 1838). Not entirely original: Tom Paine had said of Edmund Burke, 'As he rose like the rocket, he fell like the stick' – *Letter to the Addressers on the late Proclamation* (1792).

William HAZLITT English essayist (1778–1830)

2 *The Spirit of the Age.*

Hazlitt's book of essays (1825) was devoted to examinations of the work and characters of contemporary writers. The phrase had earlier been used by Shelley in a letter of 1820: 'It is the spirit of the age, and we are all infected with it.' David Hume had used it in 1752 – according to *Notes and Queries*, Vol. 236. Later, *The Pall Mall Gazette* was stating (6 August 1891): 'The Spirit of the Age is against those who put party or programme before human needs.' In 1975 the title *Spirit of the Age* was given to a BBC TV series on the history of architecture, with Alec Clifton-Taylor. The phrase translates the German word *Zeitgeist*, and is ultimately derived from that.

Denis HEALEY (later Lord Healey) British Labour politician (1917–)

3 I warn you there are going to be howls of anguish from the 80,000 rich people, people who are rich enough to pay over 75 per cent on the last slice of their income.

Speech to the Labour Party Conference (1 October 1973), when Shadow Chancellor, explaining that Labour's programme would cost money and the only way to raise it was through taxation. He promised increased income tax and a wealth tax if the party won the next election (these taxes never materialized). Not 'howls of anger', as quoted in *The Sunday Telegraph* (October 1980). In his autobiography *The Time of My Life* (1989), Healey said the phrase 'make the rich howl with anguish' still 'hangs round my neck like Wilson's phrase "the pound in your pocket", and Heath's election promise to cut prices "at a stroke". I never said either that I would "squeeze the rich until the pips squeak", though I did quote Tony Crosland using this phrase of Lloyd George's in reference to property speculators, not to the rich in general.'

'Phrase of Lloyd George's'? Surely he meant GEDDES 209:4.

4 That part of his speech was rather like being savaged by a dead sheep.

Speech, House of Commons (14 June 1978). As Chancellor of the Exchequer, on being attacked by Sir Geoffrey Howe in a debate over his Budget proposals. In 1987 Alan Watkins of *The Observer* suggested that Sir Roy Welensky, of Central African Federation fame, had earlier likened an attack by Iain Macleod to being *bitten* by a sheep. We had to wait until 1989 and the publication of Healey's memoirs to be told that 'the phrase came to me while I was actually on my feet; it was an adaptation of Churchill's remark that an attack by Attlee was "like being savaged by a pet lamb". Such banter can often enliven a dull afternoon.'

The Churchill version remains untraced, but he was noted for his Attlee jokes (and busily denied that he had ever said most of them, see CHURCHILL 140:6). In 1990, the victim of Healey's phrase, Geoffrey Howe, also claimed that it wasn't original. 'It came from a play,' he said sheepishly. A profile of Healey in *The Sunday Telegraph* (3 November 1996) suggested that he had appropriated the phrase 'savaged by a dead sheep' without acknowledgement from the journalist Andrew Alexander, probably writing in *The Daily Telegraph* with reference to Howe during the Arab–Israeli War of 1967.

Tim HEALY Irish politician (1855–1931)

5 He is not a man to go tiger-shooting with.

This jibe was reputedly fired at the somewhat weak and vacillating Lord Rosebery by Healy, the prominent Irish Nationalist politician who sat in the Westminster Parliament (1880–1918). It is quoted by Robert Rhodes James in *Rosebery* (1963). If not the first use of this slur, it is the most famous. In 1961, Lord Montgomery of Alamein was quoted as saying: '[Chairman] Mao has a very fine strong face. He's the sort of man I'd go in the jungle with.' In 1970, I was told of a university appointments secretary who would add his own comments on the bottom of application forms he was forwarding to employers on behalf of students. On one he wrote: 'This chap would be splendid to shoot tigers with.' Compare BUCHAN 106:5.

Seamus HEANEY Irish poet (1939–)

6 Is there a life before death? That's chalked up
In Ballymurphy. Competence with pain,
Coherent miseries, a bite and sup,
We hug our little destiny again.

'Whatever You Say Say Nothing', *North* (1975). But as if this underlines the saying's Irish origins too well, bear in mind that 'Is there life before death?' had earlier been the epigraph to Chap. 9 of Stephen Vizinczey's novel *In Praise of Older Women* (1966). There, it is credited to 'Anon. Hungarian'.

1 History says, Don't hope
  On this side of the grave.
  But then, once in a lifetime
  The longed-for tidal wave
  Of justice can rise up,
  And hope and history rhyme.

The Cure at Troy (1990), a version of Sophocles's play *Philoctetes*. After the Northern Ireland peace referendum, *The Observer* (24 May 1998) ran above its masthead the words: 'The day when hope and history rhyme.' One of the first people to quote it was Mary Robinson at her inauguration as Irish President in December 1990.

(Sir) Edward HEATH British Conservative Prime Minister (1916–2005)

2 The full-hearted consent of the Parliament and people of the new member countries.

On 5 May 1970, a month and a half before he became Prime Minister, Heath addressed the Franco-British Chamber of Commerce in Paris. Looking ahead to the enlargement of the European Community through the forthcoming membership of the UK, Ireland and Denmark, he said that this would not be in the interests of the Community, 'except with the full-hearted consent ...' The statement, penned by Douglas Hurd, then a Heath aide, was seized upon subsequently by those seeking a referendum on EC entry.

3 This would, at a stroke, reduce the rise in prices, increase productivity and reduce unemployment.

A press release (No. G.E.228) from Conservative Central Office, dated 16 June 1970, concerning tax cuts and a freeze on prices by nationalized industries. The phrase 'at a stroke', though never actually spoken by Heath, came to haunt him after he became Prime Minister two days later.

4 We were returned to office to change the course of history of this nation – nothing less. If we are to achieve this task we will have to embark on a change so radical, a revolution so quiet and yet so total, that it will go far beyond the programme for a parliament to which we are committed and on which we have already embarked, far beyond the decade and way into the 80s.

Speech, Conservative Party Conference (October 1970) – shortly after his government had been formed. A 'quiet revolution' is a subtle change that does not draw attention to itself. The phrase was written by Barry Day (an advertising man), who was Heath's speechwriter at the time, but it had earlier been used to describe the operations of the Liberal government in the Canadian province of Quebec, led by Jean Lesage (1960).

5 It is the unpleasant and unacceptable face of capitalism, but one should not suggest that the whole of British industry consists of practices of this kind.

In 1973 it was revealed that a former Tory Cabinet minister, Duncan Sandys, had been paid £130,000 in compensation for giving up his £50,000 a year consultancy with the Lonrho company. The money was to be paid, quite legally, into an account in the Cayman Islands to avoid British tax. This kind of activity did not seem appropriate when the government was promoting a counter-inflation policy. Replying to a question from Jo Grimond MP in the House of Commons on 15 May, Heath, as Prime Minister, created a format phrase that has since been used to describe the 'unacceptable face of' almost anything. In the text from which he spoke (said to have been prepared by his then aide, Douglas Hurd), it apparently had 'facet'.

Reginald HEBER English bishop and hymn writer (1783–1826)

6 Brightest and best of the sons of the morning!
  Dawn on our darkness and lend us Thine aid!

Hymn (1811). Compare HALBERSTAM 225:3.

7 What though the spicy breezes
  Blow soft o'er Ceylon's isle;
  Though every prospect pleases,
  And only man is vile.

This was what Heber originally wrote in the hymn 'From Greenland's icy mountains' (1821), leading up to the lines about 'the heathen in his blindness' bowing down 'to wood and stone'. Later, however, he changed 'Ceylon's' to 'Java's'. Sir Peter Kemp, writing to *The Independent* Magazine (15 May 1993), said that he had been told there were two reasons for this change: Java, with its accent on the first syllable, goes better with the tune that is usually used. Secondly, 'the Colonial Office of the day objected to Bishop Heber's traducing of a part of the Empire and insisted on the change'. Heber became Bishop of Calcutta in 1823.

John Lloyd of Haverfordwest, Pembrokeshire, challenged the second point (1994): 'I gravely doubt this: even if a Colonial Office existed at the time, both Calcutta, where Heber was Bishop, and Ceylon, would have been within the competence of the India Office. The intervention, as I heard the story when I was in the East, was from one of Heber's clergy, who pointed out that Ceylon was in Heber's Diocese – Calcutta being the Diocese for the whole of British India at the time – and it would be prudent, if he had to refer to heathen who, in their blindness, bowed down to wood and stone, to locate them somewhat further away.

'The more appealing anecdote about the hymn is that Heber showed it to his father-in-law, the Dean of St Asaph, seeking approval for his little three verse masterpiece, the peroration of which concludes verse three. The Dean is said to have said, "It is very good, but if you think you can get the collection up in three verses, you are mistaken." This resulted in Heber adding the fourth verse, which is clearly repetitious of the earlier three.'

Piet HEIN Danish poet, designer and inventor (1905–96)

1 Losing one glove is sorrow enough
But nothing compared with the pain
Of losing one glove
Discarding the other
Then finding the first one again.

'Consolation grook'. Possibly a translation of one of his aphoristic *grooks*, though as Hein lived from 1969 to 1976 in Britain, it may have been written in English originally. In 1996, on BBC Radio *Quote ... Unquote*, Jonathan Cecil quoted the following as a 'Danish proverb', which may conceivably have been what Hein versified, or may simply be a prose remembering of what he wrote: 'It is terrible to lose a right-handed glove and to have to throw the left-handed glove away. But it is even more terrible to lose a right-handed glove and to throw the left-handed glove away and then to find the right-handed glove.'

Heinrich HEINE German poet (1797–1856)

2 *Dieu me pardonnera, c'est son metier*
[God will pardon me. It is his business].

Last words. Quoted in Alfred Meissner, *Heinrich Heine: Erinnerungen* (1856). Has also been attributed to Voltaire and to Catherine the Great: '*Moi, je serai autocrate: c'est mon métier. Et le bon Dieu me pardonnera: c'est son métier* [I shall be autocratic: that's my business. And God will forgive me: that's his business].'

Joseph HELLER American novelist (1923–99)

3 There was only one catch and that was Catch-22, which specified that a concern for one's own safety in the face of dangers that were real and immediate was the process of a rational mind ... Orr would be crazy to fly more missions and sane if he didn't, but if he was sane he had to fly them. If he flew them he was crazy and didn't have to; but if he didn't want to he was sane and had to.

Catch-22, Chap. 5 (1961; film US 1970). The title of Heller's novel – about a group of US fliers in the Second World War

– has become a widely used catchphrase. 'It was a Catch-22 situation,' people will say, as if resorting to a quasi-proverbial expression like 'Heads you win, tails I lose' or 'Damned if you do, damned if you don't.' What Heller did was to affix a name to the popular view that 'there's always a catch', some underlying law that defeats people by its brutal, ubiquitous logic. Oddly, Heller had originally called it 'Catch-18'. Robert Gottlieb, his publishers' editor, advised that this would clash with Leon Uris's *Mila 18*, being put out by the same house that season. In *Something Like Fire: Peter Cook Remembered* (1996), Heller is quoted as saying: 'I thought of *Catch-Eleven*, because it's the only other number to start with an open vowel sound. I guess we doubled that.'

4 Some men are born mediocre, some men achieve mediocrity, and some men have mediocrity thrust upon them. With Major Major it was all three.

In the same novel, Chap. 9. Alluding to SHAKESPEARE 423:1.

Lillian HELLMAN American playwright and writer (1905–84)

5 *The Watch on the Rhine.*

The title of a play (1941; film US 1943). It comes from the poem '*Die Wacht am Rhein*' by Max Schnekenburger (1840), set to music by Karl Wilhelm (1854), which became a German national song. There was a British parody in the First World War: 'When We've Wound Up the Watch on the Rhine'.

(Sir) Robert HELPMANN Australian dancer and choreographer (1909–86)

6 The trouble with nude dancing is that not everything stops when the music stops.

After the opening night of *Oh, Calcutta!*. Quoted in *The Frank Muir Book* (1976). Also in the form: 'No. You see there are portions of the human anatomy which would keep swinging after the music had finished', when asked if the fashion for nudity on stage would extend to dance – Elizabeth Salter, *Helpmann* (1978).

Felicia HEMANS English poet (1793–1835)

7 The boy stood on the burning deck
Whence all but he had fled;
The flame that lit the battle's wreck
Shone round him o'er the dead.

'Casabianca' (1849). A famous recitation poem and based on a true incident. During the Battle of the Nile (1798), Louis de Casabianca was commander of the French ship *L'Orient*. His son, aged about 13, remained at his post when the vessel caught fire and perished with it.

See also COWARD 157:2.

Ernest HEMINGWAY American novelist (1899–1961)

1 *The Sun Also Rises*.

Title of novel (1926). See BIBLE 75:6.

2 Grace under pressure.

In an interview with *The New Yorker* (30 November 1929), Hemingway gave this as a definition of 'guts'. It was based on the Latin *'fortiter in re, suaviter in modo* [gentle in manner, strong in practice]', which was adopted by the Jesuits and was later invoked by John F. Kennedy at the start of his book *Profiles in Courage* (1956).

3 *F. Scott Fitzgerald*: The very rich are different from you and me.
Hemingway: Yes, they have more money.

In *Burnam* (1980) the facts are neatly established about this famous exchange, said to have occurred between Hemingway and F. Scott Fitzgerald. In his short story 'The Rich Boy' (1926), Fitzgerald had written: 'Let me tell you about the very rich. They are different from you and me.' Twelve years later in *his* short story 'The Snows of Kilimanjaro' (1938), Hemingway had the narrator remember 'poor Scott Fitzgerald', his awe of the rich and that 'someone' had said, 'Yes, they have more money.'

When Fitzgerald read the story, he protested to Hemingway, who dropped Fitzgerald's name from further printings. In any case, the put-down 'Yes, they have more money' had not been administered to Fitzgerald but to Hemingway himself. In 1936 Hemingway said at a lunch with the critic Mary Colum: 'I am getting to know the rich.' She replied: 'The only difference between the rich and other people is that the rich have more money.'

Also discussed in *Scott and Ernest* (1978) by Mathew J. Bruccoli. Compare: 'The Rich aren't like us – they pay less taxes' – Peter de Vries, in *The Washington Post* (30 July 1989).

4 *A Farewell To Arms*.

Title (1929). This is a title applied to the verses beginning 'His golden locks time hath to silver turn'd ...' by George Peele (1556–96), found by Hemingway when trawling through Sir Arthur Quiller-Couch's *Oxford Book of English Verse* (1900) searching for a title. The phrase 'a farewell to arms' also occurs in D.B. Haseler's poem beginning, 'Now that the king has no more need of me' (1919).

5 An unhappy childhood is a writer's gold mine.

Attributed remark probably based on Hemingway's article 'Monologue to the Maestro: A High Seas Letter', *Esquire* (October 1935), which contained advice to a would-be writer in this exchange: 'Mice [short for Maestro]: What is the best early training for a writer? / Y.C. [Your Correspondent, i.e. Hemingway]: An unhappy childhood.'

6 Did the earth move for you?

Jokily addressed to one's partner after sexual intercourse, this appears to have originated as 'Did thee feel the earth move?' in Hemingway's *For Whom the Bell Tolls* (1940). It is not spoken in the 1943 film version, however. Headline from *The Sport* (22 February 1989): 'SPORT SEXCLUSIVE ON A BONK THAT WILL MAKE THE EARTH MOVE.' From the same novel comes the other interesting inquiry on the subject of kissing: 'Where do the noses go? I always wondered where the noses would go.'

7 *The Old Man and the Sea*.

Title of novel (1952; film US 1958) – presumably alluding to 'The Old Man *of* the Sea', the name of a troublesome character in *The Arabian Nights* who climbs on the back of Sinbad the Sailor and is hard to dislodge, hence, the phrase for 'a burden'.

8 If you are lucky enough to have lived in Paris as a young man, then wherever you go for the rest of your life, it stays with you, for Paris is a moveable feast.

Epigraph, *A Moveable Feast* (1964). In the ecclesiastical world, a moveable feast is one that does not fall on a fixed date but, like Easter, occurs according to certain rules. This title was applied posthumously to Hemingway's Paris memoirs after his widow came across the passage in one of his letters. Titles that Hemingway himself had considered for the book included *The Eye and the Ear, To Write It Truly, Love Is Hunger, It Is Different in the Ring* and *The Parts Nobody Knows*.

See also JACKSON 252:1.

Jimmy HENDRIX American rock musician (1942–70)

9 Once you're dead, you're made for life.

This attributed remark, dating from about 1968, was certainly prescient in Hendrix's own case: his success was enhanced following his early death in September 1970, and within six weeks he had a No. 1 hit in the UK with 'Voodoo Chile'. *The Independent* (21 April 1995) added 'It's funny the way most people love the dead' before the remark.

The pattern of a surge of interest – indeed, *increased* popularity – after death has been accorded to any number of pop stars who have died relatively young. Elvis Presley in 1977, for example, and John Lennon in 1980 benefited in this way. A graffito following Presley's death – reported in *Time Magazine* (8 April 1985) – commented: 'Good career move.' Compare VIDAL 478:1.

W.E. HENLEY English poet (1849–1903)

1 In the fell clutch of circumstance,
   I have not winced nor cried aloud:
   Under the bludgeonings of chance
   My head is bloody, but unbowed.

'Invictus. In Memoriam R.T. Hamilton Bruce' (1875). Hence, 'bloody but unbowed' has become a phrase in general use, often as an unascribed quotation, meaning 'determined after having suffered a defeat'. It was a phrase much applied to Londoners in the press after the terrorist bombings of 7 July 2005, as it had been during the Blitz of 1940–1. 'Bloody but unbowed, veteran discount retailers Gerald and Vera Weisfeld have hit out at the new £56m rescue deal agreed between struggling Poundstretcher owner Brown & Jackson and South African group Pepkor' – *Daily Mail* (10 May 1994).

2 It matters not how strait the gate,
   How charged with punishments the scroll,
   I am the master of my fate:
   I am the captain of my soul.

In the same poem. Winston Churchill said in a speech to the House of Commons (9 September 1941): 'Today we may say aloud before an awe-struck world, "We are still masters of our fate. We are still captain of our souls."' Compare P.G. Wodehouse, 'Lord Emsworth and the Girl Friend', *Blandings Castle and Elsewhere* (1935): 'It is always unpleasant for a proud man to realize that he is no longer captain of his soul; that he is to all intents and purposes ground beneath the number twelve heel of a Glaswegian head-gardener.'

3 Madam Life's a piece in bloom
   Death goes dogging everywhere:
   She's the tenant of the room,
   He's the ruffian on the stair.

'To W.R.' (1877). Hence, *The Ruffian On the Stair*, title of a radio play (1964) by Joe Orton.

4 What have I done for you,
   England, my England?
   What is there I would not do,
   England, my own?

'Pro Rege Nostro', *For England's Sake* (1900). Hence, many allusions: *England My England*, title of a book of short stories

by D.H. Lawrence (1922); A.G. MacDonell's satire on country life, *England, Their England* (1933); a posthumous book of George Orwell's essays, *England, Your England* (1953); and *England, Our England*, title of a revue by Keith Waterhouse and Willis Hall (London 1962).

HENRI IV (Henri of Navarre) French King (1553–1610)

5 *Paris vaut bien une messe* [Paris is well worth a mass].

Said either by Henri or his minister Sully (in conversation with him), though no real evidence exists. Henri had led the Protestant forces in the Third Huguenot War (1569–72) as King of Navarre, and in 1589 he marched on Catholic-held Paris and became King of France. In 1593 he renounced Protestantism and converted to Catholicism, hence this cynical if pragmatic remark, which was first recorded in 1622.

In 1681 Hardouin de Péréfixe commented in *Histoire de Henry le Grand*: 'The Politiques ... said to him that of all canons, the Canon of the Mass was the best to reduce the towns of his kingdom.'

6 *Je veux qu'il n'y ait si pauvre paysan en mon royaume qu'il n'ait tous les dimanches sa poule au pot* [I will make sure that there will be no labourer in my kingdom without the means of having a chicken in his pot].

A remark recorded by a contemporary lawyer, Pierre de l'Estoile. Péréfixe (1681) later recorded it in the above French version. 'A chicken in every pot' accordingly became one of the earliest political slogans. In 1928, running for the US Presidency, Herbert Hoover said, 'The slogan of progress is changing from the "full dinner pail" to the full garage', and by 1932 this was sometimes interpreted as 'a chicken in every pot and two cars in every garage'. In 1960 John F. Kennedy misquoted Hoover as having uttered the slogan 'Two chickens for every pot'.

7 *Toujours perdrix* [Always partridge].

Or, in Latin, *semper perdrix*, meaning 'too much of a good thing'. The King was reproved by his confessor for his marital infidelities, so he ordered the priest to be fed on nothing but partridge. When the priest complained that it was 'always partridge', the King replied it was the same if you had only one mistress.

HENRY II English King (1133–89)

8 Will no man rid me of this turbulent priest?

Henry II's rhetorical question regarding Thomas Becket – which was unfortunately acted upon by the Archbishop's murderers in 1170 – is ascribed to 'oral tradition' by *ODQ*

(1979) in the form: 'Will no one revenge me of the injuries I have sustained from one turbulent priest?' The King, who was in Normandy, had received reports that the Archbishop was ready 'to tear the crown' from his head. 'What a pack of fools and cowards I have nourished in my house,' he cried, according to another version, 'that not one of them will avenge me of this turbulent priest!' Yet another version has '... of this upstart clerk'. Henry would have said whatever he said in a western version of medieval French, strongly contaminated by Provençal. His native dialect was that of Maine. It has been suggested that the Rolls series records the exact words used.

An example of the phrase used allusively in conversation was played on tape at the conspiracy-to-murder trial involving Jeremy Thorpe MP in 1979. In one recording, Andrew Newton speaking of the alleged plot said: 'They feel a Thomas à Beckett was done, you know, with Thorpe sort of raving that would nobody rid me of this man.'

HENRY IV English King (1367–1413)

1 Lauds be given to the Father of heaven, for now I know that I shall die here in this chamber, according to the prophecy of me declared, that I should depart this life in Jerusalem.

The last words of Henry IV, according to Raphael Holinshed's *The Chronicles of England, Scotland and Ireland* (1587). He had just been told that he was lying in the Jersualem Chamber of Westminster Abbey. He had been preparing for an expedition to the Holy Land and was visiting the Abbey on the eve of his departure when taken ill. Shakespeare in *Henry IV, Part 2* takes this situation almost word for word from the chronicle (see 408:12). After the dissolution of the Abbey, the Jerusalem Chamber became the meeting place of the Dean and Chapter. Its name derives from mention of Jerusalem in inscriptions round the fireplace or from the original tapestry hangings.

HENRY VIII English King (1491–1547)

2 The things I've done for England.

In Sir Alexander Korda's film *The Private Life of Henry VIII* (1933), Charles Laughton as the King is just about to get into bed with one of his many wives when, alluding to her ugliness, he sighs: 'The things I've done for England.' The screenplay was written by Lajos Biro and Arthur Wimperis. There is no historical precedent.

The phrase caught on, to be used ironically when confronted with any unpleasant task. In 1979, Prince Charles on a visit to Hong Kong sampled curried snake meat and, with a polite nod towards his ancestor, exclaimed: 'Boy, the things I do for England.'

Patrick HENRY American statesman (1736–99)

3 I know not what course others may take; but as for me, give me liberty or give me death!

Henry was the foremost opponent of British rule and the leading orator of American independence. His speech in the Virginia Convention (23 March 1775) helped carry the vote for independence. He became Governor of the new state and was four times re-elected. Compare Joseph Addison, *Cato*, Act 2, Sc. 5 (1713): 'Chains or conquest, liberty or death.'

Philip HENRY English clergyman (1631–96)

4 *All This and Heaven Too.*

Title of a novel (1939, film US 1940) by Rachel Field. As acknowledged in the book, Matthew Henry, the nonconformist divine and Bible commentator (who died in 1714), attributed the saying to his minister father in his *Life of Mr Philip Henry* (1698). Compare the title *All This and World War II* (film US 1976) and the *Daily Express* front-page headline on Coronation Day (2 June 1953): 'ALL THIS – AND EVEREST TOO' – announcing the fact that a British-led expedition had been the first to conquer the world's highest mountain.

HERACLITUS Greek philosopher (?540–?480BC)

5 The past and present
Are as one –
Accordant and discordant
Youth and age
And death and birth –
For out of one came all
From all comes one.

Edith Sitwell is buried in St Mary's churchyard extension, Weedon Lois, Northamptonshire, under a headstone designed by Henry Moore. It bears this, her own version of words from Heraclitus, which she had quoted in the concluding lines of her poem 'The Wind of Early Spring'.

(Sir) A(lan) P. HERBERT English writer and politician (1890–1971)

6 The portions of a woman that appeal to man's depravity
Are fashioned with considerable care.

Authorship of this bawdy poem, indeed something of a classic of the genre, was owned up to by Herbert. In Reginald Pound's biography (1976) he is quoted as saying: 'Many such works have been put down to me with which I had nothing to do ... this was the only one to which I confess.' He was 'neither ashamed nor proud of it', had penned it after a visit to the ship's doctor on a homeward voyage from Ceylon in the 1920s, and afterwards feared that 'by the perversity of fate it would survive as the sole proof of his poetic powers'.

George HERBERT English poet and clergyman (1593–1633)

1 Church-bells beyond the stars heard, the soul's blood,
The land of spices; something understood.

'Sonnet' (1633). Hence, *Something Understood*, the title of an autobiography (1986) by Gerald Priestland, a former BBC religious affairs correspondent, and then of a BBC Radio 4 series about 'the whole universe of religious sensation'.

Louis HEREN English journalist and editor (1919–95)

2 Why is this lying bastard lying to me?

Maxim, often attributed to Heren, the former messenger boy on *The Times* who rose to be deputy editor of the London paper. The idea is that a journalist when interviewing officials or politicians should keep asking himself this question. Latterly, the saying has been attributed to such other journalistic figures as Auberon Waugh and Jeremy Paxman, and also to that quirky *Times* figure of an earlier era, Claud Cockburn (though not quite his style). It proved difficult to pin this saying down, but prospects brightened when Paul Vallely, an associate editor of *The Independent*, wrote (8 July 2003): 'When I was a young reporter on *The Times*, one of the paper's most legendary figures, Louis Heren ... took me out to lunch [at the Garrick Club in the mid-1980s]. He wanted to pass on a tip that he'd had from an even more legendary American journalist when he was a Washington correspondent. "When you are interviewing someone," he said, "you need always to keep in the back of your mind the question: 'Why is this lying bastard lying to me?'"'

Well, many of the best quotes are remembered in a variety of forms and may also be ascribed to more than one source even by their originators. I at last found a written version in Heren's own book, *Growing Up On* The Times, Chap. 1 (1978): 'I learned to be sceptical, or rather my natural scepticism was sharpened, very early in my career when, just out of the army, I helped to cover the 1946–7 fuel crisis. One of the main sources of information was the old Ministry of Labour, and the officials were defensive and unhelpful ... I was even refused handouts, which are the official version of the truth, and was dependent for a sight of them upon a nice man who was the industrial correspondent of the old *Daily Worker* ...

'The *Worker* man was also a mentor of sorts. One day, when I asked him for some advice before interviewing the permanent secretary, he said, "Always ask yourself why these lying bastards are lying to you." I still ask myself that question today.' So, there we have it: not Heren's own maxim and to do with interviewing civil servants or officials rather than ministers or politicians. But it still counts.

HERODOTUS Greek historian (?485–425BC)

3 Neither snow nor rain nor heat nor gloom of night stays these couriers from the swift completion of their appointed rounds.

Words inscribed on the stone face of the New York City Post Office (all in capitals, and with a dot between each word), being adapted from the *Histories* of Herodotus, Bk 8, Chap. 98. He is describing how King Cyrus the Great of Persia set up what is thought to have been the first organized system of mounted messengers (in the 6th century BC). But the New York inscription has given rise to the comment, 'Well, what is it then?'

George Rawlinson's 1858 translation of the original is: 'Nothing travels so fast as these Persian messengers ... and these men will not be hindered from accomplishing at their best speed the distance which they have to go, either by snow, or rain, or heat, or by the darkness of night.'

Michael HESELTINE (later Lord Heseltine) English Conservative politician (1933–)

4 I knew that, 'He who wields the knife never wears the crown.'

Interviewed in *New Society* (14 February 1986). He later went on to prove it by standing against Mrs Thatcher, only to see John Major succeed her as Prime Minister. No other instance of this expression has so far been turned up and, at the moment, it would appear to have been an 'instant proverb', a vivid coinage to illustrate a political fact. David Whayman prefers 'The hand that bears the sword seldom wears the crown' as the original of this putative proverb and traces the *idea* back to the assassination of Julius Caesar – with Brutus doing the wielding and Augustus doing the wearing. He also notes that, post-Heseltine, Andrew Roberts in *Salisbury* (1999) has: 'In denouncing his Party leader for lack of principle in the 1860s, Salisbury had after all only attempted unsuccessfully to do what Disraeli had managed to do to Peel twenty years earlier. They constitute two rare examples of politicians who both wielded the knife and also wore the crown.'

In his autobiography, *Life In the Jungle* (2000), Heseltine wrote: 'I had once over lunch in February 1986 encapsulated my position to the *New Society* journalist David Lipsey ... I am amused by my early and uncharacteristic flash of modesty. It turned out to be a prophetic, if injudicious, comment.'

Gordon HEWART (later Viscount Hewart) British
lawyer and politician (1870–1943)

1 Justice should not only be done, but should man-
ifestly and undoubtedly be seen to be done.

The origin of this noted legal observation is contained in a
ruling by Hewart (King's Bench Reports, 1924). A man
named McCarthy in Hastings had been accused of dangerous driving. There had been an accident in which people
were injured. He was convicted, but it was later discovered
that a partner in the firm of solicitors who had demanded
damages against him was also clerk to the Hastings justices. As Robert Jackson noted in *The Chief* (1959), no one
believed that the clerk had acted improperly during the
case, but the circumstances warranted an application by
McCarthy's solicitor for the conviction to be quashed in a
Divisional Court. Hewart ruled in his favour in the case of
Rex *v.* Sussex Justices (9 November 1923).

When a fellow-judge joked that 'be seen' was a misprint for
'seem', Hewart made it clear that justice must always be
seen to be done in view of the defendant and of the world.
Compare MORTON 329:6.

2 If it's only wind, I'll call it ...

F.E. Smith, 1st Earl of Birkenhead, taunted Hewart, when
Lord Chief Justice, about the size of his stomach. 'What's
it to be – a boy or a girl?' Replied Hewart: 'If it's a boy I'll
call him John. If it's a girl I'll call her Mary. But if, as I suspect, it's only wind, I'll call it F.E. Smith.'

I printed that anecdote in my book *Quote ... Unquote*
(1978). The story had come to me the previous year from
a *Quote ... Unquote* listener who said it had been told to her
brother 'by a stranger in a bus queue in Harrogate in 1923'.
Smith died in 1930, Hewart in 1943.

According to Humphrey McQueen in *Social Sketches of
Australia* (1978), the Antipodean version has Sir George
Houstoun Reid (1845–1918) replying, in answer to the ques-
tion, apropos his stomach, 'What are you going to call it,
George?': 'If it's a boy, I'll call it after myself. If it's a girl,
I'll call it Victoria after our Queen. But if, as I strongly sus-
pect, it's nothing but piss and wind, I'll call it after you.'

According to *Pass the Port Again* (1981 edn) the exchange
occurred between Lord Haldane and Winston Churchill,
as also in John Parker, *Father of the House* (1982), in which
the exchange is specifically located at the Oxford Union in
1926. *The Faber Book of Anecdotes* (1985) has the US version: President Taft (who died in 1930) making the retort
to Senator Chauncey Depew (who died in 1929).

Joe HILL Swedish-born songwriter and industrial
organizer in US (1879–1915)

3 You will eat, bye and bye,
In that glorious land above the sky;
Work and pray, live on hay,
You'll get pie in the sky when you die.

'The Preacher and the Slave', in *Songs of the Workers* (1911),
published by the Industrial Workers of the World. Sung to
the tune of 'In the Sweet By and By', this added 'pie in the
sky' to the list of common expressions. Hill contributed
songs, essays and letters to the IWW's *Industrial Workers
and Solidarity* from 1910 until his execution (on a murder
charge). See also ALI 6:2.

Patty Smith HILL American teacher (1868–1946)

4 Happy Birthday to You.

Originally entitled 'Good Morning to All' and published in
Song Stories for Children (1893), Hill's well-known song with
this title was eventually copyrighted in 1935. The music was
written by her sister, Mildred J. Hill (1859–1916). What we
have here is the 'most frequently sung phrase in English',
according to *The Guinness Book of Records* (which also lists
'For He's a Jolly Good Fellow' and 'Auld Lang Syne' as the
top songs of all time). 'Happy Birthday to You' was the first
line of the second stanza of the original song. It has had a
chequered legal history because of the widespread belief
that it is in the public domain and, therefore, out of copyright. It is not.

Rowland HILL English preacher (1744–1833)

5 Why must the devil have all the best tunes?

According to E.W. Broome's biography of Hill, what he said
was: 'I do not see any good reason why the devil should
have all the good tunes.' He was referring to Charles
Wesley's defence of the practice of setting hymns to the
music of popular songs. The phrase is now used generally
to rebut the necessity for the virtuous and worthy to be dull
and dreary. This Revd Hill is not to be confused with Sir
Rowland Hill (1795–1879), originator of the English penny
postage system.

A perhaps better known – but later – use of the phrase
concerns William Booth (1829–1912), the founder of the
Salvation Army. It was his practice to use established tunes
to accompany religious lyrics. In this way, more than 80
music-hall songs acquired religious lyrics, 'Champagne
Charlie is My Name', for example, became 'Bless His Name
He Sets Me Free'. When Booth was challenged on the suit-
ability of such a process, he was doubtful at first, but then
exclaimed, 'Why should the Devil have all the best tunes!'

Reference to the Booth use is made by the composer Percy Grainger in the Preface to *Spoon River* (1930): 'Salvation Army Booth objected to the devil having all the good tunes. I object to jazz and vaudeville having all the best instruments!'

(Sir) Edmund HILLARY New Zealand mountaineer (1919–)

1 Well, we knocked the bastard off!

The first two climbers to reach the summit of the world's highest mountain, Mount Everest, in the Himalayas, were Hillary and his Sherpa companion, Tenzing Norgay. They were members of the British-led expedition of 1953. In his autobiography *Nothing Venture, Nothing Win* (1975), Hillary described what happened when they came down from the summit on 29 May: 'George [Lowe] met us with a mug of soup just above camp, and seeing his stalwart frame and cheerful face reminded me how fond of him I was. My comment was not specially prepared for public consumption but for George ... He nodded with pleasure ... "Thought you must have!"'

Among the frequent misrenderings of the remark is, 'We done the bugger!' – as in *PDMQ* (1971), where it is even ascribed to Tenzing Norgay (who did not speak English).

Lady (Alice) HILLINGDON Wife of 2nd Baron Hillingdon (1857–1940)

2 Close your eyes and think of England.

The source that *Partridge/Catch Phrases* (1977) gives for this saying – in the sense of advice to women when confronted with the inevitability of sexual intercourse, or jocularly about doing almost anything unpalatable – is the *Journal* (1912) of Lady Hillingdon: 'I am happy now that Charles calls on my bedchamber less frequently than of old. As it is, I now endure but two calls a week and when I hear his steps outside my door I lie down on my bed, close my eyes, open my legs and think of England.'

There *was* a Lady Hillingdon who married the 2nd Baron in 1886. He was Conservative MP for West Kent (1885–92) and, according to *Who's Who*, owned 'about 4500 acres' when he died (in 1919). A portrait of Lady Hillingdon was painted by Sir Frank Dicksee PRA in 1904. A rose was also named after her.

But where her journals are, if they ever existed, is unknown. Jonathan Gathorne-Hardy also quotes the 'journal' in *The Rise and Fall of the British Nanny* (1972), but just to complicate matters, he refers to her as Lady 'Hillingham', though *ODMQ* (1991) and *ODQ* (1992) in picking up this reference do not appear to have noticed.

Salome, Dear, Not In the Fridge!, ed. Arthur Marshall (1968),

has it instead that the newly wedded Mrs Stanley Baldwin is supposed to have declared: 'I shut my eyes tight and thought of the Empire.' We may discount Bob Chieger's assumption in *Was It Good for You, Too?* (1983) that 'Close your eyes and think of England' was advice given to Queen Victoria on *her* wedding night. In 1977 there was a play by John Chapman and Anthony Marriott at the Apollo Theatre, London, with the title *Shut Your Eyes and Think of England*.

Sometimes the phrase occurs in the form 'lie back and think of England' but this is a conflation with 'she should lie back and enjoy it'.

HIPPOCRATES Greek physician (?460–357BC)

3 *Ars longa vita brevis* [Life is short, the art long].

Aphorisms. As a suggested epitaph for one Thomas Longbottom who died young, '*Ars longa, vita brevis*' was contributed to BBC Radio *Quote ... Unquote* (17 May 1978). In the same edition, Richard Stilgoe suggested rather that *Punch* in its early days had reproduced the death announcement of a man called 'Longbottom' and put over it the headline 'Vita brevis'. Unverified. Hence, also, 'Ars Longa, Vita Sackville-West', which was used as a chapter heading in the book *Quote ... Unquote* (1978).

Raymond HITCHCOCK American comedian (?1870–1929)

4 All dressed up and nowhere to go.

The phrase comes from a song popularized by Hitchcock in *The Beauty Shop* (New York 1914) and *Mr Manhattan* (London 1915):

> When you're all dressed up and no place to go,
> Life seems dreary, weary and slow.
> My heart has ached as well as bled
> For the tears I've shed,
> When I've had no place to go
> Unless I went back to bed ...

The words gained further emphasis when they were used by newspaper editor William Allen White to describe the Progressive Party following Theodore Roosevelt's decision to retire from presidential competition in 1916. He said the party was: 'All dressed up with nowhere to go.'

OED2 has this phrase starting life in a song by 'G. Whiting' (1912), 'When You're All Dressed Up and Have No Place to Go', but Lowe's *Directory of Popular Music* ascribes it to Silvio Hein and Benjamin Burt.

Cole Porter wrote a parody in 1914 concluding with the words '... and don't know Huerto Go'.

Adolf HITLER German Nazi leader (1889–1945)

1 It was no secret that this time the revolution would have to be bloody ... When we spoke of it, we called it 'The Night of the Long Knives [*Die Nacht der langen Messer*]'.

During the weekend of 29 June to 2 July 1934, there occurred in Nazi Germany the so-called Night of the Long Knives. On this original occasion, Hitler, aided by Himmler's black-shirted SS, liquidated the leadership of the brown-shirted SA. The SA, undisciplined storm troopers, had helped Hitler gain power but were now getting in the way of his dealings with the German army. Some 83 were murdered on the pretext that they were plotting another revolution. Hitler's explanation (above) to the Reichstag on 13 July does not make it clear whether he himself coined the phrase. Indeed, it seems that he may have been alluding to an early Nazi marching song.

Hence, the phrase 'Night of the Long Knives' now in common use for any kind of surprise purge (usually without bloodshed). Compare, *Verschwörung der langen Messer* ('conspiracy of the long knives', translating the much older Welsh phrase *twyll y cyllvyll hirion*), which had previously been used as the name of a pre-meditated massacre of unarmed and unprepared men. To be precise it described the supposed murder by Hengist and his Saxons of a party of British nobles at a peace conference, as described by Nennius, Geoffrey of Monmouth, and various other pseudo-historical sources. The German phrase is used in Geoffrey of Monmouth's *Historia Regum Britanniae* (ed. San-Marte, 1854).

2 War is the father of all things.

To add to his many other atrocities, Hitler was apparently a misquoter. In *The War Path: Hitler's Germany 1933–9* (1978), David Irving says that Hitler's favourite quotation was the above, which he attributed to Karl von Clausewitz. But, according to Mr Irving, it was in fact uttered by 'Heracles'. Unverified.

In a speech at Chemnitz (2 April 1938), Hitler said: 'Man has become great through struggle ... Struggle is the father of all things.'

3 A last appeal to reason.

On 19 July 1940 Adolf Hitler made a speech to the Reichstag. Following, as it did, the Fall of France, it somewhat surprisingly appeared to contain an offer of peace to the British (though Hitler tried to draw a distinction between ordinary British folk and their warmongering leaders, principally Winston Churchill).

The speech and the peace proposal, although reported prominently in *The Times* next morning, were largely ignored, and the Germans were much annoyed by the British rejection of the peace offer that followed. In an attempt to appeal to the British people, literally over the heads of the leadership, copies of the speech were dropped on England by the Luftwaffe in a leaflet-raid on the night of 1–2 August. The Imperial War Museum in London displays an actual copy of the tabloid-sized leaflet dropped over Somerset a little later, on 11 August. It is headed 'A LAST APPEAL TO REASON / BY / ADOLF HITLER / Speech before the Reichstag 19th July 1940', and makes very tedious reading.

A correspondent wrote (1988): 'I saw a copy myself at the time and tried to read it. Nearly half was taken up, I remember, by long lists of appointments, transfers and promotions in the German armed forces and civil administration ... Needless to say, public opinion generally regarded the leaflet as beneath contempt. I remember hearing about an item on the subject in a cinema newsreel, which ended by showing a pair of hands cutting up the leaflet into small rectangles, threading a string through the corners, and hanging the bundle on a hook on a tiled wall. Very explicit for those prudish days: the audience, I was told, roared approval.'

4 *Nacht und Nebel* [Night and Fog].

Name of a 1941 decree issued over Hitler's signature describing a simple process: anyone suspected of a crime against occupying German forces was to disappear into 'night and fog'. Such people were thrown into the concentration-camp system, in most cases never to be heard of again. Alain Resnais, the French film director, made a cinema short about a concentration camp and called it *Nuit et Brouillard* (1955). Although there might seem to be an echo in the title of Woody Allen's film *Shadows and Fog* (1992), this alludes rather to features of German expressionist films of the 1920s and 30s.

The phrase comes from Wagner's opera *Das Rheingold* (1869): '*Nacht und Nebel niemand gleich*' is the spell that Alberich puts on the magic Tarnhelm, which renders him invisible and omnipresent. It means approximately 'In night and fog no one is seen' or 'Night and fog is the same as being no one, a non-person' or 'Night and fog make you no one instantly.'

5 The Final Solution [*Endlösung*] of the Jewish Problem.

A euphemistic term given by Nazi officials from the summer of 1941 onwards to Hitler's plan to exterminate the Jews of Europe. A directive (drafted by Adolf Eichmann) was sent by Hermann Goering to Reinhard Heydrich on 31 July 1941: 'Submit to me as soon as possible a draft showing ... measures already taken for the execution of the intended final solution of the Jewish question.' Gerald Reitlinger in *The*

Final Solution (1953) says that the choice of phrase was probably, though not certainly, Hitler's own. Before then it had been used in a non-specific way to cover other possibilities, such as emigration. It is estimated that the 'final solution' led to the deaths of up to six million Jews.

1 *Brennt Paris?* [Is Paris burning?]

Following the D-Day landings on the northern coast of France in 1944, the next target was the liberation of Paris. The Allied forces managed to reach the French capital ahead of German Panzer divisions, which would have tried to destroy the city. When Hitler put the above inquiry to Jodl at Oberkommando der Wehrmacht at Rastenberg (25 August 1944) – after Paris had been recaptured by the Allies – he received no reply. Later, the phrase was used as the title of a book by Collins and Lapierre (1965) and of a film (US 1965).

Thomas HOBBES English philosopher (1588–1679)

2 No arts; no letters; no society; and which is worst of all, continual fear and danger of violent death; and the life of man, solitary, poor, nasty, brutish, and short.

This description of the natural state of man prior to the emergence of the state was given by Thomas Hobbes in *Leviathan, or the Matter, Form, and Power of a Commonwealth, Ecclesiastical and Civil*, Chap. 13 (1651). In this treatise of political philosophy, Hobbes sees man not as a social being but as a selfish creature.

The last portion of this bleak view has fallen victim to over-quoting, as Philip Howard, Literary Editor of *The Times*, noted on 15 August 1984. He warned of the danger that: 'We become so fond of hackneyed quotation that we trot it out, without thinking, at every opportunity.' He gave, as his example, 'the one about the life of man being "solitary, poor, nasty, brutish, and short," just to let everybody know that I am an intellectual sort of chap who reads Hobbes in the bath'.

Curiously, later that year, on 1 November, when *The Times* had a first leader on the assassination of Mrs Indira Gandhi, it began by observing that world figures know all too sickeningly well 'the continual fear and danger of violent death' that Thomas Hobbes identified as a condition of man. And added: 'With that awful daily awareness, now goes for some a reminder of his definition of life as nasty, brutish and short.' Compare GIBBONS 212:3.

Ralph HODGSON English poet (1871–1962)

3 'Twould ring the bells of Heaven
The wildest peal for years,
If parson lost his senses
And people came to theirs,

And he and they together
Knelt down with angry prayers
For tamed and shabby tigers
And dancing dogs and bears,
And wretched, blind, pit ponies,
And little hunted hares.

'The Bells of Heaven' (1917). Hence, *Shabby Tiger*, the title of Howard Spring's first novel (1934). But why? It is a tale of bohemian goings-on in Manchester, but the relevance of the title is not immediately apparent (and no mention of the poem is made as an epigraph or in any other way). Professor John Morris commented (2000): 'The use of the expression in Hodgson's poem is a direct reference to cruelty to animals used for human purposes: work and entertainment. In this sense "shabby tigers" is referential and unambiguous (*unless*, that is, it was already a saying before Hodgson wrote his verse). In Spring's novel, it seems to me that the title refers to its central character, Nick Faunt, who is literally shabby but is determined to fight for the right to follow his destiny, as he sees it, to be a great artist – despite his bourgeois upper-class moneyed origins. I suppose the expression refers to a person or creature whose splendour is hidden by subservience.'

How odd authors are in applying allusive, not to say obscure, phrases like this as titles. In the end one is forced to conclude that Spring chose it because it was catchy – if near meaningless. But it certainly served him well, launching his career as a popular novelist. Elizabeth Knowles then commented on the two (subsequent) uses of the phrase in Dorothy L. Sayers, *Busman's Honeymoon*, Chaps. 1 & 3 (1937), where, 'in a pre-marital exchange between Harriet Vane and Lord Peter Wimsey, the tiger represents her capacity for response – which they pleasurably discover to be neither shabby nor (as far as I can remember) daunted'. Angela Koenig pointed out that Lord Peter had feared Harriet's sexual drive might have been inhibited by her being put on trial for the murder of her former lover.

Gerard HOFFNUNG English cartoonist and musician (1925–59)

4 Have you tried the famous echo in the Reading Room of the British Museum?

Suggestion to tourists visiting Britain for the first time. Speech, Oxford Union debating society (4 December 1958), on the motion 'Life begins at 38'. Most of the 'Faulty Advice for Foreigners' derived from *New Statesman* competitions. 'Notices like "Keep Left" and "No Right Turn" are political slogans, and should be ignored by motorists' and 'Zebra parking places will be found anywhere' were both appropriated by Hoffnung for his speech. The nearest the *NS* collections of competition winners get to the Reading Room remark is: 'Cheering is permitted in the public gallery of the House of Commons.'

1 '[Dear Sir or Madam,] Having freshly taken over the propriety of this notorious house, I am wishful that you remove to me your esteemed costume. Standing amongst savage scenery, the hotel offers stupendous revelations. There is a french widow in every bedroom, affording deliteful prospects. I give personal look to the interior wants of each geust. Here you shall be well fed-up and agreeably drunk! [Having once sampled our fooding, you will surely wish to enlarge your stays! Numerous bad-rooms! Full drainage!!] Our charges for weakly visitors are scarcely creditable! Peculiar arrangements for gross parties! Our motto is ever "Serve You Right!"'

'Letters from Tyrolean Landlords', in the same speech. In 2001, Charlotte Halliday revealed the extent of Hoffnung's unacknowledged borrowings from Competition No. 281 in *The Spectator* for this. As most storytellers do, he personalized the account by saying that he and his wife had 'received' the letters. In fact, he was merely reading extracts from Mervyn Horder's report on a competition for 'the most amusing reply in "English" to a holiday inquiry from the keeper of a small inn high up in the Dolomites'. R. Kennard Davis, in particular, seems to require belated credit for his entry, here printed in its entirety (above), with Hoffnung's minimal omissions in brackets. Charlotte added quietly, 'We always thought it was very hard on the original competitors that they were never mentioned!'

Lancelot HOGBEN English scientist (1895–1975)

2 This is not the age of pamphleteers. It is the age of engineers. The spark-gap is mightier than the pen. Democracy will not be salvaged by men who talk fluently, debate forcefully and quote aptly.

Epilogue, *Science for the Citizen* (1938). The art of quotation cannot put off the end of civilization – according to this scientist anyway.

Henry Scott HOLLAND English Anglican clergyman (1847–1918)

3 Death is nothing at all ... I have only slipped away into the next room.

Hardly a day passes without newspaper reports of memorial services noting that 'so-and-so read from the works of Canon Henry Scott Holland'. The passage in question is the one

beginning, 'Death is nothing at all', and judging by its popularity, the words have a message capable of comforting many who are bereaved. It comes from a sermon on death entitled 'The King of Terrors' Holland delivered in St Paul's Cathedral (of which he was a Canon) on 15 May 1910, at which time the body of King Edward VII was lying in state at Westminster. The context is important:

There is another aspect altogether which death can wear for us. It is that which first comes to us, perhaps, as we look down upon the quiet face, so cold and white, of one who has been very near and dear to us. There it lies in possession of its own secret. It knows it all. So we seem to feel. And what the face says in its sweet silence to us as a last message from one whom we loved is: 'Death is nothing at all. It does not count. I have only slipped away into the next room. Nothing has happened. Everything remains exactly as it was. I am I, and you are you, and the old life that we lived so fondly together is untouched, unchanged. Whatever we were to each other, that we are still. Call me by the old familiar name. Speak of me in the easy way which you always used. Put no difference into your tone. Wear no forced air of solemnity or sorrow. Laugh as we always laughed at the little jokes that we enjoyed together. Play, smile, think of me, pray for me. Let my name be ever the household word that it always was. Let it be spoken without an effort, without the ghost of a shadow upon it. Life means all that it ever meant. It is the same as it ever was. There is absolute and unbroken continuity. What is this death but a negligible accident? Why should I be out of mind because I am out of sight? I am but waiting for you, for an interval, somewhere very near, just around the corner. All is well. Nothing is hurt; nothing is lost. One brief moment and all will be as it was before. How we shall laugh at the trouble of parting when we meet again!'

So the face speaks. Surely while we speak there is a smile flitting over it; a smile as of gentle fun at the trick played us by seeming death ...

The sermon was published posthumously in a collection entitled *Facts of the Faith* (1919). There is a basic similarity of thought contained in a sermon by a Dean of St Paul's, with whose works one assumes Holland must have been familiar: John Donne. Preaching about death (as he did so often), on Easter Day 1627, Donne said in St Paul's (the earlier building): 'Though death have divided us ... yet we do live together already, in a Holy Communion of Saints ... If the dead, and we, be not upon one floor, nor under one story, yet we are under one roof. We think not a friend lost, because he is gone into another room, nor because he is gone into another Land; And into another world, no man is gone; for that Heaven, which God created, and this world, is all one world.'

Oliver Wendell HOLMES Jr American judge
(1841–1935)

1 The question in every case is whether the words used are used in such circumstances and are of such a nature as to create a clear and present danger that they will bring about the evils that Congress has a right to prevent.

Ruling in the US Supreme Court in the case of Schenk *v.* United States (1919). This concerned free speech and included Holmes's claim that the most stringent protection of same would not protect a man in falsely shouting fire in a theatre and causing panic. Hence, *Clear and Present Danger*, title of film (US 1994) from a Tom Clancy novel about a CIA agent in conflict with his political masters in Washington.

HOME See DOUGLAS-HOME.

HOMER Greek poet (8th century BC)

2 Rosy-fingered dawn.

The Odyssey, Bk 2, line 1. It was Alexander Pope who introduced this translation. The phrase occurs frequently throughout the epic.

3 Gray-eyed Athena sent them a favourable breeze, a fresh west wind, singing over the wine-dark sea.

In the same work, Bk 2, line 420. Homer's word *oinos* literally means something like 'sunset red', but 'wine-dark' was the coinage of the translators Lang, Lees and Myers in the 1880s, and it caught on where others ('wine-blue', for example) did not. The image evokes a sea painted wine-red by the setting sun. Hence, Hugh MacDiarmid, in *A Drunk Man Looks at the Thistle* (1926): 'Whilst I, pure fule, owre continents unkent / And wine-dark oceans waunder like Ulysses'; and *The Wine-Dark Sea*, the English translation (1985) of Leonardo Sciascia's collection of stories, *Il mare colore del vino* (1973). The image is also used in *The Iliad*, Bk 23, when Achilles grieves over Patroclus.

4 But night is already at hand; it is well to yield to the night.

The Iliad, Bk 7, line 264. This is but one translation – others include: 'And now 'tis late; we must submit to night' and 'The light is failing. We should do well to take the hint.' Either way, in the original Greek, Maurice Baring used to say that it was the most beautiful line in Homer. Hence, just possibly, *Yield to the Night*, title of a film (UK 1956) – the actress Diana Dors's finest hour as a condemned murderess – based on a novel by Joan Henry.

5 As the woman with the dog's eyes would not close my eyelids for me as I lay dying into Hades.

In the same work, Bk 11. The speech of Agamemnon's shade to Odysseus. Hence, *As I Lay Dying* (1930), title of a novel by William Faulkner.

Thomas HOOD English poet (1799–1845)

6 There is a silence where hath been no sound,
There is a silence where no sound may be,
In the cold grave – under the deep, deep sea.

Sonnet, 'Silence'. These were the last words heard in the film *The Piano* (1993) by the New Zealand writer and director, Jane Campion. They are 'spoken' by the dumb heroine who has just consigned her piano to the bottom of the sea and who has also come near to death herself by being dragged down with it.

Theodore HOOK English writer, hoaxer and joker
(1788–1841)

7 I beg your pardon, sir, are you anyone in particular?

Said to an imposing gentleman, after bowing low to him. Quoted in W.D. Adams, *Treasury of Modern Anecdote* (1886). Hook or not, 'Please, are you anybody?' was the caption to a cartoon by Lewis Baumer in *Punch* (16 February 1938). It showed a little girl with an autograph book approaching an impressive gentleman.

Herbert HOOVER American Republican 31st President
(1874–1964)

8 We are challenged with a peacetime choice between the American system of rugged individualism and a European philosophy of diametrically opposed doctrines – doctrines of paternalism and state socialism.

So said Hoover, running for the Presidency, in a speech in New York on 22 October 1928. Six years later he commented: 'While I can make no claim for having introduced the term "rugged individualism", I should have been proud to have invented it. It has been used by American leaders for over half a century in eulogy of those God-fearing men and women of honesty whose stamina and character and fearless assertion of rights led them to make their own way in life.'

9 The grass will grow in the streets of a hundred cities, a thousand towns.

From a speech (31 October 1932) on proposals 'to reduce the protective tariff to a competitive tariff for revenue'. The image had earlier been used by William Jennings Bryan in his 'Cross of Gold' speech (106:4): 'Burn down your cities and leave our farms, and your cities will spring up again as if by magic; but destroy our farms and the grass will grow in the streets of every city in the country.' Compare from Anthony Trollope, *Doctor Thorne*, Chap. 15 (1858): '"Why, luke at this 'ere town," continued he of the sieve, "the grass be a-growing in the very streets; – that can't be no gude."'

Anthony HOPE (Sir Anthony Hope Hawkins)
English novelist (1863–1933)

1 Oh, for an hour of Herod!

At the first night of J.M. Barrie's play *Peter Pan* (1904). Quoted in Denis Mackail, *The Story of JMB* (1941). Compare: 'There are moments when one sympathizes with Herod' – Saki, 'Reginald on House-Parties' (1904).

2 His foe was folly & his weapon wit.

This is inscribed on W.S. Gilbert's memorial on the Victoria Embankment, London, and the line was provided in 1915 by Hope, who recalled: 'Whilst on the committee of the Authors' Society I had something to do with the memorial. The words on the memorial are mine, except that I put them first into prose – "Folly was his foe, and wit his weapon", – then somebody (I forget who) pointed out that transposed they would make a line, and this was adopted.'

3   TO
                THE BEAUTIFUL MEMORY
                   OF KENNETH GRAHAME
                    HUSBAND OF ELSPETH
                               AND
                   FATHER OF ALASTAIR
                 WHO PASSED THE RIVER
                   ON THE 6TH OF JULY 1932
                             LEAVING
               CHILDHOOD & LITERATURE
                       THROUGH HIM
                       THE MORE BLEST
                         FOR ALL TIME.

Epitaph on the grave of Kenneth Grahame, author of *The Wind in the Willows*, in St Cross churchyard, Oxford. Hope was his cousin. The use of the phrase 'passing the river' for death is absolutely appropriate for an author who wrote so enchantingly of the river bank and 'messing about in boats'. It may also be taken to allude to the crossing of the rivers of Styx, Acheron, Lethe and so on, the classical symbol of death, but it chiefly refers to the Christian use: in John Bunyan's *The Pilgrim's Progress* (1678) Christian passes through the River of Death (which has no bridge) and quotes Isaiah 43:2, 'When thou passest through the waters, I will be with thee, and through the Rivers, they shall not overflow thee.'

HORACE Roman poet (65–8BC)

4 *Atque inter silvas Academi quaerere verum* [And seek for truth in the groves of Academe].

Epistles, II.ii.45. Hence, the phrase 'groves of Academe' for the academic community or the world of university scholarship. *The Groves of Academe* was the title of a novel (1952) by Mary McCarthy.

5 *Nil desperandum* [Never despair].

Odes, I.vii.27. Literally, 'there is nought to be despaired of'; also translated as 'never say die'. The context is '*nil desperandum est Teucro duce et auspice Teucro* [nothing is to be despaired of with Teucer as leader and protector]'. Hence, *nil carborundum* ... (as in the title of a play by Henry Livings, 1962), though this alludes rather to the cod-Latin phrase *Illegitimi non carborundum*, supposed to mean 'Don't let the bastards grind you down', used by US General 'Vinegar Joe' Stilwell as his motto during the Second World War, though it is not suggested he devised it. *Partridge/Catch Phrases* gives it, rather, as '*Illegitimis*' and its origins in British army intelligence very early on in the same war. Something like the phrase has also been reported from 1929. 'Carborundum' is, in fact, the trade name of a very hard substance composed of silicon carbide, used in grinding. Perhaps because it is a made-up one, the phrase takes many forms, e.g.: '*Nil illegitimis ...*', '*Nil bastardo illegitimi ...*', '*Nil bastardo carborundum ...*' etc. When the Rt Revd David Jenkins, the Bishop of Durham, was unwise enough to make use of the phrase at a private meeting in March 1985, a cloth-eared journalist reported him as having said, '*Nil desperandum illegitimi ...*'

6   *Dum loquimur, fugerit invida*
Aetas: carpe diem, quam minimum credula postero.
[While we are talking, envious time is fleeing: seize the day, put no trust in the future.]

Odes, I.xi.7. Accordingly, '*carpe diem*' has become a motto meaning 'enjoy the day while you have the chance' or 'seize the opportunity, make the most of the present time'.

7 *Eheu fugaces, Postume, Postume,*
Labuntur anni.
[Ah me, Postumus, Postumus, the fleeting years are slipping by.]

Odes, II.xiv.1. Note how Byron quotes this cry in his diary: 'It is three minutes past twelve ... and I am now thirty-three! *Eheu, fugaces, Posthume, Posthume, / Labuntur anni,* – but I don't regret them so much for what I have done, as for what I *might* have done' – entry for 22 January 1821.

1 *Dulce et decorum est pro patria mori* [It is sweet and honourable to die for one's country].

Odes, III.ii.13. '*Pro patria mori*' is an epitaph frequently put on the graves of those killed on active service. It has also been used as a family motto. See OWEN 350:12.

2 Even Homer nods.

Meaning 'even the greatest, best and wisest of us can't be perfect all the time, and can make mistakes', this phrase was not, naturally, coined by Homer himself. Current by the 18th century at least is the form: 'Let Homer, who sometimes nods, sleep soundly upon your shelf for three or four years' – letter of Lord Chesterfield to Lord Huntingdon (31 August 1749). *Mencken* has 'Even Homer sometimes nods' as an English proverb derived from Horace, *Ars Poetica* (?8BC): '*Indignor quandoque bonus dormitat Homerus* [I am indignant when worthy Homer nods]' – and familiar since the 17th century. Longinus (AD ?213–273) evidently added: 'They say that Homer sometimes nods. Perhaps he does – but then he dreams as Zeus might dream.'

See also CORY 155:4.

A.E. HOUSMAN English poet (1859–1936)

3 Into my heart an air that kills
From yon far country blows;
What are those blue remembered hills,
What spires, what farms are those?

That is the land of lost content,
I see it shining plain,
The happy highways where I went,
And cannot come again.

A Shropshire Lad, No. 40. Hence, *Blue Remembered Hills*, title of a TV play about childhood (1979) by Dennis Potter. The last word in the first line has been queried. Did Housman originally intend it to be 'chills'? Certainly 'chills' would be more apposite and one wonders what point the use of 'kills' is supposed to have. But in *The Manuscript Poems of A.E. Housman*, ed. Haber (1955), 'Into my heart an air that kills' is given as appearing in the printer's copy of *A Shropshire Lad* in 1896. This is presumably what also appears on Housman's manuscript in Trinity College, Cambridge.

4 Be still, my soul, be still: the arms you bear
are brittle,
Earth and high heaven are fixt of old and
founded strong.

In the same work, No. 48. Hence, *Earth and High Heaven*, title of a novel (1944) by Gwethalyn Graham.

5 But since the man that runs away
Lives to die another day.

In the same work, No. 56. Housman is putting a typically lugubrious spin on the traditional proverb, 'He who fights and runs away, lives to fight another day.' Hence, presumably, *Die Another Day*, the title of the 20th James Bond film (UK/US 2002).

6 When summer's end is nighing
And skies at evening cloud,
I muse on change and fortune
And all the feats I vowed
When I was young and proud.

Last Poems, No. 39 (1922). Hence, *Change and Fortune*, the title of the memoirs (1980) of the former Labour Cabinet minister, Douglas Jay (later Lord Jay).

7 I had a visit not long ago from Clarence Darrow, the great American barrister for defending murderers. He had only a few days in England but he could not return home without seeing me, because he had so often used my poems to rescue his clients from the electric chair. Loeb and Leopold owe their life sentence partly to me; and he gave me a copy of his speech, in which, sure enough, two of my pieces are misquoted.

From a letter to Basil Housman (dated 29 December 1927), included in *The Letters of A.E. Housman* (1971).

8 Ensanguining the skies
How heavily it dies
Into the west away;
Past touch and sight and sound,
Not further to be found,
How hopeless under ground
Falls the remorseful day.

More Poems (1936), No. XVI. Hence, the title of the final 'Inspector Morse' crime novel, *The Remorseful Day* (1999) by Colin Dexter. Although Dexter ascribes the phrase to A.E. Housman, Shakespeare had already used it, also to describe a sunset, in *Henry VI, Part 2*, IV.i.1 (1590–1): 'The gaudy, blabbing and remorseful day / Is crept into the bosom of the sea.'

1 Some can gaze and not be sick,
But I could never learn the trick.
There's this to say for blood and breath,
They give a man a taste for death.

Additional Poems, No. 16 (1937). Hence, *A Taste for Death*, the title of a crime novel (1986) by P.D. James.

2 Oh who is that young sinner with the handcuffs
on his wrists?
And what has he been after that they groan and
shake their fists?
And wherefore is he wearing such a conscience-
stricken air?
Oh they're taking him to prison for the colour of
his hair.

In the same collection, No. 18. The young sinner was homo-sexual and the 'colour of his hair' denotes his sexual orientation. The poem was apparently written in 1895, year of the trials of Oscar Wilde.

3 That is indeed very good. I shall have to repeat that
on the Golden Floor.

So Housman said to his doctor, who had told him a risqué story to cheer him up before he died (quoted in *The Daily Telegraph*, 21 February 1984). 'Golden floor' is an expression for heaven, possibly derived from 'threshing floor', as in various Old Testament verses. Current by 1813 (Shelley, 'Queen Mab'). The phrase also occurs in the Harvest Festival hymn 'Come ye thankful people, come'.

Julia Ward HOWE American preacher (1819–1910)

4 Mine eyes have seen the glory of the coming of
the Lord:
He is trampling out the vintage where the
grapes of wrath are stored.

'The Battle Hymn of the Republic' (1862). Written at the height of the Civil War after Howe had seen President Lincoln reviewing Union troops outside Washington in 1861. She thought they should have an anthem more suitable to sing than 'John Brown's Body' – but fitted her words to the earlier tune. Hence, *The Grapes of Wrath*, title of the novel (1939; film US 1940) by John Steinbeck.

Mary HOWITT English writer (1799–1888)

5 'Will you walk into my parlour?' said the spider
to the fly.
''Tis the prettiest little parlour that ever you did
spy.'

'The Spider and the Fly' (1834). Sometimes it has been insisted that the original was 'said *a* spider to *a* fly' – as in *ODQ* 1941–2004 – but this appears not to have been the case. A *Punch* parody of the poem (4 July 1868) is quite clearly entitled 'The Spider and the Fly'. There have been several musical settings of this poem. The Rolling Stones song called 'The Spider and the Fly' (written by Nanker and Phelge, recorded 1971) contains, however: 'Don't say Hi! like a spider to a fly' and 'I said my, my, my, like a spider to a fly, / Jump right ahead in my web.' Films entitled *The Spider and the Fly* (UK 1949; US 1995) have concerned themselves with policeman/thief pursuit and rival mystery writers.

The verse was parodied by Lewis Carroll in *Alice's Adventures in Wonderland* (1865) as: '"Will you walk a little faster?" said a whiting to a snail.'

Elbert HUBBARD American writer and editor
(1856–1915)

6 Never Explain – your friends do not need it and
your enemies will not believe you anyway.

The Motto Book (1907). Compare GRACIAN 218:4.

7 Life is just one damned thing after another.

In *The Philistine* (December 1909). Also attributed to Frank Ward O'Malley (1875–1932), though the saying may pre-date them both. It has become a general expression of dismay at a series of misfortunes – also rendered as 'ODTAA'. John Masefield published his novel *Odtaa* in 1926. Compare: 'History is one bloody thing after another', attributed to (Sir) Herbert Butterfield, English historian (1900–79). Alan Bennett, speaking of his play *The History Boys* (2004), was quoted thus in arts.telegraph (online) (21 June 2004): 'In the words of Rudge in the play, "History is just one fucking thing after another," which seems quite a brutish thing to say but was actually not said by him originally, but by Herbert Butterfield who was Professor of History at Cambridge in the '40s, only as he put it: "History is one bloody thing after another." The difference between the "bloody" and the "fucking" is what has happened in public discourse in the last 50 years.'

8 Editor: a person employed by a newspaper whose
business it is to separate the wheat from the chaff
and to see that the chaff is printed.

The Roycroft Dictionary (1914). See also STEVENSON 447:2.

Langston HUGHES American poet (1902–67)

1 What happens to a dream deferred?
Does it dry up
Like a raisin in the sun?

'Harlem' (1951). Hence, *A Raisin in the Sun*, the title of a play (1959; film US 1961) by Lorraine Hansberry.

Robert HUGHES Australian-born art critic (1938–)

2 *The Shock of the New.*

Title of TV series and book (1980) about modern art. As acknowledged, this was taken from the title of Ian Dunlop's 1972 book on 'seven historic exhibitions of modern art'. Compare Thomas Crawford's use of the idea in *Longer Scottish Poems* (1987), in connection with the best efforts of Robert Burns – which represent, 'the perfection of the old achieving the shock and immediacy of the new'.

Ted HUGHES English Poet Laureate (1930–98)

3 Even amidst fierce flames
The golden lotus can be planted.

Not words written by Hughes but chosen by him and inscribed on the grave of his wife Sylvia Plath, the American-born poet (1932–63), in the churchyard at Heptonstall in West Yorkshire. She is described as 'Shirley Plath Hughes', although at the time of her death, she was estranged from her husband. He arranged for her burial in his home village and indeed chose the somewhat obscure epitaph on her grave. It used to be asserted that the words were a translation from the Hindu poem, the Bhagavad-Gita, but Hughes said in *The Guardian* (20 April 1989) that the epitaph was merely a 'translation from the Sanskrit'. In fact, it comes from the book *Journey to the West*, also known as *Monkey*, written by Wu Ch'Eng-En in the middle of the 16th century. It is spoken by a Patriarch who is teaching Monkey the way of long life. The full quote is: 'To spare and tend the vital powers, this and nothing else is sum and total of all magic, secret and profane. All is comprised in these three, spirit, breath and soul; guard them closely, screen them well; let there be no leak. Store them within the frame; that is all that can be learnt, and all that can be taught. I would have you mark the tortoise and snake, locked in tight embrace. Locked in tight embrace, the vital powers are strong; *even in the midst of fierce flames the Golden Lotus may be planted*, the five elements compounded and transposed, and put to new use. When that is done, be which you please, Buddha or Immortal.'

Now our only question would appear to be why Hughes would refer to something authored by Wu Ch'Eng-En as 'a translation from the Sanskrit'. Anne Stevenson, author of

Bitter Fame (1989), a Plath biography, commented (2001): 'Its significance is obvious. Sylvia was burning in a private hell of her own for most of her short life. The golden lotus is the poetry planted in the fierce flames of Sylvia's incipient fury.'

Thomas HUGHES English novelist (1822–96)

4 If ever you go to Dolgelley,
Don't stay at the —— HOTEL;
There's nothing to put in your belly,
And no one to answer the bell.

Attributed verse. 'Dolgelley' used to be the official spelling of what is now 'Dolgellau' in Wales. The key to the verse is that the name, however spelt, is pronounced 'Dolgethly' – and so 'belly' must be pronounced 'bethly'. At the time, 'belly' was considered a distasteful word and so this was a polite way of uttering it. *The Faber Book of Comic Verse*, ed. Michael Roberts (1974 edn), ascribes it to 'Thomas Hughes', and one assumes that this is the novelist (1822–96) better remembered as the author of *Tom Brown's Schooldays*. Some versions have 'Lion Hotel', and there was indeed an establishment with this name (on the west side of the market square in Dolgellau), but it no longer exists. Thomas Firbank in his book *A Country of Memorable Honour* (1953) states that he saw the verse hanging in the 'Royal Lion Hotel' (in about 1951), when it was attributed, rather, to Wordsworth following his stay. There have been many other suggested inventors of the verse.

Victor HUGO French novelist (1802–85)

5 *On résiste à l'invasion des armées; on ne résiste pas à l'invasion des idées* [An invasion of armies can be resisted, but not an invasion of ideas].

Histoire d'un crime (written 1852, published 1877), conclusion. This quotation has, in a way that is not clear, gradually been re-translated as: 'No army can withstand the strength of an idea *whose time has come*' – Mencken (1942); 'There is one thing stronger than all the armies in the world; and that is an idea whose time has come' – in the *Nation* (15 April 1943). Compare: 'Stronger than an army is a quotation whose time has come' – W.I.E. Gates, quoted in Laurence J. Peter, *Quotations for Our Time* (1977).

David HUME Scottish philosopher (1711–76)

6 It is much more likely that human testimony should err, than that the laws of nature should be violated.

In *My Early Life*, Chap. 9 (1930), Winston Churchill quotes this passage without attribution. Many readers assume that it must be from Hume but have been unable to find the exact words in that man's works. From his *Philosophical Essays Concerning Human Understanding*, 'Of Miracles' (1748), Sect. 90, there is this: 'A miracle is a violation of the laws of nature.' Sect. 91 has (as a maxim in quotation marks): 'That no testimony is sufficient to establish a miracle, unless the testimony be of such a kind, that its falsehood would be more miraculous than the fact which it endeavours to establish.' And Sect. 99 has: 'A miracle can never be proved, so as to be the foundation of a system of religion. For I own, that otherwise, there may possibly be miracles, or violations of the usual course of nature, of such a kind as to admit of proof from human testimony.' Perhaps what Churchill quoted was a conflation or paraphrase by himself or another of all this.

The Revd Dr L.M. Brown of Edinburgh offered this instead, from Thomas Paine's *The Age of Reason* (1793): 'If we are to suppose a miracle to be something so entirely out of course of what is called nature, that she must go out of that course to accomplish it, and we see an account of such a miracle by the person who said he saw it, it raises a question in the mind very easily decided; which is, is it more probable that nature should go out of her course, or that a man should tell a lie? We have never seen, in our time, nature go out of her course ... it is therefore at least millions to one that the reporter of a miracle tells a lie.'

Dr Brown commented: 'It is perhaps not impertinent to remark that this argument, though deserving serious consideration, is not so unanswerable as Thomas Paine seems to imagine.' Compare James Boswell, *Life of Johnson* (for 21 July 1763): 'I mentioned Hume's argument against the belief of miracles, that it is more probable that the witnesses to the truth of them are mistaken, or speak falsely, than that the miracles should be true'; and again (for 22 September 1777): 'Hume's argument against miracles, "That it is more probable witnesses should lie, or be mistaken, than that they should happen".'

There is also a letter of Lord Byron (13 September 1811): 'As to miracles, I agree with Hume that it is more probable men should lie or be deceived, than that things out of the course of nature should so happen.'

Leigh HUNT English writer and editor (1784–1859)

1 Stolen sweets are always sweeter,
Stolen kisses much completer.
'Song of Fairies Robbing an Orchard' (1830). The idea that 'stolen pleasures are sweetest' really goes back to Proverbs 9:17: 'Stolen waters are sweet'. Compare CIBBER 144:2; TRENET 468:3.

2 ... I pray thee then,
Write me as one that loves his fellow-men.
'Abou Ben Adhem' (1838). Hence, 'WRITE ME AS ONE / THAT LOVES HIS FELLOW MEN', inscribed as an epitaph on Hunt's grave in Kensal Green Cemetery, London.

3 Jenny kissed me when we met,
Jumping from the chair she sat in;
Time, you thief, who love to get
Sweets into your list, put that in:
Say I'm weary, say I'm sad,
Say that health and wealth have missed me,
Say I'm growing old, but add,
Jenny kissed me.
'Rondeau' (1838). The 'Jenny' was Jane Carlyle, wife of Thomas Carlyle. Hunt was a neighbour of theirs in Cheyne Row, Chelsea, and had been told that she was anxious about him during a flu epidemic. So he went to see her and the nature of her greeting was uncharacteristic. She was not the kissing sort.

Herman HUPFELD American songwriter (1894–1951)

4 You must remember this, a kiss is still a kiss,
A sigh is just a sigh;
The fundamental things apply,
As time goes by.
Song, 'As Time Goes By', *Everybody's Welcome* (1931). Also in the film *Casablanca* (1943; see 127:1–3). Hence, *You Must Remember This*, the title of a novel (1987) by Joyce Carol Oates.

Saddam HUSSEIN Iraqi President (1937–)

5 The great, the jewel and the mother of battles has begun.
Said at the start of the Gulf War (6 January 1991, quoted in *The Independent*, 19 January 1991). Although, as a result, 'the mother of —— ' became a catchphrase format in the West, Hussein was simply using the commonplace Arabic 'mother of' construction.

Robert M. HUTCHINS American educator (1899–1977)

6 Whenever I feel like exercise, I lie down until the feeling passes.
Untraced, but apparently said by the former University of Chicago President rather than all the other candidates (Wilde, Twain, W.C. Fields and so on). Ascribed by J.P. McEvoy in *Young Man Looking Backwards* (1938). However, Hutchins's biographer, Harry S. Ashmore, ascribes it to *McEvoy* and says that it was merely one of many sayings

Hutchins collected to use when appropriate. In the film *Mr Smith Goes to Washington* (US 1939), Thomas Mitchell speaks the line: 'Every time I think of exercise, I have to lie right down till the feeling leaves me.'

In his introduction to the *Speeches* volume of the Oxford Mark Twain (1996), the actor Hal Holbrook, noted for his performances 'as' Mark Twain, mentions an attributed remark: 'When the urge to exercise comes over me I lie down until it passes away.' He does not say where he got this from, however.

Aldous HUXLEY English novelist and writer (1894–1963)

1 The proper study of mankind is books.
Crome Yellow (1921). Alluding to POPE 363:5.

2 The Gioconda Smile.
Title of short story included in *Mortal Coils* (1922), and later dramatized (1948). It refers to Leonardo da Vinci's portrait of a young woman, known as the *Mona Lisa* (?1503), now in the Louvre, Paris, which has a curious, enigmatic, unsmiling smile, almost a smirk. '*La Gioconda*' and '*La Joconde*', the titles by which the painting is also known, may either be translated as 'the jocund lady', as might be expected, or refer to the sitter's actual surname. She may have been the wife of Francesco del Giocondo (whose name does, in fact, derive from 'jocund').

The smile was already being mentioned by 1550 in Giorgio Vasari's life of the painter. Vasari probably made up the story that Leonardo employed 'singers and musicians or jesters' to keep the sitter 'full of merriment'. Any number of 19th-century writers were fascinated by the smile, some seeing it as disturbing and almost evil. More recently, Lawrence Durrell commented: 'She has the smile of a woman who has just dined off her husband', and Cole Porter included 'You're the smile / On the Mona Lisa' in his list song 'You're the Top!' (1934). Ponchielli's opera *La Gioconda* (1876), after Victor Hugo's drama, and a D'Annunzio play (1898) are not connected with da Vinci's portrait (except in that they feature jocund girls).

Thomas Henry HUXLEY English biologist (1825–95)

3 Try to learn something about everything and everything about something.
This advice was said by the *Collins Dictionary of Quotations* (1995) to be on a 'memorial stone' to Huxley. It is not on his gravestone in St Marylebone Cemetery, East End Road, Finchley, London. A search in 2001 eventually traced the 'stone' to a memorial tablet that used to be in the public library at Ealing, West London. When the old central library was demolished, the tablet was transferred to T.H. Huxley College, Acton – but in time that was demolished, too. Its whereabouts, if any, are not known. However, a photograph of the memorial shows these words flanking a relief of his head: 'THE RIGHT HON THOMAS HENRY HUXLEY BORN AT EALING 4TH MAY 1825 DIED AT EASTBOURNE 29TH JUNE 1895 TRY TO LEARN SOMETHING ABOUT EVERYTHING AND EVERYTHING ABOUT SOMETHING.' It is possible that the injunction may not actually be a quotation of Huxley's own words but merely an established saying that he subscribed to. The journal *Nature*, Vol. 66 (30 October 1902), while reporting the unveiling of the memorial, gives no clue as to any particular reason for the quotation's inclusion.

Laurence J. Peter, *Quotations for Our Time* (1977), attributes the injunction to Lord Brougham (1778–1868) in this form: 'Try to know everything of something and something of everything.' This seems quite likely, as Brougham was a great champion of popular education. Whatever the case, it is clear that the observation was known before Huxley's death in 1895, if only because *Notes and Queries* was discussing it in 1889. Other authors mentioned have included Augustus de Morgan, William Whewell and Aristotle. Indeed, in the latter's *Ethics*, Bk 1, Chap. 3, is this: 'It is the part of an educated man to require exactness in each class of subjects, only so far as the nature of the subject admits ... In each particular science, therefore, he is a good judge who has been instructed in them; and universally, he who has been instructed in all subjects.'

Then in Pascal's *Pensées* is: '*Puisqu'on ne peut être universel en sachant tout ce qui se peut savoir sur tout, il faut savoir peu de tout. Car il est bien plus beau de savoir quelque chose de tout que de savoir tout d'une chose; cette universalité est la plus belle. Si on pouvait avoir les deux, encore mieux* [Since we cannot be universal and know all that is to be known of everything, we ought to know a little about everything. For it is far better to know something about everything than to know all about one thing.]'

Compare Vladimir Nabokov, *Strong Opinions* (1973): 'You can know more and more about one thing, but you can never know everything about one thing: it's hopeless'; and Ambrose Bierce, *The Devil's Dictionary* (1911): 'Connoisseur, n. A specialist who knows everything about something and nothing about anything else.'

I

Dolores IBARRURI ('La Pasionaria') Spanish
Communist leader (1895–1989)

1 Fascism will not pass, the executioners of
October will not pass.

Radio speech given in Madrid (18 July 1936). As *'No pasarán
[They shall not pass]'* it became a Republican slogan in the
Spanish Civil War (1936–9). Compare PÉTAIN 358:1.

2 It is better to die on your feet than to live on your
knees.

Said in a radio speech from Paris calling on the women of
Spain to help defend the Republic (3 September 1936).
According to her autobiography (1966), she had used these
words earlier, on 18 July, when broadcasting in Spain (see
above). Emiliano Zapata (?1877–1919), the Mexican guer-
rilla leader, had used the expression before her, in 1910:
'Men of the South! It is better to die on your feet than to
live on your knees! [... *Es mejor/es preferible morir a pie que
vivir en rodillas!*]' Franklin D. Roosevelt picked up the expression in his message accepting an honorary degree from
Oxford University (19 June 1941): 'We, too, are born to freedom, and believing in freedom, are willing to fight to maintain freedom. We, and all others who believe as we do, would
rather die on our feet than live on our knees.'

Henrik IBSEN Norwegian playwright (1828–1906)

3 *An Enemy of the People.*

Title of play – in Norwegian, *En Folkefiende* (1882). Ibsen's
play is about a health resort, where a doctor warns that the
water is polluted. He is seen as an 'enemy of the people'
for obstructing the town's economic development. So the
use is ironical, as in the same playwright's *Pillars of Society*. Ibsen made the title quote famous, but it had occurred

earlier in Norwegian, e.g. in a newspaper debate in 1843,
and may be traced back to the French Revolution. The phrase
was used by Marat in 1790 in a pamphlet against Necker,
and on 10 June 1794 a notorious law was passed by the
National Convention, proposed by Robespierre and Couthon,
making the action of the existing Revolutionary Tribunal
more rigorous and ruthless; Article 4 of the law read: *'Le
Tribunal révolutionnaire est institué pour punir les ennemis du
peuple.'* Almost anybody could be an enemy of the people,
and the rights of the accused were negligible. The members of the jury were expected to judge on the basis of what
their conscience told them, enlightened by love for *'la patrie'*.
The only possible punishment was the guillotine. This
started the Great Terror, which ended on July 28 with the
execution of Robespierre and Couthon themselves (and
over 1300 others in the meantime). The phrase occurs in
French texts from the early 18th century.

A more modern use of the phrase, indicating an internal
enemy, a 'class enemy', occurred in the Soviet Union, where
anyone whom the authorities did not like could be branded
an 'enemy of the people' – though it seems unlikely they
were inspired by Ibsen's ironic use of the phrase. (Source:
Jaap Engelsman.)

(Sir) Bernard INGHAM English civil servant (1932–)

4 *Kill the Messenger.*

Title of memoirs (1991). Ingham was Chief Press Secretary to the Prime Minister, Margaret Thatcher, from 1979 to
1990. The somewhat surprising title of his book was an
apparent allusion to what reputedly happened to messengers
bringing bad news in classical times. Ingham's implication
would seem to be that press officers get blamed for their
master's – or in his case, mistress's – doings, just as the
media are often blamed for the news that they report rather

than initiate. As early as Sophocles, *Antigone* (line 277), a sentinel was saying to Creon: 'None love the messenger who brings bad news.' Compare the maltreatment of messengers in several Shakespeare plays: in *Antony and Cleopatra*, a messenger says, 'The nature of bad news infects the teller' (I.ii.92); elsewhere Cleopatra threatens a messenger with a knife, and the messenger says, 'It is never good to bring bad news' (II.v.85). In *Henry IV, Part 2* (I.i.100), there is: 'Yet the first bringer of unwelcome news / Hath but a losing office.'

As for precisely 'killing the messenger', the American journal *RQ* (read by reference librarians) has been agonizing over this question since 1981. One suggested original is the biblical story of David killing the man who brought the news of Saul's death in 2 Samuel 1:1–15 (though he was killed not for the news but for boasting he had killed Saul himself). Another is Plutarch's 'Life of Lucius Lucullus' in *Lives of the Noble Grecians and Romans*, which in Sir Thomas North's translation (1579) has the marginal note, 'Tigranes slue the first messenger that brought the newes of Lucullus approach' and the line: 'Now for Tigranes, the first man that ventured to bring him newes of Lucullus comming, had no joy of it: for he cut off his head for his labor.'

Washington IRVING American writer (1783–1859)

1 The almighty dollar, that great object of universal devotion throughout our land.

'The Creole Village', *Wolfert's Roost* (1855), first printed in *Knickerbocker Magazine* (12 November 1836). This use was soon followed by another pronouncement on the currency's all-powerful role in American life: 'The almighty dollar is the only object of worship' – *Philadelphia Public Ledger* (2 December 1836). Mark Twain took up the theme in his *Notebooks* (published 1935): 'We Americans worship the almighty dollar! Well, it is a worthier god than Hereditary Privilege.'

Christopher ISHERWOOD English-born American writer (1904–86)

2 The common cormorant (or shag)
Lays eggs inside a paper bag,
You follow the idea, no doubt?

It's to keep the lightning out.

But what these unobservant birds
Have never thought of, is that herds
Of wandering bears might come with buns
And steal the bags to hold the crumbs.

'The Common Cormorant' (?1925). This was usually described as being by Anon., for example in Wavell's *Other Men's Flowers* (1944), but the ascription to Isherwood appeared in *ODQ* (1979). Line 6 has been given in this form since *ODQ* (1999 edn), whereas formerly it was 'Have never noticed is ...'

Peter Parker in *Isherwood* (2004) explained that Isherwood wrote the rhymes to accompany cartoons drawn by Sylvain Mangeot in 1926 (he was working for Mangeot's parents at the time). These were never intended for publication, but the poem about the cormorant gained popular currency after being included in *The Poet's Tongue* (1935), co-edited by Auden and John Garrett. 'Typically, Auden reproduced the poem from memory and so not entirely accurately (incidentally improving the scansion). It was frequently republished in this version, and *without the author being identified*, until 1966, when Isherwood included the original version in *Exhumations*.'

3 I am a camera with its shutter open, quite passive, recording, not thinking.

'A Berlin Diary', *Goodbye to Berlin* (1939), opening words. According to Peter Parker in the *Dictionary of National Biography 1986–1990*, 'the famous sentence ... (to Isherwood's increasing irritation) was often quoted as a summation of his fictional method'. In his biography, Parker added: 'Although exaggerated for literary effect, this famous sentence not only described his working methods as a writer quite accurately, but also made clear his policy of non-involvement.' John van Druten wrote a play (1951) entitled *I Am a Camera*, based on Isherwood's stories. This was turned into a film (UK 1955), where Isherwood's line became: 'I am a camera, with its shutter open, just watching it, quite detached, taking pictures of it all, to be developed sooner or later and printed.' Then the play was turned into the musical *Cabaret* (1966; film US 1972).

J

T.J. 'Stonewall' JACKSON American Confederate general (1824–63)

1 Let us cross over the river, and rest under [the shade of] the trees.

Dying words, Jackson had been shot in error by his own troops (May 1863) during the American Civil War. *Across the River and Into the Trees* was the title of a novel (1950) by Ernest Hemingway. Accordingly, E.B. White's noted parody of Hemingway's style (collected 1954) was called 'Across the Street and Into the Grill'. Often used allusively: 'Then we began to notice, as we lazily cropped the grass, that it was greener across the river at Shepperton Studios than at Pinewood. It was time for The Archers and their followers to move across the river and into the trees' – Michael Powell, *Million-Dollar Movie* (1992).

Joe JACOBS American boxing manager (1896–1940)

2 We was robbed!

Believing that his client Max Schmeling had been cheated of a heavyweight title by Jack Sharkey (21 June 1932), Jacobs shouted this protest into a microphone. Quoted in Peter Heller, *In This Corner* (1975). Compare Jack Dempsey's 'I was robbed of the championship' when defeated controversially by Gene Tunney in 1927.

3 I should have stood in bed.

Jacobs left his sick-bed to attend the baseball World Series in October 1935. He bet on the losers. Quoted in John Lardner, *Strong Cigars and Lovely Women* (1951). Leo Rosten in *Hooray for Yiddish* (1983) puts his own gloss on the expression: 'The most celebrated instance of this usage was when Mike [sic] Jacobs, the fight promoter, observing the small line at his ticket window, moaned, "I should of stood in bed!" *Stood* is a calque [loan translation] for the Yiddish *geshtanen*, which can mean both "stood" and "remained". Mr Jacobs' use of "of" simply followed the speech pattern of his childhood.'

(Sir) Mick JAGGER and Keith RICHARD English rock musicians and songwriters (1943–) and (1943–)

4 It's Only Rock 'n' Roll.

Title of song (1974). Subsequently adopted as an expression meaning 'It doesn't matter; the importance should not be exaggerated.' In a 1983 *Sunday Express* interview Tim Rice was quoted as saying, "It would be nice if [the musical *Blondel*] is a success but I won't be upset if it isn't. It is only rock 'n' roll after all and it doesn't really matter a hoot.'

JAMES I (James VI of Scotland) Anglo-Scottish King (1566–1625)

5 Have I three kingdoms and thou must needs fly into my eye?

To a fly. Quoted in John Selden, *Table Talk* (1689). Compare Laurence Sterne, *Tristram Shandy*, Bk 2, Chap. 12 (1759–67): '"I'll not hurt thee," says my uncle Toby, rising from his chair, and going across the room with the fly in his hand ... lifting up the sash, and opening his hand as he spoke ... "go, poor devil, get thee gone, why should I hurt thee? – This world surely is wide enough to hold both thee and me."'

6 Dr Donne's verses are like the peace of God; they pass all understanding.

Archdeacon Plume (1630–1704) recorded this remark of James I's about the poet and cleric, John Donne. Alluding to Philippians 4:7 – see BIBLE 85:3.

JAMES II English King (1633–1701)

1 When King James II observed that the new St Paul's Cathedral was amusing, awful and artificial, he implied that Sir Christopher Wren's creation was 'pleasing, awe-inspiring, and skilfully achieved'.

Simeon Potter, *Our Language* (1976). Unverified remark employing three adjectives that were complimentary once but are for the most part pejorative now. In William Kent's *An Encyclopedia of London* (1937) it is Charles II who in 1675 is credited with approving a new design for St Paul's because it was 'very artificial, proper and useful'. Other monarchs up to Queen Anne have also been credited with the saying, or something like it. A tourist booklet, *The Pictorial History of St Paul's Cathedral: the Official Record* by the Revd W.M. Atkins MA, Librarian of St. Paul's (no date, post-1951), has the heading 'Very artificial, proper and useful' and states that after a beautiful design by Wren had been turned down, 'Wren, in desperation, produced what has been called the "Nightmare" design, in which the body of the building is normal enough, but superimposed upon it is a shallow dome, surmounted by a drum and cupola upon which rises a pagoda-like spire supporting three pommels and a cross. The Commissioners approved this piece of fantasy, the King [not specified] endorsed it as "very artificial, proper and useful", at the same time giving Wren liberty to make "variations, rather ornamental than essential, as from time to time he shall see proper", a permission of which Wren availed himself to the full.'

Carwyn JAMES British sports coach (1929–83)

2 Get your retaliation in first.

'The Government was trying to get its retaliation in first, as we realized it would. The phrase, by the way, comes from the late Carwyn James, the coach to the British Isles rugby team who beat New Zealand in 1971. It is now freely used by people who would be hard put to tell the difference between a rugby ball and a boiled egg. James, who liked Chekhov and gin-and-tonic, would have been pleased to be remembered in the dictionaries of quotation as well as in the record books' – Alan Watkins, *Independent on Sunday* (18 February 1996). Also recorded in *The Guardian* (7 November 1989) and applied to other sports, possibly before this.

Henry JAMES American novelist (1843–1916)

3 Cats and monkeys, monkeys and cats – all human life is there.

'The Madonna of the Future' (1879). What is the connection, if any, with the *News of the World*, which used 'All

human life is there' to promote itself in 1958–9? In 1981 Maurice Smelt, the advertising copywriter, explained: '"All human life is there" was my idea, but I don't, of course, pretend that they were my words. I simply lifted them from *The Oxford Dictionary of Quotations*. I didn't bother to tell the client that they were from Henry James, suspecting that, after the "Henry James – who he?" stage, he would come up with tiresome arguments about being too high-hat for his readership. I did check whether we were clear on copyright, which we were by a year or two ... I do recall its use as baseline in a tiny little campaign trailing a series that earned the *News of the World* a much-publicized but toothless rebuke from the Press Council. The headline of that campaign was: "'I've been a naughty girl', says Diana Dors." The meiosis worked, as the *News of the World* knew it would. They ran an extra million copies of the first issue of the series.'

4 So here it is at last, the distinguished thing.

After suffering a stroke (2 December 1915), James reported that he had heard a voice saying this – as recounted in Edith Wharton, *A Backward Glance* (1934). These are not his dying words, however. He did not die until 28 February. His last recorded words, said to Alice James, were, 'Tell the boys to follow, to be faithful, to take me seriously' – H. Montgomery Hyde, *Henry James at Home* (1969).

William JAMES American psychologist (1842–1910)

5 We do not weep because we are sad, we are sad because we weep.

Summary of a passage from Chap. 25 ('The Emotions') from *The Principles of Psychology* (1890): 'My theory is that the bodily changes follow directly the perception of the exciting fact, and that our feeling of the same changes as they occur *is* the emotion. Common-sense says, we lose our fortune, are sorry and weep ... the hypothesis here to be defended says that this order of sequence is incorrect ... and that the more rational statement is that we feel sorry because we cry, angry because we strike, afraid because we tremble, and not that we cry, strike or tremble, because we are sorry, angry or fearful as the case may be.' This is the classical statement of what became known as the James–Lange theory of emotion, because it was proposed almost simultaneously by James and by the Danish physiologist Carl Lange.

6 The moral flabbiness born of the exclusive worship of the bitch-goddess Success. That – with the squalid cash interpretation put on the word success – is our national disease.

Letter to H.G. Wells (11 September 1906). In *Lady Chatterley's Lover* (1928), D.H. Lawrence uses the term 'bitch-goddess Success' on no less than ten occasions – and then attributes it to William James's brother, Henry.

1 Hogamous, higamous
Man is polygamous
Higamous, hogamous
Woman monogamous.

ODQ gives *The Oxford Book of Marriage* (1990) as the source for the James attribution. Its editor, Helge Rubinstein, introduces the verse as follows: 'James ... woke one night feeling he had solved the ultimate mystery of life. The following morning he found that this doggerel was the great insight he had written down.' In fact, the earliest reference would seem to be Gibbons & Connelly, *Selected Readings in Psychology* (1970), where the added information is given that James produced the lines after a drug-induced dream when experimenting with opium in order to increase his creativity and powers of insight. Other accounts of these experiments mention nitrous oxide (laughing gas) and also quote sentences that supposedly resulted – but not the 'Higamous' verse. One might mention two other *aperçus* similarly arrived at. In his *History of Western Philosophy* (1945), Bertrand Russell told how James himself had described another man experiencing a 'vision of truth' from laughing gas: 'Whenever he was under its influence, he knew the secret of the universe, but when he came to, he had forgotten it. At last, with immense effort, he wrote down the secret before the vision had faded. When completely recovered, he rushed to see what he had written. It was: "A smell of petroleum prevails throughout."' According to *The Sunday Telegraph* (12 March 1961): 'Arthur Koestler once told the following story about the ultimate mystery of life, told to him by George Orwell: A friend of Orwell's, while living in the Far East, smoked several pipes of opium every night, and every night a single phrase rang in his ear, which contained the whole secret of the universe; but in his euphoria he could not be bothered to write it down and by the morning it was gone. One night he managed to jot down the magic phrase after all, and in the morning he read: "The banana is big, but its skin is even bigger."'

Douglas JAY (later Lord Jay) English Labour politician (1907–96)

2 Fair Shares for All is Labour's Call.

His slogan for the Battersea North by-election (June 1946), which he won. In *Change and Fortune* (1980), Jay wrote: 'My excellent agent ... asked me to send him a brief rhyming North Battersea slogan. I suggested "Fair Shares for All is

Labour's Call"; and from this by-election "Fair Shares for All" spread in a few years round the country.' *OED2* has no citation of the phrase 'fair shares' before this date, though 'fair share' was common in the 19th century.

3 For in the case of nutrition and health, just as in the case of education, the gentleman in Whitehall really does know better what is good for people than the people know themselves.

The Socialist Case (1947 edn). From Tam Dalyell's obituary of Jay in *The Independent* (7 March 1996): 'It is one of the misfortunes of life that a public figure can forever be associated with one inaccurate remark, taken out of context, and never intended to carry an immortal interpretation. For half a century Douglas Jay suffered as the originator of the sinister aphorism "the man in Whitehall knows best" ... [where, in fact, he said,] "the Gentleman in Whitehall is usually right".' As will be apparent, even Dalyell in trying to set the record straight, got it wrong.

In *The Downing Street Years* (1993), Margaret Thatcher commented on Jay's view: 'A disinterested civil service, with access to the best and latest information, was better able to foresee economic eventualities and to propose responses to them than were the blind forces of the so-called "free market". Such a philosophy was explicitly advocated by the Labour Party. It gloried in planning, regulation, controls and subsidies.'

Thomas JEFFERSON American polymath and 3rd President (1743–1826)

4 We hold these truths to be self-evident; that all men are created equal; that they are endowed by their creator with certain unalienable rights; that among these are life, liberty, and the pursuit of happiness.

From the Declaration of Independence (4 July 1776), which Jefferson drafted. Note, not 'inalienable'. George Mason had already drafted the Virginia Declaration of Rights (1774), which stated that 'all men are by nature equally free and independent and have certain inherent rights'.

5 You retire from the great theatre of action with the blessings of your fellow citizens.

From the President of Congress's remarks at the resignation of George Washington as Commander-in-Chief (23 December 1783), probably penned by Jefferson. On that occasion, Washington himself said: 'Having now finished the work assigned me, I retire from the great theatre of action.' Compare WALPOLE 482:1.

1 A little rebellion now and then is a good thing.

Letter to James Madison (30 January 1787). When he addressed both Houses of Parliament on a visit to Britain in June 1982, President Reagan recalled that Margaret Thatcher had earlier quoted these words apropos a portrait of George III in the British Embassy in Washington, coupled with the thought that Britons and Americans would wish to let bygones be bygones.

2 I have sworn upon the altar of God, eternal hostility against every form of tyranny over the mind of man.

In an 1800 letter (just before he became president). One of the quotations written up on the Jefferson memorial in Washington. Quoted in the film *Born Yesterday* (US 1950).

3 Avoid all foreign entanglements.

Not quite what Jefferson said in his first inaugural address (4 March 1801) – rather, 'Peace, commerce, and honest friendship with all nations, entangling alliances with none ...' – but a cornerstone of American foreign policy for generations.

4 Few die and none resign.

Letter to E. Shipman and others (12 July 1801). The actual text reads: 'If a due participation of office is a matter of right, how are vacancies to be obtained? Those by death are few; by resignation none.'

5 Advertisements contain the only truths to be relied on in a newspaper.

Letter to Nathaniel Macon (1819). Compare BEVAN 67:2.

6 To attain all this [universal republicanism], however, rivers of blood must yet flow, and years of desolation pass over; yet the object is worth rivers of blood, and years of desolation.

Letter to John Adams (4 September 1823). Compare POWELL 367:1.

7 HERE WAS BURIED
THOMAS JEFFERSON
AUTHOR OF THE
DECLARATION
OF
AMERICAN INDEPENDENCE,
OF THE
STATUTE OF VIRGINIA
FOR
RELIGIOUS FREEDOM,
AND FATHER OF THE
UNIVERSITY OF VIRGINIA.

Jefferson devised his own epitaph, 'because by these, as testimonials I have lived, I wish most to be remembered'. He omitted that he had been US president for two terms. His draft, of course, left the date of death to be inserted. The epitaph is now to be found inscribed on an obelisk over Jefferson's grave in the family cemetery near his house, Monticello, Virginia.

Roy JENKINS (later Lord Jenkins) Welsh-born Labour, then Social Democrat, then Liberal Democrat politician (1920–2003)

8 The permissive society has been allowed to become a dirty phrase. A better phrase is the civilized society.

Speech, Abingdon (19 July 1969). Jenkins had previously been Home Secretary (1965–7) in a Labour government, in which post he had a notably liberal record, presiding over or setting the tone for liberalization of divorce, abortion and anti-homosexual laws, the abolition of theatre censorship, and much else. It is impossible to say precisely when the phrase 'permissive society' had come to be applied to Britain in the 1960s – *OED2*'s first citation dates only from January 1968.

9 The politics of the left and centre of this country are frozen in an out-of-date mould which is bad for the political and economic health of Britain and increasingly inhibiting for those who live within the mould. Can it be broken?

Speech, Commons Press Gallery lunch (8 June 1980). The following year, when the Social Democratic Party was established, there was much talk of 'breaking the mould of British politics' – i.e., doing away with the traditional two-party system. In a speech to the SDP Conference at Cardiff in October 1982, its President, Shirley Williams, specifically said: 'That is why we must break the mould of politics.' This was by no means a new way of describing political change and abolishing an old form of government in a way that prevented its being reconstituted. Indeed, Jenkins had quoted Andrew Marvell's 'Horatian Ode Upon Cromwell's Return from Ireland' (1650) – 'And cast the kingdoms old, / Into another mould' – in his book *What Matters Now*, as early as 1972.

A.J.P. Taylor in his *English History 1914–1945* (1965) had written: 'Lloyd George needed a new crisis to break the mould of political and economic habit.' The image evoked, as in the days of the Luddites, was of breaking the mould from which iron machinery is cast so completely that no further machines can be cast, unless a new mould is made.

Jerome K. JEROME English writer (1859–1927)

1 Love is like the measles; we all have to go through it.

Idle Thoughts of an Idle Fellow (1886). Compare BILLINGS 88:5; JERROLD 256:3.

2 I like work: it fascinates me. I can sit and look at it for hours.

Three Men In a Boat, Chap. 3 (1889). As Jerome also wrote *Idle Thoughts of an Idle Fellow*, how appropriate that the inscription on his grave in St Mary's churchyard, Ewelme, Oxfordshire, is: 'For we are labourers together with God' (1 Corinthians 3:9).

Douglas JERROLD English writer (1803–57)

3 Love's like the measles – all the worse when it comes late in life.

'Love', *The Wit and Opinions of Douglas Jerrold* (1859). Compare BILLINGS 88:5; JEROME 256:1.

Joseph Jacques Césaire JOFFRE French general (1852–1931)

4 Troops that can advance no farther must, at any price, hold on to the ground they have conquered and die on the spot rather than give way.

Joffre, as French Commander-in-Chief, issued his order for the start of the (first) Battle of the Marne on 5 September 1914. In his memoirs (1932), he recalled that his staff were installed in an ancient convent of the Order of Cordeliers, 'and my own office was in what had formerly been a monk's cell. It was from here that I directed the Battle of the Marne and it was in this room that, at half past seven next morning, I signed the following order addressed to the troops ...' The text was apparently written by General Maurice Gustave Gamelin (1872–1958). Together, the French and British managed to push the Germans back along the 200-mile front of the Marne river, preventing the enemy from reaching Paris as it had threatened to do.

JOHN OF THE CROSS Spanish mystic, poet and saint (1542–91)

5 *La Noche oscura del alma* [The dark night of the soul].

Treatise based on his poem 'Songs of the Soul Which Rejoices at Having Reached Union with God by the Road of Spiritual Negation' (?1578). Hence, the phrase denoting mental and spiritual suffering prior to some big step. See FITZGERALD 195:9. Douglas Adams wrote *The Long Dark Tea-time of the Soul* (1988) – see ADAMS 2:5.

Augustus JOHN Welsh artist (1878–1961)

6 We have become, Nina, the sort of people our parents warned us about.

This was recorded about the time Michael Holroyd's two-volume biography of John appeared (1974–5), but it is not in that work. It was quoted in the form 'We are the sort of people, Nina, our fathers warned us against' on BBC Radio *Quote ... Unquote* (11 May 1977). Holroyd confirms it *was* addressed to Nina Hamnett (1890–1956), the painter and something of a figure in London Bohemia, but says that he encountered it only *after* he had written his biography. He first used it in 1981 in his entry on John in *Makers of Modern Culture*. In the 1996 revision of the biography, he gives it as 'We are the sort of people our fathers warned us against.'

When my version appeared in the second *Quote ... Unquote* book, Bernard Davis wrote in 1981 from Turkish Cyprus, saying: 'An acquaintance of mine, York-Lodge, a close friend of Claud Cockburn and Evelyn Waugh, was continually saying, "We are the sort of people our parents warned us against", and claiming it as his own. This was about 1924.'

It was probably a common expression dating from between the wars, if not before. In Brendan Behan's *Borstal Boy* (1958), there is: 'We're all good kids. We're all the kids our mothers warned us against.' The saying was reported as graffiti from New York City in the early 1970s ('We are the people our parents warned us about') and a placard carried at a demonstration by homosexuals in New York in 1970 asserted, 'We're the people our parents warned us against.' In 1968 Nicholas Von Hoffman brought out a book on hippies with the title *We Are the People Our Parents Warned Us Against*. He gives the source as 'graffito, coffeehouse wall, Summer 1967'.

Hiram JOHNSON American all-party senator (1866–1945)

7 The first casualty when war comes is truth.

Speech to the US Senate (in about 1917) – according to Burton Stevenson's *Home Book of Quotations* (1948), but untraced. This was also quoted in Albert Johnson, *Common English Quotations* (1963). Aeschylus has been mentioned as possible forerunner. Curiously, yet another Johnson – Samuel – said much the same thing less pithily in *The Idler*, No. 30 (11 November 1758): 'Among the calamities of war, may be justly numbered the diminution of the love of truth, by the falsehoods which interest dictates and credulity encourages.' At the time of the First World War, Arthur (later Lord) Ponsonby used, 'When war is declared, Truth is the first casualty' (unattributed) as the motto of *Falsehood in Wartime* (1928). Hence, whatever the source, *The First Casualty*, title of a book (1975) by Phillip Knightley on propaganda in wartime.

Lyndon B. JOHNSON American Democratic
36th President (1908–73)

1 Come now, let us reason together.
Frequent exhortation. Based on Isaiah 1:18.

2 We Americans know, although others appear to forget, the risks of spreading conflict. We still seek no wider war.
Broadcast address (4 August 1964). 'No wider war' is misleadingly reminiscent of the German phrase *Nie wieder Krieg* ('never again war'), a slogan of the 1920s and 30s. 'No more war' and 'Never again', although recurring slogans, were probably not much heard before the 20th century. At the UN in 1965 Pope Paul VI quoted President Kennedy 'four years ago' to the effect that 'mankind must put an end to war, or war will put an end to mankind ... No more war, never again war.' (The Pope quoted this in Italian.) Earlier, the phrase was used by Winston Churchill at the end of a letter to Lord Beaverbrook in 1928 (quoted in Martin Gilbert's biography of Churchill, Vol. 5). A.J.P. Taylor in his *English History 1914–1945* suggests that the slogan was 'irresistible' at the end of the First World War. David Lloyd George had said in an interview with *The Times* (29 September 1916): '"Never again" has become our battle cry.' Churchill in his *The Second World War* (Vol. 1) said of the French: 'with one passionate spasm [they cried] never again.'
In *Goodbye to Berlin* (1939), Christopher Isherwood describes a Nazi book burning. The books are from a 'small liberal pacifist publisher'. One of the Nazis holds up a book called '*Nie wieder Krieg* [never again war]' as though it were 'a nasty kind of reptile'. 'No More War!' a fat, well-dressed woman laughs scornfully and savagely. 'What an idea!'
Later, in the mid-1960s, 'Never again' became the slogan of the militant Jewish Defence League – in reference to the Holocaust. A stone monument erected near the birthplace of Adolf Hitler at Braunau, Austria, in 1989 (the centenary of his birth) bore the lines 'For Peace, Freedom and Democracy – Never Again Fascism [*Nie wieder Faschismus*] – Millions of Dead are a warning'.

3 We are not about to send American boys nine or ten thousand miles away from home to do what Asian boys ought to be doing for themselves.
Broadcast address (21 October 1964). Compare ROOSEVELT 386:7.

4 For the world which seems to lie out before us like a land of dreams.
In the summer of 1965 the poet Robert Lowell had outraged Johnson by refusing to attend a Festival of the Arts at the White House, in protest at America's involvement in the Vietnam War (Lowell had been jailed during the Second World War for conscientious objection). A few weeks later, in an address to a gathering of students, Johnson said: 'Robert Lowell, the poet, doesn't like everything around here. But I like one of his lines where he wrote ...'
Unfortunately for Johnson, the above was not a line of Lowell's but from Matthew Arnold's 'Dover Beach'. Lowell had used the line as an epigraph to his book *The Mills of the Kavanaughs*. Also, Arnold did not write 'lie out', simply 'lie'. Stand up the speechwriter who landed the president in this soup.

5 That Gerald Ford. He can't fart and chew gum at the same time.
Quoted in Richard Reeves, *A Ford Not a Lincoln* (1975) and J.K. Galbraith, *A Life in Our Times* (1981). This is the correct version of the euphemistic: 'He couldn't walk and chew gum at the same time.'

6 I'd much rather have that fellow inside my tent pissing out, than outside my tent pissing in.
On why he kept J. Edgar Hoover at the FBI. Quoted in David Halberstam, *The Best and the Brightest* (1972). The same sentiment is attributed to Laurence Olivier about employing Kenneth Tynan, a critic, at the National Theatre, in John Dexter, *The Honourable Beast* (1993).

7 It is true that a house divided against itself is a house that cannot stand. There is a division in the American house now and believing this as I do, I have concluded that I should not permit the Presidency to become involved in the partisan divisions that are developing in this political year. Accordingly, I shall not seek, and I will not accept, the nomination of my party for another term as your President.
Distressed by the scale of domestic opposition to the Vietnam War, Johnson surprised everyone by announcing in a TV address on 31 March 1968 his intention not to stand again as president. Even an hour before the broadcast he did not know whether he would use the passage announcing his retirement. Apart from the biblical reference to a 'house divided' (St Mark 3:25, which perhaps had come to Johnson by way of a Lincoln speech in 1858 on the circumstances that had led to the American Civil War), there is also an echo of General Sherman's words to the Republican convention in 1884 (see 430:6).

See also GOLDWATER 217:5.

Philander Chase JOHNSON American writer
(1866–1939)

1 Cheer up! the worst is yet to come!

Everybody's Magazine (May 1920). It seems that the idea was probably formed long before. It was possibly quoted by Mark Twain in a letter to his wife (1893/4) – see TWAIN 471:1.

Dr Samuel JOHNSON English writer and lexicographer
(1709–84)

2 The only thing the good Lord has distributed fairly is Intelligence. Everyone is quite sure that they have more of it than anyone else.

Attributed remark. But it is equally possible that the real origin of the thought is in the opening words of René Descartes, *Le Discours de la méthode* (1637): 'Common sense is the most widely distributed commodity in the world, for everyone thinks himself so well endowed with it that those who are hardest to please in every other respect generally have no desire to possess more of it than they have.' Compare Thomas Hobbes, *Leviathan*, Pt 1, Chap. 13 (1651): 'For such is the nature of man, that howsoever they may acknowledge many others to be more witty, or more eloquent, or more learned; Yet they will hardly believe there be many so wise as themselves ... But this proveth rather that men are in that point equal than unequal. For there is not ordinarily a greater sign of the equal distribution of any thing, than that every man is contented with his share.' La Rochefoucauld, *Maxims*, no. 89 (1678) has: '*Tout le monde se plaint de sa mémoire, et personne ne se plaint de son jugement* [Everyone complains of his memory, and no one complains of his judgement].'

3 When learning's triumph o'er her barbrous foes
First rear'd the Stage, immortal Shakespeare
    rose;
Each change of many-colour'd life he drew,
Exhausted worlds, and then imagin'd new:
Existence saw him spurn her bounded reign,
And panting Time toil'd after him in vain.

'Prologue spoken at the Opening of the Theatre in Drury Lane' (1747). According to *DNB*, when Jack de Manio, the British broadcaster, finally retired from presenting BBC Radio's breakfast-time *Today* programme in 1971 – a role in which he had become famous for frequently giving inaccurate time-checks – he was presented with a clock inscribed with the words: 'And *parting* time toiled after him in vain'. One wonders whether this misquotation was, for some reason, intentional?

4 I'll come no more behind your scenes, David; for the silk stockings and white bosoms of your actresses excite my amorous propensities.

To David Garrick. In Boswell's *Life* (1791), relating to 1750. In Appendix G to the *Life,* John Wilkes recalls this statement in the form: '... the silk stockings and white bosoms of your actresses do make my genitals to quiver'.

5 Is not a Patron, my Lord, one who looks with unconcern on a man struggling for life in the water, and, when he has reached ground, encumbers him with help?

From Johnson's magisterial and rebuking letter to the Earl of Chesterfield (February 1755). When Johnson's *Dictionary* was nearing publication, Chesterfield (who might have fancied it would be dedicated to him) attempted to insinuate himself into the learned doctor's favour, having done nothing to help until that time. Johnson made it clear to him what the position was in a devastating letter. Reproduced in Boswell, *Life of Johnson* (1791).

6 Every quotation contributes something to the stability or enlargement of the language.

Preface, *A Dictionary of the English Language* (1755). Here Johnson is referring to the citations – the examples of words used in context by other authors – rather than to quotations when employed to illustrate or decorate a theme. This method reached its greatest fulfilment in the extensive citations used by the later *Oxford English Dictionary* (1884–1928).

7 *Lexicographer.* A writer of dictionaries, *a harmless drudge.*

Johnson's celebrated definition in the same work. Other definitions in his *Dictionary* are noted for their playfulness or subjectiveness, e.g.: '*Network.* Anything reticulated or decussated at equal distances, with interstices between the intersections'; '*Oats.* A grain, which in England is generally given to horses, but in Scotland supports the people'; '*Patron.* Commonly a wretch who supports with insolence, and is paid with flattery.'

8 Ignorance, Madam, pure ignorance.

Largely working alone on his great *Dictionary* (1755), Johnson committed one or two errors. In the first edition he wrongly defined the word 'pastern' as 'the knee of a horse'. In fact, in a horse, it is rather the equivalent of the *ankle* in humans. It was corrected in later editions, but when a woman asked how he had come to make this mistake, he splendidly forbore to give an elaborate defence – as reported in Boswell's *Life*, for 1755.

1 No, *you* smell, *I* stink.

In response to someone who had said to Johnson, 'You smell!' Probably apocryphal. The stink/smell distinction is of long standing. In the film *The Philadelphia Story* (US 1940), a character says: 'Don't say "stinks", darling. If absolutely necessary, "smells" – but only if absolutely necessary.'

2 Consider, Sir, how insignificant this will appear a twelvemonth hence.

Quoted in Boswell, *Life of Johnson* (1791), relating to 6 July 1763. When Boswell talked of some temporary setback as a serious distress, Johnson laughed and promulgated this excellent piece of advice. Compare DICKENS 171:1.

3 Sir, let me tell you, the noblest prospect which a Scotsman ever sees, is the high road that leads him to England!

In the same work, relating to 6 July 1763. Johnson no doubt enjoyed baiting the Scotsman Boswell in this fashion, but his biographer records how 'this unexpected and pointed sally produced a roar of applause'.

4 Sir, a woman's preaching is like a dog's walking on his hinder legs. It is not done well; but you are surprised to find it done at all.

A saying of Johnson's often invoked to describe something about which there is little complimentary to be said. In Boswell's *Life* (1791), relating to 31 July 1763, when Boswell mentions that, 'I had been that morning at a meeting of the people called Quakers, where I had heard a woman preach.'

5 It matters not how a man dies, but how he lives. The act of dying is not of importance, it lasts so short a time.

In the same work, relating to 27 October 1769: 'To my question, whether we might not fortify our minds for the approach of death, he answered, in a passion, "No, Sir, let it alone ..."' This neatly provided an epitaph on a later memorial in the crypt of St Paul's Cathedral, London:

GORDON HAMILTON-FAIRLEY
DM FRCP
FIRST PROFESSOR OF CLINICAL ONCOLOGY
1930–1975
KILLED BY A TERRORIST BOMB
It matters not how a man dies but how he lives.

Professor Hamilton-Fairley was head of the medical oncology unit at St Bartholomew's Hospital, London, and one of Britain's leading cancer experts. He was killed in Campden Hill Square, London, as he passed a car containing an IRA bomb intended for his next-door neighbour, Hugh Fraser, a Conservative MP.

6 It was the triumph of hope over experience.

When told that a gentleman who had been very unhappy in marriage, married immediately after his wife died. One of the anecdotes collected by Johnson's friend, the Revd Dr Maxwell, and inserted by Boswell in the *Life of Johnson* (1791) in the year 1770. Johnson had a very positive view of marriage (though it is sometimes forgotten that he was himself married for a while), hence his remarks: 'Even ill assorted marriages were preferable to cheerless celibacy' (in the *Life*) and 'Marriage has many pains, but celibacy has no pleasures' (in *Rasselas*, 1759).

7 Read over your compositions, and where ever you meet with a passage which you think is particularly fine, strike it out.

Recalling the advice of a college tutor. In the same work, for 30 April 1773. Compare QUILLER-COUCH 374:2.

8 Patriotism is the last refuge of a scoundrel.

In the *Life*, for 7 April 1775. Boswell adds that, of course, he means 'pretended patriotism which so many, in all ages and countries, have made a cloak for self-interest'.

9 *OLIVARII GOLDSMITH, Poetae, Physici, Historici, qui nullum fere scribendi genus non tetigit, nullum quod tetigit non ornavit* [Of Oliver Goldsmith, A Poet, Natural Philosopher, and Historian, who left no species of writing untouched by his pen, and touched none that he did not adorn].

Goldsmith's epitaph in Poets' Corner, Westminster Abbey, was written by Johnson, but not without dissent among Goldsmith's other friends and admirers. As Boswell records in the *Life*, the 'Epitaph gave occasion to a *Remonstrance* to the MONARCH OF LITERATURE'. Various emendations were suggested to Johnson's draft and presented to him in the form of a round robin. Sir Joshua Reynolds took it to Johnson 'who received it with much good humour, and desired Sir Joshua to tell the gentlemen, that he would alter the Epitaph in any manner they pleased, as to the sense of it; but *he would never consent to disgrace the walls of Westminster Abbey with an English inscription*'. Johnson argued further that, 'the language of the country of which a learned man was a native, is not the language fit for his epitaph, which should be in an ancient and permanent language. Consider, Sir; how you should feel, were you to find at Rotterdam an epitaph upon Erasmus *in Dutch*!'

And so it remained in Latin, despite the protest from Goldsmith's friends. The above is an extract only.

1 Depend upon it, Sir, when a man knows he is to be hanged in a fortnight, it concentrates his mind wonderfully.

In the *Life*, for the same date. This was said about the unfortunate Dr Dodd. In fact, Johnson was prevaricating because it was *he* who had written most of Dodd's sermons to his fellow inmates when lying condemned at Newgate. A Mr Seward had suspected something of the sort, and Johnson misled him with the famous quotation. 'I did not *directly* tell a lie,' he later told Boswell, 'I left the matter uncertain.'

2 Sir, when a man is tired of London, he is tired of life; for there is in London all that life can afford.

In the *Life*, for 20 September 1777. One of the worst examples of 'quote abuse' I have ever come across was something attributed to Robert Moses, a New York Parks Commissioner, by Barbara Rowes in *The Book of Quotes* (1979): 'Every true New Yorker believes with all his heart that when a New Yorker is tired of New York, he is tired of life.'

3 There are no snakes to be met with throughout the whole island.

As a joke, Johnson used to boast of being able to repeat a complete chapter of *The Natural History of Iceland* by a Dane called Horrebow (1758). He would then say this sentence which is, indeed, the entire contents of Chapter 72 of Horrebow's book. In the *Life*, for 13 April 1778. Sometimes, in telling the story, *Ireland* rather than Iceland is mistakenly put into the joke, presumably out of confusion with the fact that St Patrick traditionally drove out all the snakes of that country by ringing a bell.

4 I am willing to love all mankind, *except an American*.

In the *Life*, for 15 April 1778. Johnson was not a supporter of the American Revolution – the Declaration of Independence had been signed less than two years previously. He went on to characterize Americans as 'Rascals – Robbers – Pirates'.

5 In the character of his [Gray's] Elegy I rejoice to concur with the common reader ... The churchyard abounds with images which find a mirror in every mind, and with sentiments to which every bosom returns an echo.

'Thomas Gray', *Lives of the English Poets* (1779–81). Hence, *The Common Reader*, the title of two volumes of Virginia Woolf's collected essays, published in 1925 and 1932.

6 An exotic and irrational entertainment, which has been always combated, and always has prevailed.

'John Hughes', in the same work. This is not Dr Johnson's definition of 'opera' in his *Dictionary* (1755), as is sometimes supposed. He is referring in particular to *Italian* opera. Johnson was self-admittedly unmusical but had no objection to *English* opera.

In Kenneth Clark's *Civilization* (1969, and in the TV original), he says: 'Opera, next to Gothic architecture, is one of the strangest inventions of western man. It could not have been foreseen by any logical process. Dr Johnson's much quoted definition, which as far as I can make out he never wrote, "an extravagant and irrational entertainment", is perfectly correct; and at first it seems surprising that it should have been brought to perfection in the age of reason.' Clark is quite right that Johnson did not call it an 'extravagant and irrational entertainment', but how interesting that he did not go so far as to check and find out what Johnson *did* say.

In his *Dictionary* Johnson does not in fact define the word 'opera' himself, but merely quotes Dryden: 'An *opera* is a poetical tale or fiction, represented by vocal and instrumental musick, adorned with scenes, machines and dancing.'

7 At this man's table I enjoyed many cheerful and instructive hours ... with David Garrick, whom I hoped to have gratified with this character of our common friend; but what are the hopes of man! I am disappointed by that stroke of death, which has eclipsed the gaiety of nations, and impoverished the public stock of harmless pleasure.

Johnson was Garrick's great friend (and one-time schoolteacher in Lichfield) and they continued to see each other when Garrick had become the foremost actor of the age. The 'epitaph' appears in the life of Edmund Smith, one of Johnson's *Lives of the English Poets* (published in 1779, the year of the actor's death). Eva Maria, Garrick's widow, had the words engraved below his memorial bust in the south transept of Lichfield Cathedral. John Wilkes had his doubts about the tribute and made an 'attack' on the phrase about eclipsing the gaiety of nations. Boswell relayed this to Johnson, who replied: 'I could not have said more nor less, for 'tis truth; "eclipsed", not "extinguished", and his death did eclipse; 'twas like a storm.'

'But *why* nations?' Boswell continued. 'Did his gaiety extend farther than his own nation?' Johnson deftly tossed in the Scots ('if we allow the Scotch to be a nation, and to have gaiety'), but Boswell pressed on, 'Is not *harmless pleasure* very tame?' To which Johnson replied: 'Nay, Sir, harmless pleasure is the highest praise. Pleasure is a word of dubious import; pleasure is in general dangerous, and pernicious to virtue; to be able therefore to furnish pleasure that is harmless, pleasure pure and unalloyed, is as great a power as men can possess.' Boswell's initial account of this exchange appears in his journal for 24 April 1779 and appears in substantially the same form in his *Life of Johnson* at this date.

When Charles Dickens died in 1870, Thomas Carlyle wrote: 'It is an event world-wide, a *unique* of talents suddenly extinct, and has "eclipsed" (we too may say) "the gaiety of nations".'

1 BOSWELL. 'Should you not like to see Dublin, Sir?' JOHNSON. 'No, Sir! Dublin is only a worse capital.' BOSWELL. 'Is not the Giant's Causeway worth seeing?' JOHNSON. 'Worth seeing? yes; but not worth going to see.'

In the *Life*, for 12 October 1779. Johnson always had an aversion to visiting Ireland. In fact, he never went there, though the strength of his views as here – and next – might lead one to suppose that he had.

2 Dublin, though a place much worse than London, it is not so bad as Iceland.

In a note to Boswell's *Life* (but not in the first edition). It comes from the continuation of a letter from Mrs Smart, but is not actually printed in the *Life*. Johnson never visited either place.

3 [Quotation] is a good thing; there is a community of mind in it. Classical quotation is the *parole* of literary men all over the world.

In the *Life*, for 8 May 1781. Comment on the art of quotation. *Parole* = way of speaking, conversing.

4 At night ... I thought with uncommon earnestness, that however I might alter my mode of life, or whithersoever I might remove, I would endeavour to retain Levett about me; in the morning my servant brought me word that Levett was called to another state, a state for which, I think, he was not unprepared, for he was very useful to the poor. How much soever I valued him, I now wish that I had valued him more.

Letter from Johnson to Captain Langton – in the *Life* (dated 20 March 1782), in which he mournfully relates the loss of his 'very dear old friend, Mr Levett'. Denis Norden quoted the last sentence in a eulogy for his friend and colleague, the writer Frank Muir, in January 1998: 'I think the impetus for it – besides the sentiment it embodies – was that it incorporates one of those 18th-century words Frank was so fond of' (though, in fact, Boswell puts 'how much soever' as three words).

5 Sir, there is no settling the point of precedency between a louse and a flea.

Johnson's reply when asked to decide which of two poets – Derrick and Smart – was the better. Recounted in the *Life*, for 1783. It was, in fact, a standard figure of speech at that time for pedantically nit-picking comparisons. It had earlier been used by John Eachard and, in Latin, by Daniel Heinsius –according to *Notes and Queries*, Vol. 239.

6 Madam, a fool would have swallowed that.

To his shocked companion after spitting out a hot potato at dinner. Untraced and also ascribed to Thomas Carlyle, Winston Churchill and others. In *The 'Quote ... Unquote' Newsletter* (July 1996) Leonard Miall, the BBC's first postwar Washington correspondent, recalled attending a press conference at the State Department when the Secretary of State, Dean Acheson, was asked a very cleverly loaded question. 'None of us could imagine how the Secretary of State could answer it without getting himself into trouble. Acheson stroked his guardsman's moustache for a moment and then replied, "My late law partner, Judge Covington, once attended an oyster roast on the Eastern shore of Maryland. He was given a very hot oyster which he immediately spat on to the floor, remarking, 'A bigger damn fool would have swallowed that one.'" There were no supplementaries.'

Al JOLSON American entertainer (1888–1950)

7 Wait a minute, wait a minute. You ain't heard nothin' yet! Wait a minute, I tell ya, you ain't heard nothin'! You wanna hear 'Toot, Toot, Tootsie'? All right, hold on.

It seems that when Jolson exclaimed this in the first full-length talking picture *The Jazz Singer* (1927), he was not just ad libbing – as is usually supposed – but was promoting the title of one of his songs. He had recorded 'You Ain't Heard Nothing Yet', written by Gus Kahn and Buddy de Sylva, in 1919. In addition, Martin Abramson in *The Real Story of Al Jolson* (1950) suggests that Jolson had also uttered the slogan in San Francisco as long before as 1906. Interrupted by noise from a building site across the road from a café in which he was performing, Jolson had shouted, 'You think that's noise – you ain't heard nuttin' yet!'

Listening to the film soundtrack makes it clear that Jolson did not add 'folks' at the end of his mighty line, as Bartlett (1992), *PDMQ* (1980) and *ODQ* (1979) all say he did. Rather curiously, A.J.P. Taylor in *English History 1914–1945* (1965) seems to think that the ad-libbed words were 'Come on, Ma, listen to this.'

Erica JONG American novelist (1942–)

1 The zipless fuck is the purest thing there is. And it is rarer than the unicorn. And I have never had one.

Fear of Flying (1973). Jong coined the phrase 'zipless fuck' for a 'brief and passionate sexual encounter' (*OED2*) and, in her novel, explained her choice of the word 'zipless', 'because when you come together zippers fell away like petals'.

Ben JONSON English playwright and poet (1572–1637)

2 Ramp up my genius, be not retrograde;
But boldly nominate a spade a spade.

The Poetaster, Act 5, Sc. 1 (1601). See PLUTARCH 361:3.

3 O Rare Ben Johnson.

Jonson's epitaph in Westminster Abbey was composed in the year he died. According to Abbey tradition and as recounted in the *Official Guide* (1988 edn), Jonson died in poverty and was buried upright to save space. So he was, in the north aisle of the nave, with a small square stone over him. The stone, with the inscription spelt as above, was set upright in the north aisle wall in 1821 to save it from being worn away, and it may still be found there. There is also a wall plaque 'O RARE BEN IOHNSON', erected before 1728, in Poets' Corner.

Another tradition, according to John Aubrey, had it that the original epitaph was 'done at the charge of Jack Young, afterwards knighted, who, walking here when the grave was covering, gave the fellow eighteen pence to cut it'. The inscription has also been ascribed to the playwright Sir William D'Avenant (1608–68), who succeeded Jonson as unofficial Poet Laureate. His own gravestone set in the floor of Poets' Corner reads, 'O RARE S. WILLIAM DAVENANT' (or 'O rare Sir Will. Davenant' as Aubrey has it, 'in imitation of that on Ben Johnson').

Either way, the spelling is not at fault – 'Jonson' is merely an alternative that has become accepted. An attempt has been made to suggest that what the epitaphist meant to say was '*Orare Ben Jonson*' – 'pray for Ben Jonson' – but this is questionable Latin.

JOSEPH II Holy Roman Emperor (1741–90)

4 Too many notes.

The Emperor's comments were directed at Mozart's opera *Die Entführung aus dem Serail* ('The Abduction from the Seraglio'), first performed in 1782. Unwilling to concede, Mozart replied that it had 'just as many as are necessary'. Franz Xaver Niemetschek's biography of the composer

(1798) provides the context: 'The monarch, who at heart was charmed by this deeply stirring music, said to Mozart nevertheless: "Too beautiful for our ears and an extraordinary number of notes, dear Mozart." "Just as many, Your Majesty, as are necessary," he replied with that noble dignity and frankness which so often go with great genius.'

James Agate, *Ego 6* (1944), has the opera as *Le Nozze di Figaro* and Mozart's reply as: 'Not one too many, your Majesty.'

Jenny JOSEPH English poet (1932–)

5 When I am an old woman I shall wear purple
With a red hat which doesn't go, and doesn't
suit me,
And I shall spend my pension on brandy and
summer gloves
And satin sandals, and say we've no money
for butter.

'Warning', in *New Poems*, a PEN anthology (1965). In a 1996 poll by BBC TV to find Britain's most popular postwar poem, this came first. Indeed, it is widely known and can be found printed on tea towels and other gift-fodder. The success of the poem apparently irritates Jenny Joseph, who does not regard it as typical of her work.

William JOYCE Irish-American propagandist (1906–46)

6 Germany calling, Germany calling.

Joyce broadcast Nazi propaganda from Hamburg during the Second World War, was found guilty of treason (on the technicality that he held a British passport at the beginning of the war) and was hanged in 1946. He had a threatening, sneering, lower-middle-class delivery, which made his call-sign sound more like 'Jarmany calling'. Although Joyce was treated mostly as a joke in wartime Britain, he is credited with giving rise to some unsettling rumours. No one seemed to have heard the particular broadcast in question, but it got about that he had said the clock on Darlington Town Hall was two minutes slow, and so it was supposed to be.

His nickname of 'Lord Haw-Haw' was inappropriate as he did not sound the slightest bit aristocratic. *That* soubriquet had been applied by Jonah Barrington, the *Daily Express* radio correspondent, to Joyce's predecessor who *did* speak with a cultured accent but lasted only a few weeks from September 1939. This original was Norman Baillie-Stewart. He is said to have sounded like Claud Hulbert or one of the Western Brothers. An imaginary drawing appeared in the *Daily Express* of a Bertie Woosterish character with a monocle and receding chin. Baillie-Stewart said that he understood there was a popular English song called 'We're

Going to Hang Out the Washing on the Siegfried Line' which ended 'If the Siegfried Line's still there'. 'Curiously enoff,' he said, 'the Siegfried Line is still they-ah.'

JULIAN OF NORWICH English religious recluse (1343–?1416)

1 Sin is behovely, but all shall be well and all shall be well and all manner of thing shall be well.
Revelations of Divine Love. Part-quoted by T.S. Eliot in *Four Quartets*, 'Little Gidding' (1942).

Carl JUNG Swiss psychologist (1875–1961)

2 Liverpool is the pool of life.
Returning to my home town in 1982, I was intrigued to find a sign in Mathew Street – sacred site of the erstwhile Cavern Cub – saying: 'Liverpool is the pool of life. / C.J. JUNG 1927'. An agreeable compliment, but is there any record of the Swiss psychologist ever having set foot in the fair city? None. His *Memories, Dreams, Reflections* (1963) makes clear that he was simply describing a dream he had had. He saw a round pool, and in the middle of it a small island. While everything round about was obscured by rain, fog, smoke and dimly lit darkness, the little island blazed with sunlight. 'I had had a vision of unearthly beauty,' Jung says, 'and that was why I was able to live at all. Liverpool is the "pool of life". The "liver", according to an old view, is the seat of life – that which "makes to live".'

Unfortunately, even here, Jung is basing his supposition on fanciful etymology, presumably just hearing the name 'Liverpool', and never having been there. The derivation of the place name is 'pool with clotted, thick or muddy water', rather more to the point than 'pool of life'.

The sign had been taken down by 1987. A somewhat wobbly allusion occurs in Beryl Bainbridge, *An Awfully Big Adventure* (1989): 'O'Hara reminded him that Jung had considered Liverpool the centre of the Universe. "How interesting," said Potter. "I take it he didn't live here."'

JUVENAL Roman satirist (AD60–130)

3 *Sed quis custodiet ipsos Custodes?* [But who is to guard the guards themselves?]
Satires, No. 6. A key question to be asked of people in any sort of authority – who are *they* answerable to?

4 *Panem et circenses* [Bread and circuses].
In the same work, No. 10 – on what the citizen is chiefly concerned about. It was the fashion for the Roman emperors and others in authority to bribe the citizens of Rome with public entertainments and free food, as a way of avoiding popular discontent. Circuses here means chariot races and games in a stadium – the Circus in Rome was an oval-shaped racecourse.

5 *Mens sana in corpore sano* [A sound mind in a healthy body].
In the same work, No. 10. One of the most famous of proverbial Latin sayings and much used as a motto – e.g., of Chelsea College of Physical Education, Eastbourne, and Summer Fields School, Oxford. *ODQ* (1953) gives this translation of the context: 'Your prayer must be that you may have a sound mind in a sound body. Pray for a bold spirit, free from all dread of death; that reckons the closing scene of life among Nature's kindly boons.'

K

Pauline KAEL American film critic (1919–2001)

1 *Kiss Kiss Bang Bang.*
Title of a book (1968) of her collected criticism. Kael says the words came from an Italian poster – 'perhaps the briefest statement imaginable on the basic appeal of movies'. Usually, they are taken to refer to the James Bond movies. Indeed, Bond's creator Ian Fleming himself described his books in a letter (in about 1955) to Raymond Chandler as 'straight pillow fantasies of the bang-bang, kiss-kiss variety'. John Barry, composer of music for most of the Bond films, named one of his themes 'Mr Kiss Kiss Bang Bang' (for *Thunderball*, 1965). Compare, however, this from the American anthropologist Hortense Powdermaker in *Hollywood, The Dream Factory* (1951): 'South Sea natives who have been exposed to American movies classify them into two types, "kiss-kiss" and "bang-bang".'

Alphonse KARR French novelist and editor (1808–90)

2 *Plus ça change, plus c'est la même chose* [The more things change, the more they remain the same].
Les Guêpes (1849). Presumed origin of the phrase. Compare LAMPEDUSA 278:1.

George S. KAUFMAN American playwright (1889–1961)

3 Everything I've ever said will be credited to Dorothy Parker.
Quoted in Scott Meredith, *George S. Kaufman and the Algonquin Round Table* (1974). The lament of the incorrectly misappropriated.

4 God finally caught his eye.
Of a dead waiter. Quoted in the same book. As 'By and by / God caught his eye' this epitaph is attributed to David McCord, the American poet and university fund-raiser (1897–1997), in his 'Remainders' from *Bay Window Ballads* (1935).

5 *You Can't Take It With You.*
Title of play (1936), written with Moss Hart, from the saying that suggests that there is no point in holding on to money as it will be no good to you when you are dead (as in the expression, 'There are no pockets in shrouds'). An early appearance is in Captain Marryat's *Masterman Ready* (1841). An American version is 'You can't take your dough when you go.' 'You can always take one with you' was a slogan suggested by Winston Churchill when invasion by the Germans threatened in 1940.

Nikos KAZANTZAKIS Greek novelist (1883–1957)

6 I hope for nothing, I fear nothing, I am free.
Translation of the inscription on his grave at Iraklion, Crete. He was buried by the southern bastion of the city when the Orthodox Church refused him sacred ground as a non-believer – source: Hagg & Lewis, *Guide to Greece* (1986). Compare, from Torquato Tasso, *Jerusalem Delivered* (1580–1): '*Brama assai, poco spera, e nulla chiede* [He desired much, he hoped little, and asked for nothing]', which, in turn, was written by Edward Elgar at the end of his score for the *Enigma Variations* (1899) in the form: 'I long for much, I hope for little, I ask for nothing.'

Denis KEARNEY Irish-born American labour leader
(1847–1907)

1 Horny-handed sons of toil.

Kearney used this expression describing labourers who
bear the marks of their work in a speech at San Francisco
(?1878). He was leading a 'workingman's protest movement against unemployment, unjust taxes, unfair banking
laws, and mainly against Chinese labourers' – Stuart Berg
Flexner, *Listening To America* (1982). Earlier, the American
poet J.R. Lowell had written in 'A Glance Behind the Curtain'
(1843): 'And blessèd are the horny hands of toil.' The 3rd
Marquess of Salisbury, the British Conservative Prime Minister, had earlier used the phrase 'horny-handed sons of
toil' in *The Quarterly Review* (October 1873).

John KEATS English poet (1795–1821)

2 My ear is open like a greedy shark,
To catch the tunings of a voice divine.

'Imitation of Spenser' (1817). In the novel *Gaudy Night*
(1935) by Dorothy L. Sayers, Lord Peter Wimsey quotes the
shark remark and describes it as 'the crashing conclusion of
a sonnet by Keats'.

3 Much have I travelled in the realms of gold,
And many goodly states and kingdoms seen ...
Then felt I like some watcher in the skies
When a new planet swims into his ken;
Or like stout Cortez when with eagle eyes
He star'd at the Pacific – and all his men
Look'd at each other with a wild surmise –
Silent, upon a peak in Darien.

'On First Looking Into Chapman's Homer' (1817). There
are two minor errors of fact here. It was, in fact, Balboa, a
companion of Cortez, who became the first European to
set eyes on the Pacific Ocean at Darien on the Isthmus of
Panama in 1513. Nor was he silent: he exclaimed, '*Hombre!*',
an expression of surprise, the equivalent of the modern
'Man, look at that!'
   In a postscript to *The Clicking of Cuthbert* (1922), P.G.
Wodehouse wrote that, after making an allusion to 'Stout
Cortez' in the book, he had received an anonymous letter
from a correspondent: 'You big stiff, it wasn't Cortez, it was
Balboa.' He added: 'This, I believe, is historically accurate.
On the other hand, if Cortez was good enough for Keats,
he is good enough for me. Besides, even if it *was* Balboa,
the Pacific was open for being stared at about that time,
and I see no reason why Cortez should not have had a look
at it as well.'

4 And other spirits there are standing apart
Upon the forehead of the age to come:
These, these will give the world another heart,
And other pulses. Hear ye not the hum
Of mighty workings?

Sonnet, 'Addressed to the Same' (i.e. the painter Benjamin
Robert Haydon) (1817). Hence, *Another Heart and Other
Pulses* (1984), title of Michael Foot's account of his leadership
of the British Labour Party during the 1983 general
election.

5 I had a dove and the sweet dove died;
And I have thought it died of grieving.

'I had a dove and the sweet dove died' (written 1818). See
PYM 373:2.

6 A thing of beauty is a joy forever.

Endymion, Bk 1, line 1 (1818). Compare ROWLAND 389:4.

7 Old Meg she was a Gipsy,
And liv'd upon the Moors:
Her bed it was the brown heath turf,
And her house was out of doors.

Her apples were swart blackberries,
Her currants pods o' broom;
Her wine was dew of the wild white rose,
Her book a churchyard tomb.

'Old Meg' (1818). It has been urged that this was never
intended as serious poetry. It was included in a letter from
Scotland to Fanny Keats, then aged 15. Writing from Dum-
fries in July 1818, Keats says, 'We are in the midst of Meg
Merrilies' country [in Scott's *Guy Mannering*, published
1815] of whom I suppose you have heard ...' Then follows
'Old Meg' and another nonsense verse 'There was a naughty
boy'. Neither was intended for publication, but only for
circulation among his family.

8 Oh, what can ail thee knight at arms
Alone and palely loitering?
The sedge has withered from the lake
And no birds sing! ...
For she looked at me as she did love
And made sweet moan ...
La belle dame sans merci
Thee hath in thrall.

'La belle dame sans merci' (1820). Keats took the title of his tale
of a knight fatally in thrall to an elfin woman from a 15th-cen-
tury poem *La belle dame sans mercy*. In *The White Goddess*
(1948), Robert Graves argues that La Belle Dame represents

'Love, Death by Consumption ... and Poetry all at once'. The poem inspired a number of Victorian painters – including John William Waterhouse, Frank Dicksee, Arthur Hughes and Walter Crane – to produce works with the same title.

1 My heart aches, and a drowsy numbness pains
My sense, as though of hemlock I had drunk.

'Ode to a Nightingale' (1820). The first draft of the poem in Keats's own hand (1819) in the Fitzwillian Museum, Cambridge, shows clearly that poet entitled it 'Ode to *the* Nightingale'.

2 Already with thee! tender is the night.

In the same poem. Hence, *Tender is the Night*, title of a novel (1943; film US 1961) by F. Scott Fitzgerald.

3 But when the melancholy fit shall fall
Sudden from heaven like a weeping cloud,
That fosters the droop-headed flowers all,
And hides the green hill in an April shroud.

'Ode to Melancholy' (1820). Hence, *An April Shroud*, title of a Dalziel and Pascoe novel (1975) by Reginald Hill.

4 You I am sure will forgive me for sincerely remarking that you might curb your magnanimity and be more of an artist, and 'load every rift' of your subject with ore.

Letter to Shelley (August 1820). The quotation marks are taken to indicate a reference to Edmund Spenser's *The Faerie Queene*, Bk 2, Canto 7, St. 28 (1596): 'And with rich metal loaded every rift.'

5 Here lies One
Whose Name was writ in Water.

Keats's own choice of epitaph on his anonymous grave in the English cemetery, Rome. A few days before he died, Keats said that on his gravestone there should be no mention of his name or country. As he lay dying, listening to the fountain outside on the Spanish Steps in Rome, it is said he kept being reminded of the lines from Beaumont and Fletcher's play *Philaster*: 'All your better deeds / Shall be in water writ, but this in marble.' Robert Gittings in his biography of Keats (1968) comments: 'The quotations that may have suggested this phrase are many; but the gentle sound of the fountain, which had been his companion for so many nights as he lay in the narrow room above the square, may have seemed the right symbol for his end.'

One of the possible sources? Shakespeare, in *Henry VIII* (IV.ii.45) has: 'Men's evil manners live in brass; their virtues / We write in water.'

The self-written epitaph of Robert Ross, a friend of Oscar Wilde, was: 'Here lies one whose name was writ in hot water' – source: Osbert Sitwell, *Noble Essences* (1950).

Ned KELLY Australian outlaw (1855–80)

6 Ah well, I suppose it has come to this! ... Such is life!

Last words, quoted in Frank Clune, *The Kelly Hunters* (1958). Kelly was the son of a transported Irish convict and himself became a horse thief. He was hanged in Melbourne. The last phrase *Partridge/Slang* calls a 'world-old, world-wide truism', and *Partridge/Catch Phrases* adds 'world-weary'. W.J. Temple wrote in his diary (7 April 1796): 'This interruption is very teasing; but such is Life.' From Charles Dickens, *Martin Chuzzlewit*, Chap. 29 (1846): '"Sairey," says Mrs Harris, "sech is life. Vich likeways is the hend of all things!"' The British pop singer and political clown Screaming Lord Sutch felicitously entitled his autobiography *Life as Sutch* (1992).

Walt KELLY American cartoonist (1913–73)

7 We have met the enemy and he is us.

Kelly's syndicated comic strip featured an opossum called Pogo. This phrase appeared in a 1970 Pogo cartoon used on the 1971 Earth Day poster. Kelly had taken some time to get round to this formulation. In his introduction to *The Pogo Papers* (1953) he wrote: 'Resolve then, that on this very ground, with small flags waving and tinny blasts on tiny trumpets, we shall meet the enemy, and not only may he be ours, he may be us.'

There may be an allusion here to what US Captain Oliver Hazard Perry (1785–1819) said at the Battle of Lake Erie (10 September 1813): 'We have met the enemy and he is ours' or 'and they are ours'.

KEMPIS See THOMAS À KEMPIS.

John F. KENNEDY American Democratic 35th President (1917–63)

8 We stand today on the edge of a New Frontier ... But the New Frontier of which I speak is not a set of promises – it is a set of challenges. It sums up not what I intend to offer the American people, but what I intend to ask of them.

Accepting the Democratic nomination in Los Angeles (15 July 1960). Theodore C. Sorensen in *Kennedy* (1965), suggests that Kennedy had a hand in coining the slogan for the forthcoming administration: 'I know of no outsider who suggested the expression, although the theme of the Frontier was contained in more than one draft.' In 1964 Harold Wilson said in a speech in Birmingham: 'We want the youth of Britain to storm the new frontiers of knowledge.'

The last sentence of Kennedy's speech quoted above is a clear pre-echo of a theme in his inaugural address (see 267:3 below).

1 Let the word go forth from this time and place, to friend and foe alike, that the torch has been passed to a new generation of Americans, born in this century, tempered by war, disciplined by a hard and bitter peace, proud of our ancient heritage, and unwilling to witness or permit the slow undoing of those human rights to which this nation has always been committed, and to which we are committed today at home and around the world.

Let every nation know, whether it wishes us well or ill, that we shall pay any price, bear any burden, meet any hardship, support any friend, oppose any foe to assure the survival and the success of liberty.

Inaugural address, Washington DC (20 January 1961). As preparation, Kennedy told Sorensen to read all the previous inaugural speeches, and suggestions were also solicited from the likes of Adlai Stevenson, J.K. Galbraith and Billy Graham. Kennedy laid down basic rules: the speech was to be as short as possible, to deal almost exclusively with foreign affairs, to leave out the first person singular and to emulate Lincoln's Gettysburg address by using one-syllable words wherever possible.

The sentence beginning 'Let every nation ...' was later inscribed on the Kennedy memorial at Runnymede, near London.

2 All this will not be finished in the first one hundred days. Nor will it be finished in the first one thousand days, nor in the life of this Administration, nor even perhaps in our lifetime on this planet. But let us begin.

In the same speech. The phrase 'hundred days' is used to refer to a period of intense political action (often immediately upon coming to power). The allusion is to the period during which Napoleon ruled between his escape from Elba and his defeat at the Battle of Waterloo in 1815. Hence, the title of Arthur M. Schlesinger's memoir, A Thousand Days (1965), referring also to the 1056 days of Kennedy's presidency. Compare WILSON 501:1.

3 And so, my fellow Americans, ask not what your country can do for you; ask what you can do for your country.

In the same speech. Kennedy's speech employed a number of phrases that had been used by the president (and others) before. The 'Ask not ...' idea, for example, had been used by him three times during the election campaign. In a TV address during September 1960, Kennedy had said, 'We do not campaign stressing what our country is going to do for us as a people. We stress what we can do for the country, all of us.' In his memoir A Thousand Days (1965), Arthur M. Schlesinger, a Kennedy aide, traced the president's interest in the 'Ask not' theme back to a notebook he had kept in 1945, which included the Rousseau quotation, 'As soon as any man says of the affairs of state, What does it matter to me?, the state may be given up as lost.'

Other antecedents that have been cited include Kahlil Gibran, writing in Arabic after the First World War: 'Are you a politician asking what your country can do for you or a zealous one asking what you can do for your country? If you are the first, then you are a parasite; if the second, then you are an oasis in the desert.' Warren G. Harding said at the Republican National Convention in Chicago (1916): 'We must have a citizenship less concerned about what the government can do for it and more anxious about what it can do for the nation.' The Mayor of Haverhill, Massachusetts, said at the funeral of John Greenleaf Whittier (1892): 'Here may we be reminded that man is most honoured, not by that which a city may do for him, but by that which he has done for the city.' Oliver Wendell Holmes's Memorial Day Address 1884 contained the words: 'It is now the moment when by common consent we pause to become conscious of our national life and to rejoice in it, to recall what our country has done for each of us, and to ask ourselves what we can do for our country in return.'

In Britain, meanwhile, in October 1893, the Hon. St John Broderick MP told an audience in the Tennant Hall, Leeds: 'Clergymen do well to preach the neglected doctrine that the first duty of a citizen is to consider what he can do for the state and not what the state will do for him.'

It was Kennedy's inverted use of 'Ask not', however, that made what was obviously not a new concept eminently memorable.

4 I wonder how it is with you, Harold? If I don't have a woman for three days, I get a terrible headache.

To Harold Macmillan, at their third or fourth meeting (in about 1961). Remark, quoted in Alistair Horne, Macmillan 1957–1986 (1989). In a letter from Venice (3 July 1961), Nancy Mitford told her sister the Duchess of Devonshire (who was related by marriage to the president): 'They say on the beach that if [Kennedy] doesn't ... every day he has a headache.'

1 There is always inequity in life. Some men are killed in a war and some men are wounded, and some men never leave the country ... It's very hard in military or personal life to assure complete equality. Life is unfair.

Remark at news conference (23 March 1962). Compare FRASER 202:2.

2 He mobilized the English language and sent it into battle.

At a ceremony granting honorary US citizenship to Sir Winston Churchill on 9 April 1963 (at which Churchill was not present), Kennedy used this phrase, but it was not his own. See MURROW 333:1.

3 All free men, wherever they may live, are citizens of Berlin, and, therefore, as a free man, I take pride in the words *Ich bin ein Berliner.*

On 26 June 1963 Kennedy proclaimed a stirring slogan outside the City Hall of West Berlin, two years after the erection of the Berlin Wall. Ben Bradlee noted in *Conversations with Kennedy* (1975) that the president had to spend 'the better part of an hour' with Frederick Vreeland and his wife before he could manage to pronounce this and the other German phrases he used. It detracts only slightly to know that the president need only have said, '*Ich bin Berliner*' to convey the meaning 'I am a Berliner'. It could be argued that the '*ein*' adds drama because he was saying not 'I was born and bred in Berlin' or 'I live in Berlin', but 'I am one of you.' But by saying what he did, he drew attention to the fact that in Germany '*ein Berliner*' is a doughnut.

4 According to the ancient Chinese proverb, 'A journey of a thousand miles must begin with a single step.'

In the same speech. According to Burton Stevenson, *Book of Proverbs* (1949), it is a saying of Lao-tzu and is Maxim 64 in *Tao-te Ching* ('The Way of Virtue') (?550 BC). It is also sometimes said to be an Arab proverb.

5 Forgive but never forget.

Remark attributed by Ted Sorensen in 1968 TV interview. This thought turned up in an elaborated form in the 'Personal Conduct' section of *The Second Sin* (1973) by Thomas Szasz, the Hungarian-born psychiatrist: 'The stupid neither forgive nor forget; the naïve forgive and forget; the wise forgive but do not forget.' Earlier appearances of this probably proverbial view are so far untraced, though it is said that the moral of Aesop's tale 'The Man and the Serpent' is 'Injuries may be forgiven but not forgotten.'

Joseph P. KENNEDY American politician and businessman (1888–1969)

6 When the going gets tough, the tough get going.

On the election of John F. Kennedy as US president in 1961, attention was focused on several axioms said to come from the Boston-Irish political world, and more precisely from Joseph P. Kennedy, his father. At this distance, it would be impossible to say for sure whether this wealthy, ambitious businessman/ambassador/politician originated the expressions, but he certainly instilled them in his sons. This one is quoted in J.H. Cutler, *Honey Fitz* (1962). In due course, the saying was used as a slogan for the film *The Jewel of the Nile* (US 1985), and a song with the title sung by Billy Ocean and the stars of the film was a No. 1 hit in 1986. The joke slogan 'When the going gets tough, the tough go shopping' had appeared on T-shirts in the US by 1982.

7 Don't get mad, get even.

Quoted in Ben Bradlee, *Conversations with Kennedy* (1975), and attributed to 'the Boston-Irish political jungle'. *Don't Get Mad Get Even* became the title of a book (1983), 'a manual for retaliation' by Alan Abel.

8 If you want to make money, go where the money is.

Quoted in Arthur M. Schlesinger, *Robert Kennedy and His Times* (1979), as is 'Kennedys don't cry.' Other similar sayings included: 'Only winners come to dinner' and 'We don't want any losers around here. In this family we want winners. Don't come in second or third – that doesn't count – but win' (sometimes shortened to 'Kennedys always come first').

Jomo KENYATTA Kenyan President (?1889–1978)

9 Originally, the Africans had the land and the English had the Bible. Then the missionaries came to Africa and got the Africans to close their eyes and fold their hands and pray. And when they opened their eyes, the English had the land and the Africans had the Bible.

This saying was attributed to Kenyatta on BBC Radio *Quote ... Unquote* (13 October 1984), but later *The Observer*, 'Sayings of the Week' (16 December 1984), had Desmond Tutu, then Bishop of Johannesburg, saying it. A version relating to the American Indians had earlier been said by Chief Dan George (who died in 1982): 'When the white man came we had the land and they had the Bibles; now they have the land and we have the Bibles' – *Bloomsbury Dictionary of Quotations* (1987).

Alice KEPPEL (Mrs George Keppel) English mistress of King Edward VII (1869–1947)

1 Things were done better in *my* day.

Remark made on the day of Edward VIII's abdication, according to Janet Flanner writing in the magazine *Travel & Leisure* and quoted by Bryan & Murphy, *The Windsor Story* (1979). Flanner (1892–1978) was Paris correspondent for *The New Yorker* from 1925 to 1975.

What Keppel meant to convey was, 'The King didn't have to abdicate in order to carry on with Mrs Simpson. He could have married properly and then taken whoever he fancied as a mistress.' The remark has also been attributed to Miss Maxine Elliott, the Edwardian actress and another former mistress of Edward VII, in the form, 'We did it better in my day.' According to Andrew Barrow, *Gossip* (1978), Elliott said it to Winston Churchill at a dinner with the Duke and Duchess of Windsor near Cannes on 7 January 1938.

Compare a similar lament from Laurence Sterne (see 445:1): 'They order, said I, this matter better in France', which, by 1818, had become in Lady Morgan's *Autobiography* (not published until 1859): 'So you see, my dear Olivia, they manage these things better in France.' In a letter to former President Eisenhower (20 July 1965), Harold Macmillan moaned: 'Naturally, people consult me, but they never take my advice, so I give it without much sense of responsibility. Yes, indeed, we managed things much better in our time.'

Joseph KERMAN American musicologist and critic (1924–)

2 Tosca, that shabby little shocker.

Description of Puccini's opera *Tosca*, in *Opera as Drama* (1956). 'This must be the most often quoted remark in all musicology' – *The Sunday Times* (10 March 1991). In Kerman's 1989 revision of the book, he cites Bernard Shaw's evaluation (previously unknown to him) of Sardou's original play *La Tosca*: 'Such an old-fashioned, shiftless, clumsily constructed, empty-headed turnip ghost of a shocker. Oh, if it had but been an opera!'

Jack KEROUAC American novelist (1922–69)

3 The Beat Generation.

The Guardian (4 April 1988) announced in an obituary: 'Although a novelist, poet and lecturer at many universities, John Clellon Holmes was chiefly known for giving the Beat Generation its name. The phrase first appeared in his 1952 novel *Go*.' The headline to the piece (by William J. Weatherby) was, 'The naming of a generation'. This came as news to those who had believed until then that it was Kerouac who was not only the presiding genius of that 1950s

phenomenon, but had given it its name. Indeed, in the book *The Origins of the Beat Generation* and in *Playboy* (June 1959), Kerouac admitted to borrowing the phrase from a broken-down drug addict called Herbert Huncke.

Turning to Randy Nelson's *The Almanac of American Letters* (1981), we discover a description of the moment of coinage. He reports Kerouac as saying: 'John Clellon Holmes ... and I were sitting around trying to think up the meaning of the Lost Generation and the subsequent existentialism and I said, "You know, this is really a beat generation": and he leapt up and said, "That's it, that's right."' Holmes actually attributed the phrase directly to Kerouac in *The New York Times* Magazine of 16 November 1952.

When I put these versions to Weatherby in 1988, he replied: 'I based my comment on what Holmes told me close to the end of his life. It's possible his memory was shadowed by then or he had oversimplified the past, but the majority view seems to be he fathered the phrase or at least it emerged in a conversation in which he was involved. I don't believe Kerouac himself thought it up or even cared much for it.'

Francis Scott KEY American lawyer (1779–1843)

4 O, say, can you see, by the dawn's early light,
What so proudly we hailed at the twilight's last
   gleaming.

'The Star-Spangled Banner' (1814) – latterly an American national anthem. Hence, *So Proudly We Hail*, title of film (US 1943) and *Twilight's Last Gleaming*, title of a film (US/West Germany 1977).

Nikita KHRUSHCHEV Soviet Communist Party leader (1894–1971)

5 If anyone believes that our smiles involve abandonment of the teaching of Marx, Engels and Lenin he deceives himself. Those who wait for that must wait until a shrimp learns to whistle.

On the likelihood of the Soviet Union rejecting communism. Speech at Moscow (17 September 1955). Hence, *When Shrimps Learn to Whistle – Signposts for the Nineties*, title of a book (1990) by Denis Healey.

6 We say this not only for the socialist states who are more akin to us. We base ourselves on the idea that we must peacefully co-exist. About the capitalist states, it doesn't depend on you whether or not we exist. If you don't like us, don't accept our invitations, and don't ask us to come and see you. Whether you like it or not, history is on our side.

We will bury you. [*Applause from colleagues. Laughter from Mr Gomulka.*]

Said to Western diplomats at a Moscow reception for the Polish leader Władisław Gomulka at the Polish Embassy in Moscow (18 November 1956). The last two sentences were not reported at the time by either *Pravda* or *The New York Times*, but they were by *The Times* of London (on 19 November 1956), perhaps because the previous night at a Kremlin reception the British Ambassador, Sir William Hayter, had walked out when Khrushchev described Britain, France and Israel as 'fascists' and 'bandits' (over the Suez affair).

'We will bury you' can also be translated as 'We will be present at your funeral', i.e. outlive you, and Khrushchev made several attempts in later years to make plain that he meant 'outstrip' or 'beat' in the economic sense, rather than anything more threateningly literal. The remark may have been exaggerated by Western commentators.

1 The survivors will envy the dead.

Of nuclear war. Robert Debs Heinl's *Dictionary of Military and Naval Quotations* (1966) has no supporting information but gives Khrushchev saying in 1962, 'The survivors would envy the dead.' John F. Kennedy reportedly made the ascription at a 1963 press conference. 'Will the Survivors Envy the Dead?' had appeared earlier as a heading to Chap. 2 of Herman Kahn's study *On Thermonuclear War* (1960). As such this seems to be a popular saying from those fearful times that Kahn has adopted without comment. Compare Lady Jane 'Speranza' Wilde (Oscar's mother) writing in 'The Enigma' (1864): 'Yet the living might envy the dead their sleep, / So bitter is life in that mourning land.' 'The land', though not named, is, of course, Ireland.

Søren KIERKEGAARD Danish philosopher (1813–55)

2 Life must be lived forwards, but it can only be understood backwards.

Quoted as an epigraph by John Mortimer in his novel *Paradise Postponed* (1986), and used as a promotional line for George Melly's volume of autobiography *Scouse Mouse* (1984), this obscure thought can be found in Kierkegaard's *Journals and Papers*, Vol. 1 (1843): 'Philosophy is perfectly right in saying that life must be understood backward. But then one forgets the other clause – that it must be lived forward.' Compare 'History is lived forward but it is written in retrospect', attributed to C.V. Wedgwood by Salman Rushdie in *The Jaguar Smile* (1987), Epilogue.

Joyce KILMER American poet and journalist (1886–1918)

3 I think that I shall never see
A poem lovely as a tree.

'Trees' (1913). Famously set to music by Oscar Rasbach in 1922. Compare NASH 337:1.

Martin Luther KING Jr American clergyman and Civil Rights leader (1929–68)

4 I have a dream that one day this nation will rise up and live out the true meaning of its creed – 'We hold these truths to be self-evident that all men are created equal'. I have a dream ...

The largest protest rally in US history took place on 28 August 1963, when nearly 250,000 people joined the March on Washington. The Civil Rights demonstration reached its climax near the Lincoln Memorial with a 16-minute speech by King in which he applied the repetitions and rhythms of a revivalist preacher to a clear challenge on the lack of African-American progress since the Emancipation Proclamation of exactly one hundred years before. King used his familiar technique of delivering almost ritualistic invocations of the Bible and American lore in a sob-laden voice. He summoned up themes and phrases from his own speeches dating back to 1956. In Detroit, as recently as the 23 June, he had used the 'I have a dream' motif – 'I have a dream this evening that one day we will recognize the words of Jefferson that all men are created equal ...'

5 Free at last, free at last, thank God Almighty, we are free at last!

His peroration (in both the Washington and Detroit speeches) came, as he acknowledged, from an old negro spiritual. On his grave in South View Cemetery, Atlanta, Georgia, is carved a slightly altered version of these words: 'Thank God Almighty, I'm free at last.'

6 I've been to the mountain top ... I've looked over, and I've seen the promised land. I may not get there with you, but I want you to know tonight that we as a people will get to the promised land. So, I'm happy tonight. I'm not worried about anything. I'm not fearing any man. Mine eyes have seen the glory of the coming of the Lord.

On the night before he was assassinated, King said this in a speech at Memphis (3 April 1968). Did he have a premonition? The original 'promised land' (not called as such in the Bible, but referring to Canaan – western Palestine – and by association, Heaven) was promised to the descendants of Abraham, Isaac and Jacob. In Numbers 14:39–40: 'Moses told these sayings unto all the children of Israel ... And they rose up early in the morning and gat them up into the top of the mountain, saying, Lo, we be here, and will go up unto the place which the Lord hath promised.' There is also a reference to Moses' failure to reach the promised land, which he saw from the summit of Pisgah, but died on the mountain: 'Get thee up into the top of Pisgah, and lift up thine eyes westward, and northward, and southward, and eastward, and behold it with thine eyes: for thou shalt not go over this Jordan' – Deuteronomy 3:27. Compare HOWE 246:4.

Philip KING English playwright (1904–79)

1 Sergeant, arrest several of these vicars!

Tom Stoppard once claimed this as the funniest line anywhere in English farce. Alas, King's *See How They Run* (first performed in 1944) does not have quite that line in it. For reasons it would be exhausting to go into, the stage gets filled with various people who are, or are dressed up as, vicars, and the order is given: 'Sergeant, arrest most of these people.'

Charles KINGSLEY English novelist and poet (1819–75)

2 For men must work, and women must weep,
And there's little to earn, and many to keep,
Though the harbour bar be moaning.

'The Three Fishers' (1858). 'Bar' here means 'a ridge of sand, mud, shingle', but the line has given rise to many a pun. '[Lord Simon] was not popular with his fellow barristers who proclaimed, "There'll be no moaning at the Bar when he puts out to sea"' – John Colville, *The Fringes of Power*, Vol. 2 (1985). Compare TENNYSON 456:6.

3 When all the world is young, lad,
And all the trees are green ...
Young blood must have its course, lad,
And every dog his day.

'Young and Old', song from *The Water Babies* (1863).

Hugh KINGSMILL English writer (1889–1949)

4 [Friends are] God's apology for relations.

Quoted in Michael Holroyd, *The Best of Hugh Kingsmill* (1970). Hence, the title *God's Apology* for Richard Ingrams's book about Kingsmill and his circle (1977). The origin of the saying has been said to lie in a Spanish proverb.

Neil KINNOCK (later Lord Kinnock) Welsh-born Labour politician (1942–)

5 I warn you, if Margaret Thatcher wins on Thursday, I warn you not to be ordinary. I warn you not to be young. I warn you not to fall ill. And I warn you not to get old – if Thatcher wins on Thursday.

Speech, Bridgend (7 June 1983), two days before that year's general election. Checked against a sound recording. Labour lost the election but Kinnock's fine speech may well have contributed to his becoming the party's leader four months later.

There is a mild, ironical, echo – almost certainly unconscious – of a passage from Bernard Shaw's bibliographical appendix to *The Intelligent Woman's Guide to Socialism and Capitalism* (1928) in which Shaw recalls a point he had made in the various prefaces to his plays: 'I ... made it quite clear that ... under Socialism you would not be allowed to be poor. You would be forcibly fed, clothed, lodged, taught, and employed whether you liked it or not ... Also you would not be allowed to have half a crown an hour when other women had only two shillings, or to be content with two shillings when they had half a crown. As far as I know I was the first Socialist writer to whom it occurred to state this explicitly as a necessary postulate of permanent civilization; but as nothing that is true is ever new I daresay it had been said again and again before I was born.'

6 Why am I the first Kinnock in a thousand generations to be able to get to university? Why is Glenys [his wife] the first woman in her family in a thousand generations to be able to get to university? Was it because *all* our predecessors were 'thick'? ... Of course not. It was because there was no platform upon which they could stand ... no method by which the communities could translate their desires for those individuals into provision for those individuals.

Speech, Llandudno (15 May 1987), and also used in a Party Political Broadcast (21 May). Later in that year it was famously plagiarized by US Senator Joe Biden, who was shaping up to run for the Democratic ticket in the 1988 presidential election. At other times Biden had credited Kinnock with the words, but not on 23 August when he said: 'Why is it that Joe Biden is the first in his family ever to go to university? ... Is it because our fathers and mothers were not so bright? ... It's because they didn't have a platform upon which to stand.' His rivals pounced, the speeches were reproduced side by side, and Biden, who had little chance of winning any primaries, was soon out of the race.

Rudyard KIPLING English poet and novelist (1865–1936)

1 And a woman is only a woman, but a good Cigar is a Smoke.

Poem, 'The Betrothed' (1886). Lest Kipling, as usual, take more blame than he should for what one of his characters says – now seen as an outrageous example of male chauvinism – it is worth pointing out that the man in question (the poem is in the first person) is choosing between his cigars and his betrothed, a woman called Maggie. The situation arose in an actual breach-of-promise case, in about 1885, in which the woman had said to the man: 'You must choose between me and your cigar.'

The poem ends: 'Light me another Cuba – I hold to my first-sworn vows. / If Maggie will have no rival, I'll have no Maggie for Spouse!'

2 But that's another story ...

Plain Tales from the Hills (1888). The catchphrase, popular from around 1900, derives from Kipling, though not exclusively – earlier it had appeared in Laurence Sterne's Tristram Shandy (1760), intended to prevent one of the many digressions with which that novel is full.

3 The Man Who Would Be King.

Title of a story (1888; film US 1975) about two adventurers in India in the 1880s who find themselves accepted as kings by a remote tribe. Compare The Man Born To Be King – Jesus Christ – a verse drama for radio (1942) by Dorothy L. Sayers (a title already used by William Morris for a part of his poem The Earthly Paradise, 1868–70); and 'the lad that's born to be king' in 'The Skye Boat Song' (1908) by Sir Harold Edwin Boulton.

4 Oh, East is East, and West is West, and never the twain shall meet,
Till Earth and Sky stand presently at God's great Judgement Seat;
But there is neither East nor West, Border, nor Breed, nor Birth,
When two strong men stand face to face, though they come from the ends of the earth!

'The Ballad of East and West' (1889). Kipling had a curious knack for coining popular phrases, of which 'East is East and West is West' is but one. George Orwell noted in Horizon (February 1942): 'Kipling is the only English writer of our time who has added phrases to the language. The phrases and neologisms which we take over and use without remembering their origin do not always come from writers we admire ... [but] Kipling deals in thoughts that are both vulgar and permanent.' Hence, East Is East, the

title of a film (UK 1999) set in a Northern town about a family with a Pakistani father and a white English mother.

5 And what should they know of England who only England know?

'The English Flag' (1892). Based on an incident when the Union Jack was once (apparently) burnt by a mob in Cork, Ireland. A denunciation of Little Englanders. 'The English had been given opportunity to take part in a new era of adventure and expansion. The world was opening up, making it possible for people to see places and experience ways of life that earlier generations could only hear and read about' – taken from a companion to Kipling's verse. Compare such uses as: 'What do they know of cricket who only know of cricket?' – C.L.R. James (attributed remark).

6 For the wind is in the pine trees, and the temple-bells they say:
'Come you back you British soldier; come you back to Mandalay!'
... On the road to Mandalay
Where the flyin'-fishes play,
An' the dawn comes up like thunder outer China 'crost the Bay!

'Mandalay' (1892). Famously set to music by Oley Speaks (1874–1948) in 1907. It has been objected that the last line quoted here is a geographical impossibility: Mandalay in Burma is land-locked, some 400 km from the Bay of Bengal, and even if it were moved to the coast, looking across the Bay of Bengal from Burma would lead the eye towards India and the west, the direction in which the sun sets, not rises. [An even more pedantic pedant writes: Indo-China includes neither India nor China: it is the peninsula of SE Asia incorporating Burma, Thailand, Laos, Vietnam, Cambodia and Malaya.] Jane Keskar, Secretary of the Kipling Society, commented (2005): 'Apart from poetic licence, it is plausible to consider that the British soldier is not physically in Burma and on the road to Mandalay but is thinking about his Burmese girl and his romantic memories, and is either in India or on a boat looking across the bay of Bengal. In which case the "dawn" is geographically correct.' And, one might add, the 'China' referred to is Indo-China, the peninsula of Southeast Asia that includes Burma.

7 Ship me somewheres east of Suez, where the best is like the worst,
Where there ain't no Ten Commandments an' a man can raise a thirst.

In the same poem. Hence, 'East of Suez' as a phrase to denote, especially, the British Empire as it was in India and the East, which was usually reached through the Suez Canal (opened in 1869). Somerset Maugham entitled a play *East of Suez* (1922), while John Osborne wrote a play set on a 'sub-tropical island, neither Africa nor Europe' with the title *West of Suez* (1971).

1 Gentlemen rankers out on the spree,
Damned from here to Eternity.
'Gentlemen-Rankers' (1892). Hence, *From Here to Eternity*, title of a novel (1951; film US 1953) by James Jones.

2 He wrapped himself in quotations – as a beggar would enfold himself in the purple of emperors.
'The Finest Story in the World', *Many Inventions* (1893). One way of looking at the art of quotation.

3 There are nine and sixty ways of constructing tribal lays,
And – every – single – one – of – them – is – right!
'In the Neolithic Age' (1893). In the article mentioned at 272:4, George Orwell notes that, in his book *Adam and Eve* (1944), John Middleton Murry had incorrectly ascribed this quotation to Thackeray, and adds: 'This is probably what is known as a "Freudian error". A civilized person would prefer not to quote Kipling – i.e. would prefer not to feel that it was Kipling who had expressed his thought for him.'

4 The Long Trail.
Title of the envoi to Barrack-Room Ballads. Hence, *The Long Trail*, the title of a book by John Brophy and Eric Partridge on First World War songs and slang (1965).

5 The tumult and the shouting dies;
The captains and the kings depart:
Still stands Thine ancient sacrifice,
An humble and a contrite heart.
Lord God of hosts, be with us yet,
Lest we forget – lest we forget!
From Kipling's poem 'Recessional' (1897), written as a warning on Queen Victoria's Jubilee Day that while empires pass away, God lives on. Kipling himself may have agreed to the adoption of 'Lest we forget' as an epitaph during his work for the Imperial War Graves Commission after the First World War. Another use to which the phrase has been put: it was the title of the Fritz Lang film *Hangmen Also Die* (US 1943) when it was re-issued. The alliterative coupling of captains and kings had been used earlier by Tennyson in 'A Dream of Fair Women' (1832): 'Melting the mighty hearts / Of captains and of kings.' Hence, *Captains and the Kings*, title of a novel (1972) by Taylor Caldwell (about an immigrant

orphan boy who founds a US political dynasty – based on the Kennedy family) and *The Tumult and the Shouting*, title of the autobiography (1954) of Grantland Rice.

Margaret Thatcher had a seemingly inexhaustible supply of quotations – never more so than when she had just returned in triumph to 10 Downing Street. She quoted 'Recessional' on being re-elected for a third term in June 1987. So much did she enjoy it that she repeated the words at that year's Conservative Party Conference. See also KNOX 276:3.

6 A fool there was and he made his prayer
(Even as you and I!)
To a rag and a bone and a hank of hair
(We called her the woman who did not care)
But the fool he called her his lady fair –
(Even as you and I!)
'The Vampire' (1897). Hence, the film title *A Fool There Was* (US 1914). It was through this film that Theda Bara popularized the notion of the female 'vamp'.

7 Lalun is a member of the most ancient profession in the world.
'On the City Wall', *In Black and White* (1888). The first reference found, in these terms, to prostitution. In 'In the House of Suddhoo' from *Plain Tales from the Hills* (also 1888), Kipling has: 'Janoo and Azizun are ... Ladies of the City and theirs is an ancient ... profession.' Latterly, it has perhaps been more commonly referred to as 'the word's oldest profession'. From Alexander Woollcott, *Shouts and Murmurs* (1922): 'The Actor and the Streetwalker ... the two oldest professions in the world – ruined by amateurs.' This last has also been attributed to Sir Henry Irving who, on being approached by a prostitute in London, is said to have remarked: 'You and I, madam, are members of the world's two oldest professions, and both of them, if I may say so, are being ruined by a bunch of damned amateurs.'

8 Nursed the pinion that impelled the steel.
'An Unsavoury Interlude' (1899), in *Stalky & Co*. Little Hartopp quotes about King that he 'nursed the pinion that impelled the steel' but does not explain the allusion. It is from Byron, *English Bards and Scotch Reviewers*, line 846 (1809).

9 The book was amazing, and full of quotations that one could hurl like a javelin.
In the *Stalky & Co*. stories, the lads fall to reading 'Uncle Remus'.

1 Each to his choice, and I rejoice
The lot has fallen to me
In a fair ground – in a fair ground –
Yea, Sussex by the sea!

'Sussex' (1902). Kipling lived there. But the phrase 'Sussex by the sea' also occurs in a song with this title – words and music by W. Ward-Higgs (who died in 1936):

We plough and sow and reap and mow,
And useful men are we ...
You may tell them all that we stand or fall
For Sussex by the sea.

This song was not published until 1908, so it looks as though Kipling got there first. (Incidentally, the English county has since been cut in two. It is still by the sea, however.)

2 The flannelled fools at the wicket or the muddied oafs at the goals.

'The Islanders' (1902) – where the 'fools' are, of course, cricketers. Hence, *Flanelled Fool*, title of book (1967), 'a slice of life in the 30s', by the critic T.C. Worsley, and *Flanelled Fool and Muddied Oaf*, title of the memoirs (1986) of the sports commentator Peter West.

3 And so *that* was all right, Best beloved.

The Just-So Stories (1902), 'The Beginning of the Armadillos'. This phrase is repeated thrice at the start of the tale and at the conclusion, once in the form, 'So *that's* all right, Best Beloved.' As such, it is a precursor of the more recent ironic expression, 'so that's all right then ...' – a comment when a feeble or self-serving explanation has been advanced for some state of affairs. This was popularized by the satirical magazine *Private Eye* in the 1980s. The earliest citation is from *The Guardian* (5 November 1984): "'In summary, therefore, TV-am's failure to achieve all of its starting aims by March 1983, came down simply and solely to the very bad audience ratings in the first few weeks and the effect of this on the nerves of some of those whose money was at stake. Those poor ratings were not due to any flaw in the conception of the franchises, or TV-am's application for it, or the role and talent of the original presenters." So that's all right then. But who says? Peter Jay himself.' From *The Times* (18 June 1988): 'A charming letter from Teddy Tinling, the tennis person, corrects a terrible error I made recently when I quoted him as saying of Gabriela Sabatini: "She's beautiful but she walks like John Wayne." Mr Tinling tells me he said that Sabatini walks likes Robert Mitchum. That's all right, then.'

4 The Cat That Walked By Himself.

Title of story, in the same work. 'I am the cat that walks alone' was a favourite expression of Lord Beaverbrook.

5 Five and twenty ponies
Trotting through the dark –
Brandy for the Parson
'Baccy for the Clerk;
Laces for a lady, letters for a spy,
And watch the wall, my darling, while the
    Gentlemen go by!

'A Smuggler's Song', *Puck of Pook's Hill* (1906). Hence, *Brandy for the Parson*, title of a film comedy (UK 1951) about smuggling.

6 If you can keep your head when all about you
Are losing theirs and blaming it on you ...
If you can meet with Triumph and Disaster
And treat those two impostors just the same ...
If you can talk with crowds and keep your virtue,
Or walk with Kings – nor lose the common
    touch ...

The poem 'If — ' from *Rewards and Fairies* (1910) is one of the most plundered and parodied poems in the language: the second two lines are inscribed over the doorway to the Centre Court at Wimbledon; 'As someone pointed out recently, if you can keep your head when all about you are losing theirs, it's just possible you haven't grasped the situation' – Jean Kerr, *Please Don't Eat the Daisies* (1958); also, 'If you can keep your girl when all about you / Are losing theirs and blaming it on you ...' – is the beginning of a mildly scurrilous version of the kind that says it is written 'with apologies to Rudyard Kipling Esq.' Lord Wavell quoted only the first two lines in *Other Men's Flowers* (1944). He also averred that Kipling had George Washington in mind when he wrote the original.

It is also the most popular poem in the language – or, at least, is the one people most often mention when asked what their favourite poem is. It came top of a British poll taken by the BBC TV programme *Bookworm* in 1995. In *The Ultimate Spin Doctor* (1996), Mark Hollingsworth recounts how when Tim Bell first met Margaret Thatcher in 1978, she asked him what his favourite poem was. He, of course, replied 'If —' – which accorded with her view – and she concluded that they would get on very well together. He became her advertising and public-relations adviser. The film *If...* (UK 1968) clearly borrows the title.

7 If you can fill the unforgiving minute
With sixty seconds' worth of distance run,
Yours is the Earth and everything that's in it,
And – which is more – you'll be a Man, my son!

In the same poem. Hence, *The Unforgiving Minute*, title of the autobiography (1978) of Beverley Nichols. The announced sequel *Distance Run*, covering the remaining years of the author's life, did not appear.

1 For the female of the species is more deadly than the male.

'The Female of the Species' (1911). Hence, the films *The Female of the Species* (UK 1917) and *Deadlier Than the Male* (UK 1967) – the latter based on Sapper's novel *The Female of the Species* (1927). *The Female of the Species* was also the title of an unrelated novel (1981) by Jessica Mann. A much-quoted line, though sometimes the quoter takes the teeth out of the remark. In 1989 Margaret Thatcher said: 'The female of the species is rather better than the male.'

2 So when the world is asleep, and there seems
    no hope of her waking
Out of some long, bad dream that makes her
    mutter and moan,
Suddenly, all men arise to the noise of fetters
    breaking,
And every one smiles at his neighbour and tells
    him his soul is his own!

'The Dawn Wind' – 'the fifteenth century', in the same work. Margaret Thatcher was a great quoter – Kipling was top of her source list – though sometimes she misquoted, twisted or ignored the fact that she was speaking some-one else's lines. When a newspaperman queried the source of the above lines, which Mrs Thatcher had used to indicate how things were going in her 1979 election campaign, it was duly reported that the Prime-Minister-to-be had recalled his request in the small hours of the morning and taken the trouble to write him a note explaining their provenance.

3 *A Diversity of Creatures*.

Title of a collection of stories (1917). Kipling has as epigraph: '*Praised be Allah for the diversity of His creatures – Arabian Nights*.'

See also BALDWIN 50:5.

Henry KISSINGER American Republican politician (1923–)

4 Power is the ultimate aphrodisiac.

An unverified remark, diagnosing his success as a 'swinger'. Quoted in *The Guardian* (28 November 1976). Also, in the form 'power is the great aphrodisiac', this was quoted in *The New York Times* (19 January 1971). Compare BELLOW 60:6; NAPOLEON 336:1.

5 We are [all] the President's men and we must behave accordingly.

Saying at the time of the 1970 Cambodia invasion. Quoted in Kalb and Kalb, *Kissinger* (1974). Hence, *All the President's Men*, title given by Carl Bernstein and Bob Woodward to their first book on Watergate (1974; film US 1976). It might seem also to allude to the lines from the nursery rhyme 'Humpty Dumpty' (first recorded in 1803):

All the king's horses
And all the king's men
Couldn't put Humpty together again.

There was also a Robert Penn Warren novel (1946, film US 1949) based on the life of southern demagogue Huey 'King-fish' Long and called *All the King's Men*.

See also NANSEN 334:4.

Fred KITCHEN British entertainer (1872–1950)

6 Meredith, we're in!

The catchphrase originated as a shout of triumph in a music-hall sketch called 'The Bailiff' (or 'Moses and Son') per-formed by Kitchen, the leading comedian with Fred Karno's company. The sketch was first seen about 1907, and the phrase was used each time a bailiff and his assistant looked like gaining entrance to a house. Kitchen has the phrase on his gravestone in West Norwood cemetery, south London, together with the suggestion that he died, not in 1950 as recorded above, but in 1951 aged 77.

Friedrich Maximilian von KLINGER German playwright (1752–1831)

7 *Sturm und Drang* [Storm and stress].

Title of play (1777). Hence, the name given to the German literary movement of the late 18th century that chiefly consisted of violently passionate dramas by the likes of Goethe and Schiller. Said to have been applied by Goethe himself.

John KNOX Scottish religious reformer (1505–72)

8 The First Blast of the Trumpet Against the Mon-strous Regiment of Women.

Title of pamphlet (1558). The critic George Saintsbury remarked that the title was the best part of it. *The Oxford Companion to English Literature* (1985) comments: 'The phrase is often now misapplied: "Regiment" here has its old sense of "rule, magisterial authority", and has no con-nection with the later sense of "large body of troops".'

Ronald KNOX English priest and writer (1888–1957)

1 As no less than three of [these poems] wear the aspect of a positively last appearance [i.e. a promise not to write more], they have been called in the words of so many eminent preachers 'ninthlies and lastlies'.

Knox's *Juxta Salices* (1910) includes a group of poems he had written when still at Eton and the book prefaced with the above. The expression 'ninthlies and lastlies' – or at least the idea behind it – is, as he indicates, not original. 'In Ambush', published 1898, one of Kipling's *Stalky & Co.* stories has: 'Ninthly, and lastly, they were to have a care and to be very careful.' *OED2* has Thomas B. Aldrich writing in *Prudence Palfrey* (1874–85) of 'The poor old parson's interminable ninthlies and finallies', and there is a 'fifthly and lastly' dated 1681. Benjamin Franklin, in 1745, concluded his *Reasons for Preferring an Elderly Mistress* with: 'Eighth and lastly. They are so grateful!!' Ultimately, the origin for all this must be the kind of legal nonsense-talk parodied by Shakespeare's Dogberry in *Much Ado About Nothing* (1598): 'Marry, sir, they have committed false report; moreover, they have spoken untruths; secondarily, they are slanders; *sixthly and lastly*, they have belied a lady; thirdly, they have verified unjust things; and to conclude, they are lying knaves.' In Sir Walter Scott, *Kenilworth*, Chap. 4 (1821), there is this, of a collection of old books: 'They are popish trash, every one of them, – private studies of the mumping old Abbot of Abingdon. The nineteenthly of a pure gospel sermon were a cart-load of such rakings of the kennel of Rome.'

2 The tumult and the shouting dies,
  The captains and the kings depart,
  And we are left with large supplies
  Of cold blancmange and rhubarb tart.

'After the Party', included in Laurence Eyres, *In Three Tongues* (1959). Compare KIPLING 273:5.

See also REAGAN 377:6.

Arthur KOESTLER Hungarian-born writer (1905–83)

3 *Darkness at Noon.*

Title of novel (1940) about the imprisonment, trial and execution of a Communist who has betrayed the Party. It was originally going to be called *The Vicious Circle*. Though originally written in German and translated for Koestler, the book's title appears always to have been rendered in English (Koestler was dealing with a London publisher). As such, it echoes Milton's *Samson Agonistes* (1671): 'O dark, dark, dark, amid the blaze of noon' and Cowper's 'The Progress of Error' (1782): 'Judgement drunk, and brib'd to lose his way / Winks hard, and talks of darkness at noonday.' *Darkness at Noon, or the Great Solar Eclipse of the 16th June 1806* was the title of an anonymous booklet published in Boston, Mass. (1806).

The KORAN

4 Say to the unbelievers: 'You shall be overthrown, and mustered into Gehenna – an evil cradling.'

3:8. Has also been translated as: ' ... and driven into Hell – an evil resting-place.' Hence, the title of Brian Keenan's account – *An Evil Cradling* (1992) – of his four-and-a-half-year incarceration by fundamentalist Shi'ite militiamen in Lebanon in 1985.

Milan KUNDERA Czechoslovakian-born French novelist (1929–)

5 *The Unbearable Lightness of Being.*

English title of Kundera's novel (1984; film US 1987). In Czech it is *Nesnesitelná lehkost bytí* (which means, more literally, 'the unbearable easiness/facility of being'). An allusion: 'The unbearable rightness of being PC [politically correct]', headline in *The Guardian* (24 September 1992).

L

Lady Caroline LAMB English wife of 2nd Viscount Melbourne (1785–1828)

1 Mad, bad and dangerous to know.

Diary entry on first meeting Lord Byron at a ball in March 1812. Quoted in Elizabeth Jenkins, *Lady Caroline Lamb* (1932).

Charles LAMB English writer (1775–1834)

2 Mary, where are all the naughty people buried?

As a boy in the 1780s, to his sister, on observing the fulsome epitaphs in a churchyard in the 1780s. Quoted in Leonard Russell, *English Wits* (1940). William Wordsworth, in the second of his essays on epitaphs (possibly written about 1812), recalls the story (old even in his day, one imagines) of the person who, tired of reading so many fulsome epitaphs on 'faithful wives, tender husbands, dutiful children and good men of all classes', exclaimed, 'Where are all the *bad* people buried?' Perhaps he was referring to Lamb? Whoever first made the comment, Wordsworth argues that there is a lot to be said for having, 'in an unkind world, one enclosure where the voice of Detraction is not heard ... and there is no jarring tone in the peaceful concert of amity and gratitude'.

3 The greatest pleasure I know, is to do a good action by stealth, and to have it found out by accident.

'Table Talk by the late Elia', in *The Athenaeum* (4 January 1834). Compare POPE 363:11.

Norman LAMONT (later Lord Lamont) English Conservative politician (1942–)

4 The turn of the tide is sometimes difficult to discern ... What we are seeing is the return of that vital ingredient – confidence. The green shoots of economic spring are appearing once again.

Speech to the Conservative Party Conference at Blackpool (9 October 1991). As Chancellor of the Exchequer he was earnestly endeavouring to convince his audience that Britain was coming out of a recession. It had not obviously done so before he was relieved of his responsibilities in 1993. John Smith, on his election as Labour leader (18 July 1992) commented: 'You don't have to be a paid-up member of the Royal Horticultural Society to know that the Chancellor's green shoots and his promised recovery are as far away as ever.' In *The Independent* (30 November 1993), Lamont reflected: 'My wife tried to talk me out of that phrase, but only because I used it in October, the wrong season for green shoots.'

Compare this use: in a letter to a lover (6 May 1962), the poet Philip Larkin wrote: 'Spring comes with your birthday, and I love to think of you as somehow linked with the tender green shoots I see on all the trees and bushes ... and I wish I could be with you and we could plunge into bed.'

5 We give the impression of being in office but not in power.

Lamont was sacked as Chancellor of the Exchequer in June 1994 and caused a slight stir in the House of Commons during his 'resignation' statement, by saying this of the government. A nice dig, but not new. As A.J.P. Taylor noted in his *English History 1914–1945* (1965), writing of Ramsay MacDonald as Prime Minister of a minority government in 1924: 'The Labour government recognized that they could make no fundamental changes, even if they knew what to make: they were "in office, but not in power".' Hence, the title of Lamont's autobiography, *In Office – The Chancellor's Story* (2000).

Giuseppe Di LAMPEDUSA Italian writer (1896–1957)

1 *Se vogliamo che tutto rimanga come è, bisogna che tutto cambi* [If we want everything to remain as it is, it will be necessary for everything to change].

The Leopard, Chap. 1 (1957). In the first chapter, this 'ambiguous' observation is said to have originated with his nephew and heir, Tancredi, but is now well comprehended by Prince Fabrizio. In an introductory title to the film (Italy/US 1963), it is given as the Prince's own credo, but translated into English as 'Things will have to change in order that they can remain the same.' Compare KARR 264:2.

Bert LANCE American Democratic politician (1931–)

2 If it ain't broke, don't fix it.

On government reorganization as President Carter's Director of the Office of Management and Budget. Quoted in *The Nation's Business* (27 May 1977) – what may be the first citation of a modern proverb, if not its actual coinage. Has also been ascribed to the motor magnate Henry Ford and picked up by Margaret Thatcher as an argument against unnecessary governmental intervention. From the film *Beauty and the Beast* (US 1991): '*Cogsworth (making tour of castle)*: This is yet another example of the late neo-classical baroque period and, as I always say, if it's not baroque, don't fix it!'

See also CARTER 126:7.

Andrew LANG Scottish poet and scholar (1844–1912)

3 Not in the waste beyond the swamps and sand
The fever-haunted forest and lagoon,
Mysterious Kor, thy walls forsaken stand,
Thy lonely towers beneath a lonely moon.

Lines written to his friend Rider Haggard. Hence, 'Mysterious Kor', title of a story (1944) by Elizabeth Bowen in which a girl working in bombed-out wartime London sees these lines as the ghost of a poem she had once read. Discussed in John Bayley, *Iris* (1998).

4 He uses statistics as a drunken man uses lampposts – for support rather than illumination.

Quoted in *The Treasury of Humorous Quotations*, eds Esar & Bentley (1951). Lang seems to have been the actual originator (in 1910) of this oft-quoted joke.

Julia LANG British broadcaster (1921–)

5 Are you sitting comfortably? Then I'll [*or* we'll] begin.

This way of beginning a story on *Listen With Mother*, BBC

Radio's daily spot for small children, was used from the programme's inception in January 1950. Lang, the original presenter, recalled in 1982: 'The first day it came out inadvertently. I just said it. The next day I didn't. Then there was a flood of letters from children saying, "I couldn't listen because I wasn't ready."' It remained a more or less essential part of the proceedings until the programme ended its long run in 1982.

In *The Times* obituary of Frieda Fordham, an analytical psychologist (18 January 1988), it was claimed that *she* had actually coined the phrase when advising the BBC's producers.

LAO-TZU Chinese philosopher and founder of Taoism (?604–531BC)

6 Heaven and Earth have no pity; they regard all things as straw dogs.

Tao-te Ching. Hence, *Straw Dogs*, title of film (UK 1971). Another translation: 'Heaven and Earth are ruthless, and treat the myriad of creatures as straw dogs; the sage is ruthless and treats the people as straw dogs ... Is not the space between Heaven and Earth like a bellows?'

Philip LARKIN English librarian and poet (1922–85)

7 *The Less Deceived.*

Title of his second collection of verse (1955), in which the poem 'Deceptions' tells of a 'ruined' Victorian girl: '... for you would hardly care / That you were less deceived, out on that bed ...' (than the man who had ruined her). Probably an allusion to *Hamlet*: Ophelia thought that Hamlet loved her and in this she was the 'more deceiv'd' (III.i.119).

8 Sexual intercourse began
In nineteen sixty-three
(Which was rather late for me) –
Between the end of the *Chatterley* ban
And the Beatles' first LP.

'Annus Mirabilis', in *High Windows* (1974). The Chatterley ban (i.e. on the publication of D.H. Lawrence's novel) ended in 1960; the Beatles' first LP was *Please, Please Me* (released 22 March 1963). Two significant landmarks of popular culture.

9 The headed paper, made for writing home
(If home existed) letters of exile.

'Friday Night in the Royal Station Hotel', in the same work. Hence, probably, *Writing Home*, title of book (1994) by Alan Bennett.

1 This Be the Verse.

Title of poem, in the same work. Taken from STEVENSON 447:5.

2 They fuck you up, your mum and dad.
They may not mean to, but they do.
They fill you with the faults they had
And add some extra, just for you.

... Man hands on misery to man.
It deepens like a coastal shelf.
Get out as early as you can,
And don't have any kids yourself.

'This Be the Verse', in the same work. Larkin later mourned the popularity of this poem which, he said, would 'clearly be my "Lake Isle of Innisfree". I fully expect to hear it recited by a thousand Girl Guides before I die' – letter of 6 June 1982, in *Selected Letters* (1992). Compare YEATS 510:1.

Harold LASKI English political scientist (1893–1950)

3 In that state of resentful coma that they dignified by the name of research.

In one of his letters to Oliver Wendell Holmes Jr (dated 10 October 1922, published 1953), Laski recounted how he had recently spoken at a Conference on Workers' Education at Oxford: 'I made an epigram in my address which pleased me. A trade-unionist attacked Oxford for being slow to respond to the workers' demand for education. I said that I was amazed at the speed of the response in dons who spent most of their days in ...' Laski was so pleased with his epigram that he used it soon afterwards in *three* other letters to Holmes without any apparent awareness that he was repeating himself.

In *The Lyttelton Hart-Davis Letters* (for 27 October 1955), it is suggested that 'Laski produced it – mendaciously – as his own in a letter to Judge Holmes.' If the remark was not his own, the originator remains untraced.

In *Geoffrey Madan's Notebooks*, eds Gere & Sparrow (1981 – but Madan died in 1947), there is the uncredited quotation: '"Research" is a mere excuse for idleness.' Compare what Benjamin Jowett (who died in 1893) said: '"Research!" the Master exclaimed. "Research!" he said. "A mere excuse for idleness; it has never achieved, and will never achieve any results of the slightest value"' – Logan Pearsall Smith, *Unforgotten Years* (1938).

4 De mortuis nil nisi bunkum.

Quoted in *PDMQ* (1971). Based on the maxim '*De mortuis nil nisi bonum* [Speak nothing but good of the dead – or not at all]', this remark of Laski's is to the effect that one may – or, rather, one does – only speak nonsense, emptily, or rubbish about the dead. In fact, Laski appears to have been resurrecting a joke from *Punch* (25 March 1865): 'RULE IN FUNERAL ORATIONS. *De mortuis nil nisi bunkum.*'

5 While there is death there is hope.

The Oxford Dictionary of Political Quotations (1997) ascribes this to 'Richard Crossman, speaking on the death of Hugh Gaitskell in 1963' on the say-so of Tam Dalyell in *Dick Crossman* (1989). However, in Crossman's own introduction to his *Diaries of a Cabinet Minister*, Vol. 1 (1975), he has: 'But as Harold Laski used to remind us, in British politics while there is death there is hope.'

Hugh LATIMER English bishop and martyr (1485–1555)

6 Be of good comfort, Master Ridley, and play the man. We shall this day light such a candle, by God's grace in England, as I trust shall never be put out.

On being burned at the stake with Nicholas Ridley in Oxford. Quoted in Barnaby Conrad, *Famous Last Words* (1961).

(Sir) Harry LAUDER Scots entertainer (1870–1950)

7 It's a braw bricht moonlicht nicht.

Song, 'Just a Wee Deoch-an-Doris' (1912). In fact, though Lauder did write some of his own songs – and though he did popularize this one – the words are by R.F. Morrison, to music by Whit Cunliffe. Later, the line was notably interpolated in an otherwise instrumental number, 'Hoots Mon', a UK No. 1 hit, by Lord Rockingham's XI (1958).

8 O ye'll tak' the high road, and I'll tak' the low road,
And I'll be in Scotland afore ye,
But me and my true love will never meet again,
On the bonnie, bonnie banks o' Loch Lomond.

By yon bonnie banks and by yon bonnie braes,
Where the sun shines bright on Loch Lomond ...

Traditional song, part of Lauder's repertoire. It was first collected in *Vagabond Songs and Ballads of Scotland*, ed. Robert Ford (1904). *The Dictionary of Scottish Quotations* (1996) has it that: 'The speaker in the song is thought to be a Jacobite soldier awaiting execution after the retreat from Derby: it is his spirit that will be travelling the low road.'

See also *PUNCH* 370:3.

Andrew Bonar LAW Canadian-born British Conservative Prime Minister (1858–1923)

1 I must follow them; I am their leader.

Quoted in Edward Raymond, *Mr Balfour* (1920). See also LEDRU-ROLLIN 281:5.

D.H. LAWRENCE English novelist and poet (1885–1930)

2 *Homo sum!* the Adventurer.

Essay, 'Climbing down Pisgah', published posthumously. It is quoted on Lawrence's memorial (1985) in Poets' Corner, Westminster Abbey. At a ceremony in the Abbey to mark Lawrence's birthday in September 1987, Professor James T. Boulton gave an address in which he explained his choice of this epitaph. He quoted Lawrence as saying, 'Man is nothing ... unless he adventures. Either into the unknown of the world, of his environment. Or into the unknown of himself.' Boulton added: 'The very essence of man and human life, in Lawrence's view, is bound up with the act of knowing and the nature of knowledge ... That commitment to adventure, in Lawrence's view, is what should motivate all human beings.' See also TERENCE 456:8.

T.E. LAWRENCE English soldier and writer (1888–1935)

3 I loved you, so I drew these tides of men into
   my hands
   and wrote my will across the sky in stars
   to earn you freedom, the seven pillared
      worthy house,
   that your eyes might be shining for me when
      we came.

Epigraph, *The Seven Pillars of Wisdom* (1926), and with the dedication 'To S.A.' this has been taken to refer to Selim Ahmed, an Arab friend who died in 1918. The innocent suggestion that 'S.A.' stands for 'Saudi Arabia' is thus a little wide of the mark.

4 I am proudest of my thirty fights in that I did not have any of our own blood shed. All our subject provinces to me were not worth one dead Englishman.

Introductory chapter in the same work. Compare other 'not worth one — ' constructions: Bismarck said of possible German involvement in the Balkans, 'Not worth the healthy bones of a single Pomeranian grenadier'; Thomas P. "Tip" O'Neill ... said the bombing should stop because "Cambodia is not worth one American life"' (1973) – quoted in William Shawcross, *Sideshow* (1986); 'I don't believe the

unity of Ireland is worth a single death' – Lord (Gerry) Fitt, quoted in *The Observer* (4 August 1985).

See also BIBLE 74:8.

Emma LAZARUS American poet (1849–87)

5 Give me your tired, your poor,
   Your huddled masses yearning to breathe free,
   The wretched refuse of your teeming shore,
   Send these, the homeless, tempest-tossed, to me:
   I lift my lamp beside the golden door.

'The New Colossus' (1883), inscribed on the Statue of Liberty, New York. Although Lazarus was not an immigrant herself – she was born in New York – she championed oppressed Jewry. Her sonnet echoed George Washington's letter to newly arrived immigrants in December 1782: 'The bosom of America is open to receive not only the Opulent and respectable Stranger; but the oppressed and persecuted of all Nations and Religions.'

Edward LEAR English poet and artist (1812–88)

6 How pleasant to know Mr Lear!
   Who has written such volumes of stuff!
   Some think him ill-tempered and queer,
   But a few think him pleasant enough.

Preface, *Nonsense Songs* (1871). Hence, *How Pleasant To Know Mr Lear*, title of a one-man show by Charles Lewsen (1968).

7 On the coast of Coromandel
   Where the early pumpkins blow,
   In the middle of the woods,
   Lived the Yonghy-Bonghy-Bò.
   Two old chairs, and half a candle;–
   One old jug without a handle,–
   These were all his worldly goods.

'The Courtship of the Yonghy-Bonghy-Bò' (1871). This poem was itself parodied in 1943 by Sir Osbert Sitwell, who wrote: 'On the coast of Coromandel / Dance they to the tunes of Handel.'

   The alliterative phrase 'on the coast of Coromandel' has long been around – not surprising when one considers that Coromandel is mostly coast and nothing else, and that it was the scene of the Franco-British struggle for supremacy in India in the 18th century. *OED2* has citations from 1697, 'On the coast of Coromandel ... they call them catamarans', and from 1817, 'The united fleet appeared on the coast of Coromandel', and several others. The phrase had also been used by Macaulay in his essay 'Frederick the Great' (1842).

1 Below the high Cathedral stairs,
Lie the remains of Agnes Pears.
Her name was Wiggs; it was not Pears.
But Pears was put to rhyme with stairs.

This is but one form of the 'forced rhyme' epitaph. It occurs in Lear's diary (entry for 20 April 1887). With 'Susan Pares' replacing 'Agnes Pears', the rhyme was first published without date in *Queery Leary Nonsense* (1911), edited from manuscripts by Lady Constance Strachey. The most usual form ends: 'Her name was Smith; it was not Jones; / But Jones was put to rhyme with Stones.'

Dr Timothy LEARY American hippie guru (1920–96)

2 Turn on, tune in, drop out.

Title of lecture (1966), summing up his philosophy of 'the game of life'. Later Leary ascribed the phrase to Marshall McLuhan.

John LE CARRÉ English novelist (1931–)

3 *The Spy Who Came In from the Cold.*

Title of novel (1963), about a spy from the West getting even with his East German counterpart around the time of the erection of the Berlin Wall. Hence, the journalistic format, not so say cliché, 'the — who came in from the cold'. After this, any person or any thing, coming in from any kind of exposed position, or returning to favour, might be described as 'coming in from the cold'. From the *Financial Times* (21 March 1984): '[London Stock Exchange] Oils and leading Engineerings were well to the fore. Stores also joined in the recovery, while Life Insurances came in from the cold after a particularly depressing spell before and after abolition of Life Assurance premium relief.' On 22 June 1990, Douglas Hurd, British Foreign Secretary, speaking in Berlin, said: 'We should not forget the reason for which Checkpoint Charlie stood here for so many years but no one can be sorry that it is going. At long last we, we are bringing "Charlie" in from the cold.' 'Baritone who came in from the cold' – headline over article about Dmitri Hvorostovsky who hails from Siberia in *The Independent* (19 January 1998). In *Keep Taking the Tabloids* (1983), Fritz Spiegl noted these much earlier headline uses: 'Explorer comes in from cold', 'Stranger who flew in from the cold', 'Spy who came in from the Cold War', 'Dartmoor sheep come in from the cold', 'Quarter that came in from the cold'.

LE CORBUSIER (Charles Edouard Jeanneret)
Swiss-born French architect (1887–1965)

4 *La maison est une machine à habiter* [A house is a machine for living in].

Vers une Architecture (1923). Some feel that Le Corbusier's description of the purpose of a house is a rather chilling one but in the context of his expanded explanation, it is not so bleak. He wrote in *Almanach de l'Architecture* (1925): 'The house has [three] aims. First it's a machine for living in, that is, a machine destined to serve as a useful aid for rapidity and precision in our work, a tireless and thoughtful machine to satisfy the needs of the body: comfort. But it is, secondly, a place intended for meditation and thirdly a place whose beauty exists and brings to the soul that calm which is indispensable.'

Compare from Leo Tolstoy, *War and Peace*, Bk 10, Chap. 29 (1865–9): '*Notre corps est une machine à vivre* [Our body is a machine for living].'

Alexandre Auguste LEDRU-ROLLIN French politician (1807–74)

5 I must follow them for I am their leader.

Ledru-Rollin became Minister of the Interior in the provisional government during the 1848 Revolution in Paris. He was looking from his window one day as a mob passed by and he said: '*Eh, je suis leur chef, il fallait bien les suivre* [Ah well, I'm their leader, I really ought to follow them].' It is said that 'he gave offence by his arbitrary conduct' (of which this would seem to be a prime example) and had to resign.

The remark was being quoted by 1857 and is now a frequently invoked form of political abuse. Winston Churchill is supposed to have said of Clement Attlee: 'We all understand his position. "I am their leader, I must follow them."' See also LAW 280:1.

Gypsy Rose LEE American striptease entertainer (1913–70)

6 God is love – but get it in writing.

Quoted in *The Guardian* (24 June 1975). Compare what US Secretary of State George Shultz commented after the Washington summit between Mikhail Gorbachev and Ronald Reagan in December 1987: '"Trust but verify" is really an ancient saying in the United States, but in a different guise. Remember the storekeeper who was a little leery of credit, and he had a sign in his store that said, IN GOD WE TRUST – ALL OTHERS CASH?' Referring to the verification procedures over arms reductions signed by the leaders in Washington, Shultz said, 'This is the cash.'

Laurie LEE English writer (1914–97)

7 *As I Walked Out One Midsummer Morning.*

Title of book (1969). In *Cider With Rosie*, Lee refers to a folk song 'As I Walked Out (One May Morning)', and this would appear to be a conflation with a line from another folk song entitled 'Primroses' – 'As I rode out one Midsummer's morning'. Robert Burns collected and improved a poem/song with the title, 'As I Went Out Ae [= one] May Morning'.

Robert E. LEE American general (1807–70)

1 I determined to avoid the useless sacrifice of those whose past services have endeared them to their countrymen.

Lee put this in 'General Order No. 9', a written address dated 10 April 1865, at the conclusion of the American Civil War. He was explaining to the Confederate troops he was leading why he had surrendered to General Grant at Appomattox Court House, Virginia, the previous day. The army of North Virginia had been compelled to yield to overwhelming numbers, and Lee also said, 'It is our duty to live. What will become of the women and children of the South if we are not here to protect them?'

In March 1976 the British Labour politician Roy Jenkins was quoted as saying, 'I am determined to avoid the useless sacrifice' when, not making progress in his bid for the party leadership, he withdrew from the race. In his memoirs, *A Life at the Centre* (1991), Jenkins states, 'I quoted (or more probably misquoted) Lee's message', and then goes on to quote a substantial passage from Lee's order, though pointedly omitting the actual 'useless sacrifice' phrase.

Ernest LEHMAN American writer (1920–)

2 *Sweet Smell of Success.*

Title of novel and film (1957), and origin of the phrase – compare OLIVIER 347:4.

C.A. LEJEUNE English film critic (1897–1973)

Of the film I Am a Camera (*UK* 1955):

3 Me no Leica.

A small joke, but a good one. There was a vogue for dismissive one-line criticisms of plays and films, especially in the 1930s, '40s and '50s, when suitable opportunities presented themselves. It was either when Christopher Isherwood's Berlin stories were turned first into a play, *I am a Camera* (1951), or subsequently into a film, that one critic summed up his/her reaction with the words '(Me) no Leica'. This has been variously attributed to Caroline Lejeune, George Jean Nathan, Walter Kerr and Kenneth Tynan. It is a comment on the transitory nature of much criticism that one cannot say for sure who did originate the joke.

In fact, it transpires that, although Miss Lejeune was noted for her one-line put-downs of films, it is unlikely that she

wrote this one. A review of the film by the critic of the *Sunday Dispatch* (16 October 1955) quotes: 'No Leica, snarled a New York critic.' This may well take us back to the likes of George Jean Nathan, who was ascribed the quote in a book review by Frederic Raphael.

LENIN (Vladimir Ilyich Ulyanov) Russian revolutionary and Soviet leader (1870–1924)

4 *Shag vpered dva shaga nazad* [One step forward two steps back].

In 1904 Lenin wrote a book about 'the crisis within our party' under this title. Apparently it contains this comment on the phrase: 'It happens in the lives of individuals, and it happens in the history of nations and in the development of parties.' Note that in *Conducted Tour* (1981), Bernard Levin refers to Lenin's 'pamphlet' under the title *Four Steps Forward, Three Steps Back*. Vilmos Voigt pointed out in *Proverbium Yearbook of International Proverb Scholarship* (1984) that just after the publication of his work, Lenin referred to the 'current German form, *Ein Schritt vorwärts, zwei Schritte zurück* [one step forwards, two steps back]', and Voigt wondered what precisely the source of Lenin's phrase was and in which language.

5 Communism is Soviet power plus the electrification of the whole country.

Report to the 8th Congress (1920). Could this have been alluded to in *The Electrification of the Soviet Union*, the title of an opera with libretto by Craig Raine and music by Nigel Osborne, first presented at Glyndebourne in 1986? The opera is based on a novella by Boris Pasternak called *The Last Summer*, but the only hints in the published text are two quotations: 'And the neat man / To their east who ordered Gorki to be electrified' (W.H. Auden) and 'Next, he introduced electricity to Ethiopia, first in the palaces and then in other buildings.'

6 Those who make revolutions by halves are digging their own graves.

Sometimes attributed to Lenin, this had been said earlier by the French revolutionary, Saint-Just, to the National Convention in 1794, in the form: '*Ceux qui font des révolutions à moitié n'ont fait que se creuser un tombeau.*' George Büchner quoted it, too, in *Dantons Tod* (1835), but ascribed it to Robespierre: '*Wer eine Revolution zur Hälfte vollendet, gräbt sich selbst sein Grab.*'

7 A good man fallen among Fabians.

On Bernard Shaw. Quoted in Arthur Ransome, *Six Weeks in Russia in 1919* (1919). See BIBLE 82:6.

1 Give us the child for eight years and it will be a Bolshevik forever.

Lenin *may* have said this to the Commissars of Education in Moscow in 1923, but the earliest source is tainted – it is *100 Things You Should Know About Communism* published by the Committee on Un-American Activities in 1951.

Compare, however, 'Give us a child until it is seven and it is ours for life', a saying usually attributed to the Jesuits, founded in 1534 by St Ignatius Loyala, but possibly wished on them by their opponents. Another version is: 'Give us the child, and we will give you the man.' *Lean's Collecteana*, Vol. 3 (1903), has, as a 'Jesuit maxim', 'Give me a child for the first seven years, and you may do what you like with him afterwards.'

Muriel Spark in her novel *The Prime of Miss Jean Brodie* (1962) has her heroine, a teacher, say: 'Give me a girl at an impressionable age and she is mine for life.'

2 Useful idiots.

On people in the West who supported the Russian Revolution, as in 'We will find many useful idiots to further our cause.' Sometimes 'necessary idiots'. No source has been found for this phrase, it was not known in the former USSR and it would appear to have been concocted by anti-Communists in the US. A 1948 citation (with no mention of Lenin) has apparently been found in *The New York Times*.

See also BEVAN 67:1.

John LENNON English singer and songwriter (1940–80)

3 Christianity will go. It will vanish and shrink. I needn't argue about that. I'm right and I'll be proved right. We're more popular than Jesus now.

In interview with Maureen Cleave of the London *Evening Standard* (4 March 1966). The remark lay dormant for several months, but when The Beatles paid a visit to the US it was reprinted and caused an outcry. The Beatles were burned in effigy and their records banned by radio stations in Bible-belt states. Lennon subsequently withdrew the remark: 'I just said what I said – and I was wrong' (press conference, Chicago, 11 August 1966).

An interesting pre-echo occurs in a remark by Zelda Fitzgerald, recorded in Ernest Hemingway's *A Moveable Feast* (1964): 'Ernest, don't you think Al Jolson is greater than Jesus?'

4 Imagine there's no heaven
It's easy if you try
No hell below us
Above us only sky

Imagine all the people
Living for today.

Song, 'Imagine' (1975). Yoko Ono quoted this as 'There is no hell below us, above us only sky' at the renaming of Liverpool's airport as Liverpool John Lennon Airport (in 2001).

5 Life is what happens to you while you're busy making other plans.

In the lyrics of Lennon's song 'Beautiful Boy' (included on his *Double Fantasy* album, 1980), this is one of two quotations (the other is the slogan 'Every day in every way I'm getting better and better', see COUÉ 155:5). So it is wrong to credit Lennon with either line, as has been done.

Barbara Rowe's *The Book of Quotes* (1979) ascribes the 'Life is ...' saying to Betty Talmadge, divorced wife of Senator Herman Talmadge, in the form: 'Life is what happens to you when you're making other plans.' Dr Laurence Peter in *Quotations for Our Time* (1977) gives the line to 'Thomas La Mance', who remains untraced.

6 Reality is for people who can't cope with drugs.

Katharine Whitehorn confidently ascribed this to Lennon in *The Observer* (29 January 1995). Rosalie Maggio, editor of *Quotations By Women* (1996), commented that 'Lily Tomlin said, "Reality is a crutch for people who can't cope with drugs" on the television show *Rowan and Martin's Laugh-In* in the 1960s', but concluded that the coinage should be attributed rather to Jane Wagner, the American writer, actor, director and producer (1935–), in *Appearing Nitely* (1977).

7 Love is the answer.

'Mind Games' (1973). The line itself became the title of a song written by Ralph Cole and performed by Island Lighthouse (1974). The question 'Is love the answer?' occurs in Liz Lochhead's poem 'Riddle Me-Ree' (1984). A much-alluded-to view: 'Love is the answer, but while you are waiting for the answer, sex raises some pretty good questions' – Woody Allen, 1975; 'If love is the answer, could you rephrase the question?' – Lily Tomlin, 1979; both quoted in Bob Chieger, *Was It Good For You Too?* (1983).

See also next entry.

John LENNON and (Sir) Paul McCARTNEY English singers and songwriters (1940–80) and (1942–)

8 Yeh-yeh-yeh.

Song, 'She Loves You' (1963). 'Yeh' as a common corruption of 'yes' has been current (and derived from the US) since the 1920s. But whether spelt 'yeh-yeh-yeh', as in the published lyrics, or 'yeah-yeah-yeah' (which captures the Liverpudlian pronunciation better), this phrase became a hallmark of the Beatles after its use in their song 'She Loves You'. The record they made of the song was in the UK charts for 31 weeks from August 1963, and was for 14 years Britain's all-time best-selling 45 rpm record. Though most commonly associated with The Beatles, the phrase was not new. Some of the spadework in Britain had been done by the non-Liverpudlian singer Helen Shapiro, who had a hit in September 1961 with 'Walking Back to Happiness', which included the refrain 'Whoop bah oh yeah yeah'. The Beatles had toured with Shapiro topping the bill before their own careers took off. Following The Beatles' use, there was a French expression in the early 1960s – 'yé yé' – to describe fashionable clothing.

1 It's been a hard day's night.

The title of The Beatles' first feature film *A Hard Day's Night* (UK 1964) was apparently chosen towards the end of filming when Ringo Starr used the phrase to describe a 'heavy' night out (according to Ray Coleman, *John Lennon*, 1984). What, in fact, Ringo must have done was to use the title of the Lennon and McCartney song (presumably already written if it was towards the end of filming) in a conversational way. Indeed, Hunter Davies in *The Beatles* (1968) noted: 'Ringo Starr came out with the phrase, though John had used it earlier in a poem.' It certainly sounds like a Lennonism and may have had some limited general use subsequently as a catchphrase, meaning that the speaker has had 'a very tiring time'.

2 Yesterday, all my troubles seemed so far away,
Now it looks as though they're here to stay
Oh I believe in yesterday.
Suddenly, I'm not half the man I used to be,
There's a shadow hanging over me,
Oh yesterday came suddenly.

Song, 'Yesterday' (1965). Hence, *Yesterday Came Suddenly*, the title of a memoir (1993) by Francis King.

3 Being for the Benefit of Mr Kite.

Title of song on the album *Sergeant Pepper's Lonely Hearts Club Band* (1967), from a standard 19th-century phrase used in advertising 'testimonial' performances. Compare the title of Chap. 48 of *Nicholas Nickleby* (1838–9) by Charles Dickens: 'Being for the benefit of Mr Vincent Crummles, and Positively his last Appearance on this Stage'. As for the lyrics, largely written by John Lennon, though credited jointly to him and Paul McCartney, they derive almost word for word, as Lennon acknowledged, from the wording of a Victorian circus poster he bought in an antique shop. Or that was the story, until Derek Taylor revealed in *It Was*

Twenty Years Ago Today (1987) that the poster was 'liberated' from a café during the filming of promotional clips for the 'Penny Lane/Strawberry Fields Forever' record. Headed 'Pablo Fanque's Circus Royal' in the Town Meadows, Rochdale, the poster announces:

> Grandest Night of the Season!
> And Positively the
> Last Night But Three!
> Being for the Benefit of Mr. Kite,
> (late of Wells's Circus) and
> Mr. J. Henderson,
> the Celebrated Somerset Thrower!
> Wire Dancer, Vaulter, Rider, &c.
> On Tuesday Evening, February 14th, 1843.

('Somerset' is an old word for somersault.)

4 A Day in the Life.

Title of song on the same album, presumably taking its name from that type of magazine article and film documentary that strives to depict 24 hours in the life of a particular person or organization. In 1959 Richard Cawston produced a TV documentary that took this form, with the title *This Is the BBC*. In 1962 the English title of a novel (film UK 1971) by Alexander Solzhenitsyn was *One Day in the Life of Ivan Denisovich*. Lennon and McCartney's use of the phrase for the description of incidents in the life of a drug-taker may have inspired the subsequent regular *Sunday Times* Magazine feature 'A Life in the Day', and also the play *A Day in the Death of Joe Egg* by Peter Nichols (1967; film UK 1971).

5 I heard the news today oh boy
four thousand holes in Blackburn, Lancashire
and though the holes were rather small
they had to count them all
now they know how many holes it takes
to fill the Albert Hall.

In the same song. The inspiration for these lines can be traced directly to the *Daily Mail* (17 January 1967). Lennon had the newspaper propped up on his piano as he composed. The original brief story, topping the 'Far & Near' column, stated: 'There are 4,000 holes in the road in Blackburn, Lancashire, or one twenty-sixth of a hole per person, according to a council survey. If Blackburn is typical there are two million holes in Britain's roads and 300,000 in London.'

6 *Magical Mystery Tour.*

Title of film (1967). Hence, the phrase now given to a winding journey, caused by the driver not knowing where he is going. A 'Mystery Tour' is a journey undertaken in a coach from a holiday resort when the passengers are not told of the intended destination (and known as such probably from the 1920s onwards). The 'magical' derives from the Beatles' title for a largely unsuccessful attempt at making their own film. In *The Next Horizon* (1973), Chris Bonington writes: 'Climbing with Tom Patey was a kind of Magical Mystery Tour, in which no one, except perhaps himself, knew what was coming next.' From the *Daily Express* (12 April 1989): 'On and on went the city bus driver's magical mystery tour. Passengers point out their way home – and get a lift to the door.' From McGowan & Hands's *Don't Cry for Me, Sergeant-Major* (1983) – about the Falklands war: 'Then at Midnight *Canberra* slipped out, or as Lt Hornby so eloquently put it, "buggered off on the second leg of our magical mystery tour".'

Ruggiero LEONCAVALLO Italian composer and librettist (1858–1919)

1 *Vesti la giubba* [On with the motley].
I Pagliacci (1892). 'Giubba' in Italian means simply 'jacket' (in the sense of costume), and 'the motley' is the old English word for an actor or clown's clothes, originally the many-coloured coat worn by a jester or fool (as mentioned several times in Shakespeare's *As You Like It*). The popularity of the phrase in English probably dates from Enrico Caruso's 1902 recording of the aria, which became the first gramophone record eventually to sell a million copies.

Partridge/Catch Phrases suggests that, as a result, 'On with the motley!' is what one says to start a party or trip to the theatre. It may also mean 'on with the show, in spite of what has happened'. In the opera, the Clown has to 'carry on with the show' despite having a broken heart. So it might be said jokingly nowadays by anyone who is having to proceed with something in spite of difficulties. Laurence Olivier used the phrase in something like its original context when describing a sudden dash home from Ceylon during a crisis in his marriage to Vivien Leigh: 'I got myself on to a plane ... and was in Paris on the Saturday afternoon. I went straight on home the next day as I had music sessions for *The Beggar's Opera* from the Monday; and so, on with the motley' – *Confessions of an Actor* (1982).

See also RABELAIS 375:4.

Alan Jay LERNER American songwriter and playwright (1918–86)

2 *My Fair Lady.*
Title of musical (1956; film US 1964), with music by Frederick Loewe. It was understandable when Lerner and Loewe wished to make a musical out of Shaw's *Pygmalion* that they

should seek a new title. After all, not even in Shaw's Preface (only in his Afterword) does he allude to the relevance of the Greek legend to his story of a Covent Garden flower-girl who gets raised up and taught to 'speak proper' just like an upper-class lady.

Lerner and Loewe turned, it seems, to the refrain of a nursery rhyme (first recorded in the 18th century):

London Bridge is broken down,
Broken down, broken down,
London Bridge is broken down,
My fair lady.

It has also been suggested that they were drawn to the title because 'my fair lady' is how a cockney flower-seller would pronounce the phrase 'Mayfair lady'.

3 The rain in Spain stays mainly in the plain.
Song, 'The Rain in Spain', in the same musical. According to Jonathan Cecil (1996), this elocutionary phrase was invented by Anthony Asquith, director of the 1938 film version of *Pygmalion*. It received Shaw's approval. Actually in the film it is used with 'mainly in the *plains*' – see SHAW 426:1. However, Rosemary Hewett suggested (1996) that the phrase was proposed by Professor Edmund Tilley, who was the adviser on phonetics for the production. She added that the set for Higgins's study was based on Professor Tilley's study at Robert College, Constantinople.

Whatever the case, the rhyming of 'rain' and 'Spain' is a venerable activity. In *Polite Conversation* (1738), Jonathan Swift has this exchange:

I see 'tis raining again.
Why then, Madam, we must do as they do in Spain.
Pray, my Lord, how is that?
Why, Madam, we must let it rain.

'Rain, rain, go to Spain' was a proverbial expression, current by 1659.

4 How To Handle a Woman.
Title of song, in *Camelot* (1960; film US 1967). In *Crying With Laughter* (1993), the British comedian Bob Monkhouse describes convincingly how the title was derived from a remark he once made about Erich Maria Remarque's way of handling the tantrums of his wife, Paulette Godard. Alan Jay Lerner suggests rather in his *The Street Where I Live* (1978) that he was told directly by Remarque.

5 Camelot ...
Where once it never rained till after sundown
By eight a.m. the morning fog had flown
Don't let it be forgot
That once there was a spot

For one brief shining moment that was known
As Camelot ...

Title song, in the same musical. *Camelot* was first produced
on Broadway in December 1960 just before President
Kennedy took office. Hence, the name 'Camelot' came to
be applied to the romantic concept of his presidency. As
Lerner wrote in *The Street Where I Live* (1978), when Jackie
Kennedy quoted the lines in an interview with *Life* Magazine after her husband's assassination in 1963, '*Camelot*
had suddenly become the symbol of those thousand days
when people the world over saw a bright new light of hope
shining from the White House ... For myself, I have never
been able to see a performance of *Camelot* again.'

In 1983, on the 20th anniversary of President Kennedy's
death, William Manchester wrote a memorial volume with
the title *One Brief Shining Moment*.

Alfred LESTER English comedian (1872–1925)

1 Always merry and bright.

Lester – who was always lugubrious – was especially associated with this phrase. He played 'Peter Doody', a jockey
in the Lionel Monckton/Howard Talbot/Arthur Wimperis
musical comedy *The Arcadians* (1909), and had the phrase
as his motto in a song, 'My Motter'. *Punch* quoted the phrase
on 26 October 1910. Somerset Maugham in a letter to a
friend (1915) wrote: 'I am back on a fortnight's leave, very
merry and bright, but frantically busy – I wish it were all
over.' An edition of *The Magnet* from 1920 carries an advertisement for a comic called *Merry and Bright*. P.G. Wodehouse used the phrase in *The Indiscretions of Archie* (1921).

Larry Grayson suggested (1981) that it was later used as
the billing for Billy Danvers, the red-nosed music-hall comedian (who died in 1964). However, there may have been
confusion with Danvers's undoubted bill-matter, 'Cheeky,
Cheery and Chubby' (in about 1918). Note the second, a
song by Irving Berlin for the film *Holiday Inn* (US 1942)
verse of 'White Christmas':

I'm dreaming of a white Christmas
With every Christmas card I write
May your days be merry and bright
And may all your Christmases be white.

William Hesketh LEVER (1st Viscount Leverhulme)
English soap-maker and philanthropist (1851–1925)

2 Half the money I spend on advertising is wasted,
and the trouble is I don't know which half.

Quoted by David Ogilvy in *Confessions of an Advertising Man*
(1963), this observation has also been fathered on John
Wanamaker and, indeed, on Ogilvy himself. Ogilvy says 'as
the first Lord Leverhulme (and John Wanamaker after him)

complained ...' Leverhulme remains the most likely originator – he made his fortune through the manufacture of
soap from vegetable oils instead of from tallow. Ogilvy had
Lever Brothers as a client and could presumably have picked
up the remark that way. However, Wanamaker, who more or
less invented the modern department store in the US, was
active by the 1860s and so possibly could have said it first.

Duc de LÉVIS French writer and soldier (1764–1830)

3 *Noblesse oblige* [Nobility has its obligations].

Maximes et réflexions (1812). That is to say, privileged ancestry entails responsibility and honourable behaviour. Some
hope. Hence, *Noblesse Oblige* (1956), title of a book by Nancy
Mitford, subtitled 'An enquiry into the identifiable characteristics of the English aristocracy'.

4 *Gouverner, c'est choisir* [To govern is to make
choices].

In the same work. As 'to govern is to choose', this was
ascribed to Pierre Mendès-France, the French politician
(1907–82), by Nigel Lawson, the former Chancellor of the
Exchequer, in a speech to the House of Commons (25 March
1991). He was attacking the British Government, from
which he had resigned, about the extent to which it was
making consultations without making clear-cut decisions on
certain issues. Could he have made a mistake? The remark
is so ascribed to Mendès-France in *PDMQ* (1971).

LEWIS See DAY LEWIS, C.

C.S. LEWIS English scholar, religious writer and novelist
(1898–1963)

5 Then Aslan [the great Lion] turned to them and
said: '... You are – as you used to call it – in the
Shadow Lands – dead. The term is over; the
holidays have begun. The dream is ended: this is
the morning.'

The Last Battle (1956) – the final 'Narnia' book. Hence, the
title *Shadowlands* of a BBC TV film (1985), a play (1989)
and a film (UK 1993) by William Nicholson, all about Lewis's
late-flowering relationship with the woman who became
his wife and died shortly after of cancer. In Act 1 of the play,
the meaning of the term 'shadowlands' seems to have been
transferred from death to what has not been attained in
life: 'For believe me, this world that seems to us so substantial, is no more than the shadowlands. Real life has not
begun yet.' In Nicholson's script for the film, the Lewis
character says: 'Shadows ... It's one of my stories. We live
in the shadowlands. The sun is always shining, somewhere

else, round a bend in the road, over the brow of a hill.' So, what 'shadowlands' refers to is not completely clear. It seems to imply that where we are in this world is the shadowy place and that death is where the light is (and thus a preferable place to be).

Sinclair **LEWIS** American novelist (1885–1951)

1 *It Can't Happen Here.*
Title of novel (1935), adapted for the stage the following year, warning against fascism in the United States. A self-deluding catchphrase, a short-sighted response to external threats. Appropriately, Kevin Brownlow and Andrew Mollo's film about what would have happened if the Germans had invaded England in 1940 was entitled *It Happened Here* (UK 1963).

Robert **LEY** German Nazi official (1890–1945)

2 *Kraft durch Freude* [Strength through joy].
On 2 December 1933, Ley announced the name of the Nazi organization *NS-Gemeinschaft Kraft durch Freude* – a department of the German Labour Front – though it has also been ascribed to Adolf Hitler himself. It was a sort of mock trade union, providing regimented leisure.

George **LEYBOURNE** English songwriter (?–1884)

3 He'd fly through the air with the greatest of ease
A daring young man on the flying trapeze.
Song, 'The Man on the Flying Trapeze' (1868). Music by Alfred Lee. The person referred to was Jules Léotard (who died in 1880), the French trapeze artist. He also gave his name to the tight, one-piece garment worn by ballet dancers, acrobats and other performers. *The Daring Young Man on the Flying Trapeze* is the title of a volume of short stories (1934) by William Saroyan; *The Middle-Aged Man on the Flying Trapeze* is a James Thurber title (1935).

LIBERACE (Wladziu Valentino Liberace) American pianist and entertainer (1919–87)

4 I cried all the way to the bank.
The flamboyant pianist discussed criticism of his shows in his *Autobiography* (1973): 'I think the people around me are more apt to become elated about good reviews (or depressed by bad ones) than I am. If they're good I just tell them, "Don't let success go to your head." When the reviews are bad I tell my staff that they can join me as I cry all the way to the bank.' In Alfred Hitchcock's film *North by Northwest* (US 1959), the Cary Grant character gets to say: '... while we cry about it all the way to the bank'.

Richard Keyes, in *Nice Guys Finish Seventh* (1992), suggests that the accepted version is now 'I *laughed* all the way to the bank', which is questionable. Whatever the form, it became a catchphrase meaning that the speaker is in a position to ignore criticism.

It has been suggested that Liberace's use of the phrase dates back to his 1959 libel action in London against the *Daily Mirror*, whose columnist Cassandra (William Connor) had described him as 'fruit-flavoured'. This was taken to imply that he was homosexual. Liberace won the case and £8000. However, Liberace gave currency to the saying before this – see *Collier's* Magazine (17 September 1954). As early as June 1954, he was apparently saying in response to critics after a concert in New York: 'What you said hurt me very much. I cried all the way to the bank' (quoted in Nat Shapiro, *An Encyclopedia of Quotations about Music*, 1977). Even so, the phrase existed before Liberace. From the *Waterloo Daily Courier* (Iowa) (3 September 1946): 'Eddie Walker perhaps is the wealthiest fight manager in the game ... The other night when his man Belloise lost, Eddie had the miseries ... He felt so terrible, he cried all the way to the bank!'

Abraham **LINCOLN** American Republican 16th President (1809–65)

5 If you once forfeit the confidence of your fellow citizens, you can never regain their respect and esteem. You may fool all the people some of the time; you can even fool some of the people all the time; but you can't fool all of the people all the time.
There is so much Lincolniana – and so much that can't be verified – but this has the authentic ring about it. The saying first appeared in Alexander K. McLure, *Lincoln's Yarns and Stories* (1904). Lincoln reportedly made this remark during a senatorial campaign speech in Clinton, Illinois (September 1858), but was not quoted at the time, and it does not appear in his published works. *ODQ* (1992) states that it has also been ascribed to P.T. Barnum – this, however, presumably out of confusion with 'There's a sucker born every minute' (53:1).

6 People who like this sort of thing will find this the sort of thing they like.
What has been called 'the world's best book review' – by Hilary Corke in *The Listener* (28 April 1955) – can only loosely be traced back to Lincoln. G.W.E. Russell had it in his *Collections and Recollections*, Chap. 31 (1898). *Bartlett* has steadily ignored it in recent years.
As recounted by S.N. Behrman in *Conversations with Max*

(1960), Max Beerbohm once mischievously invented a classical Greek source for the remark, and passed it off in a letter to the press under Rose Macaulay's signature. Earlier, in *Zuleika Dobson*, Chap. 11 (1911), Beerbohm puts it into the mouth of Clio who, when asked by Pallas what she thought of *The Decline and Fall of the Roman Empire*, replies in Greek (with this translation): 'For people who like that kind of thing, that is the kind of thing they like.' See also BEERBOHM 57:3.

1 In giving freedom to the slave, we assure freedom to the free – honourable alike in what we give and what we preserve. We shall nobly save or meanly lose the last, best hope of earth.

Referring to the act of giving freedom to the slaves, the phrase 'last, best hope of earth' comes from Lincoln's Second Annual Message to Congress (1 December 1862). It is not 'on earth', but has been endlessly quoted and alluded to by later presidents and politicians. One example: in President Kennedy's inaugural speech (1961), the United Nations was 'our last best hope'.

2 Four score and seven years ago our fathers brought forth [up]on this continent a new nation, conceived in liberty, and dedicated to the proposition that all men are created equal. Now we are engaged in a great civil war, testing whether that nation or any nation so conceived and so dedicated can long endure. We are met on a great battlefield of that war. We have come to dedicate a portion of that field, as a final resting place for those who here gave their lives that that nation might live. It is altogether fitting and proper that we should do this. But, in a larger sense, we cannot dedicate – we cannot consecrate – we cannot hallow – this ground. The brave men, living and dead, who struggled here, have consecrated it far above our poor power to add or detract. The world will little note nor long remember what we say here, but it can never forget what they did here. It is for us, the living, rather to be dedicated here to the unfinished work which they who fought here have thus far so nobly advanced. It is rather for us to be here dedicated to the great task remaining before us – that from these honoured dead we take increased devotion to that cause for which they gave the last full measure of devotion; that we here highly resolve that these dead shall not have died in vain; that this nation, under God, shall have a new birth of freedom; and that government of the people,

by the people, [and] for the people, shall not perish from the earth.

The Federal victory at the Battle of Gettysburg (1–3 July 1863) in the American Civil War foreshadowed the ultimate defeat of the Confederacy. But what immortalized the battle was Lincoln's address, as president, at the dedication of the battlefield cemetery at Gettysburg on 19 November 1863. Lincoln's prophecy that the world would 'little note or long remember' what he said seemed likely to be true, judging by initial reaction to the speech. One American paper spoke of the President's 'silly remarks'. *The Times* of London (as did many American papers) ignored the speech in its report of the ceremony. Later *The Times* was to say: 'Anything more dull and commonplace it wouldn't be easy to reproduce.' The *Chicago Tribune* wrote, however, that the words would 'live among the annals of man'. There is a legend that Lincoln jotted down the Gettysburg Address on the back of an envelope on a train going to the battlefield, but the structure of the words is so tight that this seems unlikely, and *Burnam* (1980) suggests that there were some five drafts of the speech. Also, the Associated Press was apparently given an advance copy. He spoke it mostly from memory.

The text, as above, though now (literally) carved in stone, is only an approximation of what Lincoln actually said. Gore Vidal in writing his novel *Lincoln* (1984) chose to draw instead on the notes made by Charles Hall of the Boston *Daily Advertiser*, who had the advantage of actually hearing the speech delivered, but the differences are very minor.

Thirty-three years before Lincoln delivered the Gettysburg Address, Daniel Webster had spoken of 'The people's government, made for the people, made by the people, and answerable to the people' (Second Speech on Foote's Resolution, 26 January 1830).

According to Bartlett (1992), Theodore Parker, a clergyman, had used various versions of this credo in anti-slavery speeches during the 1850s. Lincoln's law partner William H. Herndon gave him a copy of Parker's speeches. Before composing Gettysburg, Lincoln marked the words 'democracy is direct self-government, over all the people, by all of the people, for all of the people' in a Parker sermon dating from 1858.

3 He ain't heavy, he's my brother.

King George VI concluded his 1942 Christmas radio broadcast by reflecting on Britain's European allies and the benefits of mutual cooperation, saying: 'A former President of the United States of America used to tell of a boy who was carrying an even smaller child up a hill. Asked whether the heavy burden was not too much for him, the boy answered: "It's not a burden, it's my brother!" So let us welcome the future in a spirit of brotherhood, and thus make a world in which, please God, all may dwell together in justice and peace.'

Benham (1948) suggests that the American president must have been Lincoln – though it has not been possible to trace a source for the story. In fact, the King's allusion seems rather to have been a dignification of an advertising slogan and a charity's motto. As a headline, 'He ain't heavy ... he's my brother' may have been used first by Jack Cornelius of the BBD&O agency in a 1936 American advertisement for the 'Community Chest' campaign ('35 appeals in 1').

But it is difficult to tell what relationship this has, if any, with the similar slogan used to promote the Nebraska orphanage and poor boys' home known as 'Boys Town'. In the early 1920s, the Revd Edward J. Flanagan – Spencer Tracy played him in the film *Boys Town* (1938) – admitted to this home a boy named Howard Loomis who could not walk without the aid of crutches. The larger boys often took turns carrying him about on their backs. One day, Father Flanagan is said to have seen a boy carrying Loomis and asked whether this wasn't a heavy load. The reply: 'He ain't heavy, Father ... he's m'brother.' In 1943 a 'two brothers' logo (similar to, though not the same as, the drawing used in the Community Chest campaign) was copyrighted for Boys Town's exclusive use. Today, the logo and the motto (in the 'Father/m'brother' form) are registered service marks of Father Flanagan's Boys' Home (Boys Town).

It seems likely that the saying probably *does* predate the Father Flanagan story, though whether it goes back to Lincoln is anybody's guess. More recent applications have included the song with the title, written by Bob Russell and Bobby Scott, and popularized by The Hollies in 1969. Perhaps the brief Lennon and McCartney song 'Carry that Weight' (September 1969) alludes similarly? – 'Boy – you're gonna carry that weight, / Carry that weight a long time.'

1 You cannot bring about prosperity by discouraging thrift. You cannot strengthen the weak by weakening the strong. You cannot help small men up by tearing big men down. You cannot help the wage earner by pulling down the wage payer. You cannot further the brotherhood of man by encouraging class hatred. You cannot help the poor by destroying the rich. You cannot establish sound security on borrowed money. You cannot keep out of trouble by spending more than you earn. You cannot build character and courage by taking away man's initiative and independence. You cannot help men permanently by doing for them what they could and should do for themselves.

That Lincoln never said any of this is a fact that few people seem obliged to accept, especially if they are proponents of free enterprise. The playwright Ronald Millar described in *The Sunday Times* (23 November 1980) what had happened when he wrote his first speech for Margaret Thatcher as Prime Minister: 'I dashed off a piece including the quote from Abraham Lincoln, "Don't make the rich poorer, make the poor richer." I gave her the first draft and she immediately delved into her handbag for a piece of yellowing paper on which was written the very same Lincoln quotation. "I take it everywhere with me," she said. And from then on I've worked for her whenever she's asked me.'

Ex-President Ronald Reagan attributed the line 'You cannot strengthen the weak by weakening the strong' to Lincoln in an address to the Republican Convention in August 1992. When it was pointed out that this had in fact been uttered by 'a Rev. William Boetcker of Pennsylvania', a spokeswoman for Mr Reagan 'said it was not really his fault; he had found the line, attributed to Lincoln, in a handbook of quotes' – *The Independent* (20 August 1992). On the other hand, if he had referred to the Congressional Research Service's authoritative *Respectfully Quoted*, he would have found that President Calvin Coolidge had said, 'Don't expect to build up the weak by pulling down the strong' in a speech to the Massachusetts State Senate on 7 January 1914.

The misattribution to Lincoln of all or part of the 'Ten Points' was most likely first made by a member of the US Congress, but the list has been widely distributed since the 1940s. In *Harper's* Magazine (May 1950), Albert A. Woldman claimed that the quotation came rather from *The Industrial Decalogue*, a pamphlet published in 1911 by one William Boetcker (sometimes described as the Revd William J.H. Boetcker).

It is possible that Lincoln did say, 'I don't believe in a law to prevent a man getting rich; it would do more harm than good', and, 'That some should be rich shows that others may become rich, and hence is just encouragement to industry and enterprise.'

2 He has managed to wring one last spectacular defeat from the jaws of victory.

Attributed remark about one of his generals in the Civil War – possibly Ambrose Burnside – and so cited in Stephen Pile, *The Book of Heroic Failures* (1979). Sean O'Connor noted in 1999: 'Burnside never missed an opportunity to give up strategic positions and was never known to win an engagement. I think Lincoln's comment came after the Battle of Fredericksburg when the Civil War was as good as won. It was completely unnecessary for Burnside to fight the engagement but, needless to say, he lost and I always thought that Lincoln had said that he had taken "one last glorious opportunity to snatch defeat from the very jaws of victory".' Others agree that Burnside is the most likely recipient of the barb, but suggest that it was after Petersburg rather than Fredericksburg. There is still no definite agreement that it was Lincoln who said it, some preferring Grant.

1 I have always plucked a thistle and planted a flower where I thought a flower would grow.

In William H. Herndon's biography of Lincoln (1888) there is quoted a statement by Joshua F. Speed, a friend of the president, dated 6 December 1866, in which he relates a good turn done not long before the assassination. Lincoln released two draft-dodgers from gaol as a result of a mother's and a wife's pleas. '"The mother spoke out in all the features of her face [said Lincoln]. It is more than one can often say that in doing right one has made two people happy in one day. Speed, die when I may, I want it said of me by those who know me best, that I always plucked a thistle and planted a flower when I thought a flower would grow". What a fitting sentiment [Speed adds]! What a glorious recollection!'

2 [Laughter is] the joyous, beautiful, universal evergreen of life.

Quoted in The Boys' Life of Abraham Lincoln (1906) by Helen Nicolay. But was there an earlier source? As always with Lincoln, there is so much attributed wordage to grapple with. In Recollected Words of Abraham Lincoln (1996) by Don E. & Virginia Fehrenbacher, the memoranda are mentioned of John G. Nicolay (1832–1901), who was Lincoln's private secretary throughout his presidency and co-author of a ten-volume 'official' biography (1890). In these notes, Nicolay describes Lincoln making the comment in a lecture on 'Discoveries and Inventions' at Springfield, Illinois (26 April 1860).

See also SIMON 431:7; STEVENSON 446:2.

R.M. LINDNER American psychologist (1914–56)

3 *Rebel Without a Cause.*

According to ODMQ (1991), this was the title of a book published by Lindner in 1944 subtitled 'The hypnoanalysis of a criminal psychopath'. In ODQ (1992) he is described as a 'novelist'. The phrase became famous later when used as the title of a film (1955), for which the screenplay credit is given to Stewart Stern 'from an original story by the director, Nicholas Ray'. The Motion Picture Guide (1990) gives the provenance of the script, however, as 'based on an adaptation by Irving Shulman of a story line by Ray inspired from the story The Blind Run by Dr Robert M. Lindner.'

The film's study of adolescent misbehaviour had little to do with what one would now think of as psychopathic, but it helped popularize the phrase 'rebel without a cause' to describe a certain type of alienated youth of the period. It was the film that projected its star, James Dean, to status as chief 1950s rebel, a position confirmed when he met his premature end soon after.

Eric LINKLATER Scottish writer (1899–1974)

4 At my back I often hear Time's winged chariot changing gear.

Juan in China (1937). Alluding to MARVELL 314:5.

David LIVINGSTONE Scottish missionary and explorer (1813–73)

5 The most wonderful sight I had witnessed in Africa ... It had never been seen before by European eyes; but scenes so lovely must have been gazed upon by angels in their flight.

On the Victoria Falls, on the border of what are now Zambia and Zimbabwe. *Missionary Travels and Researches* (1857). In fact, the Falls had been seen by Portuguese eyes before Livingstone's. He renamed them after his sovereign – 'the only English name I have affixed to any part of the country'. Sometimes this passage is said to come from his journal of the 1855 expedition, but that only contains his more prosaic impressions. This was written up when he returned home for a book of his travels.

6 All I can add in my solitude is, may heaven's rich blessing come down on everyone, American, English, or Turk – who will help heal this open sore of the world.

These words (referring to the slave trade) are quoted on Livingstone's gravestone in Westminster Abbey. They are taken from a letter he had addressed to the *New York Herald* (1 May 1872). 'Loneliness' rather than 'solitude' may have been in the original.

Richard LLEWELLYN Welsh novelist (1907–83)

7 *None But the Lonely Heart.*

Title of novel (1943; film US 1944). Apparently an original coinage, but compare, 'None But the Weary Heart', the English title often given to a song by Tchaikovsky (Op. 6, No. 6). The lyrics of this song have been translated into English as, 'None but the weary heart can understand how I have suffered and how I am tormented'. It originated as 'Mignon's Song' in the novel *Wilhelm Meister* by Goethe – '*Nur wer die Sehnsucht kennt* [Only those who know what longing is]' – which was translated into Russian by Mey.

Marie LLOYD English music-hall entertainer
(1870–1922)

1 She sits among the cabbages and peas.

Line from song supposedly made famous by Marie Lloyd,
but untraced. According to the story, when forbidden by a
watch committee (local guardians of morals) to sing 'She
sits among the cabbages and peas,' she substituted, 'She
sits among the cabbages and leeks.' The story was told, for
example, by John Trevelyan, the British film censor – *TV
Times* (23 April–9 May 1981) – and is alluded to in the 'Battle
of Spion Kop' episode of the BBC Radio *Goon Show*
(29 December 1958). There is some doubt as to whether
the song really exists beyond the confines of this story –
and whether it has any connection with a song written in
1929, after Lloyd's death, called 'Mucking About in the
Garden'. This was written by Leslie Sarony, the British entertainer (1897–1985), using the *nom de plume* 'Q. Cumber'
or 'Q. Kumber'. Unfortunately, I have been unable to find the
sheet music (published by Lawrence Wright) to see if it
really does contain the immortal lines, 'She sits among the
cabbages and peas / Watching her onions grow', as has
been suggested. The only recording I have heard of the
song, by George Buck, does not have the couplet. I suspect
that the recording by Sarony himself with Tommy Handley and Jack Payne (on Columbia 5555), which I have not
heard, does not have it either.

**David LLOYD GEORGE (later 1st Earl Lloyd George
of Dwyfor)** British Liberal Prime Minister (1863–1945)

2 This is the leal and trusty mastiff which is to watch
over our interests, but which runs away at the first
snarl of the trade unions? A mastiff? It is the right
hon. Gentleman's Poodle. It fetches and carries
for him. It barks for him. It bites anybody that he
sets it on to.

Lloyd George spoke in the House of Commons on 26 June
1907 in the controversy over the power of the Upper House.
He questioned the House of Lords' role as a 'watchdog' of
the constitution and suggested that A.J. Balfour, the Conservative leader, was using the party's majority in the Lords
to block legislation by the Liberal government (in which
Lloyd George was President of the Board of Trade). As such
it is encapsulated in the phrase 'Mr Balfour's poodle'.

3 Ninepence for fourpence.

A political slogan dating from 1908–9, when the Welfare
State was being established in Britain. The phrase indicated
how people stood to benefit from their contributions to the
new National Health Insurance scheme. Associated with

Lloyd George and said by A.J.P. Taylor (in *Essays in English
History*) to have been snapped up from an audience interruption and turned into a slogan by him.

4 Sporting terms are pretty well understood wherever English is spoken ... Well, then. The British
soldier is a good sportsman ... Germany elected
to make this a finish fight with England ... The
fight must be to a finish – to a knock out.

As Secretary of State for War, Lloyd George gave an interview to Roy W. Harris, President of the United Press of
America. It was printed in *The Times* (29 September 1915).
Lloyd George was asked to 'give the United Press, in the
simplest possible language, the British attitude toward the
recent peace talk'. Hence, the particular form of the above
remarks. In his memoirs, Lloyd George entitled one chapter 'The Knock-out Blow' – which is how this notion came
to be popularly expressed.

5 What is our task? To make Britain a fit country for
heroes to live in.

This is precisely what Lloyd George said in a speech at
Wolverhampton (24 November 1918). It turned into the
better-known slogan 'A land fit for heroes' or, occasionally,
'A country fit for heroes'. By 1921, with wages falling in all
industries, the sentiment was frequently recalled and
mocked.

6 The world is becoming like a lunatic asylum run
by lunatics.

In *The Observer* (8 January 1933). See also ROWLAND 389:5;
STALLINGS 441:2.

7 A good mayor of Birmingham in an off-year.

On Neville Chamberlain (who came to national politics
after long experience in local government). Quoted in A.J.P.
Taylor, *English History 1914–1945* (1965). Also, in the form:
'He might make an adequate Lord Mayor of Birmingham in
a lean year', quoted in Leon Harris, *The Fine Art of Political Wit* (1965). In *Future Indefinite* (1954) Noël Coward
ascribes to Lord Birkenhead (F.E. Smith), 'The most we can
hope for from dear Neville is that he should be a good Lord
Mayor of Birmingham in a lean year.'

Also attributed (and possibly more correctly) to Lord
Hugh Cecil, in the form: 'He is no better than a Mayor of
Birmingham, and in a lean year at that. Furthermore he
is too old. He thinks he understands the modern world.
What should an old hunk like him know of the modern
world?' – quoted in Lord David Cecil, *The Cecils of Hatfield
House* (1973).

1 Simon has sat on the fence so long that the iron has entered into his soul.

On Sir John Simon who had been Attorney-General and Home Secretary in Asquith's Liberal government but had resigned by the time Lloyd George became PM in 1916. He formed a division of the Liberal Party in the 1920s which Lloyd George scorned. Quoted in A.J.P. Taylor, *English History 1914–1945* (1965). Alluding to BOOK OF COMMON PRAYER 97:11.

2 Lloyd George knew my father.

Even before Lloyd George's death in 1945, Welsh people away from home liked to claim some affinity with the Great Man. In time, this inclination was encapsulated in the singing of the words 'Lloyd George knew my father, my father knew Lloyd George' to the strains of 'Onward Christian Soldiers', which they neatly fit. In Welsh legal and Liberal circles the credit for this happy coinage has been given to Tommy Rhys Roberts QC (1910–75), whose father did indeed know Lloyd George. Arthur Rhys Roberts was a Newport solicitor who set up a London practice with Lloyd George in 1897. The partnership continued for many years, although on two occasions Lloyd George's political activities caused them to lose practically all their clients.

The junior Rhys Roberts was a gourmet and wine-bibber, and of enormous girth. Martin Thomas QC, a prominent Welsh liberal of the next generation, recalled (1984): 'It was, and is a tradition of the Welsh circuit that there should be, following the after-dinner speeches, a full-blooded singsong. For as long as anyone can remember, Rhys Roberts's set-piece was to sing the phrase to the tune of "Onward Christian Soldiers" – it is widely believed that he started the practice ... By the 'fifties it had certainly entered the repertoire of Welsh Rugby Clubs. In the 'sixties, it became customary for Welsh Liberals to hold a Noson Lawen, or sing-song, on the Friday night of the Liberal Assemblies. It became thoroughly adopted in the party. I recall it as being strikingly daring and new in the late 'sixties for Young Liberals to sing the so-called second verse, "Lloyd George knew my mother". William Douglas-Home's play *Lloyd George Knew My Father* was produced in London in 1972. One of the leading Welsh Silks recalls persuading Rhys Roberts to see it with him.'

From Robert Robinson, *Landscape with Dead Dons* (1956): 'He had displayed a massive indifference to the rollicking scientists who would strike up *Lloyd George Knew My Father* in a spirit of abandoned wickedness.'

Frank LOESSER American songwriter (1910–69)

3 See What the Boys in the Back Room Will Have.

Title of song, *Destry Rides Again* (1939). See also BEAVERBROOK 292:4.

4 Finally found a fellow
He says 'Murder!' – he says!
Every time we kiss he says 'Murder!' – he says!
Is that the language of love?

Song, '"Murder" He Says', *Happy Go Lucky* (1943). *Murder He Says* became the title of a film (US 1945).

5 *How To Succeed in Business Without Really Trying.*

Title of musical (1961). Taken from Shepherd Meade's non-fiction self-help book of that title.

Christopher LOGUE English poet (1926–)

6 Come to the edge.
We might fall.
Come to the edge.
It's too high!
COME TO THE EDGE!
And they came,
and he pushed,
and they flew.

'Come to the Edge', *New Numbers* (1969). In a profile of Tom Stoppard in *The New Yorker* (19 December 1977), Kenneth Tynan described the playwright addressing a class of drama students in Santa Barbara: 'What is the real dialogue that goes on between the artist and his audience? [Stoppard asks at the end]. By way of reply, he holds the microphone close to his mouth and speaks eight lines by the English poet Christopher Logue ... A surge of applause. In imagination, these young people are all flying.'

Many people have, however, seen the lines attributed to the surrealist French poet Guillaume Apollinaire (1880–1918). For example, Anthony Powell in his *Journals 1982–1986* (1995 – entry for 26 October 1982) has: 'At Royal Academy Banquet [not of this date] when [Margaret Thatcher] spoke, quoting Guillaume Apollinaire in a speech (something about a man walking blindfold over a cliff), passage I did not recognize, tho' I know Apollinaire's works fairly well ... Mrs T knew roughly about Apollinaire, a bit vague about quotation (which I still can't find).'

Accordingly, in 1995, I asked Christopher Logue for his comments. He had an intriguing explanation for the confusion: 'In 1961 or '62, Michael English and I were asked by Michael Kustow to design a poster/poem for an Apollinaire exhibition he was mounting at the ICA [Institute of Contemporary Arts in London].

'I wrote "Come to the Edge" and put the words "Apollinaire said" at the beginning of it; a cross between a title and a first line. On the poster, the poem, plus "Apollinaire said:" framed an illustration of clouds. Later, when the poem was reprinted, I dropped the trope. Last year, though, the US "magician" David Copperfield projected a garbled version of the poem on to a screen as part of his show, as well as printing it in his "tour-book" – the show's programme. I believe the poem has been reprinted in at least one US book without my permission. Maybe it had the trope attached to it still.' Indeed, a David Copperfield TV special shown in the UK in 1995 concluded with an approximation of the poem ... attributed to Apollinaire.

Mary McAleese recited the poem at her inauguration as President of the Irish Republic in November 1997. Indeed, according to *The Observer* (23 November 1997), she even had it written into the silk lining of her inaugural evening gown. By all accounts, the poem was properly attributed to Logue on this occasion.

Vince LOMBARDI American football coach (1913–70)

1 Winning isn't everything. It's the only thing.

Various versions of this oft-repeated statement exist. Lombardi, coach and general manager of the Green Bay Packers team from 1959 onwards, claimed *not* to have said it in this form but, rather, 'Winning is not everything – but making the effort to win is' (interview 1962). The first version of Lombardi's remarks to appear in print was in the form, 'Winning is not the most important thing, it's everything.' One Bill Veeck is reported to have said something similar. Henry 'Red' Sanders, a football coach at Vanderbilt University, *does* seem to have said it, however, in about 1948, and was so quoted in *Sports Illustrated* (26 December 1955). John Wayne, playing a football coach, delivered the line in the 1953 film *Trouble Along the Way*.

Compare: 'Winning in politics isn't everything; it's the only thing' – a slogan for the infamous 'Committee to Re-Elect the President' (Nixon) in 1972.

Huey LONG American politician (1893–1935)

2 Everyman a king but no man wears a crown.

The Louisiana Governor (and demagogue) found this slogan for his Share-the-Wealth platform – which he espoused from 1928 until his assassination – in William Jennings Bryan's 'Cross of Gold' speech (1896) – see BRYAN 106:4. He suggested that only 10 per cent of the American people owned 70 per cent of the wealth. As *Safire* (1978) points out, the full slogan used 'everyman' as one word.

Henry Wadsworth LONGFELLOW American poet (1807–82)

3 Life is real! Life is earnest!
And the grave is not the goal;
Dust thou art, to dust returnest,
Was not spoken of the soul.

... Lives of great men all remind us
We can make our lives sublime,
And, departing, leave behind us
Footprints on the sands of time.

Let us, then, be up and doing,
With a heart for any fate;
Still achieving, still pursuing,
Learn to labour and to wait.

'A Psalm of Life' (1838). Longfellow is probably the most parodied poet. There are several parodies of this poem – and the following one dates from 1996:

> Lives of criminals remind us
> We can make our lives sublime
> And, in parting, leave behind us
> Fingerprints on the files of crime.

4 The Wreck of the Hesperus.

Title of poem (1839) about an actual incident involving a schooner off the coast of New England. Hence, the expression, 'to look/feel like the wreck of the *Hesperus*', meaning, 'in a mess, in a sad state' – known in the US and UK since the 19th century. 'The Wreck of the Hesperus' is also referred to in the song 'Lydia, the Tattooed Lady', with lyrics by E.Y. Harburg and music by Harold Arlen (1939), as though it were commonly known as a picture.

5 Look not mournfully into the Past. It comes not back again. Wisely improve the Present. It is thine. Go forth to meet the Future, without fear, and with a manly heart.

This appears as such on the title page of *Hyperion*, a prose romance (1839) by Longfellow. It occurs again in Chap. 7 as a marble inscription on a chapel wall. The 15th (though not the 16th) edition of *Bartlett* helpfully gives the original German source as 'inscription on Chapel of St Gilgen near Salzburg'.

6 The shades of night were falling fast,
As through an Alpine village passed
A youth, who bore, 'mid snow and ice,
A banner with the strange device,
Excelsior!

'Excelsior' (1841). The poem, of which this is the first verse, became a favourite recitation of the parlour poetry school, and was also set to music more than once. It has been suggested that Longfellow was inspired by the ungrammatical motto on the state shield of New York, 'Excelsior', which is the comparative, meaning 'higher', of the adjective *excelsus*, rather than, presumably what was intended, *excelsius*, the comparative (meaning 'more loftily') of the adverb *excelse*. Strange device, indeed. It gave rise to a delightful parody 'The Shades of Night', which was written, apparently, by A.E. Housman:

> The shades of night were falling fast,
> And the rain was falling faster,
> When through an Alpine village passed
> An Alpine village pastor ...

1   Thy fate is the common fate of all,
    Into each life some rain must fall,
    Some days must be dark and dreary.

'The Rainy Day' (1842). Hence, 'Into each life some rain must fall, / But too much is falling in mine', from the song 'Into Each Life A Little Rain Must Fall' (as it is sometimes worded, but which also contains 'some rain' in the lyrics), written by Allan Roberts and Doris Fisher (1944).

2   Underneath the spreading chestnut tree
    The village smithy stands;
    The smith a mighty man is he
    With large and sinewy hands
    And the muscles of his brawny arms
    Are strong as iron bands.

'The Village Blacksmith' (1842) – one of the most parodied and plundered of verses. In the 19th century there were musical settings by several composers, but that by W.H. Weiss (1820–67), dating from 1854, was the most popular. There was then a lull until a song was written called 'The Chestnut Tree' in 1938. This was a joint effort by Jimmy Kennedy, Tommie Connor and Hamilton Kennedy:

> Underneath the Spreading Chestnut Tree
> I loved her and she loved me.
> There she used to sit upon my knee
> 'Neath the Spreading Chestnut Tree.
>
> There beneath the boughs we used to meet,
> All her kisses were so sweet.
> All the little birds went tweet tweet tweet
> 'Neath the Spreading Chestnut Tree.

The actual blacksmith only manages to make an appearance in this song by exclaiming 'Chest ... nuts!' – which gave rise to interesting gestures by performers. Instructions as to how to do these were given on the sheet music for this 'novelty singing dance sensation'.

In George Orwell's novel *Nineteen Eighty-Four* (1949) there is another variation:

> Under the spreading chestnut tree
> I sold you and you sold me:
> There lie they, and here lie we
> Under the spreading chestnut tree.

3   And the night shall be filled with music
    And the cares that infest the day
    Shall fold their tents, like the Arabs,
    And as silently steal away.

'The Day is Done' (1844). At the conclusion of his case for the defence in the Jeremy Thorpe trial (1979), Mr George Carman QC said to the Old Bailey jury: 'I end by saying in the words of the Bible: "Let this prosecution fold up its tent and quietly creep away."' His client should not have got off after that.

4   Sail on, Oh Ship of State!
    Sail on, Oh Union, strong and great.
    Humanity with all its fears,
    With all the hope of future years,
    Is hanging breathless on thy fate!

'The Building of the Ship' (1849). On 20 January 1941, before the US had entered the Second World War, President Roosevelt sent a letter to the British Prime Minister, Winston Churchill, containing this extract (with minor differences in spelling and punctuation) from Longfellow's poem. He commented: 'I think this verse applies to your people as it does to us.' For Churchill's response, see CLOUGH 147:6.

5   Lo! in that hour of misery
    A lady with a lamp I see
    Pass through the glimmering gloom,
    And flit from room to room.
    And slow, as in a dream of bliss
    The speechless sufferer turns to kiss
    Her shadow, as it falls
    Upon the darkening walls.

'Santa Filomena' (1857). Florence Nightingale (1820–1910), philanthropist and nursing pioneer, was dubbed 'the Lady with a Lamp' in commemoration of her services to soldiers at Scutari during the Crimean War (1854–6). She inspected hospital wards at night, carrying a lamp – a Turkish lantern consisting of a candle inside a collapsible shade. The phrase appears to have been coined by Longfellow in his poem, which was written very shortly after the events described.

On her death, Moore Smith & Co. of Moorgate, London, published a ballad with the title 'The Lady with *the* Lamp', which begins:

The Lady with the Lamp –
Let this her title be
Remembered through the ages
That will dawn and flee.

Straight to an Empire's heart
Her noble way she trod.
She lives, she lives for ever
Now she rests, she rests with God.

The film biography (1951), with Anna Neagle as Miss Nightingale, was called *The Lady with a Lamp* and was based on a play by Reginald Berkeley.

1 **Though the mills of God grind slowly, yet they grind exceeding small.**

Longfellow's translation of a line of verse (1654) by Friedrich von Logau, a German poet – in turn, a translation of a verse in Latin. The meaning of this saying is that the ways in which reforms are brought about, crime is punished, and so on, are often slow, but the end result may be perfectly achieved.

2 **A boy's will is the wind's will
And the thoughts of youth are long, long
thoughts.**

'My Lost Youth' (1858). Hence, *A Boy's Will* – title of the first volume of poetry (1913) by Robert Frost.

3 **Between the dark and the daylight,
When the night is beginning to lower,
Comes a pause in the day's occupations,
That is known as the Children's Hour.**

'The Children's Hour' (1859). This became the name for the period between afternoon tea and dressing for dinner, particularly in Edwardian England. When the long-running and fondly remembered BBC Radio programme *Children's Hour* began in 1922, it was known as 'The Children's Hour', which suggests that it ultimately derived from the title of Longfellow's poem. Lillian Hellman also wrote a play called *The Children's Hour* (1934), variously filmed, about a schoolgirl's allegations of her teachers' lesbianism.

4 **Ships that pass in the night, and speak each
other in passing;
Only a signal shown and a distant voice in the
darkness;
So on the ocean of life we pass and speak one
another,
Only a look and a voice; then darkness again
and silence.**

'The Theologian's Tale: Elizabeth', Pt 4, *Tales of a Wayside Inn*, Pt 3 (1874). The origin of the expression 'ships that pass in the night', referring to acquaintanceship (with people) that is only of short duration.

Alice Roosevelt LONGWORTH American political hostess (1884–1980)

5 **If you haven't got anything nice to say about anyone, come and sit by me.**

Embroidered on a cushion at Longworth's Washington DC home. The daughter of Theodore Roosevelt, she had a reputation for barbed wit, but many of her 'sayings' were not entirely original.

6 **[Calvin Coolidge] looked as if he had been weaned on a pickle.**

She admitted hearing this 'at my dentist's office. The last patient had said it to him and I just seized on it. I didn't originate it – but didn't it describe him exactly?' – *The New York Times* (25 February 1980). It first appeared as an 'anonymous remark' quoted in Longworth's *Crowded Hours* (1933).

7 **[Thomas E. Dewey] looks like the bridegroom on the wedding cake.**

A description that helped destroy Dewey when he stood against President Truman in 1948. It actually came from one Grace Hodgson Flandrau. Longworth admitted: 'I thought it frightfully funny and quoted it to everyone. Then it began to be attributed to me.' Sometimes just 'the man on the wedding cake', Dewey did indeed have a wooden appearance, and a black moustache.

Anita LOOS American novelist (1893–1981)

8 *Gentlemen Prefer Blondes.*

Title of novel (1925), to which a sequel was added: *But Gentlemen Marry Brunettes* (1928). Irving Berlin wrote a song with the title very shortly after this, and it was sung in London in the revue *RSVP* (23 February 1926). And a B.G. de Sylva and Lewis Gensler song, with the same title, was performed on Broadway in *Queen High* (2 November 1926).

9 **Kissing your hand may make you feel very very good but a diamond and safire bracelet lasts forever.**

In the same novel, Chap. 4. A caption to the frontispiece of the original edition has this slightly different version: 'Kissing your hand may make you feel very good but a diamond bracelet lasts forever.' Either way, this was the inspiration for the Jule Styne/Leo Robin song 'Diamonds Are a Girl's Best Friend' in the 1949 stage musical and 1953 film based on the book.

LORCA See GARCIA LORCA.

Edward LORENZ American meteorologist (1917–)

1 Predictability: Does the Flap of a Butterfly's Wings in Brazil Set Off a Tornado in Texas?

Title of a paper on predictability in weather forecasting delivered to the American Association for the Advancement of Science, Washington DC (29 December 1979). Apparently, Lorenz originally used the image of a seagull's wing flapping. What is now called 'The Butterfly Effect' – how small acts lead to large – appeals to chaos theorists. J. Gleick gives another example in *Chaos: Making a New Theory* (1988), also from weather forecasting: 'The notion that a butterfly stirring the air today in Peking can transform storm systems next month in New York.'

11th Marquess of LOTHIAN British Conservative politician (1882–1940)

2 The only lasting solution is that Europe itself should gradually find its way to an internal equilibrium and a limitation of armaments by political appeasement.

Letter to *The Times* (4 May 1934). Hence, the term 'appeasement' given to the policy of conciliation and concession towards Nazi Germany, around 1938. The word had been used in this context since the end of the First World War. On 14 February 1920 Winston Churchill was saying in a speech: 'I am, and have always been since the firing stopped on November 11, 1918, for a policy of peace, real peace and appeasement.' The 1930s use of the term probably dates from Lothian's letter, however.

LOUIS XIV French King (1638–1715)

3 *L'état c'est moi* [I am the state].

Alleged remark to parliament on 13 April 1655, but there is no contemporary evidence for it. Some of his personal edicts were being challenged in the interests of the state. Louis is said to have strode into the chamber wearing his hunting clothes and brandishing a riding crop.

LOUIS XVI French King (1754–93)

4 *Rien* [Nothing].

His complete diary entry made at Versailles on the evening of 14 July 1789 – the day of the storming of the Bastille. In fact, he wrote '*Rien*' on most of the days that July, and made only one-line entries most of the time, anyway. Quoted in Simon Schama, *Citizens*, Chap. 10 (1989). A similar story

has been told that on 4 July 1776, when the American Declaration of Independence was signed, King George III wrote in his diary: 'Nothing of importance happened today.' There appears to be absolutely no evidence for this.

5 Frenchmen, I die innocent: it is from the scaffold and near appearing before God that I tell you so. I pardon my enemies: I desire that France ...

Louis's last words before execution (21 January 1793) are given here as reported by Thomas Carlyle in *The French Revolution – A History*, Pt 3, Chap. 2 (1837). The remainder of the last sentence was drowned out by the sound of drumming, but others have it that he went on: 'Pray God that my blood fall not on France!' or 'I hope that my blood may cement the happiness of the French people.'

Joe LOUIS American boxer (1914–81)

6 He can run, but he can't hide.

In the *New York Herald Tribune* (9 June 1946), before a World Heavyweight Championship fight with the quick-moving Billy Conn (whom he beat by a knock-out on 19 June).

In the wake of the hijacking of a TWA airliner to Beirut in the summer of 1985, President Reagan issued a number of warnings to international terrorists. In October he said that America had 'sent a message to terrorists everywhere. The message: "You can run, but you can't hide."' Coming from a former sports commentator, the allusion was clear, but one suspects that the saying possibly pre-dates Louis in any case. On the other hand, it has been suggested that John L. Sullivan said it before his fight with 'Gentleman Jim' Corbett in 1892. It was apparently quoted in the 1942 film *Gentleman Jim*, based on Corbett's autobiography *The Roar of the Crowd* (1925).

Richard LOVELACE English poet (1618–58)

7 Stone walls do not a prison make,
Nor iron bars a cage.

'To Althea, From Prison' (1649). When combined with a phrase from SHAKESPEARE 400:6, this produced a delightfully lunatic allusion in *The Kenneth Williams Letters* (1994): 'I must say I fell about at your line – "Age shall not wither her, nor iron bars a cage" – how true that is even today' – Kenneth Williams to John Hussey (2 October 1971) – however, others recall this line as having been in the BBC Radio show *Much Binding in the Marsh* (1947–53).

James LOVELL American astronaut (1928–)

1 OK, Houston, we have had a problem here ... Houston, we have had a problem.

The *Apollo 13* space mission took off at 13.13 Houston time on 11 April 1970. Two days into the mission – i.e. on the 13th – and 200,000 miles from Earth, an oxygen tank exploded, seriously endangering the crew. Lovell, the commander, noted the happening with notable understatement. It is hard to decipher precisely what he said from the recording of the incident. *The Times* (15 April) had, 'Hey, we've got a problem.' Asked to repeat this, Lovell said: 'Houston, we've had a problem. We've had a Main B Bus Undervolt' (referring to a loss of voltage in an electrical circuit, caused by the explosion). Emergency procedures allowed the crew to make a safe return to earth – although it was a close shave. The words have also been ascribed to another crew member, John L. Swigert Jr – as in *Time* Magazine (10 January 1983). A TV movie in 1974 was entitled *Houston, We've Got a Problem*, as was a documentary (1994). In the feature film *Apollo 13* (US 1995), based on a book by Lovell, Swigert gets to say, 'Hey, we've got a problem here' and Lovell follows this with, 'Houston, we have a problem.'

In fact, combining a transcript (which Lovell has apparently confirmed) with listening to the slightly unclear recording of what was said, the correct form of the exchange is:

Swigert: OK, Houston, we've had a problem here.
Mission Control: This is Houston. Say again please.
Lovell: Oh, Houston, we've had a problem. We've had a Main B Bus Undervolt.
Mission Control: Roger, Main B Undervolt.

James Russell LOWELL American poet (1819–91)

2 New occasions teach new duties: Time makes
    ancient good uncouth;
They must upward still, and onward, who would
    keep abreast of truth.

'The Present Crisis' (1844). Probably the first formulation of the phrase 'onwards and upwards'. The first lines of the 19th-century hymn 'Onward! Upward!' – words by F.J. Crosby, music by Ira D. Sankey – are:

Onward! upward! Christian soldier.
Turn not back nor sheath thy sword;
Let its blade be sharp for conquest
In the battle for the Lord.

Sankey also set the words of Albert Midlane in 'Onward, Upward, Homeward!', of which the refrain is:

Onward to the glory!
Upward to the prize!
Homeward to the mansions
Far above the skies!

Or could the words be from a motto? The Davies-Colley family of Newfold, Cheshire, have them as such in the form 'Upwards and Onwards'. Now it has become a light-hearted catchphrase. Nicholas Craig in *I, An Actor* (1988) asks of young actors: 'Will you be able to learn the language of the profession and say things like "onwards and upwards", "Oh well, we survive" and "Never stops, love, he *never stops*"?'

See also KEARNEY 265:11.

Robert LOWELL American poet (1917–77)

3 If we see light at the end of the tunnel,
    It's the light of the oncoming train.

'Since 1939' (1977), but probably not original. Paul Dickson cited 'Rowe's Rule: the odds are five to six that the light at the end of the tunnel is the headlight of an oncoming train' in *The Washingtonian* (November 1978). On BBC Radio *Quote ... Unquote* (1980), John Lahr said it had been a favourite remark of his father – the actor, Bert Lahr (who died in 1967).

George LUCAS American film director and writer (1944–)

4 May the Force be with you.

Film, *Star Wars* (US 1977), scripted by Lucas. A benediction and valediction used several times. At one point, Ben Obi-Wan Kenobi (Alec Guinness) explains what it means: 'The Force is what gives the Jedi their power. It's an energy field created by all living things. It surrounds us, it penetrates us, it binds the galaxy together.'

The phrase turned up in Cornwall a short while after the film was released in Britain – as a police-force recruiting slogan. Later, President Reagan, promoting his 'Star Wars' weapon system, said: 'It isn't about fear, it's about hope, and in that struggle, if you'll pardon my stealing a film line, "The force is with us."'

Compare 'The Lord be with you' from Morning Prayer in the Anglican Book of Common Prayer.

5 *The Empire Strikes Back.*

Title of film (US 1980). This was the fictional 'evil empire' vaguely alluded to by Ronald Reagan in his remarks about the Soviet Union (378:4). The phrase caught on in other ways, too. In about 1981 the proprietors of an Indian restaurant in Drury Lane, London, considered it as a name before rejecting it in favour of 'The Last Days of the Raj'. In 1982 *Newsweek* Magazine gave it as the title of a cover story about Britain's attempt to recapture the Falkland Islands. *The Umpire Strikes Back* was the title of a memoir (1982) by baseball umpires Ron Luciano and David Fisher.

Martin LUTHER German Protestant theologian
(1483–1546)

1   *Hier stehe ich. Ich kann nicht anders. Gott helfe mir.
Amen* [Here I stand. I can do no other. God help
me. Amen].

Speech at the Diet of Worms (18 April 1521). Attributed.
According to Büchmann's *Geflügelte Worte* (all recent editions), a thorough study of contemporary sources by Karl
Müller in 1907 has shown that all Luther said was *'Gott helf
mir, Amen'*, which was a common formula for ending a
speech. Apparently, the long version first shows up around
1546 in the Wittenberg edition of Luther's works.

   Following Luther's attack on the doctrinal system of the
Church of Rome, a papal bull was issued against him. He
burned it in Wittenberg. When the Emperor Charles V con-
vened his diet at Worms, an order was issued for the destruction of Luther's books and he was summoned to justify
himself before the diet.

2   Wine women and song.

As Wolfgang Mieder describes in *Proverbs Are Never Out of
Season*, Chap. 4 (1993), although Martin Luther is often
credited with the saying, 'Who does not love wine, woman
and song, / Remains a fool his whole life long', there is not
the slightest evidence that he did. Besides it was not until
1775 that the attribution was made, and there are many
proverbs in Latin and German using the proverb format:
'Night, women, wine are for the adolescent man', 'Dice,
wine, love are three things that have made me destitute',
'Three things make much joy: / Wine, women and strum-
ming', among them. 'Wine, Women and Loud Happy Songs'
is the title of a track on Ringo Starr's LP *Beaucoup of Blues* –
possibly written by Kingston/Essex.

(Sir) Edwin LUTYENS English architect (1869–1944)

3   The piece of cod passeth all understanding.

When Lutyens's son, Robert, was attempting to write a book
about his father, they met for lunch at the Garrick Club in
London so that Sir Edwin could make known his views on
the project and its author. When the matter was broached,
however, Sir Edwin, embarrassed, merely exclaimed, 'Oh,
my!' Then, as the fish was served, he looked at his son over
the *two* pairs of spectacles he was wearing and made the
above comment. Recounted in Robert Lutyens, *Sir Edwin
Lutyens* (1942). Compare BIBLE 85:3; JAMES I 252:6.

4   The answer is in the plural and they bounce.

Said to have been the euphemistic response given by
Lutyens to a Royal Commission, quoted without source in
PDMQ (1971). However, according to Robert Jackson, *The
Chief* (1959), when Gordon (later Lord) Hewart was in the
House of Commons, he was answering questions on behalf
of David Lloyd George. For some time, one afternoon, he
had given answers in the customary brief parliamentary
manner – 'The answer is in the affirmative' or 'The answer
is in the negative'. After one such non-commital reply, several members arose to bait Hewart with a series of rapid
supplementary questions. He waited until they had all finished and then replied: 'The answer is in the plural!' Additionally, Howard Carter is said to have debunked
speculation about his work on the tomb of Tutankhamun
with: 'The answer is spherical, and in the plural.'

H.F. LYTE English clergyman and hymnwriter
(1793–1847)

5   Change and decay in all around I see;
O Thou, who changest not, abide with me.

Hymn 'Abide With Me' (?1847). Possibly inspired by Luke
24:29: 'Abide with us: for it is toward evening, and the day
is far spent.' Hence, *Change and Decay In All Around I See*,
the title of a novel (1978) by Allan Massie. The hymn was
sung by Edith Cavell the night before her execution, and
has been a fixture at FA cup finals since 1927.

M

Douglas MacARTHUR American general (1880–1964)

1 I shall return.

During the Second World War, MacArthur was forced by the Japanese to pull out of the Philippines, leaving Corregidor on 11 March 1942. On 20 March he made his commitment to return when he arrived by train at Adelaide. He had journeyed southwards across Australia and was just about to set off eastwards for Melbourne. So, although he had talked in these terms before leaving the Philippines, his main statement was delivered not there but on Australian soil. At the station a crowd awaited him, and prior to addressing them he had scrawled a few words on the back of an envelope: 'The President of the United States ordered me to break through the Japanese lines and proceed from Corregidor to Australia for the purpose, as I understand it, of organizing the American offensive against Japan, a primary object of which is the relief of the Philippines. I came through and I shall return.'

MacArthur had intended his first words to have the most impact – as a way of getting the war in the Pacific a higher priority – but it was his last three words that caught on. The Office of War Information tried to get him to amend them to 'We shall return', foreseeing that there would be objections to a slogan that seemed to imply that he was all-important and that his men mattered little. MacArthur refused. In fact, the phrase had first been suggested to a MacArthur aide in the form 'We shall return' by a Filipino journalist, Carlos Romulo. 'America has let us down and won't be trusted,' Romulo had said. 'But the people still have confidence in MacArthur. If he says he is coming back, he will be believed.' The suggestion was passed to MacArthur who adopted it – but adapted it.

MacArthur later commented: '"I shall return" seemed a promise of magic to the Filipinos. It lit a flame that became a symbol which focused the nation's indomitable will and at whose shrine it finally attained victory and, once again, found freedom. It was scraped in the sands of the beaches, it was daubed on the walls of the *barrios*, it was stamped on the mail, it was whispered in the cloisters of the church. It became the battle cry of a great underground swell that no Japanese bayonet could still.'

As William Manchester wrote in *American Caesar* (1978): 'That it had this great an impact is doubtful ... but unquestionably it appealed to an unsophisticated oriental people. Throughout the war American submarines provided Filipino guerillas with cartons of buttons, gum, playing cards, and matchboxes bearing the message.'

On 20 October 1944 MacArthur *did* return. Landing at Leyte, he said to a background of still continuing gunfire: 'People of the Philippines, I have returned ... By the grace of Almighty God, our forces stand again upon Philippine soil.'

2 The world has turned over many times since I took the oath on the Plain at West Point, and the hopes and dreams have long since vanished. But I still remember the refrain of one of the most popular barrack ballads of that day, which proclaimed, most proudly, that old soldiers never die. They just fade away. And like the old soldier of that ballad, I now close my military career and just fade away – an old soldier who tried to do his duty as God gave him the light to see that duty. Goodbye.

Speech to Congress (19 April 1951), conclusion. In fact, the ballad quoted by MacArthur and which he dated as 'turn of the century' was a British Army song of the First World War. It is a parody of the gospel hymn 'Kind Words Can Never Die'. J. Foley copyrighted a version of the parody in 1920. The more usual form of the words is, 'Old soldiers never die – they simply fade away.'

Thomas MACAULAY (1st Baron Macaulay) English
historian, poet and politician (1800–59)

1 The gallery in which the reporters sit has become
a fourth estate of the realm.

In 1828 Macaulay wrote this in *The Edinburgh Review* of the
representatives of the press in the House of Commons –
the 'fourth estate' after the Lords Spiritual, the Lords Temporal, and the Commons – but a number of others have
also been credited with the coinage. Edmund Burke, for
example, is said to have pointed at the press gallery and
remarked: 'And yonder sits the fourth estate, more important than them all.'

The phrase was originally used to describe various forces
outside Parliament – such as the army (as by Falkland in
1638) or the mob (as by Fielding in 1752). When William
Hazlitt used it in *Table Talk* in 1821, he meant not the press
in general but just William Cobbett. Two years later, Lord
Brougham is said to have used the phrase in the House of
Commons to describe the press in general. So when
Macaulay wrote, it was obviously an established expression.
Then Carlyle used it several times – in his article on
Boswell's *Life of Johnson* in 1832, in his *History of the French
Revolution* in 1837 and in his lectures 'On Heroes, Hero-
Worship, & the Heroic in History' in 1841. But he attributed
the phrase to Burke (who died in 1797). It has been sug-
gested that the BBC (or the broadcast media in general)
now constitute a *fifth* estate, as also, at one time, did the
'trade unions'.

2 As every schoolboy knows.

Robert Burton wrote 'Every schoolboy hath the famous testament of Grunius Corocotta Porcellus at his fingers' ends'
in *The Anatomy of Melancholy* (1621), and Bishop Jeremy
Taylor used the expression 'every schoolboy knows it' in
1654. In the next century, Jonathan Swift had 'to tell what
every schoolboy knows'. But the most noted user of this
rather patronizing phrase was Macaulay, who would say
things like 'Every schoolboy knows who imprisoned Mon-
tezuma, and who strangled Atahualpa' – in his essay on
'Lord Clive' (January 1840).

3 Lars Porsena of Clusium
By the nine gods he swore
That the great house of Tarquin
Should suffer wrong no more.

'Horatius', *Lays of Ancient Rome* (1842). Hence, *Lars Porsena,
or the Future of Swearing and Improper Language*, title of a
short study (1920) by Robert Graves.

4 We know of no spectacle so ridiculous as the British
public in one of its periodical fits of morality.

'Moore's *Life of Byron*', in the same collection. A frequently
paraded observation, not least during Britain's 'Profumo
scandal' in 1963. Has been misattributed to Oscar Wilde –
whose treatment might well have been another occasion
for quoting it.

Anthony C. McAULIFFE American general (1898–1975)

5 Nuts!

In December 1944 the Germans launched a counteroffen-
sive in what came to be known as the Battle of the Bulge.
'Old Crock' McAuliffe was acting commander of the American 101st Airborne Division and was ordered to defend the
strategic Belgian town of Bastogne in the Ardennes forest.
This was important because Bastogne stood at a crossroads
through which the advancing armies had to pass. When
the Americans had been surrounded like 'the hole in a
doughnut' for seven days, the Germans said they would
accept a surrender. On 23 December, McAuliffe replied:
'Nuts!'

The Germans first of all interpreted this one word reply as
meaning 'crazy', and took time to appreciate what they were
being told. Encouraged by McAuliffe's spirit, his men managed to hold the line and thus defeat the last major enemy
offensive of the war.

McAuliffe recounted the episode in a BBC broadcast on 3
January 1945: 'When we got [the surrender demand] we
thought it was the funniest thing we ever heard. I just
laughed and said, "Nuts", but the German major who
brought it wanted a formal answer; so I decided – well, I'd
just say "Nuts", so I had it written out: "QUOTE, TO THE
GERMAN COMMANDER: NUTS. SIGNED, THE AMERICAN
COMMANDER UNQUOTE."'

When Agence France Presse sought a way of translating
this it resorted to, '*Vous n'êtes que de vieilles noix* [You are
only old fogeys]' – although '*noix*' in French slang also carries the same testicular meaning as 'nuts' in English. When
McAuliffe's obituary came to be written, *The New York Times*
observed: 'Unofficial versions strongly suggest that the
actual language used by the feisty American general was
considerably stronger and more profane than the comparatively mild "Nuts", but the official version will have to
stand.'

Paul McCARTNEY See LENNON and McCARTNEY.

Peter Dodds McCORMICK Scottish-born Australian songwriter (1834–1916)

1 Australia's sons, let us rejoice,
For we are young and free,
We've golden soil and wealth for toil,
Our home is girt by sea;
Our land abounds in nature's gifts
Of beauty rich and rare;
In hist'ry's page, let ev'ry stage
Advance Australia Fair,
In joyful strains then let us sing
Advance Australia fair.

The song 'Advance Australia Fair' was first performed in Sydney in 1878, but the alliterative phrase 'Advance Australia' had existed much earlier, when Michael Massey Robinson wrote in the *Sydney Gazette* (1 February 1826): '"ADVANCE THEN, AUSTRALIA", / Be this thy proud gala / ... And thy watch-word be "FREEDOM FOR EVER!"'

'Advance Australia' became the motto of the Commonwealth of Australia when the states united in 1901. In the 1970s and 1980s, as republicanism grew, it acquired the force of a slogan and was used in various campaigns to promote national pride (sometimes as 'Let's Advance Australia'). In 1984 'Advance Australia Fair' superseded 'God Save the Queen' as the national anthem. The first line became 'Australians all let us rejoice ...' McCormick's second verse was mostly ignored:

When gallant Cook from Albion sailed
To trace wide oceans o'er,
True British courage bore him on
Till he landed on our shore.
Then here he raised Old England's flag,
The standard of the brave.
With all her faults we love her still
Britannia rules the wave.
In joyful strains then let us sing
Advance Australia Fair.

Compare line 7 with COWPER 157:7.

John McCRAE Canadian poet (1872–1918)

2 In Flanders fields the poppies blow
Between the crosses, row on row,
That mark our place; and in the sky
The larks, still bravely singing, fly
Scarce heard amid the guns below.

From 'In Flanders Fields', written after the second Battle of Ypres and sent anonymously to *Punch*, where it was published on 8 December 1915. McCrae was a Canadian academic turned volunteer medical officer. He himself died of wounds in a Normandy hospital in May 1918. His poem was the inspiration for the Poppy Day appeals which became an annual event from 1921, raising money for ex-servicemen. These appeals have been described as the best marketing idea in the history of charities.

3 If ye break faith with us who die
We shall not sleep, though poppies grow
On Flanders fields.

McCrae's own reputed last words ('Tell them this: If ye break faith with us who die we shall not sleep') are taken from the last lines of the same poem.

Carson McCULLERS American novelist (1917–67)

4 *The Heart Is a Lonely Hunter.*

Title of novel (1940; film US 1968), about a deaf mute. Taken from 'The Lonely Hunter' – 'My heart is a lonely hunter that hunts on a lonely hill' – by the Scottish novelist and poet William Sharp (1855–1905).

Donald McGILL English comic postcard artist (1875–1962)

5 Can't see my little Willy.

McGill drew his first comic postcard in 1905 and, judging by the style and appearance of one of his most famous cards, it probably dates from within the next ten to 15 years. The card shows a fat man with an enormous stomach (or 'corporation') which prevents him from seeing the small boy seated at his feet. The double-entendre in the caption is signed prominently by the artist.

A TV play (UK 1970) by Douglas Livingstone had the title *I Can't See My Little Willie*. 'I've lost my little Willie!' (which rather obscures the joke) was used as the title of a 'celebration of comic postcards' (1976) by Benny Green. This book title may have been taken from the caption to a re-drawing of the idea by another cartoonist.

6 'Do you like Kipling?'
'I don't know, you naughty boy, I've never kippled.'

This caption to one of McGill's postcards – undated, but possibly from the 1930s – might just be the origin of a little joke. However, J.K. Stephen (1859–92) had already seen the possibilities in the name in his poem 'To R.K.' which ends:

When the Rudyards cease from kipling
And the Haggards ride no more.

Niccolò MACHIAVELLI Florentine politician and philosopher (1469–1527)

1 There is nothing more difficult to take in hand, nor perilous to conduct, or more uncertain in its success, than the introduction of a new order of things, because the innovator has for enemies all those who have done well under the old conditions, and lukewarm defenders in those who may do well under the new.

The Prince, Chap. 6 (1532). Marmaduke Hussey, a beleaguered Chairman of the BBC, admitted in an interview with the *Independent on Sunday* (16 December 1991) that he clung to this quotation, which was 'provided by an ally [I] turned to for advice'.

2 *Divide et impera* [Divide and rule].

All sorts of people have subscribed to this way of overcoming opposition – by breaking it down and then conquering it. Philip of Macedon and Louis XI of France are among the many who have paid heed to it, but Machiavelli is generally credited with having popularized the maxim.

(Sir) James MACKINTOSH Scottish historian and philosopher (1765–1832)

3 The commons, faithful to their system, remained in a wise and masterly inactivity.

Vindiciae Gallicae (1791). Mackintosh was writing about the 'third estate' at the first session of the Estates General summoned in France in 1789. Alan Watkins in *The Observer* (19 February 1989) ascribed the phrase to the 3rd Marquess of Salisbury (the British Prime Minister), when writing of 'Mr Nigel Lawson's display of masterly inactivity'. In the US, Vice-President John C. Calhoun told the South Carolina legislature in 1831: 'If the Government should be taught thereby, that the highest wisdom of a State is a "wise and masterly inactivity", an invaluable blessing will be conferred.' *Benham* (1948) compares Horace – '*strenua nos exercet inertia* [strenuous inertia urges us on]'.

Archibald MACLEISH American poet (1892–1982)

4 To see the earth as it truly is, small and blue and beautiful in that eternal silence where it floats, is to see ourselves as riders on the earth together, brothers on that bright loveliness in the eternal cold – brothers who know they are truly brothers.

Written for *The New York Times* (25 December 1968) after an Apollo space mission returned with a photograph that showed the earth as seen from beyond the moon. Macleish revised the wording to provide an epigraph for his *Riders on the Earth* (1978): 'To see the earth as we now see it, small and blue and beautiful in that eternal silence where it floats, is to see ourselves as riders on the earth together; brothers on that bright loveliness in the unending night – brothers who *see* now they are truly brothers.'

Iain MACLEOD British Conservative politician (1913–70)

5 History is too serious to be left to historians.

Quoted in *The Observer* (16 July 1961). See also BENN 61:5; CLEMENCEAU 146:1; DE GAULLE 165:4.

6 It is some measure of the tightness of the magic circle on this occasion that neither the Chancellor of the Exchequer nor the Leader of the House of Commons had any inkling of what was happening.

On the method of choosing the Conservative Party leader in 1963. Article in *The Spectator* (17 January 1964). Sometimes rendered as 'magic circle of Old Etonians'. Macleod was describing the way in which the leader, although supposedly just 'emerging', was in fact the choice of a small group of influential Tory peers and manipulators. In the present case, they ensured that Alec Douglas-Home succeeded Harold Macmillan over the claims of R.A. Butler. Macmillan had said: 'I hope that it will soon be possible for the customary process of consultation to be carried out within the party about its future leadership.' A year or two later, and as a result of this experience, the Tory leadership came to be decided instead by a ballot of Conservative MPs.

Presumably Macleod was influenced in his choice of phrase by the stage magicians' Magic Circle (founded 1905) and the ancient use of the term in necromancy. The phrase has continued to be applied to other semi-secret cabals to which those wishing to belong are denied access.

7 This new victory for the Nanny State represents the wrong approach. It is certainly the duty of ministers to make sure that there is a full knowledge of risks thought to be involved in heavy cigarette smoking – and this duty was discharged by Conservative ministers of health and education. If this is done, the decision to smoke or not is for the individual, and it should be left to him.

In *The Spectator* (12 February 1965). On over-protective government. In the 1980s the derogatory term 'Nanny State' came to be adopted by Thatcherites, who deplored the socialist Welfare State, and believed that people should be left to sink or swim in the face of the normal forces acting upon society.

8 We now have the worst of both worlds – not just inflation on the one side or stagnation on the other

side, but both of them together. We have a sort of 'stagflation' situation.

Speech, House of Commons (17 November 1965). Coinage of another standard term in British politics for stagnant demand coupled with severe inflation.

Norman MACLEOD Scottish theologian (1812–72)

1 Courage brother! do not stumble,
Though thy path be dark as night;
There's a star to guide the humble;
Trust in God, and do the Right.

From 'Trust in God'. This may be the source of the expression 'Trust in God, and do the right', which has been much used subsequently as a gravestone inscription. For example, it appears in the form, 'HE TRUSTED IN GOD / AND TRIED TO DO THE RIGHT' on the grave of Douglas Haig, 1st Earl Haig (1861–1928), in the ruins of Dryburgh Abbey, Berwickshire (Borders). Haig was Commander-in-Chief of British forces in France and Flanders for most of the First World War. The headstone, at Haig's request, as a plaque nearby suggests, 'is the same as those placed in many lands over his comrades who fell in the Great War'. 'For God and the right' is another form of this motto-like idea. Compare also *Dieu et mon droit*, the British royal.

Marshall McLUHAN Canadian writer (1911–80)

2 The new electronic interdependence recreates the world in the image of a global village.

The Gutenberg Galaxy (1962). Hence, *David Frost's Global Village*, title of an occasional Yorkshire TV series (from 1979) in which Frost discussed global issues with pundits beamed in by satellite.

3 The medium is the message.

Understanding Media (1964). McLuhan's basic tenet: that the form of the media has a more significant effect on society than anything they say.

See also LEARY 281:2.

Ed McMAHON American broadcaster (1923–)

4 Here's Johnny!

Said with a drawn-out, rising inflection on the first word, this was McMahon's introduction to Johnny Carson on NBC TV's *Tonight* show in the US (from 1961 until 1992). In full, what McMahon (a former circus clown) said was: [Drum roll] 'And now ... heeeeere's Johnny!' It was emulated during Simon Dee's brief reign as a chat-show host in Britain during the 1960s. The studio audience joined in the rising

inflection of the announcer's 'It's Siiiiiimon Dee!' Jack Nicholson, playing a psychopath, chopped through a door with an axe and cried 'Here's Johnny!' when attempting to catch his wife in the film *The Shining* (US 1981).

Comte Maurice de MACMAHON French general (1808–93)

5 *J'y suis et j'y reste* [Here I am, and here I stay].

Said at the taking of the Malakoff fortress during the Crimean War (8 September 1855). In his home at the Château de Sully is an engraving of Macmahon standing on the parapet of a Russian gun position at Sebastopol, which has just been captured after heavy opposition. An English sailor, approaching the general to warn him that the position is mined, receives the reply: '*Libre à vous porter où vous voulez, quant à moi, j'y suis et j'y reste* [Up to you to go where you like, as for me, here I am and here I stay].'

Harold MACMILLAN (later 1st Earl of Stockton) English Conservative Prime Minister (1894–1986)

6 *The Middle Way.*

Title of book (1938), setting out the arguments for a middle course in politics, that is to say, one occupying 'the middle ground' between extremes. Not unexpectedly, the phrase had been used before – indeed, it dates back to the 13th century. See also ADAMS 3:1. Winston Churchill ended an election address on 11 November 1922 by saying: 'What we require now is not a period of turmoil, but a period of stability and recuperation. Let us stand together and tread a sober middle way.' In the 16th century Elizabeth I's religious policy was described as a *via media*, shaping the Anglican Church as a synthesis of Roman Catholicism and Protestantism. The 'Middle Way' is also a tenet of Buddhism, advocating a course between self indulgence on the one hand and extreme asceticism on the other.

7 We ... are Greeks in this American empire ... We must run the Allied Forces HQ as the Greeks ran the operations of the Emperor Claudius.

Sometimes rendered as 'The British are the Greeks in the Roman Empire of the Americans.' In 1944, after French North Africa had become an American sphere of influence with Dwight Eisenhower as Supreme Allied Commander, Macmillan said this to Richard Crossman – quoted in *The Sunday Telegraph* (9 February 1964). In June 1995 a biographer of Churchill, John Charmley, made this rejoinder to Macmillan: 'Even a Balliol man should have recalled that the Greeks had been slaves.' In the same month, a writer in *The Daily Telegraph* said more soothingly: 'Macmillan's classical background meant that he had a sense of history, of proportion and of the vanity of human affairs. When he said that the future role of the British was to be the Greeks in the Americans' Roman Empire, this may have been fatuously defeatist, or it may have been plain realism. But at least it indicated that he tried to understand the present in relation to the past, and was capable of some long-term strategy.'

1 There ain't gonna be no war.

As Foreign Secretary to Prime Minister Eden, Macmillan attended a four-power summit conference at Geneva where the chief topic for discussion was German reunification. Nothing much was achieved, but the 'Geneva spirit' was optimistic and on his return to London Macmillan breezily said this to a press conference on 24 July 1955. The phrase is, without doubt, a direct quote from the Edwardian music-hall song, which was sung in a raucous cockney accent by a certain Mr Pélissier (1879–1913) in a show called *Pélissier's Follies*:

> There ain't going to be no waar
> So long as we've a king like Good King Edward.
> 'E won't 'ave it, 'cos 'e 'ates that sort of fing.
> Muvvers, don't worry,
> Not wiv a king like Good King Edward.
> Peace wiv honour is 'is motter [*snort*] –
> Gawd save the King!

The former diplomat Sir David Hunt confirmed (1988) that it was the Pélissier song that Macmillan had in mind. In fact, he (Hunt) had sung it to him on one occasion. Coincidentally, some time before December 1941, an American called Frankl *did* write a song called, precisely, 'There Ain't Gonna Be No War'.

2 A Foreign Secretary – and this applies also to a prospective Foreign Secretary – is always faced with this cruel dilemma. Nothing he can say can do very much good, and almost anything he may say may do a great deal of harm. Anything he says that is not obvious is dangerous; whatever is not trite is risky. He is forever poised between the cliché and the indiscretion.

Speech, House of Commons (27 July 1955). In *Newsweek* Magazine (30 April 1956) Macmillan was also quoted as having said that his life as Foreign Secretary was 'forever poised between a cliché and an indiscretion'. Compare RUNCIE 390:3.

3 Let's be frank about it. Most of our people have never had it so good. Go around the country, go to the industrial towns, go to the farms, and you'll see a state of prosperity such as we have never had in my lifetime – nor indeed ever in the history of this country. What is beginning to worry some of us is 'Is it too good to be true?' or perhaps I should say 'Is it too good to last?' For amidst all this prosperity, there is one problem that has troubled us, in one way or another, ever since the war. It is the problem of rising prices. Our constant concern is: Can prices be steadied while at the same time we maintain full employment in an expanding economy? Can we control inflation?

Speech at Bedford (20 July 1957). 'You've never had it so good' is a phrase that will forever be linked with Macmillan's name but, as will be clear from the above, his first use of the idea was in the context not of a boast but a warning.

Macmillan is said to have appropriated the phrase from Lord Robens (a former Labour minister who had rejected socialism and who had used the phrase in conversation with the Prime Minister not long before). Further back, as 'You Never Had It So Good', it had been a slogan used by the Democrats in the 1952 US presidential election. As early as 1946 *American Speech* (Vol. 21) was commenting on the phrase: 'This is a sardonic response to complaints about the Army; it is probably supposed to represent the attitude of a peculiarly offensive type of officer.'

In his memoirs Macmillan commented: 'For some reason it was not until several years later that this phrase was taken out of its context and turned into a serious charge against me, of being too materialistic and showing too little of a spiritual approach to life ... curiously enough these are the inevitable hazards to which all politicians are prone.'

Given the way the phrase came to dog him, it would have been surprising if it had ever been used as an official Tory party slogan. It was rejected – in so many words – for the 1959 general election by the Conservatives' publicity group, partly because it 'violated a basic advertising axiom that statements should be positive, not negative'. There was, however, an official poster that came very close with, 'You're Having It Good, Have It Better'.

4 I thought the best thing to do was to settle up these little local difficulties, and then turn to the wider vision of the Commonwealth.

Statement at London Airport, as Prime Minister, before leaving for a tour of the Commonwealth (7 January 1958). A characteristically airy reference to the fact that his entire Treasury team, including the Chancellor of the Exchequer, had resigned over a disagreement about budget estimates. So 'little local difficulties' became a phrase used to demonstrate a dismissive lack of concern.

1 Jaw-jaw is better than war-war.

On 30 January 1958 in Canberra, Australia, Macmillan consciously echoed a saying of Winston Churchill's – 'To jaw-jaw is always better than to war-war' – which Churchill had uttered at a White House luncheon in Washington DC on 26 June 1954.

2 What matters is that Mr Macmillan has let Mr [Selwyn] Lloyd know that at the Foreign Office, in these troubled times, enough is enough.

Report, *The Times* (1 June 1959). Having fed this view to the newspaper, Macmillan was prevented by the fuss it caused from firing Lloyd, and the Foreign Secretary remained in place for a further year. This helped popularize the phrase 'enough is enough' – a basic expression of exasperation often employed in political personality clashes – though usually without result. Compare *DAILY MIRROR* 161:3.

3 Exporting is fun.

A Macmillan slogan that misfired, though in this instance he never actually said it. The phrase was included in a 1960 address to businessmen, but when Macmillan came to read the passage he left out what was later considered to be a rather patronizing remark. The press, however, printed what was in the advance text of the speech as though he had actually said it.

Compare the earlier Labour slogan, 'We must export – or die', which arose out of a severe balance-of-payments problem under the Labour government in 1945–6.

4 The most striking of all the impressions I have formed since I left London a month ago is of the strength of this African national consciousness. In different places it may take different forms, but it is happening everywhere. The wind of change is blowing through this continent. Whether we like it or not, this growth of national consciousness is a political fact.

Speaking to both houses of the South African parliament on 3 February 1960, Macmillan gave his hosts a message they cannot have wanted to hear. The phrase 'wind of change' – though not, of course, original – was contributed to the speechwriting team by the diplomat (later Sir) David Hunt (1913–98). *OED2* acknowledges that the use of the phrase 'wind(s) of change' increased markedly after this speech. When Macmillan sought a title for one of his volumes of memoirs he plumped for the more common, plural usage – *Winds of Change*. Compare BALDWIN 51:1.

5 As usual, the Liberals offer a mixture of sound and original ideas. Unfortunately none of the sound ideas is original and none of the original ideas is sound.

Speech to London Conservatives (7 March 1961). Compare what is ascribed to Dr Samuel Johnson: 'Your manuscript is both good and original; but the part that is good is not original, and the part that is original is not good' – quoted in *The Treasury of Humorous Quotations*, eds Esar & Bentley (1951); it has also been loosely ascribed to Johnson's '*Letters 1777*'. If confirmed, this might be the first English example of a critical formula.

Next in time comes Richard Brinsley Sheridan (1751–1816), commenting on a minister's speech in the House of Commons: 'It contained a great deal both of what was new and what was true, but unfortunately what was new was not true and what was true was not new' – quoted in Hesketh Pearson, *Lives of the Wits* (1962).

Notes and Queries, 7th series, 4 and 6 (1887), looked into the question and suggested that in the 1830s a saying was abroad: 'Some things the lady's said are new, / And some things she has said are true; / But what are true, alas! they are not new, / And what are new, alas! they are not true.' It also suggested that Daniel Webster criticized the platform of the American Free Soil Party in 1848 with the words: 'What is valuable is not new, and what is new is not valuable.' Precisely this form is also ascribed to Lord Brougham in an 'Essay: The Work of Thomas Young' in *Edinburgh Review* (?1839). Lord Macaulay (1800–59) apparently said: 'There were gentlemen and there were seamen in the navy of Charles II. But the seamen were not gentlemen, and the gentlemen were not seamen.' Charles Darwin said of something in 1858: 'All that was new was false, and what was true was old.' Somewhat later, A.J. Balfour made a similarly structured remark, 'In that oration there were some things that were true, and some things that were trite: but what was true was trite, and what was not trite was not true' – quoted in Winston Churchill, *Great Contemporaries*, 'Arthur James Balfour' (1937).

Possibly the Johnson citation is misleading. He definitely said, 'I found that generally what was new was false' (as Boswell records for 26 March 1779), but there is no confirmation yet of his using the other, formulaic saying. In any case, *The Oxford Dictionary of English Proverbs* (1975) has an entry for 'What is new is not true and what is true is not new', suggesting that the formula is proverbial anyway. Its earliest citation is from the German author J.H. Voss (1751–1826) in the *Vossischer Musenalmanach* (1772 – actually this should be 1792): '*Auf mehrere Bücher. / Nach Lessing. / Dein redseliges Buch lehrt mancherlei Neues und Wahres, / Wäre das Wahre nur neu, wäre das Neue nur wahr!* [On several books. / After Lessing. / Your garrulous book teaches many things new and true, / If only the true were new, if only the new were true!]' Compare BALFOUR 52:1.

1 She didn't say yes, she didn't say no ...
The song 'She Didn't Say Yes' by Otto Harbach and Jerome Kern from the musical *The Cat and the Fiddle* (1931) was memorably quoted by Macmillan when Prime Minister in October 1962. Speaking to the Conservative Party Conference at Llandudno he referred to the Labour Party's attitude to the government's attempts (from July 1961) to open negotiations for Britain's entry to the European Common Market: 'What did the socialists do? ... They solemnly asked Parliament not to approve or disapprove, but to "take note" of our decision. Perhaps some of the older ones among you [oh, wonderful Macmillanism!] will remember that popular song –

She didn't say yes, she didn't say no,
She didn't say stay, she didn't say go.
She wanted to climb, but dreaded to fall,
She bided her time and clung to the wall.'

Private Eye – perhaps inspired by a recent American record that had taken President Kennedy's inaugural speech and added a music track – put out a record of Macmillan 'singing' the song to a tinny 1960s backing. Very droll it was, too, and now sadly evocative of a bygone era.

2 Power? It's like a Dead Sea fruit; when you achieve it, there's nothing there.
Quoted in *Queen* Magazine (22 May 1963). Compare Thomas Moore, *Lalla Rookh* (1817): 'Like Dead Sea fruits, that tempt the eye, / But turn to ashes on the lips!' In *Brewer's Politics* (1995), Macmillan's saying is delightfully misquoted as, 'like a *seafront*; when you achieve it, there's nothing there.'

3 I do not live among young people fairly widely.
Speech, House of Commons (17 June 1963). Explaining why he accepted that John Profumo's statement that the letter to Christine Keeler beginning 'darling' was quite harmless. *Hansard*'s version is: 'I believe that that might be accepted – I do not live among young people much myself.'

4 Events, dear boy, events.
On being asked what gave him most problems as Prime Minister. Although widely known, a source for this comment has not been found. It is possible, of course, that the 'dear boy' has been grafted on to the remark in the re-telling, though I have heard an interview in which he does call the interviewer this. Macmillan did apparently use the phrase 'the opposition of events' to describe 'the force of punishing happenings unforeseen by any election manifesto', according to David Dilks, *The Office of Prime Minister in Twentieth*

Century Britain (1993). Professor Dilks told Peter Hennessy – for *The Hidden Wiring* (1995) – that this was a phrase 'of which he [Macmillan] was rather fond' at the time when Dilks was helping him with his memoirs.

5 There are three bodies no sensible man directly challenges: the Roman Catholic Church, the Brigade of Guards and the National Union of Mineworkers.
Quoted in *The Observer* (22 February 1981). Compare BALDWIN 51:5.

6 After a long life I have come to the conclusion that when all the establishment is united it is always wrong.
Speech, Carlton Club (October 1982). Compare: 'When a line of action is said to be supported "by all responsible men" it is nearly always dangerous or foolish' – in his book *The Past Masters* (1975).

7 [The sale of assets is common with individuals and the state when they run into financial difficulties ...] First of all the Georgian silver goes, and then all that nice furniture that used to be in the saloon. Then the Canalettos go.
Summarized as 'selling off the family silver', meaning 'to dispose of valuable assets which, once gone, cannot be retrieved', this allusion was memorably used in a speech to the Tory Reform Group by Macmillan, by then Earl of Stockton, on 8 November 1985. He was questioning the government's policy of privatizing profitable nationalized industries.

8 Memorial services are the cocktail parties of the geriatric set.
Quoted in Alastair Horne, *Macmillan 1957–1986* (1989). In Ruth Dudley Edwards, *Harold Macmillan: a life in pictures* (1983), Macmillan (who is purported to have written the picture captions) states: 'I rather agree with Ralph Richardson [the actor] that Memorial Services are the "cocktail parties of the geriatric set".' So that is where he got it from.

Louis MacNEICE British poet (1907–63)

9 Or will one's wife also belong to that country
And can one never find the perfect stranger?
'Eclogue Between the Motherless' (1937). Hence, *The Perfect Stranger*, title of a volume of autobiography by P.J. Kavanagh (1966), dealing in part with the death of his young wife. This is its epigraph. The phrase 'perfect stranger' – as in 'I'm a perfect stranger to this part of the world' (meaning 'complete, entire' rather than 'possessing perfection') had

already been found in Vanbrugh, *The False Friend* (1699). From Wilkie Collins, *No Name*, Pt 2, Chap. 1 (1862–3): "'You are mistaken," she said quietly. "You are a perfect stranger to me.'"

Maurice MAETERLINCK Belgian poet and playwright (1862–1949)

1 The living are just the dead on holiday.

Quoted in *The Treasury of Humorous Quotations*, eds Esar & Bentley (1951). Unverified. In his play *L'Oiseau bleu* (1908) there is the line, 'There are no dead.' In a 1980 episode of BBC TV's *Dr Who* ('Destiny of the Daleks'), scripted by Terry Nation, there is the question: 'Who was it that said the living are the dead on holiday?'

(Sir) John MAFFEY (later 1st Baron Rugby) British diplomat (1877–1969)

2 This temperamental country [Ireland] needs quiet treatment and a patient, consistent policy. But how are you to control Ministerial incursions into your china shop? Phrases make history here.

As British Ambassador in Dublin, in a letter to the Dominions Office in London (21 May 1945), quoted in Robert Fisk, *In Time of War* (1985). Hence, the book *Phrases Make History Here*, subtitled *A Century of Political Quotations on Ireland 1886–1987*, by Conor O'Clery (1986). Maffey's official title was UK Representative to Eire, which he was from 1939 to 1949. John Betjeman, the poet, was his press attaché (1941–3).

John Gillespie MAGEE Anglo-American air force pilot and poet (1922–41)

3 Oh! I have slipped the surly bonds of Earth,
   And danced the skies on laughter-silvered
       wings;
   ... And, while with silent lifting mind I've trod
   The high untrespassed sanctity of space,
   Put out my hand, and touched the face of God.

From 'High Flight', a sonnet written by Magee, a pilot with the Royal Canadian Air Force in the Second World War. He came to Britain, flew in a Spitfire squadron, and was killed at the age of 19 on 11 December 1941 during a training flight from the airfield near Scopwick, Lincolnshire (where the first and last lines appear on his grave). Magee had been born in Shanghai of an American father and an English mother, both missionaries. He was educated at Rugby and at a school in Connecticut. The sonnet was written on the back of a letter to his parents, in which he stated, 'I am enclosing a verse I wrote the other day. It started at 30,000

feet, and was finished soon after I landed.' The parents were living in Washington DC at the time of his death and, according to *Respectfully Quoted* (1989), the poem came to the attention of the Librarian of Congress, the poet Archibald MacLeish, who acclaimed Magee as the first poet of the war.

'High Flight' was published in 1943 in a volume called *More Poems from the Forces* (which was 'Dedicated to the USSR'). Copies of the poem – sometimes referred to as 'the pilot's creed' – were widely distributed, and plaques bearing it were sent to all RCAF airfields and training stations. It became very much the pilot's poem the world over. The lines became even more famous when President Reagan quoted them on 28 January 1986 in his TV broadcast to the nation on the day of the space shuttle *Challenger* disaster.

Two footnotes: in his lyrics for the English version of the musical *Les Misérables* (1985), Herbert Kretzmer blended Magee's words with something from Evelyn Waugh's *Brideshead Revisited* ('to know and love another human being is the root of all wisdom') to produce the line: 'To love another person is to see the face of God.' Magee's original words are curiously reminiscent of Oscar Wilde's lines prefixed to his *Poems* (Paris edition, 1903):

> Surely there was a time I might have trod
> The sunlit heights, and from life's dissonance
> Struck one clear chord to reach the ears of God.

René MAGRITTE Belgian Surrealist painter (1898–1967)

4 *Ceci n'est pas une pipe* [This is not a pipe].

Written beneath the profile of a tobacco pipe in an oil painting called '*La trahison des images* [The treachery of images]' (1929). Magritte's interest was in words as images, and in achieving a realization in paint of his belief that 'everything tends to suggest that there is little connection between an object and what represents it'. Magritte also painted *Ceci est un morceau de fromage*, in which a painting of a piece of cheese is shown inside a glass cheese dome.

William H. MAGUIRE American sailor (1890–1953)

5 Praise the Lord and pass the ammunition!

Said in 1941, and subsequently used as the title of a song by Frank Loesser (1942). The authorship of this saying is disputed. It may have been said by an American naval chaplain during the Japanese attack on Pearl Harbor. Lieutenant Howell M. Forgy (1908–83) is one candidate. He was on board the US cruiser *New Orleans* on 7 December 1941 and encouraged those around him to keep up the anti-aircraft barrage when under attack. His claim is supported by a report in *The New York Times* (1 November 1942).

Another name mentioned is that of Captain W.H. Maguire.

At first Captain Maguire did not recall having used the words, but a year later said he might have done. *Bartlett* favours Maguire and makes no mention of Forgy. Either way, the expression may actually date from the time of the American Civil War.

(Sir) John MAJOR British Conservative Prime Minister (1943–)

1 The harsh truth is that if the policy isn't hurting it isn't working. I know there is a difficult period ahead but the important thing is that we cannot and must not fudge the determination to stop inflation in its tracks.

Major had to deliver this speech at Northampton (27 October 1989) on suddenly becoming Chancellor of the Exchequer following the resignation of Nigel Lawson. It had probably been written for his predecessor. In 1996 the Conservative Party tried to capitalize on this 'harsh truth' by producing poster advertisements declaring, 'YES, IT HURTS. YES, IT WORKS.'

The phrase is much older, however. Adlai Stevenson said in his speech accepting the Democratic presidential nomination (26 July 1952): 'Let's talk sense to the American people. Let's tell them the truth, that there are no gains without pains.' 'No pain(s), no gain(s)' is, indeed, a proverb (it dates back at least to 1577), and is perhaps more commonly known in the US. In the form 'no pain, no gain' it was used by Jane Fonda in her fitness workouts (by 1984).

2 Well – who would have thought it?

What Major is alleged to have said when opening his first Cabinet meeting. Invariably, bathos is the hallmark of Major's sayings – as in, 'Gentlemen, I think we had better start again, somewhere else', which is what he said after an IRA mortar-bomb attack on Downing Street had caused a large explosion during a Cabinet meeting on 2 February 1991. For a while, he also had a verbal mannerism, 'Oh, yes ... oh, yes.'

3 Fifty years on from now, Britain will still be the country of long shadows on county [cricket] grounds, warm beer, invincible green suburbs, dog lovers and – as George Orwell said – old maids bicycling to Holy Communion through the morning mist.

In a speech on 22 April 1993 to the Conservative Group for Europe, Major sought to show that, though the future of Britain lay within Europe, the character of Britain would survive 'unamendable in all essentials'. As his speechwriter acknowledged (for one finds it hard to think that Major

spotted it himself), one of Major's lyrical certainties was derived from George Orwell's essay, 'The Lion and the Unicorn: Socialism and the English Genius: Part 1: England Your England', published in *Horizon* (December 1940). The socialist Orwell was, rather, talking about specifically *English* civilization – actually 'old maids *biking* to Holy Communion through the mists of the autumn morning' – which was 'somehow bound up with solid breakfasts and gloomy Sundays, smoky towns and winding roads, green fields and red pillar-boxes'. Orwell also talked rather of the beer being bitterer, the grass greener, and mentioned 'the queues outside the Labour Exchanges' which, for some reason, Major forbore to do.

4 The message from this Conference is clear and simple. We must go back to basics ... The Conservative Party will lead the country back to those basics, right across the board: sound money; free trade; traditional teaching; respect for the family and the law.

A political cliché now, but the alliterative phrase (sometimes 'back to *the* basics') may first have surfaced in the US, where in the mid-1970s it was the slogan of a movement in education advocating priority to the teaching of the fundamentals of reading, writing and arithmetic. On 8 October 1993, however, Major launched it as a slogan in a speech to the Conservative Party Conference. This text has been checked against a recording of the speech. A number of government scandals in the ensuing months exposed the slogan as hard to interpret or, at worst, suggested a going back to 'the bad old days'.

5 The Conservative Party must make its choice. Every leader is leader only with the support of his party. That is true of me as well. That is why I am no longer prepared to tolerate the present situation. In short, it is time to put up or shut up.

Statement (22 June 1995). Resigning leadership of the Conservative Party, while Prime Minister, in order to stand for re-election. In other words: 'Either make good your argument or stop talking about it.' In America, this translates as 'put up your money (as though for a bet)' but in Britain, 'put up your fists (as though for a fight)'. Both uses probably date from the 19th century.

See also GLADSTONE 214:5.

Stéphane MALLARMÉ French poet (1842–98)

6 *L'Après-midi d'un faune* [The afternoon of a fawn]. Title of poem (begun in 1865 and published in 1876). Debussy gave the title *Prélude à l'après-midi d'un faune* to

his 1894 orchestral work inspired by Mallarmé's poem. The reason Debussy called it a *Prélude* was because he originally envisaged it as the first part of a larger work, which would also include an *Interlude* and a *Paraphrase finale*, but he never got round to writing them.

George Leigh MALLORY English mountaineer (1886–1924)

1   Because it's there.

Mallory disappeared in 1924 on his last attempt to scale Mount Everest. The previous year, during a lecture tour of the US, he had frequently been asked why he wanted to achieve this goal. On one such occasion he replied: 'Because it's there.'

In 1911, at Cambridge, A.C. Benson had urged Mallory to read Carlyle's life of John Sterling – a book that achieved high quality simply 'by being *there*'. Perhaps that is how the construction entered Mallory's mind. On the other hand, Tom Holzel and Audrey Salkeld in *The Mystery of Mallory and Irvine* (1986) suggest that 'the four most famous words in mountaineering' may have been invented for the climber by a reporter named Benson in *The New York Times* (18 March 1923). A report in *The Observer* (2 November 1986) noted that Howard Somervell, one of Mallory's climbing colleagues on the 1924 expedition, declared 40 years later that the 'much-quoted remark' had always given him a 'shiver down the spine – it doesn't smell of George Mallory one bit'. Mallory's niece, Mrs B.M. Newton Dunn, claimed in a letter to *The Daily Telegraph* (11 November 1986) that the mountaineer had once given the reply to his sister (Mrs Newton Dunn's mother) 'because a silly question deserves a silly answer'.

The saying has become a catchphrase in situations where the speaker wishes to dismiss an impossible question about motives and also to express his acceptance of a challenge that is in some way daunting or maybe foolish. In September 1962 President Kennedy said: 'We choose to go to the moon in this decade, and do the other things, not because they are easy but because they are hard; because that goal will serve to organize and measure the best of our energies and skills ... Many years ago the great British explorer George Mallory, who was to die on Mount Everest, was asked why did he want to climb it, and he said, "Because it is there." Well, space is there, and ... the moon and the planets are there, and new hopes for knowledge and peace are there.'

There have been many variations (and misattributions). Sir Edmund Hillary repeated it regarding his own attempt on Everest in 1953. It was quoted in John Hunt, *The Ascent of Everest* (1953), which may have contributed to the remark's modern popularity.

(Sir) Thomas MALORY English writer (died 1471)

2   *Hic jacet Arthurus, rex quondam rexque futurus* [Here lies Arthur, the once and future king].

This is what, according to Malory in *Le Morte d'Arthur* (1469–70), was written on the tombstone of the legendary king. Hence, the title of T.H. White's Arthurian tetralogy, *The Once and Future King* (1958). If a King Arthur did exist (possibly in the 6th century AD), there is a notice in the ruins of Glastonbury Abbey, Somerset, which claims to mark the site of his tomb – but no inscription is available.

Nelson MANDELA South African nationalist leader and President (1918–)

3   I have made my choice. I will not leave South Africa, nor will I surrender. Only through hardship, sacrifice and militant action can freedom be won. The struggle is my life. I will continue fighting for freedom until the end of my days.

'Letter from the underground' (released to South African newspapers, 26 June 1961). The phrase 'The struggle is my life' is quoted beneath the bronze bust installed when Mandela was still a prisoner, outside the Royal Festival Hall, London (1985).

Joseph L. MANKIEWICZ American film producer and writer (1909–93)

4   My native habitat is the theatre. I toil not, neither do I spin. I am a critic and a commentator. I am essential to the theatre – as ants to a picnic, as the boll weevil to a cotton field.

Spoken by George Sanders as the critic Addison de Witt in the film *All About Eve* (1950). The allusion in the second sentence is to the BIBLE 80:5.

William MANN British music critic (1924–89)

5   The outstanding English composers of 1963 must seem to have been John Lennon and Paul McCartney ... the slow sad song about 'That Boy' ... is expressively unusual for its lugubrious music, but harmonically it is one of their most interesting, with its chains of pandiatonic clusters ... so natural is the Aeolian cadence at the end of 'Not a Second Time' (the chord progression which ends Mahler's *Song of the Earth*) ... autocratic but not by any means ungrammatical attitude to tonality ... the quasi-instrumental vocal duetting ... the melismas with altered vowels ...

Reviewing the music of The Beatles in *The Times* (27 December 1963). Not to be confused with BUCKLE 107:2 or PALMER 351:5.

Olivia MANNING English novelist (1908–80)

1 *Fortunes of War.*
Manning's Balkan Trilogy and Levant Trilogy form a single narrative with this overall title, which was also used for the BBC TV adaptation (1985) of the six. One of the individual titles is *The Great Fortune* (1960). The earliest citation in *OED2* for the phrase 'fortunes of war' is 1880, but it had long been known in the singular: in Caxton's *Aesop* (1484); 'After uncertain fortune of war, on both sides' was written by John Selden in 1612; Charles Dickens, *Sketches by Boz*, Chap. 12 (1833–6) has this cry from a street game: 'All the fortin of war! this time I vin, next time you vin'; a rhyme from the time of the Crimean War goes: 'The fortunes of war I tell you plain / Are a wooden leg, or a golden chain'; the war memorial at the cemetery of El Alamein (following the battle of 1942) is dedicated 'to whom the fortune of war denied a known and honoured grave'.

Neville and June Braybrooke commented on Manning's use of the phrase in *Olivia Manning: a Life* (2004), Chap. 13: 'Olivia managed to get a job as a press attaché to the American Embassy [in Cairo, 1941] ... Looking at the map one day, an American officer said to her, "Fortunes of war are like a see-saw, ma'am." She was to remember this when she began her Levant Trilogy in 1976.' Chap. 26 – 'Her overall title for these six books was *Fortunes of War* – a phrase used in the final volume of the Balkan Trilogy and again twice in the Levant Trilogy.'

The MAN OF LA MANCHA American musical play (1965; film 1972). Lyrics by Joe Darion, music by Mitch Leigh, based on a play by Dale Wasserman.

2 To dream the impossible dream,
To fight the unbeatable foe,
To bear with unbearable sorrow,
To run where the brave dare not go.
Song, 'The Impossible Dream'. See also NIXON 343:6.

MAO ZEDONG (Mao Tse-tung) Chinese revolutionary and Communist leader (1893–1976)

3 Every Communist must grasp the truth, Political power grows out of the barrel of a gun.
In *Quotations from Chairman Mao Tse-tung* (1966) – dated 6 November 1938. The 'Little Red Book' of the Great Helmsman's 'thoughts' was issued during the ideological purge

known as the Cultural Revolution (1966–9). It seems likely to have had the widest circulation of any book of quotations ever produced – and certainly of one devoted to a single author. Back in 1960, Lin Piao, Minister of Defence, had produced a set of sayings, which Mao revised. Next Lin started printing quotations from Mao in the *Liberation Army Daily*. In 1964 a pocket edition was produced for soldiers to carry about with them in their packs, and this formed the basis of the first regular edition of the *Quotations* published on 1 August 1965. While not pithy or particularly well expressed, the quotations echoed themes that Mao had promoted over a much longer period. As far as one can tell, Mao thought his own 'thoughts' and did not need to have his writings and speeches ghosted. After all, in his younger days he had been a prolific writer on public affairs, and wrote poetry almost all his life. To him, therefore, can be ascribed many of the slogans and catchwords of Chinese Communism.

4 All reactionaries are paper tigers. In appearance, the reactionaries are terrifying, but in reality they are not powerful.
In the same book, from an interview with an American journalist (1946). A 'paper tiger' is a person who appears outwardly strong but is, in fact, weak. *Paper Tiger* was also the title of a film (UK 1975) about a coward (David Niven) who pretended to be otherwise until he is finally put to the test. In *Kai Lung Unrolls His Mat* (1928), Ernest Bramah writes: 'Even a paper leopard can put a hornless sheep to flight', and as early as 1900 Bramah uses the precise expression in *The Wallet of Kai Lung*: 'If it is the wish of this illustriously endowed gathering that this exceedingly illiterate paper tiger should occupy their august moments with a description of ... Chee Chou ...' It should be stressed that Bramah was a lover of chinoiserie rather than an expert Sinologist, and must undoubtedly have come across the phrase in English or some other western language rather than in Chinese.

5 'He who is not afraid of death by a thousand cuts dares to unhorse the emperor' – this is the indomitable spirit needed in our struggle to build socialism and communism.
In the same book, though Mao appears to be using a proverbial saying. An eastern source for the phrase may be hinted at in what Jaffar the villainous magician (Conrad Veidt) says in the 1940 film version of *The Thief of Baghdad*: 'In the morning they die the death of a thousand cuts.' The film comedy *Carry On Up the Khyber* (1968) has the phrase, too. Now, the phrase 'death of/by a thousand cuts' is used to mean 'the destruction of something by the cumulative effect of snipping rather than by one big blow'.

1 I hope that everybody will express his opinions openly. It's no crime to talk, and nobody will be punished for it. We must let a hundred flowers bloom and a hundred schools of thought contend and see which flowers are the best and which school of thought is best expressed, and we shall applaud the best blooms and the best thoughts.

Mao's statement at a meeting of officials and party leaders in May 1956 invited intellectual criticism of the regime and outlined an experiment allowing freedom of dissent. A period of self-criticism was duly launched on 27 February 1957 in a major speech to an audience of 1800 influential Chinese. It had the title 'On the Correct Handling of Contradictions Among the People', but Mao found that his proposal did not have the support of the whole party and the press. When the official text was published on 19 June in the *People's Daily*, the horticultural image was given a sinister and revealing twist: 'Only by letting poisonous weeds show themselves above ground can they be uprooted.'

The campaign ran from 1 May, but so great was the amount of criticism stirred up that it was ended by 7 June and reprisals taken against some of those who had spoken out. These people were attacked as bourgeois rightists. Leaders of student riots were executed. Understandably, therefore, the passage about 'flowers blooming' is not included in the 'Little Red Book' of *Quotations from Chairman Mao Tse-tung* (1966).

2 People of the world, unite and defeat the US aggressors and all their running dogs!

In a 'Statement Supporting the People of the Congo Against US Aggression' (28 November 1964), Mao provided a vivid weapon in the coinage 'running dogs', for use against the 'lackeys' of the US during the Vietnam War. Edgar Snow had earlier recorded him using the term in 1937.

3 Don't be a gang of four.

Apparently, on one occasion, Mao gave this warning to Jiang Qing, his unscrupulous wife, and her colleagues. They became labelled as the Gang of Four in the mid-1970s when they were tried and given death sentences for treason and other crimes (later commuted to life imprisonment). The other three members were Zhang Chunqiao, a political organizer in the Cultural Revolution; Wang Hogwen, a youthful activist; and Yao Wenyuan, a journalist.

MARIE-ANTOINETTE Queen of France (1755–93)

4 *Qu'ils mangent de la brioche* [Let them eat cake].

This remark is commonly ascribed to Marie-Antoinette, an Austrian disliked by the French people, after she had arrived in France to marry King Louis XVI in 1770. More specifically she is supposed to have said it during the riots caused by a bread shortage in Paris (October 1789), though no evidence exists that she did. In the form, '*Qu'ils mangent de la brioche*', the saying refers to *brioche*, a type of sponge cake. *Brewer* (1923) has it that the Duchesse de Polignac was the culprit, exclaiming to Marie-Antoinette, 'How is it that these silly people are so clamorous for *bread*, when they can buy some nice brioches for a few sous?' And, 'It is said that our own Princess Charlotte avowed "that she would for her part *rather eat beef than starve*," and wondered that the people should be so obstinate as to insist upon having bread when it was so scarce.'

The saying is to be found in Bk 6 of Rousseau's *Confessions*, published posthumously in 1781–8 but written during the 1760s. Rousseau's version, referring to an incident in Grenoble about 1740, goes: 'At length I recollected the thoughtless saying of a great princess who, on being informed that the country people had no bread, replied, "Let them eat cake."' *ODQ* (1979) notes that Louis XVIII in his *Relation d'un Voyage à Bruxelles et à Coblentz en 1791* (published 1823) attributes to Marie-Thérèse (1638–83), wife of Louis XIV, 'Why don't they eat pastry? [*Que ne mangent-ils de la croûte de pâté?*]'

Burnam (1975) adds that Alphonse Karr, writing in 1843, recorded that a Duchess of Tuscany had said it in 1760 or before. Later, it was circulated to discredit Marie-Antoinette. Similar remarks are said to date back to the 13th century, so if Marie-Antoinette did ever say it, she was quoting.

Leo MARKS English cryptographer, screenwriter and bookseller (1920–2000)

5 The life that I have is all that I have,
And the life that I have is yours.
The love that I have of the life that I have
Is yours and yours and yours.

A sleep I shall have
A rest I shall have,
Yet death will be but a pause,
For the peace of my years in the long green grass
Will be yours and yours and yours.

'Code Poem for the French Resistance' (1941). The poem was of the type written to be used as the basis for codes used by Special Operations Executive agents in the Second World War. It could also be used as an *aide-mémoire* for these codes, and Marks, who was in charge of agents' cyphers, considered it better for security if the poems were original. He composed dozens of them. This one was specifically written for use by Violette Szabo, the British wartime agent, before she was dropped into occupied France in 1944. She was eventually captured, tortured and executed by the Gestapo. Hence, its use in the biographical film *Carve Her Name With Pride* (1958). In *Between Silk and Cyanide* (1998), Marks revealed that the poem had originally been written for his fiancée, who died in a plane crash. On learning of this on Christmas Eve in 1943, he went up on the roof of the buildings where he worked and 'looking up at God's pavement for signs of new pedestrians, I transmitted a message to her which I'd failed to deliver when I had the chance'. Marks was the son of the owner of Marks & Co., the booksellers featured in Helene Hanff's book *84, Charing Cross Road* (1971).

1 A twisted nerve, a ganglion gone awry
Predestinates the sinner and the saint.

Epigraph to film *Twisted Nerve* (UK 1968), for which Marks wrote the script. This was a thriller, controversial at the time of its release because it implied a link between Down's Syndrome and psychosis. It starred Hayley Mills and was directed by Roy Boulting (more usually known for comedies), who also co-wrote the screenplay with Marks. Attempts have been made to trace this quotation to another source but, although Marks's authorship is unconfirmed, I feel confident that it is by him.

Sarah Duchess of MARLBOROUGH English wife of the 1st Duke (1660–1744)

2 His Grace returned from the wars today and pleasured me twice in his top-boots.

ODQ (1979) had 'The Duke returned from the wars today and did pleasure me in his top-boots', acknowledging 'oral trad. Attr. in various forms'. When and where the remark first appeared in print is impossible to say. One source is I. Butler, *Rule of Three* (1967). Another is James Agate, *Ego 4* (1940) – for 28 July 1938 – who, talking of pageants, writes: 'How can yonder stout party hope to be Sarah, Duchess of Marlborough – "His Grace returned from the wars this morning and pleasured me twice in his top-boots" – when we know her to be the vicar's sister and quite unpleasurable?'

Christopher MARLOWE English playwright (1564–93)

3 Is it not passing brave to be a king,
And ride in triumph through Persepolis?

Tamburlaine the Great, Pt 1, Act 2, Sc 5 (?1587). Tamburlaine speaking. Some texts prefer 'passing fair'. These lines were appropriated by Pistol in Laurence Olivier's film of Shakespeare's *Henry V* (UK 1944). He speaks them on leaving the Boar's Head tavern following the similarly interpolated death of Falstaff. In no sense could Pistol have been 'quot-

ing' Marlowe's mighty line because, of course, the events of *Henry V* pre-date the Elizabethan playwright – as also applies to the following:

4 Holla, ye pampered jades of Asia!
What, can ye draw but twenty miles a day ... ?

In the same play, Pt 2, Act 4, Sc. 3. Misquoted by Pistol in *Henry IV, Part 2*, II.iv.161 (1597) – see SHAKESPEARE 408:8.

5 Thus methinks should men of judgement frame
Their means of traffic from the vulgar trade,
And, as their wealth increaseth, so enclose
Infinite riches in a little room.

The Jew of Malta, Act 1, Sc. 1 (?1592). 'The OED database is one of the wonders of the modern world – to paraphrase Christopher Marlowe, "infinite riches in a little ROM"' – Erich Segal in *The Times Literary Supplement* (1992). See also SHAKESPEARE 401:9.

6 Fornication? But that was in another country: and besides, the wench is dead.

In the same play, Act 4, Sc. 1. Barabas to Barnadine. Hence, *The Wench Is Dead*, title of a crime novel (1989) by Colin Dexter. This phrase is also used as the epigraph of T.S. Eliot's 'Portrait of a Lady' (1917). John Bayley has said that his novel *In Another Country* (1954) was *not* consciously taken from this quotation. See also SPRING-RICE 440:5.

7 Was this the face that launched a thousand ships,
And burnt the topless towers of Ilium?
Sweet Helen, make me immortal with a kiss!
Her lips suck forth my soul: see where it flies.
Come, Helen, come, give me my soul again.
Here will I dwell, for heaven is in those lips,
And all is dross that is not Helena.

Doctor Faustus, Act 5, Sc. 1 (?1594)– referring to Helen of Troy. Marlowe's mighty line had almost appeared in his *Tamburlaine the Great*, Pt 2, Act 2, Sc. 4 (1587): 'Helen, whose beauty ... / Drew a thousand ships to Tenedos.' Accordingly, Shakespeare must have been alluding to Marlowe when in *Troilus and Cressida*, II.ii.82 (?1601) he wrote of Helen: 'Why she is a pearl / Whose price hath launch'd above a thousand ships.' He also alludes to it in *All's Well That Ends Well* (1603).

The consistent feature of these mentions is the figure of a 'thousand', which was a round number probably derived from the accounts of Ovid and Virgil. *Burnam* (1975) quotes from Lucian's *Dialogues of the Dead*: 'This skull is Helen ... Was it then for this that the thousand ships were manned from all Greece?'

Much alluded to and played upon. Chips Channon records (23 April 1953) in the House of Commons: '[Aneurin] Bevan looked at poor, plain Florence Horsburgh [Independent MP for the Combined English Universities] and hailed her with the words "That's the face that sank a thousand scholarships."'

'Make me immortal with a kiss!' had also made an earlier appearance – in Marlowe's *Dido, Queen of Carthage*, Act 4, Sc. 4 (1594), in which Dido says of Aeneas: 'For in his looks I see eternity, / And he'll make me immortal with a kiss.'

1 **My men, like satyrs grazing on the lawns,**
Shall with their goat-feet dance an antic hay.

Edward II, Act 1, Sc 1 (1593). Gaveston speaking. Antic hay = a grotesque country dance. Hence, the title of Aldous Huxley's novel *Antic Hay* (1923).

2 **Whoever lov'd that lov'd not at first sight?**

A 'saw' (saying) from Marlowe's poem *Hero and Leander*, which was published in 1598, though probably written in 1593, the year of his death. Phebe, the shepherdess in Shakespeare's *As You Like It* (1598), quotes the line (III.v.82).

3 *Quod me nutrit me destruit* [That which nourishes me, destroys me].

This motto appears in capital letters at the top left-hand corner of a portrait of a young man that was rescued from builders' rubbish at Corpus Christi College, Cambridge, in the 1950s. On the basis that lettering next to the motto describes him as being aged 21 in 1585, the man is thought to be Christopher Marlowe, the future playwright, who obtained his BA at the college in that year and at that age. The Latin words have not been found in classical texts but bear a resemblance to some lines by Shakespeare (written a few years later): 'Consum'd with that which it was nourish'd by' – Sonnet 73 – and 'A burning torch that's turned upside down; / The word, *Qui me alit, me extinguit* [Who feeds me extinguishes me]' – *Pericles*, II.ii.33 (1609). A.D. Wraight wrote in 1965 that, if the portrait is of Marlowe, then the motto refers to his poetic muse 'which both inspired and nourished him, and yet consumed him with its fiery genius'.

Frederick MARRYAT English novelist (1792–1848)

4 **We always took care of number one.**

Scenes and Adventures in the Life of Frank Mildmay (1829). That is, we always gave ourselves priority, we were self-centred. An early appearance of this phrase. Compare: 'Whenever a person proclaims to you "In worldly matters I'm a child" ... you have got that person's number and it's Number One' – Charles Dickens, *Bleak House*, Chap. 57 (1853).

5 **If you please, ma'am, it was a very little one.**

Of an illegitimate baby. *Mr Midshipman Easy*, Chap. 3 (1836). Although often given as the source of this limp excuse, it is not. For example, in a letter of 9 March 1811 to William Godwin, William Wordsworth wrote: 'You remember the story of the poor Girl who being reproached with having brought forth an illegitimate Child said it was true, but added that it was a very little one: insinuating thereby that her offence was small in proportion. But the plea does not hold good.' What a characteristic it is of the humourless to explain the joke, though this does not apply, of course, to Mark Twain who (later) merely put, 'The girl who was rebuked for having borne an illegitimate child excused herself by saying, "But it is such a little one"' – in *Europe and Elsewhere*, ed. James Brander (1923). This pales besides the version of the story that Frank Muir found for *The Oxford Book of Humorous Prose* in *Gratiae Ludentes* – of which the date is 1638 ...

Arthur MARSHALL English writer and entertainer (1910–89)

6 **It's all part of life's rich pageant.**

The origin of this happy phrase – sometimes 'pattern' or 'tapestry' is preferred to 'pageant' – was the subject of an inquiry by Michael Watts of the *Sunday Express* in 1982. The earliest he came up with was from a record called 'The Games Mistress', written and performed by Marshall in about 1935. The monologue concludes: 'Oh My! Bertha's got a bang on the boko. Keep a stiff upper lip, Bertha dear. What, knocked a tooth out? Never mind, dear – laugh it off, laugh it off. It's all part of life's rich pageant.' Consequently, Marshall called his autobiography, *Life's Rich Pageant* (1984), but it seems a touch unlikely that he really originated the phrase. In 1831, Thomas Carlyle had talked of 'the fair tapestry of human life'.

Thomas R. MARSHALL American Democratic Vice-President (1854–1925)

7 **What this country needs is a really good five-cent cigar.**

Said to John Crockett, the chief clerk of the Senate, during a tedious debate in 1917 and quoted in the *New York Tribune* (4 January 1920). Another version is that it was said to Henry M. Rose, assistant Secretary of State. The remark is mentioned in a caption in *Recollections of Thomas R. Marshall* (1925). At about that time, 'Owls' cigars cost six cents and 'White Owls', seven cents.

John MARSTON English poet and playwright (1576–1634)

1 'My kingdom for a horse' – look thee I speak play scraps.

From his play *What You Will* (1607) – a clear example of quotation by a contemporary of Shakespeare. Marston's play is thought to have appeared in 1601 and Shakespeare's *Richard III* in 1591. ('What You Will' is also, of course, the subtitle of Shakespeare's *Twelfth Night* (1600).) See SHAKESPEARE 420:6.

MARTIAL Spanish-born Latin epigrammatist (AD?40–?104)

2 *Rus in urbe* [Country in the town].

Epigrammata, Bk 12, No. 57. Remark applied, for example, to a garden which provides rustic simplicity within the sophistication of the town. In May 1969 I visited a friend who had a cottage in the country near Bradford-on-Avon – but it wasn't a very rustic place. Indeed, it had almost a suburban or even an urban aspect to it. And so I pronounced it '*urbs in rure*'. Subsequently, I have found that exactly the same joke was a regular feature in *Punch* at the turn of the last century. It appeared, for example, on 30 November 1895, 3 July 1901 and 28 September 1904.

Andrew MARVELL English poet and politician (1621–78)

3 He nothing common did, or mean
Upon that memorable scene.

On the execution of Charles I. 'An Horatian Ode upon Cromwell's Return from Ireland' (written 1650). Quoted by Winston Churchill concerning Edward VIII's conduct at the Abdication in 1936 (also in his 'Finest Hour' speech, House of Commons, 18 June 1940).

4 Had we but world enough, and time,
This coyness, lady, were no crime.

'To His Coy Mistress' (1681). Hence, *World Enough and Time* (1950), title of a novel by Robert Penn Warren.

5 But at my back I always hear
Time's wingèd chariot hurrying near:
And yonder all before us lie
Deserts of vast eternity.

In the same poem. Compare LINKLATER 290:4.

6 Then worms shall try
That long preserved virginity:
And your quaint honour turn to dust;
And into ashes all my lust.
The grave's a fine and private place,

But none, I think, do there embrace.

In the same poem. Hence, *A Fine and Private Place*, title of a collection of epitaphs (1977) by Joan Bakewell and John Drummond, and of a novel (1982) by John Simpson.

7 O let our voice his praise exalt,
Till it arrive at Heaven's vault:
Which thence (perhaps) rebounding, may
Echo beyond the Mexique Bay.

'Bermudas' (?1653). Hence, *Beyond the Mexique Bay*, title of a travel book (1934) by Aldous Huxley.

See also JENKINS 255:8.

Groucho MARX American comedian (1895–1977)

8 Please accept my resignation. I don't care to belong to any club that will have me as a member.

Zeppo Marx recalled that this was about The Friars Club, a theatrical organization, for which his brother did not have much use. Hector Arce added that Groucho had some misgivings about the quality of the members – 'doubts verified a few years later when an infamous card-cheating scandal erupted there'. The wording varies, but the one here is taken from Arthur Sheekman's introduction to *The Groucho Letters* (1967). The actual letter unfortunately does not survive. In *Groucho and Me* (1959), he himself supplied the version: 'PLEASE ACCEPT MY RESIGNATION. I DON'T WANT TO BELONG TO ANY CLUB THAT WILL ACCEPT ME AS A MEMBER.' Woody Allen in *Annie Hall* (1977) appears to suggest that the joke first appeared in Freud and alludes to it in this passage: 'I would never want to belong to any club that would have someone like me for a member. That's the key joke of my adult life, in terms of my relationships with women.'

Compare this earlier use of the formula: in about 1836, Abraham Lincoln was introduced to a potential wife who was over-size, had a weather-beaten appearance and skin too full of fat, and wanted teeth (his descriptions). He convinced himself that someone with so little to recommend her could hardly refuse his proposal. He was therefore surprised and mortified when she did just that. In a letter to Mrs O.H. Browning (1 April 1838), Lincoln wrote: 'I have now come to the conclusion never again to think of marrying, and for a reason; I can never be satisfied with any one who would be block-headed enough to have me.'

Then again, compare this from the novel *Madder Music* (1977) by Peter de Vries: '[Dr. Josko is diagnosing Swirling, who believes he is Groucho Marx] "No, I mean I'm curious about something. Something generally attributed to you. Possibly your most famous wisecrack. Did you really say you wouldn't belong to a club that would have you for a member?" "Yeah, but I stole it from Henry James." "?" "In *The Princess Casamassima* the hero, what's his face, Hyacinth, tells somebody he'd never marry a girl who'd have him for a husband. Same gag."' Indeed, in Chapter 10 of that work (1886), Hyacinth [*sic*] Robinson says to Amanda Pynset (Pinnie), the dressmaker who looks after him: "Do you think I'd marry anyone who would marry me? The kind of girl who'd look at me is the kind of girl I'd never look at."'

1 My regiment leaves at dawn.

A line spoken by Groucho in the film *Monkey Business* (1931), preceded by the words, 'Come, Kapellmeister, let the violas throb!' Presumably this is a cliché of operetta, but no precise example has been traced. It was certainly the situation in many romantic tangles, even if the line itself was not actually spoken. The writer of the film, S.J. Perelman, was quoted in *Quest* Magazine (November 1978) as having said the following about Groucho: 'I saw him as a verbal clown with literary overtones. For instance, when he kissed Margaret Dumont, I'd have him say: "Goodbye, my little mountain flower. My regiment leaves at dawn." "What's this about a regiment?" he'd say [to me]. "It's a parody of *The Merry Widow*," I'd say. And he'd worry over the intricacies of the line like a medieval schoolman. "How can an audience laugh at a joke about something they never even heard of?" he would complain.' Perhaps the phrase does actually appear in a version of *The Merry Widow* libretto, or perhaps as a screen title from the silent film version (US 1925).

2 Be a lamp in the window for my wandering boy.

A line spoken by Groucho in the film *Horse Feathers* (1932). What is it? Probably a conflation of a cliché from a parlour songbook and a traditional custom. 'Where is my wand'ring boy tonight?' is the first line of a poem/song written and composed by the (presumably American) Revd R. Lowry in 1877. Under the title 'Where Is Your Boy Tonight?' it is No. 303 in Ira D. Sankey's *Sacred Songs and Solos*. No mention of a lamp in the window, however. The allusion is most probably to the silent film entitled *Where Is My Wandering Boy Tonight?* (US 1922) of which nothing is known to me, however. Putting a light or lamp in a window is a traditional sign of devotion to a cause, or of welcoming someone home. In a speech in Scotland on 29 November 1880 Lord Rosebery said of Gladstone: 'From his home in Wales to the Metropolis of Scotland there has been no village too small to afford a crowd to greet him – there has been no cottager so humble that could not find a light to put in his window as he passed.'

Groucho returned to the theme in *At the Circus* (1939). About to become a ringmaster, he is being helped by Chico into a tailcoat that he finds rather tight. 'You'd have to be a wizard to get into this coat,' he says. Chico comments: 'That's-a-right, it belonged to a wizard.' At this point, a pigeon flies out of the tail pocket. Chico: 'It's a homing pigeon.' And Groucho says: 'Then there'll always be a candle burning in my pocket for my wandering pigeon.' He had also said, 'Keep a light burning in the window – if you can find a window' in *The Cocoanuts* (1929).

3 They say a man is as old as the woman he feels. In that case I'm eighty-five ... I want it known here and now that this is what I want on my tombstone: Here lies Groucho Marx, and Lies and Lies and Lies. P.S. He never kissed an ugly girl.

The Secret Word is Groucho (1976). Presumably Groucho was alluding to the proverb 'A man is as old as he feels, and a woman as old as she looks' (known by 1871).

Karl MARX German political theorist (1818–83)

4 Religion ... is the opium of the people.

A Contribution to the Critique of Hegel's Philosophy of Right, Introduction (1843–4). This is a translation of '*Die Religion ... ist das Opium des Volkes.*' Sometimes it has been translated as 'opiate of the people', though if he had meant 'opiate', Marx would presumably have used the German word *opiat*. Either way, it has become a catchphrase suggesting that religion is like a drug releasing people from the reality of their lives. Marx is actually less critical of religion than the abbreviated version might lead us to believe. A fuller version of his text reads: 'Religion is the sigh of the oppressed creature, the heart of a heartless world and the soul of soulless conditions. It is the opium of the people.' Compare the modern graffito observed in Harrow in about 1979: 'Nicholas Parsons [then a TV quizmaster] is the neo-opiate of the people.'

5 A spectre is haunting Europe – the spectre of communism.

The Communist Manifesto (1848), opening paragraph. Written with Friedrich Engels. When the tract was first translated into English, different words were chosen. The weekly magazine *The Red Republican* serialized it from 9 to 30 November 1850 and said it was written by 'Citizens *Charles Marx* and *Frederic Engels*'. The translation – actually rather a good one by Helen MacFarlane, a Chartist – nevertheless gets off to a wobbly start with: 'A frightful hobgoblin stalks throughout Europe. We are haunted by a ghost, the ghost of Communism.'

1 The workers have nothing to lose in this [revolution] but their chains. They have a world to gain. Workers of the world, unite!

Closing words of the same work. Jaap Engelsman commented (2002): 'The League of the Just (later League of Communists) held a party congress in London on 2–9 June 1847. On June 9, the congress produced draft articles (rediscovered only in 1968 and headed by the motto *Proletarier aller Länder, vereinigt Euch!* [Proletarians of all countries, unite!] This is the earliest known instance of the slogan. The first public use of the slogan dates from September 1847, when it served as motto to a trial issue of the *Kommunistische Zeitschrift* (Communist Journal), edited by Karl Schapper. At another congress, in December 1847, a final version of the articles, with the same motto, was established. These early documents say nothing as to the inventor of the slogan. Marx is a very unlikely candidate, as he was not present at the congress. Friedrich Engels was present, but if there were any indication that he introduced the slogan, I'm sure the Communist historians would have pointed this out. No trace of that in the notes to the East German publication (1970) of those draft articles. Also, when in 1885 Engels himself described the history of the movement, he merely stated that the old slogan had been replaced by the new one. Karl Schapper on the other hand is a good candidate, but there is no confirmation of his authorship. Also, the slogan may simply be the outcome of general discussion at the congress. In 1980, A.M. Kuhnigk wrote a biography of Schapper, in which he strongly opposed the way Schapper had been written out of history by Communist historians; Kuhnigk reluctantly concludes that the matter of the attribution of the slogan cannot be solved.' See also 317:1 below.

2 History repeats itself – the first time as tragedy, the second time as farce.

In *The Eighteenth Brumaire of Louis Napoleon* (1852). Marx provides the context: 'Hegel says somewhere that all great events and personalities in world history reappear in one fashion or another. He forgot to add: the first time as tragedy, the second as farce.' Hence, the title of a book on the theatre by the playwright David Edgar, *The Second Time As Farce* (1988).

3 Prominent because of the flatness of the surrounding countryside.

This aspersion is to be found cast against John Stuart Mill, the English philosopher and social reformer, in *Das Kapital*, Vol. 1, Chap. 16 (1867). After having demolished one of Mill's arguments, Marx says: 'On a level plain, simple mounds look like hills; and the insipid flatness of our present bourgeoisie is to be measured by the altitude of its "great intellects".'

4 From each according to his ability, to each according to his needs.

Usually attributed to Marx, but not from either *Das Kapital* or *The Communist Manifesto*. The slogan appears in his *Critique of the Gotha Programme* (1875), in which he says that after the workers have taken power, capitalist thinking must first disappear. Only then will the day come when society can 'inscribe on its banners: from each according to his ability, to each according to his needs'.

John Kenneth Galbraith commented in *The Age of Uncertainty* (1977): 'It is possible that these ... twelve words enlisted for Marx more followers than all the hundreds of thousands in the three volumes of *Das Kapital* combined.'

There is some doubt whether Marx originated the slogan or whether he was quoting Louis Blanc, Morelly or Mikhail Bakunin. The latter wrote: 'From each according to his faculties, to each according to his needs' (declaration, 1870, by anarchists on trial after the failure of their uprising in Lyons).

Also, Saint-Simon (1760–1825), the French reformer, had earlier said: 'The task of each be according to his capacity, the wealth of each be according to his works.' And, much earlier, Acts 4:34–35 had: 'Neither was there any among them that lacked: for as many as were possessors of lands or houses sold them, and brought the prices of things that were sold, and laid them down at the apostles' feet: and distribution was made unto every man according as he had need.'

5 Capitalism contains within it the seeds of its own destruction.

Attributed remark. Perhaps based on: 'Not only has the bourgeoisie forged the weapons that bring death to itself; it has also called into existence the men who are to wield those weapons – the modern working class – the proletarians' – *The Communist Manifesto*, Pt 1 (1848). Or on: 'The capitalist mode of appropriation, the result of the capitalist mode of production, produces capitalist private property. This is the first negation of individual private property, as founded on the labour of the proprietor. But capitalist production begets, with the inexorability of a law of nature, its own negation. It is the negation of negation ...' – *Das Kapital*, Vol. 1, Chap. 32. Compare: 'He bears the seed of ruin in himself' – Matthew Arnold, *Merope* (1858); and (writing about the political constitution of the Anglo-Saxon kingdoms): 'The democratic character of the old Teutonic system contained the seeds of its own destruction whenever it should be applied to districts of any great extent' – Edward Freeman, *History of the Norman Conquest*, Vol. 1 (1867).

1 The philosophers have only interpreted the world in various ways. The point however is to change it.

Theses on Feuerbach (1888). Marx, though German-born, lived in London from 1849 onwards. He was buried in Highgate Cemetery on 17 March 1883. His ill-kept grave remained in a far corner of the cemetery until 1956 when the Soviet Communist Party paid for a monolithic marble block to be installed, with two quotations inscribed upon it: 'Workers of all lands unite' from 316:1 (at the top) and this quotation below it.

MARY I English Queen (1516–58)

2 When I am dead and opened, you shall find Calais lying in my heart.

'Bloody Mary' or 'Mary Tudor', who ruled 1553–8, reputedly said this, according to *Holinshed's Chronicles* (1577). She was referring to the re-capture by the French of Calais in 1558, a notable defeat for England, as the town had been an English possession for more than 200 years and was its last territory in France. Compare SELLAR AND YEATMAN 398:9.

MARY British Queen of King George V (1867–1953)

3 Well, Prime Minister, here's a pretty kettle of fish.

Queen Mary's eldest son reigned for less than a year as Edward VIII. He abdicated in order to marry the American divorcée, Wallis Simpson. For most of 1936 the British public was kept in ignorance of the manoeuvres going on behind the scenes to resolve this crisis. The Prime Minister, Stanley Baldwin, steered matters to their conclusion. He subsequently told his daughter of a meeting he had had with Queen Mary as the storm grew: 'I had a tremendous shock. For, instead of standing immobile in the middle distance, silent and majestic, she came trotting across the room *exactly like a puppy dog*: and before I had time to bow, she took hold of my hand in both of hers and held it tight. "Well, Prime Minister," she said, "here's a pretty kettle of fish"' – quoted in Frances Donaldson, *Edward VIII* (1974).

Years later, meeting Queen Mary at a dinner party, Noël Coward boldly asked, 'Is it true, Ma'am, that you said, "Here's a pretty kettle of fish?"' She replied, 'Yes, I think I did' – reported in Cole Lesley, *The Life of Noël Coward* (1978).

In the form, 'This is a nice kettle of fish, isn't it?', the Queen's remark was noted on 17 November 1936 in the diary of Nancy Dugdale, whose husband was Baldwin's Parliamentary Private Secretary. Extracts from the diary were published in *The Observer* (7 December 1986). 'Well, Mr Baldwin! *this* is a pretty kettle of fish!' is the version given in James Pope-Hennessy, *Life of Queen Mary* (1959). Queen Mary did not invent the expression 'pretty kettle of fish' – it was already current by 1740.

4 Oh, *that's* what hay looks like, is it? I never knew that.

The Duchess of Beaufort told James Pope-Hennessy about Queen Mary's evacuation to Badminton House during the Second World War: 'When she came here, she didn't even know what hay was – when I pointed to a hayfield and said look at our hay, she replied [as above], studying it ... She was totally urban, but got used to the country.' Pope-Hennessy reported this in his official biography *Queen Mary* (1959), and also in a memoir of the interview with the Duchess, included in *A Lonely Business, A Self-Portrait of James Pope-Hennessy* (1981).

Eric MASCHWITZ English songwriter (1901–69)

5 The sigh of midnight trains in empty stations ...
The smile of Garbo and the scent of roses ...
These foolish things
Remind me of you.

Song, 'These Foolish Things' (1936) – once cited by John Betjeman as evidence of poetry in popular culture. The song was originally published as by 'Holt Marvell' (with music by Jack Strachey) because Maschwitz had to conceal his identity as a BBC executive. This has led to such oddities as *PDMQ* (1980) crediting the whole song to Strachey alone. In *ODQ* (1992), it is still credited to 'Holt Marvell', as also in *ODMQ* (1991), where the music credit is shared between Jack Strachey and 'Harry Link', whoever he might be.

Picked up by Michael Sadleir for a book called *These Foolish Things* in 1937, and by Bertrand Tavernier as the title of a film (1990) which included the song on the soundtrack.

6 A Nightingale Sang in Berkeley Square.

Title of a song first sung in the revue *New Faces* (1940). Music by Manning Sherwin. As Maschwitz acknowledged in his autobiography, *No Chip on My Shoulder* (1957), the title was derived from a short story called 'When the Nightingale Sang in Berkeley Square' in Michael Arlen's *These Charming People* (1923). Nightingales are last reported to have sung in Berkeley Square in 1850 – according to Victoria Glendinning, *Trollope* (1992).

John MASEFIELD English Poet Laureate (1878–1967)

1 I must go down to the seas again, to the lonely sea and the sky.

An early draft of Masefield's poem 'Sea Fever' (1902) has this first line *without* any 'go' before 'down'. Indeed, it pursues a different course, beginning, 'I must down to the roads again, to the vagrant life.' The original manuscript of the poem is lost but the repeated line was also 'I must down' in the first published version of *Salt Water Ballads* in 1902. Heinemann Collected Editions of Masefield's poetry had just 'down' in 1923, 1932 and 1938, but changed to 'go down' in 1946. *Selected Poems* in 1922 and 1938 both had 'go down'. No one knows why this divergence occurred, but the pull of Psalm 107 – 'They that *go down to the sea* in ships, that do their business in great waters' – may have been a factor. John Ireland's musical setting of the poem has had the 'go down' since its first publication (1915). Some editions of the poem also cannot make up their minds whether it is 'lonely sea' or 'lonely seas'. Curiously, *ODQ* (1999) has a singular 'sea', for example. Note also, *The Lonely Sea and the Sky* – the title given to the memoirs (1964) of Sir Francis Chichester, the solo round-the-world yachtsman.

Some of the foregoing information is drawn from an article by Agnes Whitaker in *The Times* (5 December 1980). She commented on 'the inspired economy' of 'I must down' and added: 'It is disconcerting that standard editions, and works of reference which we treat almost like sacred texts, should contradict each other, especially over such an immensely well-known poem.' But she was ignorant of the poet's own wishes. In 2001, three listeners to my radio show wrote to say that they had (separately) asked Masefield about the matter before he died in 1967 and received letters back saying that the third word should indeed be 'go'. The reply to June Mack (14 August 1951) stated: 'As to the word "go", in the verses; it was there at first; then, later, somehow, it dropped out; then, later, was restored.' The final proof comes from the Poet Laureate's own reading of 'Sea Fever, Cargoes and other poems' on a Caedmon disc (TC1147 – no longer available, nor broadcastable either, though I have heard it, and an oddly plummy patrician voice Masefield brings to it). The 'go' is clearly audible, not to mention a plural 'seas', in the opening phrase of each of the three verses. This version must presumably reflect the poet's own wishes on both points.

See also HUBBARD 246:7.

Abraham MASLOW American professor of psychology (1908–70)

2 It is tempting, if the only tool you have is a hammer, to treat everything as if it were a nail.

The Psychology of Science: a Reconnaissance (1966). However, in Arthur Bloch's third *Murphy's Law* book (1982), this view is listed as 'Baruch's Observation' with no clue who Baruch is or was.

(Sir) James MATHEW Irish judge (1830–1908)

3 In England, Justice is open to all, like the Ritz hotel.

Attributed to Mathew by R.E. Megarry in *Miscellany-at-Law* (1955). Also attributed to Lord Bowen 30 years before, to Lord Justice Chitty and subsequently to Lord Birkett. However, the thought is old enough. In *Tom Paine's Jests* (1794) there is: 'A gentleman haranguing on the perfection of our law, and that it was equally open to the poor and rich, was answered by another, "So is the London Tavern."' In William Hazlitt's *The Spirit of the Age* (1825), this jest was specifically ascribed to the radical politician John Horne Tooke (1736–1812).

A.E. MATTHEWS English actor (1869–1960)

4 I always wait for *The Times* each morning. I look at the obituary column, and if I'm not in it, I go to work.

Quoted in Leslie Halliwell, *The Filmgoer's Book of Quotes* (1973). Matthews's own obituary appeared on 26 July 1960. Several people have adopted the line subsequently. In *The Observer* (16 August 1987), William Douglas-Home, the playwright, was quoted as saying: 'Every morning I read the obits in *The Times*. If I'm not there, I carry on.'

W. Somerset MAUGHAM English novelist and short-story writer (1874–1965)

5 *Of Human Bondage.*

Title of novel (1915). From the title of one of the books in Spinoza's *Ethics* (1677).

6 *The Moon and Sixpence.*

Maugham took the title of his 1919 novel from a review of his earlier book – *Of Human Bondage* (1915) – in *The Times Literary Supplement*. It had said that the main character was: 'Like so many young men ... so busy yearning for the moon that he never saw the sixpence at his feet' – source: Ted Morgan, *Somerset Maugham* (1980).

1 I [Death] was astonished to see him in Baghdad, for I had an appointment with him tonight in Samarra.

Sheppey, Act 3 (1933). Hence, the expression 'an appointment in Samarra', meaning an appointment with Death or one that simply cannot be avoided. Presumably a tale acquired by Maugham from some other source (possibly Arabic), in which a servant is jostled by Death in the market at Baghdad. Terrified, he jumps on a horse and rides to Samarra (a city in northern Iraq) where he thinks Death will not be able to find him. When the servant's master asks Death why he treated him in this manner, Death replies that he had merely been surprised to encounter the servant in Baghdad ... 'I had an appointment with him tonight in Samarra.' The novel *Appointment in Samarra* (1934) by John O'Hara alludes to the incident. The tale is told in the film *Targets* (US 1967).

The story appeared earlier in Jean Cocteau, *Le Grand Écart* (1923) – translator not known:

A young Persian gardener said to his Prince: 'Save me! I met Death in the garden this morning, and he gave me a threatening look. I wish that by tonight, by some miracle, I might be far away, in Ispahan.'
The Prince lent him his swiftest horse.
That afternoon, as he was walking in the garden, the Prince came face to face with Death. 'Why,' he asked, 'did you give my gardener a threatening look this morning?' 'It was not a threatening look,' replied Death. 'It was an expression of surprise. For I saw him there this morning, and I knew that I would take him in Ispahan tonight.'

Jaap Engelsman noted (2004): 'All these writers took their versions from a Persian tradition, in which an influential element was the poetic version of the legend by Jalal ad-Din ar-Rumi (also Jalal-ud-din Rumi, or Rumi for short, 1207–73), founder of the Sufi sect of the Whirling Dervishes, in his didactic epic *Masnavi-ye Ma'navi*. Here the protagonists were a nobleman, King Solomon (a prophet in Muslim eyes), and 'Izra'il, the Angel of Death. By means of the wind, the nobleman fled (from Jerusalem, presumably) to India, where the Angel of Death was expecting him. The story had already been told by some of the earliest Islamic authors, in the 8th century. They got it from the older, Jewish *Haggada* tradition (from the 5th century BC onwards); in one of their versions of the story, two of Solomon's scribes (Eliharaf and Abiyah) meet the Angel of Death; they flee from Jerusalem to some unspecified locality. This is based on a very thorough article by the Dutch orientalist J.T.P. de Bruijn, who states that Samarra was first introduced in the story by Somerset Maugham.'

2 *The Trembling of a Leaf.*

Title of collection of short stories (1921). From Sainte-Beuve: 'Extreme happiness separated from extreme despair by a trembling leaf, is that not life?' – source: Ted Morgan, *Somerset Maugham* (1980).

3 *The Razor's Edge.*

Title of a novel (1944; film US 1946). It comes from the Katha-Upanishad: 'The sharp edge of a razor is difficult to pass over; thus the wise say the path to Salvation is hard' – source: Ted Morgan, *Somerset Maugham* (1980).

4 I stand in the very first row of the second-raters.

Said by *The Oxford Companion to English Literature* (1985) to be in his autobiography *The Summing Up* (1938), though this view has not been found in that work. Compare the similar self-estimation of Arnold Bennett – quoted in *The Lyttelton Hart-Davis Letters* for 18 January 1956 – 'My work will never be better than third-rate, judged by the high standards, but I shall be cunning enough to make it impose on my contemporaries', and the view of Maugham as 'a good writer of the second rank' put forward by Karl G. Pfeiffer in his *Somerset Maugham, a Candid Portrait* (1959). And compare also this estimate of Chester Arthur, 21st US President: 'First in ability on the list of second-rate men' – Anon. in *The New York Times* (20 February 1872).

See also BEERBOHM 57:2; DAVIS 163:1.

Hughes MEARNS American writer (1875–1965)

5 As I was walking up the stair
I met a man who wasn't there.
He wasn't there again today.
I wish, I wish he'd stay away.

Lines written for an amateur play, *The Psycho-Ed* (1910). Mearns also appears to have written several parodies of the verse. *Verse and Worse*, ed. Arnold Silcock (1958 edn), credits him with: 'As I was letting down my hair / I met a guy who didn't care; / He didn't care again today – / I *love* 'em when they get that way!' (1939) – and – 'As I was sitting in my chair / I *knew* the bottom wasn't there, / Nor legs nor back, but *I just sat*, / Ignoring little things like that.'

2nd Viscount MELBOURNE British Whig Prime Minister (1779–1848)

6 A damned bore.

Of the premiership. We have only Charles Greville's word for it, but when William IV offered the premiership to Melbourne in 1834, 'He thought it a damned bore and was in many minds what he should do – be minister or no.' His secretary urged him to accept, however, with the words: 'Why damn it, such a position was never occupied by any Greek or Roman, and if it only lasts two months, it is well worth while to have been Prime Minister of England.' The words were quoted by Clement Attlee while ironically congratulating Anthony Eden on becoming Prime Minister (in 1955) when an election was imminent – source: Robert Blake, *The Prime Ministers*, Vol. 2 (1975).

H.L. MENCKEN American journalist and linguist (1880–1956)

1 Every normal man must be tempted, at times, to spit on his hands, hoist the black flag, and begin slitting throats.

Prejudices: First Series, Chap. 6 (1919), 'The New Poetry Movement'. Mencken is writing of Ezra Pound: 'Pound, it seems to me, is the most picturesque man of the whole movement – a professor turned fantee, Abelard in grand opera. His knowledge is abysmal; he has it readily on tap; moreover, he has a fine ear, and has written many an excellent verse. But now all the glow and gusto of the bard have been turned into the rage of the pamphleteer: he drops the lute for the bayonet. One sympathizes with him in his choler. The stupidity he combats is actually almost unbearable. Every normal man must be tempted, at times, to spit on his hands, hoist the black flag, and begin slitting throats. But this business, alas, is fatal to the moods and the fine other-worldliness of the poet. Pound gives a thrilling show, but ...'

2 As democracy is perfected, the office [of President] represents, more and more closely, the inner soul of the people. We move toward a lofty ideal. On some great and glorious day the plain folks of the land will reach their heart's desire at last, and the White House will be adorned by a downright moron.

In the *Baltimore Evening Sun* (26 July 1920). Written during the presidency of Woodrow Wilson, this was much quoted during the presidency of George W. Bush.

3 If after I depart this vale you ever remember me and have thought to please my ghost, forgive some sinner and wink your eye at some homely girl.

Mencken suggested this epitaph for himself in *Smart Set* (December 1921). After his death, it was inscribed on a plaque in the lobby of the offices of the Baltimore *Sun* newspapers (with which he had been associated most of his working life).

4 No one ever went broke underestimating the intelligence of the American people.

In fact what Mencken wrote (about journalism) in the *Chicago Tribune* (19 September 1926) was: 'No one in this world, so far as I know ... has ever lost money by underestimating the intelligence of the great masses of the plain people. Nor has anyone ever lost public office thereby.' Compare Bernard Shaw commenting on the growing public distaste for melodrama, in *The Saturday Review* (20 April 1895): 'This is an inevitable reaction against the artificialities, insincerities and impossibilities which form about three-fourths of the stock-in-trade of those playwrights who seek safety and success in the assumption that it is impossible to underrate the taste and intelligence of the British public.'

5 The only really happy people are married women and single men.

Quoted in *The 'Quote ... Unquote' Book of Love, Death and the Universe* (1980), but otherwise unverified.

6 Only presidents, editors and people with tapeworms have the right to use the editorial 'we'.

Precise wording and source untraced. Sometimes in the form: 'There are two kinds of people entitled to refer to themselves as "we". One is an editor, the other is a fellow with a tapeworm.' Also attributed to Bill Nye and Mark Twain.

Felix MENDELSSOHN German composer (1809–47)

7 Calm Sea and Prosperous Voyage.

The pleasing title of this overture, Op. 27 (1832), was taken from two poems by Goethe, with whom Mendelssohn was personally acquainted. One, '*Meeresstille*', the other, '*Glückliche Fahrt*'. (Beethoven also made a choral and orchestral setting of these poems.) Nowadays one might wish a 'calm sea and a prosperous voyage' to a friend off on a sea cruise, but *Meerestille* refers to that more sinister prospect for anyone on a vessel with sails – a becalmed sea.

George MEREDITH English novelist and poet (1828–1909)

8 Ah, what a dusty answer gets the soul
When hot for certainties in this our life!
Modern Love (1862). See also GLASGOW 215:1.

9 The Lark Ascending.

Title of poem (1881) – taken by Vaughan Williams for his piece for solo violin and orchestra (1914).

Dixon Lanier MERRITT American writer (1879–1972)

1 Oh, a wondrous bird is the pelican!
His beak holds more than his belican.
He takes in his beak
Food enough for a week.
But I'll be darned if I know how the helican.

In the *Nashville Banner* (22 April 1913). A version is to be
found in a letter from Oswald Mosley to his wife Cimmie
(17 February ?1921), quoted in Nicholas Mosley, *Rules of the
Game*, Chap. 4 (1982): 'A wonderful bird is the pell-i-can /
His beak holds as much as his belly can / Some say that he
can pass / This beak right up his ass / But I'm damned if
I see how the hell-he-can!'

Prince METTERNICH Austrian statesman (1773–1859)

2 When Paris sneezes, Europe catches cold.

Untraced. This comment, said to date from 1830, cannot
be found in his *Mémoires*, for example. Another form is:
'When France has a cold, all Europe sneezes.'

3 *Italien ist ein geographischer Begriff* [Italy is a
geographical concept].

Discussing the Italian question with Palmerston in 1847
(also in a letter dated 19 November 1849). Italy was indeed
no more than a group of individual states until Victor
Emmanuel II was proclaimed King in 1861. Later, Metternich said it about Germany.

Ludwig MIES VAN DER ROHE German-born architect
(1886–1969)

4 Less is more.

Statement about design, meaning that less visual clutter
makes for a more satisfying living environment. It was
quoted at Mies van der Rohe's death in the *New York Herald
Tribune*. In David A. Spaeth, *Ludwig Mies van der Rohe: An
Annotated Bibliography and Chronology* (1979), it is described
as 'the statement which is improperly credited to him'.
Spaeth does not say, however, when it first came to be associated with Mies van der Rohe, although he lists an article
headed 'Less Is More' (in quotation marks) from *Time* Magazine (14 June 1954), which adds: 'The essence of Mies's
architectural philosophy is in his famous and sometimes
derided phrase, "Less is more." This means, he says, having
"the greatest effect with the least means". Some of the best
examples of the less-is-more approach are among the buildings Mies has designed for the Illinois Tech campus –
simple clean-lined constructions of glass ribbed with steel,
which well serve their uncomplicated purpose as lighted
areas for study.' It is possible to confirm that Mies van der

Rohe did actually talk of 'greatest effect with smallest use
of means': in June or July 1923, he wrote in the first issue of
the magazine *G*, on a *Bürohaus* (office building), '*Größter
Effekt mit geringstem Aufwand an Mitteln*'.

An even earlier (unverified) use of the phrase is in P. Johnson, *Mies van der Rohe* (1947). Robert Browning had used
the phrase in a different artistic context in 'Andrea del Sarto'
(1855). Before this, there had been an interesting German
parallel. Lessing, in his play *Emilia Galotti* (1772), has 'the
Prince' say: '*Nicht so redlich, wäre redlicher* [Not so reasonable would be more reasonable]'. This was alluded to in
January 1774 by Wieland in his *Teutsche Merkur*, where he
wrote: '*Und minder ist oft mehr, wie Lessings Prinz uns lehrt*
[And less is often more, as Lessing's Prince teaches us].'
This has become a familiar phrase in German in the form
'*Weniger wäre mehr gewesen* [Less would have been more]',
which Mies, being originally German, presumably knew.

5 Der liebe Gott steckt im Detail [The dear God is
in the details].

The architect's obituary in *The New York Times* (1969) attributed the saying 'God is in the details' to Mies van der Rohe,
but it also appears to have been a favourite of the German art
historian Aby Warburg (though E.M. Gombrich, his biographer, is not certain that it originated with him). In the
form '*Le bon Dieu est dans le détail*', it has also been attributed
to Gustave Flaubert (1821–80). Compare Arthur Miller:
'Generalization is the death of art. It is in the details where
god resides' – quoted in *The Observer*, 'Sayings of the Week'
(9 April 1995).

Subsequently there has arisen the saying 'The devil is in
the detail', which has been described as a maxim of the
German pop musician Blixa Bargeld. He probably did not
invent it himself, as it is mentioned in Lutz Röhrich's
Lexikon der sprichwörtlichen Redensarten (1994) – as '*Der
Teufel steckt im Detail*'.

Arthur MILLER American playwright (1915–2005)

6 For a salesman, there is no rock bottom to the life
… He's a man way out there in the blue, riding on
a smile and a shoeshine … A salesman is got to
dream, boy. It comes with the territory.

'Requiem' at the end of play *Death of a Salesman* (1948).
Since at least 1900, 'territory' has been the American
term for the area a salesman covers. Miller's use may, however, be a possible origin for the late 20th-century expression, 'It comes/goes with the territory', meaning 'it's all
part and parcel of something, what is expected'. From *The
Washington Post* (13 July 1984): '[Geraldine Ferraro as
prospective Vice-President] will have to be judged on her
background, training and capacity to do the job. That goes

with the territory.' From the film *Father of the Bride* (1991), where Steve Martin says: 'I'm a father. Worrying comes with the territory.' From the London *Evening Standard* (17 February 1993): 'Why go on about the latest "award-winning documentary maker"? If you get a documentary on television, you win an award: it goes with the territory.'

Max MILLER American journalist (1899–1967)

1 *I Cover the Waterfront.*

Title of book (1932) about Miller's experiences as a 'waterfront reporter' on the *San Diego Sun* during the late 1920s and early 1930s. Filmed (US 1933) as a story about a journalist who exposes a smuggling racket. Hence, 'cover' is in the journalistic sense. The song with the title (by Johnny Green and Ed Heyman), sung notably by Billie Holiday, was originally unconnected with the film – written merely to cash in on the association – and sounds as if it might be about laying paving stones or some other activity. However, so successful was it that it was subsequently added to the soundtrack. Since the film, the phrase 'to cover the waterfront' has meant 'to cover all aspects of a topic' or merely 'to experience something'. A woman going in to try a new nightclub in the film *Cover Girl* (1944) says: 'This is it. We cover the waterfront.' In *The Wise Wound* (1978) by Penelope Shuttle and Peter Redgrove, 'she's covering the waterfront' is listed among the many slang expressions for menstruation.

A.A. MILNE English writer (1882–1956)

2 Sydney Smith, or Napoleon or Marcus Aurelius (somebody about that time) said that after ten days any letter would answer itself. You see what he meant.

Untraced. In fact, it was Arthur Binstead, in *Pitcher's Proverbs* (1909), who said, 'The great secret in life … [is] not to open letters for a fortnight. At the expiration of that period you will find that nearly all of them have answered themselves.'

See also BIERCE 88:3; CASSANDRA 128:1; SIMON 431:7; STOPPARD 448:6.

John MILTON English poet (1608–74)

3 Come, knit hands, and beat the ground,
In a light fantastic round.

Comus, line 143 (1637). Compare BROOKER 102:6.

4 Sabrina fair,
Listen where thou art sitting
Under the glassy, cool, translucent wave,
In twisted braids of lilies knitting
The loose train of thy amber-dropping hair.

In the same poem, line 859. Billy Wilder's 1954 film *Sabrina*, based on a play by Samuel Taylor, was about the daughter (Audrey Hepburn) of a chauffeur who gets wooed by both the two brothers who employ her father. Known simply as *Sabrina* in the US, the film was released as *Sabrina Fair* in Britain. This could have been because the distributors thought that English cinema-goers would relish an allusion to the poetic name for the River Severn, as applied to the nymph in Milton's masque *Comus*. On the other hand, the distributors might have been sending them a message that the film had nothing at all to do with Sabrina, a busty (41-18-36) model, who was at that time featured on TV shows with Arthur Askey, the comedian.

Alas, this second theory does not fit, as Norma Sykes (her real name) did not start appearing until 1956 and, in fact, actually took her stage name from the title of the film. So, it must have been the allusion to Milton after all.

5 To sport with Amaryllis in the shade,
Or with the tangles of Neaera's hair?
Fame is the spur that the clear spirit doth raise
(That last infirmity of noble mind)
To scorn delights, and live laborious days.

'Lycidas', line 68 (1638). Hence, *Fame Is the Spur*, title of a novel (1940, film UK 1946) by Howard Spring about an aspiring politician.

6 Look homeward, Angel, now, and melt with ruth.

In the same poem, line 163. Ruth = pity, the quality of being compassionate. Hence, *Look Homeward, Angel!*, the title of a novel (1929) by Thomas Wolfe, and of a song by Johnnie Ray (1957).

7 At last he rose, and twitched his mantle blue:
Tomorrow to fresh woods and pastures new.

In the same poem, line 192. Often remembered as 'Tomorrow to fresh *fields* and pastures new'. The misquotation probably gained hold because of the alliteration – always a lure in phrase-making. There may be tautology in the fields and pastures, but how likely is it that a shepherd would lead his flock into a wood where the sheep would be liable to get lost, lose their wool on bushes, eat poisonous plants and so on?

8 A good book is the precious life-blood of a master spirit, embalmed and treasured up on purpose to a life beyond life.

From *Areopagitica* (1644). A sentiment used for many years to promote the Everyman's Library series of classic reprints. Compare ANONYMOUS 15:1; SIDNEY 431:3.

1 Come, and trip it as ye go
On the light fantastic toe.

'L'Allegro', line 33 (1645). Compare BROOKER 102:6.

2 Far from all resort of mirth,
Save the cricket on the hearth.

'Il Penseroso', line 81 (1645). Compare DICKENS 169:3.

3 Blest pair of sirens, pledges of heav'n's joy,
Sphere-born harmonious sisters.

'At a Solemn Music' (1645) – the sirens are 'Voice' and 'Verse'. Notably set to music (1887) by Sir Hubert Parry.

4 Cromwell, our chief of men, who through a cloud
Not of war only, but detractions rude,
Guided by faith and matchless fortitude,
To peace and truth thy glorious way has ploughed.

Sonnet, 'To the Lord General Cromwell' (written 1652). Hence, *Cromwell: Our Chief of Men*, title of Antonia Fraser's biography (1973). Fraser's book was known in the US, however, as *Cromwell the Lord Protector*.

5 Of man's first disobedience, and the fruit
Of that forbidden tree, whose mortal taste
Brought death into the world, and all our woe,
With loss of Eden.

Paradise Lost, Bk 1, line 1 (1667). Milton's sonorous opening statement of his theme – Adam's disobedience and the Fall.

6 No light, but rather darkness visible
Served only to discover sights of woe.

In the same poem, Bk 1, line 63. Hence, the title of William Golding's novel, *Darkness Visible* (1979).

7 Let none admire
That riches grow in hell; that soil may best
Deserve the precious bane.

In the same poem, Bk 1, line 690. Hence, *Precious Bane*, title of the novel (1924) by Mary Webb.

8 Chaos umpire sits,
And by decision more embroils the fray
By which he reigns; next him high arbiter
Chance governs all.

In the same poem, Bk 2, line 907. Hence, *Chance Governs All*, the title of the memoirs (2002) of Marmaduke Hussey, a Chairman of the Governors of the BBC.

9 God is thy law, thou mine; to know no more
Is woman's happiest knowledge and her praise.
With thee conversing I forget all time.

In the same poem, Bk 4, line 637. Eve to Adam, a delicate compliment. As 'With Thee conversing we forget all time, and toil, and care, / Labour is rest, and pain is sweet, / If Thou my God, art there', it became a hymn by Charles Wesley – No. 460 in *The Methodist Hymnal*.

10 Wherefore with thee
Came not all hell broke loose.

In the same poem, Bk 4, line 917. The Archangel Gabriel speaks to Satan. Hence, 'all hell broke loose', a popular descriptive catchphrase for when chaos occurs. Milton had, however, been anticipated in this by the author of a Puritan pamphlet, *Hell Broke Loose: or, a Catalogue of Many of the Spreading Errors, Heresies and Blasphemies of These Times, for Which We are to be Humbled* (1646). Also in Robert Greene's play *Friar Bacon and Friar Bungay* in about 1589, the character Miles has the line: 'Master, master, master up! Hell's broken loose.' As an idiomatic phrase it was certainly well established by 1738 when Swift compiled his *Polite Conversation*. When there is 'A great Noise below', Lady Smart exclaims: 'Hey, what a clattering is there; one would think Hell was broke loose.'

11 Unmoved,
Unshaken, unseduced, unterrified,
His Loyalty he kept, his Love, his Zeal;
Nor number, nor example with him wrought
To swerve from truth, or change his constant
mind.

In the same poem, Bk 5, line 898. A quotation to be found on the memorial tablet to the Liberal Prime Minister, H.H. Asquith, in Westminster Abbey. The lines were chosen 'after much thought by his family', according to Asquith's biographer, Roy Jenkins.

12 Ask for this great deliverer now, and find him
Eyeless in Gaza, at the mill with slaves.

Samson Agonistes, line 40 (1671). Hence, *Eyeless in Gaza* (1936), title of a book by Aldous Huxley.

13 And calm of mind, all passion spent.

In the same poem, line 1758. Last line of poem. Having lived through or experienced the catharsis of Samson's life and death, this is what people should feel. Hence, *All Passion Spent*, the title of a novel (1931) by Vita Sackville-West (a study of ageing and independence in old age).

R.J. MINNEY English writer (1895–1979)

1 *Carve Her Name With Pride.*

As Michael Powell comments in *Million-Dollar Movie* (1992), the title of Minney's book (1956; film UK 1958), 'sounds like a quotation, and probably is'. But I think not. Minney makes no reference to the title in his somewhat soupy biography of Violette Szabo, the wartime agent who was executed by the Germans and became the first British woman to receive the George Cross (gazetted posthumously in 1946). The notion of carving an epitaph is, of course, an old one. Robert Browning has 'If ye carve my epitaph aright' in his poem 'The Bishop Orders His Tomb' (1845).

Margaret MITCHELL American novelist (1900–49)

2 My dear, I don't give a damn.

Gone With the Wind, Chap. 57 (1936). Popularly remembered, however, as in the last scene of the film (US 1939) where Scarlett O'Hara is finally abandoned by her husband, Rhett Butler. Although Scarlett believes she can win him back, there occurs the controversial moment when Rhett replies to her entreaty:

> *Scarlett:* Where shall I go? What shall I do?
> *Rhett:* Frankly, my dear, I don't give a damn.

These words were allowed on to the soundtrack only after months of negotiation with the Hays Office, which controlled film censorship. In those days, the word 'damn' was forbidden in Hollywood under Section V (1) of the Hays Code, even if it was what Mitchell had written in her novel (though she hadn't included the 'frankly'). Sidney Howard's original draft was accordingly changed to: 'Frankly, my dear, I don't care.' The scene was shot with both versions of the line, and the producer, David Selznick, argued at great length with the censors over which was to be used. He did this not least because he thought he would look a fool if the famous line was excluded. He also wanted to show how faithful the film was to the novel. Selznick argued that the *Oxford Dictionary* described 'damn' not as an oath but as a vulgarism, that many women's magazines used the word, and that preview audiences had expressed disappointment when the line was omitted. The censors suggested 'darn' instead. Selznick finally won the day – but because he was technically in breach of the Hays Code he was fined $5000. The line still didn't sound quite right: Clark Gable, as Rhett, had to put the emphasis unnaturally on 'give' rather than on 'damn', though some would argue that this is the natural American emphasis.

3 After all, tomorrow is another day.

The last words of the film, spoken by Vivien Leigh as Scarlett O'Hara, are: 'Tara! Home! I'll go home, and I'll think of some way to get him back. After all, tomorrow is another

day!' The last sentence is as it appears in Mitchell's novel, but the idea behind it is proverbial. In John Rastell's *Calisto and Melebea* (?1520) there occurs the line: 'Well, mother, tomorrow is a new day.'

See also DOWSON 177:1.

Nancy MITFORD English author (1904–73)

4 I loathe abroad, nothing would induce me to live there ... and, as for foreigners, they are all the same, and they all make me sick.

The Pursuit of Love, Chap. 10 (1945). Compare 'Frogs ... are slightly better than Huns or Wops, but abroad is unutterably bloody and foreigners are fiends', from Chap. 15. Mitford wrote both these passages in the character of Uncle Matthew, apparently modelled on her own father, Lord Redesdale. This low opinion of foreigners is put down to Uncle Matthew's four years in France and Italy between 1914 and 1918. It certainly does not reflect her own view – she lived in France for many years until her death. Compare GEORGE VI 211:1.

5 *Love in a Cold Climate.*

Title of novel (1949). This caused Evelyn Waugh to write to Mitford (10 October): '[It] has become a phrase. I mean when people want to be witty they say I've caught a cold in a cold climate and everyone understands.' The title was suggested by Bennett Cerf, the book's American publisher. In the novel, Chap. 15, is this: 'Polly and the Lecturer appeared to view. It was not a happy picture, but that may have been the fault of the climate. No aimless dalliance hand in hand under warm skies for poor English lovers who, if circumstances drive them to making love out of doors, are obliged to choose between the sharp, brisk walk and the stupefying stuffiness of the cinema.'

Earlier, George Orwell wrote in *Keep The Aspidistra Flying*, Chap. 6 (1936): 'There are so many pairs of lovers in London with "nowhere to go"; only the streets and the parks, where there is no privacy and it is always cold. It is not easy to make love in a cold climate when you have no money. The "never the time and the place" motif is not made enough of in novels'; and Robert Southey, the poet, writing to his brother Thomas (28 April 1797) said: 'She has made me half in love with a cold climate.'

See also ROSS 388:2.

François MITTERRAND French socialist President (1916–96)

6 She has the eyes of Caligula and the lips of Marilyn Monroe.

Of Margaret Thatcher. Attributed, for example, by Anthony Powell in his *Journals 1982–1986* (1995) – entry for 28 March

1985. In Hugo Young, *One of Us* (1989), the remark is attributed to Mitterand when briefing his new European Minister, Roland Dumas (which would have been in 1983), and is given in French: '*Cette femme Thatcher! Elle a les yeux de Caligule, mais elle a la bouche de Marilyn Monroe.*'

Emilio MOLA Spanish Nationalist general (1887–1937)

1 *La quinta columna* [The fifth column].

In October 1936, during the Spanish Civil War, Mola was besieging the Republican-held city of Madrid with four columns. He was asked in a broadcast whether this was sufficient to capture the city and he replied that he was relying on the support of the *quinta columna* ('the fifth column'), which was already hiding inside the city and which sympathized with his side. Hence, the term 'fifth columnists' meaning 'traitors, infiltrators'. It was also the title of Ernest Hemingway's only play (1938).

Some doubt has been cast on the ascription to Mola. Lance Haward (1996) has noted that in the *Daily Express* of 27 October 1936, Moscow Radio was quoted as having attributed the phrase to General Franco. In the *Daily Mail* of 7 November, the Guardia Civile in Madrid, disaffected from the Republican cause, was being referred to as 'General Franco's now famous "Fifth Column".'

In Hugh Thomas, *The Spanish Civil War* (1961), it is reported that the expression has been found in *Mundo Obrero* (3 October 1936) and that Lord St Oswald had used the term several weeks earlier in a report to the *Daily Telegraph*.

Jaap Engelsman has commented: 'In 1870, when Bismarck's armies invaded France, the French author Prosper Mérimée wrote to the Spanish mother of the French Empress: '*Malheureusement, alors même que l'invasion serait victorieusement repoussée, le danger ne serait pas encore conjuré. Il y a la quatrième armée de M. de Bismarck, et celle-là est à Paris.*' This fourth army, he suggests, is the foolish *Corps législatif*. As this Mérimée letter was first published in 1930, it might have been known to whoever coined 'fifth column' in 1936 – *Lettres de Prosper Mérimée à Madame de Montijo*, Vol. 2 (1995).'

Walter MONDALE American Democratic Vice-President (1928–)

2 Where's the beef?

A slogan borrowed by Mondale in 1984, when he was seeking the Democratic presidential nomination, to describe what he saw as lack of substance in the policies of his rival for the nomination, Gary Hart. Hence, a classic example of an advertising slogan turning into a political catchphrase.

The Wendy International hamburger chain promoted its wares in the US, from 1984, with TV commercials, one of which showed elderly women eyeing a small hamburger on a huge bun – a Wendy competitor's product. 'It certainly is a big bun,' asserted one. 'It's a very big fluffy bun,' the second agreed. But the third asked, 'Where's the beef?' Mondale took it from there.

Nicholas MONSARRAT English novelist (1910–79)

3 *The Cruel Sea.*

Title of novel (1951). According to more than one source, Monsarrat derived the title of his novel from Captain Gilbert Roberts of the Royal Navy, who said: 'It is the war of the little ships and the lonely aircraft, long patient and unpublicized, our two great enemies – the U-Boats and the Cruel Sea.' However, Winston Churchill used the phrase in *The World Crisis*, Pt 3, Chap. 9 (1923–9): 'And indeed the spectacle of helpless merchant seamen, their barque shattered and foundering, left with hard intention by fellow mariners to perish in the cruel sea, was hideous.'

4 You English ... think we know damn nothing *but I tell you we know damn all.*

In the same book. Compare this: in the second volume of David Niven's autobiography – to which he gave the title *Bring On the Empty Horses* (1975) – he talked of Michael Curtiz, the Hungarian-born American film director (1888–1962). During the filming of *The Charge of the Light Brigade* (1936), Curtiz ordered the release of a hundred riderless steeds by shouting: 'Bring on the empty horses!' David Niven and Errol Flynn fell about with laughter at this. Curtiz rounded on them and said, 'You and your stinking language! You think I know f*** nothing. Well, let me tell you, I know f*** all!' In fact, this is a frequently told tale and may pre-date Curtiz as well.

Lady Mary Wortley MONTAGU English writer (1689–1762)

5 It has all been very interesting.

Lady Mary's wonderful 'dying words' (as given, for example, in Barnaby Conrad, *Famous Last Words*, 1961) have, unfortunately, not been authenticated. Robert Halsband in his *Life of Lady Mary Wortley Montagu* (1956) remarks that 'they are nowhere unequivocally recorded', and notes that the source – Iris Barry's *Portrait of Lady Mary Montagu* (1928) – is 'clearly fictitious'.

Michel de MONTAIGNE French essayist (1533–92)

1 I quote others only the better to express myself.

Essays, Bk 1, Chap. 26 (1580). The French original might be more accurately rendered as: 'I do not speak the minds of others except to speak my own mind better.'

2 It could be said of me that in this book I have only made up a bunch of other men's flowers, and provided nothing of my own but the string to bind them [*Comme quelqu'un pourrait dire de moi que j'ai seulement fait ici un amas de fleurs étrangères, n'y ayant fourni du mien que le filet à les lier*].

In the same essays, Bk 3, Chap. 12. Hence, *Other Men's Flowers*, title of a poetry anthology by Lord Wavell (1944).

Hugh MONTEFIORE British Anglican clergyman (later bishop) (1920–2005)

3 Why did He not marry? Could the answer be that Jesus was not by nature the marrying sort?

At a conference, Oxford (26 July 1967). Compare Anthony Powell's autobiographical volume *Infants of the Spring* (1976), in which he writes of an entertainer called Varda that she 'had been married for a short time to a Greek surrealist painter, Jean Varda, a lively figure ... but not the marrying sort'. It is not quite clear what is to be inferred from this. However, when Hugh Montefiore used the phrase about Jesus people were outraged at the suggestion that He might have been a homosexual.

Usually encountered in the negative sense, 'marrying sort' has nevertheless existed in its own right. From Shaw's *Pygmalion* (1916): (Professor Higgins to Liza) 'All men are not confirmed old bachelors like me and the Colonel. Most men are the marrying sort (poor devils!)' *The Marrying Kind* is the title of a play (1957) by Garson Kanin and Ruth Gordon.

Bernard MONTGOMERY (later 1st Viscount Montgomery of Alamein) English field marshal (1887–1976)

4 Who is this chap? He drinks, he's dirty, and I know there are women in the background!

On Augustus John, who had been sent to paint him in about 1944. Quoted in *The Times Literary Supplement* (21 March 1975). Also told by C.P. Dawnay in *Montgomery at Close Quarters*, ed. T.E.B. Howarth (1985). Hence, *Women in the Background*, title of a novel (1996) by Barry Humphries.

5 Consider what the Lord said to Moses – and I think he was right.

For a time, it seemed that this was something that Montgomery – that blushing violet – had *actually* said. Then it was traced to a line in a sketch called 'Salvation Army', performed by Lance Percival as an army officer with a Montgomery accent on BBC TV's *That Was the Week That Was* (1962–3). Hence, it is simply a joke, though totally in character.

Compare *The Lyttelton Hart-Davis Letters* (Vol. 4 – relating to 1959), where the same joke occurs in the form, 'Did you hear of the parson who began his sermon: "As God said – and rightly ..."' No mention of Montgomery. Compare also a remark made by Donald Coggan, Archbishop of Canterbury, on 7 June 1977, during a sermon for the Queen's Silver Jubilee service at St Paul's Cathedral: 'We listened to these words of Jesus [St Matthew 7:24] a few moments ago.' Then he exclaimed: 'How right he was!'

One is reminded irresistibly of Lorenz Hart's stripper's song 'Zip' from *Pal Joey* (1940):

I was reading Schopenhauer last night,
And I think that Schopenhauer was right.

Compare, yet further, what William Jackson, Bishop of Oxford, once preached – according to *The Oxford Book of Oxford* (1978): 'St Paul says in one of his Epistles – and I partly agree with him.'

Henri de MONTHERLANT French novelist and playwright (1896–1972)

6 Happiness writes white. It does not show up on the page.

Attributed remark. Remark much-quoted by other writers to explain the roots of their creativity – i.e. unhappiness, pessimism and misfortune spur them on. An early ascription to de Montherlant is by Andrew Motion in *Philip Larkin: A Writer's Life*, Chap. 28 (1993). Based on what Larkin had told him personally, Motion has: 'In the past, long periods of silence had been produced by too much misery; now, for the only time in his life, he was fractionally too happy – and happiness, as he was fond of saying (quoting Montherlant), "writes white".' A precise source in de Montherlant has yet to be found.

MONTY PYTHON'S FLYING CIRCUS British TV comedy series (BBC), from 1969 to 1974. Written and performed by Graham Chapman, John Cleese, Terry Gilliam, Eric Idle, Terry Jones and Michael Palin.

7 *Praline*: It's not pining, it's passed on. This parrot is no more. It's ceased to be. It's expired. It's gone to meet its maker. This is a late parrot. It's a stiff.

Bereft of life it rests in peace. It would be pushing up the daisies if you hadn't nailed it to the perch. It's rung down the curtain and joined the choir invisible. It's an ex-parrot.

'Parrot Sketch' (7 December 1969), in which a man who has just bought a parrot that turns out to be dead registers a complaint with the pet-shop owner. From this came the later expression 'dead parrot' for anything one wished to describe as 'undoubtedly moribund, quite incapable of resuscitation'. Somewhat belatedly, in early 1988, there were signs of the phrase becoming an established idiom when it was applied to a controversial policy document drawn up as the basis for a merged Liberal/Social Democratic Party. Then *The Observer* commented (8 May 1988): 'Mr Steel's future – like his document – was widely regarded as a "dead parrot". Surely this was the end of his 12-year reign as Liberal leader?' In October 1990 Margaret Thatcher belatedly came round to the phrase (fed by a speechwriter, no doubt) and called the Liberal Democrats a 'dead parrot' at the Tory Party Conference. When the Liberals won a by-election at Eastbourne the same month, the Tory party chairman Kenneth Baker said the 'dead parrot' had merely 'twitched'. On 6 October 1998 *The Sun* carried a front-page photo of a dead parrot with the head of the then Conservative Party leader William Hague. The headline was: 'This party is no more ... it has ceased to be ... this is an EX-party.'

1 Nobody expects the Spanish Inquisition!

Spoken by Cardinal Ximenez of Spain, played by Michael Palin (22 September 1970). In turn used as a catchphrase in the film *Sliding Doors* (UK 1998).

2 *Leader of Judea People's Front*: All right. *Apart from the aqueducts, the sanitation, the roads, the medicine, the irrigation, the education, the wine, the public order, what have the Romans ever done for us?*

In film *Monty Python's Life of Brian* (UK 1979). Hence, a BBC TV documentary series *What the Romans Did For Us* (2004) and also *What the Ancients Did For Us, What the Tudors Did For Us* and *What the Victorians Did For Us*.

George MOORE Irish novelist (1852–1933)

3 The difference between my quotations and those of the next man is that I leave out the inverted commas.

Quoted in Laurence J. Peter, *Quotations for Our Time* (1977), but unverified. Moore also said the similarly untraced:

'Taking something from one man and making it worse is plagiarism' – quoted in *A Treasury of Humorous Quotations*, eds Esar & Bentley (1951).

Thomas MOORE Irish poet (1779–1852)

4 Oh! ever thus, from childhood's hour,
I've seen my fondest hopes decay;
I never lov'd a tree or flow'r,
But 'twas the first to fade away.
I never nurs'd a dear gazelle,
To glad me with its soft black eye,
But when it came to know me well,
And love me, it was sure to die!

'The Fire Worshippers', Pt 1, in *Lalla Rookh* (1817): Moore's lines are parodied in Charles Dickens, *The Old Curiosity Shop*, Chap. 56. See PYM 373:2.

5 'Come, come,' said Tom's father, 'at your time of life,
'There's no longer excuse for thus playing the rake –
'It is time you should think, boy, of taking a wife' –
'Why, so it is, father – whose wife should I take?'

'A Joke Versified', *Miscellaneous Poems* (1840). The joke would appear originally to have been cracked by the politician John Horne Tooke (1736–1812) who, on being told he should take a wife, replied, 'With all my heart. Whose wife shall it be?'

McKinley MORGANFIELD (Muddy Waters)
American lyricist and blues singer (1915–83)

6 Got My Mojo Workin'.

Title of song, meaning 'I have got my spell/charm working.' In the mid-1950s, Muddy Waters, the American blues singer (1915–83) recorded a song with the refrain, 'Got my mojo workin', but it just don't work on you.' This was his version of a song (composition of which is often credited to him under his real name, McKinley Morganfield) that he had picked up from a singer called Ann Cole. Her version is usually now credited to Preston Foster. *DOAS* defines 'mojo' simply as 'any narcotic', but a sleeve note to an album entitled *Got My Mojo Workin'* (1966) by the jazz organist Jimmy Smith is perhaps nearer to the meaning of the word in the song. It describes 'mojo' as 'magic – a spell or charm guaranteed to make the user irresistible to the opposite sex'. Sometimes it is an amulet (a little cloth bag) that contains extremely personal items from the object of one's affection or desire (e.g. pubic hair). Known by 1926. Indeed, it seems that 'mojo' could well be a form of the word 'magic' corrupted through Afro-American pronunciation, though *OED2* finds an African word 'mojuba' meaning 'magic, witchcraft' that is similar. *OED2* derives the narcotic meaning of the word from the Spanish *mojar*, 'to celebrate by drinking'.

Lord MORLEY (3rd Earl of Morley) English Liberal politician and writer (1838–1923)

1 Although in Cabinet all its members stand on an equal footing, speak with equal voice, and, on the rare occasions when a division is taken, are counted on the fraternal principle of one vote, yet the head of the Cabinet is *primus inter pares*, and occupies a position which, so long as it lasts, is one of exceptional and peculiar authority.

Life of Walpole (1889). Lord Morley may have been the first to use the phrase *primus inter pares* ('first among equals') in this context, but the otherwise anonymous Latin saying has also been used about the position of politicians in a number of countries, and also of the Pope. *The Oxford Dictionary of Colloquial English* (1985) defines it as an idiom meaning 'the one of a group who leads or takes special responsibility but who neither feels himself, nor is held by others to be, their superior'. The Round Table in Arthurian legend was meant to show not only that there was no precedence among the knights who sat at it but also that King Arthur was no more than first among equals.

Used specifically regarding the British Prime Minister within the Cabinet, the phrase cannot pre-date Sir Robert Walpole (in power 1721–42), who is traditionally the first to have held that position. *First Among Equals* was the title of Jeffrey Archer's novel (1984) about the pursuit of the British premiership. In 1988 Julian Critchley MP was quoted as having referred to Margaret Thatcher as '*prima donna inter pares*'.

Desmond MORRIS English zoologist and anthropologist (1928–)

2 *The Naked Ape.*

Title of book (1967). Morris begins: 'There are one hundred and ninety-three living species of monkeys and apes. One hundred and ninety-two of them are covered with hair. The exception is a naked ape self-named *Homo sapiens*.'

Jan MORRIS (formerly James Morris) Welsh writer (1926–)

3 Say farewell to the trumpets!
You will hear them no more.
But their sweet sad silvery echoes

Will call to you still
Through the half-closed door.

Some book, film and TV titles are quasi-quotations or are, rather, quasi-poetic in sound – titles like *By the Sword Divided, Carve Her Name With Pride, To Serve Them All My Days, A Horseman Riding By, God Is an Englishman, Only the Valiant*, and so on. (All of these are dealt with elsewhere in this book.) Morris has admitted that, having thought up the title *Farewell the Trumpets* (1978) for the final volume of her *Pax Brittanica* trilogy, she then wrote a poem to quote it from. The poem duly appears as the book's epigraph.

William MORRIS English poet and craftsman (1834–96)

4 Forget six counties overhung with smoke,
Forget the snorting steam and piston stroke,
Forget the spreading of the hideous town;
Think rather of the pack-horse on the down,
And dream of London, small, and white, and
    clean.

Prologue to *The Earthly Paradise* (1868–70). Morris's friend, Edward Burne-Jones, once commented: 'You cannot find short quotations in him, he must be taken in great gulps' – Georgiana Burne-Jones, *Memorials of Edward Burne-Jones* (1904).

See also BELL 59:2.

Herbert MORRISON (later Lord Morrison) British Labour politician (1888–1965)

5 Go to it!

On 22 May 1940, Morrison, as Minister of Supply, concluded a radio broadcast calling for a voluntary labour force with these words. They echoed the public mood after Dunkirk, and were subsequently used as a wall-poster slogan – in vivid letters – in a campaign run by the S.H. Benson agency (which later indulged in self-parody on behalf of Bovril, with 'Glow to it' in 1951–2). 'Go to it', meaning 'to act vigorously, set to with a will', dates from the early 19th century at least. In Shakespeare, *King Lear*, IV.vi.112 (1605), it had already been used as a specific euphemism:

Die for adultery! No:
The wren goes to't, and the small gilded fly
Does lecher in my sight.

Herbert MORRISON American broadcaster (1905–89)

6 Oh, the humanity!

'Toward us, like a great feather ... is the *Hindenburg*. The members of the crew are looking down on the field ahead of them getting their glimpses of the mooring mast ...' On 6 May 1937 radio commentator Morrison was describing the scene at the naval airbase in Lakehurst, New Jersey, as the German airship made its first arrival there that year (having made ten round trips to the US the previous year). 'It is starting to rain again ... the back motors of the ship are just holding it just enough to keep it from – It's burst into flames! ... It's crashing, terrible! ... Folks, this is terrible, this is one of the worst catastrophes the world ever witnessed ... It's a terrific sight, ladies and gentlemen, the smoke and the flames now. And the plane is crashing to the ground ... Oh, the humanity! All the passengers! ... I can't talk, ladies and gentlemen ...' (transcribed from a recording).

A few seconds later, Morrison managed to continue describing what *Time* Magazine called 'the worst and most completely witnessed disaster in the history of commercial aviation'. Although the *Hindenburg* was destroyed (virtually ending airships as a commercial venture), there were survivors.

(Sir) John MORTIMER English author, playwright and lawyer (1923–)

1 *Clinging to the Wreckage.*
Title of autobiography (1982) – explained in an epigraphic paragraph or two: 'A man with a bristling grey beard [a yachtsman], said: "I made up my mind, when I bought my first boat, never to learn to swim ... When you're in a spot of trouble, if you can swim you try to strike out for the shore. You invariably drown. As I can't swim, I cling to the wreckage and they send a helicopter out for me. That's my tip, if you ever find yourself in trouble, cling to the wreckage!"' Mortimer concludes: 'It was advice that I thought I'd been taking for most of my life.'

2 In the beginning was the Word. It's about the only sentence on which I find myself in total agreement with God.
Quoted in *The Observer* (1 July 1984). Alluding to John 1:1: 'In the beginning was the Word, and the Word was with God, and the Word was God.'

3 The shelf life of the modern hardback writer is somewhere between the milk and the yoghurt.
Quoted in *The Observer* (28 June 1987) and picked up by *ODMQ* (1991). As he had, in fact, said at the time, Mortimer was quoting the American humorous columnist Calvin Trillin (1935–), who had said, rather, 'A shelf life somewhere between butter and yoghurt' in *The New York Times* on the 14 June.

4 Champagne socialist.
ODQ (1992) attributes to Mortimer this description of himself and, indeed, *The Sunday Telegraph* (3 July 1988) stated that 'he once described himself as a "champagne socialist".' The phrase might, it is true, have been coined with Mortimer in mind – he likes a bottle or two, goes around calling everyone 'darling' and doesn't see why the good things in life should be denied him just because he is a 'bit Left' – but to what extent he has applied the phrase to himself, if at all, is not totally clear. From *The Independent* (2 September 1991): '[On the set of his latest television serial *Titmuss Regained*] Mortimer relaxed in the catering bus with a bottle of Moët (apparently determined not to disappoint those who think of him as a champagne socialist).'

The earliest use of the phrase found to date is in connection with that other larger-than-life character, the late tycoon and criminal, Robert Maxwell. From *The Times* (2 July 1987): 'Robert Maxwell, *Daily Mirror* newspaper tycoon and possibly the best known Czech in Britain after Ivan Lendl, has long been renowned for his champagne socialist beliefs.' At around that time, the phrase was also applied to socialist figures such as Clive Jenkins and Derek Hatton.

But maybe the phrase has even earlier beginnings: a similarly alliterative phrase was applied to a more admirable and larger-than-life socialist, Aneurin Bevan. Randolph Churchill (who was something of a champagne Conservative) recalled in the *Evening Standard* (8 August 1958) how Brendan Bracken had once 'gone for' Bevan: '"You Bollinger Bolshevik, you ritzy Robespierre, you lounge-lizard Lenin," he roared at Bevan one night, gesturing, as he went on, somewhat in the manner of a domesticated orang-utang. "Look at you, swilling Max's champagne and calling yourself a socialist."'

J.B. MORTON (Beachcomber) British humorous writer (1893–1979)

5 The man with the false nose had gone to that bourne from which no hollingsworth returns.
'Another True Story', *Gallimaufry* (1936). Alluding to Shakespeare *Hamlet*, III.i.79 (1600–1) – 'the undiscover'd country, from whose bourn / No traveller returns'(405:6). Bourne & Hollingsworth was a noted London department store.

6 Justice must not only be seen to be done but has to be seen to be believed.
Attributed by Peter Cook on BBC Radio *Quote ... Unquote* (5 June 1980) – and, consequently, attributed to Cook himself.

1 Wagner is the Puccini of music.

PDMQ (1971) attributes this to Beachcomber, and Rupert Hart-Davis concurs, saying that the announcement 'summed up the jargon-bosh of art- and music-critics beautifully' – *Lyttelton Hart-Davis Letters* (for 5 February 1956). But no precise source is available. On the other hand, James Agate in *Ego 6* (for 13 October 1943) has: 'I do not doubt the sincerity of the solemn ass who, the other evening, said portentously: "Wagner is the Puccini of music!"' As Agate was addressing a group of 'school-marms' and as he generally had an after-dinner speaker's way with attribution, it may well still have been a Beachcomber coinage. The original remark may be a parody of 'Wagner is the Marat of music, and Berlioz is its Robespierre' – Auguste de Gasperin in *Le Siècle* (1858).

Thomas MORTON English playwright (?1764–1838)

2 Approbation from Sir Hubert Stanley is praise indeed.

A Cure for the Heartache, Act 5, Sc. 2 (1797). This became a reasonably common proverbial phrase. Charles Dickens has 'Praise from Sir Hubert Stanley' in *Dombey and Son*, Chap. 1 (1847–8). P.G. Wodehouse uses the expression as 'this is praise from Sir Hubert Stanley' in *Psmith Journalist*, Chap. 15 (1915) and *Piccadilly Jim*, Chap. 18 (1918). It is alluded to in Dorothy L. Sayers, *Gaudy Night*, Chap. 15 (1935): 'At the end of the first few pages [Lord Peter Wimsey] looked up to remark: "I'll say one thing for the writing of detective fiction: you know how to put your story together; how to arrange the evidence." "Thank you," said Harriet drily; "praise from Sir Hubert is praise indeed."'

3 *Speed the Plough.*

Title of play (1798), but a very old phrase indeed: in the form 'God speed the plough', it was what one would say when wishing someone luck in any venture (and not just an agricultural one). The phrase was in use by 1500 at least, and is also the title of a traditional song and dance. *Speed-The-Plow* was the title of a play (1988) by David Mamet, about two Hollywood producers trying to get a project off the ground.

4 What will Mrs Grundy say?

Repeated question in the same play. Hence, the expression 'Mrs Grundy' for 'a censorious person; an upholder of conventional morality'. Compare the later names of Mrs Ormiston Chaunt, an actual woman who campaigned in the late 19th century against immorality in the music hall, and Mrs (Mary) Whitehouse who attempted to 'clean up' British TV from 1965 onwards.

(Sir) Oswald MOSLEY English politician (1896–1980)

5 When fire meets oil, then springs the spark divine.

Quoted in Nicholas Mosley, *Rules of the Game*, Chap. 1 (1982): 'When, years later, people used to ask him how it was that someone like himself had emerged from such a family background he would say – as if it were a quotation and poking fun at himself ... fire being his father and oil his mother – and then he would laugh.' An instant proverb perhaps, like HESELTINE 237:4.

John Lothrop MOTLEY American historian (1814–77)

6 Give us the luxuries of life, and we will dispense with its necessities.

Quoted in Oliver Wendell Holmes, *Autocrat of the Breakfast-Table*, Chap. 6 (1857–8). Miles Kington wrote in *The Independent* (3 May 2001) that recently this has been attributed to Frank Lloyd Wright, the American architect. *ODQ* (1953) noted that it was 'Often mistakenly attributed to Oscar Wilde'. Kington pointed out that in Théophile Gautier's preface to his novel *Mademoiselle de Maupin* (1835), there is something similar: 'Personally, I count myself among those for whom the superfluous is absolutely necessary ... I like people and things in inverse proportion to their usefulness to me.' *The Treasury of Humorous Quotations*, eds Bentley & Esar (1951), attributes to Wilde: 'We live in an age when unnecessary things are our only necessities'; and 'Take care of the luxuries and the necessities will take care of themselves' is attributed to Wilde by John Keats in *You Might as Well Live*, Pt 2, Chap. 1 (1970), though not otherwise found.

Earl MOUNTBATTEN OF BURMA British military commander and Viceroy (1900–79)

7 In my experience, I have always found that you cannot have an efficient ship unless you have a happy ship, and you cannot have a happy ship unless you have an efficient ship. That is the way I intend to start this commission, and that is the way I intend to go on – with a happy and efficient ship.

From Mountbatten's initial address to the crew of HMS *Kelly* after he became the destroyer's captain in 1939. When Noël Coward wrote the script of his film *In Which We Serve* (1942), based on Mountbatten's association with HMS *Kelly* and its sinking during the Battle of Crete, the speech was adopted almost *verbatim*. Coward delivered it.

Daniel Patrick MOYNIHAN American diplomat and Democratic politician (1927–2003)

1 The time may have come when the issue of race could benefit from a period of 'benign neglect'. The subject has been too much talked about … We may need a period in which negro progress continues and racial rhetoric fades.

As a counsellor to President Nixon, Moynihan quoted the phrase 'benign neglect' in a memorandum dated 2 March 1970. This was leaked to *The New York Times*, and the inevitable furore ensued, though all he was suggesting was that racial tensions would be lessened if people on both sides were to lower their voices a little. He was quoting an 1839 remark by John George Lambton, 1st Earl of Durham, to Queen Victoria regarding Canada, of which he was governor general. It had done so well 'through a period of benign neglect' by the mother country that it should be granted self-government.

Wolfgang Amadeus MOZART Austrian composer (1756–91)

2 I write [music] as a sow piddles.

Quoted by Laurence J. Peter in *Quotations for Our Time* (1977). Source untraced, but using imagery of which Mozart was typically fond. Compare John Aubrey's memoir of Dr Kettle who, 'was wont to say that "Seneca writes, as a boare doth pisse", *scilicet*, by jirkes' – *Brief Lives* (?1690).

Kitty MUGGERIDGE English writer (1903–94)

3 He rose without trace.

Of David Frost. A notable remark, made in about 1965. Curiously delighting in it, Frost provides the context in the first volume of his autobiography (1993). Malcolm Muggeridge (Kitty's husband) had predicted that after *That Was the Week That Was*, Frost would sink without trace. She said, 'Instead, he has risen without trace!'

Malcolm MUGGERIDGE English writer and broadcaster (1903–90)

4 Twilight of empire … a phrase which occurred to me long ago.

Diaries (entry for 21 December 1947). Referring to Britain at any time after the death of Queen Victoria in 1901, but particularly when the colonies started moving towards independence. A phrase fashioned, presumably, after 'twilight of the gods' (German *Götterdämerung*).

5 Only dead fish swim with the stream.

Proverbial saying that became linked to Muggeridge through his frequent use of it. In 1957 he was sacked by the BBC after the huge scandal following his controversial article, 'Does England Really Need a Queen?' that was published in the *Saturday Evening Post*. Somewhere along the line, Muggeridge protested, 'Only dead fish swim with the stream.' But was this original? David Williams of the Malcolm Muggeridge Society recounted his own researches (2004): '[After the monarchy scandal] Malcolm quickly got himself a new job with Granada Television, based in Manchester, his old haunt with the *Guardian*, and it was whilst staying in a hotel right by the station that someone said to him consolingly, "Only dead fish swim with the stream." Malcolm related this story himself – but knowing that he did not invent it, the question of its source remains. I have now managed to find a saying by W.C. Fields which certainly predates Malcolm's adoption: "Remember, a dead fish can float downstream, but it takes a live one to swim upstream." I have also found in use, "Only dead fish go with the flow" and "Only dead fish swim with the current." There is also a similar saying by Josh Billings [1818–85], "Some folks are so contrary that if they fell in a river, they'd insist on floating upstream."'

See also *The TIMES* 466:5.

Frank MUIR English writer and broadcaster (1920–98)

6 Oh, infamy, infamy! Yes, they've all got it in for me!

In *A Kentish Lad* (1997), Muir says this line was first uttered by Dick Bentley as Julius Caesar, attacked by Brutus and Co., in the BBC Radio show *Take It From Here* (1948–59). However, it also appeared in a contribution 'by' Jimmy Edwards, who starred in the same show, to *Radio Fun Annual 1951*. The line is often ascribed to Talbot Rothwell, because of his use of the joke in his script for the film *Carry On Cleo* (UK 1964), where Kenneth Williams as Julius Caesar exclaims it after an attempted stabbing. Muir wrote to *The Guardian* (22 July 1995) quietly asserting that it was indeed the product of his and Denis Norden's joint pen. Moreover, he said, Talbot Rothwell had very properly asked their permission to use the line, so it was a bit much always hearing Rothwell praised for writing it. Muir's letter concluded, 'Please may we have our line back.'

7 Many are cold but few are frozen.

On the service sheet at Frank's funeral on a wintry day in January 1998 was inscribed, 'Many are cold but few are frozen: F. Muir.' It does not appear to be the concluding line to any of his published stories from the *My Word* radio programme, as might be expected, so it is not clear when he produced the biblical allusion. Just a footnote, though: the line occurs in (the American) Howard Engel's thriller *Death on Location* (1983); it was available on a T-shirt printed in the US (1982); and was also listed under 'whimsy' in Reisner & Wechsler's *The Encyclopedia of Graffiti* (1974). In Wolfgang Mieder, *Talk Less and Say More: Vermont Proverbs* (1986), we have (undated): 'There's many a chill, but few are frozen' (which rather misses the joke). A Scots version (remembered from the 1930s), 'Many are cauld, but few are frozen', seems to suggest that it was a proverbial expression before it was a joke.

Count Georg MÜNSTER Hanoverian diplomat (1794–1868)

1 Despotism tempered by assassination.

So replied Lord Reith, the BBC's first Director-General, when asked by Malcolm Muggeridge in the TV programme *Lord Reith Looks Back* (1970) what he considered the best form of government. The phrase was not original. For example, *Quotations for Speakers and Writers* (1969) quotes the remark of a Russian noble *to* Count Münster on the assassination of Tsar Paul I in 1800: 'Despotism tempered by assassination, that is our Magna Carta.' *ODQ* (1992) prefers a direct quote from Count Münster's *Political Sketches of the State of Europe, 1814–1867* (1868): 'An intelligent Russian once remarked to us, "Every country has its own constitution; ours is absolutism moderated by assassination."' Bartlett (1980) attributes 'Absolutism tempered by assassination' direct to the earlier Ernst Friedrich Herbert von Münster (1766–1839).

The dates are rather important. How else is one to know whether Thomas Carlyle in his *History of the French Revolution* (1837) was alluding to the saying, when he wrote: 'France was long a despotism tempered by epigrams'? In a speech to the International Socialist Congress (Paris, 17 July 1889), the Austrian, Victor Adler, followed up with: 'The Austrian government ... is a system of despotism tempered by casualness.'

Notes and Queries, Vol. 202 (1957), has earlier sources, including Mme de Staël.

(Dame) Iris MURDOCH English novelist and philosopher (1919–99)

2 I don't believe in God, but I do believe in religion.

Encapsulation (in *The Observer*, 4 July 1999) of a view apparently expressed about the time she won the Booker Prize for her 1978 novel *The Sea, The Sea*. That view was quoted in *The Times Higher Educational Supplement* (19 July 1996) in these words: 'I am not a believer in the sense of believing in God the Father or Jesus Christ as divine. But I believe

that religion is terribly important in people's lives, because it tries to look at the world not veiled by the obsessions, fears and egoism of everyday life. Various priests now tell me that this is what they believe. If only they work fast enough, Christianity can become like Buddhism, before people forget it entirely.'

3 A bad review is even less important than whether it is raining in Patagonia.

Quoted in a profile of her in *The Times* (6 July 1989).

(Sir) James MURRAY Scottish lexicographer (1837–1915)

4 The traditional practice of dictionary makers is 'to copy shamelessly from one dictionary to another'.

When *The Century Dictionary* (1889) seemed to plagiarize Murray's work, it was his friends who reminded him of this. He did not necessarily subscribe to it himself. Quoted in Elizabeth Murray, *Caught in the Web of Words* (1977).

5 Have thy tools ready. God will find thee work.

According to Elizabeth Murray in the same biography, this was his favourite text. It supposedly came from Charles Kingsley and, curiously, Murray hung it in his bedroom.

See also BACON 47:1.

Edward R. MURROW American broadcaster (1908–65)

6 This ... is ... London.

Standard beginning to his wartime reports (1940s). A greeting that became familiar to American radio listeners to reports given by Murrow from London. It was a natural borrowing from BBC announcers who had been saying 'This is London calling' from the earliest days of station 2LO in the 1920s. One of them, Stuart Hibberd, entitled a book of his broadcasting diaries, *This Is London* (1950). Murrow added the distinctive pauses.

7 I knew something of your [England's] history and more of your literature. But to me England was a small, pleasant, historical, but relatively unimportant island off the coast of Europe. It was different and therefore interesting. Your country was a sort of museum piece – pleasant but small. You seemed slow, indifferent and exceedingly complacent – not important ... I admired your history, doubted your future, and suspected that the historians had merely agreed upon a myth. But always there was something that

escaped me. Always there remained in the back of a youthful mind the suspicion that I might be wrong.

A Reporter Remembers, BBC Radio broadcast (24 February 1946). At this date, Murrow was returning to the US after reporting from Europe on the Second World War. He began by reflecting on his first visit to Britain 16 years previously.

1 He [Churchill] mobilized the English language and sent it into battle to steady his fellow countrymen and hearten those Europeans upon whom the long dark night of tyranny had descended.

Broadcast (30 November 1954). This was a frequent trope of Murrow's. In *A Reporter Remembers* (cited above), he also spoke of 'Mr Churchill, who mobilized the language and made it fight.' However, it has been suggested that 'He mobilized the English language' was the coinage of the English writer Beverley Nichols (1899–1983). At some stage, either at the height of the Second World War, or perhaps at the end of it, he and other writers were asked to summarize Churchill's contribution in 250 words or so. Nicholls, reputedly, did it in just these five. In his memoir *The Unforgiving Minute* (1978), Nichols wrote: 'I met [Churchill], shortly after the war, and ... he did me the honour of paying me a compliment. An American newspaper was compiling a syndicate in which various European authors were asked to give their opinions of Churchill's greatest service to the Allied cause. We were offered a dollar a word, which is not to be sneezed at, even though we were limited to five hundred words. I gave my opinion in a sentence of only five words, but they put it top of the list and paid five hundred dollars for it. The five words were ... "He mobilized the English language." The phrase had come to Winston's attention; he had remembered it; and when we met he quoted it back to me ... Why not? the words were true; they went to the heart of the matter. They dated from the days of Dunkirk ... I [had] turned on the radio. Through the room echoed Winston's voice, in one of the classic speeches of the war. (I cannot be sure but I think it was the one about "fighting on the beaches".) It was not a beautiful voice, and certainly not a golden voice, it was a voice of brass ... calling the whole free world to battle.' There we are then: Nichols putting in a bid for a coinage in 1940 whereas the earliest use we have by Murrow is 1946. So did Murrow appropriate the line from Nichols, or did he not? See also KENNEDY 268:2.

2 Anyone who isn't confused doesn't really understand the situation.

Ascribed to Murrow on the subject of Vietnam by Walter Bryan, *The Improbable Irish* (1969). Then applied to the situation in Northern Ireland. 'Anyone who isn't confused here doesn't really understand what's going on' was ascribed to a 'Belfast citizen, 1970' in my book *Quote ... Unquote* (1978).

Benito MUSSOLINI Italian Fascist leader (1883–1945)

3 I will make the trains run on time and create order out of chaos.

Efficiency may be the saving grace of a Fascist dictatorship, but did Mussolini ever actually make this boast? Or did he merely claim afterwards that this is what he had done? One of his biographers (Giorgio Pini, 1939) quotes Mussolini exhorting a stationmaster: 'We must leave exactly on time ... From now on everything must function to perfection.' The improvement was being commented on by 1925. In that year, HRH Infanta Eulalia of Spain wrote in *Courts and Countries after the War* that 'the first benefit of Mussolini's direction in Italy' is when you hear that 'the train is arriving on time'. In Elliott Paul's *The Life and Death of a Spanish Town* (1937), he describes San Eulalia on Ibiza, in which he had been resident for a few years. Referring to Primo de Rivera, the Prime Minister and virtual dictator of Spain under the monarchy: 'So Miguel Tur, when chased out of his home by Primo (I know he built wonderful roads and the trains ran on time), was fully equipped ...'

Quite *how* efficient the trains really were is open to doubt. Perhaps they just ran *relatively* more on time than they had done before. But they had managed all right for the famous 'March on Rome' (October 1922) which – despite its name – was largely accomplished by train.

4 It is better to have lived one day as a tiger than a thousand years as a sheep.

'Tibetan saying' quoted by Jim Ballard, husband of the British climber Alison Hargreaves who was killed on K2 in August 1995. It may have been one of her favourite sayings but, in fact, it is better known as a slogan of Mussolini's in the form: '*È meglio vivere un giorno da leone che cent'anni da pecora* [It is better to live one day as a lion than a hundred years as a sheep]' (?1930), quoted in Denis Mack-Smith, *Mussolini's Roman Empire* (1967), though a photograph of a graffito with this text dating from the Battle of Piave (1918) is in existence. Another form, from the film *The King of Comedy* (US 1983): 'Look, I figure it this way: better to be a king for a night than a schmuck for a lifetime.'

N

Vladimir NABOKOV Russian-born novelist
(1899–1977)

1 Lolita, light of my life, fire of my loins. My sin, my soul. Lo-lee-ta: the tip of the tongue taking a trip of three steps down the palate to tap, at three, on the teeth. Lo. Lee. Ta.

Lolita (1955). Opening words. In *The Independent* Magazine (26 October 1996), the screenwriter Andrew Davies selected this as 'My Favourite Opening Paragraph', adding: 'There's a certain tantalizing purity about it ... There's a lot of play on the actual sound of the words. It's an exquisitely sensual piece of writing.'

V.S. NAIPAUL (later Sir Vidia) Trinidadian novelist
(1932–)

2 *In a Free State.*

Title of a novel (1971), set in a 'free state' in Africa. The phrase had earlier been used as the title of a sketch performed on record by Peter Sellers (1959). The latter is a take-off of an interview with a drunken Brendan Behan, the playwright, and thus the title here alludes to the Irish Free State.

Fridtjof NANSEN Norwegian explorer (1861–1930)

3 We will find in the lives of men who have done anything, of those whom we call great men, that it is this spirit of adventure, the call of the unknown, that has lured and urged them along on their course ... All of us are explorers in life, whatever trail we follow ... It is the explorers with the true spirit of adventure we now need if human-ity shall really overcome the present difficulties ... Ah, youth. What a glorious word! Unknown realms ahead of you, hidden behind the mists of the morning. As you move on, new islands appear, mountain summits shoot up through the peering mists, one behind another, waiting for you to climb; dense new forests unfold for you to explore, free boundless plains for you to traverse.

Speech on being installed as Rector of the University of Aberdeen in November 1926. *The Scotsman* reported: 'Dr Nansen was cheered to the echo when he resumed his seat after speaking for about an hour and twenty minutes.'

4 The cold of the polar regions was nothing to the chill of an English bedroom.

Quoted in *The Laughing Diplomat* (1939) by Daniele Varè. Nansen made several voyages in the Arctic regions. He was also the first Norwegian Ambassador to London (1906–8), which is when he presumably acquired his knowledge of the bedrooms.

5 The difficult is what takes a little time; the impossible is what takes a little longer.

Quoted – as said by Nansen – in *The Listener* (14 December 1939). *Bartlett* (1980) places this slogan specifically with the US Army Service Forces, but the idea has been traced back to Charles Alexandre de Calonne (1734–1802), who said: '*Madame, si c'est possible, c'est fait; impossible? cela se fera* [If it is possible, it is already done; if it is impossible, it will be done]' – quoted in J. Michelet, *Histoire de la Révolution Française* (1847). Earlier this quotation had appeared in Carlyle's *French Revolution* (1837), Pt 1, Bk 3, Chap. 2: 'If it is but difficult, it is done, if it is impossible, it shall be done.' Compare 'The Difficult is that which can be done immediately; the Impossible that which takes a little longer' – George Santayana, American poet and philosopher (1863–1952), quoted in *The Treasury of Humorous Quotations*, eds Esar & Bentley (1951). Henry Kissinger once joked: 'The illegal we do immediately, the unconstitutional takes a little longer' – quoted in William Shawcross, *Sideshow* (1979).

NAPOLEON I French Emperor (1769–1821)

1 As to moral courage, I have very rarely met with two o'clock in the morning courage: I mean unprepared/instantaneous courage [*le courage de l'improviste*].
Remark, 4/5 December 1815 – from E.A. de Las Cases, *Mémorial de Ste-Hélène* (1823). Compare 'The three o'clock in the morning courage which Bonaparte thought was the rarest' – H.D. Thoreau, *Walden*, Chap. 4 (1854).

2 *L'Angleterre est une nation de boutiquiers/marchands* [England is a nation of shopkeepers].
Most of Napoleon's attributed sayings are, like Abraham Lincoln's, impossible to verify now. This remark was quoted by Barry E. O'Meara in *Napoleon in Exile* (1822). Earlier, however, Samuel Adams, the American Revolutionary leader, *may* have said in his *Oration in Philadelphia* (1 August 1776): 'A nation of shopkeepers are very seldom so disinterested.' In the same year, Adam Smith was writing in *The Wealth of Nations*: 'To found a great empire for the sole purpose of raising up a people of customers, may at first sight appear a project fit only for a nation of shopkeepers.'

3 Every soldier has the baton of a field marshal in his knapsack.
This is the anglicized form of a saying frequently attributed to Napoleon. E. Blaze in *La Vie Militaire sous l'Empire* (1837) has it thus: '*Tout soldat français porte dans sa giberne le bâton de maréchal de France*' (which should be more accurately translated as, 'Every French soldier carries in his cartridge-pouch the baton of a marshal of France'). This was how the saying first appeared in English in 1840. The meaning is: 'Even the lowliest soldier may have leadership potential.'
Mencken (1942) ascribes the saying to Louis XVIII (1755–1824) and, indeed, the French king who reigned after Napoleon said in a speech to cadets at Saint-Cyr (9 August 1819): 'Remember that there is not one of you who does not carry in his cartridge-pouch the marshal's baton of the Duke of Reggio; it is up to you to bring it forth [*Rappelez-vous bien qu'il n'est aucun de vous qui n'ait dans sa giberne le bâton de Maréchal du duc de Reggio; c'est à vous à l'en faire sortir*].'

4 An iron hand in a velvet glove.
Napoleon is supposed to have said, 'Men must be led by an iron hand in a velvet glove', but this expression is hard to pin down as a quotation. Thomas Carlyle wrote in *Latter-Day Pamphlets* (1850): 'Soft speech and manner, yet with an inflexible rigour of command ... "iron hand in a velvet glove", as Napoleon defined it.' The Emperor Charles V (1519–56) may have said it earlier. Sometimes an iron 'fist' rather than 'hand' is evoked. Either way, the image is of unbending ruthlessness or firmness covered by a veneer of courtesy and gentle manners.

5 From the sublime to the ridiculous there is but one step.
Nowadays most often used as a phrase without the last five words. The proverbial form most probably came to us from the French. Napoleon is said to have uttered on one occasion (probably to the Polish Ambassador, De Pradt, after the retreat from Moscow in 1812): '*Du sublime au ridicule il n'y a qu'un pas.*'
However, Thomas Paine had already written in *The Age of Reason* (1795): 'The sublime and the ridiculous are often so nearly related, that it is difficult to class them separately. One step above the sublime, makes the ridiculous; and one step above the ridiculous, makes the sublime again.' Indeed, the chances are that 'from the sublime to the ridiculous' may have been a standard turn of phrase in the late 18th century. 'Dante, Petrarch, Boccacio, Ariosto, make very sudden transitions from the sublime to the ridiculous' – Joseph Warton, *Essay on the Genius and Writings of Pope*, Vol. 2 (1772).

Of St Mark's Square, Venice:

6 *Le plus beau salon d'Europe* [Europe's most beautiful salon].
There is no proof that Napoleon said this – nor that he added: 'And it has the sky for ceiling.'

7 An army marches on its stomach [*Une armée marche à plat ventre*].
Attributed remark, encapsulating a report in E.A. de Las Cases, *Mémorial de Ste-Hélène* (1823).

8 Not tonight, Josephine.
Napoleon did not, as far as we know, ever say the words that have become popularly linked with him. The idea that he had better things to do than satisfy the Empress Josephine's famous appetite, or was not inclined or able to do so, must have grown up during the 19th century. There was also a saying, attributed to Josephine, apparently,

'*Bon-a-parte est Bon-à-rien* [Bonaparte is good for nothing]', which may be relevant.

The film *I Cover the Waterfront* (US 1933) has been credited with launching the phrase, though it merely popularized it. A knockabout sketch filmed for the Pathé Library in about 1932 has Lupino Lane as Napoleon and Beatrice Lillie as Josephine. After signing a document of divorce (which Napoleon crumples up), Josephine says, 'When you are refreshed, come as usual to my apartment.' Napoleon says (as the tag to the sketch), 'Not tonight, Josephine', and she throws a custard pie in his face.

A British song with the title had appeared in 1915 (sung by Florrie Forde and written by Worton David and Lawrence Wright), and an earlier American song (sung by Ada Jones and Billy Murray) was recorded on an Edison wax cylinder (?1901–10). Neither of these songs is about the historical Josephine: the British one is about a man who has promised his mother he will not kiss his bride before their wedding day, and the American one is about a stenographer. The saying may well have been established in music hall and vaudeville by the end of the previous century.

A melodrama produced at the Lyceum Theatre, London, was written by W.G. Wills and called *A Royal Divorce*. It concerned the divorce of Napoleon and Josephine. A mention of this play in *Punch* (19 September 1891) enabled a text to be tracked down in the collection of plays submitted to the Lord Chamberlain for censorship purposes and now lodged in the British Library. Wills (1828–91) was an Irish playwright, poet and songwriter who specialized in historical dramas. As passed for production, the play does not contain the famous line but it might conceivably have been grafted on subsequently. A film with the title *A Royal Divorce* (UK 1938), produced by Herbert Wilcox and starring Ruth Chatterton and Pierre Blanchar, is said to be based, rather, on the novel *Josephine* by Jacques Thiérry (date unknown, as also whether it contains the catchphrase).

Indeed, A.E. Wilson's history of the Lyceum Theatre, *The Lyceum* (1952), does contain a photo from the 1911 revival of the play with Ethel Warwick and Frank Lister in the leading roles. The caption to the picture is: 'Not tonight, Josephine!' Confirmation of a possible link between this play and the phrase might also be hinted at by Ursula Shaw, writing to the *Daily Mail* (18 December 1997): 'Veteran stage director Basil Dean recalled that at the turn of the 19th century, an impresario called W.W. Kelly had been running provincial tours of [*A Royal Divorce*] starring his wife as the empress, for so many years "that certain lines, particularly 'Not tonight, Josephine' became bywords with the audience." The catchphrase was profitable enough for Kelly to buy a Liverpool theatre, which he renamed after himself, in the era before World War I.'

1 [Women] belong to the highest bidder. Power is what they like – it is the greatest of all aphrodisiacs.

Attributed to Napoleon by Constant Louis Wairy (his valet) in *Mémoires de Constant, premier valet de l'empereur* (1830–1). Compare KISSINGER 275:4.

2 In victory you deserve it: in defeat you need it.

A saying of Napoleon's (unverified) on the subject of champagne. On the other hand, 'Aid is ... like champagne: in success you deserve it, in failure you need it' is ascribed to Lord Bauer (born 1915), British economist, in *Lords of Poverty* (1989) by Graham Hancock.

3 China? There lies a sleeping giant. Let him sleep! For when he wakes he will move the world.

Often attributed, but unverified. Attributed to Napoleon in the form, 'There lies a sleeping giant, do not wake him', by Harold Macmillan in a TV interview (20 October 1983). There is a tradition of 'sleeping giant' remarks. As a proverb, 'Wake not a sleeping lion' dates back to 1580. One is also reminded that 'Jack and the Beanstalk' (first Englished in 1807) turns very much on what happens when a giant is asleep. In 1843 Astolphe Marquis de Custine wrote his *La Russie en 1839*, a very critical report of a voyage to Russia, which in translation includes this claim: 'One day the sleeping giant will arouse himself and violence will put an end to the reign of speech.' D.H. Lawrence wrote in *Kangaroo*, Chap. 16 (1923): 'Australian Sydney, with a magic like sleep ... a vast, endless, sun-hot, afternoon sleep with the world a mirage ... But surely a place that will some day wake terribly from this sleep.' Compare YAMAMOTO 509:2.

4 Plans are nothing, but planning is everything.

Attributed to Napoleon, but unverified. He does, however, appear to have said: 'Unhappy the general who comes on the field of battle with a system.' This is said to be included in his *Maxims 1804–15*; it also appears in *Napoleon in His Own Words*, compiled by Jules Bertaut (1916). A favourite maxim of Dwight D. Eisenhower, quoted by Richard M. Nixon in *Six Crises* (1962), was: 'In preparing for battle I have always found that plans are useless, but planning is indispensable.'

Petroleum V. NASBY (David Ross Locke) American humorist (1833–88)

5 The late unpleasantness.

Ekkoes from Kentucky (1868). A euphemism for a previous war or recent hostilities. Nasby referred to the recently ended Civil War as 'the late onpleasantniss', and the coinage spread. It still survives: 'Here, for instance, is Dan Rather,

America's father-figure, on the hot-line to Panama during the late unpleasantness [the US invasion]' – *The Independent* (20 January 1990).

Ogden NASH American poet (1902–71)

1 I think that I shall never see
A billboard lovely as a tree.
Perhaps unless the billboards fall,
I'll never see a tree at all.

'Song of the Open Road', *Happy Days* (1933). Compare KILMER 270:3.

2 Every Englishman is convinced of one thing, viz. That to be an Englishman is to belong to the most exclusive club there is.

'England Expects', *I'm a Stranger Here Myself* (1938). Possibly the first encapsulation of a frequently used format. Compare the similar views expressed about membership of the British Parliament: Mr Twemlow in Charles Dickens, *Our Mutual Friend*, Bk 2, Chap. 3 (1864–5), says of the House of Commons: 'I think ... that it is the best club in London'; *Punch* described specifically the House of Commons as 'the Best Club in the World' (2 April 1887); and Winston Churchill called it 'the best club in Europe' – quoted in Leon Harris, *The Fine Art of Political Wit* (1965). This last phrase was also used (as though well established) by Lady Astor in a talk on the BBC Empire Service in November 1937.

George Jean NATHAN American drama critic (1882–1958)

3 The test of a real comedian is whether you laugh at him before he opens his mouth.

In *The American Mercury* (September 1929). Now a cliché. Fred Lawrence Guiles said of Stan Laurel in *Stan* (1980): 'Very early on in his stage career Stan had made an interesting discovery: he found that audiences laughed at him before he ever said or did anything.' In November 1987 Robert McLennan of the SDP said of Barry Humphries as Sir Les Patterson: 'Like all great comic creations, he makes you laugh before he opens his mouth.'

Bill NAUGHTON English playwright (1910–92)

4 It seems to me if they ain't got you one way then they've got you another. So what's it all about, that's what I keep asking myself, what's it all about?

Alfie (1966) – the film script of his earlier radio and stage play. The phrase 'What's it all about, Alfie?' was chiefly

popularized by Burt Bacharach and Hal David's song. This was not written for the film, which had a jazz score (with no songs) by Sonny Rollins, but Cher recorded it and this version was added to the soundtrack for the American release of the picture. Cilla Black then recorded it in Britain and Dionne Warwick in the US.

When Michael Caine, who played Alfie in the film, published his autobiography in 1992, it was naturally entitled *What's It All About?* – as was Cilla Black's in 2003.

J.M. NEALE English clergyman and hymnwriter (1818–66)

5 Good Christian men, rejoice
With heart, and soul and voice.

From the hymn 'Good Christian Men, Rejoice'. Hence, *With Hearts and Hymns and Voices* (1996), title of a BBC *Songs of Praise* book, compiled by Pam Rhodes.

Jawaharlal NEHRU Indian politician (1889–1964)

6 There is no easy walk-over to freedom anywhere, and many of us will have to pass through the valley of the shadow again and again before we reach the mountain-tops of our desire.

'From Lucknow to Tripuri' (1939). This line of Nehru's is quoted by Nelson Mandela in *Long Walk to Freedom*, Chap. 19 (1994), referring to a speech that had to be delivered for him when he was banned from political activities in South Africa in the early 1950s: 'In that speech, which subsequently became known as "The No Easy Walk to Freedom" speech, I said that the masses now had to be prepared for new forms of political struggle.' Presumably the title of Mandela's own book was influenced by Nehru's phrase.

7 History is almost always written by the victors and conquerors and gives their viewpoint.

The Discovery of India (1946). Compare: 'History is written for the victors and what they leave out is the losers' – Arthur Drexler, American arts administrator (Director of Architecture and Design at the Metropolitan Museum of Art, New York) in *The New York Review* (27 November 1975). In the film *Crimes and Misdemeanors* (US 1989), Anna Berger delivers the line: 'Remember, history is written by the winners.' 'Anyone can make history. Only a great man can write it' – Oscar Wilde, 'The Critic As Artist', *Intentions* (1891). A 'Zimbabwean proverb' is also said to state: 'Until lions have their own historians, history will always glorify the hunter.'

Horatio NELSON (Viscount Nelson) English admiral
(1758–1805)

1 The Nelson touch.

Denoting any action bearing the hallmark of Horatio Nelson,
his quality of leadership and seamanship, this term was
coined by Nelson himself before the Battle of Trafalgar. In
letters to Lady Hamilton (25 September and 1 October 1805),
he wrote: 'I am anxious to join the fleet, for it would add to
my grief if any other man was to give them the Nelson
touch, which WE say is warranted to fail' and that, when
he came to explain it to his men, 'it was like an electric
shock'. *The Oxford Companion to Ships and the Sea* (1976)
describes various manoeuvres to which the term could be
applied, but adds: 'It could have meant the magic of his
name among officers and seamen of his fleet, which was
always enough to inspire them to great deeds of heroism
and endurance.' The British title of the film *Corvette K-225*
(US 1943) was *The Nelson Touch*.

2 I owe all my success in life to having been always
a quarter of an hour before my time.

I.e. early. Chiefly in sea battles rather than in private life,
one expects. We have this statement by courtesy of
Samuel Smiles in *Self-Help* (1859). In *The Dictionary of War
Quotations* (1989) the wording is: 'I have always been a
quarter of an hour before my time, and it has made a
man of me.'

3 Before this time tomorrow I shall have gained a
peerage, or Westminster Abbey.

At the Battle of the Nile (1798) – reported in Robert Southey,
The Life of Nelson (1860 edn). Earlier, at the Battle of Cape St
Vincent (1797), he is reported to have said: 'Westminster
Abbey or victory!' Both of these echo Shakespeare, *Henry
VI, Part 3*, II.ii.174 (1590–1): 'And either victory, or else a
grave.'

4 I have only one eye – I have a right to be blind
sometimes ... I really do not see the signal!

At the Battle of Copenhagen in 1803, Nelson 'put the tele-
scope to his blind eye', 'turned a blind eye', as the modern
allusion would have it – that is to say he made sure he did
not see what he did not want to see (a signal ordering him
to desist from action) and had a decisive victory. His exact
words, according to Robert Southey's *Life of Nelson* (1813),
were as above. The point of the gesture is sometimes misunderstood: Admiral Sir Hyde Parker had told Nelson that
he would fly a signal of recall if the battle seemed to be
going badly. He would have to decide himself whether he
would obey it (as discussed in Robert Birley, *The Undergrowth of History*, 1955).

Alan Watkins, writing in *The Observer* (27 June 1993): 'Mr
[John] Major then indulged in some misquotation of his
own involving Lord Nelson, who is supposed to have said
at the Battle of Copenhagen: "I really do not see the signal,"
though the more popular version is: "Danger? I see no
danger." Mr Major took the latter version and replied, referring to the press: "Assault? I see no assault."' (Is Watkins
right about the popularity of the 'danger' version?)

5 England expects that every man will do his duty.

At 11.30 a.m. on 21 October 1805 the British Fleet approached
Napoleon's combined French and Spanish fleets before the
Battle of Trafalgar. Nelson told one of his captains: 'I will
now amuse the fleet with a signal.' At first it was to be,
'Nelson confides that every man will do his duty.' But it was
suggested that 'England' would be better than 'Nelson'. Flag
Lieutenant Pasco then pointed out that the word 'expects'
was common enough to be in the signal book, whereas
'confides' would have to be spelt out letter by letter and
would require seven flags, not one.

When Admiral Lord Collingwood saw the signal coming
from HMS *Victory*, he remarked: 'I wish Nelson would stop
signalling, as we all know well enough what we have to do.'

Mencken (1942) finds an American saying from 1917 –
during the First World War – 'England expects every American to do his duty.' In Britain, at about the same time, there
was a recruiting slogan: 'England Expects that Every Man
will Do His Duty and Join the Army Today.'

6 Kiss me, Hardy.

What exactly did Nelson say as he lay dying on HMS *Victory* at Trafalgar in 1805, having been severely injured by a
shot fired from a French ship? It has been asserted that,
according to the Nelson family, he was in the habit of saying
'Kismet' (fate) when anything went wrong. It is therefore
not *too* unlikely that he said 'Kismet, Hardy' to his Flag
Captain, and that witnesses misheard, but there is no real
reason to choose this version.

In fact, the recording angel had to work overtime when
Nelson lay dying, he said so much. The first reliable report
of what went on was by Dr Beatty, the ship's surgeon,
included in *Despatches and Letters of Lord Nelson*, ed. Nicholas
(1846): 'Captain Hardy now came to the cockpit to see his
Lordship a second time. He then told Captain Hardy that
he felt that in a few minutes he should be no more, adding
in a low tone, "Don't throw me overboard, Hardy." The
Captain answered, "Oh, no, certainly not." Then replied his
Lordship, "You know what to do. Take care of my dear Lady
Hamilton. Kiss me, Hardy." The Captain now knelt and
kissed his cheek, when his Lordship said, "Now I am
satisfied. Thank God I have done my duty."'

This seems to be quite a reasonable description and, if Hardy did actually kiss him (a gesture that surely could not be mistaken), why should Nelson not have asked him to? Was there something wrong with a naval hero asking for this gesture from another man? Robert Southey in his *Life of Nelson*, published earlier, in 1813, also supports the 'kiss me' version (his account is almost identical to Beatty's). In Ludovic Kennedy's *On My Way to the Club* (1989) he recalls his own investigations into the matter: 'I was delighted to receive further confirmation from a Mr Corbett, writing from Hardy's home town of Portesham [in 1951]. He said that Nelson's grandson by his daughter Horatia had recently paid him a visit, at the age of over ninety. "He told me he had asked his mother what exactly had happened when Nelson was dying. She said she herself had asked Hardy, who replied, 'Nelson said, "Kiss me, Hardy" and I knelt down and kissed him.'"'

It is also possible to argue that 'kiss' can mean no more than 'touch' – a reasonable and usual request from a dying man who needs some last physical contact.

NERO Roman Emperor (AD37–68)

1 *Qualis artifex pereo!* [What a great artist dies with me!]

As he drove a dagger into his throat rather than be taken alive. Nero had poetic and artistic ambitions (hence the expression about him fiddling while Rome burned – probably he was playing the lyre). Quoted in Suetonius, *Lives of the Caesars* and in Barnaby Conrad, *Famous Last Words* (1961).

Gérard de NERVAL French poet (1808–55)

2 Well, you see, he doesn't bark and he knows the secrets of the sea.

Explaining his penchant for taking a lobster for a walk in the gardens of the Palais Royal, Paris, on a long blue leash (pink, in some versions). Théophile Gautier, *Portraits et souvenirs littéraires* (1875), has an elaborate version of the explanation, which translates as: 'Why should a lobster be any more ridiculous than a dog? Or any other animal that one chooses to take for a walk? I have a liking for lobsters; they are peaceful, serious creatures; they know the secrets of the sea; they don't bark, and they don't gnaw upon one's *monadic* privacy like dogs do. And Goethe had an aversion to dogs, and he wasn't mad.' An unanswerable conclusion, surely?

Allan NEVINS American writer and teacher (1890–1971)

3 The former allies had blundered in the past by offering Germany too little and offering even that too late, until finally Nazi Germany had become a menace to all mankind.

In *Current History* (May 1935). On 13 March 1940 the former Prime Minister David Lloyd George said in the House of Commons: 'It is the old trouble – too late. Too late with Czechoslovakia, too late with Poland, certainly too late with Finland. It is always too late, or too little, or both.' From there the phrase passed into more general use, though usually political. From the *Notting Hill & Paddington Recorder* (25 January 1989): 'Junior Transport Minister, Peter Bottomley, came to West London last week to unveil plans for a £250 million relief road that will cut a swathe through the heart of the area ... But Hammersmith and Fulham councillors are furious about the government consultation exercise which they claim is "too little too late".' From *The Guardian* (30 January 1989): 'The Home Office is preparing a video to warn prisoners of the dangers [of AIDs] – but is it too little, too late?'

(Sir) Henry NEWBOLT English poet (1862–1938)

4 *The Island Race.*

Title of book of poems (1898) – though not of any actual poem in it – the first prominent appearance of the phrase. In Newbolt's first book, *Admirals All and Other Verses* (1897), there is a poem called 'The Guides at Cabul 1879' whose first line is: 'Sons of the Island Race, wherever ye dwell.' The characterization of Britain as an 'island race' understandably reached its apogee in the Second World War, but at big patriotic moments there has always been a tendency to draw attention to the fact of Britain being an island, from John of Gaunt's 'sceptr'd isle' speech in Shakespeare's *Richard II* onwards. Winston Churchill said, 'We shall defend our Island, whatever the cost may be' in his 'We shall fight on the beaches' speech of 4 June 1940. The flag-waving film *In Which We Serve* (1942) refers specifically to the 'island race'. Churchill used the phrase as the title of Bk 1, Vol. 1 of his *History of the English-Speaking Peoples* (1956). In *The Second World War*, Vol. 5 (1952), he also quotes the 'island story' phrase from Tennyson's 'Ode on the Death of the Duke of Wellington' (1852):

Not once or twice in our rough island story
The path of duty was the way to glory.

5 There's a breathless hush in the Close to-night – ... 'Play up! play up! and play the game!'

'Vitaï Lampada', in the same collection. The title of the poem refers, roughly speaking, to 'the torch of tradition' that the generations hand on like runners. Newbolt combines a cricket match with some military action in the desert to produce an imperial-sounding message.

(Sir) Isaac NEWTON English scientist (1642–1727)

1 O Diamond! Diamond! thou little knowest the mischief done!

To his dog who is said to have knocked over a candle and set fire to Newton's papers, thus destroying the labour of many years. Probably apocryphal, though recounted by 1772. Another version renames the dog: 'Ah, poor Fidele, what mischief hast thou done!' From P.G. Wodehouse, *The Code of the Woosters* (1938): 'I don't know if you were ever told as a kid that story about the fellow whose dog chewed up the priceless manuscript of the book he was writing. The blow-out, if you remember, was that he gave the animal a pained look and said: "Oh, Diamond, Diamond, you – or it may have been thou – little know – or possibly knowest – what you – or thou – has – or hast – done." I heard it in the nursery, and it has always lingered in my mind.'

2 If I have seen further it is by standing on the shoulders of giants.

In a letter to Robert Hooke (5 February 1676) in the context of their dispute over light and colours. Newton was attempting to conciliate his correspondent. However, the letter has also been interpreted as an insult to Hooke, one of Newton's bitterest enemies, whose main crime seems to have been to criticize Newton's work. Hooke was very short, if not actually a dwarf, and unprepossessing in appearance (he was described by John Aubrey as '... but of middling stature, something crooked ... his eye full and popping ...'). Newton's reference to giants was (according to this interpretation) to make it clear, albeit in outwardly courteous terms, his utter contempt for Hooke and his complete lack of any intellectual debt to him.

An earlier appearance of the saying occurs in Robert Burton's *Anatomy of Melancholy*, 'Democritus to the Reader' (1621): 'Though there were many giants of old in physic and philosophy, yet I say with Didacus Stella, "A dwarf standing on the shoulders of a giant may see farther than a giant himself."' Long before this, in 1159, Bernard of Chartres, the French philosopher, had been quoted as saying, 'We are like dwarfs on the shoulders of giants, so that we can see more than they ... not by virtue of any sharpness of sight on our part ... but because we are carried high and raised up by their giant size.' The proverbial expression 'A dwarf on a giant's shoulders sees the further of the two' appears to have been established by the 14th century. 'Standing on the shoulders of giants' has been engraved on the £2 coin from 1998 – apparently referring to Newton's use of the phrase.

John NEWTON English hymnwriter (1725–1807)

3 Amazing grace! how sweet the sound,
That saved a wretch like me!
I once was lost, but now am found,
Was blind, but now I see.

Most people are familiar with 'Amazing Grace' from the great popular success it had when sung and recorded by Judy Collins in the early 1970s, but it is quite wrong for record companies to label the song 'Trad.' – as, for example, on the CD 'Amazing Grace' (Philips 432–546-2), by Jessye Norman. It was a hymn written in the 17th century by John Newton, a reformed slave-trafficker. He (together with the poet William Cowper), wrote the *Olney Hymns* of 1779, and this is but one example from that work.

The slightly complicated thing is that the *tune* to which 'Amazing Grace' now gets sung *is* a traditional tune – it is an old American one – but that is hardly any excuse for denying Newton his credit for the words. (Some people say that before it was an anonymous American tune it was an anonymous Scottish tune.)

NEW YORK SUN See *The SUN*.

NICHOLAS I Russian Tsar (1796–1855)

4 Russia has two generals – *Janvier and Février*.

Attributed remark. The only evidence that he said such a thing comes from the caption to a *Punch* cartoon (10 March 1855) at the time of his death. He meant, of course, that the bitter cold winter months of January and February saw off Russia's enemies (like Napoleon) as effectively as any general. He was referring to the Crimean War – he died in the middle of it.

Peter NICHOLS English playwright (1927–)

5 That Bernadette Shaw? What a chatterbox! Nags away from asshole to breakfast-time but never sees what's staring her in the face.

Privates on Parade, Act 1, Sc. 5 (1977). Acting Captain Terri Dennis speaking. Not Nichols's own view.

Vivian NICHOLSON English pools winner (1936–)

6 I'm going to spend, spend, spend, that's what I'm going to do.

Nicholson and her husband Keith, a trainee miner, were bringing up three children on a weekly wage of £7 in Castleford, Yorkshire. Then, in September 1961, they won £152,000 on Littlewoods football pools. Arriving in London by train to collect their prize (recounted in her autobiography *Spend, Spend, Spend*, 1977), she made this off-the-cuff remark to reporters. It made newspaper copy – as in the *Daily Herald* (28 September 1961) – and was used as the title of a TV play. The win was the prelude to misfortune. Keith died in a car crash and Viv worked her way through a succession of husbands until the money was all gone. A musical based on the autobiography was staged in London in 1999.

(Sir) Harold NICOLSON English writer and politician (1886–1968)

1 One of the minor pleasures in life is to be slightly ill.

Quoted in *The Observer*, 'Sayings of the Week' (22 January 1950). Compare this from C.S. Lewis, *Surprised by Joy*, Chap. 12 (1955): 'Perhaps I ought to have mentioned before that I had had a weak chest ever since childhood, and had very early learned to make a minor illness one of the pleasures in life, even in peace-time.' The point about the last phrase is that it comes in the context of the First World War, when the convalescent home was particularly attractive as an alternative to the trenches.

2 The BBC's unerring instinct for the second-rate.

Letter to Lady Violet Bonham Carter (dated 28 August 1943) in *Harold Nicolson: Diaries and Letters*, Vol. 2 (1967). He was threatening to resign as a Governor of the BBC over the appointment of William Haley as Editor-in-Chief. Compare his own low view of the activity in which he had some success: 'The gift of broadcasting is, without question, the lowest human capacity to which any man could attain' – quoted in *The Observer* (5 January 1947).

Reinhold NIEBUHR American Protestant theologian (1892–1971)

3 God give us the grace to accept with serenity
   the things that cannot be changed;
   Give us the courage to change what should be
   changed;
   Give us the wisdom to distinguish one from
   the other.

Bartlett (1980) calls this 'The Serenity Prayer', dates it 1934, and in the 15th (but not 16th edition) notes that it was 'written for a service in the Congregational church of Heath, Massachusetts, where Dr Niebuhr spent many summers. The prayer was first printed in a monthly bulletin of the Federal Council of Churches. Enormously popular, it has been circulated in millions of copies.' One place where it could be found was Dale Carnegie's book *How To Stop Worrying and Start Living* (1944), in which Niebuhr is described as Professor of Applied Christianity at New York's Union Theological Seminary.

But there is a question mark over the authorship. The prayer was immensely popular in Germany after the Second World War, and was credited to the 18th-century theologian Friedrich Oetinger. This name was actually a pseudonym of Theodor Wilhelm, a writer who later admitted that he had simply translated Niebuhr's words. Curiously, another version has been attributed to one Johann Christoph Oetinger (that name again), a deacon in Weinsberg from 1762 to 1769: '*Gib mir Gelassenheit, Dinge hinzunehmen, die icht nicht ändern kann, Den Mut, Dinge zu ändern, die ich ändern kann, und die Weisheit, das eine vom andern zu untersheiden.*'

Niebuhr was often asked where he had found the prayer but, in January 1950, he was telling *The A.A. Grapevine*: 'It may have been spooking around for years, even centuries, but I don't think so. I do honestly believe that I wrote it myself.' He stuck to this line and accepted copyright fees from Hallmark Cards from 1962. And yet, *American Notes and Queries* (June 1970) stated that: 'Niebuhr has acknowledged, more than once, both in seminar and publicly that he was not the original author of the Serenity Prayer.'

Well, God, give us the serenity to see that it doesn't really matter who wrote it. It exists, and many people obviously find it very helpful. A shortened version was adopted by Alcoholics Anonymous, the self-help group, which has two million members and 67,000 groups in 114 countries: 'God grant me the serenity to accept the things I cannot change; the courage to change the things I can; and the wisdom to know the difference.'

Martin NIEMÖLLER German Protestant pastor and theologian (1892–1984)

4 When Hitler attacked the Jews, I was not a Jew, therefore, I was not concerned. And when Hitler attacked the Catholics, I was not a Catholic, and therefore, I was not concerned. And when Hitler attacked the unions and the industrialists, I was not a member of the unions and I was not concerned. Then, Hitler attacked me and the Protestant church – and there was nobody left to be concerned.

Comment attributed to Niemöller, the former German U-boat commander turned pastor, on the extent to which he had spoken out against Hitler (and for which he was imprisoned until 1945). This is the version printed in *The Congressional Record* (14 October 1968) and cited by *ODQ* and others. Several versions exist, often doctored to reflect more current concerns. On Britain's first Holocaust Memorial Day in January 2000, Channel 4 showed a documentary in which a Jewish academic was critical of the American Holocaust Museum in Boston. He claimed that the text displayed in the museum had been doctored, bringing 'the Jews' to the start of the list, and also adding 'the Catholics' (because Boston is a heavily Catholic city).

So how did it enter circulation? *Chambers Dictionary of Quotations* (1996) gives the above version, word for word, and states that it comes from the foreword to Niemöller's *Children of Light and the Children of Darkness* (1944). It does not. For a start, that book was written by Reinhold Niebuhr, not Niemöller, and for another thing, the quotation is not mentioned in either the foreword or the rest of the book ...

Sue Critchfield of the Bay Area Reference Center at San Francisco Public Library approached Niemöller, who responded to her inquiries in a letter dated 2 June 1971, sent from Wiesbaden, and in English. He referred to 'a passage from my interviews or discussions, which may have happened about 3 years ago [this accords with the 1968 *Congressional Record* quotation]. You have not been the first with this request for information. My answer is this: I have pronounced my regret for our standing up against Hitler's concentration camps so late, and have compared our hesitation to do so with our being concerned in the first line [of the quotation] with our interest for ourselves (the "church"). But I never have spoken of Roman Catholics as having been persecuted by the "Führer" earlier than the Protestants; for this time the Protestants have been first!'

In addition, Niemöller made changes in the quotation submitted to him, with his pen. He moved the second stanza (about Jews) *after* the one about trade unionists and crossed out the stanza about the Roman Catholics. This version reflects Niemöller's corrections:

In Germany, they came first for the Communists,
And I didn't speak up because I wasn't a Communist;

And then they came for the trade unionists,
And I didn't speak up because I wasn't a trade unionist;

And then they came for the Jews,
And I didn't speak up because I wasn't a Jew;

And then ... they came for me ...
And by that time there was no one left to speak up.

Niemöller did not indicate the time or place when he had first said or printed the statement, except for the allusion to 'interviews or discussions ... about 3 years ago'. Presumably, the *Congressional Record* took its version from reports of one of these, which might explain why Niemöller was not able to reach back to a written-down original of the statement. I wonder, in fact, whether the whole matter might have its roots back in Niemöller's first speaking tour

of the United States in 1946, a year after the so-called Stuttgart Declaration of Guilt in which German Evangelicals accused themselves 'of not having borne witness more courageously [against the National Socialist terror-regime]' – which would seem to be borne out by Niemöller's widow (see below).

Whatever the case, all this makes plain that neither the *Congressional Record* version, nor the one marked 'Attributed' in *Bartlett* (1992), accords with Niemöller's wishes, because of the order they give to the material and because of the 'came for the Catholics' element.

Dennis B. Roddy, a staff writer with the Pittsburgh *Post-Gazette*, contributed a significant article entitled 'The Poison of Quotation Manipulation' (2 August 1998) that inserts a different extra sentence after the first paragraph: 'Then they came for the social democrats, but I was not a social democrat, so I did nothing.' This, he states, 'is as it is remembered by Niemöller's widow, who heard him repeat it many times' and 'was historically the progression to the camps. The communists and social democrats and trade unionists all were taken in the early roundups because they were the last groups around which an opposition could coalesce. The Jews, of course, were the most victimized, 6 million killed as opposed to 5000 political opponents executed. That they do not come first in the procession of persecuted groups is a very deliberate and significant thing: Niemöller is not comparing wounds here. He is explaining how persecutions of small, sometimes less-than-sympathetic groups, gained momentum until, at last, we had to invent a new word to encompass the evil: genocide.'

Roddy also quotes Niemöller's second wife, Sybille (then living in 'suburban Philadelphia'), as saying, 'He never did write it down and now there's nothing I can do except try to correct it.' Also, apparently, Niemöller did not make the statement until after the war, when he 'was brought to the United States by Church World Services' and 'put on a lecture tour' where he used this confession as a conclusion. Mrs Niemöller 'has come across just about every variation from every group trying to hitch a ride on the Holocaust'. Her husband would get upset 'when various groups ... smuggled themselves in' to the quotation. The misquotation that irritated him most was when they would add 'they came for the Catholics' – because 'When the Gestapo rounded up individual Catholic leaders for resisting Hitler ... Niemöller brazenly asked his congregation to pray in support of them.' So in that case he could not be accused of remaining silent. Other groups that have been 'smuggled ... in include gays and gypsies – even hackers and militia members – and apparently in many cases the Communists (and less often the social democrats and trade unionists) have been left off ...'

Florence NIGHTINGALE English nurse (1820–1910)

1 Too kind, too kind.

When given the Order of Merit in 1907. Quoted in E. Cook, *Life of Florence Nightingale* (1913). In *Eminent Victorians* (1918), Lytton Strachey suggests that Nightingale *murmured* the words and adds, 'she was not ironical'. Not her last words, as sometimes suggested.

Richard M. NIXON American Republican 37th President (1913–94)

2 Would you buy a used car from this man?

Although attributed by some to Mort Sahl and by others to Lenny Bruce, and though the cartoonist Herblock denied that he was responsible, in *The Guardian* (24 December 1975), this is just a joke *about* Nixon, and one is no more going to find an origin for it than for most such. As to *when* it arose, this is Hugh Brogan, writing in *New Society* (4 November 1982): 'Nixon is a double-barrelled, treble-shotted twister, as my old history master would have remarked; and the fact has been a matter of universal knowledge since at least 1952, when, if I remember aright the joke, "Would you buy a second-hand car from this man?" began to circulate.' It was a very effective slur and, by 1968, when the politician was running (successfully) for President, a poster of a shifty-looking Nixon with the line as caption was in circulation.

Now used of anybody one has doubts about. In a Mahood cartoon of Prime Minister Edward Heath in *Punch* (7 January 1970): 'Would you buy a used boat from this man?' *The Encyclopedia of Graffiti* (1974) even finds: 'Governor Romney – would you buy a *new* car from this man?' In August 1984, John de Lorean said of himself – after being acquitted of drug-dealing – 'I have aged 600 years and my life as a hard-working industrialist is in tatters. Would you buy a used car from me?'

3 Regardless of what they say about it, we are going to keep it ... I don't believe I ought to quit because I am not a quitter.

TV address (23 September 1952). Nixon was defending himself, when running as a vice-presidential candidate, against charges that he had been operating a secret fund. He denied that any of the money had been put to his personal use: every penny had gone on campaign expenses. Then he proceeded to throw dust in the eyes of viewers by mentioning a dog called Checkers that had been given to his daughters. Was that a politically acceptable gift? He rejected any idea of disappointing his daughters by returning it. Never mind that the problem was not the dog but the 'secret fund', the so-called 'Checkers speech' saved the day for Nixon.

4 Just think about how much you're going to be missing. You won't have Nixon to kick around any more, because, gentlemen, this is my last press conference.

To the press, on losing the California gubernatorial election (7 November 1962), following his two terms as Eisenhower's vice-president. Nixon was reluctant to appear and concede defeat before newsmen, feeling that they had given him a tough time during the campaign. But he did, and bade them what turned out to be a temporary farewell. President Kennedy's comment was that Nixon must have been 'mentally unsound' to make the statement: 'Nobody could talk like that and be normal.' In 1982 John Ehrlichman attributed the Nixon performance to a 'terrible hangover'.

5 I have a secret plan to end the [Vietnam] war.

Attributed remark during the 1968 presidential election. William Safire, *On Language* (1980), declares that Nixon never said it. Compare David Halberstam, *The Best and the Brightest*, 'A Final Word' (1972): 'He did not spell out his policies, in large part because he had none. He contented himself with telling audiences that he had a plan to end the war, even touching his breast pocket as if the plan were right there in the jacket ... The truth was that he had no plan at all.'

6 I see another child tonight. He hears a train go by. At night he dreams of faraway places where he'd like to go. It seems like an impossible dream.

Speech accepting the Republican presidential nomination at Miami (8 August 1968). Nixon suddenly switched to the third person. He told of a boy growing up with limited prospects in a small town in southern California. The climax came when Nixon let the audience know that *he* was that small boy whose 'impossible dream' had become a reality. William Safire, then a Nixon speechwriter, recalled how proud his boss was of that ending, and what Nixon had had to say about it: 'I'd like to see [Rockefeller] or Romney or Lindsay do a moving thing like that "impossible dream" part, where I changed my voice. Reagan's an actor, but I'd like to see him do it' – quoted in *The Washington Post* (6 May 1984).

The phrase was taken from a song called 'The Impossible Dream' – see *MAN OF LA MANCHA* 310:2.

7 This is the greatest week in the history of the world since the Creation.

On the USS *Hornet* welcoming the Apollo 11 astronauts home from the first moon landing on 24 July 1969. Dr Billy Graham, the evangelist, told him shortly afterwards: 'Mr

President, I know exactly how you felt, and I understand exactly what you meant, but, even so, I think you may have been a little excessive.'

1 The great silent majority of my fellow Americans.
Still trying to extricate the US from Vietnam, Nixon gave a TV address on 3 November 1969 designed to show it would be wrong to end the war on less than honourable terms or to be swayed by anti-war demonstrations. He himself wrote some paragraphs calling for the support of a particular section of American opinion. The notion of a large unheard body of opinion – sometimes called the 'silent centre' or 'Middle America' – was not new, but Nixon's appeal ushered in a period of persecution of the 'vocal minority'.

Ironically, the phrases 'silent majority' and 'great majority' were used in the 19th century to describe *the dead*. *Harper's New Monthly Magazine* had 'The silent majority' as a heading in September 1874. The dying words of Lord Houghton in 1884 were: 'Yes, I am going to join the Majority and you know I have always preferred Minorities.' Compare BROWNE 104:3.

2 I brought myself down. I gave them a sword and they stuck it in and they twisted it with relish. And I guess if I'd been in their position I'd have done the same thing.
TV interview with David Frost (19 May 1977). Hence, *I Gave Them A Sword*, title of a book (1978) by David Frost about the Nixon interviews.

See also BAKER 50:1; BLACKSTONE 90:5; CONABLE 151:5; GLADSTONE 214:4; GREELEY 221:1.

Christopher NORTH (Professor John Wilson)
Scottish literary critic (1785–1854)

3 His Majesty's dominions, on which the sun never sets.
Noctes Ambrosianae in *Blackwood's Magazine* (April 1829). Hence, the idea of 'the empire upon which the sun never sets', referring to the British Empire, which was so widespread at its apogee that the sun was always up on some part of it. Earlier, the idea had been widely applied to the Spanish Empire. In 1631 the English explorer and writer Captain John Smith (of Pocahontas fame) asked in *Advertisements for the Unexperienced*: 'Why should the brave Spanish soldier brag the sun never sets in the Spanish dominions, but ever shineth on one part or other we have conquered for our king?' Also said about the Dutch Empire, possibly by Emperor Charles V. See also ANONYMOUS 19:5.

1st Viscount NORTHCLIFFE British newspaper proprietor (1865–1922)

4 When I want a peerage, I shall buy one like an honest man.
Quoted in R. Pound & G. Harmsworth, *Northcliffe* (1959), and in Tom Driberg, *Swaff* (1974). An unlikely remark, even if meant in jest. Alfred Harmsworth was created a baron in 1905 and a viscount in 1917. His battles with David Lloyd George, the principal purveyor of pay-as-you-rise ennoblement, raged throughout the First World War.

5 News is what someone, somewhere doesn't want published ... all the rest is advertising.
Unquestionably Northcliffe's view, but unverified. Compare 'Freedom of the press in Britain is freedom to print such of the proprietor's prejudices as the advertisers don't object to' – Hannen Swaffer, English journalist (1879–1962). In conversation with Tom Driberg in about 1928 and recalled in Driberg's *Swaff* (1974). Driberg suspected that Swaffer began to take this view in about 1902.

Caroline NORTON English novelist and poet (1808–77)

6 For death and life, in ceaseless strife,
Beat wild on this world's shore,
And all our calm is in that balm –
Not lost but gone before.
Poem, 'Not Lost But Gone Before'. Hence, the standard epitaph now imprinted on countless graves. According to *Benham* (1907), 'Not lost but gone before' was the title of a song published in Smith's *Edinburgh Harmony* (1829) – perhaps a setting of Norton's poem?

But the idea was not new. From *Human Life* (1819) by Samuel Rogers:

Those whom he loved so long and sees no more,
Loved, and still loves – not dead – but gone before,
He gathers round him.

According to *Mencken* (1942), the phrase occurs in one of Alexander Pope's epitaphs for 'Elijah Fenton, Easthampstead England' (?1731) – though this one is not included in *Pope's Poetical Works*:

'Weep not,' ye mourners, for the dead,
But in this hope your spirits soar,
That ye can say of those ye mourn,
They are not lost but gone before.

And to Philip Henry (1631–96) is ascribed the couplet:

They are not *amissi*, but *praemissi*;
Not lost but gone before.

Seneca wrote: '*Non amittuntur sed praemittuntur* [They are

not lost but sent before].' So the concept is, indeed, a very old one. The simple phrase 'gone before' meaning 'dead' was well established in English by the early 16th century.

Ivor NOVELLO Welsh-born composer and actor (1893–1951)

1 Keep the Home Fires Burning.

Title of song (1915). Originally entitled 'Till the Boys Come Home'. The lyrics were, in fact, written by Lena Guilbert Ford, though Novello is credited with the title line.

2 Blaze of lights and music calling, Music weeping, rising, falling, Like a rare & precious diamond His brilliance still lives on.

Lines on Novello's memorial tablet in the crypt of St Paul's Cathedral, London. They were written by Lynn S. Maury of the Ivor Novello Memorial Society, which mounted an eight-year campaign to have a plaque placed in the cathedral.

See also BURROUGHS 111:6.

Edgar Wilson ('Bill') NYE American humorist (1850–96)

3 I have been told that Wagner's music is better than it sounds.

In Mark Twain's *Autobiography* (published posthumously in 1924) he ascribes this to Nye, who had predeceased him in 1896. Given the dates involved here, it is curious that Lewis Baumer was providing this caption to a *Punch* cartoon (20 November 1918): (Two women talking) – 'Going to hear some Wagner.' 'What! – do you like the stuff?' 'Frankly, no; but I've heard on the best authority that his music's very much better than it sounds.'

See also MENCKEN 320:6.

O

Captain Lawrence Edward ('Titus') OATES
English explorer (1880–1912)

1 I am just going outside, and I may be some time.

Oates walked to his death on Captain R.F. Scott's 1912 expedition. Beaten to the South Pole by the Norwegian explorer
Roald Amundsen, the small party fell victim to terrible
weather conditions on the return journey to its ship. One
man died, and Oates, suffering from scurvy, an old war
wound and frostbitten and gangrenous feet, realized that
he would be next. He presumably thought that without him
slowing them down, the remaining three members of the
party might stand a better chance of survival. He did not
bother to spend the couple of hours' painful effort needed
to put on his boots. He made his classic stiff-upper-lip
understatement, went out in his stockinged feet and did
not return.

It was inevitable in time that iconoclasts would review
the evidence and wonder whether, in the light of Oates's
expressed criticisms of Scott, his action was truly voluntary
or whether it was the result of silent hints from the expedition leader. As the only record of what Oates said was
contained in Scott's diary, published as *Scott's Last Expedition* (1923), it has been suggested that the words were Scott's
invention. But it was an act perfectly in character and there
would have been no need for any invention.

Not only did Oates define courage for a generation, he
unwittingly provided a joke expression or catchphrase to
be used when a person is departing from company for whatever reason. When Trevor Griffiths came to write a TV drama
series about Scott's expedition called *The Last Place on Earth*
(1985), he accordingly substituted the line: 'Call of nature,
Birdie.'

2 Hereabouts died a very gallant gentleman.

Scott wrote in his diary: 'We knew that poor Oates was walking to his death, but though we tried to dissuade him, we
knew it was the act of a brave man and an English gentleman.' Oates's actual epitaph, composed later by E.L. Atkin-
son and Apsley Cherry-Garrard and recorded in the latter's
The Worst Journey in the World (1922), took up this theme
and was placed on a cairn marking the spot from where he
walked. The epitaph continues: 'Captain L.E.G. Oates of
the Inniskilling Dragoons. In March 1912, returning from
the Pole, he walked willingly to his death in a blizzard, to
try and save his comrades, beset by hardship. This note is left
by the Relief Expedition. 1912.'

Sean O'CASEY Irish playwright (1884–1964)

3 *The Silver Tassie.*

Title of play (1929), in which tassie = cup. O'Casey got it
from a Scottish ballad that begins: 'Oh bring to me a pint
of wine / And fill it in a silver tassie, / That I may drink
before I go / A service to my bonnie lassie!' This is often
attributed to Robert Burns under the title of 'The Silver
Tassie' or 'My Bonie Mary' (1788), though he may have
adapted this from an older ballad, as he often did. O'Casey
was apparently unaware of the ascription to Burns when
he first heard the verse in London. In the play it becomes
a football cup that is won by soldiers who go away to suffer
in the First World War. Hence, also the title of Mark-
Anthony Turnage and Amanda Holden's opera (2000)
based on the play.

1 English literature's performing flea.

On P.G. Wodehouse and quoted by Wodehouse in a book entitled *Performing Flea* (1953). Wodehouse commented: 'I believe he meant to be complimentary, for all the performing fleas I have met impressed me with their sterling artistry and that indefinable something which makes the good trouper.'

Adolph S. OCHS American newspaper proprietor (1858–1935)

2 All the news that's fit to print.

Slogan devised by Ochs when he bought *The New York Times*, and used in every edition since – at first on the editorial page, on 25 October 1896, and from the following February on the front page near the masthead. It became the paper's war cry in the battle against formidable competition from the *World*, the *Herald* and the *Journal*. It has been parodied by Howard Dietz as 'All the news *that fits* we print' – which, at worst, sounds like a slogan for the suppression of news. However, no newspaper prints everything.

Patrick O'KEEFE American advertising practitioner (1872–1934)

3 Say it with flowers.

This slogan was originally devised for the Society of American Florists and invented in 1917 for its chairman, Henry Penn of Boston, Massachusetts. Major Patrick O'Keefe, head of an advertising agency, suggested: 'Flowers are words that even a babe can understand' – a line he had found in a poetry book. Penn considered that too long. O'Keefe, agreeing, rejoined: 'Why, you can say it with flowers in so many words.' Later came several songs with the title – source: Julian Lewis Watkins, *The 100 Greatest Advertisements* (1959).

(Sir) Laurence OLIVIER (later Lord Olivier) English actor (1907–89)

4 Success smells like Brighton.

Quoted in *Peter Hall's Diaries* (1983) – in an entry for 1977. Unless it was a remark Olivier was fond of making, this quotation comes from a TV interview he gave to Kenneth Tynan in the BBC series *Great Acting* (26 February 1966). Talking of the tumultuous reception of his stage *Richard III* (1944), Olivier said: 'There was something in the atmosphere ... There is a phrase "the sweet smell of success" ... I have had two experiences like that and it just smells like Brighton and oyster bars and things like that.'

Eugene O'NEILL American playwright (1888–1953)

5 *Mourning Becomes Electra.*

Title of play (1931). The origin of the 'mourning becomes' expression is obscure but was apparently in existence by 3 November 1883 when *Punch* carried a cartoon entitled 'Consolation', which showed a rather plump widow gazing at her reflection in the mirror and saying (with a sigh): 'Ah, well – "mourning" always was becoming to me.'

6 *The Iceman Cometh.*

Title of play (1946) about a saloon harbouring alcoholics who would, of course, be looking forward to having some to put in their drinks. The phrase was of endless fascination to the British, to whom the concept of the 'iceman' was all but unknown and the 'cometh' wonderfully affected. In *Salad Days* (1954) there is the line 'The spaceman cometh!', and there was a song 'The Gas-Man Cometh' by Michael Flanders and Donald Swann (1963). Perhaps the 'cometh' was biblical in origin, as in 'behold this dreamer cometh' (Genesis 37:19).

Yoko ONO Japanese-born artist (1933–)

7 Woman Is the Nigger of the World.

Title of song (1972) by her husband John Lennon – from a remark she had made in an interview with *Nova* Magazine (1968). Compare Zora Neale Hurston, *Their Eyes Were Watching God* (1937): 'De nigger woman is de mule uh de world so fur as Ah can see.'

J. Robert OPPENHEIMER American physicist (1904–67)

8 I am become death, the destroyer of worlds.

Quoting from the *Bhagavad Gita*, Chap. 11, verse 32, at the explosion of the first atomic bomb, New Mexico (16 July 1945). Recalled in Giovanitti & Freed, *The Decision to Drop the Bomb* (1965).

Suzie ORBACH American-born writer (1946–)

9 *Fat Is a Feminist Issue.*

Title of book (1978). The title was so brilliantly descriptive, you hardly had to read the book.

Baroness ORCZY Hungarian-born novelist (1865–1947)

10 We seek him here, we seek him there,
    Those Frenchies seek him everywhere.
    Is he in heaven? – Is he in hell?
    That demmed, elusive Pimpernel?

The Scarlet Pimpernel, Chap. 12 (1905). The Scarlet Pimpernel is the *nom de guerre* of a seemingly foppish Englishman, Sir Percy Blakeney, who helps French aristocrats to escape the guillotine in the 1790s. He makes up this rhyme to point up the French government's predicament.

P.J. O'REILLY British lyricist (early 20th century)

1 Drake is going west, lads.

Song, 'Drake Goes West' (1910), with music by Wilfrid Sanderson. Alluded to in Noël Coward's 1952 song 'There Are Bad Times Just Around the Corner':

> In Dublin they're depressed, lads,
> Maybe because they're Celts,
> For Drake is going West, lads,
> And so is everyone else.

Spike Milligan has also used the line in parody:

> Drake is going West, lad
> Howard is going East
> But little Fred just lies in bed
> Lazy little beast.

Joe ORTON English playwright (1933–67)

2 *Prick Up Your Ears.*

Title for unmade film, suggested by his lover and murderer Kenneth Halliwell. Eventually used by John Lahr for his biography of Orton (1978), and by Alan Bennett for a film about Orton and Halliwell (UK 1987).

3 *Mike*: There's no word in the Irish language for what you were doing.
Wilson: In Lapland they have no word for snow.

The Ruffian on the Stair, revised edn (1967). What they were doing was, naturally, of a homosexual nature. The observation about Lapland amounts to artistic licence: rather the reverse is believed to be the case. Far from having no word for snow, the Laps have any number to describe all the different types of snow.

George ORWELL English novelist and journalist (1903–50)

4 I'm fat, but I'm thin inside. Has it ever struck you that there's a thin man inside every fat man, just as they say there's a statue inside every block of stone?

Coming Up for Air (1939). See also AMIS 8:3; CONNOLLY 153:3; WHITEHORN 492:1.

5 It is commonly said that every human being has in him the material for one good book, which is true in the same sense as it is true that every block of stone contains a statue.

In *New Statesman and Nation* (7 December 1940). The 'commonly said' points to a proverbial expression, but no earlier use has been found, though Italo Svevo is said to have produced a James Joyce citation. Presumably, the idea behind the saying is that all people have one story that they alone can tell – namely, the story of their life. The 'every block of stone' remark has been attributed rather loosely to Aristotle and Michelangelo. Pope wrote in *The Dunciad*, Bk 4, line 270: '...and hew the Block off, and get out the Man'. A note to this line, signed by Pope and William Warburton, reads: 'A notion of Aristotle, that there was originally in every block of marble, a Statue, which would appear on the removal of the superfluous parts.' More recently, James Sutherland has added, 'This notion is usually credited to Michelangelo. I have failed to trace it in Aristotle' (1963 edn of *The Dunciad*). Diogenes Laertius had access, however, to works of Aristotle now lost, and in his *Vitae Philosophorum*, 5:33, he wrote: 'This realization, according to [Aristotle], is twofold. Either it is potential, as that of Hermes in the wax, provided the wax be adapted to receive the proper mouldings, or as that of the statue implicit in the bronze; or again it is determinate, which is the case with the completed figure of Hermes or the finished statue' (trans. R.D. Hicks).

The Michelangelo may be a corruption of something from *Rime* (his collected poems, ?1538):

> *Non ha l'ottimo artista alcun concetto*
> *ch'un marmo solo in sè non circoscriva*
> *col suo soverchio, e solo a quello arriva*
> *la man che ubbidisce all'intelletto.*

Which, when translated, means: 'The best artist has not any project/idea that a single piece of marble does not contain in abundance; and it is only attained by the hand that obeys the mind.' Longfellow translated it thus: 'Nothing the greatest artist can conceive / That every marble block doth not confine / Within itself; and only its design / The hand that follows intellect can achieve.'

6 Mr Blunden is no more able to resist a quotation than some people are to refuse a drink.

Reviewing a book by Edmund Blunden. In the *Manchester Evening News* (20 April 1944).

7 Four legs good, two legs bad.

Animal Farm (1945). The slogan with which the animals seize control from their human master.

1 ALL ANIMALS ARE EQUAL
BUT SOME ANIMALS ARE MORE
EQUAL THAN OTHERS.

A fictional slogan from Chap. 10 of the same novel, which was a commentary on the totalitarian excesses of Communism. It had been anticipated: Hesketh Pearson recalled in his biography (1956) of the actor-manager Sir Herbert Beerbohm Tree that Tree wished to insert one of his own epigrams in a play called *Nero* by Stephen Phillips (1906). It was: 'All men are equal – except myself.' In Noël Coward's *This Year of Grace* (1928) there is the exchange:

Pellet: Men are all alike.
Wendle: Only some more than others.

The saying alludes, of course, to Thomas Jefferson's 'All men are created equal and independent', from the 'rough draft' of the American Declaration of Independence (1776) – see 254:4. It has the makings of a formula phrase in that it is more likely to be used to refer to humans than to animals. Only the second half of the phrase need actually be spoken, the first half being understood: 'You-Know-Who [Mrs Thatcher] is against the idea [televising parliament]. There aren't card votes at Westminster, but some votes are more equal than others' – *The Guardian* (15 February 1989).

2 BIG BROTHER IS WATCHING YOU.

Slogan from *Nineteen Eighty-Four* (1949). In the totalitarian state of the novel, every citizen is regimented and observed by a spying TV set in the home. The line became a popular catchphrase following the sensational BBC TV dramatization (1954). Aspects of the Ministry of Truth in the novel were derived not only from Orwell's knowledge of the BBC (where he worked) but also from his first wife Eileen's work at the Ministry of Food, preparing 'Kitchen Front' broadcasts during the Second World War (in about 1942–4). One campaign there used the slogan 'Potatoes are Good for You' and was so successful that it had to be followed by 'Potatoes are Fattening'.

3 At 50, everyone has the face he deserves.

Notebook entry for 17 April 1949 – when he was 46 and had only one year to live, quoted in *The Collected Essays*, Vol. 4 (1968).

See also MAJOR 308:3; MITFORD 324:5; WELLINGTON 486:6.

John OSBORNE English playwright (1929–94)

4 They spend their time mostly looking forward to the past.

Look Back in Anger, Act 2, Sc. 1 (1956). Hence, the title *Looking Forward to the Past*, the title of a history chat show on BBC Radio 4 (current 1991). Compare: 'What do you look forward to?' 'The past' – an exchange with the American artist Charles Demuth in 1929, quoted in David Gebhard, *Charles Demuth* (1971).

5 'Oh, the end of me old cigar, cigar, the end of me old cigar, I turned 'em round and touched 'em up with the end of me old cigar.'

The Entertainer, Act 2, Sc. 8. Frank dancing. See also WESTON AND LEE 491:3.

6 You've been a good audience. Very good. A very *good* audience. Let me know where you're working tomorrow night – and I'll come and see YOU.

Same play and scene. Archie Rice speaks the last words of the play. The last sentence is now inscribed on Osborne's grave in St George's churchyard, Clun, Shropshire.

7 Since I gave up hope, I feel so much better.

Sign displayed in the home of playwright John Osborne – reported in *The Independent* (26 April 1994). Virgil may have anticipated this with '*Una salus victis nullam sperare salutem* [Losers have one salvation – to give up all hope of salvation]' – *Aeneid*, Bk 2, verse 354.

Arthur O'SHAUGHNESSY English poet (1844–81)

8 We are the music makers,
We are the dreamers of dreams ...
Yet we are the movers and shakers
Of the world for ever, it seems.

'Ode' (1874) – set to music by Edward Elgar as *The Music Makers* (1912). Hence, the modern expression 'movers and shakers' to describe people of power and influence. From J.F. Burke's novel *Death Trick* (1975): 'Beniamino Tucci was known as the Little Godfather of the Upper West Side. A mover and shaker with many interests.' From *The Economist* (7 November 1987): 'Many of the advertised movers and shakers [in President Reagan's administration] soon resign in disgust, or bolt back to the private sector once their Washington experience can be cashed in.'

OVID Roman poet (43BC–AD17)

9 *Quod latet ignotum est, ignoti nulla cupido* [What lies hid is unknown, and there is no desire for the unknown].

Ars Amatoria, 3.397. Hence, the proverbial phrase 'for things unknown there is no desire', one of the sayings lobbed about in Tony Hancock's immortal 'Blood Donor' TV show.

David OWEN (later Lord Owen) English Labour then
Social Democrat politician (1938–)

1 We are fed up with fudging and mudging, with
mush and slush.

Speech, Labour Party Conference, Blackpool (2 October
1980). 'To fudge and mudge', meaning 'to produce the
appearance of a solution while, in fact, only patching up a
compromise', was a verb that often arose in discussions of
the Social Democratic Party and the Liberal Party in Britain
during the 1980s. Owen, one of the SDP's founders, had
used it earlier in his previous incarnation, as a member of
the Labour Party.

Robert OWEN Welsh-born socialist reformer (1771–1858)

2 All the world is queer save thee and me, and even
thou art a little queer.

On breaking up with his business partner, W. Allen, at New
Lanark (1828). Attributed remark.

Wilfred OWEN English poet (1893–1918)

3 If you could hear, at every jolt, the blood
Come gargling from the froth-corrupted lungs,
Obscene as cancer, bitter as the cud
Of vile, incurable sores on innocent tongues, –
My friend, you would not tell with such high
    zest
To children ardent for some desperate glory,
The old Lie: Dulce et decorum est
Pro patria mori.

'Dulce et Decorum Est' (written 1917), in *Poems* (1920).
Compare HORACE 245:1.

P

Tom PAINE English-born American revolutionary and political theorist (1737–1809)

1 These are the times that try men's souls. The summer soldier and the sunshine patriot will, in this crisis, shrink from the service of their country; but he that stands it *now*, deserves the love and thanks of men and women.
'The American Crisis', *Pennsylvania Journal* (1776).

2 We have it in our power to begin the world over again.
Common Sense, originally published in 1776. The words were quoted by Ronald Reagan, first at the end of his 'Evil Empire' speech at Orlando, Florida (8 March 1983), then in a televised presidential campaign debate with his challenger, Walter Mondale (7 October 1984). Possibly they were also alluded to in Reagan's 'Farewell Address to the Nation' (11 January 1989): 'Once you begin a great movement, there's no telling where it will end. We meant to change a nation, and instead, we changed a world.'

Paine's words were also quoted by Margaret Thatcher on a visit to the White House in November 1988. An odd choice of quotation, when Paine had done his best to end any possibility of a 'special relationship' between Britain and America. The passage continues: 'Independence is the only bond that can tie and keep us [Americans] together ... Let the names of Whig and Tory be extinct.'

3 *The Rights of Man.*
Title of book (1791). A treatise on government that forced Paine to flee England the following year, but earned him an honoured place as a theoretician of the French Revolution, then in progress. It seems that Paine may have been anticipated by Edmund Burke, who used the same phrase in 'On the Army Estimates' (1790). A year earlier, in August 1789, the French National Assembly had adopted the *Declaration of the Rights of Man and of the Citizen* (*Declaration des droits de l'homme et du citoyen*); it was incorporated as the preface of the French constitution of 1791. Compare the title *The Rites of a Man: Love, Sex and Death in the Making of the Male* – a book (1991) by Rosalind Miles.

Alan J. PAKULA American film director (1928–)

4 *Love and Pain and the Whole Damned Thing.*
Title of film (US 1972), script by Alvin Sargent. *Love, Pain and the Whole Damn Thing* was used as the English title of a short-story collection by the German writer and film director, Doris Dorrie (1989).

Tony PALMER English film-maker and critic (1935–)

5 If there is still any doubt that Lennon and McCartney are the greatest songwriters since Schubert ...
Reviewing The Beatles' *White Album* in *The Observer* (November 1968). Compare BUCKLE 107:2; MANN 309:5.

Lord PALMERSTON British Prime Minister (1784–1865)

6 Die, my dear doctor? That's the *last* thing I shall do.
Deathbed words. Quoted in E. Latham, *Famous Sayings and their Authors* (1961).

Emmeline and Christabel PANKHURST English suffragette leaders (mother and daughter) (1858–1928) and (1880–1958)

1 Votes for Women.

Both Pankhursts, founders of the Women's Social and Political Union, have described how this battle cry emerged. This is a synthesis of their recollections: in October 1905 a large meeting at the Free Trade Hall, Manchester, was to be addressed by Sir Edward Grey, who was likely to attain ministerial office if the Liberals won the forthcoming general election. The WSPU was thus keen to challenge him in public on his party's attitude to women's suffrage in Britain: 'The question was painted on a banner in large letters ... How should we word it? "Will you give women suffrage?" – we rejected that form, for the word "suffrage" suggested to some unlettered or jesting folk the idea of suffering. "Let them suffer away!" – we had heard the taunt. We must find another wording and we did!

'It as so obvious and yet, strange to say, quite new. Our banners bore this terse device: "WILL YOU GIVE VOTES FOR WOMEN?"' The plan had been to let down a banner from the gallery as soon as Grey stood up to speak. Unfortunately, the WSPU had failed to obtain the requisite number of tickets. It had to abandon the large banner and cut out the three words so that they would fit on a small placard. 'Thus quite accidentally came into existence the slogan of the suffrage movement around the world.'

Alas, Sir Edward Grey did not answer the question, and it took rather more than this slogan – hunger strikes, suicide, the First World War – before women got the vote in Britain in 1918. In the US, the Nineteenth Amendment, extending female franchise on a national scale, was ratified in time for the 1920 elections.

Other uses to which the slogan was put: a newspaper with the title *Votes for Women* was launched in October 1907. At a meeting in the Royal Albert Hall, someone boomed 'Votes for Women' down an organ pipe. The Independent Labour Party used to refer to it as 'Votes for Ladies'. In due course, some feminists were to campaign with the slogan 'Orgasms for women'.

Dorothy PARKER American writer (1893–1967)

2 Guns aren't lawful;
Nooses give;
Gas smells awful;
You might as well live.

'Resumé, *Enough Rope* (1927). Hence, *You Might As Well Live*, title of a biography of Parker (1970) by John Keats.

3 Scratch an actor and you'll find an actress.

Quoted in Leslie Halliwell, *The Filmgoer's Book of Quotes* (1973). Hence, *Scratch an Actor*, title of book (1969) by Sheilah Graham, the Hollywood gossip columnist. Maybe out of confusion with 'Scratch a lover, and find a foe' from 'The Ballade of Great Weariness' in *Enough Rope* (1927).

4 What fresh hell is this?

Attributed remark on hearing the doorbell or the telephone ringing – although Vincent Sheean, a foreign correspondent quoted by John Keats in his Parker biography, *You Might As Well Live*, Chap. 7 (1970), remembered, rather, that, 'If the doorbell rang in her apartment, she would say "What fresh hell *can this be?*" – and it wasn't funny; she meant it.' The phrase seems to have been crisped up at the end, by the time it was used as the title of Marion Meade's book, *Dorothy Parker: What Fresh Hell Is This?* (1988). In her Introduction, Meade says: 'Her way of looking at life was incurably pessimistic. Confronted by the unknown, she immediately prepared for the worst. Ordinary occurrences – the doorbell or a ringing telephone – made her wonder "What fresh hell is this?"' However, if Dottie herself was quoting, a thorough search through Shakespeare has so far turned up nothing, nor does it occur in Webster's *The Duchess of Malfi* or *The White Devil* (although the latter has 'O me! this place is hell').

5 This is not a novel to be tossed aside lightly. It should be thrown with great force.

Quoted in R.E. Drennan, *Wit's End* (1973). In Matthew Parris, *Scorn* (1994), this is said to refer to Benito Mussolini's novel *Claudia Particella, L'Amante del Cardinale: Grande Romanzo dei Tempi del Cardinal Emanuel Madruzzo*. When this was published in the US as *The Cardinal's Mistress*, Parker reviewed it devastatingly (15 September 1928), but did not actually include this put-down.

6 Where does she find them?

In reply to the comment (about someone else), 'Anyway, she's always very nice to her inferiors.' Quoted in *The Lyttelton Hart-Davis Letters*, Vol. 1 (1978). Told sometimes regarding Clare Boothe Luce. Compare what Boswell put in his *Life of Johnson* for 1770: '... being told that [a certain tradesman's daughter] was remarkable for her humility and condescension to inferiors, he observed, that those were very laudable qualities, but it might not be so easy to discover who the lady's inferiors were'.

7 How can they tell?

In 1933, when told that President Calvin Coolidge had died, Parker produced this, one of her two or three most quoted remarks. It is recorded in Bennett Cerf, *Try and Stop Me* (1944). As 'How do they know?', it appears in Malcolm Cowley, *Writers at Work*, Series 1 (1958). In that form it is also attributed to Wilson Mizner – in Alva Johnston, *The Legendary Mizners* (1953). The lack of contemporary sources and its omission, for example, from the Keats biography makes one wonder if the remark has drifted to Parker from Mizner.

1 Go to the Martin Beck Theatre and watch Katharine Hepburn run the whole gamut of emotions from A to B.

Reviewing *The Lake* (1933). This is only attributed. G. Carey in *Katharine Hepburn* (1985) has the famous quip merely as a remark made in the intermission on the first night. Some would say that Parker went on and stated that Hepburn put some distance 'between herself and a more experienced colleague [Alison Skipworth] lest she catch acting from her'.

2 If, with the literate, I am
Impelled to try an epigram,
I never seek to take the credit;
We all assume that Oscar said it.

'A Pig's Eye View of Literature' (1937). Referring, of course, to Oscar Wilde. A law of quotations coined by, nevertheless, the most quoted woman of the 20th century.

3 Oh, life is a glorious cycle of song,
A medley of extemporanea;
And love is a thing that can never go wrong
And I am Marie of Roumania.

'Comment', *Not So Deep As a Well* (1937). An expression of disbelief found in a recent detective novel – Val McDermid's *Clean Break* (1995): 'If what you had nicked off your wall is a Monet, I am Marie of Romania.' The rather more pressing question is, what was so funny about Marie of Romania (1875–1938) that she found herself in the verse? Marie was one of Queen Victoria's grandchildren and became the Queen of King Ferdinand I. She paid a famous visit to the US in 1926 and, apparently, carried on rather like a cross between Imelda Marcos and Fergie, the present Duchess of York. No doubt this was what captured Parker's amused attention.

4 How do people go to sleep? I'm afraid I've lost the knack ... I might repeat to myself, slowly and soothingly, a list of quotations beautiful from minds profound; if I can remember any of the damn things.

'The Little Hours', *Here Lies* (1939). A further use for quotations.

5 Pearls before swine.

To Clare Booth Luce – when going through a swing door together, Luce had used the customary phrase 'Age before beauty.' Mrs Luce described this account as completely apocryphal in answer to a question from John Keats in the book *You Might as Well Live* (1970).

6 Because he spills his seed on the ground.

On naming her canary Onan, alluding to Genesis 38:9. Quoted in the Keats book.
See also TYNAN 472:5.

C. Northcote PARKINSON English author and historian (1909–93)

7 It is a commonplace observation that work expands so as to fill the time available for its completion.

First promulgated in *The Economist* (19 November 1955), what later became known as 'Parkinson's Law' was concerned with the pyramidal structure of bureaucratic organizations. A pre-echo may be found in the 18th-century Lord Chesterfield's letters: 'The less one has to do, the less time one finds to do it in.'

Charles Stewart PARNELL Irish nationalist politician (1846–91)

8 No man has a right to fix the boundary of the march of a nation: no man has a right to say to his country – thus far shalt thou go and no further.

Speech, Cork (1885). The limit-setting phrase was of earlier coinage, however. George Farquhar, the (Irish-born) playwright has this in *The Beaux' Stratagem*, Act 3, Sc. 2 (1707): 'And thus far I am a captain, and no farther.' And then again, Job 38:11 has: 'Hitherto shalt thou come, but no further: and here shall thy proud waves be stayed.'

Blaise PASCAL French philosopher and mathematician (1623–62)

9 I have made this letter longer only because I have not had time to make it shorter.

Lettres Provinciales, No. 16 (1657).

10 If Cleopatra's nose had been shorter the whole face of the earth would have changed.

Pensées, 2.62 (1670). That is to say, if the Queen of Egypt had not attracted both Julius Caesar and Mark Antony, and become embroiled with the affairs of the Roman Empire, history might have taken a different course.

1 *Tous le malheur des hommes vient d'une seule chose qui est de ne savoir pas demeurer en repos dans une chambre* [All the troubles of men are caused by one single thing, which is their inability to stay quietly in a room].

In the same work, 2.139. The last word has been mistranslated as 'bedroom', which puts a rather different complexion on it.

2 *Le coeur a ses raisons que la raison ne connaît point* [The heart has its reasons which reason knows nothing of].

In the same work, 4.277. Hence, *The Heart Has Its Reasons*, title of the memoirs (1956) of the Duchess of Windsor.

Walter PATER English critic (1839–94)

3 Hers is the head upon which all 'the ends of the world are come', and the eyelids are a little weary.

Of the *Mona Lisa*. From 'Leonardo da Vinci', *Studies in the History of the Renaissance* (1873), first published in *The Fortnightly Review* as 'Notes on Leonardo da Vinci' (November 1869). Here Pater incorporates a quotation – from 1 Corinthians 10:11: 'Now all these things happened unto them for ensamples: and they are written for our admonition, upon whom the ends of the world are come.'

4 To burn always with this hard, gemlike flame, to maintain this ecstasy, is success in life.

Studies in the History of the Renaissance, 'Conclusion' (1873). Pater was urging the awakening of an aesthetic sense in his followers (who included Oscar Wilde), on the grounds that a desire for beauty and a love of art give a quickened sense of life.

'Banjo' PATERSON Australian poet (1864–1941)

5 Oh! there once was a swagman camped in a
    Billabong
Under the shade of a Coolabah tree;
And he sang as he looked at his old billy boiling,
'Who'll come a-waltzing Matilda with me?'

Song, 'Waltzing Matilda' (written in 1894 but not published until 1903). The title 'Waltzing Matilda' comes from the Australian phrase for carrying your 'Matilda' or backpack as a tramp does. *The Macquarie Dictionary* (1981) suggests a derivation from the German *walzen*, to move in a circular fashion 'as of apprentices travelling from master to master', and German *Mathilde*, a female travelling companion or bed roll (from the girl's name). All this has the status of an unofficial Australian national anthem, so

Australians can get quite abusive when discussing the meaning of the song. The above verse is as shown in *The Dictionary of Australian Quotations*, ed. Murray-Smith (1984). (Swagman = itinerant labourer carrying his swag, or bundle; billabong = dead water, backwater; billy = cooking pot.) Note, however, this different transcription in *ODQ* (1992):

> Once a jolly swagman camped by a billabong,
> Under the shade of a coolibah tree;
> And he sang as he watched and waited till his 'Billy' boiled:
> 'You'll come a-waltzing, Matilda, with me.'

Alan PATON South African novelist (1903–88)

6 *Cry the Beloved Country.*

Title of novel (1948). The 2001 edition has a foreword that confirms that this is not an outside quotation. Paton asked four friends to come up with a title for his book, and they all chose the same phrase from a speech given by one of the characters.

Leslie PAUL Irish social philosopher (1905–85)

7 *Angry Young Man.*

Any writer from the mid-1950s who showed a social awareness and expressed dissatisfaction with conventional values and with the Establishment – John Osborne, Kingsley Amis and Colin Wilson among them – was likely to be labelled with this phrase. Paul had called his autobiography *Angry Young Man* in 1951, but the popular use of the phrase stems from *Look Back in Anger*, the 1956 play by John Osborne, which featured an anti-hero called Jimmy Porter. Other earlier uses of phrases like it, though not necessarily with precisely this sense, include, by H.G. Wells in *Brynhild* (1937): 'I am Angry Man ... almost professionally'; by Rebecca West in *Black Lamb and Grey Falcon* (1941): 'The angry young men run about shouting'; by J.B. Priestley, *Magicians* (1954): 'He's the contemporary Angry Little Man.'

The phrase did not occur in Osborne's play, but was applied to the playwright by George Fearon in publicity material from the Royal Court Theatre, London. Fearon later told *The Daily Telegraph* (2 October 1957): 'I ventured to prophesy that this generation would praise his play while mine would, in general, dislike it ... "if this happens," I told [Osborne], "you would become known as the Angry Young Man". In fact, we decided then and there that henceforth he was to be known as that.'

In Osborne's *Almost a Gentleman* (1991), he pours the inevitable scorn on Fearon, and quotes him as saying, 'I suppose you're really – an angry young man ... aren't you?', and comments: 'He was the first one to say it. A boon to headline-writers ever after.'

James PAYN English novelist and poet (1830–98)

1 I had never had a piece of toast
Particularly long and wide,
But fell upon the sanded floor,
And always on the buttered side.

In *Chamber's Journal* (2 February 1884). This may be no
more than a proverbial expression versified (prefiguring
Murphy's Law) and is, in any case, probably a parody of
MOORE 327:4. However, in A.D. Eichardson, *Beyond Mississippi* (1867), there had already been: 'His bread never fell
on the buttered side.'

J.H. PAYNE American actor and songwriter (1791–1852)

2 Mid pleasures and palaces though we may roam,
Be it ever so humble, there's no place like home.

Song, 'Home, Sweet Home', from the opera *Clari, or, The
Maid of Milan* (1823). The origin of the expression 'There's
no place like home.'

Thomas Love PEACOCK English novelist and poet
(1785–1866)

3 A book that furnishes no quotations is, *me judice*,
no book – it is a plaything.

Crotchet Castle, Chap. 9 (1831). The quotationist's credo.

4 His eye in a fine frenzy rolling.

Nightmare Abbey (1818). This description of a character
called Mr Flosky is based in fact on an actual poet – Samuel
Taylor Coleridge, whose fine frenzy of eye-rolling had probably been brought on by having been at the opium. See
SHAKESPEARE 418:6.

Mervyn PEAKE English novelist, poet and artist
(1911–68)

5 To live at all is miracle enough.

Title line of poem (?1949). Peake is chiefly known for his
grotesque Gothic fantasies *Titus Groan* (1946), *Gormen-
ghast* (1950) and *Titus Alone* (1959). His work as a war artist
had taken him to Belsen, and he was profoundly affected
by this experience. This poem, it will be noted, was written
quite soon afterwards. The title line is also inscribed on
Peake's gravestone at Burpham, West Sussex.

Hesketh PEARSON English biographer (1887–1964)

6 Misquotation is ... the pride and privilege of
the learned. A widely read man never quotes

accurately for the rather obvious reason that he
has read too widely.

Common Misquotations (1937). Pearson was, apparently, the
first person to compile a dictionary solely devoted to misquotations. It is a slim volume and slightly muddies its own
water by claiming that certain sayings are commonly misquoted when they are not and by condemning variants of
proverbs (which surely cannot be said to have a correct
form). Pearson truly observed, however, that 'Misquotations are the only quotations that are never misquoted.'

Vladimir PENIAKOFF Belgian-born soldier and writer
(1897–1951)

7 Spread alarm and despondency.

Meaning, 'have a de-stabilizing effect, purposely or not'.
During the Second World War, Lieutenant-Colonel Peniakoff ran a small raiding and reconnaissance force on behalf
of the Allies that became known as 'Popski's Private Army'.
In his book *Private Army* (1950), he wrote: 'A message came
on the wireless for me. It said "Spread alarm and despondency" ... The date was, I think, May 18th, 1942.' When a
German invasion was thought to be imminent at the beginning of July 1940, Winston Churchill had issued an 'admonition' to 'His Majesty's servants in high places ... to report,
or if necessary remove, any officers or officials who are
found to be consciously exercising a disturbing or depressing influence, and whose talk is calculated to spread alarm
and despondency'. Prosecutions for doing this did indeed
follow. The phrase goes back to the Army Act of 1879: 'Every
person subject to military law who ... spreads reports calculated to create unnecessary alarm or despondency ... shall
... be liable to suffer penal servitude.'

Samuel PEPYS English civil servant and diarist
(1633–1703)

8 And so to bed.

Pepys's famous signing-off line for his diary entries occurs
first on 15 January 1660. However, on that occasion these are
not quite his last words. He writes: 'I went to supper, and
after that to make an end of this week's notes in this book,
and so to bed.' Then he adds: 'It being a cold day and a great
snow, my physic did not work so well as it should have
done.' Usually, the phrase is the last thing he writes, though
sometimes he just puts, 'So to bed.' The fame of the phrase
'And so to bed' is in part due to its use as the title of a play by
J.B. Fagan (1926), which was turned into a musical by Vivian
Ellis (1951).

Both *Mencken* (1942) and *Bartlett* (1980) give the date of its
first appearance as 22 July 1660 (when the phrase in fact

is just 'So to bed'); *ODQ* (1992) also has, misleadingly, '20 April 1660'. The reason for this confusion is that these books *may* have been dealing with incomplete or inaccurate transcriptions of Pepys's shorthand that were superseded by the Latham/Matthews edition of 1970–83.

Indeed, the first time I read the diaries – in an old Dent's Everyman's Library edition (1906, revised 1953) – I was more than a little surprised that the full phrase 'And so to bed' was *nowhere* to be found. It couldn't have been excised on the grounds of taste, could it?

The phrase was clearly established before Pepys took it up. It occurs, for example, in Burton's *The Anatomy of Melancholy* (1621) – Partition 3, Section 2, Member 1, Sub-section 1. An early usage is found in the poem 'Of Gnatho' in Edward Gilpin's *Skialetheia* (1598): 'There his devotion wakes till it be day, / And so to Bed: Pray wish us all Good Rest.'

1 My Lord told me that among his father's many old sayings that he had writ in a book of his, this is one: that he that doth get a wench with child and marries her afterward it is as if a man should shit in his hat and then clap it upon his head.

Diary (7 October 1660). Pepys's patron (also his first cousin once removed) was the politician, naval commander and diplomat, Edward Mountagu, created 1st Earl of Sandwich in 1660. His father had been a Royalist, whereas Mountagu espoused the Parliamentarian cause. The book in question remains untraced.

2 I went out to Charing Cross, to see Major-General Harrison hanged, drawn and quartered; which was done there, he looking as cheerful as any man could do in that condition.

In the same work (13 October 1660). Thomas Harrison was one of the regicides. Pepys reflects that not only had he seen King Charles I beheaded but now he had seen 'the first blood shed in revenge for the blood of the King'.

3 A good honest and painful sermon.

In the same work (17 March 1661). Painful here = painstaking. It was preached by 'a stranger', but Pepys does not reveal upon what text.

4 And so I betake myself to that course, which is almost as much to see myself go into my grave – for which, and all the discomforts that will accompany my being blind, the good God prepare me!

In the same work, closing words (31 May 1669). In fact, he was able to keep on working and did not die for another 30 years or so.

Horace PERCIVAL English actor (died 1961)

5 Don't forget the diver!

This – of all the many catchphrases sired by BBC Radio's *ITMA* show – is the one with the most interesting origin. It was spoken by Percival as 'the Diver' and was derived from memories that the star of the show, Tommy Handley, had of an actual one-legged man who used to dive off the pier at New Brighton, Merseyside, in the 1920s. 'Don't forget the diver, sir, don't forget the diver,' the man would say, collecting money. 'Every penny makes the water warmer, sir.' The radio character first appeared in 1940, and no lift/ elevator descended for the next few years without somebody using the Diver's main catchphrase or his other one, 'I'm going down now, sir!'

But who was the original diver? James Gashram wrote to *The Listener* (21 August 1980): 'My grandfather McMaster, who came from a farm near the small village of Rathmullen, in County Donegal, knew Michael Shaughnessy, the one-legged ex-soldier, in the late 1890s, before he left for the Boer War and the fighting that cost him his leg. About 1910, Shaughnessy, then married to a Chester girl, settled in Bebington on the Wirral peninsula ... Before the internal combustion engine, [he] used to get a lift every weekday from Bebington to New Brighton in a horse-drawn bread-cart owned by the Bromborough firm of Bernard Hughes. The driver of that cart, apparently, was always envious of the "easy" money Shaughnessy got at New Brighton – sometimes up to two pounds a day in the summer – and would invariably say to him on the return to Bebington, "Don't forget the *driver*." Shaughnessy rarely did forget. It was many years later, some time in the early 1930s, that, remembering the phrase so well, he adapted it to his own purposes by changing it to "Don't forget the diver", and shouted it to the people arriving from Liverpool.'

As for 'I'm going down now, sir', bomber pilots in the Second World War are said to have used this phrase when about to make a descent. From *ITMA*'s VE-Day edition:

Effects: Knocking
Handley: Who's that knocking on the tank?
The Diver: Don't forget the diver, sir – don't forget the diver.
Handley: Lumme, it's Deepend Dan. Listen, as the war's over, what are you doing?
The Diver: I'm going down now, sir.
Effects: Bubbles.

S.J. PERELMAN American humorist (1904–79)

6 I've got Bright's Disease. And he's got mine.

Caption to cartoon in *Judge* (16 November 1929). The disease of the kidneys was first described in 1827 by Dr Richard

Bright, who is not to be blamed for the intrinsic humour in naming diseases after specific people.

1 **'Oh, son, I wish you hadn't become a scenario writer!' she sniffed.**
'Aw, now, Moms,' I comforted her, 'it's no worse than playing the piano in a call house.'
'Strictly from Hunger' – which later became the title of his second book (1937). Quoted in Leslie Halliwell, *The Film-goer's Book of Quotes* (1979) as: 'Movie scriptwriting is no worse than playing piano in a call house.' A common enough comparison at the time. Stuart Berg Flexner, *I Hear America Talking* (1976), has as a saying from the Depression: 'Don't tell my mother I'm in politics – she thinks I play the piano in a whorehouse.'

Jacques Seguela (1934–) wrote a book with the title: *Ne dites pas a ma mere que je suis dans la publicité, elle me croit pianiste dans un bordel* (*Don't Tell Mother I Work in Advertising – She Thinks I'm a Piano-player in a Brothel*; 1979).

Carl PERKINS American singer and songwriter (1932–98)

2 **It's a-one for the money**
Two for the show
Three to get ready
Now go, cat, go,
But don't you step on my blue suede shoes.
Song, 'Blue Suede Shoes' (1956), sung notably by Elvis Presley. The opening lines are based on the form of words that children traditionally use at the start of races. A British version dating from 1888 is, 'One for the money, two for the show, three to make ready, and four to go.' Another version from 1853, is, 'One to make ready, and two to prepare; good luck to the rider, and away goes the mare.'

Frances PERKINS American politician (1882–1965)

3 **Call me madam.**
When Perkins was appointed Secretary of Labor by President Roosevelt in 1933, she became the first US woman to hold Cabinet rank. It was said that when she had been asked *in Cabinet* how she wished to be addressed, she had replied: 'Call me Madam.' She denied that she had done this, however. It was *after* her first Cabinet meeting that reporters asked how they should address her. The Speaker-elect of the House of Representatives, Henry T. Rainey, answered for her: 'When the Secretary of Labor is a lady, she should be addressed with the same general formalities as the Secretary of Labor who is a gentleman. You call him "Mr Secretary". You will call her "Madam Secretary". You gentlemen know

that when a lady is presiding over a meeting, she is referred to as "Madam Chairman" when you rise to address the chair' – quoted in George Martin, *Madam Secretary – Frances Perkins* (1976). Some of the reporters put this ruling into Perkins's own mouth, and that presumably is how the misquotation occurred.

Hence, however, *Call Me Madam*, the title of Irving Berlin's musical, first performed on Broadway in 1950, starring Ethel Merman as a woman ambassador appointed to represent the US in a tiny European state. This was inspired by the case of Pearl Mesta, the society hostess, whom President Truman had appointed as ambassador to Luxembourg.

Eva PERÓN Argentinian actress and wife of Juan Perón (1919–52)

4 **Quite so. But I have not been on a ship for fifteen years and they still call me 'Admiral'.**
This was an Italian admiral's response when Eva Perón complained to him that she had been called a 'whore' on a visit to northern Italy. Cited in an article 'The Power Behind the Glory', *Penthouse* Magazine (UK August 1977).

See also RICE 383:2.

Boscoe PERTWEE Untraced

5 **I used to be indecisive, but now I'm not so sure.**
During the second series of BBC Radio *Quote ... Unquote* (on 13 July 1977), I read out a letter from a listener. This is precisely what I said: 'M.M. Harvey from Andover sends a favourite quotation from the little-known 18th-century poet and wit, Boscoe Pertwee (with a name like that I'm surprised he existed at all). Here it is: "I used to be indecisive, but now I'm not so sure."' The following year, I put it in my first book, *Quote ... Unquote* (but without any cautionary words), and hunted high and low for evidence of Boscoe. A little later (on 21 August 1979), it was said to be a graffito and was quoted as such by Brian Johnston on my radio show. And so the years passed with no solution. Tessa Moriarty wrote to me in 2000, asking about it and saying she had been given the quote as Boscoe by a professor of English at Prince Edward Island University ...

It had not escaped my attention that the joke had been in existence before 1977 in a slightly different form. In Christopher Hampton's play *The Philanthropist* (1970), there is this: *Philip (bewildered)*: 'I'm sorry. (*Pause.*) I suppose I am indecisive. (*Pause.*) My trouble is, I'm a man of no convictions. (*Longish pause.*) At least, I think I am.' In 2005 it was pointed out to me that Boscoe's saying had been quoted in the postscript to Professor Richard L. Gregory's book, *Mind and Science: A History of Explanations in Psychology and*

Physics (1981). It is obvious from the reference that Gregory had taken it from my book. And then, none other than Umberto Eco trotted it out in the Introduction to his *Kant and the Platypus: Essays on Language and Cognition* (1997). He says quite plainly that he found it in Gregory ...

The only way to crack the nut was to go back to 'M.M. Harvey of Andover' and ask him, if he was still alive after 28 years. Using the people-finding capabilities that are now open to us in the age of CD-ROM reference tools and the internet, I discovered that there was an 'M.M. Harvey' living in Salisbury (which is not a million miles from Andover) and wrote to him. As it happens, he was the very man, and this is his tale: 'I'm afraid I cannot claim the invention as mine. In fact, Rob, the old friend whom I thought had invented it, tells me that he thinks it was invented by a close friend of his. (How long could this go on?) They used it as a way of drawing out the pretentious who always claimed to have heard of any name you could come up with. At one time they put it about that the famous *blues player* Boscoe Pertwee was coming to Abingdon. It wasn't long before people were coming up to them to tell of the impending visit by the great blues player ... I think he was also used as a name for a well-known novelist, playwright (you fill in the blank). Even managed to fool the odd college lecturer I believe.

'As for the quote, Rob tells me he thinks he read it on a toilet wall somewhere. Aah well. Still, if it has got into an Umberto Eco book, wonderful. But, my God, I suppose this means I must now read another book by Umberto Eco!'

As to how the name 'Boscoe Pertwee' came to be invented: I expect that Jon Pertwee playing Dr Who from 1970 to 1974 might have had something to do with it (and there was Michael Pertwee, playwright and screenwriter). But Boscoe seems only to have been used as a name for a bulldog ...

Henri Philippe PÉTAIN French marshal and politician (1856–1951)

1 *Ils ne passeront pass* [They shall not pass].

Slogan popularly supposed to have been coined by Pétain, the man who defended Verdun with great tenacity in 1916. He is said to have uttered it on 26 February that year. However, the first official record of the expression appears in the Order of the Day for 23 June 1916 from General Robert Nivelle (1856–1924) to his troops at the height of the battle. His words were '*Vous ne laisserez pas passer* [You will not let them pass]'. Alternatively, Nivelle is supposed to have said these words to General Castelnau on 23 January 1916. To add further to the mystery, the inscription on the Verdun medal was '*On ne passe pas.*' One suspects that the slogan was coined by Nivelle and used a number of times by him, but came to be associated with Pétain, the more famous 'Hero of Verdun'.

The slogan saw further service: as '*No pasarán*, it was used on the Republican side during the Spanish Civil War.

Laurence J. PETER Canadian writer (1919–90)

2 In a hierarchy every employee tends to rise to his level of incompetence.

The Peter Principle – Why Things Always Go Wrong, written with R. Hull (1969). Intoning his principle on TV (1982) he added, '... and stays there'.

3 The noblest of all dogs is the hot-dog; it feeds the hand that bites it.

Quotations for Our Time (1977). Although compiling a book of quotations, Peter inserted several observations of his own. This is one of the brightest. The next one, probably not: 'When you see yourself quoted in print and you're sorry you said it, it suddenly becomes a misquotation.'

PETRONIUS Roman satirist (died AD65)

4 We trained hard; but it seemed that every time we were beginning to form into teams we would be reorganized. I was to learn later in life that we tend to meet any new situation by reorganizing; and a wonderful method it can be for creating the illusion of progress while producing confusion, inefficiency and demoralization.

Gaius Petronius (also known as Petronius Arbiter in Nero's court) is said to have put this in the 'Trimalchio's Feast' section of the *Satyricon* (written in AD66), but it has not been found in the (admittedly) variable text. Indeed, doubts have been cast on the authenticity of this quotation. One suggestion is that it only dates from 1945. In *The Observer* (7 July 1996), Mark Tully quoted the statement but described Gaius Petronius rather as a Roman *centurion*. The second sentence (only) was attributed to Petronius by Robert Townsend in *Up the Organization* (1970) – this undoubtedly is the original source of most subsequent quotings of the lines. An earlier quoting of the full version is in David Willings, *The Human Element in Management* (1968). A contributor to the *Petronian Society Newsletter* (May 1981) suggested this provenance: 'Some disgruntled soldier of a literary bent, whether commissioned or noncommissioned I do not know, pinned this "quotation" to a bulletin board in one of the camps of the armies occupying Germany sometime after 1945 (the style suggests a British occupying force). Since the sentiment is impeccable, whether applied to military, governmental, or academic administration, it has enjoyed a cachet borrowed from Petronius ever since.' In other words, it is a fake.

Francesco Maria PIAVE Italian librettist (1810–76)

1 *La donna è mobile* [Woman is fickle].

The Duke of Mantua's aria in Act 3 of Verdi's opera, *Rigoletto* (1851) ... 'Woman is wayward / As a feather in the breeze / Capricious is the word.'

Pablo PICASSO Spanish artist (1881–1973)

2 *Je ne cherche pas, je trouve / Yo no busco, encuentro* [I do not search, I find].

On painting. Picasso evidently explained this remark (recorded both in French and Spanish) to the effect that if you looked for something you knew what you were looking for, whereas when he began a painting he never knew what would happen. Quoted in *PDMQ* (1971) – this would appear to be a version of what Picasso said in an interview with *The Arts* in 1923: 'To search means nothing in painting. To find is the thing.'

3 When I was the age of these children I could draw like Raphael: it took me many years to learn how to draw like these children.

Remark to Herbert Read at an exhibition of children's drawings. Quoted in a letter from Read to *The Times* (27 October 1956); also in Roland Penrose, *Picasso: His Life and Work* (1958).

Harold PINTER English playwright (1930–)

4 'But what would you say your plays were *about*, Mr Pinter?'
'The weasel under the cocktail cabinet.'

'Exchange at a new writers' brains trust', quoted in John Russell Taylor, *Anger and After* (1962).

5 I tend to believe that cricket is the greatest thing that God ever created on earth ... certainly greater than sex, although sex isn't too bad either. But everyone knows which comes first when it's a question of cricket and sex.

Interviewed in *The Observer* (5 October 1980). Pinter continued: 'You can either have sex before cricket or after cricket – the fundamental fact is that cricket must be at the centre of things.' This was discussed on BBC Radio *Quote ... Unquote* (25 December 1980) by P.D. James, the crime novelist: 'I must say I find it a very surprising opinion considering the beauty of his wife. If he had said it on the way to the register office with me, I don't think I'd have married him.' Brian Johnston, the cricket commentator, sliced through any confusion: 'What he meant was, you can play

cricket and *then* have sex. It didn't mean that cricket came before sex, as something better than the other, he meant in time. You go out, you make a hundred, you take a hat trick, you go home, you have sex!'

William PITKIN American teacher (1878–1953)

6 *Life Begins at Forty.*

Title of book (1932), in which Pitkin, who was Professor of Journalism at Columbia University, dealt with 'adult reorientation' at a time when the problems of extended life and leisure were beginning to be recognized. Based on lectures Pitkin had given, the book was a hearty bit of uplift: 'Every day brings forth some new thing that adds to the joy of life after forty. Work becomes easy and brief. Play grows richer and longer. Leisure lengthens. Life's afternoon is brighter, warmer, fuller of song; and long before shadows stretch, every fruit grows ripe ... Life begins at forty. This is the revolutionary outcome of our new era ... TODAY it is half a truth. TOMORROW it will be an axiom.' It rapidly became a well-established catchphrase. Helping it along was a song with the title by Jack Yellen and Ted Shapiro, recorded by Sophie Tucker in 1937.

The phrase seems to have caught on everywhere with great rapidity. *Life Begins at Forty* was the title of a film comedy (US 1935) about a newspaper editor campaigning to free a man jailed for a bank robbery he did not commit. Although Pitkin is credited, the film has nothing much to do with the book. *Life Begins at Oxford Circus* was the title of a Crazy Gang show at the London Palladium in 1935. *Life Begins at Eight-Thirty* followed as the title of a film (US 1942).

William PITT (1st Earl of Chatham) (Pitt the Elder) British Prime Minister (1708–78)

7 The atrocious crime of being a young man, which the honourable gentleman has, with such spirit and decency, charged upon me, I shall neither attempt to palliate nor deny; but content myself with wishing that I may be one of those whose follies cease with their youth, and not of those who continue ignorant in spite of age and experience.

Speech, House of Commons (6 March 1741) – in response to Sir Robert Walpole. Compare below 359:8.

William PITT (Pitt the Younger) British Prime Minister (1759–1806)

8 Yes, I know I am young and inexperienced, but it is a fault I am remedying every day.

In a 1987 election broadcast, James Callaghan quoted this

response in support of Neil Kinnock, the then leader of the British Labour Party. It remains untraced, though Pitt the Younger, becoming Britain's youngest Prime Minister at the age of 24, undoubtedly did have to justify himself. Another version is that when King George III commented on his extraordinary youth, Pitt replied: 'Time, Your Majesty, will take care of that.' His father had similarly had to justify his own youth (though he was not to become Prime Minister until middle age), see above 359:7. Kenneth Williams in *Acid Drops* (1980) has Pitt the Younger visiting George III in Windsor Castle in 1783. Astonished at Pitt's age – he was only 24 – the King was doubtful about his ability to run the country. 'You're very young, Mr Pitt,' muttered the King, to which Pitt replied: 'I think we can rely on time to remedy that, sire.' Williams gives no source.

1 Roll up that map; it will not be wanted these ten years.

Commenting on the map of Europe after the Battle of Austerlitz (1805). Quoted in Lord Stanhope, *Life of the Rt Hon. William Pitt* (1862). He was correct almost to the month: Napoleon's hold over Europe only lasted until 1815.

2 Oh, my country! how I leave my country!

Pitt's last recorded words refer to the breaking up of the English coalition in the wake of the defeat of Austro-Russian forces by Napoleon at the Battle of Austerlitz in 1805. Often given as '... how I love my country!' In the 1862 edition of Stanhope's life of Pitt it is 'love'; in the 1879 edition, 'leave'. Alternatively, popular tradition has it that his actual last spoken words were, 'I think I could eat one of Bellamy's veal pies.' Quoted in *ODQ* (1941).

PLATO Greek philosopher (?428–?348BC)

3 Might is right, and justice is the interest of the stronger.

Where did 'Might is right' originate? In English, this was traced by *Apperson* to 'Might makes right' in about 1311. But the thought, translated, can be found much earlier in Plautus, *Truculentus* (?190BC), as 'The more might, the more right', and in Plato, *The Republic* (?370BC), as above.

4 No good man would wish to rule, except to prevent the rule of someone worse.

A possible encapsulation of the passage from *The Republic*, Bk 1, in which Socrates debates with Thrasymachus and Glaucon (Jowett's translation): 'And this, as I imagine, is the reason why the forwardness to take office, instead of waiting to be compelled, has been deemed dishonourable. Now the worst part of the punishment is that he who refuses

to rule is liable to be ruled by one who is worse than himself. And the fear of this, as I conceive, induces the good to take office, not because they would, but because they cannot help – not under the idea that they are going to have any benefit or enjoyment themselves, but as a necessity, and because they are not able to commit the task of ruling to any one who is better than themselves, or indeed as good.'

5 When the mode of the music changes ...
The walls of the city shake.

Attributed remark, though it has also been said by Allen Ginsberg that it was Plato quoting *Pythagoras*. 'When the Mode of the Music Changes' was the title of a song by an American underground group of the 1960s named The Fugs. It appears on their album *It Crawled Into My Hand, Honest* (1968).

See also under SOCRATES.

PLINY the Elder Roman politician (AD23–79)

6 *Semper aliquid novi Africam adferre* [Africa always brings (us) something new].

Historia Naturalis, Bk 8. Pliny's version of what was originally a Greek proverb. Often rendered '*Ex Africa semper aliquid novi* [There is always something new out of Africa]'. Hence, the film *Out of Africa* (US/UK 1985), based in part on Isak Dinesen's 1938 book (originally, in Danish, *Den Afrikanske Farm*), and leading to a whole spate of 'out of ...' constructions. In 1986, *The Independent* launched a series of weekly columns entitled 'Out of Europe/Asia/etc.' The same year, Ruth Prawer Jhabvala and Tim Piggot-Smith both brought out books called *Out of India*. An allusion: in *A Kentish Lad* (1997), Frank Muir records a scene written for Jimmy Edwards as a headmaster: 'Jimmy poured tiny glasses of British sherry for the staff, then went to a globe of the world, opened a hatch in it and pulled out a bottle of whisky. "There's always something new out of Africa!" he said and poured himself half a tumblerful. "Cheers!"'

Edmund PLOWDEN English lawyer (1518–85)

7 'The case is altered,' quoth Plowden.

Proverbial expression derived from a law case in which Plowden himself featured. A Roman Catholic, Plowden was arrested some time after 1570 for the treasonable offence of attending a surreptitious mass. He defended himself and was able to prove that the priest who had presided over the mass in question was an *agent provocateur*. Accordingly, he argued that a true mass could not be celebrated by an impostor – so 'the case is altered' – and was acquitted.

Another, less likely, origin is given by Henry G. Bohn in *A Hand-Book of Proverbs* (1855): 'Plowden being asked by a neighbour of his, what remedy there was in law against his neighbour for some hogs that had trespassed his ground, answered, he might have very good remedy; but the other replying, that they were his [i.e. Plowden's] hogs, Nay then, neighbour, (quoth he), the case is altered.'

The phrase was much quoted. In Shakespeare's *King Henry VI, Part 3*, IV.iii.30 (1590–1) there occurs the following exchange:

> *King Edward*: Why, Warwick, when we parted,
> Thou call'dst me King.
> *Warwick*: Ay, but the case is alter'd:
> When you disgrac'd me in my embassade,
> Then I degraded you from being King,
> And come now to create you Duke of York.

It occurs in Thomas Kyd, *Soliman and Perseda*, II.i.292 (1592), and Ben Jonson wrote a play called *The Case Is Altered* (1598–9). The dying Queen Elizabeth I is sometimes quoted as having said in 1603: 'I am tied, I am tied, and the case is altered with me' – quoted in Elizabeth Jenkins, *Elizabeth the Great* (1958). From all this, The Case Is Altered is also the name given to a number of public houses in Britain, though the name is sometimes erroneously said to be a corruption of the Spanish *casa alta* ('high house'). In addition, 'The Case is Altered' was the provisional title of J.M. Barrie's play *The Admirable Crichton* (1902) – an allusion surviving in the line 'Circumstances might alter cases' (Act 1, Sc. 1). It is also the title of a book (1932) by William Plomer.

PLUTARCH Greek philosopher and biographer
(AD ?46–?120)

1 *Navigare necesse est, vivere non est necesse* [There is a necessity to sail, but no necessity to live].

Life of Pompey, here in Arthur Hugh Clough's translation: '[Pompey] was just ready to set sail upon his voyage home [having collected vast stores of corn], when a great storm arose upon the sea, and the ships' commanders doubted whether it were safe. Upon which Pompey himself went first aboard, and bid the mariners weigh anchor, declaring with a loud voice, that there was a necessity to sail, but no necessity to live.' Some say it was used as the motto of the Hanseatic League in the late Middle Ages. Mussolini is reported to have changed it at an aeronautics conference in 1923 to '*Volare necesse est.*'

2 Ingratitude towards their great men is the mark of strong peoples.

Quoted by Winston Churchill in *The Second World War*, Vol. 1 (1948), reflecting on his own defeat at the hands of the British electorate in 1945 following his successful leadership of the country during the Second World War.

3 Macedonians had not the wit to call a spade by any other name than a spade.

Apophthegmata – as translated from Greek to Latin by Erasmus. What was rather a trough, basin, bowl or boat in the original Greek ended up as a 'spade' and passed into English giving us the expression 'to call a spade a spade', meaning 'to speak bluntly, to call things by their proper names without resorting to euphemisms'. The phrase had entered the language by 1580.

4 He laughed at those who insisted that the descendants of Heracles should not stoop to trickery in warfare and remarked, 'Where the lion's skin will not reach, we must patch it out with the fox's.'

In the *Life of Lysander*, the Spartan naval commander (died 395BC). This has been known as a proverbial saying in English since 1573 and means 'if you can't obtain something by force, then use craft'. The novelist Olivia Manning entitled one of her earliest short stories 'A Scantling of Foxes' after a quotation that appears twice in a commonplace book she kept in her twenties: 'If the lion skin be not large enough we must e'en make it up with a scantling of foxes' – as Neville Braybrooke told me in 1999. As to where the version with that interesting word 'scantling' comes from, I know not.

5 Students are candles to be lit not vessels to be filled.

Likely summary of a passage in his *Moralia*, 'On Listening to Lectures': 'For the mind does not require filling like a bottle, but rather, like wood, it only requires kindling to create in it an impulse to think independently and an ardent desire for the truth.'

6 So reason makes all sorts of life easy, and every change pleasant. Alexander wept when he heard from Anaxarchus that there was an infinite number of worlds, and his friends asking him if any accident had befallen him, he returns this answer: Do not you think it is a matter worthy of lamentation, that, when there is such a vast multitude of them, we have not yet conquered one? But Crates with only his scrip and tattered cloak laughed out his life jocosely, as if he had been always at a festival.

'Of the Tranquillity of the Mind'. So it was not that Alexander (the Great) wept because he had run out of worlds to conquer but because he felt that he had not even managed to conquer this one. An epitaph on Alexander would seem to allude to this incident: 'A tomb now suffices him for whom the whole world was not sufficient.'

Edgar Allan POE American novelist and poet (1809–49)

1 Thy Naiad airs have brought me home,
To the glory that was Greece
And the grandeur that was Rome.

'To Helen' (1831). Hence, *The Glory That Was Greece* and *The Grandeur That Was Rome*, titles of BBC TV series in about 1960, presented by, respectively, the writer Sir Compton Mackenzie and the archaeologist Sir Mortimer Wheeler. The two titles had earlier been given to books on Greek and Roman culture and civilization (1911 and 1912) by J.C. Stobart.

2 Take thy beak from out my heart, and take
thy form from off my door!
Quoth the Raven, 'Nevermore'.

'The Raven' (1845). In the Courtauld Institute Gallery, London, there is a painting of a nude by Gauguin which has the title *Nevermore*. What bird would you say features in it? Well, no, not a raven, it is a devil's bird. You might expect it to allude to Poe's poem, but Gauguin quite clearly stated that this was not the case. See also CAMPBELL 121:1

3 What we see and what we seem,
Are but a dream, a dream within a dream.

'A Dream Within a Dream' (1849). Quoted in two films – *Picnic At Hanging Rock* (Australia 1975), unattributed, and *The Fog* (US 1979) on a screen title.

Robert POLLOK Scottish poet and clergyman (1798–1827)

4 To set as sets the morning star, which goes
Not down behind the darkened west, nor hides
Obscured among the tempests of the sky,
But melts away into the light of heaven.

The Course of Time, Bk 5 (1827) – published in the year of his early death from consumption. This passage is quoted anonymously in Thomas Hardy, *A Pair of Blue Eyes*, Chap. 29 (1873). It was alluded to – 'She sets as sets the morning star ...' – in John Brown's moving essay about the child author 'Pet Marjorie' Fleming (who died aged eight) in *Horae Subsecivae* (1858–62).

Madame de POMPADOUR Mistress of Louis XV of France (1721–64)

5 *Après nous le déluge* [After us, the flood].

Remark to Louis XV on 5 November 1757 after Frederick the Great had defeated the French and Austrian armies at the Battle of Rossbach. It carries with it the suggestion that nothing matters once you are dead and has also been inter-preted as a premonition of the French Revolution. *Bartlett* notes that this 'reputed reply' by the King's mistress was recorded by three authorities, though a fourth gives it to the King himself. *Bartlett* then claims the saying was not original anyway but was 'an old French proverb'. However, *ODP* has as an English proverb, 'After us the deluge', deriving from Mme de Pompadour. Its only citation is Burnaby's 1876 *Ride to Khiva*: 'Our rulers did not trouble their heads much about the matter. "India will last my time ... and after me the Deluge."' Metternich, the Austrian diplomat and chancellor, may later have said '*Après moi le déluge*', meaning that everything would grind to a halt when he stopped controlling it. The deluge alluded to in both cases may be a dire event like the Great Flood or 'universal deluge' of Noah's time.

Lorenzo da PONTE Italian librettist (1749–1838)

6 *Così fan tutte* [That's what all women do].

Title of Mozart's opera (1790), which literally means 'thus do all [women]', and which may also be translated as 'women are like that', referring to their infidelity. The phrase had appeared earlier in Da Ponte's libretto for *Le nozze di Figaro* (1778). In that opera, Don Basilio sings, '*Così fan tutte le belle, non c'è alcuna novità* [That's what all beautiful women do, there's nothing new in that].'

Alexander POPE English poet (1688–1744)

7 Where'er you walk, cool gales shall fan the glade,
Trees, where you sit, shall crowd into a shade:
Where'er you tread, the blushing flow'rs shall
rise,
And all things flourish where you turn your eyes.

'Summer', *Pastorals* (1709). Not to be confused with 'Where e'er you walk', a famous tenor aria from Handel's opera *Semele* (1744) – for which the libretto was by William Congreve out of Ovid's *Metamorphoses*.

8 A little learning is a dang'rous thing;
Drink deep, or taste not the Pierian spring.

An Essay on Criticism, line 215 (1711). Hence, *A Little Learning*, title of Evelyn Waugh's autobiographical volume (1964). In *Busman's Honeymoon*, Chap. 9 (1937), Dorothy L. Sayers has Lord Peter Wimsey peevishly correct a man who has said, 'A little knowledge is a dangerous thing.'

9 To err is human; to forgive, divine.

In the same work, line 525. Though crisply expressed, not an original thought. Cicero seems to have been the first to put forward the theory that humans err. In the twelfth Philippic he says: '*Cuiusvis hominis est errare; nullius nisi insipientis in errore perseverare.*' St Augustine agreed: '*Humanum fuit errare, diabolicum est per animositatem in errore manere*' – *Sermones*, 164.10.14. Henry Wotton's translation of Jacques Yver's *Courtly Controversy* (1578) has: 'To offend is human, to repent divine, to persevere devilish.'

1 For fools rush in where angels fear to tread.

In the same work, line 625. Hence, *Where Angels Fear To Tread*, title of a novel (1906) by E.M. Forster. *Fools Rush In* was the title of a play (1947; film UK 1949) by Kenneth Horne. The phrase 'Fools Rush In' was also the bill matter of the British comedians Morecambe and Wise in the 1950s.

2 With varying vanities, from ev'ry part,
   They shift the moving toyshop of the heart.

On women. *The Rape of the Lock*, Canto 1, line 99 (1714). Hence, *The Moving Toyshop*, title of Edmund Crispin's detective thriller (1946), which begins with the apparent disappearance of a toyshop in Oxford.

3 Nature, and Nature's Laws lay hid in Night:
   GOD said, *Let Newton be!* and all was Light.

'Epitaph: Intended for Sir Isaac Newton' (1730), in Westminster Abbey. Sir John Squire later suggested this response (in his *Poems*, 1926):

   It did not last: the Devil howling 'Ho!
   Let Einstein be!' restored the status quo.

4 Hope springs eternal in the human breast:
   Man never Is, but always To be blest.

An Essay on Man, Epistle 1, line 95 (1733). The origin of the proverbial expression, 'Hope springs eternal.'

5 Know then thyself, presume not God to scan;
   The proper study of mankind is man.

In the same work, Epistle 2, line 1. Compare HUXLEY 249:1.

6 Worth makes the man, and want of it, the fellow:
   The rest is all but leather or prunella.

In the same work, Epistle 4, line 203. Pope distinguishes between a cobbler (the leather) and a parson (prunella is the material from which clerical gowns were made). But through misinterpretation came about the expression 'leather and prunella', meaning something to which the speaker is entirely indifferent. In George Eliot's *Middlemarch*, Chap. 43 (1871–2), Lydgate says, 'Ladislaw is a sort of gypsy; he thinks nothing of leather and prunella' – suggesting that he cares nothing for social rank.

7 A wit's a feather, and a chief's a rod;
   An honest man's the noblest work of God.

In the same work, Epistle 4, line 247. The American agnostic, Robert C. Ingersoll (1833–99), concluded in *The Gods* (1876): 'An honest God is the noblest work of man.' ACC Robert Burns quotes Pope in 'The Cotter's Saturday Night' (1786):

   Princes and Lords are but the breath of kings,
   'An honest man's the noblest work of God.'

8 Shall then this verse to future age pretend
   Thou wert my guide, philosopher, and friend?

In the same work, Epistle 4, line 389. 'Guide, philosopher and friend' has subsequently become an ingratiating form of address. From P.G. Wodehouse, *The Inimitable Jeeves* (1923): 'Right from the first day he came to me, I have looked on [Jeeves] as a sort of guide, philosopher, and friend.'

9 Who breaks a butterfly upon a wheel?

'An Epistle to Dr Arbuthnot', line 305 (1735). Meaning 'who goes to great lengths to accomplish something trifling?' As 'Who Breaks a Butterfly on a Wheel', it was famously used as the headline to a leading article in *The Times* (1 July 1967) when Mick Jagger, the pop singer, was given a three-month gaol term on drugs charges.

10 Let the two Curls of Town and Court, abuse
    His father, mother, body, soul, and muse.
    Yet why? that Father held it for a rule,
    It was a sin to call our neighbour fool.

In the same work. Self-justificatory lines. In a series of pamphlets Edmund Curll had depicted Pope's father as being, variously, a lowly 'Mechanic, a Hatter, a Farmer, nay a Bankrupt'. Further, 'the following line, "Hard as thy Heart, and as thy Birth obscure" had fallen from a ... Courtly pen, in certain *Verses to the Imitator of Horace*'. Pope's 18th-century editors went to some trouble in footnotes to show that, on the contrary, Pope's father was 'of a Gentleman's family in Oxfordshire' and not to be sneered at. The 'Courtly pen' was probably that of Lord Hervey (1696–1743), though he may have been joined in the attack by Lady Mary Wortley Montagu, who had fallen out with Pope by this time.

11 Let humble Allen, with an awkward shame,
    Do good by stealth, and blush to find it fame.

Epilogue to the Satires, *Imitations of Horace* (1738). Compare LAMB 277:3.

1 What are the gay parterre, the chequer'd shade,
   The morning bower, the ev'ning colonnade
   But soft recesses of uneasy minds
   To sigh unheard in, to the passing winds?

'To Mr Gay, Congratulating Mr Pope on finishing his house and gardens' (1776). Hence, the title of Cyril Connolly's *The Evening Colonnade* (1973), a collection of his journalistic writings.

See also BARING 52:7.

Richard PORSON English scholar (1759–1808)

2 There were moments when his memory failed him; and he would forget to eat dinner, though he never forgot a quotation.

Edith Sitwell, *English Eccentrics* (1933). Just prior to this remark she has described how Porson, Regius Professor of Greek at Cambridge, set about a young man in a hackney coach who had produced inaccurate quotations to impress the ladies.

See also CONRAN 153:8.

Cole PORTER American composer and lyricist (1891–1964)

3 And when they ask us, how dangerous it was,
   Oh, we'll never tell them, no, we'll never tell
      them:
   We spent our pay in some café
   And fought wild women night and day,
   'Twas the cushiest job we ever had.

These words became famous during the First World War, and were brought to a new audience in the stage show *Oh What a Lovely War* (1963; film UK 1969). As such, they were a parody of the song 'They Didn't Believe Me' by Jerome Kern and Herbert Reynolds (M.E. Rourke) (1914), which goes:

> And when I told them how beautiful you are
> They didn't believe me, they didn't believe me.
> Your lips, your arms, your cheeks, your hair,
> Are in a class beyond compare,
> You're the loveliest girl that one can see.

The parody was thought to be anonymous until Robert Kimball, editor of the *Complete Lyrics of Cole Porter* (1983), was going through the composer's voluminous papers and came across the words in the 'oldest compilation Porter had preserved of his works, a set of typed miscellaneous lyrics'.

In fact, Porter's version is slightly different from the one given above – e.g., line 2 is 'We never will tell them, we never will tell them'; line 5, ''Twas the wonderfulest war you ever knew' etc. So, we do not have 100 per cent proof

that Porter wrote the parody, but it is an intriguing possibility. Note how the words 'night and day', which he was to couple in his most famous song in 1932, make an early appearance together here.

4 Night and day you are the one.

Song, 'Night and Day', *Gay Divorce* (1932). Hence, *Night and Day*, title of play (1978) by Tom Stoppard.

5 I get no kick from champagne,
   Mere alcohol doesn't thrill me at all,
   So tell me why should it be true
   That I get a kick out of you?

Song, 'I Get a Kick Out of You', *Anything Goes* (1934). According to Robert Kimball, editor of the *Complete Lyrics of Cole Porter* (1983), 'any substitutes for the lines that begin "Some get a kick from cocaine" are incorrect.'

6 You're the nimble tread of the feet of Fred
      Astaire,
   You're Mussolini,
   You're Mrs Sweeny,
   You're Camembert.

Porter's list song 'You're the Top' in the same musical has understandably had to be revised since it was first published. In this segment, in due course, Mussolini was topped rather than the tops, and Mrs Charles Sweeny (as she had been since 1933), became the infamous Margaret, Duchess of Argyll (who died in July 1993). But note: the Mussolini/Sweeny lines are not in the original version of the song but from P.G. Wodehouse's revisions for the London production of *Anything Goes* in 1935.

7 [You'd Be So] Easy to Love.

Title of song in film *Born To Dance* (US 1936), though it had been written for another show in 1934. That same year, Noël Coward has the line 'You would be so easy to love' in the play *Conversation Piece*.

8 So goodbye, dear, and amen.

'Just One of Those Things', *Jubilee* (1935). Hence, *Goodbye Baby and Amen*, title of a book of photographs (1969) by David Bailey and Peter Evans, subtitled 'A Saraband for the Sixties'.

9 Brush up your Shakespeare,
   Start quoting him now.
   Brush up your Shakespeare
   And the women you will wow ...
   If she says your behaviour is heinous

Kick her right in the 'Coriolanus'.
Brush up your Shakespeare
And they'll all kowtow.

'Brush Up Your Shakespeare', *Kiss Me Kate* (1948). Observing the play-within-a-play (a production of *The Taming of the Shrew*) are two gangsters. At one point they hymn the art of Shakespearean quotation and include a pun on the name 'Coriolanus', which is best left unexplained here.

1 Always True to You in my Fashion.

Title of song in the same show. See DOWSON 177:2.

2 Paris Loves Lovers.

Title of song in *Silk Stockings* (1955). Compare the line 'Paris is for lovers' spoken in the previous year's Billy Wilder film *Sabrina* (*Sabrina Fair* in the UK). It almost has the ring of an official slogan, though this was long before the days of such lines as 'I Love New York' (1977) and 'Virginia is for Lovers' (1981).

3 Who Wants to Be a Millionaire?

Title of song written especially for the film musical *High Society* (US 1956) and sung in it by Frank Sinatra and Celeste Holm. Hence, *Who Wants To Be a Millionaire?*, title of a British TV quiz (from 1998 onwards) whose format has been sold all over the world.

Peter PORTER Australian-born poet (1929–)

4 In Australia
Inter alia,
Mediocrities
Think they're Socrates.

Unpublished clerihew, quoted in *The Dictionary of Australian Quotations* (1984). Porter commented on BBC Radio *Quote ... Unquote* (28 November 1989) that writing these lines had meant he had recently been denied a grant by the Australian government.

Dennis POTTER English TV playwright (1935–94)

5 Vote, Vote, Vote, for Nigel Barton.

Potter was a frequent borrower for the titles of his plays – *Blade on the Feather*, *Pennies from Heaven*, *Where the Buffalo Roam*, *Follow the Yellow Brick Road*, *Cream in My Coffee* and *Lipstick on My Collar* all come from songs, while *Blue Remembered Hills* comes from HOUSMAN 245:3. But the title of this BBC 'Wednesday Play' (1965) about a Labour politician is possibly less obvious. It echoes the election song (usually sung by children to the tune of 'Tramp, tramp,

tramp, the boys are marching' and known by 1880):

> Vote, vote, vote for (Billy Martin),
> Chuck old (Ernie) out the door –
> If it wasn't for the law
> I would punch him on the jaw,
> And we don't want (Ernie) any more.

According to Iona and Peter Opie, *The Lore and Language of Schoolchildren* (1959), Sir Anthony Eden said in 1955: 'I remember how in the old days the boys used to go round singing in chorus:

> "Vote, vote, vote for So-and-so;
> Punch old So-and-so in the eye;
> When he comes to the door,
> We will knock him on the floor,
> And he won't come a-voting any more!"

6 The trouble with words is that you never know whose mouths they've been in.

In *The Guardian* (15 February 1993). Hence, *The Trouble with Words* (1994), title of a book by John Simmons. But Potter was not the first to say it. In a piece entitled 'Four Eccentrics', written in about 1950, Kenneth Tynan, after applying Carew's elegy on John Donne to the actress Hermione Gingold, added: 'But I believe I can hear her rebuking me; very coldly, with magisterial authority. She is saying: "Take those words out of your mouth: you don't know *where* they've been."'

Stephen POTTER English humorist (1900–69)

7 'Yes, but not in the South', with slight adjustments will do for any argument about any place, if not about any person.

Lifemanship (1950) – the second volume of Potter's not solely humorous exploration of the art of 'One-Upmanship', which he defined as 'how to make the other man feel that something has gone wrong, however slightly'. In discussing ways of putting down experts while in conversation with them, Potter introduces the above 'blocking phrase' with which to disconcert, if not totally silence, them. In a footnote, he remarks: 'I am required to state that World Copyright of this phrase is owned by its brilliant inventor, Mr Pound' – though which 'Pound' he does not reveal. Indeed, the blocking move was known before this. Richard Usborne wrote of it in a piece called 'Not in the South' included in *The Pick of 'Punch'* (1941). He introduced a character called Eustace who had found a formula 'for appearing to be a European, and world, pundit. It was a formula that let me off the boredom of finding out facts and retaining knowledge.' It was to remark, 'Not in the South.'

1 If you have nothing to say, or, rather, something extremely stupid and obvious, say it, but in a 'plonking' tone of voice – i.e. roundly, but hollowly and dogmatically.

In the same book. Although 'plonking' had been used in Yorkshire dialect for 'large', this would appear to be the first appearance of the term, as defined.

Eugène POTTIER French transport worker and politician (1816–87)

2 *Debout! les damnés de la terre!*
Debout! les forçats de la faim!
La raison tonne en son cratère,
C'est l'éruption de la fin ...
Nous ne sommes rien, soyons tout!
C'est la lutte finale
Groupons-nous, et, demain,
L'Internationale
Sera la genre humain.
[On your feet, you damned souls of the earth!
On your feet, inmates of hunger's prison!
Reason is rumbling in its crater,
And it's final eruption is on its way ...
We are nothing, let us be everything!
This is the final conflict:
Let us form up and, tomorrow,
The International
Will encompass the human race.]

The official anthem of the socialist movement (and the national anthem of the Soviet Union until 1944) was written in 1871 by Pottier and set to music by Pierre Degeyter (1848–1932), a woodworker from Lille. Not to be confused with 'The Red Flag' (see 152:6). The excruciating English version reproduced here goes on to include references to 'enrolled among the sons of toil' and 'arise ye starvelings from your slumber'.

Ezra POUND American poet (1885–1972)

3 Winter is icummen in,
Lhude sing Goddamm,
Raineth drop and staineth slop,
And how the wind doth ramm!
Sing: Goddamm.

'Ancient Music' (1917). Based on 'Sumer is icumen in, / Lhude sing cuccu!', the anonymous 'Cuckoo Song' (?1250).

Anthony POWELL English novelist (1905–2000)

4 *A Dance to the Music of Time.*

The overall title of Powell's novel sequence, published 1951–75 and giving a panoramic view of postwar Britain, is given in the first novel, *A Question of Upbringing*. The narrator, Nicholas Jenkins, looking at workmen round a bucket of coke in falling snow, is put in mind of the painting with this title by Nicolas Poussin, which hangs in the Wallace Collection, London. There it is known as *Le 4 stagioni che ballano al suono del tempo* – a title bestowed by Giovanni Pietro Bellori. Sometimes, however, the painting is known, less interestingly, as '*Ballo della vita humana* [the dance of human life]'.

5 *Books Do Furnish a Room.*

Title of the tenth volume (1971) of *A Dance to the Music of Time*. According to the blurb on the dust jacket of the first edition: 'The book's title is taken to some extent from the nickname of one of the characters, Books-do-furnish-a-room Bagshaw, all-purpose journalist and amateur of revolutionary theory, but the phrase also suggests an aspect of the rather bleak post-war period – London's literary world finding its feet again.'

The notion of books being looked upon as furniture – and the consequent taunt to people who regard them as such – is an old one. Lady Holland in her *Memoir* (1855) quotes the Revd Sidney Smith as joking: 'No furniture so charming as books.' And Edward Young in *Love of Fame: The Universal Passion*, Satire II (1725–8) has: 'Thy books are furniture.'

6 *To Keep the Ball Rolling.*

Overall title given to Powell's autobiographical sequence (1976–82). He says it comes from Joseph Conrad's *Chance* (1913): 'To keep the ball rolling I asked Marlow if this Powell was remarkable in any way. "He was not exactly remarkable," Marlow answered with his usual nonchalance. "In a general way it's very difficult to become remarkable. People won't take sufficient notice of one, don't you know."'

See also BURTON 112:2.

Enoch POWELL English Conservative then Ulster Unionist politician (1912–98)

7 Milk is rendered immortal in cheese.

In a broadcast talk in 1967, I quoted Powell as having said this, but have no idea where I got it from. If, indeed, Powell did say this, he had been anticipated by Clifton Fadiman in *Any Number Can Play* (1957), when he wrote of: 'Cheese – milk's leap toward immortality.'

1 As I look ahead, I am filled with foreboding. Like the Roman, I seem to see 'the River Tiber foaming with much blood'.

With these words, on 20 April 1968, Enoch Powell, the Conservative Opposition spokesman for defence, concluded a speech in Birmingham on the subject of immigration. The next day he was dismissed from the Shadow Cabinet for a speech 'racialist in tone and liable to exacerbate racial tensions'. What became known as the 'Rivers of Blood' speech certainly produced an astonishing reaction in the public, unleashing anti-immigrant feeling that had been largely pent up until this point. Later, Powell said that he should have quoted the remark in Latin to emphasize that he was only evoking a classical prophecy of doom and not actually predicting a bloodbath. In Virgil's *Aeneid* (Bk 6, line 87) the Sibyl of Cumae prophesies: '*Et Thybrim multo spumantem sanguine cerno*'.

But 'rivers of blood' was quite a common turn of phrase in English before Powell made it notorious – see JEFFERSON 255:5. Speaking on European unity (14 February 1948), Winston Churchill had said: 'We are asking the nations of Europe, between whom rivers of blood have flowed, to forget the feuds of a thousand years.'

2 All political lives, unless they are cut off in midstream at a happy juncture, end in failure, because that is the nature of politics and of human affairs.

Joseph Chamberlain (1977). Leader of the Liberal Unionists in the 1890s, Chamberlain never became Prime Minister and had to retire from public life through ill-health, with his tariff reforms (giving preferential treatment to colonial imports) not yet in place. Powell may also have had himself in mind when writing this concluding passage.

3 Every quotation is out of context because the context of everything is everything and you can't transmit that ... To be the most misquoted is to be the most quoted [man in British politics] and I'll settle for the combination.

On BBC Radio *PM* programme (December 1978). Powell had just been voted the Best Political Speaker (or some such title) in an informal poll on the programme.

William PRESCOTT American general (1726–95)

4 Men, you are all marksmen – don't one of you fire until you see the whites of their eyes.

Instruction given at the Battle of Bunker Hill (17 June 1775) in the American War of Independence. The eyes in question were those of the British army. In the short term, the command was effective and the British suffered heavy casualties, though technically they won the battle. Has also been ascribed to US General Israel Pitman (1718–90) at Bunker Hill in the form, 'Don't one of you fire until you see the white of their eyes' – so quoted in R. Frothingham, *History of the Siege of Boston* (1873).

Hence, 'Don't fire until you see the whites of their eyes' has become an expression suggesting that you should not use up your ammunition (metaphorically speaking) before it can be effective. Or, that you should wait until you are right up against a problem before you begin to deal with it. Frederick the Great had earlier said something very similar at Prague on 6 May 1757, as also did Lieutenant-Colonel Sir Andrew Agnew to the men of his regiment at the Battle of Dettingen on 27 June 1743.

Emeric PRESSBURGER Hungarian-born screenwriter (1902–88)

5 *Killing a Mouse on Sunday.*

Title of novel (1961) about a survivor from the Spanish Civil War who comes out of retirement 20 years afterwards to kill a brutal police chief. The title is from Richard Braithwaite, *Barnaby's Journal* (1638), describing Banbury, 'the most Puritan of all Puritan towns':

> To Banbury came I, O profane one!
> Where I saw a Puritane one
> Hanging of his cat on Monday
> For killing of a mouse on Sunday.

When the novel was filmed, the title became, less obscurely, *Behold a Pale Horse* (1964) – see BIBLE 86:7. In his book *Million-Dollar Movie* (1992), Michael Powell, Pressburger's long-time film collaborator, describes how 'the title was certainly no help ... Emeric had discovered that great tempter, *The Oxford Dictionary of Quotations* ... I was worried about the title. I said so ... "It is a cat and mouse story, Michael." "Great! ... why not call it *Cat and Mouse*?" "I have called it *Killing a Mouse on Sunday*, Michael."'

J.B. PRIESTLEY English novelist and playwright (1894–1984)

6 *Let the People Sing.*

Title of novel by Priestley, written so that it could first be broadcast by the BBC in (of all months) September 1939. The story, about people fighting to save a village hall from being taken over by commercial interests, was later made into a film (1942). Characters in the story write a song that goes:

> Let the people sing,
> And freedom bring

An end to a sad old story.
Where the people sing,
Their voices ring
In the dawn of the people's glory.

In December 1939 another song was recorded with this title (music by Noel Gay, lyrics by Ian Grant and Frank Eyton), and this featured in the 1940 revue *Lights Up*. Later, ENSA, the forces' entertainment organization, used it as its signature tune. On 1 April 1940 the BBC started a long-running series of programmes – again with this title – featuring 'songs of the moment, songs of the past, songs of sentiment, songs with a smile, songs with a story, songs of the people'. The phrase almost took on the force of a slogan. Angus Calder in *The People's War* (1969) wrote of Ernest Bevin, the Minister of Labour from October 1940: 'Bevinism in industry was symbolized by the growing understanding of the value of music and entertainment in helping people to work faster ... There were the BBC's *Workers' Playtime* and *Music While You Work* which "progressive" management relayed over loudspeakers several times a day ... "Let the People Sing", it might be said, was the spiritual essence of Bevinism.' The phrase appears to have originated with Priestley, though one might note the similarity to the hymns 'Let all on earth their voices raise' and 'Let all the world in every corner sing'.

See also WAUGH 483:7.

Ann Adelaide PROCTER English poet and hymnwriter (1825–64)

1 Seated one day at the organ
I was weary and ill at ease,
And my fingers wandered idly
Over the noisy keys ...
But I struck one chord of music,
Like the sound of a great Amen.

'A Lost Chord', *Legends and Lyrics* (1858). Famously set to music by Sir Arthur Sullivan as '*The Lost Chord*' in the 1870s, and has been described as 'the most popular ballad of the 19th century'.

John PROFUMO English Conservative politician (1915–)

2 There was no impropriety whatsoever in my acquaintanceship with Miss Keeler.

When rumours surfaced of a relationship between the Secretary of State for War and Christine Keeler, a 'model' who had also been sharing her favours with a Soviet military attaché in London, Profumo made a statement to the House of Commons on 22 March 1963. It later became clear that there *had* been 'impropriety' (apart from adultery, there

was the possibility of a security risk) and Profumo resigned. For many, his 'misleading' of (or 'lie' to) the House was considered a worse crime than anything else he had done.

3 I shall not hesitate to issue writs for libel and slander if scandalous allegations are made or repeated outside the House.

In the same speech. Subsequently, 'I shall not hesitate to issue writs' became, through the offices of *Private Eye* Magazine, a catchphrase associated with Harold Wilson, who became British Prime Minister in 1964. He was famously ready to say he would have recourse to the law, though he did not always do so.

Marcel PROUST French novelist (1871–1922)

4 *À la recherche du temps perdu* [In search of lost time].

Title of novel sequence (1913–27). A captivating title that expresses perfectly what the novels are about – the artist deriving creative energy from the memory of past experiences. The title *Remembrance of Things Past* given to C.K. Scott Moncrieff's 1922 translation is not an accurate translation of the French original – which is specifically about a quest or search for lost *time*. Presumably, Scott Moncrieff chose it because it was a near-enough, resonant, ready-made phrase. Shakespeare's Sonnet 30 begins: 'When to the Sessions of sweet silent thought, / I summon up remembrance of things past ...'. It is said that Proust disapproved of the English title, but was somewhat mollified to be told that it was from Shakespeare.

Incidentally, in *George Lyttelton's Commonplace Book* (2002), he attributes, 'Man without learninge and the rememberance of things past, falls into a beastly sottishness and his life is noe better to be accounted of than to be buryed alive', to 'Gavin Douglas'. I take this to be the Bishop of Dunkeld (and poet) of that name who died in 1522, and thus someone who was dead before Shakespeare was born. So the query is – where in his works is this sentence to be found? It is also possible that Shakespeare might have acquired the phrase from a translation of the Apocryphal Wisdom of Solomon 11:12: 'For a double grief came upon them, and a groaning for the remembrance of things past.' On the other hand, translations of the Apocrypha may not have been easily to hand after the Reformation, and Shakespeare makes few biblical references in his works.

5 I raised to my lips a spoonful of the tea in which I had soaked a morsel of the cake ... suddenly the memory returns. The taste was of the little crumb of madeleine which on Sunday mornings at

Combray ... my aunt Léonie used to give me, dipping it first in her own cup of real or of lime-flower tea.

Du côté du chez Swann, Overture (1913), Vol. 1 of *À la recherche du temps perdu* in the C.K. Scott Moncrieff translation. The key moment in the novel and, if truth be told, the only one most people know about.

See also BERESFORD 63:2.

Marcus Aurelius Clemens PRUDENTIUS
Spanish-born Latin Christian poet (AD348–413)

1 Take him, Earth, for cherishing,
To thy tender breast receive him.
Body of a man I bring thee,
Noble even in its ruin ...

Poem, *Hymnus Circa Exsequias Defuncti*. 'Take him, Earth, for cherishing' is the title of a motet by the English composer, Herbert Howells (1892–1983), who wrote: 'Within the year following the tragic death of President Kennedy plans were made for a dual American-Canadian Memorial Service to be held in Washington. I was asked to compose an *a capella* work and the text was mine to choose, biblical or other. Choice was settled when I recalled a poem by Prudentius. I had already set it in its medieval Latin and I now turned to Helen Waddell's faultless translation.'

Giacomo PUCCINI Italian composer (1858–1924)

2 *Che gelida manina* [Your tiny hand is frozen].
Opera, *La Bohème*, Act 1 (1896). Rodolfo to Mimi. Puccini did not write his own libretti. This one was by Giuseppe Giacosa and Luigi Ilica.

3 *Nessun dorma! Nessun dorma!*
... All'alba vincerò!
Vincerò! Vincerò!
[No man shall sleep! No man shall sleep!
... At dawn I shall win!
I shall win! I shall win!]

Opera, *Turandot*, Act 3 (1926). Calaf refers to his secret (his name), which he does not think anyone will find out before dawn. The song as sung by Luciano Pavarotti gained widespread popularity when it was chosen to accompany British television coverage of the 1990 football World Cup, held that year in Italy. The idea of winning was aptly transferred from torture, beheading and sex in old Peking to the playing field. *Turandot*'s libretto was by Giuseppe Adami (1878–1946) and Renato Simoni (1875–1952) after a play by Carlo Gozzi.

John PUDNEY English poet (1909–77)

4 Do not despair
For Johnny-head-in-air;
He sleeps as sound
As Johnny underground ...

'For Johnny' (1942) – said to have been written by Pudney on the back of an envelope during the Blitz. The lines were subsequently used in the film *The Way to the Stars* (1945) in which they were recited following the death of their supposed author, an RAF pilot.

The character 'Johnny Head-in-Air' originally appeared in English translations of *Struwwelpeter* (1845), the collection of verse tales by Heinrich Hoffmann.

PUNCH London-based humorous weekly periodical, founded 1841

5 *Peccavi – I have Sindh.*

18 May 1844. *Punch* suggested that Caesar's '*Veni, vidi, vici*' was beaten for brevity by 'Napier's dispatch to Lord Ellenborough, *Peccavi*'. *ODQ* credits the joke to Catherine Winkworth (1827–78). She was a young girl, so it was sent into *Punch* on her behalf. Later, she became a noted translator of hymns.

It seems, however, that the supposed remark was soon taken as genuine, even at *Punch* itself. On 22 March 1856 the magazine (confusing sender and receiver in the original) included the couplet: '"*Peccavi* – I've Scinde," wrote Lord Ellen, so proud. More briefly Dalhousie wrote – "*Vovi* – I've Oude."' '*Peccavi*' is the Latin phrase for 'I have sinned'. *OED* sees it as part of the expression 'to cry *peccavi*', an acknowledgement or confession of guilt. The earliest citation given by *OED* is Bishop John Fisher's Funeral Sermon at St Paul's for Henry VII (1509): 'King David that wrote this psalm, with one word speaking his heart was changed saying *Peccavi*.' This refers to Psalm 41:4: 'I said, Lord, be merciful unto me: heal my soul; for I have sinned against thee.' But the phrase occurs in a number of other places in the Bible, mostly in the Old Testament – for example, 'And Saul said unto Samuel, I have sinned' (1 Samuel 15:24).

The Latin word is often thought to have furnished the above famous pun. Here is Charles Berlitz's version in *Native Tongues* (1982): 'Sir Charles Napier, a British officer in India, was given command of an expedition to annex the kingdom of Sind in [1843] ... To announce the success of his mission, he dispatched to the headquarters of the British East India Company a one-word message, the Latin word *peccavi*, which means "I have *sinned*."' Alas, Napier did no such thing.

1 WORTHY OF ATTENTION.
ADVICE TO PERSONS ABOUT TO MARRY, –
Don't.

On the January page of the 1845 Almanack. Never mind that this is probably the most famous of all *Punch* jokes, R.G.G. Price in his history of the magazine wonders whether it is perhaps 'the most famous joke ever made' and remarks that 'it needs an effort to realize how neat, ingenious and profound it must have seemed at the time'. It was based on an advertisement put out by a house furnisher of the day, and was probably contributed by Henry Mayhew, better known for his serious surveys of *London Labour and the London Poor*, though others also claimed to have thought of it. At about this period *Punch* also ran other jokes obviously based on the same advert – 'To persons about to marry ...', 'Persons about to marry should ...' etc.

2 Collapse of stout party.

A catchphrase that one might use as the tagline to a story about the humbling of a pompous person. It has long been associated with the magazine *Punch*, and was thought to have occurred in those wordy captions that used to be given to its cartoons. But, as Ronald Pearsall explains in his book *Collapse of Stout Party* (1975): 'To many people Victorian wit and humour is summed up by *Punch* when every joke is supposed to end with "Collapse of Stout Party", though this phrase tends to be as elusive as "Elementary, my dear Watson" in the Sherlock Holmes sagas.'

At least *OED2* has managed to find a reference to a 'Stout Party' in the caption to a cartoon in the edition of *Punch* dated 25 August 1855.

3 Mun, a had na' been the-ere abune twa hoours when – *Bang* – went *Saxpence*!

5 December 1868. Said by a Scotsman who has just been on a visit to London, in caption to a cartoon. Hence, the expression, 'Bang went sixpence!', a lightly joking remark about one's own or another person's unwillingness to spend money. The saying was re-popularized by Sir Harry Lauder, the professional stage Scotsman.

4 Go directly, and see what she's doing, and tell her she mustn't!

Vol. 63 (16 November 1872). Caption to cartoon, possibly by George du Maurier, with the title 'EXPERIENTIA DOCET'. Emily, an 'elder of fourteen' is asking her nanny 'Where's baby, Madge?' 'In the other room, I think, Emily,' replies Madge. Then comes the resounding command.

5 GOOD ADVERTISEMENT. I used your soap two years ago; since then I have used no other.

26 April 1884. Caption to a cartoon by Harry Furniss showing a grubby tramp writing a testimonial. It was taken up, with permission, by Pears' Soap and widely used in advertisements during the 1880s and 1890s. The slogan was changed slightly to: 'Two years ago I used your soap *since when* I have used no other!'

Pears' Soap also used a signed testimonial (with picture) from Lillie Langtry, the actress and mistress of King Edward VII (when he was Prince of Wales). Hers read: 'Since using Pears' Soap for the hands and complexion *I have discarded all others.*' This advertisement is undated but may possibly predate the *Punch* cartoon.

6 Dropping the Pilot.

29 March 1890. Meaning 'to dispense with a valued leader', this phrase comes from the caption to a cartoon by Sir John Tenniel that shows Kaiser Wilhelm II leaning over the side of a ship as his recently disposed-of Chancellor, Otto von Bismarck, dressed as a pilot, walks down the steps to disembark. Bismarck had been forced to resign following disagreements over home and foreign policy. The phrase was also used as the title of a poem on the same subject. From *The Independent* (12 May 1990): 'Kenneth Baker, the Conservative chairman, yesterday called on Tories to stop idle speculation about the party leadership ... "We have moved through difficult waters ... We should not, we must not, we will not drop the pilot."'

7 AN ADMONITION: *Bridget*: 'Now then, Miss Effie, you must behave yourself properly, or not at all.'

This is the caption to a Bernard Partridge cartoon (24 April 1897). Curiously, George Belcher came up with this on 27 April 1932: *Indignant Young Lady*: 'If you can't behave properly, you'd better not behave at all.'

8 Nearly all our best men are dead! Carlyle, Tennyson, Browning, George Eliot! – I'm not feeling very well myself.

Caption by anonymous cartoonist (6 May 1893). The cartoon is entitled 'A Lament' and shows a depressed young man ('Little Simpkins') lolling on a chair and talking to a woman friend. Note how Mark Twain later used the same idea in a speech on 'Statistics' to the Savage Club, London (9 June 1899): 'I was sorry to have my name mentioned as one of the great authors, because they have a sad habit of dying off. Chaucer is dead, Spencer is dead, so is Milton, so is Shakespeare, and I am not feeling very well myself' – included in *Mark Twain's Speeches* (1910). According to

Cornelia Otis Sinner, *Elegant Wits and Grand Horizontals* (1962), Alphonse Allais, the French humorist and playwright, once began a lecture: 'I have been asked to talk to you on the subject of the theatre, but I fear that it will make you melancholy. Shakespeare is dead, Molière is dead, Racine is dead, Marivaux is dead – and I am not feeling too well myself.'

However, it now transpires that everyone was anticipated by an anonymous cartoonist in *Punch* (14 August 1886) whose 'The Bills of Mortality' had this caption: *Kirk Elder* (after a look at his Morning Paper). 'Poor McStagger deid! Et's vera sad to thenk o' the great number o' Destengweshed Men that's lately been ta'en! 'Deed – I no feel vera well – mysel!'

1 Oh no, my Lord, I assure you! Parts of it are excellent!

9 November 1895. Caption to cartoon entitled 'TRUE HUMILITY' in which a 'Right Reverend Host' (a bishop at the breakfast table) is saying: 'I'm afraid you've got a bad egg, Mr Jones!' The nervous young curate, keen not to say anything critical, flannels this reply. Hence, the expression 'good in parts, like the curate's egg', meaning 'patchy, of unequal quality', although the point of the cartoon is rather that the egg is completely bad and the curate is seeking a way of softening any criticism implied in pointing this out in circumstances which are inexpedient. The cartoon was drawn by George du Maurier, the French-born British artist and novelist (1834–96) during the last year of his life.

2 *Carrier:* 'Try zideways, Mrs Jones, try zideways!' *Fat Lady:* 'Lar' bless 'ee, John, I ain't got no zideways.'

Caption to cartoon drawn by L. Raven-Hill (17 October 1900). In November 1998, opera diva Jessye Norman failed in persuading the Court of Appeal in London that she had been libelled by *Classic CD* magazine. It had drawn attention to Norman's 'fat lady' status by alleging that, trapped once in swing doors and advised to turn sideways, she had said: 'Honey, I ain't got no sideways.' The story has also been told about the large contralto Ernestine Schumann-Heink (1861–1936), who ended her days as a radio star in the US. A player, attempting to be helpful as Heink threaded her way between the music stands, whispered, 'Madame, move sideways.' She snapped back, 'With me there is no sideways!' Another appearance of this old chestnut is in Maisie Ward's *Gilbert Keith Chesterton* (1944), in her account of a visit to the United States in 1930–1, when Chesterton gave a course of lectures at Notre Dame. The chauffeur there, Johnny Mangan, said: 'I brought him under the main build-

ing, he got stuck in the door of the car. Father O'Donnell tried to help. Mr Chesterton said it reminded him of an old Irishwoman: "Why don't you get out sideways?" "I have no sideways."'

3 Look here, Steward, if this is coffee, I want tea; but if this is tea, then I wish for coffee.

23 July 1902. This was the caption to a cartoon by G.D. Armour. Frequently misascribed. On BBC Radio *Quote ... Unquote* (4 September 1979), a panellist ascribed it to Charles de Gaulle. Robert Byrne in *The 637 Best Things Anybody Ever Said* (1982) gives it to Abraham Lincoln, as does *The Treasury of Humorous Quotations*, eds Esar & Bentley (1951).

4 *MR BINKS:* 'ONE OF MY ANCESTORS FELL AT WATERLOO.'
LADY CLARE: 'AH? WHICH PLATFORM?'

1 November 1905. Caption to cartoon by F.H. Townsend. To this joke is often added the further response, 'Ha, ha! As if it mattered which platform!' Shamelessly misattributed over the years. *The Best of Myles* reprints this from Flann O'Brien's Dublin newspaper column [early 1940s]: 'D'you know that my great-grandfather was killed at Waterloo ... Which platform?' A.L. Rowse writes of Lord David Cecil in *Friends and Contemporaries* (1989): 'Anything for a laugh – simplest of jokes. I think of him now coming into my room [at Christ Church in the early 1920s], giggling and spluttering with fun. Someone had said, "My grandfather was killed at Waterloo." "I'm so sorry – which platform?"'

5 Well, mum, sometimes I sits and thinks and then again I just sits.

24 October 1906. Caption to a cartoon by Gunning-King headed 'Change of Occupation', which shows a vicar's wife talking to an old, somewhat rustic gentleman who has been laid up with an injured foot. She is sympathizing with him and saying: 'Now that you can't get about, and are not able to read, how do you manage to occupy the time?' This is his reply.

Until recently this well-known saying did not feature in any dictionary of quotations. So where did it originate? On first being asked about it, people would invariably say, 'Oh, that's what my father used to say.' Pressed as to its possible origin, they would come up with a bewildering variety of suggestions – Lewis Carroll, Laurel and Hardy, Winnie-the-Pooh, Uncle Remus (it could certainly be made to sound southern American), Mark Twain. One person thought it could be found 'in Chapter 8, probably' of *Pickwick Papers* by Charles Dickens (concerning Joe, 'the fat boy'), but it could not. Several others were absolutely positive that it came from that little American book *The Specialist* (1930) by Charles Sales, the one about a man who specializes in the building of outdoor privies. The connection with sitting and thinking seemed highly likely, but, no, it does not rate a mention.

Then came reference to the novel *Anne of the Island* (1915) by L.M. Montgomery, the Canadian writer who had earlier written *Anne of Green Gables*. At one point in the book, an old woman who drives a mail cart remarks: 'O' course it's tejus [tedious]. Part of the time I sits and thinks and the rest I jest sits.' Was this the first outing for what was clearly to become a much used and popular saying? No, it was not. Such evidence-sifting probably seems a shade preposterous ... not least because the answer (when you know it) is a very obvious one.

1 Mummy, what's that man *for*?

14 November 1906. Caption to cartoon drawn by F.H. Townsend, who was art editor of the magazine at the time. It shows the remark being said by a small boy to his mother about a man carrying a bag of golf clubs. This is probably the origin of the widely used jibe, 'What is that lady/gentleman *for*?' – a remark, out of the mouth of a not-quite babe or suckling, which becomes a convenient stick with which to beat anyone the speaker wishes to reduce in importance. It is particularly useful when taunting politicians. For example, 'It was an anonymous little girl who, on first catching sight of Charles James Fox, is supposed to have asked her mother: "what is that gentleman for?" One asks the same question of Mr [Douglas] Hurd. Why is he where he is in this particular government? He has never been wholly in sympathy either with Mrs Thatcher or with her version of Conservatism' – Alan Watkins, *The Observer* (29 May 1988). See also SHAW-LEFEVRE 428:1.

Compare: 'I am reminded of the small boy who once pointed at Hermione Gingold and asked, "Mummy, what's that lady for?"' – Michael Billington (possibly quoting Kenneth Tynan) in *The Guardian* (21 July 1988). This is probably what Russell Harty refers to in *Mr Harty's Grand Tour*, Chap. 2 (1988): 'It reminds me of the story one rather famous English actress tells about herself. She was, she says, sitting in a railway carriage ... A child opposite stared at her for quite a time and then turned to the accompanying mother and said, "What's that lady for?"'

'"What," a little girl is supposed to have asked her mother, pointing at Sir John Simon, a pre-war Chancellor, "is that man for?" What, she might now ask, pointing at the Labour faithful assembling in Brighton today, is that party for?' – editorial in the *Independent on Sunday* (29 September 1991).

2 The quality of Mersey is not strained.

19 August 1931. Writing to James Agate from Liverpool on 17 April 1942, John Gielgud, the actor, who was touring in *Macbeth*, noted: 'There was a very nice misprint in the *Liverpool Echo* on Wednesday, paying tribute to our broad comedian George Woodbridge, who plays the Porter, as "an engaging Portia". I could not forbear to murmur that the quality of Mersey is not strained.' Well, this was an early appearance of the 'Mersey' joke, in *Ego 5* (1942). It had already appeared, though, in *Punch*, as here, and long before, on 15 January 1859. See SHAKESPEARE 417:3.

3 I keep thinking it's Tuesday.

Caption to cartoon of two hippopotami lazing in the water, drawn anonymously by Paul Crum (21 July 1937). The drawing is very small, but is a favourite among cartoon buffs, who see in it a strain of that surrealism more often found in *The New Yorker* at about that time. A correspondent encourages me to believe that exactly the same picture was printed three months later with the caption: 'Angela, that's a nice name.'

Aleksandr PUSHKIN Russian poet and novelist (1799–1837)

4 I loved you and it may be that my love within my soul has not yet altogether died away; howbeit, it will not trouble you any more, I do not wish to sadden you in any way. I loved you in silence and without hope, worn out now with jealousy and now with shamefastness; I loved you so truly and so tenderly as may God grant you may be loved by some other one.

Poem, 'I Loved You' (1829). As featured in Maurice Baring's introduction to *The Oxford Book of Russian Verse* (1925). Of this short poem, Baring says: 'Russian literature in the hands of an artist such as Pushkin reminds one constantly of Greek art. Pushkin's eight lines could only have been written either in Russian or in Greek.' He then gives this prose translation.

Mario PUZO American novelist (1920–99)

5 He's a businessman. I'll make him an offer he can't refuse.

Puzo's 1969 Mafia novel *The Godfather* gave to the language a new expression which, as far as can be established, was Puzo's own invention. Johnny Fontane, a singer, desperately wants a part in a movie and goes to see his godfather, Don Corleone, seeking help. All the contracts have been signed and there is no chance of the studio chief changing his mind. Still, the godfather promises Fontane he will get him the part, with these words. In the 1971 film, the exchange was turned into the following dialogue:

> *Corleone*: In a month from now this Hollywood big shot's going to give you what you want.
> *Fontane*: Too late, they start shooting in a week.
> *Corleone*: I'm going to make him an offer he can't refuse.

1 A lawyer with his briefcase can steal more than a thousand men with guns.

In the same novel. In *The Godfather Papers* (1969) Puzo singled out this as the most quoted line from the novel. 'I've had people in France, Germany and Denmark quote that line to me with the utmost glee,' he said. 'And some of them are lawyers.' Puzo mentioned it to the head of the studio, the producer, director and everyone on the film, but the line did not get spoken in it. Compare: 'Pen and ink are now my surest means of vengeance; and more land is won by the lawyer with the ram-skin [parchment], than by the Andrea Ferrara [sword] with his sheepshead handle' – Sir Walter Scott, *The Fortunes of Nigel*, Chap. 32 (1822).

Barbara PYM English novelist (1913–80)

2 *Some Tame Gazelle.*

Title of novel (1950). Pym's stories of quiet lives lived in a narrow band of middle-class society in most cases had quotations for their titles. Sometimes it was indicated in the book what the source was: *The Sweet Dove Died* (1978) (John Keats), *A Glass of Blessings* (1958) (George Herbert), *Less Than Angels* (1955) (Alexander Pope), *Civil to Strangers* (unpublished) (John Pomfret), and the short story 'So, Some Tempestuous Morn' (Matthew Arnold). At other times, Pym kept mum. The short story 'Across a Crowded Room' is presumably Oscar Hammerstein II's 'Some Enchanted Evening' – but very 1950s. *A Few Green Leaves* (1980) could be anything or nothing, as also *Excellent Women* (1952).

Some Tame Gazelle replaced 'Some Sad Turtle', and derives from a poem called 'Something to Love' by Thomas Haynes Bayly (1797–1839), a minor English poet:

> Some tame gazelle, or some gentle dove:
> Something to love, oh, something to love!

3 *No Fond Return of Love.*

Title of novel (1961). Behind it is an interesting story, which is related in Hazel Holt's memoir of Pym. Rejecting 'A Thankless Task' Pym decided she needed a title with 'love' in it, so sat down and worked her way through *The Oxford Book of English Verse* until she came to 'Prayer for Indifference' by the 18th-century Irish poet Fanny (Frances) Greville (?1724–89). She adapted the first line:

> I ask no kind return of love,
> No tempting charm to please;
> Far from the heart those gifts remove
> That sigh for peace and ease.

4 What is the future of my kind of writing? ... Perhaps in retirement ... a quieter, narrower kind of life can be worked out and adopted. Bounded by English literature and the Anglican Church and small pleasures like sewing and choosing material for this uncertain summer.

Diary entry (6 March 1972), in Holt & Pym, *A Very Private Life* (1985). This was written when one of her novels had been rejected (Pym is famous for having fallen out of favour and for then being rediscovered). The phrase 'this uncertain summer' is quintessential Pym and sounds as if it ought to have served her as a title. It had been used by Sir James E. Smith in *The English Flora* (1824–8): 'It may be observed that our uncertain summer is established by the time the Elder is in full flower.' Compare *Uncertain Glory*, the title of a film (US 1944) and taken probably from Shakespeare's *Two Gentlemen of Verona* (I.iii.85): 'O, how this spring of love resembleth / The uncertain glory of an April day.'

See also ALEXANDER 5:7.

Dan QUAYLE American Republican Vice-President (1947–)

1 Space is almost infinite. As a matter of fact, we think it *is* infinite.

As head of the Space Council. Remark, quoted in *The Guardian* (8 March 1989). George Bush's surprise choice for running mate in the 1988 election, Quayle soon became noted, when in office, for his eccentric and often idiotic statements. Of the Nazi Holocaust (quoted in the same source), he said: 'It was an obscene period in our nation's history ... No, not in our nation's but in World War II. We all lived in this century; I didn't live in this century but in this century's history.'

(Sir) Arthur QUILLER-COUCH English academic and critic (1863–1944)

2 Whenever you feel an impulse to perpetuate a piece of exceptionally fine writing, obey it – wholeheartedly – and delete it before sending your manuscript to press. *Murder your darlings.*

In 12th and final lecture 'On Style' (given at Cambridge on 28 January 1914 in a series published as *On the Art of Writing*). Hence: 'Kill your darlings' or 'throw away your babies', advice often given to aspiring journalists (and certainly in use by the 1960s). It means 'get rid of obviously impressive writing to which you may become unreasonably attached'. Hence, also, the title of Terence Blacker's novel *Kill Your Darlings* (2000). 'In writing, you must kill all your darlings' is ascribed to William Faulkner by William Goldman in *Adventures in the Screen Trade* (1983). Compare JOHNSON 259:7.

R

François RABELAIS French writer (?1494–?1553)

1 Nature abhors a vacuum.

Gargantua (1535). Rabelais quotes the maxim in its original Latin form '*Natura abhorret vacuum*'. Galileo (1564–1642) asserted it as the reason mercury rises in a barometer. See also BROWN 103:3.

2 *Fais/Fay ce que voudras* [Do what you will/do as you please].

Gargantua (1535). An appealing motto and one that has been adopted by more than one free-living soul. In the 18th century it became the motto of the Monks of Medmenham, better known as the Hell Fire Club. Sir Francis Dashwood founded a mock Franciscan order at Medmenham Abbey in Buckinghamshire in 1745, and the members of the Club were said to get up to all sorts of disgraceful activities – orgies, black masses and the like. The politician John Wilkes was of their number. The motto was written up over the ruined door of the abbey.

Aleister Crowley (1875–1947), the satanist, who experimented in necromancy, the black arts, sex and drugs, also picked up the motto. Newspapers called him the 'Wickedest Man in the World', though he fell short of proving the claim. Of his 'misunderstood commandment', Germaine Greer comments in *The Female Eunuch* (1970): '*Do as thou wilt* is a warning not to delude yourself that you can do otherwise, and to take full responsibility for what you do. When one has genuinely chosen a course for oneself it cannot be possible to hold another responsible for it.'

3 *Adieu paniers, vendanges sont faites* [Farewell baskets, the grapes are gathered].

In the same book. One of those peculiar lines that get turned into catchphrases. Friar Jean des Entommeurs is exhorting his fellow monks to stop praying and repel the soldiers who are vandalizing their vineyard – a call to arms.

4 The comedy is ended.

The dying words of Rabelais are supposed to have been: '*Je m'en vais chercher un grand peut-être; tirez le rideau, la farce est jouée* [I am going to seek a grand perhaps; bring down the curtain, the farce is played out].' The attribution is made, hedged about with disclaimers, in Jean Fleury's *Rabelais et ses oeuvres* (1877) – also in the life of Rabelais by Motteux, who died in 1718. In Lermontov's novel *A Hero of Our Time* (1840), a character says: '*Finita la commedia*', and Canio exclaims '*La commedia è finita*' at the end of Leoncavallo's opera *Pagliacci* (1892). Compare BEETHOVEN 58:1.

(Sir) Walter RALEIGH English explorer and courtier (?1552–1618)

5 But true love is a durable fire
In the mind ever burning;
Never sick, never old, never dead,
From itself never turning.

Poem, 'Walsingham' (undated). *A Durable Fire* was the title given to a volume of the letters of Duff and Diana Cooper 1913–50 (published 1983).

6 Give me my scallop-shell of quiet,
My staff of faith to walk upon,
My scrip of joy, immortal diet,
My bottle of salvation,
My gown of glory, hope's true gage,
And thus I'll take my pilgrimage.

'The Passionate Man's Pilgrimage' or 'His Pilgrimage' (1604). There is some doubt about the authorship. The scallop shell was the emblem worn by pilgrims to identify themselves as such. More particularly, it was the emblem of St James of Compostela and was adopted, according to Erasmus, because the seashore was close to the end of the pilgrimage route to the saint's shrine.

William Brighty RANDS English journalist and poet (1823–82)

1 When Love arose in heart and deed
To wake the world to greater joy,
'What can she give me now?' said Greed,
Who thought to win some costly toy.

'The Flowers', *Lilliput Levee* (1864). Rands was sometimes known as the 'laureate of the nursery'. His books were originally published anonymously or pseudonymously.

Frederic RAPHAEL English novelist and screen writer (1931–)

2 He glanced with disdain at the big centre table where the famous faces of the Cambridge theatre were eating a loud meal. 'So this is the city of dreaming spires,' Sheila said. 'Theoretically speaking that's Oxford,' Adam said. 'This is the city of perspiring dreams.'

The Glittering Prizes (1976). See ARNOLD 40:4.

Gerald RATNER British businessman (1949–)

3 We even sell a pair of earrings for under £1, which is cheaper than a prawn sandwich from Marks & Spencers. But I have to say the earrings probably won't last as long.

On how to succeed in the jewellery business, in a speech to the Institute of Directors, Albert Hall (23 April 1991). At the time Ratner was Chairman of Ratners Group plc. The company's fortunes consequently took a dive and Ratner resigned in 1992. In *The Independent* Saturday Magazine (14 February 1998), Ratner explained: 'It was a joke to make the speech more interesting. It was a dig at people who say "Our products are so cheap because we cut out the middleman" ... It's all bollocks ... we all buy our stuff the same way. So I said: "How can we sell this [decanter] at such a low price? Because it is total crap." It was just a joke that had nothing to do with what else I was saying.'

(Sir) Terence RATTIGAN English playwright (1911–77)

4 *The Way to the Stars.*

Title of film (UK 1945), set near an RAF airfield during the Second World War, and which reworked most of Rattigan's

stage play *Flare Path*. It presumably alludes to the RAF motto '*Per ardua ad astra* [Through striving/struggle to the stars]', first proposed in 1912. However, the words '*Macte nova virtute, puer, sic itur ad astra*' from Virgil's *Aeneid*, Bk 9, line 641, are often translated as: 'Go to it with fresh courage, young man; this is the way to the stars' – the words of Ascanius, son of Aeneas, before battle. In the US, perhaps to avoid any such questions, the film was called *Johnny in the Clouds* – after the line 'Johnny Head-in-air' (see PUDNEY 369:4), which is recited in the film.

5 A nice, respectable, middle-class, middle-aged maiden lady, with time on her hands and the money to help her pass it ... Let us call her Aunt Edna ... Aunt Edna is universal, and to those who may feel that all the problems of the modern theatre might be solved by her liquidation, let me add that ... she is also immortal.

Preface, *Collected Plays*, Vol. II (1953). During the revolution in English drama of the 1950s the term 'Aunt Edna' was used by the new wave of angry young dramatists and their supporters to describe the more conservative theatregoer – the type who preferred comfortable three-act plays of the Shaftesbury Avenue kind. Ironically, the term had been coined in self-defence by Rattigan, one of the generation of dramatists they sought to replace.

Irina RATUSHINSKAYA Ukrainian poet (1954–)

6 *Grey is the Colour of Hope.*

Title of book (1988) – referring to the colour of the author's uniform as an inmate of a Soviet labour camp. On her 29th birthday, Ratushinskaya was sentenced to seven years in the camp, to be followed by five years' internal exile. Her 'crime' was her poetry. She was released (after intensive campaigning) in 1986, just prior to the Reykjavik summit meeting between Presidents Reagan and Gorbachev. Compare: 'Citizens to arms! ... Let us take as our emblem green cockades, green the colour of hope' – Camille Desmoulins, French revolutionary leader, speech (14 July 1789).

John RAY English botanist and paroemiologist (collector of proverbs) (1627–1705)

7 Misery loves company.

Bartlett (1992) lists this proverb, along with five others, under Ray's name. This is surely misleading as the whole point of any proverb book – not least Ray's own *A Collection of English Proverbs* (1670) – is that it represents traditional expression of wisdom rather than an individual's. Of course, some proverb collectors and scholars (notably Benjamin Franklin) did coin proverbs and slip them into their collection, but there is no reason to believe that Ray did so. *ODP* does not include this proverb, anyway, though *CODP* finds earlier citations in about 1349 and 1578.

Man RAY French artist and photographer (1890–1976)

1 *La photographie n'est pas l'art* [Photography is not art].
Quoted in *The Independent* (3 March 1995). Misleadingly, it has been translated as 'Art is not photography.'

Ernest RAYMOND English novelist (1888–1974)

2 Tell England, ye who pass this monument,
We died for her, and here we rest content.
Tell England, Bk 2, Chap. 12 (1922): 'We had walked right on to the grave of our friend. His name stood on a cross with those of six other officers, and beneath was written in pencil the famous epitaph ... The perfect words went straight to Doe's heart. "Roop," he said, "if I'm killed you can put those lines over me."'
The book (film UK 1931) is about a group of English public school boys who end up at Gallipoli. Quite where the epitaph originated is hard to say. In *Farewell the Trumpets* (1978) James Morris finds it on a memorial from the Boer War at Wagon Hill, Ladysmith, in the form:

Tell England, ye who pass this monument,
We, who died serving her, rest here content.

Presumably this memorial was erected *before* the First World War and *before* Raymond's book popularized the couplet.
Whatever the case, the words clearly echo the epitaph by the ancient Greek poet Simonides (432:4) on the Spartans who died at Thermopylae (delaying the vastly greater Persian army at the cost of their own lives): 'Tell the Spartans, stranger, that here we lie, obeying their orders.' Indeed, Diana Raymond, the novelist's widow, wrote in 1992: 'I (and all the family) always understood from Ernest that he had taken the lines from the epitaph for the Spartans who died at Thermopylae, substituting "England" for "Sparta" and making his own translation. This leaves the problem of the Boer War memorial at Ladysmith. Either two people had the same idea; or else Ernest had somewhere at the back of his mind without realizing it a memory of this. I rather think the first answer is the right one; he was very accurate in his references.'

Charles READE English novelist (1814–84)

3 Make 'em laugh, make 'em cry, make 'em wait.
A suggested recipe for writing novels to be published in serial form (as done by Charles Dickens and many others in the 19th century). Reade, who wrote *The Cloister and the*

Hearth (1861), came up with it – or at least he did according to *PDQ* (1960). Kenneth Robinson in his biography *Wilkie Collins* (1951) attributes the remark to Reade's contemporary.

Ronald REAGAN American film actor, Republican governor and 40th President (1911–2004)

4 Win this one for the Gipper!
Bridging his film and political careers, this Reagan slogan refers to George Gipp, a character he had played in *Knute Rockne – All-American* (1940). Gipp was a real-life football star who died young. At half-time in a 1928 Army game, Rockne, the team coach, had recalled something Gipp had said to him: 'Rock, someday when things look real tough for Notre Dame, ask the boys to go out there and win one for me.' Reagan used the slogan countless times. One of the last was at a campaign rally for Vice-President George Bush in San Diego, California, on 7 November 1988. Reagan's peroration included these words: 'So, now we come to the end of this last campaign ... And I hope that someday your children and grandchildren will tell of the time that a certain President came to town at the end of a long journey and asked their parents and grandparents to join him in setting America on the course to the new millennium ... So, if I could ask you just one last time. Tomorrow, when mountains greet the dawn, would you go out there and win one for the Gipper? Thank you, and God bless you all.'

5 Randy – where's the rest of me?
Film *King's Row* (1941) – in which Reagan plays the part of Drake McHugh, and Ann Sheridan appears as Randy Monaghan. A famous moment occurs when Drake, on waking to find that his legs have been amputated by a sadistic doctor, poses this pained question. *Where's the Rest of Me?* was used by Reagan as the title of an early autobiography (1965).

6 An alimentary canal with a big appetite at one end and no responsibility at the other.
On government. *Bartlett* (1992) came under particular attack for its treatment of Reagan, the erstwhile 'Great Communicator'. While noting two of Reagan's many borrowings in footnotes ('Go ahead, make my day' and 'Evil empire'), it listed only *three* original sayings. Adam Meyerson, raising the topic in *The Washington Post* (14 February 1993), thought the choice of only three Reaganisms (compared with 28 apiece for John F. Kennedy and Franklin D. Roosevelt) was politically motivated and intended to diminish the former president. Supporters of Bartlett responded with the suggestion that Reagan relied so much on borrowings from old movie scripts and on the scribblings of speechwriters

like Peggy Noonan that his famous lines did not deserve Bartlett's form of immortality. But neither Kennedy nor Roosevelt produced their mighty lines unaided, and the rule of thumb in compiling such dictionaries should always be to recognize the person who actually went out there and spoke the lines (however arrived at) – in other words the person who popularized them. For the record: *ODQ* (1992) included *five* Reaganisms (completely different from *Bartlett's*). *Chambers Dictionary of Modern Quotations* (1993) contains 15 entries under 'Reagan', together with four cross-references to his borrowings.

In *Speaking My Mind* (1989), the book of Reagan's selected speeches, there is not a single mention of Peggy Noonan or any other speechwriter. The drafts that are reproduced in the book – spattered with emendations in the president's own hand – seem designed to convince that he really was 'speaking his own mind'.

Of the three sayings Bartlett did include, the above is a gag dating from 1965, when Reagan was campaigning for Governor of California. Bartlett gives no indication that this might be no more than a gag-writer's re-working of the definition of a baby long ascribed to Ronald Knox in the form 'a loud voice at one end and no sense of responsibility at the other'. It was so ascribed in A. Andrews, *Quotations for Speakers and Writers* (1969) and also in the 1976 BBC Reith Lectures, though Frank S. Pepper's *Handbook of 20th Century Quotations* (1984) gives the 'baby' version to 'E. Adamson'.

1 A shining city on a hill.

In a speech on 14 October 1969 Reagan quoted Governor Winthrop of the Massachusetts Bay Colony, who told new settlers in 1630: 'We shall be as a city upon a hill, the eyes of all people are upon us.' It was meant as a warning as much as a promise. Winthrop did not use the word 'shining'. A writer in *The Observer* (8 March 1987) recalled Reagan using it as early as 1976 when he had just lost the Republican nomination to Gerald Ford. He told his supporters he would be back, they would win in the end and once again America would be a 'shining city on a hill'. Later, when president, Reagan was often to use the image to describe the US as a land of security and success. He used the phrase particularly during his bid for re-election as president in 1984. In return, at the Democratic Convention, New York Governor Mario Cuomo remarked that a shining city might be what Reagan saw 'from the veranda of his ranch' but he failed to see despair in the slums. 'There is despair, Mr President, in the faces that you don't see, in the places that you don't visit in your shining city ... This nation is more a tale of two cities than it is just a shining city on a hill.'

If anything, the image is biblical. Matthew 5:14 has: 'A city that is set on a hill cannot be hid ... Let your light so shine before men that they may see your good works'; the 'holy hill' of Zion is a 'sunny mountain' according to one etymology; the New Jerusalem is the jewelled city lit by the glory of God in Revelation – source: letter to *The Observer* from Alan MacColl, University of Aberdeen (15 March 1987.)

2 Don't you cut me off. I am paying for this microphone.

Just prior to a broadcast debate at Nashua, New Hampshire, during the presidential primary there in 1980, Reagan turned the tables on George Bush (then also a challenger) by insisting that the other Republican candidates be allowed to participate. Reagan won the dispute over who should speak in the debate by declaring 'Don't you cut me off, I am paying for this microphone, Mr Green!' Never mind that the man's name was actually 'Breen', the line in the form, 'Don't you shut me off, I'm paying for this broadcast' had earlier been delivered by Spencer Tracy in the film *State of the Union* (1948). This borrowing was pointed out by Christopher J. Matthews in *The Washington Post* (6 May 1984), and by *Time* Magazine (8 February 1988).

3 Congressional Medal of Honor, posthumously awarded.

Reagan told a meeting (undated) of the Congressional Medal of Honor Society about an aircraft gunner who couldn't leave his post when his plane was crashing. He was told by his commanding officer that he would win a 'Congressional Medal of Honor, posthumously awarded'. No such incident happened in real life, though it did in the film *Wing and a Prayer* (1944). In 1985 Michael Rogin, a professor of political science at Berkeley, explored Reagan's other borrowings of film lines in a presentation entitled 'Ronald Reagan: The Movie'.

4 In your discussions of the nuclear freeze proposals, I urge you to beware the temptation of pride – the temptation blithely to declare yourselves above it all and label both sides equally at fault, to ignore the facts of history and the aggressive impulses of an evil empire.

The Soviet Union was so described by Reagan in a speech to the National Association of Evangelicals at Orlando, Florida (8 March 1983). The inspiration for this turn of phrase was made clear later the same month (23 March) when Reagan first propounded his 'Star Wars' proposal as part of a campaign to win support for his defence budget and arms-control project. The proposal, more properly known by its initials SDI (for Strategic Defence Initiative), was to extend the nuclear battleground into space. The President did not use the term 'Star Wars' but it was an inevitable tag to be applied by the media, given his own fondness for adapting lines from the movies. The film *Star Wars* and the sequel *The Empire Strikes Back* had been released in 1977 and 1980 respectively.

In the controversy over Reagan's poor showing in *Bartlett* (1992) (see above), it was argued that Bartlett was wrong in ascribing the phrase 'evil empire' to George Lucas, the creator of *Star Wars*. Apparently, in that film it appears only in the form 'evil galactic empire'. An alternative version, 'the most evil enemy mankind has ever known in his long climb from the swamp to the stars' was quoted by *The Guardian* (30 May 1988) on the occasion of Reagan's visit to the Soviet Union. Compare from *The Independent* (19 May 1990): 'Frank Salmon, an East End protection racketeer who built an "evil empire" on violence and fear, was yesterday jailed for 7½ years at the Old Bailey.'

1 **Where do we find such men?**

In 1984, on the 40th anniversary of the D-Day landings, President Reagan visited Europe and made a speech in which he eulogized those who had taken part in the event. 'Where do we find such men?' he asked. On a previous occasion he had said: 'Many years ago in one of the four wars in my lifetime, an admiral stood on the bridge of a carrier watching the planes take off and out into the darkness bent on a night combat mission and then found himself asking, with no one there to answer – just himself to hear his own voice – "Where do we find such men?"' But the very first time he had used the line he had made it clear where it came from and that it was fiction. The line comes from James Michener's novel *Bridges at Toko-Ri*, later filmed (1954) with William Holden, who asks, 'Where do we get such men?' Over the years, fiction became fact for Reagan. Perhaps he could not, or was unwilling, to distinguish between the two – source: Rogin, as above.

2 **You ain't seen nothing yet!**

On the same occasion, and during the preceding campaign. Quoted in the *Daily Express* (8 November 1984). Compare JOLSON 261:7.

3 **There is no limit to what a man can do and where he can go if he doesn't mind who gets the credit.**

The propensity for American presidents to clutter their desks with plaques bearing uplifting messages dates back to the days of Harry S Truman at least. His motto, 'The buck stops here', was apparently of his own devising. Jimmy Carter either retrieved the original or had a copy made and displayed it near his own desk when he was in the Oval Office. Enter Ronald Reagan. According to the *Daily Mail*

(18 April 1985): 'Besides a calendar, a pen set, a clock and a horseshoe, the First Desk is now home to no fewer than eight inspirational messages. They range from the consoling "Babe Ruth struck out 1330 times", through the boosting "Illegitimi Non Carborundum" [see HORACE 244:5] ... to the altruistic "There is no limit ..."'

4 **Do we get to win this time?**

So says John Rambo (a hunk bringing home American prisoners left behind in the Vietnam War) in the film *Rambo: First Blood Part Two* (US 1985) – a sequel to *First Blood* (US 1982). The terms 'Ramboesque', 'Rambo-like' and 'Ramboism' were rapidly adopted for mindless, forceful heroics. When Reagan quoted this line in a speech (undated), he did have the grace to credit it for once rather than pass it off as one of his own.

5 **We are not going to tolerate these attacks from outlaw states run by the strangest collection of misfits, looney tunes, and squalid criminals since the advent of the Third Reich.**

On the hijacking of a US plane by Shi'ite Muslims, in a broadcast (8 July 1985). Meaning 'mad person' or, as an adjective, 'mad', the phrase 'looney tune' refers to the cinema cartoon comedies called Looney Tunes, which have been produced by Warners since the 1940s. The phrase was already established and had been used, for example, in the Mel Brooks film *High Anxiety* (1977).

6 **There's a coincidence today. On this day 390 years ago, the great explorer Sir Francis Drake died aboard ship off the coast of Panama. In his lifetime the great frontiers were the oceans, and a historian later said, 'He lived by the sea, died on it, and was buried in it.' Well, today we can say of the *Challenger* crew: Their dedication was, like Drake's, complete.**

TV address on the space shuttle *Challenger* disaster (28 January 1986). The identity of the historian remained untraced for a long time. G.M. Trevelyan is supposed to have said of Nelson that he was 'Always in his element and always on his element.' H.L. *Mencken* had as a 'Japanese proverb': 'If you were born at sea, you will die on it.' Isadora Duncan wrote in *My Life* (1928): 'I was born by the sea, and I have noticed that all the great events of my life have taken place by the sea' – she also died by the sea, at Nice. Kenneth Grahame wrote in *The Wind in the Willows*, Chap. 1 (1908): 'And you really live by the river? ... By it and with it and on it and in it.'

A letter to Peggy Noonan, Reagan's chief speechwriter,

failed to elicit a reply. Not until 2004 did Joe Kralich track down that it was written by the historian Thomas Fuller (1608–61), the King's chaplain (after the Restoration) and author of *The Worthies of England* etc. In his book *The Holy State*, published along with *The Profane State* in the 1640s around the time of the English Civil War, he wrote of the ideal characteristics for different callings. Fuller chose Drake to exemplify 'The Good Sea-Captain' in a chapter with that title, and in the next (Chap. 37), wrote 'The Life of Sir Francis Drake'. Drawing lessons from the life, he noted Drake's apprehensions that 'all the good which he had done in this [final] voyage, consisted in the evil he had done to the Spaniards afar off ... accompanying if not causing, the disease of the flux, wrought his sudden death [28 January 1595]. And sickness did not so much untie his clothes, as sorrow did rend at once the robe of his mortality asunder. He lived by the sea, died on it, and was buried in it.'

1 There is nothing better for the inside of a man than the outside of a horse.

When *Time* Magazine quoted President Reagan as saying this (28 December 1987), it received many letters from readers saying such things as: 'This quotation bears a striking resemblance to a remark made by the California educator and prep school founder Sherman Thacher: "There's something about the outside of a horse that's good for the inside of a boy"'; and, 'Rear Admiral Grayson, President Woodrow Wilson's personal physician put it ... "The outside of a horse is good for the inside of a man"'; and, 'Lord Palmerston said it.'

Time sensibly replied (19 January 1988): 'Everyone is right. The origin of the saying is unknown. It is one of the President's favourite expressions.' Compare, however: 'The Squire will wind up ... with an apocryphal saying which he attributes to Lord Palmerston – "There's nothing so good for the inside of a man as the outside of a horse"' – G.W.E. Russell, *Social Silhouettes*, Chap. 32 (1906); 'Truly it may be said that the outside of a mountain is good for the inside of a man' – George Wherry, *Alpine Notes and the Climbing Foot* (1896).

See also DEMPSEY 167:1; EASTWOOD 181:1; LOUIS 296:6; MAGEE 307:3.

John REED American writer (1887–1920)

2 *Ten Days that Shook the World.*

Title of book (1919) on the Russian Revolution. Also used as the alternative, English, title of Sergei Eisenstein's 1927 film *October*.

Rosser REEVES American advertising agent (1910–84)

3 Each advertisement must say to each reader: 'Buy *this* product, and you will get *this specific benefit*' ... The proposition must be one that the competition either cannot, or does not, offer. It must be unique ... The proposition must be so strong that it can move the mass millions ... These three points are summed up in the phrase: 'UNIQUE SELLING PROPOSITION.' This is a U.S.P.

Reality in Advertising, Chap. 13 (1960). The term was coined by Reeves at the Ted Bates & Company agency, which he helped found in 1940 and which he helped become one of the largest in the world. He described the term USP as 'a theory of the ideal selling concept ... a verbal shorthand of what makes a campaign work.'

Max REGER German composer (1873–1916)

4 I am sitting in the smallest room of my house. I have your review before me. In a moment it will be behind me.

In 1906 Reger wrote what might appear to be the original of a famous type of abusive remark in a letter to the music critic Rudolph Louis. It is quoted in N. Slonimsky, *Lexicon of Musical Invective* (1953), having been translated from the German. Ned Sherrin, in *Theatrical Anecdotes* (1991), reports the similar reply from Oscar Hammerstein (grandfather of the lyricist) to a creditor: 'I am in receipt of your letter which is now before me and in a few minutes will be behind me.' In *Playboy* (October 1977), Barbra Streisand said it was by Bernard Shaw; in the *Evening Standard* (30 January 1992), Milton Shulman ascribed it to Noël Coward ...

There seems every chance that the real originator of the remark was John Montagu, 4th Earl of Sandwich. When William Eden (later Lord Auckland) defected from Sandwich in 1785 he wrote him a letter of justification. J.H. Jesse, *George Selwyn*, Vol. 1 (1843–4, or at least the 1882 edn) records: 'The reply of Lord Sandwich was sufficiently laconic: "Sir," he said, "your letter is before me, and will presently be behind."' Apparently, manufactured lavatory paper was not known in the 18th century.

(Sir) John REITH (later Lord Reith) Scottish-born broadcasting administrator (1889–1971)

5 It was in fact the combination of public service motive, sense of moral obligation, assured finance and the brute force of monopoly which enabled the BBC to make of broadcasting what no other country has made of it.

Into the Wind (1949). Reith's dour approach to broadcasting – he was the BBC's first Director-General from 1922 – set the standard and tone of British broadcasting in its early days and beyond. When he wrote these words, however, momentum was building for the 'brute force of monopoly' to be overturned by the introduction of commercial television (which eventually arrived in 1955). Commercial radio did not operate in the UK until 1973.

1 I was inordinately ambitious, I suppose, to be *fully* stretched ... inordinately ambitious to be of service.
BBC TV, *Lord Reith Looks Back* (1967). Reith was describing his youthful determination to achieve something recognizable. Initially he was an engineer before being drawn into broadcasting, about which he then knew nothing.
See also MÜNSTER 322:1.

Erich Maria REMARQUE German novelist (1897–1970)

2 *All Quiet on the Western Front.*
Title given to the English translation of Remarque's novel *Im Westen nichts Neues* [From the Western Front – nothing to report] (1929, film US 1930). 'All Quiet on the Western Front' had been a familiar phrase of the Allies in the First World War, used in military communiqués and newspaper reports and also taken up jocularly by men in the trenches to describe peaceful inactivity. *Partridge/Catch Phrases* hears in it echoes of 'All quiet on the Shipka Pass', a phrase that appeared in cartoons of the 1877–8 Russo-Turkish War, and which Partridge says had a vogue in 1915–6, though he never heard the allusion made himself. For no very good reason, Partridge rules out any connection with the US song 'All Quiet Along the Potomac'. This, in turn, came from a poem called 'The Picket Guard' (1861) by Ethel Lynn Beers – a sarcastic commentary on General George Brinton McClellan's policy of delay at the start of the Civil War. The phrase (alluding to the Potomac River which runs through Washington DC) had been used in reports from McClellan's Union headquarters and put in Northern newspaper headlines.

Pierre Auguste RENOIR French painter (1841–1919)

3 I paint with my prick.
ODQ (1992) suggested that this was possibly an inversion of 'It's with my brush that I make love', from A. André, *Renoir* (1919). D.H. Lawrence, *Lady Chatterley's Lover*, Chap. 4 (1928), has: 'Renoir said he painted his pictures with his penis ... he did too, lovely pictures! I wish I did something with mine.'

Charles à Court REPINGTON English soldier and journalist (1858–1925)

4 *The First World War 1914–18.*
Title of book (1920). Presumably this helped popularize the name for the war, ominously suggesting that it was merely the first of a series. Indeed, it was thought to be a shocking title because it presupposed another war.
Known at first as the 'European War', the conflict became known quite rapidly as the 'Great War'. By 10 September 1918, as he later described in his book, Repington was referring to it in his diary as the 'First World War', thus: 'I saw Major Johnstone, the Harvard Professor who is here to lay the bases of an American History. We discussed the right name of the war. I said that we called it now *The War*, but that this could not last. The Napoleonic War was *The Great War*. To call it *The German War* was too much flattery for the Boche. I suggested *The World War* as a shade better title, and finally we mutually agreed to call it *The First World War* in order to prevent the millennium folk from forgetting that the history of the world was the history of war.'
OED2 finds 'Great War' in use by 1914, but does not find 'First World War' until 1931.

Walter REUTHER American labour leader (1907–70)

5 If it looks like a duck, walks like a duck and quacks like a duck, then it just may be a duck.
Usually ascribed to Reuther during the McCarthyite witch-hunts of the 1950s. He came up with it as a test of whether someone was a Communist. Then it came to be applied elsewhere – but usually in politics: 'Mr Richard Darman, the new [US] Budget director, explained the other day what "no new taxes" means. He will apply the duck test. "If it looks like a duck, walks like a duck and quacks like a duck, it's a duck"' – *The Guardian* (25 January 1989). It has also been attributed to Richard, Cardinal Cushing, who, commenting on the propriety of calling Fidel Castro a Communist, said: 'When I see a bird that walks like a duck and swims like a duck and quacks like duck, I call that bird a duck' – quoted in *The New York Times* (1 March 1964). Compare Mark Twain, *A Tramp Abroad*, Chap 3 (1880): 'It looks like a hole, it's located like a hole, – blamed if I don't believe it is a hole!'

Paul REVERE American patriot (1735–1818)

6 The British are coming! The British are coming!
Doubt has been cast on Revere's reputed cry to warn people of approaching British troops during the American War of Independence. On his night ride of 18 April 1775, from Boston to Lexington, it is more likely that he cried 'The

regulars are out', and, besides, there were many other night-riders involved. Hence, however, *The Russians Are Coming, The Russians Are Coming*, the title of a film (US 1966).

Cecil RHODES British-born South African colonialist (1853–1902)

1 Remember that you are an Englishman, and have consequently won first prize in the lottery of life.

The source for this statement (much quoted in this form by Sir Peter Ustinov – in *Dear Me*, 1977, for example) is a book called *Jottings from an Active Life* (1928) by Colonel Sir Alexander Weston Jarvis. Jarvis wrote of Rhodes: 'He was never tired of impressing upon one that the fact of being an Englishman was the greatest prize in the lottery of life, and that it was the thought which always sustained him when he was troubled.'

Hence, Tom Stoppard's attribution of the words to Kipling (quoted in 1989) is probably incorrect. Compare this from Edward Gibbon, *Memoirs of My Life and Writings* (1796): 'When I contemplate the common lot of mortality, I must acknowledge that I have drawn a high prize in the lottery of life ... the double fortune of my birth in a free and enlightened country, in an honourable and wealthy family, is the lucky chance of an unit against millions.'

2 So much to do, so little done, goodbye, God bless you.

From 'Dr Robinson's sermon at Westminster' (presumably at a memorial service) comes this report of Rhodes's dying words. Also reported in Lewis Mitchell, *Life of Rhodes* (1910). The gist of what Rhodes said before he breathed his last on 26 March 1902 was indeed 'So much to do, so little done', though this is sometimes quoted with the phrases reversed. It was a theme that had obviously preoccupied him towards the end of his life. He said to Lord Rosebery: 'Everything in the world is too short. Life and fame and achievement, everything is too short.'

Tennyson had already anticipated him. *In Memoriam* (1850) has these lines in section lxxiii:

So many worlds, so much to do,
So little done, such things to be.

The actual last words of Rhodes were much more prosaic: 'Turn me over, Jack.'

Jean RHYS British novelist (1894–1979)

3 *Wide Sargasso Sea.*

Title of novel (1966). This, in modern parlance, is a 'prequel' to Charlotte Brontë's *Jane Eyre*. It recounts the previous history of Mr Rochester's mad wife before she was incarcerated in Thornfield Hall. She is described as being Antoinette Cosway, a Creole heiress from the West Indies. The Sargasso Sea, in the North Atlantic, is made up of masses of floating seaweed, creating sluggish waters.

Lord RIBBLESDALE English peer (1854–1925)

4 It [is] gentlemanly to get one's quotations very slightly wrong. In that way one unprigs oneself and allows the company to correct one.

Quoted in Lady Diana Cooper, *The Light of Common Day* (1959). On the art of gentle misquotation. Lord Ribblesdale is the subject of a notable portrait by John Singer Sargent in the National Gallery, London.

Grantland RICE American sports journalist and poet (1880–1954)

5 For when the One Great Scorer comes to mark against your name,
He writes – not that you won or lost – but how you played the Game.

'Alumnus Football', *Only the Brave and Other Poems* (1941). The 14-verse poem is little better than doggerel, and concerned with 'Life's big game' upon the 'Field of Fame'. The last two lines, all that is ever quoted, are in the voice of 'the wise old coach, Experience': 'Keep coming back, and though the world may romp across your spine, / Let every game's end find you still upon the battling line; / For when the One Great Scorer ...'

A number of odd aspects to this couplet have been pointed out. Firstly, in quotation dictionaries the initial word is sometimes given as 'But' or 'And'. Secondly, there are versions with '*write* against your name' and 'He *marks* – not that you ...' Thirdly, on the gravestone at Eyam, Derbyshire, of Harry Bagshaw, the Derbyshire and MCC cricketer who died in January 1927, the verse is inscribed (under the heading 'WELL PLAYED') with 'to *write* against your name' and 'He *writes* – not that you ...' Fourthly, in *The Manor School*, a boys' school story by one H. (Helen) Elrington (first published in 1927), the lines are given as the book's epigraph in a 'But', 'to write', 'He writes' and '*But that* you played the game' version. In addition, the name 'H. Elrington' is placed after the words, as though she were claiming authorship. Is her claim to have penned the lines fraudulent? What might have happened is that Grantland Rice's poem was first published in the New York *Tribune* – this is a fact, though there is no date for it. Rice was certainly active in writing for its sports pages in the early 1920s. His prose characterization of some footballers as 'The Four Horsemen' and a poem describing the footballer 'Red' Grange as

'The Galloping Ghost' both appeared in the *Trib* over the same weekend in October 1924.

The 'One Great Scorer' lines became known in Britain, but without acknowledgement to their author, who was not known here – hence, their unattributed appearance on the Bagshaw grave and under the novelist's own name in H. Elrington's book, both as it happens in 1927.

In Alan Bennett's parody of an Anglican sermon in the revue *Beyond the Fringe* (1961), the lines are (deliberately?) misascribed to that 'Grand old Victorian poet, W.E. Henley' (who wrote, rather, 'It matters not how strait the gate ... I am the master of my fate', see 61:7). See also DE COUBERTIN 164:4.

(Sir) Stephen RICE Irish lawyer and politician (1637–1715)

1 I will drive a coach and six horses through the Act of Settlement.

Rice, a Roman Catholic Chief Baron of the Irish Exchequer, used the courts in Dublin to get his own back on an Act of Settlement (1662), and was quoted as having said this by W. King, *The State of the Protestants of Ireland* (1672). It is presumably the origin of the expression 'to drive a coach and horses through something', meaning 'to overturn something wantonly, and to render it useless'. It is clear that by the late 17th century the phrase was based on a common metaphor (usually mentioning *six* horses) for something large: in Sir John Vanbrugh's play *The Relapse*, Act 2 (1696), there is: '*Seringe* (*viewing his wound*) Oons, what a gash is here! Why, sir, a man may drive a coach and six horses into your body.' The modern equivalent probably involves a bus or a tank. In 1843 Charles Dickens wrote in *A Christmas Carol*: 'You may talk vaguely about driving a coach-and-six up a good old flight of stairs, or through a bad young Act of Parliament ... ' (which might seem to allude to the Rice example).

(Sir) Tim RICE English lyricist (1944–)

2 Don't Cry for Me, Argentina.

Title of song, *Evita* (1976). There is an unexplained conjunction between this line and the inscription (in Spanish) that appears on Eva Perón's bronze tomb in Recoleta cemetery, Buenos Aires. It begins with words to the effect, 'Do not cry for me when I am far away.' Besides, Eva's body was not returned to Argentina until 1976, and the inscription (of which there is more than one) in Recoleta cemetery bears a date 1982. Could it have been inspired by the song rather than the other way round? Hence, whatever the case, *Don't Cry for Me, Sergeant Major*, title of a book (1983) by Robert McGowan and Jeremy Hands, giving an 'other ranks' view

on the Falklands conflict between Britain and Argentina.

The tomb also bears the words: '*Volvere y sere millones!* [I will come again, and I will be millions!]' According to Nicholas Fraser, co-author of *Eva Perón* (1980), 'She never said this last, but that doesn't keep it from being true', though some sources give it as from a speech she made towards the end of her life. It was also the title of a rival musical written by Argentinian nationalists. Eva died in 1952. That same year, Howard Fast published his novel *Spartacus*, in which the following appears (in Chap. 1, at the end of Pt 2), referring to a slave crucified as part of the vengeance of Rome: 'Do you know what was the last thing he said?' 'What?' whispered Claudia. '*I will return and I will be millions.* [Fast's italics] Just that. Fanciful, isn't it?'

The most likely origin lies in an insurrection of maltreated natives in the Peru/Bolivia area in 1780–2. On 15 November 1781, Tupac Amaru II, leader of the 1781 anti-colonial peasant uprising in the region of La Paz, today part of Bolivia, was going to be tortured to death by royalist counter-insurgents. He told his enemies: '*A mi solo me mataréis, pero mañana volveré y seré millones* [Me alone you will kill, but tomorrow I will return, and I will be millions].' Apparently this has become part of South American revolutionary legend, though there is no documentary evidence for it.

3 Oh what a circus, oh what a show!

Song, 'Oh What a Circus' in the same musical. Sung by the Che Guevara figure and referring to the obsequies surrounding the death of Evita. Hence, *Oh, What a Circus*, title of Rice's memoirs (1999).

Mandy RICE-DAVIES English 'model and show girl' (1944–)

4 Well, he would, wouldn't he?

An innocuous enough phrase (and not original to the speaker), but one still used allusively because of the way it was spoken by Rice-Davies during the Profumo affair in 1963 (Secretary of State for War John Profumo carried on with Rice-Davies's friend Christine Keeler, who was allegedly sharing her favours with the Soviet military attaché). *ODQ* (1992) describes Rice-Davies as a 'courtesan', which is rather quaint. She was called as a witness when Stephen Ward was charged under the Sexual Offences Act. During the preliminary Magistrates Court hearing on 28 June 1963, she was questioned about the men she had had sex with. When told by Ward's defence counsel that Lord Astor – one of the names on the list – had categorically denied any involvement with her, she replied, chirpily: 'Well, he would, wouldn't he?'

The court burst into laughter, and the expression passed into the language. It is still resorted to because – as a good catchphrase ought to be – it is bright, useful in various circumstances and tinged with innuendo. Hence such uses as: 'Oscar Wilde said the Alps were objects of appallingly bad taste. He would, wouldn't he?' wrote Russell Harty in *Mr Harty's Grand Tour* (1988).

ODQ was the first to elevate Mandy's *bon mot* to its pages in the 1979 edition but, in those days, did not attempt descriptions of the quotees. I led the way in *A Dictionary of 20th Century Quotations* (1987) with the ludicrously neutral 'British woman', while, in the same year, the *Bloomsbury Dictionary of Quotations* boldly (and perhaps inaccurately) went for 'British call-girl'. *ODQ* quaintly plumped for 'English courtesan' in 1992. I switched to 'British "model and show girl"' for *Brewer's Quotations* (1994). *Collins Dictionary of Quotations* (1995) opted for 'Welsh model, nightclub performer and owner'. Somehow I don't think any of us has got it right yet. The question is, I suppose, did she or did she not take money for it in the way normally associated with a prostitute? Ah well, at least such protracted musings keep me off the streets. NB: in the book *Mandy* (1980), having just described the circumstances of her famous utterance, Mandy writes of herself and Christine Keeler: 'Whatever we were, we weren't prostitutes or whores, but this was the company we were now linked with.'

RICHARD, Keith See (Sir) Mick JAGGER and Keith RICHARD.

Cardinal RICHELIEU French prelate and politician (1585–1642)

1 If you give me six lines written by the hand of the most honest of men, I will find something in them which will hang him.

Usually ascribed to Richelieu, but it may have been said, rather, by one of his agents (according to an 1867 French source).

See also BULWER-LYTTON 107:4.

Jacob RIIS Danish-born American journalist (1849–1914)

2 *How the Other Half Lives.*

Title of book (1890) describing the conditions in which poor people lived in New York City. This might appear to have given us the expression meaning 'how people live who belong to different social groups (but especially the rich)'. Indeed, the expression seems basically to have referred to the poor, but has since been used about any 'other half'. Riis alluded to the basic saying in these words: 'Long ago it was

said that "one half of the world does not know how the other half lives".' *OED2* finds this proverb in English (by 1607), and in French, in *Pantagruel* by Rabelais (1532). Alan Ayckbourn entitled a play *How the Other Half Loves* (1970).

(Sir) Boyle ROCHE Irish politician (1743–1807)

3 Mr Speaker, I smell a rat; I see him forming in the air and darkening the sky; but I'll nip him in the bud.

Attributed remark in the Irish Parliament. In F. Wills, *The Irish Nation* (1871–5), it is conceded that the Chamberlain to the Vice-Regal Court (in Dublin), as Roche later became, had a 'graceful address and ready wit', but, additionally, 'it was usual for members of the cabinet to write speeches for him, which he committed to memory, and, while mastering the substance, generally contrived to travesty the language and ornament with peculiar graces of his own'. Could this be the reason for Roche's peculiar sayings?

DNB adds that 'he gained his lasting reputation as an inveterate perpetrator of "bulls" [i.e., ludicrous, self-contradictory propositions, often associated with the Irish]'.

4 How could the sergeant-at-arms stop him in the rear, while he was catching him at the front? Could he like a bird be in two places at once?

Supposedly said in the Irish Parliament. This version is from *A Book of Irish Quotations* (1984). *Brewer* suggests that he was quoting from 'Jevon's play *The Devil of a Wife*' (untraced) and that what he said was, 'Mr Speaker, it is impossible I could have been in two places at once, unless I were a bird' – adding that the phrase was probably of even earlier origin.

5 Why should we put ourselves out of our way to do anything for posterity; for what has posterity done for us? [*Laughter.*] I apprehend you gentlemen have entirely mistaken my words, I assure the house that by posterity I do not mean my ancestors but those who came immediately after them.

Said in the Irish Parliament? Quoted in *A Book of Irish Quotations* (1984). *Benham* (1948), claiming that it is 'erroneously attributed' to Roche, notes that the words occur in John Trumbull's poetic work *McFingal* (1775):

As though there were a tie
And obligation to posterity.
We get them, bear them breed and nurse:
What has posterity done for us.
That we, lest they their rights should lose,
Should trust our necks to grip of noose.

Benham also notes that Mrs Elizabeth Montagu had earlier

written in a letter (1 January 1742): 'The man was laughed at as a blunderer who said in a public business "We do much for posterity; I would fain see them do something for us."' Stevenson's *Book of Quotations* (1974) has Thomas Gray writing in a letter to Dr Warton (8 March 1758): 'As to posterity, I may ask (with somebody whom I have forgot) what has it ever done to oblige me?' These references obviously allude to the true originator, ADDISON 3:9.

Abraham Lincoln said in a speech (22 February 1842): 'Why should we put ourselves out of the way to do anything for posterity? What has posterity done for us?' 'Why should I write for posterity – what has posterity ever done for me?' was attributed to Oscar Wilde in *The Independent* (9 November 1996). Mark English finds Hesketh Pearson in *The Life of Oscar Wilde* (1946) quoting one of Oscar's early theatrical reviews: 'What our descendants will think of [a certain farce] is an open question. However, posterity has as yet done nothing for us!' Compare 'Posterity is Right Around the Corner' (1976) by E.Y. Harburg (1898–1981):

Why should I write for posterity?
What, if I may be free
To ask a ridiculous question,
Has posterity done for me?

John Wilmot, 2nd Earl of ROCHESTER English poet (1647–80)

1 Here lies a great and mighty king
Whose promise none relies on;
He never said a foolish thing,
Nor ever did a wise one.

A familiar jesting epitaph on Charles II, quoted in *Thomas Traherne: Remarks and Collections* (1885–1921). Other versions include, 'Here lies our sovereign Lord the King ...' and 'Here lies our mutton-eating king' (where 'mutton' = prostitute). Charles II's reply is said to have been: 'This is very true; for my words are my own, and my actions are my ministers' (which is also in *Traherne* ...).

2 If I by miracle can be
This live-long minute true to thee,
'Tis all that Heav'n allows.

'Love and Life' (1680). Hence, the title of the film *All That Heaven Allows* (US 1955; screenwriter Peggy Fenwick), which has widow Jane Wyman falling for her gardener Rock Hudson to the consternation of her class-conscious friends. Despite Wyman's quoting a hefty chunk from Thoreau's *Walden*, no hint is given as to where the title of the film comes from. Rochester's poem was included in Quiller-Couch's *Oxford Book of English Verse* (1900) – that great repository of quotations later to be used as film titles.

Will ROGERS American humorist (1879–1935)

3 I never met a man I didn't like.

The folksy American 'cowboy comedian' of the 1920s and 30s suggested this epitaph for himself (by 1926). It is a little more believable in context: 'When I die, my epitaph or whatever you call those signs on gravestones is going to read: "I joked about every prominent man of my time, but I never met one I dident [*sic*] like." I am so proud of that I can hardly wait to die so it can be carved. And when you come to my grave you will find me sitting there, proudly reading it.'

According to Paula McSpadden Love, *The Will Rogers Book* (1972), the utterance was first printed in the *Boston Globe* (16 June 1930). However, the *Saturday Evening Post* (6 November 1926) had: 'I bet you if I had met him [Trotsky] and had a chat with him, I would have found him a very interesting and human fellow, for I never yet met a man that I didn't like.'

ROHE, Mies van der See MIES VAN DER ROHE.

Madame ROLAND French revolutionary (1756–93)

4 The more I see of men, the more I like dogs.

Attributed remark in *ODQ* (1979). However, later, Alphonse de Lamartine, French poet and politician (1790–1869), is reported to have said: 'The more I see of the representatives of the people, the more I admire my dogs'; and A. Toussenel wrote in *L'Esprit des bêtes* (1847): 'The more one gets to know of men, the more one values dogs [*Plus on apprend à connaître l'homme, plus on apprend à estimer le chien*].'

5 O Liberty! how many crimes are committed in thy name!

Mme Roland was about to be executed by the guillotine during the French Revolution (on 8 November 1793). According to Robert Chambers, *Book of Days* (1864), she addressed her remark to a gigantic statue of Liberty erected near it.

Mickey ROONEY American film actor (1920–)

6 Let's put on a show!

This is often taken to be a staple line from the films that the young Rooney made with Judy Garland from 1939 onwards. The expression apparently had several forms – 'Hey! I've got it! Why don't we put on a show?' / 'Hey kids! We can put on the show in the backyard!' / 'Let's do the show right here in the barn!' – though it is difficult to give a precise citation.

In *Babes in Arms* (1939) Rooney and Garland play the teenage children of retired vaudeville players who decide to put on a big show of their own. Alas, they do not actually say any of the above lines, though they do express their determination to 'put on a show'. In *Strike Up the Band* (1940), Rooney has the line: 'Say, that's not a bad idea. We could put on our own show!' – though he does not say it to Garland. In whatever form, the line has become a film and show-biz cliché, now used only with amused affection.

1 **Had I been brighter, had the gods been kinder, had the dice been hotter, this could have been a one-sentence story: Once upon a time Mickey Rooney lived happily ever after.**

I.E. An Autobiography, Chap. 1 (1965). The blurb to a British edition (possibly using material from an earlier draft) inserts the words 'had the ladies been gentler, had the Scotch been weaker' after 'Had I been brighter'.

Franklin D. ROOSEVELT American Democratic 32nd President (1882–1945)

2 **He is the Happy Warrior of the political battlefield.**

Alfred E. Smith, the Democrat politician, had this nickname bestowed on him by Roosevelt in 1924. Smith ran against Herbert Hoover for the presidency in 1928 but did not win. He subsequently fell out with Roosevelt when the latter became president. The phrase comes from WORDSWORTH 506:7.

3 **I pledge you, I pledge myself to a New Deal for the American people.**

So said Roosevelt to the 1932 Democratic Convention that had just nominated him. The 'New Deal' slogan became the keynote to the election campaign, but it was not new to politics. In Britain, David Lloyd George had talked of a 'New deal for everyone' in 1919. Woodrow Wilson had had a 'New Freedom' slogan, and Teddy Roosevelt had talked of a 'Square Deal'. Abraham Lincoln had used 'New deal' on occasions. The FDR use was engineered by either Samuel Rosenman or Raymond Moley. 'I had not the slightest idea that it would take hold the way it did,' Rosenman said later, 'nor did the Governor [Roosevelt] when he read and revised what I had written ... It was simply one of those phrases that catch public fancy and survive.' On the other hand, Moley claimed: 'The expression "new deal" was in the draft I left at Albany with Roosevelt ... I was not aware that this would be the slogan for the campaign. It was a phrase that would have occurred to almost anyone.'

4 **I ask you to judge me by the enemies I have made.**

Quoted in *The Observer* (16 October 1932). Compare CLEVELAND 147:1.

5 **Let me assert my firm belief that the only thing we have to fear is fear itself.**

Roosevelt took the presidential oath of office on 4 March 1933 and then delivered his first inaugural address. The classic sentence did not appear in Roosevelt's first draft, but appears to have been inserted by him the day before the speech was delivered. As for inspiration: a copy of Thoreau's writings was with him at this time containing the line 'Nothing is so much to be feared as fear.' Raymond Moley asserted later, however, that it was Louis Howe who contributed the 'fear' phrase, having picked it up from a newspaper advertisement for a department store.

In fact, any number of precedents could be cited – the Duke of Wellington ('The only thing I am afraid of is fear'), Montaigne ('The thing of which I have most fear is fear'), Bacon ('Nothing is terrible except fear itself'), the Book of Proverbs 3:25 ('Be not afraid of sudden fear') – but in the end what matters is that Roosevelt had the wit to utter it on this occasion.

6 **There is a mysterious cycle in human events. To some generations much is given. Of other generations much is expected. This generation of Americans has a rendezvous with destiny.**

Speech, Democratic Convention (1936). Later, in a TV address on behalf of Senator Barry Goldwater (27 October 1964), Ronald Reagan told viewers: 'You and I have a rendezvous with destiny. We will preserve for our children this, the last best hope of man on earth.'

7 **And while I am talking to you mothers and fathers, I give you one more assurance. I have said this before, but I shall say it again and again and again: Your boys are not going to be sent into any foreign wars.**

Campaign speech delivered in Boston, Massachusetts (30 October 1940). In a sense, Roosevelt kept his promise. American boys were never sent into any foreign wars. The US went to war in December 1941 after the Japanese attack on Pearl Harbor, and only later were American forces sent to Europe and elsewhere. Compare JOHNSON 257:3.

8 **Yesterday, December 7th 1941, a date which will live in infamy, the United States of America was suddenly and deliberately attacked by naval and air forces of the Empire of Japan.**

Thus Roosevelt began his address to Congress, the day after the Japanese attack on Pearl Harbor. In the draft it had said, 'a date which will live in world history' and 'simultaneously'. With such strokes did he make his speech seeking a declaration of war against Japan the more memorable. However,

Palmer & Palmer, *Quotations in History* (1976), has 'date *that shall* live in infamy', while Cole & Lass, *The Dictionary of 20th-Century Allusions* (1991), has '*day that* will live in infamy'.

Theodore ROOSEVELT American Republican
26th President (1858–1919)

1 There is a homely adage – 'Speak softly and carry a big stick – you will go far.'

In 2 September 1901, just a few days before the assassination of President McKinley, Roosevelt said this at Minnesota State Fair. He went on, 'If the American nation will speak softly and yet build and keep at a pitch of the highest training a thoroughly efficient navy, the Monroe Doctrine [which sought to exclude European intervention in the Americas] will go far.' Note that he did not claim the 'adage' to be original.

2 Good ... to the last drop.

Visiting Joel Cheek, perfector of the Maxwell House coffee blend, in 1907, the president drank a cup and passed this comment. The slogan has been in use ever since, despite those who have inquired, 'What's wrong with the last drop then?' Professors of English have considered the problem and ruled that 'to' can be inclusive and need not mean 'up to but not including'.

3 I am strong as a bull moose.

After two terms as president, Roosevelt withdrew from Republican politics and then, in 1912, unsuccessfully tried to make a come-back as a Progressive ('Bull Moose') candidate. The popular name stemmed from a remark Roosevelt had made when he was standing as vice-president in 1900. Writing to Mark Hanna he said, 'I am strong as a bull moose and you can use me to the limit.'

4 Foolish fanatics ... the men who form the lunatic fringe in all reform movements.

Autobiography (1913). Referring to a group of extremists, usually in politics. Roosevelt popularized, if he did not coin, the term.

See also BUNYAN 108:1.

Billy ROSE American impresario and songwriter
(1899–1966)

5 Does the Spearmint Lose Its Flavour on the Bedpost Overnight?

The 1924 song with this title is usually credited to Marty Bloom and Ernest Breuer 'with assistance from' Rose. 'Chewing gum' was substituted for 'Spearmint' when the song was revived in Britain in 1959, lest it seem to be advertising a particular brand.

6 The Night is Young (and You're So Beautiful).

Title of a song (1936), written with Irving Kahal. The previous year 'The Night Is Young (And So Are We)' had been written by Oscar Hammerstein II and Sigmund Romberg and included in the film *The Night is Young*. Hence the popularity of the expression, 'The night is young!' – the sort of thing one says when attempting to justify another drink. From Frank Brady, *Citizen Welles* (1989): 'At three in the morning, when a few people decided to leave, Orson, stepping into the role of clichéd host from a Grade B movie, would not hear of it: "You're not leaving already, my friends. The night is still young. Play, Gypsies! Play, play, play!"'

The expression was known before all this, however. In Sir Walter Besant's *Dorothy Forster*, Chap. 11 (1884), there is: 'They ... left the table when the night was yet young, and the bottle just beginning'; Max Beerbohm's *Seven Men* (1919) has: 'He looked at the clock. I pointed out that the night was young.'

5th Earl of ROSEBERY British Liberal Prime Minister
(1847–1929)

7 I have three ambitions in life: to win the Derby, marry an heiress, and become Prime Minister.

A legend grew up that Rosebery had said this. Robert Rhodes James comments in *Rosebery* (1963) that 'although it is quite possible that he did once make such an observation, it is extremely unlikely that it was meant seriously'. Rhodes James also quotes Algernon Cecil in *Queen Victoria and Her Prime Ministers* (1953) as saying: 'At London dinner-parties half a century ago it was rare for Rosebery to be mentioned without some allusion being made to his three declared ambitions ... Apocryphal or not, it gives if not Rosebery's measure as a man, yet certainly the measure of him given by the men of his time.'

Nevertheless, Rosebery achieved his attributed ambitions: he did win the Derby (three times, twice while Prime Minister), he married Hannah Rothschild, an heiress, and – managing to overcome his aristocratic disdain for accepting almost anything that was offered him – he succeeded Gladstone as Prime Minister in 1894. But the Liberal Party was falling apart, Rosebery himself was prey to insomnia and inaction, and he was out of office after a year. He was 48 and, despite his undoubted personal qualities, never held high office again.

8 To your tents, O Israel!

A famous – and possibly apocryphal – story concerns Rosebery saying this one evening when he felt his Rothschild in-laws had kept him up long enough. The phrase was later used by Bernard Shaw as the title of a diatribe in *The Fortnightly Review* (November 1893), expressing Fabian disillusion with Gladstone's Liberal Party on such radical matters as Irish Home Rule. Michael Holroyd in *Bernard Shaw* (Vol. 1) calls it 'the Biblical call to revolt'. It is a quotation from 1 Kings 12:16.

1 **I must plough my furrow alone.**

Rosebery said this in a speech at the City Liberal Club (19 July 1901) on breaking away from his Liberal Party colleagues. A famous declaration of independence, but it seems likely that the expression had been used by others before him. He added: 'Before I get to the end of that furrow it is possible that I may find myself not alone ... If it be so, I shall remain very contented in the society of my books and my home.' So it was to be. *Benham* (1948) has this (wrongly) as: 'I must plough my lonely furrow alone.'

Alan S.C. ROSS British academic (1907–80)

2 **U and Non-U. An Essay in Sociological Linguistics.**

Title of essay in *Noblesse Oblige*, ed. Nancy Mitford (1956). Ross had first used 'U' to denote 'upper-class' verbal usage and 'Non-U' to denote incorrect, non-upper-class usage, in a 1954 article.

Harold ROSS American editor (1892–1951)

3 **The New Yorker will not be edited for the little old lady from Dubuque.**

When Ross founded the magazine in 1925, he made this declaration. Dubuque, Iowa, thus became involved in another of those yardstick phrases on account of its being representative of Middle America – like 'It'll play in Peoria' (see EHRLICHMAN 184:4). A man called 'Boots' Mulgrew who lived there used to contribute squibs to the Chicago *Tribune* signed 'Old Lady in Dubuque'. Ross, presumably, had heard of this line and consciously or otherwise developed it to describe the sort of person he was not creating the magazine for. On the other hand, Malcolm Muggeridge once quoted a writer on the *Daily Express* who explained the huge readership of Beaverbrook newspapers in the UK by saying, 'I write for one little old reader.'

Compare: 'I think it well to remember that, when writing for the newspapers, we are writing for an elderly lady in Hastings who has two cats of which she is passionately fond. Unless our stuff can compete for her interest with those cats, it is no good' – Willmott Lewis (1877–1950), quoted in Claud Cockburn, *In Time of Trouble* (1957).

4 **Who he?**

James Thurber in *The Years with Ross* (1959) describes how Ross would customarily add this query to manuscripts (though not for publication) on finding a name he did not know in an article (sometimes betraying his ignorance). He said the only two names everyone knew were Houdini and Sherlock Holmes. Dale Kramer in *Ross and The New Yorker* (1952) had earlier noted this trait. The phrase echoes the elderly Duke of Wellington's peremptory 'Who? Who?' on hearing the names of ministers in Lord Derby's new administration (1852).

Re-popularized by *Private Eye* in the 1980s, this editorial interjection after a little-known person's name showed some signs of catching on: 'This month, for instance, has been the time for remembering the 110th anniversary of the birth of Grigori Petrovsky. Who he?' – *New Statesman*, 26 February 1988. A book with the title *Who He? Goodman's Dictionary of the Unknown Famous* was published in 1984, and the actress Billie Whitelaw entitled her memoirs *Billie Whitelaw ... Who He?* (1995) – this, however, as is made clear by an epigraph, is also an allusion to Samuel Beckett's *Play* (1963), in which occurs the line 'Who he, I said filing away, and what it?'

Christina ROSSETTI English poet (1830–95)

5 **In the bleak mid-winter**
Frosty wind made moan,
Earth stood hard as iron,
Water like a stone.

'Mid-Winter' (1875). Known particularly as a Christmas carol sung to the tune 'Cranham' by Gustav Holst. Hence, *In the Bleak Midwinter*, title of film (UK 1996), written and directed by Kenneth Branagh, about a theatrical group putting on a production of *Hamlet* in December.

Gioachino ROSSINI Italian composer (1792–1868)

6 **Wagner has beautiful moments but awful quarters of an hour.**

Letter (April 1867), quoted in E. Naumann, *Italienische Tondichter* (1883). In his *Reminiscences, Inscriptions & Anecdotes* (1913), the musician Francesco Berger attributed this to the pianist Hans von Bülow: 'Someone observed, "Well, you must admit that he has some heavenly moments." "I don't dispute the *heavenly moments*," said he, "but he has some *devilish ugly half-hours*."' Rossini is also supposed to have said: 'One can't judge Wagner's opera *Lohengrin* after a first hearing, and I certainly don't intend hearing it a second time' – quoted in *The Frank Muir Book* (1976).

Johnny ROTTEN (John Lydon) English pop singer
(1957–)

1 Love is two minutes and fifty seconds of squelching noises ... It shows your mind isn't clicking
right.

Of recent *bons mots*, one of the most quoted – but variously
so – is the opinion of Johnny Rotten, who was at one time
with the notorious punk group, The Sex Pistols. The above
original quotation derives from an article by Charles M.
Young in *Rolling Stone* (20 October 1977). Variously quoted
thereafter. My *Graffiti 3* had a photograph taken in
London (1980) of a wall bearing the legend: 'Love is three
minutes of squelching noises. (Mr J. Rotten).' Auberon
Waugh in *Private Eye* (18 November 1983) settled for 'two
and a half minutes of squelching', but provided the interesting gloss that, in an interview with Christena Appleyard
in the *Mirror*, Rotten had wished to amend his aphorism:
'It is more like five minutes now, he says, because he has
mastered a new technique.' McConville and Shearlaw in
The Slanguage of Sex (1984) claim that as a result of Rotten's
statement, 'squelching' became an expression for sexual
intercourse.

Jean-Jacques ROUSSEAU French philosopher (1712–78)

2 *L'homme est né libre, et partout il est dans les fers*
[Man was born free, and everywhere he is in
chains].

Du Contrat Social, Chap. 1 (1762).

(Dr) Martin ROUTH English scholar (1755–1854)

3 Always verify your references.

In 1949 Winston Churchill gave an inaccurate account to
the House of Commons of when he had first heard the
words 'unconditional surrender' from President Roosevelt.
Subsequently, in his *The Second World War*, Vol. 4 (1951),
Churchill wrote: 'It was only when I got home and searched
my archives that I found the facts as they have been set out
here. I am reminded of the professor who in his declining
hours was asked by his devoted pupils for his final counsel. He replied, "Verify your quotations."'

Well, not exactly a 'professor', and not exactly his dying
words, and not 'quotations' either. Martin Routh was President of Magdalen College, Oxford, for 63 years. Of the
many stories told about Routh, Churchill was groping
towards the one where he was asked what precept could
serve as a rule of life to an aspiring young man. Said Routh:
'You will find it a very good practice *always to verify your
references, Sir!*'

This story was first recorded in this form in July 1878, as

Churchill and his amanuenses might themselves have verified. In 1847 Routh gave the advice to John Burgon, later a
noted Dean of Chichester, who ascribed it in an article in
the *Quarterly Review* (and subsequently in his *Lives of Twelve
Good Men*, 1888 edn). Perhaps Churchill was recalling
instead the Earl of Rosebery's version, given in a speech on
23 November 1897: 'Another confirmation of the advice
given by one aged sage to somebody who sought his guidance in life, namely, "Always wind up your watch and verify
your quotations."'

Helen ROWLAND American columnist and writer
(1875–1950)

4 Somehow a bachelor never quite gets over the idea
that he is a thing of beauty and a boy forever.

A Guide to Men (1922). Compare the comment of Flann
O'Brien (1911–66) on the supposed youthfulness of the
Irish police force: 'A thing of duty is a boy forever.' Both
alluding to KEATS 256:6.

Richard ROWLAND American film executive
(?1881–1947)

5 The lunatics have taken over the asylum.

Quoted in Terry Ramsaye, *A Million and One Nights* (1926).
Rowland is said to have made this remark when the United
Artists film company was established in 1919 by Charles
Chaplin, Mary Pickford, Douglas Fairbanks and D.W. Griffith to exploit their own talent. Rowland was one of their
erstwhile employers at Metro. See also LLOYD GEORGE
291:6; STALLINGS 441:2.

(Sir) Henry ROYCE English motor engineer (1863–1933)

6 Small things make perfection, but perfection is
not a small thing.

Attributed remark (1924). Compare what Robert Shaunon
wrote in *The Canadian Magazine* (October 1898) about the
proper quoting of statements. 'Perhaps the reader may ask,
of what consequence is it whether the author's exact language is preserved or not, provided we have his thought?
The answer is, that inaccurate quotation is a sin against
truth. It may appear in any particular instance to be a trifle,
but perfection consists in small things, and perfection is
no trifle.' Michelangelo is also supposed to have said: 'Trifles
make perfection and perfection is no trifle.'

Jerry RUBIN American Yippie leader (1938–94)

1 Don't trust anyone over thirty.

Attributed by Stuart Berg Flexner, *Listening To America* (1982). Actually, this appears to have been first uttered by Jack Weinberg (1940–) at Berkeley in 1964/5 during a free-speech demonstration. *Bartlett* (1992) finds Weinberg saying in an interview on the free-speech movement, 'We have a saying in the movement that we don't trust anybody over thirty.' In 1970 Weinberg told *The Washington Post* (23 March) that he did not actually believe the statement, but had said it in response to a question about adults manipulating the organization. In 1969 Spiro Agnew included 'Thou shalt not trust anybody over thirty' as one of his 'Ten Commandments of Protest'. The Yippie movement, founded in 1968 by Rubin and Abbie Hoffman, was made up of politically active hippies and derived its name from the initials of the Youth International Party, a would-be anarchic protest organization.

Donald RUMSFELD American Republican politician (1932–)

2 Stuff happens ... and it's untidy, and freedom's untidy, and free people are free to make mistakes and commit crimes and do bad things.

The Secretary of Defense's response to the looting of Baghdad, at a press conference (11 April 2003). Hence, the title of David Hare's play *Stuff Happens* (2004), portraying 'the extraordinary process leading up to the invasion of Iraq'. Obviously, this phrase is a polite version of 'Shit happens', which has been current since the 1980s, meaning 'these things happen' – a statement of resignation in the face of life's vicissitudes. An early citation for this appears in the published diary of the novelist Anthony Powell (of all people). His entry for 26 October 1988 describes a visit by some friends of his to the Five Hundred Acre Fair in Oklahoma: '... including a sale of hats bearing slogans, one of these saying simply: SHIT HAPPENS (how profoundly true)'.

Robert RUNCIE (later Lord Runcie) English Archbishop of Canterbury (1921–2000)

3 My advice was delicately poised between the cliché and the indiscretion.

On discussions with the Prince and Princess of Wales prior to marrying them. Quoted in *The Times* (14 July 1981). Compare MACMILLAN 304:2.

4 I have done my best to die before this book is published.

Letter to Humphrey Carpenter quoted in the biographer's

Robert Runcie, The Reluctant Archbishop (1996). Runcie had cooperated with Carpenter (indeed, had invited him to write the biography), believing that the book would not be published until after his death.

Damon RUNYON American writer (1884–1946)

5 He is without strict doubt a Hoorah Henry, and he is generally figured as nothing but a lob as far as doing anything useful in this world is concerned.

'Tight Shoes', in *Take It Easy* (1938). Jim Godbolt adapted this to 'Hooray Henry' in 1951 to describe a sub-species of British upper-class twit.

6 The race is not always to the swift nor the battle to the strong, but that's the way to bet.

Quoted in *The Treasury of Humorous Quotations*, eds Esar & Bentley (1951). Alluding to BIBLE 76:3.

Salman RUSHDIE Indian-born novelist (1947–)

7 Naughty but nice.

Before achieving fame and misfortune as a novelist, Rushdie worked as a freelance advertising copywriter in London. In 1988, appearing on BBC Radio's *Desert Island Discs*, he claimed to have originated the use of the phrase 'Naughty but nice' to promote fresh cream in cakes for the National Dairy Council (from 1977 onwards). Advertisements being collaborative efforts, agencies – in this case Ogilvy & Mather – are reluctant to concede creative triumphs to particular individuals. Whatever his contribution on this one, however, Rushdie certainly did not coin the phrase 'Naughty but nice': it was the title of a 1939 US film about a professor of classical music who accidentally wrote a popular song. Curiously, *ODMQ* (1991) gives the coinage of the phrase to Jerry Wald and Richard Macaulay, writers of the film, on this basis. But *Partridge/Slang* glosses it as 'a reference to copulation since *c.*1900 ex a song that Minnie Schult sang and popularized in the USA, 1890s'. Indeed. There have since been various songs with the title, notably one by Johnny Mercer and Harry Warren in *The Belle of New York* (film, 1952). Compare also the similarly alliterative 'It's Foolish But It's Fun' (Gus Kahn/Robert Stolz) sung by Deanna Durbin in *Spring Parade* (1940).

Dean RUSK American Democratic politician (1909–94)

8 We're eyeball to eyeball and the other fellow just blinked.

In the missile crisis of October 1962, the US took a tough line when the Soviet Union stationed missiles on Cuban soil. After a tense few days, the Soviets withdrew. Secretary of State Rusk was speaking to an ABC news correspondent, John Scali, on 24 October and said: 'Remember, when you report this, that, eyeball to eyeball, they blinked first.' Columnists Charles Bartlett and Stewart Alsop then helped to popularize this in the above form (though sometimes 'I think' is inserted before 'the other fellow').

'Eyeball to eyeball' is black American serviceman's idiom. *Safire* (1978) quotes a reply given by the all-black 24th Infantry Regiment to an inquiry from General MacArthur's HQ in Korea (November 1950) – 'Do you have contact with the enemy?' 'We is eyeball to eyeball.'

John RUSKIN English art critic (1819–1900)

1 All violent feelings ... produce ... a falseness in ... impressions of external things, which I would generally characterize as the 'Pathetic fallacy'.
Modern Painters, Vol. 3 (1856). Hence, the concept of the 'pathetic fallacy' – the attribution of human feelings to nature or, to put it another way, the convention, common in literature as well as art, whereby nature reflects the feelings of the protagonists. So, a thunderstorm may be represented as echoing some human drama played out beneath it.

2 I have seen, and heard, much of Cockney impudence before now; but never expected to hear a coxcomb ask two hundred guineas for flinging a pot of paint in the public's face.
On Whistler's painting *The Falling Rocket, or Nocturne in Black and Gold*, in a letter (18 June 1877) and included in *Fors Clavigera: Letters to the Workers and Labourers of Great Britain* (1871–84). Whistler (an American) brought an action for libel and was awarded a farthing in damages. He was bankrupted by his legal costs; Ruskin could not pay his own either and had to be helped by friends. See WHISTLER 491:5.

3 There is nothing in the world that some man cannot make a little worse and sell a little more cheaply. Those who buy on price alone are this man's lawful prey.
Quoted (for example) in John Julius Norwich, *A Christmas Cracker* (1985). Although this has been ascribed many times to Ruskin, it really cannot be found anywhere in his writings. I doubt if it is a view he would have disagreed with, but it would seem it has been wrongly attributed to him in the past and found its way into books of quotations. In 2004

I was told of a small leather-bound volume entitled *The Thoughts of John Ruskin* (undated), where something like the quotation is said to come from his 'The Painters' (whatever that might be). Now I look into the matter, little books of Ruskiniana were once quite the thing. *Precious Thoughts* was published in New York (1874) and *Thoughts of Beauty and Words of Wisdom from the writings of John Ruskin* (Massachusetts, 1887). It would be interesting to know if these contain the rogue quotation.

Bertrand RUSSELL (3rd Earl Russell) English mathematician and philosopher (1872–1970)

4 Better Red than dead.
A slogan used by some (mainly British) nuclear disarmers. *Time* Magazine (15 September 1961) gave 'I'd rather be Red than dead' as a slogan of Britain's Campaign for Nuclear Disarmament. Russell wrote in 1958: 'If no alternative remains except Communist domination or the extinction of the human race, the former alternative is the lesser of two evils.' The counter-cry 'Better dead than red' may also have had some currency. In the film *Love With a Proper Stranger* (US 1964) Steve McQueen proposed to Natalie Wood with a picket sign stating 'Better Wed Than Dead'.

(Sir) William Howard RUSSELL British journalist (1820–97)

5 The ground flies beneath their horses' feet; gathering speed at every stride, they dash on towards that thin red streak topped with a line of steel.
So Russell wrote in a report dated 25 October 1854 (published in *The Times* on 14 November) describing a Russian charge repulsed by the British 93rd Highlanders. This was the first stage of the Battle of Balaclava in the Crimean War (the Charge of the Light Brigade followed a few hours later). *ODQ* (1979, 1992) has 'tipped' here instead of 'topped'.

By the time he wrote his book *The British Expedition to the Crimea* (1877), Russell was putting: 'The Russians dashed on towards *that thin red line tipped with steel*' [his italics]. Thus was created the jingoistic Victorian phrase 'the thin red line', standing for the supposed invincibility of spirit of the British infantry.

Compare Kipling's poem 'Tommy' from *Departmental Ditties* (1890) which goes: 'But it's "Thin red line of 'eroes" when the drums begin to roll.' *The Thin Red Line* was the title of a novel by James Jones and the two film versions thereof (US 1964, 1998).

S

Rafael SABATINI Italian-born novelist (1875–1950)

1 Born with the gift of laughter and a sense that the world was mad.

Over the inside gate at Yale University's Hall of Graduate Studies is inscribed this slight variation of the first line from Sabatini's popular novel *Scaramouche* (1921), though understandably Yale savants did not immediately recognize it as such. How this not very highly regarded literary figure came to have his work displayed in such an illustrious setting was subsequently explained in a letter to *The New Yorker* (8 December 1934) from a young architect, John Donald Tuttle. He had chosen the line, he said, as a form of protest against the neo-gothic he had been forced to use on the building. 'As a propitiatory gift to my gods for this terrible thing I was doing, and to make them forget by appealing to their sense of humour, I carved the inscription over the door' – quoted in *Burnam* (1980).

Vita SACKVILLE-WEST English novelist and poet (1892–1962)

2 They rustle, they brustle, they crackle, and if you can crush beech nuts under foot at the same time, so much the better. But beech nuts aren't essential. The essential is that you should tramp through very dry, very crisp, brown leaves – a thick drift of them in the Autumn woods, shuffling through them, kicking them up ... walking in fact 'through leaves'.

In a BBC Radio talk 'Personal Pleasures' (1950), Sackville-West explained the origin of an expression 'through leaves', used in her family to express pure happiness. That is, the sort of happiness enjoyed by young children shuffling through drifts of dry autumn leaves. It spread, at least as far as James Lees-Milne, later to become the biographer of Vita's husband, Harold Nicolson. In a diary entry for 9 January 1949, he wrote: 'I made a little more progress with my book this weekend, but no "through leaves" as I should like. Laboured, factual and stodgy stuff churned itself out' – *Midway on the Waves* (1985).

Mort SAHL American satirist (1926–)

3 Let my people go!

During viewing of the lengthy film epic, *Exodus*, about the violent establishment of the state of Israel – as told on his record album *The New Frontier* (1961). Another version is that Sahl, invited by the director, Otto Preminger, to a preview, stood up after three hours and said, 'Otto – let my people go!' – alluding to BIBLE 68:8.

SAKI (H.H. Munro) English writer (1870–1916)

4 Women and elephants never forget an injury.

'Reginald on Besetting Sins', *Reginald* (1904). The basic expression 'an elephant never forgets' is what one might say of one's self when complimented on remembering a piece of information forgotten by others. As such, it is based on the view that elephants are supposed to remember trainers, keepers and so on, especially those who have been unkind to them. A song with the title 'The Elephant Never Forgets' was featured in the play *The Golden Toy* by Carl Zuckmayer (London 1934) and recorded by Lupino Lane. *Stevenson's Book of Proverbs, Maxims and Familiar Phrases* (1949) has that the modern saying really derives from a Greek proverb: 'The camel [*sic*] never forgets an injury' – which is exactly how Saki uses it.

1 But there were other objects of delight and interest claiming his instant attention: there were quaint twisted candlesticks in the shape of snakes, and a teapot fashioned like a china duck, out of whose open beak the tea was supposed to come. How dull and shapeless the nursery teapot seemed in comparison!

'The Lumber Room', *Beasts and Super-Beasts* (1914). Hence, the title of a Minette Walters crime novel, *The Shape of Snakes* (2000).

2 Put that bloody cigarette out!

Last words. Quoted in A.J. Langguth, *The Life of Saki* (1981), having first been recorded in 'Biography of Saki' by his sister, Ethel M. Munro, in 1930. During a night march on Beaumont-Hamel in the First World War, it was said by Lance-Sergeant Munro to one of his men who had just lit up. He was killed by a German sniper.

See also HOPE 244:1.

J.D. SALINGER American novelist (1919–)

3 *The Catcher in the Rye.*

Title of novel (1951) about the emergent 17-year-old Holden Caulfield. As explained in Chap. 22, it comes from a vision he has of standing in a field of rye below a cliff where he will catch any children who fall off. He wishes to protect innocent children from disillusionment with the world of grown-ups.

3rd Marquess of SALISBURY British Conservative Prime Minister (1830–1903)

4 We are part of the community of Europe and we must do our duty as such

Speech at Caernavon (10 April 1888). Sometimes misattributed to Gladstone and Lloyd George – and on one occasion to both.

5 By office boys for office boys.

Of the *Daily Mail*. Quoted in H. Hamilton Fyfe, *Northcliffe, an Intimate Biography* (1930). Compare THACKERAY 457:8.

See also KEARNEY 265:1; SALISBURY (next) 393:6.

5th Marquess of SALISBURY British Conservative politician (1893–1972)

6 The present Colonial Secretary has been too clever by half. I believe he is a very fine bridge player. It is not considered immoral, or even bad form to outwit one's opponents at bridge. It almost seems to me as if the Colonial Secretary, when he abandoned the sphere of bridge for the sphere of politics, brought his bridge technique with him.

On Iain Macleod. Speech, House of Lords (1961). To say that someone is 'too clever by half' is to show that you think they are more clever than wise and are overreaching themselves. As such, this is a fairly common idiom. The remark seems to run in the family. The 3rd Marquess (see above) had anticipated him in a debate on the Irish Church Resolutions in the House of Commons on 30 March 1868, when he said of an amendment moved by Disraeli: 'I know that with a certain number of Gentlemen on this side of the House this Amendment is popular. I have heard it spoken of as being very clever. It is clever, Sir; it is too clever by half.'

Rodney Ackland's version of an Alexander Ostrovsky play was presented as *Too Clever by Half* at the Old Vic, London, in 1988. Of Jonathan Miller, the polymath, in the early 1970s, it was said, 'He's too clever by three-quarters.' Compare: 'Only in Britain could it be thought a defect to be "too clever by half". The probability is that too many people are too stupid by three-quarters' – John Major, quoted in *The Observer*, 7 July 1991.

Carl SANDBURG American poet (1878–1967)

7 Sometime they'll give a war and nobody will come.

The origin of this light joke appears to lie in Sandburg's epic poem *The People, Yes* (1936). It became popular in the 1960s – especially as a graffito – at the time of protests against the Vietnam War. Charlotte Keyes wrote an article in *McCall's* Magazine (October 1966) that was given the title 'Suppose They Gave a War, and No One Came?' There was also a film (US 1969) called *Suppose They Gave a War and Nobody Came?*

It is also well known in German as '*Stell dir vor, es gibt Krieg, und keiner geht hin* [Suppose they gave a war and nobody came]'. Ralf Bülow in the journal *Der Sprachdienst*, No. 27 (1983) traced it back not only to Sandburg but also to Thornton Wilder. They both lived in Chicago in the early 1930s. Bülow recounts a Wilder anecdote that Sandburg may have picked up. In the same edition of *Der Sprachdienst*, Reinhard Roche comments on how German journalists and others have ascribed the remark to Bertolt Brecht because of his poem '*Wer zu Hause bleibt, wenn der Kampf beginnt* [Who stays at home when the fighting begins?]' and argues that 'much more philological caution is needed before assigning certain popular expressions to literary figures'. Quite so.

1 Slang is a language that rolls up its sleeves, spits on its hands and goes to work.

In *The New York Times* (13 February 1959). But attributed earlier to Sandburg in the film *Ball of Fire* (US 1941).

Jean-Paul SARTRE French philosopher and writer (1905–80)

2 *L'enfer, c'est les autres* [Hell is other people].

Huis Clos (1944). Subsequently, T.S. Eliot in *The Cocktail Party* (1950) had: 'What is hell? / Hell is oneself.' A character in Henry Reed, *A Very Great Man Indeed* (1953), quotes Sartre as 'one of our modern neo-pessimists' saying 'Hell consists of other people' and adds: 'We know what Shewin's comment on that would have been ... "Yes, but so does heaven."'

Dorothy L. SAYERS English novelist (1893–1957)

3 Far from it, as the private said when he aimed at the bulls-eye and hit the gunnery instructor.

Unnatural Death (1927). This Wellerism (see DICKENS 171:9) may not be original to Sayers. However, it was a literary form that she enjoyed using. Compare, from *The Unpleasantness at the Bellona Club* (1928): '*Au contraire*, as the man said in the Bay of Biscay when they asked if he'd dined.' In this, Sayers had been anticipated by G.K. Chesterton in *The Man Who Was Thursday* (1908): '"Au contraire", as the man said when asked if he'd dined on the boat.' In his *Autobiography* (1936), Chesterton has this as, '... when asked if he'd *lunched* on the boat.'

4 I always have a quotation for everything – it saves original thinking.

Have His Carcase, Chap. 4 (1932).

5 *The Nine Tailors.*

Title of novel (1934) in which 'Tailor Paul' is the name of one of the church bells of Fenchurch St Paul, which play a significant part in the plot. What we have in the title is a blend of various elements. In bell-ringing it was possible to indicate the sex of the dead person for whom the bells were being tolled. 'Nine tailors' or 'nine tellers' (strokes) meant a man. The bell-ringing use of the phrase does, however, echo an actual proverb, 'It takes nine tailors to make a man', which apparently came from the French in about 1600, and which is quoted on the last page of the novel. The meaning would seem to be that a man should buy his clothes from various sources. Or it was something said in contempt of tailors (in that they were so feeble that it would take nine of them to equal one normal man).

Apperson (1929) shows that, until the end of the 17th century, there was some uncertainty about the number of tailors mentioned. In *Westward Hoe* by John Webster and Thomas Dekker (1607) it appeared as three.

See also DICKENS 170:3 and 172:2; KIPLING 272:3.

Wallace Stanley SAYRE American professor of political science (1905–72)

6 In any dispute, the intensity of feeling is inversely proportional to the value of the stakes at issue. That is why academic politics are so bitter.

Quoted in Charles Philip Issawi, *Issawi's Laws of Social Motion* (1973). Justin Kaplan, editor of *Bartlett* (2002), asked me whether Henry Kissinger or someone else had stated, 'The reason academic politics are so bitter is that so little is at stake', and eventually himself provided an answer: 'I finally queried Henry Kissinger who, foxy as ever, said he didn't recall saying it but that it "sounded" like him. In other words, he didn't say it but wouldn't mind if we thought he did. I've now tracked it to its source (oral rather than written): Wallace Stanley Sayre (1905–1972), professor of political science at Columbia University. It's sometimes cited by political scientists as "Sayre's Law". One version: "The politics of the university are so intense because the stakes are so low." I prefer this fuller, more formal, version as above.'

Al SCALPONE American writer (1913–)

7 The family that prays together stays together.

Devised by Al Scalpone for the Roman Catholic Rosary Crusade in the US. The crusade began in 1942 and the slogan was first broadcast on 6 March 1947, according to Father Patrick Peyton, *All For Her* (1967). The slogan is quoted in Joseph Heller, *Catch-22* (1961), which is set in the period 1944–5, but this may simply be an anachronism. It is the original of many humorous variants: 'The family that shoots together loots together', 'The family that flays together stays together' etc.

Friedrich von SCHELLING German philosopher (1775–1854)

8 *Architektur ist überhaupt die erstarrte Musik* [Architecture in general is frozen music].

Die Philosophie der Kunst (1809) – in which Schelling also describes architecture as 'music in space'. He had already used the 'frozen' phrase in a lecture in 1802–3. Goethe, perhaps aware of this, states in *Gespräche mit Eckermann* (23 March 1829), 'I have found among my papers a sheet ... in which I call architecture frozen music.' In *Maximen und Reflexionen*, Goethe attributes the saying, rather, to a 'noble philosopher' – he probably meant Schelling. Madame de Staël wrote in *Corinne* (1807) about St Peter's in Rome: '*La vue d'un tel monument est comme une musique continuelle et fixée.*' As she was in touch with leading German intellectuals – she met Goethe in 1804 – she may well have known Schelling's phrase. In the reflection following his maxim, Goethe does not refer to Madame de Staël, but he does mention Saint Peter's as a building in which this sensation can be experienced. Schopenhauer said in *Die Welt als Wille und Vorstellung* (written 1814–18) that for 30 years people had kept repeating the witticism about architecture being 'frozen [*gefrorene*] music' – the first mention of 'frozen'; *erstarrte* actually means something more like 'fixed' or 'petrified'.

Heinrich SCHLIEMANN German archaeologist (1822–90)

1 I have looked upon the face of Agamemnon.

Attributed comment on discovering a gold death mask at an excavation in Mycenae, in a telegram to the King of the Hellenes in August 1876. Quoted in W. Durant, *The Story of Civilization: The Life of Greece* (1939). He had just found the well-preserved body of a high-ranking man wearing a golden burial mask in the grave circle at Mycenae. Removing the mask, he found eyes, mouth and flesh still intact. But was it really Agamemnon, the King of Mycenae in the 13th century BC, and leader of the Achaean coalition that fought against Troy? Alas, there seems little chance. Agamemnon's burial place is not known (if indeed he existed at all), and the mask, having now been dated with accuracy, proves to be of someone even more ancient. Still, it was a wonderful telegram to have sent.

Alternatively, the wording sent to the relevant minister in Athens was, 'This one is very like the picture which my imagination formed of Agamemnon long ago.' When finally persuaded that the mask pre-dated Agamemnon, Schliemann said, 'All right, let's call him Schulze.'

Arnold SCHOENBERG German composer (1874–1951)

2 Very well, I can wait.

When told his violin concerto needed a soloist with six fingers. Quoted in *PDMQ* (1971) and Nat Shapiro, *An Encyclopedia of Quotations About Music* (1978). In Joseph Machlis, *Introduction to Contemporary Music* (1963), Schoenberg is quoted as having said of his violin concerto: 'I am delighted to add another unplayable work to the repertoire. I want the Concerto to be difficult and I want the little finger to become longer. I can wait.'

Artur SCHOPENHAUER German philosopher (1788–1860)

3 All truth passes through three stages. First, it is ridiculed. Second, it is violently opposed. Third, it is accepted as being self evident.

Attributed remark. Professor Jeffrey Shallit of the Department of Computer Science at the University of Waterloo, Ontario, sought the genuine source of this quotation in 1997. He acquired attributions to Schopenhauer (frequently), Louis Agassiz (especially), William Whewell, Gustav Le Bon, Elbert Hubbard, William James, Arthur C. Clarke and Adrienne Zihlman, but nothing solid.

Paul Cloutman provided an anonymous text of the type that has been described as 'wall fun' or 'office graffiti'. He says it emanated from the Norman Craig & Kummel advertising agency in New York (when he was working in the London office): 'The Six Phases of a Project: 1. Enthusiasm. 2. Disillusionment. 3. Panic. 4. Search for the guilty. 5. Punishment of the innocent. 6. Praise and honours for the non-participants.'

Patricia SCHROEDER American Democratic politician (1940–)

4 After carefully watching Ronald Reagan, he is attempting a great break-through in political technology – he has been perfecting the Teflon-coated Presidency. He sees to it that nothing sticks to him.

Speech in the US House of Representatives (2 August 1983). 'Teflon' is the proprietary name for polytetrafluoroethylene (first produced 1938, US patent 1945), a heat-resistant plastic chiefly known as the name given to a range of cookware coated with it that 'won't scratch, scar or mar' (1965). Hence, when President Reagan exhibited an ability during his first term (1981–5) to brush off any kind of dirt or scandal that was thrown at him (chiefly through the charm of his personality), this was the epithet applied to him. *Time* Magazine wrote (7 July 1986): 'Critics say that he is coated with Teflon, that no mess he makes ever sticks to him. That is perfectly true.' As his second term wore on, however, and as happens with an old non-stick frying pan, the story was a little different.

Schroeder made the observation first, but it turned into a political cliché used by many.

Budd SCHULBERG American writer (1914–)

5 *Terry (to Charley)*: I coulda had class! I coulda been a contender! I coulda been somebody – instead of a bum, which is what I am! Let's face it. It was you, Charley!

Film, *On the Waterfront* (US 1954). Schulberg's script was performed by Marlon Brando as Terry and Rod Steiger as

Charley, his brother. It has become a much-quoted line, not least because of Brando's delivery. Brando plays a dockyard worker fighting corruption. In this speech, he laments what has happened to his former career as a boxer and blames it on his brother's betrayal. It continues:

1 So what happens? He gets the title shot outdoors in the ball park – and whadda I get? A one-way ticket to Palookaville.

In the same film. Later, *Palookaville* was chosen as the title of yet another 'incompetents plan a heist' movie (US 1997). Although, as so often, *OED2* has 'orig. unknown' for the American word 'palooka', it does at least define it. Firstly, it means an inferior or average boxer, and secondly, a stupid or mediocre person. The coinage is generally credited, however, to an ex-baseball player and sports writer, Jack Conway (died 1928), who put the word in its original sense into the pages of *Variety* in the 1920s. It was then popularized by the name 'Joe Palooka', title of a syndicated comic strip in the 1930s. This concerned an unsophisticated and oafish prizefighter who was nevertheless a world champion and not a loser. By extension, 'Palookaville' would be the kind of town inhabited by palookas, therefore the equivalent of ignominy and oblivion. The most famous use of this word occurs, as here, in Budd Schulberg's script for the film *On the Waterfront*, which takes us back to the boxing origins.

Charles M. SCHULTZ American cartoonist (1922–2000)

2 *It Was a Dark and Stormy Night.*

Title of book (1960s). In it, the line is given to the character Snoopy in his doomed attempts to write the Great American Novel. As a scene-setting, opening phrase, this appears to have been irresistible to more than one storyteller over the years, and has now become a joke. It was used in all seriousness by the English novelist Edward Bulwer-Lytton at the start of *Paul Clifford* (1830). At some stage, the phrase also became part of a jokey children's 'circular' story-telling game, 'The tale without an end'. Iona and Peter Opie in *The Lore and Language of Schoolchildren* (1959) describe the workings thus: 'The tale usually begins: "It was a dark and stormy night, and the Captain said to the Bo'sun, 'Bo'sun, tell us a story,' so the Bo'sun began ..." And such is any child's readiness to hear a good story that the tale may be told three times round before the listeners appreciate that they are being diddled.'

E.F. SCHUMACHER German-born British economist (1911–77)

3 *Small is Beautiful. A study of economics as if people mattered.*

Title of book (1973) – the first phrase of which provided a catchphrase and a slogan for those who were opposed to the expansionist trend in business and organizations that was very apparent in the 1960s and 1970s, and who wanted 'economics on a human scale'. However, it appears that Schumacher very nearly did not bother with the phrase. According to his daughter and another correspondent (*The Observer*, 29 April and 6 May 1984), the book was going to be called 'The Homecomers'. His publisher, Anthony Blond, suggested 'Small*ness* is Beautiful', and then Desmond Briggs, the co-publisher, came up with the eventual wording.

C.P. SCOTT British newspaper editor (1846–1932)

4 Comment is free, but facts are sacred.

Scott was the influential editor of the *Manchester Guardian* for more than 59 years – the longest editorship of a national newspaper anywhere in the world. In a signed editorial on 5 May 1921, marking the paper's centenary, he wrote: 'The newspaper is of necessity something of a monopoly, and its first duty is to shun the temptations of monopoly. Its primary office is the gathering of news. At the peril of its soul it must see that the supply is not tainted. Neither in what it gives, nor in what it does not give, nor in the mode of presentation, must the unclouded face of truth suffer wrong. Comment is free, but facts are sacred.' This passage was seized upon fairly quickly by politicians and journalists who, broadly speaking, held Scott in high regard. A man of forthright ideas and integrity, he is said to have expressed surprise when it was suggested to him that not all readers immediately turned to the leader page first of all.

Paul SCOTT English novelist (1920–78)

5 *The Jewel in the Crown.*

Title of novel (1966). It would be reasonable to suppose that the 1984 television adaptation of Paul Scott's 'Raj Quartet' of novels had something to do with the popularity of this phrase, now meaning, 'a bright feature, an outstanding part of anything'. This first of Scott's novels gave its name to the whole TV series. 'The Jewel in *Her* Crown' [my italics] is the title of a 'semi-historical, semi-allegorical' picture referred to early on in the book. It shows Queen Victoria, 'surrounded by representative figures of her Indian Empire: Princes, landowners, merchants, money-lenders, sepoys, farmers, servants, children, mothers, and remarkably clean and tidy beggars ... An Indian prince, attended by native servants, was approaching the throne bearing a velvet cushion on which he offered a large and sparkling gem.' (In fact, Victoria, like Disraeli, who is also portrayed, never set foot in India.)

Children at the school where the picture is displayed have to be told that 'the gem was simply representative of tribute, and that the jewel of the title was India herself'. The picture must have been painted *after* 1877, the year in which Victoria became Empress of India. Scott probably based it on an actual picture, though, if so, the painter's name is untraced.

The *OED2* refers only to the 'jewels of the crown' as a rhetorical phrase for the colonies of the British Empire, and has a citation from 1901. The specifying of India as *the* jewel is understandable. The Kohinoor, a very large oval diamond from India, had been part of the British crown jewels since 1849.

Many writers have used the phrase in other contexts. In *Dombey and Son*, Chap. 39 (1846–8), Charles Dickens writes: 'Clemency is the brightest jewel in the crown of a Briton's head.' Earlier, in *The Pickwick Papers*, Chap. 24 (1836–7), he has (of Magna Carta): 'One of the brightest jewels in the British crown.' In the poem 'O Wert Thou in the Cauld Blast', Robert Burns has: 'The brightest jewel in my crown / Wad be my queen, wad be my queen.' And then again, Laurence Olivier was quoted in *The Scotsman* (19 July 1957) as saying: 'I have always had the greatest admiration for the work of the BBC ... By far its most valuable jewel in its crown is the Third Programme, and that is going to be cut up, we are told.'

Robert Falcon SCOTT English explorer (1868–1912)

1 Great God! This is an awful place and terrible enough for us to have laboured without the reward of priority.

Scott contrived masterly epitaphs for himself and his companions by keeping at his diary as he slowly froze to death. All these jottings were quickly published in *Scott's Last Expedition: Journals* (1913). The above was written on reaching the South Pole and finding that the Norwegian explorer, Roald Amundsen, had beaten him to it.

2 Had we lived, I should have had a tale to tell of the hardihood, endurance, and courage of my companions which would have stirred the hearts of every Englishman. These rough notes and our dead bodies must tell the tale.

Towards the end he wrote this 'Message to the public'.

3 It seems a pity, but I do not think I can write more. R. SCOTT. For God's sake look after our people.

The last entry in the diary, with the writing tapering away, was for 29 March 1912.

(Sir) Walter SCOTT Scottish novelist and poet (1771–1832)

4 If thou would'st view fair Melrose aright, Go visit it by the pale moonlight.

The Lay of the Last Minstrel, Canto 2, St. 1 (1805). Compare ANONYMOUS 36:2.

5 O Caledonia! stern and wild, Meet nurse for a poetic child! Land of brown heath and shaggy wood, Land of the mountain and the flood.

In the same poem, Canto 6, St. 2. Caledonia was the Roman name for part of northern Britain. This is the most famous poetic use of the word to describe the modern Scotland.

6 O, young Lochinvar is come out of the west, Through all the wide Border his steed was the best.

Marmion, Canto 5, St. 12 (1808). Lochinvar, the hero of a ballad, claims his 'fair Ellen' just as she is about to be married to another. He puts her on his horse and rides off. Hence, the phrase 'Young Lochinvar' to describe any dashing, heroic figure, but especially a young male eloper.

7 O what a tangled web we weave, When first we practise to deceive.

In the same poem, Canto 6, St. 17. The origin of the modern proverbial expression.

8 O Woman! in our hours of ease, Uncertain, coy, and hard to please ... When pain and anguish wring the brow, A ministering angel thou!

In the same poem, Canto 6, St. 30. Alluded to in P.G. Wodehouse, *Jeeves in the Offing*, Chap. 16 (1960): 'Like the woman in the poem I was mentioning, she sometimes inclined to be a toughish egg in hours of ease, but she could generally be relied on to be there with the soothing solace when one had anything wrong with one's brow.'

9 As he appeared through the morning mist, Brown, accustomed to judge of men by their thews and sinews, could not help admiring his height, the

breadth of his shoulders, and the steady firmness of his step.

Guy Mannering, Chap. 25 (1815). Two years later in *Rob Roy*, Scott also used the 'thews and sinews' trope. As early as 1794, Thomas Holcroft used the phrase, not as a metaphor for 'strength' but with the implication that strength comes from the thews and sinews: 'I grew strong of muscle, and my thews and sinews became alert and elastic in the execution of their office' – *Hugh Trevor*, Vol. 1, Chap. 6.

1 *The Heart of Midlothian.*

Title of novel (1818). It refers to the nickname of the Tolbooth or prison which once stood on a site near St Giles' Cathedral in Edinburgh. Heart of Midlothian (or 'Hearts') football team (founded 1873), apparently took its name from a ballroom used by the players in the early days, which in turn had taken its name from the novel.

2 I offered Richard the services of my Free Lances.

Ivanhoe (1820) – coining the word 'freelance', redolent of the Middle Ages when an unattached soldier for hire – a mercenary – would have been appropriately called a 'free lance'. Thus what is only, in fact, a 19th-century invention came to be used to describe any self-employed person, especially a writer or journalist.

3 My own right hand shall do it.

In his journal for 22 January 1826 Scott is reflecting on the fact that he has just been saddled with thousands of pounds worth of debts. He is going to raise the money by writing and not by involving anyone else. On another occasion – recorded in Lord Cockburn, *Memorials of His Time* (1856) – he said, 'This right hand shall work it all off.' And so he did, but with a deleterious effect on his health.

4 That young lady has a talent for describing the involvements and feelings and characters of ordinary life which is to me the most wonderful thing I ever met with. The Big Bow-Wow strain I can do myself like any now going; but the exquisite touch, which renders ordinary commonplace things and characters interesting, from the truth of the description and the sentiment, is denied to me.

On Jane Austen, in his journal (14 March 1826). He had just been reading *Pride and Prejudice* and was lamenting that its author had died so young. Scott may have taken his use of 'bow-wow' (dog-like, barking, snarling) from what Lord Pembroke is quoted as saying in Boswell's *Journal of a Tour to the Hebrides* (1785): 'Dr Johnson's sayings would not appear so extraordinary, were it not for his *bow-wow way*.'

Erich SEGAL American writer (1937–)

5 Love means never having to say you're sorry.

Film, *Love Story* (1970) – also used as a promotional tag for it. Ryan O'Neal says it to Ray Milland, playing his father. He is quoting his student wife (Ali MacGraw), who has just died. Segal, who wrote the script, also produced a novelization of the story in which the line appears as the penultimate sentence, in the form 'Love means *not ever* having to say you're sorry.' A graffito (quoted 1974) stated: 'A vasectomy means never having to say you're sorry'; the film *The Abominable Dr Phibes* (UK 1971) was promoted with the slogan: 'Love means never having to say you're ugly.'

W.C. SELLAR and R.J. YEATMAN British humorists (1898–1951) and (1897–1968)

6 *1066 and All That.*

Title of book (1930). Compare GRAVES 220:3.

7 Henry I ... tried to console himself [for the loss of his son] by eating a surfeit of palfreys. This was a bad Thing since he died of it and *never smiled again*.

In the same book, Chap. 13. According to chroniclers, Henry I actually was said to have died of 'a surfeit of lampreys' (a fish that looks something like an eel). A surfeit does not necessarily mean an excess – just that it did not agree with him. Hence, however, *A Surfeit of Lampreys*, the title of a detective novel (1941) by Ngaio Marsh.

8 'Honi soie qui mal y pense' ('Honey, your silk stocking's hanging down').

In the same book, Chap. 24. See EDWARD III 183:2.

9 A post-mortem examination revealed the word 'CALLOUS' engraved on her heart.

In the same book, Chap. 32. Compare MARY 317:2.

10 The Cavaliers (Wrong but Wromantic) and the Roundheads (Right but Repulsive).

In the same book, Chap. 35. A characterization of the opposing forces in the English Civil War that is worthy of being taken seriously.

11 [Gladstone] spent his declining years trying to guess the answer to the Irish Question; unfortunately, whenever he was getting warm, the Irish secretly changed the question.

In the same book, Chap. 57. The phrase 'Irish question' appears, incidentally, to have been coined by Benjamin

Disraeli, in a speech to the House of Commons (16 February 1844): 'I want to see a public man come forward and say what the Irish question is ... Thus you have a starving population, an absentee aristocracy, and an alien Church, and in addition the weakest executive in the world ... That is the Irish question in its integrity.'

1 AMERICA was thus clearly top nation, and History came to a.

In the same book, Chap. 62. Sellar and Yeatman may have been parodying a currently fashionable theory that history had come to an end, an idea that has been found in the works of Robert Graves and others, but this remains unverified. Compare FUKUYAMA 204:7.

2 Oh to be in England now that Dean Nuisance is on a Hellenic cruise.

Garden Rubbish and Other Country Bumps (1936). Captain Pontoo speaking. Dean Nuisance is the archetypal gardening bore, or something even worse: the gardening expert who gives advice without ever getting his hands dirty, and who regards all gardening as a kind of spiritual experience.

SENECA Roman philosopher and poet (?4BC–AD65)

3 *Ecce par Deo dignum, vir fortis cum mala fortuna compositus* [Behold a thing worthy of a God, a brave man matched in conflict with adversity].

From *De Providentia*, Sect. 4. An oft-alluded to and variously rendered remark. Robert Burton's *Anatomy of Melancholy* (1621) has: 'Seneca thinks the gods are well pleased when they see great men contending with adversity.' Oliver Goldsmith's *The Vicar of Wakefield* (1766) has: 'The greatest object in the universe, says a certain philosopher, is a good man struggling with adversity; yet there is a still greater, which is the good man that comes to relieve it.' The Revd Sydney Smith's 'Sermon on the Duties of the Queen' (preached in St Paul's Cathedral, undated but possibly 1837) has: 'A wise man struggling with adversity is said by some heathen writer to be a spectacle on which the gods might look down with pleasure.' It is ignored by *Bartlett* and *ODQ*.

Robert W. SERVICE Canadian poet (1874–1958)

4 Back of the bar, in a solo game, sat Dangerous Dan McGrew,
And watching his luck was his light-o'-love, the lady that's known as Lou.

'The Shooting of Dan McGrew' (1917). Written with Cuthbert Clarke.

5 Ah! the clock is always slow;
It is later than you think.

'Spring' (1921). Peter Porter commented (1999) apropos this line: 'Even Shakespeare may not have coined "Thereby hangs a tale" or Belloc "We have got the Maxim gun." These sayings are in the air and the later authority for their usage may only be the first person who recorded them in print.' Indeed, 'It is later than you think' appeared on sundials long before Service came along.

(Sir) Ernest SHACKLETON Irish explorer (1874–1922)

6 Men wanted for hazardous journey. Small wages, bitter cold, long months of complete darkness, constant danger, safe return doubtful. Honour and recognition in case of success.

This small advertisement, said to have appeared in London newspapers in 1900 signed 'Ernest Shackleton', was nominated by Julian L. Watkins in his book *The 100 Greatest Advertisements* (Chicago, 1949/59) for the simplicity and 'deadly frankness' of its copy. Watkins reports Shackleton as saying: 'It seemed as though all the men in Great Britain were determined to accompany me, the response was so overwhelming.' Shackleton led three expeditions to the Antarctic, in 1907–9, 1914–17 and 1921–2. His biographer, Roland Huntford, suggests that the advertisement would have been published before the 1914 expedition, but casts doubt on it ever appearing. Shackleton had no need to advertise for companions, he says.

(Sir) Peter SHAFFER English playwright (1926–)

7 As old Martin describes the ordeal, the men climb the Andes.

The Royal Hunt of the Sun, Act 1, Sc. 8 (1964). An ambitious stage direction in an epic play about the conquest of Peru, Atahuallpa, featuring Atahuallpa, the last Inca emperor, and the Spanish conquistador Pizarro. It is said that John Dexter agreed to direct the play only when he saw this challenge. From Robert Stephens, *Knight Errant* (1995): 'Dexter's production was a work of sheer inspiration, sparked off by the famously unhelpful but challenging stage direction of "They cross the Andes."'

William SHAKESPEARE English playwright and poet (1564–1616)

The text of all the works is as in the Arden Shakespeare (2nd Series), except for the Sonnets, which are as in the Oxford Shakespeare (1988). The dates of first performance are approximate.

ALL'S WELL THAT ENDS WELL 1603

1 *All's Well That Ends Well.*

Title. The Revd Francis Kilvert's diary entry for 1 January 1878 has: 'The hind axle broke and they thought they would have to spend the night on the road ... All's well that ends well and they arrived safe and sound.' So, is the allusion to the title of Shakespeare's play or to something else? In fact, it was a proverbial expression before Shakespeare. *CODP* finds, 'If the ende be wele, than is alle wele' in 1381, and points to the earlier form, 'Wel is him that wel ende mai.' *Apperson* has 'For al ys good that hath good ende', from Audelay, *Poems* (?1426).

A curious footnote is that the title was very nearly also bestowed on Leo Tolstoy's *War and Peace* (1863–9). See TOLSTOY 467:2.

2   'Twere all one
That I should love a bright particular star
And think to wed it, he is so above me.

I.i.83. Although one can see the point of Michael Coveney entitling his biography of the actress Dame Maggie Smith, *A Bright Particular Star* (1993), in the play the words are said by a woman (Helena) about a man (Bertram).

3 I know a man that had this trick of melancholy sold a goodly manor for a song.

III.ii.8. The expression 'for a song' was proverbial in Shakespeare's day. 'I bought it for a song' occurs in *Regulus* (1694) by John Crowne. Possibly also from the 'trifling cost' (*Brewer*) of ballad sheets sold in olden days. Hence, 'to go for a song', meaning 'to be sold very cheaply, if not for free'. *Going for a Song* was the title of a BBC TV antiques programme (from 1968).

ANTONY AND CLEOPATRA 1607

4   My salad days,
When I was green in judgement, cold in blood,
To say as I said then!

I.v.73. Cleopatra. Hence, *Salad Days*, title of a musical (1954) by Julian Slade and Dorothy Reynolds.

5 The barge she sat in, like a burnished throne,
Burned on the water ...
                    For her own person,
It beggared all description.

II.ii.191. Enobarbus on Cleopatra. Hence, the expression 'beggars all description', meaning 'is indescribable' and originating with the meaning of the verb 'to beggar' in the sense 'exhausting the resources of'.

6 Age cannot wither her, nor custom stale
Her infinite variety.

II.ii.235. Enobarbus on Cleopatra. See also LOVELACE 296:7.

7 *Cleopatra*: Give me some music; music, moody food
Of us that trade in love.
All: The music ho!
(*Enter Mardian the Eunuch.*)
Cleopatra: Let it alone; let's to billiards.

II.v.1. Hence, the title of Constant Lambert's book *Music Ho!*, subtitled 'A Study of Music in Decline' (1934). In the book he explains: 'It will be observed that Cleopatra emphatically preferred billiards to music. This attitude, though somewhat philistine perhaps, is to be praised in that it recognizes that music and billiards represent two different sides of life. Cleopatra neither confused the functions of the two diversions nor suggested that they were better combined. Today, however, she would either have the wireless turned on continually in the billiard room, or else she would have to listen to composers like Hindemith, who reduce music to the spiritual level of billiards, pingpong and clock golf.'

8 Let's have one other gaudy night: call to me
All my sad captains; fill our bowls once more;
Let's mock the midnight bell.

III.xiii.183. Antony. Hence, *Gaudy Night*, title of a detective novel (1935) by Dorothy L. Sayers, making play on the word 'gaudy', meaning an Oxford college celebration. However, Sayers – who was a great user of quotations – does not make the connection explicit in her book, but only has Lord Peter Wimsey allude to it in Chap. 23. The same passage inspired the title of a collection by the poet Thom Gunn: *My Sad Captains, and Other Poems* (1976).

9   I have yet
Room for six scotches more.

IV.vii.9. Scarus's apparently jocular remark is quite the reverse of its modern meaning. A 'scotch' is a cut, or small incision – so when he meets Antony on the battlefield he is boasting of his bravery.

10   Shall I abide
In this dull world, which in thy absence is
No better than a sty? ...
O! withered is the garland of the war,
The soldier's pole is fall'n; young boys and girls
Are level now with men; the odds is gone,

And there is nothing left remarkable
Beneath the visiting moon.

IV.xv.67. Cleopatra laments Antony's death. Rosemary Anne Sisson entitled a novel *Beneath the Visiting Moon* (1986).

AS YOU LIKE IT 1598

1 I will tell you the beginning, and if it please your ladyships, you may see the end, for the best is yet to do.

I.ii.104. Le Beau. Hence, *Beginning*, the title of an auto-biography (1989) by the youthful actor Kenneth Branagh – which might not appear to be a quotation at first glance, but is, and is suitably modest.

2 Sweet are the uses of adversity,
Which like the toad, ugly and venomous,
Wears yet a precious jewel in his head;
And this our life, exempt from public haunts,
Finds tongues in trees, books in the running
    brooks,
Sermons in stones, and good in everything.

II.i.12. Duke Senior. Compare WILDE 496:7.

3 Under the greenwood tree
Who loves to lie with me.

II.v.1. Amiens singing. Hence, *Under the Greenwood Tree*, title of a novel (1872) by Thomas Hardy.

4 And so from hour to hour, we ripe and ripe,
And then, from hour to hour, we rot and rot:
And thereby hangs a tale.

II.vii.28. Jaques, reporting the words of a motley fool (Touch-stone). As a story-telling device, 'thereby hangs a tale' is still very much in use to indicate that some tasty titbit is about to be revealed. It occurs a number of times in Shake-speare, e.g. *The Merry Wives of Windsor* (I.iv.143) and *The Taming of the Shrew* (IV.i.50). In *Othello* (III.i.8) the Clown says, 'O, thereby hangs a tail', emphasizing the innuendo that may or may not be present in the other examples.

5 If ever you have look'd on better days ...
True it is that we have seen better days.

II.vii.113 and 120. Orlando and Duke Senior. Hence, 'to have seen better days', meaning 'to have been more suc-cessful, prosperous than at present', as in 'The whole town bears evident marks of having seen better days' – Robert Forsyth, *The Beauties of Scotland* (1806).

6 All the world's a stage,
And all the men and women merely players:
They have their exits and their entrances;
And one man in his time plays many parts,
His acts being seven ages. At first the infant,
Mewling and puking in the nurse's arms.
And then the whining schoolboy, with his satchel,
And shining morning face, creeping like snail
Unwillingly to school ...

II.vii.139. Jaques speaking. Probably the second most famous speech in all Shakespeare. Hence, *Seven Ages*, title of the first volume of memoirs (1970) of the stage director Basil Dean; *Each Man In His Time*, autobiography of Hollywood film director Raoul Walsh (1974); and *All the World's a Stage*, title of a BBC TV history of the theatre (1984).

7   And then the justice,
In fair round belly with good capon lined,
With eyes severe, and beard of formal cut,
Full of wise saws and modern instances.

In the same speech. Modern instances = trite examples or cases recently presided over.

8 Blow, blow, thou winter wind,
Thou art not so unkind
As man's ingratitude.

II.vii.174. Amiens singing. Unkind = cruel, contrary to nature.

9 When a man's verses cannot be understood, nor a man's good wit seconded with the forward child, understanding, it strikes a man more dead than a great reckoning in a little room.

III.iii.9. Touchstone. Compare MARLOWE 312:5.

10 Whoever lov'd that lov'd not at first sight?

III.v.82. Phoebe quoting. See MARLOWE 313:2.

11 A poor virgin, sir, an ill-favoured thing, sir, but mine own.

V.iv.57. Touchstone. In 1985 the painter Howard Hodgkin won the £10,000 Turner prize for a work of art called *A Small Thing But My Own*. It was notable that he chose the word 'small' rather than 'poor'. In Shakespeare, Touchstone is not talking about a work of art but about Audrey, the coun-try wench he woos. The line is nowadays more likely to be used (in mock modesty) about a thing rather than a person. A pun: 'Do you know Sir Arthur Evans's reported remark on finding a fragment of pottery in Crete – "An ill-favoured thing, but Minoan"?'

1 He uses his folly like a stalking horse and under the presentation of that he shoots his wit.

V.iv.105. Duke Senior. A figurative use of the term 'stalking horse'. Originally, this was a device used in hunting to get close to game which apparently sees no danger in a four-legged beast (and recorded since 1519). The wooden horse at Troy was an even more devastating form of equine deception. Since the mid-19th century in the United States, the phrase has been used in politics about a candidate put forward to test the water on behalf of another candidate. Latterly in Britain (since about 1989) the term has been applied to an MP who stands for election as leader of his party with no hope of getting the job. His role is to test the water on behalf of other stronger candidates and to see whether the incumbent leader is challengeable.

CORIOLANUS 1608

2   Despising
For you the city, thus I turn my back.
There is a world elsewhere.

III.iii.133. Coriolanus. Lord Byron alludes to this in a letter dated 8 February 1816: 'I mean to go abroad the moment packages will permit – "There is a world beyond Rome."' In a second letter of the same date he quotes Shakespeare directly.

3 The gods look down, and this unnatural scene They laugh at.

V.iii.184. Coriolanus. The Gods (or God) laughing is a phenomenon frequently to be observed in many areas of literature. In the first book of Homer's *Iliad* there is a scene in the gods' dwelling on Olympus that has the gods roaring with laughter. This was caused by the spectacle of the crippled god of fire and metallurgy, Hephaestus, with his bobbing gait carrying round the wine cup to serve them. Homer says that this caused 'uncontrollable laughter' among the gods. This passage gave rise to the expression 'Homeric laughter', meaning an irresistible belly laugh that is cosmically dominant. That is to say, the laughter is epic rather than of the sort that Homer might have produced. It is interesting that here the laughter is directed at a cripple, reminding us that, even among the gods, there is very little laughter that is not cruel.

The Jewish God also laughs. A book called *The Day God Laughed* (1978) by Hyam Maccoby contains the story about Rabbi Eliezer disputing with the Sages who refuse to accept any sign that God approves his interpretation of Jewish law. The prophet Elijah comments on God's involvement in this dispute: 'He was laughing, and saying, "My children have defeated me, my children have defeated me."' Maccoby adds that this story was dismissed as one of the imbecilities of the Talmud in the medieval Disputation of Paris, when the Talmud was put on trial by Christians.

The Christian God laughs lots of times – not least in the works of G.K. Chesterton, especially in his poem 'The Fish':

For I saw that finny goblin
Hidden in the abyss untrod;
And I knew there can be laughter
On the secret face of God.

Blow the trumpets, crown the sages,
Bring the age by reason fed!
('He that sitteth in the heavens,
He shall laugh' – the prophet said.)

Then there is the poem by Sir Laurence Jones, 'Lines to a Bishop who was shocked (AD1950) at seeing a pier-glass [mirror] in a bathroom'. When the Bishop sees his nakedness, the poem ends:

You shrink aghast, with pained and puzzled eyes,
While God's loud laughter peals about the skies.

The poem 'Ducks' by F.W. Harvey (1888–1957) ends:

Caterpillars and cats are lively and excellent puns:
All God's jokes are good – even the practical ones!
And as for the duck, I think God must have smiled a bit
Seeing those bright eyes blink on the day he fashioned it.
And He's probably laughing still at the sound that came out of its bill!

Laughter in Paradise was the title of a 1951 film about a dead man's revenge on the beneficiaries of his will. The original idea (as in the headword quotation) also occurs in a Cole Porter song, 'I Love Him But He Didn't Love Me' (1929), whose first verse begins:

The gods who nurse
This universe
Think little of mortals' cares.
They sit in crowds
On exclusive clouds
And laugh at our love affairs.

Groucho Marx says, 'The gods look down and laugh' in *Animal Crackers* (US 1930). Additionally, a song of the 1940s called 'Tonight' (also known as 'Perfidia'), written by Milton Leeds to music by Alberto Dominguez, has: 'While the Gods of love look down and laugh at what romantic fools we mortals be.' There is here a more obvious allusion to the situation in Shakespeare's *A Midsummer Night's Dream* (III.ii.115) when the sprite Puck says to Oberon, King of the Fairies: 'Lord, what fools these mortals be!' It is but a short step from this to *The Stars Look Down*, the title of the novel (1935, filmed UK 1939) by A.J. Cronin.

CYMBELINE 1609–10

1 　　　　Boldness be my friend!
Arm me, Audacity, from head to foot.

I.vii.18. What Iachimo says when he sets off to pursue Imogen. Hence, *Boldness Be My Friend*, title of a book (1953) by Richard Pape about his exploits in the Second World War. He followed this up with *Arm Me, Audacity* (1956). In 1977, Richard Boston wrote a book called *Baldness Be My Friend*, partly about his own lack of hair.

2 Hark! hark! the lark at heaven's gate sings.

II.iii.20. Hence, *Hark, Hark, the Lark*, the title of a novel (1960) by H.E. Bates. See BLAKE 94:1.

3 Golden lads and girls all must,
As chimney-sweepers, come to dust.

IV.ii.262. Guiderius singing. Hence, possibly, the expression 'golden youth', meaning 'a young man or woman with obvious talent who is expected to do well in life and career'. Also in the form 'gilded youth', a fashionable young man or men (usually), dedicated to the pursuit of pleasure (possibly based on the French *jeunesse dorée*). 'What avail his golden youth, his high blood ... if they help not now?' – Benjamin Disraeli, *Coningsby* (1844)

HAMLET 1600–1

4 For this relief much thanks.

I.i.8. Francisco to Barnardo, the two sentinels at the very beginning of the play. 'Relief' here in the sense of relieving another person of guard duty, nothing lavatorial. In *The Lyttelton Hart-Davis Letters* (for the 1960s), reference is made to the phrase being used as the title of a book about a Victorian sanitary engineer (Thomas Crapper, presumably), but if any such volume was published, it remains untraced.

5 O! that this too too sullied flesh would melt,
Thaw and resolve itself into a dew ...
How weary, stale, flat and unprofitable
Seem to me all the uses of this world ...
Frailty, thy name is woman!

I.ii.129. Hamlet. The Arden edition describes the choice of the word 'sullied' (= dirty, soiled, tarnished) as 'the most debated reading in the play in recent years'. The First Folio has 'solid'.

6 Methinks I see my father ... in my mind's eye, Horatio.

I.ii.184. Hamlet. Hence, 'in the mind's eye', meaning 'in the imagination'. However, this is a traditional metaphor dating back to Plato.

7 'A was a man, take him for all in all;
I shall not look upon his like again.

I.ii.187. Hamlet of his late father. Now a cliché of tribute and obituary. Dorothy Parker on Isadora Duncan's book *My Life*, in *The New Yorker* (14 January 1928): 'She does not whine, nor seek pity. She was a brave woman. We shall not look upon her like again.' In *Joyce Grenfell Requests the Pleasure* (1976) the actress recalls being rung by the United Press for a comment on the death of Ruth Draper, the monologist: 'My diary records: "I said we should not see her like again. She was a genius." Without time to think, clichés take over and often, because that is why they have become clichés, they tell the truth.'

8 A countenance more in sorrow than in anger.

I.ii.231. Horatio describing a feature of the Ghost of Hamlet's father. 'More in sorrow than in anger' now means that you are doing something – like meting out punishment – in a rational rather than hot-headed way. From *The Independent* (23 April 1992): 'I told an Essex Girl Joke. A young woman turned on me as if I came from another, less advanced planet, and, more in sorrow than in anger, said she didn't think what I'd said was frightfully right-on.'

9 　　　　But good my brother,
Do not as some ungracious pastors do,
Show me the steep and thorny way to heaven,
Whiles like a puff'd and reckless libertine
Himself the primrose path of dalliance treads.

I.iii.46. Ophelia to Laertes. Hence, the title of the film *Primrose Path* (US 1940), though see also Macbeth below. There is also this from Hugh MacDiarmid, *In Memoriam James Joyce* (1955): 'Other masters may conceivably write / Even yet in C major, / But we – we take the perhaps "primrose path" / To the dodecaphonic bonfire.'

10 This above all: to thine own self be true,
And it must follow, as the night the day,
Thou canst not then be false to any man.

I.iii.78. Polonius, verging on the pompous. It would appear to have provided the somewhat unlikely title *This Above All* for a film (UK 1942) based on a novel by Eric Knight about a conscious objector/deserter in the Second World War who sees the light. The lines from *Hamlet* are read out from a copy of Shakespeare and become the last words of the film.

1   Though I am native here
And to the manner born.

I.iv.14. Hamlet. Hence, *To the Manor Born*, the title of a TV comedy series (1979–81), created by Peter Spence, about a lady of the manor. Shakespeare may have intended a play on the word 'manor', too.

2   It is a custom
More honour'd in the breach than in the
      observance.

I.iv.16. The Prince is telling Horatio that the King's drunken revelry is a custom that would be *better* 'honour'd' if it were not followed at all. Now an expression usually taken to mean that whatever custom is under consideration has fallen into sad neglect.

3 Angels and ministers of grace defend us!

I.iv.39. Hamlet on seeing his father's ghost. It is a prayer for protection from a possibly evil spirit. 'Ministers' here means 'messengers of God'.

4 Something is rotten in the state of Denmark.

I.iv.90. Hamlet. Now, as 'there is something rotten in the state of Denmark', a common way of expressing that all is not well in some situation.

5   But that I am forbid
To tell the secrets of my prison-house,
I could a tale unfold whose lightest word
Would harrow up thy soul, freeze thy young
      blood,
Make thy two eyes, like stars, start from, their
      spheres,
Thy knotted and combinèd locks to part,
And each particular hair to stand on end,
Like quills upon the fretful porpentine.

I.v.13. The Ghost of Hamlet's father talking to the Prince. Porpentine = porcupine. 'His face was flushed, his eyes were bulging, and ... his hair was standing on end – like quills upon the fretful porpentine, as Jeeves once put it when describing to me the reactions of Barmy Fotheringay-Phipps on seeing a dead snip, on which he had invested largely, come in sixth in the procession at the Newmarket Spring Meeting.' So says Bertie Wooster in *The Code of the Woosters* (1938) by P.G. Wodehouse, using one of his favourite Shakespearean images – from *Hamlet*, though Wooster probably isn't aware of this. From *Jeeves in the Offing* (1949): '[Jeeves], do you recall telling me once about someone who told somebody he could tell him something which would make him think a bit? Knitted socks and porcupines

entered into it, I remember.' In 1986, it was reported that some of the more literate regulars of the Porcupine pub in Charing Cross Road, London, would talk of repairing to 'the Fretters'.

6 *Ghost*: Murder most foul, as in the best it is,
But this most foul, strange and unnatural.

I.v.27. The Ghost. Hence, *Murder Most Foul*, title of a film (UK 1964) based on the Agatha Christie novel *Mrs McGinty's Dead* (1952), with Miss Marple substituted for Hercule Poirot.

7 There are more things in heaven and earth,
      Horatio,
Than are dreamt of in your philosophy.

I.v.174. Hamlet. Not some philosophy of Horatio's in particular, but philosophy in general.

8 To put an antic disposition on.

I.v.180. Hamlet's announcement that he is going to affect madness. Antic = grotesque, strange or odd.

9 Brevity is the soul of wit.

II.ii.90. Polonius. Meaning, that the cleverest and most effective statements are made in relatively few words.

10 Though this be madness, yet there is method
      in it.

II.ii.205. An aside by Polonius about Hamlet. Hence, the expression 'There is method in my/his/her madness.'

11 He that plays the king shall be welcome.

II.ii.318. Hamlet is talking to Rosencrantz and obviously toying with the idea of having the actors play out recent events at Elsinore. *He That Plays the King* was used as the title of a book of theatre criticism (1950) by Kenneth Tynan. The thriller *To Play the King* (1992) by Michael Dobbs, concerning a clash between a British Prime Minister and a King, might seem to allude to this, but probably owes more to 'playing the king' in chess or cards (as is shown by the other titles in the trilogy, *House of Cards* and *Final Cut*). Shakespeare quite frequently uses the 'play the — ' formula, and not just about kings.

12 I am mad north-north-west. When the wind is
southerly, I know a hawk from a handsaw.

II.ii.374. Hamlet speaking. Hence, *North by Northwest*, title of Alfred Hitchcock's film thriller (US 1959) in which Cary Grant has to feign madness as Hamlet does. There may also be an allusion to a slogan of Northwest Airlines.

1 Buzz, buzz.

II.ii.389. Hamlet speaking, when told by Polonius, 'The actors are come hither, my lord.' One commentator describes it as 'a contemptuous exclamation dismissing something as idle gossip or (as here) stale news'. Hence, *Buzz, Buzz!*, title given to a collection of his reviews (1918) by James Agate, the dramatic critic, and *Buzz-Buzz*, title of a successful London revue (1918).

2 Then came each actor on his ass.

II.ii.391. Hamlet says this to Polonius, who has just announced the arrival of the actors. It is thought that Shakespeare might have been quoting a line from a ballad. Michael MacLiammoir, the Irish actor, used the phrase *Each Actor On His Ass* as the title of one of his volumes of memoirs (1960).

3 For the play, I remember, pleased not the million, 'twas caviare to the general.

II.ii.431. Hamlet. The general = the general public. The Arden Shakespeare notes that when the play was written, caviare was a novel delicacy. It was probably inedible to those who had not yet acquired a taste for it. Hence, 'caviare to the general', a famously misunderstood phrase meaning 'of no interest to common folk'. It has *nothing* to do with giving expensive presents of caviare to unappreciative military gentlemen. Lord Jenkins, Chancellor of Oxford University, apparently committed this solecism in an obituary of Lord Zuckerman in *The Independent* (2 April 1993): 'Solly Zuckerman's taste was sharp and astringent, "Caviar for the general" (on the whole he liked generals in spite of his scepticism for conventional military wisdom), but once acquired it never palled.'

4 O, what a rogue and peasant slave am I.
Is it not monstrous that this player here,
But in a fiction, in a dream of passion,
Could force his soul so to his own conceit ...
                    ... And all for nothing!
For Hecuba!
What's Hecuba to him, or he to her,
That he should weep for her?

II.ii.544. The sorrows of Hecuba are depicted in several Greek tragedies and, as Hamlet discusses with the players what play they might perform to catch his uncle out, the Prince reflects on an aspect of the actor's craft. Acting can make the other actors (and the audience weep), but what is the point of doing so? He, Hamlet, has a much better motive for using the art. Michael MacLiammoir, the Irish actor, reduced the words to *All for Hecuba*, as the title of a volume of memoirs (1946).

5 The play's the thing
Wherein I'll catch the conscience of the king.

II.ii.600. Hamlet speaking. Hence, the somewhat watered-down use of 'the play's the thing' in contexts where theatre or drama as a whole is being promoted. Hence also, the title of P.G. Wodehouse's adaptation of Ferenc Molnar's play *Spiel Im Schloss* (1926); a book title (1941) by Joseph E. Mersand; and an untraced film title.

6 To be or not to be, that is the question:
Whether 'tis nobler in the mind to suffer
The slings and arrows of outrageous fortune,
Or to take arms against a sea of troubles
And by opposing end them? To die – to sleep,
No more; and by a sleep to say we end
The heart-ache and the thousand natural shocks
That flesh is heir to: 'tis a consummation
Devoutly to be wish'd. To die, to sleep;
To sleep, perchance to dream – ay, there's the rub:
For in that sleep of death what dreams may come
When we have shuffled off this mortal coil,
Must give us pause – there's the respect
That makes calamity of so long life.
For who would bear the whips and scorns of time,
Th' oppressor's wrong, the proud man's contumely,
The pangs of dispriz'd love, the law's delay,
The insolence of office, and the spurns
That patient merit of th'unworthy takes,
When he himself might his quietus make
With a bare bodkin? Who would fardels bear,
To grunt and sweat under a weary life,
But that the dread of something after death,
The undiscovered country, from whose bourn
No traveller returns, puzzles the will,
And makes us rather bear those ills we have
Than fly to others that we know not of?
Thus conscience doth make cowards of us all,
And thus the native hue of resolution
Is sicklied o'er with the pale cast of thought,
And enterprises of great pitch and moment
With this regard their currents turn awry
And lose the name of action.

III.i.56. Hamlet's soliloquy beginning thus is one of the most quoted passages in all literature. It is constantly alluded to, especially in the titles of works by other writers. A small selection: *To Be Or Not To Be* was used as the title of a film comedy (US 1942, 1983) about Polish actors under the Nazis. *Slings and Arrows* was a post-Second World War revue in London, with Hermione Gingold. *Outrageous Fortune* was the title of a film (US 1987), loosely about rival actresses aspiring to be in a production of *Hamlet*. *Perchance to Dream* was the title of a musical by Ivor Novello (1945). *What Dreams May Come* was the title of a film (US 1998) starring Robin Williams. *Mortal Coils* was the title of a collection of short stories (1922) by Aldous Huxley. A thriller by Cyril Hare was entitled *With a Bare Bodkin* (1982). There is a natural history book by John Hay called *The Undiscovered Country* (1982), and that title was also used for Tom Stoppard's 1980 adaptation of a play by Arthur Schnitzler. Graham Greene had a novel *The Name of Action* (1930).

1 O! what a noble mind is here o'erthrown ...
The glass of fashion, and the mould of form.

III.i.152. Ophelia is lamenting Hamlet's apparent madness and decline. This is what he once was: a person upon whom others modelled themselves and who dictated what fashion should be. *The Glass of Fashion* was used as the title of a play by Sydney Grundy, first staged at the Globe, London, in the 1880s; also as the title of a book (1954) by Cecil Beaton.

2 O! it offends me to the soul to hear a robustious periwig-pated fellow tear a passion to tatters ... I would have such a fellow whipped for o'erdoing Termagant. It out-Herods Herod. Pray you, avoid it.

III.ii.8. The Prince is instructing the actors not to go over the top. Hence, 'to out-Herod Herod', a literary allusion, often adapted in the form 'to out-something something' and meaning to go beyond the extremes of tyranny (or whatever activity is under consideration) as usually perceived. The allusion is to Herod's slaughter of all the children of Bethlehem (Matthew 2:16). Termagant and Herod both featured in medieval mystery plays as noisy violent types.

3   Give me that man
That is not passion's slave, and I will wear him
In my heart's core, in my heart of heart.

III.ii.71. Hamlet. Hence, 'in my heart of hearts', meaning 'in my deepest and most hidden thoughts and feelings' – apparently a coinage of Shakespeare's.

4 *Hamlet*: Lady, shall I lie in your lap?
Ophelia: No, my lord.
Hamlet: I mean, my head upon your lap.
Ophelia: Ay, my lord.
Hamlet: Do you think I meant country matters?
Ophelia: I think nothing, my lord.
Hamlet: That's a fair thought to lie between
    maids' legs.

III.ii.115. Shakespeare's bawdy is sometimes obscure, but few can miss that 'country matters' means physical love-making

or fail to note the pun in the first syllable – which also occurs in John Donne's poem 'The Good-Morrow' (1635) and William Wycherley's *The Country Wife* (1675). *Country Matters* was the title of a British ITV drama series (1972) presenting an anthology of stories by H.E. Bates and A.E. Coppard, linked only by their setting in the English countryside. One presumes that the producers knew what they were doing in calling it this.

5 The lady doth protest too much, methinks.

III.ii.225. Gertrude's line is often evoked to mean, 'There is something suspicious about the way that person is complaining (or denying something) more than is natural.' However, what Hamlet's mother is actually doing is giving her opinion of 'The Mousetrap', the play-within-a-play. What she means to say is that the Player Queen is promising more than she is likely to be able to deliver. Gertrude uses the word 'protest' in the sense of 'state formally' not 'complain'. Hence, also, the title of the world's longest-running play, *The Mousetrap* (1952) by Agatha Christie.

6 *Hamlet*: Methinks it is like a weasel.
Polonius: It is backed like a weasel.
Hamlet: Or like a whale.
Polonius: Very like a whale.

III.ii.373. The Prince is teasing Polonius about the shape of a cloud. Hence, the title of John Osborne's 1980 TV play *Very Like a Whale*, about a captain of industry in emotional turmoil.

7 'Tis now the very witching time of night,
When churchyards yawn and hell itself
    breathes out
Contagion to this world.

III.ii.379. Hamlet. The modern phrase 'witching hour (of midnight)' seems to have grown out of a blend of such lines as this from *Hamlet* and 'It was now the witching hour consecrated to ghost and spirit' – Lord Lytton, *Rienzi* (1835). *The Witching Hour* was the title of a play by Augustus Thomas (?1915; filmed US 1921 and 1934). From the *Daily Mirror* (3 December 1994): '9.45pm Drop in to The Midnight Shop (223 Brompton Road, SW3), which, as its name suggests, stays open until the witching hour. It claims to be London's original late-night store, and is a well-stocked grocers and delicatessen.'

8 For 'tis the sport to have the engineer
Hoist with his own petard.

III.iv.208. Hamlet. A petard was a newly invented device in Shakespeare's day, used for blowing up walls and so on with gunpowder. Thus the image is of the operative being blown up into the air by his own device. Hence, 'hoist with one's own petard', meaning 'to be caught in one's own trap', has nothing to do with being stabbed by one's own knife (poniard/poignard = dagger) or hanged with one's own rope. Compare the more recent expression 'to score an own goal'.

1 Hamlet, this deed, for thine especial safety ...
          ... must send thee hence
With fiery quickness.

IV.iii.40. King Claudius means that the commission or document sending Hamlet to England is for his own safety (ironically: as it turns out, Hamlet is supposed to be killed on the journey). Hence, 'for thine especial safety' – the motto on the safety curtain at the Theatre Royal, Drury Lane, London.

2 They say the owl was a baker's daughter.

IV.v.43. So says Ophelia, mystifyingly. The reference is to an old English legend about Christ going into a baker's shop and asking for something to eat. A piece of cake is put in the oven for Him, but the baker's daughter says it is too large and cuts it in half. The dough swells up to an enormous size, she exclaims 'Woo! Woo!' and is turned into an owl.

3 When sorrows come, they come not single spies,
But in battalions.

IV.v.78. Hence, *Single Spies*, title of stage double bill (1988) by Alan Bennett, consisting of his plays *An Englishman Abroad* and *A Question of Attribution* about, respectively, Guy Burgess and Anthony Blunt (who were indeed both single and spies).

4 There's rosemary, that's for remembrance.

IV.5.173. Ophelia. Hence, *This For Remembrance*, title of the autobiography (1978) of Rosemary Clooney, the American singer.

5 Alas, poor Yorick. I knew him, Horatio, a fellow of infinite jest, of most excellent fancy.

V.i.178. Hamlet speaking, when the Gravedigger produces the skull of Yorick, the late King's jester. To make it easier to quote, presumably, the form 'I knew him *well*, Horatio' has crept into popular use.

6 It did me yeoman's service.

V.ii.36. Hamlet. Hence, the phrase 'yeoman service' meaning 'useful service as rendered by a faithful servant'. 'Sir,

Your correspondent, Frank McDonald, who has given yeoman service to the protection of our environment ...' – letter to the editor, *The Irish Times* (9 June 1994).

7 The rest is silence.

V.ii.363. Hamlet's dying words. A 1959 German film of *Hamlet* was given the English-language title *The Rest is Silence*.

8   Goodnight, sweet prince,
And flights of angels sing thee to thy rest.

V.ii.364. Horatio at Hamlet's death. Also to be found on the grave of Douglas Fairbanks (1883–1939), the actor of swashbuckling film roles, chiefly in the silent cinema; the words are 'inscribed on the white marble sarcophagus at the head of a 125-foot lagoon in Hollywood Cemetery' – Barnaby Conrad, *Famous Last Words* (1961). *Goodnight, Sweet Prince* is the title of a biography of actor John Barrymore by Gene Fowler (1943).

9 The ears are senseless that should give us
      hearing,
To tell him his commandment is fulfilled,
That Rosencrantz and Guildernstern are dead.

V.ii.374. The line is spoken by one of the English ambassadors after Hamlet has arranged for the killing of his two old student friends (who had been set up by his uncle Claudius to kill *him*). Hence, *Rosencrantz and Guildernstern Are Dead*, the title of a play (1966) by Tom Stoppard, concerning two of the minor characters in *Hamlet*. The two characters are also referred to in a play by W.S. Gilbert, *Rosencrantz and Guildernstern* (1891).

10 Hamlet, revenge!

The title of a detective novel (1937) by Michael Innes comes *not* from Shakespeare's play but from an earlier one (which is lost to us) on the same theme. Thomas Lodge saw it in 1596 and noted the pale-faced 'ghost which cried so miserably at the theatre, like an oyster-wife, Hamlet, revenge'.

See also GILBERT 213:1.

HENRY IV, PART 1 1597

11 Let not us that are squires of the night's body be called thieves of the day's beauty: let us be Diana's foresters, gentlemen of the shade, minions of the moon.

I.ii.25. Falstaff to Prince Hal. Minions of the moon = night-time robbers. In 1984, a French film was released in the English-language market with the title *Favourites of the*

Moon. It was a quirky piece about Parisian crooks, petty and otherwise, whose activities overlapped in one way or another, but the English title hardly seemed relevant to the subject. Not surprisingly, as it was a translation back into English. The original French title was *Les Favoris de la Lune* and, as a caption acknowledged, this was a French translation of the original Shakespearean phrase.

1 By heaven, methinks it were an easy leap
To pluck bright honour from the pale-fac'd moon.

I.iii.199. Hotspur. Oddly misquoted in an official British government booklet about Combined Operations, 1940–2: 'The tradition of combined operations, which began in the reign of Elizabeth, is rapidly reaching its fullest manifestation in the reign of George VI. Men of the Commandos still go out in the night-time with darkened faces, "To win bright honour from the palefaced moon," but they are not alone.'

2 The turkeys in my panier are quite starved.

II.i.26. First Carrier. As the events of the play cannot have occurred later than 1413 (when King Henry IV died), it was anachronistic of Shakespeare to have had anyone mention turkeys. These were not known to Europeans until 1518, when the Spanish saw them in Mexico, from whence they were introduced to Europe. However, the term 'turkey-cock' had been known in England since the Crusades (referring to what we now call guinea-fowl), so perhaps this is not an error after all. And yet, the earliest *OED2* citation for 'turkey-cock' is 1541, and it is not apparent whether this term was abbreviated to 'turkey' by 1597, when *Henry IV, Part I* was first performed.

3 I tell you, my lord fool, out of this nettle, danger, we pluck this flower, safety.

II.iii.9. Hotspur commenting on a letter he is reading. Hence, 'to grasp the nettle', meaning 'to summon up the courage to deal with a difficult problem'. The latter part was quoted by Neville Chamberlain as he was about to fly off to Germany in September 1938 on a trip to see Hitler, a meeting that resulted in the Munich Agreement. This led the *Sheffield Star* to comment: 'Our Prime Minister carries a pocket Shakespeare with him wherever he travels. He put Shakespeare on the map with a quotation from *Henry IV* when he set out for the Munich conference' – quoted in Michael Bateman, *This England* (1969).

4 I would 'twere bed-time, Hal, and all were well.

V.i.125. Falstaff to Prince Hal before the Battle of Shrewsbury. 'Would it were bedtime and all were well' is how the phrase came to be used generally – as in Oliver Goldsmith, *She Stoops to Conquer*, Act 1, Sc. 2 (1773).

5 But thoughts, the slaves of life, and life,
     time's fool,
And time, that takes survey of all the world,
Must have a stop.

V.iv.80. Hotspur. Hence, *Time Must Have a Stop*, title of a novel (1944) by Aldous Huxley.

6 The better part of valour is discretion

V.iv.119. Falstaff cynically reinterprets an old maxim and this is how the words are still used. Sometimes rendered as 'Discretion is the better part of valour.'

HENRY IV, PART 2 1597

7 He hath eaten me out of house and home; he hath put all my substance into that fat belly of his.

II.i.72. Mistress Quickly of Falstaff. Hence, the expression 'to eat someone out of house and home', meaning 'to eat so much that the house-owner who has provided the fare for the guest(s) is in a seriously depleted state as a result'. Never said in complete seriousness. Parents might say to their children, 'You would eat us out of house and home, you would.' Apparently it was a proverbial expression by the time Shakespeare used it.

8   Shall pack-horses,
And hollow pamper'd jades of Asia,
Which cannot go but thirty miles a day,
Compare with Caesars ... ?
          ... Let the welkin roar.

II.iv.160. Pistol. Compare MARLOWE 312:4.

9 Uneasy lies the head that wears a crown.

III.i.31. King Henry. Hence, *Uneasy Lies the Head*, title of autobiography (1962) by King Hussein of Jordan.

10 We have heard the chimes at midnight, Master Shallow.

III.ii.209. Falstaff. A film compressing both parts of *Henry IV* (1966) and directed by Orson Welles was entitled *Chimes at Midnight*.

11 Thy wish was father, Harry, to that thought.

IV.v.2. King Henry to Prince Hal, who has presumed that his father was dead.

12 *King*: Doth any name particular belong
Unto the lodging where I first did swoon?
Warwick: 'Tis called Jerusalem, my noble lord.

King: Laud be to God! Even there my life must end.
It hath been prophesied to me, many years,
I should not die but in Jerusalem,
Which vainly I suppos'd the Holy Land.
But bear me to that chamber; there I'll lie;
In that Jerusalem shall Harry die.

IV.v.232. Compare HENRY IV 236:1.

1 Let me but bear your love, I'll bear your cares.

V.ii.58. Hal in his first speech as King Henry V. The line is placed, unattributed, below the statue of Queen Victoria in Piccadilly, Manchester. Neal Ascherson commented in *The Independent* (1995) on the incongruity of 'the suggestion that this ancient queen, by then a hermit who seldom left her dusty palaces, was still as hungry to be loved as a young princess, still as eager to purchase love with royal sympathy and good works.'

2 Under which king, Besonian? Speak or die!

V.iii.110. Pistol exclaims this to Justice Shallow, who has just said he has some special authority under the King. Besonian literally means 'raw recruit', but here means 'ignoramus'.

HENRY V 1599

3 O, for a Muse of fire, that would ascend
The brightest heaven of invention;
A kingdom for a stage, princes to act
And monarchs to behold the swelling scene! ...
Can this cockpit hold
The vasty fields of France? or may we cram
Within this wooden O the very casques
That did affright the air at Agincourt?

Prologue, line 1. Chorus speaking, in a notable appeal to the audience of the Elizabethan stage to use its imagination. 'Cockpit' reminds us that theatres like the Globe (which had probably not quite been completed when this play was written) were but a short step from that less enlightened form of entertainment, the cock fight. 'Wooden O' is a straightforward reference to the round shape of the wooden theatre building. Casques = helmets.

4 Nay, sure, he's not in hell: he's in Arthur's bosom, if ever man went to Arthur's bosom.

II.iii.9. The Hostess (formerly Mistress Quickly) is talking of the dead Falstaff. Her malapropism is for *Abraham's* bosom, meaning the place where the dead sleep contentedly. From Luke 16:23: 'And it came to pass, that the beggar died, and was carried by the angels into Abraham's bosom.'

The person alluded to is Abraham, the first of the Hebrew patriarchs. The Hostess refers to a rather more English figure, King Arthur, and thus dignifies Falstaff in death, associating him with a native chivalric tradition.

5 A' parted ev'n just between twelve and one, ev'n at the turning o' th' tide: for after I saw him fumble with the sheets and play with flowers and smile upon his fingers' end, I knew there was but one way; for his nose was as sharp as a pen, and a' babbled of green fields.

II.iii.17. The Hostess, continuing to relate the death of Falstaff. One of the most pleasing touches to be found in all of Shakespeare may not have been his at all. The 1623 Folio of Shakespeare's plays renders the last phrase as 'and a Table of green fields', which makes no sense, though some editors put 'as sharp as a pen, on a table of green field' (taking 'green field' to mean green cloth).

The generally accepted version was inserted by Lewis Theobald in his 1733 edition. As the 1954 Arden edition comments: '"Babbled of green fields" is surely more in character with the Falstaff who quoted the Scriptures ... and who lost his voice hallooing of anthems. Now he is in the valley of the shadow, the "green pasture" of Psalm 23 might well be on his lips.'

Shakespeare may well have handwritten 'babld' and the printer read this as 'table' – a reminder that the text of the plays is far from carved in stone, but rather a prey to mishaps in the printing process – as are all books and newspapers.

Francis Kilvert, the diarist, made a pleasant allusion to the phrase in his entry for 15 May 1875: 'At the house where I lodge there is a poor captive thrush who fills the street with his singing as he "babbles of green fields".'

6 Once more unto the breach, dear friends, once more,
Or close the wall up with our English dead ...
Stiffen the sinews, conjure up the blood ...
I see you stand like greyhounds in the slips,
Straining upon the start. The game's afoot:
Follow your spirit.

III.i.1. King Henry 'before Harfleur'. From this, Sherlock Holmes, in the stories by Sir Arthur Conan Doyle, had a way of saying: 'Come, Watson, come! The game is afoot' – as in 'The Adventure of the Abbey Grange' (1904).

7 Cry 'God for Harry, England, and Saint George!'

III.i.34. King Henry concludes his rousing speech. Hence, *Cry God for Larry*, title of a book (1969) by Virginia Fairweather about Sir Laurence Olivier, who notably portrayed King Henry in a 1944 film of the play.

1 Behold, as may unworthiness define,
 A little touch of Harry in the night.
IV. Chorus, line 46. Referring to the king's wandering about, disguised, in the English camp on the eve of the Battle of Agincourt. Hence, *A Little Touch of Schmilsson In the Night*, the title of a record album (US 1973) by the singer Harry Nilsson (whose first name provides the link). Nilsson/Schmilsson is a Yiddish reduplication of no great meaning (as in the joke 'Oedipus, Schmoedipus – what does it matter so long as he loves his mother?').

2 'Tis not the balm, the sceptre and the ball,
 The sword, the mace, the crown imperial
 ... That beats upon the high shore of this world.
IV.i.266. King Henry. 'Crown Imperial' was the title given to the march Sir William Walton composed for the Coronation of King George VI in 1936. 'Orb and Sceptre' followed for that of Queen Elizabeth II in 1953. In a television interview, Walton said that if he lived to write a march for a third coronation it would be called 'Sword and Mace'.

 Oddly enough, the orchestral parts of 'Crown Imperial' bear a different quotation: 'In beauty bearing the crown imperial' from the poem 'In Honour of the City' by William Dunbar. This is what Walton must have begun with, subsequently discovering the Shakespeare sequence.

3 Old men forget; yet all shall be forgot,
 But he'll remember with advantages
 What feats he did that day.
IV.iii.49. King Henry. Hence, *Old Men Forget*, title of the memoirs (1953) of Duff Cooper, 1st Viscount Norwich, published when he was a mere 63.

4 From this day to the ending of the world,
 But we in it shall be remembered;
 We few, we happy few, we band of brothers ...
 And gentlemen in England now a-bed
 Shall think themselves accurs'd they were
 not here.
IV.iii.58. King Henry before the Battle of Agincourt. Hence, *We Happy Few*, a play (2004) by Imogen Stubbs, *Gentlemen in England*, the title of a novel (1985) by A.N. Wilson, and *Band of Brothers*, the title of a history (1992) of E Company of the US 101st Airborne Division from 1942 to 1945 by Stephen E. Ambrose, subsequently turned into a TV series (US 2001).

HENRY VI, PART 2 1590–1

5 Seal up your lips and give no words but mum.
Hume speaking. Hence, 'mum's the word' meaning 'we are keeping silent on this matter'. No mother is invoked here: 'mum' is just a representation of 'Mmmm', the noise made when lips are sealed. The word 'mumble' obviously derives from the same source.

6 *Commons* (*Within*) [i.e. a rabble offstage]: An
 answer from the King, or we will all break in!
 King: Go, Salisbury, and tell them all from me,
 I thank them for their tender loving care.
III.ii.277. When people use the expression 'tender loving care' nowadays, it is a pretty fair bet that they are not quoting Shakespeare. However, Shakespeare does use the three words in the same order. In its modern sense, *OED2* recognizes the phrase as a colloquialism denoting 'especially solicitous care such as is given by nurses' and cites *The Listener* (12 May 1977): 'It is in a nurse's nature and in her tradition to give the sick what is well called "TLC", "tender loving care", some constant little service to the sick.' The catalogue of the old BBC Gramophone Library revealed a considerable list. As 'TLC', there is a song by Lehman/Lebowsky/C. Parker dating from 1960 (and translated as 'Tender loving *and* care). Also with this title there is: a Motown song by Jones/Sawer/Jerome (1971), an instrumental by R.L. Martin/Norman Harris (1975), and a song by The Average White Band and Alan Gorrie. As 'Tender Lovin' Care' there is a song written by Brooks/Stillman (1966) and one written and performed by Ronnie Dyson (1983). As 'Tender Loving Care' there is a song written by Mercer/Bright/Wilson, and recorded in 1966 by Nancy Wilson. It was also used as the title of an album by her. The song 'Music To Watch Girls By' (1967) includes the lines: 'Eyes watch / Girls walk / With tender loving care'. But there is an even earlier use of the phrase, in this sense, in the final chapter, 'T.L.C. TREATMENT', of Ian Fleming's novel *Goldfinger* (1959). James Bond says to Pussy Galore, 'All you need is a course of TLC.' 'What's TLC?' she asks. 'Short for Tender Loving Care Treatment,' Bond replies. 'It's what they write on most papers when a waif gets brought in to a children's clinic.' This may point to an American origin. Indeed, a correspondent in the US recalls being told in the 1940s that there was a study done in foundling hospitals where the death rate was very high, which showed that when nurses picked up the babies and cuddled them more frequently, the death rate went down. This led to the prescription, 'TLC *t.i.d.*' (three times a day).

1 The first thing we do, let's kill all the lawyers.

IV.ii.73. Dick the Butcher (one of Jack Cade's rebels). Hence, *Let's Kill All the Lawyers*, title of a film (US 1998).

2 And Adam was a gardener.

IV.ii.128. Cade. After Genesis 2:15 and 3:23. In *Hamlet* (V.i.31), Shakespeare refers to gardening as 'Adam's profession'.

HENRY VI, PART 3 1590–1

3 See how the morning opes her golden gates,
And takes her farewell of the glorious sun!

II.i.21. Richard, Duke of Gloucester. In 1960, when I was still at school, I had the never-to-be-forgotten experience of watching BBC TV's *An Age of Kings*. This was a series fashioned out of Shakespeare's English history plays from Richard II to Richard III and was produced by Peter Dews. All sorts of young actors made up the repertory company – Robert Hardy playing Henry V and Sean Connery as Hotspur, to name but two. The series proved to me, at an impressionable age, that Shakespeare was every bit as wonderful as my teachers were telling me he was. All the 15 fortnightly episodes had individual titles such as 'The Hollow Crown', 'The Road to Shrewsbury', 'The Band of Brothers', 'The Boar Hunt', 'The Morning's War' (some quotations, some not) and another, I have now confirmed, was 'The Sun in Splendour'. And the reason for this last, though the exact phrase is not to be found in Shakespeare, is because it was an allusion to the lines quoted above. A stage direction (added by later editors) indicates at this point that no less than three suns appear in the air. This is an allusion to an occurrence before the actual Battle of Mortimer's Cross (in 1461), when Edward IV saw three suns 'sodainly joined all together in one' (this was a rare meteorological phenomenon known as a parhelion, involving multiple images of the sun). In consequence, according to Hall, the chronicler, he 'toke suche courage that he fiercely set on his enemies, & them shortly discomfited: for which cause, men imagined, that he gave the sunne in his full brightness for his cognisaunce or badge'. Indeed he did, and the 'sun in splendour' or 'in his glory' or 'in his brightness' became a feature of heraldry. The symbol is always shown with surrounding rays and sometimes with a human face on it. So well known was this that Shakespeare could assume that his audience knew what he was on about when, in the opening lines of *Richard III*, he has Gloucester state punningly: 'Now is the winter of our discontent / Made glorious summer by this sun of York.' Ted Bell points out that when the sun's rays are shown alternately as straight and wavy, this is meant to symbolize the provision of light and heat.

Incidentally, I much prefer the old spelling of the 'sun in splendor', and can only regret that it is not the one currently favoured by the 1850s pub of that name which, as a result of all this, I find situated in the Portobello Road, just a few hundred yards from my home in London.

4 Why, I can smile, and murder whiles I smile.

III.ii.182. Richard, Duke of Gloucester speaking. One of the many interpolations used by Laurence Olivier in his film of *Richard III* (1955). In fact, in the film, the speech from which this line is taken was bolted on to 'Now is the winter of our discontent' from *Richard III* to make an even more substantial soliloquy. Also incorporated in Ian McKellen's film of *Richard III* (1996), for which the line was used as a promotional slogan on posters, in the form, 'I can smile ... and murder while I smile.'

HENRY VIII 1612

5 Had I but serv'd my God with half the zeal
I serv'd my king, he would not in mine age
Have left me naked to mine enemies.

III.ii.455. Cardinal Wolsey. See WOLSEY 504:7.

6 This is the state of man; today he puts forth
The tender leaves of hopes, tomorrow's blossoms,
And bears his blushing honours thick upon him:
The third day comes a frost, a killing frost;
And when he thinks, good easy man, full surely
His greatness is a-ripening, nips his root.

III.ii.352. Cardinal Wolsey. A passage much alluded to (usually obscurely) by P.G. Wodehouse – as here from 'Jeeves and the Unbidden Guest' in *Carry on Jeeves* (1925): 'I'm not absolutely certain of my facts, but I rather fancy it's Shakespeare – or, if not, it's some equally brainy bird – who says that it's always just when a fellow is feeling particularly braced with things in general that Fate sneaks up behind him with a bit of lead piping. And what I'm driving at is that the man is perfectly right.'

Wodehouse himself makes a similar allusion in his autobiographical volume, written with Guy Bolton, *Bring on the Girls*, Chap. 6 (1954): 'It is in a precisely similar way that Fate likes to work, waiting with the brass knucks and the sock full of sand until its victims are at the peak of one of those boom periods when life appears to be roses, roses all the way. As Shakespeare, who often hits off a thing rather neatly, once said.'

Even here, Wodehouse doesn't give chapter and verse.

JULIUS CAESAR 1599

1 Beware the ides of March.

I.ii.18. Soothsayer. In the Roman calendar, this was the 15 March. The 'Ides' was also the 15th day of May, July and October, and the 13th day of all other months.

2 I, as Aeneas, our great ancestor,
Did from the flames of Troy upon his shoulder
The old Anchises bear, so from the waves of Tiber
Did I the tired Caesar.

I.ii.111. Cassius describing how he once rescued Caesar from drowning. According to Greek mythology, Anchises and Aphrodite had a son, Aeneas. The story of Aeneas rescuing his father is told in Virgil's *Aeneid*. Shakespeare also alludes to this incident in *King Henry VI, Part 2* (V.ii.63). In his diary for 15 October 1940, Harold Nicolson is describing what happened when a bomb fell on the Carlton Club in London: 'They saw through the fog the figure of Quintin Hogg escorting old Hailsham [his father, Lord H.] from the ruins, like Aeneas and Anchises' – *Harold Nicolson: Diaries and Letters*, Vol. 2, ed. Nigel Nicolson (1967).

3 The fault, dear Brutus, is not in our stars,
But in ourselves, that we are underlings.

I.ii.138. Cassius speaking. Hence, *Dear Brutus*, title of a play (1917) by J.M. Barrie.

4 Let me have men about me that are fat,
Sleek-headed men, and such as sleep a-nights.
Yond Cassius has a lean and hungry look;
He thinks too much: such men are dangerous.

I.ii.189. Caesar. Hence, film titles *Such Men Are Dangerous* (US 1930) and *Such Women Are Dangerous* (US 1934).

5 For mine own part, it was Greek to me.

I.ii.280. Casca. The apparent origin of the expression 'It's all Greek to me', meaning 'I don't understand.'

6 Against the Capitol I met a lion,
Who glaz'd upon me, and went surly by.

I.iii.20. Casca. Together with 'A lioness hath whelped in the streets, / And graves have yawn'd and yielded up their dead' (II.ii.17), this probably leads to *A Lion Is In the Streets*, title of film (US 1953), based on the Huey Long story.

7   Yon grey lines
That fret the clouds are messengers of day.

II.i.103. Cinna. Hence, *Messengers of Day*, the title of Vol. 2 (1978) of Anthony Powell's autobiography *To Keep The Ball Rolling*.

8 Cowards die many times before their deaths;
The valiant never taste of death but once.

II.ii.32. Caesar. Could this be behind the film title *Only the Valiant* (US 1950)?

9 *Et tu, Brute?* Then fall, Caesar!

III.i.77. Caesar's dying words. See CAESAR 118:1.

10 Cry havoc and let slip the dogs of war.

Antony. Hence, the titles of the film *Cry Havoc* (US 1943) and Frederick Forsyth's novel (1974; film UK 1980).

11 Friends, Romans, countrymen, lend me your ears;
I come to bury Caesar, not to praise him.
The evil that men do lives after them,
The good is oft interred with their bones.

III.ii.75. Antony. Hence, *The Evil That Men Do*, title of film (US 1984).

12 See what a rent the envious Casca made.

III.ii.177. Antony. Hence, *Envious Casca*, title of a crime novel (1941) by Georgette Heyer.

13 This was the most unkindest cut of all.

III.ii.185. Antony. The origin of the expression for a wounding act or piece of behaviour that is especially hurtful because of the person who does it.

14 There is a tide in the affairs of men,
Which, taken at the flood, leads on to fortune;
Omitted, all the voyage of their life
Is bound in shallows and in miseries.

IV.iii.217. Brutus. Hence, *Taken at the Flood*, title of a Hercule Poirot novel (1948) by Agatha Christie (though re-titled *There Is a Tide* in the US). See BYRON 116:3.

15 To tell thee thou shalt see me at Philippi.

IV.iii.282. Caesar's ghost to Brutus. From P.G. Wodehouse, *Thank You, Jeeves* (1934): '"We shall meet at Philippi, Jeeves." "Yes, sir." "Or am I thinking of some other spot?" "No, sir, Philippi is correct." "Very good, Jeeves." "Very good, sir."'

16 This was the noblest Roman of them all ...
His life was gentle, and the elements
So mix'd in him, that Nature might stand up
And say to all the world, 'This was a man!'

V.v.68. Antony speaking about Brutus. 'This was a man' is the epitaph on the fictional 'Cassius Hueffer', one of the characters who speaks from beyond the grave in *Spoon River*

Anthology (1915) by the American poet, Edgar Lee Masters. 'Hueffer' comments on his gravestone: 'Those who knew me smile / As they read this empty rhetoric / ... Now that I am dead I must submit to an epitaph / Graven by a fool!'

KING JOHN 1596

1 Therefore, to be possess'd with double pomp,
To guard a title that was rich before,
To gild refined gold, to paint the lily,
To throw a perfume on the violet,
To smooth the ice, or add another hue
Unto the rainbow, or with taper-light
To seek the beauteous eye of heaven to garnish,
Is wasteful and ridiculous excess.

IV.ii.11. Salisbury speaking. Hence, the expression 'to gild the lily', meaning 'to attempt to improve something that is already attractive and risk spoiling it'. Arden notes that 'to gild gold' was a common expression in Shakespeare's time.

2 This England never did, nor never shall,
Lie at the proud foot of a conqueror,
But when it first did help to wound itself ...
Come the three corners of the world in arms
And we shall shock them! Nought shall make
    us rue
If England to itself do rest but true!

V.vii.113. Philip the Bastard. Last words of play. Hence, *This England*, title of a book (1969) by Michael Bateman, made up of selections from the *New Statesman* column of that name 1934–68. See also below, 419:13.

KING LEAR 1605

3 Nothing will come of nothing: speak again.

I.i.89. Lear. Compare Lucretius, '*Ex nihilo nihil fit* [Nothing comes of nothing].'

4   Edmund the base
Shall top th'legitimate – : I grow, I prosper;
Now, gods, stand up for bastards!

I.ii.20. The Bastard Edmund speaking of himself. Hence, *God Stand Up for Bastards*, title of a book (1973) by David Leitch, which is a study of the author's upbringing and the circumstances of his birth.

5 How sharper than a serpent's tooth it is
To have a thankless child!

I.iv.286. Lear. Alluded to in P.G. Wodehouse, *The Inim-*

itable Jeeves, Chap. 17 (1924): '"I might have known you would muck it up," said young Bingo. Which, considering what I had been through for his sake, struck me as a good bit sharper than a serpent's tooth.'

6 I have seen better faces in my time
Than stands on any shoulder that I see
Before me at this instant.

II.ii.90. Kent. Hence, *Faces in My Time*, the title of Vol. 3 (1980) of Anthony Powell's autobiography *To Keep The Ball Rolling*.

7   I am a man
More sinn'd against than sinning.   ·

III.ii.59. Lear. Hence, the expression meaning 'to be less guilty or responsible than other people who have done wrong' – an example being prostitutes.

8 Child Rowland to the dark tower came,
His word was still: Fie, foh, and fum,
I smell the blood of a British man.

III.iv.179. Edgar mouthing snatches of verse in his assumed madness. Shakespeare, in turn, was quoting a line from an older ballad (a 'child(e)' was a candidate for knighthood). In certain Scottish ballads of uncertain date, Childe Roland is the son of King Arthur who rescues his sister from a castle to which she has been abducted by fairies. In the *Chanson de Roland* (French, 12th century) and other tellings of the legend, he is the nephew of Charlemagne. Shakespeare probably combined material from two completely different sources – the first line from a ballad about Roland, the second two from the old story of Jack the Giant-killer.

Later, Shakespeare's use was quoted by Robert Browning in the poem 'Childe Roland to the Dark Tower Came' (1855), which concludes with the lines:

> Dauntless the slug-horn to my lips I set,
> And blew. 'Childe Roland to the Dark Tower came.'

In Thomas Nashe's satire *Have with you to Saffron-walden* (1596) there occurs this line: 'O, tis a precious apotheg-matical Pedant, who will find matter enough to dilate a whole day of the first invention of *Fy, fa, fum*, I smell the blood of an Englishman' – which just goes to show how well-established is the business of phrase-origin finding. Note how it is 'Englishman' rather than 'British man'.

Pearson (1937) states that the line is often misquoted as 'I smell the blood of an Englishman.'

9 *Lear*: We'll go to supper i'th'morning.
Fool: And I'll go to bed at noon.

III.vi.83. The Fool's last words. Hence, *I'll Go To Bed at Noon*, the title of a book (1944), subtitled 'A Soldier's

Letters to His Sons', by the actor Stephen Haggard, published posthumously. Haggard had played the Fool in the 1940 Old Vic production with John Gielgud. It is also the title of a semi-autobiographical novel (2004) by Gerard Woodward.

1 *Gloucester*: The trick of that voice I do well
    remember:
Is't not the king?
Lear: Ay, every inch a king.
IV.vi.106.

2   Men must endure
Their going hence, even as their coming hither:
Ripeness is all.

V.ii.9. Edgar. 'Men must endure their going hence' is the text on the grave of the writer C.S. Lewis (and his brother W.H. Lewis) in Headington Quarry churchyard, Oxfordshire. *Ripeness Is All* is the title of a book (1935) by Eric Linklater.

3 The wheel is come full circle.

V.iii.173. Edmund the Bastard speaking. He is referring to the Wheel of Fortune, being at that moment back down at the bottom where he was before it began to revolve. A modern example of the phrase in use: Chips Channon writes in his diary (13 October 1943), 'I turned on the wireless and heard the official announcement of Italy's declaration of war on Germany. So now the wheel has turned full circle.'

4   O! let him pass; he hates him
That would upon the rack of this tough world
Stretch him out longer.

V.iii.312. Kent. Hence, *The Rack*, the title of a novel (1958) by the English writer A.E. Ellis (Alan Beesley; died 1971) about the ordeal of a man in a sanatorium. The last page explains how the title was arrived at: 'He picked up [Benjamin] Haydon's *Journal* and turned to the entry which the latter had made just before killing himself: "22nd. God forgive me. Amen. Finis of B.R. HAYDON. 'Stretch me no more on this rough world' – Lear." Something was grotesquely wrong. He opened his Shakespeare ... "The rack," he murmured. "Haydon forgot the rack."' (He also changed 'tough' to 'rough'.)

LOVE'S LABOUR'S LOST 1592–3

5 Berowne is like an envious sneaping frost
That bites the first-born infants of the spring

I.i.101. King Ferdinand. Compare *Infants of the Spring*, the title of Vol. 1 (1976) of Anthony Powell's autobiography *To Keep the Ball Rolling*. Powell does not indicate a source, but in his published journals (for 5 November 1990) he indicates that he was thinking rather of *Hamlet* (I.iii.39):

The canker galls the infants of the spring
Too oft before their buttons be disclos'd.

6 *Honorificabilitudinitatibus.*

V.i.37. Costard speaking. The longest word in Shakespeare appears to be a schoolmasterly joke, not original to him. The context allows it no meaning, just length, though it has something to do with honourableness. *OED2* does not list it as a headword, preferring 'honorificabilitudinity' (honourableness). Samuel Johnson noted that it was 'often mentioned as the longest word known'. At 27 letters it was overtaken, in time, by 'antidisestablishmentarianism' with 28, and by 'floccipaucinihilipilification', with 29, meaning, 'the action of estimating as worthless', which was first used in 1741, and is the longest word actually in *OED2*, though there is always the more recent 'supercalifrajilisticexpialidocious' – 34 letters. Scientific words of 47 and 52 letters have also been invented, but don't really count.

Those seeking to prove that Francis Bacon wrote Shakespeare's plays claimed that the 27-letter word was, in fact, an anagram – 'Hi ludi, F Baconis nati, tuiti orbi' ('These plays, born of F. Bacon, are preserved for the world') – which surely deserves some sort of prize for ingenuity, if nothing else.

7 The words of Mercury are harsh after the songs of Apollo.

V.ii.922. Meaning 'news and information are harsh after entertainment'. It is not clear who should speak the line, and may just be a comment on the play as a whole. The First Folio adds: 'You, that way: we this way' – words addressed by an actor presumably to the audience. Hence, *Words of Mercury*, the title of an anthology (2003) of the writings of Patrick Leigh Fermor.

MACBETH 1606

8 *1 Witch*: When shall we three meet again?
In thunder, lightning, or in rain?
2 Witch: When the hurlyburly's done,
When the battle's lost and won.

I.i.1. Hence, *The Battle Lost and Won*, title of a novel (1978) by Olivia Manning.

9 What bloody man is that?

I.ii.1. Duncan speaking of a 'bleeding Captain'. Often quoted jokingly as though it was a pejorative comment.

1   If you can look into the seeds of time,
And say which grain will grow, and which will not,
Speak then to me.

I.iii.58. Banquo is talking to the witches. Demons were said to have the power of predicting which grain would grow and which would not. *The Seeds of Time* was used by John Wyndham as the title of a collection of short stories (1969).

2   Come what come may,
Time and the hour runs through the roughest day.

I.iii.148. Macbeth's aside. Hence, *Time and the Hour*, title of a novel (1975) by Faith Baldwin.

3   Nothing in his life
Became him like the leaving it; he died
As one that had been studied in his death,
To throw away the dearest thing he ow'd,
As 'twere a careless trifle.

I.iv.7. Malcolm on the executed Thane of Cawdor. Sometimes adapted and used figuratively to describe the way a person has relinquished a position with dignity. A cliché by 1900.

4   Yet do I fear thy nature:
It is too full o' th'milk of human kindness,
To catch the nearest way.

I.v.16. Lady Macbeth on compassion. The origin of the phrase 'milk of human kindness'.

5   Letting 'I dare not' wait upon 'I would,'
Like the poor cat i'th adage.

I.vii.44. Lady Macbeth. The proverbial expression referred to is 'The cat would eat fish, and would not wet her feet' or 'All cats love fish but fear to wet their paws.' In P.G. Wodehouse's Jeeves stories, this quotation is a source of endless allusion. For example: 'That is the problem that is torturing me, Jeeves. I can't make up my mind. You remember that fellow you've mentioned to me once or twice, who let something wait upon something? You know who I mean – the cat chap' – *The Code of the Woosters* (1938).

6   We fail?
But screw your courage to the sticking-place,
And we'll not fail.

I.vii.60. Lady Macbeth. Alluded to in P.G. Wodehouse, *Joy in the Morning*, Chap. 13 (1974): 'That will give you eight minutes to screw your courage to the sticking-point, one minute to break window and one to make get-away.'

7   This is a sorry sight.

II.ii.20. Macbeth. Hence, the expression 'a sorry sight', meaning 'a miserable, sad, pitiable sight'. Apparently a coinage of Shakespeare's.

8   I had thought to let in some of all professions, that go the primrose way to th'everlasting bonfire.

II.iii.18. The Porter. Hence, *Primrose Path*, title of a film (US 1940) – though see *Hamlet* 403:9 above.

9   The night has been unruly: where we lay,
Our chimneys were blown down; and, as they say,
Lamentings heard i' th'air; strange screams of death.

II.iii.53. Lennox describing the night of Duncan's murder. Hence, J.C. Trewin, *The Night Has Been Unruly* (1957), a book about 'strange exciting and often comic occasions that have passed into stage record'. *The Knight Has Been Unruly* was the punning title of a BBC TV tribute to the actor Donald Wolfit transmitted in March 1968, after his death – source: Ronald Harwood, *Sir Donald Wolfit CBE – His Life and Work in the Unfashionable Theatre* (1971).

10 After life's fitful fever he sleeps well.

III.ii.23. Macbeth speaking of the murdered King Duncan. Curiously, this quotation appears on the grave in Warrington Cemetery of George Formby Snr (died 1921) – for whom it has a certain relevance. He was a music-hall comedian who invented the Wigan Pier joke, and one of his catchphrases was 'Coughin' well tonight' – often tragically true. He had a convulsive cough, the result of a tubercular condition that eventually killed him.

11 Double, double toil and trouble:
Fire, burn: and cauldron, bubble.

IV.i.10. All the Witches speaking. Hence, *Double Double Oil and Trouble*, title of a crime novel (1978) by Emma Lathen, and *Double Double Toil and Trouble*, title of a Halloween film comedy (US 1993).

12 By the pricking of my thumbs,
Something wicked this way comes.

IV.i.44. Said by the Second Witch as Macbeth approaches. It was an old superstition that sudden pains in the body were signs that something was about to happen. Hence, *By the Pricking of My Thumbs*, title of a detective novel (1968) by Agatha Christie, and *Something Wicked This Way Comes*, title of a novel (1962; film US 1983) by Ray Bradbury.

1   O Hell-kite! – All?
What, all my pretty chickens, and their dam,
At one fell swoop?

IV.iii.219. Macduff, told that his wife and children have all
been slaughtered. Hence, 'at one fell swoop' meaning 'at
one time, in a single movement'. 'Fell' here means 'fierce'
and originally had a 'deadly' connotation. Indeed, the image
in the full phrase is of a hawk swooping on its prey. Apparently, a Shakespearean coinage.

2 Out, damned spot! out, I say!

V.i.33. Lady Macbeth. In Thomas Bowdler's *The Family
Shakespeare* (1818) – with all those words omitted 'which
cannot be read aloud in a family' – this becomes 'Out
crimson spot ...'

3 I have liv'd long enough: my way of life
Is fall'n into the sere, the yellow leaf.

V.iii.22. Macbeth. Note how Byron takes up the phrase: 'My
days are in the yellow leaf; / The flowers and fruits of love are
gone' – 'On This Day I Complete my Thirty-Sixth Year'
(1824). He died three months later.

4 To-morrow, and to-morrow, and to-morrow,
Creeps in this petty pace from day to day,
To the last syllable of recorded time;
And all our yesterdays have lighted fools
The way to dusty death. Out, out, brief candle!
Life's but a walking shadow; a poor player,
That struts and frets his hour upon the stage,
And then is heard no more: it is a tale
Told by an idiot, full of sound and fury,
Signifying nothing.

V.v.19. Macbeth speaking. Almost every phrase from this
speech seems to have been used as title material. A slight
exaggeration, but *Tomorrow and Tomorrow* was a film in
1932; *All Our Yesterdays* was the title of Granada TV's
1960–73 programme devoted to old newsreels, and *All My
Yesterdays* the title of the actor Edward G. Robinson's memoirs (1974); *The Way to Dusty Death* was the title of a novel
by Alastair Maclean (1973); *Brief Candles* was the title of a
collection of short stories (1930) by Aldous Huxley; *Told By
an Idiot* was a novel by Rose Macaulay (1923); and 'full of
sound and fury' is deliberately alluded to in the title of
William Faulkner's novel *The Sound and The Fury* (1929).

5 They have tied me to the stake, I cannot fly,
But, bear-like, I must fight the course.

V.vii.1. Macbeth. Compare *King Lear* (III.vii.54) where
Gloucester, shortly before his eyes are put out, says: 'I am
tied to th'stake, and I must stand the course.'

6 Let fall thy blade on vulnerable crests;
I bear a charmed life.

V.viii.11. Macbeth. Hence, 'a charmed life', an expression
for a life in which luck and ease are in full measure. *Charmed
Life* is the title of a book by Mary McCarthy (1956). 'Actually, the goaltender led a charmed life. Most of the danger
was involved with the fellow who played between point and
cover-point' – *Globe and Mail* (Toronto; 16 May 1967).

7   Lay on, Macduff;
And damn'd be he that first cries, 'Hold enough!'

V.viii.33. Macbeth. It would be interesting to know at what
stage people started saying 'Lead on, Macduff' to mean,
'You lead the way, let's get started.' *Partridge/Catch Phrases*
has an example from 1912, but it probably started long
before then. There has been a change of meaning along
the way. Macbeth uses the words 'lay on' as defined by *OED2*
as: 'to deal blows with vigour, to make vigorous attack, assail'.
The shape of the phrase was clearly so appealing that it was
adapted to a different purpose.

MEASURE FOR MEASURE 1604

8   Man, proud man,
Dress'd in a little brief authority,
Most ignorant of what he's most assur'd –
His glassy essence – like an angry ape ...
Plays such fantastic tricks before high heaven
As makes the angels weep.

II.ii.118. Isabella. Hence, *Ape and Essence* – title of a novel
(1948) by Aldous Huxley.

9 O cunning enemy, that, to catch a saint,
With saints doth bait thy hook! ...
     ... But this virtuous maid
Subdues me quite. Ever till now
When men were fond, I smil'd and wonder'd how.

II.ii.180. Angelo. Compare 'Set a thief to catch a thief' under
ANONYMOUS 31:2.

THE MERCHANT OF VENICE 1596

10 The devil can cite Scripture for his purpose.

I.iii.93. Antonio speaking – because Shylock has just been
doing so. Hence, the expression meaning that 'an ill-disposed person may turn even good things to his
advantage'.

1 All that glisters is not gold,
Often have you heard that told.

II.vii.65. Morocco reading the scroll in the golden casket. Meaning, 'appearances can be deceptive', the proverb was common by Shakespeare's time. *CODP* quotes a Latin version – '*Non omne quod nitet aurum est* [not all that shines is gold]' – and also an English one, in Chaucer. The now obsolete word 'glisters', rather than 'glitters' or 'glistens', was commonly used in the saying from the 17th century onwards. In poetic use, Thomas Gray, for example, used 'glisters' in his 'Ode on the Death of A Favourite Cat drowned in a tub of Gold Fishe' (1748).

Pearson (1937) has Spenser, 'Gold all is not that doth golden seem', then Shakespeare, then Middleton, 'All is not gold that glisteneth', and Dryden, 'All ... that glitters is not gold.'

2 What's here? the portrait of a blinking idiot
Presenting me a schedule!

II.ix.54. Arragon speaking on opening the silver casket. Hence, 'blinking idiot' meaning a very stupid person (with twinkling or half-opened eyes). Apparently an original coinage by Shakespeare.

3 The quality of mercy is not strain'd,
It droppeth as the gentle rain from heaven
Upon the place beneath: it is twice blest,
It blesseth him that gives and him that takes.

IV.i.180. Portia. Origin of the expression 'the quality of mercy (is not strained)'.

4 A Daniel come to judgement! yea, a Daniel!

IV.i.219. Shylock. Alluding to the story of Susannah and the Elders in the Apocrypha. Daniel was a young youth who, by a cunning ploy, saved Susannah from death after she had been condemned to death by the Elders, having rejected their advances. Hence, the expression 'a Daniel come to judgement' for people who display unusual wisdom for their years.

5 The man that hath no music in himself,
Nor is not moved with concord of sweet sounds,
Is fit for treasons, stratagems, and spoils ...
Let no such man be trusted.

V.i.83. Lorenzo. From P.G. Wodehouse, *Thank You, Jeeves* (1934): '"Jeeves," I called down the passage, "What was it Shakespeare said the man who hadn't music in himself was fit for?" "Treasons, stratagems, and spoils, sir." "Thank you, Jeeves."'

THE MERRY WIVES OF WINDSOR 1601

6 We have a nay-word how to know one another: I come to her in white, and cry 'mum'; she cries 'budget'; and by that we know one another.

V.ii.6. Slender's ludicrous planned elopement with Anne Page is to be carried out by their finding each other in the crowd with this exchange of greetings. The Arden Shakespeare adds the gloss: 'An appropriately childish greeting. "Mumbudget" ... was used of an inability or a refusal to speak ... *OED2* conjectures, with convincing citations, that it was "the name of some children's game in which silence was required". Thomas Hardy later uses "to come mumbudgeting" in the sense of "to come secretly".' In Ngaio Marsh's *A Wreath for Riviera* (1949), Inspector Alleyn whispers, 'You cry mum and I'll cry budget' when hiding from a villain.

A MIDSUMMER NIGHT'S DREAM (1594)

7 That which, withering on the virgin thorn,
Grows, lives, and dies, in single blessedness.

I.i.77. Theseus. Hence, *Single Blessedness*, title of a book (1976) by Margaret Adams, about women remaining unmarried. Note also from the film *Now, Voyager* (US 1942) – *Mother*: 'And what do you intend to do with your life?' *Daughter (Bette Davis)*: 'Get a cat and a parrot and live alone in single blessedness.'

8 Ay me! for aught that ever I could read,
Could ever hear by tale or history,
The course of true love never did run smooth.

I.i.132. Lysander. Origin of the proverbial expression.

9 So quick bright things come to confusion.

I.i.149. Lysander. Hence, *Quick Bright Things*, title of a novel by Keith Ovenden (2000).

10 Ill met by moonlight, proud Titania.

II.i.60. Oberon. Hence, *Ill Met By Moonlight*, title of a film (UK 1956, based on a book by W. Stanley Moss) about British agents in Crete during the German occupation. In the US the film was called *Night Ambush*.

11 Night and silence – Who is here?
Weeds of Athens he doth wear.

II.ii.69. Puck speaking, referring to Lysander, who is asleep with Hermia. Hence, *Night and Silence, Who Is Here?*, title of a novel (1963) – described as 'an American comedy' – by Pamela Hansford Johnson, and *Night and Silence*, title of a crime novel (1999) by Aline Templeton.

1 Follow? Nay, I'll go with thee, check by jowl.

III.ii.338. Demetrius. I.e. 'close together, side by side, in the closest intimacy'. The phrase 'cheek by jowl' predates Shakespeare, and was earlier 'cheek by cheek'. Hence, the name of the late 20th-century British theatre company Cheek By Jowl, so-named in reference to the closeness of actors and audience.

2 Lord, what fools these mortals be.

III.ii.115. Puck. See above 402:3.

3 I have a reasonable good ear in music. Let's have the tongs and the bones.

IV.i.28. Bottom to Titania, referring to the most primitive of instruments, the tongs and the bones (knackers or clappers, rattled together). When Lord Harewood, the noted opera lover and administrator, wrote his autobiography (1981) he gave it the title *The Tongs and the Bones* and put the lines as epigraph to the book.

4 Music ho, music, such as charmeth sleep!

IV.i.81. Titania. 'Soft music' follows. Compare 400:7.

5   I never heard
So musical a discord, such sweet thunder.

IV.i.117. Hippolyta. Hence, *Such Sweet Thunder*, title of Duke Ellington's Shakespeare suite (1956) and the title of a book of Benny Green's jazz writings (2001).

6 The lunatic, the lover, and the poet
Are of imagination all compact ...
The poet's eye, in a fine frenzy rolling,
Doth glance from heaven to earth, from earth to
     heaven;
And as imagination bodies forth
The forms of things unknown, the poet's pen
Turns them to shapes, and gives to airy nothing
A local habitation and a name.

V.i.7. Theseus. In Thomas Love Peacock, *Nightmare Abbey*, Chap. 8 (1818), Mr Flosky (based on the poet Coleridge) 'sate with "his eye in a fine frenzy rolling," and turned his inspired gaze on Marionetta as if she had been the ghastly ladie of a magical vision'.

7 We do not come, as minding to content you,
Our true intent is. All for your delight,
We are not here ...

V.i.113. When Quince reads the prologue of the play-within-a-play, he mispunctuates it. Hence, 'Our true intent is all

for your delight' were the words written over the entrance to the first Butlin's holiday camp to be opened, at Skegness, in 1936. One wonders how many of the campers who passed under it recognized it as a great 'unspoken' line from Shakespeare? It is also a motto that has cropped up on the programmes of countless British repertory theatres.

8 Well roared, Lion!

V.i.254. Demetrius to the Lion in the play. One of the two Shakespearean quotations on the memorial plaque to Sir Donald Wolfit (1902–68), last of the actor-managers, in St Paul's Church, Covent Garden, London. The other is 'Is't not the King? Ay, every inch a King', from *King Lear* (414:1).

9 This passion, and the death of a dear friend, would go near to make a man look sad.

V.i.277. Theseus. A forerunner of the modern format 'that and a — will get you — ', an American expression of the obvious where the object mentioned is clearly of no value: 'That, and a dollar, will get you a cup of coffee', 'That, and a token, will get you on the subway' ...

10 Come, trusty sword,
Come, blade, my breast imbrue!

V.i.330. Thisbe. Lines from the play-within-a-play and thus a consciously archaic use of the phrase 'trusty sword'. Phrase known by 1558; also in Edmund Spenser – 'His trusty sword, the servant of his might' (1596).

11 Now the hungry lion roars ...
Whilst the heavy ploughman snores,
All with weary task fordone.

V.i.358. Puck speaking. It has been objected that 'heavy' and 'weary' have been transposed, but this is surely not the case. Elsewhere, Shakespeare uses 'weary' to mean 'causing weariness' and 'heavy' to mean 'drowsy, sleepy' and these fit the sense here perfectly well.
See also CLARK 144:9.

MUCH ADO ABOUT NOTHING 1598

12 *Don Pedro*: You were born in a merry hour ...
Beatrice: A star danced, and under that I was born.

II.i.316. The actress Gertrude Lawrence entitled her autobiography *A Star Danced* (1945).

13 Is it not strange, that sheeps' guts should hale souls out of men's bodies?

II.iii.59. Benedick. Shakespeare got it right. Sheep, horse, ass, but *not* cat intestines are used in the making of strings for musical instruments. The name 'catgut' was possibly introduced as a pejorative way of describing the sound made by badly played violin strings, whatever their actual source.

1 Sigh no more, ladies, sigh no more,
Men were deceivers ever:
One foot in sea, and one on shore,
To one thing constant never.

II.iii.65. Balthasar's song. Hence, *Sigh No More*, title of a revue (1945) by Noël Coward.

2 Comparisons are odorous.

III.v.15. Dogberry. 'Comparisons are odious' had been an established proverbial expression by about 1440. This is one of Dogberry's pre-Malaprop malapropisms. Compare DONNE 175:6.

OTHELLO 1604

3 But I will wear my heart upon my sleeve,
For doves to peck at: I am not what I am.

I.i.64. Iago. 'Daws' instead of 'doves' in the First Folio (1623).

4 Put money in thy purse.

I.iii.340. Iago to Rodrigo. Michael MacLiammoir, the Irish actor, took the phrase for a volume of his diaries (1952), recounting the time he spent playing Iago to Orson Welles's Othello, in the 1951 film.

5 To suckle fools and chronicle small beer.

II.i.160. Iago to Desdemona. Small beer = trivialities.

6 Excellent wretch, perdition catch my soul,
But I do love thee, and when I love thee not,
Chaos is come again.

III.iii.91. Othello on Desdemona. Hence, the title of the rock musical *Catch My Soul* (1970), based on the play.

7   O farewell ...
Pride, pomp, and circumstance of glorious war!

III.iii.356. Othello. Hence, *Pomp and Circumstance*, the title of a set of five marches by Sir Edward Elgar (Nos. 1–4 composed 1901–7, and No. 5 in 1930).

8 Nay, we must think
Men are not gods.

III.iv.146. Desdemona. In 1936 a film about an actor playing Othello who nearly strangles his wife was called *Men Are Not Gods*.

9 Here is my journey's end, here is my butt,
And very sea-mark of my utmost sail.

V.ii.268. Othello. See SHERRIFF 430:7.

10 Speak of them as they are; nothing extenuate,
Nor set down aught in malice; then must you
speak
Of one that lov'd not wisely, but too well.

V.ii.343. Othello. Origin of the saying 'loved not wisely but too well'.

RICHARD II 1595

11 O, who can hold a fire in his hand
By thinking on the frosty Caucasus?

I.iii.294. Bolingbroke. This is a couplet that Colly Cibber shoehorns into his 1700 version of *Richard III*.

12 This royal throne of kings, this scepter'd isle,
This earth of majesty, this seat of Mars,
This other Eden, demi-paradise ...
This happy breed of men, this little world,
This precious stone set in the silver sea ...
This blessed plot, this earth, this realm, this
England.

II.i.40. John of Gaunt. Hence, *This England*, title of a film (UK 1941), known in Scotland as *Our Heritage* [sic] – but see also above, 413:2; *The Demi-Paradise*, title of a film (UK 1943), known in the US as *Adventure for Two*. *This Happy Breed*, title of a play (1943; film UK 1944) by Noël Coward. All patriotic flag-wavers (like the speech itself) and designed to promote England in the Second World War. *Set In a Silver Sea* was the title of the first volume (1984) of Sir Arthur Bryant's *History of Britain and the British People. This Sceptered Isle* was the title of a history of Britain written by Christopher Lee and broadcast on BBC Radio 4 (1997–9).

13 O, call back yesterday, bid time return.

III.ii.69. Salisbury. Hence, *Call Back Yesterday*, title of a volume of memoirs (1953) by Hugh Dalton.

1 Let's talk of graves, of worms, and epitaphs.

III.ii.145. King Richard. Hence, *Let's Talk of Graves of Worms and Epitaphs*, title of a crime novel (1975) by Robert Player.

2 For God's sake, let us sit upon the ground
And tell sad stories of the death of kings ...
For within the hollow crown
That rounds the mortal temples of a king
Keeps Death his court.

III.ii.155. King Richard. Hence, *The Hollow Crown*, title of the Royal Shakespeare Company's entertainment (1962) based on Shakespeare's kings and queens.

RICHARD III 1592–3

3 Now is the winter of our discontent
Made glorious summer by this sun of York ...

I.i.1. Richard speaking. Hence, the title of John Steinbeck's novel *The Winter of Our Discontent* (1961). See also *The SUN* 449:4.

4 I am not in the giving vein today.

IV.ii.116. Richard to Buckingham. Two lines later he emphasizes, 'I am not in the vein.'

5 The king's name is a tower of strength.

V.iii.12. Richard. See also TENNYSON 455:9. In the Bible, God is often referred to as a 'strong tower'.

6 A horse! a horse! My kingdom for a horse!

V.iv.7/13. Richard's twice-repeated cry in his last desperate moments. The actual Richard III's last words when he met Henry Tudor at the Battle of Bosworth on 22 August 1485 were, 'I will die King of England. I will not budge a foot ... Treason! treason!' That was how it was reported by John Rowe, who presumably picked it up from someone who had actually been at the battle, for he was not. Evidently, Richard then rushed on the future Henry VII and was killed.

Shakespeare's memorable cry may have been inspired by lines in other plays written about the time he wrote his (in about 1592). The anonymous *True Tragedy of Richard III* (albeit dated 1594) has: 'A horse, a horse, a fresh horse.' The only indication that Richard III might have had a similar concern at the actual battle is contained in the book of Edward Hall's chronicle called 'The tragical doynges of Kyng Richard the thirde' (1548), where it states: 'When the loss of the battle was imminent and apparent, they brought to him a swift and light horse to convey him away.' See also MARSTON 314:1.

ROMEO AND JULIET 1594

7 The strangers all are gone.

I.v.143. The Nurse. Hence, the title of Vol. 4 (1982) of Anthony Powell's autobiographical sequence *To Keep the Ball Rolling*.

8 O Romeo, Romeo, wherefore art thou Romeo?

II.ii.33. Juliet. In this famous – and famously misunderstood – line, 'wherefore' does not mean 'where'. Juliet is not *looking for* Romeo from her balcony. It means 'for what reason'.

9 What's in a name? That which we call a rose
By any other word would smell as sweet.

II.ii.43. Juliet. There is an implicit comparison here with Romeo as a rose. Hence, 'a rose by any other name', an expression indicating that the name of someone or something is unimportant, and that the quality or nature of that person or thing is the important factor.

10 A plague o' both your houses.

III.i.92. Mercutio speaking, fatally wounded in the feud between the Montagus and Capulets. Origin of the curse on all parties in a dispute.

11 O I am fortune's fool.

III.i.138. Romeo speaking, after he has just killed Tybalt. Meaning, he is the helpless victim of fortune's mockery and abuse. Hence, *Fortune's Fool*, the title given to a version of Turgenev's play also known as *Insolvency*, *Impecuniousness* and *A Poor Gentleman* (?1848).

SONNETS 1592–5

12 To the only begetter of these ensuing sonnets,
  Mr W.H.

Dedication (1609), inserted by Thomas Thorpe, the publisher. The identity of Mr W.H. is still disputed.

13 Shall I compare thee to a summer's day?
Thou art more lovely and more temperate.
Rough winds do shake the darling buds of May,
And summer's lease hath all too short a date.

Sonnet 18. Hence, the titles of two modern novels. In H.E. Bates, *The Darling Buds of May* (1958), Charlie the tax inspector recites the poem when he is drunkenly pursuing the lovely daughter, Mariette. John Mortimer's *Summer's Lease* (1988) is about goings-on in a villa rented by English visitors to Tuscany.

1 When, in disgrace with fortune and men's eyes,
I all alone beweep my outcast state.

Sonnet 29. Hence, *Fortune and Men's Eyes*, title of a play (1967) by John Herbert, about homosexuals.

2 When to the sessions of sweet silent thought,
I summon up remembrance of things past.

Sonnet 30. Hence, *Remembrance of Things Past* – see PROUST 421:4.

3 Full many a glorious morning have I seen
Flatter the mountain tops with sovereign eye,
Kissing with golden face the meadows green,
Gilding pale streams with heavenly alchemy.

Sonnet 33. From P.G. Wodehouse, *The Code of the Woosters* (1938): 'I remember Jeeves saying to me once, apropos of how you can never tell what the weather's going to do, that full many a glorious morning had he seen flatter the mountain tops with sovereign eye and then turn into a rather nasty afternoon.'

4 Like as the waves make towards the pebbled shore,
So do our minutes hasten to their end.

Sonnet 60. Hence the title of Elizabeth Longford, *The Pebbled Shore* (1988).

5 That time of year thou mayst in me behold
When yellow leaves, or none, or few, do hang
Upon those boughs which shake against the cold,
Bare ruined choirs where late the sweet birds sang.

Sonnet 73. Compare *The Rape of Lucrece*, line 871: 'The adder hisses where the sweet birds sing.'

6 They that have power to hurt and will do none ...
Lilies that fester smell far worse than weeds.

Sonnet 94. Hence, *Lilies That Fester*, title of a detective novel (2000) by Hazel Holt.

7 From you have I been absent in the spring.

Sonnet 98. Hence, *Absent In the Spring*, title of a thriller (1948), written by Agatha Christie under the name Mary Westmacott.

8 When in the chronicle of wasted time
I see descriptions of the fairest wights.

Sonnet 106. Hence, *Chronicles of Wasted Time*, title of Malcolm Muggeridge's two volumes of autobiography (1972–3).

9   My nature is subdued
To what it works in, like the dyer's hand.

Sonnet 111. Hence, *The Dyer's Hand*, title of a collection of essays and lectures (1962) by W.H. Auden.

10 My mistress' eyes are nothing like the sun.

Sonnet 130. Hence, *Nothing Like the Sun*, title of a novel (1964) by Anthony Burgess, about the life of Shakespeare, and of a record album by Sting (1987).

THE TAMING OF THE SHREW 1592–3

11 And do as adversaries do in law,
Strive mightily, but eat and drink as friends.

I.ii.277. Tranio. The apparent coining of 'striving mightily', a florid expression for great endeavour.

12 Come on, and kiss me Kate.

V.ii.181. Petruchio to Katherina. Hence, *Kiss Me Kate*, title of the Cole Porter musical (1948; film US 1953) based around a touring company's production of *The Taming of the Shrew*.

THE TEMPEST 1612

13 Hell is empty and all the devils are here.

I.ii.214. Ariel quoting Ferdinand. Hence, the title of a film, *Hell Is Empty* (UK/Czechoslovakia 1966).

14 Full fadom five thy father lies;
Of his bones are coral made;
Those are pearls that were his eyes:
Nothing of him that doth fade,
But doth suffer a sea-change
Into something rich and strange.

I.ii.399. Fadom = fathom. When Ariel sings of a sea-change he does actually mean a change caused by the sea. Now, invariably, the expression is used simply as a grandiloquent and irrelevant way of saying 'change'. *Rich and Strange* was the title of a film (UK 1932) by Alfred Hitchcock.

15 Be not afeard; the isle is full of noises,
Sounds and sweet airs, that give delight, and
    hurt not.

III.ii.133. Caliban. Hence, *The Aisle Is Full of Noises*, title of Michael Coveney's diary of a theatre critic's perambulations round the UK (1994).

1 Our revels now are ended. These our actors,
As I foretold you, were all spirits and
Are melted into air, into thin air ...
And, like this insubstantial pageant faded,
Leave not a rack behind. We are such stuff
As dreams are made on; and our little life
Is rounded with a sleep.

IV.i.148. Prospero. It is definitely 'dreams are made on'
not 'made of' (though Shakespeare did use the 'of' form
elsewhere). So, well done, the writer of *The Guardian* headline (9 May 1988), 'Stuff that dreams are made on'. Rather
less well done, Humphrey Bogart as Sam Spade in *The
Maltese Falcon* (1941): 'What is it?' he is asked before replying with the last line of the picture, 'The stuff that dreams
are made of.' Absolutely no marks to the cast of the
1964 Cambridge Footlights revue, *Stuff What Dreams Are
Made Of.*

2   This rough magic
I here abjure; and, when I have requir'd
Some heavenly music – which even now I do, –
To work mine end upon their senses, that
This airy charm is for, I'll break my staff,
Bury it certain fadoms in the earth,
And, deeper than did ever plummet sound
I'll drown my book.

V.i.49. Prospero. Hence, *This Rough Magic*, title of a 'sus-
penseful novel about British residents on a Greek island'
(1964) by Mary Stewart.

3   O brave new world,
That has such people in't!

V.i.183. Miranda's exclamation. 'Brave new world' has subsequently become a phrase for a future state, particularly
one where progress has produced a nightmarish anti-utopia:
Aldous Huxley used it as the title of his futuristic dystopian
novel in 1932. Nowadays a slightly ironic term for some
new or futuristically exciting aspect of modern life.

TROILUS AND CRESSIDA 1601–2

4 Time hath, my lord, a wallet at his back
Wherein he puts alms for oblivion.

III.iii.145. Ulysses. Hence, *Alms for Oblivion*, title of a novel
sequence (1964–84) by Simon Raven.

TWELFTH NIGHT 1600

5 If music be the food of love, play on,
Give me excess of it, that, surfeiting,
The appetite may sicken, and so die.

I.i.1. Orsino. Hence, the title of Simon Brett's 'Charles Paris'
crime novel, *Sicken and So Die* (1995).

6 O mistress mine, where are you roaming?
... Journeys end in lovers meeting.
What is love? 'Tis not hereafter,
Present mirth hath present laughter.

II.iii.40. Clown's/Feste's song. Hence, *Present Laughter*,
title of a play (1942) by Noël Coward.

7 Dost thou think because thou art virtuous, there
shall be no more cakes and ale?

II.iii.114. Sir Toby Belch to Malvolio. The Arden Shakespeare comments that cakes and ale were 'traditionally
associated with festivity, and disliked by Puritans both on
this account and because of their association with weddings, saints' days, and holy days'. In due course, 'cakes
and ale' became a synonym for enjoyment, as in the expression 'Life isn't all cakes and ale' (or 'beer and skittles', for
that matter).

On 4 May 1876 Francis Kilvert wrote in his diary: 'The
clerk's wife brought out some cakes and ale and pressed
me to eat and drink. I was to have returned to Llysdinam
to luncheon ... but as I wanted to see more of the country
and the people I decided to let the train go by, accept the
hospitality of my hostess and the cakes and ale which life
offered, and walk home quietly in the course of the afternoon' – a neat demonstration of the literal and metaphori-
cal uses of the phrase.

Hence, also, *Cakes and Ale*, the title of a novel (1930) by
W. Somerset Maugham.

8 Come away, come away death,
And in sad cypress let me be laid.

II.iv.51. From the Clown's/Feste's song. Probably referring
to a coffin made of cypress wood, or a shroud of Cyprus
lawn, i.e. linen. Hence, *Sad Cypress*, title of a Hercule Poirot
novel (1940) by Agatha Christie. *Come Away Death* is the
title of a novel (1937) by Gladys Mitchell, who wrote the Mrs
Bradley mysteries.

9 But let concealment, like a worm i'th'bud.
Feed on her damask cheek ...
                    She pin'd in thought,
And with a green and yellow melancholy

She sat like Patience on a monument,
Smiling at grief.

II.iv.112. Viola. Origin of the expression 'like Patience on a monument' for anyone waiting uncomplainingly.

1 But be not afraid of greatness. Some are born great, some achieve greatness, and some have greatness thrust upon 'em.

II.v.144. Malvolio reading from a letter. Compare HELLER 233:4.

2 Daylight and champaign discovers not more!

II.v.160. Malvolio, having finished the letter, exclaiming that its meaning is as clear as daylight. Champaign = flat open country (and not the drink). Other texts have the word as 'champain' and 'champian'. Hence, *Daylight and Champain*, title of a collection of essays (1937) by the historian, G.M. Young.

3 There is no darkness but ignorance.

IV.ii.43. Clown/Feste to Malvolio when he is incarcerated. From the *Independent on Sunday* (27 October 1996): 'Words that, like so many of the Bard's dazzlingly plain throwaways, have somehow ricocheted down the centuries and struck quite unexpected targets. If you look at the statue of Shakespeare in Leicester Square, you will find them carved into the scroll that dangles from his stone hand. If you browse through Ezra Pound's *Pisan Cantos* (written when the poet, like Malvolio, was locked up), you will find the same phrase, charged with rancour and nostalgia, used to evoke Edwardian London. You will not, however, find Feste's maxim in Trevor Nunn's screenplay for *Twelfth Night* ...'

THE TWO GENTLEMEN OF VERONA 1592–3

4 O, how this spring of love resembleth
The uncertain glory of an April day,
Which now shows all the beauty of the sun,
And by and by a cloud takes all away.

I.iii.84. Proteus. Hence, *Uncertain Glory*, title of a film (US 1944). Compare PYM 373:4.

VENUS AND ADONIS 1592–3

5 Who sees his true-love in her naked bed,
Teaching the sheets a whiter hue than white.

Line 397. The possible origin of 'whiter than white', meaning 'of extreme purity, innocence or virtue'.

THE WINTER'S TALE 1611

6 Our ship hath touch'd upon
The deserts of Bohemia.

III.iii.1. Antigonus. A supposed geographical error on Shakespeare's part. Bohemia (now part of the Czech Republic) does not have a coast. However, at certain points in history it *did* have an outlet on the Adriatic.

7 *Exit, pursued by a bear.*

III.iii.58. A famous stage direction. It refers to the fate of Antigonus, who is on the sea coast of Bohemia (see above). Most of Shakespeare's stage directions are additions by later editors, but this one may be original. The bear used could have been a real one (as bear-baiting was common in places adjacent to Shakespeare's theatres) or portrayed by a man in costume.

8 GOOD FREND FOR IESUS SAKE FORBEARE,
TO DIGG THE DUST ENCLOASED HEARE:
BLESTE BE YE MAN [THA]T SPARES THES STONES,
AND CURST BE HE [THA]T MOVES MY BONES.

Inscription on Shakespeare's grave in Holy Trinity church, Stratford-upon-Avon. According to S. Schoenbaum, *William Shakespeare: A Documentary Life* (1975), several 17th-century sources suggest that Shakespeare wrote his own epitaph. However, perhaps the point is rather that he may have *chosen* it rather than *composed* it. By the 19th century, Halliwell Phillips was curtly dismissing this 'wretched doggerel', but James Walter in *Shakespeare's True Life* (1890) was asking, 'Who dares question the words being those of the great dramatist himself?' Walter seemed to accept that because the words were 'there chiselled when the great one was laid in his grave', they must, therefore, have been written by him.

Hesketh Pearson in his biography argues that Shakespeare chose to phrase his wish simply and clearly, and not in the words of a King Lear, because of a very real fear that his remains would be removed.

9 Item I give unto my wife my second best bed with the furniture.

From his will (1616). 'Second best' here means 'next in quality to the first' and need not necessarily suggest that Shakespeare was snubbing his wife with this bequest. Peter Levi, *The Life and Times of William Shakespeare* (1988), has this comment: 'Much crazy speculation has been raised on this small foundation. It is true that most wills provide for widows and this does not, but the reason is obvious. John Hall and Susanna [son-in-law and daughter] were to move into New Place [the Stratford-upon-Avon home] and look after Anne Shakespeare as they were uniquely fitted to do. The "second best bed" was William and Anne's old marriage bed. The grander New Place bed in the best bedroom must go to John Hall and Susanna, but William remembered at the last moment to reserve his wife's bed, in which she no doubt habitually slept, for her own.' Garry O'Connor, *William Shakespeare* (1991), adds: 'Anne had asked for this, which otherwise would have gone to Susanna. A correspondent in *The Times* in 1977 suggests that this is roughly similar to a modern testator who, having disposed of the bulk of his estate, turns to his solicitor and says, "And don't forget to leave Anne the mini."'

William SHARP Scottish novelist and poet (1855–1905)

1 Green is that hill and lonely, set far in a
    shadowy place;
  White is the hunter's quarry, a lost-loved human
    face:
  O hunting heart, shall you find it, with arrow of
    failing breath,
  Led o'er a green hill lonely by the shadowy
    hound of Death?

'The Lonely Hunter' (1896), writing as 'Fiona Macleod'. Hence, *The Hound of Death* (1933), title of a novel by Agatha Christie.

Bernard SHAW Irish playwright and critic (1856–1950)

2 The Devil can quote Shakespeare for his own purposes.

Quoted in *The Treasury of Humorous Quotations*, eds Esar & Bentley (1951). Alluding to SHAKESPEARE 416:2.

3 I often quote myself; it adds spice to my conversation.

Quoted in the same collection. Shaw, with some justification, on a self-quotation habit.

4 England and America are two countries separated by the same language.

Quoted in the same collection and in *Readers' Digest* (by 1942). See WILDE 494:4.

5 A man who never missed an occasion to let slip an opportunity.

Shaw said this of Lord Rosebery, presumably in the 1890s when he was briefly Liberal Prime Minister, though it remains untraced. Robert Rhodes James in *Rosebery* (1963) has the slightly different 'man who never missed a chance

of missing an opportunity', which, he says, expresses the point of view of 'the political extrovert who turns aside with contempt from hesitation, pusillanimity, and doubt'.

6 Oh, you are a very poor soldier – a chocolate cream soldier!

Arms and the Man, Act 1 (1894). Shaw's play was later turned into an operetta known as *The Chocolate Soldier* (New York, 1909 – after the original German *Der Tapfere Soldat* ['brave soldier'], 1908). The story concerns Captain Bluntschli, a Swiss officer, who gets the better of a professional cavalry soldier. As shown here, Shaw's phrase for Bluntschli was, rather, 'the chocolate *cream* soldier'. Ian Fleming, the creator of James Bond, was nicknamed the *chocolate sailor* during the Second World War because as a Commander of the RNVR he never actually went to sea.

7 Titles distinguish the mediocre, embarrass the superior, and are disgraced by the inferior.

Man and Superman (1903). In 'Maxims for Revolutionists', included with the published text. Shaw himself did not accept any titles or honours; he even turned down the Nobel Prize for Literature he was awarded in 1925.

8 He who can, does. He who cannot, teaches.

In the same work. A development of this thought was popular as a graffito (reported, for example, from Middlesex Polytechnic in 1979): '... and those who can't teach lecture on the sociology of education degrees'.

Yet a further development is encompassed by A.B. Ramsay in 'Epitaph on a Syndic' from his *Frondes Salicis* (1935):

No teacher I of boys or smaller fry,
No teacher I of teachers, no, not I.
Mine was the distant aim, the longer reach,
To teach men how to teach men how to teach.

9 Kings are not born: they are made by artificial hallucination. When the process is interrupted by adversity at a critical age, as in the case of Charles II, the subject becomes sane and never completely recovers his kingliness.

In the same work. Sometimes misquoted as 'universal hallucination'. This section, entitled 'Royalty', also includes: 'The Court is the servants' hall of the sovereign'; 'Vulgarity in a king flatters the majority of the nation'; and 'The flunkeyism propagated by the throne is the price we pay for its political convenience.'

1 Wot prawce Selvytion nah? [What price salvation now?]

Major Barbara, Act 2 (1907). See also STALLINGS 441:3.

2 With the single exception of Homer, there is no eminent writer, not even Sir Walter Scott, whom I can despise so entirely as I despise Shakespear when I measure my mind against his ... It would positively be a relief to me to dig him up and throw stones at him.

Dramatic Opinions and Essays, Vol. 2 (1907). Quoting a view already stated in *The Saturday Review* (26 September 1896). Compare the slightly later remark by Frank Harris in *My Life and Loves*, Vol. 2, Chap. 4 (1925): 'I am annoyed whenever I hear Homer, who is not as great as Sir Walter Scott, placed among the first of men.' Robert Graves in *Goodbye To All That*, Chap. 28 (1929), reports Thomas Hardy as dividing the honours evenly: 'His taste in literature was certainly most unexpected. Once, a few years later [than 1920], when [T.E.] Lawrence ventured to say something disparaging about Homer's *Iliad*, he protested: "Oh, but I admire it greatly. Why, it's in the *Marmion* class!" Lawrence at first thought that Hardy was having a little joke.' John Buchan, *Sir Walter Scott*, Chap. 2 (1932), has Buchan calling Scott 'the chief of the later Homeridae'. That perceptive critic the Prince Regent was another who spoke of them in the same breath. As Byron told Scott, in a letter of 6 July 1812, '[the Prince] spoke alternately of Homer and yourself, and seemed well acquainted with both' – quoted in Lockhart, *Life of Walter Scott*, Chap. 24 (1837–8). And for all that, Scott didn't care much for Homer.

3 Dearest liar: I have found you out.

Letter to Mrs Patrick Campbell (4 January 1913), included in *Bernard Shaw and Mrs Patrick Campbell: Their Correspondence* (1952). Mrs Pat had claimed that Shaw had written critically of her, but when he re-read his articles he discovered they were full of praise. Hence, *Dear Liar*, title of a play (1960) by Jerome Kilty, based on the correspondence.

4 What's a five-pound note to you? And what's Eliza to me? ... You give me what I ask you, Governor: not a penny more, and not a penny less.

Pygmalion, Act 2 (1914). Alfred Doolittle to Henry Higgins. *OED2* finds the phrase 'not a penny more' in use by 1931. Before this, it may have been a phrase from market traders' patter. Compare the title of Jeffrey Archer's first novel *Not a Penny More, Not a Penny Less* (1975).

5 *Liza:* My aunt died of influenza: so they said ... But it's my belief (as how) they done the old woman in.

Act 3. The words 'as how' were inserted by Mrs Patrick Campbell in her performances as Eliza Doolittle, and were also incorporated in the 1938 film.

6 *Freddy:* Are you walking across the Park, Miss Doolittle? If so –
Liza: Walk! Not bloody likely. (*Sensation*). I am going in a taxi.

In the same act. Shaw's play is about the conversion of an illiterate, ill-spoken flower girl (Eliza Doolittle) by a professor of phonetics (Henry Higgins). It uses the same theme as part of Tobias Smollett's novel *Peregrine Pickle* (1751), in which Pickle trains a girl and then introduces her into exclusive and elegant circles. From Chap. 95: 'One evening, being at cards with a certain lady, whom she detected in the very fact of unfair conveyance, she taxed her roundly with the fraud, and brought upon herself such a torrent of sarcastic reproof, as overbore all her maxims of caution, and burst open the floodgates of her own natural repartee, twanged off with the appellations of b— and w—, which she repeated with great vehemence ... to the terror of her antagonist and the astonishment of all present: nay, to such an unguarded pitch was she provoked, that starting up, she snapt her fingers, in testimony of disdain, and, as she quitted the room, applied her hand to that part which was the last of her that disappeared, inviting the company to kiss it, by one of its coarsest denominations.'

Here, obviously, is the origin of the celebrated tea-party scene in Act 3 of Shaw's play. Audience anticipation for the first performance in London on Saturday 11 April 1914 had been whipped up by that morning's edition of the *Daily Sketch*: '*PYGMALION* MAY CAUSE SENSATION!! Mr Shaw introduces a certain forbidden word. WILL MRS PATRICK CAMPBELL SPEAK IT? Has the censor stepped in or will the word spread? If he does not forbid it then anything might happen!! It is a word which the *Daily Sketch* cannot possibly print and tonight it is to be uttered on the stage.'

When the phrase was finally uttered, the audience gasped – 'their intake of breath making a sound that could have been mistaken for a protracted hiss', according to Shaw's biographer, Hesketh Pearson (1942). 'This never happened again because all future audiences knew what was coming and roared with laughter.' This laughter often continued for a minute and a quarter, according to the stage manager's stopwatch.

Although the play was well received by the critics, the press rumbled on about the language it used. *The Times* in its review (13 April 1914), said: 'O, greatly daring Mr Shaw!

You will be able to boast you are the first modern dramatist to use this word on the stage! But really, was it worth
while? There is a whole range of forbidden words in the
English language; a little more of your usage and we suppose
that they will be heard, too. And then goodbye to the delights
of really intimate conversation.'

The *Daily Mirror* sought the view of a number of bishops. Sydney Grundy, theatre critic of the *Daily Mail*, said
there was no harm in Shaw's 'incarnadine adverb' when
informed by genius but 'on his pen it is poison'. The Theatrical Managers' Association wrote to Sir Herbert
Beerbohm Tree, who was presenting the play as well as
playing Professor Higgins, saying that a member had complained of the phrase and that 'with a view to retaining
the respect of the public for the theatre' they wanted him
to omit the words. He declined. A revue opened at the
Alhambra shortly afterwards with the title *Not ******
Likely*. In time, the euphemistic alternative 'Not Pygmalion
likely!' emerged.

Shaw concluded: 'By making a fashionable actress use
bad language in a fashionable theatre, I became overnight
more famous than the Pope, the King, the Kaiser and the
Archbishop of Canterbury.'

Pygmalion was filmed with Wendy Hiller in 1938, and
thus the word 'bloody' was heard for the first time in the
cinema. By the time *My Fair Lady* – the musical version –
was filmed in 1964, the shock effect of 'bloody' was so mild
that Eliza was given the line 'Come on, Dover, move your
bloomin' arse!' in the Ascot racing sequence. Which takes
us right back to *Peregrine Pickle* ...

1 The rain in Spain stays mainly in the plains.
   In the same work, 1938 film version only. See also LERNER
   285:3.

2 In Hampshire, Hereford and Hertford,
   Hurricanes hardly ever happen.
   Introduced for the film and adopted for *My Fair Lady*.

3 Where the devil are my slippers, Eliza?
   Last words (spoken by Higgins) in the 1938 film version
   (and of the musical adaptation *My Fair Lady* – in the order
   'Eliza, where the devil are my slippers?'), but not in Shaw's
   original stage text. The intention appears to be for Higgins
   to hint at some romantic interest in Eliza. Shaw always
   opposed this. Even his published text of the film script (1941)
   shuns the line. And although Higgins asks for his slippers
   twice during the course of Act 4 of the original play, the
   words are only once addressed to Eliza.

4 You see things; and you say 'Why?' But I dream
   things that never were; and I say 'Why not?'
   Back to Methuselah, Pt 1, Act 1 (1921). A saying that has often
   wrongly been ascribed to both John and Robert Kennedy
   (because they both used it in numerous political speeches),
   but it is, in fact, from Shaw. In the play, it is spoken by the
   Serpent, in an attempt to seduce Eve. President Kennedy
   quoted it correctly (and acknowledged Shaw) in his address
   to the Irish Dáil (parliament) in Dublin in June 1963.
   Robert's version tended to be: 'Some men see things as they
   are and say "Why?" I dream things that never were and say,
   "Why not?"' In this form it was attributed to Robert (Shaw
   going unmentioned) in the address delivered by Edward
   Kennedy at his brother's funeral in 1968.

   So frequently was the saying invoked by Robert Kennedy
   as a peroration that, on the campaign trail, the words 'As
   George Bernard Shaw once said ...' became a signal for
   reporters to dash for the press bus. Once he forgot to
   conclude with the Shaw quote, according to Arthur M.
   Schlesinger in *Robert Kennedy and His Times* (1979), and
   several reporters missed the bus. On another occasion it
   came on to rain and Kennedy told the crowd: 'It's silly for
   you to be standing in the rain listening to a politician ... As
   George Bernard Shaw once said, "Run for the buses."'

5 [Nobel Prize] money is a lifebelt thrown to a swim-
   mer who has already reached the shore in safety.
   Quoted in Hesketh Pearson, *Lives of the Wits* (1962). Shaw
   was awarded the Nobel Prize for Literature in 1925, but
   refused it. Here he is merely paraphrasing Samuel Johnson's pointed remark to Lord Chesterfield – see JOHNSON
   426:5.

6 All Americans are blind and deaf – and dumb.
   A whopping journalistic misquotation dating from the
   1930s. Shaw *did* meet Helen Keller, the American writer
   who heroically overcame deafness and blindness. According
   to Hesketh Pearson's 1942 biography of Shaw, he rather
   paid her the compliment: 'I wish all Americans were as
   blind as you.'

7 What if the child inherits my beauty and your
   brains?
   There may be some truth in the story that Shaw was once
   approached by a woman who thought herself to be a fine
   physical specimen and suggested that they combine to make
   a baby, saying: 'You have the greatest brain in the world and
   I have the most beautiful body; so we ought to produce the
   most perfect child.' His reply: 'Yes, but fancy if it were born
   with my beauty and your brains?' Alas, this was not said to
   Isadora Duncan or any of the other women who have been

woven into the tale. Hesketh Pearson in *Bernard Shaw* (1942) said the request came from 'a woman in Zurich', though no trace of a letter containing it has ever been found. Pearson's version of the reply was: 'What if the child inherits my body and your brains?'

1 *G.K. Chesterton*: To see you, Mr Shaw, one would think there was a famine in the land.
G.B. Shaw: And looking at you, Mr Chesterton, one would know who to blame.

This celebrated fat man/thin man exchange was the subject of a letter to *The Guardian* from a Mr Robert Turpin of Plymouth (14 May 1985): 'I first heard the story from a great-uncle of mine who knew both Shaw and Chesterton and actually attended the meeting at which the exchange took place.' (If so, the great-uncle was privileged to be one of those rare people to have been present at the cracking of an immortal joke.)

Caution immediately sets in, however – especially as the paper also carried a letter from Peter Black, the journalist, saying he had first encountered the story in Australia involving the portly Prime Minister, Sir Robert Menzies. *PDMQ* (1980) meanwhile, had cast Lord Northcliffe, the well-built press baron, in the Chesterton role.

The most reliable version must surely be that which appears in *Thirty Years With GBS* (1951) by Blanche Patch. Shaw's secretary says, 'One look at you, Mr Shaw, and I know there's famine in the land.' Shaw replies, 'One look at you, *Mr Hitchcock*, and I know who caused it.' This was, of course, Alfred Hitchcock, the film director.

2 The trouble, Mr Goldwyn, is that you are only interested in art and I am only interested in money.

Telegraphed version of the outcome of a conversation between Shaw and the film producer Sam Goldwyn. It appears to have been recounted first in Alva Johnson, *The Great Goldwyn* (1937). It has been said that this witticism was, in fact, the creation of Howard Dietz, but that Shaw approved it.

3 Youth is too precious/important to be wasted on the young.

Attributed in Copeland, *10,000 Jokes, Toasts, & Stories* (1939), in the form '[Youth is] far too good to waste on children.' The *Treasury of Humorous Quotations*, eds Esar & Bentley (1951), has it from Shaw in the form, 'Youth is a wonderful thing; what a crime to waste it on children.' But where is it to be found in all of Shaw?

In the film *It's a Wonderful Life* (US 1946), a proverbial-sounding line is uttered: 'Youth is wasted on the wrong people.' Later, in Sammy Cahn's lyrics for the song 'The

Second Time Around' (1960; music by Jimmy Van Heusen), there is what is presumably no more than a quotation:

It's that second time you hear your love song sung,
Makes you think perhaps, that
Love like youth is wasted on the young.

4 The question of who are the best people to take charge of children is a very difficult one; but it is quite certain that the parents are the very worst.

Everybody's Political What's What? (1944). In fact, Shaw is quoting William Morris, the designer. Compare BELL 59:2.

5 We don't stop playing because we grow old, we grow old because we stop playing.

Unverified. Quoted in *The Independent* (29 October 1996). Another version: 'People do not cease to play because they grow old, people grow old because they cease to play' – promotional material for book, *Serious Play: A Leisure Wellness Guidebook* (1994) by Martin Kimeldorf.

6 A dramatic critic is a man who leaves no turn unstoned.

Attributed in *The New York Times* (5 November 1950). According to E. Short, *Fifty Years of Vaudeville*, Arthur Wimperis, the British librettist and screenwriter (1874–1953), said of a vaudeville show: 'My dear fellow, a unique evening! I wouldn't have left a turn unstoned.' Hence, *No Turn Unstoned* (1982), title of a book of 'the worst ever theatrical reviews' compiled by Diana Rigg. However, she ascribes it to the Revd Joseph McCulloch in the form, 'A critic is a man who leaves no turn unstoned.'

See also CAMPBELL 120:5–6; FRASER 202:2; LENIN 282:7; WILDE 494:4.

(Sir) Hartley SHAWCROSS (later Lord Shawcross)
English jurist and Labour politician (1902–2003)

7 We are the masters now!

It might have seemed in poor taste for a Labour minister to crow this. After all, it had been into the mouth of an imperialist that George Orwell had earlier put these words in his novel *Burmese Days* (1934): 'No natives in this Club! It's by constantly giving way over small things like that that we've ruined the Empire ... The only possible policy is to treat 'em like the dirt they are ... We've got to hang together and say, "We are the masters, and you beggars ... keep your place."'

So quite why Shawcross, Attorney-General in Britain's first postwar Labour Government, did say something like it bears some examination. For a start, it was not said, as one might expect, on the day new Labour MPs swarmed into the House of Commons just after their sweeping election victory in 1945. It was said on 2 April 1946, almost nine months later. Then again, what Shawcross said was, 'We are the masters at the moment' – though understandably the more pungent variant has passed into the language. A look at *Hansard* reveals precisely why he chose this form of words. He was winding up for the Government in the third reading of the Trade Disputes and Trade Unions Bill and drew attention to what he saw as the Conservative Opposition's lack of support for a measure it had promised to introduce if it won the election:

> [We made this an issue at the election] when he invited us to submit this matter to the verdict of the people ... I realize that the right hon. Member for Woodford [Winston Churchill] is such a master of the English language that he has put himself very much in the position of Humpty-Dumpty in *Alice* ... 'When I use a word,' said Humpty-Dumpty, 'it means just what I intend it to mean, and neither more nor less.' 'But,' said Alice, 'the question is whether you can make a word mean different things.' 'Not so,' said Humpty-Dumpty, 'the question is which is to be the master. That's all.'
>
> We are the masters at the moment, and not only at the moment, but for a very long time to come, and as hon. Members opposite are not prepared to implement the pledge which was given by their leader in regard to this matter at the general election, we are going to implement it for them.

At the end of the debate, the votes cast were: Ayes 349; Noes 182. When the House met again after the 1950 general election – at which the Conservatives just failed to oust Labour – Churchill commented: 'I like the appearance of these benches better than what we had to look at during the last four and a half years. It is certainly refreshing to feel, at any rate, that this is a Parliament where half the nation will not be able to ride rough-shod over the other half ... I do not see the Attorney-General in his place, but no one will be able to boast "We are the masters now."'

So, by this time, the popular version of the words had already emerged. Compare BURKE 109:11.

Charles SHAW-LEFEVRE (Viscount Eversley)
English lawyer and politician (1794–1888)

1 What is that fat gentleman in such a passion about?

As a child, on hearing Charles James Fox speak in the House of Commons. Quoted in G.W.E. Russell, *Collections and Recollections*, Chap. 12 (1898). Compare *PUNCH* 372:1.

John SHEFFIELD, 1st Duke of Buckingham and Normanby English poet (1648–1721)

2 Foolish and false, ill-natur'd and ill-bred.

'Essay Upon Satire', published anonymously in 1679–80. Sheffield was Dryden's patron and Dryden was mistakenly thought to be the author by the Earl of Rochester's heavies, and they gave him a going over for his pains. The line above still sometimes appears in this form in editions of Dryden's works.

What would appear to be Sheffield's original occurs in a passage about Charles II and his mistresses:

> While sauntring Charles, between so mean a brace,
> Meets with dissembling still in either Place,
> Affected humour, or a painted face.
> Was ever Prince by two at once misled,
> Foolish and false, ill-natur'd and ill-bred.

Percy Bysshe SHELLEY English poet (1792–1822)

3 How wonderful is Death,
Death and his brother Sleep!

Queen Mab, Canto 9, line 1 (1813).

4 Many a green isle needs must be
In the deep wide sea of misery,
Or the mariner, worn and wan,
Never thus could voyage on.

'Lines Written in the Euganean Hills' (1818). Palgrave's notes to *The Golden Treasury* delicately put it: 'The leading idea of this beautiful description of a day's landscape in Italy is expressed with *an obscurity not infrequent with its author*' (my italics).

5 The winds of heaven mix for ever
With a sweet emotion.

'Love's Philosophy' (written 1819). The phrase 'wind(s) of heaven' might seem to suggest the movements and changes in our lives, as directed by heaven, but it may simply be poetic usage for 'winds' rather than religious. Shakespeare, *Hamlet* (I.ii.141), has: 'He might not beteem the winds of heaven.' From George Eliot, *Silas Marner* (1861): 'Life ... when it is spread over a various surface, and breathed on variously by the multitudinous currents from the winds of heaven to the thoughts of men.' Eliot is also quoted as having said in 1840: 'O how luxuriously joyous to have the wind of heaven blow on one after being stived in a human atmosphere.' *The Wind of Heaven* was a drama by Emlyn Williams, first performed in 1945.

1 Hail to thee, blithe spirit!
Bird thou never wert.
'To a Skylark' (1819). Hence, *Blithe Spirit*, title of Noël
Coward's comedy (1941; film UK 1945) about a spiritualist.

2 If winter comes, can spring be far behind?
'Ode to the West Wind' (1819). Hence, *If Winter Comes*, title
of a film (US 1948) based on a novel by A.S.M. Hutchinson.

3 And yours I see is coming down.
The Cenci, V.iv.162 (1819). In fact, referring to hair.

4 'My name is Ozymandias, king of kings:
Look on my works, ye Mighty, and despair!'
'Ozymandias' (1819). Words written on the pedestal of a
tyrant's monument in the desert – emphasizing that even
tyrants and power do not last forever.

5 I met murder on the way
He had a mask like Castlereagh ...
'The Mask of Anarchy', St. 2 (1819). See BYRON 116:5.

6 O world! o life! o time!
On whose last steps I climb,
Trembling at that where I had stood before;
When will return the glory of your prime?
No more – Oh, never more!
'A Lament' (1821). Thomas Hardy thought this one of the
finest passages in all English poetry.

7 The cemetery is an open space among the ruins,
covered in winter with violets and daisies. It might
make one in love with death, to think that one
should be buried in so sweet a place.
On Keats's burial place in the English cemetery in Rome.
Preface to *Adonais* (1821) – his elegy on the death of Keats,
and probably alluding to 'half in love with easeful Death'
from Keats's 'Ode to a Nightingale'. Shelley's own remains
were to be buried there, in due course, not far away from
his fellow poet's.

8 I weep for Adonais – he is dead!
O, weep for Adonais! though our tears
Thaw not the frost which binds so dear a head.
... Peace, peace! He is not dead, he doth not sleep –
He hath awakened from the dream of life.
In the same poem. Quoted by Mick Jagger of the Rolling
Stones at a concert in Hyde Park, London, following the
death of his colleague, Brian Jones (July 1969).

Philip Henry SHERIDAN American general (1831–88)

9 The only good Indian is a dead Indian.
Sheridan, mostly a cavalry commander on the Federal side
in the American Civil War, is supposed to have said this at
Fort Cobb in January 1869, but exhaustive study by Wolfgang Mieder in *The Journal of American Folklore*, No. 106
(1993), has shown that this particular racial slur may already
have been proverbial and may have been wished on Sheridan unjustly. For example, the previous year, during a debate
on an 'Indian Appropriation Bill' in the House of Representatives (28 May 1868), James Michael Cavanaugh
(1823–79), a congressman from Montana, had said: 'I will
say that I like an Indian better dead than living. I have never
in my life seen a good Indian (and I have seen thousands)
except when I have seen a dead Indian.'

Mieder adds that, though Sheridan was known as a
bigot and Indian hater, Charles Nordstrom's account of
the Fort Cobb incident in 1869 is of questionable authenticity: 'A chief of the Comanches, on being presented to
Sheridan, desired to impress the General in his favor, and
striking himself a resounding blow on the breast, he managed to say: "Me, Toch-a-way; me good Injun." A quizzical
smile lit up the General's face as he set those standing by
in a roar by saying: "The only good Indians I ever saw were
dead."'

Sheridan repeatedly denied having made any such a
statement, but, whatever the case, an imperishable formula
had been devised: 'The only good X is a dead X' is still with
us.

Richard Brinsley SHERIDAN English dramatist and
politician (1751–1816)

10 I was struck all of a heap.
The Duenna, Act 2, Sc. 2 (1775). Not, in fact, an original
phrase for 'astounded'. 'Struck of a heap' was current by
1741, and Shakespeare has 'all on a heap'.

11 Burghley's nod.
Nothing to do with the actual Lord Burghley, Elizabeth I's
chief minister. Within Sheridan's play *The Critic* (1779) is a
mock-tragedy on the Spanish Armada. In Act 3 Sc. 1, Burghley is represented as too preoccupied with affairs of state
to be able to say anything, so he shakes his head and the
character Puff explains what he means: 'Why by that shake
of the head, he gave you to understand that even though
they had more justice in their cause and wisdom in their
measures – yet, if there was not a greater spirit shown on
the part of the people – the country would at last fall a sacrifice to the hostile ambition of the Spanish monarchy ...'
'The devil! – did he mean all that by shaking his head?'

'Every word of it – if he shook his head as I taught him.'

Hence, also, the expression, 'To be as significant as the shake of Lord Burghley's head.'

1 He is the very pineapple of politeness!

The Rivals, Act 3, Sc. 3 (1775). Mrs Malaprop speaking – after whom 'malapropisms' are called. 'Her select words [are] so ingeniously *misapplied*, without being *mispronounced*' (Act 2, Sc. 2). She was not the first character to have such an entertaining affliction: Shakespeare's Dogberry and Mistress Quickly are similarly troubled. After the French phrase *mal à propos* ('awkward, inopportune'). In this instance, she is attempting to say 'the very pinnacle of politeness' (but see GOLDSMITH 217:3).

2 If I reprehend any thing in this world, it is the use of my oracular tongue, and a nice derangement of epitaphs!

In the same play, act and scene. Hence, *A Nice Derangement of Epitaphs*, title of a novel (1988) by Ellis Peters, about a medieval monk detective, Father Cadfael.

3 A man may surely be allowed to take a glass of wine by his own fireside.

On being found drinking a glass of wine in the street, when watching the Drury Lane Theatre, which he owned, burning down (24 February 1809). Reported in T. Moore, *Life of Sheridan* (1825).

William T. SHERMAN American general (1820–91)

4 Hold the fort, for I am coming.

The phrase 'hold the fort' has two meanings: 'Look after this place while I'm away' and 'Hang on, relief is at hand.' In the second sense, there is a specific origin. In the American Civil War, General Sherman signalled words to this effect to General John M. Corse at the Battle of Allatoona, Georgia (5 October 1864). What he actually semaphored from Keneshaw Mountain was: 'Sherman says hold fast. We are coming' (*Mencken*, 1942) or 'Hold out. Relief is coming' (*Bartlett*, 1980).

The phrase became popularized in its present form as the first line of a hymn or gospel song written by Philip Paul Bliss in about 1870 ('Ho, My Comrades, See the Signal!' in *The Charm*). This was introduced to the British Isles by Moody and Sankey during their evangelical tour of 1873 (and not written by them, as is sometimes supposed):

'Hold the fort, for I am coming,'
Jesus signals still;
Wave the answer back to heaven,
'By thy grace we will.'

More recently, perhaps thanks to a pun on 'union' (as in the American 'Union' and as in 'trade union'), the song has been adapted as a trade union song in Britain:

Hold the fort, for we are coming
Union men be strong
Side by side keep pressing onward.
Victory will come.

5 War is hell.

All he may have said in a speech at Columbus, Ohio (11 August 1880) was: 'There is many a boy here today who looks on war as all glory, but, boys, it is all hell.'

6 I will not accept if nominated, and will not serve if elected.

Message to the Republican Convention in 1884, sent by telegraph to General Henderson when Sherman was being urged to stand as the Republican candidate for the presidency. This version was recalled by Sherman's son in an addendum to his father's *Memoirs*, 4th edn (1891). Perhaps most usually rendered in the form: 'If nominated, I will not run. If elected, I will not serve.' Sometimes, the message is extended to: 'If asked I will not stand. If drafted I will not run. If elected I will not serve.'

R.C. SHERRIFF English playwright (1896–1975)

7 *Journey's End.*

The title of Sherriff's play (1929), set in the trenches of the First World War, might seem to nod towards Shakespeare – 'Journeys end in lovers meeting' (*Twelfth Night*, II.iii.44) or 'Here is my journey's end' (*Othello*, V.ii.268) – or towards Dryden, 'The world's an inn, and death the journey's end' ('Palamon and Arcite'). But it is impossible to be certain. In his autobiography, *No Leading Lady* (1968), Sherriff wrote of the titles he rejected, like 'Suspense' and 'Waiting', and then adds: 'One night I was reading a book in bed. I got to a chapter that closed with the words: "It was late in the evening when we came at last to our Journey's End." The last two words sprang out as the ones I was looking for. Next night I typed them on a front page for the play, and the thing was done.' He does not say what the book was. It has also been reported that Sherriff once explained that, in need of a title, he saw an advertisement for a whisky that proclaimed, 'Have a dram at your journey's end ...'

George SHULTZ American Republican politician (1920–)

8 Don't just do something, stand there.

Objecting to government meddling, in a speech (1970) as Labor Secretary, quoted in *Safire* (1978). An amusing reversal of the modern proverb (dating from the 1940s and perhaps from the services), 'Don't just stand there, do something!' In the Walt Disney cartoon version of *Alice In Wonderland* (US 1951), the White Rabbit says, 'Don't just do something, stand there!' In *Newsweek* (23 September 1985), Clint Eastwood was quoted as saying: 'My old drama coach used to say: "Don't just do something, stand there." Gary Cooper wasn't afraid to do nothing.' This has also been attributed to Peter Ustinov, chiding a Method actor who was being tiresome.

See also LEE 281:6.

Walter SICKERT German-born English painter (1860–1942)

1 Come again when you can't stay so long.

As a young man, Denton Welch paid a visit to Sickert, and later wrote a description of the oddities he had encountered. The great man persecuted and terrified him and, during tea, danced in front of him wearing boots such as deep-sea divers wear ... 'to see how Denton would react to the experience' (in Edith Sitwell's phrase). As Welch left the house, Sickert said the above to him. Welch's 'Sickert at St Peter's' appeared in *Horizon*, Vol. 6, No. 32 (1942). In *Taken Care of* (1965), Edith Sitwell comments on the article, but gives the tag as 'Come again – when you have a little less time'. Either way, this farewell was not originated by Sickert. Indeed, Welch ends his article by saying, 'And at these words a strange pang went through me, for it was what my father had always said as he closed the book, when I had finished my bread and butter and milk, and it was time for bed.'

(Sir) Philip SIDNEY English soldier and poet (1554–86)

2 Thy necessity is yet greater than mine.

Wounded at the Battle of Zutphen (1586), Sidney was 'thirsty with excess of bleeding' and called for something to drink. As he was putting the bottle to his lips, he saw a wounded soldier who eyed it enviously. 'Which Sir Philip perceiving, took the bottle from his head, before he drank, and delivered it to the poor man with these words' – a story reported by Fulke Greville, Lord Brooke, *Life of Sir Philip Sidney* (1652).

3 A tale which holdeth children from play, and old men from the chimney corner.

One of the quotations used to promote the Everyman's Library series of classic reprints. It is from *The Defense of Poetry* (1595): 'With a tale forsooth he [the poet] cometh unto you, with a tale which ... ' Compare ANONYMOUS 15:1; MILTON 322:8.

Emmanuel Joseph SIEYÈS French prelate and revolutionary leader (1748–1836)

4 *J'ai vécu* [I lived = survived].

When the Abbé Sieyès, who played an important part in the French Revolution and then lapsed into 'philosophic silence', was asked in about 1795 what he had done during the Reign of Terror, this was his reply. Recorded by 1836.

Simone SIGNORET French film actress (1921–85)

5 *Nostalgia Isn't What It Used To Be.*

Title of autobiography (1978). From a graffito chalked up on a wall in New York City. As 'Nostalgia ain't what it used to be', the remark has been attributed to the American novelist Peter de Vries.

Georges SIMENON Belgian novelist (1903–89)

6 I have made love to ten thousand women.

Simenon's best-known remark arose parenthetically in an interview *he* was conducting with an old friend Federico Fellini to publicize the latter's new film *Casanova*. Not in a calculated, premeditated or publicity-seeking way, he suddenly said: 'You know, Fellini, I think that in my life I have been even more of a Casanova than you. I did the sum a year or two ago and since the age of 13 and a half I have had 10,000 women. It was not at all a vice, I suffer from no sexual vice, but I have a need to communicate [*J'ai eu 10,000 femmes depuis l'âge de 13 ans et demi. Ce n'était pas du tout un vice. Je n'ai aucun vice sexuel, mais j'avais besoin de communiquer*].' And even the 8000 prostitutes who must be included in this total of 10,000 women were human beings, female human beings.' The interview was published in *L'Express* (21 February 1977) and the claim attracted worldwide publicity. Later, his second wife Denyse said: 'The true figure is no more than twelve hundred' – *The Sunday Times* (20 February 1983). Patrick Marnham in *The Man Who Wasn't Maigret* (1992) calls this 'Simenon's last publicity coup ... and in some ways his greatest coup of all'.

Guy SIMON English writer (1944–)

7 Jimmy Carter had the air of a man who had never taken any decisions in his life. They had always taken him.

In *The Sunday Times* (5 June 1978). Compare Pooh's words from A.A. Milne, *The House at Pooh Corner*, Chap. 9 (1928): 'Because Poetry and Hums aren't things which you get, they're things which get *you*. And all you can do is to go where they can find you'; a letter (4 April 1864) from Abraham Lincoln to A.G. Hodges: 'I claim not to have controlled events, but confess plainly that events have controlled me'. Compare also: '[*As It Happened*] is a good title [for Clement Attlee's autobiography]. Things happened to him. He never *did* anything' – Aneurin Bevan, said to have been quoted in Michael Foot, *Aneurin Bevan*, Vol. 2 (1973).

Paul SIMON American singer and songwriter (1942–)

1 Like a bridge over troubled water,
I will ease your mind.

Song, 'Bridge Over Troubled Water' (1970) by the pop group Simon and Garfunkel. It sounds positively biblical – but although waters are troubled in Psalm 46:3 and John 5:7, the word 'bridge' occurs nowhere in the Bible. In fact, the phrase may have been influenced by 'I'll be a bridge over deep water if you trust my name', spoken by the Revd Claude Jeter, lead singer of the Swan Silvertones gospel group in 'O Mary Don't You Weep'.

2 The mother and child reunion is only a motion away.

Song, 'Mother and Child Reunion' (1972). Professor Simon Frith of the University of Strathclyde confidently stated in *The Independent* (22 January 1993) that this was a reference to abortion. Lesley Bennett responded the following day: 'Paul Simon told me (in 1968 or 1969) that "Mother and Child Reunion" was the name of a dish he had eaten in Chinatown in San Francisco. The dish was a combination of chicken with egg; the reunion, presumably, happened when they were eaten and digested together.'

3 Still Crazy After All These Years.

Song and album title (1975). Hence, presumably, the title of the film *Still Crazy* (US/UK 1998).

SIMONIDES Greek poet (?556–468BC)

4 Go, tell the Spartans, thou who passest by,
That here obedient to their laws we lie.

Quoted in Herodotus, *Histories*, Bk 7. Another translation: 'Go tell the Spartans, you who read: / We took their orders, and are dead.' Hence, *Go Tell the Spartans*, title of film (US 1978). See also RAYMOND 377:2.

George R. SIMS English journalist and playwright (1847–1922)

5 It is Christmas Day in the Workhouse.
And the cold bare walls are bright
With garlands of green and holly,
And the place is a pleasant sight.

The poem 'In the Workhouse – Christmas Day' (1879)

became a popular late-Victorian recitation. It tells of a pauper rising up to challenge the 'guardians' who have come to watch the Christmas feast. He chides them for turning away a dying woman the previous year – his wife. Nowadays it is probably better known as the result of several parodies. One from the First World War (and included in the stage show *Oh What a Lovely War*, 1963) goes:

It was Christmas day in the cookhouse,
The happiest day of the year,
Men's hearts were full of gladness
And their bellies full of beer,
When up spoke Private Shorthouse,
His face as bold as brass,
Saying, 'We don't want your Christmas pudding
You can stick it up your ...'

Tidings of comfort and joy, comfort and joy,
Oh, tidings of comfort and joy!

Hence, the further version performed by the music-hall comedian Billy Bennett (died 1942).

It was Christmas Day in the cookhouse,
The troops had all gone to bed,
None of them had any Christmas pudding
'Cause the sergeant had done what they said.

(Dame) Edith SITWELL English poet (1887–1964)

6 Love is not changed by Death,
And nothing is lost and all in the end is harvest.

'Eurydice' (1940). Hence, *All In the End is Harvest*, title of an 'anthology for those who grieve' (1984), edited by Agnes Whitaker in association with Cruse Bereavement Care.

See also HERACLITUS 236:5.

(Sir) Osbert SITWELL English writer (1892–1969)

7 Great Morning.

The title of one of his volumes of memoirs (1947) may derive from fox-hunting. Compare Shakespeare, *Troilus and Cressida* (IV.iii.1): 'It is great morning; and the hour prefix'd / For her delivery to this valiant Greek'; and *Cymbeline* (IV.ii.61): 'It is great morning' – in both of which cases, the meaning is 'broad daylight'. Compare also the title of J.B. Priestley's 1946 novel, *Bright Day*.

B.F. SKINNER American psychologist (1904–90)

8 Education is what survives when what has been learned has been forgotten.

In *New Scientist* (21 May 1964). There is a much earlier formulation of this thought: 'Education is what survives when we have forgotten all that we have been taught' – George Savile, Marquess of Halifax (1633–95), according to *The Treasury of Humorous Quotations*, eds Esar & Bentley (1951).

Christopher SMART English poet (1722–71)

1 He *walks* as if he had fouled his small-clothes, and *looks* as if he smelt it.

Said about Thomas Gray, the poet. Quoted in Christopher Devlin, *Poor Kit Smart* (1961), from *Facetiae Cantabrigienses*, which appears to have been some kind of 19th-century Cambridge University rag. Compare from a letter written by Sir Walter Scott (7 September 1822) on a speech delivered by the Duke of Hamilton: 'He spoke as if he were b[eshit]t / And looked as if he smelt it.'

Alfred E. SMITH American politician (1873–1944)

2 Nobody shoots at Santa Claus.

In American politics, this is sometimes said about the folly of attacking government benefit programmes. Former Governor Smith said in 1933: 'No sane local official who has hung up an empty stocking over the municipal fireplace is going to shoot Santa Claus just before a hard Christmas.' Later Santa Claus came to represent the free lunch, the government handout, the something-for-nothing – and again, any politician had to take his courage in both hands to knock it.

3 No matter how thin you slice it, it's still baloney.

Said by Smith about Roosevelt's New Deal during campaign speeches in 1936. Roosevelt had supported him in 1928, but they fell out when Roosevelt himself ran for the presidency. *PDMQ* (1980), on the other hand, has Brendan Gill, *Here at the New Yorker* (1975), ascribing the remark to Rube Goldberg. Clare Booth Luce, in a speech to the House of Representatives (9 February 1943), said: 'Much of what Mr [H.G.] Wallace calls his global thinking is, no matter how you slice it, still globaloney.'

4 The kiss of death.

On William Randolph Hearst's support for Governor Al Smith's opponent, Ogden Mills. *Safire* (1978) defines the political use of the phrase as 'unwelcome support from an unpopular source, occasionally engineered by the opposition'. The 'kiss of death' derives from the kiss of betrayal given by Judas to Christ, which foreshadowed the latter's death. In the Mafia, too, a kiss from the boss is an indication that your time is up. Compare *Kiss of Death*, the title of a gangster film (US 1947).

In Britain, Winston Churchill used the phrase in the House of Commons on 16 November 1948. Nationalization and all its methods were a 'murderous theme'; the remarks of Government spokesman about the control of raw materials, 'about as refreshing to the minor firms as the kiss of death'.

See also ROOSEVELT 386:2.

Bessie SMITH American blues singer (1894–1937)

5 Any Woman's Blues.

Title of a song (?1929). Hence, title of a novel (1990) by Erica Jong.

Edward SMITH English sea captain (died 1912)

6 Be British, boys, be British.

Smith's reputed last words were said to his crew some time in the hours between the *Titanic* hitting the iceberg and his going down with the ship. Michael Davie in *The Titanic: The Full Story of the Tragedy* (1986) describes the evidence for this as 'flimsy', but obviously the legend was well established by 1914 when the statue to him in Lichfield was erected. It has 'Be British' as part of the inscription. The line is not spoken in the film *A Night to Remember* (UK 1958) nor mentioned in Walter Lord's book (1956), upon which the film was based. However, in the 1976 illustrated edition, a page from a 1912 edition of *The Sphere* is reproduced. It is headed: '"BE BRITISH": The Last Words of the "Titanic's" Captain.' See also WRIGHT 508:4.

F.E. SMITH (1st Earl of Birkenhead) British Conservative politician and lawyer (1872–1930)

7 *Judge*: You are extremely offensive, young man. *Smith*: As a matter of fact, we both are, and the only difference between us is that I am trying to be, and you can't help it.

In 2nd Earl of Birkenhead, *The Earl of Birkenhead* (1933). One can hardly believe that Smith really said some of the things he is supposed to have said to judges. If there is any truth in this story – as in the two following – one suspects it was polished up by Smith in the re-telling.

8 Mr George Robey is the Darling of the music-halls, m'lud.

To Mr Justice Darling who had asked, as judges do, who George Robey the comedian was. Quoted in A.E. Wilson, *The Prime Minister of Mirth* (1956).

1 I should rather say they [the Liberals] were begotten by Chinese slavery out of passive resistance, by a rogue sire out of a dam that roared.

Maiden speech in the House of Commons (12 March 1906). The last phrase would seem to have been one of the bits that Smith added to what he actually said in the House when he came to publish his speeches, because it does not appear in *Hansard*.

2 The world continues to offer glittering prizes to those who have stout hearts and sharp swords.

Rectorial address at Glasgow University (7 November 1923) – in which he suggested that the only way to preserve the peace was to prepare for war. His subject was 'Idealism in International Politics'. John Campbell in his biography of Birkenhead (1983) comments that 'for ever after, his career was seen, as it still is, as exemplifying the single-minded pursuit of "glittering prizes", from cups and scholarships to office, wealth and fame. This was not at all the context in which F.E. coined the phrase.' Campbell states additionally that there were other instances of Smith using the phrase – 'but it seems clear from [an earlier] Montreal speech that F.E. was neither plagiarizing not consciously coining an epigram'. To the Canadian Bar Association at Montreal he had said (3 September 1923): 'The glittering counter of world-dominion ... The world still holds precious and incalculable prizes for those who have the will to conquer and the manhood to die.'

Hence, *The Glittering Prizes*, the title of a BBC TV drama series (1976) by Frederic Raphael, about the fortunes of a group of Cambridge graduates.

According to Anthony Powell, the phrase occurs in *The Education of Henry Adams* (1918), and in *OED2* there are citations from F. Arnold, *Our Bishops and Deans* (1875), and from Bentley, *Rem. Sisc. Free-think* (1713).

Of Sir Samuel Hoare:

3 [He] looked as though he was descended from a long line of maiden aunts.

Attributed remark. J.A. Cross's biography of Hoare (1977) complicates this attribution: 'One of his lecturers was the distinguished medieval historian Reginald Lane-Poole of Magdalen ... Hoare later recalled that, according to the contemporary Oxford gossip, Lane-Poole was thought to have "descended through a long line of maiden aunts". Perhaps some of the scholar's passion for academic precision rubbed off on to Hoare for this was the very phrase which was applied to him by a ministerial colleague of the 1930s, Lord Birkenhead (F.E. Smith) ... Hoare, with becoming modesty, later admitted that he thought the maiden aunt gibe "not inaptly applied to me".' But the matter doesn't end there.

Elizabeth Falkner found this in John Farrow, *The Story of Thomas More*, Chap. 4 (1954): 'Holbein shows [More] long-nosed and thin-lipped, cadaverous, and somewhat bland in expression ... He had pale blue eyes and, as Lindsay in his famed book on the Reformation remarks, "the dainty hands, and general primness of his appearance" suggested descent "from a long line of maiden aunts".' This presumably refers to Thomas M. Lindsay's noted book, *The Reformation* (1907). The jibe has been applied to others, including the poet A.E. Housman.

John Alexander SMITH English philosopher (1863–1939)

4 Nothing that you will learn in the course of your studies will be of the slightest possible use to you in after life – save only this – that if you work hard and intelligently you should be able to detect *when a man is talking rot*, and that, in my view, is the main, if not the sole, purpose of education.

Opening a lecture course (1914) as Waynflete Professor of Moral and Metaphysical Philosophy at Oxford. The only source for this quotation is Harold Macmillan's article 'Oxford Remembered' in *The Times* (18 October 1975).

Logan Pearsall SMITH American writer (1865–1946)

5 An improper mind is a perpetual feast.

Afterthoughts (1931). As 'a filthy mind is a continual feast' this has also been ascribed to Edward Heron-Allen and Vyvyan Holland, respectively acquaintance of and son of Oscar Wilde. In John G. Murray's *A Gentleman Publisher's Commonplace Book* (1996) there is a version '*from* [note rather than *by*] Osbert Lancaster' with 'perpetual feast'. There is little reason to doubt that Smith was the originator, however.

6 Thank heavens, the sun has gone in, and I don't have to go out and enjoy it.

These are sometimes quoted as though they were Logan Pearsall Smith's last (dying) words – as in *A Dictionary of Famous Quotations* (1962), for example. They are not, though the misunderstanding is understandable. They appear in 'Last Words' in *All Trivia* (1933). Smith did not die until 1946 when, according to James Lees-Milne, *Caves of Ice* (1983), his actual last words were, 'I must telephone to the Pope-Hennesseys.'

Samuel Francis SMITH American clergyman and poet
(1808–95)

1 My country, 'tis of thee,
Sweet land of liberty,
Of thee I sing:
Land where my fathers died,
Land of the pilgrims' pride,
From every mountain-side
Let freedom ring.

'America' (1832). Hence, *Of Thee I Sing* was the title of a musical (1931) by Gershwin/Gershwin/Kaufman/Ryskind, about the US presidency; the title song was called 'Of Thee I Sing, Baby'. Smith's verse is sung to the tune of the British national anthem. This verse was quoted by Martin Luther King just before the peroration of his 'I have a dream' speech (1963).

Stevie SMITH English poet (1902–71)

2 *A Good Time Was Had By All.*

Title of a collection of her poems (1937). Eric Partridge asked her where she had taken the phrase from and she duly replied: from parish magazines, where reports of church picnics or social evenings invariably ended with the phrase.

3 Nobody heard him, the dead man,
But still he lay moaning:
He was much further out than you thought
And not waving but drowning.

'Not Waving, But Drowning' (1957). Hence, the modern proverbial expression used to describe any sort of situation where a gesture may be misinterpreted. When Hugh Whitemore's play *Stevie* opened in London (1977), a critic wrote that any poet 'who could encapsulate the whole irony of existence in a poem's title' deserved more than our trifling attention.

Sydney SMITH English clergyman, essayist and wit
(1771–1845)

4 If you choose to represent the various parts in life by holes upon a table, of different shapes, – some circular, some triangular, some square, some oblong, – and the persons acting these parts by bits of wood of similar shapes, we shall generally find that the triangular person has got into the square hole, and a square person has squeezed himself into the round hole.

Sketches of Moral Philosophy, Lecture 9 (1804). An early formulation of the 'square peg in a round hole' idea, meaning 'someone badly suited to his job or position'. The more familiar phrase was known by 1836. James Agate in *Ego 5* (1942) writes: 'Will somebody please tell me the address of the Ministry for Round Pegs in Square Holes?' Mark English commented (2002): 'Some light is thrown on this by Scott's *The Pirate*, Chap. 4 (1821): "A laughing philosopher, the Democritus of our day, once, in a moral lecture, compared human life to a table pierced with a number of holes, each of which has a pin made exactly to fit it, but which pins being stuck in hastily, and without selection, chance leads to the most awkward mistakes. 'For how often do we see,' the orator pathetically concluded, – 'how often, I say, do we see the round man stuck into the three-cornered hole!' This new illustration of the vagaries of fortune set every one present into convulsions of laughter, excepting one fat alderman, who seemed to make the case his own, and insisted that it was no jesting matter." The laughing philosopher is plainly Sydney Smith, so of the two earliest usages known one refers specifically back to the other. I should say that Smith's, which you cautiously only call "an early formulation", looks like the actual origin of the phrase. But how does a work of moral philosophy put a phrase into the language, as it apparently was by 1836? Well, Scott's novel would have been quite capable of getting it into circulation more quickly than anything else I can think of.'

5 My idea of heaven is eating *pâté de foie gras* to the sound of trumpets.

The source usually given for this famous remark is Hesketh Pearson, *The Smith of Smiths*, Chap. 10 (1934). *ODQ* (1979), citing Pearson, put it as ' — 's idea of heaven … ', as though Smith were quoting another. By 1992 *ODQ* was putting it in Smith's own mouth. In fact, Pearson's version is quite clearly '*His* idea of heaven …', without saying whose. *Bartlett*, although managing to include 25 of his sayings, does not include the quotation in any form.

What we have here is quite clearly *not* Smith's own conception of bliss. Although he was by far the wittiest clergyman of the 19th century and possibly of all time, he was certainly not frivolous in matters of religion. Indeed, he proudly claimed never to have made jokes on that subject.

The whole matter is neatly sorted out by Alan Bell in his short biography, *Sydney Smith* (1980): 'Probably the joke was made more than once, just as he preached a good sermon several times … [the form] "—s idea of heaven" was Saba's [his daughter and biographer, Lady Holland's] suggestion to the editor of *Recollections of the Table-Talk of Samuel Rogers* (1887), and it seems to have been made not merely to protect the reputation of a clergyman from having made humorous speculations about the hereafter. The remark is surely best applied to Sydney's friend and fellow-wit, Henry Luttrell, one of the best-known gourmets of the period, the very man whom Sydney had described as having a "soup-and-pattie look". When this friend was thought to be dying, Sydney wrote to Lady Davy that he was "going gently downhill, trusting that the cookery in another planet may be at least as good as in this; but not without apprehensions that for misconduct here he may be sentenced to a thousand years of tough mutton, or condemned to a little eternity of family dinners".'

A further curiosity: Smith died in 1845, but presumably uttered his remark a good few years before that. In Benjamin Disraeli's novel *The Young Duke*, we can read this, however: 'All paradise opens! Let me die eating ortolans to the sound of soft music.' And that was published in 1831.

1 Avoid shame, but do not seek glory: nothing so expensive as glory.

Quoted in Lady Holland, *A Memoir of Sydney Smith*, Chap. 4 (1855). His favourite motto, 'which through life he inculcated on his family', according to his daughter. Hence, *The Expense of Glory*, title of a biography of John Reith (1993) by Ian McIntyre.

2 Death must be distinguished from dying, with which it is often confused.

'Maxims and Rules of Life', in the same memoir, Chap. 6. Compare FIELDING 194:1.

3 No furniture so charming as books, even if you never open them or read a single word.

In the same memoir, Chap. 9. Compare POWELL 366:5.

Tobias SMOLLETT Scottish novelist (1721–71)

4 I am again your petitioner, in behalf of that great Cham of literature, Samuel Johnson.

Smollett's nickname for Dr Samuel Johnson occurred in a letter to John Wilkes (16 March 1759), reproduced in James Boswell, *Life of Johnson* (1791). 'Cham' is a form of 'khan' (as in Genghis Khan), meaning 'monarch' or 'prince'.

C.P. SNOW (later Lord Snow) English novelist and scientist (1905–80)

5 *Corridors of Power.*

Title of novel (1964). This phrase was reasonably well established for the machinations of government, especially the bureaucrats and civil servants of Whitehall, by the time Snow used it, but he undoubtedly popularized it. Earlier, he had written in his novel *Homecomings* (1956): 'The official world, the corridors of power, the dilemmas of conscience and egotism – she disliked them all.'

6 Two Cultures and the Scientific Revolution.

For a time, the title of Snow's 1959 Rede Lecture at Cambridge on the gap between science and literature and religion gave another much used phrase to the language. 'The Two Cultures' became a catchphrase in discussions of the inability of the two camps to speak a common language or, indeed, to understand each other at all.

Philip SNOWDEN (1st Viscount Snowden) English politician (1864–1937)

7 This is not Socialism. It is Bolshevism run mad.

An early political sensation on British radio was made in a broadcast during the 1931 general election. On 17 October, Snowden, who had been Chancellor of the Exchequer in the 1929 Labour Government and who now held the same post in the National Government, said this of the Labour Party's plans in a radio broadcast. He also said: 'I hope you have read the Election programme of the Labour Party. It is the most fantastic and impracticable programme ever put before the electors.' The plans were, of course, similar to the ones he had himself devised in 1929. He later commented: 'My effort was universally believed to have had great influence on the result of the Election. The Labour Party gave me the credit, or, as they put it, the discredit of being responsible for the tragic fate which overtook them.'

SOCRATES Greek philosopher (469–399BC)

8 Crito, we owe a cock to Aesculapius; please pay it and don't forget it.

Last words, quoted in Plato, *Phaedo*. Said to the friend with whom he had been conversing after drinking hemlock. A cock was the usual offering made to Aesculapius, the Greek god of medicine and healing, to return thanks for a recovery from illness.

9 A life that has not been tested is not worth living.

Apology of Socrates (38A, 3–5). In Benjamin Jowett's translation, this is given as: 'The unexamined life is not worth living.' In the T. Mills edition: 'For man, a life without examination is not worth living.' According to Plato, it was said after the guilty verdict had been brought at Socrates' trial.

SOLON Athenian statesman and poet (?640–?556BC)

10 *De mortuis nil nisi bonum* [Of the dead, speak kindly or not at all].

Sometimes ascribed to Solon (?600BC). 'Speak not evil of the dead' was also a saying of Chilo(n) of Sparta (one of the Seven Sages, also 6th century BC). Later Sextus Propertius (who died in AD2) wrote: '*Absenti nemo non nocuisse velit* [Let no one be willing to speak ill of the absent].' Sometimes simply referred to in the form '*De mortuis ...* ', it is a proverb that appears in some form in most European languages.

Anastasio SOMOZA Nicaraguan dictator (1925–80)

1 Indeed, you won the elections, but I won the count.

Quoted in *The Guardian* (17 June 1977). Ironically, this remark had been anticipated by Tom Stoppard in his play *Jumpers* (1972): 'It's not the voting that's democracy, it's the counting.'

Stephen SONDHEIM American songwriter (1930–)

2 Everything's coming up roses.

Title of song, in *Gypsy* (1959), with music by Jule Styne. But did the expression exist before this? *Partridge/Catch Phrases* guesses that it was around in about 1950. It is possibly adapted from the expression, 'to come out smelling of roses', but there do not seem to be any examples even of *that* before the date of the Sondheim coinage.

3 The Ladies Who Lunch.

Title of song, in *Company* (1970), words and music by Sondheim. Hence, the expression 'ladies who lunch' for (mostly middle-aged married) women who have nothing else in their lives but to organize and take part in lunches for charity.

4 Send in the Clowns.

Title of song, in *A Little Night Music* (1973), words and music by Sondheim. The tradition that the 'show must go on' grew out of circus. Whatever mishap occurred, the band was told to go on playing and the cry went up 'send in/on the clowns' – for the simple reason that panic had to be avoided, the audience's attention diverted, and the livelihood of everybody in the circus depended on not having to give the audience its money back. Perhaps 'send in' was right for the circus, 'send on' for the stage?

Similarly, 'the show must go on' seems primarily a circus phrase, though no one seems able to turn up a written reference much before 1930. In 1950 the phrase was spoken in the film *All About Eve* and, in the same decade, Noël Coward wrote a song that posed the question '*Why* Must the Show Go On?'

5 Shepherd's pie and peppered
With genuine shepherds on top.

Sweeney Todd (1979), words and music by Sondheim. Sondheim attempts to fashion a lyric out of an amusing notion.

Not the first to do so, as witness this cartoon caption from *Punch* (30 January 1918):

> *Bobbie (who is eating shepherd's pie, and has been told not to be wasteful)*: Mummie, *must* I eat this? It's such a *partickerly* nasty bit of the shepherd?

6 *Sunday in the Park with George.*

Title of musical (1983) – derived from that of a painting, *Sunday on the Island of La Grande Jatte*, and the name of the painter, Georges Seurat, who first exhibited it at the 1886 Impressionist Exhibition.

SOPHOCLES Greek playwright and poet (?496–406BC)

7 To die would be good, but never to have been born would be better.

Chorus in play, *Oedipus at Colonus* – but sometimes remembered in a German translation. Friedrich Hölderlin quoted the words on the title page of his novel *Hyperion* (1797). They occur also in Heinrich Heine's *Ruhelechzend* [Yearning for rest] (?1853–6) – '*Der Tod ist gut, doch besser wär's / Die mutter hätt uns nie geboren* [Death is good, but it is better Mother had never given birth to us]' – and in his poem 'Morphine' – '*Gut ist der Schlaf, / Der Tod ist besser, / Das beste wäre, / Nie geboren sein* [Sleep is good. Death is better. Best it were never to have been born].' Friedrich Nietzsche wrote similarly in *The Birth of Tragedy* (1872), attributing the words to Silenus, the companion of Dionysus.

Sophocles may have been anticipated by Aeschylus. In a fragment of an otherwise lost play, there is a passage which has been translated as: 'Death is rather to be chosen than a toilsome life; and not to be born is better than to be born to misery' – Loeb Classical Library edn of Aeschylus, Vol. 2 (1926).

8 Someone asked Sophocles, 'How is your sex-life now? Are you still able to have a woman?' He replied, 'Hush, man; most gladly am I rid of it all, as though I had escaped from a mad and savage master.'

When the jazz singer George Melly was on BBC Radio *Quote ... Unquote* in 1989 he quoted a 'Greek philosopher' who, on being asked if he was upset at losing his sexual appetite, replied: 'Upset, certainly not. It's like being unchained from a lunatic.' In a 1988 epistle from *The Kenneth Williams Letters*: 'Understand exactly what Plato meant when he said that after the sexual compulsion vanished with age, he felt "released from a demon".' Williams – the late comic actor – was half-right. It was in fact Sophocles who said it, but as reported by Plato in *The Republic* (Bk. 1, line 329b). It all depends on the translation from the Greek, of course.

Another is: 'I have left it behind me and escaped from the madness and slavery of passion ... a release from slavery to all your many passions.'

John SPARROW English scholar (1906–92)

1 This stone with not unpardonable pride,
Proves by its record what the world denied:
Simon could do a natural thing – he died.

Suggested epitaph for Sir John (later Viscount) Simon (1873–1954), lawyer and Liberal politician. 'Lord Simon has died ... John Sparrow wrote this epitaph many years ago ... But then John Simon helped John Sparrow to become Warden of All Souls, and the latter came to regret his epigram' – *Harold Nicolson's Diaries and Letters 1945–1962* (entry for 11 January 1954). In Sparrow's *Grave Epigrams and Other Verses* (1981), 'Simon' is replaced by '*Nemo*'.

2 Without you, Heaven would be too dull to bear,
And Hell would not be Hell if you are there.

Epitaph for Sir Maurice Bowra (1898–1971), first published in *The Times Literary Supplement* (23 June 1972) as a poem, 'C.M.B.' It was reprinted, in this altered form, in Sparrow's *Grave Epigrams and Other Verses* (1981):

Send us to Hell or Heaven or where you will,
Promise us only, you'll be with us still:
Heaven, without you, would be too dull to bear,
And Hell will not be Hell if you are there.

Bowra was a noted Oxford personality and Warden of Wadham. Sparrow was part of his circle, the Warden of All Souls, and a connoisseur of inscriptions and epitaphs. Bowra's actual grave in St Cross churchyard bears his name in suitably bold letters, but no epitaph.

Phil SPECTOR American record producer (1940–)

3 To Know Him Is To Love Him.

Song title (1958). In *The Picture of Dorian Gray* (1890), Oscar Wilde had: 'To see him is to worship him, to know him is to trust him.' Blanche Hozier wrote to Mabell, Countess of Airlie, in 1908: 'Clementine is engaged to be married to Winston Churchill. I do not know which of the two is more in love. I think that to know him is to like him.'

Thus the format existed before Spector. The words have a biblical ring to them, but whether Spector was ever aware of the words of No. 3 in *CSSM Choruses* (3rd edn, 1928, by the Children's Special Service Mission, London) we may never know. Written by R. Hudson Pope, it goes:

All glory be to Jesus
The sinner's only Saviour ...

To know Him is to love Him,
To trust him is to prove Him.

Robert Burns (1759–96) came very close to the phrase on a couple of occasions – in 'Bonnie Lesley': 'To see her is to love her / And love but her for ever'; and in 'Ae Fond Kiss': 'But to see her was to love her, / Love but her, and love for ever.' Lady Hester Stanhope in a letter of 27 June 1810 wrote to the father of her lover: 'To know him is to love & admire him, & I *do both!*' Principally, however, the words have been used in an epitaph context. Fitz-Greene Halleck (1795–1867) wrote 'On the death of J.R. Drake':

Green be the turf above thee,
Friend of my better days;
None knew thee but to love thee
Nor named thee but to praise.

Samuel Rogers (1763–1855) wrote of 'Jacqueline':

Oh! she was good as she was fair.
None – none on earth above her!
As pure in thought as angels are,
To know her was to love her.

It appears that Spector acquired the title of his song from the gravestone of his father, a suicide, where it read: 'To Have Known Him Was To Have Loved Him' – quoted in John Tobler & Stuart Grundy, *The Record Producers* (1982).

Herbert SPENCER English philosopher (1820–1903)

4 To play billiards well is the sign of a misspent youth.

Under Spencer, *ODQ* (1979) has: 'It was remarked to me by the late Mr Charles Roupell ... that to play billiards was a sign of an ill-spent youth.' On the other hand, in the archives of the Savile Club in London it is recorded that Robert Louis Stevenson, who was a member from 1874 to 1894, propounded to Spencer that 'proficiency in this game [note: probably billiards, because it was said in the Savile billiards room] is a sign of a misspent youth' – mentioned in 'Words', *The Observer* (4 May 1986).

Other clubs also claim the honour, and some people would supply the word 'snooker' or 'bridge' instead of 'billiards'. A keen billiards player, Spencer was displeased when the saying kept being ascribed to him in newspapers. He had quoted it from someone else. So he dictated a denial to Dr David Duncan, who edited his *Life and Letters* (1908), from which the *ODQ* quotation was taken. *ODQ* (1992) puts the remark under Roupell and describes him as an 'official referee of the British High Court of Justice'.

Benham (1948) notes that a similar view had earlier appeared in *Noctes Ambrosianae* in March 1827.

1 This survival of the fittest which I have here sought to express in mechanical terms is that which Mr Darwin has called 'natural selection, or the preservation of favoured races in the struggle for life.'

Principles of Biology (1864–7). In other words, Spencer, in talking of evolution and the 'survival of the fittest', was pointing to the survival of the most suitable, not of the most physically fit.

(Sir) Stanley SPENCER English painter (1891–1959)

2 Painting is saying 'Ta' to God.

Quoted in letter to *The Observer* from his daughter Shirin (7 February 1988). This remark neatly encapsulates Spencer's homely, albeit visionary, approach to religion in his works. He said he wished 'to take the inmost of one's wishes, the most varied religious feelings ... and to make it an ordinary fact of the street'. Some of his most memorable canvasses, like *The Resurrection: Cookham*, show religious images in the village where he lived.

Edmund SPENSER English poet (?1552–99)

3 That we spent, we had:
That we gave, we have:
That we left, we lost.

Epitaph of 'the Earl of Devonshire', quoted in *The Shepheardes Calendar*, 'May', line 70 (1579). Compare:

What wee gave, wee have;
What wee spent, wee had;
What wee left, wee lost.

This is the epitaph on Edward Courtenay, Earl of Devon (who died in 1419) and his wife, at Tiverton.

4 Sweet Thames, run softly, till I end my song.

This line is repeated at the end of each verse of Spenser's *Prothalamion* (1596). In *Handbook of 20th Century Quotations*, ed. Frank S. Pepper (1984), it is attributed to T.S. Eliot in *The Waste Land* (1922). As with ELIOT 186:8–9, this is another example of Eliot's magpie-like use of quotation misleading readers who do not plunge in among his fairly copious notes.

5 Sleep after toil, port after stormy seas,
Ease after war, death after life does greatly please.

The Faerie Queen, Bk 1, Canto 9, St. 40. Popular as a gravestone inscription. It was put, for example, on the bronze statue of Admiral Robert Blake (1599–1657) at Bridgwater, Somerset. It also appears on the tombstone of the Polish-born novelist Joseph Conrad (1857–1924) in the cemetery of St Thomas's Roman Catholic Church, Canterbury. The quotation had been used by Conrad as the epigraph to his last complete work, *The Rover*.

Baruch SPINOZA Dutch philosopher (1632–77)

6 Peace is not an absence of war, it is a virtue, a state of mind, a disposition for benevolence, confidence, justice.

Theological-Political Treatise (1670). Hence, *Absence of War*, title of play (1993) by David Hare, which concerns a leader of the British Labour Party losing yet another general election and asks whether a socialist government could ever gain power without compromising its principles.

William SPOONER English clergyman and academic (1844–1930)

7 Kinquering congs their titles take.

Spoonerism, the accidental transposing of the beginnings (or other parts) of two or more words, is named after a former Warden of New College, Oxford. The term had been coined by about 1885. William Hayter, in his *Spooner*, Chap. 6 (1977), says: 'New College oral tradition is that he admitted giving out the hymn in New College Chapel, as "kinquering Kongs" but denied all the rest. I asked Rosemary Spooner [his daughter] about this, and she replied "I never understood how kinquering kongs originated because we never had the hymns given out in Chapel – they were just on printed sheets."' Whatever the case, the remark – sometimes dated to 1879 – was being reported in the Oxford *Echo* (4 May 1892). It was alluded to in *Punch* (Vol. 122, 1902) in a joke about the current Ping Pong craze – 'Ponquering Pings their titles take' – and Spooner is mentioned by name.

8 Sir, you have tasted two whole worms; you have hissed all my mystery lectures and been caught fighting a liar in the quad; you will leave Oxford by the next town drain.

A surely apocryphal spoonerism, but reported in *The Oxford University What's What* (1948). Many of Spooner's reported efforts must be apocryphal. 'Which of us has not felt in his heart a half-warmed fish' is one of the more likely ones. This was being attributed simply to a 'don' by G.K. Chesterton in 'High-Brows and Humbugs' – in *Hearst's Magazine* (December 1913). Apocryphal, too, are probably the following: 'Let us drink a toast to the queer old dean', quoted in *PDQ* (1960); 'The Minx by Spoonlight' – the most remarkable sight in Egypt – quoted in Julian Huxley, *Memories* (1970); 'It popped on its little drawers' (of a cat falling from a window) and 'the well-boiled icicle', quoted in William Hayter, *Spooner* (1977); 'Yes indeed, the Lord *is* a shoving leopard', quoted in *Brewer* (1989).

1 Through a dark glassly ...

Attributed by James Laver, in conversation with the author (5 December 1969). Described by Hayter (in above book) as one of the more likely spoonerisms.

2 Loifully jawned in holy matrimony.

Hayter notes that David Butler, the Oxford don, claims that Spooner said this when he was officiating at his (Butler's) parents' wedding.

3 Was it you or your brother who was killed in the war?

Not a Spoonerism, but an eccentric remark. A joke well established at New College by 1963 was that Spooner had once inquired of an undergraduate in about 1918, 'Now, tell me, was it you or your brother who was killed in the war?' But Frank Muir in *The Oxford Book of Humorous Prose* cites this from John Taylor's *Wit and Mirth* (1630): 'A nobleman (as he was riding) met with a yeoman of the country, to whom he said, "My friend, I should know thee. I do remember I have often seen thee." "My good lord," said the countryman, "I am one of your honour's poor tenants, and my name is T.I." "I remember thee better now," (saith my lord). "There were two brothers but one is dead. I pray thee, which of you doth remain alive?"'

(Sir) Cecil SPRING-RICE English diplomat and poet (1859–1918)

4 I vow to thee, my country – all earthly things above –
Entire and whole and perfect, the service of my love.

'I Vow to Thee, My Country' (1918). Notably set to music by Gustav Holst in 1921, using the central melody from 'Jupiter', No. 4 of his *The Planets*.

5 And there's another country, I've heard of long ago –
Most dear to them that love her, most great to them that know.

In the same hymn. Hence, *Another Country*, title of a play (1981; film UK 1984) by Julian Mitchell, showing how the seeds of defection to Soviet Russia were sown in a group of boys at an English public school. In this original context, the 'other country' is Heaven, rather than the Soviet Union, of course. As the playwright has confirmed, the title was

not taken from MARLOWE 312:6. *Another Country* was earlier used as the title of a novel (1927) by Hélène de Coudray, though whether this alludes to Spring-Rice is not clear.

6 And her ways are ways of gentleness and all her paths are Peace.

In the same hymn. Compare Proverbs 3:17: 'Her ways are ways of pleasantness, and all her paths are peace.'

(Sir) John SQUIRE English poet, essayist and critic (1884–1958)

7 Whose names like a chime so sweetly call,
And high over all
The cross and the ball
On the riding redoubtable Dome of Paul.

'A New Song of the Bishop of London (On a proposal to pull down nineteen City Churches)' in *Collected Poems* (1959). It is quoted without source in A.G. MacDonell, *England, Their England* (1933).

See also POPE 363:3.

Madame de STAËL French writer (1766–1817)

8 *Tout comprendre rend très indulgent* [To be totally understanding makes one very indulgent].

Corinne (1807). Possibly best remembered in the form '*Tout comprendre, c'est tout pardonner* [To know everything is to forgive everything].'

Joseph STALIN Soviet Communist leader (1879–1953)

9 Oho! The Pope! How many divisions has he got?

Quoted in Winston Churchill, *The Second World War*, Vol. 1 (1948). Pierre Laval, French Foreign Minister, asked Stalin in 1935, 'Can't you do something to encourage religion and the Catholics in Russia? It would help me so much with the Pope.' This was Stalin's reply.

10 He who is not with us is against us.

A view popularly ascribed to the Soviet leader. *Time* Magazine (11 August 1986) also noted a corollary attributed to the Hungarian Communist Party leader, Janos Kadar (1912–89): 'He who is not against us is with us.' In fact, Stalin was quoting Jesus Christ, who said: 'He that is not with me is against me' (Luke 11:23), and Kadar was also quoting Christ, who provided the corollary: 'He that is not against us is for us' (Luke 9:50). It is not surprising that Stalin quoted Scripture. He went from a church school at Guri to the theological seminary at Tiflis to train for the Russian Orthodox priesthood. Compare BUSH 113:3.

1 The trouble with free elections is, you never know who is going to win.

This has been attributed to Leonid Brezhnev, but not traced. It is, however, just the kind of thing Stalin might have said at the Potsdam Conference in 1945 when Winston Churchill's fate in the British general election hung in the balance. Molotov has also been suggested. Consider this from Clement Attlee's autobiography *As It Happened* (1954): 'Neither Churchill nor Eden wished to return to Potsdam, so my colleague for the remainder of the Conference was the new Foreign Secretary, Ernest Bevin. Our arrival created somewhat of a sensation. Our American friends were surprised to find that there was no change in our official advisers and that I had even taken over, as my Principal Private Secretary, Leslie Rowan, who had been serving Churchill in the same capacity. Molotov kept saying, "But you said the election would be a close thing and now you have a big majority." I said, "Yes, we could not tell what would be the result." But he kept repeating the same phrase. He could not understand why we did not know the result. I am sure he thought that Churchill would have "fixed" the election and that the change-over by democratic process was a great shock to him.' I feel now that the quotation as we have it is possibly just an encapsulation of Molotov's reaction, rather than his or anybody else's actual words.

Laurence STALLINGS American writer (1894–1968)

2 Hollywood – a place where the inmates are in charge of the asylum.

Quoted in Laurence J. Peter, *Quotations for Our Time* (1977). See also LLOYD GEORGE 291:6; ROWLAND 389:5.

3 *What Price Glory?*

Title of play (1924; film US 1952) about the stupidity of war, written with Maxwell Anderson. Further popularized the 'What price — ?' format phrase, questioning the sacrifices and compromises that may have to be made in order to carry out any sort of mission. Known by 1893. *What Price Hollywood?* was the title of a film (US 1932). See also SHAW 425:1.

(Sir) Henry Morton STANLEY British explorer and journalist (1841–1904)

4 Dr Livingstone, I presume?

The most famous greeting of all time was put by Stanley to the Scottish explorer and missionary Dr David Livingstone at Ujiji, Lake Tanganyika, on 10 November 1871 (though this date has been questioned). Stanley had been sent by the *New York Herald* to look for Livingstone, who was missing on a journey in Central Africa. In *How I Found Livingstone* (1872), Stanley described the moment: 'I would have run to him, only I was a coward in the presence of such a mob – would have embraced him, only, he being an Englishman, I did not know how he would receive me; so I did what cowardice and false pride suggested was the best thing – walked deliberately to him, took off my hat and said: "Dr Livingstone, I presume?" "YES," said he, with a kind smile, lifting his cap slightly.'

One unhelpful suggestion is that Stanley was making a tongue-in-cheek reference to a moment in Sheridan's *School for Scandal*, Act 5, Sc. 1 (1777), in which, after much mutual confusion, two of the main characters finally get to meet with the line, 'Mr Stanley, I presume.' But, really, it was not such a remarkable salutation after all. In the American Civil War, General Robert E. Lee, when he entered Maryland at Williamsport on 25 June 1863, was greeted by the spokesman of a women's committee of welcome with the words, 'This is General Lee, I presume?'

In the 1960s, when Robert F. Kennedy was campaigning south of Atlanta, he said to one of the rare white men he met: 'Dr Livingstone, I presume.'

5 *Through the Dark Continent.*
Through Darkest Africa.

In 1878 Stanley published a book of reportage *Through the Dark Continent* and followed it, in 1890, with *Through Darkest Africa*. It is presumably from these two titles that we get the expressions 'dark continent' and 'darkest — ' to describe not only Africa but almost anywhere remote and uncivilized. Stuart Berg Flexner, *Listening To America* (1982), suggests that 'In darkest Africa' was a screen subtitle in a silent film of the period 1910–14. Compare from P.G. Wodehouse, *Psmith in the City*, Chap. 7 (1910): 'Through Darkest Dulwich in a Taximeter.'

Vivian STANSHALL English entertainer and eccentric (1942–95)

6 The Canyons of Your Mind.

Title of 1968 hit record, written and performed by Stanshall: 'In the canyons of your mind … I will wander through your brain to the ventricles of your heart, my dear … I'm in love with you again.' Somewhat oddly, it came from a phrase in the Val Doonican hit 'Elusive Butterfly' (1966), written by Bob Lind (who had recorded it himself in 1965).

Charles E. STANTON American soldier (1859–1933)

7 Lafayette, we are here! [*Lafayette, nous voilà!*]

Nine days after the American Expeditionary Force landed in France in 1917, Stanton, a member of General Pershing's staff, stood at the tomb of Lafayette in the Picpus cemetery in Paris and declared, 'Here and now, in the presence of the illustrious dead, we pledge our hearts and our honour in carrying this war to a successful issue. Lafayette, we are here!' This graceful tribute to the Marquis de Lafayette (1757–1834) – who enlisted with the American Revolutionary armies in 1777 and forged a strong emotional link between the United States and France – was delivered by Colonel Stanton on 4 July 1917 and repeated on 14 July. According to the *New York Tribune* (6 September 1917), Stanton may have spoken all or some of his remarks in French – '*Lafayette, nous voilà!*' As *Bartlett* (1968 and 1980) points out, the remark has also been attributed to General Pershing, though he disclaimed having said 'anything so splendid'. There is evidence, however, that he may have pronounced the phrase before Stanton and that Stanton merely picked it up.

Frank L. STANTON American journalist and poet (1857–1927)

1 Sweetest li'l feller, everybody knows;
   Dunno what to call him, but he's mighty lak' a
   rose!

Song, 'Mighty Lak' a Rose' (1901), music by Ethelbert Nevin. By 1991, when the singer Elvis Costello was entitling one of his albums *Mighty Like a Rose* (there is no title song), the southern American intonation of the original had clearly been dispensed with. There is a parody:

   Sweetest little feller,
   Wears his sister's clothes.
   Don't know what to call him,
   But we think he's one of those.

STAR TREK American science-fiction TV series, first aired 1966–9, then the basis of several feature films and various subsequent TV series. It was created by Gene Roddenberry (1921–91).

2 Space – the final frontier. These are the voyages of the starship *Enterprise*. Its five-year mission: to explore strange new worlds, to seek out new life and new civilizations, to boldly go where no man has gone before.

From the introductory voice-over commentary to the TV series. Though short-lived, the show nevertheless acquired a considerable after-life through countless repeats (not least in the UK) and through the activities of 'Trekkies'. In one of the feature films (1988) that belatedly spun off from the series, the split infinitive remained, but feminism, presumably, had decreed that it should become 'to boldly go where no *one* has gone before'.

3 Beam me up, Scotty!

In fact, 'Beam us up, Mr Scott' appears to be the nearest thing to this catchphrase ever actually spoken in the series (in an episode called 'Gamesters of Triskelion'). According to 'Trekkies', Captain Kirk (William Shatner) never actually said to Lieutenant-Commander 'Scotty' Scott, the chief engineer, 'Beam me up, Scotty!' – meaning that he should transpose body into matter, or some such thing. Another actual phrase that has been used is, 'Enterprise, beam us up' and, we are told, that in the fourth episode, 'Scotty, beam me up' *may* have been said. Somebody has probably written a doctoral thesis on all this. Was it later worked into one of the films?

4 It's life, Jim, but not as we know it.

This is Mr Spock's line from the song 'Star Trekkin' by The Firm – a No. 1 hit record in the UK (June 1987) in which impersonators of the main *Star Trek* characters simply intone would-be lines from the show to music. As far as one knows, this line was never actually spoken in any of the TV episodes or films. Other lines from this song include: 'There's Klingons on the Starboard Bow' and 'It's worse than that, he's dead, Jim.'

The catchphrase had a certain vogue in the UK in the early 1990s. A 1995 poster advertisement in London stated 'It's direct insurance, but not as we know it, Jim.' A headline from *The Independent* (19 April 1996): 'It's the weekend, Jim, but not as we know it.'

A belief still persists that something like it *was* said in one of the TV episodes but, if so, this remains to be found. Nowlan & Nowlan, *Film Quotations* (1994), confidently assert that in *Star Trek: The Motion Picture* (1979), Spock says to Kirk, 'It's life, Captain, but not life as we know it.' However, given that the Nowlans refer to '*Dr* Spock' it is hardly surprising to find that, in fact, the line is not actually uttered in the film. This is not the least of the apocryphal lines they happily include in their book.

(Sir) David STEEL (later Lord Steel) British Liberal politician (1938–)

5 I have the good fortune to be the first Liberal leader for over half a century who is able to say to you at the end of our annual assembly: go back to your constituencies and prepare for government.

Speech, Liberal Party Assembly, Llandudno (18 September 1981). Rallying cry in the first flush of enthusiasm for the alliance with the newly formed SDP. However, by the time of the next general election (1983), squabbling had broken out between the two parties, and the Falklands War had given the incumbent Conservative government an unassailable advantage.

Lincoln STEFFENS American journalist (1866–1936)

1 I have seen the future and it works.

Steffens was a muckraking journalist who paid a visit to the newly formed Soviet Union as part of the William C. Bullitt diplomatic mission of 1919. As did a number of the first visitors to the new Soviet system, he returned with an optimistic view. His phrase for it was this. However, in his *Autobiography* (1931), he phrases it a little differently. '"So you've been over into Russia?" said Bernard Baruch, and I answered very literally, "I have been over into the future, and it works."' Bullitt said Steffens had been rehearsing this formula even before he went to the Soviet Union. Later, he tended to use the shorter, more colloquial form himself.

Philip Toynbee wrote of the US in *The Observer* (27 January 1974): 'I have seen the future and it does not work.'

Gertrude STEIN American poet (1874–1946)

2 Rose is a rose is a rose is a rose.

Stein's poem 'Sacred Emily' (1913) is well-nigh impenetrable to most readers, but somehow it has managed to give a format phrase to the language. If something is incapable of explanation, one says, for example, 'A cloud is a cloud is a cloud.' What Stein wrote, however, is frequently misunderstood. She did not say 'A rose is a rose is a rose', but 'Rose is a rose is a rose is a rose' (i.e. upper case R and no indefinite article at the start and three not two repetitions). The Rose in question was not a flower but an allusion to the English painter, Sir Francis Rose, 'whom she and I regarded,' wrote Constantine Fitzgibbon, 'as the peer of Matisse and Picasso, and whose paintings – or at least painting – hung in her Paris drawing-room while a Gauguin was relegated to the lavatory' – letter to *The Sunday Telegraph* (7 July 1978). Stein also refers to 'Jack Rose' (not a 'Jack' rose) earlier in the poem.

In John Malcolm Brinnin, *The Third Rose* (1959), Stein is quoted as saying: 'Now, listen! I'm no fool. I know that in daily life we don't go around saying "is a ... is ... is ..." Yes, I'm no fool; but I think that in that line the rose is red for the first time in English poetry for a hundred years.'

Note: *ODMQ* (1991) and *ODQ* (1992) have: 'Rose is a rose is a rose is a rose, is a rose.' And, perversely, Sir Harold Acton wrote in *Memoirs of an Aesthete* (1948) of a letter from Stein: 'A silver rose adorned the writing-paper with the motto "a rose is a rose is a rose". (She had not yet discovered Francis Rose, who must have made her doubt this opinion.)'

3 To write is to write is to write is to write is to write is to write is to write is to write.

Unverified. Possibly a confusion of the 'rose' line above with another dictum of hers: 'The way to say it, is to say it' – quoted by Robert Graves in *Modern Language Quarterly*, No. 27 (Spring 1973).

4 *I Love You Alice B. Toklas.*

The film comedy with this title (US 1968) was about a lawyer (Peter Sellers) amid the Flower People of San Francisco in the 1960s. Alice B. Toklas (who came, as it happens, from San Francisco) was Stein's secretary and lover, for whom Stein 'ghosted' *The Autobiography of Alice B. Toklas* (1933). *The Alice B. Toklas Cookbook* (1954) – a mixture of memoirs and culinary hints – was, however, written by Toklas herself. Popular in the 1960s – perhaps in an 'alternative' edition – it contains, for example, Brian Gysen's recipe for 'haschich fudge'.

5 The lost generation.

Stein recorded and popularized the remark made by a French garage owner in the Midi just after the war. Rebuking an apprentice who had made a shoddy repair to her car, he said: 'All you young people who served in the war' are from 'a lost generation [*une génération perdue*]'. Ernest Hemingway used this as the epigraph to his novel *The Sun Also Rises* (1926) and referred to it again in *A Moveable Feast* (1964). I would guess, however, that the phrase is now more often used to refer to the large number of promising young men who lost their lives in the First World War rather than, as in Stein's context, to those who were not killed in the war but who survived to become part of a generation that was thought to have lost its values. John Keegan's *The First World War* (1998) begins by analysing the casualties and says of the small percentages of national populations killed or wounded: 'Even those smaller proportions left terrible psychic wounds, falling as they did on the youngest and most active sections of society's males. It has, as the war recedes into history, become fashionable to decry the lament for this "Lost Generation" as myth-making.' Here Keegan equates 'The Lost Generation' with those men killed or wounded, rather than all those men who wasted their youth in the war, which is what Gertrude Stein meant. A further redefinition of the phrase in an F. Scott Fitzgerald short story 'The Swimmers', published in *The Saturday Evening Post* (19 October 1929): 'There was a lost generation in the saddle at the moment, but it seemed to him that the men coming on, the men of the war, were better.' So that would make the lost generation the men of *before* the First World War.

John STEINBECK American writer (1902–68)

1 A man got to do what he got to do.

The Grapes of Wrath (1939). The earliest appearance traced of the expression 'a man's gotta do what a man's gotta do', though probably not original to Steinbeck.

Gloria STEINEM American feminist writer (1934–)

2 A woman without a man is like a fish without a bicycle.

Elaine Partnow's *The Quotable Woman 1800–1981* (1982) attributes this saying to Steinem, but gives no hint as to why it makes such a very dubious attribution, though it is reasonable to assume that the words must have crossed Ms Steinem's lips at some stage. It is, after all, probably the most famous feminist slogan of recent decades. Bartlett (1992) lists it anonymously as a 'feminist slogan of the 1980s'.

So, if not from Steinem, whence came the saying? Mrs C. Raikes of Moseley, Birmingham contributed it to BBC Radio *Quote ... Unquote* (1977), adding: 'I felt you had to share in this pearl of wisdom I found yesterday on a lavatory wall in Birmingham University. Written in German, it translates as ...' Indeed, the chances are that the saying may have originated in Germany, where it is known in the form, '*Eine Frau ohne Mann ist wie ein Fisch ohne Velo!*' Meanwhile, in the US in the same year, 1977, *Ms.* Magazine was advertising T-shirts with the slogan on them (in English). Perhaps this is the explanation for the Steinem attribution.

Compare, however, what Arthur Bloch in *Murphy's Law* ... (also 1977) calls 'Vique's Law': 'A man without religion is like a fish without a bicycle.' In a 1974 book called *II Cybernetic Frontiers*, Stewart Brand attributed 'A man without a God is like a fish without a bicycle' to the late *San Francisco Chronicle* columnist Herb Caen. All this seemed to suggest that the feminist slogan had merely been grafted on to an already existing phrase format.

In 1999, Charles S. Harris, a psychologist of Middletown, NJ, presented me with some well-documented research into both facets of the case. For a start, he found an earlier attribution to Steinem in *Life* (December 1979) – [it is also in Barbara Rowes, *The Book of Quotes* (1979)] – and a mention of her specifically not wearing a T-shirt with the slogan on it at the 1976 Democratic Convention in *People* (26 July 1976). But also a denial from an interview with her on National Public Radio (9 February 1992): 'Yeah, I wish I knew who said it, 'cause I think it's quite funny, but it wasn't me.'

In addition, Harris put in a reasonable bid to have (as he thinks) coined the original phrase format: 'I do know where the fish without a bicycle came from: an intro philosophy class at Swarthmore College in 1955. In reaction to our assigned reading of St Augustine, I wrote: "*A man without faith* is like a fish without a bicycle." Later, it was printed along with other quips, in my weekly humor column in the Swarthmore College *Phoenix* (8 April 1958).'

ODP has a fine example of the format in 'A man without religion is like a horse without a bridle', which occurs in *Anatomy of Melancholy* (1621); it derives from the anonymous Medieval Latin '*Homo sine religione sicut equus sine freno.*' Several proverbs of the format 'A man without a woman is like a ship without a keel' are known in German and Dutch from the 17th century onward.

Referring to her books of *Quotations by Women*, Rosalie Maggio stated (1999): 'I talked to Gloria Steinem about that quotation a few years ago – she has always maintained it wasn't original to her. Out of curiosity, she tracked it down to Irina Dunn (Patsi Dunn, born 1948, Australian educator, journalist, politician). I spoke with Dunn on the phone in 1995. She says she wrote it in at least two toilets in 1970, spinning it off from something in one of her textbooks – "Man without God is like a fish without a bicycle." Which is where we came in.'

In 1979, Arthur Marshall contributed the interesting variant: 'A woman without a man is like a moose without a hatrack.' In Haan & Hammerstrom, *Graffiti in the Big Ten* (1981), is 'Behind every successful man is a fish with a bicycle.' One of Peter Cook's contributions to *Private Eye* Magazine was 'The Memoirs of Rhandhi P'Hurr' – described as 'Rudyard Kipling meets a predecessor of the Maharishi Mahesh Yogi in the pages of the *Kama Sutra*' – and though the precise date is not known, in the 1965 'Preface' is this: 'It was Kipling, I think, who said "An India without Rhandhi P'Hurris is as hard to imagine as a fish without marmalade."'

Laurence STERNE Irish novelist and clergyman (1713–68)

3 This world surely is wide enough to hold both thee and me.

Tristram Shandy, Bk 2, Chap. 12.

4 'L––d!' said my mother, 'what is all this story about?' — 'A cock and a bull,' said Yorick, 'And one of the best of its kind, I ever heard.'

In the same novel, Bk 9, Chap. 33. Last words. As for where the phrase 'cock and bull story' comes from, suggested origins include: old fables in which animals talk, a tradition going right back to Aesop – confirmed perhaps by the equivalent French phrase '*coq à l'âne*' (literally, 'cock to donkey') – someone who hated having to listen to such fables was probably the first to dub them as such; Samuel Fisher's 1660 story about a cock and a bull being transformed into a single animal – which people would have thought a load of nonsense; somehow from the Cock and Bull public houses, which are but a few doors apart in Stony Stratford, Buckinghamshire – perhaps referring to confused tales told first in one pub, the Cock, and then retold in another, the Bull.

OED2's earliest citation of the precise form as it is now used comes (later than Sterne) from the Philadelphia *Gazette of the United States* (1795): 'A long cock-and-bull story about the Columbianum' (a proposed national college). Motteux's 1700 translation of Cervantes, *Don Quixote*, Pt 1, Bk 3, Chap. 17, has: 'Don't trouble me with your foolish stories of a cock and a bull.'

1 They order, said I, this matter better in France.

A Sentimental Journey (1768). First sentence. He is referring to the ancient *droits d'aubaine* – under which the effects of strangers who died in France (excepting the Swiss and Scots) were seized by the law. Compare KEPPEL 269:1.

2 God tempers the wind to the shorn lamb.

In the same novel, we find: 'How she had borne it ... she could not tell – but God tempers the wind, said Maria, to the shorn lamb.' That is to say, God arranges matters so as not to make them unduly harsh for the unfortunate. As such, this is possibly one of the most preposterously untrue of all proverbial sayings. For a proverb it is, not an original remark of Sterne's, as is sometimes supposed, though Sterne's wording provides the form in which it is now used. *CODP* finds a French version in 1594.

Winston Churchill, *My Early Life* (1930), in the chapter entitled 'The Fourth Hussars', remembers a widely read colonel who could not pronounce his r's: 'When, for instance, on one occasion I quoted, "God tempers the wind to the shorn lamb", and Brabazon asked "Where did you get that fwom?" I had replied with some complacency that, though it was attributed often to the Bible, it really occurred in Sterne's *Sentimental Journey*.'

Brewer (1989) points out that Sterne erred in putting 'lamb' where earlier it had said 'sheep' – lambs are never shorn.

Wallace STEVENS American poet (1879–1955)

3 Only, here and there, an old sailor,
Drunk and asleep in his boots,
Catches tigers
In red weather.

'Disillusionment of Ten O'Clock' (1923.) Hence, *Tigers in Red Weather*, the title of a memoir (2005) by Ruth Padel.

4 I do not know which to prefer,
The beauty of inflections
Or the beauty of innuendoes,
The blackbird whistling
Or just after.

'Thirteen Ways of Looking at a Blackbird' (1923). Compare *52 Ways of Looking at a Poem*, the title of a study (2002) by Ruth Padel.

Adlai STEVENSON American Democratic politician (1900–65)

5 A heartbeat away from the Presidency.

The traditional description of the position of the US Vice-President and, as *Safire* (1978) puts it, 'a reminder to voters to examine the shortcomings of a Vice-Presidential candidate'. The earliest use of the phrase *Safire* finds is Stevenson beginning an attack on Richard Nixon in 1952 with, 'The Republican Vice-Presidential candidate, who asks you to place him a heartbeat from the Presidency'. Or 'The young man who asks you to set him one heartbeat from the Presidency of the United States' – speech at Cleveland, Ohio (23 October 1952). Jules Witcover entitled a book on Vice-President Spiro Agnew's enforced resignation in 1973, *A Heartbeat Away*. The phrase was much in evidence again when George Bush selected Dan Quayle as his running-mate in 1988.

6 Dragged kicking and screaming into the twentieth century.

For a well-known phrase, this is curiously little documented and has proved impossible to track to source. The earliest example found in this precise form comes from an article by Kenneth Tynan written in 1959 and collected in *Curtains* (1961): 'A change, slight but unmistakable, has taken place; the English theatre has been dragged, as Adlai Stevenson once said of the Republican Party, kicking and screaming into the 20th century.'

Tony Benn said during a by-election in May 1961: 'It is given to Bristol in this election to wrench the parliamentary system away from its feudal origins, and pitchfork it kicking and screaming into the 20th century.' Nobel prize-winning chemist, Sir George Porter, said in a speech in September 1986: 'Should we force science down the throats of those that have no taste for it? Is it our duty to drag them kicking and screaming into the 20th century? I am afraid it is.'

Obviously, it is a 'format' phrase that lends itself to subtle modification. From *The Daily Telegraph* (11 September 1979): 'Mr Ian McIntyre, whose ambition was to bring Radio 4 kicking and screaming into the 1970s'; from *The Washing-*

ton Post (19 January 1984): 'All [President Reagan] said before he was dragged kicking and screaming into the East Room was that he wouldn't call the Soviet Union an "evil empire" any more'; and from the same paper (19 December 1988): 'Still, Jones and Hawke, prodded by other corporate-minded partners, have dragged Arnold & Porter – sometimes kicking and screaming – into a 21st-century mode of thinking, which they believe will position the firm to compete with firms that already have more than 1000 lawyers.'

The nascent form can be found in a 1913 article by J.B. Priestley in London Opinion: '[By listening to ragtime] he felt literally dragged out of the nineteenth into the twentieth century.' (His use of 'literally' suggests that the idea of dragging from one century to another was already an established one.)

1 A lie is an abomination unto the Lord and a very present help in time of trouble.

Attributed remark – an amalgamation of Proverbs 12:22 and Psalms 46:1. However, as is sometimes the case with Stevenson, his wit is by no means original to him. Philip Eden, the BBC Radio 5 weather forecaster, showed me this from Symons's Meteorological Magazine (May 1916): 'That urchin when asked for the Scriptural definition of a lie is reported to have answered glibly, "A lie which is an abomination unto the Lord is a very present help in time of trouble."' The following month, a (British) reader stated that the 'true version of what he said' was: 'A lie is an abomination to the Lord, but a very present help in trouble' – and surmised that it was said by an American 'Sunday school boy'.

2 Someone asked me as I came down the street, how I felt, and I was reminded of a story that a fellow townsman used to tell – Abraham Lincoln. They asked him how he felt once after an unsuccessful election. He felt like a little boy who had stubbed his toe in the dark. He said that he was too old to cry, but it hurt too much to laugh.

Stevenson's words after his presidential electoral defeat (5 November 1952). The actual Lincoln remark appeared in Frank Leslie's Illustrated Weekly (22 November 1862) after a defeat in the New York elections: '[I feel] somewhat like the boy in Kentucky who stubbed his toe while running to see his sweetheart. The boy said he was too big to cry, and far too badly hurt to laugh.'

3 Eggheads of the world unite; you have nothing to lose but your yolks.

Attributed. In a speech at Oakland (1 February 1956) he said, rather, 'Eggheads of the world, arise – I was even going

to add that you have nothing to lose but your yolks.' 'Egghead' as a synonym for 'intellectual' had been popularized by the columnist Joseph Alsop during the 1952 US presidential campaign. Compare MARX 316:1.

4 Aeschines – how well he spoke.

Attributed remark. In 1960 Adlai Stevenson dithered over whether he should make a third try at the US presidency. In fact, he dithered right up to the Democratic Convention that chose John F. Kennedy. Relations between the two men were somewhat guarded, and Kennedy eventually sent Stevenson as Ambassador to the UN rather than making him Secretary of State. Nevertheless, according to Bert Cochran, Adlai Stevenson (1969), Stevenson introduced Kennedy on one occasion in 1960 with these words, ruefully contrasting the young man's charisma with his own appeal: 'Do you remember that in classical times when Cicero had finished speaking, the people said, "How well he spoke", but when Demosthenes had finished speaking, they said, "Let us march."'

Stevenson's contrast has been queried on the basis that, orators and speechwriters though they undoubtedly were, Cicero and Demosthenes were neither contemporaries nor rivals. Cicero was a Roman and lived more than two hundred years after Demosthenes, an Athenian. A much more valid comparison is to be found in David Ogilvy's Confessions of an Advertising Man, first published in 1963, three years after Stevenson spoke. The Oxford-educated Ogilvy wrote: 'It is the professional duty of the advertising agent to conceal his artifice. When Aeschines spoke, they said, "How well he speaks." But when Demosthenes spoke, they said, "Let us march against Philip." I'm for Demosthenes.' So, who was Aeschines? An Athenian orator and deadly rival of Demosthenes. He advocated appeasement of Philip II of Macedon and negotiated a peace with him. Demosthenes attempted to have him tried for treason. So, all in all, this is a comparison that holds water. But how and where did either of the versions come into being? Leonard Roy Frank found this in John Stuart Mill's inaugural address as Rector of St Andrews University in Scotland (1 February 1867): 'It was not the object of Demosthenes to make the Athenians cry out "What a splendid speaker!" but to make them say "Let us march against Philip."' Sylvia Dowling found this under 'Oratory, the Effects of' in Other Men's Minds, or seven thousand choice extracts on history, science, philosophy, religion, etc, selected from the standard authorship of ancient and modern times and classified in alphabetical order by E. Davies DD (London, Frederick Warne & Co., 1894): 'When the Roman people had listened to the diffuse and polished discourses of Cicero, they departed, saying one to another "What a splendid speech our orator has made!" But when the Athenians heard Demosthenes, he so filled them with the subject matter of his oration, that they quite forgot the orator, and left him at the finish of his harangue, breathing revenge, and exclaiming "Let us go and fight against Philip!"' The book ascribes this passage to the Revd Caleb C. Colton, author of *Lacon*, who died in 1832. This takes us back to Stevenson and demonstrates that his was a valid comparison after all.

Compare what J.K. Galbraith wrote in the book version of his TV series *The Age of Uncertainty* (1977): 'Once quite a few years ago a Soviet historian visited Harvard ... He had known Lenin well ... I asked him the source of Lenin's leadership – a man so tidy, looking so much like a clerk. He replied: "When Lenin spoke, we marched."' So no comparison with Trotsky, as has been suggested.

1 **She would rather light a candle than curse the darkness, and her glow has warmed the world.**

An eloquent tribute paid by Stevenson to Eleanor Roosevelt when the former First Lady died in November 1962. Possibly he had been inspired to do so by what she had written in *My Day* (based on her newspaper column): 'Even a candle is better than no light at all.' However, Stevenson was merely quoting the motto of the Christopher Society, which came, in turn, from a Chinese proverb. 'Better to light a candle than curse the darkness' was also quoted by Peter Benenson, the founder of Amnesty International, at a Human Rights Day ceremony on 10 December 1961 and provided Amnesty International with its symbol of a burning candle (encircled by barbed wire).

2 **An editor is one who separates the wheat from the chaff and prints the chaff.**

Attributed in Bill Adler, *The Stevenson Wit* (1966), but see also HUBBARD 246:6.

See also ANONYMOUS 29:2.

Robert Louis STEVENSON Scottish writer (1850–94)

3 **For my part, I travel not to go anywhere, but to go. I travel for travel's sake. The great affair is to move.**

'Cheylard and Luc', *Travels With a Donkey* (1879). Stevenson also put this view in the words: 'To travel hopefully is a better thing than to arrive, and the true success is to labour' – 'El Dorado', *Virginibus Puerisque* (1881). Subsequently, the thought emerged in the form 'the journey not the arrival matters' (an expression used as the title of an autobiographical volume by Leonard Woolf, 1969). 'Getting there is half the fun' may have been used to advertise Cunard steamships in the 1920s and 1930s. It was definitely used to promote the Peter Sellers film *Being There* (1980) in the form: 'Getting there is half the fun. Being there is all of it.' In *Up the Organization* (1970), Robert Townshend opined of getting to the top: 'Getting there isn't half the fun – it's all the fun.'

4 **A Penny Plain and Twopence Coloured.**

Title of a noted essay in *The Magazine of Art* (1884) on the toy theatres or 'juvenile drama' of his youth. The expression referred to the prices of characters and scenery you could buy either already coloured or in black and white to colour yourself. Stevenson popularized the phrase in several pieces, but it undoubtedly existed before. George Augustus Sala, *Twice Round the Clock* (1859), has: 'The Scala [theatre, Milan] ... with its rabbit-hutch-like private boxes, whose doors are scrawled over with the penny plain and twopence coloured-like coats of arms of the ... Lombardian nobility.' *Tuppence Coloured* (on its own) was the title of a theatrical novel by Patrick Hamilton (1927) and of a revue (with Joyce Grenfell and others) in 1947.

5 **Under the wide and starry sky**
Dig the grave and let me lie.
Glad did I live and gladly die,
And I laid me down with a will.

This be the verse you grave for me:
Here he lies where he longed to be;
Home is the sailor, home from the sea
And the hunter home from the hill.

Stevenson's gravestone on Mount Vaea, Samoa, wrongly transcribes his poem 'Requiem', from *Underwoods* (1887), as above. The penultimate line should read 'Home is the sailor, *home from sea*', without the definite article. But this is a common quotation error. The two verses are also inscribed on Stevenson's memorial in St Giles's Cathedral, Edinburgh, complete with the misquotation.

The phrase 'This Be the Verse' was used by Philip Larkin as the title of the notorious poem beginning 'They fuck you up, your mum and dad', in *High Windows* (1974).

In *Across the Plains* (1892), Stevenson had composed an epitaph of which any man 'need not be ashamed': '*Here lies one who meant well, tried a little, failed much.*'

Home From the Hill was the title of a film (US 1960), based on a novel by William Humphrey. Compare *Home Is the Hero*, title of a film (UK 1959) based on Walter Macken's play. 'Home Comes the Hero' is the title of Chap. 22 of *Tom Moore* (1977) by Terence de Vere White. Otherwise the origin of this form of the phrase remains untraced. See also CRAWFORD 158:4.

1 Steel-true and blade-straight
The great artificer
Made my mate.

Poem 'My Wife', *Songs of Travel* (1896). Rather curiously, it is quoted as:

STEEL TRUE

BLADE STRAIGHT

on the grave of Sir Arthur Conan Doyle (1859–1930), the creator of Sherlock Holmes, in All Saints' churchyard, Minstead, Hampshire. Presumably, the widow – who was a spiritualist, if that is relevant – chose the epitaph.

(Sir) Tom STOPPARD British playwright (1937–)

2 The House of Lords, an illusion to which I have never been able to subscribe – responsibility without power, the prerogative of the eunuch throughout the ages.

Lord Malquist and Mr Moon (1966). See BALDWIN 50:5.

3 The bad ended unhappily, the good unluckily. That is what tragedy means.

Rosencrantz and Guildenstern Are Dead, Act 2 (1966). Compare WILDE 495:6.

4 McFee ... whose chief delusion is that Edinburgh is the Athens of the North ... McFee's dead ... He took offence at my description of Edinburgh as the Reykjavik of the South.

Jumpers (1972). Compare John Betjeman's earlier remark in a letter to Michael Rose (25 September 1955): 'As someone said, "We have often heard Cork called the Venice of Ireland, but have never heard Venice called the Cork of Italy."'

5 It seems pointless to be quoted if one isn't going to be quotable ... It's better to be quotable than honest.

Quoted in *The Guardian* (21 March 1973). An interviewer (Janet Watts) had noted his gift for quotable remarks and reminded him of something he had once said, producing a wry reaction.

6 If I knew, I'd go there.

In answer to the journalists' clichéd question 'Where do you get your ideas from?' Source – probably a *Guardian* interview. But compare what Joyce Grenfell wrote in *Joyce Grenfell Requests the Pleasure* (1976), which stated that this was her reply to the question 'Where do you get the ideas for your monologues?'

Earlier, A.A. Milne said of writing his articles for *Punch*: 'Ideas may drift into other minds, but they do not drift my way. I have to go and fetch them. I know no work manual or mental to equal the appalling heart-breaking anguish of fetching an idea from nowhere' – quoted in Ann Thwaite, *A.A. Milne* (1990). Later, the novelist Terry Pratchett was profiled in *The Observer* (8 November 1992): '"Where do you get your incredible ideas from?" asked a boy. (Someone always does.) "There's this warehouse called Ideas Are Us," Pratchett replied.'

7 Every member of the orchestra carries a conductor's baton in his knapsack.

Every Good Boy Deserves Favour (1978). Compare NAPOLEON 335:3.

Jack Trevor STORY British novelist (1917–91)

8 *Live Now, Pay Later.*

Title of screenplay (1962), based on the novel *All on the Never Never* by Jack Lindsay. As a simple graffito, the same line was recorded in Los Angeles (1970) in *The Encyclopedia of Graffiti* (1974). The same book records a New York subway graffito on a funeral parlour ad: 'Our layaway plan – die now, pay later.' 'Book now, pay later' was used in an advertisement in the programme of the Royal Opera House, Covent Garden, London, in 1977.

Back to 1962: in that year, Daniel Boorstin in *The Image* made oblique reference to travel advertisements using the line, 'Go now, pay later.' Was hire purchase ever promoted with 'Buy now, pay later'? It seems likely. These lines – in the US and UK – seem to be the starting point for a construction that has been much used and adapted since.

Harriet Beecher STOWE American novelist (1811–96)

9 I s'pect I growed. Don't think nobody ever made me.

Uncle Tom's Cabin (1852). The little slave girl, Topsy, on being asked who made her, asserts that she has no father or mother, and replies thus. Hence, the rephrased expression: 'Like Topsy – she just growed.'

Lytton STRACHEY English biographer (1880–1932)

10 I would try to get between them.

During the First World War Strachey had to appear before a military tribunal to put his case as a conscientious objector. He was asked by the chairman what, in view of his beliefs, he would do if he saw a German soldier trying to violate his sister. With an air of noble virtue, the homosexual Strachey replied, 'I would try to get between them.' A correspondent suggests that it was much more likely that Strachey would have said something more grandiloquent

– 'I would interpose my body' or some such – but the source for this anecdote is Robert Graves in *Goodbye To All That* (1929) and his version is the one given above.

Simeon STRUNSKY American writer (1879–1948)

1 Famous remarks are very seldom quoted correctly.
No Mean City, Chap. 38 (1944).

Geoffrey STUDDERT KENNEDY English clergyman (1883–1929)

2 God gave His children memory,
That in life's garden there might be
June roses in December.
'Roses in December', *Songs of Faith and Doubt*. It has been set to music by F.G. Russell. Compare BARRIE 53:5. Kennedy was known as 'Woodbine Willie' to the troops in the First World War, because of his habit of walking through the trenches and casualty stations with a haversack full of Woodbine cigarettes. As an ordained minister he was enrolled as Forces' chaplain in 1916 and served until 1919.

The SUN American New York-based newspaper, founded 1833

3 Yes, Virginia, there is a Santa Claus.
In 1897 an eight-year-old New York girl called Virginia O'Hanlon wrote a letter to *The Sun* which went, in part: 'Dear Editor: I am 8 years old. Some of my little friends say there is no Santa Claus. Papa says, "If you see it in *The Sun* it's so." Please tell me the truth, is there a Santa Claus?' The newspaper replied, in a famous piece (21 September 1897): 'Virginia, your little friends are wrong ... Yes, Virginia, there is a Santa Claus ... Not believe in Santa Claus! You might as well not believe in fairies! ... Thank God! he lives, and lives forever. A thousand years from now, Virginia, nay, ten times ten thousand years from now, he will continue to make glad the heart of childhood.' After his death, it was revealed that Francis P. Church (1839–1906) had written the editorial. There is a TV film based on the incident and entitled *Yes, Virginia, There Is a Santa Claus* (US 1991).

The SUN British London-based newspaper, founded 1964

4 WINTER OF DISCONTENT. Lest we forget ... the *Sun* recalls the long, cold months of industrial chaos that brought Britain to its knees.
This was the headline to a feature (30 April 1979) in the run-up to the general election that swept Margaret Thatcher

and the Conservatives to power. It was probably the first major use of this phrase to characterize the industrial unrest of the winter of 1978–9. It alludes to *Richard III* (SHAKESPEARE 420:3), which begins, famously, with Gloucester's punning and original metaphor, even if the editor of the Arden Shakespeare does describe the entire image as 'almost proverbial'. Probably made all the more memorable by Laurence Olivier's delivery of these lines in the 1955 film, the phrase 'winter of discontent' suffered the unpleasant fate of becoming a politician's and journalist's cliché following the winter of 1978–9, when British life was disrupted by all kinds of industrial protest against the Labour government's attempts to keep down pay rises. Most notably, rubbish remained uncollected and began to pile up in the streets, and a gravediggers' strike in one area reportedly left bodies unburied.

This 'winter of discontent' (as it is still referred to many years later) may perhaps have contributed to the Conservative victory at the May 1979 general election. The question has been asked, who first referred to it as such? *The Sun*'s earlier use of the phrase was the crucial one. (Sir) Larry Lamb, editor at the time, recalled in a Channel 4 TV programme *Benn Diaries II* (29 October 1989) that he introduced the phrase 'in a small way' during the winter itself (it was imitated by others), then 'in a big way' during the election. James Callaghan, the Prime Minister who was destroyed by the phrase, seems to have claimed that he used the phrase first (recalled in a TV programme, December 1991). Indeed, he appears to have done so on 8 February: 'I had known it was going to be a "winter of discontent".'

There is little new under *The Sun*, of course. J.B. Priestley, writing of earlier, much harder times in *English Journey* (1934) ended his fourth chapter with: 'The delegates have seen one England, Mayfair in the season. Let them see another England next time, West Bromwich out of season. Out of all seasons except the winter of discontent.'

5 GOTCHA!
Front page headline (4 May 1982). How *The Sun* 'celebrated' the sinking of the Argentine cruiser *General Belgrano* during the Falklands War, but the headline was retained for the first edition only. Other 'gung-ho' *Sun* headlines of the time included: 'STICK IT UP YOUR JUNTA' (20 April) – its attitude towards a negotiated settlement – and 'THE SUN SAYS KNICKERS TO ARGENTINA' and 'UP YOURS, GALTIERI', which sound so unlikely they must have appeared. *The Sun*'s posture was memorably parodied at the time by *Private Eye*, which suggested the headline: 'KILL AN ARGIE AND WIN A METRO.'

1 IF KINNOCK WINS TODAY WILL THE LAST PERSON IN BRITAIN PLEASE TURN OUT THE LIGHTS.

Front-page headline on the day of a British general election (9 April 1992), referring to Neil Kinnock, leader of the Labour Party, who, in fact, did not win the election. Something of an old joke. As 'Would the last person to leave the country please switch off the lights' it appeared in the book *Graffiti 2* (1980). Earlier, in Israel (in about 1966), when due to the political situation many people decided to leave the country, the story ran that at Lydda Airport near Tel Aviv a notice had been put up: 'Will the last to leave kindly turn out the light' – source: Maxime Rodinson, *Israel and the Arabs* (1969).

Willie SUTTON American bank robber (1901–80)

On being asked why he kept on robbing banks:

2 Because that's where the money is.

Attributed remark. Philip French touched on this topic in *The Observer* (8 October 2000): 'There is a mysterious kind of movie title that is not explained in the film itself and demands some special knowledge. *A Clockwork Orange*, *Straw Dogs* and *O Brother, Where Art Thou?* are examples. The amiable *Where the Money Is* … belongs in this category. Nobody uses the phrase in the film and, surprisingly, it is not in any dictionary of quotations that I possess. But it is generally attributed to the legendary American criminal Willie Sutton, who spent most of his life in jail and the rest of it planning heists. Asked in old age why he persisted in robbing banks, Willie replied: "Because that's where the money is" and it is clear that Henry, the elderly thief played by Paul Newman, is modelled on Willie Sutton.' As it happens, Sutton (who has been described as 'The most publicized bank robber since Jesse James') told CBS TV's *Sixty Minutes* (8 August 1976) that, in fact, a reporter made it up and attributed it to him. His book *I, Willie Sutton* (1953) apparently does contain the observation: 'It is a rather pleasant experience to be alone in a bank at night.'

Compare the similar-sounding proverbial sayings, 'Marry for love, but love where there is money' and 'Never marry for money, but marry where money is.' Tennyson's dialect poem 'Northern Farmer, New Style' contains this dialect version:

But I knaw'd a Quaäker feller as often 'as towd ma this:
'Doänt thou marry for munny, but goä wheer munny is!'

According to *Quotations for Our Time*, ed. Laurence J. Peter (1977), John F. Kennedy, when asked why he wanted to be President, replied: 'Because that's where the power is!'

Jonathan SWIFT Anglo-Irish writer and clergyman (1667–1745)

3 There are few wild beasts more to be dreaded than a talking man having nothing to say.

Unverified. Compare from Matthew Prior's *Alma*, Canto 2, line 345 (1718): 'And 'tis remarkable, that they / Talk most who have the least to say.'

4 Instead of dirt and poison we have rather chosen to fill our hives with honey and wax; thus furnishing mankind with the two noblest of things, which are sweetness and light.

Preface, *The Battle of the Books* (1704). Compare ARNOLD 40:8.

5 Many a true genius appears in the world – you may know him by this sign, that the dunces are all in confederacy against him.

Thoughts on Various Subjects (1706). Hence, *A Confederacy of Dunces*, the title of a novel (1980) by John Kennedy Toole.

6 Proper words in proper places, make the true definition of style.

Letter to a Young Gentleman lately entered into Holy Orders (9 January 1720). Compare COLERIDGE 150:5.

7 Their opinion is, that parents are the last of all others to be trusted with the education of their own children: and therefore they have in every town public nurseries, where all parents, except cottagers and labourers, are obliged to send their infants of both sexes to be reared and educated when they come to the age of twenty moons.

Gulliver's Travels, 'A Voyage to Lilliput', Chap. 6 (1726). Of the Lilliputians. Not quite the same as the William Morris/Bernard Shaw view, but an interesting precursor of BELL 59:2.

8 I cannot but conclude the bulk of your natives to be the most pernicious race of little odious vermin that nature ever suffered to crawl upon the surface of the earth.

In the same novel, 'A Voyage to Brobdingnag', Chap. 6. The King to Gulliver – about the British.

9 And he gave it for his opinion, that whoever could make two ears of corn or two blades of grass to grow upon a spot of ground where only one grew before, would deserve better of mankind, and do

more essential service to his country than the whole race of politicians put together.

In the same novel, 'A Voyage to Brobdingnag', Chap. 7. Compare VEBLEN 476:5.

1 So, naturalists observe, a flea
Hath smaller fleas that on him prey;
And these have smaller fleas to bite 'em,
And so proceed *ad infinitum*.
Thus every poet, in his kind,
Is bit by him that comes behind.

Referring to literary critics. 'On Poetry, a Rhapsody' (1733). Hence, the better-remembered lines from *A Budget of Para-doxes* by Professor Augustus de Morgan (1806–71):

Great fleas have little fleas
Upon their backs to bite 'em,
And little fleas have lesser fleas,
And so *ad infinitum*.

And the great fleas themselves in turn
Have greater fleas to go on,
While these again have greater still,
And greater still, and so on.

2 Here lies the body of Jonathan Swift, Professor of Holy Theology, for thirty years Dean of this cathedral church, where savage indignation can tear his heart no more. Go, traveller, and if you can, imitate one who with his utmost strength protected liberty. He died in the year 1745, on the 19th of October, aged seventy-eight.

Swift wrote this epitaph for himself (originally in Latin), and it may be found on a tablet in St Patrick's Cathedral, Dublin, where he lies buried and where he served as Dean 1713–45. The inscription includes the key phrase: '*Ubi saeva indignatio ulterius cor lacerare nequit*'. Said W.B. Yeats: 'Swift sleeps under the greatest epitaph in history.'

Algernon SWINBURNE English poet (1837–1909)

3 Thou hast conquered, O pale Galilean.

'Hymn to Proserpine' (1866). Pale Galilean = Jesus Christ. At one time, 'Galilean' (meaning a native of Galilee, but by extension, Christ or any Christian) was a term of abuse used by pagans. The line, and its follower ('The world has grown grey with thy breath!'), are quoted in Thomas Hardy's *Jude the Obscure*, Pt 2, Chap. 3 (1896).

4 All our past proclaims our future: Shakespeare's voice and Nelson's hand,
Milton's faith and Wordsworth's trust in this our chosen and chainless land,
Bear us witness: come the world against her, England yet shall stand.

'England: An Ode', Pt 2, St. 5, in *Astrophel and Other Poems* (1894). Compare SHAKESPEARE 413:2.

T

Charles Maurice de TALLEYRAND French statesman
(1754–1838)

1 *C'est une nouvelle, ce n'est pas un évènement* [It is
not an event, it is an item of news].

Remark when the news of Napoleon's death at St Helena
in 1821 reached Europe. Ignored by *Bartlett* and *ODQ*, this
quotation does, however, appear in *Benham* (1907). Quoting
the 5th Earl of Stanhope's *Conversations with the Duke of
Wellington* (for 1 November 1831), Elizabeth Longford,
Wellington: Pillar of State (1972), places the remark at 'a
Parisian party ... at Mme Craufurd's ... [and] Wellington
and Talleyrand were there to hear the startled cries'. J.F.
Bernard's *Talleyrand* (1973) dates this occasion to 14 July
1821: 'Madame Crawford broke the silence with a cry: "Oh,
good God! What an event!" She was answered by the prince's
[Talleyrand's] quiet, deep voice, from a corner of the room:
"No, madame. It is no longer an event. It is only a bit of
news."'

2 What does he mean by that?

On the death of the Turkish Ambassador to France. Unverified. Alluded to in Ben Pimlott, *Harold Wilson*, Chap. 29
(1992). However, another version is that it was said – in the
form 'Died, has he? Now I wonder what he meant by that?'
– by King Louis Philippe *about* Talleyrand. And yet another
is that Prince Metternich said, also of Talleyrand's own
death, 'What did he mean by it?' But there are no sources for
these either.

3 That fellow has a mind of inverted commas.

Said of a man who dealt in nothing but quotations. Attributed in *Punch* (16 July 1853).

Nahum TATE English hymnwriter (1652–1715)

4 Thus on the fatal banks of Nile,
Weeps the deceitful crocodile.

Dido and Aeneas, Act 3 (1689) – Tate's libretto for Henry
Purcell's opera. Dido sings the words about Aeneas just
after he has told her he is leaving her. The corresponding
scenes in Virgil's *Aeneid*, Bk 4, line 305ff and 365ff, do not
use this metaphor, so presumably it is Tate's own.

Bernie TAUPIN English lyricist (1950–)

5 It seems to me you lived your life
Like a candle in the wind.

Song, 'Candle in the Wind' (1973), music by Elton John. The
opening words 'Goodbye Norma Jean' refer to Marilyn
Monroe (who was born Norma Jean Mortenson/Baker): 'It
seems to me you lived your life / Like a candle in the wind.
/ Never knowing who to cling to / When the rain set in. /
And I would have liked to have known you / But I was just
a kid / That candle burned out long before / Your legend
ever did.' Elton John sang a revised version of the song at
the funeral of Princess Diana (7 September 1997): 'Goodbye
England's rose; / May you ever grow in our hearts ... / And
it seems to me you lived your life / Like a candle in the
wind; / Never fading with the sunset / When the rain set
in.' But where did the original title phrase come from?
Mencken (1942) gives 'Man's life is like a candle in the wind'
as a 'Chinese proverb'. A French dictionary of proverbs lists
'*La vie de l'homme est comme une chandelle dans le vent*' as
Chinese. A Dutch collection of Oriental quotations has:
'What is the life of Man? A candle in the wind, hoar frost
on the roof, the spasm of a fish in the frying pan.' A poem
by the Chinese poet Bai Juyi (772–846), describing the

illusory character of reality, contains the phrase 'a candle's flame in the wind'. A Latin emblem book by the French author Denis Lebey de Batilly (1596 edn) has a picture of a man seated at a table amidst classicist architecture. On the table is not a candle but a classical oil-lamp with burning wick. Big clouds with faces and puffed-up cheeks blow at the flame. The Latin motto is (in corrected form): '*QUID EST HOMO SICVT LVCERNA IN VENTO POSITA* [What is Man but a lamp in the wind].' The four-line Latin commentary says, in translation (from German): 'Man is like a small lamp, which in the dark night is exposed to the winds blowing from all sides. His flame of life feeds on such meagre, such unreliable oil – it is extinguished when the gale of Death grabs it.' The English novelist George Meredith later majored in wind-blown candle images in several of his novels. 'The light of every soul burns upward. Of course, most of them are candles in the wind. Let us allow for atmospheric disturbance' is from his novel, *Diana of the Crossways*, Chap. 39 (1885), where it is spoken by the heroine. Charles Joaquin Quirk, an American Catholic priest and a professor at Loyola University, published a book with the title *Candles in the Wind* in 1931. There is also a book with the same title by Maud Diver, possibly a novel (1909). Alexander Solzhenitsyn wrote a play entitled *Candle in the Wind* (1960) about moral choices in any society, either communist or capitalist. The original Russian title was *Svecha na vetru : (svet kotoryj v tehe)* [(A) candle in the wind : (the light which is in thee)], which refers to Luke 11:35. Of course, Taupin may not have been aware of any of these earlier uses. Indeed, according to Philip Norman's biography of Elton John, *Elton* (1991), Taupin heard that someone had applied the phrase to the singer Janis Joplin (1943–70), 'also doomed to early death from drugs', and took it on from there.

Ann and Jane TAYLOR English writers (1782–1866) and (1783–1824)

1 Who ran to help me when I fell,
And would some pretty story tell,
Or kiss the place to make it well?
My Mother.

One of the verses from 'My Mother', *Original Poems for Infant Minds* (1804). Sometimes this is attributed to Ann Taylor only. A parody that was widely known by at least 1978 goes:

Who took me from my bed so hot
And placed me shivering on the pot,
Nor asked me whether I should or not?
My Mother!

See also CARROLL 123:6.

Jeremy TAYLOR English divine (1613–67)

2 *Si fueris Romae, Romano vivito more; si fueris alibi, vivito sicut ibi* [If you are at Rome, live in the Roman style; if you are elsewhere, live as they live elsewhere].

Ductor Dubitantium (1660). Usually rendered: 'When in Rome, do as the Romans do.' This maxim suggests that one should adapt to prevalent customs. It appears in medieval Latin and is possibly based on an earlier remark by St Ambrose (who died in AD397). Hence, *When In Rome*, the title of a film (US 2002).

Norman TEBBIT (later Lord Tebbit) English Conservative politician (1931–)

3 [My father] did not riot. He got on his bike and looked for work. And he kept on looking till he found it.

Having just been appointed British Employment Secretary, Tebbit addressed the Conservative Party Conference on 15 October 1981. He related how he had grown up in the 1930s when unemployment was all around and gave the above comment. This gave rise to the pejorative catchphrase 'On your bike' or 'Get on your bike' from the lips of Mr Tebbit's opponents, and gave a new twist to a saying *Partridge/Slang* dates from about 1960, meaning 'go away' or 'be off with you'. Tebbit later pointed out that he had not been suggesting that the unemployed should literally get on their bikes.

4 Some thought my willingness to stand toe to toe against the more thuggish elements of the Labour Party and slug it out blow for blow rather vulgar. Others, especially in the country at large, seemed delighted at the idea of a Tory MP unwilling to be strangled by the old school tie.

Upwardly Mobile (1988). *OED2*'s oldest citation for the very British phrase 'old school tie' – symbolizing the supposed freemasonry among those who have been educated at public (i.e. private) schools in Britain – dates from 1932 (in a piece by Rudyard Kipling). The strangulation element appears to have crept in more recently. In Frederic Raphael's script for the film *Nothing But the Best* (UK 1964), the Denholm Elliott character says to the Alan Bates character, 'From now on, no one will be able to accuse you of being strangled by the old school tie' (this is just a moment before Bates strangles Elliott with just such an article of clothing). From BBC Radio's *Round the Horne* (7 April 1968): 'It's painful to be strangled by the old school tie.' *The Times* (27 September 1986) had: '[Trevor Howard] broke new ground, away from the English studio stereotypes of silly-ass eccentrics or decent but wooden chaps strangled by a combination of old school tie and stiff upper lip.'

William TEMPLE English theologian and Archbishop
(1881–1944)

1 Intellectually, stops matter a great deal. If you are getting your commas, semi-colons, and full-stops wrong, it means that you are not getting your thoughts right, and your mind is muddled.

Quoted in *The Observer* (23 October 1938). The rest of the news report is as follows: 'The Archbishop of York, Dr Temple, thinks that correct punctuation is more important – intellectually – than correct spelling. He said so yesterday when he presented the school prizes at the Royal Infant Orphanage at Wanstead. "In writing essays," said Dr Temple, "there are two things one has difficulty with – spelling and stops. Nearly everybody says it is the spelling that matters. Now spelling is one of the decencies of life, like the proper use of knives and forks. It looks slovenly and nasty if you spell wrongly, like trying to eat your soup with a fork. But, intellectually, spelling – English spelling – does not matter. Shakespeare spelt his own name at least four different ways, and it may have puzzled his cashiers at the bank. Intellectually, stops matter a great deal. If you are getting your commas, semi-colons, and full-stops wrong, it means that you are not getting your thoughts right, and your mind is muddled.'

Alfred TENNYSON (1st Baron Tennyson) English
Poet Laureate (1809–92)

2 Below the thunders of the upper deep;
Far, far beneath in the abysmal sea,
His ancient, dreamless, uninvaded sleep
The Kraken sleepeth.

'The Kraken' (1830), about a mythical sea monster, sleeping in the depths, waiting only to rise and die. The word 'kraken' is of Norwegian origin, and the monster was supposed to be of gigantic size and found off the coast of Norway. Hence, *The Kraken Wakes*, title of a science fiction novel (1953) by John Wyndham.

3 You must wake and call me early, call me
early, mother dear;
Tomorrow'll be the happiest time of all the
glad New-year;
Of all the glad New-year, mother, the maddest
merriest day;

For I'm to be Queen o' the May, mother, I'm to
be Queen o' the May.

'The May Queen' (1832). When Tennyson entered the Sheldonian Theatre in Oxford to receive an honorary degree of DCL, his long hair was in poetic disorder, dishevelled and unkempt. A voice cried out to him, 'Did your mother call you early, dear?' – recounted by Julian Charles Young in a diary note (8 November 1863).

4 Out flew the web and floated wide;
The mirror crack'd from side to side;
'The curse is come upon me,' cried
The Lady of Shalott.

In the same poem. Hence, *The Mirror Crack'd from Side to Side*, title of a Miss Marple crime novel (1962) by Agatha Christie and *The Mirror Crack'd*, title of a film therefrom (UK 1980).

5 Howe'er it be, it seems to me,
'Tis only noble to be good.
Kind hearts are more than coronets,
And simple faith than Norman blood.

'Lady Clara Vere de Vere' (1833). Hence, *Kind Hearts and Coronets*, title of film (UK 1949), about an aristocratic English family.

6 ... I dipped into the future far as human eye
could see,
Saw the Vision of the world, and all the wonder
that would be.
Saw the heavens fill with commerce, argosies of
magic sails,
Pilots of the purple twilight, dropping down
with costly bales;
Heard the heavens fill with shouting, and there
rain'd a ghastly dew.

'Locksley Hall', line 119 (1842). A rejected lover returns to his one-time home by the sea and, among other things, complains of the modern world of steamships and railways. He also makes an eerie prediction of commerce and warfare being extended to the skies. Sir John Colville's published diaries of his time as Winston Churchill's private secretary – *The Fringes of Power* (paperback editions 1986–7) – reveal the wartime Prime Minister quoting 'Tennyson's prescient lines about aerial warfare' (19 March 1941) without saying what the lines are.

1 We are not now that strength which in old days
Moved earth and heaven; that which we are,
  we are;
One equal temper of heroic hearts,
Made weak by time and fate, but strong in will
To strive, to seek, to find, and not to yield.

'Ulysses', line 44 (1842). The line 'To strive, to seek ...' appears on a memorial to Captain Scott, Captain Oates and others, at the South Pole. It was chosen by Apsley Cherry-Garrard, author of *The Worst Journey in the World* (1922), who had been a member of Scott's last expedition.

2 Rose a nurse of ninety years,
Set his child upon her knee –
Like summer tempest came her tears –
'Sweet my child, I live for thee.'

The Princess, Pt 6 (song added 1850). Hence, 'Like Summer Tempests came his Tears' – the title to Chap. 11 of Kenneth Grahame, *The Wind in the Willows* (1908). See GRAHAME 219:4. Grahame puts *'his* Tears' because it refers to Toad, but in the original Tennyson, the subject is *female*. Also, the 'tempest' is singular.

3 Now sleeps the crimson petal, now the white.

In the same poem, Pt 7, line 161 (song added 1850). Hence, *The Crimson Petal and the White*, title of a novel (2002) by Michael Faber.

4 The moan of doves in immemorial elms.

In the same poem, Pt 7, line 203. Hence, 'immemorial elms' as a cliché of quotation. 'The PM ... dreams of a Britain where we all drink warm beer in the shadow of immemorial elms, and nuns bicycle to church through the mist, and Denis Compton is still at the crease on the final day of the Oval test match' – *The Observer* (19 February 1995); 'I have driven for hours around those winding lagoon-like car parks, lovingly landscaped between clumps of immemorial elms, trying to find the exit' – *The Times Higher Education Supplement* (31 March 1995).

5 'Tis better to have loved and lost
Than never to have loved at all.

In Memoriam A.H.H., Canto 27 (1850). Several earlier expressions of this thought have been adduced. In William Congreve, *The Way of the World*, Act 2, Sc. 1 (1700), is: ''Tis better to be left than never to have been loved'; in Thomas Campbell's poem 'The Jilted Nymph' (1843): 'Better be courted and jilted / Than never be courted at all.' And compare BUTLER 115:2.

6 Though Nature, red in tooth and claw
With ravine, shrieked against his creed.

In the same poem, Canto 56. Origin of the phrase 'red in tooth and claw', which became associated with the evolutionary idea of 'the survival of the fittest' – see SPENCER 439:1.

7 So many worlds, so much to do,
So little done, such things to be.

In the same poem, Canto 73. Compare RHODES 382:2.

8 Revered, beloved – you that hold
A nobler office on the earth
Than valour, power of brain, or birth,
Could give the warrior kings of old.

'To the Queen' – the new Poet Laureate's first poem to his sovereign in March 1851. G.K. Chesterton quotes the last three lines in *The Napoleon of Notting Hill*, Chap. 3 (1904), as though they had been written by his character, Mr Quin: '... to quote a poem that I wrote in my youth ...'

9 O fall'n at length that tower of strength
Which stood four-square to all the winds that
  blew!

'Ode on the Death of the Duke of Wellington' (1852). See also SHAKESPEARE 420:5.

10 Not once or twice in our rough island story
The path of duty was the way to glory.

In the same poem. The probable origin of the 'island story' phrase. *Our Island Story, a child's history of England* (?1910) by H.E. Marshall (stories and fables from King Arthur to Queen Victoria, addressed to two Australian children) was an immensely popular history book in the early 20th century. Compare NEWBOLT 339:4.

11 Forward the Light Brigade!
Was there a man dismay'd?
Not tho' the soldier knew
Someone had blundered:
Their's not to make reply,
Their's not to reason why,
Their's but to do and die:
Into the valley of Death
Rode the six hundred.

'The Charge of the Light Brigade' (1854). 'Their's' is as written. The Charge of the Light Brigade took place at Balaclava, near Sebastopol, on 25 October 1854, during the Crimean War. Owing to a misunderstood order, 247 officers and men out of 637 were killed or wounded. Tennyson's famous poem about it was published in *The Examiner* newspaper on 9 December that same year. According to Christopher Ricks's edition of the poems, Tennyson wrote this on 2 December 1854, 'in a few minutes, after reading ... *The Times* in which occurred the phrase *someone had blundered*, and this was the origin of the metre of his poem'. In fact, *The Times* had spoken rather (in a leader on 13 November) of 'some hideous blunder'. Advised to be careful because controversy would offend the War Office, Tennyson allowed the 'someone had blundered' line to be deleted when his next collection of poems was published – *Maud, and Other Poems* (1855). But when he heard that the Society for the Propagation of the Gospel intended to circulate this *revised* poem to the troops, he had copies of the *uncut* version printed and sent to the Crimea.

Hence, *The Reason Why* (1953), Cecil Woodham-Smith's study of the Charge of the Light Brigade, and *To Reason Why*, a war memoir by Denis Forman (1991).

1 Come into the garden, Maud,
For the black bat, night, has flown.

Maud, I.xxii.1 (1855). The first line, immensely famous, was further popularized in the musical setting of the lines by Michael Balfe in 1856.

2 For why is all around us here
As if some lesser god had made the world,
But had not force to shape it as he would.

'The Passing of Arthur', lines 13–15, *Idylls of the King* (1859). Hence, *Children of a Lesser God*, the title of Marc Medoff's play (1979; film US 1986), about a relationship between a deaf girl and her speech therapist. Medoff's suggestion, presumably, is that people with a disability like deafness are regarded by some as the work of a 'lesser god'.

3 The old order changeth, yielding place to new,
And God fulfils himself in many ways,
Lest one good custom should corrupt the world.

In the same poem, line 407. The meaning of the third line has puzzled some readers. Tennyson himself indicated that what he meant was 'e.g. chivalry, by formalism of habit or by any other means'.

4 The woods decay, the woods decay and fall,
The vapours weep their burthen to the ground,
Man comes and tills the field and lies beneath,
And after many a summer dies the swan.

'Tithonus' (1860). Hence, *After Many A Summer*, title of a novel (1939) by Aldous Huxley.

5 Landscape-lover, lord of language
more than he that sang the Works and Days,
All the chosen coin of fancy
flashing out from many a golden phrase.

'To Virgil' (1882) – 'written at the request of the Mantuans for the nineteenth centenary of Virgil's death'. The rush of alliteration in the first line of this stanza possibly introduces the phrase 'lord of language'. Subsequently it has been otherwise bestowed. 'Ah, Madame Melba, I am the Lord of Language and you are the Queen of Song, and so I suppose I shall have to write you a sonnet' – Oscar Wilde, quoted in Nellie Melba, *Melodies and Memories* (1925). In *De Profundis* (published 1905), Wilde wrote of his mother's death: 'I, once a lord of language, have no words in which to express my anguish and shame.'

From this phrase may also have come such compliments as 'master of language' and 'lord of words'. The latter was used, for example, to describe the broadcaster, Sir Huw Wheldon, and the playwright, Samuel Beckett, at their deaths in 1986 and 1989, respectively. 'The Word-Lord' is a heading in *Punch* (9 June 1915).

An early appearance of the phrase: in the prologue to Chaucer's *Treatise on the Astrolabe*, he presents a justification of his decision to write it in English, ending with the clincher that Richard II is an English-speaker: 'And preie save the king, that is lord of this langage, and alle that him feith berith and obeieth ...'

6 Sunset and evening star,
And one clear call for me!
And may there be no moaning of the bar,
When I put out to sea.

'Crossing the Bar' (1889). Compare KINGSLEY 271:2.

7 I don't think that since Shakespeare there has been such a master of the English language as I. But to be sure, I have nothing to say.

Quoted in Nicholas Parsons, *The Book of Literary Lists* (1985). Compare BIERCE 88:3.

TERENCE Roman playwright (?190–159 BC)

8 *Homo sum; Humani, nil a me alienum puto* [I am a man; nothing human is alien to me].

Heauton Timoroumenos, 1,1. See also LAWRENCE 280:2.

TERESA OF AVILA Spanish mystic and saint (1515–82)

1 Let nothing disturb thee,
Let nothing affright thee,
All passeth away,
God alone will stay,
Patience obtaineth all things.
Who God possesseth, is lacking in nothing
God alone sufficeth.

In *The Art of the Possible* (1971), R.A. Butler recalled how he quoted all but the last two of these lines to Winston Churchill when the Prime Minister retired in 1955, adding 'This, like St Augustine, I have learned.' But, no, this is commonly known as 'St Teresa's Prayer', and Stephen Clissold in his biography of her (published in 1979) tells of the circumstances in which it was written.

2 Alas, O Lord, to what a state dost Thou bring those who love thee!

The Interior Castle (1577), translated by the Benedictines of Stanbrook (1921). This has also been rendered as, when caught in a great flood on the road to Burgos, she exclaimed: 'Lord if this is how you treat your friends, no wonder they are so few.'

3 More tears are shed over answered prayers than unanswered ones.

Attributed remark. Hence, *Answered Prayers*, title of an unfinished *roman à clef* (1986) by Truman Capote.

The TERMINATOR American film 1984. With Arnold Schwarzenegger as the Terminator.

4 I'll be back!

A phrase that caught on following its menacing use by Schwarzenegger playing a time-travelling robot who terminates his opponents with extreme prejudice. The phrase is only spoken once within the film, but caught on because it so perfectly caught the central threat and menace of the story.
Coincidentally, the last words of the film *Pimpernel Smith* (UK 1941) are: 'I'll be back ... we'll all be back.' These are spoken by Leslie Howard as a professor of archaeology who goes into war-torn Europe to rescue refugees.

Josephine TEY British crime novelist (1896–1952)

5 The beasts that talk,
The streams that stand,
The stones that walk,
The singing sand,
...

That guard the way
To Paradise.

The Singing Sands (1952) – in which the whole plot hinges on this fragment of verse scribbled on a newspaper by a dying man. The detective in question – Inspector Grant – is reduced to putting an advert in *The Times* to find the source, and thinks: 'It will serve me right if someone writes to say that the thing is one of the best-known lines of some Xanadu concoction of Coleridge's, and that I must be illiterate not to have known it.' But it does not appear to be an actual quotation.
'Singing sands' in itself is a long-established term for sands that appear to make a noise. The caption to a cartoon in *Punch* (22 August 1923): 'Lord Curzon's forthcoming book of travel, his publishers state, will contain "a full and picturesque study of the Singing Sands, i.e. the sand slopes and dunes which in remote and often inaccessible parts of Asia, Arabia and even America, give forth sounds which resemble the noise of trumpets and drums".'

William Makepeace THACKERAY English novelist (1811–63)

6 'Revenge may be wicked, but it's natural,' answered Miss Rebecca. 'I'm no angel.' And, to say the truth, she certainly was not.

Vanity Fair, Chap. 1 (1847–8). An early appearance of the self-deprecatory phrase, 'I'm no angel.' Compare: *I'm No Angel* (film US 1933) and *We're No Angels* (film US 1954).

7 Come, children, let us shut up the box and the puppets, for our play is played out.

In the same book, Chap. 67. Last words of novel. This only makes sense if the edition of the novel has begun with the prefatory chapter 'Before the Curtain', which is, however, omitted in some. Thackeray speaks as 'the Manager of the Performance' at a Fair ('Yes, this is VANITY FAIR'). He refers to his characters as 'Puppets' ('the famous little Becky Puppet has been pronounced to be uncommonly flexible in the joints') and 'with this, and a profound bow to his patrons, the Manager retires, and the curtain rises'.

8 The *Pall Mall Gazette* is written by gentlemen for gentlemen.

Pendennis, Chap. 32 (1848–50). Compare SALISBURY 393:5.
See also BUNYAN 107:7.

(Sir) Denis THATCHER Bart. English businessman
and husband of Margaret Thatcher (1915–2003)

1 I like everything my beloved wife likes. If she wants
to buy the top brick of St Paul's, then I would
buy it.

Quoted in *The Observer* (7 April 1985) – probably taken from
an interview in the *Sunday Express*. *Partridge/Slang* suggests that the phrase 'to give someone the top brick off the
chimney' means 'to be the acme of generosity, with implication that foolish spoiling, or detriment to the donor would
result, as in "his parents'd give that boy the ..." or "she's
that soft-hearted, she'd give you ..."' Partridge's reviser, Paul
Beale, who inserted this entry, commented that he had
heard the phrase in the early 1980s, but that it was probably
in use much earlier.

Indeed, when Anthony Trollope was standing for Parliament in 1868, he described a seat at Westminster as 'the
highest object of ambition to every educated Englishman'
and 'the top brick of the chimney'. In *Nanny Says*, Joyce
Grenfell's and Sir Hugh Casson's collection of nanny sayings
(1972), is included, 'Very particular we are – it's top brick
off the chimney or nothing.' Presumably, Denis Thatcher
was reworking this saying for his own ends. Unconsciously,
he may have been conflating it with another kind of reference, such as is found in Charles Dickens, *Martin Chuzzlewit*, Chap. 38 (1844): 'He would as soon as thought of
the cross upon the top of St Paul's Cathedral taking note of
what he did ... as of Nadgett's being engaged in such an
occupation.'

Margaret THATCHER (later Baroness Thatcher)
British Conservative Prime Minister (1925–)

2 No woman in my time will be Prime Minister or
Chancellor or Foreign Secretary – not the top jobs.
Anyway, I wouldn't want to be Prime Minister.
You have to give yourself 100%.

Interview, *The Sunday Telegraph* (26 October 1969). Mrs
Thatcher was notably dismissive of her chances of achieving
high office – before the opportunity presented itself. A little
later, when Secretary of State for Education, she was interviewed on BBC TV *Val Meets the VIPS* (5 March 1973) and
said: 'I do not think there will be a woman Prime Minister
in my lifetime ... I would not wish to be Prime Minister,
dear. I have not enough experience for that job. The only
full ministerial position I've held is Minister of Education
and Science. Before you could even *think* of being Prime
Minister, you'd need to have done a good deal more jobs
than that.'

3 Ladies and gentlemen, I stand before you tonight
in my green chiffon evening gown, my face softly
made up, my fair hair gently waved ... the Iron
Lady of the Western World. Me? A Cold War
warrior? Well, yes – if that is how they wish to
interpret my defence of values, and freedoms
fundamental to our way of life.

Speech in her Finchley constituency (31 January 1976). Earlier, on 19 January, Mrs Thatcher had said in a speech that
'The Russians are bent on world dominance ... the Russians
put guns before butter' (compare GOEBBELS 216:1). Within
a few days the Soviet Defence Ministry newspaper *Red Star*
(in an article signed by Captain Y. Gavrilov) had accused the
'Iron Lady' of seeking to revive the Cold War. The article
wrongly suggested that she was popularly known by this
nickname in the UK at that time, though a headline over a
profile by Marjorie Proops in the *Daily Mirror* of 5 February
1975 had been 'The Iron Maiden'. Now, in her Finchley
speech, she made the 'Iron Lady' sobriquet her own.

4 Let us make this a country safe to work in. Let us
make this a country safe to walk in. Let us make
it a country safe to grow up in. Let us make it a
country safe to grow old in. And [the message of
the 'other' Britain] says, above all, may this land
of ours, which we love so much, find dignity and
greatness and peace again.

Televised party political broadcast (30 April 1979) – the eve
of her first election win. Thatcher smuggled in an unacknowledged quote from Noël Coward's play *Cavalcade* (1931).
In the original, the toast is: 'That one day this country of
ours, which we love so much, will find dignity and greatness and peace again.' The hand of Sir Ronald Millar, the
playwright and her principal speechwriter, may presumably be detected in this.

5 I would just like to remember some words of
St Francis of Assisi which I think are really just
particularly apt at the moment – 'Where there is
discord, may we bring harmony; where there is
error may we bring truth; where there is doubt,
may we bring faith; and where there is despair,
may we bring hope.'

Outside 10 Downing Street on becoming Prime Minister
(4 May 1979). See FRANCIS OF ASSISI 200:5.

6 There is no easy popularity in that [harsh economic
measures already set in train by the government]
but I believe people accept there is no alternative.

Speech to the Conservative Women's Conference, London

(21 May 1980). An early appearance of the famously nannyish phrase 'There is no alternative', which became a rallying cry of the Thatcher government. It provides a good example of how it can be more difficult tracing the origins of recent quotations than of older ones. By the early 1980s, everyone in Britain knew the phrase, but how had it arisen? If she had said it in the House of Commons it would have been possible to search through *Hansard* (the electronic version makes computer-searching very simple). But she had not, apparently. So one was faced with searching through newspapers for a mention of the phrase, except that most British newspapers were not being transferred on to computer databases until the mid-1980s.

Perhaps she had said it at one of her meetings with Parliamentary lobby correspondents? But these occasions are never directly reported (hence the obscurity surrounding the coining of Harold Wilson's famous observation 'a week is a long time in politics', see 501:2), and if she had said it at one, the political correspondents consulted were unable to remember.

In 1984 Dr David Butler, the psephologist, approached me regarding the phrase, because he was revising his *British Political Facts*. Some more asking around was done and no progress was made. Patrick Cosgrave, an adviser to Mrs Thatcher before she became Prime Minister, suggested that, perhaps, the phrase had not actually been coined by her, but simply picked up, in the way she had of seizing on ideas that she fancied.

Butler wrote to Downing Street and received a letter from Mrs Thatcher's then political secretary espousing a similar view: 'I am not sure that the Prime Minister ever actually used the phrase ... and my suspicion, shared by others, is that TINA was coined by those who were pressing for a change of policy.'

This only took us further away than ever from a satisfactory conclusion. Then, in 1986, and in the time-honoured fashion, I happened to stumble upon a report of Mrs Thatcher's speech to the Conservative Women's Conference, marking the end of her first year in office, as above. So, there, she *had* said it, and publicly, too. I don't know whether this was the first time – in fact, I think she may well have said it at some stage in 1979 – but at last here was a reference.

A correspondent suggested a comparison with the old Hebrew catchphrase '*ain breira*' ('there is no choice'). The acronym 'TINA', said to have been coined by Young Conservatives, was flourishing by the time of the Party Conference in September 1981, and as a consequence some journalists gave Thatcher the nickname 'Tina'.

1 To those waiting with bated breath for that favourite media catchphrase, the U-turn, I have only one thing to say. You turn if you want to. The lady's not for turning.

Speech to the Conservative Party Conference at Brighton (11 October 1980). Here Mrs Thatcher comes up with what is, in a sense, her best-remembered formally spoken 'line'. While not convincing the hearer that she could have alluded unaided to the title of the play *The Lady's Not for Burning* (1948) by Christopher Fry, the cry had the curiously insidious memorability that most effective slogans need to have. Again, one detects the hand of Sir Ronald Millar in all this. Indeed, in *The Sunday Times* (23 November 1980), he confirmed that he had coined the phrase, but also reported that he would have 'preferred his friend the prime minister to have said "the lady's not for turning" with an elided "'s" exactly as in the original title of Christopher Fry's play.' Which is odd, because any recording of the speech will confirm that she did *not* say, 'The lady is not', but 'the lady's not ...' (just as she was told).

2 As the poet said, 'One clear morn is boon enough for being born', and so it is.

Interview on BBC Radio with Pete Murray (7 March 1982). The occasion was when, tearfully, she described her fears while it had seemed that her son Mark was lost on a Trans-Sahara car rally. She realized then, she said, that all the little things people worried about really were not worth it. Here Mrs Thatcher is relying on that old standby 'As the poet said ...' to disguise forgetfulness or genuine ignorance of the source.

I was puzzled by the quotation and wrote to Downing Street for illumination, my letter plopping on the mat just as the Falklands War broke out. When that little difficulty was resolved, I received back a photocopy of an anonymous poem which had presumably been carried about in the Thatcher handbag for many a year. Subsequently, in *Woman's Own* (17 November 1984), it was revealed that the poem had been taken from something called 'Love's Tapestry Calendar 1966':

> Life owes me nothing:
> One clear morn
> Is boon enough
> for being born;
> And be it ninety years
> or ten,
> No need for me
> to question when.
> While life is mine,
> I'll find it good
> And greet each hour
> with gratitude.

1 Failure? Do you remember what Queen Victoria once said? 'Failure? – the possibilities do not exist.'

TV news interview (5 April 1982) at the start of the war in the Falklands. Mrs Thatcher evoked the spirit of Queen Victoria with the remark that had been made at the end of 'Black Week' in 1899, during the Boer War: 'We are not interested in the possibilities of defeat; they do not exist.' *Time* Magazine (December 1982) ascribed the words to Mrs Thatcher as though they were not a quotation. See also VICTORIA 477:3.

2 Just rejoice at that news and congratulate our forces and the Marines. Goodnight. Rejoice!

Remark to newsmen outside 10 Downing Street (25 April 1982) on the recapture of South Georgia – wording confirmed by TV recordings made at the time. Usually rendered as 'Rejoice, rejoice!' From the next day's *Daily Telegraph* (26 April 1982): 'A triumphant Prime Minister declared "Rejoice, rejoice" last night ...' Much later, this is Julian Critchley MP writing in *The Observer* (27 June 1993): 'Shortly after Mrs Thatcher's defenestration in November 1990, I ran into [Sir Edward] Heath in a Westminster corridor. I quoted a Spanish proverb: if you wait by the river long enough, the body of your enemy will float by. Heath broke into a broad grin: "Rejoice, rejoice", was his reply.' In a TV interview (September 1998), Heath told Michael Cockerell that he had also communicated similarly with his office: 'I said it three times – rejoice, rejoice, rejoice. She'd only said it twice.'

However it is quoted, can one detect in it signs of her Methodist upbringing? Although 'Rejoice, rejoice!' is quite a common expression, each verse of Charles Wesley's hymn 'Rejoice! the Lord is King' ends: 'Rejoice, again I say, rejoice' (a hymn played at the 1983 Conservative Party Conference). There was also a 19th-century hymn (words by Grace J. Frances), 'Rejoice, Rejoice, Believer!' The refrain of 'O Come, O Come Emmanuel' (a hymn translated by J.M. Neale) goes, 'Rejoice! Rejoice! Emmanuel / Shall come to thee, O Israel'. But, as has been pointed out, the ultimate source is Philippians 4:4: 'Rejoice in the Lord always: and again I say, Rejoice.'

3 Victorian values ... those were the values when our country became great, not only internationally but at home.

Interview on ITV's *Weekend World* (17 January 1983). In the general election of that year and thereafter, Margaret Thatcher and other Cabinet ministers frequently commended the virtue of a return to Victorian values. The phrase appears to have been coined for her by Brian Walden in this TV interview. It was *he* who suggested to *her* that she was trying to restore 'what I would call Victorian values'. She replied: 'Very much so. Those were the values when our country became great. But not only did our country become great internationally, also much advance was made in this country – through voluntary rather than state action.' She made the phrase her own, using it several times in the next few weeks. Mrs Thatcher also said in an LBC radio interview on 15 April: 'I was brought up by a Victorian grandmother. We were taught to work jolly hard. We were taught to prove ourselves; we were taught self-reliance; we were taught to live within our income ... You were taught that cleanliness is next to godliness. You were taught self-respect. You were taught always to give a hand to your neighbour. You were taught tremendous pride in your country. All of these things are Victorian values. They are also perennial values.' On 23 April *The Daily Telegraph* quoted Dr Rhodes Boyson, the Minister for Schools, as saying: 'Good old-fashioned order, even Victorian order, is far superior to illiterate disorder and innumerate chaos in the classroom.' It also quoted Neil Kinnock, then Chief Opposition Spokesman on Education, as saying: 'Victorian Britain was a place where a few got rich and most got hell. The "Victorian values" that ruled were cruelty, misery, drudgery, squalor and ignorance.'

In a speech to the British Jewish Community (21 July 1983), Thatcher said: 'I was asked whether I was trying to restore Victorian values. I said straight out I was. And I am.' In her book *The Downing Street Years* (1993), Thatcher comments: 'I never felt uneasy about praising "Victorian values" or – the phrase I originally used – "Victorian virtues".'

4 Some say Maggie may, or others say Maggie may not. I can only say that when the time comes, I shall decide.

Speech (April 1983) – when wishing to appear coy about whether she would be calling a General Election soon. An unwise allusion to a character in the Liverpool song 'Maggie May', which dates from at least 1830. Maggie May is a prostitute who steals sailors' trousers, but, as the song goes on to relate: 'A policeman came and took that girl away. / For she robbed a Yankee whaler, / She won't walk down Lime Street any more.'

A number of groups (including The Beatles) revived the song at the time of Liverpool's resurgence in the early 1960s. In 1964 Lionel Bart and Alun Owen wrote a musical called *Maggie May*, based on her life.

5 Oh, the Right Honourable Gentleman is afraid of an election is he? Afraid, afraid, afraid, frightened, frit, couldn't take it, couldn't stand it!

A challenge to the prominent Labour minister, Denis Healey,

in the House of Commons (20 April 1983). Healey had suggested that she was preparing to 'cut and run' regarding a general election. 'Frit', as an abbreviation for 'fright/frightened', is still widely used in the north Midlands – including Grantham where she was born. The first recorded use of the word was by the Northamptonshire poet, John Clare. In 'The Village Minstrel' (1821), he wrote:

The coy hare squats nesting in the corn,
Frit at the bow'd ear tott'ring over her head.

The chief surprise in Mrs Thatcher using the word was that hitherto she had successfully concealed her linguistic roots.

1 We had to fight the enemy without in the Falklands. We always have to be aware of the enemy within, which is more difficult to fight and more dangerous to liberty.

Speech to the 1922 Committee (19 July 1984). The expression 'enemy within' refers to an internal rather than external threat. It has been suggested that it is a shortened version of 'the enemy/traitor within the gate(s)' – 'one who acts, or is thought to act, against the interests of the family, group, society, etc. of which he is a member' – but, whatever the case, it is a phrase with a long history. Charles Welsey's hymn 'None Is Like Jeshurun's God' (1742) contains the lines: 'God is thine; disdain to fear / The enemy within: / God shall in thy flesh appear, / And make an end of sin ...' In 1940 Winston Churchill said of the BBC that it was 'an enemy within the gates, doing more harm than good'.

On 22 January 1983 *The Economist* wrote of the industrial-relations scene in Britain: 'The government may be trusting that public outrage will increasingly be its ally. Fresh from the Falklands, Mrs Thatcher may even relish a punch-up with the enemy within to enhance her "resolute approach" further.' Seven months later, Mrs Thatcher was using exactly the same phrase and context regarding the British miners' strike. She 'told Tory MPs that her government had fought the enemy without in the Falklands conflict and now had to face an enemy within ... she declared that the dockers and pit strikers posed as great a threat to democracy as General Galtieri, the deposed Argentine leader' – *The Guardian*, 20 July 1984.

Earlier, in 1980, Julian Mitchell had used the phrase as the title of a play about anorexia. It was also the title of a Tony Garnett BBC TV play in 1974 and of a stage play by Brian Friel in 1962. A book (1960) by Robert F. Kennedy about 'organized corruption' in the US labour movement had the title, as did one by John Watner during/about the Second World War (untraced). The earliest *OED2* citation dates from 1608: 'The enemy within ... sporteth herself in the consumption of those vital parts, which waste and wear away by yielding to her unpacifiable teeth' – Edward Topsell,

The Historie of Serpents. Compare also Cicero on the Catilinarian conspiracy to launch a *coup d'état*: '*Intus est hostis*' – *In Catilinam*, II.v.11.

2 In church on Sunday morning – it was a lovely morning and we haven't had many lovely days – the sun was coming through a stained glass window and falling on some flowers, falling right across the church. It just occurred to me that this was the day I was meant not to see.

Mrs Thatcher expressed her feelings in a TV interview on having escaped death in an IRA bomb explosion at Brighton. She referred to Sunday 14 October 1984. *The Observer* (21 October) reported the final phrase as 'the day I was not meant to see'. *The Daily Telegraph* (17 October) had already affirmed that 'the day I was meant not to see' was the correct version, adding: 'Since they are words which may well enter future anthologies, we should get the record straight.' In 1995, *Brewer's Politics* was giving the phrase as, 'this was *a* day I was not meant to see'.

3 We must try to find ways to starve the terrorists of the oxygen of publicity on which they depend.

Speech to the American Bar Association meeting in London (15 July 1985). While the phrase 'oxygen of publicity' did not seem new at the time, this usage certainly popularized the term. Coinage of the phrase has been ascribed to Britain's then Chief Rabbi, Lord Jakobovits.

4 Stop being moaning minnies.

Remark during visit to Tyneside (11 September 1985). Mrs Thatcher was reported as accusing those who complained about the effects of unemployment of being 'Moaning Minnies'. In the ensuing uproar, a Downing Street spokesman had to point out that it was the reporters attempting to question her, rather than the unemployed, upon whom Mrs Thatcher had bestowed the title.

As a nickname, it was by no means an original coinage. Anyone who complains is a 'moaner', and a 'minnie' is a word that can be used to describe a lost lamb that finds itself an adoptive mother. From *The Observer* (20 May 1989): 'Broadcasters are right to complain about the restrictions placed on them for the broadcasting of the House of Commons ... But the Moaning Minnies have only themselves to blame.'

The original 'Moaning Minnie' was something quite different. In the First World War a 'Minnie' was the slang name for a German *Minenwerfer*, a trench mortar or the shell that came from it, making a distinctive moaning noise. In the Second World War the name was applied to air-raid sirens, which also made that noise.

1 Is he one of us?

Attributed remark when reviewing candidates for appointments (by 1985). From *The Independent* (28 January 1989): 'Mr [Kenneth] Clarke also failed the is-he-one-of-us? test applied by Mrs Thatcher to favoured colleagues.' Hence, *One of Us*, the title of Hugo Young's political study of Mrs Thatcher (1989).

2 I hope to go on and on.

On her future as Prime Minister. In a BBC Radio interview with John Cole (11 May 1987) after she had called a general election, possibly repeating an earlier remark. This is precisely what she said in answer to Cole's question about whether she expected this to be her last election as party leader. In Cole's memoir, *As It Seemed to Me* (1995), he cannot resist stating that what she said was – as popularly rendered – that she intended 'to go on and on and on'.

3 There is no such thing as Society. There are individual men and women, and there are families. And no government can do anything except through people, and people must look to themselves first. It's our duty to look after ourselves and then to look after our neighbour.

Interview, *Woman's Own* (31 October 1987) – which, in her memoirs (as above), she says 'caused a storm of abuse at the time'. What she meant was that no one could escape moral responsibility for their actions by transferring that responsibility to an abstraction. Much-alluded to, for example, from the film *Trainspotting* (UK 1996): 'There was no such thing as society and, even if there was, I most certainly had nothing to do with it.'

4 We have become a grandmother.

Remark to news reporters (3 March 1989). From this use of the royal 'we' stemmed a conviction in some observers that all was not well with Mrs Thatcher. She only remained in office another year and a half.

5 Every Prime Minister needs a Willie.

Remark at a Carlton Club dinner for the Deputy Prime Minister, Lord (William) Whitelaw when he retired. Quoted by Michael Cockerell in *The Guardian* (8 April 1989) as the 'latest' example of Thatcher's penchant for the unintended double entendre. In fact this was said a year earlier, as reported in *The Guardian* (29 January 1988).

6 The Chancellor's position is unassailable ... In this party, ministers decide and advisers only advise.

Remark in the House of Commons (26 October 1989).

She was commenting on the role of her economic adviser (Alan Walters) in relation to that of her Chancellor of the Exchequer (Nigel Lawson), who resigned next day on this issue. One of her other ministers, Norman Fowler, accordingly entitled his memoirs *Ministers Decide* (1991).

7 The President of the Commission, M. Delors, said at this conference the other day that he wanted the European Parliament to be the democratic body of the Community, he wanted the Commission to be the Executive, and he wanted the Council of Ministers to be the Senate. No. No. No.

Speech, House of Commons (30 October 1990) on her return from the Rome summit. It has been said that the stridency of her attack on this occasion contributed to the resignation of the Deputy Prime Minister, Sir Geoffrey Howe, the following month and her own removal from office the month after that.

8 I fight on: I fight to win.

Remark to reporters, as she left 10 Downing Street for the House of Commons to make a statement on a Paris summit conference (21 November 1990). The previous evening she had not received sufficient votes to ensure her re-election as Conservative Party leader and, at this moment, seemed to be going forward to a second ballot. John Cole in *As It Seemed To Me* (1995) describes her remark as 'in Joan of Arc mood'. In *The Downing Street Years* (1993), Thatcher says she 'was interested to see later on the news that I looked a good deal more confident than I felt'. The following day she withdrew from the contest and resigned.

9 It's a funny old world.

In *The Independent* (23 November 1990), Margaret Thatcher was reported as having exclaimed 'It's a funny old world' (with tears in her eyes) at the previous day's Cabinet meeting at which she announced she had been ousted from the premiership. A fairly common expression of reluctant acceptance of some blow that fate has delivered. In the 1934 film *You're Telling Me*, W.C. Fields delivers the line, 'It's a funny old world – a man's lucky if he gets out of it alive.' In 1921 Alec Kendal and Herbert Townsend wrote a monologue entitled 'It's a Funny Old World We Live In'.

10 Home is where you come to when you have nothing better to do.

Interview, *Vanity Fair* (May 1991). The meaning of this observation was disputed. Her view was that she had spoken as if addressing her children – this was the traditional attitude of children towards their homes – and had not been describing her own feelings about home. All she had meant to say was that the children's home was always there. Compare FROST 204:2. In *The Observer* (20 September 1987), Bette Davis, the actress, was quoted by Katharine Whitehorn as having said: 'Home is only where you go to when you've nowhere to go.'

See also DRAKE 178:2; KIPLING 273:5.

The THING American film 1951 (known in the UK as *The Thing From Another World*).

1 *Last speech*: I bring you a warning – to every one listening to the sound of my voice. Tell the world, tell this to everyone wherever they are: *watch the skies*, watch everywhere, keep looking – *watch the skies*!

The key phrase was later used to promote the film *Close Encounters of the Third Kind* (1977), and was the original title of that film.

THOMAS à KEMPIS German religious writer (1379–1471)

2 *Nam homo proponit, sed Deus disponit* [Man proposes and God disposes.]

De Imitatione Christi, I, 19 (?1420) – first appearance of the idea in this form. It derives from an old proverb found in Greek, Hebrew and Latin. Proverbs 16:9 in the Bible has it in the form: 'A man's heart deviseth his way; but the Lord directeth his steps.'

Man Proposes, God Disposes is the title of an extraordinary painting (1864) by Sir Edwin Landseer, showing two polar bears amid the wreckage of a ship caught in Arctic ice. In 1987 Liza Minelli said 'Man plans and God laughs' in a TV interview, which sounds like a modern development of the old proverb.

3 *O quam cito transit gloria mundi* [O, how quickly the world's glory passes away].

In the same work. More usually rendered as '*Sic transit gloria mundi* [So passes away the glory of the world].' This expression is used at the coronation ceremony of Popes when a reed surmounted with flax is burned and a chaplain intones: '*Pater sancte, sic transit gloria mundi*' to remind the new Holy Father of the transitory nature of human vanity. *ODQ* (1992) says, however, that it was used at the crowning of Alexander V at Pisa in July 1409, and is of earlier origin, which, if so, would mean that it was à Kempis who was doing the quoting.

4 Everywhere I have sought rest and not found it, except sitting in a corner by myself with a little book.

Quoted by Allen Andrews in *Quotations for Speakers and Writers* (1969). *Benham* (1948) has that, 'according to his biographer', Thomas à Kempis inscribed these words in his books: '*Im omnibus requiem quaesivi, et nusquam invei nisi in een hoecksken met een boecksken, id est angello cum libello* [In all things have I sought rest and have never found it except in a little nooklet with a booklet, that is in a small corner with a small book].'

Saint THOMAS AQUINAS Italian philosopher and theologian (1225–74)

5 How many angels can dance on the head of a needle [*or pin*]?

Attributed question. *Benham* (1948) went into this thoroughly but does not actually provide an example of what it gives as a head phrase: 'A company of angels can dance on the point of a needle.' *Benham* states that it is a saying 'attributed with variations to St Thomas Aquinas' who in *Summae Theologiae* devotes superabundant space to fanciful conjectures about the nature of angels … "Whether an angel can be in several places at once" … "Whether several angels can be in one place at the same time" … He expends much laboured argument on this and similar problems.'

Correspondents in *The Times* (20/21 November 1975) seemed to suggest that the attribution had been made, mistakenly, by Isaac Disraeli. Mention was made of the 14th-century tractate *Swester Katrei* – wrongly ascribed to Meister Eckhart – which contains this passage: 'Doctors declare that in heaven a thousand angels can stand on the point of a needle.'

Mencken (1942) has 'How many angels can dance upon the point of a needle?' – 'ascribed to various medieval theologians, *c.* 1'400'.

Dylan THOMAS Welsh poet (1914–53)

6 And Death Shall Have No Dominion.

Title of poem (1936) on immortality – a straightforward allusion to Romans 6:9: 'Christ being raised from the dead dieth no more: death hath no more dominion over him.'

7 *Portrait of the Artist as a Young Dog*.

Title of a book (1940) of mostly autobiographical short stories – probably after *Portrait of the Artist as a Young Man*, the novel (1914–15) by James Joyce, also largely autobiographical. It alludes to the customary way of describing self-portraits in art, e.g. *Portrait of the Artist with Severed Ear* (Van Gogh).

1 In my craft or sullen art
Exercised in the still night
When only the moon rages
And the lovers lie abed
With all their griefs in their arms ...

Not for the proud man apart
From the raging moon I write
On these spindrift pages.

'In my craft or sullen art' (1945). The phrase 'raging moon'
may be an original coinage to Thomas. The nearest *OED2*
gets is 'raging *noon*'. *The Raging Moon* was given to the title
of a film (UK 1970, from a novel by Peter Marshall) about
physically disabled people.

2 Time held me green and dying
Though I sang in my chains like the sea.

'Fern Hill' (1946). Part of the inscription on Thomas's
memorial in Poets' Corner, Westminster Abbey (unveiled
on St David's Day 1982). The second line is also quoted on
the statue of him and on a stone monument, both in
Swansea. On Thomas's modest grave in the Welsh town of
Laugharne there is but a wooden cross, bearing his name,
dates and 'RIP'.

3 Do not go gentle into that good night.
Rage, rage against the dying of the light.

'Do Not Go Gentle Into That Good Night' (1951). Probably
inspired by Thomas's observation of his dying father. A
combative man in earlier years, he was now, in his eight-
ies, 'soft and gentle at the last'. The poet urges him not to
acquiesce in the process of dying.

4 The land of my fathers [Wales] – my fathers can
have it.

Quoted in *Adam* (December 1953). 'Land of My Fathers'
(1860) is the Welsh national anthem.

5 In pursuit of my life-long quest for naked women
in wet mackintoshes.

When asked, 'Why have you come to America, Mr Thomas?'
Quoted in Constantine Fitzgibbon, *Dylan Thomas*, Chap.
8 (1965). Another version from the *Evening Standard* (2
May 1995): 'Asked by the hack pack the reason for his visit
to [New York] his succinct reply was: "Naked women in wet
macs."'

6 I've had eighteen straight whiskies. I think that's
the record.

Thomas made this dying boast to his girlfriend, Liz Reit-
ell, after a drinking bout in New York. Quoted in Barnaby

Conrad, *Famous Last Words* (1961). These were not his last
words, although he went into a coma shortly afterwards
and died. His biographers have subjected the bout to much
scrutiny and have watered it down to a mere four or five
whiskies. He often exaggerated.

Edward THOMAS English poet (1878–1917)

7 Yes; I remember Adlestrop –
The name, because one afternoon
Of heat the express-train drew up there
Unwontedly. It was late June.

... And for that minute a blackbird sang
Close by, and round him, mistier,
Farther and farther, all the birds
Of Oxfordshire and Gloucestershire.

'Adlestrop', *Poems* (1917). A hugely evocative description of
a moment on a hot summer's day in Oxfordshire. Adlestrop station was, in fact, in Gloucestershire, though close
to the county border.

Francis THOMPSON English poet (1859–1907)

8 Look for me in the nurseries of heaven.

'To My Godchild Francis M.W.M.' (1913). This is the text
chosen for Thompson's grave in the Roman Catholic annexe
to Kensal Green Cemetery, London.

9 The angels keep their ancient places;
Turn but a stone and start a wing!
'Tis ye, 'tis your estranged faces,
That miss the many-splendoured thing.

'The Kingdom of God' (1913). Hence, *Love Is a Many-
Splendored Thing*, the novel (1952; film US 1955) by Han
Suyin.

10 O my Hornby and my Barlow long ago!

'At Lord's'. This poem was written by Thompson when he
was in constant pain from failing health and had been
invited to see Lancashire (county of his birth) play Middlesex, but was unable to accept. The poem also refers to a
match in 1878 when 16,000 people attended the county
game between Lancashire and Gloucestershire. Everyone
is familiar with the first stanza (which is repeated at the
end) of what in fact is a four-stanza poem, found among
Thompson's papers when he died. A.N. Hornby is said to be
the most influential person, as President and player, in the
history of Lancashire County Cricket Club. R.G. Barlow was
the first great Lancashire-born professional. His grave at
Blackpool shows a set of stumps with the ball passing
through middle and leg, together with the epitaph 'Bowled

at Last'. The poem was read by Wendy Hiller at the memorial service for cricket writer and music critic Sir Neville Cardus at St Paul's, Covent Garden, in 1978. A delightful allusion by Matthew Engel in a feature on the decline of TV comedy in *The Guardian* (23 January 1999) was: 'Oh, my Eric and my Ernie long ago!'

Hunter S. THOMPSON American writer (1939–2005)

1 *Fear and Loathing in Las Vegas.*

Title of book (1972) based on his articles in *Rolling Stone* (11/25 November 1971) describing a visit to the gambling resort while under the influence of a variety of mind-expanding drugs. Apart from having a much-quoted title, the book is a prime example of what Thompson calls 'gonzo journalism', in which the writer chronicles his own role in the events he is reporting and doesn't worry too much about the facts. The word may be the same as Italian *gonzo* = a fool; foolish.

William Hale 'Big Bill' THOMPSON American politician (1867–1944)

2 [I'd] punch King George in the snoot.

On what he would do if George V were ever to set foot in Chicago (not that there was much chance of the King ever doing so). Quoted in Kenneth Allsop, *The Bootleggers* (1961). No direct quotation exists of whatever it was Thompson said when running for a third term as mayor in 1927 – 'poke in the snoot', 'bust in the snoot' are other reported versions – but his Anglophobia is not in question. 'I wanta make the King of England keep his snoot out of America … That's what Big Bill wants' – quoted in Lloyd Wendt & Herman Kogan, *Big Bill of Chicago* (1953). In the MacArthur & Hecht play, *The Front Page* (1928), the unnamed Mayor of Chicago refers to his slogan: 'Keep King George Out of Chicago.' J.P. Bean, *Verbals: The Book of Criminal Quotations*, has Mayor Thompson among the Mafia quotations: '*Mayor of Chicago, blaming King George V of England for prohibition*: "I shouldn't be surprised if the King had something to do with slipping over the Volstead Act on us so all their distillers can make fortunes selling us bootleg. If George comes to Chicago I'll punch him in the snoot."'

James THOMSON Scottish poet (1700–48)

3 When Britain first, at Heaven's command,
Arose from out the azure main,
This was the charter of the land,
And guardian angels sung this strain:
'Rule, Britannia, rule the waves;
Britons never will be slaves.'

Alfred: a Masque (1740) – which had another author called Mallet, but Thomson is thought to have written this bit. The music was by Dr Thomas Arne. Invariably misquoted. Of the several recordings of this famous patriotic song, few can match that by Cilla Black (on PCS 7103). I suspect it was recorded when Swinging London was at its height and the Union Jack flag was plastered patriotically over everything from miniskirts to tea mugs. Anyway, what she is heard to sing is:

> Rule, Britannia,
> Britannia rules the waves.
> Britons never, never, never
> Shall be slaves.

Of course, Cilla Black is not alone in preferring to sing 'rules' and 'shall'. Annually, at the Last Night of the Proms, several hundred other people can be heard singing her version – and drowning out those who may feel like sticking to Thomson.

There is a difference, however, between a poetic exhortation – 'rule' – and a boastful assertion in – 'rules'. As for the difference between 'will' and 'shall', life is really too short to go on about that at any length. But an interesting defence of the Cilla Black reading comes from Kingsley Amis and James Cochrane in *The Great British Songbook* (1986): 'When what a poet or lyric-writer wrote differs from what is habitually sung, we have generally preferred the latter … Britons never "shall" be slaves here, not "will" as James Thomson, a Scot following Scottish usage, naturally had them.'

Roy THOMSON (later Lord Thomson) Canadian-born industrialist (1894–1976)

4 You know, it's just like having a licence to print your own money.

To a neighbour in Edinburgh just after the opening of Scottish Television (a commercial TV company he had founded) in August 1957. Quoted in Russell Braddon, *Roy Thomson* (1965). Cautioned not to repeat this brash statement, he flew to Canada and repeated the *bon mot* in an interview with *Time* Magazine. 'In fact it was current in America before he used it. Having more important things to do he did not repudiate the authorship' – L. Marsland Gander (TV critic) in *The Sunday Telegraph* (6 June 1982).

5 Editorial is what keeps the ads apart.

Attributed remark. Compare NORTHCLIFFE 344:5.

Henry David THOREAU American writer (1817–62)

1 If a man does not keep pace with his companions, perhaps it is because he hears a different drummer. Let him step to the music which he hears, however measured or far away.

Walden (1854). Hence, presumably, *Different Drummer*, a ballet (1984) choreographed by Kenneth MacMillan; *The Different Drum* (1987), a work of popular psychotherapy by M. Scott Peck; and *Different Drummer*, a BBC TV series (1991) about eccentric American outsiders.

Jeremy THORPE English Liberal politician (1929–)

2 Greater love hath no man than this, that he lay down his friends for his life.

Comment on the 'Night of the Long Knives', when Harold Macmillan sacked half his Cabinet (13 July 1962). Quoted in D.E. Butler & A. King, *The General Election of 1964* (1965). Alluding to John 15:13 – see BIBLE 83:5.

3 Looking around the House, one realizes that we are all minorities now.

After a general election that resulted in no party having a clear majority. Speech, House of Commons (6 March 1974), alluding to 'We are all socialists nowadays', EDWARD VII 183:3.

James THURBER American cartoonist and writer (1894–1961)

4 A woman's place is in the wrong.

Attributed remark in speech (24 October 1953). But Thurber did not actually say this himself but merely quoted it, as here: 'Somebody has said that Woman's place is in the wrong. That's fine. What the wrong needs is a woman's presence and a woman's touch. She is far better equipped than men to set it right. The condescending male, in his pride of strength, likes to think of the female as being "soft, soft as snow," but just wait till he gets hit by the snowball. Almost any century now Woman may lose her patience with black politics and red war and let fly. I wish I could be on earth then to witness the saving of our self destructive species by its greatest creative force. If I have sometimes seemed to make fun of Woman, I assure you it has only been for the purpose of egging her on.'

The TIMES British London-based newspaper, founded 1788

5 But the truth is that when it comes to the heat [*sic*] of the matter, to the courage that supports a nation, Lord George-Brown drunk is a better man than the Prime Minister [Harold Wilson] sober.

Leading article (4 March 1976), after Brown had announced that he was quitting the Labour Party and after an incident in which he was photographed falling in the gutter outside the Houses of Parliament. *The Times* Magazine (23 May 1993), while mentioning that Woodrow Wyatt claimed to have made the remark earlier – in 1963 – also revealed that William Rees-Mogg had actually come up with the sentence, as editor, in 1976: 'I wrote it. I remember it well. Bernard Levin was sitting in my outer office. I showed it to Bernard and said: "I don't really think I can print that, do you?" Bernard replied: "If you *don't* print it, I shall never speak to you again." Perhaps Woodrow's memory is playing him up.'

Compare what Andrew Bonar Law is reported to have said: 'Asquith, when drunk, can make a better speech than any of us when sober' – quoted in *A Guide to Political Quotations* (1985). Also the story told by John Beevers in the *Sunday Referee* (19 February 1939): 'About ten years ago there was a famous scene in the House. Mr Jack Jones was speaking. Lady Astor entered and sat down opposite him. He stopped speaking, turned to her and said: "I am not drunk. I have had so many insults from this lady I resent it. She does not talk to me straight. She talks under her breath." The Deputy Speaker then said how glad he would be if the honourable lady would keep quiet. Mr Jones continued: "It is a common thing for the honourable lady to talk under her breath about drunkenness when I am speaking. I will tell her straight in her teeth that I am a better man when I am drunk than she is when I am sober." And the House laughed its head off.'

See also COCKBURN 148:4; LINCOLN 288:2; POPE 363:9.

TO HAVE AND HAVE NOT US film 1945. Script by Jules Furthman and William Faulkner after Ernest Hemingway's novel. With Lauren Bacall as Slim and Humphrey Bogart as Steve.

6 If you want anything – just whistle.

This is not a direct quotation (though sometimes given as such). What Bacall actually says *to* Bogart – and not the other way round, as in *PDMQ* (1980) – is: 'You know you don't have to act with me, Steve. You don't have to say anything, and you don't have to do anything. Not a thing. Oh, maybe just whistle. You know how to whistle, don't you, Steve? You just put your lips together and blow.'

J.R.R. TOLKIEN English novelist and academic (1892–1973)

1 Farmer Giles of Ham.

Title of story (1949). 'Farmer Giles' as the personification of the (British) farmer possibly derives from the subject of Robert Bloomfield's poem *The Farmer's Boy* (1800) – although he is a labourer rather than a farmer. Coincidentally or not, Isaac Bickerstaff in *The Maid of the Mill* (1765) has: 'I am determined farmer Giles shall not stay a moment on my estate, after next quarter day.' Accordingly, 'farmers' is rhyming slang for piles (haemorrhoids).

Leo TOLSTOY Russian novelist (1828–1910)

2 *War and Peace.*

English title of novel (1865–8). According to Henry Troyat's biography, Tolstoy did not decide on a title until very late. '*The Year 1805* would not do for a book that ended in 1812. He had chosen *All's Well That Ends Well* [see SHAKESPEARE 400:1], thinking that would give the book the casual, romantic tone of a long English novel.' Finally, the title was 'borrowed from Proudhon' – *La Guerre et la Paix* (1862).

Nicholas TOMALIN English journalist (1931–73)

3 The only qualities essential for real success in journalism are rat-like cunning, a plausible manner, and a little literary ability.

In *The Sunday Times* Magazine (26 October 1969). Tomalin was writing on careers in journalism and his view, though a touch self serving, has continued to be quoted admiringly by other journalists. The passage continues: 'Other qualities are helpful but not essential. These include a knack with telephones, trains and petty officials, a good digestion and a steady head ... The capacity to steal other people's ideas and phrases – that one about rat-like cunning was invented by my colleague Murray Sayle – is also invaluable.' Tomalin himself was killed while covering the Arab-Israeli War of 1973.

Augustus Montague TOPLADY English clergyman (1740–78)

4 Rock of Ages, cleft for me,
Let me hide myself in Thee.

Hymn, first published in *The Gospel Magazine* (1775). *Brewer* (1989) recounts two stories of its composition: one, that it was written while seated by a great cleft in the rock near Cheddar, Somerset; two, that it was written on the ten of diamonds between two rubbers of whist at Bath.

The phrase 'rock of ages' is said to be the actual meaning in Hebrew of the words 'everlasting strength' at Isaiah 26:4.

Pete TOWNSHEND English pop musician and songwriter (1945–)

5 Hope I die before I get old.

Song, 'My Generation' (1965). Andrew Motion in *The Lamberts* (1986) comments: '[Kit Lambert, manager of The Who exhorted Townshend] to use a stutter on the key chorus words "f-f-fade away", "c-c-cold" and "g-g-generation". The reason for the stutter was this: the personality portrayed in the song was supposed to be an archetypal pill-headed Mod – and amphetamines make their users stammer ... [It was] banned, initially, by the BBC, who thought it ridiculed stutterers.'

Arnold TOYNBEE English historian (1889–1975)

6 No annihilation without representation.

Pressing for a greater British voice at the United Nations (1947) when under the threat of the atomic bomb. Attributed by *PDMQ* (1971). Toynbee was, of course, echoing the cry 'No Taxation Without Representation', the North American colonists' anti-British slogan in the years before the War of Independence. In the form 'Taxation Without Representation Is Tyranny', its coinage has been attributed to the lawyer and statesman James Otis. In 1763 he opposed British taxation on the grounds that the colonies were not represented in the House of Commons.

Jack TRAIN English actor (1902–66)

7 I don't mind if I do!

Catchphrase of Colonel Chinstrap in the BBC Radio show *ITMA* (first appeared 1940–1). Spoken whenever a drink was even so much as hinted at, originally in the form, 'Thanks, I will!' The Colonel was based on an elderly friend of the announcer, John Snagge. He was a typical ex-Indian Army type, well pleased with himself. The phrase had existed before, of course. *Punch* carried a cartoon in 1880 with the following caption:

Porter: Virginia Water!
Bibulous old gentleman (seated in railway carriage): Gin and water! I don't mind if I do!

ITMA, however, secured the phrase a place in the language, as the Colonel doggedly turned every hint of liquid refreshment into an offer:

Tommy Handley: Hello, what's this group? King John signing the Magna Carta at Runnymede?
Chinstrap: Rum and mead, sir? I don't mind if I do!

Barbara TRAPIDO English novelist (1941–)

1 *Brother of the More Famous Jack.*

Title of novel (1982). It refers neither to characters in the book nor to Robert and John F. Kennedy. No, Chapter 4 has: 'Yeats, William Butler ... Brother of the more famous Jack, of course.' The Irish poet W.B. Yeats did indeed have a brother, Jack, who was a leading artist. Often alluded to. From Robert Stephens, *Knight Errant* (1995): 'The stars were Claude Hulbert, brother of the more famous Jack, his wife Delia Trevor, and another fine comedian called Sonny Hale.' From Michael Kerrigan, *Who Lies Where* (1995): 'Bankside was, of course, theatreland in the seventeenth century. Edmund Shakespeare, brother of the more famous William, is buried here.'

(Sir) Herbert Beerbohm TREE English actor-manager (1853–1917)

2 A committee should consist of three men, two of whom are absent.

Quoted in Hesketh Pearson, *Beerbohm Tree* (1956). Also attributed to Lord Mancroft (1914–87) in some anthologies. On the other hand, *The Treasury of Humorous Quotations*, eds Esar & Bentley (1951), has E.V. Lucas (1868–1938) saying, 'The best committee is a committee of two when one is absent.' Hendrik Van Loon wrote in *America* (1927): 'Nothing is ever accomplished by a committee unless it consists of three members, one of whom happens to be sick and the other absent.' Anon. said: 'A committee of one gets things done.'

On the same subject: to J.B. Hughes – in Prochnow & Prochnow, *Treasury of Humorous Quotations* (1969) – is attributed the remark, 'If Moses had been a committee the Israelites would still be in Egypt.' (Or, 'never would have got across the Red Sea' in a remark attributed in 1965 to General Booth, founder of the Salvation Army.)

The anonymous observation, 'A camel is a horse designed by a committee' – quoted, for example, in American *Vogue* (1958) – bears an interesting resemblance, surely, to 'A donkey is a horse translated into Dutch' – which Georg Christoph Lichtenberg (1742–99) had in his *Aphorisms*.

John Le Carré included in the novel *Tinker, Tailor, Soldier, Spy* (1974) the observation, 'A committee is an animal with four back legs'. See also ALLEN 6:5.

Charles TRENET French singer and songwriter (1913–)

3 *Baisers Volés* [Stolen Kisses].

Title of film (France, 1968) by François Truffaut – taken from a phrase in the song, '*Que Reste-t-il de Nos Amours*' (1943), written and performed by Trenet (and which is

featured in the film). In English, there had earlier been the song 'A Stolen Kiss' (1923) by R. Penso; also a ballad, undated, by F. Buckley, 'Stolen Kisses are the Sweetest'. See also CIBBER 144:2; HUNT 248:1.

Robert TRESSELL Irish-born novelist (1870–1911)

4 If God is powerful he is not good; if God is good he is not powerful.

This would seem to derive from a passage in Tressell's *The Ragged Trousered Philanthropists*, Chap. 4 (1914): 'Was God unaware of the miseries of His creatures? If so, then He was not all-knowing. Was God aware of their sufferings, but unable to help them? Then He was not all-powerful. Had He the power but not the will to make His creatures happy? Then He was not good.' This passage is taken from the 1955 full-text edition of the book.

Tommy TRINDER English comedian (1909–89)

5 Overpaid, overfed, oversexed and over here.

On American troops in Britain during the Second World War. Quoted in *The Sunday Times* (4 January 1976). This was Trinder's full-length version of a popular British expression of the early 1940s. He certainly did not invent it, although he may have done much to popularize it. *Partridge/Catch Phrases* makes no mention of Trinder and omits the 'overfed'.

As 'over-sexed, over-paid and over here' it is said also to have been a popular expression about American troops in Australia 1941–5 – according to *The Dictionary of Australian Quotations* (1984) and to have been revived there during the Vietnam War.

Leon TROTSKY Russian revolutionary (1879–1940)

6 You are pitiful isolated individuals; you are bankrupts; your role is played out. Go where you belong from now on – into the dustbin of history!

History of the Russian Revolution, Vol. 3, Chap. 10 (1933). Sometimes 'dust heap' or 'scrapheap of history' is put instead. Was it with reference to the fate of the decrees emanating from Kerensky's Provincial Government in the Winter Palace in 1917? Or was it to the fate of his opponents (as suggested by E.H. Carr in his *Socialism in One Country* (1958)? The latter, in fact, and specifically referring to the Mensheviks (the moderates who opposed Lenin and the Bolsheviks' call for the overthrowing of the Tsar by revolution). Earlier, in a similar coinage, Charles Dickens reflected on Sir Robert Peel's death in 1850: 'He was a man of merit who could ill be spared from the Great Dust Heap down at Westminster.' See also BIRRELL 89:1.

Harry S TRUMAN American Democratic 33rd President
(1884–1972)

1 The son of a bitch isn't going to resign on me, I
want him fired.

To Omar Bradley of General MacArthur. Quoted in Merle
Miller, *Plain Speaking: An Oral Biography of Harry S Truman*
(1974). Truman's language was notably salty for the period.
His wife had to reprimand him for frequent recourse to
's.o.b.'s'. In 1951 he sacked General Douglas MacArthur
from his command of UN forces in Korea for insubordin-
ation and repeatedly criticizing the administration's policy
of non-confrontation with China. Truman added this
remark, lest the General hear of the decision and jump
the gun.

2 If you can't stand the heat, get out of the kitchen.

Looking back in 1960, Truman wrote in his book *Mr Citizen*:
'Some men can make decisions and some cannot. Some
men fret and delay under criticism. I used to have a saying
that applies here, and I note that some people have picked
it up.' When Truman announced that he would not stand
again as president, *Time* Magazine (28 April 1952) had him
give a 'down-to-earth reason for his retirement, quoting a
favourite expression of his military jester Major General
Harry Vaughan', namely, 'If you can't stand the heat, get
out of the kitchen.' Wolfgang Mieder in *The Politics of
Proverbs* (1997) comments that the attribution of the proverb
to Vaughan was probably made in jest, 'for, after all, Truman
had known it from the first quarter of the 20th century.'
Mieder then cites this extract from a speech given by the
about-to-be ex-president (17 December 1952): 'One of the
results of the system [of the president's approval powers]
gives the President a good many hot potatoes to handle –
but the President gets a lot of hot potatoes from every
direction anyhow, and a man who can't handle them has
no business in that job. That makes me think of a saying
that I used to hear from my old friend and colleague on the
Jackson County Court. He said, "Harry, if you can't stand
the heat you better get out of the kitchen." I'll say that is
absolutely true.'

The attribution is still usually given to Truman himself, but
it *may* not be what he said at all. 'Down-to-earth' is not quite
how I would describe this remark, whereas 'If you can't
stand the stink, get out of the shithouse' would be. I have
only hearsay evidence for this version, but given Truman's
reputation for salty expressions, it is not improbable.

Bartlett (1980) quotes Philip D. Lagerquist of the Harry
S Truman Library as saying, 'President Truman has used
variations of the aphorism ... for many years, both orally
and in his writings' (1966). Note the 'variations'.

3 The buck stops here.

Truman had a sign on his desk bearing these words, indicating that the Oval Office was where the passing of the
buck had to cease. He drew specific attention to the sign
in a speech at the National War College (19 December
1952). It appears to be a saying of his own invention. As
Wolfgang Mieder notes, however, in the work cited above,
Truman spoke frequently of 'passing the buck' (first in a
1918 letter to his wife) and, latterly, specifically in connection with the presidency. In his Farewell Address to the
American People (15 January 1953), he said: 'The President – whoever he is – has to decide. He can't pass the
buck to anybody.' 'Passing the buck' is a poker player's
expression. It refers to a marker that can be passed on by
someone who does not wish to deal.

Later, Jimmy Carter restored Truman's motto to the Oval
Office. When President Nixon published his memoirs
(1978), people opposed to its sale went around wearing
buttons which said, 'The book stops here.'

4 What's a statesman anyway? I'll tell you what
he is – he's just a politician no one is afraid of
any more.

Quoted in *The Observer* (11 May 1986). Another definition:
'A statesman is a defunct politician.' Maybe based on: 'A
politician is a man who understands government, and it
takes a politician to run a government. A statesman is a
politician who's been dead ten or fifteen years' – attributed
in the *New York World Telegram and Sun* (12 April 1958).

Sophie TUCKER Russian-born American entertainer
(1884–1966)

5 I've been rich and I've been poor. Believe me,
honey, rich is better.

Unverified. Henry McNulty wrote (1995): 'Although Ms
Tucker was born in Russia, she grew up in Hartford, Connecticut, and is considered a "hometown girl" by Hart-
fordites. So as you can imagine, the files at the *Hartford
Courant* newspaper, where I am an editor, are full of stories about, and comments by, Sophie Tucker. I have diligently gone through all the stories that appeared in the
Courant from 1922 until her death in February 1966. There
was absolutely no mention of the "I've been rich" quotation – not even in her obituary. I also checked the lengthy
obituaries in *The New York Times* and the (now defunct)
Hartford Times. Again, no mention of this comment, and
you'd think there would have been if she'd said it. I then
studied Ms Tucker's 1945 autobiography *Some of These Days*
(named after one of her signature tunes.) But again,
although she wrote extensively of her early poverty, there

was no I've-been-rich-and-poor comment. (In fact, the book is amazingly free of the wisecracks she is so known for.) So I have nothing conclusive to provide except, I suppose, negative evidence (and fortunately, no one else will have to pore through her autobiography). My guess is that this is one of those comments that sounds like something "the last of the Red Hot Mamas" *would* have said, so it is attributed to her whether she said it or not.

'The most recent edition of *Bartlett* [1992], by the way, has a version of the quote calling it "attributed" to Ms Tucker. They report it as: "I have been poor and I have been rich. Rich is better." This rather more formal version, leaving out "believe me, honey" makes me think, again, that this is something that Sophie Tucker *ought to have said*, and various people quote it as they imagine she would have said it. Whether she did so is still in question, but if votes are being counted, I vote no.'

Incidentally, in *PD20* (1995) there are the following two entries: 'I've been rich, and I've been poor and believe me, rich is better' – Joe E. Lewis (died 1971), quoted in Barbara Rowes, *The Book of Quotes* (1979); 'I have been poor, and I have been rich. Rich is better' – J.R. Colombo, *The Wit and Wisdom of the Movie Makers* (1979). Compare: 'I've been rich and I've been poor; believe me rich is better' – spoken by Gloria Grahame in the film *The Big Heat* (US 1953), screenplay by Sydney Boehm from the story by William P. McGivern. Further evidence, perhaps, that it is a modern proverb that somehow became attached to Tucker, maybe without reason. In the musical *Minnie's Boys* (1970), the line was incorporated in the song 'Rich Is': 'I've been poor and I've been rich / And if anyone should ask me which / Is better – rich is better – much, much better.'

J.M.W. TURNER English painter (1775–1851)

1 The Fallacies of Hope.

Poem (?1812). Turner liked not only to give titles to his pictures – *The Fighting Témeraire*, *Slavers throwing overboard the dead and dying – typhoon coming on*, and so on, but to append portions of verse as citations or captions. As one of his biographers, Jack Lindsay, explained (1966): 'He wanted the extra heightening of consciousness which the verses provided.' However, if the verses did not quite fit his ideas, he happily rewrote them, be they by Shakespeare or Gray or whoever. He also wrote his own poetry so that he could quote from it in these captions, including a work which only survives in fragments, 'The Fallacies of Hope'. There are some who believe that the poem never actually existed.

Kenneth Clark used the phrase as the title of one of the parts of his *Civilization* TV series (1969) and explained how Ruskin had said of Turner that he was indeed 'without hope'

– especially in the face of Nature's cruelty and indifference. Turner also wrote: 'Hope, hope, fallacious hope, where is thy market now?'

Unfortunately, Turner was considerably less of a poet than he was a painter. Under his painting *Queen Mab's Grotto* he appended supposed lines from *A Midsummer Night's Dream* – 'Frisk it, frisk it, by the moonlight beam' (which appear nowhere in Shakespeare) – and from his own 'Fallacies of Hope' – 'Thy orgies, Mab, are manifold.' That should give sufficient flavour of his written art.

2 The sun is God!

Dying words. Quoted in Barnaby Conrad, *Famous Last Words* (1961).

Mark TWAIN (Samuel Langhorne Clemens)
American writer (1835–1910)

3 If you don't like the weather in New England now, just wait a few minutes.

So attributed in *A Treasury of Humorous Quotations*, eds Prochnow & Prochnow (1969), but this does not appear in the text of Twain's speech on 'The Weather' to the New England Society (22 December 1876). On the other hand, Wolfgang Mieder lists 'If you don't like the weather in New England, just wait a minute and it will change' as merely a 'New England saying' in his *Yankee Wisdom: New England Proverbs* (1989). Perhaps this proverbial saying was assigned to Twain on account of its similarity to this passage in the 1876 speech: 'There is a sumptuous variety about the New England weather that compels the stranger's admiration – and regret. The weather is always doing something there; always attending strictly to business; always getting up new designs and trying them on the people to see how they will go. But it gets through more business in spring than in any other season. In the spring I have counted one hundred and thirty-six different kinds of weather inside of four-and-twenty hours ... Yes, one of the brightest gems in the New England weather is the dazzling uncertainty of it.'

4 Earned a precarious living by taking in one another's washing

Remark customarily ascribed (with slight hesitancy) to Mark Twain. In *The Commonweal* (6 August 1887) an article entitled 'Bourgeois Versus Socialist' signed by William Morris ends: 'A bourgeois paradise will supervene, in which everyone will be free to exploit – but there will be no one to exploit ... On the whole, one must suppose that the type of it would be that town (surely in America and in the neighbourhood of Mark Twain) that I have heard of, whose inhabitants lived by taking in each other's washing.'

Two years later, Bernard Shaw wrote that 'The inhabitants [of Bayreuth] either live in villas on independent incomes or else by taking in one another's washing and selling confectionery, scrap books and photographs' – from *The Hawk* (13 August 1889). Slightly after this, 'E.W.C.' wrote in *Cornish Notes & Queries* (First Series) (1906): 'I have certainly heard the phrase in connection with the Scilly Islands. And some go so far, and are so rude, as to suggest "Hence their name".' Similarly, in the forward to his *Poems 1938–1945* (1946), Robert Graves declared: 'I write poems for poets, and satires or grotesques for wits ... The moral of the Scilly Islanders who earned a precarious livelihood by taking in one another's washing is that they never upset their carefully balanced island economy by trying to horn into the laundry trade of the mainland; and that nowhere in the Western Hemisphere was washing so well done.'

Benham (1960) lists the well-known joke with the attribution 'origin unknown', and adds: 'It is said that a society was formed (*circa* 1900) for the purpose of discovering the origin of the phrase, but without result.'

1 **Cheer up! The worst is yet to come.**

In a letter from Twain to his wife (1893/4) included in *The Love Letters of Mark Twain*. Also in *Those Extraordinary Twins* (1894). *Partridge/Catch Phrases* manages no more than 'a US c.p. of ironic encouragement since *c.*1918'. The most usual attribution, though, is to the American writer Philander Johnson (1866–1939) in his *Shooting Stars* (?1920). The similar expression, 'Cheer up ... you'll soon be dead!' appears in several British entertainments in the period 1909–18. The original non-ironic line, 'The worst is yet to come', occurs in Tennyson's *Sea Dreams* (1864).

The worst pun on the phrase concerns the man who was eating a German meal but was encouraged to continue with the words, 'Cheer up, the *wurst* is yet to come!'

2 **When I was a boy of fourteen, my father was so ignorant I could hardly stand to have the old man around. But when I got to be twenty-one, I was astonished at how much he had learned in seven years.**

Attributed in *Reader's Digest* (September 1939). As *Burnam* (1980) points out, if Twain ever said this (or words to the effect: it is untraced), there was more than a hint of poetic licence about it. His own father died when Twain was eleven.

3 **The report of my death was an exaggeration.**

Twain's reaction to a false report, quoted in the *New York Journal* (2 June 1897). Frequently over-quoted and paraphrased ever since, this has become the inevitable remark to invoke when someone's death has been wrongly reported

(most usually one's own). Twain's own version of the incident appears in A.B. Paine, *Mark Twain: A Biography* (1912): when a reporter called regarding reports of his death with an order to write 500 words if very ill, 1000 if dead, Twain responded, 'You don't need as much as that. Just say the report of my death has been grossly exaggerated.' It is also now employed in the sense of, 'You thought I was finished, but look at me now' (for example, by George Bush in February 1988 regarding the decline in his political fortunes). Variations include: 'Reports of my death have been greatly exaggerated' or 'are premature'.

A headline from *The Independent* (13 November 1993): 'Reports of Queen Mother's death exaggerated Down Under'.

4 **Homer's writings are Homer's Essays Virgil the Aeneid and Paradise Lost some people say that these poems were not written by Homer but by another man of the same name.**

In his essay 'English As She is Taught' (1887), Twain largely quotes from an unpublished collection of schoolboy howlers, among which is this one. Compare the subsequent Aldous Huxley, *Those Barren Leaves*, Chap. 5 (1925): 'It's like the question of the authorship of the Iliad ... The author of that poem is either Homer, or if not Homer, somebody else of the same name.' And also the application to Shakespeare: see ALLAIS 6:4.

5 **Everybody talks about the weather but nobody does anything about it.**

Was this said by Twain or by Charles Dudley Warner (1829–1900)? It first appeared in an unsigned editorial in the *Hartford Courant* (24 August 1897) in the form – 'A well-known American writer said once that, while everybody talked about the weather, nobody seemed to do anything about it' – but the quip has often been assigned to Twain, who lived in Hartford (Connecticut) at the time. In 1993 Henry McNulty, an Associate Editor and the Reader Representative on the *Courant* (which is 'the Oldest Newspaper of Continuous Publication in America') guided me through the minefield of attribution: 'For many years the *Courant*, quite understandably, has taken the position that Warner, not Twain, made this remark. Example: a 1947 *Courant* article on the subject was headlined, "Sorry, Mark, But Charlie Really Said It". But after studying what various experts have had to say, I am now in favour of attributing it to Twain until new evidence turns up.

'As far as I know, the "weather" remark has not been found in any of Twain's writings, so I suppose it's fair to say that *in print*, the *Courant* is the original source. But who wrote the *Courant* editorial? Then, as now, they were unsigned. In

1897, Warner was the *Courant*'s editor, so it is certain that the editorial was approved (or at least seen) by him; but did he actually write it? No one knows, and there is no way to tell for sure today.

'Assuming that Warner wrote the editorial, one possibility is that the reference was to himself. He certainly was well-known at the time; he was a prolific writer; and the phrase "Politics makes strange bedfellows" is one from one of his eighteen books. It's not impossible that this was just a further quip, a wink to his friends. But if not, the most likely suspect would be Mark Twain. Warner and Twain were friends, neighbours and literary collaborators (they wrote *The Gilded Age*). Again, the "well-known American writer" phrasing would very likely be an in-joke, since of course every *Courant* reader would be familiar with Twain.

'Some years later, several people indeed attributed the remark to Warner. Charles Hopkins Clark, editor of the *Courant* after Warner's death in 1900, is reported to have said, "I guess it's no use. They still believe Mark Twain said it, despite all my assurances that it was Warner." That seems conclusive, but could his statement be coloured both by the passage of time and by the fact that he and Warner were friends and colleagues?

'In July 1989, the New York State Bar Journal addressed the problem in a column entitled "Legal Lore". The Bar Journal decided to attribute the remark to both men. "Mark Twain ... probably did make the oral comment first to his billiard companion, Charles Dudley Warner," it said. "But ... Warner deserves the credit for having first put into writing this well-weathered statement.

'In the absence of any genuinely new historical evidence, this seems to me to be the best solution. I suppose one can't blame the *Courant* for insisting for all these years that Warner, not Twain, was the sole author of the quip, but I'm afraid that owes more to chauvinism than to scholarship.'

1 Golf is a good walk spoiled.

So attributed by Laurence J. Peter in *Quotations for Our Time* (1977). The German author Kurt Tucholsky (1890–1935) wrote: '*Golf, sagte einmal jemand, ist ein verdorbener Spazier-gang* [Golf, someone once said, is a walk spoiled]'. Otherwise unverified.

2 Always do right. This will gratify some people, and astonish the rest.

Talk to young people, Brooklyn (16 February 1901). Quoted in 'Frontispiece', *Mark Twain in Eruption*, ed. Bernard de Vote (1940). President Truman kept this saying on his desk.

3 What a good thing Adam had. When he said a good thing he knew nobody had said it before.

Mark Twain's Notebook, ed. A.B. Paine (1935). A surely unnecessary worry for a highly quotable author to have. Has also been ascribed to Bernard Shaw.

4 Love seems the swiftest but it is the slowest of all growths. No man or woman really knows what perfect love is until they have been married for a quarter of a century.

Notebooks (published 1935). Hence, *Perfect Love*, title of a novel (1995) by Elizabeth Buchan.

See also ALLEN 7:5; DISRAELI 174:7; *PUNCH* 370:8.

Kenneth TYNAN English critic (1927–80)

5 And I'll stay off Verlaine, too; he was always chasing Rimbauds.

Tynan used this quip in his very early days as a (schoolboy) critic. It earned him a rebuke from James Agate (recounted in *Ego 8*, for 20 July 1945), who wrote: 'To say that "Verlaine was always chasing Rimbauds" is just *common*. Like cheap scent.' Whether Tynan knew it or not, he had been anticipated by Dorothy Parker, who wrote the 'chasing Rimbauds' line, in 'The Little Hours', *Here Lies* (1939).

6 What, when drunk, one sees in other women, one sees in Garbo sober.

On Greta Garbo (1953), collected in *Curtains* (1961). One of the finest compliments Tynan ever paid, just as his description of Anna Neagle (in that same year) is among his most withering: 'She sings, shaking her voice at the audience like a tiny fist.'

7 They say *The New Yorker* is the bland leading the bland. I don't know if I'm bland enough.

To a journalist before leaving England to join the magazine as its drama critic (1958). Quoted in Kathleen Tynan, *The Life of Kenneth Tynan* (1987). At about the same time, J.K. Galbraith was writing in *The Affluent Society* (1958): 'These are the days when ... in minor modification of the scriptural parable, the bland lead the bland.' In Leslie Halliwell, *The Filmgoer's Book of Quotes* (1973), an anonymous definition of television is given as 'the bland leading the bland'. This probably alludes to 'Television is the bland leading the bland', which occurs in Murray Schumach, *The Face on the Cutting Room Floor* (1964). All these quips allude, of course, to BIBLE 81:3.

1 I think so certainly ... I doubt if there are any rational people to whom the word 'fuck' would be particularly diabolical, revolting or totally forbidden. I think that anything that can be printed or said can also be seen.

In answer to a question whether he would allow 'a play to be put on at the National Theatre in which, for instance, sexual intercourse took place on the stage?' Interviewed on BBC TV *BBC3* programme (13 November 1965). This was the first time the f-word had been spoken, noticeably, in a British broadcast.

2 *Sergeant Pepper* – a decisive moment in the history of Western Civilization.

In 1967. Quoted in Howard Elson, *McCartney* (1987). But see WINNER 503:1, with which it may have been mistaken.

3 *Oh! Calcutta!*

Title of Tynan's sexually explicit stage revue (1969) – it derives from a curious piece of word play, being the equivalent of the French '*Oh, quel cul t'as* [Oh, what a lovely bum you've got]'. French *cul* is derived from the Latin *culus* 'buttocks' but, according to the context, may be applied to the female vagina or male anus. In her *Life of Kenneth Tynan* (1987), Kathleen Tynan states that she was writing an article on the surrealist painter Clovis Trouille, one of whose works was a naked odalisque lying on her side to reveal a spherical backside. The title was *Oh! Calcutta! Calcutta!*: 'I suggested to Ken that he call his erotic revue *Oh! Calcutta!* ... I did not know at the time that it had the further advantage of being a French pun.'

4 I do not see the EEC as a great love affair. It is more like nine middle-aged couples with failing marriages meeting at a Brussels hotel for a group grope.

Quoted in *The Observer* (11 May 1975), but possibly misattributed as it had also been ascribed to E.P. Thompson in *The Sunday Times* (27 April 1975) in the form: 'This "going into Europe" will not turn out to be the thrilling mutual exchange supposed. It is more like nine middle-aged couples with failing marriages meeting in a darkened bedroom in a Brussels hotel for a Group Grope.'

5 *The Sound of Two Hands Clapping.*

Title of a collection of Tynan's critical writings (1975). As he acknowledged, it derives from a Zen koan ('a riddle used in Zen to teach the inadequacy of logical reasoning'): 'We know the sound of two hands clapping. But what is the sound of one hand clapping?' This koan is said to appear as the epigraph of J.D. Salinger's *For Esmé – With Love and Squalor* (1953), though not in all editions.

See also BEHAN 58:7.

U

Johann Ludwig UHLAND German lyric poet
(1787–1862)

1 Take, O boatman, thrice thy fee:
Take, I give it willingly:
For, invisible to thee,
Spirits twain have crossed with me.

An anonymous translation given in *Benham* (1907) – where also the poet's name is given as John Louis Upland. In *Mary Barton* (1848) Mrs Gaskell gives the lines in the original language: '*Nimm, nur, Fährmann, nim die Miethe, / Die ich gerne dreifach biete! / Zween, die mit mir überfuhren, / Waren geistige Naturen.*' These come from Uhland's poem '*Auf der Überfahrt*'. Lewis Carroll, in *Sylvie and Bruno Concluded*, Chap. 3 (1893), quotes the above English version, but does not name the poet.

Ralph R. UPTON American engineer (early 20th century)

2 Stop; look; listen.

Notice at US railroad crossings (from 1912). Quoted in R. Hyman, *A Dictionary of Famous Quotations* (1967). This rather esoteric piece of information stayed with me for many years, until suddenly confirmation started flooding in. The date was confirmed by Meredith Nicholson in *A Hoosier Chronicle* (1912): 'Everybody's saying "Stop, Look, Listen!" ... the white aprons in the one-arm lunch rooms say it now when you kick on the size of the buns.' The originator was confirmed by *Notes and Queries*, Vol. 195 (1950), saying that it was devised by Upton to replace the former 'Look out for the locomotive.' And any number of allusions testify to its popularity. A show with the title *Stop! Look! Listen!* (with music by Irving Berlin) opened on Broadway (27 December 1915); in 1916, George Robey introduced one of his greatest popular songs, 'I Stopped, I Looked, I Listened' in *The Bing Boys Are Here*, in London; a 1936 cheesecake advertisement for a New York supplier of artists' materials had the slogan 'Stop, Look and Kiss 'em.'

V

Paul VALÉRY French poet and writer (1871–1945)

1 A work of art/a poem is never really finished, it is merely abandoned.

This is how the quotation is usually rendered these days. The original is: '*Un texte n'est jamais achevé, mais toujours abandonné* [a *text* is never finished, but always abandoned].' It is to be found in Valéry's '*Au sujet du "Cimetière marin"*, *Œuvres, édition établie et annotée par J. Hytier*, Paris, Gallimard (1957). Compare: '[W.H. Auden] accepted Valéry's dictum "A poem is never finished, only abandoned", to which he added his own comment "It must not be abandoned too soon"' – Humphrey Carpenter, *W.H. Auden*, Pt 2, Chap. 4 (1981).

(Sir) John VANBRUGH English playwright and architect (1664–1726)

2 Under this stone, Reader, survey
Dead Sir John Vanbrugh's house of clay.
Lie heavy on him, Earth! for he
Laid many heavy loads on thee!

This epitaph was not written by Vanburgh, nor was it ever actually placed on his grave. It was written by Dr Abel Evans (1679–1737) thinking of Blenheim Palace, though it has also been ascribed to the architect, Nicholas Hawksmoor. The above version is the one in John Booth, *Metrical Epitaphs* (1868). *A Collection of Epitaphs* ... (1806) has: 'Lie *light* upon him earth! tho' he / Laid many a heavy load on thee.' Compare, on the British Prime Minister Henry Pelham (1696–1754): 'Lie heavy on him, land, for he / Laid many a heavy tax on thee.'

 Benham (1907) compares the Latin, '*Sit tibi terra gravis!* [May the earth be heavy upon thee!]', which contrasts with '*Sit tibi terra levis!* [Let the earth lie light upon you!]', sometimes abbreviated to 'S.T.T.L.'

Willard D. VANDIVER American politician (1854–1932)

3 I come from a state that raises corn and cotton and cockleburs and Democrats, and frothy eloquence neither convinces nor satisfies me. I am from Missouri. You have got to show me.

Vandiver was a representative in Congress from Columbia, Missouri, from 1897 to 1905. When he was a member of the House Naval Committee and was inspecting the Navy Yard at Philadelphia in 1899, he good-humouredly made the above statement when speaking at a dinner. 'I'm from Missouri' quickly became a way of showing scepticism and demanding proof. Missouri, accordingly, became known as the 'Show Me State'. The date of the speech is sometimes given as 1902, and the speaker's name as 'Vandiner'. Barry Popik in *Comments on Etymology* (May 1997) traced the expression back to 1896, and an attestation of the scepticism of Missourians has been found even earlier, during the Civil War.

Henry VAN DYKE American minister, essayist and poet (1852–1933)

4 Time is
Too Slow for those who Wait,
Too Swift for those who Fear,
Too Long for those who Grieve,
Too Short for those who Rejoice;
But for those who Love,
Time is not.

Music and Other Poems (1905). Van Dyke was a Presbyterian minister in Rhode Island and New York. He was appointed Professor of English at Princeton in 1900, and was American Ambassador to the Netherlands (1913–16). This passage was read by Lady Jane Fellowes at the funeral service of her sister, Diana, Princess of Wales, at Westminster Abbey (6 September 1997). At this reading, 'Time is Eternity' was substituted for the last line. Elsewhere, 'Time is an eternity' has been substituted.

VARIETY American show business newspaper, founded 1905

1 WALL ST. LAYS AN EGG.

Headline on the Wall Street crash (30 October 1929). Credited to Sime Silverman (1873–1933), who was editor at the time. *Bartlett* (1980), although correctly attributing 'WALL ST. LAYS AN EGG' to Silverman, puts it in upper and lower case as 'Wall *Street* Lays an Egg', which is not quite the same thing. This was corrected in the 1992 edition, though still not put all in upper case.

2 STICKS NIX HICK PIX.

Headline meaning that cinema-goers in rural areas were not attracted to films with bucolic themes (17 July 1935). The sub-head is: 'NOT INTERESTED IN FARM DRAMA'. Credited to Abel Green (1900–73), editor at the time. In the film *Yankee Doodle Dandy* (US 1942), James Cagney, playing George M. Cohan, rattles it off about three times, clearly sounding as if he is saying '*hicks* pix'. Even if this version makes the saying flow better, it is not what was actually printed. The wording here has been checked against the facsimile reproduced in the *Variety History of Show Business* (1993). *Bartlett* (1980) credited the headline to the paper's founder Sime Silverman ... though he had died two years previously. It also gave the headline as: 'Sticks Nix *Hicks* Pix'.

Luc de Clapiers, Marquis de VAUVENARGUES
French writer (1715–47)

3 *C'est un grand signe de médiocrité de louer toujours modérément* [It is a great sign of mediocrity always to praise moderately].

Reflections and Maxims, No. 12 (1746). Compare what John Sheffield, 1st Duke of Buckingham and Normanby (1648–1721), wrote 'On Mr Hobbes':

Such is the mode of these censorious days,
The art is lost of knowing how to praise.

Thorstein VEBLEN American economist (1857–1929)

4 Conspicuous consumption of valuable goods is a means of reputability to the gentleman of leisure.

The Theory of the Leisure Class (1899). Veblen coined the term 'conspicuous consumption' to describe the extrava

gant use of expensive goods to display status. Compare the term 'conspicuous waste' (*OED2*'s only citation is from 1969), a Marxist term to denote much the same thing but more critically.

5 The outcome of any serious research can only be to make two questions grow where one question grew before.

'Evolution of the Scientific Point of View', in the *University of California Chronicle* (1908). Veblen was clearly alluding to SWIFT 450:9.

VESPASIAN Roman Emperor (AD9–79)

6 *Pecunia non olet* [Money does not smell].

Remark in about AD70. When Vespasian imposed a tax on public lavatories, his son Titus objected on the grounds that this was beneath the dignity of the state. The Emperor – according to Suetonius, *Lives of the Caesars* – took a handful of coins and held them under his son's nose, and asked if they smelt. On being told they didn't, Vespasian said, '*Atque et lotio est* [Yet, that's made from urine].'
    As a result, public urinals in France are still sometimes called *vespasiennes*. The expression *Pecunia non olet* now means, 'Don't concern yourself with the source of money. Don't look a gift horse in the mouth.'

VICTORIA British Queen (1819–1901)

7 I will be good.

From E.V. Lucas, *A Wanderer in London* (1906): 'It was there [Kensington Palace] that on May 24, 1819, she was born; and there that she was sleeping when in the small hours of June 20, 1837, the Archbishop of Canterbury and the Lord Chamberlain awakened her to hail her queen – and "I will be good," she said, very prettily, and kept her word.'
    But no. These pious words were not said by Queen Victoria on her accession to the throne in 1837, but on 11 March 1830 when she was a mere 11 years of age. It was casually revealed precisely what lay in store for her, and this is what she said – source: Sir Theodore Martin, *The Prince Consort* (1875).

8 No woman would do that.

Commenting on the fact that the Criminal Law Amendment Act of 1885 (which outlawed indecent relations between same sex adults in public and in private) made no mention of women. Another version: originally the wording had been 'any male or female person', but when the text was shown to the queen, no one had the nerve to answer her query of 'Why women were included in the Act as surely it was impossible for them' – source: Ted Morgan, *Somerset*

Maugham (1980). Dermod Quirke commented (1999): 'There are many versions of this old chestnut – I like the lesbian one, which has Victoria saying, "I'll be damned if I'll let them spoil the fun for us girls." But they're all non-sense: there is absolutely no evidence that Victoria made any comment on the Act of 1885 ... [besides] women were never included in any draft of sect. 11 ... and they were certainly not included in the definitive text submitted to Victoria for her assent. Labouchere's draft read "if any male person ...", and it was adopted by parliament in precisely that form.

'Richard Ellman's version [in his *Oscar Wilde*, 1987] is more subtle. He recognizes that the Act referred only to men, and so has Victoria asking why women were not included. Nice try, but it still doesn't really hold water.'

1 We are not amused.

The subject was raised in *Notebooks of a Spinster Lady* (1919) written by Miss Caroline Holland (1878–1903): '[The Queen's] remarks can freeze as well as crystallize ... there is a tale of the unfortunate equerry who ventured during dinner at Windsor to tell a story with a spice of scandal or impropriety in it. "We are not amused," said the Queen when he had finished.'

The equerry in question appears to have been the Hon. Alexander Yorke. Unfortunately, the German he had told the story to laughed so loud that the queen's attention was drawn to it. Another contender for the snub is Admiral Maxse, whom she commanded to give his well-known imitation of her, which he did by putting a handkerchief on his head and blowing out his cheeks. Interviewed in 1978, Princess Alice, Countess of Athlone, said she had once questioned her grandmother about the phrase – 'I asked her ... [but] she never said it' – and affirmed what many have held, that Queen Victoria was 'a very cheerful person'.

2 He speaks to Me as if I was a public meeting.

Of W.E. Gladstone. Quoted in G.W.E. Russell, *Collections and Recollections* (1898) – 'is a complaint which is said to have proceeded from illustrious lips'. It has been objected that, if she did indeed say any such thing, Victoria would have said '... as if I *were* a public meeting'. But what we have here is only a report (albeit published while she was still alive). As her published letters and journals show, she wrote in a very emphatic manner and often referred to herself in the third person, but she did not usually capitalize 'Me' as here. It is not clear, either, how unthinkable it really is for her to have committed the solecism.

By a curious coincidence, that same year Bismarck in his memoirs *Gedanken und Erinnerungen* looked back on an unsatisfactory conversation he had had in private in 1850 with Heinrich von Gagern, former President of the first National Assembly in Frankfurt. When someone asked Bismarck what Gagern said, he replied: '*Er hat mir eine Rede gehalten, als ob ich eine Volksversammlung wäre* [He made a speech to me as if I were a public meeting].'

3 Please understand that there is no one depressed in *this* house. We are not interested in the pos-sibilities of defeat. They do not exist.

To A.J. Balfour, who was in charge of the Foreign Office. Quoted in Lady Gwendolen Cecil, *The Life of Robert, Marquis of Salisbury* (1931). During one week of the South African War in December 1899 – 'Black Week', as it came to be called – British forces suffered a series of setbacks in their fight against the Boers. Queen Victoria 'braced the nation in words which have become justly famous' – W.S. Churchill, *A History of the English-Speaking Peoples*, Vol. 4.

Margaret Thatcher quoted these words in her first television interview during the Falklands War, having seen them as a motto on Winston Churchill's desk in his Second World War bunker beneath Whitehall. See THATCHER 466:1.

Gore VIDAL American novelist, playwright and critic (1925–)

4 I'm all for bringing back the birch, but only between consenting adults in private.

Interviewed on TV by David Frost and quoted in *The Sunday Times* Magazine (16 September 1973). This refers to an edition of Rediffusion TV's *The Frost Programme* in 1966. In his memoirs, Frost suggests that the line was, 'Yes, I am in favour of birching, but only between consenting adults', and that it was not actually uttered on air: 'In the hospitality room after the programme Gore Vidal was kicking himself for having thought of one rejoinder ten minutes too late.'

5 It is not enough to succeed. Others must fail.

This was quoted as 'the cynical maxim of a clever friend' by the Revd Gerard Irvine during his 'anti-panegyric' for Tom Driberg (Lord Bradwell) after a requiem mass in London on 7 December 1976.

'It's not enough that I should succeed – others should fail,' was attributed to David Merrick, the Broadway producer, in Barbara Rowes, *The Book of Quotes* (1979).

6 Looks and sounds not unlike Hitler, but without the charm.

On William F. Buckley Jr, quoted in the same source. Which came first, this or the line used by Peter Cook about Dudley Moore ('A power-crazed ego-maniac, a kind of Hitler without the charm') in a newspaper interview of February 1979?

1 Good career move.

Remark on hearing of Truman Capote's death (1984). Confirmed by him in BBC TV *Gore Vidal's Gore Vidal* (1995). According to *Time* Magazine (8 April 1985), the graffito 'Good career move' had appeared following Elvis Presley's death in 1977.

2 Really? Well, meretricious and a happy New Year.

Riposte to the novelist Richard Adams when, on the BBC Radio show *Start the Week* (24 September 1984), Adams had described Vidal's novel about Abraham Lincoln as 'meretricious'. The exchange was recorded in Alan Bennett's diary (included in *Writing Home*, 1995), with the comment: 'That's the way to do it.' But, unusually for Vidal, it now appears he was quoting an old wish (a 'meretricious and a happy New Year') by Franklin Pierce Adams – so quoted in Scott Meredith, *George S. Kaufman and the Algonquin Round Table* (1977). It seems that Adams was not alone in anticipating Vidal's noted riposte. Ken Austin points out that in an episode of the Marx Brothers' NBC radio show *Flywheel, Shyster and Flywheel* (broadcast on 13 March 1930, the following exchange took place between Chico and an exasperated judge who is fighting for re-election:

> *Judge*: Ladies and gentlemen, my candidacy is being fought by a group of men who are dishonest, grafting and meretricious!
> *Chico*: Tank you judge, and I wish you da same.
> *Judge*: You wish me what?
> *Chico*: A meretricious. A meretricious and a happy new year!

Ah, but who came first – F.P.A. or the brothers M? Samuel Hopkins Adams, *A. Woollcott – His Life and His World* (1945), includes among wisecracks attributed to the Algonquin Round Table, 'Frank Adams' example of a sentence embodying the word "meretricious" – Meretricious 'n Happy New Year'. No date, but as the Round Table is thought to have ceased in 1932, most likely Adams takes precedence over the Marx Brothers.

Philippe-Auguste VILLIERS DE L'ISLE ADAM
French poet, novelist and playwright (1838–89)

3 *Vivre? les serviteurs feront cela pour nous* [Living? The servants will do that for us].

Play, *Axël*, Act 4, Sc. 2 (1890). This has given rise to a number of joke variations, of which 'Sex? Our servants do that for us' is probably the best known. In the film comedy *Carry On Up the Khyber* (UK 1968), Kenneth Williams as the 'Khasi of Kalabar' says to Joan Sims as 'Lady Ruff-Diamond', 'I do not make love ... I am extremely rich. I have servants to do everything for me.' Which only goes to

show how old this version must have been even then, for it to have been included in a *Carry On*.

When the film actor Victor Mature was told that he looked as though he had slept in his clothes, he is said to have replied: 'Don't be ridiculous. I pay someone to do that for me.'

François VILLON French poet (1431–?63)

4 *Mais où sont les neiges d'antan?* [But where are the snows of yesteryear?]

'Ballade des dames du temps jadis', *Le Grand Testament* (1461). This translation by D.G. Rossetti.

VIRGIL Roman poet (70–19BC)

5 *Amor vincit omnia* [Love conquers all].

Eclogues, No. 10, line 69. One of the best-known proverbial expressions of all. Chaucer's Prioress had it on her brooch, as mentioned in 'The General Prologue' to *The Canterbury Tales*. Virgil actually wrote '*Omnia vincit amor, nos et cedamus amori* [Love conquers all so let us yield to love].'

6 *Arma virumque cano* [I sing of arms and the man].

The first line of the *Aeneid* has given us the poet's phrase 'I sing ...' Robert Herrick in *Hesperides* (1648) begins: 'I sing of brooks, of blossoms, birds, and bowers'. William Cowper begins 'The Sofa' in *The Task* (1785):

> I sing the Sofa. I who lately sang
> Truth, Hope and Charity, and touch'd with awe
> The solemn chords ...
> Now seek repose upon a humbler theme.

Titles of poems by Walt Whitman include, 'One's Self I Sing', 'For Him I Sing' and 'I Sing the Body Electric' (see WHITMAN 492:5).

It also gives us the title of a play, *Arms and the Man* (1894) by Bernard Shaw – or, rather, it does so via Dryden's translation of the same: 'Arms, and the man I sing.' This version had earlier been cited by Thomas Carlyle in *Past and Present* (1843) when he wrote: 'For we are to bethink us that the Epic verily is not *Arms and the Man*, but *Tools and the Man*, – an infinitely wider kind of epic.'

7 *Timeo Danaos et dona ferentes* [I fear the Greeks, especially when they offer gifts].

In the same work, Bk 2, line 49. Hence, 'Beware Greeks bearing gifts', a warning against trickery. This is an allusion to the most famous Greek gift of all – the large wooden horse that was built supposedly as an offering to the gods before the Greeks were about to return home after besieging Troy unsuccessfully for ten years. It was taken within the city walls of Troy, but men leapt out from it, opened the gates and helped destroy the city. In the *Aeneid*, Laocoön warn the Trojans not to admit the horse, with these words. The Revd John Skinner, a Somerset rector, wrote in his diary for 28 April 1822: 'Upon my admiring some gooseberry wine at dinner, she turned to the Butler, and ordered him to send half-a-dozen to the Parsonage the following day, which I did all I could to decline, under the old feeling *Timeo Danaos, et dona ferentes.*'

1 *Decus et tutamen* [An ornament and a safeguard].

In the same work, Bk 5, line 262. This has become the Latin inscription now found on the rim of the British pound coin, which replaced the banknote in 1983. The same words, suggested by John Evelyn the diarist, had appeared on the rim of a Charles II crown of 1662–3 (its purpose then was as a safeguard against clipping). The words refer to the inscription rather than the coin – and originally were '*viro, decus et tutamen in armis*'. The last five of these words comprise the motto of the Feltmakers' Company (incorporated 1604). Also translated as 'handsome and secure'.

2   *Bella, horrida bella,*
Et Thybrim multo spumantem sanguine cerno
[I see wars, horrible wars, and the Tiber foaming with much blood].

In the same work, Bk 6, line 86. See POWELL 367:1.

3 *Facilis descensus Averno* [It is easy to go down into Hell].

In the same work, Bk 5, line 126. This phrase is employed when wanting to suggest that man is readily inclined towards evil deeds. Avernus, a lake in Campania, was a name for the entrance to Hell. The epic poem continues with: '*Noctes atque dies patet atri ianua Ditis; / Sed revocare gradum superasque evadere ad auras, / Hoc opus, hic labor est* [Night and day, the gates of dark Death stand wide; but to climb back again, to retrace one's steps to the upper air – there's the rub, that is the task].'

See also RATTIGAN 376:4.

VOLTAIRE French writer and philosopher (1694–1778)

4 I disapprove of what you say, but will defend to the death your right to say it.

A remark attributed to Voltaire, notably by S.G. Tallentyre in *The Friends of Voltaire* (1907). But Tallentyre gave the words as a free paraphrase of what Voltaire wrote in his *Essay on Tolerance*: 'Think for yourself and let others enjoy the privilege to do so, too.' So what we have is merely Tallentyre's summary of Voltaire's point of view.

Then along came Norbert Guterman to claim that what Voltaire *did* write in a letter of 6 February 1770 to a M. Le Riche was: 'Monsieur l'Abbé, I detest what you write, but I would give my life to make it possible for you to continue to write.' This reference is unverified, however.

So, whether or not he used the precise words, at least Voltaire believed in the principle behind them.

5 *Si Dieu n'existait pas, il faudrait l'inventer* [If God did not exist, it would be necessary to invent him].

Epîtres, No. 96 (1770). Hence, the formula, 'If — did not exist it would have to be invented.' Other examples include: 'If Austria did not exist it would have to be invented' (Frantisek Palacky, ?1845); 'If he [Auberon Waugh, writer, critic and journalist] did not exist, it would be unnecessary to invent him' (Desmond Elliott, literary agent, in about 1977); 'What becomes clear is that Olivier developed his own vivid, earthy classical style as a reaction to Gielgud's more ethereal one ... So if Gielgud did not exist would Olivier have found it necessary to invent himself?' – review in *The Observer* (1988); 'Had Olivier not existed – and it would have been difficult to invent him' – Anthony Holden, *Olivier*, Chap. 20 (1988); 'If Tony Benn did not exist, the old Right of the Labour Party would have had to invent him' – *The Observer* (15 October 1989).

6 In this country [England] it is thought well to kill an admiral from time to time to encourage the others [*pour encourager les autres*].

Candide, Chap. 23 (1759). This was a reference to the case of Admiral Byng who, in 1756, was sent to relieve Minorca, which was blockaded by a French fleet. He failed and, when found guilty of neglect of duty, he was condemned to death and shot on board the *Monarque* at Portsmouth.

7 All is for the best in the best of all possible worlds.

In the same book, Chap. 30. This is the motto of the bland philosopher Pangloss, through whom Voltaire is satirizing the theology of Leibniz, who held that God could not have created a more perfect world than that which he did. Compare P.G. Wodehouse, 'Lord Emsworth and the Girl Friend', *Blandings Castle and Elsewhere* (1935): 'Lord Emsworth's gloom deepened. He chafed at being called upon – by this woman of all others – to behave as if everything was for the jolliest in the jolliest of all possible worlds.'

8 'That is well said,' replied Candide, 'but we must cultivate our garden [*il nous faut cultiver notre jardin*].'

Meaning, 'we must attend to our own affairs'. In the same book, Chap. 30.

1 God is always on the side of the big battalions.

Voltaire did not say this, though he did refer to the idea. In this form it has been attributed to the French marshal, the Vicomte de Turenne (died in 1675), and to Roger, Comte de Bussy-Rabutin (in a letter to the Comte de Limoges, 18 October 1677) – the latter adding, 'and against the small ones'.

What Voltaire wrote in a letter to Le Riche (6 February 1770) was: '*They say* that God is always on the side of the big battalions', obviously referring back. Earlier, in what are called his 'Piccini Notebooks' (?1735–50), Voltaire had, in fact, written: 'God is on the side not of the heavy battalions, but of the best shots.'

2 *Je n'impose rien; je ne propose rien: j'expose* [I impose nothing; I propose nothing: I expose].

In 2003, Henry Hardy traced what is in fact a bogus 'quotation' from Voltaire to its inventor, Lytton Strachey, who was parodying scholarship in his preface to *Eminent Victorians* (1918).

Werner VON BRAUN German-born American rocket scientist (1912–77)

3 *I Aim At the Stars.*

Title of biographical film (US 1960 – with Curt Jurgens in the title role). After working on German V-2s in the Second World War, von Braun went to the US and participated in the space programme. There is no evidence that he ever used this phrase himself, though *Griff nach den Sternen* was the title of a book on which von Braun collaborated in 1962, which is more properly translated as 'reaching / grasping / groping for the stars.' Erik Berghast's 1960 biography of von Braun is entitled *Reaching for the Stars*. All these titles may allude to Virgil's *Aeneid* (as also may the RAF motto *Per ardua ad astra*).

Diana VREELAND American fashion journalist (?1903–89)

4 I love London. It is the most swinging city in the world at the moment.

Quoted in *Weekend Telegraph* Magazine (30 April 1965). The coming together of the words 'swinging' and 'London' for the first time may have first occurred publicly in this way. In addition, a picture caption declared, 'London is a swinging city.' Almost exactly one year later, *Time* Magazine picked up the angle and devoted a cover story to the concept of 'London: The Swinging City' (edition dated 15 April 1966).

5 The beautiful people.

Coinage of this term is credited to Vreeland in *Current Biography* (1978). Whether she deserves this or not is open to question. The earliest *OED2* citation, with capital letters for each word, is from 1966, though there is a *Vogue* use from 15 February 1964 that would appear to support the link to Vreeland. *OED2* makes the phrase refer primarily to 'flower people' and 'hippies', though I would prefer the 1981 *Macquarie Dictionary*'s less narrow definition of: 'Fashionable social set of wealthy, well-groomed, usually young people'. The Lennon and McCartney song 'Baby You're a Rich Man' containing the line 'How does it feel to be one of the beautiful people?' was released in July 1967.

William Saroyan's play *The Beautiful People* had been performed long before all this, in 1941, and Oscar Wilde in a letter to Harold Boulton (December 1879), wrote: 'I could have introduced you to some very beautiful people. Mrs Langtry and Lady Lonsdale and a lot of clever beings who were at tea with me.'

W

John WAIN English novelist, poet and critic (1925–94)

1 *Hurry on Down.*
Title of novel (1953). The epigraph is simply 'Hurry on down to my place, baby, / Nobody home but me. – *Old Song*'. In fact it was a song (1947) written and performed by Nellie Lutcher, the American entertainer. Wain's novel was lumped together with others in the Angry Young Men school of the early 1950s. It was about a man hurrying down from university and doing rather unlikely jobs.

James J. WALKER American politician (1881–1946)

2 Will you love me in December as you do in May?
Title of song (1905), with music by Ernest R. Ball. Walker was a future Mayor of New York. Possibly it had some influence on the coinage of the expression 'A May/December romance' or 'Spring/winter romance' to describe a union between a younger person and an older one. Compare this, from 'To the most Courteous and Fair Gentlewoman, Mrs Elinor Williams' by Rowland Watkyns (who died in 1664): 'For every marriage then is best in tune, / When that the wife is May, the husband June.' In Chaucer's 'Merchant's Tale' a young girl, May, marries an old man, January.

Lew WALLACE American novelist (1827–1905)

3 Beauty is altogether in the eye of the beholder.
The Prince of India (1893). Wallace is sometimes considered to have coined the expression in this form but, in fact, he was preceded (without the 'altogether') by Margaret Wolfe Hungerford in *Molly Bawn* (1878), and, as 'Most true is it that "beauty is in the eye of the gazer"', by Charlotte Brontë in *Jane Eyre*, Pt 2, Chap. 2 (1847). In any case, the idea that beauty is according to the beholder's estimation was not

new. In David Hume's *Essays Moral & Political* (1742) there is: 'Beauty, properly speaking, lyes ... in the Sentiment or Taste of the Reader.'

W.R. WALLACE American poet (1819–81)

4 A mighty power and stronger
Man from his throne has hurled,
For the hand that rocks the cradle
Is the hand that rules the world.
'What rules the world' (1865) – a tribute to motherhood, first appearing in *John O'London's Treasure Trove*. Hence, the slogan 'The hand that rocks the cradle can rock the system', which was employed successfully in 1990 by Mary Robinson, a feminist lawyer, in her successful campaign to become President of the Irish Republic. *The Hand That Rocks the Cradle* was the title of a film (US 1992) about a nanny from hell.

WALL STREET American film, 1987. Written by Stanley Weiser and Oliver Stone. With Michael Douglas as Gordon Gekko.

5 *Gekko*: Greed, for want of a better word, is good.
Probably inspired by the words of Ivan Boesky, the American financier (1937–): 'Greed is all right ... Greed is healthy. You can be greedy and still feel good about yourself' – part of a commencement address when receiving an honorary degree at the University of California at Berkeley on 18 May 1986. Boesky also said, 'Seek wealth, it's good.' In December 1987 he was sentenced to three years' imprisonment for insider dealing on the New York Stock Exchange. *Bartlett* (1992) has the version: 'Greed is good! Greed is right! Greed works! Greed will save the U.S.A.!'

Horace WALPOLE (4th Earl of Orford) English writer (1717–97)

1 These ... were what filled me with disgust, and made me quit that splendid theatre of pitiful passion.

Memoirs of the Reign of King George III (published posthumously). On his retirement from the House of Commons in 1767. He was trying not to pass off his anecdotes as a history of England but hoped that they contained 'the most useful part of all history, a picture of human minds'. Compare JEFFERSON 254:5.

2 This world is a comedy to those that think, a tragedy to those that feel.

Letter to the Countess of Upper Ossory (16 August 1776). Unverified. However, Blaise Pascal (1623–62) is reported to have said earlier: '*La vie, c'est une tragédie pour celui qui sent, mais une comédie pour celui qui pense.*'

3 Everything's at sea – except the Fleet.

On the state of England. Presumably he meant that the country's affairs were (as we would now say) 'all at sea'. Quoted by Malcolm Muggeridge on BBC Radio *Quote ... Unquote* in 1978, but unverified. Compare CARSON 126:1.

4 This sublime age reduces everything to its quintessence; all periphrases and expletives are so much in disuse, that I suppose soon the only way to making love will be to say 'Lie down.'

Letter to H.S. Conway (23 October 1778). A precursor of the modern expression 'Lie down, I think I love you.' This last was considered a sufficiently well-established, smart, jokey remark to be listed by *The Sun* (10 October 1984) as one of its 'Ten top chat-up lines'. It may also have been used in a song or cartoon just a little before that. Indeed, there was a song entitled 'Lie Down (A Modern Love Song)' written and performed by the British group Whitesnake in 1978. Earlier, 'Sit Down I Think I Love You', written by Stephen Stills, as in Crosby, Stills, Nash and Young, was performed by The Mojo Men in 1967. An article 'Down with Sex' was published in collected form (1966) by Malcolm Muggeridge, and in it he wrote: 'I saw scrawled on a wall in Santa Monica in California: "Lie down! I think I love you." Thus stripped, sex becomes an orgasm merely.' And then again, there was the Marx Brothers' line from *The Cocoanuts* (1929), 'Ah, Mrs Rittenhouse, won't you ... lie down?'

See also ARNOLD 40:7.

(Sir) Robert WALPOLE (1st Earl of Orford) British Whig Prime Minister (1676–1745)

5 [The gratitude of place-expectants] is a lively sense of future favours.

Quoted in William Hazlitt, 'On Wit and Humour', *Lectures on the English Comic Writers* (1819). By this century, the *Dictionary of American Proverbs* has, as simply proverbial, 'Gratitude is a lively expression of favours yet to come.' Prior to Walpole, La Rochefoucauld had said, 'The gratitude of most men is merely a secret desire to receive greater benefits [*La reconnaissance de la plupart des hommes n'est qu'une secrète envie de recevoir de plus grands bienfaits.*' – *Maxims*, No. 298 (1678).

6 They now *ring* the bells, but they will soon *wring* their hands.

On the declaration of the war with Spain (the War of Jenkins' Ear) in 1739 – which he had opposed. Robert Jenkins, a British mariner, claimed that his ear had been cut off by Spanish coastguards. The war merged with that of the Austrian Succession. Quoted in W. Coxe, *Memoirs of Sir Robert Walpole* (1798).

7 The balance of power.

An expression used by Walpole in the House of Commons (13 February 1741), which has now come to mean the promotion of peace through parity of strength in rival groups. *ODQ* (1979) gave it as though Walpole had coined the phrase, but dropped it in 1992. *Safire* (1978) states that the phrase was being used in international diplomacy as early as 1700. Initially, the phrase appears to have been 'the balance of power in Europe'. In 1715 Alexander Pope wrote a poem with the title 'The Balance of Europe': 'Now Europe's balanc'd, neither side prevails; / For nothing's left in either of the scales.'

Andy WARHOL American artist (1927?–87)

8 In the future everybody will be world famous for fifteen minutes.

Catalogue for an exhibition of Warhol's work in Stockholm (February–March 1968). More often rendered as 'In the future everyone will be famous for fifteen minutes.' Accordingly, the phrase 'to be famous for fifteen minutes' means to have transitory fame of the type prevalent since the later 20th century. It is often to be found used allusively – 'He's had his fifteen minutes.' *Famous for Fifteen Minutes* was the title of a series of, naturally, 15-minute programmes on BBC Radio 4 in 1990, in which yesterday's headline-makers were recalled from obscurity. In Warhol's published diaries (for 27 July 1978) he wrote: 'After work I just stayed in. Watched 20/20 and instead of saying, "In the future everyone will be famous for fifteen minutes," it was so funny to hear Hugh Downs say, "As Andy Warhol once said, in fifteen minutes everybody will be famous." People on TV always get some part wrong, like – "In the future fifteen people will be famous."'

Charles Dudley WARNER American journalist and writer (1829–1900)

1 Politics makes strange bedfellows.

My Summer in a Garden (1870). In 1854, however, Leigh Hunt had written a letter (published in 1862) that included this sentence: 'Politics, like "misery", certainly makes a man acquainted with strange bedfellows.' Both remarks probably allude to Shakespeare, *The Tempest*, II.ii.40 (1612) – 'Misery acquaints a man with strange bed-fellows'.

See also TWAIN 471:5.

Booker T. WASHINGTON American educationist (1856–1915)

2 No race can prosper till it learns that there is as much dignity in tilling a field as in writing a poem.

Up from Slavery (1901). As a phrase 'the dignity of labour' has proved hard to trace. *OED2*'s earliest citation is only in 1948, although Dorothy L. Sayers has the exact phrase in *Gaudy Night*, Chap. 3 (1935). Oscar Wilde states in his essay 'The Soul of Man Under Socialism' (1891) that 'a great deal of nonsense is being written and talked nowadays about the dignity of manual labour'. Shaw, in his play *Man and Superman*, Act 2 (1903), has the exchange: 'I believe most intensely in the dignity of labour' / 'That's because you never done any, Mr Robinson.'

The similar 'honest toil' is almost as elusive. Thomas Gray in his 'Elegy' (1751) spoke of the '*useful* toil' of the 'rude fore-fathers' in the countryside – GRAY 221:4). *Useful Toil* was the title of a book comprising 'autobiographies of working people from the 1820s to the 1920s' (published 1974). *OED2* finds 'honest labour' in 1941. Thomas Carlyle spoke of 'honest work' in 1866. 'Honourable toil' appears in the play *Two Noble Kinsmen* (possibly by John Fletcher and William Shakespeare, published 1634).

George WASHINGTON American 1st President (1732–99)

3 Looking at his father with the sweet face of youth brightened with the inexpressible charm of all-conquering truth, he bravely cried out. 'I can't tell a lie. I did cut it with my hatchet.'

Mason Locke Weems, Washington's first popular biographer, in *The Life of George Washington: With Curious Anec-*

dotes Equally Honorable to Himself and Exemplary to His Young Countrymen (1800). Sometimes remembered as, 'Father, I cannot tell a lie. I did it with my little hatchet.' When asked, as a boy, by his father, how a certain cherry tree had come to be cut down. A tale almost certainly invented by Weems.

See also JEFFERSON 254:5.

Evelyn WAUGH English novelist (1903–66)

4 Any who have heard the sound will shrink at the recollection of it; it is the sound of English county families baying for broken glass.

Decline and Fall, Prelude (1928). Compare BELLOC 60:5.

5 Mr Salter's side of the conversation was limited to expressions of assent. When Lord Copper was right he said, 'Definitely, Lord Copper'; when he was wrong, 'Up to a point.'

Scoop (1938). Lord Copper is a newspaper proprietor. Hence, the expression 'Up to a point, Lord Copper' used when disagreeing with someone it is not prudent to differ with. An example from *The Independent* (4 April 1990): 'We are told that [Norman Tebbit] was only trying to help ... he was out to "stop Heseltine". Well, up to a point, Lord Whitelaw.'

6 *Put Out More Flags.*

Title of novel (1942). According to Waugh, it comes from a Chinese saying: 'A drunk military man should order gallons and put out more flags in order to increase his military splendour.'

7 'I have been here before,' I said; I had been there before; first with Sebastian more than twenty years ago on a cloudless day in June, when the ditches were creamy with meadowsweet and the air heavy with all the scents of summer.

Brideshead Revisited, Chap. 1 (1945) – in which Charles Ryder says it about Brideshead (hence the 'revisited'). *I Have Been Here Before* had earlier been the title of a 'Time' play (1937) by J.B. Priestley. Then there is: 'I have been here before, / But when or how I cannot tell' – D.G. Rossetti, 'Sudden Light' (1870).

8 As I took the cigarette from my lips and put it in hers, I caught a thin bat's squeak of sexuality, inaudible to any but me.

In the same novel, Chap. 3. Charles Ryder of Lady Julia. A later use of 'bat's squeak', not otherwise much recorded: at the Conservative Party Conference in 1981, a then upwardly rising politician called Edwina Currie was taking part in a debate on law and order. To illustrate some point, she held aloft a pair of handcuffs. Subsequently, the Earl of Gowrie admitted to having felt 'a bat's squeak of desire' for Mrs Currie at that moment.

See also MAGEE 307:3.

Sidney WEBB (later Lord Passfield) English socialist (1859–1947)

1 Once we face the necessity of putting our principles first into Bills, to be fought through committee clause by clause; and then into the appropriate machinery for carrying them into execution from one end of the kingdom to the other ... the inevitability of gradualness cannot fail to be appreciated.

Presidential address to the Labour Party Conference at the Queen's Hall, London (26 June 1923). The phrase 'the inevitability of gradualness' was taken to mean that, for Labour, electoral success would come gradually but certainly, and by evolution not revolution.

2 To secure for the workers by hand or by brain the full fruits of their industry and the most equitable distribution thereof that may be possible upon the basis of the common ownership of the means of production, distribution and exchange.

Clause 4 of the party's Constitution (Party Objects), adopted 1918/1926 – believed to have been the work of Webb. The words 'socialization of the means of production &c.' had appeared in the 1900 Labour Party manifesto. The words 'distribution and exchange' were added at the 1928 conference. Clause 4 was rewritten in 1995, after Labour, under Tony Blair, had become New Labour, and the above words were abandoned.

Max WEBER German economist (1864–1920)

3 The Protestant work ethic.

Translation of part title of article, *Die protestantische Ethik und der Geist des Kapitalismus* ('The Protestant ethic and the spirit of capitalism', 1904–5). Hence, the phrase for an attitude towards business, based on the teachings of Calvin and the analysis of Weber, which suggests that it is one's duty to be successful through hard work.

John WEBSTER English playwright (?1580–?1625)

4 'Tis just like a summer birdcage in a garden; the birds that are without despair to get in, and the

birds that are within despair, and are in a consumption, for fear they shall never get out.

The White Devil, Act 1, Sc. 2 (1612). Hence, title of the novel by Margaret Drabble, *A Summer Birdcage* (1963).

5 Leave thy idle questions;
I am i'th'way to study a long silence,
To prate were idle.

In the same play, Act 5, Sc. 6 (1612). Flamineo speaking. Hence, *A Long Silence*, title of a crime novel – the last of the Van der Valk series (1972) by Nicholas Freeling.

6   I have caught
An everlasting cold; I have lost my voice
Most irrecoverably.

In the same play, act and scene.

7 I am Duchess of Malfi still.

The Duchess of Malfi, Act 4, Sc. 2 (1623). When the Philip Hensher/Thomas Ades opera *Powder Her Face* was performed (1999), containing the line 'I am a duchess still' – it was about a notorious 20th-century duchess, Margaret, Duchess of Argyll – it was assumed that this was an allusion to Webster, but Hensher said (2004) it was only a coincidence.

8 *Ferdinand*: Cover her face; mine eyes dazzle; she died young.
Bosola: I think not so; her infelicity
Seem'd to have years too many.

In the same play, act and scene. Concerning the Duchess whom Ferdinand has just strangled. Hence, *Cover Her Face*, title of a crime novel (1962) by P.D. James. The Philip Hensher/Thomas Ades opera *Powder Her Face* (1999) was also thought to take its title by way of allusion to these lines of Webster's. Again, Hensher denied this (2004), saying that it was, rather, an allusion to *La Poudreuse*, the title of the painting (1889–90) by George Seurat. It shows a woman holding a powder puff.

9 We are merely the stars' tennis-balls, struck and bandied,
Which way please them.

In the same play, Act 5, Sc. 4. Hence, *The Stars' Tennis Balls*, title of a novel (2000) by Stephen Fry – about a young man who gets taken prisoner and then seeks revenge.

Josiah WEDGWOOD English potter (1730–95)

10 Am I not a man and a brother?

Motto on Wedgwood cameo (by 1791), showing a kneeling

Negro slave in chains. The motto was adopted by the Anti-Slavery Society. It also features at the end of Chap. 6 of Charles Kingsley, *The Water Babies* (1863).

Fay WELDON English novelist and playwright (1931–)

1 Go to work on an egg.

Slogan for the British Egg Marketing Board in 1957. Hardly a profile of Weldon gets written without mention of her time as an advertising copywriter and her supposed coinage. She did indeed work for the Mather & Crowther agency, but in a 1981 letter to the author she poured a little cold water on the frequent linking of her name with the slogan: 'I was certainly in charge of copy at the time "Go to work on an egg" was first used as a slogan as the main theme for an advertising campaign. The phrase itself had been in existence for some time and hung about in the middle of paragraphs and was sometimes promoted to base lines. Who invented it, it would be hard to say. It is perfectly possible, indeed probable, that I put those particular six words together in that particular order but I would not swear to it.'

Charles E. WELLER American journalist (19th century)

2 Now is the time for all good men to come to the aid of the party.

Typewriter exercise – possibly originated by Weller, a court reporter in Milwaukee (1867) to test the efficiency of the first practical typewriter, which his friend, Christopher L. Scholes, had made. However, in his book *The Early History of the Typewriter* (1918), Weller does not claim credit for the coinage. In the Muir & Norden *My Word* stories (1973), the line is stated to be found in 'The Typewriter's Song' by Edwin Meade Robinson – though I suspect this is merely a quotation of it. Evidently, the sentence was appropriate because it was coined during 'an exciting political campaign'.

Whoever was responsible did not do a very good job, because the phrase contains only 18 letters of the alphabet. 'The quick brown fox jumps over the lazy dog', on the other hand, has all 26. This was once thought to be the shortest sentence in English containing all the letters of the alphabet, but it was superseded by: 'Pack my box with five dozen liquor jugs' (which is 3 letters shorter overall, but the initial 'the' before 'quick brown fox' could always be dispensed with) and 'Quick blowing zephyrs vex daft Jim' (which is even shorter). Even more concise 'pangrams' have been devised, but they are also shorter on sense and memorability.

The sentence has also been found in the form: 'This is the time for all good men to come to the aid of the town' – designed, so it is said, to demonstrate the fact that the key-board was laid out in such a way that most words could be typed using the fingers of alternate hands, which helped the operator to get a good rhythm and attain greater speeds.

Orson WELLES American film director, writer and actor (1915–85)

3 This is the biggest electric train [set] any boy ever had!

Remark on learning how to use a Hollywood studio. First attributed by Leo Rosten in *Hollywood* (1941). Frank Brady in *Citizen Welles* (1989) suggests that this was just prior to the filming of *Citizen Kane*, in about 1939. Penelope Houston, *Contemporary Cinema* (1963), ascribes to Nicholas Ray, 'The biggest, most expensive electric-train set anyone could be given.'

4 You know what the fellow said – in Italy, for thirty years under the Borgias, they had warfare, terror, murder and bloodshed, but they produced Michelangelo, Leonardo da Vinci and the Renaissance. In Switzerland, they had brotherly love; they had five hundred years of democracy and peace – and what did that produce? The cuckoo clock.

So says Harry Lime (played by Welles) in Carol Reed's film *The Third Man* (1949). It soon got around that Welles had added this speech to the basic script, which was written by Graham Greene and Carol Reed. Indeed, it appears only as a footnote in the published script of the film. In a letter, dated 13 October 1977, Greene confirmed to me that it *had* been written by Welles during shooting: 'What happened was that during the shooting of *The Third Man* it was found necessary for the timing to insert another sentence and the speech you mention was put in by Orson Welles.'

Whether the idea was original to Welles is another matter. After all he introduces the speech with, 'You know what the fellow said ...' Welles apparently later suggested that the lines came originally from 'an old Hungarian play'. Anthony Powell in his *Journals 1982–1986* (1995), for 21 December 1986, points out that the painter Whistler 'initially made joke about the Swiss having invented the Cuckoo Clock as chief fame in their cultural achievements. This I corroborated (Whistler's *Ten O'Clock*, 1885), so joke just over century old.'

Indeed, in *Mr Whistler's 'Ten O'Clock'* (1888), which is the text of a lecture he gave on art in 1885, Whistler spoke of: 'The Swiss in their mountains ... What more worthy people! ... yet, the perverse and scornful [goddess, Art] will none of it, and the sons of patriots are left with the clock that turns the mill, and the sudden cuckoo, with difficulty restrained in its box! For this was Tell a hero! For this did Gessler die!'

In *This Is Orson Welles* (1993), Welles is quoted as saying: 'When the picture came out, the Swiss very nicely pointed out to me that they've never made any cuckoo clocks – they all come from the Schwarzwald in Bavaria!' Actually the Schwarzwald [Black Forest] is in Baden-Württemberg.

1 Now we sit through Shakespeare in order to recognize the quotations.

Quoted in *The Treasury of Humorous Quotations*, eds Esar & Bentley (1951). In Prochnow & Prochnow, *A Treasury of Humorous Quotations* (1969), the remark is ascribed to Oscar Wilde. Easy to confuse the two, of course ...

See also *CITIZEN KANE* 144:3.

1st Duke of WELLINGTON Irish-born soldier and politician (1769–1852)

2 I don't know what effect these men will have upon the enemy, but, by God, they frighten me.

Popular summary of a despatch to Sir Colonel Torrens, military secretary at the Horse Guards (29 August 1810). This referred to some of his generals, and not to his regimental officers or to the rank and file, as is made clear from the full text. Wellington in fact said: 'As Lord Chesterfield said of the generals of his day, "I only hope that when the enemy reads the list of their names, he trembles as I do."'

3 We have in the service the scum of the earth as common soldiers.

On his men, in a despatch to Lord Bathurst, the War Minister (July 1813). This was after the Battle of Vitoria, when Wellington's troops ('our vagabond soldiers') were 'totally knocked up' after a night of looting. It was a favourite expression of Wellington: in 1831, Philip Henry Stanhope recorded him as saying of the army: 'Ours is composed of the scum of the earth – the mere scum of the earth.' But on more than one occasion Wellington spoke in complimentary terms about the common soldiers under his command.

The expression predates Wellington. Dr John Arbuthnot in *John Bull*, Act 3, Sc. 6 (1712) has 'Scoundrels! Dogs! the Scum of the Earth!' *The Scum of the Earth* is the title of a novel by Arthur Koestler (1941).

4 Up Guards and at 'em!

Popular short form of what Wellington is supposed to have said at Waterloo, namely, 'Up Guards and at them *again*.' The longer version was reported in a letter from a certain Captain Batty of the Foot Guards on 22 June 1815, four days after the battle.

Benham (1980) has this: 'In A. Tels guide-book, *Excursions*

to the Lion of Waterloo (2nd ed. 1904), a Belgian publication, this is improved as follows: "Wellington cried, 'Upright, guards! prepare for battle.'" In *The Times* (15 October 1841), appeared an "anecdote which may be relied on" quoted from *Britannia*, to the effect that lately the Duke had sat for his bust to "one of the most distinguished of living sculptors," who stated "that it would be popular and effective if it could represent his Grace at the moment when he uttered the memorable words ... at Waterloo. The Duke laughed very good-humouredly at this observation and said 'Ah! the old story. People will invent words for me ... but really I don't know what I said. I saw that the moment for action was come, and I gave the command for attack. I suppose the words were brief and homely enough, for they ran through the ranks and were obeyed on the instant ... but I'm sure I don't recollect them, and I very much doubt whether anyone else can.'"'

Again, in 1852, the Duke commented to J.W. Croker: 'What I must have said and probably did say was, Stand up, Guards! and then gave the commanding officers the order to attack.' The following year, *Notes and Queries* was already puzzling over the matter.

5 A damn close-run thing.

As with most of Wellington's alleged remarks, this was not quite what he said, but it is how it is remembered. What he told the memoirist Thomas Creevey (on 18 June 1815) about the outcome of the Battle of Waterloo, was: 'It has been a damned serious business. Blücher and I have lost 30,000 men. It has been a damned nice thing – the nearest run thing you ever saw in your life.' *The Creevey Papers*, in which this account appears, was not published until 1903. Somehow out of this description a conflated version arose, with someone else presumably supplying the 'close-run'. Hence, David Howarth, *Waterloo: A Near Run Thing* (1959).

6 The battle of Waterloo was won on the playing fields of Eton.

This view was first ascribed to the 1st Duke of Wellington in Count Charles de Montalembert's *De l'Avenir politique de l'Angleterre* in 1856. The Frenchman stated that the Duke returned to Eton in his old age and, recalling the delights of his youth, exclaimed: 'It is here that the battle of Waterloo was won' (i.e. he made no mention of playing fields). In *Self-Help* (1859), Samuel Smiles renders the remark: 'It was there that the battle of Waterloo was won!'

Burnam (1980) suggests that Sir Edward Creasy built on this in *Memoirs of Eminent Etonians* (though as this was published in 1850, and the French book not until 1856, this must have been difficult). Anyhow, Creasy had the Iron Duke passing the playing fields in old age and saying, 'There grows the stuff that won Waterloo.'

Then in 1889 a third writer, Sir William Fraser, in *Words on Wellington*, put together Montalembert's remark with Creasy's playing fields to produce the popularly known version. The 7th Duke tried to pour more cold water on the matter in letters to *The Times* sometime prior to his death in 1972:

> During his old age Wellington is recorded to have visited Eton on two occasions only and it is unlikely that he came more often. He attended the funeral of his elder brother in College Chapel in October 1842 and he accompanied the Queen when she came to Eton with Louis Philippe in October 1844. On the first occasion, he attended the ceremony only and went away when it was over: and, on the second, he is hardly likely to have talked about the battle of Waterloo. Wellington's career at Eton was short and inglorious and, unlike his elder brother, he had no particular affection for the place ... Quite apart from the fact that the authority for attributing the words to Wellington is of the flimsiest description, to anyone who knows his turn of phrase they ring entirely false. It is, therefore, much to be hoped that speakers will discontinue using them either, as is generally the case, in order to point out their snobbishness, which is so alien to ideas generally now held, or else to show that Wellington was in favour of organized games, an assumption which is entirely unwarranted.

Perhaps the nearest the 1st Duke came to any sort of compliment about the effect his old school had on him was, 'I really believe I owe my spirit of enterprise to the tricks I used to play in the garden' (of his Eton boarding house) – quoted in Vol. 1 of Elizabeth Longford's biography (1969).

But the saying, however apocryphal, still exerts its power. One H. Allen Smith (born 1906) said: 'The battle of Yorktown was lost on the playing fields of Eton' (Yorktown, in Virginia, was the scene of the surrender of British forces at the end of the War of Independence, 1781). George Orwell (an Old Etonian himself) averred: 'Probably the Battle of Waterloo *was* won on the playing fields of Eton, but the opening battles of all subsequent wars have been lost there' – *The Lion and the Unicorn* (1941).

1 **I don't care a twopenny damn what becomes of the ashes of Napoleon Bonaparte.**

Attributed, as in Farmer and Henley, *Slang and its Analogues* (1890–1904), but unverified. In *Notes and Queries* (1879), the source is given as a *Life*, ii.257 (1878 edn), presumably that by Brialmont and Gleig. Lord Macaulay in a letter of 6 March 1849 wrote: 'How they settle the matter I care not, as the duke says, one twopenny damn.' James Morris in *Pax Britannica* (1968) comments: 'a *dam* was a small Indian coin, as Wellington knew when he popularized the phrase "a twopenny dam".' *Brewer* (1989) says: 'The derivation ...

from the coin, a dam, is without foundation.' *OED2* has: 'The conjecture that ... the word is the Hindi *dam, dawm,* an ancient copper coin ... is ingenious, but has no basis in fact.'

2 **Publish and be damned!**

Quoted in Elizabeth Longford, *Wellington: The Years of the Sword* (1969). This was Wellington's comment in 1824 to a blackmailer called Stockdale, who offered not to publish anecdotes of the Duke and his mistress, Harriette Wilson, in return for payment. Legend has it that the Duke scrawled this response in bright red ink across Stockdale's letter and sent it back to him. Unfortunately for the tale, Lady Longford states that the letter, now at Apsley House, does not bear any traces of red ink upon it. Valerie Grosvenor Myer in her book *Harriette Wilson, Lady of Pleasure* (1999), pins the start of the rumour on Harriette's former friend, Julia Johnstone (and not on Stockdale). In *Confessions of Julia Johnstone In Contradiction to the Fables of Harriette Wilson* (1825), she writes: 'I should like to know of Miss Wilson, if she did not send to the Duke of Wellington for £300, threatening in case of non-compliance to write anathemas against his moral reputation; and if the Duke did not send her back her letter with "write and be d-d" written in red ink on the back of it?' Anyway, how splendidly catty. Hence, naturally, the title of *Publish and Be Damned*, a book about the press (1955) by Hugh Cudlipp. Richard Ingrams declared on several occasions in about 1977 that a suitable motto for *Private Eye*, of which he was editor, would be: 'Publish and Be Sued'.

3 **If you believe that, you will believe anything.**

Replying to a minor government official who had accosted him in Pall Mall with the words: 'Mr Jones, I believe.' The earliest source I have for this story is Elizabeth Longford, *Wellington: Pillar of State* (1972). It is said that there *was* a Mr Jones who bore a striking resemblance to Wellington – George Jones RA (1786–1869), a military painter. This likeness is referred to by W.P. Frith in *My Autobiography and Reminiscences*, Vol. 1 (1887), together with Wellington's comment on hearing that Jones was sometimes taken for him: 'Mistaken for me, is he? That's strange, for no one ever mistakes me for Mr Jones.'

Compare this caption to a cartoon that appeared in *Punch* (9 April 1864; Wellington had died in 1852):

> *Polite Oxbridge tradesman (in quest of little Nibbs of S. Boniface, and walking by mistake into the rooms of long Nobbs, who 'keeps' on the same staircase).* 'Mr. Nibbs, I believe?'
> *Nobbs (who is six feet one, and rowed a trifle over twelve stone at Putney, the other day).* 'Then, my good fellow, you'll believe anything!'

Now, it was not unknown for *Punch* cartoonists to take existing jokes and make something quite new of them, but is that what happened here? Or was the Wellington anecdote based on the cartoon situation? I note in passing that Mr Nobbs has something of a resemblance in the nose to the Great Duke, and the (anonymous) cartoonist has shaded it quite noticeably.

1 **I should have given more praise.**

Attributed remark. In the final chapter of Elizabeth Longford's book *Wellington: The Years of the Sword* (1969), she writes: 'Sir Winston Churchill told Field-Marshal Montgomery that a friend asked the aged Duke [of Wellington] whether, if he had to live his life over again, there was any way in which he could have done better. The Duke replied, "Yes, I should have given more praise."' Longford apparently took this from Montgomery's own *A History of Warfare* (1968).

H.G. WELLS English novelist and writer (1866–1946)

2 **In the country of the blind the one-eyed man is king.**

This saying has become associated with Wells because of its use by him in the story he wrote with the title 'The Country of the Blind' (1904) – though he quite clearly labelled it as an 'old proverb'. Indeed, it is that and occurs in the proverbs of many languages – as shown by *CODP* (1982.) An early appearance is in a book of *Adages* by Erasmus (who died in 1536): '*In regione caecorum rex est luscus.*' Other 16th-century uses of the saying include John Palsgrave's translation of Fullmin's *Comedy of Acolastus* and John Skelton's 'An one eyed man is Well syghted when he is amonge blunde men' (1522).

3 **The war to end wars.**

Wells popularized this notion in a book he brought out in 1914 with the title *The War That Will End War*. It was not an original cry, having been raised in other wars, but by the end of the First World War it was popularly rendered as 'the war to end wars'. On the afternoon of 11 November 1918 David Lloyd George announced the terms of the Armistice to the House of Commons and concluded: 'I hope we may say that thus, this fateful morning, came to an end all wars.' Later, Wells commented ruefully: 'I launched the phrase "the war to end war" and that was not the least of my crimes' – quoted in Geoffrey West, *H.G. Wells* (1930).

Sometimes it is is said – for example, in *The Observer* Magazine (2 May 1993) – that it was a phrase of the 1930s and that there is no evidence the words were used at the time of the First World War. Clearly not the case.

4 *The New World Order.*

Title of book (1940). Always a rather vague concept. 'New Order' had previously been the name given to programmes of Hitler's regime in Germany in the 1930s and of a Japanese Prime Minister in 1938. Additionally, Hitler said in Berlin (30 January 1941): 'I am convinced that 1941 will be the crucial year of a great New Order in Europe. The world will open up for everyone.' The phrase lingers: in an exchange of New Year's greetings with US President Bush in January 1991, President Gorbachev of the Soviet Union spoke of the serious obstacle posed to a 'new world order' by the Iraqi invasion of Kuwait. After the allied victory in the Gulf War, Bush himself proclaimed a New World Order based on law and human rights. New Order is also the name of a British pop vocal/instrumental group from about 1981.

Timberlake WERTENBAKER Anglo-French-American playwright (1928–)

5 *Our Country's Good.*

Title of play (1988) about Australian convicts putting on a production of Farquhar's *The Recruiting Officer* in 1788/9. It is taken from a stanza first published in the *Annual Register* of 1801 as written by 'a Gentleman of Leicester' and performed at the opening of 'the Theatre, at Sydney, Botany Bay, by the celebrated *Mr Barrington*'. As *The Dictionary of Australian Quotations* (1984) points out: 'The convict George Barrington was long attributed with the authorship, but that the real author was in fact a literary gentleman from the English provinces [Henry Carter who died in 1806] is now beyond dispute.' The matter is discussed in *The Australian Encyclopedia* (1927). In fact, whoever wrote it, the prologue was not actually spoken at the opening of the Sydney playhouse on 16 January 1796 and it is not clear why it should have been passed off as being by Barrington (1755–?1835), an Irish pickpocket who was transported to Botany Bay. It has become famous nevertheless and includes these couplets:

> True patriots we; for be it understood,
> We left our country for our country's good ...
> And none will doubt but that our emigration
> Has proved most useful to the British nation.

Thomas Keneally's novel *The Playmaker* (1987), upon which Wertenbaker based her play, does not contain the verse, but quotes from Farquhar's own prologue to *The Recruiting Officer*. One other note: the first production to be staged at the Sydney playhouse was not in fact by Farquhar. It was Dr Young's tragedy, *The Revenge*.

6 *Three Birds Alighting on a Field.*

Title of play (1991) about the market in modern art. It might appear to be one of those apparently arbitrarily applied titles fixed to paintings (*Cornfield with Crows* is a well-known Van Gogh one). In fact, as the play's original director, Max Stafford-Clark, explained on BBC Radio *Quote ... Unquote* (1993), Wertenbaker took the title from an interview with Francis Bacon, when he described the process of painting. He said how he started drawing a figure and how the figure became less and less important, ending up being about 'three birds alighting on a field'. 'And in the play,' Stafford-Clark added, 'Wertenbaker reverses that. The painter has fallen in love with the woman and he says, "I started off painting this picture about three birds alighting on a field but you've taken over this canvas."'

Bacon's own paintings include works with such titles as *Figure in a Landscape, Three Figures in a Room* and *Landscape with Car*.

(Sir) Arnold WESKER English playwright (1932–)

1 *Chips with Everything.*

Title of play (1962) about class attitudes in the RAF during National Service. It alludes to the belief that the working classes tend to have chips as the accompaniment to almost every dish. Indeed, the play contains the line: 'You breed babies and you eat chips with everything.' The character 'Pip' has an earlier speech, before the one in which he denounces the working class in these terms, recalling having found the title-words at the end of a menu in a greasy-spoon caff. *Partridge/Catch Phrases* dates it to about 1960 and says the phrase has 'been applied to that sort of British tourist abroad which remains hopelessly insular'.

It has a wider application than just to tourists, however, and Wesker was popularizing a phrase that had already been coined. In an essay, published as part of *Declaration* (1957), the film director Lindsay Anderson stated: 'Coming back to Britain is always something of an ordeal. It ought not to be, but it is. And you don't have to be a snob to feel it. It isn't just the food, the sauce bottles on the cafe tables, and the chips with everything. It isn't just saying goodbye to wine, goodbye to sunshine ... We can come home. But the price we pay is high.'

John WESLEY English evangelist and founder of Methodism (1703–91)

2 Cleanliness is next to Godliness.

Although this phrase appears in Wesley's Sermon 88 'On Dress', within quotation marks, it is without attribution. *Brewer* (1989) states that it is to be found in the writings of Phinehas ben Yair, a rabbi (AD ?150–200). In fact, the inspiration appears to be the Talmud: 'The doctrines of religion are resolved into carefulness ... abstemiousness into cleanliness; cleanliness into godliness.' So the saying is not from

the Bible, as might be supposed. Wesley might have found it, however, in Francis Bacon, *The Advancement of Learning*, Bk 2 (1605): 'Cleanliness of body was ever deemed to proceed from due reverence to God.'

Thomas J. Barratt, one of the fathers of modern advertising, seized upon it to promote Pears' Soap, chiefly in the UK. On a visit to the US in the 1880s, he sought a testimonial from a man of distinction. Shrinking from an approach to President Grant, he ensnared the eminent divine, Henry Ward Beecher. Beecher happily complied with Barratt's request and wrote a short text beginning: 'If cleanliness is next to godliness ...' and received no more for his pains than Barratt's 'hearty thanks'.

3 I look upon the whole world as my parish.

This expression – meaning 'I am knowledgeable about many peoples and places; I look upon the world as my oyster' – derives from a letter Wesley wrote to the Revd James Hervey (and which was included in Welsey's *Journal* for 11 June 1739). In it he defended himself against charges that he had invaded the parishes of other clergymen: 'You ... ask, How is it that I assemble Christians, who are none of my charge, to sing psalms and pray and hear the Scriptures expounded? and think it hard to justify doing this in other men's parishes, upon catholic principles ... Seeing I have now no parish of my own, nor probably ever shall ... Suffer me now to tell you my principles in this matter. I look upon all the world as my parish ... This far I mean, that, in whatever part of it I am, I judge it meet, right, and my bounden duty to declare unto all that are willing to hear the glad tidings of salvation.'

4 For what cause I know not to this day, [my wife] set out for Newcastle purposing 'never to return'. *Non eam reliqui; non dismisi; non revocabo* [I did not forsake her; I did not dismiss her; I will not recall her].

In the same journal (23 January 1771) – when his wife, Mrs Vazeile, a widow with four children and a fortune, abandoned him. Initially supporting Wesley in his work, she grew tired of the discomforts, became jealous of the people he worked with, and plagued him in every possible way. His *Journal* suggests that he was probably a difficult man to live with and in the end she left him, clearly with not much regret on his part.

5 God buries his workmen, but carries on his work.

Wesley and his hymnwriting brother Charles are commemorated by a wall plaque in Westminster Abbey. This bears three sayings: 'The best of all is, God is with us' (what John Wesley 'said emphatically' the day before he died), 'I look upon all the world as my parish' (as above) and this one. Where does it come from? There is no mention of it in *Wesley Quotations* (1990) by Betty M. Jarboe, a former reference librarian at the University of Indiana.

Samuel WESLEY English divine and poet (1662–1735)

1 Style is the dress of thought; a modest dress,
Neat, but not gaudy, will true critics please.

'An Epistle to a Friend concerning Poetry' (1700). Possibly the origin of the popular phrase 'neat, (but) not gaudy', although in 1631 there had been the similar 'Comely, not gaudy'. Shakespeare in *Hamlet* (I.iii.71) has 'rich, not gaudy; / For the apparel oft proclaims the man ...' Later, Charles Lamb wrote to William Wordsworth (June 1806), 'A little thin flowery border round, neat not gaudy.' John Ruskin, writing in the *Architectural Magazine* (November 1838): 'That admiration of the "neat but gaudy" which is commonly reported to have influenced the devil when he painted his tail pea green.' Indeed, *Partridge/Catch Phrases* cites: 'Neat, but not gaudy, as the monkey said, when he painted his tail sky-blue' and '... painted his bottom pink and tied up his tail with pea-green.'

Mae WEST American vaudeville and film actress (1893–1980)

2 You know I always did like a man in uniform. And that one fits you grand. Why don't you come up some time and see me? I'm home every evening.

Film, *She Done Him Wrong* (US 1933). To a very young Cary Grant, playing Captain Cummings (a coy undercover policeman). As a catchphrase, the words have been rearranged into 'Come up and see me some time' to make them easier to say. And that is how W.C. Fields says them *to* Mae West in the film *My Little Chickadee* (1939). She herself also took to mouthing them in the easier-to-say form.

3 Warm, dark and handsome.

In the same film. A comment to the character Serge, who has just kissed her on the hand. Obviously playing upon the established phrase 'tall, dark and handsome'. This latter description of a romantic hero's attributes (as likely to be found especially in women's fiction) had surfaced by 1906. Stuart Berg Flexner, *I Hear America Talking* (1976) puts it in the late 1920s as a Hollywood term referring to Rudolph Valentino (though, in fact, he was not particularly tall). Sophie Tucker recorded a song called 'He's Tall, Dark and Handsome' (by Tobias & Sherman) in 1928. Cesar Romero played the lead in the 1941 film *Tall, Dark and Handsome*. However, in a piece called 'Loverboy of the Bourgeoisie'

(collected in 1965), Tom Wolfe writes: 'It was Cary Grant that Mae West was talking about when she launched the phrase "tall, dark and handsome" in *She Done Him Wrong* (1933).' This appears to be an inaccurate assumption.

4 Is that a gun in your pocket or are you just pleased to see me?

Quoted in Joseph Weintraub, *Peel Me a Grape* (1975). Sometimes remembered as 'pistol', and also in connection with her play *Catherine Was Great* (1944) in the form: 'Lieutenant, is that your sword, or are you just glad to see me?' Leslie Halliwell in *The Filmgoer's Book of Quotes* (1978) has this last as West's reaction in a Broadway costume play, when the romantic lead got his sword tangled in his braid so that it stuck up at an unfortunate angle.

5 Beulah – peel me a grape!

Film, *I'm No Angel* (US 1933). A catchphrase expressing dismissive unconcern, which is uttered by West to a maid after a male admirer has just stormed out on her. It has had some wider currency since then, but is almost always used as a quotation.

6 *Leticia (to actor)*: How tall are you without your horse?
Actor: Well, Ma-am, I'm six feet seven inches.
Leticia: Well, never mind the six feet. Let's talk about the seven inches.

Famously indelicate exchange from earlier in West's career, revived in the screenplay of Gore Vidal's *Myra Breckinridge* (US 1970). West delivers the line in the film as Leticia. Quoted in Leslie Halliwell, *The Filmgoer's Book of Quotes* (1973). Tom Stoppard alluded to it in the first edition of BBC Radio *Quote ... Unquote* (1 January 1976). But it is a very old exchange: in Harriette Wilson's *Memoirs*, Chap. 2 (1825) – the book that supposedly gave rise to the Duke of Wellington's response, 'Publish and be damned!' – a stranger says to her, 'A name is not important. I stand before you, an upright man of five feet nine inches.' Lord Alvanley then quips, also in French, 'The lady knows about your five feet, but she's not sure of your nine inches.'

7 A hard man is good to find.

Attributed remark (by 1985). Used, nudgingly – though not ascribed to West – as the slogan for Soloflex body-building equipment in the US (1985): the ads in question showed a woman's hand touching the bodies of well-known brawny athletes. Earlier it was the title of a song by Eddie Green (1919). The line is an inversion of the saying 'A good man is hard to find'. Is this the same as the proverb 'Good men are scarce' found by *CODP* in 1609?

Nathanael WEST American novelist (1903–40)

1 *Miss Lonelyhearts.*

Title of novel (1933) – about a man who writes such a column under this pen name. Hence, the name given to writers of advice columns for the lovelorn (chiefly in the US). In the UK (mostly), the term 'lonely hearts column' has come to mean not an advice column but a listing service for men and women seeking partners.
See also BIBLE 78:3.

R.P. WESTON and Bert LEE British songwriters (1878–1936) and (1880–1947)

2 With her head tucked underneath her arm,
She walks the Bloody Tower.
With her head tucked underneath her arm,
At the midnight hour.

'With Her Head Tucked Underneath Her Arm' (1934). Recorded by Stanley Holloway. The 'midnight hour' phrase may first have occurred in the poetry of Robert Southey. *Thalaba the Destroyer* (written 1799–1800, published 1801), a romance set in medieval Arabia, contains (Bk 8): 'But when the Cryer from the Minaret / Proclaims the midnight hour, / Hast thou a heart to see her?' Charles Lamb's friend 'Ralph Bigod' [John Fenwick] in his essay 'The two Races of Men' (1820) has: 'How magnificent, how *ideal* he was; how great at the midnight hour ...' In the same year, John Keats, 'Ode to Psyche' has: 'Temple thou hast none, nor / Virgin-choir to make delicious moan / *Upon the* midnight hours.' Keats also wrote of '[Sleep] embalmer of the still midnight', and so on. Edward Lear's poem 'The Dong With the Luminous Nose' (1871) has 'at *that* midnight hour'. The full phrase 'at the midnight hour' is a quotation from the Weston & Lee song 'With Her Head Tucked Underneath Her Arm (She Walks the Bloody Tower)' (1934), as notably performed by Stanley Holloway. In a speech to the Indian Constituent Assembly (14 August 1947), Jawharlal Nehru said: '*At the stroke of the* midnight hour, while the world sleeps, India will awake to life and freedom.' Wilson Pickett, the American soul singer, established the phrase '*In the* Midnight Hour' with his hit single of that title (1965).

3 The End of My Old Cigar.

Title of a mildly suggestive music-hall song (1914) by R.P. Weston and Worton David, performed by Harry Champion. Sample verse and chorus: 'To help the Prince of Wales' Fund, and do our little share, / We gave a swell bazaar down at the mission room, and there / My wife was selling kisses to the dukes and earls, it's true. / She charged them half a sov'reign each, and I was helping too / [Chorus] With the end of my old cigar – Hoorah! hoorah! hoorah! / We got

the Prince of Wales a thousand pounds at our bazaar. / The wife was selling kisses to the swells at "half a bar", / And I was running a peepshow with the end of my old cigar.' Following on from this, *The End of Me Old Cigar* became the title of a play (1975) by John Osborne, and also of a song in Osborne's *The Entertainer*; see 349:5.

James McNeill WHISTLER American painter (1834–1903)

4 *Oscar Wilde*: I wish I had said that.
Whistler: You will, Oscar, you will.

Quoted in L.C. Ingleby, *Oscar Wilde* (1907), and Douglas Sladen, *Twenty Years of My Life* (1915). Sladen says that the exchange was in response to a remark by a woman that Wilde had rather taken a fancy to, but Hesketh Pearson, *The Life of Oscar Wilde* (1946), states, more convincingly, that it was something said by Whistler himself that Wilde was obviously going to make his own. In Frank Harris, *Oscar Wilde, His Life and Confessions*, Chap. 4 (1930), is this: 'The art critic of *The Times*, Mr Humphry Ward, had come to see an exhibition of Whistler's pictures. Filled with an undue sense of his own importance, he buttonholed the master and pointing to one picture said: "That's good, first-rate, a lovely bit of colour; but that, you know," he went on, jerking his finger over his shoulder at another picture, "that's bad, drawing all wrong ... bad!"

'"My dear fellow," cried Whistler, "you must never say that this painting's good or that bad, never! Good and bad are not terms to be used by you; but say, I like this, and I dislike that, and you'll be within your right. And now come and have a whiskey for you're sure to like that."

'Carried away by the witty fling, Oscar cried: "I wish I had said that."

'"You will, Oscar, you will," came Whistler's lightning thrust.'

5 No, I ask it for the knowledge of a lifetime.

Replying to the question (in a court of law), 'For two days' labour, you ask two hundred guineas?' Quoted in the same book. See RUSKIN 391:2.

See also WELLES 485:4.

E(lwyn) B(rooks) WHITE American humorist (1899–1985)

6 I say it's spinach.

Caption devised by White for a cartoon by Carl Rose in *The New Yorker* (8 December 1928). The cartoon shows a mother at table saying: 'It's broccoli, dear.' Her little girl replies: 'I say it's spinach, and I say the hell with it.' Harold Ross, then editor of the magazine, remembered that when White asked his opinion of the caption the writer was clearly uncertain that he had hit on the right idea. 'I looked at the drawing and the caption and said, "Yeh, it seems okay to me", but neither of us cracked a smile.' The use of the word 'spinach' to mean nonsense (mostly in the US) stems from this – as in the title of Irving Berlin's song 'I'll Say It's Spinach' from the revue *Face the Music* (1932) and as in *Fashion is Spinach*, title of the autobiography (1933) of the American designer Elizabeth Dawes.

1 Across the Street and Into the Grill.

Title of pastiche of Ernest Hemingway (collected 1954). See JACKSON 252:1.

Katharine WHITEHORN English journalist (1928–)

2 Outside every thin girl there is a fat man trying to get in.

Revived by her on BBC Radio *Quote ... Unquote* (27 July 1985). Compare ORWELL 153:3.

William WHITELAW (later Viscount Whitelaw)
British Conservative politician (1918–99)

3 Harold Wilson is going around the country stirring up apathy.

Whitelaw was holder of the office of Deputy Prime Minister until ill-health forced him to retire in 1988, and was famous for his informal sayings. The essence of these 'Whitelawisms' or 'Willieisms' is a touching naivety that may conceal a certain truth.

The most notable is his description of the then Prime Minister, Harold Wilson, during the 1970 General Election 'going around the country stirring up apathy'. On the face of it, a nonsensical remark, but conveying, oddly, just what Wilson was doing. In *The Independent* (14 July 1992), Whitelaw told Hunter Davies: 'It's a strange thing. I did say those words, but the real meaning has been lost. For a start, I meant to say "spreading apathy" not "stirring it up" ... Wilson was so sure of victory that he was going round the country calming people down, telling everyone not to worry, leave it all to him. I was really attacking him for encouraging people not to want a change, not saying people were apathetic to him.'

4 One must be careful not to prejudge the past.

Of Irish politics, on becoming Secretary of State for Northern Ireland (25 March 1972). Quoted in *The Times* (3 December 1973).

See also GILBERT 213:2.

Walt WHITMAN American poet (1819–92)

5 I Sing the Body Electric.

Title of poem (1855), in *Leaves of Grass* (various editions 1855–97). The phrase was later used by Ray Bradbury as the title story in a collection called *I Sing the Body Electric* (1970). Compare VIRGIL 478:6.

6 We Two Boys together Clinging.

Title of poem, in the same work. Hence, the title of David Hockney's 1961 painting *We Two Boys Together Clinging*. The picture shows two figures indeed clinging together and surrounded by various inscriptions, including the numerals '4.2'. This is code for 'Doll Boy' – i.e., Cliff Richard. Hockney had been amused to come across a newspaper headline that stated: 'TWO BOYS CLING TO CLIFF ALL NIGHT LONG'. Although the article concerned a climbing accident and not a sexual fantasy, the reference gives an added resonance to the picture. Quoted in Marco Livingstone, *David Hockney* (1981).

7 Out of the Cradle Endlessly Rocking.

Title of poem, (1859), in the same work. Later used as a silent film subtitle in the epic *Intolerance* (1916), written and directed by D.W. Griffith. It accompanies a shot of Lillian Gish rocking a cradle and is repeated many times during the course of the long film. The Gish character is billed as 'The Woman Who Rocks the Cradle'.

8 I Hear America Singing.

Title of poem, in the same work. Hence, *I Hear America Talking*, title of a study of the American language (1976) by Stuart Berg Flexner.

9 When Lilacs Last in the Dooryard Bloom'd.

Title of poem, in the same work. It was written a few weeks after the April 1865 assassination of President Lincoln, which it commemorates. Whitman also wrote a prose description of the assassination, which was included in his *Memoranda During the War* (1875) and reprinted in *The Faber Book of Reportage* (1987). This might give the impression that he was actually present, but he was away from Washington DC at the time. In it, however, he says: 'I find myself always reminded of the great tragedy of that day by the sight and odour of these blossoms.' Hence, *When Elephants Last In the Doorway Bloomed*, title of a poetry collection (1973) by Ray Bradbury.

10 The untold want by life and land ne'er granted, Now voyager, sail thou forth to seek and find.

'The Untold Want', in the same work. Hence, *Now Voyager*,

title of a novel (1941; film US 1942) by Olive Higgins Prouty. 'Now voyager' also appears in Whitman's 'Now Finalè to the Shore' as: 'Now Voyager depart (much, much for thee is yet in store').

1 Darest thou now O soul,
Walk out with me toward the unknown region,
Where neither ground is for the feet nor any
path to follow?

'Darest Thou Now O Soul', *Whispers of Heavenly Death* (1870). Hence, 'Toward the Unknown Region', title of a song setting of the poem by Vaughan Williams (1907).

2 'Pioneers! O Pioneers!'

Title of poem (1865). Hence, *O Pioneers!* – title of a novel (1913) by Willa Cather.

J(ohn) G(reenleaf) WHITTIER American poet (1807–92)

3 For of all sad words of tongue or pen,
The saddest are these: 'It might have been!'

Ah, well! for us all some sweet hope lies
Deeply buried from human eyes.

Maud Muller (1854). Parodied by Arthur Guiterman (1871–1943) in 'Prophets in Their Own Country': 'Of all cold words of tongue and pen / The worst are these: "I knew him when ..."' Also parodied by Bret Harte in 'Mrs Judge Jenkins' (1867): 'If, of all words of tongue and pen, / The saddest are, "It might have been," / More sad are these we daily see: / "It is, but hadn't ought to be!"'

4 Dear Lord and Father of mankind,
Forgive our foolish ways.

'The Brewing of Soma' (1872) – later immensely popular in Britain as a hymn, especially in schools. Hence, *Forgive Our Foolish Ways*, title of a BBC TV drama series (1980) by Reg Gadney about goings-on in an English public school.

Robert WHITTINGTON English teacher (?1480–?1530)

Of Sir Thomas More (1478–1535):

5 More is a man of angel's wit and singular learning; I know not his fellow. For where is the man of that gentleness, lowliness and affability? And as time requireth, a man of marvellous mirth and pastimes; and sometimes of as sad a gravity: as who say a man for all seasons.

Whittington wrote the passage for schoolboys to put into Latin in his book *Vulgaria* (?1521). It translates a comment on More by Erasmus – who wrote in his preface to *In Praise of Folly* (1509) that More was '*omnium horarum hominem*'. Hence, *A Man for All Seasons*, Robert Bolt's title for his 1960 play about More (film UK 1967), and the now clichéd phrase for an accomplished, adaptable, appealing person. From Laurence Olivier, *On Acting* (1986): '[Ralph Richardson] was warm and what the public might call ordinary and, therefore, quite exceptional. That was his ability, that was his talent; he really was a man for all seasons.' Jean Rook wrote of Margaret Thatcher in the *Daily Express* (in 1982–3): 'She has proved herself not the "best man in Britain" but the "Woman For All Seasons".'

Cornelius WHUR English clergyman and poet (1782–1853)

6 What lasting joys the man attend
Who has a polished female friend.

'The Female Friend', from *Village Musings on Moral and Religious Subjects* (1837), which was published anonymously. In fact these lines are a conflation of those in the original – as in *ODQ* (1941), which also got the title wrong and spelled the poet's name as 'Whurr'. The last three verse endings are (correctly):

... On firmer ties his joys depend
Who has a polished female friend.

...While both arise, and duly blend
In an accomplished female friend!

... While lasting joys the man attend
Who has a faithful friend!

Poem and poet make an appearance in *The Stuffed Owl*, the anthology of bad verse, but neither is without charm.

Ella Wheeler WILCOX American poet (1855–1919)

7 Laugh and the world laughs with you;
Weep and you weep alone.

'Solitude', published in the *New York Sun* (25 February 1883) and, as *CODP* points out, an alteration of the sentiment expressed by Horace in his *Ars Poetica*: 'Men's faces laugh on those who laugh, and correspondingly weep on those who weep.' Another alteration is: '... weep, and you sleep alone'. In this form it was said to the architectural historian James Lees-Milne and recorded in his diary on 6 June 1945 – published in *Prophesying Peace* (1977). In the form ' ... snore and you sleep alone', it occurs in Anthony Burgess, *Inside Mr Enderby* (1963), though he did not claim it as original – despite its appearance under his name in *PDMQ* (1971).

Oscar WILDE Irish playwright, poet and wit (1854–1900)

1 There was no fog in London before Whistler painted it.

Quoted (but without a source) in the art historian Ernst Gombrich's *Art and Illusion* (1960). Gombrich may have taken this passage from Wilde's essay, 'The Decay of Lying' (January 1889) and crisped it up into a quotation:

> *Cyril*: Nature follows the landscape painter, then, and takes her effects from him?
> *Vivian*: Certainly. Where, if not from the Impressionists, do we get those wonderful brown fogs that come creeping down our streets, blurring the gas-lamps and changing the houses into monstrous shadows? To whom, if not to them and their master, do we owe the lovely silver mists that brood over our river, and turn to faint forms of fading grace curved bridge and swaying barge? The extraordinary change that has taken place in the climate of London during the last ten years is entirely due to a particular school of Art.

On the other hand, I wouldn't have said myself that Whistler really painted fogs. Mists, maybe. Here is what Whistler himself said on the subject in his 1885 'Ten O'Clock' lecture: 'And when the evening mist clothes the riverside with poetry, as with a veil, and the poor buildings lose themselves in the dim sky, and the tall chimneys become campanili, and the warehouses are palaces in the night, and the whole city hangs in the heavens, and fairy-land is before us – then the wayfarer hastens home; the working man and the cultured one, the wise man and the one of pleasure, cease to understand, as they have ceased to see, and Nature, who, for once, has sung in tune, sings her exquisite song to the artist alone, her son and her master – her son in that he loves her, her master in that he knows her.' Even he calls it 'mist' rather than 'fog'.

2 I have nothing to declare except my genius.

At the New York Custom House, on arriving in the United States (1882) and asked by the customs officer if he had anything to declare. Quoted in Frank Harris, *Oscar Wilde, His Life and Confessions*, Chap. 5 (1930). No contemporary account exists.

3 Please don't shoot the pianist; he is doing his best.

Wilde reported having seen this notice in a bar or dancing saloon in the Rocky Mountains ('Leadville', from *Impressions of America*, pub. 1906). Hence, the film *Tirez Sur Le Pianiste* (France, 1960), translated as *Shoot the Pianist/Piano-Player*, and Elton John's 1972 record album, *Don't Shoot Me, I'm Only the Piano-Player*.

4 Two nations separated by a common language.

Of the UK and the US. The 'origin request' most frequently received. Sometimes the inquirer asks, 'Was it Wilde or Shaw?' The answer *appears* to be: *both*. In *The Canterville Ghost* (1887), Wilde wrote: 'We have really everything in common with America nowadays except, of course, language.' However, *The Treasury of Humorous Quotations*, eds Esar & Bentley (1951), quotes Shaw as saying: 'England and America are two countries separated by the same language', but without giving a source. The quote had earlier been attributed to Shaw in *Reader's Digest* (November 1942).

Much the same idea occurred to Bertrand Russell, as published in the *Saturday Evening Post* (3 June 1944): 'It is a misfortune for Anglo-American friendship that the two countries are supposed to have a common language', and in a radio talk prepared by Dylan Thomas shortly before his death – and published after it in *The Listener* (April 1954) – European writers and scholars in America were, he said, 'up against the barrier of a common language'.

Inevitably: 'Winston Churchill said our two countries were divided by a common language' – *The Times* (26 January 1987) and *The European* (22 November 1991).

5 *Mrs Allonby*: They say, Lady Hunstanton, that when good Americans die they go to Paris.
Lady Hunstanton: Indeed? And when bad Americans die, where do they go to?
Lord Illingworth: Oh, they go to America.

A Woman of No Importance, Act 1 (1893). Earlier, this exchange had appeared in *The Picture of Dorian Gray*, Chap. 3. The originator of the remark 'Good Americans, when they die, go to Paris' was Thomas Gold Appleton (1812–84). He was so quoted by Oliver Wendell Holmes in *The Autocrat of the Breakfast Table* (1858).

6 The English country gentleman galloping after a fox – the unspeakable in full pursuit of the uneatable.

In the same play and act. Origin of a much-quoted characterization.

7 *Lord Illingworth*: The Book of Life begins with a man and a woman in a garden.
Mrs Allonby: It ends with Revelations.

In the same play and act. Hence, *It Ends With Revelations*, title of a novel (1967) by Dodie Smith.

1 Children begin by loving their parents; after a time they judge them; rarely, if ever, do they forgive them.

In the same play, Act 2. This line had earlier appeared, almost exactly in this form, in *The Picture of Dorian Gray*, Chap. 5. It is sometimes quoted as 'First they love us, then they judge us.'

2 *Salomé dances the dance of the seven veils.*

Stage direction, *Salomé* (pub. 1893), though originally written in French. Salome so beguiled Herod by her seductive dancing that he gave her the head of St John the Baptist, as she requested. In neither Matthew 14:6 nor Mark 6:22 is she referred to by name – only 'as the daughter of Herodias', nor is the nature of her dancing described. The name Salome was supplied by Josephus, the 2nd-century Jewish historian. One must assume that the particular nature of the dance originated with Wilde, from whose play Richard Strauss took the idea for his opera *Salome* (1905). A little earlier, in Gustave Flaubert's 'Hérodias' – in *Trois contes* (1877) – only one veil is mentioned. See also BIBLE 71:6.

3 I have invented an invaluable permanent invalid called Bunbury, in order that I may be able to go down into the country whenever I choose.

The Importance of Being Earnest, Act 1 (1895). Algernon speaking. Hence, the name 'Bunbury' for an imaginary person who is invoked in order to furnish an excuse not to do something. The activity is accordingly known as 'Bunburying'. Bunbury is the name of an actual village in Cheshire but, in fact, Wilde took the name from a friend of his youth, Henry S. Bunbury – who lived in Gloucestershire – source: Richard Ellman, *Oscar Wilde* (1987).

4 To lose one parent, Mr Worthing, may be regarded as a misfortune; to lose both looks like carelessness.

In the same play. Lady Bracknell speaking. The origin of a format phrase, 'To lose one — is a misfortune, to lose two looks like carelessness', and variations on same. From *The Observer* (6 July 1997): 'To lose two Hollywood legends in the space of a week is worse than misfortune: it begins to look something like a final curtain.'

5 All women become like their mothers. That is their tragedy. No man does. That's his.

In the same play. Algernon speaking. The same words occurred before this (in dialogue form) in *A Woman of No Importance* (1893). Compare BENNETT 62:1.

6 The good ended happily, and the bad unhappily. That is what fiction means.

In the same play, Act 2. Miss Prism. Compare STOPPARD 448:3.

7 I never travel without my diary. One should always have something sensational to read in the train.

In the same play, and Act. Gwendolen. Hence, *Something Sensational To Read In the Train*, an examination of modern diary-keeping, BBC Radio (21 July 1970). Note it is 'in' rather than 'on' the train.

8 Yet each man kills the thing he loves,
By each let this be heard,
Some do it with a bitter look,
Some with a flattering word.
The coward does it with a kiss,
The brave man with a sword!

The Ballad of Reading Gaol, 1 (and slightly altered in 6) (1898). The first line has become a proverbial saying.

9 And alien tears will fill for him
Pity's long-broken urn,
For his mourners will be outcast men,
And outcasts always mourn.

In the same poem, 4 (1898). These words are carved on Jacob Epstein's monument (1909) over Wilde's grave in Père Lachaise cemetery, Paris.

10 In the world, madam.

Reply to an actress, not noted for her good looks, who had said to him: 'Mr Wilde, you are looking at the ugliest woman in Paris.' Quoted on BBC Radio *Quote ... Unquote* (5 April 1978) and in Richard Ellman, *Oscar Wilde*, Chap. 13 (1987). Before this in Frank Harris, *Oscar Wilde, His Life and Confessions*, Chap. 20 (1930): 'Mdlle. Marie Anne de Bovet ... was a writer of talent and knew English uncommonly well; but in spite of masses of fair hair and vivacious eyes she was certainly very plain. As soon as she heard I was in Paris, she asked me to present Oscar Wilde to her. He had no objection, and so I made a meeting between them. When he caught sight of her, he stopped short: seeing his astonishment, she cried to him in her quick, abrupt way: "*N'est-ce pas, M. Wilde, que je suis la femme la plus laide de France* [Come, confess, Mr Wilde, that I am the ugliest woman in France]?" Bowing low, Oscar replied with smiling courtesy: "*Du monde, Madame, du monde* [In the world, madam, in the world]." No one could help laughing; the retort was irresistible. He should have said: "*Au monde, madame, au monde*," but the meaning was clear.'

1 No good deed goes unpunished.

This is a consciously ironic rewriting of the older expression 'No *bad* deed goes unpunished' and has been attributed to Wilde, but remains unverified. Joe Orton recorded it in his diary for 13 June 1967: 'Very good line George [Greeves] came out with at dinner: "No good deed ever goes unpunished."' James Agate in *Ego 3* (for 25 January 1938) states: '[Isidore Leo] Pavia was in great form today: "Every good deed brings its own punishment."' Note that neither of these sources mentions Wilde.

2 He has fought a good fight and has had to face every difficulty except popularity.

Of W.E. Henley, in an unpublished sketch, quoted in William Rothenstein, *Men and Memories* (1931). In Wilde's *The Duchess of Padua*, Act 1 (1883), the Duke remarks: 'Popularity / Is the one insult I have never suffered.'

3 He hasn't an enemy in the world – and none of his friends like him.

Of G.B. Shaw. Shaw himself quoted this remark in *Sixteen Self Sketches* (1949). An early appearance occurs in Irvin S. Cobb, *A Laugh a Day Keeps the Doctor Away* (1921), in which someone says of Shaw, 'He's in a fair way to make himself a lot of enemies.' 'Well,' replies Wilde, 'as yet he hasn't become prominent enough to have any enemies. But none of his friends like him.' Hesketh Pearson in *The Life of Oscar Wilde* (1946) wonders whether Shaw did not adapt to himself the following from *Dorian Gray*: 'Ernest Harrowden, one of those middle-aged mediocrities so common in London clubs, who have no enemies, but are thoroughly disliked by their friends.'

4 I am the love that dare not speak its name.

I.e. homosexual love, particularly between men. This expression is so much bound up with the Wilde case that it is sometimes assumed that he coined it. Not so. It was the person who had helped land him in his predicament, Lord Alfred Douglas (1870–1945), who wrote the poem 'Two Loves' (1892–3), which concludes with the line. In both his trials, Wilde was asked about the poem. In the second (April–May 1895) he was asked to explain the line and gave a spontaneous explanation: 'In this century [it] is such a great affection of an elder for a younger man as there was between David and Jonathan, such as Plato made the very basis of his philosophy, and such as you find in the sonnets of Michelangelo and Shakespeare. It is that deep, spiritual affection that is as pure as it is perfect ... It is in this century misunderstood, so much misunderstood that it may be described as the "Love that dare not speak its name", and on account of it I am placed where I am

now.' Wilde's words produced an outburst of applause from the gallery, which inevitably rattled the judge.

5 Most people are other people. Their thoughts are some one else's opinions, their lives a mimicry, their passions a quotation.

De Profundis (1905).

6 People thought it dreadful of me to have entertained at dinner the evil things of life, and to have found pleasure in their company. But then, from the point of view through which I, as an artist in life, approach them they were delightfully suggestive and stimulating. It was like feasting with panthers; the danger was half the excitement.

In the same work – in a passage about his life before he was sent to Reading gaol for homosexual offences. Hence, *Feasting with Panthers*, title of play devised and directed by Peter Coe at the 1981 Chichester Festival about Wilde's trials. The idea has been traced back to Balzac who, in *Illusions perdues* (1837–9) wrote: '... *je soupe avec des lions et des panthères* ...' – source: *Notes and Queries*, Vol. 240.

7 Wordsworth went to the Lakes, but he was never a Lake poet. He found in stones the sermons he had already hidden there.

'The Decay of Lying', *Intentions* (1891). Alluding to SHAKESPEARE 401:2.

8 Work is the curse of the drinking classes.

Quoted in Frank Harris, *Oscar Wilde, His Life and Confessions*, Chap. 11 (1930).

9 'Ah, well then,' said Oscar, 'I suppose that I shall have to die beyond my means.'

R.H. Sherard, *Life of Oscar Wilde* (1906). Alternatively, 'I am dying, as I have lived, beyond my means', said as he called for champagne when he was approaching death in 1900. Quoted in Barnaby Conrad, *Famous Last Words* (1961). Richard Ellman, *Oscar Wilde* (1987), has: 'I am dying beyond my means, I will never outlive the century', as said to Wilde's sister-in-law. Frank Harris, *Oscar Wilde, His Life and Confessions*, Chap. 26 (1930), has the words said to Robbie Ross, on one of the last drives they took together. Whatever way, they were not his 'dying words'. He lived for another month or so.

10 This wall paper'll be the death of me – one of us'll have to go.

This remark about the furnishings in his room was indeed said by Wilde, but not *in extremis*. The jest was first recorded in Sherard (as above). Another version is that Wilde said to Claire de Pratz: 'My wallpaper and I are fighting a duel to the death. One or the other of us has to go' – reported in Guillot de Saix, '*Souvenirs inédits*', also in Frank Harris, *Oscar Wilde, His Life and Confessions* (1930).

See also ANONYMOUS 9:5; DICKENS 171:4; MAGEE 307:3; WHISTLER 491:4.

Billy WILDER American film director and writer (1906–2002)

1 You have Van Gogh's ear for music.

Appearing on BBC Radio *Quote ... Unquote* in 1977, Kenneth Williams came up with a rather good showbiz story. He quoted the above as what Orson Welles had reputedly said of the singing of Donny Osmond (then a popular young star). In fact, Orson Welles did not say it, nor was it about Donny Osmond, but the reasons why the joke had been re-ascribed and redirected are instructive. It was in fact Billy Wilder, the film director, who made the original remark. He had a notably waspish wit but is, perhaps, not such a household name as Orson Welles. He lacks, too, Welles's Falstaffian stature and his, largely unearned, reputation in the public mind for having said witty things. And Wilder said it about *Cliff* Osmond, an American comedy actor who had appeared in the film director's *Kiss Me Stupid*, *The Fortune Cookie* and *The Front Page*. As far as one knows, he is not related to Donny Osmond but, apparently, he had to be replaced in the anecdote because he lacked star status. The correct attribution was given in Leslie Halliwell, *The Filmgoer's Book of Quotes* (1973).

Tom Stoppard included something very similar in *The Real Inspector Hound* (1968): 'An uncanny ear that might [have] belonged to a Van Gogh.'

Thornton WILDER American playwright (1897–1975)

2 But soon we shall die and all memory of those five will have left the earth, and we ourselves shall be loved for a while and forgotten. But the love will have been enough; all those impulses of love return to the love that made them. Even memory is not necessary for love. There is a land of the living and a land of the dead, and the bridge is love, the only survival, the only meaning.

The Bridge of San Luis Rey, Pt 5 (1927). Quoted by Tony Blair, the British Prime Minister, when speaking at a service of prayer in St Thomas's Church on Fifth Avenue, New York (20 September 2001), following the terrorist attacks on the United States. The words, deemed by *The Independent* 'almost unbearably apposite', are from the closing pages

of the novel that meditates on the deaths of five people 'falling through the air' after the collapse of the Peruvian bridge.

WILHELM II German Kaiser (1859–1941)

3 We have fought for our place in the sun and won it. Our future is on the water.

Speech at Hamburg (18 June 1901), echoing the phrase referring to German colonial ambitions in East Asia that had been coined by Count Bernard von Bülow (1849–1929), the German Chancellor, in a speech to the Reichstag (6 December 1897): 'In a word, we desire to throw no one into the shade, but we also demand our own place in the sun [*Platz an der Sonne*].' Subsequently, the notion was much referred to in the run-up to the First World War. Hence, probably, *A Place in the Sun* – the title given to the 1951 film of Theodore Dreiser's *An American Tragedy*. A much earlier appearance occurred in the *Pensées* of Blaise Pascal (Walker's translation, 1688): 'This Dog is mine, said those poor Children; That's my place in the Sun. This is the beginning and Image of the Usurpation of all the Earth.' The phrase is now hardly ever used in this precise sense, but simply to indicate a rightful piece of good fortune, a desirable situation, for example: 'Mr Frisk could bring Aintree punters their place in the sun' – headline in the *Independent on Sunday* (1 April 1990).

4 It is my Royal and Imperial command that you concentrate your energies for the immediate present upon one single purpose, and that is that you address all your skill and all the valour of my soldiers to exterminate first, the treacherous English [and] walk over General French's contemptible little army.

British Expeditionary Force (BEF) Routine Orders for 24 September 1914 contained what was claimed to be a copy of orders issued by the German Emperor on 19 August. The greatest canard of the First World War was that Kaiser Wilhelm had described the 1914 BEF as 'a contemptibly little army' – referring to its size rather than to its quality. The British Press was then said to have mistranslated this so that it made the Kaiser appear to have called the BEF 'a contemptibly little army'. Rank and file thereafter happily styled themselves 'The Old Contemptibles'.

The truth as revealed by Arthur Ponsonby in *Falsehood in War-Time* (1928) is that the whole episode was a propaganda ploy masterminded by the British. The Kaiser's alleged words became widely known, but an investigation during 1925 in the German archives failed to produce any evidence of the order ever having been issued. The ex-Kaiser himself said: 'On the contrary, I continually emphasized the high value of the British Army, and often, indeed, in peacetime gave warning against underestimating it.' It is now accepted that the phrase was devised at the War Office by Sir Frederick Maurice.

1 Hang the Kaiser!

During the Versailles Peace Conference and for some time afterwards, Britain's Northcliffe newspapers and others kept up this cry. Candidates at the 1918 general election are said to have lost votes if they did not subscribe to the policy. The Allies committed themselves to try the ex-Kaiser in the Treaty of Versailles (28 June 1919), but the government of the Netherlands refused to hand him over for trial in June 1920. Arthur Ponsonby (as above) argued that casting the Kaiser as villain of the piece had been a put-up job anyway: 'When, as months and years passed, it was discovered that no responsible person really believed, or had ever believed, in [his] personal guilt, that the cry "Hang the Kaiser" was a piece of deliberate bluff, and that when it was over and millions of innocent people had been killed, he, the criminal, the monster, the plotter and initiator of the whole catastrophe, was allowed to live comfortably and peacefully in Holland, the disillusionment to simple, uninformed people was far greater than ever realized.' The ex-Kaiser died in 1941.

John WILKES English politician (1727–97)

2 *4th Earl of Sandwich*: 'Pon my soul, Wilkes, I don't know whether you'll die upon the gallows or of the pox.
Wilkes: That depends, my Lord, whether I first embrace your Lordship's principles, or your Lordship's mistresses.

A famous exchange, which made an early appearance in Sir Charles Petrie, *The Four Georges* (1935), but is quite likely apocryphal. Where did Petrie get it from, and where had it been for the intervening two centuries? In *Memoirs of the Life and Writings of Percival Stockdale, Written by Himself* (1809) the exchange is given as between Sandwich and Samuel Foote, the actor, playwright and wit (1720–77).

Sandwich and Wilkes were certainly acquainted but there seems no evidence that he took part in this exchange. It is frequently misapplied. George E. Allen in *Presidents Who Have Known Me* (1950) has it between Gladstone and Disraeli. It is difficult to imagine the circumstance in which either Disraeli or Gladstone could have made either of the remarks.

See also ANONYMOUS 22:5.

Geoffrey WILLANS British writer (1911–58)

3 There is no better xsample of a goody-goody than fotherington-tomas in the world in space. You kno he is the one who sa Hullo Clouds Hullo Sky and skip about like a girly.

How To Be Topp (1954). The earliest citation available containing something like the cry 'Hello birds, hello clouds, hello trees, hello sky!' – a joke expression of joy in nature, as though spoken by a poet, aesthete or other fey character dancing round the countryside. In a later book about the schoolboy character Nigel Molesworth, Willans returns to the theme: 'And who is this who skip weedily up to me, eh? "Hullo clouds, hullo sky," he sa. "Hullo birds, hullo poetry books, hullo skool sossages, hullo molesworth 1." You hav guessed it is dere little basil fotherington-tomas' – *Back in the Jug Agane* (1959). There is an unconfirmed appearance in a 1941 Warner Bros cartoon.

Lloyd S. WILLIAM American soldier (early 20th century)

4 Retreat? Hell, no! We just got here!

An attributed remark, made by Captain William when advised by the French to retreat, shortly after his arrival at the Western Front in the First World War. Or, specifically referring to the retreat from Belloar (5 June 1918). Untraced and unverified. Margaret Thatcher quoted it at a Confederation of British Industry dinner in 1980. Compare: 'Retreat, hell! We're just fighting in another direction' – attributed to General Oliver Prince Smith, US Marine Corps, at Changjin Reservoir, North Korea (autumn 1950). When trapped by eight divisions of Chinese Communists in North Korea he led the 20,000-man 1st Division on a bloody, 13-day, 70-mile breakthrough to the sea and rescue – source: *Partridge/Catch Phrases* (1985). However, when the title *Retreat, Hell!* was bestowed on a film of this event (US 1952), a different ascription was given by the screenwriters Milton Sperling and Ted Sherdeman: 'The Colonel' says: 'We've been ordered to withdraw.' Soldier: 'You mean retreat?' Colonel: 'Retreat? Hell, we're just attacking in another direction.'

Tennessee WILLIAMS American playwright (1911–83)

5 *Blanche Dubois*: I have always depended on the kindness of strangers.

A Streetcar Named Desire, Act 2 (1947). Her last words in the play. Blanche is about to be taken off to an institution. Christopher Isherwood once said that to his mind this was the finest single line in modern letters (source: Gore Vidal, *New World Writing No. 4*, 1953). Hence, the frequent use of the phrase 'the kindness of strangers' as the title of: Donald

Spotto's biography of Williams (1990), Bernard Braden's autobiography (1990), John Boswell's account of 'the Abandonment of Children in Western Europe from Late Antiquity to the Renaissance' (1988) and TV news reporter Kate Adie's memoirs (2002).

There may be some allusion to a passage from W. Somerset Maugham's novel *The Narrow Corner* (1932): 'Everyone is so nice. Nothing is too much trouble. You cannot imagine the kindness I've received at the hands of perfect strangers.' Williams had certainly read this novel – see Gore Vidal, *A View from the Diner's Club* (1993).

Not to be confused with the film titles *The Comfort of Strangers* (1990, based on Ian McEwan's novel) and *The Company of Strangers* (1991).

1 *Cat On a Hot Tin Roof.*

Title of play (1955; film US 1958) – derived from the (mostly US) expression 'as nervous as a cat on a hot tin roof', which derives, in turn, from the common English expression 'like a cat on hot bricks', meaning 'ill-at-ease, jumpy'. John Ray in his *Collection of English Proverbs* (1670–8) has 'To go like a cat upon a hot bake stone'. An expression 'nervous as cats' appeared in *Punch*'s Almanack for 1903.

In the play, the 'cat' is Maggie, Brick's wife, 'whose frayed vivacity', wrote Kenneth Tynan, 'derives from the fact that she is sexually ignored by her husband'. The title phrase is referred to by Maggie in Act 1: 'What is the victory of a cat on a hot tin roof? ... Just staying on it, I guess, as long as she can'; by Brick/Big Daddy in Act 2: 'Nervous as a couple of cats on a hot tin roof?' / 'That's right, boy, they look like a couple of cats on a hot tin roof'; and the last words of the play (Broadway version) in Act 3 are: 'Nothing's more determined than a cat on a hot tin roof – is there? Is there, baby?'

2 *Sweet Bird of Youth.*

Title of play (1959). A librarian from the University of Delaware Library, where the Tennessee Williams papers are kept, commented (2001): 'I have looked at the *Sweet Bird* manuscripts in our collection as well as a number of secondary sources. The motto in the front of the play is a quote from Hart Crane which is taken from the poem "Legend" in the work *White City* ["Relentless caper for all those who step / The legend of their youth into the noon"]. Some authors make reference to the title as echoing the legendary bird in TW's later *Orpheus Descending*. As to the actual title, the librarians I spoke with here believe that it is not a direct quote from another source.' Compare: 'To the Nightingale' from *Poems* (1802) by Mrs John Hunter: 'Why from these shades, sweet bird of eve / Art thou to other regions wildly fled? / ... / Oh, simple bird! where art thou flown? / What distant woodland now receives thy nest?'

Charles E. WILSON American Republican politician (1890–1961)

3 What's good for General Motors is good for the country.

President Eisenhower wished to appoint Wilson as Secretary for Defense. At hearings of the Senate Committee on Armed Services in January 1953, the former President of General Motors was asked about any possible conflict of interest, as he had accepted several million dollars' worth of General Motors shares. When he was asked whether he would be able to make a decision against the interests of General Motors and his stock, what Wilson in fact replied was not the above, but: 'Yes, sir, I could. I cannot conceive of one because for years I thought what was good for our country was good for General Motors, and vice versa. The difference did not exist.'

Wilson was finally persuaded to get rid of his stock, but he never quite lived down his (misquoted) remarks. Note how the formula had earlier surfaced in the film *Stagecoach* (US 1939) – 'And remember this, what's good for the banks is good for the country.'

4 [It gives] a bigger bang for a buck.

Wilson said this of the new type of H-bomb tested at Bikini in 1954 and was so quoted in *Newsweek* Magazine (22 March 1954). *PDMQ* (1980) misinterprets a passage in David Halberstam's *The Best and the Brightest* (1973) and attributes the remark to President Eisenhower.

(Sir) Harold WILSON (later Lord Wilson) British Labour Prime Minister (1916–95)

5 The school I went to in the north was a school where more than half the children in my class never had any boots or shoes to their feet. They wore clogs, because they lasted longer than shoes of comparable price.

Speech as President of the Board of Trade at Birmingham (July 1948). Newspaper reports wrongly suggested he had claimed that when he was at school some of his classmates had gone *barefoot*. A former teacher at the school, reacting to the abbreviated report, denied that any of Wilson's schoolmates had ever gone barefoot, and soon the politician was being widely reported as having said that he himself had had to go barefoot to school. This gave rise to the jibe by Ivor Bulmer-Thomas (see 107:3). The incident was the first of many misunderstandings between Wilson and the press.

1 All these financiers, all the little gnomes in Zurich and the other financial centres, about whom we keep on hearing.

Speech, House of Commons (12 November 1956). 'The gnomes of Zurich' was a term used to disparage the tight-fisted methods of speculators in the Swiss financial capital who questioned Britain's creditworthiness and who forced austerity measures on Wilson's Labour Government when it came to power in 1964. George Brown, Secretary of State for Economic Affairs, popularized the term in November of that year, and it is often associated with him. Wilson himself had, however, used it long before. In 1958, Andrew Shonfield wrote in *British Economic Policy Since the War*: 'Hence the tragedy of the autumn of 1957, when the Chancellor of the Exchequer [Peter Thorneycroft] adopted as his guide to action the slogan: I must be hard-faced enough to match the mirror-image of an imaginary hard-faced little man in Zurich. It is tough on the Swiss that William Tell should be displaced in English folklore by this new image of a gnome in a bank at the end of a telephone line.'

2 Every time Mr Macmillan comes back from abroad, Mr Butler goes to the airport and grips him warmly by the throat.

Quoted in Leslie Smith, *Harold Wilson, The Authentic Portrait* (1964). Undated but made, obviously, before 1963, when Harold Macmillan resigned as British Prime Minister. Possibly 1957, when Macmillan had beaten Butler to the premiership. In the 1964 Broadway version of *Beyond the Fringe*, the Duke of Edinburgh was given the similar line, 'I was very well received [in Kenya, at Independence]. Mr Kenyatta himself came to the airport to greet me and shook me warmly by the throat as I got off the plane.'

3 The Labour Party is like a stagecoach. If you rattle along at great speed, everybody inside is too exhilarated or too seasick to cause any trouble. But if you stop, everybody gets out and argues about where to go next.

Quoted in Leslie Smith, in the same book. In Anthony Sampson, *The Changing Anatomy of Britain* (1982), it appears as: 'This party is a bit like an old stagecoach. If you drive along at a rapid rate, everyone aboard is either so exhilarated or so seasick that you don't have a lot of difficulty.'

4 Whichever party is in office, the Treasury is in power.

Quoted in Anthony Sampson, *The Changing Anatomy of Britain* (1982). In *The Oxford Dictionary of Political Quotations* (1996), the editor Antony Jay included this line but

also states in his introduction that he had been unable to trace the saying, 'Whoever is in office, the Conservatives are always in power.' Perhaps a solution to the problem is that Harold Wilson may have made use of a sort of epigram format with several variables. In an essay contributed to *The Establishment* (ed. Hugh Thomas, 1959), Thomas Balogh (later Wilson's economic adviser) wrote: 'The fact that the Treasury controls senior appointments, and that Ministers are busy men, does the rest. Mr Harold Wilson aptly put it: "Whoever is in office, the Whigs are in power" [Whigs here meaning 'the old established interest']'.

5 I have always deprecated – perhaps rightly, perhaps wrongly – in crisis after crisis, appeals to the Dunkirk spirit as an answer to our problems because what is required in our economic situation is not a brief period of inspired improvisation, work and sacrifice, such as we had under the leadership of the Rt Hon. Member for Woodford [Winston Churchill], but a very long, hard prolonged period of reorganization and redirection. It is the long haul, not the inspired spirit that we need.

Speech, House of Commons (26 July 1961). No sooner had he become Prime Minister than he said in a 'hastily compiled' speech to the Labour Party Conference on 12 December 1964: 'I believe that the spirit of Dunkirk will once again carry us through to success.' Neatly pointed out by Paul Foot in *The Politics of Harold Wilson* (1968).

6 We are redefining and we are restating our socialism in terms of the scientific revolution ... the Britain that is going to be forged in the white heat of this revolution will be no place for restrictive practices or outdated methods on either side of industry.

Speech, Labour Party Conference in Scarborough (1 October 1963). Usually encapsulated as 'the white heat of the technological revolution'.

7 After half a century of democratic advance, the whole process has ground to a halt with a four-teenth Earl.

On the Earl of Home's appointment as Prime Minister. Speech, Belle Vue, Manchester (19 October 1963). See also DOUGLAS-HOME 176:5.

8 [I am] a Bolshevik leader of a Menshevik government.

Remark (date unknown), except that like many Wilsonisms he repeated it. The year before he became Prime Minister in

1964, he remarked to Barbara Castle and Richard Crossman (who recorded it in his *Backbench Diaries* for 12 March 1963): 'You must understand that I am running a Bolshevik Revolution with a Tsarist Shadow Cabinet.' Another time he said that running his heavily Gaitskellite Shadow Cabinet was 'like Krushchev trying to govern through a Tsarist Cabinet'. The meaning is clear: he thought himself to be a radical leading reactionaries.

1 What I think we are going to need is something like what President Kennedy had when he came in after years of stagnation in the United States. He had a programme of a hundred days – a hundred days of dynamic action.

Labour Party political broadcast (15 July 1964). In fact, Kennedy had specifically ruled out a 'hundred days', saying in his inaugural address that his programmes could not be carried out even in a thousand days – compare KENNEDY 267:2.

2 A week is a long time in politics.

In 1977, I asked the then recently retired Prime Minister when he had first uttered his most-quoted dictum. Uncharacteristically, he was unable to remember. For someone who used to be able to cite the column numbers of *Hansard* in which his speeches appeared, this was a curious lapse. Inquiries among political journalists led to the conclusion that in its present form the phrase was probably first uttered at a meeting between Wilson and the Parliamentary lobby in the wake of the sterling crisis shortly after he first took office as Prime Minister in 1964. However, Robert Carvel, then of the London *Evening Standard*, recalled Wilson at a Labour Party Conference in 1960 saying, 'Forty-eight hours is a long time in politics.' One might note here that in his *The Second World War*, Vol. 1 (1948), Winston Churchill had written: 'But in war seven months is a long time ...' In addition, it is said that Joseph Chamberlain said to Arthur Balfour in 1886, 'In politics there is no use looking beyond the next fortnight.'

Apart from dating, there has been some dispute as to what precisely the dictum means. Most would take it to be along the lines of, 'Just give a problem time and it will solve itself', 'What a difference a day makes', 'Wait and see', and 'Don't panic, it'll all blow over.' But when I consulted Wilson in 1977, he challenged the accepted interpretation. 'It does not mean I'm living from day to day,' he said. 'It was intended as a prescription for long-term strategic thinking and planning, ignoring the day-to-day issues and pressures which may hit the headlines but which must not be allowed to get out of focus while longer-term policies are taking effect.'

The phrase caught on: from the late 1980s, Channel 4

TV has carried a weekly review with the title *A Week in Politics*, clearly alluding to Wilson's phrase. From *The Independent* (19 May 1989), on the outgoing editor of the TV programme *Forty Minutes*: 'His successor will have to work hard, though, to keep the formula fresh. 2400 seconds is a long time in television.'

When Wilson took his peerage, he chose as his motto: '*Tempus Rerum Imperator* [Time is the ruler of all things]', which is also the motto of the Worshipful Company of Clockmakers of London (founded in 1631) and is written beneath their armorial bearings. Wilson was a member of the company and is believed to have requested the motto be put on his grave because of this association.

3 Weeks rather than months.

Now an idiom meaning 'sooner rather than later', this echoes Wilson's use of the phrase at the Commonwealth Prime Ministers' Conference (12 January 1966). He had first used it in an unreported speech on that day, and it was later included in the final communiqué: 'In this connection [the use of military force in Rhodesia] the Prime Ministers noted the statement by the British Prime Minister that on the expert advice available to him, the cumulative effect of the economic and financial sanctions [against Rhodesia] might well bring the rebellion to an end within a matter of weeks rather than months.' As was to be discovered, this was a little wide of the mark. The return to legality took until 1980 to achieve.

4 It is difficult for us to appreciate the pressures which are put on men I know to be realistic and responsible, not only in their executive capacity but in the highly organized strike committees in the ports, by this tightly knit group of politically motivated men who, as the last general election showed, utterly failed to secure acceptance of their views by the British electorate, but who are now determined to exercise backstage pressures, forcing great hardship on the members of the union and their families, and endangering the security of the industry and the economic welfare of the nation.

Speech, House of Commons (22 June 1966) – during the sixth week of a national seamen's strike. He later explained: 'I did not use the word "Communist", though no one in the House or in the press ... had any doubts whom I had in mind.' Compare what his namesake Woodrow in the US had said earlier about Senate isolationists who filibustered a bill to allow the arming of merchant vessels (4 March 1917): 'A little group of wilful men representing no opinion but their own, has rendered the great government of the United States helpless and contemptible.'

1 From now on the pound abroad is worth 14 per cent or so less in terms of other currencies. That doesn't mean, of course, that the pound here in Britain, in your pocket or purse or in your bank, has been devalued.

Broadcast address (19 November 1967), after a devaluation of the pound sterling. In *The Labour Government 1964–70* (1971), he said this was the only part of the Treasury draft speech he had incorporated in his final version – 'Though I was cautioned by a civil service adviser, I was reinforced by the words of one of my own staff whose maiden aunt had telephoned to express concern that her Post Office Savings Bank holdings had been slashed by three shillings in the pound.'

The following evening, the Opposition leader, Edward Heath, quoted Wilson's reference to the 'pound in your pocket' as a misleading pledge that prices would not rise as a result of devaluation. The charge was taken up by many others.

2 Get your tanks off my lawn, Hughie.

According to Peter Jenkins, *The Battle of Downing Street* (1970), Wilson said this to Hugh Scanlon, the trade union leader, at Chequers, the prime ministerial country residence, in June 1969, during the battle between the government and the trade unions over reform. Scanlon was head of Britain's second largest union, the engineers. Jenkins reports that Wilson was enraged at the intransigence and arrogance of Scanlon and Jack Jones, another union leader. In an exchange of views, Scanlon said, 'Prime Minister, we don't want you to become another Ramsay Macdonald' (that is, betraying the Labour movement). Wilson replied, 'I have no intention of becoming another Ramsay Macdonald. Nor do I intend to become another Dubček. Get your tanks off my lawn, Hughie!'

As such, this is the first recorded use of a political metaphor for 'back off, don't threaten me'. Subsequently it has entered the lexicon of British politics and journalism. From the *Financial Times* (6 November 1982) on the Harrods/Lonrho dispute: '[Professor Roland Smith, chairman, House of Fraser:] If this is your idea of a game, please play somewhere else in the future ... To make it absolutely clear: get your tanks off my lawn.' From *The Observer* (14 April 1991): 'It is true, of course, that the Home Secretary does not park his tanks on [BBC Director-General] Checkland's lawn ... That is not the British way.' From a speech made by John Major to the Conservative Party Conference, 8 October 1993: 'Let me say to some of our European colleagues, "You're playing with fire [on GATT world free-trade talks]," or to put it more bluntly, "Get your tractors off our lawn."'

3 You can't guarantee being born a Lord. It is possible – you've shown it – to be born a gentleman.

When President Nixon came to dinner with Wilson at Downing Street in 1969, the first year of his presidency, he had to sit down at table with John Freeman, the British Ambassador to Washington. So far Nixon had managed to ignore the man who had once written of him as 'a man of no principle whatsoever except a willingness to sacrifice everything in the cause of Dick Nixon'. As it turned out, Nixon proposed a toast and graciously said he hoped all that was behind them. As Henry Kissinger recorded in his *Memoirs* (1979), Wilson scribbled the above note to Nixon on a menu card.

Compare what King James I is reputed to have said: 'I can make a Lord, but only God Almighty can make a gentleman' (but see also BURKE 109:5).

Woodrow WILSON American Democratic 28th President (1856–1924)

4 The world must be made safe for democracy. Its peace must be planted upon trusted foundations of political liberty.

Speech to Congress (2 April 1917), asking for a declaration of war against Germany. The words might never have been remembered had not Senator John Sharp Williams of Mississippi started clapping and continued until everyone joined in. In 1937 James Harvey Robinson commented: 'With supreme irony, the war to "Make the world safe for democracy" ended by leaving democracy more unsafe in the world than at any time since the collapse of the revolutions of 1848.'

Duchess of WINDSOR (formerly Mrs Wallis Simpson) American-born wife of the Duke of Windsor (1896–1986)

5 I married him for better or worse, but not for lunch.

This rather pleasing play on the words from the Anglican marriage service was reported in an article by Ludovic Kennedy in *The Observer* (2 December 1979), based on *The Windsor Story* by J. Bryan III and Charles J.V. Murphy, in the context: '[The Duke of Windsor] usually lunched alone on a salad while the duchess went out ("I married the Duke for better or worse but not for lunch").'

But *Partridge/Catch Phrases* (1977) has it listed as an 'Australian catchphrase used by a woman whose husband has retired, works at home or comes home for his midday meal', dating it from the 1940s and 'familiar to Britons since at least the latish 1960s'.

Langdon WINNER American writer (20th century)

1 The closest western civilization has come to unity since the Congress of Vienna in 1815 was the week the *Sgt. Pepper* album was released ... for a brief while the irreparably fragmented consciousness of the West was unified, at least in the minds of the young.

On The Beatles' *Sergeant Pepper* album of 1967. Quoted in *The* Rolling Stone *Illustrated History of Rock and Roll*, ed. Jim Miller (1976). Compare TYNAN 473:2.

Owen WISTER American writer (1860–1938)

2 Therefore Trampas spoke. 'You bet, you son-of-a — '. The Virginian's pistol came out, and ... he issued his orders to the man Trampas: – 'When you call me that, *smile!*'

Novel, *The Virginian*, Chap. 2 (1902). However, in the film version (1929) – based on the play and the novel by Wister – what Gary Cooper says, standing up to Walter Huston, is: 'If you want to call me that, smile.' *Halliwell's Film Guide* (1987) nevertheless has the cliché as: 'Smile when you say that.' Hence, the generally used phrase when giving a warning about an incident that could lead to a fight.

(Sir) P(elham) G. WODEHOUSE English-born novelist and lyricist (1881–1975)

3 To my daughter Leonora, without whose never-failing sympathy and encouragement this book would have been finished in half the time.

Dedication, *The Heart of a Goof* (1926). Not the first use by Wodehouse of this formula. In the first edition of *A Gentleman of Leisure* (1910) appears: 'To Herbert Westbrook, without whose never-failing sympathy and encouragement this book would have been finished in half the time.'

4 Begin at the beginning and omit no detail, for there is no saying how important some seemingly trivial fact may be.

Summer Lightning (*Fish Preferred* in the US) (1929). A parody of Sherlock Holmes's invitation to a consulting client to put him in possession of the facts, but not a direct quotation. Conan Doyle never exactly put it like that, preferring rather: 'Little things are infinitely the most important' and 'Pray let me have the details.' Wodehouse returned to the idea repeatedly. As early as 1902 he wrote, 'He would frequently observe, like the lamented Sherlock Holmes, the vital necessity of taking notice of trifles.' Wodehouse used the above format identically many times from 1939 to 1974.

5 'What's that thing of Shakespeare's about someone having an eye like Mother's?'
'"An eye like Mars, to threaten and command", is possibly the quotation for which you are groping, sir.'

The Mating Season (1949) – Bertie's question and Jeeves's reply. The reference is to Shakespeare, *Hamlet*, III. iv. 57. Few writers have employed literary allusions to the same extent as Wodehouse in his novels and short stories featuring Bertie Wooster and Jeeves, his gentleman's gentleman. Wodehouse was undoubtedly well-read but he seems also to have used a short cut to mighty lines: he admitted that he used a well-thumbed copy of *Bartlett*. 'Hullo, fathead ... what news on the Rialto?' – unusually, this is Bertie's Aunt Dahlia plucking a line from *The Merchant of Venice* in *Aunts Aren't Gentlemen*. Usually, it is Bertie who is fumbling for the apt quotation and, more often than not, believing that Jeeves invented all the best lines. When Jeeves quotes 'It is a far, far better thing', Bertie comments: 'As I said before, there is nobody who puts these things more neatly than he does.' A quotation from Shakespeare is frequently accompanied by, 'As I have heard Jeeves put it' or 'To quote one of Jeeves's gags'. For example: 'Leaving not a wrack behind, as I remember Jeeves saying once.' Although we all know that Jeeves is quite capable of reading Spinoza's *Ethics* (indeed he gets a complete edition of the Annotated Works), such faith in his ability to coin a neat phrase is strange in a Wooster educated at Eton and Oxford and who once won the Scripture Knowledge prize. But as Richard Usborne pointed out in *Wodehouse at Work* (1961), Bertie's frame of reference is no more than one would expect of an educated man in the early 20th century. There are lapses, though: 'The next moment I was dropping like the gentle dew upon the place beneath. Or is it rain? Jeeves would know.' Occasionally Bertie resorts – as so many of us do – to 'as the fellow said'. In one book, he refers to the 'works of somebody called Wordsworth'. Some quotations recur throughout the Jeeves canon. 'With a wild surmise' probably crops up most often. Bertie worries obsessively and understandably over 'the cat i' the adage' and 'fretful porpentine'. What is more, Wodehouse larded the novels with more and more literary allusions as he grew older. *Jeeves in the Offing* (1960) contains some fifty. It is a delight when Bertie alludes to 'Shakespeare and those poet Johnnies' by way of attribution or when he scrambles his allusions, as in 'One man's caviare is another man's major-general, as the old saw has it.' He would have found this book invaluable.

See also DOYLE 177:5 and 177:9.

Charles WOLFE Irish poet and clergyman (1791–1823)

1   Not a drum was heard, not a funeral note,
    As his corse to the rampart we hurried ...
    We carved not a line, and we raised not a stone –
    But we left him alone in his glory.

'The Burial of Sir John Moore at Corunna' (1817). From an incident in Spain during the Peninsular War (1808–14). Moore was in command of an outnumbered British army when he was forced to retreat by the unexpected arrival of Napoleon and 200,000 Frenchmen. Hence, *Not a Drum Was Heard: the War Memoirs of General Gland*, title of a radio play (1959) by Henry Reed.

2   Go, forget me – why should sorrow
    O'er that brow a shadow fling?
    Go, forget me – and tomorrow
    Brightly smile and sweetly sing.

'Go, Forget Me'. Samuel Beckett's Winnie scrabbles for this quotation in *Happy Days*, Act 2 (1961): 'What are those exquisite lines? Go forget me why should something o'er that something shadow fling ... go forget me ... never hear me ... sweetly smile ... brightly sing ... One loses one's classics ... A part remains ... That is what I find so wonderful, a part remains, of one's classics, to help one through the day.'

James WOLFE English general (1727–59)

3   The General ... repeated nearly the whole of Gray's Elegy ... adding, as he concluded, that he would prefer being the author of that poem to the glory of beating the French tomorrow.

Said on the eve of the Battle of Quebec, during which Wolfe was fatally wounded. Quoted in J. Playfair, *Biographical Account of J. Robinson* (1815).

Tom WOLFE American novelist and writer (1931–)

4   *The Right Stuff.*

Title of book (1979; film US 1983) – referring to the qualities needed by test pilots and would-be astronauts in the early years of the US space programme. But the 'right (sort of) stuff' had been applied much earlier to qualities of manly virtue, of good officer material and even of good cannon fodder. *Partridge/Slang* has an example from the 1880s. In this sense, the phrase was used by Ian Hay as the title of a novel – 'some episodes in the career of a North Briton' – in 1908.

  It is now a handy journalistic device. An *Independent* headline over a story about the ballet *Ondine* (13 May 1988) was 'The Sprite Stuff'; the same month, *The Magazine* (London) had 'The Right Stuff' as the title of an article on furnishing fabrics; in 1989, there was an ITV book programme called *The Write Stuff*.

  It has also been used as an expression for alcohol (compare 'the hard stuff').

5   *The Bonfire of the Vanities.*

Title of novel (1987; film US 1990). Derived from Savonarola's 'burning of the vanities' in Florence, 1497. The religious reformer – 'the puritan of Catholicism' – enacted various laws for the restraint of vice and folly. Gambling was prohibited, and Savonarola's followers helped people burn their costly ornaments and extravagant clothes.

6   A liberal is a conservative who has been arrested.

In two places in *The Bonfire of the Vanities*, Wolfe quotes this, but is clearly referring to an established saying. In the Fall 1993 issue of the American *Policy Review*, James Q. Wilson is credited with a similar (though reverse) observation: 'There aren't any liberals left in New York. They've all been mugged.'

Thomas WOLSEY English prelate (?1475–1530)

7   I see the matter against me how it is framed. But if I had served God as diligently as I have done the King, he would not have given me over in my grey hairs.

Cardinal Wolsey's remark was made to Sir William Kingston, Constable of the Tower of London, when Wolsey was under arrest for high treason, in November 1530. These were not his actual 'last words', as is sometimes suggested, though they were spoken on his deathbed. His last words appear to have been: 'Master Kingston, farewell. My time draweth on fast. Forget not what I have sent and charged you withal. For when I am dead you shall, peradventure, understand my words better.' Wolsey was not executed but died in Leicester on his way to the Tower. Compare SHAKESPEARE 411:5.

Kenneth WOLSTENHOLME English TV and radio sports commentator (1920–2002)

8   They think it's all over ... It is now!

Commentating for BBC Television on the World Cup Final at Wembley between England and West Germany on 30 July 1966, Wolstenholme ad-libbed what has come to be regarded as the 'most famous quote in British sport'. After a disputed third goal, the England team was 3–2 in the lead as the game continued in extra time. 'Some people are on the pitch,' Wolstenholme began before the final whistle, 'They think it's all over.' Then Geoff Hurst scored England's fourth goal (and his third) and decisively won the game. So that was why Wolstenholme added, 'It is now!'

It took until the 1990s for the phrase really to catch on. By 1992, a jokey BBC Radio sports quiz had the title *They Think It's All Over*, and this transferred to TV in 1995. Some accounts have the commentator saying, '*Well*, it is now. It's four.' According to *The Guardian* (30 July 1991), Wolstenholme himself used to complain if the 'well' was omitted, but then a replay of his commentary showed that he had not said the word after all.

Mrs Henry WOOD English novelist (1814–87)

1 **Dead! ... and never called me mother!**

This line is recalled as typical of the three-volume sentimental Victorian novel, yet nowhere does it appear in Wood's *East Lynne* (1861), where it is supposed to. Nevertheless, it was inserted in one of the numerous stage versions of the novel (that by T.A. Palmer in 1874) that were made between publication and the end of the century. Act 3 has, 'Dead, dead, dead! and he never knew me, never called me mother!' Mrs Wood's obituary writer noted in 1887: 'At present, there are three dramatic versions of *East Lynne* nightly presented in various parts of the world. Had the author been granted even a small percentage on the returns she would have been a rich woman ... The adapters of *East Lynne* grew rich and Mrs Henry Wood was kept out of their calculations.' Thus did *East Lynne* become 'a synonym for bad theatrical melodrama' – Colin Shindler, *The Listener* (23–30 December 1982).

The line arises in a scene when an errant but penitent mother who has returned to East Lynne, her former home, in the guise of a governess, has to watch the slow death of her eight-year-old son ('Little Willie'), unable to reveal her true identity. Whether the line was carried through to any of the various film versions of the tale, I do not know, but expect so.

Tommy WOODROOFFE English radio commentator (1899–1978)

2 **The Fleet's lit up.**

Woodrooffe committed the most famous British broadcasting boob on the night of 20 May 1937. As a former naval officer and now a leading outside broadcast and sports commentator, he had been due to give a 15-minute BBC Radio description of the illumination of the Fleet on the night of the Coronation Naval Review at Spithead. What he actually said, in a commentary that was faded out after less than 4 minutes, began like this: 'At the present moment, the whole Fleet's lit up. When I say "lit up", I mean lit up by fairy lamps. We've forgotten the whole Royal Review. We've for-

gotten the Royal Review. The whole thing is lit up by fairy lamps. It's fantastic. It isn't the Fleet at all. It's just ... it's fairyland. The whole Fleet is in fairyland.'

He concluded: 'I was talking to you in the middle of this damn – in the middle of this Fleet. And what's happened is the Fleet's gone, disappeared and gone. We had a hundred, two hundred, warships all around us a second ago and now they've gone. At a signal by the morse code – at a signal by the Fleet flagship which I'm in now – they've gone ... they've disappeared. There's nothing between us and heaven. There's nothing at all.' (Text checked against the BBC recording.)

Eventually, an announcer said: 'The broadcast from Spithead is now at an end. It is eleven minutes to eleven, and we will take you back to the broadcast from the Carlton Hotel Dance Band.' That familiar BBC figure, A. Spokesman, commented later: 'We regret that the commentary was unsatisfactory and for that reason it was curtailed.' Naturally, many listeners concluded that Woodrooffe himself had been 'lit up' as the result of too much hospitality from his shipmates on board HMS *Nelson*. But he denied this: 'I had a kind of nervous blackout. I had been working too hard and my mind just went blank.' He told the *News Chronicle*: 'I was so overcome by the occasion that I literally burst into tears ... I found I could say no more.'

The phrase 'The fleet's lit up' became so famous that it was used as the title of a 'musical frolic' at the London Hippodrome in 1938 and of a song by Vivian Ellis within that show.

ODQ (1979) misspells Woodrooffe's surname, states that he said, 'The Fleet *is all* lit up', which he did not, and describes the occasion as his 'first live outside broadcast', which it was not. The 1992 edition repeats the first and last of these errors. The second error derives from a misquotation in Asa Briggs, *A History of Broadcasting in the United Kingdom*, Vol. 2 (1965). *Chambers Dictionary of Quotations* (1996) compounds the third error by describing the occasion as 'Britain's first live outside broadcast', which it certainly was not.

Virginia WOOLF English novelist (1882–1941)

3 *A Room of One's Own.*

Title of book (1929) – in which Woolf asserts that 'a woman must have money and a room of her own if she is to write fiction'.

4 **We are only lightly covered with buttoned cloth; and beneath these pavements are shells, bones and silence.**

The Waves (1931). Hence, *Bones and Silence*, title of a Dalziel and Pascoe novel (1990) by Reginald Hill.

Alexander WOOLLCOTT American writer and critic
(1887–1943)

1   All the things I really like to do are either illegal,
immoral, or fattening.

The Knock at the Stage Door (1933). W.C. Fields uttered the
line, 'According to you, everything I like to do is either illegal, immoral or fattening' in the film *Six of a Kind* (US
1934). Hence, presumably, the song, 'It's Illegal, It's Immoral
Or It Makes You Fat' by Griffin, Hecht and Bruce, and popularized in the UK by the Beverley Sisters (1950s).

2   For all his reputation [he] is not a bounder. He is
every other inch a gentleman.

Of Michael Arlen. Quoted in R.E. Drennan, *Wit's End* (1973).
The same remark has also been attributed to Rebecca West
– by Ted Morgan in *Somerset Maugham* (1980) – about the
same subject. *Every Other Inch a Lady* was the title of the
autobiography (1973) of Beatrice Lillie, the actress who was
Lady Peel in private life. The basic expression 'every inch
a gentleman' occurs, for example, in William Thackeray,
Pendennis, Chap. 54 (1848–50), and Shakespeare, *King Lear*,
IV.vi.107 (1605) has 'Every inch a king'.

See also BENCHLEY 60:8.

Christopher WORDSWORTH English journalist and
critic (1914–98)

3   A legend in his own lunchtime.

On the famously bibulous sports journalist and editor Clifford Makins (1924–90). Remark made by 1976, in an
Observer review of a thriller Makins had co-authored. Alternatively, according to Ned Sherrin, *Theatrical Anecdotes*
(1991), 'David Climie, the witty revue and comedy writer
... claims to have invented the phrase "A legend in his own
lunchtime" and to have lavished it on the mercurial BBC
comedy innovator, Dennis Main Wilson.'

4   *Travels* by Edward Heath is a reminder that *Morning Cloud's* skipper is no stranger to platitude and
longitude.

Book review in *The Observer* (18 December 1977). The conjunction had been made earlier by Christopher Fry in his
play *The Lady's Not For Burning* (1949): 'Where in this small-
talking world can I find / A longitude with no platitude?'

William WORDSWORTH English poet (1770–1850)

5   Enough of science and of art;
Close up these barren leaves;
Come forth, and bring with you a heart

That watches and receives.

'The Tables Turned' (1798). Hence, *Those Barren Leaves*
(1925), a novel by Aldous Huxley.

6   Some random truths he can impart, –
The harvest of a quiet eye
That broods and sleeps on his own heart.

'A Poet's Epitaph' (1800). Hence, *The Harvest of a Quiet Eye*,
ed. Alan L. Mackay (1977), title of a selection of scientific
quotations.

7   Who is the happy Warrior? Who is he
That every man in arms should wish to be?

'Character of the Happy Warrior' (1807). Hence, 'Happy
Warrior', the nickname of Alfred E. Smith, US Democrat
politician; see ROOSEVELT 386:2.

8   The glory and the freshness of a dream.
It is not now as it hath been of yore.

'Ode, Intimations of Immortality from Recollections of
Early Childhood', St. 1 (1807). In the work as a whole, Wordsworth explores the way in which the intensity of childhood
experiences of the natural world fades into the 'light of
common day' as adulthood takes over.

9   The Rainbow comes and goes,
And lovely is the Rose ...

The cataracts blow their trumpets from the steep;
No more shall grief of mine the season wrong.

At length the Man perceives it die away,
And fade into the light of common day ...

In the same poem, Sts. 2, 3, 5. Hence, *The Rainbow Comes
and Goes* (1958), *The Light of Common Day* (1959) and
Trumpets from the Steep (1960), titles of volumes of autobiography by Lady Diana Cooper.

10   But trailing clouds of glory do we come
From God, who is our home.
Heaven lies about us in our infancy!
Shades of the prison-house begin to close
Upon the growing Boy.

In the same poem, St. 5. Hence, *Shades of the Prison House*,
title of a book about prison life by 'S. Wood' (1932). Note
also the opening lines of 'Marlborough', a poem written
about his old school by John Betjeman for a TV programme
(1962): 'Shades of my prison house, they come to view, /
Just as they were in 1922: / The stone flag passages, the
iron bars ...'

1 Though nothing can bring back the hour
Of splendour in the grass, of glory in the flower;
We will grieve not, rather find
Strength in what remains behind.

In the same poem, St. 10. Hence, *Splendour in the Grass*, title of a film (US 1961).

2 To me the meanest flower that blows can give
Thoughts that do often lie too deep for tears.

In the same poem, St. 11. Much alluded to. 'Sympathies that lie too deep for words, too deep almost for thoughts, are touched, at such times, by other charms than those which the senses feel and which the resources of expression can realize' – Wilkie Collins, *The Woman in White*, First Epoch, Chap. 8 (1860).

3 Bliss was it in that dawn to be alive,
But to be young was very heaven!

'The French Revolution as it Appeared to Enthusiasts' (1809). Also included in *The Prelude* (1850).

4 I wander'd lonely as a cloud
That floats on high o'er vales and hills.
When all at once I saw a crowd,
A host, of golden daffodils;
Beside the lake, beneath the trees,
Fluttering and dancing in the breeze.

'I wandered lonely as a cloud', also known as 'The Daffodils' (1815). In her journal for 15 April 1802, the poet's sister Dorothy described a windy walk she had taken with him from Eusemere during which they had encountered a huge number of daffodils on the shores of Ullswater. She wrote: 'We saw that there was a long belt of them along the shore, about the breadth of a country turnpike road. I never saw daffodils so beautiful. They grew among the mossy stones about and about them; some rested their heads upon these stones as on a pillow for weariness; and the rest tossed and reeled and danced, and seemed as if they verily laughed with the wind, that blew upon them over the lake; they looked so gay, ever glancing, ever changing.'

It is interesting that William's poem makes direct use of phrases from this description, though always enhancing them. Dorothy's 'a long belt' becomes 'a crowd, a host'; her 'tossed and reeled and danced' becomes 'tossing their heads in sprightly dance'. This is not to suggest that William in any way 'stole' his ideas from Dorothy's diary. He recognized how often his poems originated in her own vivid experiences:

She gave me eyes, she gave me ears;
And humble cares, and delicate fears.

But she jotted down descriptions that more than once were used by William as a reminder of experiences. Colette Clark in her comparison of the poems with the journal, *Home at Grasmere* (1960), asks: 'Was it Dorothy or William who first spoke the phrases which seem so spontaneous in the Journal and then reappear in the poems? Sometimes we know it to be Dorothy ... Such a lively chronicle close at hand would have been irresistible to any poet, and William seems to have used it again and again. It was not until two years after that heavenly walk from Eusemere that he wrote "The Daffodils", but there is no doubt that he first re-read Dorothy's account and tried to recapture the joy and delight of her description in his own poem.'

5 The presence even of a stuffed Owl for her
Can cheat the time.

Miscellaneous Sonnets, 13 (1827). The object in question gave pleasure to a Miss Jewsbury when long confined to her bed by sickness. Hence, the expression 'stuffed owl' to describe poetry that deals with trivial or inconsequential matters in a high-flown way. *The Stuffed Owl* was the title given to an anthology of notably bad verse by otherwise good poets (1930), compiled by D.B. Wyndham Lewis and Charles Lee.

6 Ministry of pain and evil.

'The Borderers' (1842). Hence, *Ministry of Fear*, title of a novel (1943; film US 1944) by Graham Greene, about a spy hunt in wartime London. Greene wrote: 'The title ... I took from a poem by Wordsworth ... and the novel was bought unseen by an American film company on the strength of Wordsworth's title' – *Ways of Escape* (1980). This is the only relevant line.

7 Those were the days
Which also first emboldened me to trust
With firmness ...
... that I might leave
Some monument behind me which pure hearts
Should reverence.

The Prelude, Bk 6, line 52 (1850). Referring to his time at Cambridge. Hence, the phrase 'Those were the days', which has had any number of uses: as the title of a BBC Radio show of 1943–74 about old-time dancing; a compilation of books by A.A. Milne (1929); the song sung by Mary Hopkin in 1968; title of a film (UK 1934) about 1890s music hall, and of another film (US 1940) about looking back to college days; and so on. An expression of regret for times past.

(Sir) Henry WOTTON English diplomat and poet (1568–1639)

1 An ambassador is an honest man sent to lie abroad for the good of his country.

Wotton was England's envoy to Venice in the reign of King James I. His punning view of the diplomat's calling very nearly cost him his job. As Izaak Walton recounted in his *Reliquiae Wottonianae* (1651), Wotton had managed to offend a Roman Catholic controversialist called Gasper Scioppius. In 1611 Scioppius produced a book called *Ecclesiasticus*, which abused James I and related an anecdote concerning Wotton: on his way out to Italy in 1604, Wotton had stayed at Augsburg where a merchant, Christoper Fleckmore, invited him to inscribe his name in an album. Wotton wrote: '*Legatus est vir bonus peregre missus ad mentiendum Reipublicae causa*' – 'which he would have been content should have been thus Englished: An ambassador is an honest man, sent to lie abroad for the good of his country.' Scioppius, on the basis of this joke, accused James I of sending a confessed liar to represent him abroad.

According to *DNB*, 'Wotton's chances of preferment were ruined by the king's discovery of the contemptuous definition of an ambassador's function ... James invited explanations of the indiscreet jest. Wotton told the king that the affair was "a merriment," but he was warned to take it seriously, and he deemed it prudent to prepare two apologies.'

James said that one of these 'sufficiently commuted for a greater offence', but the joke had done its damage, and, although Wotton was later to be given further diplomatic work and become Provost of Eton, he continued to suffer for it. A Dutch source suggests that Wotton may have had in mind Socrates' statement in Plato's *Republic* that the leaders of the state may lie both in their own country and abroad, provided this benefits the commonwealth; others may not lie. The saying is sometimes misquoted as 'sent to lie for his country'. 'Sent to lie *abroad*' is a pun on terminology used in relation to the disposition of the fleet.

(Sir) Christopher WREN English architect (1632–1723)

2 *LECTOR, SI MONUMENTUM REQUIRIS, CIRCUMSPICE ...*
[Reader, if you seek his monument, look around].

The last two lines of Wren's epitaph on a wall tablet by his burial place in the crypt of St Paul's Cathedral, London, which he designed. His actual gravestone has a factual description. The famous epitaph was reputedly composed by his son. Horace Smith (1779–1849) commented dryly that it would 'be equally applicable to a physician buried in a churchyard'.

Lawrence WRIGHT (also known as Horatio Nicholls) English music publisher and songwriter (1888–1964)

3 Are we downhearted? – no!

A phrase connected with the early stages of the First World War, although it had political origins before that. Joseph Chamberlain (1838–1814) said in a 1906 speech: 'We are not downhearted. The only trouble is, we cannot understand what is happening to our neighbours.' The day after he was defeated as candidate in the Stepney Borough Council election of 1909, Clement Attlee, the future Prime Minister, was greeted by a colleague with the cry, 'Are we downhearted?' (He replied, 'Of course, we are.')

On 18 August 1914 the *Daily Mail* reported: 'For two days the finest troops England has ever sent across the sea have been marching through the narrow streets of old Boulogne in solid columns of khaki ... waving as they say that new slogan of Englishmen: "Are we downhearted? ... Nooooo!" "Shall we win? ... Yessss!"'

Wright merely incorporated the phrase in a song.

4 Be British! was the cry as the ship went down,
Ev'ry man was steady at his post,
Captain and crew, when they knew the worst:
Saving the women and children first,
Be British! was the cry to ev'ry one,
And though fate had prov'd unkind
When your country to you pleaded,
You gave freely what was needed,
To those they left behind.

'Be British' was written and composed by Wright (with Paul Pelham) in 1912 to commemorate the sinking of the *Titanic*. It is in march tempo and, if nothing else, demonstrates that it was believed very soon after the event that Commander Smith had said 'Be British' – see SMITH 433:6.

Peter WRIGHT British intelligence officer (1916–95)

5 I have loved justice and hated iniquity: therefore I die in exile.

Wright was author of a book on the security services – *Spycatcher* – which the British Government tried and failed to ban in 1986. Wright had already gone to live in Australia, where he quoted this remark, made originally by Hildebrand, Pope Gregory VII, on his deathbed in May 1085. Hildebrand died at Salerno after a long struggle with the Holy Roman Emperor, Henry IV, over the rival claims of spiritual and temporal powers.

X Y Z

XENOPHON Greek historian (?428–?354BC)

1 *Thalatta, thalatta!* [The sea, the sea!]

Anabasis, IV.vii.24. *Thalatta* is Attic Greek, otherwise it would be *thalassa*. Xenophon tells how Greek mercenaries retreated to the Black Sea following their defeat in battle (401BC). When they reached it, the soldiers gave this cry. Hence, *The Sea, The Sea*, title of a novel (1978) by Iris Murdoch.

Compare the poem 'The Sea' (1851) by Barry Cornwall (B.W. Procter) (1787–1874), which begins: 'The Sea! the Sea! the open Sea! / The blue, the fresh, the ever free!' The Chevalier Sigmund Neukomm (who died in 1858) wrote a song with this title, which was parodied in H.J. Byron's version of *Aladdin*, with reference to tea-clippers, in 1861:

> The Tea! The Tea!
> Refreshing Tea.
> The green, the fresh, the ever free
> From all impurity.

And then, anonymously in *Punch* (19 August 1843), there is a suggested temperance song, beginning: 'The tea – the tea – the grateful tea, / The black – the green – the strong Bohea.' And before that in R.H. Barham, *The Ingoldsby Legends*, 'Mr Peters's Story' (collected 1840): 'The Sea! the Sea! the open Sea! – / That is the place where we all wish to be, / Rolling about on it merrily!'

Isoroku YAMAMOTO Japanese admiral (1884–1943)

2 I fear we have only awakened a sleeping giant, and his reaction will be terrible.

Said after the Japanese attack on Pearl Harbor (1941), which he, as Commander-in-Chief of the Combined Fleet, devised. Attributed by A.J.P. Taylor in *The Listener* (9 September 1976). The Library of Congress's *Respectfully Quoted* makes clear that the only suggestion that Yamamoto said any such thing is in the screenplay of *Tora! Tora! Tora!* (US 1970), in which the words are: 'I fear all we have done is to awaken a sleeping giant and fill him with a terrible resolve.' However, the month after Pearl Harbor, he *did* write in a letter: 'A military man can scarcely pride himself on having "smitten a sleeping enemy"; in fact, to have it pointed out is more a matter of shame.' Yamamoto had studied and worked in the US and earlier was opposed to Japanese participation in the Second World War. Compare NAPOLEON 336:3.

W.F. YEAMES British painter (1835–1918)

3 *And When Did You Last See Your Father?*

Title of painting (1878) that Yeames first exhibited at the Royal Academy; the original is now in the Walker Art Gallery, Liverpool. There can be few paintings where the title is as important as (and as well known as) the actual picture. This one was even turned into a tableau at Madame Tussaud's, where it remained until 1989. In Roy Strong's book *And When Did You Last See Your Father? – The Victorian Painter and British History* (1978), he notes: 'The child ... stands on a footstool about to answer an inquiry made by the Puritan who leans across the table towards him ... To the left the ladies of the house ... cling to each other in tearful emotion. They, it is clear, have not answered the dreaded question.'

All Yeames himself recalled of the origin of the painting was this: 'I had, at the time I painted the picture, living in my house a nephew of an innocent and truthful disposition, and it occurred to me to represent him in a situation where the child's outspokenness and unconsciousness would lead to disastrous consequences, and a scene in a country house occupied by the Puritans during the Rebellion in England suited my purpose.'

The title of the painting is often remembered wrongly as *When Did You ... ?* but has become a kind of joke catchphrase, sometimes used nudgingly, and often allusively – as in the title of Christopher Hampton's 1964 play *When Did You Last See My Mother?* and the 1986 farce by Ray Galton and John Antrobus, *When Did You Last See Your ... Trousers?* The poet Blake Morrison entitled his memoir of his father and his family, *And When Did You Last See Your Father?* (1993).

R.J. YEATMAN See SELLAR and YEATMAN.

W.B. YEATS Irish poet (1865–1939)

1 I will arise and go now, and go to Innisfree,
And a small cabin build there, of clay and
    wattles made;
Nine bean rows will I have there, a hive for the
    honey bee,
And live alone in the bee-loud glade.

'The Lake Isle of Innisfree' (1893). According to Peter Warlock, Yeats had an aversion to having his poetry set to music (though a great deal of it has been), 'born of his horror at being invited by a certain composer to hear a setting of his "Lake Isle of Innisfree" – a poem which voices a solitary man's desire for greater solitude – sung by a choir of 1000 boy scouts' – source: *The Independent* (3 February 1997). Compare LARKIN 279:2.

2 *The Celtic Twilight.*

Title of collection of stories (1893) on Celtic themes. The phrase came to be used (by others) to describe the atmosphere and preoccupations of Celtic Britain – particularly in the sense that they were on the way out (compare the phrase 'twilight of empire', MUGGERIDGE 331:4).

3 Tread softly because you tread on my dreams.

'He Wishes for the Cloths of Heaven' (1899). Alluded to in the title *Tread Softly for you Tread on My Jokes* (1966), a collection of articles by Malcolm Muggeridge.

4 When I was young,
I had not given a penny for a song
Did not the poet sing it with such airs
That one believed he had a sword upstairs.

'All Things Can Tempt Me' (1910). Hence, *A Penny for a Song*, title of play (1951) by John Whiting.

5 Things fall apart; the centre cannot hold;
Mere anarchy is loosed upon the world ...
The best lack all conviction, while the worst
Are full of passionate intensity.

'The Second Coming' (1921). Hence, *Things Fall Apart*, title of a novel (1958) by Chinua Achebe. Of all the quotations used by and about politicians, the most common by far in recent years in Britain has been this one. The trend was probably started by Kenneth Clark, the art historian, at the conclusion of his TV series *Civilization: a Personal View* (1969). Roy Jenkins in his BBC TV Dimbleby Lecture of 23 November 1979 (which pointed towards the setting up of the centrist Social Democratic Party) followed suit. In *The Listener* (14 December 1979), Professor Bernard Crick threatened to horsewhip the next politician who quoted the poem. On the very next page, Neil Kinnock (later to become Labour Party leader) could be found doing so. The threat has had no lasting effect, either.

6 And what rough beast, its hour come round
    at last,
Slouches towards Bethlehem to be born?

In the same poem. Hence, *Slouching Towards Bethlehem*, title of a book (1968) by Joan Didion.

7 I write it out in a verse –
MacDonagh and MacBride
And Connolly and Pearse
Now and in time to be,
Wherever green is worn,
Are changed, changed utterly:
A terrible beauty is born.

'Easter 1916' (1921) – reflecting Yeats's view of the Dublin Rising against British rule at that time. The four names are of leaders of the Rising who were subsequently executed for their part in it. Hence, *Now And In Time To Be*, title of a record album (1997) made up of musical settings of various Yeats poems, and *Ireland: A Terrible Beauty*, title of a book (1976) by Jill and Leon Uris.

8 We were the last romantics – chose for theme
Traditional sanctity and loveliness.

'Coole Park and Ballylee, 1932' (1933). Hence, *The Last Romantics*, title of an appraisal (1949) of Morris, Rossetti, Yeats and Ruskin, by Graham Hough.

9 Under bare Ben Bulben's head
In Drumcliff churchyard Yeats is laid ...
On limestone quarried near the spot
By his command these words are cut:

Cast a cold eye
On life, on death.
Horseman, pass by!

Yeats's epitaph is to be found on his grave in Drumcliff churchyard, Co. Sligo, Ireland, and was written by himself. The wording and the proposed place of burial were described in 'Under Ben Bulben', written on 4 September 1938, a few months before the poet's death. (Ben Bulben is the mountain above Drumcliff.) Yeats died in France, and because of the Second World War his remains were not brought back for burial at the designated spot until 1948. Hence, *Horseman, Pass By*, title of books by Dennis Parry (1954), Larry McMurtry (1961) and Diana Raymond (1977).

Andrew YOUNG Scottish poet (1807–89)

1 There is a happy land,
   Far, far away,
   Where saints in glory stand,
   Bright, bright as day.

   Hymn (1838). Included in C.H. Bateman's *Sacred Song Book* (1843). Hence, *There Is a Happy Land*, title of a novel (1957) by Keith Waterhouse.

Edward YOUNG English poet and playwright (1683–1765)

2 Some, for *renown*, on scraps of learning dote,
   And think they grow immortal as they *quote*.

   The Love of Fame, Satire 1, line 89 (1725–8). A cautionary thought for all quotationists.

3 Procrastination is the thief of time.

   Night Thoughts, line 393 (1742–5). The origin of the now proverbial expression.

ZHOU ENLAI (Chou Enlai) Chinese politician (1898–1976)

4 It's too soon to tell.

   When asked, 'What do you think has been the effect of the French Revolution?' A look at a British newspaper database turned up numerous ascriptions to Zhou Enlai. However, the earliest citation (in a 1984 *Guardian* review) awards the palm to Mao Zedong. So no firm source for this delightful anecdote.

Émile ZOLA French novelist (1840–1902)

5 *J'accuse* [I accuse.]

   See CLEMENCEAU 145:4.

not a d. was heard, 504:1

drummer: hears a different d., 466:1

drums: with d. and guns, 36:3

  without d. or trumpets, 53:6

drunk: riposte by d., 140:3

  what when d. one sees, 472:6

drunken: as d. man uses lamp-posts, 278:4

drunks: God protects fools d., 90:3

dry: drink Canada d., 58:6

  into a d. martini, 60:8

  keep your powder d., 158:7

Dublin: D. is only worse capital, 261:1

  D. not so bad as Iceland, 261:2

Dubuque: little old lady from D., 388:3

duchess: D. of Malfi still, 484:7

  Hell said D., 133:3

duck: honey I just forgot to d., 167:1

  if it looks like a d., 381:5

  son of a d. is a floater, 32:1

dulce: d. et decorum est, 245:1, 350:3

dump: what a d., 163:2

dunces: d. all in confederacy, 450:5

Dunkirk: appeals to D. spirit, 500:5

Dunn, Miss J. Hunter: 65:3

durable: true love is d. fire, 375:5

durance: in d. vile here must I wake, 111:3

dusk: in d. with light behind her, 212:7

dust: dig d. enclosed here, 423:8

  fear in a handful of d., 186:7

  palm without d., 155:4

  provoke silent d., 221:6

dustbin: d. of history, 468:6

dust-heap: great d. called history, 89:4

duty: d. of opposition to oppose, 134:5

  every man will do his d., 338:5

dwelt: d. at peace within habitation, 142:1

dyer: like d.'s hand, 421:9

dying: act of d. not of importance, 259:5

  against d. of light, 464:3

  as I lay d., 243:5

  death distinguished from d., 436:2

  d. with help of physicians, 5:5

  not death but d., 194:1

  unconscionable time d., 130:7

  what is d., 100:9

E

Eagle: E. has landed, 38:6

eagles: mount up with wings as e., 77:5

ear: e. is open like greedy shark, 265:2

Van Gogh's e. for music, 497:1

earl: halt with fourteenth E., 500:7

early: e. to bed, 14:3

  vote e. and vote often, 88:6

earned: e. precarious living, 470:4

earrings: e. cheaper than prawn sandwich, 376:3

ears: keep both e. to ground, 29:1

  prick up your e., 348:2

earth: did e. move for you, 234:6

  e. and high heaven, 245:4

  e. receive an honoured guest, 43:4

  heaven on e., 103:1

  here lies Fuller's E., 205:6

  I will move e., 37:3

  last best hope on e., 288:1

  lie heavy on him e., 475:2

  passenger on Spaceship E., 205:4

  riders on e. together, 302:4

  salt of e., 79:8

  scum of e., 486:3

  slipped surly bonds of e., 307:3

  take him e., 369:1

earthquake: small e. in Chile, 148:4

ease: to be always ill at e., 196:4

easier: e. for a camel to go through, 81:6

east: e. is e., 272:4

  e. of Eden, 68:3

  somewheres e. of Suez, 272:7

eastward: e. in Eden, 68:3

easy: e. to go down into Hell, 479:3

  e. to love, 364:7

  life is not meant to be e., 202:2

eat: could not e. that night, 10:2

  e. drink and be merry, 77:3

  e. someone out of house and home, 408:7

  let them eat c., 311:4

  never e. at place, 6:1

  one day you'll e. a beefsteak, 120:6

eating: e. *pâté de foie gras*, 435:5

  e. people is wrong, 196:3

ecce: e. homo, 88:1

echo: famous e. in Reading Room, 241:4

eclipsed: e. gaiety of nations, 260:7

economic: green shoots of e. spring, 277:4

  when have to read e. documents, 176:4

economical: e. with *actualité*, 144:6

  e. with truth, 39:2

economy: commanding heights of e., 67:1

  it's e. stupid, 147:3

ecstasy: melon for e., 112:1

Eden, Sir Anthony: best Prime Minister, 114:1

Eden: eastward of E., 68:3

edge: come to e., 292:6

Edinburgh: Athens of North, 448:4

edition: brilliant e. of universal fact, 49:6

  first e. rare, 2:6

  in a new beautiful e., 201:6

editor: definition of, 246:8

  e. is one who separates, 447:2

  to born e. news is great fun, 121:6

editorial: e. is what keeps ads apart, 465:5

Edna: Aunt E. is universal, 376:5

Edom: over E. will I cast out my shoe, 73:2

education: e. is what survives, 432:8

  e. of own children, 450:7

  e., e., e., 91:2

  sole purpose of e., 434:4

Edward VIII, King: lack of awareness, 94:5

EEC: view of, 473:4

effect: alienation e., 100:7

  butterfly e., 296:1

efficient: e. ship unless you have, 330:7

  more e. conduct of war, 25:1

effluent: e. society, 206:3

effortless: e. superiority, 41:4

egg: curate's e., 371:1

  eat a boiled e. at ninety, 62:4

  go to work on an e., 485:1

  Wall Street lays an e., 476:1

eggheads: e. of world unite, 446:3

eggs: lays e. inside paper bag, 251:2

ego: e. et in Arcadia e., 14:4

Egypt: fleshpots of E., 68:9

  not at war with E., 182:3

eheu: e. fugaces, 244:7

eighty: e. in shade, 213:3

Einstein: let E. be, 363:3

elderly: e. man of , 41:1

elected: if e. will not serve, 430:6

elections: trouble with f. elections, 441:1

  you won e. but, 437:1

Electra: mourning becomes E., 347:5

electric: electric: e. tidings came, 45:5

  sing body e., 492:5

electrification: e. of whole country, 282:5

Elegy, Gray's: envied, 504:3
view of, 260:5

elementary: e. my dear Watson, 177:9

elephant: hot breath of pursuing e., 11:2

elephants: e. never forget injury, 392:4

eleventh: at e. hour, 81:7

elms: immemorial e., 455:4

elsewhere: images of e., 220:4
is a world e., 402:2

emotions: in one word e., 205:5
run gamut of e., 353:1

empire: Britain has lost e., 1:2
e. strikes back, 297:5
Greeks in American e., 303:7
how is E., 210:5
impulses of evil e., 378:4
sun never sets on British E., 19:5
twilight of e., 331:4

employee: every e. tends to rise, 358:2

emptied: e. of its poetry, 43:4

enchantments: e. of Middle Age, 40:3

encourage: to e. others, 479:6

encumbers: e. him with help, 258:5

end: all good things come to e., 97:12
all in e. is harvest, 432:6
e. is bitter as wormwood, 74:7
e. is near, 9:3
e. of all things is at hand, 86:4
e. of history, 204:7
e. of me old cigar, 349:5, 491:3
here is my journey's e., 419:9
in my e. is my beginning, 188:2
journey's e., 430:7
not even beginning of e., 138:7
now e. is near, 9:3
of making books there is no e., 76:7
war to e. wars, 488:3

endless: e. night, 92:9

enemies: e. shall lick dust, 73:4
judge me by e. I have made, 386:4
love him for e. he has made, 147:1
naked to mine e., 411:5
who needs e., 15:8

enemy: and with wrong e., 99:4
aware of e. within, 461:1
effect men will have upon e., 486:2
e. nearly slew ye, 36:3
e. of people, 250:3
hasn't e. in world, 496:3
his own worst e., 67:3
last e. that shall be destroyed, 84:7

met e. and he is us, 266:7
my friend's friend is e., 25:4

enfants: e. terribles, 209:2

engine: a Really Useful E., 46:1

England: apple falling towards E., 43:1
close eyes and think of E., 239:2
cry God for Harry E., 409:7
E. and America language, 424:4
E. home and beauty, 99:5
E. is land without music, 57:5
E. is mother of parliaments, 101:5
E. is nation of shopkeepers, 335:2
E. is island off coast of Europe, 332:7
E. expects man will do duty, 338:5
E. my E., 235:4
E. to itself do rest but true, 413:2
E. waste, 184:2
E. with all thy faults, 157:7
E. yet shall stand, 451:4
gentlemen in E., 410:4
in E.'s green and pleasant land, 93:3
oh to be in E., 105:3, 399:2
only have to survive in E., 62:4
road that leads him to E., 259:3
speak for E., 7:7
stately homes of E., 157:2
tell E. ye who pass, 377:2
that is for ever E., 102:5
things I've done for E., 236:2
this E. never did, 413:2
this E., 419:12
wake up E., 210:2

English: chill of E. bedroom, 334:4
E. literature's performing flea, 347:1
E. unofficial rose, 102:3
mobilized E. language, 268:2
raped and speaks E., 16:4
under an E. heaven, 102:5

Englishman: E. belongs to exclusive club, 337:2

Englishman: God is an E., 166:3
not trust E. in dark, 19:5
not worth one dead E., 280:4
remember you are an E., 382:1
smell blood of E., 413:8

Englishmen: mad dogs and E., 156:6

enigma: inside an e., 135:8

enjoy: don't have to go out and e. it, 434:6
e. smell of their own farts, 44:4

enough: e. is e., 161:3, 305:2
one is e., 140:2
patriotism is not e., 128:7
world is not e., 197:5

entanglements: avoid foreign e., 255:3

enter: ye who e. here, 162:3

enterprises: impediments to great e., 48:1

enthusiasm: nothing without e., 149:6

envious: e. Casca, 412:12

envy: survivors will e. dead, 270:1

epigram: day of jewelled e., 9:4

epitaph: greatest e. in history, 451:2
let no man write my e., 190:9

epitaphs: nice derangement of e., 430:2
of graves worms e., 420:1

eppur: e. si muove, 207:2

equal: doubt six his e. in Boston, 16:2
some more e. than others, 349:1

equals: first among e., 328:1

era: e. of four-letter word, 9:4

err: to e. is human, 362:9

erred: e. and strayed from thy ways, 96:2

Esau: E. is a hairy man, 68:6
E. selleth his birthright, 68:5

escaped: e. from mad and savage master, 437:8

especial: for thine e. safety, 407:1

essays: e. have been most current, 47:2

essence: e. like an ape, 416:8

essential: I am e. to theatre, 309:4

Establishment, The: coinage of, 192:1

establishment: when e. united, 306:6

estate: fourth e. of realm, 300:1

estate: ordered their e., 5:7

et: e. in Arcadia ego, 14:4
e. tu Brute, 412:9

état: é. c'est moi, 296:3

eternal: hope springs e., 363:4

eternity: from here to e., 273:1

ethic: protestant work e., 484:3

Eton: motto of, 53:4
on playing fields of E., 486:6

Étonne-moi: 167:5

eunuch: prerogative of e., 448:2

eunuchs: like e. in harem, 58:7

Eureka: 37:4

Europe: E. catches cold, 321:2
lamps out all over E., 223:3
most beautiful salon in E., 335:6
off coast of E., 332:7
part of community of E., 393:4
set E. ablaze, 137:1

even: don't get mad get e., 268:7
e. unto half my kingdom, 71:6

evening: e. colonnade, 364:1

event: it is not an e., 452:1

generation: beat g., 269:3
  lost g., 443:5
generations: first in thousand g., 271:6
genitals: make my g. to quiver, 258:4
genius: g. capacity for taking pains,
  122:6
  g. does what it must, 52:8
  g. one per cent inspiration, 182:4
  nothing except my g., 494:2
gentle: do not go g. into night, 464:3
gentleman: died very gallant g., 346:2
  every other inch a g., 506:2
  fat g. in passion, 428:1
  g. able to play flute: 38:3
  g. in Whitehall, 254:3
  g. knows how to play accordion, 149:1
  give breast to g. opposite, 52:6
  king cannot make a g., 109:5
  not quite a g., 41:1
  once a g. always a g., 170:4
  to be born a g., 502:3
gentlemen: both ladies and g., 44:6
  g. do not take soup at luncheon,
  160:2
  g. in England now a-bed, 410:4
  g. prefer blondes, 295:8
  g. rankers out on spree, 273:1
  keep them all like g., 14:2
  while g. go by, 274:5
  written by g. for g., 457:8
geographical: Italy is g. expression,
  321:3
geography: g. is everywhere, 167:3
George V, King, snoot of, 465:2
  told me, 42:1
George: G. don't do that, 223:1
  Lloyd G. knew my father, 292:2
  Sunday in park with G., 437:6
George-Brown, Lord: drunk, 466:5
Georgie: G. Porgie pudding and pie,
  15:7
geriatric: cocktail parties of g. set, 306:8
Germans: G. to pay every penny, 209:4
Germany: calling, 262:6
Gestapo: fall back on form of G., 139:3
getting: g. of wisdom, 74:6
  g. there is half fun, 447:3
ghastly: g. good taste, 65:1
giant: awakened sleeping g., 509:2
  China sleeping g., 336:3
  g. leap for mankind, 39:1
  G.'s Causeway, view of, 261:1
giants: standing on shoulders of g.,
  340:2

Gibbon, Edward: scribbler, 215:2
giftie: some pow'r g. gie us, 110:3
gifts: Greeks bearing g., 478:7
gigantic: g. system of outdoor relief,
  101:4
gild: g. refined gold, 413:1
gilded: g. youth, 403:3
Gilead: balm in G., 77:8
gin: notoriously a bottle of Gordon's
  g., 95:5
Gioconda: G. Smile, 249:2
Gipper: win this for G., 377:4
girl: and g. is mine, 27:1
  g. at impressionable age, 283:1
  kissed g., 15:7
  g. me girl at impressionable age, 283:1
  g. me liberty or g. me death, 236:3
  g. me your tired your poor, 280:5
  g. peace in our time, 96:5
  g. us tools, 138:2
  recited by thousand G. Guides, 279:2
given: g. thee to half of kingdom, 71:6
giving: I am not in g. vein, 420:4
glad I tell you g. g. g., 163:1
glad: never g. confident morning, 105:5
Gladstone, William: and Irish, 398:11
  in hurry, 134:4
  speaks, 477:2
  verbosity, 174:4
Glasgow: never played G. Empire
  Saturday, 175:3
glass: baying for broken g., 483:4
  g. of blessings, 373:2
  g. of fashion, 406:1
  liked sound of broken g., 60:5
  see through a g. darkly, 84:67
glassly: through a dark g., 440:1
gleaming: twilight's last g., 269:4
glen: monarch of g., 34:5
glimmer: g. of twilight, 105:5
glimmering: fades g. landscape, 221:3
glint: g. of gold, 126:3
glisters: all that g. is not gold, 417:1
glittering: g. prizes, 434:2
glitters: g. is not gold, 417:1
global: g. village, 303:2
glorious: full many g. morning, 421:3
  g. morning for America, 3:4
glory: g. and freshness of dream,
  506:8
  g. that was Greece, 362:1
  nothing so expensive as g., 436:1
  paths of g. lead but to grave, 221:5
  power and g., 96:4

uncertain g. of April day, 423:4
  what price g., 441:3
  yields true g., 178:2
glove: iron hand in velvet g., 335:4
  losing one g. is sorrow, 233:1
gloves: about people in g. as such,
  154:6
glow: g. has warmed world, 447:1
gnomes: little g. in Zurich, 500:1
go: g. anywhere I damn well please,
  67:4
  g. extra mile, 80:3
  g. to it, 328:5
  g. up thou bald head, 71:3
  G. West young man, 221:9
  in name of God g., 7:8
  let my people g., 68:8, 392:3
  to boldly g. were no man, 442:2
goat: g. in wilderness: 69:4
god: as if some lesser g., 456:2
  cry G. for Harry, 409:7
  don't believe in G., 332:2
  further from G., 8:8
  G. alone will stay, 457:1
  G. bless us every one, 169:2
  G. buries his workmen, 489:5
  G. created heaven and earth, 68:1
  G. created man in own image, 68:2
  G. disposes, 463:2
  G. does not play dice with universe,
  185:2
  G. finally caught his eye, 264:4
  G. gave Noah rainbow sign, 50:2
  G. give us grace to accept, 341:3
  G. if powerful not good, 468:4
  G. is an Englishman, 166:3
  G. is in details, 321:5
  G. is love, 281:6
  G. is not mocked, 84:9
  G. made country, 157:6
  G. made them high or lowly, 5:7
  G. moves in a mysterious way, 157:5
  G. on side of big battalions, 480:1
  G. planted a garden eastward, 68:3
  G. protect me from my friends, 15:8
  G. protects fools, 90:3
  G.'s in his heaven, 105:1
  G. save king, 70:1
  G. tempers wind to shorn lamb, 445:2
  G. first garden made, 157:3
  G. will pardon me, 233:2
  G. wouldn't trust Englishman in
  dark, 19:5
grace of G. goes G., 140:4

mouths: whose m. they've been in, 365:6

moutons: revenons à ces m., 30:4

move: but it does m., 207:2

did earth m. for you, 234:6

I will m. earth, 37:3

ladies never m., 160:4

moveable: Paris is a m. feast, 234:8

movers: we are m. and shakers, 349:8

movies: m. should have beginning, 215:4

moving: m. finger writes, 195:7

m. peacefully towards, 163:3

m. toyshop of heart, 363:2

MP: being an MP, 1:1

Mrs Grundy, what will M.G. say, 330:4

much: so m. to do, 382:2, 455:7

muckrake: man with m. in his hand, 108:1

mucus: m. of a good idea, 217:8

mud: longing to be back in m., 44:8

muddied: m. oafs at goals, 274:2

muddled: somewhere in m. middle, 65:6

mudging: fed up with fudging and m., 350:1

Muffet, Little Miss: 24:2

muffled: with m. drum, 43:3

mugwump: m. is sort of bird, 25:3

mulberry: here we go round m. bush, 17:3

mum: cry 'm.' she cries 'budget', 417:6

give no words but m., 410:5

mummy: M. what's that man for, 372:1

murder: I met m. on way, 429:5

m. he says, 292:4

m. most foul, 404:6

m. your darlings, 374:2

m. whiles I smile, 411:4

see how love and m. will out, 152:2

Murphy's Law, 19:1

muscles: seventy-two m. to frown, 21:3

muse: O for a m. of fire, 409:3

muses: house m. haunt, 203:3

museum: British M. had lost, 211:3

mushroom: life too short to stuff m., 153:8

music: architecture is frozen m., 394:8

brave m. of distant drum, 195:5

dance to m. of time, 366:4

do not interrupt m., 79:2

don't know anything about m., 57:32

how potent cheap m. is, 156:3

I write m. as sow piddles, 331:2

if m. be food of love, 422:5

land without m., 57:5

man that hath no m., 417:5

mode of m. changes, 360:5

m. has charms to soothe, 152:3

m. ho, 400:7, 418:4

m. in air, 185:4

Wagner is Puccini of m., 330:1

Wagner's m. better than sounds, 345:3

we are m. makers, 349:8

musical: sex with man was m., 135:7

music-halls: darling of m., 433:8

must: m. it be, 57:4

word m. not used to princes, 189:3

mutual: our m. friend, 171:7

mysterious: God moves in m. way, 157:5

m. Kor, 278:3

mystery: magical m. tour, 284:6

where there is m. there is power, 166:1

N

N or M, 97:3

nacht: n. und nebel, 240:4

nail: for want of n., 15:5

treat everything as n., 318:2

naked: n. ape, 328:2

n. into conference chamber, 66:6

n. to mine enemies, 411:5

n. women in wet mackintoshes, 464:5

name: as long as you spell my n. right, 148:6

love dare not speak n., 496:4

my n. is George Nathaniel, 25:6

my n. is legion, 82:2

n. liveth for evermore, 79:5

n. of action, 405:6

n. of rose, 182:1

spell my n. right, 10:1

to mark against your n., 382:5

whose n. was writ in water, 266:5

nanny: n. state, 302:7

Napoleon: ashes of N. Bonaparte, 487:1

N. of crime, 177:8, 188:1

narrow: n. is way, 80:7

nasty brutish and short, 212:3, 241:2

nasty: something n. in woodshed, 212:2

nation: happy n. that has no history, 185:7

n. of shopkeepers, 335:2

n. shall not lift up sword against n., 76:10

n. shall speak peace unto n., 78:4

one n. under God, 60:1

this n. under God, 288:2

nations: eclipsed gaiety of n., 260:7

n. end committing suicide, 3:2

separated by language, 494:4

n. touch at their summits, 49:4

two n., 173:3

natural: twice as n., 125:4

nature: laws of n. be violated, 247:6

n. abhors straight line, 103:3

n. abhors vacuum, 375:1

n. red in tooth and claw, 455:6

naught: n. for your comfort, 132:3

struggle n. availeth, 147:6

naughty: n. but nice, 390:7

n. people buried, 277:2

naval: n.tradition, 141:2

navies: nations' airy n., 454:6

navy: n.'s here, 25:7

nearer: n. church, 8:8

n. my God to thee, 3:5

neat: n. but not gaudy, 490:1

necessary: is it n., 20:2

n. to destroy it, 34:1

necessities: dispense with its n., 330:6

necessity: n. to sail, 361:1

thy n. is greater than mine, 431:2

needful: is it n., 20:2

needle: quick Watson n., 177:5

through eye of a n., 81:6

needs: each according to his n., 316:4

your country n. you, 193:5

neglect: benign n., 331:1

neiges: n. d'antan, 478:4

neighbour: death is my n., 191:1

love thy n., 69:5

shalt not covet thy n.'s wife, 69:2

neighbours: good fences make good n., 204:1

Nell, Little: fate of, 171:4

Nelson: N. touch, 338:1

nessun: n. dorma, 369:3

nest: one flew over cuckoo's n., 27:2

nettle: out of n. danger, 408:3

network: definition of, 258:7

never: n. again war, 257:2

n. complain and n. explain, 51:6, 174:5

n. despair, 244:5

n. eat at place called Mom's, 6:1

T

XYZ